THE OXFORD HANDBOOK OF

DANCE AND THEATER

THE OXFORD HANDBOOK OF

DANCE AND THEATER

Edited by

NADINE GEORGE-GRAVES

OXFORD

UNIVERSITY PRESS

OXFORD
UNIVERSITY PRESS

Oxford University Press is a department of the University of
Oxford. It furthers the University's objective of excellence in research,
scholarship, and education by publishing worldwide.

Oxford   New York
Auckland   Cape Town   Dar es Salaam   Hong Kong   Karachi
Kuala Lumpur   Madrid   Melbourne   Mexico City   Nairobi
New Delhi   Shanghai   Taipei   Toronto

With offices in
Argentina   Austria   Brazil   Chile   Czech Republic   France   Greece
Guatemala   Hungary   Italy   Japan   Poland   Portugal   Singapore
South Korea   Switzerland   Thailand   Turkey   Ukraine   Vietnam

Published in the United States of America by
Oxford University Press
198 Madison Avenue, New York, NY 10016

Library of Congress Cataloging-in-Publication Data
The Oxford handbook of dance and theater / edited by Nadine George-Graves.
    pages cm
Includes bibliographical references and index.
ISBN 978–0–19–991749–5 (hardcover : alk. paper)   1. Dance—Handbooks, manuals, etc.   2. Theater—
Handbooks, manuals, etc.   3. Performing arts—Handbooks, manuals, etc.   I. George-Graves, Nadine., editor.
GV1594.O94 2015
790.2—dc23
2014046000

1 3 5 7 9 8 6 4 2
Printed in the United States of America
on acid-free paper

This one's for Cebra
Looking at 25 years together
And counting . . .

CONTENTS

SECTION III GENUS (PART 2)

SECTION IV HISTORIOGRAPHICAL PRESENCE AND ABSENCE

SECTION VII   UNRULY BODIES

SECTION VIII   BIOPOLITICS

SECTION IX   NATIONAL SCALES
AND MASS MOVEMENTS

SECTION X INFECTION

ACKNOWLEDGMENTS

THIS anthology has been many years in the making and I am indebted to the people who have devoted their time, energy, and intellectual acumen to its creation. What began as an observation about the importance of a certain type of performance led me to many like-minded scholars—so many, in fact, that the possibilities for these discussions could only be held by this large volume. I would like to express my gratitude to all the contributors for trusting my curatorship of their research.

Anthea Kraut was a valuable early collaborator on these ideas when we co-chaired the 2010 conference *Embodying Power: Work Over Time*. Susan Manning has been a mentor since graduate school and her work in theater and dance has influenced many of these discussions. I'm thankful that we have continued the conversations on the intersections of theater and dance at working group sessions at the 2012 and 2014 ASTR conferences. Thanks to Ira Murfin and Tara Rodman for helping us orchestrate these meetings. I look forward to more such provocative forums.

Scholarly organizations play an important role in the generation and dissemination of ideas. I am fortunate to have found a number of supportive professional associations during my academic and creative journey. Behind all the acronyms (CORD, ASTR, SDHS, ATHE, BPT, BTA, BTN, CADD, PSi, IFTR, ASA, etc.) lie brilliant scholars and artists pushing back the frontiers of ignorance. During the creation of this volume, I was honored to serve as president of the Congress on Research in Dance. Many thanks to the board of directors and the many scholars and artists I met and worked with during my term.

Thanks to my colleagues and students at my home institution UC San Diego, particularly the students in my Dance Theater graduate seminar.

Scholars don't thank enough artists working in theater and dance around the world creating the aesthetics and traditions that inspire our humanist inquiries and insights. We are privileged to participate in your work as witnesses, collaborators, performers, investigators, and disseminators. The complex nexus of artistry and scholarship around the phenomena of performance is a prolific site that I am proud to call home.

Thank you to the folks at Oxford University Press who have patiently worked with me on the publishing of this work. Norm Hirschy is a remarkable editor who guided me from proposal to print, patiently answering (and sometimes re-answering) all my questions. Assistant editor, Lisbeth Redfield, helped us keep the ship afloat and sailing. And thank you to the anonymous readers for their support of the project and advice for improvement.

I could not have pulled this off without the administrative support of Maiya Murphy. She deftly choreographed the movement of drafts, permissions, and artwork all while moving from PhD student to assistant professor.

Nothing is possible or worth it without the love and support of my family. My husband, Cebra Graves, is the smartest person I know and my intellectual partner since our late night dorm-room debates. We've been on an odyssey of love, art, curiosity, and geography, and I wouldn't have it any other way. Our beautiful children, Gideon, Maya, and Zora, make life fun and work easy. Watching them discover and grow are constant reminders of the impetus to understand. My rock is my aunt, Ruby Rowe, whose balance of grace, peace, and righteousness is a model for excellence. And I honor my mother, Lorna George, in whose memory I do everything.

Contributors

Patrick Anderson is director of critical gender studies, and associate professor in the departments of ethnic studies and communication, at the University of California, San Diego. He currently serves as vice president of the American Society for Theatre Research, and is co-editor (with Nicholas Ridout) of the Performance Works book series at Northwestern University Press. He has published two books: *Violence Performed* (co-edited with Jisha Menon) and *So Much Wasted: Hunger, Performance, and the Morbidity of Resistance*. He is currently completing two new books, *Empathy's Others* and *Autobiography of a Disease*.

Virginia Anderson is assistant professor of theater at Connecticut College, where she serves on the steering committee for the Holleran Center for Community Action and Public Policy and is a faculty fellow for the Ammerman Center for Arts and Technology. Her work has appeared in *Theatre History Studies, Text and Presentation, The 1980s*, and *The Oxford Handbook of the American Musical*. Her current book project, *Beyond Angels: Broadway Theatre and the AIDS Epidemic* grew from years of research concerning creative, social, and political representations of the AIDS epidemic. Her investigations have taken her to England, China, and Cuba, and her work in advocacy and the arts has been recognized by the National Center for HIV, STD, and TB Prevention, Centers for Disease Control and Prevention (CDC), and the AIDS Action Committee of Massachusetts.

Ann Cooper Albright A dancer, improviser, and a scholar, Ann Cooper Albright is professor of dance and chair of the Department of Dance at Oberlin College. Combining her interests in dancing and cultural theory, she is involved in teaching a variety of dance, performance studies, and gender studies courses that seek to engage students in both practices and theories of the body. She is the author of *Engaging Bodies: The Politics and Poetics of Corporeality* (2013); *Modern Gestures: Abraham Walkowitz Draws Isadora Duncan Dancing* (2010); *Traces of Light: Absence and Presence in the Work of Loie Fuller* (2007); and *Choreographing Difference: The Body and Identity in Contemporary Dance* (1997), and co-editor of *Moving History/Dancing Cultures* (2001) and *Taken by Surprise: Improvisation in Dance and Mind* (2003). The book *Encounters with Contact Improvisation* (2010) is the product of one of her adventures in writing and dancing and dancing and writing with others. Ann is founder and director of *Girls in Motion*, an award-winning afterschool program at Langston Middle School now in its tenth year, and co-director of *Accelerated Motion: Towards a New Dance Literacy*, a National Endowment for the Arts–funded digital collection of materials about dance. She is president of the Society of Dance History Scholars and is currently working on an interdisciplinary book titled *Gravity Matters: Finding Ground in an Unstable World*.

Jane Baldwin, a longtime faculty member of the Boston Conservatory, taught modern drama, acting, and humanities. She is a recipient of the Canadian Heather McCallum Award for her English essay on Jean Gascon and of the French language Prix André G. Bourassa.

Her books and articles include *Michel Saint-Denis and the Shaping of the Modern Actor*; *Theatre: The Rediscovery of Style and Other Writings*, which she edited; and *Vie et morts de la creation collective/Lives and Deaths of Collective Creation*, co-edited with Jean-Marc Larrue and Christiane Page. Her essay "Michel Saint-Denis: Training the Complete Actor" is published in *Actor Training*, edited by Alison Hodge. Her chapter "The Accidental Rebirth of Collective, Jacques Copeau, Michel Saint-Denis, Léon Chancerel, and Improvised Theatre" appears in *A History of Collective Creation*, edited by Kathryn Mederos Syssoyeva and Scott Proudfit. Dr. Baldwin is a theater critic for www.capitalcriticscircle.com.

Marie C. Percy is an assistant professor in residence at the University of Connecticut, where her primary responsibility is movement training for actors in the BFA and MFA program. She received her MFA from Virginia Commonwealth University in 2012 and became a certified movement analyst through the Laban Institute for Movement Studies in New York City in 2013. In addition to her academic work she is also an actor, dancer, choreographer, movement analyst, acrobat, aerialist, and continual student of the intersection between the body, movement, and performance.

Darcey Callison, PhD, is a choreographer, teacher, and scholar whose research includes postmodern dance/theater histories, dancing masculinity, and dance dramaturgy. Recently Callison co-edited the "Dance and Movement Dramaturgy" issue for *Canadian Theatre Review* and is in the process of co-editing a collection of articles focusing on practices of the dramaturgy of dance. An established choreographer, Callison continues to create dance and most recently collaborated with choreographers Carol Anderson and Holly Small on a re-visioning of Igor Stravinsky's *Sacre du Printemps*, set in the wilds of northern Ontario and titled *Rite Redux*. Callison continues to pursue the fusion of studio and scholarly research as a dance artist; for the last six years has served as graduate program director for York University's MFA in contemporary choreography and dance dramaturgy.

Royd Climenhaga is on the arts faculty at Eugene Lang College/The New School University in New York City. He recently published an essay on Pina Bausch's American Legacy in the book *Inheriting Dance: An Invitation from Pina* (2014), the book *Pina Bausch* (2009), and the *Pina Bausch Sourcebook* (2013), an edited collection of essays that explores Bausch's legacy and places her work in cultural and aesthetic context. He writes on performance and intersections between dance and theater, including essays on Anne Theresa de Keersmaeker, Big Dance Theater, and Anne Bogart and SITI Company. He is currently working on a new book, *20th Century Performance: A History of Interdisciplinary Artistic Practice*, integrating influences from theater, dance, music, and the visual arts. Royd also works as a development consultant and grant writer for several arts organizations, serves as development director for Monica Bill Barnes & Company, and develops and produces new physical performance works as co–artistic director of Human Company.

Amy Cook (associate professor) specializes in the intersection of cognitive science and theories of performance and early modern drama. She has published *Shakespearean Neuroplay: Reinvigorating the Study of Dramatic Texts and Performance through Cognitive Science* (2010); essays in *Theatre Journal, TDR, SubStance, Journal of Dramatic Theory and Criticism*; and several edited volumes, including *Bloom's Modern Critical Interpretations, Affective Performance and Cognitive Science* and the forthcoming *Shakespeare and Consciousness*. She is currently co-editing a book with Rhonda Blair called *Languages,*

Bodies, and Ecologies: Theatre, Performance and Cognition. She taught from 2008 to 2014 at Indiana University, Bloomington, where she was an associate professor in the Department of Theatre, Drama, and Contemporary Dance and an adjunct professor in the Cultural Studies Program and the Cognitive Science Program. She was a Mellon Fellow at Emory University in Atlanta. She has directed and assistant directed in New York and San Diego. She got her PhD in theater and drama at University of California, San Diego, and her BA from University of Michigan, Ann Arbor.

Miriam Felton-Dansky is assistant professor of theater and performance at Bard College. Her writing has appeared in *Theater* magazine, where she is also a contributing editor, as well as in *Theatre Journal, PAJ,* and *TDR,* and she is a regular contributor to the theater section of the *Village Voice.* She is currently preparing a book manuscript on the subject of viral performance.

Ann Dils, professor and chair of the Department of Dance at the University of North Carolina at Charlotte, is a dance historian with interests in movement analysis, feminist theory and research methods, and cultural studies. Her recent essays appear in the edited collection *Investigating Dance on Its Own Terms: Histories and Methodologies* (Bales and Eliot, eds.) and in the *International Journal of Screendance.* Dils co-edited *Intersections: Dance, Place, and Identity* (2009) and *Moving History/Dancing Cultures: A Dance History Reader* (2001) and co-directs Accelerated Motion: Towards a New Dance Literacy, a National Endowment for the Arts–funded digital collection of materials about dance (http://acceleratedmotion. wesleyan.edu). Dils has taught in the Department of Dance and the Women's and Gender Studies Program at the University of North Carolina, Greensboro, and at Teacher's College, Columbia University. She received the Dixie Durr Award for Outstanding Service to Dance Research from the Congress on Research in Dance (CORD) in 2010 and has been editor of *Dance Research Journal* and president of the Congress on Research in Dance.

Lisa Doolittle is professor in theatre arts at the University of Lethbridge. A dancer, choreographer, and director, her recent university/community collaborations integrate participatory research and activism in workshops and performance events. Her research, which has been presented and published internationally, focuses on the roles of performance in social change including work on folk and social dance, dance and human rights, theater and dance for community development, and arts-based pedagogy. With Anne Flynn, she co-edited the anthology *Dancing Bodies, Living Histories: New Writing about Dance and Culture* (2000) and was co-investigator on multiyear research, funded by the Social Sciences and Humanities Research Council of Canada, examining indigenous and "folk" dance in Canada, and Canadian multicultural policy. Currently co-investigator on a five-year national partnership funded by SSHRC, *Art for Social Change: An Integrated Research Program in Teaching, Evaluation, and Capacity Building,* Doolittle leads the Teaching and Learning component. She regularly partners with health sciences colleagues to join the Museums of Malawi in arts-based health promotion in rural primary schools. She is also developing performances and advocacy events with people living with developmental disabilities and the nongovernmental organizations who support them in southern Alberta.

Colleen Dunagan, PhD, is associate professor of dance at California State University, Long Beach. Her research on dance aesthetics and Susanne Langer's concept of the virtual appears in *Topoi: An International Journal of Philosophy.* Dunagan's writing on dance in television advertising and film has appeared in *Dance Research Journal* and *The International Journal of Arts in Society*. She has co-authored essays with Roxane Fenton that are forthcoming in *The Oxford Handbook of Dance and the Popular Screen* and *Movies, Moves, and Music: The Sonic World of Dance Film*. Currently, she is working on a book manuscript that analyzes the discourse of dance within television commercials.

Susan Leigh Foster, choreographer and scholar, is distinguished professor in the Department of World Arts and Cultures/Dance at the University of California, Los Angeles. She is the author of *Reading Dancing: Bodies and Subjects in Contemporary American Dance, Choreography and Narrative: Ballet's Staging of Story and Desire, Dances That Describe Themselves: The Improvised Choreography of Richard Bull*, and *Choreographing Empathy: Kinesthesia in Performance*. She is also the editor of three anthologies: *Choreographing History, Corporealities*, and *Worlding Dance*. Three of her danced lectures can be found at the Pew Center for Arts and Heritage website http://danceworkbook.pcah.us/susan-foster/index.html.

Anne Flynn is professor of dance in the School of Creative and Performing Arts, and the Faculty of Kinesiology at the University of Calgary. A graduate of the State University of New York, Brockport, and Wesleyan University, Flynn has been involved in the Calgary dance community as a performer, artistic director, teacher, scholar, administrator, and dance education advocate. Her research on multiculturalism and identity, women in dance, health promotion through dance, and dance education has been presented and published internationally. She is co-editor, with Lisa Doolittle, of *Dancing Bodies, Living Histories: New Writing about Dance and Culture* (2000) and co-recipient of a Social Sciences and Humanities Research Council Standard Research Grant (SSHRC) (2004-2009). Flynn is the director of Urban Dance Connect, a communty dance component of the Dance Division created in 2005 that involves partnerships with numerous community groups, and practicum opportunities for dance students. Flynn has served on the boards of the Congress on Research in Dance, Society of Canadian Dance Studies, Alberta Dance Alliance, *Dance Connection Magazine*, Dancers' Studio West, and Dance in Canada Association. Currently, she is co-investigator on a SSHRC partnership grant focusing on arts for social change.

Sondra Horton Fraleigh, professor emeritus of dance and somatic studies at the State University of New York, Brockport, is the author of *BUTOH: Metamorphic Dance and Global Alchemy* (2010). Her other books include *Dancing Identity: Metaphysics in Motion* (2004); *Dancing into Darkness: Butoh, Zen, and Japan* (1999); *Researching Dance: Evolving Modes of Inquiry* (1998); and *Dance and the Lived Body* (1987). Her book on the founders of Japanese butoh is *Hijikata Tatsumi and Ohno Kazuo* (2006). She has also published numerous articles and book chapters. Fraleigh was chair of the Department of Dance at SUNY Brockport for nine years and later head of graduate dance studies there. She was also selected as a faculty exchange scholar for the State University of New York. Her innovative choreography has been seen in New York, Germany, Japan, and India. Fraleigh is the founding director of Eastwest Somatics Institute for the study of dance, yoga, and somatic bodywork. For more information on Fraleigh and her work see her website: www.eastwestsomatics.com

Liza Gennaro choreographed the critically acclaimed Broadway revival of *The Most Happy Fella* directed by Gerald Gutierrez and the Broadway revival of *Once upon a Mattress* starring Sarah Jessica Parker. She has choreographed off-Broadway and in regional theaters across America including: Roundabout Theatre, Actor's Theatre of Louisville, The Old Globe, Hartford Stage, Guthrie Theater, The Goodspeed Opera House, Pittsburgh Civic Light Opera, Paper Mill Playhouse, and The St. Louis "Muny" Opera. She collaborated with Stephen Flaherty and Frank Galati on their chamber musical *Loving, Repeating: A Musical of Gertrude Stein* for the About Face Theater in Chicago. In 2013 she choreographed *Elf: The Musical* at Pioneer Theatre and the 20th Anniversary Concert of *Titanic: The Musical* at Avery Fisher Hall and she created a dance-pantomime of *A Charlie Brown Christmas* for the New York Pops Christmas Concert at Carnegie Hall. She is a member of the Tony Award Nominating Committee and on the executive board of the Stage Director and Choreographers Society. Liza has taught at Barnard College, Princeton University, and Yale University and is currently on faculty at Indiana University. Her essay "Evolution of Dance in the Golden Era of the American 'Book Musical'" appears in *The Oxford Handbook of the American Musical*.

Nadine George-Graves (BA, Yale; PhD, Northwestern) is professor of theater and dance at the University of California, San Diego. Her work is situated at the intersections of African American studies, gender studies, performance studies, theater history, and dance history. She is the author of *The Royalty of Negro Vaudeville: The Whitman Sisters and the Negotiation of Race, Gender, and Class in African American Theater, 1900–1940* and *Urban Bush Women: Twenty Years of Dance Theater, Community Engagement and Working It Out* as well as numerous articles on African American theater and dance. Her recent creative projects include directing Suzan-Lori Parks's *Topdog/Underdog*, adapting and directing *Anansi the Story King*, an original dance theater production of African American folk stories using college students, professionals, and fourth graders, and *Architectura*, a dance theater piece about the ways in which we build our lives. She currently serves as president of the Congress on Research in Dance (CORD).

William Given is a writer, photographer, filmmaker, and performer. He is currently a PhD candidate in the Department of Theatre and Dance at the University of California, San Diego, where his research focuses on the interplay between spectator and performer. His dissertation examines how illusionists created new performative spaces through the construction of hyperreal identities and the utilization of the new mediums of photography and film during the belle époque in Paris. William teaches writing, theater, and film at UC San Diego, and has also lectured at UC Irvine and the Washington Symposium on Magic History. He has written the articles "*Allegiance* and the Construction of a New American Musical" and "Reimagining Chekhov's Lost Work *Platonov*" for *TheatreForum*. As a dancer, William had the unique opportunity to study briefly with two of the originators of the Lindy Hop, Frankie Manning and Norma Miller.

Anita Gonzalez is professor of theater and drama at the University of Michigan. Her research and publication interests are in the fields of intercultural performance and ethnic studies, particularly the way in which performance reveals histories and identities in the Americas and in transnational contexts. Her books include a co-edited anthology with Tommy DeFrantz, *Black Performance Theory* (2014); *Afro-Mexico: Dancing between Myth and Reality* (2010); and *Jarocho's Soul: Cultural Identity and Afro-Mexican Dance* (2004). Other publications include articles about cruise ship culture ("Maritime Scenography and the Spectacle of Cruising," *Performance Research International*, 2013), utopia in urban bush women performance (*Modern Drama*, 2004), archetypes of African identity in Central America ("Mambo and the Maya," *Dance Research Journal*, 2004), and the pedagogy of teaching African American drama (*Theatre Topics*, 2009). Gonzalez is also a director who has staged more than fifty productions during the course of her career.

Neal Hebert is a PhD Candidate in theater history and historiography at Louisiana State University. He received his MA in philosophy in 2008, and has taught theater and philosophy at Louisiana State University while pursuing his PhD. Hebert is an experienced director, acting coach, and dramaturg, whose productions have been produced in academic, nonprofit, and for-profit theaters throughout Louisiana. His dissertation, *Professional Wrestling: Local Performance Tradition, Global Performance Praxis*, will be completed under the direction of Alan Sikes in December 2014. Hebert's work combines approaches from masculinity studies, performance studies, analytic philosophy, and theater historiography. A Louisiana native, Hebert received Louisiana State University's 2014 Dissertation Year Fellowship and was selected to receive one of the American Theatre and Drama Society's 2013 graduate student fellowships.

Amy Strahler Holzapfel is associate professor of theater at Williams College, where she teaches courses in theater history and literature, performance studies, and dramaturgy. Her principal research interests include nineteenth-century European theater, theater and visual culture, theater and science, dance-theater, and contemporary performance. Her monograph *Art, Vision, and Nineteenth-Century Realist Drama: Acts of Seeing* (2014) explores how modern theories of vision in art and science impacted the rise of the realist movement in theater. She has published articles in the journal *Contemporary Theatre Review, PAJ: A Journal of Performance and Art*, the *Journal of Dramatic Theory and Criticism, Modern Drama, and Theater*, and the anthology *Spatial Turns: Space, Place and Mobility in German Literary and Visual Culture* (2010). She received her MFA (2001) and DFA (2006) in dramaturgy and dramatic criticism from the Yale School of Drama and her BA from Brown University (1996). She is the recipient of a Fulbright Award, a Hellman Fellowship, a Lehman Fellowship from the Oakley Center for the Humanities and Social Sciences, and a Research Fellowship from the American Society of Theatre Research, as well as two honorable mentions for her published essays.

Odai Johnson is professor in theater history and head of the PhD program at the University of Washington School of Drama. He took his MFA from the University of Utah and his PhD from the University of Texas at Austin. His articles have appeared in *Theatre Journal, Theatre Survey, New England Theatre Journal, Theatre Symposium*, and the *Virginia Magazine of History* as well as in numerous anthologies. His books include *Rehearsing the Revolution* (1999), *The Colonial American Stage: A Documentary Calendar* (2001) and *Absence and Memory on the Colonial American Stage* (2005). He is currently finishing a work on classical theater, titled *Ruins*. Professor Johnson holds the Floyd and Delores Jones Endowed Professorship in the Arts.

Ketu H. Katrak (originally from Bombay) is professor in the Department of Drama at the University of California, Irvine (UCI). She was UCI's founding chair of the Department of Asian American Studies (2002). Katrak specializes in drama, dance, performance theory, postcolonial, Asian American and diasporic literature, third world women writers, and feminist theory. She is the author of *Contemporary Indian Dance: New Creative Choreography* *in India and the Diaspora* (2011), *Politics of the Female Body: Postcolonial Women Writers* (2006), and *Wole Soyinka and Modern Tragedy: A Study of Dramatic Theory and Practice* (1986). Her essays on South Asian American Literature and expressive arts (mainly on Indian dance) appear in journals such as *Amerasia* and *South Asian Popular Culture* among others. Katrak is the recipient of a Fulbright Research Award to India (2005–06); University of California, Humanities Research Institute Fellowship (2002); Bunting Fellowship (1988–89) (Harvard/Radcliffe), and other awards. Katrak is currently on the Fulbright Senior Specialist roster (2010–2015).

Petra Kuppers is a disability culture activist, a community performance artist, and professor of English, women's studies, art and design and theater. She also teaches on Goddard College's low residency MFA in interdisciplinary arts. She leads The Olimpias, a performance research collective (www.olimpias.org). Her books include *Disability and Contemporary Performance: Bodies on Edge* (2003), *The Scar of Visibility: Medical Performance and Contemporary Art* (2007) and *Community Performance: An Introduction* (2007). Edited work includes *Somatic Engagement* (2011), and *Community Performance: A Reader* (2007). Her *Disability Culture and Community Performance: Find a Strange and Twisted Shape* (2011, paperback 2013) explores The Olimpias's arts-based research methods and won the Biennial Sally Banes Prize by the American Society for Theatre Research. She is also the author of a new textbook for undergraduate classrooms, *Studying Disability Arts and Culture: An Introduction* (2014).

Esther Kim Lee is associate professor in the School of Theatre, Dance, and Performance Studies at the University of Maryland, College Park. She is the author of *A History of Asian American Theatre* (2006), which received the 2007 Award for Outstanding Book given by Association for Theatre in Higher Education and the editor of *Seven Contemporary Plays from the Korean Diaspora in the Americas* (2012). She was the editor of *Theatre Survey*, the flagship journal of the American Society for Theatre Research. She is currently working on a book project on the Chinese American playwright David Henry Hwang.

Daphne P. Lei is professor of drama at the University of California, Irvine. Her research and expertise include Chinese opera, intercultural performance, Asian American theater, and diasporic and postcolonial studies. She is the author of many articles and two books: *Operatic China: Staging Chinese Identity across the Pacific* (2006) and *Alternative Chinese Opera in the Age of Globalization: Performing Zero* (2011). She has also served on the editorial board of *Theatre Survey* and as an executive committee member of the American Society for Theatre Research. She is committed to diversity and multiculturalism in academia, and she founded Multicultural Spring (2007) and Dramatic Transformations (2012) at UCI for such purposes.

Erika T. Lin is an associate professor of English at George Mason University. She is the author of *Shakespeare and the Materiality of Performance*, which won the 2013 David Bevington Award for Best New Book in Early Drama Studies. She is currently working on a study of seasonal festivities and early modern commercial performance. In support of this project, she received a 2014–15 Andrew W. Mellon Long-Term Fellowship at the Folger Shakespeare Library.

Michael Lueger received his PhD from Tufts University in 2014. He has published articles on representations of women in Eugene O'Neill's short plays and on Jesuit drama. His current research centers on constructions of celebrity in nineteenth-century American theater. He holds a BA in English and theater from the College of the Holy Cross.

Kim Marra is professor of theater arts and American studies at the University of Iowa, where she is also affiliate faculty in the Department of Gender, Women's, and Sexuality Studies. Her books include *Strange Duets: Impresarios and Actresses in American Theatre, 1865–1914* (winner of the 2008 Joe A. Callaway Prize), and the co-edited volumes *Passing Performances: Queer Readings of Leading Players in American Theater History* (1998), its sequel *Staging Desire: Queer Readings of American Theater History* (2002), and *The Gay and Lesbian Theatrical Legacy: A Biographical Dictionary of Major Figures in American Stage History in the Pre-Stonewall Era* (2005). "Horseback Views: A Queer Hippological Performance," her autobiographical solo piece, appears in *Animal Acts: Performing Species Today* (2014). Her article about that performance as research, "Riding, Scarring, Knowing: A Queerly Embodied Performance Historiography," *Theatre Journal* 64, no. 4 (December 2012): 489–511, received the 2013 Outstanding Article Award from the Association for Theatre in Higher Education and the honorable mention for the Oscar G. Brockett Essay Prize from the American Society for Theatre Research.

Marianne McDonald, Distinguished Professor of Theatre and Classics at the University of California, San Diego, and a member of the Royal Irish Academy, is a pioneer in the field of modern versions of the classics in films, plays, and opera. She has translated all extant Greek tragedies and some comedies and has over 250 publications to her credit, including *Euripides in Cinema: The Heart Made Visible* (1983); *Ancient Sun, Modern Light: Greek Drama on the Modern Stage* (1992); *Sing Sorrow: Classics, History and Heroines in Opera* (2001); *The Living Art of Greek Tragedy* (2003); and *The Craft of Athol Fugard: Space Time and Silence* 2012); and edited with J. Michael Walton *Amid Our Troubles: Irish Versions of Greek Tragedies* (2002) and *The Cambridge Companion to Greek and Roman Theatre* (2007). Her nationally and internationally performed prize-winning translations and original plays include: Aeschylus's *Prometheus Bound*; Sophocles' *Antigone, Ajax, Oedipus Tyrannus*, and *Oedipus at Colonus*; Euripides' *Hecuba, Trojan Women, Iphigenia at Aulis, Bacchae, Phoenician Women*, and *Children of Heracles*; Seneca's *Thyestes*; Aristophanes's *Lysistrata*; *The Trojan Women*; *Medea, Queen of Colchester*; *The Ally Way*; . . .*and then he met a woodcutter; The Last Class; Fires in Heaven; A Taste for Blood*; and *Peace*.

Vida L. Midgelow, dance artist/academic, joined Middlesex University as professor in dance and choreographic practices in 2012. Prior to this position she was professor and director of research at University of Northampton, where, over many years, she established the taught programs in dance and performance studies and developed the postgraduate research provision.

Ray Miller is a professor in dance studies and theater arts in the Department of Theatre and Dance at Appalachian State University. In addition, he serves as the director for strategic initiatives for the College of Fine and Applied Arts. He has directed and choreographed productions for the Cincinnati Playhouse in the Park and the Octagon Musical Theatre in New York City. Since coming to ASU in 2005, he has directed and choreographed numerous productions including *The Fantasticks, The Exonerated, Metamorphoses, Stop Kiss*, and *The Trojan Women*, among others. As a scholar, he has served as president for the Congress on Research in Dance and has published in the areas of musical theater, dance dramaturgy, and dance pedagogy. Dr. Miller served on the editorial board and was a contributor to *Broadway: An Encyclopedia of Theater and American Culture* (2010) and collaborated with folk singer Doris Bazzini, who contributed music to a play Dr. Miller wrote on the tragic killing of students on the Kent State campus in 1970. His most recent publication is a chapter, "Tappin' Jazz Lines," in *Jazz Dance: A History of the Roots and Branches* (2014), edited by Lindsay Guarino and Wendy Oliver.

Krista K. Miranda is a PhD candidate (ABD) in performance studies at New York University. Her dissertation, "Queer-Cripping 'Whole': Performing the Variable Body," examines performances of embodiment on and off the stage that remap the body, its meanings, its taxonomies, and its possibilities to expose the network of forces that create the fantasy of the "whole" body and flesh out what is at stake when the body is revealed to be (always) partial. She was the recipient of the Congress on Research in Dance's "2010 Outstanding Graduate Research" award for her essay "Staring at the (Clitoral) Sun: Arousing Abjection in Ann Liv Young's *The Bagwell in Me*." Her prior graduate work includes an MA in humanities and social thought with a concentration in gender politics (New York University) and an MA in writing and publishing (Emerson College). Her research interests include theories of embodiment, queer and feminist theory, critical disability studies, psychoanalysis, dance studies, and performance art.

Michael J. Morris is an artist/scholar and PhD candidate in the Department of Dance at the Ohio State University, working in and between dance, performance studies, and sexuality studies. Morris has presented research at a number of national and international conferences, including the Congress on Research in Dance; the Society of Dance History Scholars; Queer Places, Practices, and Lives; Meanings and Makings of Queer Dance; Staging Sustainability: Arts Community Culture Environment; and the EcoSex Symposium II. Morris was a participant in the Mellon Dance Studies Summer Seminar at Stanford University in 2014. Morris's work has also been published in the *European Journal of Ecopsychology*. Morris teaches courses in writing about dance, dance history, yoga, butoh, modern dance, and ballet technique, and received the Writing Across the Curriculum Outstanding Writing Instruction Award at OSU in 2013. Morris studied butoh at the Kazuo Ohno Studio in Yokohama, Japan, and is certified in Labanotation through the Dance Notation Bureau in New York.

J. L. Murdoch earned her PhD at Bowling Green State University. Her dissertation received the Miesle Award for Outstanding Scholarship in Theatre and was the department nomination for the university-wide Distinguished Dissertation Award. She received a Fulbright fellowship to South Korea to conduct research on the folk masked dance-drama of Talchum. She has taught and presented in the Philippines, South Africa, South Korea, Jamaica, and the United States and has had work published in *Theatre Journal, Theatre Topics, The Arts in Psychotherapy*, and in the Fulbright Korea publications *Infusion* and *Review*. She is currently teaching at Yongsan International School of Seoul, where she is developing a theater program.

Maiya Murphy is an assistant professor in the Theatre Studies Programme at National University of Singapore's English Language and Literature department. Her research centers on physical theater, theories of the body, and cognitive science. In addition to contributing a chapter to *Collective Creation in Contemporary Performance* (Kathryn

Syssoyeva and Scott Proudfit, eds., 2013), Maiya has presented papers to the American Society for Theatre Research's working groups Practice as Research (2009), Cognitive Science in Theatre and Performance (2010 and 2013), and Working between Theater and Dance Studies (2012). Maiya also served as the founding administrative director for Naropa University's MFA theater program. She received her BA from Yale in theater studies with a concentration in performance, trained in Lecoq-based physical theater at the London International School for Performing Arts (LISPA), and received her PhD in theatre and drama at the University of California, San Diego, where she was a 2012–2013 UC President's Graduate Fellow.

Sally Ann Ness is professor of anthropology at University of California, Riverside. She has worked in urban provincial centers in the Philippines as well as in Indonesia and the United States. Her research has focused on various forms of symbolic action, both in the practice of everyday life and in extraordinary ritual and secular performances. She has written on the semiotics of festival life, dance, and sport, and on tourism development and its consequences for cultural practice and cultural identity. Her current research, funded in part by a 2006 Guggenheim Fellowship, focuses on choreographic aspects of visitor practice in Yosemite National Park, drawing in part on the work of Gregory Bateson and Charles S. Peirce to illuminate connections between place, embodiment, and movement.

Halifu Osumare is professor of African American and African studies at the University of California, Davis, and has been involved with dance and black popular culture internationally for over thirty years as a dancer, choreographer, teacher, administrator, and scholar. She holds an MA in dance ethnology and a PhD in American studies. She has been a 2008 Fulbright Scholar and has published two books: *The Africanist Aesthetic in Global Hip-Hop: Power Moves* (2007) and *The Hiplife in Ghana: West African Indigenization of Hip-Hop* (2012). Having taught and researched in Malawi, Kenya, Ghana, and Nigeria, her work has spanned traditional African performance and ritual to contemporary African American dance and performance.

Sandy Peterson is a PhD candidate in interdisciplinary theater studies at the University of Wisconsin-Madison. Her work focuses broadly on the relationship between politics, performance, and culture in the 20th and 21st centuries. Her dissertation examines the performance of contemporary American conservatism, and argues that conservative belief systems and identities are not only reified through performance, but that they become increasingly immoderate through repetition. She has presented her work at several national conferences, including the Association for Theatre in Higher Education, the American Society for Theatre Research, and the American Conference for Irish Studies. Peterson teaches Theatre for Cultural and Social Awareness at UW-Madison, and has taught practical and scholarly courses in theater at UW-Madison; the University of Nevada, Las Vegas (UNLV); and the College of Southern Nevada (CSN), and courses in women's studies at UNLV and CSN. In addition to her research, she is a practicing director, dramaturg, and producer and is a founding member of Our Initial Dissent, a local theater company dedicated to producing work that addresses racial and economic disparities in Dane County, Wisconsin. She has been a Mellon-Wisconsin Fellow and is currently a Chancellor's Fellow at UW-Madison.

Thomas Postlewait, a professor emeritus from Ohio State University, has also taught at Cornell University, MIT, University of Georgia, Indiana University, and University of

Washington. He served as president of the American Society for Theatre Research (1994–97). Between 1991 and 2014 he edited over forty books for the series Studies in Theatre History and Culture. His publications include *Prophet of the New Drama: William Archer and the Ibsen Campaign* (1986) and *The Cambridge Introduction to Theatre Historiography* (2008). He co-edited *Interpreting the Theatrical Past* (1989), *Theatricality* (2003), and *Representing the Past: Essays in Performance Historiography* (2009). He also contributed to *The Cambridge History of American Theatre* (1999), *The Cambridge History of British Theatre* (2004), and the *Oxford Handbook of Early Modern Theatre* (2009). Forthcoming is his edition of *The Correspondence of Bernard Shaw and William Archer* (2015).

VK Preston is a postdoctoral Social Sciences and Humanities Research Council (SSHRC) fellow at McGill University's Institute for the Public Life of the Arts and Ideas. She is a graduate of Stanford University's Department of Theatre and Performance Studies, and she works in collaboration with the Sense Lab's research project Immediations. She comes to scholarship on baroque and contemporary performance through dance, theater, and visual performance practices. Her article with Alanna Thain, "Tendering the Flesh: the ABCs of Dave St-Pierre's Contemporary Utopias," won the 2013 Canadian Association of Theatre Research's Richard Plant Award for best article. She joins Brown University's Theatre Arts and Performance Studies department as a visiting assistant professor in 2015–16.

Jade Y. Power Sotomayor Jade is a code-switching, hyphen-jumping, border-crossing, Cali-Rican educator, dancer, actor, and scholar of performance who engages embodied practices of remembering and creating community as a lens for theorizing performative constructions of *Latinidad*. She has a Master's degree in Latin American studies and a PhD in theater from the University of California, San Diego. Her research focuses on epistemologies of the body, the intersections between race, gender and language, and on the intercultural dance practices of Chicana/os and members of the Latin Caribbean diaspora. Her work has been published in *e-misférica*, *Latin American Theatre Review*, and *Gestos*. She also has performed with and codirected the San Diego–based Puerto Rican *bomba* group *Areito Borincano* since 2005 (*Bomba Liberté* since 2011) and has performed and collaborated with the all women's *bomba* group *Bomberas de la Bahia* since 2008.

Marlis Schweitzer is associate professor in the Department of Theatre at York University. She is the author of *When Broadway Was the Runway: Theater, Fashion and American Culture* (2009), and *Transatlantic Broadway: The Infrastructural Politics of Global Performance* (2015) and co-editor with Joanne Zerdy of *Performing Objects and Theatrical Things* (2014). Marlis's work has appeared in a range of scholarly journals including *Theatre Journal*, *Theatre Survey*, *Theatre Research International*, *TDR*, *Performance Research*, *Canadian Theatre Review*, *Theatre Research in Canada*, and the *Journal of American Drama and Theatre*. She is the general editor of *Theatre Research in Canada/Recherches théâtrales au Canada*. The research represented in her essay was made possible by a SSHRC Insight Grant from the Social Sciences and Humanities Council of Canada.

E. J. Westlake is an associate professor of theater and drama and associate professor of English language and literatures at the University of Michigan. She is the author of *Our Land Is Made of Courage and Glory: Nationalist Performance in Nicaragua and Guatemala* (2005) and co-editor of *Political Performances: Theory and Practice* (2009). She is working on a book-length study and new translation of *El Güegüence*, the national dance drama of Nicaragua. Her research focuses on performance in the Americas, including nationalist drama, public art, community-based theater, pedagogy, and the interplay between public identity, political discourse, and performance narrative. Westlake's articles have appeared in *Theatre Annual, Latin American Theatre Review, TDR*, and *Youth Theatre Journal*. Chapters have appeared in Lengel and Warren's *Casting Gender* (2005), Bial and Magelssen's *Theatre Historiography: Critical Questions* (2010), and Haedicke and Nellhaus' *Performing Democracy* (2001). She volunteers her services as peer reviewer for *Modern Drama* and serves on the editorial board of *Youth Theatre Journal*. She is also the book review editor for *Theatre Annual*.

Stacy Wolf is professor of theater and director of the Princeton Arts Fellows in the Lewis Center for the Arts at Princeton University. She is the author of *Changed for Good: A Feminist History of the Broadway Musical* (2011) and *A Problem Like Maria: Gender and Sexuality in the American Musical* (2002) and the co-editor of *The Oxford Handbook of the American Musical* (with Raymond Knapp and Mitchell Morris, 2011).

Praise Zenenga holds an interdisciplinary PhD in theater and drama from Northwestern University and is an associate professor in the Africana Studies Program at the University of Arizona. He teaches courses on the history, politics, and aesthetics of Pan-African theater, drama, and dance. His research and teaching focus on interdisciplinary approaches to understanding issues of identity, race, social change, and social justice in the literature and performance of Africa and African diaspora communities. He has published more than a dozen journal articles and book chapters on masculinities, identities, censorship, avant-gardism, political expression, and modes of protest in Zimbabwean theater, dance, sport, and everyday life performance. He recently completed a book monograph on contemporary popular theater in Zimbabwe focusing on the relationship between artists, donors, and the state. He has also delivered papers at scholarly gatherings and has been invited to present guest lectures at campuses across the nation on various aspects of African and diaspora theater, dance, and performance.

ABOUT THE COMPANION WEBSITE

www.oup.com/us/ohdt

Oxford has created a website to accompany *The Oxford Handbook of Dance and Theater*. Material, like video clips and website links, that cannot be made available in a book is provided here. The reader is encouraged to consult this resource in conjunction the chapters. Examples available online are indicated in the text with Oxford's symbol ⏵.

THE OXFORD HANDBOOK OF

DANCE AND THEATER

CHAPTER 1

....

MAGNETIC FIELDS
Too Dance for Theater, Too Theater for Dance

....

NADINE GEORGE-GRAVES

In 2011, the English theater company Punchdrunk's production of *Sleep No More* caused much sturm and drang over the genre to which this breathless performance belonged. Requiring audience members to wear masks and follow the action (sometimes at break-neck speeds) in a choose-your-own-adventure tour through *Macbeth* set in a fictitious hotel, the performance was simultaneously dance, theater, site-specific installation art, and architectural meditation. The performers worked very hard for us, dancing and emoting this loose adaptation of a classic story. We audience members dutifully made room so that they could move, though occasionally we came into contact with their sweating, panting bodies. They, oblivious to us (for the most part), silently (for the most part), maintained the fourth wall even as we voyeuristically occupied the playing spaces. Occasionally, an audience member became a part of the actual action and world of the performance (helping to lift the dead body of Lady Macduff for example) but we were always an embodied part of any given audience members' experience (as obstacles, co-sojourners, new characters). The narrative relied on our Shakespearean cultural literacy—Lady Macbeth pushes her husband to murder the king and others with rightful claims to the throne so he can become king, then they both feel very guilty, seeing daggers and ghosts and such. There were three witches who make Macbeth think he is destined for greatness only to have him meet his doom in the end. Lady Macbeth kills herself, and Macbeth is killed in battle. Arguably, not even this much detail was necessary for *Sleep No More*. Instead, Punchdrunk created a consuming, encompassing experience for the audience members, asking us to commit with our bodies to the journey of the performance, believing that there would be an end to the labyrinth and we could feel free to make of the experience what we would.

This is an important contemporary example of the meeting of dance and theater that sparks a provocative new aesthetic. Choreographer Maxine Doyle called the production "a theater show with a dance company in the middle"[1] Seventeen of the twenty performers had dance training and all summoned intense expressionist passion. The play text clearly informed the movement choices:

> In one of the most powerful duets of the show, Lady Macbeth persuades her husband to murder the king. Ms. Doyle worked with the dancers to examine Shakespeare's text, in terms of its rhythm and imperative quality, to gain a sense of its energy. Anatomically, she relied on the mechanics of opposition: pushing and pulling.[2]

And it comes through in performance. Even if one does not have command of the text, the poetry of the movement echoes the poetry of the text. The danger of the performance lies not only in the seemingly precarious (though undoubtedly meticulously controlled) thrashing about of passionate characters, but also in the liberties taken with traditional definitions of the "pure" genres of dance and theater.

Though I value my affective response to the experience, appreciate the labor involved, was pushed to consider not only the story but also qualities such as greed, passion, and personal space, and though I quite liked the performances, I was and am baffled by the continued interest in how to define this kind of performance. There have been a number of examples of immersive, embodied, theatrical dance/movement pieces since the late twentieth century (De La Guarda's *Learn to Fly, Fuerza Bruta, The Donkey Show*, and *Here Lies Love*, to name a few). So why do we still marvel at genre/genus? Is it because we have yet to find a pithy label and we need classifications and categories to contain and comprehend?

These conversations around genre echo responses to Susan Stroman's work for the 1999 production of *Contact*. Stroman, who worked with playwright John Weidman, created three pieces to make up a largely wordless evening about the ups and downs of heteronormative love. The first piece has Jean-Honoré Fragonard's lovers from the painting "The Swing" captured midswing and brought to life in a display of acrobatic lovemaking. In the second, a stereotypical 1950s-era housewife fantasizes about a more passionate life. And in the final piece, a contemporary middle-aged middle manager in midlife crisis is "rescued" by a blond bombshell who can swing dance.

Though *Contact* is referred to as a "dance play," this label seems inadequate. On the surface, the cognitive disconnect for viewers and reviewers lay in the fact that these pieces were dramatic (i.e., there were characters, plots, narrative arcs, conflict, rising tension, denouement, etc.) They had other elements of a traditional play (costumes, representative sets and props, lighting that aided in telling the stories). They had stories (not requisite in contemporary dance). They were also theatrical: The performers/characters accessed and made manifest heightened emotional and affective responses to the situations in an acting style that was more like method acting (the style most contemporary Western audience members are used to from television, movies, and theater) than the emotive styles of ballet, opera, musicals, or contemporary dance (which might be thought of as nonemotive or antiemotive).[3] What the pieces lacked, for the most part, were words—ironic for a dance *play*. Indeed, silent method acting and virtuosic dancing in a variety of styles made *Contact* stand out. What the show had that does not exist in a traditional play, for the most part, was dance. The substitution of orality with corporeality was the signal difference. Story ballet has always done this but is perhaps too staid with its traditional "highbrow" technique or too steeped in a certain acting style to be of interest in the way that contemporary dance is experimenting with theatricality, presence, and embodiment.

These experiments are perhaps most obvious in contemporary dance theater with the work of more comfortably defined and labeled aesthetics like tanztheater, contemporary dance, performance art, and butoh and even with outliers like Elizabeth Streb or Ann Liv Young. Artists from the late twentieth century up until today have called our attention to the body and the affective power of performance in new ways. But the term "dance theater" does not completely help our understanding (with or without a hyphen and even though every new company seems to attach itself to that label). The contemporary aesthetic dance theater, with its varied examples, is just one manifestation of the intersection between dance and theater. "Dance theater" is inadequate at defining all of the ways in which dance and theater meet.[4]

Though dance theater is arguably more a subgenre of dance than theater, contemporary theater artists are also interested in heightened physicality in performance. Physical theater techniques are well established (biomechanics, Grotowski, viewpoints, Lecoq, Suzuki, and others), and theater artists have pushed the boundaries of physical meaning for some time now (Robert Wilson, Annie Sprinkle, The Wooster Group, Barbara Ann Teer, Guillermo Gomez Peña, Coco Fusco, Elevator Repair Service, Ntozake Shange, Goat Island).

The genre buzz around contemporary performance may lead one to believe that this is a historic moment of convergence between theater and dance. (Indeed, aesthetic experimentation, notably with the use of new media technology, is advancing a liberating freedom from labels for contemporary artists.) And though we pick up the conversation at a contemporary moment with a focus mainly on Western stage performance, opening the lens and stepping back allows us to recognize that dance and theater have met in many important ways historically and globally. Indeed, there are aesthetics that not only resist the separation between dance and theater but also never accepted it.

In my own research in African American performance, I've found that most examples blur the lines between performative genres. For a people rooted in diasporic African traditions, historically denied written literacy, forced to dissemble and signify to preserve the archive and the repertoire of culture, there is little surprise that these aesthetics resist discrete boundaries. For example, focusing on gender, I have written about Negro vaudeville as a discursive site where theater, dance, comedy, music, etc., came together to imagine a new black subjectivity. I have also written about the contemporary dance theater company Urban Bush Women and the ways in which the choreography "works" elements like blended dance styles, narrative, and spirituality to work through social issues and engage communities. My work on black performance theory and subjectivity is firmly rooted in and spidered out from the body.

Indeed, all of the performance that interests me as a scholar and artist take on the mix of theater and dance. This has not always meant a smooth navigation of the profession, and I have often felt too theater for dance and too dance for theater.[5] And for all the academy's talk of interdisciplinarity, the persistent resistance against more synergies between the fields of theater and dance are vexing. We should even trouble this conversation—is this interdisciplinarity or disciplinarity? Dance and theater are both embodied performing arts, natural bedfellows, with many genres that straddle the lines between the two forms. There are many departments of theater and dance, though the scholarly fields too seldom communicate. But in my fields of interest I've found many sites of convergence.

So I was thrilled when in 2008 Ric Knowles, then vice president for the American Society for Theater Research (ASTR), approached me to chair a joint conference with the Congress on Research in Dance (CORD) in 2010. Then he asked me to find someone on "the dance side" to co-convene. I sighed a bit, though I understood the impulse. My degree is in theater and drama. I am hired in the theater PhD area of a theater and dance department. Nevertheless, I was reminded once more of the disciplinary boundaries that we create and navigate. I have always attended both theater and dance conferences, and depending on funding and timing (ASTR's and CORD's are often on the same weekend) some years I have had to choose. So when Ric asked me, I said yes immediately and admittedly selfishly, not just to save on conference fees but also to have the opportunity for these two fields to be in more direct conversation with each other particularly around issues of corporeality and the negotiations of power—issues that have always been central to my interests and, judging from the response to the proposal, of interest to others as well.

Working with Anthea Kraut, a scholar whose work also troubles disciplines, to develop the program further pushed my thinking about the liminal space between theater and dance and the affective relationship between corporeal power and discursive subjectivity. We had a record number of proposals from grad students, artists, and junior and senior faculty from diverse geographical locations including the United States, the United Kingdom, Canada, Australia, Japan, South Africa, Brazil, and Singapore. We had a range of home departments—not only dance, theater, and performance studies but also anthropology, English, music, etc.

We were blessed with a great program committee that took on the task of blind-vetting more quality proposals than we had anticipated. In the end, the committee's selections reflected an exciting range. Panel presentations featured an array of topics—from spectatorship in the seventeenth-century French theater, to early twentieth-century Cuban dance academies, to Chilean military parades, to the labor of Michael Jackson—while working sessions mapped the relationships between theater and dance, considered the performance of violence, and explored the theories and practices of specific aesthetics. Over the four days of the conference, we heard about a host of bodies—individual and collective, absent and present, mediated and live, on stage and off—that are both resistant to and complicit with the workings of power.

We pushed the proof in the pudding of embodied knowledge by encouraging performative presentations beyond the typical conference lecture format. These were not evening dance performances meant as entertainment after a long day of thinking. These were presentations advancing knowledge through performance. Not new to CORD but newer to ASTR, these panels aimed to further arguments that gestures are rhetorical and movement epistemological. Surprisingly, this intersectional conference attracted a greater number of attendees than the sum of what the separate conferences typically attract, which further encouraged my interest in this nexus. Beyond interesting synergies, it became clear to me that focusing on the interstices and overlaps between theater and dance afforded critical insight into not only performance history, theory, epistemology, historiography, and ontology but also the humanities, social sciences, and the arts. I was inspired.

In 2011 I began the process of proposing this book project. In 2012 Susan Manning, a mentor and leading dance scholar, and I convened a working session at the ASTR conference on working between theater studies and dance studies. (We convened the group again in 2014 and hopefully every other year going forward.) In 2013 I taught a graduate seminar on the topic. Also in 2013 I was invited to attend the Mellon Summer Dance Seminar (held that year at Brown) as a senior scholar to work with the next generation of dance scholars and speak on the "Beside Dance Studies Roundtable." In 2014 I directed/choreographed *Architectura*, a dance theater piece about architecture, home, longing, loss, leaving, support, structure, and the ways in which the buildings we build help define who we are. Working with artists in this way drove home both the practicalities and the philosophies behind these genres. Finding artists who could give to this kind of creative process across lines was important. As was the language on grant applications, programs, and promotional materials. But most important was the access to ideas around my theme that was afforded by this perspective. In other words, neither theater nor dance alone was adequate for my exploration, and only at the nexus could we begin to make discoveries. As an artist and a scholar I am provoked by the possibilities for the arts and humanities at these interstices.

And now as I finish editing this volume of insightful and provocative essays on the intersections of dance and theater and am in my second year as president of CORD, I hope to continue to investigate the territories of these boundaries while strengthening institutional ties. I build on the work of many important scholars in this and related fields (Susan Manning, Susan Foster, Ann Cooper Albright, Selma Jeanne Cohen, Helen Thomas, and many others) and I hope to advance interest in exploring and defining the contours of these associations.

The Oxford Handbook of Dance and Theater collects a critical mass of border-crossing scholarship toward the goal of erasing many of the lines of demarcation between the two fields and encouraging less respect in the future for historical disciplinary boundaries. In foregrounding the politics and poetics of moving bodies, and by focusing on performative embodiment as a negotiation of power dynamics, this book hopes both to widen the horizons of scholarship in the performing arts and to move the fields of dance and theater closer together. This undertaking promises to challenge the two disciplines to take a closer look at the histories, theories, and practices of physical performance.

Taking corporeality as an idea that unites the work of dance and theater scholars, these essays focus on the moving body in performance and examine how this energy has worked on, through, and with bodies throughout history. Contemporary stage performances have sparked global interest in new experiments between dance and theater, and this volume situates this interest in its historical context by extensively investigating other such moments from early modern England to Bolshevik Russia to contemporary flash mobs.

This volume bids to define an emerging field. Scholars of theater and scholars of dance worked for most of the twentieth century in isolation from each other, developing different theories and analytical methodologies. For the past few years, however, we have begun to identify and explore common ground and to develop common methodologies that enrich each field. The scope of this work (the book and companion website) hopes to establish this research field and lay out its salient dialogues.

There are a number of theoretical implications for working between theater and dance, many of which are taken up in the essays to follow. I want to take a moment here to unpack a few that impact all of the work in this volume. Specifically, it becomes clear that new insight is gained into theories of embodiment and theatricality by attending to performances (on and off stage, professional, personal, social, or cultural) that are at the nexus of theater and dance.

What does it mean to be embodied, to be "in your body," to be aware (or hyperaware) of your body's movement in time and space and to exert corporeal energy or power (work over time) for an aesthetic end? The same question goes for witnessing another body moving to such ends. This cuts to the core of embodied performance practices. We move in everyday life for survival-based objectives—I get out of bed in the morning because I am hungry. I move to take a shower to remain socially acceptable and I drive to work to earn a paycheck to buy food and shelter. Hopefully, my activities bring me great happiness and I am surrounded by loved ones to share in this joy and I move in order to achieve the desired level of happiness for me and my loved ones. Then why do we move for reasons other than those? Why do we dance, for example?[6] Why do you dance? Why don't you dance more? Why are you interested in dance—at least enough to read this far? And why do we make pretend? Why embody an other—either a specific character or a distinctly human emotion that we are pretending to feel? Why try out other circumstances? And why do we watch others dance and make pretend, sometimes spending money that could be used for survival? Audience members commit their bodies and attentions for a period of time in order to be "enriched" by art—enriched beyond basic survival.

As evidenced by their longevity, these different ways of being in our bodies and movement for reasons other than survival are important. Dance and theater artists experiment with bodily presence, absence, and perception. Our phenomenological human experience of the world is made manifest corporeally and, as Drew Leder explains, our bodily presence is essentially characterized by absence. In other words, one is usually unaware of one's body even as it is the most important thing in one's life. "That is, one's own body is rarely the thematic object of experience."[7] Except in dance.[8] Even in something like sports, another non-survival-based movement genre, attention is usually more on the opponent or target than on embodiment. And in sports spectatorship there is usually a goal of "winning" that holds our attention. In dance, attention is "moved" to the body. In everyday life the body tends to recede from direct experience. In dance and theater (other than staged readings to some extent), the body is part and parcel of direct experience. There are activities such as exercise, yoga, or getting back to nature, for example, that (perhaps as reactions to the more disembodied lifestyles of advanced economies) have us focus on the body, but these activities rarely involve an audience.

Dance and theater serve as correctives to the Cartesian emphasis on "cogito" experience, advancing embodied knowledge that is not easily explained in a Cartesian paradigm of disembodied reason. And moments when these two ways of knowing are more closely aligned call on us to pay even more attention. Theater and dance remind us that the human body is not just another physical object but (after Husserl, Merleau-Ponty, Noë, Lakoff, and other philosophers and cognitive scientists) the mechanism by which the world is made manifest and, indeed, existent. If the distinction between perception and movement is an artificial divide of what is always united in lived experience[9] then dance and theater afford us perhaps a more direct access to knowledge than is usually recognized. Intentionality in movement (as complicated as it is), for example, takes a different shape in performance. As do motivation, organization, and the means to ends. If we push the heresy and rely on Merleau-Ponty and Leder's assertions that consciousness is a matter of doing rather than thinking we might argue that "I can therefore I am"—I can walk, speak, gesture, etc.[10] Even if I can't (walk, speak, gesture), I can do something (breathe, think, feel) or I would not be alive. Leder borrows from Heidegger in employing the term "ecstasis" to describe the operation of the lived body. This ecstatic body "stands" "out" from a determinate stance that locates and defines. "But the very nature of the body is to project outward from its place of standing."[11] Paradoxically for Leder this happens by disappearance and absence. Again, one is unaware of most of the action of one's body, and dance and theater more acutely call these actions forth. Raising an arm in dance and theater is no benign action as it might be in everyday life and we (artists and audience members) are asked to consider the significance of raising an arm in this particular way.

Not all ways of being in the world face this tension. Various ethics of humanist philosophy recognize the epistemological importance of embodiment especially in terms of social ontology and intersubjectivity (Ubuntu, Confucianism, meditation practices). And different intellectual fields recognize (or are beginning to recognize) not only the mind-body connection but also the importance of the body for their inquiries (e.g., psychology, cognitive science, neuroscience, "traditional" medicine). Indeed, one gets the sense that those with a better sense of embodiment are better off medically, socially, intellectually, and spiritually.

Why then are theater studies and dance studies (fields that directly engage embodiment) still so suspect in the academy in terms of the epistemological insight they have to offer? Why are dance and theater as humanities and social sciences as well as arts such a difficult sell? I believe it is because there is something dangerous and destabilizing in the work that happens here. Perhaps it revolves around the myth of certainty and absolute truths in the sciences and the acknowledgment of contingency and persuasion in the arts. The arts disrespect, trouble, shift, and challenge absolute meaning—sometimes in serious ways and sometimes in playful, snarky, or irreverent ways. Artists have the power to manipulate feeling, empathy, memory, happiness, and pain—perhaps sincerely, perhaps as a ruse. As Amy Cook argues here, the "pretend play frame allows for a wider range of beings." And the bringing together of theater and dance is even more threatening to academic hegemonic knowledge structures (perhaps this is the root of the genre angst discussed above as well as the difficult tenure paths for those who teach in theater or dance departments at Research 1 universities in the United States). But this coming together is also a unique and uniquely important lens through which we can analyze a host of subjects—many of which are detailed here. Ultimately, theater and dance get at experience, perception, and knowledge in significant bodily ways.

Like embodiment, insight is gained into the concept of theatricality when we focus our lenses on the crossroads of dance and theater. Theatricality has become a principal theory in performance studies though it impacts many other disciplines. And though definitions of theatricality differ, we can point to many of the tenets at play to investigate how the kinds of performances that concern us here use and are influenced by notions of theatricality. At the heart of the crossing of theater and dance is an awareness of and manipulation of theatricality.

The introduction to Tracy C. Davis and Thomas Postlewait's influential collection of essays, *Theatricality*, provides a guiding primer on the concept, and it is from here that we can theorize the concepts' usefulness in examining dance/theater. They provide a genealogy of the term and theories behind it and argue that "the concept is comprehensive of all meanings yet empty of all specific sense."[12] In some regards the same could be said of performance between dance and theater. Indeed, the resistance of simple definition is part of the appeal of much of this work. In the video *European Dance Theater*, for example, many of the artists interviewed struggle to define their aesthetics acknowledging both attraction and resistance to the term "tanztheater." The "heightened states when everyday reality is exceeded by its representation,"[13] one of the many definitions proffered by Davis and Postlewait, is particularly useful in thinking about the intersection between dance and theater. Though I take issue with some of the moves of this introduction to assert a purer form of theater, I do agree that, despite the protean nature of the term "theatricality," we should aim to be as specific as possible. This volume aims to answer this call.

I agree because I think the stakes are very high. Rooted in a Christian suspicion/fear of the body, antitheatricalism as a sentiment is still quite pervasive in modern ideology. The paradox of the lies that get at truth (perhaps making the false seem true), the emptiness and fullness of the theatrical, and the unruliness of the body that does not always adhere to the dictates of reason get at the source of the wariness as well as the epistemological well-spring. Aligned with a general suspicion of the embodied arts in the academy and a general anti-intellectualism in the performing arts (and sometimes in the academy, paradoxically), we still need to argue for these conversations to be taken seriously.

The many definitions and competing meanings of theatricality are well rehearsed and I will not exhaust the discussion here. What is most salient is to assert that when theatricality is deployed corporeally and choreographically there are important affective relationships created, the significance of which is explored in this volume. Theatricality can be the essence of the form of theater used on or off stage. It can be a metaphor for interpreting human behavior. It can be a constellation of signs and significations. It can be an indistinct floating signifier (after Fisher-Lichte) but it is not void. It is resource. It is a wake-up call. Artists and social actors use it for a host of reasons, and attending to the specificity of different uses is at the heart of this project. Every age has a different idea of what "lifelike" performance is (and, we might say, what theatricality is). So theatricality depends on perception, not just intention. It is located both on the stage and in the perceiver as well as in the situation and ethos of the generation. A literacy among participants and/or audience members is implied, as well as a legibility on the part of the performance. And this relationship is necessarily raced, gendered, and classed. This relationship gets "worked" in different ways at different times in different genres.

In instantiations as culturally diverse as dance theater, tanztheater, musical theater, butoh, viewpoints, Kabuki, African total theater, performance art, Chinese Opera, state-sponsored mass political spectacle, popular political protest, court performances, ritual, staged ritual, staged social dance, early twentieth-century "isms" (expressionism, dadism, futurism, etc.), modern dance, postmodern dance, choreomania, gay pride parades, flash mobs, circus performance, Korean Talchum, Nazi movement choirs, explicit body performance, story ballet, early modern alchemic theater, hip-hop, clowning, krumping, and turfing, (to name a but a few), there exists this heightened state, this heightened awareness of embodiment, this heightened theatricality, but there is also an uncanniness between stage and life, even in the most abstract pieces. They are simultaneously lifelike, not lifelike, but not not lifelike. And in that uncanniness where is subjectivity? As Marvin Carlson deftly articulates what we know to be true, performances are haunted by prior performances. But performances are also haunted by life, and the ghosting destabilizes what we know of history, relationships, physics, etc. Are these performances the topsy-turvy type that restores order or the type that leads to revolution? This suspicion and threat relies on an assumption that there is any selfhood other than performed selfhood—performed with many layers visible differently in different situations perhaps, but performed nonetheless. As Davis and Postlewait say, "this defense of an inner sanctum of identity and sincerity is a dubious proposition."[14] I exist because I can and (not *or*) I exist because others exist. Dance and theater teach us this acutely.

For example, writing about Pina Bausch, Susan Manning examines the trope of discarded costumes in her work:

Discarded costumes often appear among the stage debris. In fact, constant costume changes mark the performers' shifting roles, suggesting that the performers' roles are like costumes to be put on and taken off at will. The performers often dress and undress onstage, frequently assisted by one another. Even when they change offstage, they often reenter still adjusting their undergarments, zipping their last zipper, or buttoning their last button. At times the performers, usually the women, are forced into layers and layers of costumes.[15]

A straightforward metaphor perhaps, but the idea of the shifting roles we each play and the interest in fluid identity is inextricably linked to ontology. Of course Bausch is not the only artist to explore this, nor do all dancers/performers explore identity this way, but the uncanny ghosting of identity is part and parcel of the embodiment and theatricality of dance/theater. And in this ontological turn, the stakes revealed are the most vital.

Organization of the Book

I've discussed a few possible genres and theories that this work engages. The project of this volume is to unpack these and other sites and theorize on the significance of this nodality. The book is organized into ten miniconversations of four or five chapters within the broader conversation at the meeting of dance and theater. Many of these chapters could fit into other conversations, and I invite the reader to rearrange them into such dialogues.

The first section is a conversation about theory and practice, oftentimes odd adversaries in theater and dance studies. Here we take on those who would advocate the rigid separation between theory and practice. Many of us even argue that the two have never been separated—indeed cannot be. Do we gain more insight by reading about or by doing? Is there a way to do both? How do we theorize practice and practice our theories? Is the divide more pronounced in dance than theater? This section (and the entire volume) pushes for a more nuanced understanding of theory and practice in the embodied arts beyond an antagonistic binary. The very definitions of theory and practice and the relationships between the two are challenged. The assumptions, arguments, and methodologies in the five chapters in this section demonstrate the tenuousness and flexibility of the binary set-up. Ann Cooper Albright opens the book, taking on corporeality as the wellspring for creativity by examining the move from the interior life of identity to the focus on bodily training practices. Anita Gonzalez looks at the ways in which two neighboring communities of working-class citizens in two different case studies negotiate shifting relationships through "theatrical dance and dancing theatrics." Though this essay could fit neatly into the biopolitics discussion, it appears here because of the significant way she theorizes these practices, especially around notions of presence, identity, dialogic performance, and race. VK Preston takes us into her process as a scholar in an early modern ballet archive working with a material artifact, attempting to access the 1582 *Balet comique de la Royne* by Balthazar de Beaujoyeulx. One comes to understand the distance not just in terms of the years between his hands writing the manuscript and hers turning pages to read it but also in terms of their understanding of not only dance, theater, and choreography/staging but also what is valuable in terms of the recording of process and product. Why the rich details about staged flora and fauna but fewer about movement? What results is an understanding of a kind of sorcery that enchants until today. Ray Miller discusses the history and importance of the role of the dance dramaturg in the creation of performance. Even though it is a burgeoning field, dance dramaturgy already has developed guiding tenets and multiple proven techniques. These practices provide productive sites for interrogating the communicative power of bodies in performance, the aesthetic possibilities for reworking genres and the relationships possible between the moving body and the spoken word. Miller is careful to lay out the points of divergence and well as the points of convergence between theater dramaturgy and dance dramaturgy and he lays out the most salient issues in the profession. Ultimately, his attention to detail on a number of fronts sets the stage for future scholarship. Vida L. Midgelow brings us into her process as an artist/scholar. This performative paper IS theory in practice as she stages a dialogue between her self qua dancer and her self qua practice. She works somatically, and her process dovetails with later conversations on affect, somatics, and cognition, but ultimately she is giving us insight into how the body experiences and knows by doing. This practice IS research—an important burgeoning idea in the academy. Midgelow gives us an important example of how this works despite naysayers. The essays in this section also set up our conversation as located on the stage, outside, in communities, in the archive, in the studio, in the mind, and, of course, in the body.

The next discussion is divided into two sections looking at genus and takes on some on the many genres that cut across dance and theater. First, Maiya Murphy lays out the genealogies of the simultaneous developments of contemporary physical theater practices and techniques of postmodern dance from the mid-twentieth century to today and makes aesthetic links between the two forms highlighting their shared cultural and historical influences. Stacy Wolf and Liza Gennaro take on seemingly the most obvious genre in our discussion, musical theater, but their examination lends new insight particularly in terms of the varied and variable functions in the relationship between dance and the text and the many ways in which dance has "served" the musical and gets at meaning in a way not available to the score, lyrics, dialogue, design, etc. Colleen Dunagan takes us in a perhaps unexpected but exciting direction by looking at the implications for theatricality, liveness, spectacle, and social identity from dance in popular television (reality shows, primetime hits, and commercials) and extends her analysis to ontological proportions. Susan Leigh Foster pushes the "usual suspects" of dance analysis even further by examining flash mobs and dance mobs, Internet culture, public spaces, spectacle, politics, ethics, and consumer capitalism.

The second part of the Genus section takes a more global approach, though many of the other chapters in the book are international, intercultural, and transnational. By no means am I arguing that these examples are totally representative of national zeitgeists. Rather, I find it interesting to examine aesthetic choices from this worldly perspective. Royd Climenhaga looks at German tanztheater icon Pina Bausch and the ways in which her work challenges notions of presence, expression, drama, obstacle, individuality, and the "convenient boundaries between dance and theater [that] are collapsed at the site of the performer's body." Praise Zenenga shows us that in African total theater performative elements (theater, music, dance, etc.) are always already integrated in a complex aesthetic matrix and theorizes the key elements of total theater and the conscious decision on the part of African artists to resist the separation and hierarchization of these elements. He pushes the definition of theater itself and highlights the attention necessary to understand the dynamics of the history of these practices and values. Jane Baldwin looks at Jean Gascon's work that traverses not only theater and dance but also French Canada and English Canada. She shows how the quest for unity in a national theater is borne acutely on the body of the performer by giving us the history of this important artist. Marianne McDonald navigates time and aesthetics by tracing not only the importance of dance in ancient Greek drama but also how Martha Graham and Ariane Mnouchkine adapt ancient texts with uniquely modernist takes on the body.

The next section takes on historiography at the site of theater and dance. These articles are more than essays on figures or events of the past. Beyond that, these articles investigate the implications of history-making and the ways in which we remember and re-member the past. Ketu H. Katrak looks at the female Indian performance group of artist/scholars The Post Natyam Collective and the work *Sunoh! Tell Me Sister* and studies the work the collective does in creatively recreating the past of mid-eighteenth-century South Asian courtesans and linking that history to contemporary South Asian women in domestic violence situations through movement, script, and multimedia. This mash-up of past and present mirroring the fragmented history provides rich terrain for drawing conclusions about memory, morality, training, emotion, and stereotypes and ultimately leads to engaging communities and raising awareness about social injustice. Odai Johnson looks at the resistance of paganism in the face of early Christian eradication as a performative embodiment of identity and as a dancerly resistance. As the Christian order swept the land, pagan culture located in dancer's bodies proved more difficult to destroy than temples, statues, books, and idols. In this new look at the relationship between the archive and the repertoire, Johnson examines the power dynamics of performances and the survival of mimes in late antiquity despite the association with heathenism. Erika T. Lin sets the stage for the historiographical implications of theater and dance in early modern performance by examining the transformation of hobbyhorse and morris dances from social contexts to the professional stage. She looks at the theaters of Shakespeare and his contemporaries to get at these complex meanings. Touching on the alchemical and transformative discussed in Preston's chapter, Lin points to the transgressive sexuality possible in festive mirth through transformative onstage performance in *The Witch of Edmonton*. The morris becomes a mechanism for queer eroticism and licensed licentiousness made manifest onstage though seeping into everyday life. Esther Kim Lee participates in recuperative analytic history and writes a wrongfully neglected important figure in dance and theater back into the archive by detailing and contextualizing the career of costume designer Willa Kim. She extends from a discussion of Kim to analyze costume history in Asian American performance and make an argument for the inclusion of costume design in the study of theater, dance, and performance. Lee meditates on the ways in which Kim's ethnicity and gender helped, rather than hurt her career even if her reputation was linked to exoticized readings of her talent. Finally, Ann Dils looks at two creative examinations of Lincoln's legacy, Ken Burns's 1990 documentary series, *The Civil War*, and Bill T. Jones's 2009 piece *Fondly Do We Hope . . . Fervently Do We Pray*. By comparing the two pieces, Dils is able to make claims about the choices artists and scholars make and the implications on history making. Burns's noble vision of white American masculinity and patriotic duty and Jones's critique of public institutions, the ways in which we treat and mistreat each other, and the fixity of identity, though not exhaustive representations of the same past, hint at the range of historical interpretations and the stakes embedded in the processes of such meaning making.

In "Place, Space, and Landscape" four authors attend to the particulars of environment as constitutive of meaning in dance and theater. Amy Strahler Holzapfel unpacks the term "landscape" and, using Gertrude Stein's conception of "play as landscape," traces

the affective meeting of theater and dance through landscape in three contemporary performance examples. Anne Flynn and Lisa Doolittle provide an ethnographic and historical study of the tradition of Blackfoot dance, the effects of colonial oppression, the bitterly
ironic practice of destruction of these bodily practices for their original identitarian purposes and the state-sanctioned reconstruction of these practices as theatricalized event for
tourists, and ultimately, the persistence of those original purposes through the generations.
Like Midgelow and Preston, they demonstrate a particularly impressive facility with navigating different voices (performance theorists, creative writers, ethnographers, and historians). Sally Ann Ness then asks us to consider the constitution of subjectivity in touristic
ritual sojourns. These pilgrimages (in this case to Yosemite's Half Dome) present liminoid
spirituality and a vocational identity. Ness's intervention is to recognize the significance and
nuance of performance in these settings ultimately detailing the choreography (and improvisation) of her own experience climbing Half Dome in a dangerous (though seemingly safe
as orchestrated by the National Park Service) encounter with nature. Michael Morris pushes
the composition of spirituality cum love, performance, and environment by examining Love
Art Laboratory (Annie M. Sprinkle and Elizabeth M. Stephens) and their performative marriage to the sea. Morris articulates their living life as love and art through an ecosexual identity as emblematic of an intra-action that portends the manifestation of a new ontology or at
least a new ideology of ontology.

In "Affect, Somatics, and Cognition" the writers engage various methodologies for getting at our subjectively experienced feelings about performance. Either holistic, imagistic,
or parsed out neuron by neuron, these theories all scan the body to get at meaning. Petra
Kuppers asks us to become aware of our own bodies as we read her essay and view her examples. After theorizing on somatic work in communities, she details her own work as artist, facilitator, flaneur, and participant. She deeply engages relationality, embodiment, and
counterpublics in terms of disability, community performance, and flanerie. Amy Cook
details the possibilities for a cognitive approach to examining the nexus of theater and dance.
Taking as a point of departure her flinch and squirm when a performer stabbed a horse
puppet in *Warhorse*, she deploys theories of embodied cognition and conceptual blending to analyze two contemporary performances. She lends insight into the science of emotion and empathy by linking performance to agency and selfhood. Sondra Horton Fraleigh
looks at two important affective relationships (love and power) in the works of Pina Bausch,
Elizabeth Streb, and butoh in terms of the embodiment of imagery. The image-making process is a complex network of relationships between artist, audience member, performer, art,
and meaning. From kinesthetic awareness to conscious cognition, our experiences of art
become part and parcel of us, our projects of self-making and utopic imaginings. Taking up
the theme of imagery, Darcey Callison analyzes the relationship between narrative and spectacle in the evocation of emotional response in Robert Lepage's work. Relying on the ocularcentrism of certain cultures, the typical elements of dramatic structure (story, character, and
text) no longer hold the same weight. Instead, images become discursive and the technology
and choreography of the images shape intellectual meaning and power relations and challenge audiences to look, feel, and think differently.

Patrick Anderson's essay could easily fit into the previous section and it opens the dis-
cussion on unruly bodies as a bridge between affect and dissent from normative processes.
He writes about the "ruses of empathy" located in several moments of Althusserian turns.
He defines a "choreographic imperative" by examining the definitions of dance by the court

system around several public encounters with police that involved movement and examples of bodies moving or not moving in public spaces as aesthetic practices of political discourse. The essay also serves to foreshadow our discussion of biopolitics. But ultimately, these bodies refuse to behave themselves and the results have important implications for what choreography can "set forth." Picking up on Zenenga's articulation of African total theater, Halifu Osumare demonstrates the survival of Africanist aesthetic practices in one of the Diaspora's latest manifestation, hip-hop. This body-based epistemology is part and parcel of a long tradition of embodied historiography, public "voice," and layered significance. Through the amalgamation of text, music, and dance, Osumare argues that hip-hop participates in this theatrical conjuring of magic as survival making way for performance as social movement. Thomas Postlewait examines a particularly provocative example of a body that resisted "rule." Postlewait, like Lee, delivers a recuperative analytical history of a surprisingly ignored yet important figure in London theater. Jeffrey Hudson was a dwarf who performed before kings and queens, had parts written for him by Ben Jonson and William Davenant, and was the most famous court performer in the 1630s. His absence from performance histories, no doubt because he was a dwarf, exposes a bias in historiography, and this chapter could certainly join the earlier conversation on history and historiography. But the voyeurism of his body that simultaneously captivated contemporaneous audiences and betrayed a scholarly blind spot is of primary interest here. Postlewait rectifies some of this erasure by analyzing Hudson's unruly body in performance. Finally, Krista K. Miranda discusses another immersive space on experimental performance in which the audience directly engages heightened "life" through dance theater. Her essay discusses the movement from "real" to "hyper-real" in Ann Liv Young's *Michael* and the dis-ease of the uncanny in this experience of the development of female sexuality and subjectivity.

Though many essays in this volume address a type of biopolitics, the essays in the next section directly engage the encounters between the body and political or cultural ideology. Daphne P. Lei argues that focus on the body of Chinese performers in Western spaces over the orality of the sounds of storytelling or singing was a willing act on the part of the West to render Asian subjectivity as body over voice and these muted bodies dominate the representation of the East to the West. Lei looks at Chinese dancing bodies in Chinese opera on international stages and argues that political moves served to other the Asian body and misread Oriental performing bodies as fixed dancing bodies thereby equating culture, ethnicity, and dance. E. J. Westlake gives a case study of Diana Taylor's archive and repertoire by discussing performances of the Nicaraguan dance drama El Güegüence. As a contested site of communal and cultural memory, reworkings of the dance spark dialogue about the "authenticity" of the tradition and the resistive and restorative power of embodied tradition over the erasure of the remains of the artifact of the original dance and the original body/subjectivity. Jade Power Sotomayor outlines the national and racial corporeal "conversations" embedded in the practice and performance of *bomba* music and dance as repertoire. She contrasts theatricalized representations of the form with community-based counterparts and details the nuances of the different power dynamics and narratives of race and nation created in these spaces. She defines the "speaking body" to show how *bomba* as improvised, embodied music-making relies on both theater and dance in a complex politicized matrix of signification. William Given then adds to the body of scholarship around the politics of appropriation of African American performance tropes. By focusing in on the Lindy Hop, Given is able to provide a detailed analysis of the implications of the new layers of meaning created when the dance form moved from being Harlem-identified to being American-identified. The liminal space of the integrated dance floor of the Savory Ballroom cum imagined community is unpacked, and the process and social politics of shifting the dances identity is theorized.

The next section pushes these politicized conversations to larger scales. We look at performative moments that exist on extreme, intense, or national proportions. Sandy Peterson begins with a look at a 1920 spectacle in Petrograd (a.k.a. St. Petersburg, Leningrad) involving over 100,000 spectators and over 8,000 performers. This example of total theater serves a very different purpose from the African total theater discussed by Zenenga. Peterson argues that these complex displays were attempts to narrativize and mythologize the Bolshevik regime. This involved not only revolutionary reimaginings of the performer/audience relationship and experience but also reimaginings of the ultimate purpose of performance. She shows how communities are created in these processes with the goal of articulating a shared past, present, and future as a grand narrative defining national identity. Marie C. Percy looks at the incorporation of Nazi politics through choreographic strategies during the 1936 Berlin Olympics. She details Rudolf von Laban's relationship with the Third Reich in general and the Reich Chamber of Culture in particular to contextualize the use of theater and dance in Nazi pursuits and add to the conversation on embodying power. *Talchum*, the Korean masked folk dance-drama, also works to create, define, and strengthen community by blurring lines between audience and performer but with very different goals than the previous two examples in this section. Though it was nearly wiped out by the Japanese occupation, large efforts have been made since the 1960s to preserve the tradition. J. L. Murdoch becomes a participant observer to embody understanding and provide details of the local differences and the implications for cohesive understanding of the regional and national import of this performance practice. Following the equine affective power that sparks Cook's examination, Kim Marra brings her embodied knowledge as a rider to explore the immensity of large-scale equestrian performances that are choreographed syntheses of human and equine movement capacity. She focuses on the work of Bartabas, the enigmatic founder and principal performer of the equestrian dance-theater troupe Zingaro. She provides a complex investigation around issues of zooesis, race, gender, sexuality, species, ethics, intensity, power, privilege, and aesthetics. And lastly, Neal Hebert examines the larger-than-life drag Mardi Gras Bal Masques in contemporary Louisiana and untangles the far-reaching implications of performances by the Krewe of Apollo, a gay male community in the city-parish of Baton Rouge. Hebert resists simple interpretations and instead recognizes the complexities of class, Camp(s), and consumer capitalism in these spectacular embodied performances of sexuality writ large.

From unconsciously tapping our feet to a song to sympathetic emotional responses to the plight of a character to dance mania resulting in death, embodied performances are infectious. The articles in the last section interrogate some important moments in history where dance and theater meet around contagion. Miriam Felton-Dansky discusses the Living Theatre's attempt to stage Antonin Artaud's plague (a totalizing event resulting in extinction or purification). The turning point in the company's aesthetic in terms of dramaturgy, staging, and audience participation was inextricably linked to a turn away from using texts in the ways they had before and a turn toward embodiment of poetry and ritual. The "mercilessly contagious epidemic" that is a part of performance became more important to the work. So much so that when the performers "died" in the audience and audience members "caught" their plague and died with them and allowed themselves to be piled on the heap of dead bodies, there was more than just benign play-acting happening. Felton-Dansky unpacks this attempt to make gesture communicable, plague revolutionary, and pacifist anarchy contagious. Marlis Schweitzer investigates the "epidemic" of Salome performances that surfaced in the beginning of twentieth century. Salome's dancing, state of dress, eroticism, and deadly mission were the stuff of both derision and obsession. The discourse surrounding this "fad" suggests the joy and threat of the infectious desire to witness "Salomania." The fear was that good Victorian women would catch this disease through performance and the social order of respectability would unravel with dire consequences for health, sanity, morality, sexuality, and (for some) the very foundation of society. Schweitzer focuses in on the contradictory meanings for the dance that were shaped by anti-Semitism and homophobic assumptions about the degeneracy of Jewish sexuality. Virginia Anderson looks at Broadway's philanthropic response to the HIV/AIDS epidemic. She defines the "philanthroproduction" as a professionally produced and fully mounted performance event that raises money for nonprofit organizations. By looking at Broadway Bares and analyzing the theater and dance in the performances alongside the socioeconomic situations, she shows how this annual burlesque offers important clues about the shifting attitudes about HIV. Like Felton-Dansky, Michael Lueger begins with Artaud but he directly ties Artaud's theories to epidemic choreomania. He defines choreomania not only as a transmittable uncontrollable impulse to dance but also as performance and follows out some of the undertheorized aspects of Artaud's philosophies. He looks at three instances of these "dancing plagues" and considers the results that lead to either death or purification.

It is fitting that we end with choreomania, a topic that has always interested me—the compulsion of large numbers of bodies to move, to perform. It illustrates the affective and effective power of embodied performance. It also hints at one of my earliest influences as a young child. I hesitated to include such a seemingly prosaic example alongside the profound articles you are about to read, but the more I engaged with these conversations as I curated the book, the more apt it seems. In the 1980 movie *Fame*, a movie about the hopes and dreams of students at New York's High School of the Performing Arts, the father of a young music student, a New York City cab driver, stops his cab in front of the school, pops in his son's tape, puts a speaker on top of the cab and plays his son's music. Kids come pouring out of the school, take to the streets, and dance. They stop traffic (read the city) with their art while Bruno Martelli (the music student) and the cab driver play out a scene of dramatic father/son conflict. This early flash mob paved the way to understanding the characters' journeys. Everyone in the city seemed to catch the fever. The state, in the form of a mounted police officer, was helpless. These bodies would not be contained. This moment displayed the possibilities of the performing arts in theory and practice—the boundless coming together of bodies. Utopic and hopeful? Forgive me. Did I just want to do fouetté turns on a New York City cab? Perhaps. But from the promise of this early moment, through the gritty and sometimes tragic stories that unfolded, to graduation, where they sing the body electric, this performance helped inspire me to think deeply about embodied performance as an artist and as a scholar. I hope this volume, ostensibly on the body electric, inspires the reader to do the same.

NOTES

1. Gia Kourlas, " 'Sleep No More,' but Move Nonstop," *New York Times*, September 6, 2011, http://www.nytimes.com/2011/09/07/arts/dance/sleep-no-more-is-theater-embedded-with-dancers.html? (accessed May 20, 2013).
2. Ibid.
3. These affective barometers are debatable, of course. My point is that in the spectrum of theatricality *Contact* pairs dance with method acting, a novel choice that was a key difference in the pieces' aesthetic and an important factor in the show's acclaim.
4. Wikipedia provides an apt metaphor for this rabbit hole, as a search for "dance theater" gets redirected to "tanztheater." If one spells theater with "re" and searches for "dance theatre" Wikipedia redirects you to "contemporary dance," an entirely different entry.
5. A colleague joked with me once about referring to me as a dance scholar only to be corrected by another who informed her that I was a theater scholar.
6. It is beyond this project to try to answer these questions or others, such as What is dance? or What is theater? But it would do for me to ask you, reader, and leave it to you to unravel, for surely there are many valid answers.
7. Drew Leder, *The Absent Body* (Chicago: University of Chicago Press, 1990), 1.
8. For Leder, illness and aging are the important moments when our focus shifts acutely to our bodies.
9. See Erwin Straus, *The Primary World of Senses*, trans. Jacob Needleman (Glencoe, NY: The Free Press of Glencoe, 1963), 233–36; Hans Jonas, *The Phenomenon of Life* (Chicago: University of Chicago Press, 1966), 152–56; Leder, *The Absent Body*, 17–20.
10. We could push this further to argue circuitously "I can think therefore I am" if we understand thought as embodied mental activity in a nonmetaphorical sense.
11. Leder, *The Absent Body*, 22.
12. Tracy C. Davis and Thomas Postlewait, eds., *Theatricality* (New York: Cambridge University Press, 2003), 1.
13. Ibid., 6.
14. Ibid., 10.
15. Susan Manning, "An American Perspective on Tanztheater," *The Drama Review: TDR* 30, no. 2 (Summer 1986), 68.

BIBLIOGRAPHY

Davis, Tracy C., and Thomas Postlewait, eds. *Theatricality*. New York: Cambridge University Press, 2003.

Jonas, Hans. *The Phenomenon of Life*. Chicago: University of Chicago Press, 1966.

Kourlas, Gia. " 'Sleep No More,' but Move Nonstop." *New York Times*, September 6, 2011. Accessed May 20, 2013. http://www.nytimes.com/2011/09/07/arts/dance/sleep-no-more-is-theater-embedded-with-dancers.html?

Leder, Drew. *The Absent Body*. Chicago: University of Chicago Press, 1990.

Manning, Susan. "An American Perspective on Tanztheater." *Drama Review: TDR* 30, no. 2 (Summer 1986): 57–79.

Straus, Erwin. *The Primary World of Senses*. Translated by Jacob Needleman. Glencoe, NY: The Free Press of Glencoe, 1963.

SECTION I

IN THEORY/
IN PRACTICE

CHAPTER 2

SPLIT INTIMACIES

*Corporeality in Contemporary Theater
and Dance*

ANN COOPER ALBRIGHT

I recently had what many would call a classic moment of catharsis at the theater. I had been to see a local production of *The Laramie Project*, and while I was describing the show to a friend afterward, I broke down crying. I was profoundly affected by the production—something that does not happen very often when I go to see a play. My position as a resistant (read feminist, queer) spectator who is highly suspicious of traditional theater (particularly the convention of the fourth wall) usually disrupts many of the pleasures inherent in realist drama. This time, however, I was completely caught up in the events unfolding onstage. What I found compelling about the performance was not so much the dramatic relationships between characters or the language of the script per se, but rather the layering of dynamic and bodily exchanges that led me to reflect on the very slippery way that bodies carry meaning in contemporary performance. Attending to corporeality allows us to chart the split intimacies of embodiment and representation across forms of theater and dance that are not anchored in the usual codes of realistic mimesis or expressive movement.

One classic explanation of my experience in the theater that evening would be to attribute my response to the production itself, claiming it was the kind of magical effect that a successful combination of visionary directing and highly competent acting would inspire in anyone. On the other hand, I could connect my reaction to the fact that I attended the performance during a time when there had been a recent spate of vicious gay bashing in France in reaction to the country's marriage equality vote and even more egregious homophobic violence in Russia and the Republic of Georgia that may have been abetted by Russian Orthodox priests no less. In addition, since I had just taught a course in which we read a review of the sequel to *The Laramie Project* based on a series of interviews done ten years later, I was deeply familiar with the whole context of the production. Clearly the personal stakes were high for me as I entered the theater that night. Nonetheless, I was surprised by my reaction—I was truly moved.

This chapter hinges on the reverberations of that last word, "moved," the meaning of which splits across the psychic and physical to encompass both an emotional and a visceral responsiveness to the world. Being moved by a performance represents an intertwining of somatic feeling and political urgency that characterizes much of the contemporary performance work that I have attended over the past two decades. There is, I believe, something vital in these works that leads the audience from passive spectators into the role of active witnesses, raising the stakes of our viewing experience. As I have argued in another context, to witness a performance suggests a response/ability, which includes both an ability to respond to the events onstage and a sense of being implicated in their outcome.[1] This particular sensibility, however, departs significantly from two classic theories of audience reception: the Aristotelian notion of catharsis in the theater and the modernist concept of kinesthesia in dance most fully articulated in the work of the mid-twentieth-century dance critic John Martin. In the writing that follows, I explore the possibilities of an affective relationship with the audience that engages neither a direct psychological identification with the protagonist(s) onstage nor a conventional notion of physical empathy but rather prioritizes other kinds of exchanges, bringing attention to corporeality as encompassing somatic embodiment as well as cultural representation.

I define corporeality here as an intertwining of sensation and perception where the body remains anchored as the central scope of awareness. In order to use corporeality as a category of reception, it is crucial to think beyond the most obvious effects of vision and language. We need to learn to appreciate the elusive contours of somatic meaning. Although embodiment is enjoying a renaissance in contemporary cultural theory these days, it is most often elided with discussions of affect. I want to resist this well-trodden path, however, and branch off into a territory that is not as clearly charted. That is, I want to conceptualize feeling as the practice of sensing (I am feeling) rather than the object of possession (I have feelings). Keeping the verb fully active without letting it settle into the stable structure of a noun not only helps us to resist the psychological construction of an interior self so endemic to discourses of affect, but also disrupts any easy equation of physical corporeality with social identity. Within the context of performance, corporeality circulates between the bodies onstage and those in the audience; but those relationships of power and exchange are rarely predictable. This is not to suggest, however, that they are entirely subjective either. Audience members and performers can share the process of feeling together without necessarily imbuing that experience with the same meaning. My task in this chapter is to incorporate a critic's sensibility within a theoretical inquiry such that I both describe onstage events and conceptualize their impact without assuming a normative, universal audience reaction or a completely random series of individual responses.

Located in the intersection of reportage and ethnography, *The Laramie Project* is not exactly standard theatrical fare. It is what one might call a "reality drama."[2] The script is based on a series of interviews conducted by the Tectonic Theater Project with local community members after the 1998 brutal beating, hospitalization, and subsequent death of Matthew Shepard. Shepard, a gay student who attended the University of Wyoming in Laramie, became a cause célèbre as candlelight vigils were held in his honor around the world. Each performer in the cast takes on the persona of different characters, each of which narrates their experience of the events surrounding Shepard's assault. News reporting blurs into storytelling, truth into fiction, and life into performance as the actors weave individual responses (both those of the community members as well as their own) within discussions of the media's representations and misrepresentations of the community. The fact that the same actors play homophobic as well as gay community members unsettles any easy or direct correspondence between dramatic characters and their respective physical bodies, complicating the audience's ability to empathize with any one character. The performance progresses like a series of switchbacks, zigging and zagging through multiple interpretations of what happened and why. In the end, there is no resolution to the tragedy and the audience is left on its own to sort out the larger ethical ramifications of the community's response to the event.

This particular production of *The Laramie Project* was directed by Caroline Jackson Smith, whose theatrical vision is influenced by both African American performance traditions and her experience with Suzuki actor training. The minimal set allowed for a very dynamic staging, which beautifully reflected the multiple voices and points of view of the community members. The actors were constantly moving around the raked stage, entering from the far reaches of upstage or downstage and then abruptly crossing to the center to replace one another like billiard balls ricocheting across a pool table. There was a sense of movement flow to each scene that held its own integrity and operated like a separate physical script, at once splitting from the storytelling and yet intimately connected to it.

I am noticing a similar integrated corporeal sensibility in many theatrical productions these days. It is not uncommon for directors such as Anne Bogart or Peter Sellars to suspend the narrative structure of the dramatic action in order to incorporate moments of individual abstract movement or group gestural sequences as a dynamic intersection with the spoken text. This postmodernist approach is distinctly different from the usual models of theatrical blocking or staging of dramatic action, where individual gestures or movements are crafted in the service of portraying a character. In this more traditional approach to staging, it is rare that the whole stage becomes caught up in one dynamic movement or rhythmic sequence that sweeps across the stage space and pulls the audience out of their normal mode of attending to the story. The same kind of parallel yet split physical text also threads through much contemporary dance, where a kinetic texture is woven in ways that operate very differently than traditional choreographies, affecting the audience's bodily sensibility without necessarily registering as an obviously choreographed sequence.

In his survey of contemporary theater practices, Hans Thies Lehman maps out the contours of an international range of contemporary performance work that both confuses and refuses any simple distinctions between theater as strictly focused on a text and dance as movement-based performance. Throughout his book *Postdramatic Theatre*, Lehman catalogs the many aesthetic and ideological differences between mimetic dramas, where the script is the clear priority for the staging, and more experimental productions in which the frame of realistic representation is disrupted. "Wholeness, illusion, and world representation are inherent in the model 'drama'; conversely, through its very form, dramatic theatre proclaims wholeness as the *model* of the real."[3] One of the major differences that Lehman outlines in his survey is the difference for the audience between the experience of watching a traditional narrative, in which the final scene almost always stages a resolution before "the end" of the script, and that of witnessing the multilayered, often conflicting and unresolvable aspects of much contemporary performance work. While his discussion of these performance elements is descriptive rather than prescriptive, Lehman insists that there is a fundamentally different audience dynamic within postdramatic theater. This is not just a question of a new style of staging but rather a new conception of what constitutes the performance experience. He writes, "it becomes more presence than representation, more shared than communicated experience, more process than product, more manifestation than signification, more energetic impulse than information."[4]

The Laramie Project is a telling example of postdramatic theater precisely because it refuses any personal dénouement or larger political statement. In Lehman's taxonomy, *The Laramie Project* would be categorized as "documentary theatre," which he claims is "less the desire for direct political action, and even less its conventional dramaturgy."[5] Rather, it disrupts the ideologies of either discourse. In this kind of theater, Shepard's death is not the tragic event that results in any kind of resolution or classical sense of enlightenment. The emphasis and delivery of the text communicates more disruption and confusion than illustration or explanation of the historical events or even of any individual's motivation. Moments of dramatic dialogue between characters quickly dissolve into citations of various news reports and discussions of the growing media sensation around the event. As Debby Thompson writes in her review of the November 2000 Wyoming premiere, "The deliberate accumulation of fragments, by turns colorful, understated and conflicting, gradually documents the complexity of the Laramie community."[6]

As staged by Jackson-Smith, *The Laramie Project* confounds any easy identification between certain bodies and their respective political positions. The cast members play a dizzying array of roles and engage with one another only briefly before turning to address the audience directly, often with a metacommentary on the scene they have just enacted. This self-referential aspect cuts through any mimetic interpretation, highlighting instead the complex mechanisms of individual posturing and institutional justification, not to mention the tensions between local and global media depictions of the situation being enacted onstage. To put it bluntly, there are no good or bad guys, no feel-good redemptions, no final realizations that serve to make the world (or even the town of Laramie) a better place in the end. Thompson concludes her review by comparing the production to the Names Project's collective quilt commemorating friends and relatives who have died of AIDS. "Its [*The Laramie Project*'s] strategy of sewing together fragments captures the community's unresolved struggles, the variety of its individual personalities, and, finally, its ultimate resistance to ever being wholly contained within any representation."[7]

In the course of reading various reviews of both the New York premiere and the Wyoming production, I was struck by how quickly many of the articles moved past the specifics of the performance itself into discussions of antigay bias, homophobia in the West, and the status of hate crime legislation. Although it is understandable that these writers would highlight the ongoing connection between the source story and the resulting upswing of gay activism, I was disappointed at how often the theatrical contours of the production were collapsed into pedestrian journalism, making Matthew Shepard, as critic Ben Brantley succinctly put it, "a poster boy for the casualties of anti-gay violence" (*New York Times*, May 19, 2000). With a few wonderful exceptions, the theatrical experience, with all its nuances of kinetic exchange, echoes of images, rhythmic phrasing of dialogue, and spatial dynamics, seemed to carry little meaning outside of the direct references to the original scene. Looking at the critical responses to *The Laramie Project*, I realize that this production is an example of how the narrative text still registers as the most significant element, even in the midst of a calculated splintering of any one story line. Although his death is the stone that breaks the placid surface of this small town community where people supposedly "live and let live," Matthew Shepard is never depicted. Instead, the production focuses the audience's awareness on how his absence ripples out to affect us all.

If *The Laramie Project* is part of what Lehman calls "documentary theatre," then many of the performances put together by Liz Lerman and the Dance Exchange could similarly be considered "documentary dance." As artistic director of a multifaceted dance organization, Lerman piloted a number of important collaborations that address ethical issues through the creation and production of work that combines movement, text, and video images. In her book *Hiking the Horizontal*, Lerman articulates the possibilities as well as the challenges inherent in what she terms "subject matter choreography." Subtitled *Field Notes from a Choreographer*, this reflection on her working process locates meaning in performance as an interweaving of critical issues and the somatic insights accrued by moving, witnessing, and experiencing those ideas in an embodied way. "In subject matter choreography, various thinking processes are subjected to physical examination."[8] In a section titled "What Is the Dancing About?" Lerman explains: "Subject matter dancing doesn't feel less than, or like a crutch, or like some simplistic pretend game. It offers, rather, a fantastic dialogue of intellect and impulse, feeling and the matter of the mind, gathered in a weird kinesthetic wrapping."[9]

Small Dances about Big Ideas (2006) was commissioned by the Harvard Law School as part of an international conference on human rights and the legacy of the Nuremburg Trials. In a lengthy program note for the inaugural performances, Lerman details a conversation between herself and Martha Minow, the dean of Harvard Law School at the time and one of the organizers of the event. In this exchange, Lerman asks Why? Why choose dance to address the atrocities of genocide? Minow's reply is remarkably insightful about the potential of performance to saturate the audience with the corporeal experience of ethical discussions.

> These are my hopes: that a dance would reach people who seldom think about mass atrocities—students, lawyers—with the chance to be drawn in emotionally and intellectually, with the pacing that can allow people to absorb or begin to absorb the incomprehensible scales of atrocity . . . For those who think about these matters often . . . the chance to imagine images and voices about these things, and to have a shared experience with others who seldom attend to these issues.[10]

Small Dances about Big Ideas begins in the dark. As a single light brightens, it reveals three women of different ages and ethnicities slowly rising and reaching upward as if awakening from a long sleep. These sister-witches, with long loose hair and flowing skirts, move across the space silently. Looking out through the darkness, they seem frightened. One by one, they venture out to explore the unknown and then rush back to the embrace of the others, their contorted faces reflecting the horrors of the other side of the night. At times instigators, at other times healers, these three crone figures will take on the role of otherworldly witnesses to the human stories and judicial proceedings that make up the rest of the evening's performance.

Soon, the mysterious and somber music abruptly changes to loud shots, sirens, and the sound of a helicopter overhead as the rest of the cast darts frantically across the stage, hoping to escape the shots that fell each one in turn. Over and over again people flail as if they have been shot, fall, and then get up to run again. The repetitive effect of each body arching backward and then crumpling forward into the ground reflects the bittersweet layering of a provocatively beautiful movement sequence with powerfully devastating consequences, splitting our attention between mimesis and abstraction, the literal and the figurative. Eventually the cast lines up with their back to the audience and we can't tell if they are facing an unseen firing squad upstage, or if we, as the audience, are being implicated in that position. This opening scene dissolves as three people come downstage to sit on benches and tell their stories of persecution and survival. A young black man, an older white woman, and a young white woman relate three different experiences in three different languages, weaving a tapestry of voice and gesture that is echoed in the movements of the dancers behind shadowing them. The personal and lyrical quality of that scene shifts into the stark angular gestures of the men in ties who enter with chairs and set up the repetitive structure of judicial proceedings.

Throughout this dance, institutional narratives are juxtaposed to individual memories. In one of the most extraordinary sequences, a young woman dances to a recitation from Clea Koff's memoir *The Bone Woman*, creating a gestural counterpoint to the horrifying forensic descriptions of collecting fragments of human bones at sites in Rwanda. As the voice-over details her desire to both document the atrocities of that war and to gather the bone fragments to send back to the families, the silent dancer shifts back and forth, edging closer to a pile of bodies onstage, as if she were being pushed by the incoming tide. This contrast between moving figures and still prone bodies speaks its own corporeal language that intersects with the textual progression of historical details of Nuremburg, Rwanda, and Bosnia. For Liz Lerman, dancing is not an escape from but rather a process through which we can deal with the recognition and memories of these atrocities.

About halfway through the evening-length work, the cast members drop their performance personas and all come downstage as the lights come up on the audience. What follows is a dialogue between the performers and the audience (basically a talk-back in the middle of the evening) that begins with small group discussions about the issues of justice, retribution, and reconciliation that animate the performance. One of the performers acts as a master of ceremonies and suggests that people begin a conversation by asking themselves "What it is that we teach our children about questions of justice in the world?" After a while, the cast comes back onstage to report on their conversations. Intentionally repeating many of the gestures used by the original speaker as they actively remembered a comment from the audience discussion, the dancers build a gestural sequence from everyone's contributions, adding a few of their own. One that was particularly striking was "looking back to the past and moving forward" which translated into a turning movement and sweeping of the arm in a big arc from behind to forward. Another striking moment was a description of events unfolding while the hands revolved around one another in front of the chest. It was interesting to me to realize how many audience members were doing the sequence along with the cast onstage. Indeed it was quite an amazing experience to see hundreds of hands doing the unfolding gesture more or less in unison, especially as someone spoke about remembering the feeling that sponsored the original gesture. In this way (admittedly a tad bit pedantic), the audience was drawn into the theatrical process of the work as both civic and corporeal witnesses. Merging ideas and ethics with the fleshy substance of their implications, *Small Dances about Big Ideas* insists that our sense of justice—as it is played out across the world's bodies—is inherently connected to our physical selves.

I want to pause for a moment in the midst of this analysis of various contemporary theater and dance productions to think about the nature of the communication I just described. Even though I did not participate in learning the gestural sequence, I could not help but be affected by the movement rippling across the rows of spectators in that performance. Here, for me, was a moment of "communitas," a term that I learned from Richard Schechner, who, in turn, has adapted it from the work of anthropologist Victor Turner. Schechner uses "communitas" to describe similar sweeps of energy that are a palpable aspect of many ceremonial gatherings, including theatrical productions, religious rites, political demonstrations, or rituals of transformation such as a wedding or a bar mitzvah. The term suggests a sense of heightened receptivity that is never only intellectual or even strictly emotional but is also always rooted in a bodily awareness. These situations can be quite magical and remind me of the fact that the etymological root for "communication" is "commune," a word that—like feeling—also splits into a verb and a noun, echoing both the act and the experience. It is in the intimate vibrations between the doing and the being that we find the "communitas" of corporeality.

I realize that it may seem to some readers as if I am edging pretty close to describing a moment of dramatic catharsis, the Aristotelian telos of ancient Greek tragedy that has long been the aesthetic yardstick of Western theater. Many scholars point to the passage in his *Poetics* where (depending on the translation) Aristotle declares, "[T]ragedy is the imitation of men in action [. . .]; tragedy through pity and fear effects a catharsis of such misfortunes."[11] One of the distinctions that I want to draw in this chapter is the difference between a descriptive perspective and a prescriptive one. Although the moment of "communitas" that I am describing may sound similar to catharsis, it is not necessarily the same kind of psychological "purging" of emotion that resolves the conflicts onstage. Nor is it necessarily a "universal" experience. Rather, I want to assert the real possibility of *feeling* together without insisting that we all *feel* the same way.

In a postscript to his erudite essay "On Catharsis, or Resolution," literary scholar Kenneth Burke unpacks the etymological root of the Greek word "peran," which most often gets translated as "opposite shore." He suggests a more appropriate term might be something like "beyonding," rather than the conventional use of catharsis as "purge," to signify the cleansing of the emotions of fear or pity. Burke points out the kinetic tension in the fact that pity is conceived as a movement toward and fear as a movement away. Traditionally, catharsis is seen as an experience that transcends that opposition and leads the audience toward a resolution. Burke notes, "Such an order of development gives the feeling of *going somewhere*, [. . .] The curative effect that comes from a sense of direction in the unfolding of an implicational structure may explain why purgative rituals are so often built around a *procession*."[12] But if we keep the notion of "beyonding" alive, we can replace the implicit teleology of a resolution with an ongoing somatic resonance. That is to say, we could replace an emphasis on dramatic action with a focus on theatrical states of being, which is precisely what Lehman identifies as an essential aspect of postdramatic theater. "The theatre here showed less a succession, a development of a story, more an involvement of inner and outer states."[13]

I am intrigued by Burke's use of "beyond" as a gerund, for *beyonding* reverberates past the prepositional or even nominal uses of the word to indicate at once a sense of possibility and the *im*possibility of ever arriving there. This tension between textual and corporeal meaning animates the power and the complexities of much contemporary performance work, insisting that what happens in the theater actually makes a difference. Indeed, as Burke reminds us, the original experiences of Greek tragedy were civic ceremonies in which the political and the familial were constantly echoing one another such that the human body, the world's body, and the body politic all reflected and refracted one another.

My own initiation to Greek tragedy was the Theatre du Soleil's mythic 1992 production of the *Oresteia* (*Les Atrides*). Directed by Ariane Mnouchkine and produced by the Brooklyn Academy of Music in the Park Slope Armory, this four-play cycle (Mnouchkine included

Euripides's telling of *Iphigeneia at Aulis* to set up Clytemnestra's motivation in the Oresteia trilogy) ran ten hours and was presented in repertory with afternoon and evening performances. My notes from the October 11, 1992, performances indicate that I was in the Park Slope Armory from 1 p.m. to 8:30 p.m. with a small break for dinner served inside that space. Everything in this production was epic in scale: from the massive space of the Armory itself to the Indian Kathakali-inspired costumes and the elaborate make-up that the actors were putting on under the bleachers as the audience was entering the space and from the spell-binding movement of the large chorus to the classical use of oratory in the recitations of the text in French. The stage was defined by a series of connected wooden walls that created both a cityscape and an enduring sense of claustrophobia. The chorus used these walls in different ways; sometimes the walls served as percussive instruments and sometimes the chorus would rush over and throw themselves up the walls in order to quickly clear the space so that they could witness the interactions between the main characters. More than one reviewer likened this stage environment to a "bull ring," particularly in the scene where Orestes is chasing a frantic Clytemnestra around the enclosed space.

Anchored in Aeschylus's text, this production did not attempt to humanize the larger-than-life characters of Agamemnon, Clytemnestra, Orestes, and Electra but rather chose to accentuate the ritualistic and civic aspects of the whole event. The plot and dramatic action seemed less important than the highly theatrical display of repetitive gesture and circular movements of the chorus (who at times looked like whirling dervishes), as well as the rhythmic chanting, and the mixture of human and nonhuman figures onstage. Frank Rich sums up Mnouchkine's approach in his review of the performances: "Yet in the Theatre du Soleil rendition, the storytelling is neither modern nor archaic in the presumed manner of the fifth century B.C. but timeless. Ms. Mnouchkine fulfills her idea of a cosmopolitan, ritualistic theater that is beyond language, plot or any kind of realism and that instead digs deep into the primordial passions, many of them ugly, that seem the eternal, inescapable legacy of the human race" (*New York Times*, October 6, 1992).

Some of the most powerful moments for me in this production were times of riveting chaos, moments when the stage space was flooded by the whirling movements of the chorus and the frantic rushing here and there of the main characters, accompanied by the clashing of the large acoustical percussion orchestra. All these elements created the feeling of a kind of apocalyptic tremor in the Armory. Attempting to describe the affect of this corporeal tension, Rich calls it "a subterranean, not easily articulated pull on a viewer's psyche" (ibid.). Rather than resolving this chaos with a miraculous dénouement that crystalizes into a clear tableau before the dramatic blackout, Mnouchkine chose to methodically unravel this frenzied action layer by layer. This created the effect of rewinding the whole event, a dramaturgical strategy that allowed the audience to witness the way the chaos was built, fracturing even further any sense of realistic representation. By thus folding the dramatic plot into a total theatrical spectacle, Theatre du Soleil's production of the Oresteia creates what Lehman, quoting Jean-Francois Lyotard, describes as "Energetic Theatre." "This would be a theatre not of meaning but of 'forces, intensities, present affects'. [. . .] Energetic theatre would be theatre beyond representation—meaning, of course, not simply without representation, but not governed by its logic."[14]

At once epic and chaotic, William Forsythe's *Decreation* (2003) is an intriguing example of an "energetic" theatrical movement event that is clearly not governed by the usual rules of dance composition. In this dance there is no unifying narrative or coherent visual picture. Its medium is neither abstract motion nor pedestrian movement, but rather a strangely inter-twined hybrid of textual and physical nonsequiturs that trace the scars of combative inter-personal relationships. *Decreation* is a good example of Lehman's discussion of the charged corporeality in many contemporary performances in which "[t]he body becomes the centre of attention, not as a carrier of meaning but in its physicality and gesticulation."[15] Embracing French theorist Julia Kristeva's distinction between language and voice (the latter vibrating with the turbulence of the somatic), Lehman points out the underlying shift in perception where "The body no longer demonstrates anything but itself, the turn away from a body of signification and towards a body of unmeaning gesture (dance, rhythm, grace, strength, kinetic wealth) turns out as the most extreme charging of the body with significance con-cerning the social reality."[16]

Created at the end of his twenty-year career as artistic director of Ballett Frankfurt and right before he established his own company, *Decreation* was inspired by poet Anne Carson's essay of the same name. Her elegiac discussion of "undoing"—that dissolution of one's self through intense passion—gets translated quite differently onstage. Under Forsythe's direc-tion, the unmaking here revolves around the inverse relationship of passion and passivity. *Decreation* was originally staged at the Bockenheimer Depot, a cavernous old tram station that evokes a hollow empty feeling. This slightly existential quality remained even when the dance was performed at the main stage at Brooklyn Academy of Music. In *Decreation*, angu-lar, intense, and neurotic movements are matched by equally discordant sounds, many of which are created by manipulating the performers' voices into surreal high or low pitches. The effect is to unsuture the mimetic connection of voice to body such that movement and speech shift unpredictably, like cadences that never quite match up. For instance, at the beginning of the dance it is clearly Dana Caspersen talking even as she physically splits her-self in order to enact both sides of a bitter lover's quarrel. But that narrative soon fragments across a barrage of isolated figures and raw interactions that flash from detached attraction to jealous rage. Dance critic Roslyn Sulcas describes the movement in *Decreation* as "both powerful and disturbingly strange—emphatic, extreme propulsions of the body; grotesquely angled, impossible-looking coordinations; faces grimacing as if being pulled by invisible forces."[17]

In an essay that documents the experience of making and performing this work, veteran Forsythe dancer and artistic collaborator Dana Caspersen details the complexity at stake in the creation of the movements.

> *Decreation* was a tricky process; it was full of deep-dwelling things that were reluctant to sur-face. It seemed to be composed of impossible things; contradictory and divided things. We began the process of considering the state of jealousy that arises from fragmentation and the fragmentation that arises from jealousy. We thought about the nature of the contiguous and the singular, the nature of restraint and communication.[18]

Translating those ideas onto the body requires a complete somatic shift from willfully and articulately executing the movement phrases to allowing that motion to carry one's body across the space. Caspersen describes a movement method called "shearing" in which "the body becomes a proliferation of angular currents flowing backwards out from the point of desire; the body enters into a state of complex, fragmented reaction."[19] This physical ricochet is only sustainable if Caspersen can learn to "think" her body in a radically different way, giv-ing up the usual effort in executing movement in order to ride the kinetic currents already traversing the space. "I realized, for example, that the task of creating this physical ricochet of eyes, jaw, rib cage, hips, and so on, actually became possible if I allowed it, in my thought, to be not an activity, not something that I constructed, but rather a state that traveled through my body and connected me to the room."[20]

It is rare that we scholars have access to such a clear articulation of the experience of dancing complex multiperspectival work such as *Decreation*, and this short essay by Caspersen gives us insights into the uncomfortable beginnings of a movement technique that has now, I would argue, become increasingly codified over the past decade. I am struck by the parallels with other movement techniques such as Merce Cunningham's or Trisha Brown's. Cunningham used chance procedures to unravel a certain physical coherency and expand the palette of movement possibilities available to him. Eventually, however, he was able to dispense with throwing the I Ching to do so because he had internalized how to choreograph multiple facings and nonsequitur combinations directly. Similarly, much of Trisha Brown's movement style came out of her choreographic investigations but also eventually became a movement technique. Although less codified than Cunningham technique (for instance there are no "fundamentals" classes at the studio), Brown's idiosyncratic style of moving, the loose, multidirectional movement that has become her trademark is taught by her company members.

Interestingly enough, if we compare Caspersen's dancing in *Decreation* with a later Forsythe piece, *I Don't Believe in Outer Space* (which premiered in Frankfurt in 2008, and was presented at the Brooklyn Academy of Music in 2013), we can see that her dancing, while retaining the same awkward intensity, feels much less disjointed. Indeed, it seems as if she and the other dancers have found a way to ride the kinetic ricochets across the space without becoming distraught, even as they dance through a cacophony of text, motion, sound, and various dada-esque objects littering the floor. The fantastic elements in *I Don't Believe . . .* include the oddly shaped moon rocks made from crumpled up gaffer tape, which dancers sometimes pick up and insert in their costumes to create weird bulges on their bodies, as well as a large playing card animating the random quality of the stage set. Equally random (albeit fascinating) is Dana Caspersen's compelling and extremely virtuosic opening monologue where she both narrates and takes on the personas of a meek host and a ferocious guest.

As the dance proceeds and little hints of its existential underpinnings appear (including the repetitive mantra "As if by chance" and the awkward, spastic solo to a tortured rendition of Gloria Gaynor's "I Will Survive"), it becomes clear that this dance is also a meditation on human mortality. Ironically, the performance is much more light-hearted than *Decreation*, and there are amazing moments of complete unison ("as if by chance") that establish a sweet community even in the midst of a kinetic bedlam. At the end of the work, as two dancers move in intricate alignment upstage, Dana Caspersen intones series of "no mores." ("No more sky. No more standing by a lake with your friend.") As she moves toward the audience, her voice and address becomes increasingly intimate. She ends by tracing her own collarbone from one side to the other as she says almost whispering, "no more this."

Emotionally speaking, *I Don't Believe . . .* ends on a radically different register than it began. The boisterous chaos at the beginning has been distilled to a final quiet image of absence as the lights fade. Nonetheless, I would argue that this last moment is not exactly a dramatic resolution in the usual sense, especially given the frenetic action still reverberating in some of the bodies onstage. It is, however, an indication that the somatic underbelly of this kind of high-impact, high intensity "Energetic Theatre" contains the possibility of a more intimate exchange in which the spectacular is linked to the personal. Throughout Forsythe's work, rather than looking for the more traditional shapes or poses of the body, the audience has to attend to fierce states of moving energy that wash over us, pushing us to reckon with our own corporeal habitus.

John Jasperse's *Fort Blossom Revisited* (2000/2012) begins even before the house lights go off, as a man enters and casually walks across the stage close to the audience to lie, belly down, on the white floor. His face is turned away from the audience, and he just waits while the house lights go dark and the stage lights come up. The viewing priority set up by this first sequence in *Fort Blossom* is familiar to most of us who have watched and been involved in contemporary dance over the past three decades. Many of us are completely used to seeing bodies, even naked bodies, walking casually around on stage and we have been taught the patience to observe the minute details of a still body's breath, tracing the small contraction and expansion of the chest, possibly even noticing how the inhale causes a slight external rotation in the limbs. The intimate size of the theater, the casual delineation between audience and performers, the frank, pedestrian address (even though highly intentional) creates a sensibility in the audience that attunes us to the sticky vulnerability of the body. We are watching this body lie in front of us, but with a sense of open expectations, we are not meant to judge or to look too carefully for instance, at the crop of red pimples across the skinny guy's buttocks. This act of witnessing is based on a model of mutual responsiveness—literally, an ability to respond. We are watching as participants because our bodies are engaged in a receptive, somatic manner. We are looking from one body to another.

This tension between embodiment and representation is what John Jasperse, in reference to *Fort Blossom Revisited*, frames as "how we experience the body as both owners and spectators." Simultaneously connected and separated by the conjunction *and*, these binaries as well as ones such as self/other, feeling/seeing, and movement/stillness form the interpretive scaffolding of this dance, helping it to slip through any easy categorization of the work as expressive modern dance, formalist postmodern, or even pastichey post-postmodern performance. What we do know is that the dancers are deeply serious about performing the movement phrases; that the women wear red dresses and the men perform naked; that the inflatable chairs serve as humorous Laurel and Hardy props at one point and as pointed commentary on sexual safety and intimacy at another. In this dance there is a tension between inside and outside, between corporeal sensation and spatial definition, between red dresses and naked asses that is intriguingly provocative and opens *Fort Blossom* up to various frequencies of interpretation including both a corporeal one and a queer reading.

About halfway through the dance, two men engage in a duet—naked. Although, the dancers face away from one another, rarely acknowledging the other's gaze, there is a mutual awareness of the comforting pressure of another's touch as one partner sits on the other's shoulder or leg. At times this sweet and chaste exchange is punctuated by an explicit focus on the open, available asshole as a site of erotic possibilities. Usually, this shift in attention (both the performers' and the viewers') coincides with a slow, sensuous stroke of a butt down one's partner's arm or leg. These moments, however, are mini starbursts within a larger constellation of formal choreographic considerations such as the interesting geometry made by the joining of this body part to that body shape. As the duet progresses and the eerie mechanical sounds get louder, the men's interactions paradoxically become less sensual, less about the experience of touching and more about the physical dynamic of their exchanges of weight. As they perch on one another, their physicality morphs and they begin to appear more like a pair of animals, or like they are doing Contact Improvisation, albeit without the usual clothing. Eventually they slow down again, but then separate and go off to dance with the women waiting patiently upstage.

The Symmetry Project (2009) begins with many of the same features as *Fort Blossom*, including the casual entrance while the audience is still milling around and the focused demeanor of the dancers, open to being seen yet attentive to their internal experience. This collaborative and improvisational duet by Jess Curtis and Maria Francesca Scaroni is based on, to quote the press materials, "investigating and embodying symmetrical (homologous) movement practice." This dance (described as "physically based work"—a code that tries to complicate our gaze by insisting on the sticky nakedness of the nudity) has moved from the theater to a gallery space, although the audience is still set up very much like a proscenium stage. The press release tells us that this shift "reframes" the work, "affording the viewers the possibility to see the body and its metaphorical possibilities through different filters, with different types of attention, expectation, and association."

In this piece, however, the addition of fur coats over the naked bodies hints at a whole other series of cultural associations, including Neanderthal, porn, bourgeois, or just funky thrift store costuming. Although the two dancers' physical attitude stays with the task-based demeanor of much postmodern dance, that pedestrian frame is shattered very quickly when Maria spreads her legs and leans back to present the audience with a very unambiguous crotch shot. Immediately, the background chatter in the audience dies down (in fact, on the video you can hear a woman's faint "Oh my god" in the background) as this provocative address continues to be tempered by both dancers' very matter of fact physical adjustments of spine and limbs and a clear awareness of their breath. It's a pretty weird moment, with the somatic attentiveness that informs our viewing priorities in this work at odds with the patently sexual frame of this "mystère du monde."

Jess and Maria move on their own for a while, wriggling out of the fur coats without unbuttoning them and then tentatively trying out the "homologous" movement like newborn bunny rabbits.[21] Eventually they end up facing one another, naked and sweaty by now, breasts and balls swaying as they work through their mirrored or parallel movements with quiet seriousness. Even when they are not touching, their movement is very intimate. But this is a result of the close atmosphere and their symmetrical movement, not the result of any erotic tension or an implied romantic narrative. Why is this, I ask myself? Here we have a naked woman and a naked man and yet there is not the slightest frisson of sexual desire or intrigue. Their embodiment works precisely against the cultural proscription of a heteronormative narrative, refusing the "normal" priorities of viewing in the abstract gestural dance sequences executed side by side, or with the preciousness usually accorded to a romantic duet. The space in between the bodies in this duet vibrates with an unfamiliar frequency as the meaning of their dancing is rendered askew. What are these two doing together, at once split and yet intimately connected?

Splitting and connecting—in pairs or as a larger group—is one of the underlying structures in Bebe Miller's *Landing/Place* (2005), a work that I was fortunate enough to see in performance several times over the course of its development. Originally inspired by a trip to the small African country of Eritrea, *Landing/Place* merges text, projected images, and a live sound score with the flow of exquisite dancing into a woven texture of landscape, memory, and human interactions. The central text across the top of the Bebe Miller Dance Company's website's home page says: "I've always been interested in the space between people." This choreographic focus, which she also defines as "the paradox of describing something from both the inside and the outside" has become increasingly intentional as Miller and her dramaturge, Talvin Wilkes, research creative methods to document and archive her artistic process and that of her collaborators. The director's notes for *Landing/Place* describe the central tension of the work: "LANDING/PLACE explores sensory, spatial and cultural dislocation, the yearning towards order in the apprehension of difference," and this sense of place and displacement is carried throughout the evening-length piece.

The dance begins as the plaintive sounds of an eerie stringed instrument sounds in the darkness. As the lights brighten on a small wooden house in the center of this space, we notice a video projection of an open window with curtains blowing upstage. Already this setting evokes a feeling of time passing and a sense of return. A woman, Angie Hauser, walks across the stage, stopping to look for or maybe at something. The tentative suspensions of her movement forward suggest that she has been here before, although maybe not for a long time. Soon a man, Darrell Jones, follows in her path and touches her back to begin the first of a series of duets that punctuate the larger journey of the piece. These duets, the result of extended improvisations of the theme of "circumnavigation," are marked by the same theme of connection and disconnection that animates the rest of the work. Reflecting on the process of making the movement, Hauser describes her and her partner's "adjacent but perpendicular" relationship: "it has to do with each of us maintaining the integrity of our individual 'score' while in intimate relationship to the other." Much of their dancing relies on the physically intimate and yet abstract partnering of the kind derived from Contact Improvisation, in which a reach of the arm motivates a pull from one's partner leading into an exchange of weight. Leaning over one another or riding the crest of someone else's movement, these movement interchanges register as meaningful mininarratives (especially when they actually look at one another), even though their expression eludes any easily definable relationship.

Throughout *Landing/Place* the dancing shifts from group interactions and extended duets into moments of sustained individual solos, pulling the audience's focus from large sweeps of movement across the landscape to quirky gestural behaviors. Sometimes the group gets caught up in a rhythm that carries its own sense of celebration as the straggler on the other side of the stage finally joins in the communal beat. Or maybe there is a clear leader, as in the moment where Kathleen Fisher is downstage dancing her heart out, and the rest of the group is shadowing her movement. At other times, there is more of a sense of group interdependence that gives the space a meditative quality, a sense of being alone while sharing space. Occasionally this togetherness carries a more mysterious, ritualistic tone, as in a moment when the stage is flooded with red light, and all the dancers arch up in wonder to look at something magical in the sky. Throughout much of the dance, video projections of landscapes, animated cityscapes, and motion capture figures provide a ghostly visual presence that echoes the live action onstage, but also (paradoxically) displaces it, incorporating a weightless visual realm that illustrates the impossibility of actually landing anywhere.

I am curious about the diacritical slash in *Landing/Place*, and the relationship of the small wooden house in the center and the movement streaming across the stage. What does movement have to do with finding a place to land? In her book, *The Cultural Politics of Emotion* (2004) Sara Ahmed offers a perspective that, interestingly, tells us a lot about this work.

> The relationship between movement and attachment is instructive. What moves us, what makes us feel, is also that which holds us in place, or gives us a dwelling place. Hence

movement does not cut the body off from the "where" of its inhabitance, but connects bodies to other bodies: attachment takes place through movement, through being moved by the
proximity of others.[22]

As a phenomenologist, Ahmed is attuned to the lived experience of interpersonal exchanges,
including communal ones. Her book also tries to shift the emphasis of affective studies from
"feelings" to the activity of feeling itself. As Ahmed points out, emotion is derived from the
Latin term *emovere*, which literally means to move away. Attending to feeling as the movement in between people rather than the psychological possession of emotion, Ahmed offers
"[a]n analysis of affective economies, where feelings do not reside in subjects or objects,
but are produced as effects of circulation."[23] Although Ahmed is much more interested in
how power relations become embedded in somatic exchanges, her emphasis on the circulation of feeling highlights the social work accomplished in the contemporary genre of
community-based performance.

A Life Without was the culmination of a three-month-long collaboration between the
educational outreach arm of Cleveland Public Theatre and Y-Haven, a transitional housing
and recovery program in Cleveland's west side. Performed by an intergenerational cast of
twelve men, this devised theater piece was staged in a variety of venues, including a church, a
high school auditorium, a community center, and at an experimental black box theater. The
event itself was framed by casual introductory remarks by the directors before the performance began, as well as by the final talk-back with the performers themselves after the show.
While these discussions highlighted the "professional" standards of the work (which meant
showing up on time, memorizing the text, and being able to repeat the scenes with consistency), *A Life Without* was clearly embedded within a specific situational and therapeutic
context. Although some men had more dramatic personas than others, and some had a clear
appetite for performing, all the men helped facilitate the group transitions and joined in the
choral moments, which were especially strong.

The narrative scaffolding of the play is a story of a sister's accidental death and the way
that loss creates choices and the possibility of community in the face of individual isolation. In their "Directors' Note" in the program, Adam Seeholzer, Chris Seibert, and Darius
Stubbs write, "Experiencing loss—the loss of an opportunity, a job, a loved one—any kind of
loss, can amplify our experience of choice. [. . .] It's ironic; to have such agency at the precise
moment when loss leaves us feeling powerless, cheated, even devastated." For me, the melodramatic recitation of the plot was distracting and the character embodiment felt forced
much of the time. Nonetheless, the cumulative effect of the whole experience transcended
the lack of theatrical mastery or skill. This was due, in part, to the corporeal subtext embedded in the communal moments of stillness, unison gesture, and song. In *A Life Without*, the
deep intimacy and sense of kinship among the men came to the fore when they all sang spirituals together, or in moments of group motion, such as the time they crossed the stage slowly,
rocking back and forth and singing as they marched along to signify a funeral procession.

Collaborations between theater practitioners and people in a specific community often
stage a performance to mark the completion of a project. This immersion in a process of
making something together is a rite of passage, a baptism of sorts (*Wade in the Water* was one
of the spirituals that the men sung) that insists that each man confront his own vulnerability and willingness to trust and compromise within the group dynamic. The talk-back after
every performance in which the men share individual stories of survival and transformation

highlights this aspect of the process. Indeed, this last stage was crucial in acknowledging the power of the exchange between performers and the importance of the audience's role as witnesses. Renewed applause and verbal affirmations followed each person's discussion of his particular challenges and achievements, including the response to one man's declaration that this was the first time he has ever finished anything in his life. The audience's role as witness in performances such as *A Life Without* raises the stakes of our own participation, allowing us to recognize the real social labor involved.

I began this chapter with a description of a recent production of *The Laramie Project* and ended it with one of a community-based collaboration entitled *A Life Without*. Both of these performances navigate the space between mimesis and abstraction, life and art, in ways that call upon a very different engagement with the audience. My discussion of corporeality in this writing is an attempt to expand how we might think about the circulation of embodied energies in performances that are based neither on the cathartic reception of a literary text in a traditional play nor on the belief that a legible kinesthetic impulse underlies all forms of expressive movement. I am interested in the less theorized and often invisible exchanges of somatic and cultural meaning that affect us in ways that we find hard to articulate and conceptualize. Often this is because our primary remembrance traces the elusive experience of being moved by the current of events (feeling), not necessarily the residue of emotion left behind after it is over (feelings). The examples of work presented here deploy theatrical elements of text, image, and motion in ways that confound our usual modes of audience reception. Splitting across the corporeal registers of language and movement, contemporary performance can take us beyond ourselves, leading the audience to develop new response-abilities toward what is happening onstage. As someone who is deeply committed to the intimacy of body-to-body interactions, I think that is a good thing.

NOTES

1. See the introduction to Ann Cooper Albright, *Choreographing Difference: The Body and Identity in Contemporary Dance* (Middletown, CT: Wesleyan University Press, 1997).
2. This quasi-ethnographic approach to telling stories and reimagining local, individual experiences of highly politicized events is a theatrical genre pioneered by performance studies scholars such as Dwight Conquergood and made popular by performers such as Anna Deavere Smith and ensembles like the Tectonic Theater Project.
3. Hans Thies Lehman, *Postdramatic Theatre* (New York and London: Routledge, 2006), 22.
4. Ibid., 85.
5. Ibid., 56.
6. Debby Thompson, "The Laramie Project," *Theatre Journal* 53, no. 4 (December 2001): 644.
7. Ibid., 645.
8. Liz Lerman, *Hiking the Horizontal* (Middletown, CT: Wesleyan University Press, 2011), 74.
9. Ibid., 74.
10. Ibid., 88.
11. Quoted in Edward Chute, "Critics, Catharsis and Colonus," *Comparative Drama* 5, no. 4 (Winter 1971–72): 283.
12. Kenneth Burke, "On Catharsis, or Resolution," *Kenyon Review* 21, no. 3 (Summer 1959): 366.

13. Lehman, *Postdramatic Theatre*, 68.
14. Ibid., 37–38.
15. Ibid., 95.
16. Ibid., 96.
17. Roslyn Sulcas, "Watching the Ballett Frankfurt," in *William Forsythe and the Practice of Choreography*, edited by Steven Spicer (London: Routledge, 2011), 16.
18. Dana Caspersen, "Decreation: Fragmentation and Continuity," in *William Forsythe and the Practice of Choreography*, edited by Steven Spicer (London: Routledge, 2011). 97.
19. Ibid., 98.
20. Ibid.
21. In the 1970s this movement might have resonated with Simone Forti's animal observations, but in the twenty-first century, many of us associate this with Bonnie Bainbridge Cohen's development movement sequences in her Body-Mind Centering work.
22. Sara Ahmed, *The Cultural Politics of Emotion* (New York: Routledge, 2004), 11.
23. Ibid., 8.

BIBLIOGRAPHY

Ahmed, Sara. *The Cultural Politics of Emotion*. New York: Routledge, 2004.

Albright, Ann Cooper. *Choreographing Difference: The Body and Identity in Contemporary Dance*. Middletown, CT: Wesleyan University Press, 1997.

Burke, Kenneth. "On Catharsis, or Resolution." *Kenyon Review* 21, no. 3 (Summer 1959): 337–375.

Caspersen, Dana. "Decreation: Fragmentation and Continuity." In *William Forsythe and the Practice of Choreography*, edited by Steven Spicer, 93–100. London: Routledge, 2011.

Chute, Edward. "Critics, Catharsis and Colonus." *Comparative Drama* 5, no. 4 (Winter 1971–72): 283–300.

Lehman, Hans Thies. *Postdramatic Theatre*. New York and London: Routledge, 2006.

Lerman. Liz. *Hiking the Horizontal*. Middletown, CT: Wesleyan University Press, 2011.

Sulcas, Roslyn. "Watching the Ballett Frankfurt." In *William Forsythe and the Practice of Choreography*, edited by Steven Spicer, 4–19. London: Routledge, 2011.

Thompson, Debby. "The Laramie Project." *Theatre Journal* 53, no. 4 (December 2001): 644–645.

CHAPTER 3

···

NEGOTIATING THEATRICS
Dialogues of the Working Man

···

ANITA GONZALEZ

IN working-class performance, bodies communicate, negotiating nontextual dialogues that invigorate cultural exchanges across language barriers. In working-class dialogues, the performing body prevails as a multilingual instrument. Scripts and texts locate theatrical practice on formal stages, but for working-class people work, not performance, is primary. I am interested in the way in which laboring workers communicate through song-and-dance practices where identity is at stake. What happens in moments of "down time" when song, dance, or storytelling become a way of bridging communities? This chapter uses maritime performance as a case study in dialogic performance practices that situate themselves in worker communities. Histories and current practices demonstrate that intercultural exchanges girded in dance/song theatricality are part and parcel of the maritime world as workers cross national boundaries. Indeed, ocean travel and seaports primarily nurtured transfer of theatrical dance culture prior to the mid-twentieth century.

Maritime performances are acts at sea—theater, music, and dance activities on ships, along shipping routes, or within port environments. The genre values money making through individual performing talent rather than serving aesthetic principles of high art. Because ships travel through international waters, maritime performance must supersede language boundaries. As a result, it privileges dance and song over text and literature. Narrative emerges through oral and gestural storytelling. In maritime settings, performers play with cultural difference. I posit that traveling artists encountering difference on ships or in ports modulate artistic praxis to adjust to shifting racial and cultural norms. The artist entrepreneur experiments with performance aesthetics until they result in lucrative artistic practice. Bringing a maritime lens to theatrical performance foregrounds points of cultural encounter. Each landing of a ship in a port provides an opportunity for workers to engage with a different culture. When a work break becomes a dance or storytelling break, liaisons and social commentary manifest through the performing gesture. Moments of restful play allow voyagers from differing class, national, or ethnic backgrounds to collaboratively negotiate identity associations within a transitional space.

In this chapter, I focus on transatlantic maritime performance with the understanding that the maritime world is not limited to hemispheric considerations. A topnotch nineteenth-century whaler, for example, could easily work the Atlantic and Pacific oceans over the course of a single whaling trip. Merchant and passenger ships of the same century generally worked across a single route—Liverpool to New York or Jamaica to Charleston to Boston. Today, in the new millennium, maritime performance is an equally viable way of passing time at sea while forming cross-cultural alliances. The cruise industry in particular uses performance to entertain and unify passengers and crew on ocean-going voyages.

Prior to the twentieth century all international performers, particularly those traveling between Europe and the Americas arrived by ship. Both career sailors and temporary travelers used time at sea to acquaint themselves with others on the ship. Onboard performance equalized voyagers trapped on a boat seeking respite from the monotony of the ocean. Nineteenth-century maritime working-class performance included dance/music competitions, crossing-the-line ceremonies, wrestling, sea chanteys, and "yarning." Each of these performance acts in some way staged identity through nontextual performance. Wealthier passengers, captains, or military officers participated in more formalized productions, watching minstrel shows, viewing short entertainments, or dancing at balls or parties. For example, scholar Mary Isbell, in her study of "ship theatricals," describes multiple performances of farces and melodramas staged on naval vessels, where sailors could develop and participate in amateur performance.[1] Modern cruise vessels replicate the idea of "play at sea" with cruise passengers.[2]

Performances on boats easily transfer ashore and most clearly manifest in similar kinds of cross-cultural terrestrial exchanges. Landed reinventions of working-class maritime performance are evident in pub dance competitions, carnival masquerades, and a plethora of metatheatrical street hawking, busking activities. While it is common to consider the port as a landing point for shore-based activities, for maritime travelers, notions of voyage and destination invert. Maritime people find a temporary respite at a port or pursue trade at a point of entry or exit. For example, early Dutch and Spanish settlers of the sixteenth century deliberately created outposts rather than populated settlements. They understood port as exchange point, not home. Any play of word or gesture was designed for profit, and the most lucrative act was to collect wealth and transfer to another point. Maritime performers work within this theoretical frame. Strict definitions of theater or dance are rendered irrelevant if the goal of the performing act is to encourage the audience to "put-money-in-the-hat." Experienced voyagers know the idiosyncrasies of each port and skillfully craft their acts to suit local practices.

A quick scan of mid-nineteenth-century newspapers from US port cities of New Bedford, Providence, Philadelphia, and Baltimore show vastly different types of entertainments.[3] New England harbors, founded by Quakers and Puritans, frowned on most types of theatrical activity. Consequently, newspapers from these active shipping ports primarily reference merchant exchange news and cargo reports. In contrast, sources like the "racy newspaper,"[4] working-class periodicals popular in mid-Atlantic ports, advertised lowbrow entertainments such as circuses or boxing matches. They also announce performances of visiting actors and minstrel companies, offering critical commentary about the nature or content of the shows (fig. 03.1).

During the age of sail, any shipboard performer with theatrical abilities would need to carefully assess the character of any specific port's culture before presenting his act. This was especially true if the performer were black or ethnic. These same paradigms of distinctive port cultures still affect maritime performance. Maritime performance acts, as

FIGURE 03.1 Billboard advertisement for a minstrel show next to a pier. Photographer unknown. Photo courtesy of Mander and Mitchenson/University of Bristol Theatre Collection/ArenaPAL.

an entertainment genre, readily transfer from ship to shore and back again, supporting or resisting local cultures.[5]

Dance/Music Competitions

Lithographs and drawings from the nineteenth century depict various onboard music and dance exchanges. The foc'sle or forward section of the ship was where common sea hands gathered. In its cramped, tight, low-ceiling space, each man was confined to a bunk or a hanging hammock. Sailors slept and worked in four-hour shifts, spending limited leisure time in the foc'sle. Nevertheless, this was an unsupervised space where mariners could freely tell stories (yarns) or share adventures either verbally or through their instruments. Personal memorabilia or instruments stored in trunks or bags brought from home might prompt a sailor to remember and share a folk song or melody. This under-the-deck storytelling established bonds between sailors and allowed workers from different countries to learn about customs and culture in other ports. Sailor's logs seldom describe the details of foc'sle entertainments, however they do include descriptions of conversations or exchanges between sailors. Most often they articulate frustration about the dangers of hard sea labor or express boredom with the monotony of working in a contained location, surrounded by a repeating landscape.[6]

The most frequent visual image of entertainment at sea that appears as the visual archive depicts two or three sailors performing a jig or hornpipe. Dancers, with knees lifted high, appear with a fiddler who accompanies the stepping (Henderson and Carlisle, 131–54). Jig dancing probably originated in Great Britain, although many nations have dance traditions that emphasize high-stepping knees and foot beats. In the maritime world, it makes sense that a dance like the jig that features sounding against a wooden deck, would become a popular form of shipboard play. The wooden deck provides a natural acoustic surface for amplifying complex foot beats. With a fiddle to carry the melody and propel the song along, a danced rhythm exchange could pass away long hours on the water. The easily transportable fiddle, often coupled with a flute, captured a variety of international folk song traditions: Irish, Italian, French, British, and American. Learning songs and dancing to them was popular during the age of sail. The physicalized exchange of foot to deck, hand to instrument, opened a forum for theatricalized communications that superseded language constraints.[7]

Jig dancing persisted as an entertainment on shore. Images similar to shipboard performance visuals also situate sailors at port locations. For example, a 1878 painting by the English painter George Green titled *Dancing the Hornpipe* depicts a sailor dressed in blue navy colors performing before a mixed-gender crowd in a low-ceiling pub. A well-dressed civilian accompanies the dance. As the men and their ladies witness the dance, they show silent respect for the dancing soloist. Other visual images of port sailors dancing jigs are much less flattering. A hand-colored engraving titled *Portsmouth Point* from 1784 portrays a rowdy port scene where prostitutes kiss, drunks grovel, and dockworkers laboriously roll barrels and sacks of goods. Amid the entire hubbub, a sailor with a wooden leg plays the fiddle and dances on his one good leg. Nobody watches his disabled busking. The theatricality of his peg leg performance is inextricably linked with his physical representation of marginal maritime life. Illustrated scenes of decadent port life capture fears and imaginations about maritime communities even as they document the real hardships of sailor's lifestyles.[8]

Undoubtedly the most widely publicized dance competitions were the 1845 exchanges between John Diamond and William Henry Lane (also known as Master Juba). Both of these performers built their careers on an ongoing battle of the feet. The two performers, one Irish and one of African descent, performed rhythmic and jig dancing in challenge acts that traversed the Atlantic Ocean. The dancers competed in both London and New York, charging money for spectators to bet on their performance speed and accuracy. Their spirited performances were but one of many types of ethnic performance trade-offs. In 1841 Charles Dickens witnessed jig competitions at the black-owned Almack's club on Orange Street in the Little Five Points district of New York. Five Points housed many dance clubs and drinking establishments. In both singing and dancing exchanges, the stakes were high. Successful entertainers received monetary awards of as much as five hundred dollars and were given the chance to travel and perform in Liverpool, London, and other British cities. Later, more structured entertainments like touring acts and variety shows would popularize the vernacular dances. Local audiences began to attend public spectacles, and the spectacles became forums for exchanges between ethnic communities. Part of the theatricality of the

FIGURE 03.2 *Jarocho* dancers from the coast of Mexico perform on a raised wooden platform or *tárima*. Photo by George O. Jackson Jr.

Diamond/Juba competitions lay in advertisements pitting the infamous contenders against one another. The notoriety of the performer partially determined his potential audience draw. Consequently the two performers crafted their stage personalities to accommodate the moneybox.[9]

Rhythmic board dances circulated through the maritime world affecting nonprofessional performers as well. Novices dancing a jig or sounding a board entertained one another. In some Latin American port towns dancing rhythmically on wooden platforms was a social rather than professional act. Jarocho, originating in Veracruz Mexico, brought together mariners from seaside towns to participate in *fandangos*, or collective gatherings of rhythmic play. In Jarocho song and dance musicians play stringed instruments like the guitar, *jarana*, or violin while dancers create percussive accompaniment on a *tarima*, or raised wooden platform. When performers turn this rhythmic play into competitive exchange, dancers circle one another in complex patterns. Couples, either male/male or male/female, display prowess through the accuracy of their foot beats and, perhaps more importantly, the demeanor of their characters as they face off on the platform. Jarocho is associated with maritime fishing communities and with black presence along the gulf coastal area. Today, in the twenty-first century, Latino communities dance Jarocho as a way of maintaining cultural connections with Mexican heritage (fig. 03.2).[10]

CROSSING THE LINE

"Crossing the Line" ceremonies were another rich source of maritime play. This masquerade, like initiation ceremonies of medieval guilds, inaugurates a novice sailor into an experienced sailor social network. The enactment, drawing from mythologies of the ocean involves, masking, role playing, degradation, subservience, and ultimately acceptance. Hazing of initiates is an important component of the ritual. When a boat passes over the equator, or the artic circle, a senior sailor bedecked like a sea god plays the role of King Neptune. As officiator of the ritual, he inducts younger sailors through pranks, beatings, or devised tortures such as shaving in salt water with a dull blade. Race and gender are commonly inverted in these ceremonies so that men dress up as mermaids, while lowly cooks or stewards can become a part of Neptune's "court." Bronner argues that the ceremony incorporates myths and legends from various nations (witches, mermaids, turtles), severs ties with the homeland, and instates a maritime culture where gender roles shift.[11]

The ceremony takes place over two days. Davy Jones, who represents lost sailors, appears the night before the celebration as a kind of omen for what is to come. The following day Neptune appears with his entourage. Often he has a wife, a senior sailor dressed in outrageous female garb. Together they enter on a chariot that may be pulled by younger, "pollywog" sailors. Once Neptune arrives, he obtains permission from the captain to take over the ship so that he may cleanse the vessel of uninitiated pollywogs. After enduring a series of tests and trials, the pollywogs or novice sailors will be able to earn their way into the ranks of the "shellbacks" or veteran sailors—they will have "crossed the line" both metaphorically and physically. Bronner writes at length about how the maritime ceremony, through its initiation activities, inculcates sailors into a new set of social relationships that affirm masculine codes even as they give permission for sailors to engage in feminine activities. For example, a later phase of the ritual has sailors dress in drag and lick egg yolk off one another's bellies. Sexualized female behaviors are forced onto sailors, so that they will understand the new gender codes and boundaries of onboard life.[12]

Distinct racial or ethnic identities are conflated in the maritime act of Crossing the Line. Photographs and drawings depicting the ceremony reflect the ethnic diversity of the maritime world. When sailors put on the garb of cannibals, beasts, gods, witches, and unruly women they experiment with a cross-section of archetypal images. The very unstructured nature of the world they recreate allows for new mythologies, imaginatively constructed and uniquely formulated to each ship's crew and architecture. Through embodiment within a ritual ceremonial act, an alternative maritime culture replaces the customs or cultural backgrounds of each individual sailor. Now each voyager can reference two realities, the one they knew before and the one that binds them to the endless sea.

Merchant and navy ships still practice Crossing the Line ceremonies. Despite public outcry against hazing in the military, the ritual persists as a valued component of maritime culture. Mass communication specialist Andrew B. Church, writing about the ceremony in 2013, quotes a Navy man and explains, "The tradition has carried on, but it's carried out so that it is in line with our Navy Core Values . . . the purpose of the ceremony is to have fun, but it is strictly voluntary and Sailors can leave at any time. We keep it safe." Today's masquerades struggle to locate female sailors within a very masculine paradigm, yet both Bronner and Church cite women sailors who seem to enjoy the shellback status they earn through the initiation rites. One wonders if antics like licking the belly or biting the buttocks have the same significance in the mixed gender rendition of the at-sea play.

Sea initiation rites transfer to shore as maritime activities that maintain guild associations or activities in port towns. The Seaman's Church Institute in Newport, Rhode Island, for example, is a sailor's service organization that connects mariners at sea with a community of mariners living in port cities. "Serving those connected with the sea," the institution offers "compassionate assistance to seamen and their families."[13] The restored historical building housing the institute sits near the docks in a highly gentrified section of an upscale New England town. If you are a mariner, the Seaman's Church can offer inexpensive housing, meals, and camaraderie. Seaman's homes are part of a matrix of port institutions that support lifestyles of sailors once they land. Like pubs and maritime service depots, they enable sailors to continue camaraderie on shore and to maintain maritime identities forged on the boat through Crossing the Line rituals and other work activities.

Upstairs at the Seaman's Church a reclusive space, the Chapel of the Sea, sometimes draws visitors. This small chapel, full of iconic, symbolic sea imagery, honors men and women who died at sea. Within the chapel an expansive blue mural painted on all four walls of the space, is peppered with images of maritime saints from various nations. Visitors can leave offerings to lost loved ones on an altar that resembles intricately carved sailcloth embedded with knots. At the center of the small, slightly cramped area, an image of a seashell is engraved into the floor. It symbolically marks the ultimate resting ground of many a mariner. Sitting in the chapel gives the impression of stepping underwater; it offers space to for those connected with the maritime community to commemorate the loss of maritime lives through embodied pilgrimage to the chapel. The cornice of the Chapel of the Sea displays a verse from Psalms 107: "They that go down to the Sea in ships, and occupy their business in great waters; these men see the works of The Lord and His wonders in the deep. For He maketh the storms to cease so that the waves thereof are still. Then are they glad because they are at rest, and so He bringeth them unto their desired haven." The Seaman's Church Institute provides a land-based safe house for sailors. Religious rituals that take place in the chapel of the seaman's home can be seen as extensions of rituals like the Crossing the Line ceremony that unify seamen. The act of coming to the chapel and paying homage to dead sailors is performative in that individuals or groups can come to a place that recognizes the unique maritime community and displays symbols that are especially meaningful to sailors. The chapel helps mariners come to terms with the dangers and losses of life at sea and provides a place where sailors can continue to honor the ritual traditions established at sea.

Downstairs there are lively maritime performance activities that contrast the solemn symbols of the upstairs memorial site. The Aloha Café (the name evokes a far- flung port) hosts a monthly musical event called "Food Folk and Fun," where local singers share songs and stories. The sessions, populated by locals, invoke memories of seaside sessions old and new. Gathering spaces like the Aloha Café allow mariners to trade stories or sing songs that validate their maritime histories. But seaman's institutes uniquely sanitize the maritime space. Activities at the Rhode Island institute build on a tradition of seaman's homes that, during the mid to late nineteenth century, sought to evangelize mariners. Victorian agencies tried

r or ine Emancipator.

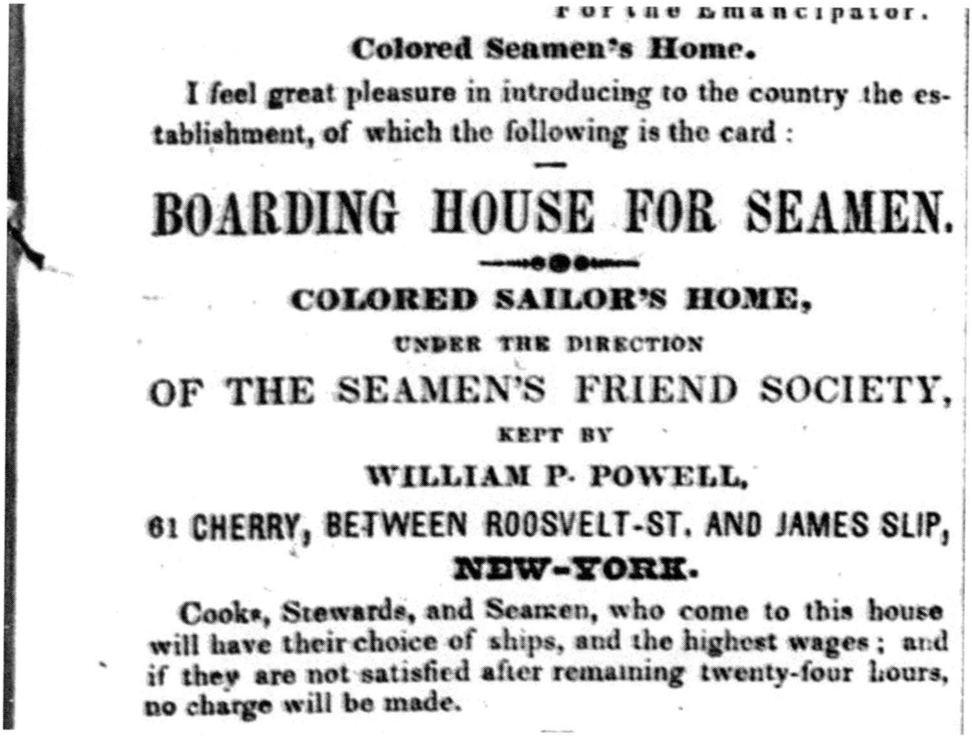

Colored Seamen's Home.

I feel great pleasure in introducing to the country the establishment, of which the following is the card :

—

BOARDING HOUSE FOR SEAMEN.

———•⊙•———

COLORED SAILOR'S HOME,

UNDER THE DIRECTION

OF THE SEAMEN'S FRIEND SOCIETY,

KEPT BY

WILLIAM P. POWELL,

61 CHERRY, BETWEEN ROOSVELT-ST. AND JAMES SLIP,

NEW-YORK.

Cooks, Stewards, and Seamen, who come to this house will have their choice of ships, and the highest wages ; and if they are not satisfied after remaining twenty-four hours, no charge will be made.

FIGURE 03.3 Image of a mid-nineteenth-century advertisement introducing William Powell's Colored Seaman's Home. Photo courtesy of Anita Gonzalez.

to contain and control port activities of sailors, who were renowned for living itinerant and uncouth lives. While seaman's homes provided cheap food and shelter, sailors using the facilities were also expected to learn the Bible and abstain from unsavory activities. Similar types of organizations included the Marine Temperance Society, and the Colored Seaman's Home (fig. 03.3).

Each of these institutions took a three-pronged approach to maritime activism: pastoral care, maritime education, and legal advocacy to protect the health and well-being of sailors.[14] Even though seaman's homes attempted to restrictively shape seaman lifestyles, they provided a space for performance of sacred and secular rituals that solidified and validated maritime culture.

SEA SHANTIES

If ever you go to Liverpool
To Liverpool the Packet School
Yankee Sailors there you'll see
With red-topped boots an' short cut hair

> There's Liverpool Pat with his tarpaulin hat
> And 'Frisco Jim the packet rat.
> Wake up yer bitch 'n' let us in
> Get up yer bitch 'n' serve us gin
> Oh I wisht I wuz in Liverpool Town
> Them Liverpool judies I'd dance around.
> O long Stormy-stormalong
> O long Stormy-stormalong[15]

Lyrics of the shanty "Stormalong, Lads Stormy"[16] reference a history of transatlantic travel and performance harkening back to a time when interracial sailors sang songs to unite their efforts while executing shipboard tasks. Yet the practice of singing sea songs persists in folk-life festivals and contemporary shanty sing-alongs. From Alaska to Mystic Seaport, folk activists write lyrics and participate in tributes to the maritime world through song. "Stormalong, Lads Stormy," one of the more popular shanties, evokes red-haired sailors on packet ships traveling to and from Liverpool and demanding "bitch" service from ladies who dance to entertain the crew of the sailing vessel. Shanty practitioners who sing this song and songs like this revitalize discussions of transnational maritime with each reiteration of the shanty tale.

Liverpool is a useful site to begin discussions of race within the maritime world. The British town is a port city with a long history of maritime multicultural encounters. In 1664, the small village was merely a shipping stop along the rugged western coast of Great Britain. One hundred years later, as the physical infrastructure of the port improved and more sailors migrated into the area, Liverpool was poised to become the major slave port of the English-speaking world. The slave trade ignited a triangular exchange of goods that brought prosperity to the city, particularly during the eighteenth century. Some maintain that Liverpool was built on the backs of slave labor. As mariners navigated through Atlantic waters meeting demands for slaves and goods, the Liverpool docks evolved into a multilingual site of cultural meetings. By the mid-nineteenth century, passenger services between England and the Americas replaced slave trading as a primary source of maritime employment.

Transatlantic passenger trade accelerated as sailors learned to sail faster and more efficiently. Liverpool Packets, established in 1818 by the Black Ball shipping line, increased traffic along this lucrative route.[17] "Stormalong, Lads Stormy" references this shipping line when it describes Frisco Jim as a Packet Rat. Packet ships were the first to sail along a fixed route on a regular schedule. This meant that the vessels would sail regardless of weather. The tough sailors who were able to manage the sails along the cold northern Atlantic route regardless of the weather were know as "Packet Rats." This tight community of maritime workers valued strength and expertise over racial divisions; they were willing to work with anyone who could endure the grueling work.

Hugill, in his book *Shanties from the Seven Seas* credits his knowledge of the sea shanty "Stormalong" to "a fine old coloured seaman who hailed from Barbadoes." He describes the colored seaman as one who sailed on British, American, Scandinavian, and West Indian Traders. "He was a master of the 'hitch'—the singing of wild yelps at certain points in a hauling song . . . he would give vent to many wild 'hitches,' absolutely impossible for a white man to copy, although white sailors did execute a poor shadow of the negro yelps."[18] Hugill's description of singing yelps underscores a core aspect of sea shanty performance—its origins in African American work song practices.

A sea shanty differs from a foc'sle song in that a shanty is specifically meant to accompany work. Foc'sle songs, in contrast, are usually ballads or storytelling songs that would be sung during "down time" for idle entertainment. Most sea shanty historians consider West African work songs absolute forerunners of sea shanties. Rhythmic percussive singing is pervasive in South and West Africa, and sailors traveling to the gold coast in the seventeenth and eighteenth centuries quickly realized that singing while working could unify a crew and help to make time pass more quickly. Even though sea shanties tell stories, they are limited in content since the primary intent of the singing is to do the work. At the same time, they provide an opportunity to trade off song ideas or improvise around verses. The type of work performed defines the type of sea shanty that will be sung. If sailors are turning the capstan then they sing a capstan shanty. If they are doing a long pull, like hauling up an anchor or using a pulley to move cargo onto the ship, then they might sing a "hand over hand" song, where the verses of the song help to coordinate one hand passing over the other onto the rope.[19]

The multicultural origins of sea shanties are well established. Even Hugill, who questions the solely African origins of sea shanties, is quick to reference the multicultural dimensions of the songs. Black West Indian influences on sea shanties are particularly easy to trace because mariners in the Caribbean still actively sing them. What is most important to this discussion is the type of dialogic exchange that occurs when sailors sing shanties. As the songs travel with sailors through global ports, they are enhanced and adapted each time they are sung. Hugill, for example describes how "coolie" ships that traveled through the West Indies mixed Hindustani language from the Lascari of East India with pidgin English to develop the song *Eki Dumah (Kay, Kay, Kay)*.[20]

Global circulation of sea shanties is evident at the Sea Music Festival. Mystic, Connecticut, supports this annual summer event that draws hundreds of sea shanty singers to a single location. Mystic Seaport uniquely allows sea music enthusiasts to embody sea shanties by pulling ropes or turning halyards while singing the songs. The historic museum houses whale boats, sailing vessels, and simulated ropes pulls, enabling experiential immersive practice in sea shanty singing. The international music festival draws some of the world's best chanticleers, and its high-profile concert performance events ensure dialogue and exchange between artists. New forms for singing songs also emerge at the festival. A sea music symposium is a part of the festival, and the 2013 academic session introduced poet/singers from an Alaskan fishing village as well as artists from communities in New Zealand, Australia, and other far-flung ports. Many of the festival participants are historical reenactment enthusiasts and not seamen; nevertheless, the festival demonstrates that storytelling and exchange still unites some maritime communities.

Negotiating Race in Nineteenth-Century Maritime Performance

My discussion of maritime performance views acts at sea as opportunities for sailors from diverse cultural communities to negotiate status and exchange cultural practices. African negotiations of racial identity in the nineteenth-century maritime world exemplify shifting modes of identity expressed through performance. Sailing while black during the nineteenth century was a precarious undertaking. Each port offered a completely different landscape for black identities. A colored seaman traveling on a merchant ship in 1840 might venture from the Caribbean islands with their primarily black populations, to Charleston port, a slaveholding city where it might be safer to stay on the ship. From there, traveling north, the sailor might arrive in Northern ports such as Philadelphia, New York, or Boston, where free black mariner communities thrived. In the United States, the status of black mariners changed drastically between the beginning and the end of nineteenth century. The war of 1812 offered opportunities for African-descendant peoples to learn maritime skills by working and fighting on British ships. When the war ended and they had earned their freedom, they were free to travel and work throughout the maritime world. Increasing demand for maritime workers on passenger ships and Liverpool packets also offered opportunities. In the 1820s, newspapers freely advertised for black stewards and waiters, yet by 1850 jobs for free black mariners were nearly nonexistent. Archival papers from the Colored Seaman's Home run by William Powell describe an increasingly desperate stream of impoverished black sailors passing through Powell's establishment on Cherry Street in New York City.[21] The most prevalent occupations for sailors of African descent were the positions of steward or cook (fig. 03.4).

The steward or cabin boy would personally attend to the needs of the captain and his mates. Unlike the common seamen who hovered in the foc'sle, the steward and cook would stay in quarters closer to the captain so that they could respond to his daily demands. I view

FIGURE 03.4 1889 photograph of the crew of the *Moel Eilian* passenger ship with a black cook. The ship was built in 1877 and sailed between Liverpool and Australia. Photographer unknown. Photo courtesy National Museums Liverpool (Merseyside Maritime Museum).

this arrangement as one similar to the Pullman Porters. The African sailing staff could quietly witness conversations in the captain's quarters while attending to his duties. Many cooks and stewards were also abused, and by the end of the century some would work without pay as if they were enslaved. Yet the status of a conscripted African sailor and a conscripted white sailor differed little in the later nineteenth century. And some stewards did very well.[22]

Historian Sokolow carefully researched the life of Charles Benson, an African American mariner from the city of Salem, Massachusetts, who worked for over 40 years as a steward, traveling primarily to the east coast of Africa with merchant ships. He was one of the few African American sailors to keep a complete record about his travels in a journal. In the book *Charles Benson: Mariner of Color in the Age of Sail*, Sokolow chronicles the life of this man who, while successful in his maritime career, lost connections with his family and with African American social and political movements. Even though Benson travels freely throughout the Atlantic and Indian oceans, he does not use his position to promote social activism. Instead, the daily drudgery of his shipboard life prevents him from pursuing social or cultural interests. Sokolow maintains that Benson's greatest pride and greatest achievements lay in his skill as a mariner. Toward the end of his voyages the steward was left in charge of purchasing food and goods for ship at each port, and he earned more money than other common seamen on the vessel.

Understanding the position of the steward helps explain the emergence of the African Grove Theatre in New York City in 1821. Afro-Caribbean William Wells Brown came to know about the art of theater through his service on ships that sailed between the Caribbean, New York, and Liverpool. James Hewlett, the actor that he hired for performances in his summer African Grove, was also a steward along this line. Hewlett's skills as a tailor, coupled with his first-hand knowledge of British Shakespeare performances allowed him to introduce theatrical performances to the "free colored people" of New York.[23] One accomplishment of the African Grove was the production of the first African American play, *King Shotaway*. This play told the story of the Native American chief Chatoyer, who, working with enslaved Africans, attempted to overthrow British rule on the island of St. Vincent. Brown's connection to St. Vincent makes sense if he arrived in New York on the ocean currents that move cargo and people from south to north. Actors of the African Grove were probably not the only performers to fluctuate between service work and performance work. As I mentioned earlier, images of black buskers dancing or playing fiddles appear in multiple archival documents. I'm interested in how African descendants shifted and negotiated identity as they moved along maritime routes.[24]

One clear example is Ira Aldridge. He was not a mariner, even though the steward actors of the African Grove inspired him to pursue his career. He took advantage of increasingly frequent passenger opportunities to travel to the United Kingdom by ship, and he was able to develop and maintain a long and lucrative career as an actor in Europe. In the process, he renamed himself the African Roscius and crafted an identity that differed greatly from the minstrelsy that was popular in the United States. By playing a cross-section of character types, ranging from the black doctor Fabian to the comic slave Mungo to the noble Othello, he was able to demonstrate cultural fluency in performance practice. This working-class man successfully used the shifting potentials of the maritime world to craft a new livelihood.[25]

Dialogic Conversations
in Blackface Minstrelsy

Not all performers succeeded in making this shift. Another example of a maritime exchange was the 1866 tour to Liverpool of Mr. Hague's Slave Troupe of Georgia Minstrels. Hoping to build on the successes of "real negro impersonator" black minstrel companies in the United States, Mr. Hague decided to bring a troupe of emancipated African Americans to Liverpool. The results were disastrous. When they traveled to Liverpool in 1866 the black entertainers were not well received. The heavily Irish city of Liverpool preferred to see interpretations of blackness designed and performed by whites. The entrepreneur eventually fired his black actors, leaving several behind to become integrated into the local black Liverpudlian community.[26] Nineteenth-century minstrelsy and its performance had different meanings on each side of the Atlantic Ocean. While US minstrelsy developed within a highly segregated slave economy, black minstrelsy in England reflected and commented on a distant and exotic social "type." Working-class artists like Sam Hague's troupe, who engaged in transnational minstrelsy, understood cultural distinctions in the reception of their performance and adjusted characters, venues, and performance styles to match shifting social environments for their acts. Unfortunately African American artists performing caricatures of black lifestyles were not a winning formula.

When innovative white performers like the Virginia Minstrels developed blackface minstrelsy, the working-class communities in both England and the United States embraced the genre as a mechanism for distancing themselves from popular imagery that personified immigrants as poor, uncouth, outsiders. Minstrelsy was ideally suited for this transformation; it was a revue-style performance format that could be used for political ends. Not only could the show's contents be adapted for local social commentary but also the genre itself, by ridiculing southern African American lifestyles, served a political purpose. The supposed ignorant and uncouth manners of the southern Negro provided strong contrast for the humanity and relative whiteness of immigrants.[27]

Lower class Irish- and British-descendant performers created US minstrel shows as a way of capitalizing their art. The revue format of the shows made them easily adaptable to varying talents and acting abilities. Furthermore the format and structure of the shows referenced busking and troubadour traditions long popular with the European working class. Uniquely North American versions of the "show" cast African Americans as ignorant creatures content with the slow and lazy life of the American south. While there was some variety in the depiction of character types, all were derogatory and simplistic. It is no coincidence that Irish immigrants were often participants in American minstrelsy performances. The Irish themselves had often been represented as animalistic creatures, "bog trotters," ogres, or pigs, in derogatory British cartoons and comedy acts. Thomas Nast's cartoon drawings of the Irish in New York City (published in *Harper's Weekly*) are just one example of this type of negative stereotyping. United States minstrelsy provided an opportunity for Irish and other lower class citizens to elevate themselves while denigrating and ridiculing African Americans.[28]

Minstrel performances persisted throughout the nineteenth and into the early twentieth centuries, becoming featured acts in port towns and on merchant/passenger ships.[29] While researching popular theater acts in the Mander and Micheson archives in Bristol, I came across a photograph of a troupe of blackface minstrels (fig. 03.5).[30]

Nineteen men are sitting on the deck of a ship just beneath the ropes of the upper deck. They wear biblike white shirts and white gloves that contrast their dark clothes and shoes. Tambo and Bones, the end men of the show still hold their sticks and tambourine. The image is labeled "The Nubian Minstrels taken on board the training Ship Exmouth, 1888." You can't tell whether the performers are black or white from the photograph. Even if you could see skin tones or examine crew lists, descriptive labels used in maritime logs—"black," "brown," "dark," "colored," "swarthy"—are elusive. The photograph underscores the fluency of voyages and returns. A performance genre originating in the United States travels in circular routes within very material boats that sail or steam along very prescribed ocean currents. Each stopping-off point initiates a dialogue about race, ethnicity, and culture that regenerates and transforms. Port towns with their mobile and multilingual constituencies thrive on dialogues expressed through performance acts that blur lines between theater and dance. When verbal language fails, call or shouts or dances or impersonations communicate.

FIGURE 03.5 Photograph of minstrels sitting on a ship after a 1889 performance by the Nubian minstrels on the training ship *Exmouth*. Photographer unknown. Photo courtesy of Mander and Mitchenson/University of Bristol Theatre Collection/ArenaPAL.

CODA

Roatán, Honduras. The pilot boats have finished guiding the cruise ship into its slot of the extended pier at Coxen Hole. This island, once an extension of Honduras's banana coast, now markets scuba diving and snorkeling trips along the barrier reef. Its cruise pier, partially owned by Royal Caribbean, opened in 2008. Because the cruise ship company owns the pier, it can control access and select appropriate activities for the guests. Today, as the passengers disembark, a collective of dancers dressed in traditional Garinagú regalia greet the guests by playing drums and dancing shuffling steps slightly reminiscent of the ceremonial *punta* dancing that characterizes Black Caribe culture. The Garífuna[31] were one of the earliest settlers of the island of Roatan. An early community migrated to the coast of Honduras in 1797, when they were ousted from the island of St. Vincent's after joining with Taino islanders to rebel against British rule. King Chatoyer, the subject of the play *King Shotaway*, was a part of this rebellion. Garinagú culture is one of the few black cultures of the Americas that maintain an indigenous language.

Roatán, located on the banana coast, provides a useful window for discussion of cruise maritime history. An inventive and entrepreneurial sailor named Dow Baker first imagined transporting bananas in 1878, when he brought a load of bananas up the coastal currents to Boston and resold them for a profit. Recognizing a business opportunity, he formed the Boston Banana Company with partners.

Later, United Fruit Company acquired the business, introducing the Great White Fleet in 1907. To improve business efficiency and to prevent fruit from rotting, the corporation installed air-conditioned holds on their vessels and innovatively marketed a "Tropical Fruit Steamship" company that could transport both bananas and passengers aboard air-conditioned vessels. While transatlantic passenger trade was well established by the second half of the nineteenth century, the notion of cruising through warm waters for the experience of the ocean was a unique innovation of the banana industry.[32] Rozwadowski writes, "Between 1840 and 1880, the ocean ceased being a wasteland and a highway and was transformed into a destination, a frontier, an uncivilized place ripe for conquest and exploration."[33] Open water and nautical thoroughfares accommodated late-nineteenth and early-twentieth-century leisure travelers who could afford free time and transport fees. The deep blue ocean unfolded as a backdrop for scales of human desires and potentialities. Sixty years later, in 1966, Ted Arison expanded the idea of upscale leisure travel. Capitalizing on consumer urges for uncomplicated, exotic travel experiences, he founded Norwegian Cruise lines. By 1972 Arison had acquired Carnival Cruises, whose empire of corporate subsidiaries expanded and merged into clusters of cruise ship ownership that consists of Costa Cruises, Royal Caribbean, and Celebrity enterprises.[34] The banana coast that first spawned the idea of Caribbean leisure cruising continues to market bananas and island life.

In the new millennium, dancing Garífuna port performers differ little from predecessors who might have entertained these early tourists. The ensemble on the dock uses song, dance, and local customs to earn money and to communicate their heritage. A Great White Fleet advertisement from 1927 depicts black people carrying baskets of fruits on their heads as they welcome passengers landing in dinghies from a great white ship. Today the Garífuna dancers similarly carry baskets on their heads as they demonstrate ethnic artistry. I can easily see through the artifice of the performance. The dancers execute the more energetic dance steps between 9:00 and 10:00 a.m. as the bulk of the passengers disembark. They collect tips and financial offerings in a painted red pail. If anyone wants to take a picture they pay more. Later in the day the performers will sporadically hit the drum once or twice if it looks as if a passenger might be inclined to donate. The ensemble includes two or three women and a couple of men so that the performers are able to trade off. No one wants to exert herself too much in the midday heat. I'm not sure what the dancers do when they leave the port. This dance performance is an adaptation of their life to accommodate port trade. Maybe next week they will be in New York helping an aunt or uncle manage another business. Maritime economies are managing the ebb and flow of their performances.

Theater and dance, viewed through the lens of a maritime life, are fluid exchanges that easily blur genre distinctions. In a stinky port on a hot day no one cares to analyze where text and narration ends and dance begins. The gestalt of the experience either deserves compensation or it doesn't. For the performer, disciplinary boundaries unravel in the effort to entertain, communicate, and earn elusive currency. Hardscrabble struggles for social mobility are more important than genres. If knowing other cultural art forms or performing in more lucrative social spaces can be achieved by shifting performance modes, then the working-class performer will respond. Performance serves as a template for negotiating identities against a backdrop of work.

NOTES

1. Mary Isbell, "P(l)aying Off Old Ironsides and the Old Wagon: Melville's Depiction of Shipboard Theatricals in White Jacket," *Leviathan: A Journal of Melville Studies* 15, no. 1 (2013): 8–16.
2. Activities staff on contemporary cruise ships often organize events where passengers can dance, sing, cook, or otherwise cavort with the crew during sea days. Cruise ships also offer professional staged productions to entertain guests.
3. In this survey of port newspapers I focused on clippings from 1845 to 1850 using collections at the New Bedford Public Library in New Bedford, Massachusetts, and the American Antiquarian Society's newspaper collection in Worcester, Massachusetts.
4. "Racy newspapers" are a collection of low-brow, working-class newspapers that circulated in mid-Atlantic port cities such as New York, Philadelphia, or Boston. A few extant issues are collected as microfilm rolls. Their content includes community events such as fires, brawls, dances, or spectacles as well as complaints against vagrant women. Some of the newspapers include reprints of popular novels.
5. Adrian Jarvis and W. Robert Lee, *Trade, Migration, and Urban Networks in Port Cities, c. 1640–1940* (St. John's, Newfoundland: International Maritime Economic History Association, 2008); and Robert Greenhalgh Albion and Jennie Barnes Pope, *The Rise of New York Port 1815–1860* (New York: C. Scribner's Sons, 1939).
6. Frederick Pease Harlow, *The Making of a Sailor; or, Sea Life aboard a Yankee Square-rigger* (Salem, MA: Marine Research Society, 1928), Print; *Journal of the Barque Keoka: New York to San Francisco*: Mystic Seaport Research Center, 1849; John Holstead Mead, *Sea Shanties and Fo-c-sle Songs, 1768–1906* (Lexington: University of Kentucky, 1973), dissertation; Clement Cleveland Sawtell, *Captain Nash DeCost and the Liverpool Packets* (Mystic,

CT: Marine Historical Association, 1955); and Michael Sokolow, *Charles Benson: Mariner of Color in the Age of Sail* (Amherst: University of Massachusetts Press, 2003).

7. Kevin McManus, *Ceilis, Jigs, and Ballads: Irish Music in Liverpool* (Liverpool: Institute of Popular Music, University of Liverpool, 1994).

8. J. Welles Henderson and Rodney P. Carlisle, *Marine Art and Antiques: Jack Tar; a Sailor's Life 1750–1910* (Woodbridge, England: Antique Collectors' Club, 1999), 149, 130.

9. Tyler Anbinder, *Five Points: The 19th-Century New York City Neighborhood That Invented Tap Dance, Stole Elections, and Became the World's Most Notorious Slum* (New York: Free Press, 2001); W. James Cook, "Master Juba, the King of All Dancers: A Story of Stardom and Struggle from the Dawn of the Transatlantic Culture Industry," *Discourses in Dance* 3, no. 2 (2006): 7–20; V. James Hatch and Errol G. Hill, *A History of African American Theatre*. Cambridge Studies in American Theatre and Drama (New York: Cambridge University Press, 2003); Hans Nathan, *Dan Emmett and the Rise of Early Negro Minstrelsy*. New ed. (Norman: University of Oklahoma Press, 1977); and Marian Hannah Winter, "Juba and American Minstrelsy," *Dance Index* 6 (1947): 28–48.

10. Anita Gonzalez, *Jarocho's Soul: Cultural Identity and Afro-Mexican Dance* (Lanham, MD: University Press of America (Rowman and Littlefield), 2004) and *Afro-Mexico: Dancing between Myth and Reality* (Austin: University of Texas Press, 2010).

11. Dan Bryant, *A Comical Ethiopian Sketch in Four Scenes* (New York: Dewitt, 1874), 8–15.

12. Bryant, *A Comical Ethiopian Sketch in Four Scenes*; Andrew Church, "From 'Wog to Shellback." Story Number: NNS130704-01. *America's Navy*. July 4, 2013. http://www.navy.mil/submit/display.asp?story_id=75241 (accessed January 31, 2014); Henderson and Carlisle, *Marine Art and Antiques*; Isbell, "P(l)aying Off Old Ironsides and the Old Wagon"; and Harry Miller Lydenberg, *Crossing the Line: Tales of the Ceremony during Four Centuries* (New York: New York Public Library, 1957).

13. From the website of the Newport Seaman's Church Institute.

14. "Colored Sailors Home Reports, 1855 to 1866," American Seaman's Friends Society. Manuscript Collection of Mystic Seaport. Collection 158, Box 2, Folder 2, (New York, 2012); A. Paul Gilje, *Liberty on the Waterfront: American Maritime Culture in the Age of Revolution* (Philadelphia: University of Pennsylvania Press, 2004); Benjamin Woods Labaree, *America and the Sea: A Maritime History* (Mystic, CT: Mystic Seaport, 1998); W. Alex Roland, Jeffrey Bolster, and Alexander Keyssar, *The Way of the Ship: America's Maritime History Re-envisioned, 1600–2000* (Hoboken, NJ: Wiley, 2008).

15. Shanty singers sing the chorus "O Long Stormy Storm-along" between each line of verse recorded here.

16. Stan Hugill, *Shanties from the Seven Seas: Shipboard Work-Songs and Songs Used as Work-Songs from the Great Days of Sail* (Mystic, CT: Routledge & Kegan Paul, 1961). Reprint, 1994, 70.

17. Roland, Bolster, and Keyssar, *The Way of the Ship*, 160–162; Albion and Barnes Pope, *The Rise of New York Port 1815–1860*, 38–54.

18. Hugill, *Shanties from the Seven Seas*, 71.

19. Horace Palmer Beck, *Folklore and the Sea*. 1st ed. (Middletown, CT: Published for the Marine Historical Association, Mystic Seaport, by Wesleyan University Press, 1973); Hugill, *Shanties from the Seven Seas*; Craig Edwards, Personal interview. July 16, 2012; Mead, *Sea Shanties and Fo-c-sle Songs*; Robert Young Walser, *The Shantyman's Canon*. Master's thesis, University of Wisconsin-Madison, 1995.

20. Hugill, *Shanties from the Seven Seas*, 361.

21. W. Jeffrey Bolster, *Black Jacks: African American Seamen in the Age of Sail* (Cambridge, MA: Harvard University Press, 1997); "Colored Sailors Home Reports, 1855 to 1866"; Carla L. Peterson, *Black Gotham: A Family History of African Americans in Nineteenth-century New York City* (New Haven, CT: Yale University Press, 2011); Sokolow, *Charles Benson*; Shane White, *Stories of Freedom in Black New York* (Cambridge, MA: Harvard University Press, 2002), Print.

22. Charles Brown, "Steward." Letter 1873 by Charles E. Brown. H.H. Brown of Providence RI. Whaling Bark Courser, New Bedford. Aug. 27, 1873. Speech; "Colored Sailors Home Reports, 1855 to 1866"; Sokolow, *Charles Benson*.

23. Marvin McAllister, *Whiting Up: Whiteface Minstrels and Stage Europeans in African American performance* (Chapel Hill: University of North Carolina Press, 2011), 43–47

24. Jonathan Dewberry, "The African Grove Theatre and Company," *Black American Literature Forum* 16 (1986); Marvin McAllister, *White People Do Not Know How to Behave at Entertainments Designed for Ladies and Gentlemen of Colour: William Brown's African and American Theater* (Chapel Hill: University of North Carolina Press, 2003) and *Whiting Up*.

25. Courtney Kujawinska and Maria Lukowska, *Ira Aldridge 1807–1967* (Frankfurt: Peter Lang, 2009); Bernth Lindfors, *Ira Aldridge: The African Roscius*. Rochester Studies in African History and the Diaspora (Rochester: University of Rochester Press, 2007); Herbert Marshall and Mildred Stock, *Ira Aldridge: The Negro Tragedian* (Washington DC: Howard University Press, 1993); Jack Shalom, "The Ira Aldridge Troupe: Early Black Minstrelsy in Philadelphia," *African American Review* 26, no. 4 (1994).

26. Eileen Southern, *The Music of Black Americans: A History*. 3rd ed. (New York: Norton, 1997), 10.

27. Lynn Abbott, *Out of Sight: The Rise of African American Popular Music, 1889–1895* (Jackson: University Press of Mississippi, 2002); Ann Marie Bean, James Hatch, and Brooks MacNamara, *Inside the Minstrel Mask: Readings in Nineteenth-Century Blackface Minstrelsy*. 1st ed. (Middletown, CT: Wesleyan University Press, 1996); Bryant, *A Comical Ethiopian Sketch in Four Scenes*; Louis Chude-Sokei, *The Last "Darky": Bert Williams, Black-on-Black Minstrelsy, and the African Diaspora (a John Hope Franklin Center Book)* (London: Duke University Press, 2006); Eric Lott, *Love and Theft: Blackface Minstrelsy and the American Working Class* (London: Oxford University Press, 1995); Nathan, *Dan Emmett and the Rise of Early Negro Minstrelsy*; Robert C. Toll, *Blacking Up: The Minstrel Show in Nineteenth-Century America* (New York: Oxford, 1974).

28. Mary Kells, "Ethnicity in the 1990s: Contemporary Irish Migrants in London." *Landscape, Heritage and Identity: Case Studies in Irish Ethnography*; John Belchem, "Whiteness and the Liverpool Irish," *Journal of British Studies* 44, no 1 (2005): 146–152; Noel Ignatiev, *How the Irish Became White* (New York: Routledge, 1995).

29. I combine categories here because by the mid-nineteenth century Liverpool packets and other passenger ships increased their profits by transporting both passengers and goods. Any component of the cargo could be offloaded and replaced to gain a competitive edge at port.

30. Mander and Mitcheson/University of Bristol Theatre Collection Archive: MM/B12/R1/S3 Box #4 Minstrels.

31. *Garinagú* refers to the culture of the people while *Garífuna* refers to the people. During a 1992 Fulbright fellowship I spent several months living and working with Garífuna artists. The folklore of the region reflects a matrilineal society. The Punta dance, now widely regarded as a popular club dance, originated as a fertility ritual performed by women when a relative died.

32. A. Elizabeth Doyle, *Banana Boats: A Missing Link in the Rise of Cruise Vacationing 1881–1958*. Unpublished manuscript, 2004.

33. Helen M. Rozwadowski, *Fathoming the Ocean: The Discovery and Exploration of the Deep Sea* (Cambridge, MA: Belknap Press of Harvard University Press, 2005), 62.

34. Kristoffer A. Garin, *Devils on the Deep Blue Sea: The Dreams, Schemes, and Showdowns That Built America's Cruise Ship Empires* (New York: Viking, 2005); Roland, Bolster, and Keyssar, *The Way of the Ship*.

Bibliography

Abbott, Lynn. *Out of Sight: The Rise of African American Popular Music, 1889–1895*. Jackson: University Press of Mississippi, 2002.

Albion, Robert Greenhalgh, and Jennie Barnes Pope. *The Rise of New York Port 1815–1860*. New York: C. Scribner's Sons, 1939.

Anbinder, Tyler. *Five Points: The 19th-Century New York City Neighborhood That Invented Tap Dance, Stole Elections, and Became the World's Most Notorious Slum*. New York: Free Press, 2001.

Bean, Ann Marie, with James Hatch and Brooks MacNamara. *Inside the Minstrel Mask: Readings in Nineteenth-Century Blackface Minstrelsy*. 1st ed. Middletown, CT: Wesleyan University Press, 1996.

Beck, Horace Palmer. *Folklore and the Sea*. 1st ed. Middletown, CT: Published for the Marine Historical Association, Mystic Seaport, by Wesleyan University Press, 1973.

Belchem, John. "Whiteness and the Liverpool Irish." *Journal of British Studies* 44, no. 1 (2005): 146–152.

Bolster, W. Jeffrey. *Black Jacks: African American Seamen in the Age of Sail*. Cambridge, MA: Harvard University Press, 1997.

Bronner, Simon J. *Crossing the Line: Violence, Play, and Drama in Naval Equator Traditions*. Amsterdam: Amsterdam University Press, 2006.

Brown, Charles. "Steward." Letter 1873 by Charles E. Brown. H.H. Brown of Providence RI. Whaling Bark Courser, New Bedford. Aug. 27, 1873. Speech; "Colored Sailors Home Reports, 1855 to 1866."

Bryant, Dan. *A Comical Ethiopian Sketch in Four Scenes*. New York: Dewitt, 1874.

Chude-Sokei, Louis. *The Last "Darky": Bert Williams, Black-on-Black Minstrelsy, and the African Diaspora (a John Hope Franklin Center Book)*. London: Duke University Press, 2006.

Church, Andrew. "From 'Wog to Shellback." Story Number: NNS130704-01. *America's Navy*. July 4, 2013. Accessed Jan. 31, 2014. http://www.navy.mil/submit/display.asp?story_id=75241.

"Colored Sailors Home Reports, 1855 to 1866." American Seaman's Friends Society. Manuscript Collection of Mystic Seaport. Collection 158, Box 2, Folder 2, New York. Accessed July 18, 2012.

Cook, James W. "Master Juba, the King of All Dancers: A Story of Stardom and Struggle from the Dawn of the Transatlantic Culture Industry." *Discourses in Dance* 3, no. 2 (2006): 7–20.

Dewberry, Jonathan, "The African Grove Theatre and Company." *Black American Literature Forum* 16 (1986).

Doyle, A. Elizabeth. *Banana Boats: A Missing Link in the Rise of Cruise Vacationing 1881–1958*. Unpublished manuscript, 2004.

Edwards, Craig. Personal interview. July 16, 2012.

Garin, Kristoffer A. *Devils on the Deep Blue Sea: The Dreams, Schemes, and Showdowns That Built America's Cruise Ship Empires*. New York: Viking, 2005.

Gilje, Paul A. *Liberty on the Waterfront: American Maritime Culture in the Age of Revolution.* Philadelphia: University of Pennsylvania Press, 2004.

Gonzalez, Anita. *Afro-Mexico: Dancing between Myth and Reality.* Austin: University of Texas Press, 2010.

Gonzalez, Anita. *Jarocho's Soul: Cultural Identity and Afro-Mexican Dance.* Lanham, MD: University Press of America (Rowman and Littlefield), 2004.

Harlow, Frederick Pease. *The Making of a Sailor; or, Sea Life aboard a Yankee Square-rigger.* Salem, MA: Marine Research Society, 1928. Print.

Hatch, James V., and Errol G. Hill. *A History of African American Theatre.* Cambridge Studies in American Theatre and Drama. New York: Cambridge University Press, 2003.

Henderson, J. Welles, and Rodney P. Carlisle. *Marine Art and Antiques: Jack Tar; a Sailor's Life 1750–1910.* Woodbridge, England: Antique Collectors' Club, 1999.

Hugill, Stan. *Shanties from the Seven Seas: Shipboard Work-Songs and Songs Used as Work-Songs from the Great Days of Sail.* Mystic, CT: Routledge & Kegan Paul, 1961. Reprint, 1994.

Ignatiev, Noel. *How the Irish Became White.* New York: Routledge, 1995.

Isbell, Mary. "P(l)aying Off Old Ironsides and the Old Wagon: Melville's Depiction of Shipboard Theatricals in White Jacket." *Leviathan: A Journal of Melville Studies* 15, no. 1 (2013): 6–30.

Jarvis, Adrian, and W. Robert Lee. *Trade, Migration, and Urban Networks in Port Cities, c. 1640–1940.* St. John's, Newfoundland: International Maritime Economic History Association, 2008.

Journal of the Barque Keoka: New York to San Francisco: Mystic Seaport Research Center, 1849.

Kells, Mary. "Ethnicity in the 1990s: Contemporary Irish Migrants in London." *Landscape, Heritage and Identity: Case Studies in Irish Ethnography.*

Kujawinska, Courtney, and Maria Lukowska. *Ira Aldridge 1807–1967.* Frankfurt: Peter Lang, 2009.

Labaree, Benjamin Woods. *America and the Sea: A Maritime History.* Mystic, CT: Mystic Seaport, 1998.

Lindfors, Bernth. *Ira Aldridge: The African Roscius.* Rochester Studies in African History and the Diaspora. Rochester: University of Rochester Press, 2007.

Lott, Eric. *Love and Theft: Blackface Minstrelsy and the American Working Class.* London: Oxford University Press, 1995.

Lydenberg, Harry Miller. *Crossing the Line: Tales of the Ceremony during Four Centuries.* New York: New York Public Library, 1957.

Mander and Micheson Collection, Theatre Collection at the University of Bristol, UK.

Marshall, Herbert. *Ira Aldridge: Negro Tragedian.* London: Southern Illinois University Press, 1958.

Marshall, Herbert, and Mildred Stock. *Ira Aldridge: The Negro Tragedian.* Washington DC: Howard University Press, 1993.

McAllister, Marvin. *White People Do Not Know How to Behave at Entertainments Designed for Ladies and Gentlemen of Colour: William Brown's African and American Theater.* Chapel Hill: University of North Carolina Press, 2003.

McAllister, Marvin. *Whiting Up: Whiteface Minstrels and Stage Europeans in African American performance.* Chapel Hill: University of North Carolina Press, 2011.

McManus, Kevin. *Ceilis, Jigs, and Ballads: Irish Music in Liverpool.* Liverpool: Institute of Popular Music, University of Liverpool, 1994.

Mead, John Holstead. *Sea Shanties and Fo-c-sle Songs, 1768–1906.* Lexington: University of Kentucky, 1973. Dissertation.

Nathan, Hans. *Dan Emmett and the Rise of Early Negro Minstrelsy*. New ed. Norman: University of Oklahoma Press, 1977.

Peterson, Carla L. *Black Gotham: A Family History of African Americans in Nineteenth-century New York City*. New Haven, CT: Yale University Press, 2011.

Roland, Alex, W. Jeffrey Bolster, and Alexander Keyssar. *The Way of the Ship: America's Maritime History Re-envisioned, 1600–2000*. Hoboken, NJ: Wiley, 2008.

Rozwadowski, Helen M. *Fathoming the Ocean: The Discovery and Exploration of the Deep Sea*. Cambridge, MA: Belknap Press of Harvard University Press, 2005.

Sawtell, Clement Cleveland. *Captain Nash DeCost and the Liverpool Packets*. Mystic, CT: Marine Historical Association, 1955.

Shalom, Jack. "The Ira Aldridge Troupe: Early Black Minstrelsy in Philadelphia." *African American Review* 26, no. 4 (1994).

Sokolow, Michael. *Charles Benson: Mariner of Color in the Age of Sail*. Amherst: University of Massachusetts Press, 2003.

Southern, Eileen. *The Music of Black Americans: A History*. 3rd ed. New York: Norton, 1997.

"The Seamen's Church Institute." *The Seamen's Church Institute*. Accessed January 31, 2014. http://www.seamenschurch.org/.

Toll, Robert C. *Blacking Up: The Minstrel Show in Nineteenth-Century America*. New York: Oxford, 1974.

Walser, Robert Young. *The Shantyman's Canon*. Master's thesis, University of Wisconsin-Madison, 1995.

White, Shane. *Stories of Freedom in Black New York*. Cambridge, MA: Harvard University Press, 2002. Print.

Winter, Marian Hannah. "Juba and American Minstrelsy." *Dance Index* 6 (1947): 28–48.

CHAPTER 4

"HOW DO I TOUCH THIS TEXT?" OR, THE INTERDISCIPLINES BETWEEN

Dance and Theater in Early Modern Archives

VK PRESTON

Et personne ne lit ses vers,
De qui l'âme ne soit charmée:
C'est enfin l'Apollon François,
La gloire et l'honneur de cest aage,
De qui les reigles et les loix
Ont mis les Muses hors de page.

—"A Monsieur de Malherbe," Balet comique de la Royne
(Lacroix I, 86) [original spelling]

I *will* read for an "illegitimate" history

—Rebecca Schneider

I am sitting in the Paris Opera library, with Balthazar de Beaujoyeulx's 1582 *Balet comique de la Royne* on the wooden desk in front of me, pinching myself.[1] The text is a quarto edition bound in folded, semilucent animal skin so viscerally organic it seems to have pores. I hesitate, uncertain whether to touch the book. Until this afternoon, my guides to collections have distributed research tools with an unspoken *noli me tangere*, setting out cotton or latex gloves, velvet book supports, lead weights, and magnifying glasses. Here I am left alone, without props. Realizing no bar on touch is forthcoming, I take the plunge, open the cover, touch the book. The grain of the page is rough, satisfying. I set to work with the text. In my hands, this slim 1582 *livret* (*libretto*)—often cited as the first ballet[2]—becomes an object of mystery, indexing the alterity of early ballet's pasts.[3]

Leafing through the book's cut pages, the making of the document begins to expose itself. My eyes and fingers linger on faint bleeds of the print, ink pooling at the edges of illustrations and eddying in plate marks pressed into the pages. Engrossed, I annotate scans on a glassy, electronic screen, hesitating over unfamiliar, sixteenth-century French spellings (õ, u for v, f for s, i for j) since standardized in Paul Lacroix's nineteenth-century edition of the text. The rhythm of this labor opens porosities between past and present understandings of movement and its representations—both on the stage and in the book.

Going back and forth between sixteenth- and nineteenth-century versions of the work, I mark out images, music, and texts missing from Lacroix's 1868 anthology. "We have suppressed [*supprimé*], as redundant [*inutile*]" an '*Other Allegory of Circe, according to the opinion of Sieur Gordon*' due to its length,"[4] Lacroix writes. What has been suppressed, or omitted, is the 1582 *livret*'s conclusion, an interpretation of the ballet's female lead Circe (as desire) and a rare commentary on the performances of women in the cast.[5] The passage illuminates what is and is not transmitted from the archives, and it marks the grounds of Stephen Orgel's call for performance scholars to return to work with them.[6]

What do scholars bring and miss, I ask myself, when we apply conceptual categories like "dance" and "theater," or indeed "performance," to archival work? Does this distinction open up or occlude such documents' self-stylings as printed archives, "live" events, and practices? And what do we make of unfamiliar notions of performance and performativity in the historical past—ones whose conceptions of doing defamiliarize media in the present? The *Balet comique*'s text provides almost nothing in the way of instructions for dances and no movement notation. Its flights of detail seek to pack performance into print, spilling between descriptions of set and staging, theoretical texts, verse, images, music notation, and allegories. Offering a distributed authorship, the published elements offer contributions from at least a dozen voices, many of which are anonymous.

In what follows—working with the material culture of the book (as an object and as an image)—I address records of historical performances that combine dance and theater, finding myself aware of (and drawn to) the archives' metamorphoses. The two pieces I take up in this exploration, the *Balet comique de la Royne* (1581, published in 1582) and *Le Ballet de la Délivrance de Renaud* (1617),[7] are among the most extensively documented early French theatrical dances—rare instances of records that combine music, texts, and images with detailed accounts of the performance, production, and reception of the work.

My methodology, for which a simple, dancerly process of tracing my actions becomes a kind of score, brings the task of historiography into the sensorium and the realm of materially concrete acts. Addressing these records' accounts of perception, I piece together the *livret*'s references to blurring and illusion by drawing upon early modern writings on artifice, alchemy, and the witch. The sorceress figure, Circe, drives the performance, and I approach her here as a "living emblem"[8] performed in the midst of the witch trials in France.[9]

The influence of illusions on perception is a recurring preoccupation in early modern writing on witchcraft and demonology.[10] The *livrets*' baroque descriptions of blurred and bedazzled senses reflect and interpret motifs of transformation. As descriptions, they address at least two kinds of artificial doubles: likenesses and duplications that surpass nature, created through "generative" or "perfective" mixtures in alchemy.[11] This slippery pair subtly confounds perception, introducing epistemic uncertainties into their confoundings of artifice and the real. To take up the trail of enchantment's destabilizing effects, I begin with Beaujoyeulx's address to the reader from the preface to the *Balet comique*.

To the Reader (*Au Lecteur*)

The *Balet comique*'s mixture of texts, images, and music notation opens with pithy texts that include an address to the reader ("*Au lecteur*"), describing the performance as a "modern invention" that "confounds" and "interlaces" dance and theater to make "Balet speak" and comedy "sing and resonate."[12] Describing ballets as "only geometric mixtures," Beaujoyeulx compares this composite production to the fashioning of a "well-proportioned" artificial and dramaturgical body, preferring the "tranquil" endings of comedy to tragedy's blood-baths, that generate a "*meslange*" ("mixing") of artistic forms.[13] His equation of "mixture" and what we might retrospectively term an alchemical dramaturgy imagines mixture as a dramaturgical body yoked to the rhetorical contest of alchemy and art-making. This pro-cessual context brings nuance to the *livret*'s statements on metamorphoses, performing the order and disorder of interdisciplinary creation in artificial, lifelike form:

AU LECTEUR	TO THE READER
Pourtant, amy Lecteur, que le tiltre & inscription de ce liuvre est sans exemple, & que lon n'a point veu par cy deuant aucun Balet auoir esté imprimé, ny ce mot de Comique y estre adapté: ie vous prieray ne trouuer ny l'un ny l'autre estrange. Car quant au Balet, encores que ce soit une invention moderne, ou pour le moins, repetee si loing de l'antiquité, que lon la puisse nommer telle: n'estant à la verité que des meslanges geometriques de plusieurs personnes dansans ensemble sous une diuerse harmonie de plusieurs instruments: ie vous confesse que simplement representé par l'impression, cela eust eu beaucoup de nouueauté, & peu de beauté, de reciter une simple Comedie: aussi cela n'eust pas esté ny bien excellent, ny digne d'une si grande Royne, qui vouloit faire quelque chose de bien magnifique & triomphant. Sur ce ie me suis advisé qu'il ne seroit point indecent de mesler l'un & l'autre ensemblément, & diuersisier la musique de poesie, & entrelacer la poesie de musique, & le plus souvent les còfondre toutes deux ensemble: ainsi que l'antiquité ne recitoit point ses vers sans musique, & Orphee ne sonnoit iamais sans vers. I'ay toutesfois donné le premier tiltre & honneur à la dance & le second à substàce, que i'ay inscrite Comique, plus pour la belle, tràquille, & heureuse conclusion où elle se termine, que pour la qualité des personnages, qui sont presque tous dieux & deesses ou autres personnes heroiques. Ainsi i'ay animé & fait parler le Balet, & chanter & resonner la Comedie: & y adioustant plusieurs rares & riches representations & ornements, ie puis dire auoir contenté en un corps bien propotionné, l'oeuil, l'oreille, & l'entendement [...] sans faire tort à la Comedie, distinctement representee par ses scenes & actes: ny à la Comedie sans preiudicier au Balet, qui honore, esgaye & remplit d'harmonieux recits le beau sens de la Comedie [sic]	*Nevertheless, friend Reader, the title and inscription of this book are unprecedented, & never before have we seen a ballet having been printed, nor [such an] adaption of the word Comedy: I pray you not to find either one or the other strange. Because, as regards the Balet [sic], even as it is a modern invention, or at the least, one repeated at such a distance from Antiquity we might name it such: being in truth only geometric mixtures (meslanges) of several people dancing together under the diverse harmony of many instruments: I confess to you, that re-presented simply by impression [print] there was much novelty, & little beauty, in reciting a simple Comedy: there was little excellent, nor dignified of a great queen, who wanted to make something magnificent & triumphant. On this I advised myself it would not be indecent to mix [mesler] one & the other together, & diversify music with poetry, & interlace poetry with music, & as often as possible confound the two together: just as antiquity never recited verse without music, & Orpheus never sounded without verse. I always gave the first title and honor to dance, and the second to the substance, which I have written as Comedy, for the beautiful, tranquil, & happy conclusion where it ends, and for the quality of the characters, who are almost all gods and goddesses, or other heroic persons. Thus I animated and made Balet speak, & Comedy sing and resonate: & adding many rare & rich representations & ornamentations, I could be said to be contented in a well-proportioned body, eye, ear, and understanding [...] without doing an injustice to Comedy, distinctly represented in scenes an acts, nor to Comedy without prejudicing the Balet, which honors, enlivens (engaye) & fills out with harmonious narratives (recits) the beautiful sense of Comedy.* (No page numbers in original; translation mine.)

Hybrid Codex: *Le Balet comique de la Royne* (1582)

The *Balet comique*'s chimerical structure leaps between verse, prose, and ekphrastic description, intercutting elaborate narratives with beautifully engraved images, staves of music, poetry, and prose. As a result, Beaujoyeulx's *livret* is a difficult text to follow, not only because the work crosses epistemological and disciplinary boundaries but also because it makes the crossing of categories its meaning. Epistemic shifts regarding the body in performance contribute to the volume's alien effect. Its preoccupation with metamorphoses goes beyond the mixture and mutability of categories themselves, "leaking"[14] between natural and artificial worlds. The work's lead role, the antagonist-sorceress Circe gives a key to the work's mutabilities, fueling these with the controversy of bodies' susceptibilities to magic and spells. Until she is defeated at the end of the ballet, and she relinquishes her tools for enchantment to the king and cardinal seated in the audience,[15] Circe diagetically influences the work's movements and sounds with her wand.

The transdisciplinary effect of this text, and of its continual ruptures, overwhelms. It presents a five-and-a-half-hour work—seemingly image by image and scene by scene—in a rhapsodic, discontinuous register without a clear formal or narrative through-line. Texts, images, and music notation jam the book's pages.[16] Diamond-shaped notes ascend and descend jittery musical staves. Fonts, scales, and narrative forms change in rapid succession,[17] and scenes appear distinctly, one after another, with little linking or transition. Among these discontinuous fragments, insects move among artificial leaves, a Ulysses-like gentleman flees Circe, demi-mortals sing ethereal dialogues, chimerical creatures play instruments, and Mercury enters on a cloud, suspended over an ensemble of enchanted, immobilized nymphs. In the scenes glimpsed through these stanzas in the text's accumulations of description and verse, this "Fugitive" and his companions escape the enchantress Circe, who holds their bodies and perceptions captive on her enchanted island. The ballet concludes with the collapse of her illusions and geometric dances celebrating the captives' disenchantment from her spells.

Bristling with attempts to convey a live event in print,[18] the *Balet comique*'s detailed descriptions draw the reader's attention impossibly close to objects in the scenery, highlighting rather than concealing surprising miniatures: counterfeit insects, flowers, berries, and lizards as well as the trembling nuance of performers' affect, amplifying sensorial aspects of spells. Even scale proliferates, as the text describes details beyond the possible perception of a spectator. Beaujoyeulx tells of a perplexing "infinity of *connils* [rabbits]" that runs to and fro in the extremities of Circe's garden,[19] while both extremes of this fecund ecology, a *faux* night sky and an artificial sun, present an alchemical world lush with enchanted, sensory detail. Glass oil lamps cast "a hundred thousand colors," he suggests, such that those watching (*des regardans*) could neither guess the lights' sources nor grasp the diversity of what he oddly terms its "represented colors."[20]

Beaujoyeulx's attention to the eye blinds and tricks it with illumination, reflecting epistemes of reception that blur artifice and nature. This slipping of focus, marking magic in early modern texts, signals the effects of spells, composing perceptions of an artificially fashioned world.[21] This world-loss[22] of discernment between reproduction and production mirrors competing discourses in the history of alchemy, shifting over the course of centuries from instructions on the imitation and use of faux gems and ornaments, in Egyptian antiquity, to the perfective claim of duplicating nature, disputed in Arabic philosophy, and the "generative mixture" imagined in early modern European alchemists' promise to create bodies, intelligences, and life-forms. The discourse of a competition between art and nature flows through the whole of this narrative, setting out alchemy as a model for interdisciplinary creation while evoking, within the enchanted sphere of Circe's garden, a fluid spectacle of imitations that seem to move and swarm. In the enchanted sphere of Circe's garden[23] this liveliness of illusion claims the immersive power of spells, making seemingly lifelike things analogues for artistic ingenuity. Artists' ambition to lay claim to this enchanted, sensory sphere tips a philosophical discourse on perception and illusion into the discursive claims of art's ability to perfect nature, channeling a conception of futurity (indeed reproduction) onto the political present of the court.[24]

In contrast to this flux of artifice, the ballet evidences a threatening and precarious present. Circe describes this in a remarkable *harangue*—a performative form of spoken denunciation in verse. Giving a harrowing account of her sorcery from within a *tableau vivant* of paralyzed nymphs, Circe calls on the return of a mythic golden age as a contrast to the cold and catastrophic present under her spells, anachronizing not just a past and present, but a future as well.[25]

LE BALET COMIQUE DE LA ROYNE (1581): PERFORMANCE

The *Balet comique* was an astonishing work by any measure. It was performed from ten at night until almost four in the morning on October 15, 1581, in the *grande salle de Bourbon*, a theater and assembly room, later destroyed in expansions of the Louvre.[26] The production was part of two weeks of festivities for the wedding of the queen's sister with king Henri III's favorite, the Duc de Joyeuse, construed in a largely hostile historiographical tradition as the king's male lover.[27]

"Scabrous" poetry regarding Henri's sexuality and "queer failure"[28] to produce a Valois heir fueled seamy histories of the régime, portraying the king as "the most reviled of all French monarchs [. . .] loathed, despised and demonized—most famously by the Protestant Agrippa d'Aubigné, who compared him to a 'made-up whore' (*une putain fardee* [*sic*]) and 'a King-woman or a man Queen.' "[29] This homophobic legacy of Henri III's repudiation, born in the shaming texts of his political opponents,[30] significantly influences ballet history, I suggest, rerouting the medium's myths of origin toward the later reign of Louis XIV. Virulent, often little-studied attacks on sex and gender accompany dance history's silences regarding this era of social, religious, and political crises, contributing to what Erwin Panofsky has described as an emphatic disapproval of the baroque from the Enlightenment to the mid-twentieth century.[31] The haunted "infidelity" and perceived "inauthenticity" of baroque representations, he writes, stems from their "breaking, "liquidation," and "rupture" of codes.[32]

The "Fugitive Gentleman" who enters the playing space at the beginning of the *Balet comique*, introduces Circe in direct address. "[She] was not a woman, or not one who breathes air [. . .],"[33] he begins, describing the enchantress in sensual and yet maleficent terms.[34] Her eyes shoot painful darts of love, and her beauty, like poison and as thick as honey, "flows from her mouth as words (*paroles*)."[35] While the eroticization of such beauty remains potent as a staging of desire in the verse, the dramaturgical efficacity of the character's magic will be drained of force with the undoing of Circe's spells—and it is not for nought that Beaujoyeulx declares the dancers of geometrical performance at the end of the ballet "*desenchantees*" [sic]. This dramaturgical trajectory toward enacting disenchantment may be read as anticipatory, projecting the tendency of this medium to both found itself within and abjure stagings of witchcraft and sorcery.[36]

Circe's activation of magic, like the ballet's "artificial" and metamorphic bodies, ultimately performs the receding of the enchantress's powers. Blurrings of gender, sexuality, and the stability of the body's shape, made mutable by Circe's spells, vanish in Lacroix's cuts, as do many of its allegories on sexual avarice, generation, corruption, and desire.[37] Nonetheless, "artificial" and metamorphic bodies remain central preoccupations of this medium, in descriptions of spectators' febrile doubt regarding the truth or artifice of what they see, troubling conventional distinctions between subjects, illusions, and things. Such sensorial deception, highlighting the entangling of subject and sensation through bodies' susceptibilities to spells, marks an important site of early modern disputation engaged in performance as well as law and doctrine, notably on the body's capacity to change shape.

Artifice: The Dance Is in the Details

Taking a shot at posterity, early modern French artists moved to perform for the book as well as the stage, fueling works with subjects and themes that activated controversies of their eras. As I leaf delicately through the 430-year-old codex, marveling at the volume's leaps and transitions, the ambition of Beaujoyeulx's descriptions of immersion unfold themselves in an avalanche of detail. Its sensorial allure rejoices in the confusion of viewers' perceptions with crafted things. The book's reach seeks to lay out simultaneous elements, conjuring "a place where all places are—seen from every angle, each standing clear, without any confusion or blending."[38]

Through this blurring of discernment between "natural" and "artificial" things I focus on passages that slip between descriptions of objects and viewers' senses, honing in on his example of artificial grapes so artfully fashioned that "the most alert would take them for natural."[39] Here, the author's allusion to the Greek artist Zeuxis,[40] who famously painted grapes so seemingly real they fooled the birds, aligns Beaujoyeulx's work with the arterial currents of early modern thinking on matter, representation, and embodiment. Celebrating (rather than seeking to hide) this fashioning of illusions, the *Balet comique*'s narrative seizes on mimetic delight and losses of bearing, investigating fascinations with the body's nonmastery of the real.

This uncertainty of perception takes a particularly visceral and frightening corporeal form in stanzas for the Fugitive Gentleman, describing the temporary loss of his reason as his limbs became those of a lion under Circe's spells. These anxious perceptions, as Robert Muchembled writes, describe reflections of "the human body as an object of fright,"[41] prompting affective and corporeal disorder as they trouble the belief that discernment between artifice and natural things remains ontologically possible. Lusciously muddying descriptions of object and sense, the verse invites the possibility of a "*lack* of differences between faux and real."[42]

Why might an account of an artificial cucumber—or a grape—receive more of the author's attention than any of the dances in this introduction to the *Balet*? Lifelike *things*—plants and vegetables (even berries, herbs, cucumbers) as well as "creatures" (*bestes*) fashioned with "counterfeit" materials thickly populate his description, appearing in a kind of rhapsody in which Beaujoyeulx seeks to describe things all at once. Illusionary animals and plants in Circe's artificial garden dwell within the pleasures of fooling and being fooled, competing with the natural world through artifice and illusion. The temporal, nearly unreadable intensity of these descriptions highlights what Edward Soja, through Jorge Luis Borges, describes as the sequential character of language,[43] resulting in an unfamiliar, even bewildering density of images, texts, music notation, and ekphrasis that exceeds contemporary habits of continuous reading.[44] A readerly movement of the sensorium, therefore, rather than a sense of geometric dancing, characterizes Beaujoyeulx's opening account, marking ontologies of perception and spectatorship pointedly differing from lay models of disciplined movement. Here the entangling of disorder and order mixes life and things together, inviting transformations of corporeal sense, temperament, and even shape: "[a]n object becomes a thing," Robin Bernstein writes coyly, "when it invites a person to dance."[45]

"Monstrous," chimerical bodies and materials confound and confuse the spectator, Beaujoyeulx writes, delving into simulacral possibilities of the counterfeit and illusion. His attention to crafted matter comes enveloped in reflections on perception that dwell in minute detail on the artificial status of objects, highlighting their crafting from silks, paints, metals, and feathers. These materials re-mediate performative and symbolic registers of staging alchemical simulacra, offering extended metaphors for the mixing and crossing of the arts and perception.

Witchcraft, alchemy, and magic are central to the ballet's composition, both on the stage and in the book, shifting between ontologies of dance that resonate with popular and learned early modern theories of embodiment. "Local," involuntary or "nonrational" qualities of sense and subjectivity—in particular pain, paralysis, and sexual attraction—could (and did) serve in these cosmologies as legal proof and even evidence of sorcery. In demonological disputes and notably in the witch-hunt manuals, the sensorium, and in particular the female sensorium, is dangerously susceptible to the harmful performance of magic (*maleficium*).

Who dances, how one dances, and the perceived order (or disorder) of the dancing body could define, and moreover distinguish between, a legitimate and illegitimate subject in the world. Regulation of magical knowledge and belief thus, surprisingly, intervenes into the life-world of sixteenth- and seventeenth-century subjects with profound and historical effects, as women in particular were characterized as disorderly, lacking, and susceptible to magic and sorcery.

In this context, gender is a central preoccupation of the early modern demonology tracts. In Institoris's *Malleus Maleficarum* (*The Hammer of Witches*)[46] female inferiority begins with Creation. Woman is formed of a lesser material, Institoris argues: the imperfectly "curved" or bent shape of Adam's rib. His false, and widely cited, etymology of the word *femina* ("from *fe* and *minus* ["less in faith"]) appears in a passage in which he also claims woman "is an unfinished animal"[47] whose touch may cause harm to both humans and beasts.[48] The surrogation of a "lesser creature" with a "more perfect" (implicitly male) form is used routinely in the early modern period to distinguish between unlearned, female witchcraft and the learned magic and alchemical pursuits of educated male elites.

TEXT AS HOMUNCULUS

Beaujoyeulx's ambition becomes his creation—an artificial, "well-proportioned" dramaturgical body that realizes an interdisciplinary mixture of forms. These stagings of transformation go beyond the mixing of arts disciplines, however, contributing to a centuries-long rhetorical dispute comparing the powers and limits of art and nature.[49] Beaujoyeulx's appeal to sorcery suggests magic can successfully mediate relationships between material and immaterial worlds, making bodies, perceptions, and passions susceptible to the performance of harmful magic (*maleficium*).[50] In so doing, he celebrates the labor of the artist, holding out his greatest praise for the magic of visual deception, the tricking of the eye that complicates the very categories of the alive and the lifelike (or the *vrai* and the *vrai-semblable*). This vision of theatrical illusion, which takes a metaphorical form in the introduction to the *Balet comique*, gives extraordinarily dense attention to a creation both enlivened and fashioned through a mixture of forms. This "modern invention"[51] accompanies Beaujoyeulx's boast of committing the ballet to print (well before Shakespeare and many of the early modern dramatists), promising, in a prefatory letter to the king, to save heroic action from time, a threat that he deploys metonymically as Saturn's devouring "teeth of oblivion."[52]

The print version of the *Balet comique* opens with a theoretical preamble comparing dance and theater to a fictional body, mind, and its senses.[53] Beaujoyeulx likens this "interlacing" of media (ballet and comedy) to the "well-proportioned" coherence of an imagined body whose coordination across "eye, ear, and understanding" becomes a dramaturgical model.[54] This fashioning of an artificial body re-members the arts as a species of early modern *Gesamtkunstwerk*,[55] an imagined homunculus whose coordination of sense organs, reflection, and perception signifies a dramaturgy of interdisciplinary forms. This metaphorical, performing body "inter(in)animates"[56] parts and whole, articulating hierarchy through a harmonic converging of disciplines that resembles Hobbes's composite body in *Leviathan*.[57] Thus Beaujoyeulx participates in early modern rhetorical debates, presenting performance as a body, alchemy as artifice, and the book as its system of survivance.[58]

COUNTERFEIT AND MIMESIS

Beaujoyeulx's loquacious, seemingly encyclopedic ambition to narrate each detail of the ballet may seem odd to contemporary readers, since the tiny scale of his descriptions extends beyond any spectator's viewing distance. His approach suggests that the drive animating his account is textual (rather than a fact-based record of performance), generating roving descriptions that are difficult to distinguish from the artist's mind's eye.

Within the surpassingly detailed text, Beaujoyeulx's insistence on spectators' uncertainty regarding what they see returns again and again to descriptions of "singular artifice" and counterfeit things.[59] The lush attraction to imitation put forward here presents a destabilizing mixture of fashioned objects and living forms. This subtle blurring or scrambling (*bruuage*) associated with witchcraft[60] engages a play of epistemological and ontological uncertainty, slipping between descriptions of light and objects, perception and things.[61] This approach, laid out in nonlinear flights of detail, counters Plato's ontological riddle, in the tenth book of the *Republic*, of a man with a mirror who can represent all things at once without fashioning them.[62]

Beaujoyeulx's description of a vivarium of lifelike things lingers appreciatively on the made, and he pointedly celebrates the counterfeit fruit of artisans' labor in the seemingly natural grapes of the enchantress' garden (*raisins tresbeaux & contrefaicts au naturel*).[63] Circe's island—the setting of the ballet—is both an everywhere and a no-place: a paradigmatic and even dystopian "utopia" in which the enchantments of an ostensibly "Persian" sorceress serve as vehicles of an opulent *mise-en-scène*.[64] This imagining of the garden as a simulacral, permeable world evidences an entangling of copy, image, and simulation. We might engage it here through a cross-temporal reading of Rebecca Schneider as not only relative to the theatrical but central to theatricality.[65] Its baroquely heterogeneous composition raises the anxious rhetoric of the double, seeking to deploy theatrical magic as spectacle while eschewing the infection of enchantment. Book ten of the *Republic* is an important key to the *Balet comique*'s dramaturgy, here, as "Socrates begins by promising that insight into *mimêsis* operates as a countercharm (595b). People need countercharms because the imitator is a 'sorcerer [*goêtes*]' and thereby a deceiver (598d; cf 602d)," Nickolas Pappas suggests, and just as "the English 'charm' does, this noun *kêlêsis* can mean 'appeal' but also something explicitly magical, a spell or conjuration. Poetry works magically to draw in the audience that it then degrades."[66]

Addressing antitheatrical fears of imitations "that cannot copy themselves" and that "degrade" preexisting categories, Laura Levine brings the question of imitation and the copy to bear directly on the early modern performer. Magic, she observes, "is most profoundly a copy,"[67] threatening in the concern that it might affect (or infect) the thing it represents.[68] "Anti-theatrical tracts," Levine observes, are "dominated by both explicit and implicit claims about magic,"[69] whereas, in contrast to these writings, early modern artists also embraced what she terms an "*anti-anti-theatricality*,"[70] rerouting antitheatrical sentiment by conspicuously *doing imitation* and code-switching between categories. Seen from this perspective as performative, Circe's lush and sense-deceiving garden adheres to antitheatrical orthodoxies as it flaunts them, (re)doubling the performance's recourse to stage magic while conspicuously unbinding its spells.

Circe's source in the tenth book of Homer's *Odyssey* offers one genealogy of this enchantress. Yet traditions of learned commentary, from Augustine to Boccaccio, situate her in conversations on the flexibility of the human form that extend over centuries.[71] The result is a temporally and geographically complex discourse, rife with anachrony, regarding the proof and evidence of human metamorphosis.

Jean Bodin, leading early modern theorist of sovereignty and author of the witch treatise *De la Démonomanie des sorciers* (1580) addresses Circe in his chapter on corporeal transformations.[72] He claims that the witch trials, and indeed "the divine and human histories of all peoples," give undeniable proof that human bodies can change shape, and yet arguing that Circe's power to transform remains limited to perceptions rather than material bodies. Addressing Circe in his chapter on the werewolf (*lupos varios*) and other metamorphic figures,[73] he writes, "[the] most difficult thing to believe, and the most wonderful," he continues, "is the changing of the human figure into a beast and even more from one body into another."

While disorder and disorderly bodies appear central to the *ballets de cour*, later histories of the medium marginalize both. We might account for this in the way that metamorphic and potentially improvised performances of disorderly movement serve as recurring sites of dramatic interest, even as they are superseded by spectacles of order. This move from disorder to order, staged in a shifting of dramaturgical emphasis from metamorphic to geometric bodies, suggests that figures ideologically construed as disorderly (and frequently subjected to either a return to orderliness, expulsion, abjection, defeat, or destruction) are important complements and counter memories to the official, "noble style" in theatrical dance.

THE KING AND THE WITCH

Jacques Patin's widely reproduced "*Figure de la salle*" (fig. 04.1) from the opening of the *Balet comique* shows a distant Circe, her wand raised like a scepter, evoking the gesture with which she immobilizes the cast and musicians.[74] Spectators look down from above on the polarized *mise-en-scène*, while the king and the witch, seated opposite one another, divide the expanse of the theater between them. In contrast with the microscale of Beaujoyeulx's descriptions, Patin's cavernous view of the theater seeks to confine Circe to the deepest part of perspective. At the deep end of the venue, she leads enchanted animals in a dance. This visual representation of the production arranges space and time diagrammatically, as if laid out for the sovereign's view.[75] Within the same image, a figure approaches Henri III for protection, echoing the opening scene of the performance, while Circe's ballet, from late in the production, plays out as a temporal montage on the threshold of perspective, at the farthest point of the theater.[76]

Muchembled, cultural historian of the sorceress and witch-hunts, offers a compelling analysis of the king-and-witch dyad in his historical studies of the trials.[77] The witch is an "exact and inverted image of the king," he argues, "within a dualistic conception of things both political and religious."[78] The sovereign and the enchantress occupy poles of a hierarchy, Muchembled argues, configuring the world of the witch as an impression-in-negative, a binary double or counter-state menacing the République (Res publica). Circe's compelling of human-animal bodies to perform confirms her problematic role as an inversion of the sovereign's authority.[79] Barely visible beneath the vanishing point, she leads a strutting stag, a pint-sized elephant, and a parade of unrecognizable animals in a dance, suggesting an anti-court that Mercury decries in the ballet's verse as subjugation.

While the figure of the sovereign is pivotal in political analyses of court performance, notably in the works of Jean-Marie Apostolidès, Mark Franko, and Louis Marin, the king's female double, the enchantress or witch, receives considerably less scholarly attention. Marie-Thérèse Mourey's recent study of dance at the height of the witch-hunts in France and Germany makes inroads into this neglected history. Taking an interdisciplinary approach to textual and visual archives, as well as to histories of the witch trials, she notes that official publications, such as the *Gazette de France*, never mention scenes of witches' sabbaths or sorceresses' balls in their accounts of *ballets de cour*, even where documentation of the dances shows such stagings have been central to their dramaturgy.[80] Elite bodies displaced and concealed proscribed ones, her observation suggests, even in the "eyewitness" accounts that serve as primary sources on these productions.

Figure de la Salle.

FIGURE 04.1 "*Figure de la Salle*," copperplate after drawings by Jacques Patin. Courtesy: Bibliothèque National de France (BnF), Beaujoyeulx, *Balet comique*, 4r. RES4-LN27-10436 (EPSILON).

Circe is an apt, codified figure for organizing reflection on early modern magic and gender, as she is not born a witch but becomes one.[81] In the *livret* she slips between terminologies and temporalities, from the multivalent "enchantress," to the immortal deity of Greek Antiquity,[82] to the Medieval *Fée*,[83] and early modern *sorcière*.[84] "Circe's power derives from grace," Franko writes, from "the power to move people subliminally, to reposition and realign them politically, in short, to manipulate them." "This political use of grace," he continues, "is symbolized dramatically by her power to hold men captive or to metamorphose them,"[85] changing their bodies' shape. Descriptions of her power run the proverbial gamut from the benign to the malign, suggesting political and Christian grace as well as their opposites. As desire personified, she embodies flexibilities of feeling and affect (terror as well as love), engendering narratives of corporeal disarray dominated by forces of disorder and lack.[86]

The enchantress's ability to paralyze and disarray bodies (freezing the dancers and turning men into dancing animals) delays and waylays a framework borrowed from the epic, male journey of conquest and return. As an allegory of desire, however, Circe's dances vehicle a more carnal body of reference, notably in the voyeuristic and explicit dimensions of witch narratives representing *sorcières* cavorting sexually with nonhuman figures while metamorphosing between human and animal forms.[87]

In her essay "Animal Sex," Elizabeth Grosz addresses attractions as "the coming together of surfaces," "the appeal and power of desire, its capacity to shake up, rearrange, reorganize the body's forms and sensations, to make the subject and body as such dissolve into something else, something other than what they are habitually."[88] This capacity for affective and corporeal reorganization appears in the foreground of Beaujoyeulx's stagings of movement and metamorphosis. While desire's capacity to transform bodies and objects in the *Balet comique* feeds feverish, textual description, its authors give strikingly few descriptions of the dancers' movements as repeatable (or even knowable) steps.[89]

Of the few passages in the *livret* that focus on dances, however, most give emphasis to ensembles. In the first of these, quite late in the *livret*, twelve "*danseresses*"[90] perform geometric dances while Circe freezes them one by one with her wand.[91] After immobilizing the nymphs she moves on to the violinists, causing the music to fall, by subtraction, into silence. Then the mutable god Mercury enters on a cloud, decrying the *sorcière*'s spells.[92] Spilling a "tincture of Moly" over the figures,[93] he brings them back to sound and movement: prompting Circe to repeat the whole of the scene again, this time freezing the god for good measure.[94] Then, surrounded with a tableau of statue-like figures, Circe speaks in verse, addressing substantive conceptual themes ("man," time, the gods, and the arts), before moving on to the recent storms of war and the promise of a future golden age for France. Detailing the effects of her sorcery on a frightening "present," she then describes an age of iron in which "vagabond peoples," sterile lands, cold, and food scarcity exhaust all art and work.[95] "I am the sole cause of all this change," she claims, invoking storms and war as her weapons.[96] Contrasting the stillness of the figures around her to Niobe's stony grief, she loosens her spell on the statue-like tableau, leading the dancers out of the garden and locking them away. Then the stage scene flares with "thousands of kinds of fires and lights"—and, with the opening of a curtain, "a great stag appears from the garden and dances before Circe." This stag, a man transformed into a beast,[97] is "followed by a dog, the dog followed by an elephant, the elephant by a lion, the lion by a tiger, the tiger by a hog, and the hog by other beasts all following one another (*s'entresuyvans*)."[98] While the sequence involves staged, likely acrobatic movement, the account eschews textually repeatable steps,[99] unfolding dramaturgically in accounts of performed paralysis, immobility, and animal embodiments, as well as through danced patterns.

Following this metamorphic animal dance, a *grand ballet* of seventeen women asserts a reverse entropy as nymphs released from Circe's spells, staging a shift from disorder and metamorphosis toward order and geometric spectacle.[100] The description's emphasis on danced patterns evokes a "science" of law and order across and between bodies in motion, triumphantly disavowing Circe's metamorphic and paralyzing effects.[101] Beaujoyeulx imagines the Greek geometer Archimedes as a cross-temporal witness to this dance, confounding the mathematical revenant with its dynamic precision of danced figures and shapes.

Important in the performance of this disenchantment, however, is its conclusion. The "Madamoyselle de Saincte Mesme,"[102] playing "*La Circe*," is alone among the performers in keeping her character's name until the last page of the text. Breaking with her theatrical role as she gives a golden present to the Cardinal de Bourbon, seated in the audience, she makes the gift of an emblem, on a medal, signifying the unbinding of spells. This scene performatively reorders the ballet's codes in breaking them, accomplishing the subjection of her magic at the end of the ballet.

The performer playing Circe is the last of the female performers to render such an object, joining the cast in (re)crossing the threshold Michael Kirby has described as that between matrixed and nonmatrixed performance[103]—here between her interpretation of narrative and character and that of social "rank." "Circe" thus re-members herself within the French elite as "de Saincte Mesme," the king's gendered and aristocratic subject, offering a dancerly and material transmission of the golden *objet d'art* to a powerful (yet potentially threatening) spectator.[104] This reordering of the ballet's performative codes marks a genealogical slip, perhaps from hand to hand, of an object putting image, text, and thing in play, "undoing" performances and spells within a performative rendering of the dancer's magic to the spectator's religion.

BETWEEN BALLETS AND TEXTS: 1581/2 AND 1617

In the next, elaborate *livret* taken up in this chapter, the role of the enchantress repeats with a difference, played *en travestie* by the celebrated and male-identified professional performer, clown, and dancer Marais.[105] At the center of this ballet is another adaptation of the *sorceress*: the stage witch Armide. This gender-crossing version of theatrical witchcraft appears alongside an intriguing reinflection in the language of the *livrets*, asserting a relationship of dominance between the performer and role. While the sixteenth-century *Balet comique* states that "Circe *was represented by* the damoyselle de Saincte Mesme," the poet Estienne Durand, the author of the 1617 *Discours au Vray*, writes of "*Marais as the one who represented* Armide [Circe's avatar]." This subtle surrogation, inverting the gendered labor and primacy of the performing artist and the stage witch, invites us to speculate about what the tradition of gender-crossing witch roles *does* in the era and context of the early modern witch-hunts.[106]

Charles Zika observes that while "it is inappropriate to identify this [learned discussion of] Circe in any simple fashion with traditions of popular witchcraft, it is also difficult to believe that the theatrical presentation of an ancient female sorcerer as the embodiment of all the vices in the France of 1581 had no relationship at all to contemporary discussions of witchcraft."[107] Writing of failure among dance historians to take up links to sorcery in ballets from the time of the trials, he then criticizes Frances Yates and Margaret McGowan for eliding Circe's incarnation of the early modern witch. This relationship is perhaps more pointed in the gender-crossing performance of Armide, suggesting a gendered inflection of embodiment at work in early modern performance dramaturgy[108]—an anxiety regarding ontological and corporeal instability in its proximity to women's dances and magic.[109]

Gone too from the *Ballet de la Délivrance* are the *Balet comique*'s large ensembles of dancing women.[110] The all-male cast of the *Délivrance* implies a shifting perception of female performers, particularly those enacting stage magic during the rule of powerful queen regents.[111] The well-established cross-dressing tradition of male-identified virtuosos performing as witches persists, moreover, in twenty-first century ballet repertoire, reiterating uneasy associations of gender, witchcraft, and punishment entangled with the history of the trials. The performative potencies of witchcraft and dance, unmooring transformations of perception and the sensorium, thus also troubles and upsets a master narrative of early ballet's secure display of a hegemonic body politic.

While the role of the stage witch seems to recur with features of parody in the later performance, it continues to solicit religious and political comparisons as the ballet and its documentary *livret* straddle the 1617 plotting of political assassinations that displaced queen Marie de Medici and her allies.[112] Mutability, here, performs an insurrection of the spirits, mocking (and also demarcating) the limits of the sorceress' powers. Replaying force as farce here again enacts tropes of the witches' sabbath and its ballets of shapeshifting animals, notably at a legal turning point of the witch prosecutions in France.

The move towards the decriminalization of witchcraft in Paris in this period offers a compelling lens through which to consider the ballet in the context of changing configurations of knowledge and power struggling over the ethics and legality of such trials.[113] The stage witch figure thus offers multiple performative valences, intertwining gender performance and danced satires of female authority with a history of sovereignty and law. Here the logic of ridding the world of "foreign" sorcery becomes "deliverance," and the spectacular rupturing of the witch's spells offers theaters of remarkable mutability as well as of shifting authority.

DISCOURS AU VRAY (1617): NARRATING DANCING

Rather than "lacking dances" in the absence of notated steps, Durand's *livret* teems with nuanced accounts of political power guised in descriptions of movement and light.[114] While the ballet's source is poetry, Torquato Tasso's *Jerusalem Delivered* (*La Gerusalemme liberata*, 1581), set in the eleventh-century First Crusade in Palestine, the shapeshifting scenes in the ballet's records repeat sixteenth- and seventeenth-century European accounts of the witches' sabbath.[115] Given the multiplicity of allusions at play in these staged metamorphoses, I refrain from attributing gendered binaries to roles in what follows as records do not offer them.[116] These dances offer mutable *travesti(e)s* between human and non-human forms rather than single trajectories from one fixed gender category into another.

Two anonymous engravings from the *Discours au Vray* (figs. 04.2 and 04.3) present Marais, cross-dressed as Armide the "Muslim sorceress,"[117] surrounded by shape-shifting

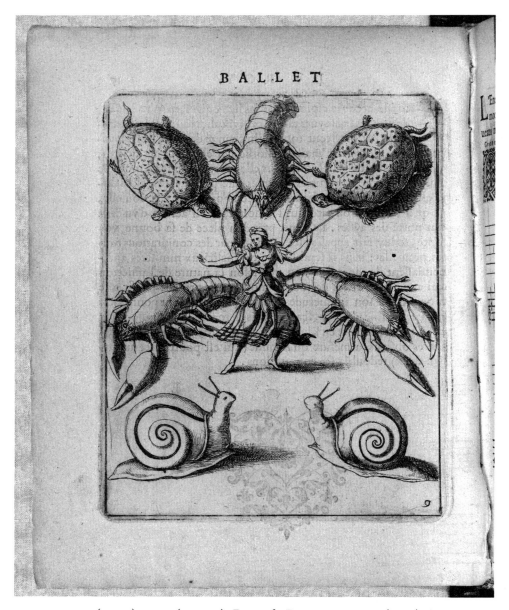

FIGURE 04.2 (LEFT)–04.3 (RIGHT) Durand, *Discours au vray* (1617) Anonymous engravings of Marais as Armide. Courtesy: BnF. RES VM7-683 (2) 17v and 19v, plates 9 and 10.

demons. In the first of these, "mocking spirits" in the form of tortoises, snails, and lobsters perform her failure to control her invocations and spells. In the second, upon emerging from their shells, the dancers take the shape of "*Vieilles*" (old women)—stereotypical targets of the witch-hunt treatises.[118] Durand designates these *Vieilles* as female from the bellybutton (*nombril*) up, wearing out-of-fashion women's head-dresses, and male from the waist

FIGURE 04.2 (LEFT)–04.3 (RIGHT) (*Continued*)

down, dressed in satin incarnadine pants, gold embroidery, and men's boots.[119] This sartorial top-and-bottom mixture performs what Pierre de Lancre, an author of witch treatises and judge during the trials, described as "transmutation of sex,"[120] writing that the dancers during the witches' sabbaths moved back and forth between male and female forms.[121] Such accounts of metamorphosis and movement flaunt gendered binaries while redoubling motifs of prohibition: from parodies of Jewish and Islamic dietary law to mutable gender. The characters' metamorphoses from shelled creatures to boisterous "androgynes" parodies Armide's inability to transform a world of spirits according to her will—asserting norms of gender and embodiment beyond a human realm as well as a failure of "feminine" authority within a more-than-human cosmology of spirits.

These unexpected stagings of religious dietary laws and prohibitions conjure infelicitous embodiments.[122] As in Leviticus, they "creep upon the earth," "crawl on their stomachs," and live in the sea "without fins and scales."[123] Such modes of locomotion parody prohibition in Abrahamic religions, performing living beings set apart as neither halal nor kosher. These illuminate how early modern performance might dance an antonym to the "noble style," a theme that also appears in the "dance histories" penned by the demonologists and prosecutors of the witch hunts.

The "*Vieilles*" also instantiate an early modern trope Natalie Zemon Davis describes as the "Woman on Top," a practice of inverting gender hierarchies, both visually and performatively, in accusatory shaming rites[124] targeting dominant women, nonnormative gender, and relationships in which husbands appeared to be submissive to their wives.[125] Such "minor roles" and figures have a long and largely unexamined history in early theatrical dance, offering transversal passages and metamorphic performances charged with religious satire and opprobrium at fault-lines between Christian "deliverance" and a more Ovidian mutability. Artificed embodiments and costumes performing such transformations open up histories of "minor figuration" and satire in early modern European theatrical dances that complicate and disclose (as political) a distinction between "illegitimate" and "legitimate" or "disorderly" and "orderly" bodies and hierarchies. Dancing on the "belly," or on single or multiple "feet," they parody both scripture and the *danse noble*, performing metamorphoses-in-process beyond binaries of species and sex that are also satires of flaunting religious law.

Pierre de Lancre's *Tableau de l'Inconstance* (1612) published "eye-witness" details of the witches' sabbath for readers in Paris. These dances "almost render men mad (*furieux*) and very often make women abort,"[126] de Lancre writes—giving voyeuristic, often highly theatricalized accounts of demons and witches coupling while metamorphosing between human and animal as well as male and female forms.[127]

This *Tableau* is packed with descriptions of the witches' dances, tracing wild and improvisational movements from *pirouettes* to "Hercules strengths." The author and judge of French witch trials on the border with Spain alleges that what he calls these "*sale*" (dirty) dances come from the south, bringing with them incest and abortions. The Basque and Labourd, among whom he unleashed brief but deadly mass prosecutions in 1609, do not have a *danse noble*, he explains. Their dances "agitate and torment" the body, disfigure it, and make it indecent. He is remarkably particular, moreover, about dangerous and indecent dance forms, counting among these "Pyrrhic and Moresque [or 'Moorish'] dances, perilous leaps, tightrope dances (*les danses sur les cordes*), falls, flights (with false wings), Pirouettes, dances in half piques [. . .] *Canaries* of the feet and hands [. . .] as well as the Chaconne and Sarabande."[128] Such ways of moving the body, outside normative, vertical codes and gaits appear in the witch-hunter's writings as offenses to legal, theological, and cultural prohibitions that were nevertheless clearly and widely performed. Enacting these while satirically reinforcing norms against such movements, the ballets seem to try to have it both ways, performing a wide range of (possibly improvised) steps.

Durand's account of the king's entrance[129] in the *Délivrance* as the Demon of Fire—clothed in reflective enamel, scattering light—addresses a performance of the king's desire for the queen as well as of his political vengeance on disruptive subjects.[130] His descriptions of sound and illumination give legal and political force to tropes of fire and light, ornamenting the motif of a celestial body enflaming senses and desires at the risk of burning spectators' bodies. "[His] Majesty wishes to have the queen his wife see some representations of the fires he felt for her," Durand writes, evoking "his strength to his enemies, and his Majesty to strangers."[131] The poet then extends this alchemical metaphor further, writing that "what is proper to fire is to purify impure bodies & to reunite things into homogeneity and likeness."[132] This allusion to alchemy's violent punishments of "mixed" corporeal forms reasserts "order" and homogeneity, serving "to remind his subjects to their duties, & to purge from them all pretexts of disobeying him."[133] This danced motif of alchemical vengeance touched each spectator, at least metaphorically, with fiery light, extending the consequence of rebellion as burning by fire, that in *Ancien Règime* laws of *Leze Majesté* were meted out to witches as well as those who rebelled against the king.[134] Among these rebellious subjects would be the author of the *livret*, Durand himself, who was broken on the wheel and executed, ostensibly for publishing illicit pamphlets in the exiled queen's support.

Cultural (as opposed to legal) representations of alchemy and magic are key here, foregrounding the changing, political meaning of the magical at the threshold of France's decriminalization of witchcraft.[135] As acts of sorcery largely ceased to be tried in the courts, witchcraft installed itself in political and artistic discourse in the imaginary of absolute power, cleaving to its performative scope. While the trials caught up both men and women in accusations, as well the very young and the very old, the role of the stage witch in the ballet canon remains a living avatar of the trials' most stereotypical targets, the *real-and-imagined* "*Vieilles*" of demonological literature, performing the excluded knowledges as well as the trauma of the witches' dances and their punishments at the center of dance-theatrical dramaturgy.

WITCHES' DANCES

Gerhild Scholz-Williams's study of the witch trial judge de Lancre critically pursues a "historiography of magical beings,"[136] exploring eroticized descriptions of dancers as an "ethnography of the witch-hunter" during the 1609 trials. The complicated ethical and historiographical context of witch-hunt literature thus erupts from the page as a dance archive. The writer's paranoid analyses and accounts of witnesses' testimony and confessions to the witches' dances share important structures and *topoi* with theatrical dances and balls. Participation in, and even merely witnessing witches' dances, as de Lancre's litany of dance description in his *Tableau* shows, could and did serve to accuse individuals and serve as evidence against them, haunting the virtual of the dance. If accusations of participation in the witches' sabbath could potentially lead to torture, prosecution, and execution—as de Lancre suggests it did in France's borderlands—the question remains as to why these dances appear with such frequency in early ballets. Can it be that the dances enacted complex cultural entanglements of witness and witch, accuser and victim? I suggest that we take up the traces of staged witches' sabbaths as volatile political and media archives saturated with theorizations of the performative; these articulate and challenge cultural histories of both popular and theatrical dances, rehearsing an ontologically precarious cultural trauma. Making the audience the witness to the witches' sabbath also troubles conceptions of evidence and the witness, staging what in the late sixteenth and early seventeenth centuries remained both contemporary and potentially proximal violence. These witches' dances enacted relations of force, coercion, and marginalization, as well as spectacle, placing dance's epistemologies and spectatorship profoundly in question.

MAGIC (EPISTEMES)

The witch hunter Institoris suggests that magic immediates relationships between material and nonmaterial worlds. He limits many of the effects of sorcery, however, to tricking perception rather than transforming or generating objects or bodies. Of particular note are his descriptions of sorcery on sensations. Sorcery's effects on the body, and in particular on involuntary feelings (numbness, paralysis, prickling, and sexual arousal) contributed discourses of evidence and even epistemologies of feeling to spells deeply entangled with conceptions of the performative.[137] Comparing witches' illusions to counterfeit gold,[138] he proposes that their influence on "the shape of illusions"[139] can throw minds into confusion[140] without changing bodies or substances themselves. This understanding of witchcraft's effects on sense, perception, and dreams rests on a hierarchical epistemology of mind and body in which bodies our bodies "are moved by our souls"[141] and in which sensation provides reservoirs of memory drawn upon by the imagination.[142] Localized movement and these "forms in the imagination" are thus particularly susceptible to magical manipulation, such that devils, witches, and demons appeal to *"peoples' intellect or to their interior or exterior senses"*[143] through illusions transmuted by inner and outer movements. In this epistemology of the body, dreams of flight, erotic desire and, most infamously, the loss of the penis (which he argues is still there but cannot be sensed) follow from the performance of harmful magic (*maleficium*). These come to attention through both a lack and an excess of sensation, that is, as that which may feel like movement but does not move.

Disconcerting bodily events attributed to witchcraft thus appear in ballets' founding discourses, precisely through their recourse to magical "epistemes." These ways of knowing and performing magic, both on and off stage, unsettle epistemological certainties as they destabilize subjects, bodies, and perceptions. The cultural representation of magic is key here. French superior courts were beginning to undo the criminal foundations of the witch trials, almost eradicating prosecutions for witchcraft in Paris's jurisdiction during the passage of time between the two ballets. Yet allegations of sorcery in political life, as well as in theater and performance, played intensifying roles in political defamation and propaganda. Sorcery and bewitchment animated such dramaturgies, repeating disavowed knowledges that could only accede to the stage if the dances' performative status could be contained. Despite the claims of demonologists like de Lancre, dance had to be perceived to be largely inefficacious, a secular disordering of the body and sense, to be performed.[144] Such early modern accounts of perception and feeling open the door to approaching a phenomenology of history through movements, performances, and embodiments whose delineations as media can change considerably over time. Historical accounts of senses, gestures, and feeling are disclosed here *in extremis* in complex relationships to histories of injustice, illness, and marginalization within mediatic, disciplinary definitions of live arts.

MISE-EN-ABYME: BOOK WITHIN A BOOK

On the wooden desk in front of me, Beaujoyeulx's account of the *Balet comique* ends with an image of an open book scattered with occult signs, propped toward the reader (fig. 04.4). Taking the object before me and the image within it together, I observe how this doubling draws attention to the mediality of the codex, rendering it as both a visual and textual emblem transferred onto the page with copper plates. The trace of this impression leaves grooves and messy ink marks on the page, memorializing an absent, golden object—the medal offered by the performer playing Circe, the "Madamoyselle de Saincte Mesme," to the Cardinal de Bourbon at the end of the ballet. Promising the doing and undoing of spells, this evocation of the emblem as a material thing seems to shift a procedure from ephemeral to material form, inviting the reader into a performative relation to the world and text. Making the world anew, it seems to promise or require a decryption, utterance, or procedure performed with the signs on the page.

The hybrid ingredients of this magic, however, refuse to be stitched together. The scattered symbols on the pages of the open book remain unavailable to the viewer. This dispersion of inscrutable signs both confirms and waylays the emblem's dispersion of magics, suggesting the possibility of a modification of the world glimpsed, as if through a round window, beyond the codex. This printed version of Circe's gift highlights Beaujoyeulx's transdisciplinary experiment with the "modern invention" of ballet as a print form. The perpetually open pages of Patin's engraved book, "*Le Livre*," emphasize an ongoing potential for a transformation in the doing of representation, complicating the certainty of the artifact, the page, and memory in an ecology of imperfect things. The phrase beneath this emblem, "*Fatorum arcana resignat*"[145] creates a visual solicitation to parse or reconstruct its elements, as if ink's stamping of events and acts onto paper might still time and memory, saving these, as Beaujoyeulx writes, from Saturn's "teeth of oblivion,"[146] and inviting a performative capacity for transformation in a future that is not yet here.

Observing that the power to define the magical led to extraordinary powers over the accused, Gerhild Scholz Williams argues magic "is always, even etymologically, associated with *Macht* ('power')."[147] Magic, she writes, "does not conform to Michel Foucault's concept of the episteme as a new and epoch-making epistemology or to his concept of an archive [. . .] a paradigm that transcends centuries and surfaces."[148] It "is both of these concepts at once," an *archive* and *episteme*: "a discourse of contemporary violence, fears, and marginalization in the context of a century-old cosmology and theology."[149] These virtualities give the lie to a "linear flow of secular Enlightenment time"[150] that is undeniable in its effects on the accused and yet is all too easily written off as superstition and past belief.

This seemingly blasphemous, certainly unusual gift from the hands of a stage witch to the king's potential surrogate seems to wish to take purchase in a mixture of materiality and durability, on the one hand, and the performative elusiveness of spells on the other. It points to the relation between the viewer and a windswept, forbidding world—beyond the book—one, perhaps, to be performatively reimagined by the reader. This fashioning

BALET COMIQVE

Madamoyſelle de Sainte Meſme à monſieur
le Cardinal de Bourbon,

LE LIVRE.

Fatorum arcana reſignat.

FIGURE 04.4 *"Le Livre,"* copperplate after drawings by Jacques Patin. Print of the gold medal given to the Cardinal de Bourbon by the "Madamoyselle de Sainte Mesme," playing Circe, at the end of the *Balet comique de la Royne*. Courtesy: BnF, Beaujoyeulx, *Balet comique*, 73v. RES4-LN27-10436 (EPSILON).

of transmission entangles magic's performance with its records, cleaving the archive and the repertoire[151] and messing with a culture-bound division of knowledges that Schneider describes as "inter(in)animating" one another, drawing the notion of the performative into the image (in turn an object) and the image into the performative. In this book within a book—as object, image, text, and gift—Beaujoyeulx's emphasis on his ballet as a "modern invention" in print appears here as if distilled on the last page of the performance text.

CODA

Studying this image of a book within a book compels a return to the question of touch that opens and closes this study. I observe the vellum skin of the binding, the inert body of the text and its remarkably well preserved pages, reflecting on Beaujoyeulx's spectacular ambition to set protean performance in print in the midst of an era of destabilizing violence and change. I am reminded of his promise, in his introduction to the king, that suggests text and print might "protect" acts and memory.

Returning the book to the curators and librarians, I retrieve my belongings and leave the library. Slipping down the opera house's famous stairs, and pausing on the landing among the caryatids, I sense ballet's latent techniques in my limbs: recognizing an incorporation, however nonlinearly, of its histories in my alignment. My bones and sensory world remember the techniques, acts, and experiences of my own version of the medium as I move in this space, activating the kinesthetic imaginary with which I trace my own exit from the building. Leaving through the bookshop, I feel a defamiliarizing slip—as if my immersion in print were just beginning to dissolve, confronted with the everyday speech of another century, revealing a sense of temporal dislocation. Past conceptions of sense serve as tricky holds and grips for these reflections, as to be subject to spells offers accounts of subjection, time, and relation well beyond cause and effect.

Leaving the opera house I then slip underground, sliding a ticket into a machine and entering the subway, still juggling with this disjuncture between image and spell. As I travel underground eastward, I fumble in my bag and pull out a digital reader. At a touch, my scan of Lacroix appears on the electronic screen, and I see more clearly, rendered in light, the keen complexity of the scanned image and its represented dimensions: the grain of the page, the shadow of the fold, and the soft dimpling between its pages—holding the work together with the image of a stitch. Taking in the image on the screen, I observe a new format in the archives, another species of picture that "resembles memory."[152] As I read by the screen's cold light, the precious copy in the archives hurtles disconcertingly away behind me. I browse passages with my fingers on chilled glass, tracing notes like a scryer.

Touching icons, I move from Lacroix's nineteenth-century version of the text, stripped bare of images and allegories, emblems and music notation, and then to my photographs of the seventeenth-century book. Now, in my mind's eye, the screen appears as a tricky dance across time, technologies, and material supports, disclosing the prescience of Beaujoyeulx's insistence on proliferating artifice. Then I scroll to "Le Livre," examining the emblem on the screen, with its promise the text is always open, its pages frozen, facing the reader.

The very valuable book, paradoxically confined in archives that I have just touched, seems almost astonishingly accessible as this ghostly, digital surrogate—and yet it is disconcertingly, affectively cold.[153] I "know" which copy of Beaujoyeulx this copy is a copy of, and yet what becomes "my" copy increasingly becomes what I do to it. I reread my un-inky, scarlet red, digital marginalia scrawled and saved over a surface of images: its ghosts of stilled pages. The emblem in the *livret*, reflecting alchemically on the materialization of the event, seems torn out of the *mise-en-abyme* in which it performs (or invites) its copying as a codex. Now I read it with a gesture that cannot touch the text itself, replacing Circe's appeal to the material world with what Sherwin calls a "mediatized dematerialization:" a digital baroque.[154]

Poised between digital and historical turns, I find myself on a cusp between media, reflecting on a then-new and now-new technology of the book. In today's context, in which the scarce and collectible *livret* is quickly becoming a "free" electronic resource (whose "digital" moniker ironically transforms and distanciates touch), I absorb these changes in access to texts, memory, and works' recirculations across centuries—discovering excesses of artifices and multiplications of surface that are recursive and progressive, precarious and historical. The book, like the archive, performs, as does this thinking through (inter)disciplines in movement.

Here on the train, under the city, technology's transformation dawns disconcertingly upon me as I hold the emblem of the image-book, displaying the absent object on its screen. I look at the emblem's stormy skies and rocky horizon, registering its drama of a precarious potential that seems to invite reinventing relationships of subjects and objects, viewers and texts. Slitheringly evocative in this concatenation of act, image, book, and emblem is the flicker of the book's clasp, moving like a serpent's tail behind the open pages of the book. Beaujoyeulx's tentative steps toward this emergence and immersion trigger another kind of imagining, reigniting this instability of artifice and real. The question of perception, here, is no longer one of truth or illusion, but an invitation to perform—glimpsing an as-yet unconjured relation to an imperfect world glimpsed beyond the unbinding of the codex—behind the serpent's tail.

NOTES

1. See Balthazar de Beaujoyeulx, Nicolas de la Chesnaye, and René Bordier. *Le Balet comique de la Royne*, with engravings by Jacques Patin, music by Lambert Beaulieu with Jacques Salmon, and contributions in poetry and prose by multiple authors. My thanks to the editors of this volume and to Gabrielle Ann Moyer, Elizabeth Claire, Patrick Riley, Janice Ross, and Mark Franko.

2. Scholars have established a long history of ballets before the *Balet comique de la royne*. For earlier works in France, see Jean Dorat (1573).

3. Key English-language monographs on the early court ballets include Mark Franko, *Dance as Text: Ideologies of the Baroque Body*; Margaret McGowan, *Dance in the Renaissance*; and Frances Yates, *Astraea* and *French Academies of the Sixteenth Century*. French-language scholarship on this period includes Bernadette Dufourcet and Anne Surgers, *Corps dansant*; Marie-Françoise Christout, *Le Ballet de cour au XVIIe siècle*; Margaret McGowan, *L'Art du ballet de cour en France, 1581–1643*; Henry Prunières, *Le ballet de cour en France avant Benserade et Lully*; Paul Lacroix, *Les ballets et masquerades de cour sous Henri IV*

et Louis XIII; and Victor Fournel, "Théâtre de la cour (ballets et mascarades)" in *Les Contemporains de Molière.*

4. Lacroix, *Les ballets et mascarades,* vol. 1, 1–86, omits all of the music and images as well as 74v–75v from the 1582 edition. While omitting the descriptions of female dancers and allegories of desire from the first edition, Lacroix nevertheless adds verse by the renowned author François de Malherbe not found in the published source. I cite Malherbe's poem in the epigraph of this essay. For facsimiles see Baltasar de Beaujoyeulx, *Balet Comique de la Royne,* and Margaret McGowan, *Le Balet Comique by Balthazar de Beaujoyeulx, 1581: A Facsimile.* Digital versions of the Beaujoyeulx and Estienne Durand *livrets* are available from the web portal Gallica. Accessed May 1, 2013. <http://visualiseur.bnf.fr/CadresFenetre?O=IFN-8608300&I=1&M=chemindefer> and <http://bibliotheque-numerique.inha.fr/collection/4836-discours-au-vray-du-ballet-danse-par-le/>.

5. Circe, as desire, controls the living, writes Gordon: "it seems to me it would not be unreasonable to take Circe (*la Circé*) for desire in general, which reigns over and dominates all that has life & is mixed with divinity and sense (*le sensible*) [. . .] & leads some to virtue and others to vice." Sieur Gordon in Beaujoyeulx et al., *Ballet comique,* 74r–75v. All translations mine.

6. In Peter Holland and Stephen Orgel, *From Script to Stage in Early Modern England.*

7. Estienne (Étienne) Durand, Réné Bordier, and Pierre Guédron, *Discours au vray du ballet dansé par le Roy* (1617).

8. Orgel, *The Illusion of Power,* 11.

9. On France's witch-hunts and their quickly changing legal frameworks at the turn of the seventeenth century, see Soman, *Sorcellerie et justice criminelle,* 28; Bodin, *On the Demon-mania of Witches.*

10. Newman, 54–55:

    > the first folio of the most famous witch-hunting manual of all time [was] the *Malleus Maleficarum* published by the two Dominican inquisitors Heinrich Kramer and Jakob Sprenger in 1487. This extraordinary fact has gone virtually unnoticed by historians and yet it demonstrates—as nothing else could—the reality that alchemy and witchcraft were linked in the minds of the most influential proponents of the Great Witch Hunt of early modern Europe.

11. Newman traces a long-running rhetorical dispute between art and nature through Arabic, North African, and Greco-Roman texts on the competition between "imitative" (painting, mechanics, and illusion) and "perfective arts" (conceived as transformations). On the artificial production of human life as a "crowning pinnacle of human art" that subsumes all others, see 24–44, 195, and 236.

12. Beaujoyeulx, "*Au lecteur,*" *Balet comique,* n.p. [6v–7r]; translation mine.

13. Of these, Beaujoyeulx writes that he gives pride of place to dancing and to the scripting of futurity—in the pleasures of comedy's happy endings.

14. Rebecca Schneider uses the apt term "leak" to describe temporal phenomena and the effects of one time upon another. Schneider, 9–10.

15. Following Henri III's 1589 assassination, the Cardinal de Bourbon was hailed as king by the Catholic League, but he is no longer acknowledged as a king of France in genealogies of royal power, and Charles Philippe of France took his name as sovereign in 1830, thereby erasing it.

16. For reconstructions of the production's music, see Beaulieu, *Le Balet comique de la Royne de Baltazar de Beaujoyeulx,* compact disc.

17. Such font changes designate passages set to music as well as changes of authorship—though these rarely seem systematic.
18. Franko, *Dance as Text*, 34.
19. Beaujoyeulx et al., *Balet comique*, 5r–6v.
20. Beaujoyeulx et al., *Balet comique*, 6v.
21. See Stuart Clark, *Vanities of the Eye* and *Thinking with Demons*.
22. See Richard K. Sherwin, "*Performer la Loi*," n4. Translation provided by author.
23. Newman, 51.
24. On sovereignty, the body natural and the body politic, see Franko, "Fragment of the Sovereign," 120–121; "Figural Inversions of the King's Dancing Body," 35–51; and Kantorowicz, *The King's Two Bodies*. On Henri III and Queen Louise's attempts to have a child, see Crawford, *Sexual Culture of the French Renaissance*, 226–230.
25. See Didi-Huberman, 88.
26. The building stood by the Seine between an early footprint of the Louvre and the Church of Saint-Germain l'Auxerrois. Before its destruction, the theater premiered major seventeenth-century works including *le Ballet de la nuit* (1653) and works by Molière and Corneille.
27. The wedding was satirized in the sixteenth century in an anonymous pamphlet, claiming "one has never seen the like of such marriages as these: Men marry men and women marry women." Zorach, 226.
28. See Halberstam (2011).
29. Wintroub, 387.
30. See Crawford, "Love, Sodomy, and Scandal," 513–542; Wintroub, 395.
31. Panofsky, 45.
32. The terms "Renaissance," "baroque," and "mannerism" are markedly elastic, Franko suggests, and I follow his arguments regarding periodicity. Franko, xiii and 3–4.
33. Beaujoyeulx et al., 8r.
34. On stage witches and early modern racialization, see Purkiss, 251.
35. Beaujoyeulx et al., *Balet comique*, 8v.
36. Addressing "invalidated" pasts in *The Queer Art of Failure*, Halberstam refers by way of Michel Foucault to "forms of knowledge that have not simply been lost or forgotten [but] disqualified, rendered nonsensical or nonconceptual or 'insufficiently elaborated'" (11). This approach to discredited and "subjugated knowledges" underlies my approach to magic and alchemy in the artistic discourses of the era of the witch trials.
37. McIlvenna, 181–208.
38. Jorge Luis Borges qtd. in Soja, 55.
39. Beaujoyeulx et al., *Balet comique*, 6r–v.
40. On Zeuxis see Newman, 12–14.
41. Muchembled, 36.
42. Schneider, 41; Purkiss, 260.
43. Borges qtd. in Soja, 54–57.
44. On religion, denomination, and discontinuous reading see Stallybrass, 48.
45. Bernstein, 70.
46. See Maxwell Stuart's introduction to Institoris [Kramer], *The Malleus Maleficarum*, 17. On this infamous work, first published in 1487 and republished in multiple editions in the late sixteenth and seventeenth centuries, see Purkiss, 8–11; Muchembled, 38–43; and Williams, 1–8, for different readings of the impact of the text.

47. Institoris, 8 and 75; Isidore of Seville, *Etymologiae* XI.2.17–24.

48. On the witch's capacity to inflict harm through sight and touch, see Institoris, part 1, question 9 and 217.

49. Newman, 9.

50. "Passions operate on an all-or-nothing principle," writes Joseph Roach, addressing spirits of movement and the mind. They are "either quiescent or firing full bore like the discharge of a musket." See Roach, 26–31 and 64–65.

51. Beaujoyeulx et al., "*Au lecteur*," *Balet comique*, no page numbers in the original [xi].

52. Beaujoyeulx et al., [ii] and [iv].

53. Beaujoyeulx et al., [xi].

54. Beaujoyeulx et al., [xi–xii].

55. The "real theater of ideological tensions," Franko writes, is "a vertiginous complexity of collateral arts," *Dance as Text*, 1–2 and 32.

56. Schneider uses the term "inter(in)animation," which she elaborates cross-temporally from Fred Moten and John Donne, to address the "tangling" of objects, representations, and temporalities. See Schneider, 1, 139, and 167–168.

57. Like the "magic" of the moving body, the organization of the limbs, senses, and understanding was an early modern commonplace for describing the socius. See Apostolidès, 7–15.

58. On the entanglement of theater and print histories in early modern Europe, see Peters (2000).

59. In early modern usage, the term "*contrefait*" (counterfeit) can also signify the "imitation" or the performance of gestures, positions, and stock characters.

60. "[Through] a kind of scrambling (*bruuage* [sic])," writes the Sieur de Gordon, "[she] changes men into beasts [and returns] them to their true being and human form," in Beaujoyeulx, *Balet comique*, 75r.

61. Beaujoyeulx's preface suggests an intriguing epistemology of the senses as a distance from objects and their qualities. See, for example, Thomas Hobbes's reflections on sense in *Leviathan*, "For if those Colours, and Sounds, were in the Bodies, or Objects that cause them, they could not bee severed from them, as by glasses, and in Ecchoes by reflection, we see they are; where we know the thing we see, is in one place; the appearance, in the other." Hobbes, 86 [3–4].

62. Plato, *Republic* X, 596b–596e.

63. Beaujoyeulx et al., 6v.

64. The evident question of how the ballet deploys and performs these "Persian" "Indes" remains open. *Balet comique* predates most contemporary scholarship on Orientalism, though poetry in the *livret*'s introduction praises the work for helping spectators to "see" the "Indians" "without peril" (n.p.). Nicholas Dew addresses a "baroque Orientalism" in *Orientalism in Louis XIV's France*, 5–16. Ina Baghdiantz McCabe calls for research on early modern orientalisms before the 1630 lifting of the ban on Middle Eastern languages in France. In McCabe, 2–42. Susan Leigh Foster addresses the proliferation of such utopias in European theatrical dance. In *Worlding Dance*, 14.

65. Schneider, paraphrasing Aristotle's retort to Plato, writes "*mimesis* is what we *do*." "[To] ask how to do things with mimesis might be to ask how to engage with historical process—with history," Schneider, 18.

66. Pappas, "Plato's Aesthetics," *The Stanford Encyclopedia of Philosophy* (2012). Accessed May 1, 2013. http://plato.stanford.edu/archives/sum2012/entries/plato-aesthetics/.

67. Levine, 117.
68. Levine, 108.
69. Levine, 12.
70. Levine, 3.
71. The ballet's references exceed its classical source in the tenth book of Homer's *Odyssey*. See Charles Zika on Circe's early modern iconography from Boccaccio, Boethius, Virgil, and Saint Augustine. In "Images of Circe and Discourses of Witchcraft, 1480–1580," 5.
72. Bodin, 128.
73. Bodin, 87 and 122–124.
74. In *Balet comique*, 7v and 16v.
75. Beaujoyeulx et al., *Balet comique*, 4v and 7v.
76. "[We] are before the image as if *before a complex of time*, time considered provisionally, dynamically, and from its own movements." Didi-Huberman, 39. Translation mine.
77. Muchembled, 6.
78. Muchembled, 10.
79. Sovereignty "demands the completion of the image of the sovereign, as tyrant," writes Walter Benjamin. In *The Origin of German Tragic Drama*, 69.
80. Mourey, 111.
81. See Bodin, 128; Yarnall, "Renaissance Circe" in *Transformations of Circe*.
82. Purkiss, *The Witch in History*, 250–275; Didi-Huberman, 99 and 106.
83. In Williams, *Defining Dominion*, 12–13.
84. See Arie Graafland on Circe's resemblances to Armide, Calypso, and other stage enchantresses. In *Versailles*, 15; Purkiss, 267.
85. "Inasmuch as the king is an actor rather than merely a spectator, allegory becomes history as its own representation, its power to transform itself in the understanding glance of its prime mover." Franko, *Dance as Text*, 38–39.
86. Franko specifies that "her theatrical presence [. . .] is dramaturgical." Franko, *Dance as Text*, 39.
87. See "Whether Witches Have Copulation with Demons," following Bodin's analysis of Circe in *Demon-mania*, 128 and 130–135.
88. Grosz, 289 and 290–294.
89. Beaujoyeulx et al., *Balet comique*, 22v and 55.
90. This plural form for female dancers is rare and no longer in use.
91. See Franko, *Dance as Text*, 45–46.
92. Beaujoyeulx et al., *Balet comique*, 24r–v.
93. Hermes gives Moly to Odysseus in Homer to protect him from Circe's spells; the unidentified herb is also the referent for the character name Molly Bloom in James Joyce's *Ulysses*.
94. On *tableaux vivants*, repetition, and "simulacral soup" see Schneider, 145–147.
95. On the thesis of the Little Ice Age, witchcraft, and baroque climactic crisis, see Dillinger, 100–101, 209, and 267; Behringer, 1–27.
96. Circe's *harangue* claims a full suite of harmful magic associated with witches: crop failure, storms, hail, famine, and the sterility of humans and animals. See Beaujoyeulx et al., *Balet comique*, 25r–26r; Levack, 219–220, 153–154, and 273.
97. The stag, often described as the devil, is a recurring figure of witches' sabbath narratives.
98. Beaujoyeulx et al., *Balet comique*, 26v–27r.
99. Franko, *Dance as Text*, 44–47. The *Balet comique* predates Thoinot Arbeau's *Orchésographie* (1589).

100. Beaujoyeulx et al., *Balet comique*, 56 and 63v; Franko, *Dance as Text*, 34–51; Lepecki, 1–18.

101. The dances, Beaujoyeulx writes with praise, were performed by the women with the rigor and order of a battle corps, while Archimedes was also renowned as a military strategist and inventor of projectiles. See also Billard in Beaujoyeulx et al., *Balet comique*, [iv].

102. Though the names of the female cast appear in the *livret*, very little is known about the "Madamoyselle de Sainte Mesme." She may have been a member of the de l'Hôpital family. See Beaujoyeulx et al., *Balet comique*, 64r and 73v.

103. Kirby, 30.

104. Henri III subsequently kept the Cardinal in prison for the remainder of his reign.

105. On the celebrated dancer and musician Marais, see Georgie Durosoir, *"Illustre . . . et Inconnu: Quelques notes sur Marais"* in Garden, *La Délivrance de Renaud*, 157.

106. Examples of the persistence of the *travestie* witch figure in ballet repertoire include *Les Sylphides'* Madge and *Sleeping Beauty's* Carabosse.

107. Zika, 30.

108. Sara Beam points out women did not perform in farce, with ballets taking the place of rowdy farce practices such as *Mère folle*. In Beam, 26.

109. On the mutability of affects, passions, and humors, see Roach, 39–43.

110. Though women did perform in ballets at this time, they are pointedly less prominent than in the *Balet comique*. See Brooks (2007). Stephen Orgel subtly addresses this context, writing of England, arguing that while "our evidence does not support any blanket claim that women were excluded from the stages of Renaissance England [. . .] it may certainly indicate that the culture, and the history that descends from it, had an interest in rendering them unnoticeable." Stephen Orgel, *Impersonations*, 8–9.

111. See McIlvenna, "Stable" (2013). The allegory concluding with an insistence on the female dancers' impeccable morality, that was omitted in the nineteenth-century Lacroix edition of the text, leaves a trace of the considerable cultural controversy over women's political and cultural reach in the Valois court. Beaujoyeulx, *Balet* comique, 75v. Both the *Balet comique* and *Ballet de la Délivrance* were works commissioned by queens, and both writers reflect on conversations with women on dramaturgy in the introductions to their texts.

112. On the ballet's political context and the *livret's* likely date of publication after the coup, see Garden, 15–28; McGowan, *L'Art du ballet de cour*.

113. Alfred Soman overturns many widespread perceptions of the trials, arguing that the period following Henri IV's assassination, during Marie de Medici's rule, "inaugurated a period of accelerated decriminalization" of witchcraft (196). The last execution of a witch in the jurisdiction of Paris's *Parlement* was that of Catherine Bouillon in 1625 (404). In *"La décriminilasation de la sorcellerie en France"* and "Decriminalizing Witchcraft," reprinted in *Sorcellerie et justice criminelle* (1992).

114. See Durand et al., *Discours au vray*, 17r–20r; and Franko (1999).

115. See, for example, Pierre de Lancre's chapter on the witches' Sabbath and his citations from testimony and interrogations describing this event in the course of trials he presided over as a judge. In Lancre, *Tableau de l'inconstance des mauvais anges et démons*, [1612] 1982.

116. The roles of Armide, her spirits, and the nymphs were performed on one hand by a cast of male performers and on the other by "machines" and automata. On machines, fountains, and designer Tommaso Francini's simulacra, see Garden, *La Délivrance de Renaud*, 46. On the identification of the cast, see ibid., 7–13. On early modern hydraulic robots, mimesis, and Daedalus' moving statues, see Newman, 12–3.

117. Charles T. Downey in Garden (ed.), 54.

118. See Fox, "Authorizing the Metamorphic Witch: Ovid in Reginald Scot's *Discoverie of Witchcraft*" in *Metamorphosis*, 170.
119. Durand et al., *Discours au vray*, 19r.
120. See Parker, 337–364; Soyer, "Inquisitors and Hermaphrodites," 50–95; McClive, 45–68; Long (2006); Pardo Tomás (2003); Orgel, "Nobody's Perfect," 7–29.
121. On gender hierarchies, nonhuman figures, and early modern witchcraft, see Levack, 219–220 and 35; Soman; Sluhovsky.
122. Historian Jean-François Dubost addresses this era as one of "state xenophobia," addressing expulsion orders given for Jews in 1615. In Dubost (2009); Anchel, 45–60.
123. Leviticus 11:9–10 and 42.
124. Davis, 124–151.
125. A "world turned upside down can only be righted, not changed." Davis, 131. On gender and witchcraft, see Levack 40–44; Garrett, 32–72; Purkiss (1996); Williams (1999).
126. Lancre, 190.
127. These dances "turn shoulder to shoulder" in circles, Durand writes, "with the back of each turned to the center of the round [. . .] *en dehors.*" In Lancre, 194, 141–169, 188–196, and 209.
128. Lancre, 190–193.
129. On dancing kings and critical theories of political power, see Franko's "Jouer avec le feu," 161–169; "Fragment of the Sovereign," 119–133; and "The King Cross-Dressed," 64–84.
130. No one, writes Durand, who saw such "persons so inventively masked and dressed" could but believe themselves to be in a dream "in which we might take for true Demons those who were only portraying them (*qui ne creut estre en quelque agreable songe, ou qui ne prit pour Démons veritables ceux qui les representoyent seulement*)." Durand et al, *Discours au vray*, 4v. See also translation in Garden (ed.), *Ballet de la Délivrance*, 245.
131. Durand et al., 5v.
132. Durand et al., 5v.
133. Durand et al., 5v; Franko, *Dance as Text*, 70; "Jouer avec le feu," 167–169; "Fragment of the Sovereign," 126; Rogers, 5.
134. Durand's insight into this power to punish was uncannily prescient. The author was imprisoned the following year, ostensibly for writing a pamphlet in support of his exiled patron and ordered to kneel in front of the cathedral of Notre Dame in an *amende honorable*. Then he was broken on the wheel (*roué*) at the *place du Grève* and, according to his sentence, burned along with his writings. This terrifying execution of a leading artist sent an unambiguous message. On the *amende honorable* and codification of public punishment, see Foucault, "The Body of the Condemned," in *Discipline and Punish*, 3–16.
135. "The crime of witchcraft was always irreconcilable with traditional standards of legal proof," writes Alfred Soman, observing a "sudden and permanent downturn in witchcraft executions—tantamount to *de facto* decriminalization" in early seventeenth-century France. Soman, 4 and 13.
136. Williams, 12.
137. On the performance of magic, see Sofer, 1–21.
138. Institoris, 51.
139. Institoris, 51.
140. Institoris, 68.
141. Institoris, 79.
142. Institoris, 17.

143. Institoris, 79.
144. On the witch's recurrence in later European dances, from Romantic ballet to Mary Wigman, see Glon (2012).
145. Amy Wygant suggests "Fatorum arcana resignat" (it opens the secrets of the fates), signifies the unbinding of a spell. In *Medea*, 14–15.
146. Beajoyeulx, "*Au Roy,*" *Balet comique*, no page number in original [ii].
147. Williams, 14.
148. "The magic underlying this system is *archive* and *episteme*, unchanging and constantly in flux, at the same time." Williams, 9 and 63.
149. See Williams, 9.
150. Schneider, 171.
151. "The rift," Diana Taylor writes, "does not lie between the written and spoken word, but between the *archive* of supposedly enduring materials (i.e., texts, documents, buildings, bones) and the so-called ephemeral *repertoire* of embodied practice/knowledge (i.e., spoken language, dance, sports, ritual)." See Taylor, 19–20; Schneider, 108.
152. Derrida (1993).
153. Magical metaphors persist in conceptions of new forms of media. See Mike Daisey on the iPad in the controversial *The Agony and the Ecstasy of Steve Jobs*: "He's never actually seen one on, this thing that took his hand. I turn it on, unlock the screen, and pass it to him. He takes it. The icons flare into view, and he strokes the screen with his ruined hand, and the icons slide back and forth. And he says something to Cathy, and Cathy says, "He says it's a kind of magic." Mike Daisey, "Mr. Daisey and the Apple Factory," *This American Life*. Transcript episode 454. Accessed May 1, 2013. http://www.thisamericanlife.org/radio-archives/episode/454/transcript.
154. See Sherwin, [n.p.] on Ulrich Gumbrecht.

BIBLIOGRAPHY

Anchel, Robert. "The Early History of the Jewish Quarters in Paris." *Jewish Social Studies* 2, no. 1 (1940): 45–60.

Apostolidès, Jean-Marie. *Le roi-machine: spectacle et politique au temps de Louis XIV.* Paris: *Editions de minuit*, 1981.

Banes, Sally. *Dancing Women: Female Bodies on Stage.* New York: Routledge, 1998.

de Beaujoyeulx, Baltasar. *Balet Comique de la Royne* 1582 [facsimile]. Turin: Bottega d'Erasmo, 1965.

de Beaujoyeulx, Balthazar, Nicolas de la Chesnaye, and René Bordier. *Le Balet comique de la Royne, faict aux nopces de monsieur le duc de Joyeuse & madamoyselle de Vaudemont sa soeur. Par Baltasar de Beaujoyeulx, valet de chambre du Roy.* Bibliothèque-musée de l'opéra [BnF Bmo: RES-659 (BIS)]. Paris: Adrian Le Roy, Robert Ballart, & Mamert Patisson, 1582.

de Beaulieu, Lambert. *Le Balet comique de la Royne de Baltazar de Beaujoyeulx.* Longeville les Metz [Ensemble Elyma; Chief of Orchestra Gabriel Garrido], K617 080, 1998, compact disc.

Beam, Sara. *Laughing Matters: Farce and the Making of Absolutism in France.* Ithaca: Cornell University Press, 2007.

Behringer, Wolfgang. "Weather, Hunger and Fear: Origins of the European Witch-Hunts in Climate, Society and Mentality." Translated by David Lederer. *German History* 13, no. 1 (1995): 403–24.

Benjamin, Walter. *The Origin of German Tragic Drama*. Translated by John Osborne. London and New York: Verso, [1963] 2009.

Bernstein, Robin. "Dances with Things: Material Culture and the Performance of Race," *Social Text 101* 27, no. 4 (2009): 67–94.

Bodin, Jean. *On the Demon-mania of Witches*. Translated by Randy A. Scott, intro by Jonathan L. Pearl. Toronto: Centre for Reformation and Renaissance Studies, [1580] 1995.

Brooks, Lynn Matluck. *Women's Work: Making Dance in Europe before 1800*. Madison: University of Wisconsin Press, 2007.

Christout, Marie-Françoise. *Le Ballet de cour au XVIIe siècle*. Geneva: Minkoff, 1987.

Clark, Stuart. *Thinking with Demons: The Idea of Witchcraft in Early Modern Europe*. Oxford: Oxford University Press, 1999.

———. *Vanities of the Eye: Vision in Early Modern European Culture*. Oxford: Oxford University Press, 2007.

Crawford, Katherine. "Love, Sodomy, and Scandal: Controlling the Sexual Reputation of Henri III," *Journal of the History of Sexuality*, 12, no. 4 (2003): 513–42.

———. *Sexual Culture of the French Renaissance*. Cambridge: Cambridge University Press, 2010.

Davis, Natalie Zemon. *Society and Culture in Early Modern France: Eight Essays*. Stanford: Stanford University Press, 1965.

Daisey, Mike. "Mr. Daisey and the Apple Factory," *This American Life*. Transcript episode 454. Accessed May 1, 2013. http://www.thisamericanlife.org/radio-archives/episode/454/transcript.

Derrida, Jacques. *Mal d'archive: une impression Freudienne*. Paris: Galilée, 1993.

Dew, Nicholas. *Orientalism in Louis XIV's France*. Oxford: Oxford University Press, 2009.

Didi-Huberman, Georges. *L'Image survivante: histoire de l'art et temps des fantômes selon Aby Warburg*. Paris: Éditions de minuit, 2002.

Dillinger, Johannes. *"Evil People": A Comparative Study of the Witch Hunts in Swabian Austria and the Electorate of Trier*. Translated by Laura Stokes. Charlottesville: University of Virginia Press, 2009.

Dorat, Jean. "*Ballet des Polonais*," *Magnificentissimi spectaculi a regina regum* [. . .] at the Bibliothèque nationale de France (BnF) [BnF: RES M-YC-748]. Paris: F. Morel, 1573.

Dubost, Jean-François. *Marie de Médicis: La Reine dévoilée*. Paris: Payot, 2009.

Dufourcet, Bernadette, and Anne Surgers, *Corps dansant—corps glorieux: Musique, danses et fêtes de cour en Europe au temps d'Henri IV et de Louis XIII*. Les cahiers d'artes, 7. Pessac: Presses Universitaires de Bordeaux, 2011.

Durand, Estienne (Étienne), Réné Bordier, and Pierre Guédron, *Discours au vray du ballet dansé par le Roy, le dimanche XXIXe jour de janvier. M. Vlc.XVII. Avec les desseins, tant des machines & apparances differentes, que de tous les habits des masques)*, 19r. Bibliothèque nationale de France, Réserve des livres rares [BnF: RES-YF-1217]. Paris: Pierre Ballard, 1617.

Foster, Susan Leigh. *Worlding Dance*. London: Palgrave Macmillan, 2009.

Foucault, Michel. *Discipline and Punish: The Birth of the Prison*. New York: Vintage, 1977.

Fournel, Victor. "Histoire du ballet de cour." In *Les Contemporains de Molière*, 173–221. Paris: Firmin Didot, 1866.

Fox, Cora. "Authorizing the Metamorphic Witch: Ovid in Reginald Scot's *Discoverie of Witchcraft*." In *Metamorphosis: The Changing Face of Ovid in Medieval and Early Modern Europe*, 165–78. Edited by Alison Keith and Stephen Rupp. Toronto: University of Toronto, 2007.

Franko, Mark. "'Fragment of the Sovereign as Hermaphrodite: Time, History and the Exception in *Le Ballet de Madame*.'" *Dance Research* 25, no. 2 (2007): 119–33.

———. "Majestic Drag: Monarchical Performativity and the King's Body Theatrical." *TDR* 47, no. 2 (2003): 71–87.

———. "Figural Inversions of the King's Dancing Body." In *Acting on the Past: Historical Performance across Disciplines*, 35–51. Hanover, NH: Wesleyan University Press, 2000.

———. "Jouer avec le feu" in *"La Jérusalem délivrée" du Tasse: Poésie, peinture, musique, ballet: Actes du colloque, Musée du Louvre*, 159–77. Paris: Klincksieck, 1999.

———. *Dance as Text: Ideologies of the Baroque Body*. New York: Cambridge University Press, 1993.

Garden, Greer, ed. *La Délivrance de Renaud: Ballet Danced by Louis XIII in 1617*. Turnhout: Brepols, 2010.

Garrett, Julia M. "Witchcraft and Sexual Knowledge in Early Modern England." *Journal for Early Modern Cultural Studies* 13, no. 1 (2013): 32–72.

Glon, Marie, ed. "Sorcières," *Repères: Cahier de danse* 30 (November 2012).

Graafland, Arie. *Versailles and the Mechanics of Power*. Rotterdam: 010 Publishers, 2003.

Grosz, Elizabeth. "Animal Sex: Libido as Desire and Death." In *Sexy Bodies: The Strange Carnalities of Feminism*, 278–99. New York: Routledge, 1995.

Halberstam, Jack. *The Queer Art of Failure*. Durham, NC: Duke University Press, 2011.

Hobbes, Thomas. *Leviathan*. London: Penguin, [1651] 1968.

Holland, Peter, and Stephen Orgel, *From Script to Stage in Early Modern England*. New York: Palgrave Macmillan, 2004.

Institoris [Kramer], Heinrich. *The Malleus Maleficarum*. Edited and trans. by P.G. Maxwell-Stuart. Manchester: Manchester University Press, [1486; 1588 edition] 2007.

Kantorowicz, Ernst. *The King's Two Bodies: A Study in Medieval Political Theology*. Princeton: Princeton University Press, [1957] 1997.

Kirby, Michael. *Happenings: An Illustrated Anthology*. London: Sidgwick and Jackson, 1965.

Lacroix, Paul. *Les ballets et masquerades de cour sous Henri IV et Louis XIII (de 1581 à 1659)*, 6 vols. Paris: Gay et fils, [1868] 1968.

de Lancre, Pierre. *Tableau de l'inconstance des mauvais anges et démons, où il est amplement traité des sorciers et de la sorcellerie*. Introduction by Nicole Jacques-Chaquin. Paris: Palimpseste, [1612] 1982.

Lepecki, André. *Exhausting Dance: Performance and the Politics of Movement*. New York: Routledge University Press, 2006.

Levack, Brian. *The Witch-hunt in Early Modern Europe*. Harlow: Pearson Longman, [1987] 2006.

Levine, Laura. *Men in Women's Clothing: Anti-theatricality and Effeminization, 1579–1642*. Cambridge: Cambridge University Press, 1994.

Long, Kathleen P. *Hermaphrodites in Renaissance Europe*. Aldershot: Ashgate, 2006.

McCabe, Ina Baghdiantz. *Orientalism in Early Modern France: Trade Exoticism and the Ancien Regime*. Oxford: Berg, 2008.

McClive, Cathy. "Masculinity on Trial: Penises, Hermaphrodites and the Uncertain Male Body in Early Modern France," *History Workshop* 61, no. 1 (2009): 45–68.

McGowan, Margaret. *Dance in the Renaissance: European Fashion, French Obsession*. New Haven: Yale University Press, 2008.

———. *Le Balet Comique by Balthazar de Beaujoyeulx, 1581: A Facsimile*. Binghamton: Medieval and Renaissance Texts, 1982.

———. *L'Art du ballet de cour en France, 1581–1643*. Paris: Editions du CNRS, 1963.

McIlvenna, Una. "'A Stable of Whores'?: The 'Flying Squadron' of Catherine de Medici." In *The Politics of Female Households: Ladies-in-Waiting across Early Modern Europe*. Edited by Nadine Akkerman and Brigid Houben, 181–208. Leiden: Brill, 2013.

Mourey, Marie-Thérèse. "Le Corps et le Diable—le Diable au corps? De la transe à la danse, entre croyances, légendes, et représentations (XVIe–XVIIIe siècles)." In *Diables et spectres: Croyances et jeux littéraires*. Vol. 1. Edited by Françoise Knopper and Wolfgant Fink, 95–117. Cahiers d'études germaniques, 62. Aix-en-Provence: University of Provence, 2012.

Muchembled, Robert. *Culture populaire et culture des élites dans la France moderne (XVe–XVIIIe siècles): Essai.* Paris: Flammarion, 1978.

———. *Le Roi et la sorcière: L'Europe des bûchers XVe–XVIIIe siècle.* Paris: Desclée, 1993.

Newman, William. *Promethean Ambitions: Alchemy and the Quest to Perfect Nature.* Chicago: University of Chicago Press, 2004.

Orgel, Stephen. *Impersonations: The Performance of Gender in Shakespeare's England.* Cambridge: Cambridge University Press, 1995.

———. "Nobody's Perfect: Or, Why Did the English Stage Take Boys for Women?" *South Atlantic Quarterly* 88 (1989): 7–29.

———. *The Illusion of Power: Political Theater in the English Renaissance.* Berkeley: University of California Press, 1975.

Panofsky, Erwin. "What Is Baroque?" In *Three Essays on Style*, 17–90. London: MIT Press, 1995.

Pappas, Nickolas. "Plato's Aesthetics." *Stanford Encyclopedia of Philosophy.* 2012. Accessed May 1, 2013. http://plato.stanford.edu/archives/sum2012/entries/plato-aesthetics/.

Pardo Tomás, José. "Physicians' and Inquisitors' Stories? Circumcision and Crypto-Judaism in Sixteenth-Eighteenth-Century Spain." In *Bodily Extremities: Preoccupations with the Human Body in Early Modern European Culture*, 168–94. Aldershot: Ashgate, 2003.

Parker, Patricia. "Gender Ideology, Gender Change: The Case of Marie Germain." *Critical Inquiry* 19, no. 2 (Winter 1993): 337–64.

Peters, Julie Stone. *Theatre of the Book, 1480–1880: Print, Text, and Performance in Europe.* Oxford: Oxford University Press, 2000.

Prunières, Henry. *Le ballet de cour en France avant Benserade et Lully.* Paris: Laurens, 1914.

Plato. *Republic.* In *Complete Works*, 971–1223. Translated by John M. Cooper and D. S. Hutchinson. Indianapolis: Hackett: 1997.

Purkiss, Diane. *The Witch in History: Early Modern and Twentieth-Century Representations.* New York: Routledge, 1996.

Roach, Joseph. *The Player's Passion: Studies in the Science of Acting.* Ann Arbor: University of Michigan Press, 1993.

Rogers, Hoyt. "Etienne Durand et les flammes de l'amour." In *Etienne Durand: Poésies complètes*, 1–22. Geneva: Droz, 1990.

Schneider, Rebecca. *Performing Remains: Art and War in Times of Theatrical Reenactment.* New York: Routledge, 2011.

Seville, (Saint) Isidore of. *The Etymologies of Isidore of Seville.* Translated by Stephen A. Barney. Cambridge: Cambridge University Press, 2006.

Sherwin, Richard K. *"Performer la Loi: Présences et simulacres, sur scène et au tribunal"* [Law as Performance: Presence as Simulation inside the Theater/Courtroom"]. *Revue Communications* (2013): n4. Translation provided by author.

Sluhovsky, Moshe. *Believe Not Every Spirit: Possession, Mysticism, and Discernment in Early Modern Catholicism.* Chicago: University of Chicago Press, 2007.

Sofer, Andrew. "How to Do Things with Demons: Conjuring Performatives in *Doctor Faustus*." *Theatre Journal* 61, no. 1 (March 2009): 1–21.

Soja, Edward. *Thirdspace: Journeys to Los Angeles and Other Real-and-Imagined Places.* Malden: Blackwell, 1996.

Soman, Alfred. *Sorcellerie et justice criminelle, 16e–18e siècles.* Aldershot: Variorium, 1992.

Soyer, Françoise. "Inquisitors and Hermaphrodites." In *Ambiguous Gender in Early Modern Spain and Portugal*, 50–95. Leiden: Brill, 2012.

Stallybrass, Peter. "Books and Scrolls: Navigating the Bible." In *Books and Readers in Early Modern England: Material Studies*, eds. Jenny Anderson and Elizabeth Sauer, 42–79. Philadelphia: University of Pennsylvania Press, 2002.

Taylor, Diana. *The Archive and the Repertoire: Performing Cultural Memory in the Americas*. Durham, NC: Duke University Press, 2003.

Williams, Gerhild Scholz. *Defining Dominion: The Discourses of Magic and Witchcraft in Early Modern France and Germany*. Ann Arbor: University of Michigan Press, 1999.

Wintroub, Michael. "Words, Deeds, and a Womanly King." *French Historical Studies* 28, no. 3 (Summer 2005): 387–413.

Wygant, Amy. *Medea, Magic, and Modernity in France: Stages and Histories, 1553–1797*. Aldershot: Ashgate, 2007.

Yarnall, Judith. *Transformations of Circe: The History of an Enchantress*. Champaign: University of Illinois Press, 1994.

Yates, Frances. *Astraea*. London: Routledge, 1975.

———. *French Academies of the Sixteenth Century*. London: Routledge, [1947] 1988.

Zika, Charles. "Images of Circe and Discourses of Witchcraft, 1480–1580." *Zeitenblicke* 1, no. 1 (2002): 5. Accessed October 1, 2011. http://www.zeitenblicke.historicum.net/2002/01/zika/zika.html

Zorach, Rebecca. *Blood, Milk, Ink, Gold: Abundance and Excess in the French Renaissance*. Chicago: University of Chicago Press, 2006.

CHAPTER 5

DANCE DRAMATURGY
Definitions, Perspectives, Projections

RAY MILLER

DANCE dramaturgy is a relatively new and emerging area within the field of dance studies. In the literature, there is little agreement on what exactly constitutes dance dramaturgy. There is little agreement even on its definition. While many recognize its potential, others seriously question its role, function, and value within dance production. The discussions about and around dance dramaturgy are often contentious. Some dance dramaturgs see their role as activist co-creators with choreographers, designers, performers, and others engaged in dance making. Others see themselves as dispassionate observers who might gently insert their ideas or points of view delicately into the creative process—often acting more as sounding boards for ideas than as co-creators themselves. The field is in flux, and therein lies its interest for today's dance artists and their constituencies and its potential as dance negotiates its way into an uncertain future.

This chapter looks at the development of dance dramaturgy as it emerges from and in reaction to that of theater dramaturgy. While it is most commonly understood as a response to the changing aesthetics in dance performance of the 1980s and 1990s, dance dramaturgy began more as a series of questions regarding dance as process and dance as performance. Rather than mimic the often literary basis for much of what is understood in the practice and expectations of the theater dramaturg, dance dramaturgs often functioned more as critics and commentators with choreographers, designers, and others who were actively interrogating among themselves fundamental questions, such as what is dance, how is dance, where is dance, to what end is dance, and so on. In some aspects, this development might be viewed as an extension of the postmodern experiments of the late 1960s and early 1970s.

From another perspective, the field of dance dramaturgy may be seen more as an evolutionary extension of modern dance making as it confronts the same challenges as do other performing arts at the beginning of the twenty-first century. In contemporary art practice, the distinction between the arts often loses much of its appeal and they merge and overlap by sharing vocabulary, means of production, and aesthetic expectations. In addition, digital technologies invade, extend, and alter the field of dance as performance, distribution, and literature. For many, the terminology of dance studies not only reflects a broader perspective on dance and related fields but also fosters a deepening understanding of dance across a multitude of fields of study from the social sciences to the digital and performing arts and from the sciences to the humanities. Finally, the expectations of audiences for the performing and visual arts, and dance in particular, are just as ephemeral. The notion of following a choreographer's work over a lifetime, or of purchasing a season ticket to support a particular theatrical venue and its goal to provide over time a consistent high quality series of artistic performances is giving way to an audience that is more individualistic and expects more choice, more flexibility, and more emphasis on a spontaneity in selecting which events or performances they will support at any one time. Dance, like theater performance and music concerts, are in serious competition with other forms of mediated, interactive, digital experiences from blogging and YouTube to Internet performance and gaming.[1] It is within this highly dynamic and fluid environment that dance dramaturgy is negotiating its way into dance performance and dance studies scholarship.

A HISTORICAL PERSPECTIVE

In terms of a historical understanding of dance dramaturgy, many would cite the partnership between Pina Bausch and Raimund Hoghe in the mid-1990s as the pivotal collaboration that featured this unique relationship between a choreographer and a dance dramaturg and that spawned others to develop their own dyadic configurations. Others would point to a familiar line in the Western theatrical tradition that begins with Aristotle's *Poetics*, extends to Gotthold Ephraim Lessing's *Hamburg Dramaturgy*, and then focuses on the collaboration between Bertolt Brecht and his fellow dramaturgs. From that point onward, the field of theater dramaturgy quickly permeated European theater and, following World War II, made its way into American theatrical production. To more fully understand the development and future potential for dance dramaturgy, it is necessary to place the particular Bausch-Hoghe collaboration within this wider context. To that tend, it is important to review briefly the development of theater dramaturgy, particularly as it is understood since the Age of Enlightenment.

Many who write about the history of theater dramaturgy, particularly in the modern era, will start with the first resident dramaturg at the Hamburg National Theatre in Germany, Gotthold Ephraim Lessing. His work as a poet and playwright helped to inform his work as a dramaturg in Germany's first permanent repertory theater from 1767 to 1769. His essays on theatrical productions of the time were collected and printed as the *Hamburg Dramaturgy*. In these essays, we find a passionate intelligence that interrogates not only the playwriting of his time but also the production values that were challenging the French Neoclassic rule-laden approach to theatrical production.

Lessing used his position as dramaturg to advocate for a new approach to the stage, one that favored the bourgeois rather than aristocratic theater, and which ultimately better anticipated what would latter be termed the Storm and Stress movement. Lessing set a high standard in which the dramaturg was not solely focused in a myopic way with the particular needs of any one single production but also was expected to engage with the wider cultural and intellectual currents of his time. The dramaturg as thinker and critic demanded an engagement with the full breadth of the movements and ideas of the time period in which he and his audience lived. At the same time, the dramaturg was expected to have a thorough knowledge of history as it informs the artistic, political, and philosophical questions of the day. For example, Lessing was a strong advocate for a more emotionally charged and engaged production of the plays of Shakespeare. Dispassionate classicism gave way to emotional engagement with ideas, stories, characters, and metaphors that resonated with his contemporaries. For Lessing, keeping his intellectual antennae attuned to the currents of his time and to the repercussions of historical movements informed his day to-day dialogue with his fellow theater practitioners in choices they would make from conception to direction and from design to performance. Lessing and his contemporaries helped audiences and producers of their time to see theatrical production within a wider lens of influence and meaning. For Lessing, theater was not created in a vacuum for a lucky few but was intended, as it had been for the Greeks, to be an artistic production that engaged an informed community of sponsors, participants, and audiences. In addition, this community was seen to extend beyond the immediate audience for any one particular production and through his writing to cross national boundaries and, over time, generations. In that regard, the dramaturg could facilitate and inform a conversation that might have its origins in a historically past performance but that would inform a contemporary production.

Other prominent German dramaturgs followed in his footsteps, such as Johann Ludwig Tieck (1773–1853), who was a strong advocate for Romantic drama. He would later be superseded by Otto Brahm (1856–1912), who, with the support of his famous avant-garde theater, the Freie Bhune, promoted starkly realistic approaches to theatrical productions. These, along with others, encouraged Germany to embrace the role of the dramaturg in theatrical production and to lead the way for other European countries to emulate their success. The culmination of this first stage for theater dramaturgy was evident in the work and example Germany's preeminent theater artist, Bertolt Brecht.

This prolific playwright and poet served his apprenticeship as a dramaturg himself under several of Germany's most creative and inventive theatrical artists—Max Reinhardt and Erwin Piscator. He served as an assistant dramaturg at Max Reinhardt's famous Deutsches Theater. While there, he broadened his theatrical dramaturgical experience with a wide range of plays, including the Reinhardt-directed production of Luigi Pirandello's *Six Characters in Search of an Author* and George Bernard Shaw's *Saint Joan*, among others. With Piscator, he dramaturged one of the twentieth century's most important productions—*The Good Soldier Schweik*, based on the novel by Jaroslav Hašek.[2]

While Lessing had started with his emphasis on the dramaturg as literary interpreter for dramatic production, a role that often took place within the library or carefully crafted production meetings or simply on the page as preproduction research or postproduction analysis, Brecht moved into the dynamics of the rehearsal hall, thereby creating what has become known as "production dramaturgy."

According to Cathy Turner, Brecht moved the dramaturg from the private study into the rehearsal process so that he could work alongside the director " offering advice on textual changes, researching contextual information, offering comment on the evolving work and so on."[3] Brecht had learned from his previous collaborators Reinhardt and Piscator that playwriting and theater making were not to be conventionally set in stone but rather were to be dynamically engaged with the contemporary world. Consequently, what was written, how it was written, and the methods by which it was realized on the stage needed to adapt and respond to this changing world. For Brecht, this experience resulted in the development of the epic theater, or what he would later call dialectical theater, a form of playwriting and production values in which it was imperative that the theater of illusion be replaced with a distancing approach in which the audience becomes aware of the constructs of theatrical contrivance so that they might engage with the ideas and the subject matter as a part of their responsibility as fully conscious and participatory audience members. This idea was carried into the rehearsal process by the construction of what Brecht called the gestus, that is, an approach to acting that placed emphasis on the actor selecting one or more aspects of character that relates to some larger social interaction with other characters and with the larger themes of the play.

Again, Brecht subverts the psychological realism of Stanislavski as a way in which to engage the audience. His overall dramaturgical mission was not to create the illusion of reality but to respect the audience's given situation and offer them ways in which to examine more closely, more realistically, the world around them. The complexity of the world and its often violent changing dynamics demanded that an audience take responsibility. The psychological depth suggested in Stanislavski's approach was not enough. The theater, according to Brecht, would be better served by concentrating on its sociological contextualizing of the drama, in which the audiences would be expected to argue and debate the merits of the production within their lived experience. For Brecht, the role of the dramaturg was essential to interrogating the process of theatrical production so that it remained "honest" and provided the audience with an authentic theatrical experience that did not dismiss their intelligence nor absolve them of their social responsibilities.

This idea of the production dramaturg remained, for many, a peculiarity to Brecht and the Berliner Ensemble up through the 1950s. For many dramaturgs throughout Europe, the dramaturge as literary manager, or literary advisor, tended to dominate theater production. The literary was often preferred to the political, and the audience was often more open to being informed rather than being asked to question and then to take an action. It was not until the later 1960s that the role of the dramaturg began to be more widely questioned and evaluated. As story-based plays with strong, easily recognizable characters gave way to experiments in theatrical language, form, and structure, the role and function of the theater dramaturg was thrown into question.

Certainly by the 1970s and 1980s there seemed to be a gradual shift from the notion of dramaturg as literary consultant or respondent to the idea of a production dramaturg initially inspired by Brecht but different in spirit; that is, someone who is invited into the creative theatrical process in order to interrogate the ideas, to question theories and practices related to the productions, to collaborate in a creative way with the construction of the piece along with the director. The overtly political and sociological emphasis of Brecht and his imitators were replaced with dramaturgs who were not asked to think in terms of "the big picture" but rather to focus on the process of theater making. What defined "the theatrical experience" was tested by many on the fringes of theatrical production. Jean Claude van Italie's *The Serpent*, directed by Joseph Chaikin and his Open Theatre, was not Elia Kazan's production of Tennessee Williams's *A Streetcar Named Desire*. Jed Harris's direction of the Arthur Miller play *The Crucible* was challenged by The Performance Group's production of *Dionysius in '69* directed by Richard Schechner. The Harold Clurman approach to directing was far removed from that of Robert Wilson. Even on the musical theater stage, the book-based musical, like the iconic *Oklahoma!*, was being replaced with the concept musical, like *Cabaret*. The theater was breaking apart.

This transition mirrored the movement away from the play as sacred text to the idea that the physicalization and visualization aspects of productions are not simply interpretative but creative. This coincides with the increasingly popular notion of the concept musical, physical theater, and devised theater. Directors and other artistic personnel started to see themselves as collaborators with playwrights rather than a kind of hired hand who primarily functioned as an interpretive craftsman. This dichotomy between the literary and "hands-off" theater dramaturg, who often serves as a kind of representative of the playwright and who offers to translate that to the production team, versus the production-centered dramaturg who engages with the director, actors, designers, and others to provide a theatrical experience that demands audience participation reflects a tension that describes much of contemporary theater dramaturgy even today. It was this cauldron of creative energies mixed with destructive impulses that informed what would become dance dramaturgy.

BEGINNINGS

This development in the theater world coincided with experimental developments in the concert dance world, particularly those from the modern dance area. Instigated initially by the Judson Dancers and their contemporaries, mostly young modern dance choreographers, dancers, and collaborators from various fields such as music, film, visual arts, and theater, interrogated not only conventional forms of choreography and performance but also the nature of what makes a movement a dance and who gets to dance and what is technique and what relationship audiences can have with the performer. These experimental forms of modern dance, later characterized under the umbrella term "postmodern dance," ranged from the most abstract and nonlinear to the most didactic and nonsequential forms of story-telling narrative, from silent pantomime to dancers talking on stage, from dancers in street clothes to dancers without cloths, and from the conventional concert venues into museum locations and public outdoor spaces. It was inevitable that the fringes from the dance and the theater worlds would mix, collaborate, and create new forms of dance and theater. In that intersection, some dramaturgs approached choreographers and some choreographers approached dramaturgs to begin a relationship of cross-pollenization. Within that milieu arose the dance dramaturg.

As previously stated, the most famous collaboration in dance between choreographer and dramaturg was that of Raimond Hoghe and Pina Bausch with her Tanztheater Wuppertal. Their collaboration dominated the 1980s.[4] In an interview with Bonnie Maranca, Hoghe explained that his role as dance dramaturg with Pina Bausch was "a personal collaboration. I brought some music, and texts sometimes, which she used in the performances. But most of all I was there to help with the structure, to put things together."[5] For Hoghe, there is the idea that the dramaturg brings to the choreographer a wealth of images, associations, slivers of music or design elements, historical documents, or contemporary perspectives as ways in which to further stimulate the choreographic imagination of the artist as she conceives, tests out, draws forth the materials she needs to construct the dance.[6] Hoghe continues to bring his dramaturgical experience with Bausch into his work with his own dance company. He is known to begin rehearsals with tea and conversation with his dancers and collaborators, and in rehearsal "he gives almost no feedback to dancers while they are working, what comes to the surface appears to be a quiet watchfulness, underlined by the conviction of knowing what is 'right.'"[7] This patient "observance" that he brings to his own dancers is a quality that he contributed to his collaboration with Bausch and it is a quality that is emphasized by many dance dramaturgs when describing "what they do." Since then, there have been a growing number of choreographers who have chosen to work with dance dramaturgs. Among them are Meg Stuart with André Lepecki, Anne Teresa de Keersmaeker with Marianne van Kerkhoven, William Forsythe with Heidi Gilpin and Freya Vass-Rhee, Alain Platel with Hildegard de Vuyst, and many, many others.

DEFINITIONS AND PRACTICES: DRAMATURGY FROM THEATER TO DANCE

Today, for many, theater dramaturgy "denotes the multi-faceted study of a given play: its author, content, style, and interpretive possibilities, together with its historical, theoretical, and intellectual background."[8] The dramaturg functions as someone who can serve as literary advisor or consultant and, at the same time, as a performance confidant to the director, the designers, and the actors.

Many will prepare elaborate casebooks for the production team and for the actors. These "books" can include an abbreviated production history of the play, research source materials on related primary sources and appropriate imagery in the form of photographs or art reproductions. Some will provide their "books" in digital format, which allows the easy inclusion of video material and sound or music elements. These "books" can easily be consulted by directors, designers, and others who are engaged in developing and implementing a "production concept." They may also serve as resource materials for actors and performers as they develop performance techniques and stylistic choices that support the production concept. In some cases, the dramaturg's job is completed once these documents are provided. He or she is seldom invited into the rehearsal hall.

For others, like the script itself, these "books" are simply a beginning and the dramaturg engages with the director, the production team, and the performers throughout the rehearsal process. Their advice, points of view, and ideas are continually sought out, particularly in those productions in which investigation and discovery is valued over that in which a regimented implementation of a predetermined clearly articulated vision sets the parameters for the rehearsal process and, ultimately, the production. This combination of observing, writing, conferring, and collaborating was also at the heart of the Bausch-Hoghe creative relationship. One of Bausch's dancers, Meryl Tankard, aptly describes what it was like. "Quietly, intensely observing our rehearsals and performances, taking notes, taking photos. Raimund was always by Pina's side. Deeply concentrated on every move, every detail, occasionally whispering in Pina's ear. He was a comforting presence during that very vulnerable creation period."[9] When the production becomes more about investigation rather than clever execution of a preconceived aesthetic, the role of the theater or dance dramaturg becomes more critically important in the creative process.

In this context, the dramaturg serves three constituencies. First, he or she serves those immediately engaged in the production of a play—from the director and production team to the performers, or, in the case of a dance, from the choreographer and their collaborators to the dancers and their technicians. This is the role that most people might be familiar with when they think about the purpose of a dramaturg.

The second constituency the dramaturg serves is the producing organization, which is sponsoring the production. In the United States, this would most often be the repertory theater company or a university theater department. In this role, the dramaturg may well take on the function of literary manager in which role they supervise and coordinate the reading and advocacy of new plays and the selection and coordination of a season of plays. While the choosing of plays may be varied, they often coalesce around common themes or questions that inform the season selection process. This has been characterized as "the big picture" function of the dramaturg.

In dance, this role is more often practiced in European or Canadian venues than it is in the United States. One of the most interesting and unique examples of this is "Carol's Dance Notes," which was conceived in the tradition of music CD liner notes or art museum catalogs that accompany various exhibitions, as a way in which to engage audience to be "in dialogue" with new dance pieces and their creators. Originally conceived by Lawrence Adams, co-founder of Dance Collective Danse, in conjunction with DanceWorks, a producing organization for independent dance making in Toronto, it called on Carol Anderson to write 500-word essays or "notes" that would accompany the production of new work by selected choreographers. The intent is not to tell audiences what to see nor how to see a new work but rather to invite them "into the act of witnessing dance"[10] by providing a lens, a hint, a suggestion by which to engage with the choreography and the performance of new and innovative work. After sitting in on rehearsals, reviewing DVDs of the work and/or talking with the choreographer, Anderson would try to combine brief and selected descriptions with poetic evocations as a way in which to invite audiences into a more informed engagement with the performance of the dance. In that way, she carries on some of the approach used by American dance philosopher and critic, George Beiswanger, who wrote essays about early American modern dance artists like Martha Graham and Doris Humphrey for *American Theatre Magazine* in the 1930s and 1940s. Beiswanger's writing served to educate American theater and dance audiences about what was then a new and important dance art form. In both cases, Anderson and Beiswanger became "activists" in their work by serving as apologists for the new and as conduits for audiences to discover a vocabulary by which they too could engage in their own right with new and emerging art forms or styles.[11]

This front-loading of the role of the dramaturg with a producing organization is further refined by the dramaturg's third constituency—the audience and the community in which the theater exists. To that extent, dramaturgs will write dramaturgical notes to be included in the program and serve as preshow informants or postperformance facilitators for talk-backs with the audience. They can coordinate their efforts with the front of house operations to give talks to community groups on the plays and/or their themes, offer readings of new work, and initiate publicity engagements on television, radio, or the Internet that not only promotes the production but also engages the wider audience in the role and function of theater within their community.

All of this supports the observation by Mary Luckhurst that at least in the West, "the history of dramaturgy exposes persistent struggles over the control of creative territories and profound cultural resistances to the idea that play-making processes, dramatic literature and repertoire can be objects of intellectual enquiry, it also highlights a deep-rooted suspicion of working models that insist on a dynamic relationship between critical reflection and artistic practice."[12] For many, theater dramaturgy centers around the text as literary artifact and the idea of history, which can relate to the history of the previous productions of this play, the historical period in which it occurs or will occur in the re-visioning of the director, history of style, and so on. Literary and historical concerns become central to the specific contributions of the theater dramaturg.

This emphasis on the word as script or text is sometimes seen as privileging the printed page over that of the performance on stage. In many American universities, for example, there are more professors teaching drama and Shakespeare in English departments than those who teach drama and Shakespeare in theater departments.[13] There is this notion that someone needs to represent the best interests of the playwright as if he or she functioned as the conscience of authentic responsibility. Moving from page to stage apparently is fraught with the potential to turn the text into an excuse for the director and others to create their own theatrical vision of the play, irrespective of the play itself.

Dance dramaturgy arose within this dynamically changing conception of the role of the theater dramaturg in modern theatrical production. Moving from modern dance to post-modern dance and from modern theater to postmodern theater created a cavernous arena in which the conventional role of choreographer or director as being capable of dramaturging their own work started to give way to a bifurcation of roles in relation to creative work.[14] What has its roots in the 1950s theater and the 1960s dance world accelerated by the 1980s when text, narrative, and "the talking dancer" started to regularly invade the stage. This coincided with the breaking down of performance conventions, not only in dance, but in theater, music, and the visual arts as well. Cross-pollination between and among the visual and performing arts created interesting and strange hybrids of performance that required facilitators to negotiate the various vocabularies for the mediums involved. Sometimes, those facilitators provided a conduit between the artists from these various mediums with their often interested but confused audiences in the form of talk-backs, written critiques, and scholarly articles. Sometimes, that facilitation was incorporated into the business of art making itself.

Some theater dramaturgs were initially brought in, for example, to advise dancer/choreographers on their use and execution of text. Of course, some of the dramaturgs had background, experience, and interests in movement and began to advocate for a broader definition of what could be "dramaturged." There was a precedent set in the theater when experts in period dance would be employed not only to choreograph dances appropriate to the period of the play but also to work with the director and actors to seek and find ways in which to advance plot or reveal character. This back and forth between movement and text would, by the late 1930s and early 1940s, become standard practice in the American musical theater. What was happening in the musical theater genre was a recognition that rather than dance being solely at the service of theater production, that the theater could contribute in some way to dance production. As the conventions of dance itself were being challenged, room was made for an invitation for dramaturgy to step in and take a place in the creation of new work in the studio and on the concert stage. One clear example of this is documented in the work of Clare Croft. She writes about her experience with a narrative dance work titled *Changuita Perla* created at the University of Texas in Austin by choreographer Rachel Murray. In her role as dramaturg, she brought a critical feminist theoretical perspective to the creation of the piece. Her primary function was to challenge assumptions on which the dance was based, to ask questions to the choreographer throughout the process including those directed to the performers to help them clarify their choices, and to develop a rehearsal language that would break open caricature to allow for a more developed and nuanced performance. What is also interesting to note here is the role the dramaturg plays in relationship to the audience. She makes clear that "as an advocate for the audience, the dramaturge helps work toward one of the most difficult goals of dance: to help people experience their bodies more fully and to recognize others' experience of their bodies."[15] As with Beiswanger in the 1930s and 1940s and Anderson in contemporary Canada, Croft articulates an important function for the dramaturg in that she advocates for the audience in a way that is not unlike how some theater dramaturgs think of themselves as advocates for the playwright. Each fills a responsibility to represent the interests and perspective of that part of the performance equation that may not be weighted as heavily by the directors, choreographers, performers, and designers when actually engaged in the production of a play or dance. The dramaturg in each case provides a kind of balance among the many constituencies that contribute to any one theater or dance production.

Dance Dramaturgy Charts Its Own Path

While some see dance dramaturgy as an extension of this historical development, others are reluctant to do so.[16] Some hesitate to separate dance dramaturgy from choreographing, producing, dancing, and so on. This latter group sees dance dramaturgy more as a perspective on, or function of, dancing-making with an emphasis on critiquing with a "third eye." This perspective or function is not placed on the shoulders of a particular individual with the title of dance dramaturg, but rather it is a role shared by the producer, designers, dancers, and even the choreographer. Some have cited the role Diaghilev played as he constructed unique collaborative partnerships that lit the fuse for a modern ballet aesthetic as just one example of many.[17] For others, it is not so much about assembling varied ingredients to foster a creative spark or creation; rather, the role of the dramaturg, unlike producers, designers, and composers, should dissolve into the process. As Liesbeth Wildschut points out, the dramaturg role might resemble that of a coach—whose contribution is not to make decisions but to reflect and respond to what is essential in the creative process.[18] It is important to note, however, that the word "coach" can be problematic when discussing dramaturgy. The dance coach in the Netherlands, for example, is a well-respected position that is more often associated with amateur dancing and is viewed more from the perspective of its educational value in developing the artistic potential of choreographers and dancers.[19]

In many ways, the role of the contemporary dance dramaturg harkens back to her or his role or responsibility "to teach." We are not referring here to the common model of theater dramaturg associated with many university theater programs as "the in-house academic of the theater profession."[20] For many, the role functions more as the researcher who brings materials relevant to the production to the production staff and then politely steps back to let the artists resume their role of creating a piece out of them. For some departments, there is a patronizing acknowledgment that the dramaturg serves a function but it is seen as more preparatory to the "real work" of "creating theater." In many cases, the dramaturg is even discouraged from attending production meetings or rehearsals. There is a fear that they may

overstep their bounds and challenge the authority of the director or designer or the autonomy of the actor. This is certainly not the case universally, but it occurs often enough that you
hear this anthem repeated when dramaturgs get together to present workshops at theater
conferences and they anecdotally share their personal experience with their colleagues.

For the dance dramaturg—at least for the moment—the emphasis on the responsibility
of teaching recalls the notion of the didaskalos from early Greek theater, in which the playwright and/or director of the plays would function not only as a coordinator for all of the
production aspects of the play but also serve as an inspiration or example of how to interrogate the production from the ground up. His focus was not just on the performers and
those who helped to produce the play but, more importantly, on the audience and the city
officials who supported the production. A play was not simply an entertaining diversion but
was a community-sponsored event, which all strata of society were encouraged to attend and
to participate in. There was a teaching purpose here that was shared by everyone. It was not
so much that the artists were charged with delivering dramatic, choreographic, and musical
pronouncements on the themes of the play but rather that the audience was invited into a
relationship that was cathartic; that is, their emotional empathies, intellectual curiosities,
and active imaginations were in sympathy with the imagery and text of the performance.
The need for audiences to connect in meaningful ways with contemporary dance and theater productions is no less important; however, the way in which we experience ourselves
and others around us is fundamentally changed and therefore the role of teacher-as-teacher
to the wider culture is changed as well. Now, we live in a time that has accelerated well past
Alvin Toffler's *Future Shock* of forty years ago to what New York University media theorist
Douglas Rushkoff so aptly defines as Present Shock, that is, the notion that we have for-
saken the futurism of Alvin Toffler's late-twentieth-century perspective for what he calls a
twenty-first-century presentism—everything must be known and understood within a
much shorter span of time.[21] Within this context, the dance dramaturg may not be a luxury
but a necessity in contextualizing dance making as it occurs for the time in which it is to be
performed.

To provide an additional sense of perspective, it may be important to note that although
we are missing one of Aristotle's final writings, *Didascaliai*, in which he addressed the specifics of his exposure and his thinking regarding the tragic and comic plays of his time as well
as the dithyrambs, we do have from his extant writings ideas that help us understand how
he viewed the dramaturgical values of his time related to the plays he valued the most. Many
are familiar with his notion of the three unities and their impact on Western classical drama;
however, it is his insistence on the importance of plot over character that may have stronger
impact on dance dramaturgical understanding.

For Aristotle, tragedy, at its heart, was "an imitation, not of men, but of actions." This idea
placed the plot over character as the primary essence of successful tragic plays. His idea was
that plays were not so much character driven as they were "personified passions" determined
by plot construction.[22] Choreographers and dance dramaturgs certainly understand this as
it relates to the creation and construction of dances. Even in the most literal of dances, such
as those from traditional narrative ballet or musical theater production, there is a recognition that movement choices placed together in certain sequences and patterns and further
informed by other factors such as rhythm, space, and energy, will generate a sense of cohe-
siveness that creates a unified whole that can stand on its own merit.[23] This does not describe
all dance by any means, but many dance dramaturgs talk about their role as "objectivists"

in relation to the function of the choreographer; that is, their observations of process, their descriptions of dance movement, and their ability to question along with the choreographer in a shared vision frees the choreographer from having to serve more than one role at a time. In addition, the dance dramaturg functions as an important empathetic sounding board for the dance as it develops over time. In that context, collaboration is not viewed as a servant to the choreographer as the apex of an hierarchical structure in which one individual is responsible for "visioning forth" the dance; rather, the dance dramaturg joins a team of creative artists who privilege the dance over hard and fast definition of the various roles that each plays in the making of that dance.

Nonetheless, dance dramaturgs function in a wide variety of ways with their choreographers. André Lepecki describes the process with Meg Stuart, who requests that he be present often in the rehearsal studio. "After that we talk a great deal. She asks me about what I see happening in a scene, and I come up with what I call 'metaphorical explosions'—where I see relations and connections, etc. Towards the latter part of the process we work together to make it more cohesive."[24] Scott deLahunta offers an alternative view on the role of the dance dramaturg. In the same structured conversation on dance and dramaturgy held in 1999 in Barcelona, he notes that while there may be many theater dramaturgs who view their role as helping the director to make more clear the choices in a production, for him, "the role of the dance dramaturge as I see it is decidedly not to provide an interpretation or explanation of the dance for the audience."[25] This hands-off approach to interpreting and clarifying for the audience how to view or understand the dance may be peculiar to dance itself. Unlike many theatrical productions that start with text and rely on a kind of informed predetermined or "discovered" interpretation of that text as a barometer for determining the authenticity or value of a production, the choreographer in collaboration with the dramaturg is looking, at best, for "metaphorical explosions" to further interrogate the choreographic enterprise and to offer the audience multiple levels of access to their experience of the dance in performance. [26] These are simply two divergent perspectives on the role of dance dramaturgs in dance performances. Others are inventing their roles as the opportunities arise to engage dramaturgy in the creative process of dance making.[27]

CONTEMPORARY ISSUES AND PRACTICES

Within the last 10–15 years, there has been an upsurge of interest in dance dramaturgy. It is not unusual to see a dramaturg listed as collaborator for many concert dance events in Europe and increasingly in Canada. Though not nearly as widely accepted, there is a growing interest in this area by choreographers here in the United States. Scholars and historians have taken notice of this growing interest and involvement of dance dramaturgs in dance practice.

In 1999, a series of "Conversations on Choreography" with a focus on dance dramaturgy were held in Europe and published in *Dance Theatre Journal*. As recently as 2010, there was an enthusiastic response to a panel facilitated by this author at a joint ASTA/CORD/TLA (The American Society for Theatre Research/The Congress on Research in Dance/The Theatre Library Association) conference in Seattle on a dialogue between theater dramaturgs and dance dramaturgs. The following year, SDHS (The Society of Dance History Scholars) sponsored a conference devoted solely to an exploration of dance dramaturgy. Publications from

Ballet International, Contemporary Theatre Review, Theatre Topics, Women and Performance, and others are publishing articles by and about dance dramaturgy. The most recent issue of *Canadian Theatre Review* (2013) has devoted itself solely to dance dramaturgy.

Potentially, one of the most exciting areas for dance dramaturgy now and into the future is how it might serve dance and theater production in a university setting. There are a number of examples of ways in which to model this kind of collaboration in higher education environments. One such example occurred recently at Yale University.

A team-taught seminar course taught by Joseph Cermatori, Emily Coates, Kathryn Krier, Bronwen MacArthur, Angelica Randle, and Joseph Roach, among others, "culminated in a production, applying the research done in and by the class to the creation of a musical that was simultaneously a multimedia event."[28] The process and the product focused on a retelling of the Orpheus myth informed by their questions and research of popular music and dance forms of the 1950s and 1960s. Among the issues that this project addressed was the process of bringing forward African American popular dance forms into what the authors described as a postracial generation. The body-kinesthetic was equally interrogated along with text and music. While there were dramaturgs involved, the collaborators emphasized the shared responsibility for dramaturgy by all of the participants. In many ways, this approach echoed what we have come to expect from devised theater making. In this model, dance dramaturgy functions more as a verb rather than as a noun.

Another example of possible future directions for contemporary dance dramaturgy is provided by Clare Croft in her discussion of feminism as it informs dance dramaturgy, particularly for the undergraduate experience. She identifies the primary role or function of the dance dramaturg when she writes, "the dance dramaturg asks questions about how dance creates worlds through the intersection of image, movement, space and sound."[29] That simple yet direct statement with its emphasis on questioning is important. Some would even say that it is the questioning itself that serves a critical function within contemporary dance practice. She makes it clear that feminist theory advocates for a dissemination of power and that results in the dance dramaturg recognizing the importance of the audience as active respondents rather than passive recipients of a dance performance. She argues that "the dramaturg helps work toward one of the most difficult goals of dance: to help people experience their bodies more fully and to recognize others' experiences of their bodies."[30] Based on this experience, Croft makes a strong case for bringing dance dramaturgs into dance departments in higher education. They become a logical connection between the theorizing and the making of dance in the classroom, the studio, and the stage. At a time when everything from devised theater practice to contact improvisation is more common than rare, it is evident that performing artists are continually engaged in the act of critiquing the basic assumptions that undergird dance and theater making of all kinds. Dramaturgs provide a natural crossover between theory and practice, between history and choreography, and between performance and audience response.

Within the academic setting, theater dramaturgy has enjoyed an increasing presence as a part of many theater programs. It is not unusual today to have a faculty member designated as the department dramaturg. Often, but not always, this person serves as a theater historian. Many departments engage the dramaturg not only as a member of particular production of a play or musical but also as a sitting member of a season selection committee advising and guiding the department in its overall choice for a theme for its productions for a particular academic year.

The same has not necessarily been the case in dance programs. While a number of professional ballet and modern dance companies employ a dance dramaturg and some graduate level dance programs offer at least one course in dance dramaturgy, there are few undergraduate dance programs that do the same. As programs move toward a dance studies model, I suspect that opportunities will emerge for a dance dramaturg to serve the department in ways that are similar to those of the theater dramaturg. That is not common practice now but it may well be so in the future. Dance dramaturgs may well function as "cultural workers," what Paulo Freire underscores as "those who dare to teach," those who dare to question, those who dare to collaborate in the process of creating dance that continues to be meaningful to our audience now and tomorrow.

Those of us who "do dance" can sometimes be made to feel as though we have been pushed down Alice's rabbit hole. Maybe, we have. Maybe the role of dramaturg helped to negotiate the birthing of a modern theater aesthetic at a time of tremendous change when Lessing took on his role at German National Theatre Hamburg. Maybe the same could be said in dance when Raimond Hoghe assisted Pina Bausch in creating her own unique approach to contemporary dance. We ask questions when we don't know and particularly when we know we don't know. If that is the case, then the role of the dance dramaturg may well be with us for the foreseeable future not as a luxury but as a necessity.

The focus on dance dramaturgy comes at a time when there is a confluence of ideas and influences having a direct impact on dance-making today. Everything from a plethora of forms of mediated performance to the decentering of who gets to make a dance to an exploration of a more interactive role between the performer and the audience—all demand a much more fluid collaborative style and a more conscientious engagement with performance itself. Within this context, it is not unusual now for there to be a shared collaborative relationship between individuals who contribute to "shared authorship" in bringing a dance into existence. The collaboration may even cross time zones and take place in a myriad of virtual realities. The dance dramaturg provides, at the very least, a conduit that allows these various constituencies to create, to give meaning to, and to engage audiences in ways that are both informative and cooperative. Confidence and empathy between the dance dramaturg and her collaborators are essential.[31] As we move away from the notion of choreographer as artist-auteur, we are creating room for a conscientiously conceived role for dramaturgy in our dance making, our dance performance, and our dance understanding.

Just as Lessing in his Herculean creation of the thinker-as-thinker who was not afraid to engage the literary, dramatic, intellectual and political movements and ideas of his time and bring that to bear in theater productions with his peers, the role of the dance dramaturg today extends beyond the studio and the concert hall to the wider, dynamically changing culture in which we live. One of the most consistently recognized examples of this is demonstrated in the varied roles that dance dramaturgs have played in the dances created by William Forsythe. Elizabeth Waterhouse, a dancer with his company, has documented how this "collective of people who live, dance and perform meaningful spatial relationships" work in terms of research, process, and performance.[32] One of his well-known dance dramaturgs, Heidi Gilpin, describes the way her collaboration with Forsythe worked in creating the dance "Limb's Theorem" in 1990. "I combined mathematical, architectural, and physical terms with terms of action and motion, change, form, order, dimensions, quantity, relation, difference, and time to construct an extensive series of directives called U-lines. These short phrases were then given to the dancers to be applied as operations onto various movement material in a virtually infinite number of ways."[33] Clearly, Rudolph Laban's work in spatial possibilities informs this exploration and the dramaturg is able to find a connection between the theoretical and the kinesthetic in a way that contributes to the choreography of this Forsythe piece. Finally, the dramaturgical investigation that permeates the method by which Forsythe and his dancers and collaborators work with dramaturgs extends beyond the performance into related areas of interest to dance scholars and others in the work of another of his dramaturgs—Freya Vass-Rhee. She has written widely on Forsythe's work as related to everything from his use of visuosonic choreographic processes to include the emerging field of cognitive dance studies. Forsythe has made the widest possible use of multiple dramaturgs to investigate, create, and disseminate the wide net of investigation that has informed his dance-making career for over thirty years. It is model to be envied and one that can recommend future directions for dramaturgs and artists into the future.

The field of dance dramaturgy today is still more verb than noun. It is both vital and elusive. Though it has a nearly 40-year history and is well informed by the much longer history of theater dramaturgy, it is still seeking to define itself and to find its place in dance performance and dance studies. It is actively engaged with the shifting dynamics of contemporary dance and it seeks to make connections with the wider global cultures in which it is framed. Dance dramaturg Marianne Van Kerkhoven succinctly summarizes how she sees dramaturgy, whether it serves the theater or the dance. She writes: "There is no essential difference between theater and dance dramaturgy, although the nature and history of the material used differs. Its main concerns are: the mastering of structures; the achievement of a global view; the gaining of insight into how to deal with the material, whatever its origin may be—visual, musical, textual, filmic, philosophical etc."[34] As more opportunities present themselves and as more questions are asked regarding the nature of dance itself, dance dramaturgs will find a way in which to contribute their voice, their perspective, and their empathic encouragement for daring artists and for hungry audiences.

NOTES

1. To understand how these forces are being interpreted and played out in the field of literature, David Shields in his book, *Reality Hunger: A Manifesto*, delivers an incisive "experience" of the blurring of fictive and nonfictive forms as they relate to how readers see, understand, experience, and interact with emerging forms of literature—much of which does not recognize nor hold sacred conventional boundaries between genres and styles of writing. As we look forward in terms of how dance dramaturgy might inform dance performance, it may be helpful to examine the work of Alan Kirby, particularly his book *Digimodernism: How New Technologies Dismantle the Postmodern and Reconfigure Our Culture*. Theater dramaturgy clearly finds its home base in literary analysis, and that basis may have been a strength when theatrical practice privileged the playwright over all other theater practitioners. In contemporary theater practice, however, those theater dramaturgs who center their work in drama as literature may now be held hostage by that point of view. Contemporary theater practice is as much informed by performance studies, the scenographic imagination, and

crossover experimentation with traditional and newly emerging art forms, so that its literary base is one of several instigators for production. Paying homage to the text is not always the best way to create vital, meaningful theatrical experiences. This is a flashpoint at which dance dramaturgs may be able to "take the lead" to help theater dramaturgs open up their arsenals of understanding and contribute to theater production.

2. See http://www.poemhunter.com/bertolt-brecht/biography/.

3. Cathy Turner, *Dramaturgy and Performance*, p. 7.

4. For a brief contemporary biography of the work of Raimund Hoghe since his collaboration with Pina Bausch, see http://www.raimundhoghe.com/english.php.

5. See http://www.raimundhoghe.com/en/en_dancing_the_sublime.html.

6. Wim Wenders's recent movie *Pina* is able to capture a sense of the creative process that informs the aesthetic associated with Pina Bausch.

7. Mary Kate Connolly, *Throwing the Body into the Fight: A Portrait of Raimund Hoghe*, (Chicago: Intellect, the University of Chicago Press), 15.

8. Bert Cardullo, "Enter Dramaturgs," in *What Is Dramaturgy?*, edited by Bert Cardullo (New York: Peter Lang), 3.

9. Connolly, 114.

10. Carol Anderson, "Writing Dramaturgical Notes for Dance: 'Carol's Dance Notes' 1996–2012," *Canadian Theatre Review* 155 (Summer 2013): 59. To read some examples of "Carol's Dance Notes," please go to the author's website at: http://finearts.yorku.ca/about-us/our-faculty/carol-anderson.

11. See article by Raphael F. Miller, "George Beiswange and Dance Criticism," in *Dance Chronicle* 16 (January 1993): 45–71.

12. Mary Luckhurst. *Dramaturgy: A Revolution in Theatre* (New York: Cambridge University Press, 2006), 2.

13. This is an age-old problem, particularly in the Western theater tradition, which has been excellent documented and analyzed in

14. The reader is advised to look a Philip Auslander's chapter on postmodernism and performance, which can be accessed at: http://lmc.gatech.edu/~auslander/publications.html. For a more detailed analysis of postmodern dance, one can consult Sally Banes's seminal work, *Terpsichore in Sneakers: Postmodern Dance*, and for a clear analysis of postmodern theater as it emerges from its modern roots, one can look at Elinor Fuch's award-winning book *The Death of Character: Perspectives on Theater after Modernism*.

15. Croft, Clare. "A Mutually Satisfying Pas de Deux: Feminist Dramaturgy and Dance in the Undergraduate Dance Curriculum," *Theatre Topic* 19, no. 2 (September 2009): 183.

16. See Ken Pierce's paper "Using a Dance Historian's Approach as a Guiding Concept in Stage Direction," *Proceedings: Thirty Fourth Annual Conference, York University and University of Toronto, June 23–26, 2011* (Riverside, CA: Society of Dance History Scholars, 2011), 191–200, as an example of this more commonly understood interpretation of the role of the dramaturg-as-historian in dance performance.

17. See Elizabeth Kattner's paper "Diaghilev: Ballet's Great Dramaturge," in *Proceedings: Thirty Fourth Annual Conference, York University and University of Toronto, June 23–26, 2011* (Riverside, CA: Society of Dance History Scholars, 2011), 69–76, for an explanation of Diaghilev's contribution to the works created for his ballet company. She delineates the role of the dramaturg from that of the producer.

18. See Liesbeth Wildschut's "Reinforcement for the Choreographer: The Dance Dramaturg as Ally," in *Contemporary Choreography: A Critical Reader*, edited by Jo Butterworth and Liesbeth Wildschut (New York: Routledge, 2009), 383–98.

19. Dumon, Dirk. "Choreography Coaching in the Field of Amateur Dance in the Netherlands," in *Contemporary Choreography: A Critical Reader*, edited by Jo Butterworth and Liesbeth Wildschut (New York: Routledge, 2009), 235–47.

20. Shannon Jackson, *Professing Performance: Theatre in the Academy from Philology to Performativity (Theatre and Performance Theory)*.

21. Rushkoff, Douglas. *Present Shock: When Everything Happens Now* (New York: Current, 2013), 3.

22. See http://www.imagi-nation.com/moonstruck/spectop007.html.

23. This idea may best be illustrated in the contemporary work of theater director Anne Bogart and choreographer Mary Overlie and further developed by Tina Landau in the development of their unique approach to theatrical production known as Viewpoints. It is a compositional technique that acknowledges the importance of movement to creating viable and interesting theatrical performances based on exercises that addresses the elements of space, shape, time, emotions, and bodily movement. See Anne Bogart and Tina Landau's *The Viewpoints Book* published by Theatre Communications Groups in 2005.

24. See http://www.sdela.dds.nl/conv3/article.html.

25. See http://www.sdela.dds.nl/conv3/article.html.

26. It is important to note here that this discussion is based on most concert dance forms. This may not be so important when redoing *The Nutcracker* from one year to the next, nor when offering a reinterpretation of familiar choreography for a musical such as *West Side Story*, or *Oklahoma!*.

27. There are many examples. Two that may be of particular interest are: Ruth Ben-Tovim collaborating with Charlotte Vincent in Britain serving as the dramaturg for the Vincent Dance Theatre (http://www.vincentdt.com/), and Hildegard de Vuyst from Belgium working with Les Ballets C de la B and its director Alain Platel.

28. See Joseph Cermatori, Emily Coates, Kathryn Krier, Bronwen MacArthur, Angelica Randle, and Joseph Roach, "Teaching African-American Dance/History to a 'Post-Racial' Class: Yale's Project o," *Theatre Topics* 19, no. 1 (2009): 1.

29. See Clare Croft, "A Mutually Satisfying Pas de Deux: Feminist Dramaturgy and Dance in the Undergraduate Dance Curriculum," *Theatre Topics* 19, no. 2 (2009): 181.

30. Croft, 183.

31. See Jean Lee's paper "Between Meaning and Significance, and Beyond," in *Proceedings: Thirty Fourth Annual Conference, York University and University of Toronto, June 23–26, 2011* (Riverside, CA: Society of Dance History Scholars, 2011), 99–110, for a fuller discussion of the paradigm shift in contemporary dance practice that requires a new approach to dramaturgical engagement.

32. Elizabeth Waterhouse, "Dancing amidst the Forsythe Company: Space, Enactment and Living Repertory," in *Theatre without Vanishing Points: The Legacy of Adolphe Appia; Scenography and Choreography in Contemporary Theatre*, edited by Gabriele Brandstetter and Birgit Wiens (Berlin: Alexander Verlag Berlin, 2010), 153.

33. Heidi Gilpin, "Aberration of gravity," in *William Forsythe and the Practice of Choreography: It Starts from any Point* (New York: Routledge, 2011), 124.

34. Marianne Van Kerkhoven, "Looking without Pencil in the Hand," accessed at: http://sarma.be/docs/2858.

BIBLIOGRAPHY

Adolphe, Jean-Marc. "Dramaturgy of Movement: A Plea for a Dramaturgy of Perception." *Ballet International* 6 (1998): 27–29.

Anderson, Carol. "Writing Dramaturgical Notes for Dance: 'Carol's Dance Notes' 1996–2012." *Canadian Theatre Review* 155 (Summer 2013): 58–62.

Barton, Bruce. "'Stop Looking at Your Feet': Bluemouth's 'Dance Marathon' and Inter/Actual Dramaturgy." *Performance Research—A Journal of Performing Arts*, 14, no. 3 (September 2009): 13–25.

Barton, Bruce. "Navigating Turbulence: The Dramaturg in Physical Theatre." *Theatre Topics* 15, no. 1 (2005): 103–19.

Behrndt, Synne K. "Dance, Dramaturgy and Dramaturgical Thinking." *Contemporary Theatre Review* 20, no. 2 (2010): 185–96.

Bogart, Anne, and Tina Landau. *The Viewpoints Book*. New York: Theatre Communications Group, 2005.

Cermatori, Joseph, Emily Coates, Kathryn Krier, Bronwen MacArthur, Angelica Randle, and Joseph Roach. "Teaching African-American Dance/History to a 'Post-Racial' Class: Yale's Project 0." *Theatre Topics* 19, no. 1 (2009): 1–14.

Connolly, Mary Kate, ed. *Throwing the Body into the Fight: A Portrait of Raimund Hoghe*. Chicago: Intellect, the University of Chicago Press, 2013.

Croft, Clare. "A Mutually Satisfying Pas de Deux: Feminist Dramaturgy and Dance in the Undergraduate Dance Curriculum." *Theatre Topics* 19, no. 2 (2009): 181–92.

DeLahunta, Scott. "Dance Dramaturgy: Speculations and Reflections." *Dance Theatre Journal* 16, no. 1 (April 2000): 20–24.

Dumon, Dirk. "Choreography Coaching in the Field of Amateur Dance in the Netherlands." In *Contemporary Choreography: A Critical Reader*, edited by Jo Butterworth and Liesbeth Wildschut, 235–47. New York: Routledge, 2009.

Eckersall, Peter. "Toward an Expanded Dramaturgical Practice: A Report on 'The Dramaturgy and Cultural Intervention Project.'" *Theatre Research International* 31, no. 3 (2006): 283–97.

Gandrow, Kristen. "Dramaturgy: Quirky and Productive." *Theatre Topics* 13, no. 1 (March 2003): 79–80.

Gilpin, Heidi. "Aberrations of Gravitiy." In *William Forsythe and the Practice of Choreography: It Starts from Any Point*, edited by Steven Spier, 112–27. New York: Routledge, 2011.

Gilpin, Heidi. "Shaping Critical Spaces: Issues in the Dramatury of Movement Performance." In *Dramaturgy in American Theater: A Source Book*, edited by Susan Jonas, Georff Proehl, and Michael Lupu, 83–87. Belmont, CA: Thomson Wadsworth, 1997.

Hamera, Judith. "The Romance of Monsters: Theorizing the Virtuoso Body." *Theatre Topics* 10, no. 2 (2000): 145–54.

Hansen, Pil. "Dance Dramaturgy: Possible Work Relations and Tools." In *Space and Composition: A Nordic Symposium on Physical/Visual Stage Dramaturgy*, edited by Miriam Frandsen and Jesper Schou-Knudsen, 124–41. Copenhagen: NordScen and Statens Teatrerskole, 2005.

Hickey-Moody, Anna. "Becoming-Dinosaur: Collective Process and Movement Aesthetics." In *Deleuze and Performance*, edited by Laura Cull, 161–82. Edinburgh, UK: Edinburgh University Press, 2009.

Imschoot, Myriam van. "Anxious Dramaturgy." *Women and Performance: A Journal of Feminist Theory* 13, no. 2 (2003): 57–68.

Kunst, Bojana. "The Economy of Proximity: Dramaturgical Work in Contemporary Dance Performance Research." *Performance Research—A Journal of Performing Arts* 14, no. 3 (September 2009): 81–88.

Langley, Elizabeth. "The Role of the Dramaturge: The Practical Necessities." *Proceedings: Thirty Fourth Annual Conference, York University and University of Toronto, June 23–26, 2011*, 93–98. Riverside, CA: Society of Dance History Scholars, 2011.

Lee, Jean. "Between Meaning and Significance, and Beyond." *Proceedings: Thirty Fourth Annual Conference, York University and University of Toronto, June 23–26, 2011*, 99–110. Riverside, CA: Society of Dance History Scholars, 2011.

Lepecki, Andre. "Dance without Distance." *Ballet Tanz International* 2 (2001): 29–31.

Leverett, James. "Dramaturgy: An Embarrassment of Job Descriptions." *Performing Arts Resources*, 26 (2008): 1–10.

Lynn, Kirk, and Shawn Sides. "Collective Dramaturgy: A Co-Consideration of the Dramaturgical Role in Collaborative Creation." *Theatre Topics* 13, no. 1 (2003): 111–15.

Mazer, Cary. "Dramaturgy in the Classroom: Teaching Undergraduate Students Not to Be Students." *Theatre Topics* 13, no. 1 (March 2003): 135–41.

McNeilly, Jodie. "Methods for a New Dramatury of Digital Performances." *Proceedings: Thirty Fourth Annual Conference, York University and University of Toronto, June 23–26, 2011*, 141–56. Riverside, CA: Society of Dance History Scholars, 2011.

Miller, Raphael F. "George Beiswange and Dance Criticism." *Dance Chronicle* 16 (January 1993): 45–71.

Mylona, Stefania. "Curating Dance: Dramaturgy as a Multiplicity of Perspectives." *Proceedings: Thirty Fourth Annual Conference, York University and University of Toronto, June 23–26, 2011*, 157–66. Riverside, CA: Society of Dance History Scholars, 2011.

Pierce, Ken. "Using a Dance Historian's Approach as a Guiding Concept in Stage Direction." *Proceedings: Thirty Fourth Annual Conference, York University and University of Toronto, June 23–26, 2011*, 191–200. Riverside, CA: Society of Dance History Scholars, 2011.

Portanova, Stamatia. "The 'Minor' Arithmetic of Rhythm: Imaging Digital Technologies for Dance." In *Deleuze and Performance*, edited by Laura Cull, 240–60. Edinburgh, UK: Edinburgh University Press, 2009.

Proehl, Geoffrey S. "Dramaturgy and Silence." *Theatre Topics* 13, no. 1 (2003): 25–33.

Profeta, Katherine. "Geography at Yale Repertory Theatre." In *The Production Notebooks: Theatre in Process*, Vol. 2, edited by Mark Bly, 193–278. New York: Theatre Communications Group, 2001.

Quick, Robyn. "Dramaturgy: A Case Study of Expanded Access to Twenty-First-Century Pedagogy." *New England Theatre Journal* 20 (2009): 113–21.

Richardson, Sally. "Dramaturgical Dance." *Dance Australia* 149 (April–May 2007): 44–49.

Rushkoff, Douglas. *Present Shock: When Everything Happens Now*. New York: Current, 2013.

Stalpaert, Christel. "A Dramaturgy of the Body." *Performance Research* 14, no. 3 (2009): 121–25.

Turner, Cathy, and Synne Behrndt. "The Production Dramaturg in Dance: An Emerging Field." In *Dramaturgy and Performance*, 165–66. New York: Palgrave, 2008.

Van Kerkhoven, Marianne. "Looking without Pencil in the Hand." Accessed at: http://sarma.be/docs/2858.

Vass-Rhee, Freya. "Dancing Music: The Intermodality of the Forsythe Company." In *William Forsythe and the Practice of Choreography: It Starts from Any Point*, edited by Steven Spier, 73–89. New York: Routledge, 2011.

Vass-Rhee, Freya. "Turning the Tables: William Forsythe's *AntipodesI/II*." In *Theatre without Vanishing Points: The Legacy of Adolphe Appia; Scenography and Choreography in Contemporay Theatre*, edited by Gabriele Brandstetter and Birgit Wiens, 293–301. Berlin: Alexander Verlag, 2012.

Waterhouse, Eilizabeth. "Dancing Admidst the Forsythe Company: Space, Enactiment and Living Repertory." In *Theatre without Vanishing Points: The Legacy of Adolphe Appia; Scenography and Choreography in Contemporay Theatre*, edited by Gabriele Brandstetter and Birgit Wiens, 153–81. Berlin: Alexander Verlag, 2012.

Wildschut, Liesbeth. "Reinforcement for the Choreographer: The Dance Dramaturg as Ally." In *Contemporary Choreography: A Critical Reader*, edited by Jo Butterworth and Liesbeth Wildschut, 383–98. New York: Routledge, 2009.

Zelenak, Michael X. "Why We Don't Need Directors: A Dramaturgical/Historical Manifesto." *Theatre Topics* 13, no. 1 (2003): 105–9.

Zimmerman, Mary. "The Archaeology of Performance." *Theatre Topics* 15, no. 1 (2005): 25–35.

CHAPTER 6

....

SOME FLESHY THINKING
Improvisation, Experience, Perception

....

VIDA L. MIDGELOW

INTRODUCTION AND A FEW
CONTEXTUAL THOUGHTS

CONCEIVED as a playful conversation between myself as dancer and as practice, the performative form of the duologue is used to explore how somatically based dance improvisation practices might be said to be a way of thinking and to question how this critically embodied thought is recognized and understood by both dancer and viewer. In doing so, I tussle with ideas based in phenomenology to illuminate the ways that deeply internalized experiential movement practices enter and expand perceptual fields. What follows thereby entails a consideration of the relationships between body, experience, perception, and knowledge.

Drawing on my own dance improvisation practice, which is underpinned by Skinner releasing technique and other somatically informed approaches, I emphasize image- and sensation-based anatomical exploration and interior impulse as a basis for, and as developed through, improvised compositional activities. This practice is a phenomenological "knowing in doing" formed through what French philosopher Maurice Merleau-Ponty names intercorporeal being. I propose that this somatically based performance practice activates a perceptional consciousness in the dancer and viewer.

Another frame of reference for these deliberations is that of performance practice as a mode of research. The debates surrounding practice-as-research have developed in the United Kingdom, Australia, and across Europe, such that there is now a substantive body of researchers and PhD candidates undertaking and presenting live and mediated artistic work with the equivalent academic status to that of the written word. Building on this approach to research, I address notions of embodied knowledge, for this has been a core and recurring debate for the field.

The mode of embodiment I refer to throughout encompasses a dancer's bodily knowledge—that is, the deep understanding of the body at rest and in particular forms of action attained and shaped through years of practice and experience. And also a bodily ontology in which experiencing, conceptual ideas, and physical practices are embedded and embodied, existing in and emanating from movement practices in reflexive and critical ways. Thereby embodied forms of knowing and knowledge are understood to be varied and interconnected—abstract and concrete, experiential and conceptual, physical and visual. These interconnections form a complex nexus, for, as Les Todres nicely puts it, "One could say that embodying is where being and knowing meet" (20).

In this meeting of knowing and being I am interested in the bodymind at work—knowledge in the making. Thereby through this discussion there is a consideration of the nature of knowledge that as movement artist and academic, I hold, carry, draw on, and engender in and through dancing. These multifarious knowings often remain implicit, but I suggest that they can be recognized and are locatable, and therefore it is possible (at least in part) to form languages for, and from, them. Further, I seek to understand the ways in which others, the viewers of improvised performances, may come to know and make "sense" of these embodied knowings.

In what follows I suggest there are processes that occur across key interconnected two stages as I ask:

> First: How, as an improviser, is it possible to know "something" of the dancing body while "in-action"?
> Second: How is improvisation, as a mode of embodied research and knowing, developed with, and made "sense" of, by an audience?

And so, to the dialogue between dancer and practice . . .

Mindbody knowing in action

Dancer and Practice lay supine on the studio floor.
Eyes closed.
They spend time easing into the floor that raises up to support their bodies.
As air comes in and out of their lungs, they work to release muscle tension and their bones begin to sit more lightly in their sockets. Dancer lets the weight of her head roll to the side and notices the tension in the left side of her neck.

DANCER: You know this stuff is difficult.
PRACTICE: Well that is why we are here, resting on the floor, and talking about it isn't it?
DANCER: It is nice down here, I can feel my body sinking, easing, and melting into the wooden surface.

Both Dancer and Practice rest a while in a comfortable silence.

DANCER: So how is it that we really come to know "of" or "through" the body? It is one thing to have a body, another to know something of it. That is, it is one thing to dance and another to be able to know what your body is doing, to have an interior sensibility of it, and to recognize your own practices at work. It is yet another thing to be able to share that knowing, for knowledge also entails an interaction, an agreement of sorts, between perceiver and perceived.

I am tussling with this, as you can tell. There is in dance something important about the ways in which the particular (my interior experiential knowing of the act of dancing) relates to and can illuminate the general (as a shared recognition and understanding of that knowing with others). How, I might ask, is it possible, through somatic improvisation forms, to extend a circle of meaning or understanding?

Resting on her elbow Dancer picks up a marker pen and begins to draw three concentric circles, radiating outward. She draws each circle with a dotted line and writes within and around each circle. Her hand hovers as she considers the "right" words to describe things: bodily, reflexivity, intersubjectivity—She muses: Are these the words?

DANCER: [She finishes the diagram and rests back on her elbows (see fig 6.1)] I'm thinking in circles. I'm visualizing this set of things as three layers of awareness and interaction. In the center lays the phenomenal body, around the edge of that we have processes of/for heightened awareness—reflexivity, if you will. This provides the basis for a bodily empathy and knowing of self and other. This in turn enables a fluid merging of a fuller embodied intersubjective exchange. Within and between each layer there is a porosity and a process of learning—a considering and expanding of how and what we perceive. There is in this process a constant (re)checking in with the bodily experience and a sliding back and forth between this and knowingness.

PRACTICE: OK, this schema seems useful. But to open it up I think we need to go a bit further. It seems to me that these questions, as well your dance practice, writing, and methodology, might all be seen to tend toward a phenomenological approach. And I know you have been drawn (like many others before you) to phenomenological insights as a way to research, frame, and articulate your ideas—ideas like those embedded in your diagrammatic sketch. Would it be useful for you to rehearse this thinking? Could you say a little something more about this approach?

Dancer rolls to sitting. Resting on her knees she turns to address Practice. Her eyes cast upward and to the side as she considers the question, organizing her thoughts before tentatively starting to speak.

DANCER: OK. I guess it would help.

Phenomenology (like improvisation) develops unpredictably, for, drawing on immediate experience, it is not a "reflection of pre-existing truth but, like art, the act of bringing truth into being" (Merleau-Ponty 1962: xxi). I find that phenomenology offers a method through which to consider lived experience and study firsthand accounts providing a useful and appropriate way to illuminate and articulate somatically based practices, which, in and of themselves, prioritize experiential first-person modes of knowing.

Merleau-Ponty suggested that it is the body as lived, as lodged in the world, which is the basis of being and knowing. Reflecting and analyzing the lived experience, through the human capacity for self-reflexivity, Merleau-Ponty made it clear that the body is not just an object in the world, but through acts of perceiving, it is the very medium whereby our world comes in being. This thinking

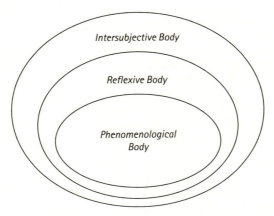

FIGURE 06.1   The phenomenological to the intersubjective body.

forms the basis of his phenomenology, wherein the embodied self is understood as an integrated being that lives, breathes, perceives, acts, speaks, reasons and, yes, dances (although Merleau-Ponty himself never directly discusses dance).

Significantly, in Merleau-Ponty's last (incomplete and poetically tantalizing) work, *The Visible and the Invisible* (1968), he offers a radicalized phenomenology of embodiment. Here he proposes intercorporeal being as a kind of corporeal reflexivity that eliminates the ontological dualism of body subject and body object:

> One can say that we perceive the things themselves, that we are the world that thinks itself—or that the world is at the heart of our flesh. In any case, once a body-world relationship is recognized, there is a ramification of my body and a ramification of the world and a correspondence between its inside and my outside and my inside and its outside.
>
> (Merleau-Ponty 1968: 136)

In other words, this is the phenomenal body, the living-lived body, which participates and is inextricably entangled with the world. Significantly the intercorporeal body understands its worlds without recourse to symbolic or representational processing, that is, without explicit symbol, sign, and image manipulation as aligned to representational thinking. This is significant, I think, for understanding largely experiential movement practices and sits alongside those approaches that are more representationally directed.

This interconnection with the world offers insights of how I come to "know" (my/our) dancing selves and how we connect with others. It is such foundational concepts, alongside the words of Les Todres (2007), Drew Leder (1990) and Alva Noë (2007 and 2004), that resonate for me. They each, in their differently nuanced ways, give space for bodily-lived-experiences, that often reside before, inside, and around representational or symbolic references, to be the basis of understanding. This "feels" right, "feels" akin to how I come to know something of (my) dancing while improvising.

While this sounds very subjective, indeed in some ways it is, it is an attempt to "bracket" pre-expectations and assumptions in order to consider things anew. As dancer and phenomenologist Sondra Fraleigh writes, "Phenomenology seeks the intangible obvious, that which lies before our eyes and in our hearts however obscured through habit, even as its existential conscience reminds us that innocence, the river of our body's memory, is not naivete" (2000: 55). So, while emanating from an internal place, the aim is not to rest on or valorize the singular uniqueness of experience. Like improvised performance itself, the draw of phenomenology is that it is intersubjective—connecting self and other, dance and dancer, viewer and performer, establishing ever-looping hermeneutic circles.

PRACTICE: Hummm. I am glad you mentioned Fraleigh and dance-focused writings here. Philosophy is all very interesting and fine as far as it goes, but movement artists have been developing practices that have fundamentally challenged the notion of body as object, valuing instead the whole person and bodily awareness too.

DANCER: Indeed, the contemporary currency of somatically based dance practices is a testament to these developments. Practices as promoted in dance by artists and teachers such as Joan Skinner (Skinner Releasing Technique), Bonnie Bainbridge Cohen (Body-Mind Centering), and Mary Starks Whitehouse and Janet Adler (Authentic Movement), alongside Contact Improvisation (Steve Paxton and Nancy Stark-Smith) and Alexander Technique–informed practices (as developed by dancers such as Eva Karczag), cultivate a deep attentiveness to the body, working within principles of body-mind integration and the connectedness of soma to kinesthetics, psyche, imagination, aesthetics, and the world.

These developments in the field of dance built on the work of "first-generation" practitioners such as F. M. Alexander, M. Feldenkrais, and I. Rolf, among others (Behnke 2009; Eddy 2009). Thomas Hanna drew the work of these practitioners, each of whom developed distinctive approaches to bodywork, into the rubric of "somatics" in the 1970s. Describing typical features of a somatic approach, Martha Eddy writes:

Each person and their newly formed "discipline" had people take time to breath, feel and "listen to the body," often by beginning with conscious relaxation on the floor or lying down on a table. From this gravity-reduced state, each person was guided to pay attention to bodily sensations emerging from within and move slowly and gently in order to gain deeper awareness of "the self that moves". Students were directed to find ease, support, and pleasure while moving—all the while paying attention to proprioceptive signals. Participants were also invited to experience increased responsiveness as they received skilled touch and/or verbal input as "fresh stimuli" from a somatic educator or therapist.

(Eddy 2009: 6)

Principles such as these, developed by the pioneers of somatics, became "a canon inclusive of exercises, philosophies, methods, and systems of inquiry" (Eddy 2009:7). Enhanced by the concurrent developments in phenomenology, Thomas Hanna defined the "soma" of "somatics" as "the body experienced from within" (in Behnke 2009: 11). Through such thinking the interface between phenomenological thought and somatic (dance) practice is evident.

PRACTICE: It seems that these particularized practices and ideas enable us to experience and perceive the body differently—differently that is from what might be our everyday usage and awareness. Further, they each implicitly seek to address how hard it is to stay connected and present in our bodies.

DANCER: That is true and it is difficult. Difficult to stay connected, for the body (my body) has a habit of disappearing.

PRACTICE: Drew Leder in *The Absent Body* (1990), heavily influenced by Merleau-Ponty, describes the paradoxical nature of bodily presence. The "fuzziness" that surrounds your body in any moment, the difficulty in being really aware of it, is described as the receding of the body, reflecting the erasure of the body from perception. Even in moments of extreme physicality—for example when playing a sport—we may not attend to our own embodiment—caught instead in the game or the result of an action.

Pointing to the ways in which we are generally present in the body in only limited ways, Leder argues that it is often through dysfunction and discomfort that we can become aware of otherwise latent bodily processes or functions. So, in everyday usage we only note for example the expansion of the ribs on the intake of the breath in to the lungs when we take an extraordinary breath—be it short, sharp, or long. You might try it—go on—take in an extra deep breadth. *[Both Dancer and Practice take a deep intake of breath, and on the exhale Dancer makes a long hissssing sound, squeezing the air out of her lungs.]* It is in this passing moment that the body, the lungs and ribs, become what Leder calls "ecstatic" and the fleshly body is present to us. While I find the emphasis on the body in discomfort uncomfortable (!), the relationship to our bodies Leder describes is very resonant.

DANCER: Yes, Leder's ideas work for me. In somatic improvisational practices it is this ecstatic body that is to the fore. In these moments and through improvisation I am "paying attention" and dancing in such a way that the body retains its ecstatic state for extended periods.

Given the difficulties of perceiving the body, of bringing it into an ecstatic state, it is perhaps not surprising that many somatic approaches (and certainly in releasing practices—the basis of my own approach) tend to begin in stillness and often in a supine position. The stilling of the body, and the support of the floor, reduces the number things one has to concern oneself with, and allows attention to dwell in the detail, for example, on the temperature of the skin, the movement of the rib cage, the shape of the collarbone, or the weight of the pelvis. As a session develops, the dancer works to maintain these interior images and sensations—carrying them into extended movement through improvisational activities. This adds another layer of difficultly, but with practice it is possible while experimenting improvisationally to note, in the moment, shifts between ecstatic and recessive states that occur in and across different parts of the body at any one time.

LET ME ELABORATE A LITTLE: *[As she speaks, Dancer begins to trace movement through her body: An opening of the shoulder ripples in a successive flow to her fingers, and a dip forward in the head triggers pulses down her spine]* Training in releasing techniques—particularly Skinner- and Alexander-based approaches—has led me to follow and develop an improvisational form that focuses on a muscular releasing and deep listening as a basis for moving. This approach to improvisation practice is based in "lividness," in sensation and in anatomically based imagery. When improvising, I am not performing precomposed movement, rather I am responding through an embodied reflexivity to internal and external information as part of a complex nexus of "data" arising for the being in/of the world. This interoceptive and exteroceptive data includes proprioceptive information about positions of the body—of limbs in relation to torso, of torso in relation to the floor, of floor in relation to the roof of the mouth—drawing on mechanical receptors in the muscles, joints, vision, and inner ear. Dancing with an awareness of my movement and relationship to space and through duration, I rotate and shift my kinesphere and follow different paths.

This sounds all well and good as I say it, but it is also true to say that I struggle to pay attention to all these pieces of sensory information and to draw on all these skills at the same time. It is much easier without distractions, without trying to talk at the same time, and without an audience watching. This "paying attention," enabling an ecstatic state, is most easily achieved in a quiet studio (with ideally a partner's hands or voice to guide me) when there is the time and space to focus on the interior workings of the body. [*Dancer lays prone on the floor, and Practice lays her hands onto her back, her hands feeling, and at the same time drawing attention to, the expanding and deflating of the torso as Dancer breathes*].

Even in these quiet moments it is important to recognize that the body, like improvisation itself, is in perpetual flux, for as Leder writes:

> The lived body constantly transforms its sensorimotor repertoire by acquiring novel skills and habits. [. . .] A phenomenological anatomy cannot then be thought of as fixed over time, or even confined by the physical boundaries of the flesh. It must take account of the body as living process.
>
> (Leder 2007: 30)

Such is the quandary of knowing in relation to the body. However through somatically based improvisation it is possible, I think, to continually explore the changing phenomenology of the body—to take account of the body in process.

PRACTICE: Would you say, then, that your somatically based improvisation entails a consciousness of action? [*Her hands move to the sides of Dancers ribs and then begin to shift her body side to side.*]

DANCER: Humm, Yes. There is an emphasis on strategies that foreground a heightened awareness of the body in stillness and in motion, the interconnectedness to that which we are made of and that which is around us. Tracing this relationship through somatic practice places the emphasis on the living body that integrates the physical, emotional, and cognitive realms.

While, for example, it is clear that we cannot actually "see" the interior of our own bodies in any remotely normal circumstance, it is possible to activate a lived kinesthetic consciousness of the dancing body. Through recognizing the pre-articulations of the human body—"its sensory organs, its forward directedness, its muscular capacities" (Leder 1990: 29), we can categorize the lived body into its usual forms of absence and presence, tracing out a "phenomenological anatomy" (Leder 1990: 29). As such, we can note that the surface of the body is knowable through the interaction of sensorimotor capabilities. I can, for instance, gaze on parts of my own skin—I can look at my hands, but I cannot see my own eyes or the back of my neck. Also, my hands can touch each other and I can feel the shape of my ribs under my skin. But the internal spaces of the body—organs, joints, and tissues—cannot be observed or touched. Exploring this interceptive field relies on inner sensations, imagination, and the application of conceptual understanding.

PRACTICE: So how does this work in practice when dancing?

DANCER: Well let's see . . . [*Dancer and Practice come together and lay side by side*]. I might for example look at an image of the rib cage, touch a skeleton and locate the ways it moves. I can, through my imagination and my cognitive abilities, place these images inside my own body—enhancing my appreciation of the structure and viscera of the body. As such, this perceptual field is known indirectly, and while relationally ambiguous and discontinuous, it can be sensed through metaphor and through images, giving rise to renewed understandings of our embodiment.

This sensing of the body, the tracing out my "phenomenological anatomy," it just one of the fields of awareness that I draw on while dancing. Others are in the territory of the body as located in space and time, the purposeful tracking of the dance (just) past—or compositional memory and the implicit and explicit (body) memory of my own history, images, and knowledge. These areas of awareness are not singular or hierarchical in nature but are experienced as a nexus, each informing, layering, and weaving into the other.

PRACTICE: We might say, then, that in developing what you are calling "fields of awareness" through various senses and through imaginative acts, the interaction between self, body, and world become more evident. This is a pro-active process—a perceptual mode of practice even. For perceiving is, Alva Noë (2004) argues, something we "do," and it requires a purposeful engagement. In order that the lived experience when dancing be more present in you and to you, your perceiving must be active—it is not done to you, nor it is a prenatural state of awareness.

To take it a bit further, and as Noë suggests (2004: 1), in a perceptual mode of practice, it is not enough merely to have sensations, rather it is necessary to have sensations that we understand. Further, I think you would subscribe to the view that it is not enough to recognize what any particular movement feels like, but important to be able to thematize their inner logic with other experiences and contexts.

DANCER: Certainly. The thematizing of inner logic is a crucial part of my practice and of practice as research per se. Rather than trying to fit within a preexisting theoretical scheme, as an improviser I am drawn toward materials that emerge within the process of dancing. Through listening to these experiences (from) within the act of dancing, clustered themes begin to take shape, forming an inner logic. Taking account of experience (which incorporates experiencing the physical, sensate, emotional, philosophical, and conceptual) allows the phenomena of improvising to be articulated and understood "as actually had rather than laying some invented theoretical scheme on experience" (Gendlin in Todres 2007: 27).

PRACTICE: So—so far we have suggested that coming to know what we know of somatic practices requires attention to sensation to the body while in action. We might usefully describe this process of coming to a thematized logic as a mode of embodied reflexive learning.

DANCER: Hum, yeah, that feels right—what you describe feels akin to what I experience when improvising as a critical and curious mode of enquiry. This embodied reflexivity happens both in the moment and upon reflection.

PRACTICE: In the moment reflexivity, though, might seem to go against the grain of improvisation practices. Many improvisers value the ability to "be present" and to "go with the flow" and, as such, a reflective approach might seem to suggest a distancing of self from the doing, leading to a generally undesired level of "objectivity."

DANCER: This is true. Indeed Todres points to this paradox too, noting that "embodied understanding," on the one hand, forges "a fruitful distance from the specific embodied occasion," while, on the other hand, it requires that "they remain responsively connected to the aliveness of the specific experiential occasion" (2007: 29).

With this in mind, I think I would want to say that developing a reflexive sensibility, a reflection in the midst (as Merleau-Ponty might say), doesn't intervene in "the flow" but enables me to remain immersed, deepening the kinesthetic experience in a purposeful mode. Though small intersecting loops, and with practice, this embodied-reflectivity deepens the experience—for through this process it is possible to become more present in more multifaceted ways. It is this reflective practice that enables concepts to be drawn out of raw experience.

The interior thematizing and naming of experience and sensation is achieved through the finding of "good words" (Todres 2007: 28) to make fresh sense of lived experience, opening the said, as well as the unsaid, life of improvisation. These "good words" are then a significant part of developing the synergy between somatic and conceptual knowledge—for in tight multidirectional looping circles experience, words, and knowledge intersect.

PRACTICE: And so for me a picture of improvisation as a thinking research practice is emerging, and it becomes possible to recognize improvisation as both a way of practicing thinking and a way of making present embodied thought.

We might try it together.

Dancer and Practice come to standing. Taking time, they work to note that which draws their attention and, noting anatomical "glitches" and the sounds around them, they ease into movement. Following these small beginnings, exploring and elaborating, their dance emerges as they both dwell in curiosities and traverse through space. Sliding around each other, never in contact, but always aware—they dance their duet.

Seeing/Sensing the (in)visible and knowing the other's body

Dancer and Practice sit on a mat in the far corner of the studio. Leaning back to back, they share their weight, the warmth of each other's backs passing between them, as they are at the same time touching and being touched.

DANCER: I want to shift focus from what I know as a dancer to what others can come to know through watching. This requires a further consideration of the seer/seen and touched/touching relationship, evoking a challenge to conventional modes of reception, leading to an expanded notion of dancer/ viewer exchange.

PRACTICE: OK.

DANCER: I am aware, for instance, that some aspects of the particularized perceptual field that is my internal embodied knowing while improvising are available to viewers and are some not.

PRACTICE: What do you mean?

DANCER: Well, my dear Practice, if I stand here in front of you, *[Dancer stands]* I guess you can *see* that I am standing with my weight spread evenly between my two feet. You might also perceive that as I say these very words I am beginning to pay more attention to the nature of that standing. I am trying "let go" of muscular tension in my shoulder girdle, I am deepening my breathing to enable my ribs to soften and drop downward, I am shifting the balance of weight across my feet, which requires an easing of the muscular grip in the thighs and buttocks. But can you tell that the coffee I drank earlier is causing my stomach to churn and is pressing on my bladder, or that my heart, which usually pumps away without my awareness, is beating hard and thereby calling my attention to it?

Further, I would think that many of the images and remembered sensations that I use to enrich my bodily actions are obscured to you too. For instance, the image I use of a man's suit being filled and emptied to deepen the breath is hidden, my memory of the sensation of hands on my pelvis as a partner encourages the loosening of the legs is hidden. These sensations and images are in the interior of my body, and unless I share them in some way these aspects of body knowledge remain largely out of view but are no less experientially resonant for me. So bodies certainly contain knowings, but the details of my body's knowings might not always be communicated to you in precise ways. Even if we accept this fact, I suggest that something resonates between bodies that can be perceived—perhaps in the softness of the body and or the focus on easing into moving. So while a viewer doesn't have the same image bank or sensorial memory as me, there is perhaps a sense of this through the textures in the movement that reverberate with my knowings, these might be found in the sense of weight or the differing quality of action at play.

PRACTICE: It might be useful to go to phenomenological accounts and Merleau-Ponty again to help us think through the nature of bodily exchange and empathy. *[Extending her hand toward Dancer, they firmly grasp each other's hands and lean away from each other and, in counterbalance, they lower to the floor].*

I am reminded of the analogy of touching hands—in which hands both touch and are touched (and in the studio I might call attention to the such sensations as back rests on back, as we were sitting earlier, or point to our interconnectedness as air in my lungs is exchanged with the air in your lungs). This interconnectedness is, I think, important to the way in which the dancing exceeds the representational or projected image and how the perceived and perceiver become intertwined.

Yet Merleau-Ponty surpasses even this position. His articulation of intercorporeal intersubjectivity enables the relationship to the other (in our case other dancers and the audience) to begin with our bodies but suggests that intercorporealities are not constructed through a seeing or touching of the other. Rather, by recognizing that our bodies are in constant intercorporeal contact, he enables us to recognize that we do not passively sense or actively observe the behaviors of the other, but are coparticipant beings in the world.

DANCER: Hum, yeah. These ideas are picked up by dancer writer April Flakne, who in a reconsideration of Derrida's reading of Merleau-Ponty playfully illuminates them through contact improvisation. She writes that intercorporeal intersubjective interactions, understood as a form of choreography, suggest mutual marking and constitute a space between bodies or among bodies:

> The other body impacts my body, even when there is no direct touch, because my body is in constant contact—even if indirect—with other bodies that share and inscribe the space comprising heres and theres.
>
> (Flakne 2007: 45)

Through this we can start to understand that being-in-relation is always subject to multiple and shifting sensibilities that are in contact (if not literal touch) in with others.

PRACTICE: I like that essay and the way she brings phenomenology into the processes of contact improvisation.

She describes how in contact improvisation "the body and self as self-same, is/are not assumed in advance. Rather, they are a perpetually improvised centering and de-centering, of balancing and falling in contact with the improvisations of others in an open, dynamic space, a chora-graphic field" (2007: np). As such, she argues, our sense of the body is a performative accomplishment, one that requires continual reenactment in intercorporeal, intersubjective, imaginary, and rational chora-graphies (spatial practices) (Flakne 2007: np). As such, the body radiates beyond itself.

DANCER: In *The Visible and the Invisible* Merleau-Ponty talks about the intercorporeal and develops the somewhat ambiguous notion of "flesh." I think this idea is relevant here too.

PRACTICE: Go on.

DANCER: Flesh, as Merleau-Ponty speaks of it, is not simply synonymous with the body per se. It might be more useful to think of flesh as the shared corporeal condition between oneself and the world. So, flesh is not limited to the individual body, it is a more encompassing, even elemental, state of the world. Merleau-Ponty writes, "The flesh is not matter, is not mind, is not substance" (1968: 139).

Exploring this in relation to movement, dancer and author Susan Kozel writes that we are "porous beings, and we are part of flesh as well as being flesh" (2007: 33). Flesh for Merleau-Ponty is always immanent, it always exceeds, remaining beyond grasp. For, when flesh is understood as my body, your body and, importantly, the space between bodies it becomes possible to recognize that flesh is "capable of weaving relations between bodies" . . . and that this will not only enlarge "but will pass definitively beyond the circle of the visible" (Merleau-Ponty 1968: 144).

PRACTICE: Hum. Passing beyond the visible—that sounds like it could offer a tantalizing way to consider an embodied response.

DANCER: I think so . . . It leads us toward an understanding of how the body functions as a locus of transaction and how the relation between dancer, dance, spectator, and the visible world constitutes the trajectory of meaning-making in relation to dance. An audience might be thought of as been in a quasi-immersive state in relation to the dance, for a phenomenological view assumes that the viewer is not merely physically located in relation to the dance, but is incorporated in it, and formulated as a viewing subject through this corporeal relation (a coparticipant in a virtual (contact) improvisation).

PRACTICE: So, this idea of flesh is, in Merleau-Ponty's writings, intertwined with the relation between the seer and seen, such that he states, "the flesh that one sees and touches is not all there is to flesh" (Merleau-Ponty 1968; 144). Through reversibility of the seer/seen relationship (I can see that I am also seen), the exchange between flesh is understood to be constantly sliding and twisting, reaching beyond the purely visual to acknowledge touch-in-vision. The resonance of reversibility gives us a way to describe perceiving the world and others in it:

> not to see the outside, as others see it, the contour of the body one inhabits, but to be seen by the outside, to exist within it, to emigrate into it, to be seduced, captivated . . . So that the seer and the visible reciprocate one another and we no longer know which sees and which is seen.
>
> (Merleau-Ponty 1968: 139)

Read materially, as by Kozel, "Merleau-Ponty acknowledges that there is "that which reaches the eye directly," the frontal, but also that which reaches vision from below ("profound postural latency") and from above ("of flight, of swimming, of movement"). Through these designations he introduces not only corporeal routes of vision but also kinetic and kinaesthetic qualities" (Kozel 2007: 41)

DANCER: Yet Merleau-Ponty doesn't seek a full fusion between the comprehending of the known and knower; rather he describes this as a chiasmic encounter. I suggest flesh at once surrounds and is "held" by the chiasm, for the chiasm represents a moment of exchange or overlap between an individual and the world (and within an individual herself). The model of the chiasm becomes a way to understand reciprocal perceiving/perceived that, having started with seeing/seen, visible/invisible, extends through the phenomenal body. The chiasm is further developed, and complicated, as a process that occurs between senses—"not only between the touched and the touching, but also between the tangible and the visible" (Merleau-Ponty 1968: 134)—and ultimately pertains to an individual's entire inhabitation of the world:

> the idea of chiasm, that is: every relation with being is simultaneously a taking and a being taken, the hold is held, it is inscribed and inscribed in the same being that it takes hold of.
>
> (Merleau-Ponty 1968: 266)

Through this thinking the gap between the dancer and the viewer could be described as chiasmic. Obscure and resisting full disclosure, the chiasm is a pulsing space that animates the visible, offering us the possibility of slippage and allusion, for, as Kozel very nicely describes it, the invisible gives depth and texture to what we see (2007: 40).

PRACTICE: I wonder, then, if we might consider strategies through which the phenomenological chiasmic space of flesh might be activated, made more present? Akin to the dancer's heightened interior awareness that enables a more extended presencing of the ecstatic body (to recall Leder), perhaps flesh can be bought forth too in the shared space of dancer and viewer. Perhaps this activation is found in the emergent nature of improvisation that incorporates the (at times tacit) inclusion of the audience?

DANCER: Yes, and perhaps if we recognize that improvisatory performance only becomes fully present through the copresencing of/with the audience, it becomes possible to understand the way knowings and knowledges are generated in this sharing.

While Practice watches, Dancer rolls along the floor, shifting between radiating her limbs outward, extending out in differing directions, and letting her weight drop, she uses the momentum of each roll to propel her into the next.

A self-revealing practice: Spiraling processes of movement, perception, and excess

PRACTICE: So what does all this mean, really, in relation to an audience's viewing? What potentials do the inherent blurring of viewer/performer positions and the tacit inclusions of the viewer in improvisation enable? What are the resonances, reverberations, and repercussions that carry between bodies? Is it possible that there are "things" that exceed the visible frame of dancing to be perceived by the audience such that a phenomenological experience can unfold?

DANCER: Yes. In my experience there is, in this unfolding, such an excess. There is sense in which improvisation exceeds readability, exceeds full comprehension. Yet it is also overflowing with potential. To paraphrase Alva Noë, and his discussion of embodied perception, nothing and everything is hidden—there is too much to take in. As such we might say, that everything is available to us, but it is difficult (if not impossible) for viewers to perceive everything that is present. Further, just as I said earlier, it is not enough to experience the body, but we must understand those experiences too. It is also not enough for an audience to merely have sensory stimulation. Rather, they need ways to grasp and apprehend those sensory stimulations (Noë 2007: 180).

PRACTICE: Noë argues that to fully experience, one must be able to appreciate *how* the experience presents things as being, writing that "the world shows up for us in experience in so far as we understand, that is, know or anticipate it" (Noë 2007, 121). The implication of this is that the viewer needs some framing mechanism in order to perceive and apprehend improvisation.

DANCER: So, to bring this closer to the practice and into a diagrammatic form, I wonder if perceiving a somatically based improvisation might it be visualized as a spiraling process that encompasses multiple surfaces—off which echoes resound as the sensations and images of the improvisation roll outward, entering the dancer and audience from different directions and allowing differentiated echoes to reside in the bodymind?

I visualize it something like this: (see fig 6.2)

Taking up a marker pen, Dancer beings to draw a series of intersecting circles. The long looping spirals forming mobile a spinelike center—within which each element, each vertebra is able to rotate and curve, intersecting with its partners. Then, in a sweep of the hand, she draws two large looping semicircles at either side of the spine, these connect and enfold the central spine while encompassing and holding the wider spatial terrain—a circle that suggests the ways in which the central spine reaches out to encompass much more than it can physically touch.

Putting down the pen, Dancer traces the shape of this organic structure. She muses on how the central spinelike curves radiate out in circular tendrils that reach out to touch others and in turn they are touched, rotating back to her body in an exchange of interconnected flesh.

PRACTICE: This gives us a framework through which it is possible to understand the way in which embodied knowledge might be formed, with improvisation operating as a self-revealing form. In the central "spine" you have the dancer's interior processes, which are developed through self-reflective processes including expanding perceptions and the "finding of good words" in order to give structure to awareness.

DANCER: Yes. And the outer circle seeks to map out how these interior processes interconnect with exterior ones, foregrounding the immediacy of improvisation and the use of choreographic strategies as a route through which the interior becomes visible. In doing so, I am proposing that improvisations offer special kinds of processes in which creation/performance become the same generative occurrence. Similarly, activities of making and viewing, experiencing and interpreting, are collapsed into each other, activating the intercorporeal encounter.

In this thinking I am drawing on Lisa Nelson's "Tuning Scores" (or rather Noë's discussion of this score at work). Noë describes a process in which the improvisational structure provides a method through which the dancers (as both participants and observers) "attune themselves" to the other dancers and the environment. Developing this analysis, Noë uses Wittgenstein's language games as an example of how we might learn through the practice itself to perceive.

Through language games, Wittgenstein sought to reveal the nature of language, asking us to think of language games as a way to build a primitive language that exhibited the elements essential for developing more complex linguistic exchanges. To use Noë's own example, while listening to an unfamiliar language may be perceived as sound, what is being said (the words themselves) is

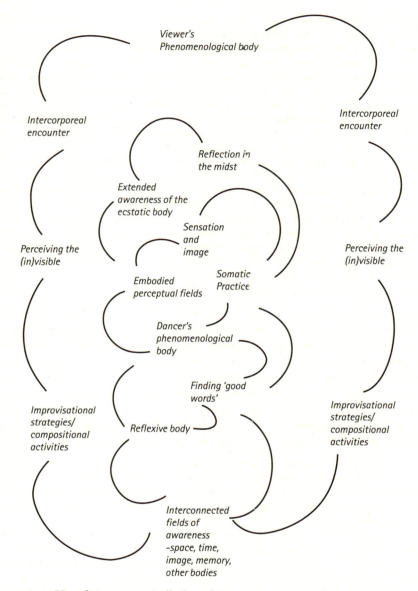

FIGURE 06.2   Visualising somatically based improvisation as a looping process.

invisible. Yet it is possible to start to "make sense" of that which is at first unfamiliar (the new language) by building blocks from small modules and couplings.

Following this argument, he suggests that Nelson's turning scores offer the dancer/viewer a way through which to navigate experience—a way through which to come to "make perspicuous our mode of perceptual being-in-the-world" (Noë 2007: 126). In this way, he argues, "A Tuning Score, like a grammatical exercise, is an occasion to being to acquire the skills necessary for access to the world. [...] It is an activity of bringing the world into focus for perceptual consciousness" (2007: 127).

Through his analysis Noë begins to open up ways improvisation practices unfold perceptions, by offering building blocks and strategic tools to the viewer as a route toward shared understanding.

DANCER: Yes, by offering strategic tools, combined with our understanding that the depth of bodily experience is relational and exceeds precise formulation, improvisation might provide ways to activate the invisible space of flesh. For, just perhaps, it might it be possible that the emergent nature of improvisation, in that it reveals itself for and with the audience in the moment, could allow an audience "to learn its way about," enabling a skillful consciousness to be developed. Therefore we might think of somatic dance improvisation as a tool for the study of a perceptual phenomenological consciousness.

DANCER: Yes. I think so.

In this process the audience enters a somatic and choreographic relationship with me as a dancer. As movement ideas unfold, they come with me on a journey. Entering a kind of somatic mirroring, audience members may begin by recognizing small building blocks, or the DNA of the dance, which forms the basis of that which follows. Thereby a viewer engages with the practice of improvisation and learns their way about at the same time as I do. As I dancer, I am sharing with my fellow dancers and my audience my thinking/moving, and they are a part of my thinking/moving. We are in it together—entwined in something akin to a pedagogical process. So I think it is possible to see and learn through the thinking-in-action processes that are being played out in front of/with the viewer.

Physical possibilities are "found," explored, and developed together.

Spaces are animated and made more present together.

Time is expanded and truncated together.

One at a time, Dancer and Practice support each other's movement—stroking, holding, guiding, following each other with their hands. Through this touch they guide the emerging solo and echo it with their touch and in their bodies.

After a while they exchange roles—passing from guide to guided.

As the dance between them develops and extends, a duet takes shape. The roles of following and leading blur, and a dance with or without touch/contact is formed. They notice how this dance resides within them, how one movement possibility is explored and transformed, how an image forms between them, becoming more present through their mutual yet unspoken manipulations.

Then, after a time, Dancer and Practice drift away from each other to explore this dance as a solo, each tracing their own path, Informed by their previous duetting and altered by their own curiosities and bodily practices.

They work to notice what has changed, how things have moved on and been transformed.

DANCER: Through the intercorporeal encounter processes of watching emerge that draw on the sensory basis of perception and lived experience. These experiential processes are activated through the use of one's body as a locus of sensory appreciation and critical engagement. Through such processes knowings and knowledges occur in relation to the improvisation as it is formed, as the dance unfolds. In this way improvisation evokes relations wherein an embodied experience is cultivated and viewers are encouraged to pay more attention to the phenomenology of their experiences to access the "world" presented before them.

PRACTICE: So to complete the circle of perception—even while recognizing it is messy and porous, the important task of phenomenology, and of experiential movement practices, ought not to be so much to depict or represent or describe experience but rather to catch experience in the act of making the world available, drawing an audiences attention to an activity, to dance thought in the making.

DANCER: Nice. So, perhaps we should dance?

BIBLIOGRAPHY

Behnke, Elizabeth A. "The Human Science of Somatics and Transcendental Phenomenology." *Man and the Word/Zmogus ir zodis* 11, no. 4 (2009): 10–26.

Eddy, Martha. "A Brief History of Somatic Practices and Dance Historical Development of the Field of Somatic Education and Its Relationship to Dance." *Journal of Dance and Somatic Practices* 1, no. 1 (2009): 5–27.

Flakne, April. "Contact/Improv: A Synaesthetic Rejoinder to Derrida's Reading of Merleau-Ponty." *Philosophy Today* 51, SPEP Supplement (2007): 42–49.

Fraleigh, Sondra. "Consciousness Matters." *Dance Research Journal* 32, no. 1 (Summer 2000): 54–62.

Kozel, Susan. *Closer: Performance, Technology, Phenomenology.* Cambridge, MA: MIT Press, 2007.

Leder, Drew. *The Absent Body.* Chicago: University of Chicago Press, 1990.

Merleau-Ponty, M. *Phenomenology of Perception.* Translated by C. Smith. London: Routledge and Kegan Paul, 1962.

Merleau-Ponty, M. *The Visible and the Invisible.* Translated by A. Lings. Evanston, IL: Northwestern University Press, 1968 (first published 1964).

Noë, Alva. "Making Worlds Available." In *Knowledge in Motion: Perspectives of Artistic and Scientific Research in Dance,* edited by S. Gehm, P. Huseman, and K. von Wilcke. New Brunswick and London: Transaction, 2007.

Noë, Alva. *Action in Perception.* Cambridge, MA: MIT Press, 2004.

Todres, Les. *Embodied Enquiry: Phenomenological Touchstones for Research, Psychotherapy and Spirituality.* Houndsmills, Basingstoke, England: Palgrave Macmillan, 2007.

SECTION II

GENUS (PART 1)

....

CHAPTER 7

FLESHING OUT
Physical Theater, Postmodern Dance, and Som[e]agency

....

MAIYA MURPHY

ALLIED through a shared commitment to the body,[1] physical theater and postmodern dance took sometimes distinct and sometimes intertwined journeys to claim territories[2] of engagement beyond aesthetics. This broad arena, fully realized, reaches from the aesthetic into the ontological and boldly asserts that through the body we can see, understand, and exert agency. When I refer to physical theater and postmodern dance, I am referring to a particular moment and place: the mid-twentieth century through the present in North America, Australia, and Western Europe. "Agency," in this context, is the ability—comprising power, structure, and authorization—to act on that environment. While agency emphasizes the locus of the power to act, it also implies an inextricable relationship of this locus to the environment because it is expressed only insofar as it makes an impression on the environment. Physical theater and postmodern dance evolved in response to similar cultural and historical influences and shared points of reference and might even be considered one in the same field at certain points. Considering how the two body-based performance forms developed both through their own theatrical and dance traditions, and where they cross paths, reveals how their shared preoccupations with the body are ultimately about the theatrical and dancing body's ability to expand from the aesthetic outward to multiple registers. These registers include basal levels of aesthetic structure and ontological states. These artists "flesh out" in two ways: First, like the exaggerated attention and enjoyment given to food in the notion of "pigging out," they revel in expanding and/or heightening the role of corporeal privilege in training and creation; second, through celebrating this privilege, they press out and extend the borders of what the body can access. Through "fleshing out" and articulating somatic agency, postmodern dance and physical theater expand the body's territory all the way to agency's frontiers.

AN OUTLINE OF THE TERRAIN

The particular paths I will be following for this discussion are between Western Europe and the United States. This overall moment and location have global reference points, influences, and diasporas, but I circumscribe this Western flashpoint as the core of this particular dance/theater convergence. Physical theater practices tended to emerge in Europe and travel to North America and Australia. While we often think of the spread of postmodern dance practice as a United-States-to-the-world phenomenon, scholars such as Ramsay Burt remind us that postmodern practices were developing in Europe not only according to American influence but also in response to their own domestic artistic and cultural conversations.[3] When referring to both physical theater and postmodern dance, I am drawing attention to performer training systems just as much as performance practices, as performer preparation became (and continues to be) one of the great needs and preoccupations of both traditions.

Outlining the details of these histories and influences is important because postmodern dance and physical theater can be easily misunderstood in one of two ways: as superficial isolated aesthetic practices or as a generalized mob of motley conventions united only around the body as vacuous, virtuosic tool. Detailing significant elements of these practices' histories reveals the deeper commitment to what the body affords. Highlighting where these practices crossed paths, shared influences, or embraced common goals uncovers the salient theoretical and historical reasons to coalitionize them. Without this explicit explanation, the reader may miss the driving undercurrent of these practices as a movement, just as artists in these traditions may miss the opportunity to gather enough focused power to make pervasive effects on practice, pedagogy, and theory.

"Physical theater" is a contested term that always seems not entirely accurate but nevertheless useful. Under this umbrella can reside visually based theater, dance theater, mime, circus, movement theater, commedia dell'arte, and pedagogical traditions of theater artists such as Jacques Copeau, Vsevolod Meyerhold, Jerzy Grotowski, Tadashi Suzuki, Anne Bogart, Jacques Lecoq, Philippe Gaulier, and Monica Pagneaux, to name a few. What these diverse forms share is a physical privilege in performance and performer preparation. Some may see postmodern dance as a subgroup that fits under this umbrella. However, because of the way that postmodern dance is in conversation with and reacting to the Western dance tradition of ballet and modern dance, I wrench it out from underneath to better see it in relation to how it interfaces with body-based forms that came out of a Western theatrical conversation.

To outline the borders of the physical theater traditions to which I refer, I will mark several important milestones in theater from the late nineteenth century through the present. These milestones mark a heightened focus on physicality, spotlighting the body's potential as a rallying point for change in theater. The first milestone is the impulse to systematize Western actor training in the late nineteenth and early twentieth centuries. This is important for both actor-training and performance because it reveals the desire to define what an actor should be able to do and by extension what kind of theater should be made. Naturally, the body is always involved in actor preparation, but the extent to which it is privileged demonstrates whether the technique or system might be considered "physical" theater. Constantin Stanislavsky and Jacques Copeau were among the first westerners to create exercises and training regimens for the actor, and both men considered many ways to account for the body in actor training, from sport to yoga. As the wildly popular work of Stanislavsky was disseminated (in particular the way Americans began to teach and misinterpret it), it began to emphasize the psychological and emotional aspects over the physical and aimed acting toward a theater of realism. As the twentieth century barreled forward, psychologically based acting technique became and continues to be the mainstream paragon.

I mark the second milestone at the ensuing strong reaction against the predominance of psychologically based acting practices, starting at the beginning of the twentieth century, around fifteen years after Stanislavsky's work took hold. Some theater practitioners became dissatisfied with psychological acting, citing its limit to realism and its reliance on unwieldy human capacities such as emotion and memory. In response, many theater artists—including Michael Chekhov, Vsevolod Meyerhold, Antonin Artaud, and, later on, Jacques Lecoq and Anne Bogart—focused on the more overtly physical as a corrective to what they saw as deficiencies in actor training and theater theory. They developed new physical practices and theories, imported them from other fields, and harked back to body-centric historical theatrical forms such as commedia dell'arte. At this milestone, privileging the body was the solution, and that which constitutes "physical" theater began to take shape.

The third milestone, which I locate in the 1960s, is where the cultural climate of the West saw bodies play an important role in manifesting political popular opinion, with the popularity of the demonstration. Theater too began to emphasize the body, whether it was through literally exposing it in performance or distilling theatrical performance into only a few elements but still featuring the body as essential. The 1960s also brought about the cooperation of bodies in collective forms of theater making. Inspired by the riots in Paris in 1968, where college students and other supporters took to the streets in rebellion against the stringent control of governmental authority, Jacques Lecoq's school ⊙ made a permanent and prominent place in its pedagogy for student-authorized collaborative creation called *auto-cours*. The milestone of the 1960s again brought the body to the fore by both stripping it bare, literally and conceptually, and putting it into contact with other bodies. In this milestone, the body gained more energy and potential beyond that of representation in theater—for it could also simultaneously create a greater degree of political traction. While political theater artists, including those such as Bertolt Brecht, had long since been making political theater, it was in the 1960s that the body's potential, to simultaneously do multidimensional theatrical and political work, expanded greatly.

I situate the fourth milestone in the 1980s, where physical theater started to coalesce into a loose group of related body-based performers that, despite their focus on physical performance, did not quite assign themselves to the dance world. The phrase "physical theater" can be traced to various groups before then, but it was in the 1980s that the term came into circulation, particularly in the UK, along with the birth of what would be considered exemplary companies such as Complicite ⊙.[4] The term came into North American circulation around a decade later.[5] To mark one of the many overlaps and slippages in distinguishing physical theater and dance, the first prominent company to use the term in its title is the UK's DV8 Physical Theatre, a group known as a dance company. Simultaneously, Complicite, who openly acknowledge the pedagogy of Jacques Lecoq as a major influence, have at times resisted being categorized by the term.[6]

I mark the fifth milestone at the turn from the twentieth to the twenty-first century. At that moment enough festivals and workshops of physical and visual theater had occurred, and the term had been in circulation in Europe, North America, and Australia for long enough, that theater artists began writing practical books about it. As they did so, they often acknowledged the challenges in using the term, but "physical theater" began to usefully point to a recognizable group of practitioners and practices. It is important to recognize that masters Jacques Lecoq and Jerzy Grotowski both passed away within five days of each other in January of 1999. While the body of written work about these men's practical work was consistently growing (there already existed a significant amount of writing about Grotowski), perhaps their deaths marked a significant moment in body-based theater practices. With an impulse to memorialize or record their work, or perhaps a recognition that people would no longer have the opportunity to learn firsthand from these two masters, writers began to even more vigorously disseminate physical theater practices and examine them in relationship to a wider context. The two-volume book set on physical theater published in 2006 and 2007 by Simon Murray and John Keefe, *Physical Theatres: A Critical Introduction* and *Physical Theatres: A Critical Reader*, marked an academic arrival of physical theater as a genre. It was the first comprehensive look at physical theater from multiple angles: its practices, its histories, and its theoretical entanglements. The fact that Murray and Keefe could write in this broader capacity suggests that an intensified coalescence of practices and principles had occurred. In addition, the traditional modes for transmitting physical theater practice—private workshop and studio conservatory—were joined by the university degree format. Physical theater practices started entering university training programs as supplements to Stanislavsky-based methods. This turn of the century saw the establishment of full-fledged physical theater programs in the university context. Through the institutionalization of these practices, artists have gathered various physical theater practices to shape their curricula. Even if they follow a consistent pedagogy as the spine of the program, such as a Lecoq-based approach, they often supplement it with other physical training, such as acrobatics or martial arts. The institutionalization of the work serves to not only train performers but also offer a more widely legible certification process. This certification may become important if the performers choose to also work at universities, which may require a postgraduate degree even to apply to a position. Some longtime private studios, such as Dell'Arte in northern California and East 15 Acting School in London, created supplemental programs that actually offer undergraduate and/or graduate degrees. Conversely, existing universities developed physical theater programs such as the MFA program at Naropa University in the United States, and UK-based MA programs St. Mary's University College Twickenham and Royal Holloway University. This institutionalization of physical theater suggests both a high level of demand for this kind of work and a need for a legitimation process to authorize it within the context of academia.

For this discussion, I will mark postmodern dance as the work that was generated by Judson Dance Theater through the present. ▶ ▶ I take the Judson work as a point of departure, but recognize that the exact definitions of modern and postmodern dance are complicated.[7] I embrace the Judson marker for two reasons. The first is because SITI company director Anne Bogart has overtly cited postmodern dance and Judson Dance Theater—along with a later group whose origins can be found in Judson's work, The Grand Union—as inspirational and foundational to the tradition in which she works.[8] Bogart has directly transferred and applied practices and principles for dance to theater,

FIGURE 07.1 Photo by Peter Moore © Estate of Peter Moore/Licensed by VAGA, NY. The Getty Research Institute, Los Angeles. An example of postmodern dance in performance: *The Mind is Is a Muscle* by Yvonne Rainer at Judson Church in 1966.

exemplifying the wide reach of postmodern dance practices. Second, because much of the connection between physical theater and dance is evident and developed within performer training, I follow Melanie Bales's argument that postmodern dance training was indelibly marked by the Judson work.[9] In other words, before and after Judson Dance Theater there were very different assumptions about what dancers needed to be able to do and how training should prepare them. In this way, postmodern dance training was in many ways defined by what Judson suggested dance could be. In fact, Bales's dance training working group, which first used the term "postmodern" to describe the kind of training that they were investigating, eventually settled on the term "post-Judson" as a more "fitting" description.[10] Because, in this light, there is a certain equivalency in dance training between what is considered "postmodern" in dance training and what is considered "post-Judson," I retain the useful marker of the Judson era as the beginning of postmodern dance. Even so, for the purposes of this discussion, I turn away from using the term "post-Judson" *instead* of "postmodern," despite its more nuanced accuracy. This is to enable the discussion to acknowledge other points of postmodern dance origin beyond the United States.

The features of postmodern dance training mirrored the major features of postmodern dance. Just as postmodern dancers, like the Judson Dance Theater, often rebelled against traditional technique to embrace the potential of less formalized dance movement, dance training since the Judson era does not see technique as the be-all and end-all of dancer preparation. While dance training still includes technique, it also includes work that functions through undoing body patterns and making associations within the body that are not expressed through outward technique. "Release technique" became and remains central to postmodern dance training. While the definition remains contested, release technique encompasses a wide range of practices and focuses not on the acquisition of formal aesthetic technique but on accessing deeper corporeal practices.[11] These practices function to either release unwanted corporeal habits, such as tension, or to access the body's capacities via deeper corporeal systems including the skeletal, muscular, energetic, and organ-based. These release techniques work in a different (and sometimes opposing) direction than aesthetic technique. They are designed to reveal corporeal capacities of the body by undoing negative habits and modes of movement. Release technique is a practice of what Bales, taking a cue from Elizabeth Dempster, refers to as "deconstruction," a major theme of post-Judson training.[12] Release technique from dance has also found its way into physical theater training, such as the Feldenkrais and Alexander Technique training offered to all of the students at the London International School of Performing Arts (LISPA). Bales follows Dempster further to categorize the two-pronged approach to post-Judson dance training as "deconstruction" and "bricolage."[13] "Bricolage" is the act of patching together different kinds of training. For a dancer this might mean taking ballet along with jazz, hip-hop, and tap. Despite the fact that ballet placement (upward-pulled with a balanced stance) works in the opposite way as hip-hop placement (low to the ground and capable of extreme asymmetry), dancers have to negotiate these conflicts within their own bodies and are responsible for dancing like a ballet dancer in ballet and dancing like a hip-hop dancer in hip-hop. The postmodern dancer is required to simultaneously put on vastly different movement techniques while stripping away unwanted habits—mastering working in both an additive and subtractive mode. The ideal dancer's body is one that is fluent in many forms, and can participate in the creation process.

During this Western moment in Europe and the United States, the visible body became a primary tool for political change, offering the promise of transforming even some of the most intractable social problems. The late nineteenth through the twentieth centuries saw particularly bloody wars and the failure of longstanding political structures. This time period also saw movements that began to transform deeply rooted social injustices. One of the major features of both the civil rights and feminist movements in the mid-twentieth century were the marches, protests, and displays of corporeal visibility. Television could broadcast these images of visible bodies beyond their immediate locations and local languages. To take a political stand was to strategically place the body in a visible location. Unseen political work often built the foundation for acts of visibility. Rosa Parks's visible moment of defiance on the famous bus, for example, was a reaction from a woman highly involved in and educated about the civil rights movement, not a naïve and pure human response to injustice, as the story is often mythologized. Parks's ability to respond in such a way, and the manner in which that act could come to symbolize civil disobedience, was the fruit of dogged and diligent political planning and strategizing by a large number of people. Corporeal acts, however, precisely because of their visibility, were able to become symbols for their causes, circulating as reminders of what they stood for. In this environment, displaying the body did political work. Exposing bodies both exposed power structures and offered the promise of transformation. Just as the visible corpses in the media enraged people over the injustice of the Vietnam War, citizens made their own bodies visible through corporeal protest in hopes of political change. Increasingly throughout the twentieth century, in a globalizing world, the visible body was synonymous for making power visible and envisioning alternatives.

Physical Theater Case Studies: SITI Company and Lecoq-Based Pedagogy

This discussion interfaces postmodern dance, as the work conceived from the Judson moment onward, with physical theater. While the "postmodern" label in dance, like the term "physical theater," connotes a wide umbrella of disparate yet loosely linked practices, artists and scholars have spent longer reconciling what "postmodern dance" means. Because this is a rather new pursuit for the genre of physical theater, I will use two different case studies within physical theater to demonstrate its range in relating to postmodern dance: the American-based, yet internationally inclined, SITI Company ⊙ and training based on the pedagogy of the late-twentieth-century French theater artist Jacques Lecoq ⊙. Both of these case studies include an actor-training tradition along with a performance tradition.

While SITI Company, established in 1992 by Anne Bogart and Tadashi Suzuki, both performs and hosts training sessions under its own auspices, Lecoq-based pedagogy has spawned performance companies around the world without formal continuing ties to Lecoq-based training programs. In addition to the school that Jacques Lecoq founded in 1956 and led for nearly half a century, École Internationale de Théâtre Jacques Lecoq, I include schools and programs led by students he officially instructed as teachers of his pedagogy in the term "Lecoq-based." While all of these schools and programs, including the original Paris school, continue to grow and develop in ways that interest the teaching staff and students, by gathering them together under the term "Lecoq-based," I am acknowledging that they share both a common interest in the creative power of the moving body and many pedagogical formats and exercises.

I will be focusing on SITI Company because of its acknowledged debt to postmodern dance practice ⊙. I will outline how directly applying postmodern dance practices bears on the body's ontological potential. Because I want to show the relationship of postmodern dance to the entirety of the physical theater field, I will also explore physical theater traditions that did not develop in direct connection to postmodern dance practices, such as Lecoq-based pedagogy, a practical and philosophical physical approach to creating theater born out of a European corporeal and theatrical heritage. By circumscribing the wide berth of physical theater, I will show how the two umbrellas of physical theater and postmodern dance were responding to similar aesthetic and cultural obsessions, both when there is a direct lineage of practices and even when there is not. In this way I can reveal that the commonality between postmodern dance and physical theater is not simply bound up in shared practices but rather shared philosophical embattlements.

FIGURE 07.2 Photo by Megan Wanlass. Actors training in the Suzuki actor training method at SITI Company.

THE PATH TO AGENCY

Throughout the development of physical theater and postmodern dance, both of these projects sought not a superficial change of style, but a much deeper change within the process of creating art itself—the demand for the performer to be endowed with a greater creative agency than traditional forms of Western theater and dance had allowed. Agency, the ability to act on the environment, is a power that is shaped by implicit authorizing principles. In traditional Western twentieth-century dance and theater, the most common authorizing principles were concentrated in the choreographer, director, music, or text. While the power to act may emanate from intrinsic faculties of the performer, it is deployed, shaped, and validated by the authorizing principles at work. In this way, the relationship between the performer and her context determines the agency of the performer; agency is not an isolated inherent quality that the performer unleashes at will. Both postmodern dance and physical theater envisioned performers as figures capable of asserting agency on three levels–performing their role in the piece, creating their portion of the piece, and creating the piece's overall aesthetic structure. This shared push toward expanding the role of the performer in the creative process might appear on the surface to be a reflection of a mid-twentieth-century political demand for democracy. However, democracy is too specific a formulation to describe what they actually sought. In both postmodern dance and physical theater companies structured authorial power in multiple ways. Many experimented in democratic collective creation, but many did not. Some of these body-based artists worked as interpretive performers in some pieces and as authors in others. Some collectives were run with strong leadership centered in the hands of a single person or a few, and some refused to predetermine their power structure of creative leadership altogether. In this way, these experiments are only united around the effort to unlock authoritative power from the hands of a single, stable and unquestioned source. These postmodern dance and physical theater practices made room for, and created structures within which it was possible for, the performers to determine the outcome of their creative agency. In this light, the actual impact of these practices is their refusal to take creative power structures for granted, and a commitment to the individual artist's ability to determine her own degree and expression of agency. These physical artists may choose to employ traditional relationships between performers, directors, choreographers, texts, and music, but because of the legacy of postmodern dance and physical theater, this is now a *choice*, not a given. Not actually a democratic move, these efforts merely define creative agency as something any body can access to any degree. How the individual then harnesses and shapes that creative agency is not foreclosed upon. This attitude produces not a democratic vision, but one committed to the creative agency of the individual, and refuses to define the ideal outcome of this agency. Therefore this commitment to individual creative agency necessarily circulates in a measure of uncertainty and ambiguity. Postmodern dance and physical theater carve out the path to creative agency as a two-pronged approach of cultivating creative empowerment while removing restrictions on output. This approach of putting positive pressure on creative empowerment while evacuating the output expectation creates a vacuum—an empty space brimming with potential—into which the performer/creator is poised to enter. This creative agency, however, is constantly carved within the context of a world where social agency is necessarily limited. Just as larger social and political forces shape individual agency in the world, the possibility of even participating in these aesthetic experiments is realized only because of larger forces that enable certain people to have the resources to participate in such creative endeavors. An experiment in reshaping power forces—endowing agency and releasing restriction—is made possible, in a sense, through the hypothetical context of aesthetic work because it encourages the reimagination of social vectors where the intractability of actual social forces resists it.

To try to categorize the work at Judson Dance Theater becomes quite difficult because there was no collective agreement, artistic aim, or goal. While Judson resides in the cultural memory as a *group* of innovators, they did not set out to function, nor end up functioning, as a unified artistic unit. It was the performance space at the church (the entire package of space to both rehearse and perform free of charge) that was the unifying element of the work—the potential to show it, the reason to create it, and the vacuum to fill. Initially the performances began because the students of Robert Dunn's workshop wanted to publicly show their work. In this way these were artists who knew each other and had been working together but functioned together in a loose way, not with the aim of being a formal company. While there was a certain curatorial process that initiated what work would be shown, Steve Paxton explained to Banes, "it was largely reasons of necessity that determined what had to follow what; who had time to be where when, who needed to be free at a certain time, so they could make their changes."[14] Therefore the organizing element had nothing to do with overt artistic agenda, but to more workaday personnel demands. The church was the literal and creative space that, because of its undetermined nature, allowed innovation to take place. Again, there was no democratic imperative in this project. Burt suggests that, rather than democratic, Judson and postmodern dance in the 1960s could be best described as "anarchic."[15] This does not refer to an anarchy that equals complete, unrelenting disorganized chaos. This refers rather, to the rejection of an overt organizing principle. The Grand Union, many of whom met through Judson or related work, functioned more as an ensemble but created a working structure loose enough to allow individual members to assert creative agency within the context of the group. Banes explains that as the group continued to work together, each of the group members began to develop as recognizable characters, "It is tempting to characterize Nancy [Green] as the floppy clown, David [Gordon] as the flamboyant rock star-provocateur, Barbara [Dilley] as the humorless mystic, Trisha [Brown] as the deadpan punster in words and movement, Steve [Paxton] as a gentle Jesus, and Doug [Dunn] a cross between Fred Astaire and John Wayne. All stock characters."[16] Banes goes on to warn that the focus of The Grand Union's performances was what went on in between the dancers, not the phenomenon of stock characters itself.[17] However, it is key that The Grand Union's work, in the context of an experimental ensemble with an anarchic spirit, could rely so heavily on such a traditional theatrical format as the stock character. This gives credence to the notion that what postmodern dance as a whole was working toward was an openness of possibility, not the categorical refutation of the traditional. This feature of The Grand Union's work suggests that innovation is not just the total invention of the new, but also the reapplication of the old to new contexts. In this way the true innovation is the vacuum, the potentiality, that is created through empowering the performers in an unrestricted field of possibility.

Physical theater also operates through the dynamic of the vacuum. Both SITI Company and Lecoq-based training envisions actors who are more than interpreters. Both of these pedagogical systems function via two main poles: actor empowerment and creative expansion. They both cultivate in the actor the ability to also create theatrical material, and simultaneously hold novelty as the creative ideal. In this sense "novelty" can include reinterpretations of classic work or engagements with traditional practices, but these training systems do not aim to preserve any particular tradition, and value producing the new in creative activities. SITI Company's mission statement pledges to "offer new ways of seeing and of being as both artists and global citizens."[18] Lecoq envisioned his pedagogy as that which shapes actor-creators who produce the theater of the future, theater that is relevant to his young students and will be capable of addressing the demands of a world that is not even yet in existence.[19] In this way physical theater practices, like postmodern dance practices, see their goal as a body-based reconfiguration of creative agency, emboldening performers to approach an empty space and create something new.

In both postmodern dance and physical theater, this desire for a more pervasive creative agency was born out of frustration with limitations of creative agency in existing dance and theater. In this sense, both postmodern dance and physical theater stemmed from a rebellious spirit—one that turned away from the frozen concentration of creative power. While modern dance rebelled against the strict codification of ballet to find new forms, postmodern dance rebelled against the imperative of formal codification, expressivity, and creation methods altogether. This rebellion, however, was a broad rebellion against the mandate of style, form, and content. That is to say that these artists might use codified form or certain creation techniques of their predecessors, but they blasted apart the system of authority that permitted some forms and not others. Banes writes:

> perhaps the most important legacy the Judson Dance Theater bequeathed to the story of dance was its intensive exploration and expansion of possibilities for choreographic method . . . for the generations that have followed their message was clear: not only any movement or any body, but also any method is permitted.[20]

For postmodern dance, the only imperative was that there were no imperatives.

Physical theater was born out of a moment when theater was actively searching for a technique suitable for acting. Physical theater's rebellion against the dominant technique—psychologically based acting—however, was symptomatic of a longer and increasing rebellion against concentrated and fixed power in the theatrical process, which often manifested as the director or the text. Mainstream theater often emphasized realism and therefore necessitated a focus on both the character's and the actor's psychology and emotion during the creation process. One objection to this is that since realistic acting depends on the actor's actual psychological and emotional resources, it can produce for the actor at best a narcissism and at worst a psychological harm. A second objection to the dominance of psychologically based training is that it was simply too limited. Wildly successful for plays based in realism, this training did not successfully translate into the performance of a wide array of styles. Theater artists yearned for either a technique that could function across styles, or multiple techniques that could access a variety of styles. Proponents of physical theater techniques felt that this limit was a reflection of the limited way that psychologically based training addressed the actor's instrument. Focused on the embrained mind, psychologically based technique saw the body as secondary, a servant to the creatively generative faculties of psychology and emotion. Physical theater practitioners saw this as, in effect, excluding the body from the creative process. This limitation on the actor's participation in the creative process produces just another anxiety over creative restriction that had been exacerbating Western theater for some time. Antonin Artaud (1896–1948) raged over "our superstitious valuation of texts and *written* poetry,"[21] decrying how as the written structure dictates and defines poetry, it ossifies the actual poetic energy that springs from underneath. Likewise physical theater artists rail against how the playtext clamps down a literary hold over the theater, immobilizing a physical art by the constraints of a literary one. As theater artists who saw the power of a text over a production as detrimental, including Jerzy Grotowski, they began to look to forms that privileged the body as exemplary forms of theater, such as Balinese dance and commedia dell'arte. Texts themselves were not necessarily the enemy. What physically oriented artists came to reject is the text as the only acceptable theatrical organizing principle. Similarly, physical theater artists began to reject the authority of the director as the only acceptable power structure for theatrical creation. The experimental work in collectively created formats, such as that of the Open Theater and the Living Theater in the 1960s, challenged the authority of the director in the creation process. Physical theater training, such as the work happening at Lecoq's Paris school around the same time, included permanent and significant modules in non-director-based creation in their programs. To physical theater practitioners, an actor as merely an interpreter of some text, a director's vision, or external imperative was too constrictive. The body, for these corporeally inclined artists, became the solution to combat the actor's limited creative agency. This joint desire of postmodern dance and physical theater to rebel against limited creative agency led both groups to experiment with new processes of creation, but ultimately led to the question of performer training. In order to have dancers and actors who can assume a greater creative agency and work without the restrictions of text, choreographer, and director, these dancers and actors had to be forged. In this light, technique lost its priority in performer training. It was not abandoned altogether, but it was made secondary to the ability of both the dancer and actor to become simultaneous authors and interpreters of their own work. This is why performer training is essential to the histories, strategies, and goals of postmodern dance and physical theater. While the Judson group, for instance, did not create a formal training school, the advent of the Judson group, just as Bales explained, shifted dance training dramatically and decisively. Similarly, because of these preoccupations central to physical theater, training holds a key spot, either as an in-house component to theater companies, such as SITI, or as a launching pad dedicated to proliferating a variety of companies and artists, such as the Lecoq-based schools (see fig. 07.2). For postmodern dance and physical theater, the path to agency became a path of forging performers-as-creators able to thrive in a vacuum, recognizing it not as empty, but as a space of potential.

This vacuum configuration creates agency because of the nature of its structure. External authority is removed from the vacuum, and only two factors remain: an empty space and a pressure pulling the creator toward the space. In physically based performer pedagogy, this configuration is at first artificially created in the training conditions. For example, when students in Lecoq-based training programs are working on improvisation exercises, the instructor may ask for a certain number of students to enter the performance space before telling them what they will be working on. After gathering the appropriate number of students and assigning them the improvisation activity, they begin. Here the students who are working most often volunteer—the instructors rarely tell students that it is their turn to perform. In this way the students learn that if they are going to work, they first have to throw themselves in the middle of the space, of their own volition, without knowing what they are going to do. When performers can thrive in this pedagogical situation, they are able to work without external authority, without the promise of resources or support from the outside, and develop a creative instinct to enter the center of creativity with very little feedback. This instinct forges the ability to assert agency, to self-authorize. This configuration of the vacuum teaches that the body's presence is the only requirement for creative authority, and the starting point for creative action. The effect of this vacuum is that it extends the political mandate of the visible body-as-acting body into the realm of performance.

A Philosophy of Embodiment
and Antitheory Theory

Both postmodern dance and physical theater inherently function based on the theoretical premise that the body has the ability to generate meaning, not only interpret it or act as a symbol for something else. They endow the body with a more profound and more far-reaching value than mainstream philosophy. This stance is rather radical in the twentieth-century mainstream philosophical climate where a Cartesian privilege of the mind still reigns. Physical theater and postmodern dance envision the body as agent through multidimensional capability. These artists espouse an embodied philosophy in two ways: through the way in which they actively engage the body in the creation and performance process and the way in which they reject traditional theory. Rejecting theory, in this case, refers to the various ways that these artists take a stance against the intellectual. This does not mean that they work without intellectual faculties or with no theoretical bases. This antitheory stance is actually a way to claim a positive philosophical investment in the body's capabilities. The antitheory stance does not refer to all theory, per se, but rather reacts to and encompasses the linguistic- and text-based tradition of semiotics. This tradition, both born from and sustaining of a Cartesian devaluation of the body, takes theory into a realm where capacities of the intellect and even subjectivity proper are traced back to an investment in the disembodied mind. In this tradition the body is often absent, and if present, is in a theoretical position of abjection as a foil to the capacities of the mind. For postmodern dancers and physical theater practitioners, taking an antitheory stance means to distance themselves from this anticorporeal tradition, rejecting its foundation as invalid.

Manifestations of this stance are both acts of speaking out against this theoretical tradition and simply not acknowledging it or making room for it in the creative process. In her book *Through the Body: A Practical Guide to Physical Theatre*, Dymphna Callery titles a section "There Is No Theory" to describe physical theater's overarching approach.[22] The heart of this section is that practical embodied engagement is the primary entry point into physical theater, as opposed to an overarching analytical system to which practices must be faithful. Callery goes on to distance the act of understanding from the mind: "It is only through 'doing' that you will understand."[23] While physical theater tended to collapse the literary, the textual, the intellectual, the theoretical, and the analytical into a single "threatening mind" category, postmodern dance had a more nuanced relationship with each of these categories. However, postmodern dance still took care to keep a distance from that which aligns with the "mind" node of the Cartesian mind/body binary. Even from the most nascent stages of the Judson Dance Theater at Robert Dunn's workshops, the literary tradition was regarded as a threat. In an interview with Banes, Dunn remarked that his classes explored all types of artistic activity, but purposefully paid the least attention to literature, "dance had been so super-literary in a very destructive way."[24] Dunn does not go on to say exactly what is at risk of being destroyed, but makes clear that their project was to turn away from that literary tradition.

While these stances against theory and literary engagement may seem on the surface to be an agenda of refusal for both physical theater and postmodern dance, they are actually sophisticated maneuvers toward a positive thesis. By taking an antitheoretical stance in both the articulation of their work and in their action, these artists are distancing themselves from the Cartesian binary, the bifurcation of the mind and body, and the devaluation of the body in that context. Through creating this distance, they make room for the body—they produce a philosophical space to assert an embodied, practically based, and process-oriented theoretical position. These artists advocate for the value of the body in response to a context that dismisses it by demonstrating it in space and time. This act is therefore far from a rejection of theory altogether; it is in fact an assertion of a new theoretical proposition: embodied theory. Nor is it a categorical rejection of writing or even theoretical writing. While many physical theater artists produced very little writing about their work, and most of it in the form of handbooks for exercises, many of the prominent postmodern dancers followed in the tradition of visual arts to write extensively about their work. This clarifies that the general antitheory stance does not have to do with theory as a whole, but with how the twentieth-century Western discursive-based theory left no room for the generative body. Taking an antitheory stance creates a wedge to make room for its literal and ensuing philosophical reemergence. Part of this embodied philosophy is that the body, in the act of doing, becomes the primary generator of meaning. It is through the body's work that the meaning and value are both constructed and created. An example can be seen in the way Bogart outlines the SITI Company's pedagogical debt to postmodern dance:

> These postmodern pioneers forged the territory upon which we now stand. They rejected the insistence by the modern dance world upon social messages and virtuosic technique, and replaced it with internal decisions, structures, rules, or problems. What made the final dance was the context of the dance. Whatever movement occurred while working on these problems *became* the art. This philosophy lies at the heart of both Viewpoints and Composition.[25]

If this philosophy is at the core of SITI's training, then what they borrowed from postmodern dance, by borrowing practices and principles, is a body fully endowed with creative agency.

RECASTING VIRTUOSITY

As Bogart alludes to in the above quotation, part of this move to work based on a theory of embodiment involves a recasting of virtuosity. Both postmodern dance and physical theater challenge traditional notions of virtuosity—ultimately retaining it as a value—but completely transform it. Ballet is the quintessential example of traditional virtuosity in Western dance. The ballerina has mastered a technique that is totally inaccessible to the common person. To successfully perform as a ballet dancer requires an already high level of mastery as the technique gives the illusion of working against gravity and quotidian anatomical function. The ballerina masks incredible physical effort with a style that values fluidity and lightness, making her look unbound to the earth. The virtuoso ballerino, on top of this standard level of mastery, shines through technical prowess or particularly charismatic stage presence and artistry. This style of dance is cultivated to look superhuman: above and beyond the capabilities of human bodies. In ballet, the celebration of virtuosity is a celebration of rigorous training, of an excess of the quotidian. Modern dance rebelled against this kind of virtuosity and shifted the value invested in movement. For Isadora Duncan, "natural" movement and movement inspired by images on Grecian urns became the ideal. Later on, Martha Graham embraced the body's subservience to gravity and exploited the torso's ability to contract and release. Throughout these changes in dance, virtuosity still existed, but was defined in a different manner, shifting the content of the virtuosic. In one sense, postmodern dance seemed to reject the virtuosic. Inspired by visual arts and calling on Dadaist artist Marcel Duchamp in particular, postmodern dance used everyday movement—people walking around as they do in the street, or ironing clothes—and cast nondancers in their performances (as shown in fig. 07.1). In performance this quotidian content functioned similarly to Duchamp's readymade objects by taking the everyday and framing it as "art." By virtue of the content's relationship to the privileging frame of "art," this suggests that anything can be art, and it is the frame that makes it so. In this sense the act of using the quotidian as art does two opposite things at once: it rejects that there are essential internal qualities to art that can authorize it and it deems the everyday as worthy of being categorized as "art." Postmodern work with the quotidian, like the readymades, unsettles the relationship between art, value, and authority. Far from removing value from art, postmodern dance's work with everyday movement simply denaturalized the traditional authority of value, and in so doing rejected the narrowness of traditional codified technical virtuosity in dance. Postmodern dance did, however, transfer the value of virtuosity to more basal creative faculties, as evidenced by the development of post-Judson dance training. One of the main features of postmodern dance training is that dancers are required to be able both to perform within a variety of styles and to contribute to the choreographic process. Instead of possessing a mastery of one dance style, dancers have to exhibit a virtuosity in flexibility, able to move between styles of dance and registers of creative activity.

One drawback to the demand for this flexibility is an anxiety of smorgasbordism[26] in training. Smorgasbordism is taking a little from this training, and a little from that, without delving deeply into any single system. The problem with this approach is that when an actor enters a system, they will definitely arrive at certain obstacles that will frustrate them. Much of the value of training is to learn how to deal with these obstructions and move through them. This is where training shapes the abilities and sensibilities of the performer. While smorgasbordism might give the impression that a performer can have it all, it also allows her to avoid the development that is only accomplished through challenging a sustained difficulty. Bogart suggests that smorgasbordism is "dangerous. In a way, I think it doesn't really matter what you choose to study, but you have to stick with it. The word I look for in actor training is *rigor*."[27] Joshua Monten writes about how eclecticism effects postmodern dance and acknowledges that the result may hinder the dancer more than it helps her: "to the extent that technical training is about instilling *instincts*—patterns of movement so consistent that the body can respond correctly in an instant—having too many training techniques can be quite problematic."[28] Monten recounts Twyla Tharp's attitude toward her own training: "I had been given too many options."[29] Just as such smorgasbordism in training may result in short-circuiting the individual training forms, Monten suggests that another downside to this type of training is that dancers deal with this by simply working toward a flexible body that is generalized and, as a result, "bland."[30] The responsibility to navigate an eclectic training without falling into the trap of smorgasbordism falls to the individual performer.

One of the main misconceptions of physical theater is that the goal is a physically virtuosic performance. Some of the most visible and commercial outgrowths of physical theater features amazing acts of physical virtuosity. Cirque du Soleil, for instance, highlights the work of extensively technical performers of acrobatics and other physical specializations. Despite the fact that Jacques Lecoq's school once contained the word "mime" in it, this pedagogy has long fought the misconception that it is a mime school. Mime, in Lecoq-based pedagogy, is a stylistic reference point, but more importantly it is an embodied technique of epistemological investigation. For Lecoq, mime-as-performance form is limited, only finding value in virtuosity: "Mime became ossified as soon as it separated itself from theatre. It closed in upon itself and only an emphasis on virtuosity could give it any meaning."[31] However, mime as a foundational tool for investigation, or "open mime,"[32] forms the heart of Lecoq's practical and philosophical work. "To mime is literally to embody and therefore to understand better ... miming is a way of rediscovering a thing with renewed freshness. The action of miming becomes a form of knowledge."[33] On the one hand then, Lecoq's turn away from frozen mime might be construed as a turn away from virtuosity, but, as in postmodern dance, this is simply a turn away from technical virtuosity to turn toward virtuosity in more fundamental levels of creativity. The ideal figure of the actor-creator in Lecoq-based pedagogy not only performs in various styles but also possesses the capability to understand the "motor"[34] of dramatic styles. This also includes the ability to invent new styles. In a manner similar to the Lecoq-based performer and the postmodern dancer, the actor trained in Viewpoints and Composition is valuable for her ability to work in an ensemble and contribute to the theatrical composition process in addition to working as a focused performer. All of these corporeally inclined artists engage the body beyond the surface level to recast the value of virtuosity as a somatic intelligence defined by creative flexibility, resourcefulness, and generativity.

CORPOREAL INVESTIGATIONS INTO FORM

A major expression of this joint interest in basal levels of creativity is the dedication to exploring the compositional form of performance. In the cases of both theater and dance prior to physical theater and postmodern dance, the performer only held an interpretive role: the actor had to act and the dancer had to dance. In the era of physical theater and postmodern dance, understanding form and being capable of participating in its creation becomes a necessary skill. In both of these artistic realms, form was not just a container for content; form and content could enjoy many relationships—sometimes the form was the content. Therefore, investigating form was not simply exploring structure but an entry point into all aspects of the work. Mary Overlie is a dancer from the postmodern tradition who invented the Six Viewpoints, an embodied "artistic and philosophical process, composed of the isolation of the practical materials of theater and their languages, conceptual frames and established physical and mental practices."[35] Through these Six Viewpoints (movement, story, space, time, shape, and emotion), the dancer could investigate the form and content of dance. This approach to making dance is emblematic of a new way for both dancers and actors to participate in the act of creation. Performers do not simply take for granted the form and content in which they work, but are developing techniques for making investigation of form and content part and parcel of the training and creation process. Overlie suggests:

> I sometimes refer to the Six Viewpoints as a process of "inventing the wheel backwards," because it has taken the highly organized and established idea of theater—what it is and what it is for—and inverted it, bringing the actor back to the raw materials.[36]

This process, like many other physical theater and postmodern dance strategies, sees working "backward" as a way to forge the performer and to make new work. They enter the creative process through interrogating form and content whereby performers are engaging in training and authorial activities simultaneous to their corporeal investigations, working at a foundational level of creativity.

Main strategies of this interrogation, for both postmodern dance and physical theater, are the cultivation of composition and improvisation skills. Dancers of the post-Judson era are often called on to create choreography within the dance creation process. They may be just as likely to function as the main choreographer as they are to contribute choreography to a small section or collaborate in conjunction with other dancers to the overall dance structure. This generalized ability to compose dance, not just execute it, became a mandatory skill for dancers, and they needed to be comfortable entering dance process through form. An interest in composition is what drew together the Judson dancers in the first place. The founding members, having met in Robert Dunn's workshop, were trained within a music composition tradition transposed to dance. Dunn, originally an accompanist, took composition courses from John Cage and transformed Cage's pedagogical attitude and techniques into a dance composition course that gave students wide berth to produce new dance pieces. Dunn would give the students certain prompts or constraints such as "Make a dance about nothing special."[37] This technique of giving sparse or vague constraints led the students to make a wide variety of pieces during the course. This process of making work through limited constraints became embedded into postmodern dance. The ability to work in this way became important not just for choreographers but also for all dancers, inaugurating composition skills as mandatory for the postmodern dancer.

Part of the SITI Company's creation process is Composition. Just as Bogart has acknowledged her overall creative debt to postmodern dance, she also acknowledges that Composition is an outgrowth of the work that her professor at Bard College, Aileen Passloff, wrought in applying dance composition strategies to theater.[38] Bogart's Composition is a loosely systematized process akin to how dancers in Dunn's class would work or how Judson dancers might create performance pieces. Jacques Lecoq's *auto-cours* is a similar process, whereby instructors deliver theme prompts to students, who are given an extended period of time (one week, for instance) with which to create a theater piece. As with Composition, the performers are given neither specific roles—i.e., actor, writer, director, designer—nor instructions regarding how to come up with a finished piece by the end of the rehearsal period. In this way, students forge, through struggle and experimentation, a collection of collaborative processes to create a final product. Through this repetitive exercise of creating material, physical theater practitioners mold themselves into creators, not just actors, and the physical theater field becomes shaped around this figure rather than the actor-interpreter.

Corporeal improvisation compliments compositional activity in both postmodern dance and physical theater. Brenda Dixon Gottschild argues that the overall aesthetic deployment of postmodern dance reflects the deep Africanist presence in American culture. Gottschild sheds light on the Africanist aspects of postmodern dance that may traditionally be attributed to European or Asian influences, such as "coolness, relaxation, looseness, and laid-back energy."[39] Improvisation is another example of an Africanist presence in both postmodern dance and physical theater, as African corporeal practices and African American dances, such as the cakewalk, had long incorporated improvisation. Improvisation in both physical theater and dance can be deployed as performance, creation processes, or training methods. Postmodern dance credits Anna Halprin and James Waring, teachers with whom many of the prominent postmodern dancers studied, with developing improvisation as a key component of dance. While the work in the Judson group was not focused on improvisation, The Grand Union used it extensively in both the creation process and during performance. Improvisation, not just an open-ended practice authorizing any result, functions with a variety of internal structures, and often requires the performer to be responsible to other performers, improvisational constraints, and the conditions of the performing space. The widespread use of improvisation in postmodern dance and physical theater practices demonstrates how they endowed the body with a self-authorizing creative capability. In the theater, improvisation is most typically thought of as a comic device, however physical theater technique also uses it to generate material and train performers. In Lecoq-based pedagogy, improvisation compliments modules of movement analysis and collective creation. This kind of improvisation is always accompanied by pedagogical constraints to shape the improvisation and allow the actor to develop certain capabilities during the course of the improvisation. For example, a basic Lecoq-based improvisation for the actor is "The Childhood Home." The constraint of this theme, a short narrative instruction about returning home after a long absence, along with a spatial blueprint of the home provides something for the actor to react against and something to shape the improvisation. While some dance and theater improvisations may embrace the equality of all possible results of improvisation, Lecoq's vision of the creative body in improvisation and theater stopped short of what Lecoq-trained instructor Amy Russell called "conceptual art," where postmodern dance certainly treads.[40] "Anything is possible, but not anything goes," Lecoq would say, suggesting that the territory of his poetics, while aimed at broad creativity, envisioned certain borders of theatrical activity.[41] Therefore, improvisation itself is a flexible enough tool that it functions in different ways, moving from the permissive to the strict. Both permissive and rigid structures of improvisation function through the tension between constraint and potential output. Bogart's extrapolation of Overlie's Six Viewpoints, which adds vocal viewpoints and more specific viewpoints within the space and time categories, also functions based on the improvisatory principle of constraints colliding with a field of possibility. Improvisation has the ability to create new relationships, new hierarchies, and therefore new systems of value. Improvisation and composition activities complement one another. Just as improvisation focuses on generating material, composition focuses on the act of making choices and shaping content. These are often paired to exercise the agency of the creator. The dancer and actor can access this creative agency through investing in the process of creating the form and content of both individual performance and overall performance structure.

Another formal feature of physical theater and postmodern dance alike is the convention of "showing the strings." This phrase refers to the practice of puppetry where the strings of the puppet are visible, therefore constantly marking the fact that the puppets are neither real nor animating themselves and that the power of their animation comes from elsewhere. This practice actively traces power through the visual. In other forms of performance, this practice is a way to feature the mechanism that both performs and produces the art. Banes places "showing the strings," or what she calls "baring the device," in the category of techniques of defamiliarization as articulated by Russian Formalist Viktor Shklovsky.[42] Banes describes how this technique articulated by Shklovsky, designed for "reinvigorating perception," is applicable to the many strategies of postmodern dance to make strange things familiar and familiar things strange. [43] She connects it primarily to the way that postmodern dance puts the quotidian on stage.[44] Showing the strings of the puppeteer and revealing how power is conducted in performance puts a hiccup in the illusion that the puppet is real. It defamiliarizes both ideas of an inert piece of wood and an animated person. The strings and the puppet together constantly agitate total illusion or total reality. Physical theater and dance both profit from this technique. In the 2011 London International Mime Festival, Compagnie 111/Aurélian Bory's piece "Sans objet" centered around a huge industrial robot, a moving machine with a rotating platform, and two men ⏵ ⏵. The star of the show was the machine, as the men supported the action through exploring the object. Only through the changing relationships between the moving machine and the men were tensions and emotional moments born. Throughout the entire piece, the machine shifted, disassembled, and reassembled itself. Therefore whenever a dramatic "moment" was created, the audience saw that it was made through object manipulation and the relationship of the object to space, time, sound, and performer. In effect, micronarratives, emotions, and relationships were born through shape and movement. Part of the impact of this production was the way that it completely revealed its own mechanism, quite literally in this case. Similarly, Cirque du Solei's *Kà* is performed on a massive stage that tilts, changes shape, and sprouts set pieces ⏵. The drama of scaling a mountain is created by the floor literally tilting and the actors struggling to keep from falling. Here as well, the object reveals how dramatic dynamic is being made through space and time. The Grand Union often "showed the strings" of their performance by stopping the action to talk about it or to try the action in different ways as if demonstrating how they make choices.[45] The Grand Union shows how their pieces are made as part of the piece itself. What is significant about strategies of showing the strings is that they feature the "madeness" of the performance. That is to say that these artists destroy the illusion that the piece inhabits a world of its own laws. By emphasizing the way that the piece is made, they are emphasizing *that* it is made. In this way they demonstrate their own creative powers and responsibilities as performers, pointing to agency as the heart of creative matter. Banes suggests that, "showing their own seams and process of construction, these works showed how the aura of culture could be dissipated—how art could be secularized, so to speak, brought down to earth and made part of daily life."[46] Whether "showing the strings" is an intentional political act, made to resonate beyond the purely aesthetic realm, its very fact of "madeness" makes the device press out into politics and ontology. When revealing how both something is made and power flows, the art demonstrates how it inhabits the world and how power shapes that position. It demonstrates and defines ontology as a fact of bodies existing in relation to environments.

The focus on structure and form through composition, improvisation, and showing the strings exposes the demand for performers to work at the foundations of creativity. The deeper these artists reach into the creative process, the closer they come to working toward exposing agency in general, not just agency in the creative process. By centering on the body—the material reality of participant and observer alike—and its ability to create, these physically based artists demystify the creative process, and in so doing uncover the impact the body can make on its environment and that it in fact *makes* its environment.

CONCLUSION

This demand reflects the focus of physical theater and postmodern training: the individual-as-creative engine. Instead of training dancers and actors in these traditions to be exceptional at one thing, they instill a virtuosity of creative flexibility to access the most basal levels of creativity through invention, collaboration, and performance.

Because individual agency is the goal of the performers within postmodern dance and physical theater, the performer herself, not just the performances, had to be redefined. Creative and pedagogical agency forges a democratic vision in that each creator is not limited to a single role in the creative process and can access and channel creativity in a limitless number of ways. This vision is not, however, an imperative to democratic dance and theater. Rather, it is a call for confidence in the body to fully flesh out the creative process. It is a call for the promise of unbounded individualistic agency to boldly yield new methods, new work, and a relentless present- and future-focused dance and theater.

This corporeally accessed agency is gained through transforming the performing body from a mere instrument of interpretation into one capable of determining, generating, and participating in epistemology and ontology. Lecoq is clear about how mime, in particular, is employed as an epistemological process in his pedagogy. One of postmodern dance's most significant contributions to dance is the reorientation of technique and virtuosity. By demonstrating that they have the power to determine what technique is, including the quotidian to which all people have access, they validated dance knowledge as accessible to anyone. Postmodern dancers demonstrated that anyone can be an arbiter of dance knowledge. Epistemological acts such as these are pushed into the realm of ontology because of the weight given to the foundations of creativity and pedagogy in these corporeal arts. To be so concerned with basal creativity and pedagogy is to renegotiate power in the creative process. This renegotiation focuses attention on how relationships give way to and sustain power. Therefore these acts do not look at the body in isolation, they always take into account relationality. Even in a physical theater or postmodern dance performance about isolation, it would only be given meaning because of its relationship to relationality.

In addition to their preoccupation with the "madeness" of corporeal performance, these artists employ physically based pedagogical techniques that are animated by expansive philosophical concepts. Lecoq-based pedagogy makes use of essentialism—such as an the search for essential "treeness," "wateriness," or "neutrality."[47] Lecoq does, however, acknowledges its limits:

> Starting from an accepted reference point, which is neutral, the students discover their own point of view. Of course there is no such thing as absolute and universal neutrality it is merely a temptation. This is why error is interesting. There can be no absolute without error.[48]

Overlie's Six Viewpoints, the foundation for Bogart's version, is also animated through essentialism. Overlie describes how what she calls "solid-state theater"—what we think of as a finished production—is deconstructed through the Six Viewpoints.[49] She classifies this process as an emancipation of the "the six materials or languages."[50] Through this description, Overlie suggests that "the six materials or languages" are distinct because of their essential qualities and, through these qualities, combine to produce "solid-state" theater. While the Six Viewpoints was born from and fed into postmodern dance, it might be surprising to highlight such essentialism considering the overall nonessentialist mandate of postmodern dance. However, in addition to such directly essentialist strategies of postmodern dance, even the most radical nonessentialism reveals itself to be essentialist. In her discussion of constructivism versus essentialism in feminism, Diana Fuss argues, "constructionism (the position that differences are constructed, not innate) really operates as a more sophisticated form of essentialism."[51] By classifying the Judson legacy as "not only any movement or any body, but also any method is permitted," Banes inadvertently highlights postmodern dance's version of a nonessentialism so radical it is essentialist.[52] By inherently making use of broad philosophical concepts such as essentialism and neutrality, both physical theater and post-modern dance situate themselves, their art, their process, and their pedagogy in relation to ontological issues. Because their work advocates an embodied philosophical viewpoint through enacting one, they are not just putting themselves into relation with ontological issues but also staking a claim in them. As they inherently work in this ontological register, they demonstrate how the body and aesthetics can simultaneously work through and beyond art, politics, and epistemology to ontology itself. These revolutionary philosophical acts, even when overtly confined to the aesthetic, function as attempts to overthrow the legacy of the Cartesian binary. By centering on the body, something that all people possess, physical theater and postmodern dance practitioners boldly flesh out a philosophy that embraces an ontology tapped through corporeal creativity revealing the vast reach of somatic agency.

This reach takes shape an as ontology that claims that being there *is* being. Here the fact of physicality, anchored to its environment, composes its own ontological state. This is also the ontology of the mandate of corporeal visibility—to show up is the first and most important step toward taking a political and social stand. This ontology forces a perceptual acknowledgment of the body's inherent complexities including race, gender, class, and ability. It also acknowledges that these complex bodies are given meaning through their relationship to their environment. The punch line to a joke that fails to elicit a laugh, "I guess you had to be there," suggests that being there—being physically present in context of the narrative—is the only way of actually understanding and fully participating in the world. "Fleshing out," is the battle cry of this ontological mandate for the visible body. It is a call to use the body to first find and then exceed limitation through physical struggle. This physical struggle extends to an epistemological and ontological one, resulting in a body that seeks to throw off external restriction, determine itself, assert its own ability to act, and claim its own right to authority.

NOTES

1. Thank you to the 2012 ASTR Between Theatre Studies and Dance Studies Working Group for their input on a previous version of this essay.
2. In using the term "territory," I am borrowing Jacques Lecoq's word to describe the different styles of theater that his pedagogy investigates including melodrama, commedia dell'arte, Greek tragedy and clown. Inspired by the way Lecoq's usage encourages thinking through style in spatial, almost cartological manner, I borrow this term to think about the intersection of aesthetics and philosophy as a space that has borders that can be approached, broached, penetrated, and contested.
3. Burt, *Judson Dance*, 1–2.
4. Keefe and Murray, *Physical Theatres*, 14.
5. Keefe and Murray, *Physical Theatres*, 16.
6. Keefe and Murray, *Physical Theatres*, 14.

7. Many contours of this issue are outlined by Burt in his book, *Judson Dance Theater: Performative Traces*, including the so-called "Terpsichore in Combat Boots" debate between Sally Banes and Susan Manning. Burt, *Judson Dance Theater: Performative Traces*, 7–10.

8. Diamond, "Balancing Acts," 33.

9. Bales and Nettl-Fiol, *The Body Eclectic*, 1.

10. Bales and Nettl-Fiol, *The Body Eclectic*, ix.

11. Bales and Nettl-Fiol, *The Body Eclectic*, 157.

12. Bales and Nettl-Fiol, *The Body Eclectic*, 2.

13. Ibid.

14. Banes, *Democracy's Body*, 38.

15. Burt, *Judson Dance Theater*, 11.

16. Banes, "The Grand Union," 45.

17. Ibid.

18. SITI Company website.

19. Lecoq, *The Moving Body*, 18.

20. Banes, *Writing Dancing in the Age of Postmodernism*, 211.

21. Artaud, *The Theater and Its Double*, 78.

22. Callery, *Through the Body*, 13.

23. Callery, *Through the Body*, 14.

24. Banes, *Democracy's Body*, 3.

25. Bogart and Landau, *The Viewpoints Book*, 4.

26. Thanks to Amy Russell for coining the term "Smorgasbordism."

27. Diamond, "Balancing Acts," 34.

28. Bales and Nettl-Fiol, *The Body Eclectic*, 61.

29. Ibid.

30. Bales and Nettl-Fiol, *The Body Eclectic*, 63.

31. Lecoq, *The Moving Body*, 21–22.

32. Lecoq, *The Moving Body*, 21.

33. Lecoq, *The Moving Body*, 22.

34. Lecoq, *The Moving Body*, 98.

35. Overlie, "The Six Viewpoints," 190.

36. Overlie, "The Six Viewpoints," 193.

37. Banes, *Democracy's Body*, 4.

38. Bogart and Landau, *The Viewpoints Book*, 5.

39. Dixon Gottschild, *Digging the Africanist Presence in American Performance*, 51.

40. Russell in discussion with the author, January 31, 2011.

41. Ibid.

42. Banes, "Gulliver's Hamburger," 4.

43. Ibid.

44. Banes, "Gulliver's Hamburger," 3–19.

45. Banes, "The Grand Union," 44.

46. Banes, *Reinventing Dance in the 1960s*, 12.

47. Lecoq, *The Moving Body*, 20.

48. Ibid.

49. Overlie, "The Six Viewpoints," 197.

50. Ibid.

51. Fuss, *Essentially Speaking*, ix.

52. Banes, *Writing Dancing in the Age of Postmodernism*, 211.

BIBLIOGRAPHY

Artaud, Antonin. *The Theater and Its Double*. New York: Grove Press, 1958.

Bales, Melanie, and Rebecca Nettl-Fiol, eds. *The Body Eclectic: Evolving Practices in Dance Training*. Urbana and Chicago: University of Illinois Press, 2008.

Banes, Sally. *Democracy's Body: Judson Dance Theater 1962–1964*. Ann Arbor: University of Michigan Research Press, 1983.

Banes, Sally. "The Grand Union: The Presentation of Everyday Life as Dance." *Dance Research Journal* 10, no. 2 (1978).

Banes, Sally. "Gulliver's Hamburger: Defamiliarization and the Ordinary in the 1960s Avant-Garde." In *Reinventing Dance in the 1960s: Everything Was Possible*, edited by Sally Banes with the assistance of Andrea Harris. Madison: University of Wisconsin Press, 2003.

Banes, Sally. *Writing Dancing in the Age of Postmodernism*. Hanover, NH: University Press of New England, 1994.

Bogart, Anne, and Tina Landau. *The Viewpoints Book: A Practical Guide to Viewpoints and Composition*. New York: Theatre Communications Group, 2005.

Burt, Ramsay. *Judson Dance Theater: Performative Traces*. New York: Routledge, 2006.

Callery, Dymphna. *Through the Body: A Practical Guide to Physical Theatre*. New York: Routledge, 2001.

Diamond, David, moderator. "Balancing Acts." *American Theatre* (January 2001).

Dixon Gottschild, Brenda. *Digging the Africanist Presence in American Performance: Dance and Other Contexts*. Westport, CT: Greenwood Press, 1996.

Fuss, Diana. *Essentially Speaking: Feminism, Nature, and Difference*. New York: Routledge, 1989.

Keefe, John, and Simon Murray, eds. *Physical Theatres: A Critical Reader*. New York: Routledge, 2007. Kindle edition.

Lecoq, Jacques. *The Moving Body: Teaching Creative Theatre*. New York: Routledge, 2000.

Overlie, Mary. "The Six Viewpoints." In *Training of the American Actor*, edited by Arthur Bartow. New York: Theatre Communications Group, 2006.

Russell, Amy (Deputy Director of Pedagogy, London International School of Performing Arts). Discussion with the author, January 31, 2011.

SITI Company website. Accessed August 28, 2012. www.siti.org/#.

CHAPTER 8

....

DANCE IN MUSICAL THEATER

....

LIZA GENNARO AND STACY WOLF

INTRODUCTION

....

A Chorus Line, Michael Bennett's groundbreaking 1975 musical about Broadway dancers' lives, begins in darkness. The audience hears a simple, even stereotypical vamp played on a single piano, a man's voice calls, "Again!," and the lights bump up to their full power, bright and unfiltered. The performers, their backs to the audience, face an upstage wall of mirrors, allowing those seated in the Shubert Theatre to see their bodies reflected as multiple, inevitably distorted shapes. The voice calls out, "Step kick kick leap kick touch. Again. Step kick kick leap kick touch. Again. Step kick kick leap kick touch. Again," and the dancers follow the instructions, moving almost together but not quite in unison. "Okay, let's do the whole combination, facing away from the mirror," instructs the voice, which the audience might surmise is the director's: "A five six seven eight!"[1] A full orchestra joins the piano, filling the theater with composer Marvin Hamlisch's brassy, half-step-rising, excitement-inducing melody. The dancers turn 180 degrees and explode into a combination etched in Broadway musical theater's cultural memory.

A Chorus Line, a collaboration among director and choreographer Bennett, composer Hamlisch, lyricist Edward Kleban, and book writers James Kirkwood and Nicholas Dante, won nine Tony Awards, five Drama Desk Awards, and the Pulitzer Prize for Drama. It became the longest running musical on Broadway for almost 20 years until it was surpassed by *Cats* in 1997. It bankrolled the Public Theatre where it was workshopped and premiered well into the 21st century, launched actor Priscilla Lopez to stardom, reignited Donna McKechnie's career, and gave performance opportunities to hundreds of dancer-actors over its fifteen-year run.[2] The 2006 revival made virtually no changes in the script, music, or choreography and became a kind of performed love letter to Bennett, whose life was cut tragically short by AIDS in 1987.[3] Add the hundreds of national and international touring companies and the thousands of regional, semiprofessional, community, and high school productions, and *A Chorus Line* has been performed by many performers who no doubt deeply identify with the roles they take on. Moreover, the show has been seen by countless more who are touched by the representation of hard-scrubbing, relentlessly determined, dedicated, and passionate dancers and who likely make the analogy with any situation where few are chosen from the many who aspire to be chosen.

In addition to its unique, deceptively casual opening moment, *A Chorus Line* broke other musical theater conventions that had solidified (or to some, ossified) by the mid-1970s. Its set, designed by Robin Wagner, consisted only of a simple white line painted across the stage parallel to the proscenium and a series of three-sided flats that rotated to a blank wall, a mirror, and the art deco design used in the glittery finale of "One." Its lighting design by Tharon Musser shaped the show's emotional journey and signified each character's private moment of contemplation and memory with a special saturated color. *A Chorus Line* was also the first show to use a computerized light plot and among the first to eschew an overture, a front curtain, and an intermission.

The musical's workshop process, as well, was completely unique to Broadway at the time and was even considered experimental in more avant-garde circles. Veteran Broadway dancers Tony Stevens and Michon Peacock invited a number of their peers, many of them out of work in the depressed economy of New York City in the early 1970s, to gather to eat, drink, and tell stories about their lives. They intended to create an opportunity for dancers to develop work of their own and included Michael Bennett, whom the dancers respected and who had a successful track record and could get things done. The meeting encouraged Bennett to pursue an idea he had for a "dancers' musical," and he began editing and shaping the stories into a series of monologues, each to be delivered in the fictitious setting of an audition in which the director requires the dancers trying out for the chorus and bit speaking parts to talk about themselves.[4] The conceit provides a psychologically realistic way for characters to sing solo numbers about themselves and how they came to be dancers. In this way, every song in *A Chorus Line* functions as a character's typical first number according to mid-20th-century Broadway musical theater conventions: the "I am/I want" song, which tells the audience who the character is, how she sounds—both in terms of the music and the lyrics—and what she wants. The songs and stories are ordered by the dancer's age, from three-years-old to now, so that they trace a larger trajectory of a Broadway dancer's life from childhood through adolescence and adulthood. Near the end of the show, one of the dancers gets injured and is carried out to the hospital, and the remaining auditioners must face the painful question, which Zach the director asks, "What you would do if you had to stop dancing?" The ensemble answers, led by the feisty, irreverent Diana in a moment of dark melodious contemplation, "What I Did For Love."

The finale of *A Chorus Line*, an elaborate, Busby Berkeley–style production number, is at once a rousing celebration and an ironic comment on what has occurred over the preceding ninety minutes. The chorus sings how "she's the one," referring to the leading lady whom the audience never meets. And this crew, each of whom the audience has grown to care about, is virtually undistinguishable from one another in their identical top hats and tails. After an entire show that values each individual person's story, life, hopes, and desires, the ending reminds the audience that the Broadway chorus dancer's ultimate role is to blend in, all differences and distinctions erased.[5]

A Chorus Line made Broadway dance and a gypsy's life visible in a new way. Though the producers, creators, and audiences recognized the metaphorical power of the audition, of striving to be seen as an individual, of dreams fragile and possibly unfulfilled, the show featured dance as the subject as well as the means of communication and an element of beauty.

In some ways, then, *A Chorus Line* might be seen as the crystallization of Broadway dance history from the 1940s to then.

Though the field of musical theater studies has exploded since the early 2000s, little has been written about dance in the context of the Broadway musicals. Scholarly examinations of the genre have focused, for example, on people and their roles, especially composers and lyricists, librettists, directors, producers, and performers, and on the musicals in their historical context, whether to trace the creative process or to analyze from various identities' positions. This essay seeks to redress that absence, with a focus on Broadway musicals since the "Golden Age" of the 1940s.[6] If musicals are made of music, lyrics, spoken word, design, and dance, how does dance function in the form?

Like all Broadway musicals of the mid-twentieth century, *A Chorus Line* tells a story, and the script (also referred to as the book or the libretto) serves as its key organizing document. As Richard Rodgers and Oscar Hammerstein II—possibly the most important and influential creators of Broadway musicals—asserted, the book is everything. Even when a choreographer's style is idiosyncratic and unique—such as Agnes de Mille's privileging a woman's point of view, Jerome Robbins's comic virtuosity, or Bob Fosse's gender-bending distortions—the dance emerges from and supports the musical's text. Every musical theater choreographer, from George Balanchine to Andy Blankenbuehler, creates movement material related to the libretto.[7] Dance in musical theater, then, is always created in relation to the musical's story or its narrative, and since the 1940s, choreographers have used dance in a number of ways, including (1) dance to reveal a character's psychology; (2) dance to tell a piece of the story; (3) dance to express an unspoken aspect of the libretto; (4) dance to transition to another scene; (5) dance to allow the characters to express themselves; and (6) dance to present an idea or feeling metaphorically or abstractly. In many cases, a specific dance functions in more than one way.

Analyzing dance in musical theater is particularly challenging.[8] First, like all dance, musical theater dance is fleeting and ephemeral. What does the scholar see to analyze the work? What is the archive that remains for analysis and interpretation? Must a scholar experience the show—in person or on tape—to be able to write about it responsibly? Second, musicals are, as Bruce Kirle argues, always in process and constantly reinvented with each new production.[9] The nominal opening night of a musical, the day after which the *New York Times* publishes the review of the show, is only one show among many.[10] The Broadway cast album, frequently the only remaining document of the show, is typically taped before the show opens. Which performance, then, is the best one to study? Opening night? Closing night? And how does a scholar get access to a certain performance? Third, the choreographer is only one among many collaborators. *A Chorus Line* may have been Michael Bennett's brainchild, but the show is ultimately the result of complex collaborations among the choreographer and a score of others: composer and lyricist, director and designers, producers and marketers, and of course, the audience. (Interestingly and perhaps not surprisingly, some of the most successful and influential choreographers were also directors: Agnes de Mille, Jerome Robbins, Gower Champion, Bob Fosse, and Michael Bennett. By combining the role of choreographer and director, the creative team is reduced by one artist and unified around one central vision, thus reducing the degree of contentiousness among the collaborators.) In the commercial theater world of Broadway, the expense of the production and need to sell tickets above all puts a certain pressure on the artistic team and gives the producers more power than anyone.[11] On whom does the scholar focus? Whose point of view is authoritative in the musical's creation?[12] Finally, because musical theater is a popular form of entertainment that aims to communicate directly with its audience, every element of a musical is functional and meant to be legible. Every gesture, every movement phrase, every dance number intends to communicate something specific about the character, the world, and the story.

In what follows, we offer some answers to these questions. How does dance function in musical theater from the 1940s to today? What does dance do? How does it communicate? How does it work in tandem with the other communicative and expressive modes of the musical theater, including spoken script, music, lyrics, and design? Our examples are organized by choreographer, although we realize that each dancer's actualization of choreography—such as Donna McKechnie's incomparable "Mirror Dance" as Cassie in *A Chorus Line*—is essential. Still, we credit Bennett as both the imagination behind the dance and director of the dancer. Our examples are loosely chronological to convey how choreographers, consciously and not, respond to what's preceded them, though we frequently loop back to de Mille, who originated many of Broadway dance's functions. Dance, in the words of theater scholar Marvin Carlson, is "haunted."[13] Some choreographers overtly quote their predecessors; others strive to create new movement vocabularies; some use dance conventionally; others work to find new purposes for dance.

DANCE TO EXAMINE CHARACTER IN PSYCHOLOGICAL TERMS

In her *Oklahoma!* (1943) dream ballet, "Laurey Makes Up Her Mind," Agnes de Mille expands and enhances the character of Laurey, the musical's female principal and ingénue. De Mille's inventive movement schemes and her insistence on casting the ballet with dancer-actors rather than with Broadway chorus dancers introduced a new kind of dance to the commercial theater.

The ballet explores Laurey's subconscious sexual desires and internal struggle in her attraction both to Curly, the play's hero, and to Jud, the villain. Though de Mille didn't invent the use of dance to examine a character's psychology—George Balanchine, Albertina Rasch, and Seymour Felix created psychological dream ballets in musicals prior to *Oklahoma!*—her dream ballet humanized Laurey by exposing her hidden desires.[14] De Mille posits the revelation that Laurey, while frightened and repulsed by Jud, is also sexually attracted to him. Absent the ballet, this aspect of Laurey's character would not be explored in the musical and so is necessary for the audience to understand Laurey's feelings and actions.

The ballet is structured as a dream that begins with a pas de deux between Laurey and Curly, culminates in their wedding, and turns into a nightmare when Laurey realizes that she has in fact married Jud. Jud carries Laurey to a saloon, where she is taunted by the "Post Card Girls," who are Laurey's imaginings of saloon hall girls. Rather than simply creating a rowdy saloon dance, de Mille employed Louis Horst's method of introspection-expression and created a modernistic representation of a dance hall girl. Horst, influenced by Freudian psychology and the study of the subconscious, developed the method as a technique for discovering movement. Using Freudian analysis as his map, he devised a system for the choreographer to examine inner feelings, to delve into personal interior landscapes, and to discover "inward-turning," "in-pointing" movement. Just as a psychoanalyst leads a patient back to childhood in order to discover suppressed feelings, Horst developed the method of introspection-expression to guide the choreographer to develop movement that originated from an essential, personal emotion.[15] With the monumental success of de Mille's *Oklahoma!* dances, the psychological ballet became a standard element in musical theater.

De Mille also used dance in musicals to make personal and political statements. Due to a highly attuned dramaturgical approach and a consummate ability to analyze text, de Mille could put forth her point of view while never diverting from the narrative goals of the libretto. From her earliest days as a self-producing female soloist, she engaged in a highly autobiographical approach to her work, making dances that addressed the concerns of women. Her "Venus in Ozone Heights" ballet from *One Touch of Venus* (1944), for example, is a scathing parody of the stultifying lives of women in World War II suburbia. In Act II scene 3, the Goddess Venus is about to embark on a life with a mid-twentieth-century American, Rodney. He regales her with his description of all the fun they are going to have as a married couple living in Ozone Heights, a new real estate development on Staten Island:

> Rodney: Every bungalow's just the same; they got an electric incinerator, and a radio, that looks like a fireplace. And a fireplace that looks like a radio ... The most important thing of all—a dandy big yard for the kiddies when they start to come along.
> Venus: (wryly) You better look for something with a lake; with me, you might get swans.[16]

Rodney sings, "Waiting for our wooden wedding, Golly how the time will fly, Stealing kisses in the kitchen, Holding hands while the dishes dry." After the song Venus questions if she is in fact the right wife for Rodney: "I can't sew or weave or milk a goat." Rodney replies, "When I get through with you, you'll be a Number One homebody!" Venus asks, "What will it be like—you and I—in five years?"[17] The stage directions describe the beginning of the ballet:

> The life of Ozone Heights closes in on her—the neighbors, the children; Rodney dividing his attention between the lawnmower and the comics. Stealthily the creatures of her magic world invade the scene. She resists them, but they will not be resisted; now ancient Greece is real and Ozone Heights the myth. Rodney vanishes, the humdrum houses vanish, only the vast open sky remains. Venus, once again the goddess, returns to her people.[18]

De Mille depicts "the creatures of the magic world" as nymphs and satyrs engaged in a bacchanalia that culminates in Venus being carried aloft to Olympus.

The ballet is less a psychological examination of character than it is a dance-pantomime depicting the culmination of Venus's twentieth-century visit to earth from her point of view. As the sole means by which the audience gains information about Venus's life in Ozone Heights, the dance functions as both narrative tool and, for the women in the audience, as a means of identification with the character and a cathartic release from lives of children and housekeeping.

As the ballet begins, children's voices are heard and Venus is revealed in ordinary housewife garments seated in front of one of three identical suburban homes.[19] De Mille's original choreographic scenario indicates that Venus, along with two more wives in their respective houses, perform household chores as children play outdoors and an adolescent couple engages in a flirtation all to the accompaniment of a pastoral arrangement of "Wooden

PHOTO 08.1 Mary Martin in *One Touch of Venus* amid nymphs and satyrs in the "Bacchannale" section of Agnes de Mille's, "Venus in Ozone Heights." The far left of the photo includes the romantic couple from the act one ballet "Forty Minutes for Lunch."

Wedding." The wives' husbands return home from work, kiss them on the cheek, and settle in with their evening newspapers and beers while the women sew, knit, or darn. Suddenly a women's vocal chorus is heard from offstage and nymphs appear in the yard calling eerily and rolling in the grass—there is a flash of heat lightning. Photographs of the original production depict the nymphs writhing on the floor, backs arched, heads thrown in sexual abandon. The husbands become jumpy and close windows against the impending storm as the stage fills with Baccantes and bewitched mortals. De Mille's notes indicate that Venus, called from every direction, "Dances wildly and tears off her clothes ... Rodney brings her a shawl ... She stands up with an ancient and terrible cry." As the suburban houses fade away the scene changes to "a wilderness ... ancient Greece."[20] As the ballet continues, more satyrs and nymphs enter, executing a primitive foot stomping as Venus exits. De Mille writes, "The enormous and terrible figures of the Zodiac appear in the heavens ... Venus appears naked, translucent, Olympian, awful and walks in wreathings of mist against the stars."[21] Finally, she is carried off high overhead by two satyrs in a whirl of dancing bodies.

The first half of the ballet depicting Venus in suburbia is at once a severe condemnation of bourgeois utopias, a stark depiction of contemporary marriage, and an insightful but tragic foreshadowing of what was to become the accepted role of women in the 1950s. It is no surprise that de Mille, a newlywed war bride, was preoccupied with the idea of domesticity; it is to her credit, however, that she discovered a way to express her preoccupation in a musical. Both "Venus in Ozone Heights" and "Laurey Makes Up Her Mind" offer a side of the play's heroine that would go unacknowledged minus the ballets. De Mille supplies voyeuristic thrills inviting audiences to experience Laurey's dream life and Venus's alternate universe. As an artist who moved between the dance and theater worlds, de Mille created innovative movement vocabularies for dance. Compelled by modernist movement invention prevalent at the time, she challenged herself to invent movement and developed a distinct dance style.

DANCE TO NARRATE THE STORY

De Mille and Robbins established musical theater's choreographic paradigms and paved the way for a new breed of choreographer on Broadway.[22] They both explored how to insert dance seamlessly into a musical play, but for Robbins, that smooth integration eventually took precedence over movement innovation and personal social commentary.

In Jerome Robbins's first two shows, *On the Town* (1944) and *Billion Dollar Baby* (1945), he followed de Mille's example and created psychological dream ballets that explored a character's psyche. His early imitation led a critic in the *Evening Bulletin* to describe his work as "Run of de Mille."[23] As reviewer Edwin Denby wrote of the dances in *On the Town*, "They generally tell a little pantomime story but you don't think of them as distinct from the rest of the show. They generally emerge from the stage action and melt into it again so as to give value to a scene rather than a hand to the dance. Often they express a sentiment too, much as Miss de Mille's musical comedy dances do."[24]

In time, though, Jerome Robbins focused less on movement innovation and social commentary and more on creating dances that developed organically from the text, employing Group Theater and Method acting principles and techniques.[25] Maintaining a strict adherence to time and place, Robbins's dances emerged out of the fabric of the libretto. Whereas de Mille manipulated texts in order to insert her ideas, Robbins developed his dances as a natural extension of the text.

By 1948 audiences were becoming weary of the dream ballet, and as Robbins gained his footing he developed a system of choreographing for musicals that was separate from de Mille's. For example, he wrote and co-directed with George Abbott *Look Ma I'm Dancin'* (1948), a musical based on his experiences touring with a ballet company. Critic Jerry Gaghan wrote of the dances, "For once in a musical, someone doesn't have to go into a dream, a trance, or a funk to start a ballet sequence. The people in 'Look Ma' dance because they are dancers."[26]

In *High Button Shoes* (1947), Robbins's "Keystone Ballet" demonstrated what would become a defining aspect of his work: comic virtuosity and showmanship. The *New Yorker* reported, "Mr. Robbins probably hasn't Miss de Mille's intensity of purpose, but he is certainly her superior as a conscious humorist."[27] The show takes place in 1913 and revolves around con men Harrison Floy and Mr. Pontdue, who cheat an unsuspecting family, the Longstreets, out of a large sum of money, and take Fran Longstreet to Atlantic City, where they are discovered and pursued by police. The ballet advances the plot in narrative pantomime. It begins with Keystone Cops on patrol and a group of turn-of-the-century bathing beauties out for a day at the beach. A family of crooks appears, tricks Floy and Pontdue into giving them the absconded money, and a chase ensues. With a line of bathhouse doors as the primary element of the chase hijinks, the characters run in and out, and what begins as amusing combinations of characters appearing through the doors becomes riotous until finally, a gorilla emerges.

Original cast member Helen Gallagher recalled, "When that gorilla came through it was like a blow. It was almost as if the audience had socked you the laughter was so enormous."[28] Richard P. Cooke reported in the *Wall Street Journal* that the ballet "reduced the audience to a pulp of laughter."[29] Dance critic John Martin wrote in the *New York Times*, "During the first half of its foolery, when it follows the Mack Sennett tradition fairly closely, it may not cause you to break any ribs laughing, but when it gets along toward the end and goes berserk in a tradition nearer to Dali than Sennett it becomes cock-eyedly hilarious."[30]

Robbins's sharp storytelling, perfectly timed jokes, and embodiment of comic ideas and the number's precise structure make the ballet a tour de force. Still, its movement draws on standard period lexicons and pastiche and makes no attempt at innovation. Rather, Robbins immersed himself and his dancers in silent film comedies and tried to "capture the rhythm, style and content" of the old movies.[31] From early in his career, when as a member of Gluck-Sandor's Dance Center he was exposed to actors from the Group Theater and introduced to acting techniques developed by Constantine Stanislavsky, Robbins always researched extensively before choreographing a musical.[32] Consequently, his musical theater dances, with the exception of *West Side Story* (1957), lack an identifiable movement style.

Robbins's brand of dance integration became the primary choreographic method in the "Golden Age" of musicals, with strict adherence to time, place, and the plausibility of dance in the scripted context as primary goals. De Mille also relied on these techniques of using the script and building on it to create a danced, realistic world, for example, in "The Farmer and the Cowman" from *Oklahoma!* Engaging American country dance expert May Gadd to coach her dancers in authentic square dance, de Mille then employed distortion techniques and layered the square dance with her own personal movement style.[33] The result is a musical number that feels entirely natural even as it builds to a dance break in which de Mille's original movement lexicon dominates.

Robbins used a similar approach for his "Small House of Uncle Thomas" ballet in the *King and I* (1951). Assisted by Cambodian dance scholar, Mara Von Sellheim, Robbins drew on the authentic steps of Cambodian dance while at the same time injecting considerable humor to make the form palatable for an American commercial theater audience. He was able to create US-based choreography that seemed to be authentically "other" and also insert vaudeville and borscht belt gags and jokes, even in a movement form as defined and austere as Cambodian dance.[34]

Most choreographers embraced Robbins's story-driven paradigm for making musical theater dance during and after the "Golden Age." In an interview with Svetlana Mckee Grody, for example, Michael Bennett explained, "A dance number has to get you from what happened before to what happens next . . . dances are never arbitrary."[35] Still, some "arbitrary" dance numbers, according to Bennett's long-time collaborator Bob Avian, had "value because of dynamics alone." He added:

> If a show or film needs a goose, you try and build a number that's maybe a tangent, but it will give you a lift . . . . We did this in the show *Promises, Promises* (1968), at the end of the first act. We put in a number called the "Turkey, Lurkey" number. It was the big number that ended the first act because we needed it, in terms of entertainment.[36]

The number occurs at an office party when three secretaries, played by Donna McKechnie, Baayork Lee, and Margo Sappington, break into a dance based on 1960s social dances. By the end of the number the entire office party is dancing. Though the dance does not extend or enhance the plot, it's crucial to provide a moment of delightful, nonsensical dance fun, and an energy jolt at the end of the act.

DANCE TO EXPRESS AN UNSPOKEN
ASPECT OF THE LIBRETTO

Using dance to express an unspoken aspect of the libretto is one of the most sophisticated uses of dance in the musical theater. In 1966, twenty-three years after de Mille created the "Post Card Girls" in *Oklahoma!*, Bob Fosse presented another version of the dance hall girl in the musical number "Big Spender" in Cy Coleman and Dorothy Fields's *Sweet Charity* with a group of taxi dancers at work in a Times Square dance hall. ⊙ Following the paradigm established by de Mille, Fosse privileged the dance's dramaturgical integrity and was also keen to develop a unique movement style. Moreover, Fosse created the role for his then-wife, Gwen Verdon, a brilliant jazz dancer trained by Jack Cole.[37] The plot of *Sweet Charity* revolves around a dance hall hostess, Charity Hope Valentine, and her search for love. Dramaturgically, the number presents the dance hall girls at work in the Fandango Ballroom, as Fosse explained in an interview with dance critic Arthur Todd: "Before I started my choreography I spent a great deal of time observing what really went on in the remaining half-dozen dance halls in New York. They are as close to prostitution as anything you can find."[38] Fosse's depiction of the women in "Big Spender" is, as actor Helen Gallagher (Nickie in the original production) said, "As close as the show got to saying we were hookers"[39] because the show's dialogue or lyrics never overtly state dance hall hostesses' work as prostitution, but only hint as much. As Nickie tells a new girl, "A cute lookin' thing like you can always go into the extra-curricular business,"[40] and there are several other mentions in the script of an "other business," a vague allusion to prostitution. In "Big Spender," lyricist Dorothy Fields allows the audience to literally fill in the blanks:

What do you say to a ...
How's about a ...
Laugh.
I could give you some ...
Are you ready for some ...
Fun.
How would you like a ...
Let me show you a ...
Good time.[41]

Fosse's choreography, though, makes it clear. The women's work is stripped of its musical comedy sugar coating and a gritty, explicit exposition—the physicalization of Charity's admission that the Fandango Ballroom is "not-a-nice-place"—is presented.[42] The women, displayed against a rail at the downstage edge of the stage, stand gazing aggressively at the audience. Their insolence is palpable as they squirm from one distorted pose to the next appearing as painted, broken dolls with an attitude. They mount the rail splaying their legs and daring prospective customers to buy what they are selling. *New Yorker* critic Joan Accocella wrote of the taxi-dancers, "You sense that anyone who spent a little time with one of these women would have to go to the doctor afterward."[43] Charity doesn't appear in the number, and later insists, "All I sell is my time."[44] Her innocent, hopeful nature is the key marker of her character in spite of the realities of her life, and she remains isolated from any association with the sex trade. That she does not appear in "Big Spender" supports the musical's assertion that she is different from her co-workers.[45]

De Mille's *Oklahoma!* choreography in "Many a New Day" offers another example of a dance that provides information apart from what is written in the text. In the scene leading into "Many a New Day," Laurey and her girlfriends have just witnessed Curly walking with another girl. Laurey sings "Many a New Day" to save face in front of the women and to promote the image of herself as not tied down to any one man.[46] The lyric demonstrates how Laurey covers her feelings of disappointment after Curly has chosen another girl. The women listen, then they join in the singing, and the vocal section of the song ends in a clean musical button that signals applause. Laurey then moves to the side of the stage as the dancing chorus begins an extended dance break in which each woman's personality is expressed in moments of solo, duet, or trio dancing. Dramaturgically, the content of the dance is not an obvious choice, but de Mille expands the moment by presenting a community of women in consort with Laurey. They support her statement of independence and express sisterhood in singing, but then in dance they also demonstrate their individual personalities within the group, presenting different models of vanity as they primp and take pride in their appearances. One movement phrase, performed by a small group, emphasizes their calculated flirtatiousness as they lift their skirts, flick their feet, and adjust their corsets, pretending that they have no awareness of how attractive these movements make them to men. "The Girl Who Falls Down," originated by Joan McCracken, appears as a giddy child in her awkward and inappropriate glee, not yet fully a woman, as she tries to fit in with the group. A stern mother hen character watches her closely, shooting her glances that insist she give up her childlike behavior and conform to the group. Finally, a "sexually adventurous" woman races through the group shaking a red petticoat. The women ignore this aberration from their homogeneous community, except for the child, who imitates her shaking petticoat movement with abandon. Laurey returns to center stage to complete the song, swats at the girl to stop her silly behavior, and the mother hen offers another determined glance that insists that the child return to the fold. She does so, however, as the women exit in a flock stage right, the child is momentarily left behind, then follows them, executing a joyous leap just before exiting the stage.

The dance reveals much about Laurey, about the women in this community, and about societal expectations. The sung music in combination with the dance break expands the audience's knowledge of Laurey's experience in a place where the population lives by a set of circumscribed mores but where, in keeping with the pioneering spirit of the American west, individual strength of character is prized.

WEST SIDE STORY: INTEGRATED DANCE, CHARACTER EXPRESSIVENESS, AND MOVEMENT INNOVATION

West Side Story, which Robbins created with Leonard Bernstein, Arthur Laurents, Stephen Sondheim, and co-choreographer Peter Gennaro, stands as an aberration in Robbins's musical theater career because the dances, while adhering to Robbins's requirements of coherence with the time, place, and period, were also examples of movement innovation in a modernistic sense. Robbins's fusion of ballet, jazz, and 1950s social dance idioms was so astonishing and revolutionary that after the opening of *West Side Story*, he formed a new company, Ballets: USA, and continued to develop *West Side Story*'s movement vocabulary for the concert stage.[47]

More than any other book musical, *West Side Story* employs dance as a narrative tool equal to book, music, and lyric. The opening danced prologue establishes the territorial conflict between the opposing gangs, the Jets and Sharks. Originally conceived to be sung, the opening's lyrics were eventually eliminated in favor of a pure (that is, only) danced narrative that establishes from the very start of the show that dance will function as a storytelling device.[48] In addition to the "Prologue," "The Dance at the Gym," which uses dance at a social gathering to express animosity and competition between the Jets and Sharks, illustrates the immediate attraction between Tony and Maria, the beginning of their romance, and the disapproval of their communities. The "Somewhere (Ballet)," which depicts a utopian community in which Jets and Sharks exist together in peace and harmony, is another moment of pure dance. These numbers are not radical or unprecedented in terms of musical theater dance; Agnes de Mille created ballets with similar narrative and characterological functions, as had Robbins. What is different is that *West Side Story* contains three major dance sequences that advance the plot without any spoken or sung words. These extended moments of dance are not intended to provide comic release or social commentary, or even psychological investigation of character. In addition, "America," with choreography by Peter Gennaro, and "Cool" present extended dance breaks in a more conventional manner.

Finally, in *West Side Story*, Robbins developed an original movement style by using modernist distortion methods to create a dance lexicon rooted in the social dances of urban 1950s America. Anna Sokolow was also experimenting with a fusion of jazz and modern dance at the time, and Robbins was likely aware of her work. Artists influence each other, and those with considerable expertise, like Robbins, would readily absorb, transmit, and transmute choreographic ideas. This sharing and borrowing does not at all diminish artistic achievement.

DANCE TO TRANSITION TO ANOTHER SCENE AND A CINEMATIC SENSIBILITY

Dance as a transitional device evolved in conjunction with scenic technology over the second half of the twentieth century. From the mid-1940s to the mid-1960s, the "in one"—a dance or short scene that occurs far downstage in front of a drop—was the typical technique for a scene change or reveal. "Steam Heat," the number in *The Pajama Game* (1954) that launched Bob Fosse's Broadway career, is an "in one." Positioned at the top of Act II, the number occurs during a union rally, where three pajama factory workers (played by Buzz Miller, Carol Haney, and Peter Gennaro) perform a song and dance about "Gettin' Hot" in response to employee demands. Though it serves no narrative purpose, the show-stopping number reengages the postintermission audience and provides a seamless reveal when the drop flies out and the next scene begins.

As stage technology advanced, Robbins's use of dance as a transitional device evolved, too. In *West Side Story*, for example, the transition from the bridal shop to the "Dance at the Gym" was seamless and occurred "a-vista" in full view of the audience. As the bridal shop set withdrew, the stage became populated with dancers and magically the audience was transported to a new scene.

Gower Champion advanced the technique of "continuous staging" further by introducing a cinematic sensibility to the stage.[49] Describing his concept for *Carnival* (1961), Champion wrote, "There are no bridging scenes-in-one for set changes, no blacking-out for set changes, no house curtain, no show curtain."[50] He conceived of the ensemble as a troupe of "Roustabouts" who performed "a-vista" transitions between scenes. Champion's dancers were "instruments, like keys on a typewriter, to tell a story," notes John Anthony Gilvey.[51] Champion stated emphatically, "I hate dancing for the sake of dancing in a show. It should be used to aid the story line,"[52] echoing de Mille and Robbins's core methods. Champion added, "In one scene in *Carnival*, dancers are used to suggest a kaleidoscopic view of a carnival through the eyes of a disillusioned girl,"[53] just as de Mille led the audience into Laurey's mind. As a director, Champion was theatrically innovative and astute, and as a choreographer he depended on tried and true musical theater dance routine-making. While his dances were entertaining, were well structured, served the play's narrative and character development, and functioned as effective transitional devices, they were not innovative in a modernistic sense. Gilvey, in *Before the Parade Passes By*, describes Champion's movement vocabularies in *Carnival* as "vaudeville and social dance steps merged with marching, acrobatics, and a range of circus routines in a deceptively simple narrative."[54] When asked to describe "the source of his psychokinetic impulse," Champion replied, "I just go for the hand."[55]

With Champion, dance on Broadway broke from a modernistic approach that used modern dance methods, distortion, and introspection-expression. The artistic environment that encouraged the movement innovations of de Mille, Fosse, Jack Cole, and Michael Kidd was replaced by Robbins's trend toward dance realism. The question, Why are they dancing? required an answer that supported a diegetic approach to movement. Choreographers favored dance in which characters knew that they were dancing, in scenes where dance actually took place. For Champion, this approach meant using known showbiz dance lexicons.

Champion's ascendance as one of the most important director-choreographers on Broadway occurred as Robbins transitioned to full-time ballet-maker at New York City Ballet and as de Mille became preoccupied with writing and running her own company. Over the course of Robbins's theatrical career, he gained more authority as director-choreographer, and, after *West Side Story*, his use of dance in musicals decreased as he focused on the musical's spoken and sung drama. In his last two Broadway book shows, *Gypsy* (1959) and *Fiddler on the Roof* (1964), dance exists fundamentally as a realistic extension of the libretto.[56] The vaudeville numbers in *Gypsy*, featuring child star Baby June, are choreographed as if designed by June's overbearing mother, Rose, with classic vaudeville dance vocabularies of basic tap and acrobatics.[57] The brilliance of the numbers is not found in innovative movement expression but in Robbins's witty ability to tell the story using a "common fund" of dance lexicons.[58] Similarly, the dances in *Fiddler on the Roof* are diegetic, emerging organically out of the dramatic scene and employing Jewish traditional dance.[59]

With *A Chorus Line* (1975), Michael Bennett succeeded in creating the ultimate dance show within the Robbins's inside out, realistic, Stanislavskian paradigm. The show tells the story of a group of dancers at an audition. The audience sees them dance and hears them tell their stories in dialogue and song. The characters dance because they are dancers, in dance clothes at a dance audition.

A Chorus Line's "Mirror Dance," performed by the character Cassie—an almost starlet who, after failing in Hollywood, returns to New York to reclaim her career as a Broadway chorus dancer—offers an opportunity for the audience to experience and identify with Cassie's relationship with dance.⏵ She tells Zach, "I'm putting myself on the line," belts out her war cry, "God I'm a dancer, a dancer dances!" and performs a solo tour de force in front of a massive, three-way mirror reflecting multiple images of her. Like Robbins's ballet "Afternoon of a Faun," a pas de deux in which two ballet dancers meet in a studio and perform a duet while maintaining their gaze on a mirror reflection of themselves, Cassie demands, "All I ever needed was the music and the mirror and the chance to dance for you."[60] She then performs a dance for herself, and the audience sees the required narcissism of the trained dancer. The number is both fascinating and disturbing in Cassie's desperate striving for perfection over an ephemeral form in a tragically short career. The "Mirror Dance" is a six-minute marathon, a feat of stamina and tenacity that ends in a sequence of technically precise double turns performed along the line on stage. Moreover, Cassie is balanced on the line between success and failure and triumphs in her execution of the dance, baring her soul and left gasping for air. Much of the dance is performed facing up stage, her back to the audience and her front reflected in the mirror that not only captures her image but also the image of the audience watching her. In the performance, Donna McKechnie danced for the Shubert audience while Cassie danced for the audience in her mind. When Cassie is among the dancers finally cast in the "musical," the audience is likely to notice and celebrate her achievement. The "Mirror Dance" gives the audience a visceral, real-time experience of Cassie's life force in dance.

In the finale of A Chorus Line, the audience witnesses all of the characters they have come to know performing a flashy, showbiz chorus number, replete with top hats and tails, a pre–de Mille, Busby Berkley–, or for some spectators, Ned Wayburn– or Chester Hale–inspired precision dance in which each individual subsumes into the greater whole of the line. However, the audience has just completed an intimate journey with each dancer, and as they appear one at a time and fall into line, the audience celebrates their achievement. They are no longer cogs in a wheel, they are individuals and the audience experiences the sure-fire thrill attached to any number of this kind, but all the more intensely for knowing the dancers. And yet, as the bodies multiply on stage, it becomes increasingly difficult and then impossible for the audience to identify who is who. The number gains velocity and energy and becomes more beautiful and thrilling. The dancers make precise formations, pinwheels, and the requisite kicklines, and the whole subsumes the individual in a bittersweet expression of the chorus line's and A Chorus Line's raison d'être. Bennett succeeds in fusing Robbins's diegetic approach with his own expression of the individual characters.

DANCE AS METAPHOR

Dance as metaphor, frequently composed from non-naturalistic movement, is another function of musical theater dance. In Bloomer Girl (1944), de Mille created "The Civil War

Ballet."[61] A thinly disguised piece of American propaganda, *Bloomer Girl* depicted an idealized re-vision of American freedom. Set in 1861 in the northeastern city of Cicero Falls, New York, the show advances three major themes: freedom for women, freedom for a runaway slave, and freedom of political choice. While de Mille was interested in the Broadway musical's formal integration, she also believed in dance's expressive power capable of delivering complex ideas. "The Civil War Ballet" is a self-contained dance, unconnected to the musical play. In fact, the dance is so self-contained that it was often cut in revivals. After the dance, the narrative resumes when the eligible male population of Cicero Falls departs for battle. Frustrated by the ballet's lack of connection to the libretto, a critic writing for *The Commonweal* noted:

> In a Civil War Ballet she [de Mille] presents the war in its entirety with balance, feeling, striking design, some beautiful dancing. In an exact space of time the struggle is experienced and emerged from by the audience. Nevertheless, when the curtain again rises, on the final scene, what is our surprise to discover that for the characters of the play the war has not even begun . . . . The facts of the just previous ballet are denied; its technical significance is denied; it has not been.[62]

Though it is an isolated moment, the ballet foreshadows the experience of women during war; it is a metaphoric dance in which the townsmen bid farewell and depart for battle, the women cope in their daily lives absent the men, long for husbands and sons, and ultimately rejoice at the men's return. In the final section of the ballet, de Mille stages a joyous reuniting of the men and women, using American country-dance vocabulary and formations. By the 1840s, country dances had been replaced by the polka, the mazurka, and the waltz.[63] Why then, does de Mille choose the historically inaccurate American country dance as the basis for her movement inventions? The answer lies in what de Mille is trying to convey. She uses American country dance to create a metaphoric dance language evoking democratic ideals. In *The Playford Ball: 103 Early English Country Dances*, Kate Van Winkle Keller and Genevieve Shimer explain its symbolic patterns:

> The country dance is a group dance in which there is interaction between two or more couples and it is a democratic dance in that the couples often change positions in the set and take turn leading the figures. Only in a culture in which the absolute power of the king had been tempered by the demands of democracy could such a dance form flourish. And flourish it did! From 1650–1850 it was a significant medium of social expression for rising bourgeois society.[64]

De Mille uses the country dance to serve as a metaphor for American democracy; in 1944, the image of freedom resonated strongly with audiences.

Michael Bennett's "Tick Tock" dance from *Company* (1970) is another example of dance as metaphor as well as dance to express the unspoken. ▶ *Company* explores the marriages of a group of couples and their relationship with their bachelor friend Robert. In Act II Robert takes April, an airline stewardess, to his apartment to have sex. April and Robert engage in an awkward (spoken) exchange, and they hurriedly undress. The stage directions read, "Kathy [an ex-girlfriend of Robert's played by Donna McKechnie] appears and begins to dance.[65] Throughout the number Robert and April's voices are audible; Kathy's dance expresses the difference between "having sex" and "making love";[66] and the title, "Tick Tock," represents the short time April and Robert have together and their rushed need to connect. The following spoken lines are interspersed throughout the dance.

APRIL: I think I could love him.
ROBERT: If only I could remember her name.
APRIL: He smells so good.
ROBERT: She tastes so good.
APRIL: I love you, I love you . . .
ROBERT: I . . . I . . . [67]

The audience witnesses April's initial excitement and eventual disappointment and Robert's intimate, private, and unflattering side. After declaring her love in a moment of passion, April is frozen by Robert's stumbling, "I . . . I . . . ." and McKechnie stands with her back to the audience, arms raised over head, lowering her arms after each "I." April's pain is palpable as McKechnie's arms descend; Robert's words are body blows. His inability to connect emotionally continues with the song that follows, "Barcelona," during which he half-heartedly

PHOTO 08.2 Michael Bennett's "Tick Tock" created for *Company*. The solo dance, performed by Donna McKechnie, depicts a woman experiencing sexual intercourse. (The costume in the photo was changed during previews).

invites April to stay with him and skip her flight to Barcelona. To his surprise, she agrees, and he is faced with spending more time with a woman for whom he has no affection.[68]

As with "Laurey Makes Up Her Mind" and "Big Spender," dance is used in "Tick Tock" to express the taboo subject of sex. What is deemed to be too explicit for the spoken word to express finds "voice" in dance. Each number serves a different function, though. "Laurey Makes Up Her Mind" examines Laurey's psyche, revealing her sexual desires and thereby enhancing her character; "Big Spender" explicitly tells the audience in movement that the women at work in the Fandango Ballroom are selling more than a dance; and "Tick Tock" translates the act of sex and April's disappointment and resignation into movement while addressing one of the primary themes in *Company* regarding Robert's love life: why he can't or won't find a mate and whether a psychological issue is blocking his ability to have a relationship.

ABSTRACT DANCE IN A MUSICAL'S NARRATIVE

If de Mille introduced a modern dance aesthetic to the commercial stage, Bill T. Jones in *Spring Awakening* (2006) and Steven Hoggett in *Once* (2012) ushered in a postmodern/contemporary dance aesthetic. For *Spring Awakening*, the story of repressed youths in pre–World War I Germany, Jones introduced a movement phrase in the first moments, performed by the ingénue, Wendla. The movements demonstrate Wendla's absentminded exploration of her developing body and sexual awareness. Throughout the show, the phrase is reperformed, morphing on different characters as a bodily illustration of their sexual confusion and frustration. Dance adds a layer of meaning; thus Jones returns to de Mille's system, rejecting Robbins's realistic approach and embracing the potential of innovative and abstract movement as metaphor.

Similarly, Hoggett's dance expands emotional content. While the use of dance to intensify meaning and emotion of sung text is standard practice in musical theater, Hoggett's movement lexicon is abstract and more evocative than literal. As comparison, in *West Side Story*, Robbins stages "Officer Krupke" as a vaudeville number, drawing on what would have been a familiar movement lexicon to 1950s audiences. The Jets perform broad comic gestures, smacking each other over the head with a newspaper, dropping to their knees in a "Mammy" finish, all the while tossing off a litany of 1950s psychobabble on the crisis of juvenile delinquency. The vaudeville "schtick" supports the comic irony of Stephen Sondheim's lyrics and gives the audience permission to laugh (while it articulates a harsh indictment of the system in which these boys are stuck). In contrast, Hoggett's abstracted choreography does not signify a specific place or time or presume a certain response; like the lyrics, the movement is poetic, its meaning veiled. Each audience member must interpret both lyric and movement, as they're not necessarily related to each other but rather independently explore and express the emotional content of the dramatic moment. This practice moves the staging away from literal representation and allows for an abstract movement experience that enhances meaning through the medium of movement.

Once tells the story of how a man, called Guy, and woman, Girl, each recovering from a failed romance, form a healing bond through a shared passion for music. As their relationship deepens they sing, "If You Want Me." Guy disappears in to the shadows while Girl and two other women perform a trio dance, each in her own world executing fluid movement phrases that evoke longing. The lyric speaks of Girl's ambivalence, doubt, and caution while her body expresses her longing:

> Are you really here or am I dreaming
> I can't tell dreams from truth
> For it's been so long since I have seen you
> I can hardly remember your face anymore
> When I get really lonely and the distance causes only silence
> I think of you smiling with pride in your eyes a lover that sighs
> If you want me satisfy me[69]

Does each woman represent an embodiment of Girl? Or do they represent anyone who experiences the conflict among passion, desire, and doubt? Hoggett does not attempt to answer questions; instead he presents a visual palate to be interpreted at will. Moreover, in this dance, it's impossible to assess whether the characters are consciously motivated to dance or not. In *A Chorus Line*, Cassie dances consciously and she bares her soul. In *Oklahoma!*, Laurey dances unconsciously, in a dream, revealing thoughts she can't admit to herself. In contrast to Robbins's aesthetic and methodology, which aimed for explicit narrative clarity above all, Hoggett's method is the newest installment in the methodologies developed by de Mille, adopted by Bob Fosse and later by Bill T. Jones.

CONLUSION

In the twenty-first century, musical theater choreographers continue to build on the uses of dance invented and practiced by de Mille and Robbins, by Fosse and Champion, and by Jones and Hoggett. As artists explore the relationships among the different elements of musical theater—spoken text, music and lyrics, dance, and design—they continue to reemploy old uses of dance and imagine new ones. Every musical—even those that revel in dance's ambiguities—communicates with its audience. Every musical employs movement with purpose: dance tells a story, dance reveals character, dance represents place and time, dance expresses emotion, dance evokes a metaphor. It is up to the dance scholar of musical theater to decipher, interpret, and analyze those meanings.

NOTES

1. Kirkwood, Bennett, et al., 7.
2. See McKechnie; Turan.
3. See *Every Little Step*.
4. Viagas, Lee, and Walsh, 24–38.
5. On *A Chorus Line*, see, for example, Mandelbaum; Wolf, *Changed for Good*, 117–126; Sandoval-Sánchez, 83–102; *Broadway: The American Musical*.
6. We have chosen the 1940s as the starting point for this chapter. While much wonderful and important dance happened in Broadway musicals before the 1940s, conventions were newly established after Agnes de Mille's *Oklahoma!* in 1943. We're also using the term

"Golden Age" as a chronological marker and not an assessment of certain shows' aesthetic value. Scholars continue to debate the usefulness of the label and whether *Oklahoma!* should be credited as the beginning of a new stage in the Broadway musical's development. Many look to *Show Boat* (1929), to *Pal Joey* (1940), or reject this narrative altogether. This chapter is bracketing that debate. See, for example, Sternfeld and Wollman, 111–124.

7. On Dunham, see http://www.pbs.org/wnet/freetodance/biographies/dunham.html (accessed December 3, 2012). On Blankenbuehler, see http://www.ibdb.com/person. php?id=32280 (accessed December 3, 2012).

8. See Gennaro, "Evolution," 45–61.

9. See Kirle.

10. Moreover, now reviewers typically see a show in the last few nights of previews. No longer do they actually write about the opening night's performance.

11. See Adler.

12. Each of the four creators of *West Side Story* famously credited himself for the idea; moreover, co-choreographer Peter Gennaro's crucial contribution was written out of the musical's history, and only now is he receiving credit for his work. See Herrera, 231–47.

13. See Carlson.

14. On "dream ballets" see McClung; Kislan.

15. Horst, 89. Introspection-expression, this "inward-turning," abounds in the work of Martha Graham and is one of the principle defining physical characteristics of the early American modern dance canon.

16. Weill, Perelman, and Nash, 2.3.25.

17. Weill, Perelman, and Nash, 2.3.25.

18. Weill, Perelman, and Nash, 2.3.27.

19. The ballet "Venus in Ozone Heights" was not recorded in its entirety; only "The Bacchanale," the second part of the dance, was taped for the *de Mille Project* in a studio reconstruction. The analysis of the ballet's first part is based on photographs and stage directions from the original production, examination of the original dance music, and letters from Agnes de Mille to Kurt Weill describing her plans for the ballet scenario. Taking into account de Mille's admission that "my scenarios always simplify as I get into rehearsal," sources have been cross-referenced to assemble an understanding of the ballet. See Agnes de Mille to Kurt Weill.

20. De Mille to Weill.

21. De Mille to Weill.

22. For complete analysis of two central paradigms established by de Mille and Robbins see Gennaro, "Evolution," 45–61.

23. *Philadelphia Evening Bulletin.*

24. Denby.

25. See Gennaro, "Evolution," 51.

26. Gaghan.

27. *The New Yorker.*

28. Gallagher.

29. Cooke.

30. Martin.

31. Rice.

32. Gennaro, "Evolution," 51.

33. Easton, 256.

34. Gennaro, "Evolution," 52.
35. Grody and Lister, 95.
36. Grody and Lister, 95.
37. See Wolf, *Changed*, 53–90.
38. Todd.
39. Gottfried, 179.
40. Simon, 92.
41. Simon, 16–18.
42. Simon, 94.
43. Accocella, 324.
44. Simon, 99.
45. See Gennaro, "Broken Dolls." This analysis of "Big Spender" is based on the 1969 Universal Pictures film version of *Sweet Charity* directed and choreographed by Bob Fosse.
46. This analysis of "Many a New Day" is based on the 1979 Broadway revival of *Oklahoma!*, NYPL for the Performing Arts, *MGZIC9-5246.
47. For further reading on Ballets: USA, see Jowitt, 293–318.
48. For further discussion of the creation of "The Prologue" see Wells, 69.
49. Gilvey, 88.
50. Gilvey, 88.
51. Gilvey, 108.
52. Gilvey, 88.
53. Gilvey, 88.
54. Gilvey, 104.
55. Gilvey, 72.
56. Gennaro, "Evolution," 53.
57. Gennaro, "Evolution," 53.
58. On de Mille's employment of a "common fund" of dance and modernist distortion practices, see Beiswanger, 609–614.
59. Lawrence, 338.
60. Bennett et al, 95–96.
61. Gennaro, "Evolution," 54.
62. "Review of *Bloomer Girl*."
63. Keller and Shimer, viii.
64. Keller and Shimer, viii.
65. This analysis of the "Tick Tock" dance is partly based on Donna McKechnie's performance in the 1993 Concert Version of *Company*. http://www.youtube.com/watch?v=jyiZH4HjU98 (accessed May 31, 2013).
66. Sondheim and Furth, 94.
67. Sondheim and Furth, 94.
68. See Wolf, "Keeping Company."
69. Walsh, Hansard, and Irglová, 31–32.As of 2013, one of dance's primary functions is as transition; for example, Steven Hoggett employs dance regularly to move from scene to scene, as does Andy Blankenbuehler in *Bring It On* (2012) and the revival of *Annie* (2012).

BIBLIOGRAPHY

Accocella, Joan. "Dancing in the Dark." *Twenty-eight Artists and Two Saints*. New York: Pantheon Books, 2007.

Adler, Steven. *On Broadway: Art and Commerce on the Great White Way*. Carbondale: Southern Illinois University Press, 2004.

Beiswanger, George. "New Images in Dance: Martha Graham and Agnes de Mille." *Theatre Arts* (October 1944): 609–14.

Broadway: The American Musical. DVD. Directed by Michael Kantor. Public Broadcasting System, 2004.

Carlson, Marvin A. *The Haunted Stage: The Theatre as Memory Machine*. Ann Arbor: University of Michigan Press, 2003.

Cooke, Richard P. *The Wall Street Journal* (October 11, 1947). Karl Bernstein Collection, *High Button Shoes* Scrapbook, MWEZ x n.c.22,058-22,059. New York Public Library.

De Mille, Agnes, to Kurt Weill, 14 and 16 July 1943. De Mille Collection, Dem A, Folder 7, Dance Collection. New York Public Library.

Easton, Carol. *No Intermissions: The Life of Agnes de Mille*. New York: Little, Brown, 1996.

Edwin, Denby. *Herald Tribune* (January 21, 1944). Karl Bernstein Collection scrapbook, Clippings, MWEZ x n.c.22,076-22,077. New York Public Library.

Every Little Step. DVD. Directed by James D. Stern and Adam Del Deo, 2009.

Gaghan, Jerry. George Abbott scrapbooks, MWEZ, n.c. 19,581. New York Public Library.

Gallagher, Helen. 2006. Interview by Liza Gennaro. Transcript. New York Public Library Oral History Collection.

Gennaro, Liza. "Broken Dolls: Representations of Dancing Women in the Broadway Musical." Accessed May 31, 2013. http://www.bodiesofwork.info/Bob%20Fosse.html.

Gennaro, Liza. "Evolution of Dance in the 'Golden Age.'" In *The Oxford Handbook of the American Musical*, edited by Raymond Knapp, Mitchell Morris, and Stacy Wolf, 45–61. New York: Oxford University Press, 2011.

Gilvey, John Anthony. *Before the Parade Passes By: Gower Champion and the Glorious American Musical*. New York: St. Martin's Press, 2005.

Gottfried, Martin. *All His Jazz: The Life and Death of Bob Fosse*. Cambridge, MA: Da Capo Press, 1998.

Grody, Svetlana McLee, and Dorothy Daniels Lister. *Conversations with Choreographers*. Portsmouth, NH: Heinemann, 1996.

Herrera, Brian Eugenio. "Compiling *West Side Story's* Parahistories, 1949–2009." *Theatre Journal* 64, no. 2 (2012): 231–47.

Horst, Louis. *Modern Dance Forms: In Relation to the Other* Arts. New York: Dance Horizons, 1961.

Internet Broadway Database. "Andy Blankenbuehler." Accessed December 3, 2012. http://www.ibdb.com/person.php?id=32280.

Jowitt, Deborah. *Jerome Robbins: His Life, His Theater, His Dance*. New York: Simon & Schuster, 2004.

Keller, Kate Van Winkle, and Genevieve Shimer. *The Playford Ball: 103 Early Country Dances*. Pennington, NJ: A Capella Books; Northampton, MA: Country Song and Dance Society, 1990.

Kirkwood, James, Michael Bennett, Nicholas Dante, Marvin Hamlisch, and Edward Kleban. *A Chorus Line: The Complete Book of the Musical*. New York: Applause, 1995.

Kirle, Bruce. *Unfinished Show Business: Broadway Musicals as Works-in-Process*. Carbondale: Southern Illinois University Press, 2005.

Kislan, Richard. *Hoofing on Broadway: A History of Show Dancing*. New York: Prentice Hall Press, 1987.

Lawrence, Greg. *Dance with Demons: The Life of Jerome Robbins*. New York: Berkley Books, 2001.

Mandelbaum, Ken. *"A Chorus Line" and the Musicals of Michael Bennett*. New York: St Martin's Press, 1989.

Martin, John. "The Dance: Musicals." *New York Times* (November 9, 1947). Karl Bernstein Collection, *High Button Shoes* Scrapbook, MWEZ x n.c.22,058-22,059. New York Public Library.

McClung, Bruce D. *Lady in the Dark: Biography of a Musical*. New York: Oxford University Press, 2007.

McKechnie, Donna, with Greg Lawrence. *Time Steps: My Musical Comedy Life*, with Greg Lawrence. New York: Simon and Schuster, 2006.

PBS. "Katherine Dunham." *Free to Dance: Biographies*. Accessed December 12, 2012. http://www.pbs.org/wnet/freetodance/biographies/dunham.html.

Philadelphia Evening Bulletin (September 16, 1947). *High Button Shoes* Scrapbook, MWEZ x n.c.22,058-22,059. Billy Rose Theatre Collection. New York Public Library.

"Review of *Bloomer Girl* by Harold Arlen and Yip Harburg." *The Commonweal*, October 27, 1944.

Rice, Vernon. "Robbins Viewed Old Films for Mack Sennett Ballet." *New York Post* (October 14, 1947). Karl Bernstein Collection. *High Button Shoes* Scrapbook, MWEZ x n.c.22,058-22,059. New York Public Library.

Sandoval-Sánchez, Alberto. *José, Can You See? Latinos On and Off Broadway*. Madison: University of Wisconsin Press, 1999.

Simon, Neil. *Sweet Charity*. New York: Random House, 1966.

Sondheim, Stephen, and George Furth. *Company: A Musical Comedy*. New York: TCG, 1996.

Sternfeld, Jessica, and Elizabeth L. Wollman. "After the 'Golden Age.'" In *The Oxford Handbook of the American* Musical, edited by Raymond Knapp, Mitchell Morris and Stacy Wolf, 111–24. New York: Oxford University Press, 2011.

The New Yorker, Karl Bernstein Collection, *High Button Shoes* Scrapbook, MWEZ x n.c.22,058-22,059, NYPL.

Todd, Arthur. *Dancing Times* (London, March 1996). Bob Fosse, Clipping File. New York Public Library.

Turan, Kenneth. *Free for All: Joe Papp, the Public, and the Greatest Story Ever Told*. New York: Doubleday, 2009.

Viagas, Robert, Baayork Lee, and Thommie Walsh. *On The Line: The Creation of "A Chorus Line."* New York: William Morrow, 1990.

Walsh, Enda, Glen Hansard, and Markéta Irglová. Once. New York, TCG, 2012.

Weill, Kurt, S. J. Perelman, and Ogden Nash. *One Touch of Venus*. New York: Little, Brown, 1944.

Wells, Elizabeth A. *West Side Story: Cultural Perspectives of an American Musical*. Toronto: Scarecrow Press, 2011.

Wolf, Stacy. *Changed for Good: A Feminist History of the Broadway Musical*. New York: Oxford University Press, 2011.

Wolf, Stacy. "Keeping *Company* with Sondheim's Women." In *The Oxford Handbook of Sondheim Studies*, edited by Robert Gordon, 365–83. New York: Oxford University Press, 2014.

....

CHAPTER 9

DANCE AND THEATER
Looking at Television's Deployment of
Theatricality through Dance

....

COLLEEN DUNAGAN

INTRODUCTION

....

THE inclusion of dance across various genres of television programming dates back to its commercial beginnings, and dance, as a result, has played a fundamental role in television's assimilation of theatrical conventions. In this chapter, I argue that on television, dance's association with theatrical performance and its conventions is so strong that it calls to mind the notion of live performance whenever recognizable dance movement vocabularies appear, even when obvious theatrical conventions and/or contexts are not immediately apparent. Dance's ability to indicate theatrical performance is directly linked to the history of television production and content as well as to choreographic conventions and the history of popular representations of dance in the United States.

The chapter first addresses how television's appropriation of theatrical content affected and was informed by early production practices and technology. I demonstrate how television's early practice of one-camera, static, frontal shots and live broadcasts echoed the perspective and performer/audience relationship found in the proscenium theater, as well as how production quickly moved to three-camera shoots, on location shooting, and the ability to broadcast prerecorded shows.[1] Throughout the chapter I employ examples that reveal how, despite these shifts, dance tended (and still often tends) to be shot in accordance with theatrical conventions and performed in a manner more closely aligned with the direct address of live performance. Looking at both historical and contemporary examples, I reveal how dance is often filmed so that it is framed on three sides by profilmic elements and/or other characters—much like a narrative ballet in which the corps de ballet are arranged along the sides of the stage, framing the choreography and serving as an on-stage audience.[2] In addition, the dancing is often staged to signal that there is one front to the space in which the characters perform, even when the action is filmed from additional angles. Further, choreographic conventions such as body facing, the direction of the gaze, and the direction and angle of the movement all work to reinforce this frontal perspective and mimic the dynamics of live performance.

I then turn to the concept of *liveness* as an element of theatrical performance, arguing that this sense of liveness joins forces with another kind of liveness within the television format. This secondary, or perhaps parallel, sense of liveness is one that arises in association with the presentation of *real* people doing *real* things—the presence or display of reality. I place these concepts of liveness and reality in conversation with those of performance, examining the ways in which performance is about presenting something for and to one's audience that is, at once, both an illusion (a role being embodied) and a truth (an actual person performing). Drawing on both television shows and commercials, I draw attention to how the presence of performance, the not "real," simultaneously signals the embodiment of a crafted role and the presence of "reality," of "real" people performing.[3]

Despite this connection to the "real," film musical studies scholars have argued that the staging of dance as a performance suspends the linear logic of the visual text to indulge in a moment of associative meaning, a moment of qualitative excess.[4] These qualitative moments align with Maya Deren's concept of *verticality*, moments in which the horizontal logic of the narrative is suspended in order to explore the qualities of images, ideas, or other aspects of the televisual text.[5] This creation of excess and investment in the qualitative is due, in part, to the manner in which moments of *verticality* present themselves as moments of display, as moments in which actors quit pretending to be the character and perform. However, performance both serves as the crafting and embodiment of excess and signals the embodiment of subjective interiority and expression.

On television, dance as performance not only creates moments in which characters perform *expression* through movement but also allows for moments of televisual expressivity, a chance for the medium and individual television shows to shape their own identities through the movement. However, while dance on television draws attention to the medium of television as a kind of formal presentation, it also participates in and benefits from the naturalization of performance through filmic acting styles in order to engage television viewers in popular discourses about social identities and their expression through movement. I argue that, through its deployment of theatrical conventions, dance on television sets the stage for understanding reality and identity as constructed and embodied through actions, encouraging viewers to understand social identity as a performance. As a result, television serves as a site of negotiation, a space for modeling different possible realities.

This relationship between dance and television—in particular dance's ability to invoke theatrical conventions within a variety of television genres—is significant because it points to the ways in which mass media in the United States has affected twentieth-century discourses surrounding performance and identity. While concepts of performance and identity are widely theorized, less work has been done on the intersections between dance and television and their respective strategies and conventions. As a result, the role of dance and the effect of its presence within television genres have been absent from much of television studies and theories of its genres and their conventions. This chapter offers an analysis of dance's role in bringing theatrical performance conventions to a variety of television genres in an effort to highlight the previously unaddressed significance of dance within this broadcast medium and contribute to a growing body of literature on televised dance.

TELEVISION AND THEATRICAL PERFORMANCE

All television was broadcast live for the first three years of production because it was not practical to record the television signal.[6] While there were occurrences of stations live-broadcasting filmed materials, the technology was limited in its capacity, and the process of procuring films was costly.[7] Thus, as television developed, like radio, it favored live programming and in fact modeled its programming largely on that of radio.[8] As a result, live performance forms have comprised a significant portion of television's content, dating as far back as the late 1920s and the 1930s, when the medium was still an experimental form. During this initial experimental period, broadcasts were often visual versions of radio programs; one such example is the *Fox Trappers Orchestra* (CBS 1928).[9] Furthermore, when commercial television finally began in the mid-1940s the influence of radio was still prominent.[10]

During the early years of commercial television (1948–52) most programming still consisted of live broadcasts such as sporting competitions, newsworthy events, operas, and symphony concerts.[11] However, programming also included shows based on other forms of live entertainment, such as vaudeville, variety, and theater.[12] This early programming was performed in studio in a manner that followed the conventions of live theater. Vaudeville acts, variety shows, dramas, and comedies were staged with a clear frontal perspective and were formats that tended to employ forms of direct address. In addition, vaudeville and variety shows relied on hosts who introduced the acts and created a through-line. The shows' hosts were clearly situated on a studio sound stage and used direct address to speak and perform to and for the television audience. This emphasis on live performance and its theatrical conventions as a model for television content was reinforced by programming such as news broadcasts, where newscasters would speak directly to the audience, and by the airing of sports events, which while not directed at the television audience, called to mind the experience of being a spectator sitting on the sidelines, or in the stands, and witnessing the game.

Unlike film, which recorded events both fictional and actual as they happened in order to allow viewers to voyeuristically peer into worlds other than their own, television consciously directed its content to the viewers and emphasized its ability to bring disparate spaces together into the same *time*. While narrative film conventions developed around the idea of maintaining the "fourth wall," and thus the illusion of a fictional world, television conventions were modeled after live performance and, as a result, included both performing to and breaking the fourth wall.[13] The sense of performance conveyed by television's production conventions and the theatrical conventions of its broadcast content instilled a sense of liveness by association—the liveness associated with theatrical entertainment and presentation—into the television medium.[14]

To demonstrate television programming's appropriation of the theatrical, I offer an analysis of an excerpt from *The Lawrence Welk Show,* featuring the polka "Shall We Dance." The opening shot of the sequence reveals Welk in his suit with his conducting baton in hand, standing in front a slightly sparkly blue curtain and looking directly at the viewers as he announces the act.

Welk tells the in-studio and the television audiences it's a "pleasure to have a polka with Barbara Boylen, naturally we call on Myron Floren to provide the music with the title song

FIGURE 09.1 *The Lawrence Welk Show*—Welk introduces Barbara Boylen dancing the polka to Myron Floren's accordion performance of "Shall We Dance." Screen shot.

of his album *Shall We Dance.*"[15] He then turns to his left and slightly upstage to ask Floren if he's ready and counts him off with a 1, 2, 3, 4 accented by his baton; the camera cuts to a frontal shot of Myron centered in the shot and facing the camera as he smiles and begins to play "Shall We Dance" on his accordion. As he continues to play, Welk and others dance the polka around him.

The scene is shot largely from downstage center; however, close-ups and highlights are shot on an angle from a downstage left perspective. At various points, an audience is heard clapping and/or laughing at the antics of the dancers, who ham it up a bit at the end. Thus, the whole presentation of the musical act is framed as just that—a presentation, a performance both for the in-studio audience and the at-home television audience. While the dance performed is a social form that is typically intended for participation rather than spectatorship, the history of social and ballroom dances in the United States includes a long practice of exhibition dances performed in social dance venues.[16] In addition, musicals, such as those of Fred Astaire and Ginger Rogers, draw on this practice and feature ballroom forms as performance (for example, *Shall We Dance*, RKO 1937).[17] At the same time, this example demonstrates the blurring of television roles and everyday identity, as the show is named after its host, Lawrence Welk, and the congenial atmosphere of the show and its cast members' interactions create a sense of personal relationship.

As the Welk example demonstrates, within US mass media social dances have historically functioned as both participatory social activities and as performance forms. Furthermore, when viewed within the context of television programs, such as the *Lawrence Welk Show*, social dancing participates in the modeling of social identity, providing tangible markers of class, gender, and ethnicity. While these markers may serve as way of establishing a shared identity between the performers and some of the viewers, the markers also provide audience members with a clear set of bodily skills that may be acquired through practice and thus offer a means of allowing viewers to *change* their identity.[18] Clearly, changing *how* one moves is not going to change one's biological gender, race, or ethnicity; however, it can allow viewers to assume some of the social markers of these forms of identity, as well as to *perform* a class identity other than their own.[19]

Television commercials and their use of dance have become particularly apt demonstrations of this dynamic. Advertising began incorporating dance as early as 1948 (Lucky Strikes), and dance has continued to play a role in advertising up to the present day. Even when the programming formats that had once provided a venue for dance on television died down in the 1970s, TV spots continued to feature dance.[20] Advertising has promoted a notion of identity as something one performs, which it does by providing the viewer with new possibilities and asking the viewer to consider whether or not what the ad offers suits the viewer's perception of who she/he is or wants to be and offering the product as a sign of that identity. In this way commercials promote identity as a construction, as a conglomeration of signs that can be picked up or discarded at will.[21] Thus, I argue that advertising has played a prominent role in promoting the notion of identity as a performance. This notion of identity as a performance complicates the deployment of theatrical conventions and its relationship to liveness and reality, which can be seen in the following analysis.

Pepsi's Shakira Tango commercial (2003) demonstrates this dynamic as it is achieved through dance and its deployment of theatrical conventions.[22] The Pepsi spot feels like a minifilm; it appears to be shot on location, and it offers the television viewer a voyeuristic lens into the world of the ad. The opening shot reveals the outside of a small grocery store at night and then quickly cuts to the inside of the store to reveal a slightly "nerdy" grocery clerk restocking the shelves after hours. When the radio announces Shakira's new song, he stands and looks down the aisle. The camera cuts to a shot from his perspective, revealing the object of his gaze: a life-size cardboard cutout of Shakira wearing low-riding black leather pants, a black bra, and a sheer lace and mesh overcoat. He slinks down the aisle toward her (the cutout), taking her into his arms and dipping her.

When she whips up out of the dip to face him, she is suddenly flesh and blood, which she emphasizes by gazing at him with a kind of lazy, sultry hunger as she runs her right hand down the side of his face. He responds by cautiously peering out toward the television audience before they begin their tango.

While much of the dance is shot from one side of the couple or the other, so that they are both visible in the shot, there are two very distinct moments where a shot-reverse-shot is used so that first Shakira and then the man dance facing the camera directly, which stands in for the partner who is not visible.

Near the end of the ad the viewer sees the couple dancing in a ballroom embrace as they travel, turning around themselves, down an aisle. The ad cuts to a shot from outside the window as the man dances into view while embracing the cardboard cutout of Shakira. As he casually turns his head, he suddenly realizes that there is a group of people standing outside the window staring at him, and he does a double-take.

FIGURE 09.2 Pepsi's "Tango" commercial—The grocery store clerk slinks toward the cardboard cutout of Shakira. Screen shot.

FIGURE 09.3 Pepsi's "Tango" commercial—As the cutout of Shakira comes to life in his arms, the clerk breaks the fourth wall to look hesitantly at the television audience. Screen shot.

FIGURE 09.4 Pepsi's "Tango" commercial—Employing the shot-reverse-shot to create direct address, Shakira dances toward the clerk and the at-home television viewers. Screen shot.

FIGURE 09.5 Pepsi's "Tango" commercial—Employing the shot-reverse-shot to create direct address, the clerk dances toward Shakira and the at-home television viewers. Screen shot.

FIGURE 09.6 Pepsi's "Tango" commercial—Caught in the act, the clerk realizes he is being watched through the window of the store as he dances with Shakira's likeness. Screen shot.

He pauses, staring at them as the music dies down, until the music abruptly restarts and he runs off in embarrassment with the cardboard Shakira in his arms.

THE INVOCATION OF THE REAL

On the one hand, the Pepsi commercial's structure and content encourage viewers to feel as though they are voyeuristically watching the interaction. The establishing shot creates the impression that the camera allows the audience to enter into the clerk's world, rather than the clerk performing for the audience. This impression is reinforced by his actions; in the first few shots of the ad, he looks around to make sure he is alone before approaching the Shakira cutout. In other words, even though viewers know that what they are watching is fictional, the filmic conventions employed encourage viewers to watch the commercial as though it were real. Additionally, the commercial appears to be shot on location, and the clerk performs, initially at least, with a filmic acting style that naturalizes actions by performing them in a pedestrian manner, which avoids the outward projection and excessive movement qualities of theatrical performance.[23]

In contrast, subtle aspects of the choreography's staging and movement vocabulary work in collaboration with the camera and casting to evoke the theatrical, rather than the filmic, and encourage viewers to view the dance as a performance. Theatricality begins to take hold when the clerk starts to slink toward the Shakira cutout (and the camera). In facing off to the camera, the clerk positions not only the Shakira cutout but also the television viewer as the direct targets of his gaze, creating a form of direct address. The repetition of these direct address moments during the shot-reverse-shot structure enhances the movement's ability to generate theatricality.

The looks he casts in the camera's direction, when she first comes to life and then again when he is caught dancing, further anchor the theatricality of the dance. The first look actually is a form of intentional direct address that occurs both in the movement and how it is filmed, and the second look's addressing of the television audience is enhanced and reinforced by his storefront audience. This sense of the theatrical is strengthened even more by the choreography, which includes several "flashy" tango movements (e.g., ochos, off-balance partnering) [24] and a dramatic, self-consciously exaggerated performance.

Furthermore, by casting Shakira in the commercial, the Pepsi/BBDO spot draws on Shakira's existing career and reputation as a pop music singer and performer who regularly performs in both live concerts and music videos. Since Shakira is known to study dance and tends to dance in her concerts and videos, television viewers are used to viewing her dancing as a part of a performance and also are invited to think of her dancing as a part of who she is, as a facet of her life or personality. In other words, there is the expectation that she will perform and that her dancing is intended as a form of entertainment. However, at the same time, viewers have prior knowledge of her, the celebrity, and her existence outside the world of this particular ad. Despite the fact that television viewers do not know Shakira personally, she doubles as both a real person and a performer because she exists for viewers prior to appearing in the Pepsi TV spot and the content of the spot refers to an aspect of her "real" life. She is, on one level, literally performing herself. This dynamic points to the way in which performers in American culture are often understood to be "pretending" in their performance while at the same time being seen as somehow the same as the roles they play. [25]

The difference/distinction between mediated images and live performance allows for a sort of double-coding in which actors can signal live performance as a mark of artifice based in the real even as they perform inside of what is already a mediated form. [26] In addition, the common practice of crossover between live entertainment and mediated forms further confuses the distinction between life and performance. As seen in the Shakira Tango Pepsi ad, she is known as a performer of both live (concerts, public appearances) and mediated (music videos) entertainment, and so in the context of the ad she is there as herself, as an aspect of the real, and as a performer. This idea is overtly demonstrated by having her cardboard cutout come to life.

As seen in the above examples, the inclusion of dance in television triggers theatricality through the incorporation of and/or allusion to theatrical conventions and live performance. In addition to facilitating a kind of double-coding or insertion of the live, or real, into the mechanical reproduction of mass media, the deployment of theatrical conventions instills television performances with a sense of *expressive subjectivity*. [27] I argue that one way in which expressive subjectivity has become linked to theatrical performance in American culture is through the incorporation of the structural dynamics of film musicals and their predecessor, musical theater.[28]

THE EXPRESSION OF IDENTITY

In film musicals, while dance sometimes occurs within the narrative itself in the form of social dance events or rehearsals, the presence of dance within the musical numbers is more pertinent to my argument and plays an important role in the genre as a form of excess that signals the transition from narrative to number. The transition to the number is symbolic of the transition within the musical from literal action to expressive action.[29] Obviously, the performers are still literally doing things, but the audience is expected to understand their actions as a performance of expression, or as a performance of feelings/emotions/thoughts. Dance transforms interior subjectivity into outward display and expression. Thus, theatrical conventions serve as a sign of performance, and, in addition to indicating illusion or make-believe, they signal moments of expression. I argue that this aspect of dance's function in film musicals is evidence of how American mass media has, over the course of the twentieth and twenty-first centuries, participated in the construction of an ideology in which performance and the theatrical are a part of social identity.

In terms of genres, dance in TV shows and commercials often drew from Broadway and social dance; however, concert dance, such as ballet and modern, also aired on television as early as the late 1930s, and subsequent decades from the 1950s up to the present (2013) have included one or more programs that broadcast the concert forms of ballet and modern.[30] Early television variety shows, even when the studios were too small to accommodate a live audience, were structured as live performances and often included laugh and applause tracks to simulate the presence of an audience for the at-home viewer.[31] One example of an early variety show format in which dance evokes liveness and embodies theatrical conventions is Jack Cole and Chita Rivera's appearance on "Tip Toe Thru TV" (*The Revlon Revue* 1959/60) in Cole's group choreography. The dancing is presented as part of the show's efforts to answer the question "What is jazz?" posed by host Sid Caesar.[32] In "Tip Toe Thru TV" Cole and Rivera are backed by a chorus of male and female dancers as they "demonstrate" what jazz is. The dancers start off in a simple line formation upstage of Caesar and begin with unison, relatively simple, gestures, such as snapping their fingers to the pulse of the live music, as Caesar introduces the segment. As he exits, the dancers begin to take up more of the stage space. As Cole struts/slinks downstage to perform a solo, the chorus moves in unison until Cole and the chorus quickly arrange themselves in lines along either side of Rivera, making her the focus of the shot. As she begins to sing, Cole and the chorus accent her movements by providing complementary contrast, framing her, or moving in unison with her. The choreography uses much of Cole's jazz dance style: snapping fingers, pulsing crouched stances, and fast turns that end in an accent, etc.

The entire choreography is filmed from a clear frontal perspective, though the location of front is determined as much by the location of the camera as the stage space. While the choreography on these types of programs often indicates one frontal perspective, there are numerous examples of switching between camera angles in order to film movement from a frontal perspective when the dancers employ variations in facing (such as facing the

FIGURE 09.7 Tip Toe Thru TV's *The Revlon Revue* and Chita Rivera in Jack Cole's choreographic response to the question "What is jazz?". Screen shot.

downstage left corner). Thus, the camera often stands in for or creates a frontal perspective. The dancers project their movement and energy out toward the television audience and wear coordinated costumes that unite them as a group. At times, the at-home audience can hear what sounds like an in-studio audience laughing at Caesar's jokes and applauding both him and the dancers.

These various elements work to position the dancing as a performance and also to call to mind the role and function of dance in musicals; it resembles a musical number itself and features dancers known for their work in both stage and film musicals. Furthermore, it is significant that the show offers dance as the answer to the question "what is jazz?" because it suggests that jazz expresses a particular way of being in the world, which the show conveys through movement and choreography. The inclusion of concert and theatrical forms of dance in television has further strengthened the connection between dance and theatrical performance as well as reinforced the use of theatrical conventions for staging and shooting dance for television. In addition, this example demonstrates some of the ways in which movement's role in identity was negotiated on commercial television and how mainstream mass media introduced television audiences to an array of ways of being in the world.

This blending of social and theatrical dance on television continued throughout the twentieth century and, during the late twentieth and early twenty-first centuries dance often made appearances in sitcoms or dramas. Often in this manifestation, shows have included moments where social and theatrical dance are thoroughly combined within a given number, where theatrical dance is an integral part of the show, and where the conventions of musicals literally take over the formatting of the show, either for the entire episode or during portions of the episode that are presented as musical numbers. Shows like *Fame* (NBC 1982–1987) and *Glee* (Fox 2009–present) function as kinds of televisual adaptations of the musical genre, presenting dramas or comedies that combine narrative television with musical numbers by grounding the show in theatrical practices: a high school for the arts in *Fame* and a high school glee club in *Glee*. While in both programs dance sometimes occurs within the context of the narrative (in a class, at a club etc.), dance tends to join forces with music and singing to create elaborate production numbers that evoke film musical numbers and clearly exceed the everyday, pedestrian world of the show. Thus, the at-home television audience is continually positioned as an audience for dance/music performances.

This positioning of the at-home viewers as the audience for dance within television shows is then further amplified by the insertion of dance into sitcoms that follow the standard format. In these cases, choreography unexpectedly interrupts the normal narrative structure to temporarily carry the show into a hybrid space in which cast members perform directly for the television audience. Examples of shows that have used song and dance in this manner include *Ally McBeal* (John's dance to Barry White's "You're the First, You're the Last, You're my Everything,"[33] which occurred in a few different formats), *Buffy the Vampire Slayer* (which transformed a whole episode into a musical with each scene being a different number), *Scrubs* (which has inserted dance in a variety of ways but often uses the associations generated by dance and performance as means to create parodies or ironic humor), and *Psych* (which parodies older television shows and music videos through its main characters' constant citing of these forms, not only through dialogue but also through song and dance).

Dance in these contexts often reveals, expresses, and/or reinforces aspects of the characters and/or narrative. For example, John in *Ally McBeal* is a quiet, socially awkward man for whom Barry White and particularly his song "You're the First . . ." is a source of extreme pleasure. His choreography to the song is initially a private resource that he draws on in moments when he needs to summon confidence and inspiration. Once his dance is discovered by the other characters, it gradually becomes a more prominent part of the show, including episodes where the whole cast performs it together, such as when John's girlfriend hires White to sing the song for him on his birthday. Thus, in this example, dance allows the television audience to learn more about a specific character, and dance serves as a means of expressing things that John doesn't feel capable of expressing in other ways.

A more recent example of a television show that positions the at-home viewer as an audience for dance and uses dance to corporealize identity and narrative themes is the sitcom *Bunheads*, which premiered summer 2012. The show revolves around an ex-Las Vegas showgirl/ex-ABT dancer who moves to a small town where she becomes a dance instructor in her mother-in-law's dance studio.[34] Dance plays a major role in the show with scenes that feature the students dancing in both class and performances.[35] One example of the role of dance as an embodiment of identity, specifically gender/sexuality is the number "Makin' Whoopee" in "Next," the final episode of the first season. This final dance of the episode sums up themes from the season by capturing the transition from adolescent girl to woman.

While how dance is incorporated and staged differs in each of these television shows, the performance of song and dance expresses both aspects of the narrative and the subjective interiority of the show's characters. Dance in sitcoms aptly demonstrates the ways in which theatrical conventions and performance are used in television to signal the performance of identity through expressive movement. Dance helps the television viewer see *who* the characters *are* and *how* movement informs, shapes, and transforms that identity.

However, I argue that in American culture even as spectators consciously recognize that the "actors" are performing—that it is their job to assume a given persona, character, or part—television and film have taught American audiences to conflate the "person" and the "performer." Evidence of this confusion can be found in the media texts themselves, as well as the dynamics of fandom and in the contemporary creation of reality TV shows. Television *encourages* audiences to slide easily into the belief that on some level performers present their "real," authentic, true selves.

Evidence of this conceptual slippage between performance and reality can be found throughout television's history. For example, on *This Is Your Life* (ABC 1952–1961) each show spotlighted a given individual, whose friends and family would be brought in to help present the individual's life; *The Arthur Murray Show* (CBS 1952, NBC 1953–1962) invited couples to the show to help demonstrate the latest social dance styles and was hosted by Murray and his wife Kathryn; *Candid Camera* (ABC 1948, NBC 1949–1959, CBS 1960–1967) caught people in embarrassing situations or hoaxes that were introduced and narrated by the show's host. However, this conflation of performance and reality was also achieved through shows such as *The Adventures of Ozzie and Harriet* (ABC 1952-–1966), whose stars were in reality a married couple who then played a married couple on television—even to the point that their real children played their children on television, and *I Love Lucy* (CBS 1951–1961), which starred the real-life couple of Lucille Ball/Desi Arnaz and featured her real life pregnancy and the birth of their son, Desi Jr., in 1953. These overlaps between real people and the characters they played were public knowledge and allowed for a kind of casual conflating of the fictional and the "real." The presence of these shows and their popularity points to the way in which reality has always been a feature of television, joining forces with the nature of live broadcasting to bring at-home viewers into the presence of people and things that they would otherwise not have access to and allowing the actors to perform for a wider audience.[36]

Shakira's presence in the Pepsi ad also speaks to the relationship between theatrical performance, liveness, reality, and consumption. Commercials like this one reveal how television uses theatrical conventions to suggest that the spectator, or viewer, has the capacity to construct reality through the consumption of both products and corporeality. The Pepsi commercial uses dance to signal performance, which in turn highlights the distinction between the theatrical and the real. I suggest that the commercial, in fact, insinuates that reality is a performance by holding forth the potential to change who one is by physically embodying one's desired reality (i.e., by performing differently).[37] Thus, viewers can choose to identify with the store clerk and his fantasy of being with Shakira, or choose to identify with Shakira, her corporeality, and her status as a famous performer. As a result, the ad suggests that by drinking Pepsi, as well as by learning to dance, television viewers can define themselves through their consumption.

This idea can be seen in the store clerk's behavior as he tries on a new persona through movement. The commercial portrays the store clerk as a little socially awkward (he does a very exaggerated, rough version of the tango and dances with a cardboard cutout as though it is really Shakira), but within the ad as he dances the tango he plays at being the confident male full of machismo and seduction. However, also inherent within the ad is the sense that this energy, this way of being, is already in him; thus, consumption is more about acting on a potential.[38] In other words, the ad suggests that consuming Pepsi is about embracing desire and acting on one's potential, even if that means being a bit of a maverick at times. Ultimately, the sense of performance evoked by dance sets the stage for the construction of reality and identity through embodied actions.

The Spectacle of Our Expressive Selves

The fascination with the immediacy and affect of live performance has surfaced in different genres over the course of television's history. Shows modeled after or thematically based on vaudeville and variety shows combined the interest in reality with the conventions, format, and content of theatrical performance; they were common television show formats starting around 1946 and running up through the 1970s. The content of vaudeville and variety television shows has varied widely, but many of these shows have included dance as a featured performance or as a part of musical performances.[39] While these formats dwindled severely in the 1980s and 1990s, they resurfaced in the 2000s in the form of competition-based reality TV talent shows.[40]

Other show formats have provided a more prominent presence of dance on television, such as *The Arthur Murray Party* (1950–1962), *American Bandstand* (1952–1989), and *Soul Train* (1971–2006). Arthur Murray's half-hour program highlighted dance, demonstrating ballroom dances and featuring professional dancers, but the other two programs tended to feature new music that was accompanied both by professional dancers and by audience members who were invited to dance to the musical performances.

The ideology of identity as a performance achieved through the conflation of live performance and the "real" is amply evident in the proliferation of dance-based reality TV shows. Shows like *So You Think You Can Dance* (*SYTYCD*) and *Dancing with the Stars* (*DWTS*) explicitly join live performance with mediation, featuring a live audience on the set that can be heard throughout the performances by the at-home television audience and which is intentionally shown at times during the broadcast. This style of reality show clearly harkens back to the "origins" of television in terms of both production and content, while at the same time reflecting current production practices and a televisual emphasis on style and exhibitionism.[41]

The competitive format of the dance-based reality TV shows (*SYTYCD* and *DWTS*) calls to mind both the variety show and game show formats of early television. Both shows feature hosts who connect one performance to the next, interview the contestants, and serve as intermediaries between judges, contestants, and audience. These hosts function as a low-key substitute for the variety show hosts of television's early years, who were stars in their own rights and played a much bigger role in the show's content. However, both styles of hosts serve as MCs that introduce performances.

Live broadcasting adds the sensation of being present, of witnessing events as they happen in the moment, even when in reality the viewer might be thousands of miles away sitting at home in her/his living room. Thus, live broadcasts create presence through their ability to allow viewers to access realities other than their own and to witness real people doing things. In that sense reality becomes a kind of performance—it begins to take on aspects of theatrical performance because it shares with theater this sense of presence, the sense of seeing people perform and share a part of themselves in real time. The (re) presentation of live performance alludes to and simulates the effect produced by seeing something happen as it happens, of witnessing real effort, real people—of being there.

The discussion of liveness within television scholarship has been a lively one, serving as a key debate affecting the discussion of the differences and similarities between television and cinema.[42] One element of television that encouraged the sense of liveness associated with the medium was the perceived "immediacy" and "spontaneity" of the form.[43] In illustrating this affinity Misha Kavka draws on the work of earlier media theorists such as Stephen Heath and Gillian Kirrow, who argued that this concept of liveness was operative during the 1970s and informed the differences in reception between television and film.[44] Much of television theory has continued to emphasize the *nowness* of television's perceived temporality. Thus, the sense of theatricality generated by performance forms on television reinforces and/or encourages the viewers' perception of TV as occurring in the present and as direct for them.

Recent studies on reality television have once again raised this specter of liveness in the context of television. Kavka is interested in making an argument that grounds the allure and effects of reality shows in a form of affect and intimacy created between the show's participants and the at-home audience:

> In this way, the "electronically constituted society" of TV viewers (Rath, 1989, p.89) expands to include intimacy with the TV performers, precisely because the effect of liveness forecloses any preceding period in which they would have been able to practice a performance which has no prequel. They are there, doing what they would do, the cameras are on, and we are watching. The actuality strengthens the effect of immediacy; immediacy strengthens the effect of social community; and the community creates a sense of intimacy amongst viewers as well as performers.[45]

My analysis of the power of dance to evoke performance within the television medium and the effect of that evocation resonates with Kavka's theory of reality television. Her description of the performance quality of reality TV speaks to how liveness functions in contemporary television. In defining the effect and attraction of reality TV shows, Kavka points to this fascination with people "performing" (i.e., being) themselves:

> This is less a matter of "acting" in the sense of simulation than of "acting out," a performance of the self which creates feeling. This is one way to describe the performative economy of reality TV: the performance of reality generates reality effects, just as the performance of intimacy generates intimacy effects. To push this further, however, is to see that reality television, as an extension of the televisual technology of intimacy, involves a performance of reality which generates intimacy as its affect.[46]

In essence, Kavka argues that the intimacy generated by the performance of reality creates a sense of liveness without employing theatrical conventions. In contemporary dance-based reality television programs this sense of liveness is enhanced by the liveness brought on by dance's association with performance and theatrical conventions.

The contemporary reality television dance shows, *SYTYCD* and *DWTS*, create liveness by basing their content in live performance, much as early variety shows did, and emphasizing theatrical conventions through set design. Both shows take place in a studio setting that has a clearly delineated stage and a separate space for the audience. Both employ

EVERY LITTLE THING SHE DOES IS MAGIC
STING

FIGURE 09.8 *SYTYCD* Season 7—Mia Michaels's "Alice in Mia-land" set to Sting's "Every Little Thing She Does Is Magic" demonstrates the use of theatrical production elements on the show. Screen shot.

theatrical lighting and elaborate costuming, and in the case of *SYTYCD* props and set design are included as appropriate.

The major distinction between the two programs, in terms of how they employ theatrical conventions, occurs at the level of the stage design; however, this variation reflects the differences in the shows' content and basic premises.

So You Think You Can Dance holds auditions nationally prior to each season in order to select a group of male and a group of female dancers to compete on the show. When the program first started there seemed to be at least an implicit understanding that these dancers were young and looking for their big break. As the show progressed it became clear that the competitors often, not always, but often, had some form of professional dance experience. So there is a conflation here between the sense of the real (as in real people, amateurs, people like those watching at home) and the theatrical (as in professional performers, who also happen to be real people). This overlapping of the real and the theatrical continues into the show's format through the mix of interviews with the contestants (whom the audience will later see in the role of performers), rehearsal footage (a site where the real of the contestant and the theatrical of the performer are in the process of "merging"), and performance footage (wherein the contestants step onto the stage to perform live for the in-studio audience, which will seem live for the television viewers). What happens afterward finalizes this merger, as the judges talk to the contestants/performers about their performance in terms of personal growth, emphasizing the way in which their mastery of dance styles, their ability to embody different styles of movement and choreographic content demonstrates their "real" personal growth and transformation. Thus, the show presents dance as a site of performance that is both spectacular and "real."

FIGURE 09.9 *SYTYCD* Season 9—Hampton Williams gets feedback from the judges after auditioning for them with his Exorcist style of dance. Screen shot.

Furthermore, the dance signals performance and expression, both in terms of choreography and movement style/vocabulary. While several styles of dance (jazz/lyrical/contemporary, hip-hop, ballroom, and musical theater, predominately) are performed and contestants are required to be or learn to be proficient and then excel in each, the choreography tends to highlight precision and the display of the body and its movements. The movement possesses a kind of excess of clarity as the dancers project their energy outward, and the choreography frequently relies on a crisp movement quality that emphasizes visual design, direct energy, and abbreviated (sharp, clean) transitions. The choreography is staged to use a variety of facings while regularly reorienting the dancers to face the audience, so that often couples are dancing side by side facing front while looking at and/or relating to each other.

When they do dance facing each other, the choreography adjusts for the proscenium by having them face each other in a horizontal line on the stage so that both bodies are visible from the center of the audience.

Thus, choreography and movement both work to produce theatrical conventions and a sense of performance. This employment of theatrical conventions is reinforced through the stage design, which resembles a traditional proscenium stage.

Dancing with the Stars is similar in many ways but modifies the basic structure and content to provide a marketable variation on the program. On this program the basic premise is that professional DanceSport (competitive ballroom) dancers are paired with amateur dancers who also happen to be celebrities of one ilk or another. Sometimes the celebrities are sports stars or have some dance experience, but they are just as often actors or other public figures who do not possess a high level of skill in a physical form. In this sense, the celebrities function as an odd hybrid of professional and amateur—not like the audience in the sense of being public figures but like the audience in that they are not highly trained dancers. Thus, they provide a slightly different merging of the "real" and the "theatrical."

FIGURE 09.10 *SYTYCD* Season 5—Jason Glover and Jeanine Mason perform Travis Wall's choreography set to Jason Mraz's "If It Kills Me" (The Casa Nova Sessions). Screen shot.

FIGURE 09.11 *SYTYCD* Season 7—Lauren Froderman and Pasha Kovalev perform choreography by Tony Meredith and Melanie LaPatin set to Christina Aguilera's "Not Myself Tonight." Screen shot.

FIGURE 09.12 *DWTS* (US) Season 16—Zendaya Coleman and Valentin Chmerkovskiy dance jive to Bobby Day's "Rockin' Robin." Screen shot.

The stage setting on *DWTS* also employs a clear delineation between the stage and the audience; however, the show honors its DanceSport/ballroom theme by using a dance floor that is bordered on three sides by the audience in tiered seating that begins at the same level as the dance floor.

The dimly lit orchestra forms a backdrop for the dance floor, or stage space. Both the use of a dance floor, rather than a raised stage, and the presence of the orchestra are reminiscent of the ballroom dance venues where it would have been possible to watch exhibition ballroom dancers perform in the early twentieth century, while also calling to mind the structure of DanceSport competition venues.[47] While this physical setting is perhaps less indicative of theatrical performance than the proscenium structure of *SYTYCD*, the sense of live performance is maintained or reasserted through the clear presence of the audience and its separation from the dance space. In addition, *DWTS* participates in a similar sense of the theatrical through its staging of the choreography and the movement vocabulary/style.

While a greater variety of facings are employed, partially due to the rectangular shape of the stage and having the audience on three sides, the choreography continuously orients the dancers into a side-by-side formation that looks toward stage "front."

In addition, the idea of a stage front is reinforced by the positioning of the orchestra upstage of the dancers and by the tendency of the cameras to shoot from positions that are opposite the orchestra and in line with the judges. The movement vocabulary aligns itself with the highly codified forms of the dances seen in DanceSport, rather than with the dance forms as they are practiced socially.[48] As a result, the choreography is crafted to emphasize skill and visual design and often includes steps that are not included in the dance forms when practiced socially. This emphasis on visual design is then further theatricalized through a similar emphasis on precision and clarity combined with a strong sense of projecting the

FIGURE 09.13 *DWTS* (US) Season 16—Zendaya Coleman and Valentin Chmerkovskiy dance jive to Bobby Day's "Rockin' Robin." Screen shot.

energy outward. However, as with *SYTYCD*, while the dancing and setting employ theatrical conventions, the show grounds this sense of live performance within the context of watching real celebrities really learn how to dance in a new way. Thus, performance is a means of accessing a visible sign of an interior transformation, a means of accessing the real.

Concluding Thoughts: Identity as Performance

What these reality shows demonstrate most proficiently, I argue, is that performance and theatrical conventions have become a regular presence on television. However, while dance on television draws attention to the medium of television as a kind of formal presentation, it also participates in and benefits from the naturalization of performance. This naturalization of performance creates a dynamic in which dance on television is read simultaneously as both *real* expression and spectacular excess. As a result, dance conveys cultural ideologies and social identity through movement, and the association between dance and spontaneous expression encourages viewers to see these ideologies as personal choices. By evoking theatrical performance, dance works with television to conceptualize identity as a conscious performance (at once both real and constructed) and expression as the spectacle of excess in movement.

In American culture performers play an essential role in the construction of both national and individual identity by modeling possible identities and encouraging viewers to understand identity as a kind of performance. Examining specific examples of dance on television reveals how television uses dance and theatrical conventions to evoke performance and how performance, in turn, creates immediacy, affect, and notions of the real.

Notes

1. Phillip Auslander, *Liveness: Performance in a Mediatized Culture* (New York: Routledge, 1999); Barbara Moore, Marvin R. Bensman, and Jim Van Dyke, *Prime-time Television: A Concise History.* Westport, CT: Praeger, 2006).

2. Elizabeth Burns, *Theatricality: A Study of Convention in the Theatre and in Social Life* (London: Longman Group Limited, 1972); Susan Leigh Foster, *Reading Dancing: Bodies and Subjects in Contemporary American Dance* (Berkeley: University of California Press, 1986).

3. Misha Kavka and Amy West. "Temporalities of the Real: Conceptualising Time in Reality TV," in *Understanding Reality Television*, edited by Su Holmes and Deborah Jermyn (New York: Routledge, 2004), 136–53; Auslander, *Liveness*; Burns, *Theatricality.*

4. Rick Altman, *The American Film Musical* (Bloomington: Indiana University Press, 1987); Jane Feuer, "The Concept of Live Television: Ontology as Ideology," in *Regarding Television: Critical Approaches—An Anthology*, edited by Ann Kaplan (Frederick, MD: University Publications of America, 1983), 12–22.

5. Erin Brannigan, *Dancefilm: Choreography and the Moving Image* (New York: Oxford University Press, 2011), 104–11, 142–43.

6. Moore, Bensman, and Van Dyke, *Prime-time Television*, 44.

7. Gary R. Edgerton, and Peter C. Rollins, eds., *Television Histories: Shaping Collective Memory in the Media Age* (Lexington: University Press of Kentucky, 2001); Moore, Bensman, and Van Dyke, *Prime-time Television.*

8. Moore, Bensman, and Van Dyke, *Prime-time Television.*

9. Television broadcasts aired for the first time as early as 1928; however, the first regular seven-day per week schedule was not broadcast until 1931 by W2XAB (CBS). In these early years, live broadcasts were really for experimental purposes only, not for commercial audiences. However, the broadcast technology (though it shifts during this time from "mechanical" to electronic) and content during this period aligned with the practices seen with the onset of commercial television in 1940. TV sets were not really being manufactured at this point, and so commercial broadcasting was still in the early stages in 1941, at which point, World War II disrupted production. Within a couple of years after the war's end, the commercial industry really began to produce television sets, which quickly became a coveted commodity. For more information on the early years of experimental television and its content, see Moore, Bensman, and Van Dyke, *Prime-time Television*, 28–33.

10. Moore, Bensman, and Van Dyke, *Prime-time Television*, 34–37, 44–65.

11. Moore, Bensman, and Van Dyke, *Prime-time Television*, 45, 54, 79.

12. For example, the first televised variety show, "Hour Glass," premiered May 9, 1946, and included a chorus line (http://www.imdb.com/title/tt0128878/plotsummary); Moore, Bensman, and Van Dyke, *Prime-time Television.*

13. Kavka, *Reality Television.*

14. Auslander, *Liveness*; Moore, Bensman, Van Dyke, *Prime-time Television*; Kavka, *Reality Television*; Feuer, "The Concept of Live Television"; Stephen Heath and Gillian Skirrow, "Television: A World in Action," *Screen* 18, no. 2 (1977): 7–59; Foster, *Reading Dancing*; and Burns, *Theatricality.*

15. *Lawrence Welk Show*, "Summer by the Shore" (1967) http://www.tvrage.com/shows/id-12013/episodes/624246 (accessed June 27, 2012).

16. Several theorists have written more on the history and relationship between social dance and exhibition ballroom within the United States; I have listed three examples here: Susan Cook, "Passionless Dancing and Passionate Reform: Respectability, Modernism, and the Social Dancing of Vernon and Irene Castle," in *The Passion of Music and Dance: Body, Gender, and Sexuality*, edited by William Washbaugh (New York: Berg, 1998), 133–50; Julie Malnig, "Athena Meets Venus: Visions of Women in Social Dance in the Teens and Early 1920s," *Dance Research Journal* 31, no. 2 (Autumn 1999): 34–62; and Danielle Robinson, "Performing American: Ragtime Dancing as Participatory Minstrelsy," *Dance Chronicle* 32, no. 1 (2009): 89–126.

17. While a number of scholars have written analyses and histories of film musicals, detailed studies on dance within the genre are limited; scholars who have offered more substantial treatments of dance within film musicals include Jerome Delamater, Sherril Dodds, and Larry Billman.

18. This understanding of dance and bodily comportment as a means of social identity (class, gender, ethnicity, sexuality) and as a way of transforming one's person has been discussed by theorists in relationship to both concert and social dance. Two examples that speak to the formation of these concepts within the early part of the twentieth-century in America are Ann Daly, *Done into Dance: Isadora Duncan in America* (Bloomington: Indiana University Press, 1995); and Malnig, "Athena Meets Venus."

19. Evidence of the assumption of social markers of racial, ethnic, and gender identity abound in popular culture. One needs only to look at the performance of gender in drag culture or the embodiment of hip-hop and rap culture within white communities. The foundation of this argument was laid by Judith Butler in *Gender Trouble: Feminism and the Subversion of Identity* (New York: Routledge, 1990) but has been taken up, revised, and extended by various scholars, for example, Susan Foster's "Choreographies of Gender," *Signs: Journal of Women in Culture and Society* 24, no. 1 (1998) 1–33.

20. In addition to Lucky Strikes, other cigarette brands featured dance vocabulary in the early 1950s. The 1960s is, perhaps, the low point of dance in commercials; however, examples from the period include commercials for Great Shakes and National Airlines. The 1970s included, among others, the well-known series of Dr. Pepper ads; the 1980s saw a slight increase (e.g., the series of Bounce commercials choreographed by Louis Falco), and the late 1990s are known for sparking a sudden proliferation of dance in advertising (beginning with Gap's khaki TV spots). These are not the only examples, but this list gives a sense of dance's continued presence.

21. Colleen Dunagan, "The Changing Face of Dance: Televisual Excursions into the World of the Aesthetic," *International Journal of the Arts in Society* 1, no. 4 (2007): 9–14; Robert Cooper, "Interpreting Mass: Collection/Dispersion," in *The Consumption of Mass*, edited by Nick Lee and Rolland Munro (Malden, MA: Blackwell, 2001), 16–43.

22. The music for the commercial is Shakira's "Objection: Tango" (2004); the ad is part of Pepsi's Dare for More campaign. Additional information regarding the ad can be found here: http://www.tvspots.tv/video/20388/PEPSI--TANGO (accessed June 13, 2012).

23. Historically, the differences between film and theater have been discussed within film theory (for example, the work of Andre Bazin, Leo Braudy, and Susan Sontag). I also draw on Thompson's summary of acting styles found in Debby Thompson, "Is Race a Trope?: Anna Deavere Smith and the Question of Racial Performativity," *African American Review* 37, no. 1 (2003): 127–38.

24. For a complex history and an analysis of tango and its diasporic journeys as a dance form that reveals the transformations of the dance within various cultural contexts and its

complex history as a form of exotic spectacle, see Marta Savigliano, *Tango and the Political Economy of Passion* (Boulder, CO: Westview Press), 1995.

25. See André Bazin's "Theatre and Cinema," Leo Braudy's "Acting: Stage vs. Screen," and Susan Sontag's "Film and Theater," respectively, in *Film Theory and Criticism: Introductory Readings*, 4th ed., edited by Gerald Mast, Marshall Cohen, and Leo Braudy (New York: Oxford University Press, 1992).

26. Auslander, *Liveness*; Kavka, *Reality Television*.

27. In using this term, "expressive subjectivity," I refer to the ways in which Enlightenment notions of the subject play out in twentieth-century understandings of performance and expression. Specifically, I am arguing that on one level television encourages a liberal humanist understanding of performance in which characters are understood to have "an essential core of interior objectives and the character's (or actor's) bodily acts [are viewed] as the outward manifestation of the character's interior identity." Thompson, "Is Race a Trope?", 128.

28. However, I suggest that whether or not viewers have seen live musical theater or other theatrical performances, experiences with live performances of one kind or another are ubiquitous enough that most viewers possess a pragmatic conceptual understanding of live performance and its conventions.

29. Martin Rubin, "Busby Berkeley and the Backstage Musical," in *Hollywood Musicals: The Film Reader*, edited by Steven Cohan. (New York: Routledge, 2002/2006), 53–61; Altman, *American Film Musical*; Feuer, "The Concept of Live Television."

30. A quick and very much abbreviated list of historical examples of programs airing concert dance on television includes the following: a series called *Choreotones* (CBS 1945), *Omnibus* (CBS 1952–1961), the "Dance USA" series (WNET/New York 1966), the "Dance in America" series (PBS *Great Performances* 1976–) and "Alive from Off Center" (PBS 1985–1996).

31. Auslander, *Liveness*, 22.

32. While early television programming has presented the concert forms of modern and ballet, my decision to use the Cole/Rivera performance reflects two things. First, I intentionally chose not to privilege what might be viewed as the canon of ballet and modern dance. Two, I have found that the concert forms of ballet and modern dance have not been the biggest influences on television content and production style.

33. Recorded and released by Barry White in 1974 on the 20th Century Records label, the single was written by Peter Radcliffe, Tony Sepe, and Barry White.

34. The show ended up running for only one season (2012–2013). The plot is slightly more complicated than what I lay out in the text. While the newlyweds arrive in the small town together, the husband dies in the second episode, leaving his mother's dance studio and house to his new wife in his will—both of which appear to have been in his name rather than his mother's—making the ex-Vegas showgirl the owner of the dance studio.

35. While the name, *Bunheads*, is a colloquial term for ballet dancers, and ballet is a staple of the show's dance studio, the numbers performed range from ballet to musical theater to jazz and lyrical. Given that the show's choreographer is Marguerite Derricks, who studied ballet but has choreographed for commercials, television shows, and films in a wide variety of genres and styles, the mix of dance forms on the show is not surprising.

36. Moore, Bensman, and Van Dyke, *Prime-time Television*, 39–120.

37. While I am not drawing on one specific theorist, the ideas regarding performance and the construction of identity that I employ here are grounded in theories of performance, performativity, and theatricality arising out of performance, theater, and dance studies

including the work of Janelle Reinelt, "The Politics of Discourse: Performativity Meets Theatricality," *Substance* 31, no. 2/3 (2002): 201–15; Miranda Joseph, "The Performance of Production and Consumption," *Social Text* no. 54 (Spring 1998): 25–61; Jill Dolan, "Geographies of Learning: Theatre Studies, Performance, and the 'Performative,'" *Theatre Journal* 45, no. 4 (December 1993): 417–41; and Sue-Ellen Case, "The Emperor's New Clothes: The Naked Body and Theories of Performance." *Substance* 31, no. 2/3, Issue 98/99 (2002): 186–200. Many of the ideas from these texts are in conversation with the notion of performativity put forth by Butler in *Gender Trouble*.

38. The use of humor and socially awkward behavior is complex in this ad, as it is in many of them. The ad calls on viewers to recognize aspects of themselves in his behavior, even if they do not completely identify with him. However, the commercial also uses humor and the breaking of social taboos as forms of spectacle and accessible meaning-making that attract and hold the consumers' attention. While he may end up looking silly within the reality of the commercial, he enacts a desire that viewers can identify with even if they choose not to act on it.

39. Evidence of dance's appearance on variety shows is wide ranging, but examples include everything from the Herb Ross Dancers appearing on an episode of the *Texaco Star Theatre* (1954, http://www.texacostartheater.com/page3.html), to Jack Cole and Chita Rivera's appearance on the "Tip Toe Thru TV," an episode of *The Revlon Revue* (Dale Grover remembers performing as part of the production number and cites it as airing in 1959; however, IMDB gives it as 1960 http://www.imdb.com/title/tt0894656/), to a polka "Shall We Dance" (1967) on *The Lawrence Welk Show*, to the *Dean Martin Show* (NBC, 1965–1974), to *In Living Color* (Fox, 1990–1994), to *The Mickey Mouse Club* (1955–1959).

40. Richard M. Huff, *Reality Television* (Westport, CT: Praeger, 2006); Kavka, *Reality Television*; Moore, Bensman, and Van Dyke, *Prime-time Television*.

41. Caldwell states, "Televisuality was a stylizing *performance*—an exhibitionism that utilized many different looks . . . Conceived of as a *presentational attitude*, a display of knowing *exhibitionism*, any one of many specific visual looks and stylizations could be marshaled for the spectacle. The process of stylization rather than style—an activity rather than a static look—was the factor that defined televisual exhibitionism" (*Televisuality*, 5, author's emphasis). Caldwell's language and his distinction between "style" as a look and "style" as an activity seems to speak to "style" as kind of performance and thus once again to evoke not only theatricality but also the notion of television as "alive."

42. Misha Kavka and Amy West. "Temporalities of the Real: Conceptualising time in Reality TV," in *Understanding Reality Television*, edited by Su Holmes and Deborah Jermyn (New York: Routledge, 2004), 136–53. They cite several of the key theorists engaged in this debate, including Heath and Skirrow, "Television: a World in Action"; Feuer, "The Concept of Live Television"; and Caldwell, *Televisuality*.

43. As Kavka states, "For example, Guy Simpson, a director of NBC in 1955, connected the trope of television as a vast window with the appeal of spontaneous transmission . . . The intimacy of television is thus bound to its *actuel/aktuell* presentation as something of the moment—'live,' lived, and living. The insistent presentism of television brings time to the fore, so that Morse's designation of television as a 'fiction of presence' must be understood not only in intersubjective but also in temporal terms," *Reality Television*, 14.

44. Heath and Skirrow, "Television."

45. Kavka, *Reality Television*, 19.

46. Kavka, *Reality Television,* 35.
47. This structure also bears similarities to the physical setting of the ballrooms and the presentation of early ballet/baroque spectacles. See Foster, *Reading Dancing*; and Julie Malnig, ed., *Ballroom, Boogie, Shimmy Sham, Shake: A Social and Popular Dance Reader* (Chicago: University of Illinois Press, 2009).
48. McMains, "Reality Check;"; Carline Jean S. Picart, *From Ballroom to DanceSport: Aesthetics, Athletics, and Body Culture* (New York: State University of New York Press, 2006).

BIBLIOGRAPHY

Altman, Rick. *The American Film Musical.* Bloomington: Indiana University Press, 1987.

Auslander, Phillip. *Liveness: Performance in a Mediatized Culture.* New York: Routledge, 1999.

Bazin, André. "Theatre and Cinema" (reprint). In *Film Theory and Criticism: Introductory Readings,* 4th ed., edited by Gerald Mast, Marshall Cohen, and Leo Braudy, 375–86. New York: Oxford University Press, 1992.

Bellour, Raymond. "Segmenting/Analysing." In *Genre: The Musical,* edited by Rick Altman, 102–33. London: Routledge & Kegan Paul, 1981.

Benjamin, Walter. *Illuminations: Essays and Reflections.* New York: Schocken Books, 1969.

Billman, Larry. *Film Choreographers and Dance Directors.* Jefferson, NC: McFarland, 1997.

Brannigan, Erin, *Dancefilm: Choreography and the Moving Image.* New York: Oxford University Press, 2011.

Braudy, Leo. "Acting: Stage vs. Screen" (reprint). In *Film Theory and Criticism: Introductory Readings,* 4th ed., Ed. Gerald Mast, Marshall Cohen, and Leo Braudy, 387–94. New York: Oxford University Press, 1992.

Burns, Elizabeth. *Theatricality: A Study of Convention in the Theatre and in Social Life.* London: Longman Group, 1972.

Butler, Judith. *Gender Trouble: Feminism and the Subversion of Identity.* New York: Routledge, 1990.

Caldwell, John Thorton. *Televisuality: Style, Crises, and Authority in American Television.* New Brunswick, NJ: Rutgers University Press, 1995.

Case, Sue-Ellen. "The Emperor's New Clothes: The Naked Body and Theories of Performance." *SubStance* 31, no. 2/3, Issue 98/99 (2002): 186–200.

Cook, Susan. "Passionless Dancing and Passionate Reform: Respectability, Modernism, and the Social Dancing of Vernon and Irene Castle." In *The Passion of Music and Dance: Body, Gender, and Sexuality,* edited by William Washbaugh, 133–50. New York: Berg, 1998.

Cooper, Robert. "Interpreting Mass: Collection/Dispersion." In *The Consumption of Mass,* edited by Nick Lee and Rolland Munro, 16–43. Malden, MA: Blackwell, 2001.

Daly, Ann. *Done into Dance: Isadora Duncan in America.* Bloomington: Indiana University Press, 1995.

Delamater, Jerome. "Dance in the Hollywood Musical." Dissertation. Ann Arbor: University of Michigan Research Press, 1981, 1978.

Deleuze, Gilles. *Cinema 1: The Movement-Image.* Minneapolis: University of Minnesota Press, 1986, 1996.

Dodds, Sherril. *Dance on Screen: Genres and Media from Hollywood to Experimental Art.* New York: Palgrave, 2001.

Dolan, Jill. "Geographies of Learning: Theatre Studies, Performance, and the 'Performative.'" *Theatre Journal* 45, no. 4 (December 1993): 417–41.

Dunagan, Colleen. "The Changing Face of Dance: Televisual Excursions into the World of the Aesthetic." *International Journal of the Arts in Society* 1, no. 4 (2007): 9–14.

Edgerton, Gary R., and Peter C. Rollins, eds. *Television Histories: Shaping Collective Memory in the Media Age.* Lexington: University Press of Kentucky, 2001.

Egginton, William. *How the World Became a Stage: Presence, Theatricality, and the Question of Modernity.* New York: State University of New York Press, 2003.

Feuer, Jane. "The Concept of Live Television: Ontology as Ideology." In *Regarding Television: Critical Approaches—An Anthology,* edited by Ann Kaplan, 12–22. Frederick, MD: University Publications of America, 1983.

———. *The Hollywood Musical.* 2nd ed. Bloomington: Indiana University Press, 1993.

Foster, Susan Leigh. "Choreographies of Gender." *Signs: Journal of Women in Culture and Society* 24, no. 1 (1998): 1–33.

———. *Reading Dancing: Bodies and Subjects in Contemporary American Dance.* Berkeley: University of California Press, 1986.

Heath, Stephen, and Gillian Skirrow. "Television: A World in Action." *Screen* 18, no. 2 (1977): 7–59.

Huff, Richard M. *Reality Television.* Westport, CT: Praeger, 2006.

Joseph, Miranda. "The Performance of Production and Consumption." *Social Text* no. 54 (Spring 1998): 25–61.

Jordan, Stephanie, and Dave Allen. *Parallel Lines: Media Representations of Dance.* London: John Libbey, 1993.

Kavka, Misha. *Reality Television: Affect and Intimacy.* New York: Palgrave Macmillan, 2008.

Kavka, Misha, and Amy West. "Temporalities of the Real: Conceptualising Time in Reality TV." In *Understanding Reality Television,* edited by Su Holmes and Deborah Jermyn, 136–53. New York: Routledge, 2004.

Lury, Celia. "Style and the Perfection of Things." In *High Pop: Making Culture into Popular Entertainment,* edited by Jim Collins. Malden, MA: Blackwell, 2002.

Malnig, Julie. "Athena Meets Venus: Visions of Women in Social Dance in the Teens and Early 1920s." *Dance Research Journal* 31, no. 2 (Autumn, 1999): 34–62.

———. *Dancing till Dawn: A Century of Exhibition Ballroom Dance.* New York: New York University Press, 1992.

Malnig, Julie, ed. *Ballroom, Boogie, Shimmy Sham, Shake: A Social and Popular Dance Reader.* Chicago: University of Illinois Press, 2009.

McMains, Juliet. "Dancing Latin/Latin Dancing: Salsa and DanceSport." In *Ballroom, Boogie, Shimmy Sham, Shake,* edited by Julie Malnig, 302–22. Chicago: University of Illinois Press, 2009.

———. "Reality Check: *Dancing with the Stars* and the American Dream." In *The Routledge Dance Studies Reader,* 2nd ed., edited by Alexandra Carter and Janet O'Shea, 261–72. New York: Routledge, 2010.

Moore, Barbara, Marvin R. Bensman, and Jim Van Dyke. *Prime-time Television: A Concise History.* Westport, CT: Praeger, 2006.

Picart, Carline Jean S. *From Ballroom to DanceSport: Aesthetics, Athletics, and Body Culture.* New York: State University of New York Press, 2006.

Reinelt, Janelle. "The Politics of Discourse: Performativity Meets Theatricality." *Substance* 31, no. 2/3 (2002): 201–15.

Robinson, Danielle. "Performing American: Ragtime Dancing as Participatory Minstrelsy." *Dance Chronicle* 32, no. 1 (2009): 89–126.

Rubin, Martin. "Busby Berkeley and the Backstage Musical." In *Hollywood Musicals: The Film Reader*, edited by Steven Cohan, 53–61. New York: Routledge, 2002/2006.

Savigliano, Marta. *Tango and the Political Economy of Passion*. Boulder, CO: Westview Press, 1995.

Sontag, Susan. "Film and Theatre" (reprint). In *Film Theory and Criticism: Introductory Readings*, 4th ed., edited by Gerald Mast, Marshall Cohen, and Leo Braudy, 362–74. New York: Oxford University Press, 1992.

Thompson, Debby. "Is Race a Trope?: Anna Deavere Smith and the Question of Racial Performativity." *African American Review* 37, no. 1 (2003): 127–38.

CHAPTER 10

··

WHY NOT "IMPROV EVERYWHERE"?

··

SUSAN LEIGH FOSTER

THIS chapter focuses on the recent emergence of a new kind of performance, flash mobs, in order to examine what these events say about our current experiences of public and private space and our current conceptions of theater, dance, and performance. Situated between play, disruption, the carnivalesque, and social protest, flash mobs typically originate as an invitation circulated through social media to participate in an event whose location and choreography are specified. At the appointed time, an unpredictable number of people, mostly strangers to one another, arrive at a public site, perform as instructed, oftentimes documenting their own actions through hand-held cameras, twitter, or texting, and then they disperse back into anonymity. Afterward, they upload video versions of the event onto the Web, where an unspecified number of viewers will watch what occurred.

Most frequently taking place in large public spaces, such as train stations, shopping malls, or street intersections, flash mobs disconnect and redirect the normal trajectories of all those passing through the area. They stop what had been in motion; they claim a new focus for attention; they make it difficult to get on with what one was doing.[1] As Georgiana Gore has remarked, the mobs create a scene, in the sense of a kind of drama that intervenes in the normal actions of the place in which it occurs, and at the same time, they construct a kind of stage through the coordinated positions and actions of all participants (Gore, 125). By mutually establishing the performance space and subsequently uploading documentation of the event, sometimes carefully edited, flash mobsters create three distinct audiences: the passersby who are taken unawares by what is happening, the performers themselves, and the mostly anonymous group of online viewers who happen on the videos.

Although mobsters are sometimes costumed in a specific and identifiable way, the majority of flash mobs make use of untrained and nonprofessional participants who resemble everyone else in the area. Part of the shock, puzzlement, or delight that the mobs provoke in those around them comes from the sudden awareness that not all the people in the space have the same status or purpose. It is initially baffling and sometimes impossible even over the course of the entire event to determine who is a "performer" and who is not. Still, the mobs function, in part, as creators of new but very transitory communities among both participants and surprised passersby, all of whom experience an abrupt if brief reconfiguration of their pedestrian itineraries.

In their organization, flash mobs model themselves on social media structures that provide an opportunity to connect, then share, participate, and comment, and eventually disperse (Brejzek, 112). They have even been described as a "physicalization of viral culture" (Brejzek, 111). However, rather than merely corporealizing social media, I would argue that flash mobs cycle in and out of the Internet. Transitory in the moment of their implementation, flash mobs garner a more enduring presence on the Web, which initially facilitated their existence. Indeed, in some cases, as John Muse argues, flash mobs are "premediated," that is, designed for the Web even before being performed (Muse, 19). In this sense, they vacillate between the physical and the virtual and between the ephemeral and the somewhat more permanent.

Additionally, flash mobs are located at the interstices of theater, dance, and spectacle, calling into question the boundaries between these mediums. They frequently call on participants to engage in dialogue as well as orchestrated movement, and they locate themselves within space so as to pull focus toward their commotion and away from the complex visual and aural stimulation that constitutes urban space. A subgenre of the flash mob, the dance mob, has emerged, seeming to reinstantiate the distinction between theater and dance, in that the choreography, learned in live or online rehearsals, is far more complex and detailed. Often beginning with a soloist or small group of dancers and then expanding incrementally until a large group is present, the dancers perform in unison in evenly spaced lines, oriented toward the presence of a camera that is filming the action. The routines are frequently formulaic, relying on canon, as in a rolling of motion through the crowd from one end to the other, and traveling toward and away from center to enliven a bland and simplistic vocabulary, usually derived from hip-hop. Less interactive than other flash mobs, dance mobs emphasize the display of skills and enthusiasm more than any disruption or commentary on the space itself and its typical uses. Still, they share with the other types of flash mobs the unexpected appropriation of a public space for a new purpose, the use of diversely trained and untrained participants, and the ability to gather an audience and instill in them a sense of wonderment at best and annoyance at worst.

In what follows, I want to consider how flash mobs articulate with metropoles and their public spaces and what kinds of politics they embody. I will also assess the complex set of ethical issues concerning the participation of passersby that the flash mobs engender. I will focus in particular on some of the works of Improv Everywhere, a New York–based group of self-named "pranksters" coordinated by Charlie Todd, examining what they claim they are doing as well as what they refrain from mentioning about their pranks. I will also consider the experiences of those who decide to participate in a given event and how their voluntary presence subtly disturbs the foundations of consumer capitalism.

THE POLITICS OF/IN URBAN SPACES

Resuscitated in the Renaissance, the Greek agora and Roman forum served as models in the West for the development of public spaces, areas within cities designated as open and accessible to the public. Typically hosting markets, public debate, and recreational pursuits, public

spaces evolved in the seventeenth, eighteenth, and nineteenth centuries as architectural signifiers for a notion of the public as a people who share a set of beliefs and etiquettes defining
the comportment of citizens interacting in common. Conceptualized as existing in opposition to private spaces, such as homes and businesses, public space suggested the possibility
of an egalitarian exchange among residents of and visitors to a region, or for the purposes of
this essay, a city.[2]

In recent years, the status of public space has been interrogated from within the fields of
urban planning, landscape architecture, art history, technology studies, and performance
studies, to name but a few. A variety of scholars in all these disciplines agree on the decline
or erosion of urban public space over the last thirty years brought on by the rise of global
capitalism and the branding of public space by corporations or even individual donors.
Following Lefebvre, critics have argued that public spaces have been homogenized and
fragmented so as to become capable of exchange as commodity. Following Debord, critics
have proposed that public space has become the container for an endless series of spectacles,
prompting the visual artist Wodiczko to call Union Square, the space for which he designed
one of his projections, "fake architectural real estate theater" (quoted in Deutsche, 33). The
square, already thoroughly corporatized even as it has been designed to appear as free and
open, becomes the stage, the host, and the performer of real estate theater.[3]

At the same time, new technologies such as the smartphone and the iPod have introduced
the private into the public thereby blurring and blending the two in unprecedented ways.
On the one hand, pedestrians navigating public spaces can now insulate themselves aurally
through the use of ear buds from any public pronouncements or attempts at interaction. On
the other hand, cell phone users frequently divulge the intimate details of their personal lives
while chatting with friends or conducting business as they move through the city. Taken
together, the claiming of public space by private corporations and the selective introduction
of personal information into the social sphere by individuals have significantly eroded and
perhaps thoroughly eradicated earlier experiences of public space and its function.[4]

In tandem with this overhaul of public space, comportment within public space in cities
in the West has been profoundly altered by terrorist tactics that have targeted these spaces so
as to advance their political critique of the West and promote fear and heightened anxiety.
In the United States, especially since the 2001 attacks on the World Trade Center, citizens
have been exhorted to surveil one another, to assess any impropriety in appearance or non-
normative activity in order to anticipate and guard against a possible attack. The climate of
suspicion engendered by these events has further docilized and alienated all those passing
through public spaces.[5]

Flash mobs, in particular, and urban hacking, more generally, have been interpreted as
articulating a resistance to the hegemonic and anonymous organization of power that now
organizes and defines public space. Embodying De Certeau's distinction between the tactical and the strategic, a huge variety of projects and initiatives have been instigated to repur-
pose urban public space or reanimate its earlier function as a public forum. From spray
paint–based graffiti, one of the earliest examples of tactical resistance, beginning in the early
1980s, to more contemporary efforts at urban gardening; from city-based parcours to urban
and suburban planking; from elderly women exercising in parking lots to installation artists
exploring the intersection between gallery and public space by creating sites where viewers in the very act of participating become performers, a variety of groups are endeavoring
to resist this new status of public space.[6] These initiatives challenge the transformation of

public space into corporately owned space available for advertising and the relentless and aggressive efforts to attract consumers and derive information about their preferences. They also endeavor to intervene in public anonymity and alienation.

Improv Everywhere's *Frozen Grand Central* provides a powerful example of flash mobs' efforts to revitalize public space.[7] Responding to an online invitation to show up on a Saturday afternoon in February 2007, approximately two hundred volunteers met in a bitterly cold Bryant Park to receive instructions from Todd and synchronize their watches. They then entered the large lobby of the Grand Central Train Station and at the appointed time froze into statue-like poses for five minutes. The number of volunteers was sufficient to make a clear visual statement throughout the entire lobby, forcing all passengers commuting to or from the trains to go around the individual statues. The volunteers had stilled themselves into postures that revealed actions interrupted: starting to sneeze, waving toward a friend, searching in one's handbag, etc., and as such, they presented a marvelous range of human actions, halted for contemplation. Initially alarmed by so many people suddenly screeching to a stop, viewers slowly relaxed and began to enjoy the newly created performance space.

Todd and some of the Improv Everywhere team moved among the frozen people pretending to be passersby and setting a tone for responses by casually asking others if they knew what was happening, and in Todd's case, even poking gently at one of the statues. The team's movements through the space also enabled them to record visually and aurally the general response including the hilarious request for assistance sent by one of the workers in the station who was trying to transport garbage. Others surmised that the event was either a protest or an acting class. These responses were then carefully edited and uploaded into a document of the entire performance that went viral as soon as it was posted to You-Tube. What was its appeal?

The video invites online viewers into the event, encouraging them to imagine it happening to them and documenting a range of responses from startled apprehension to intrigue and delight. Wandering amid the statues and appreciating the diverse actions they depicted, one might have experienced the train station transforming into theater or museum. The statues were haphazard and funky enough to be nonthreatening, since all participants wore regular street clothes and the actions they were staging were familiar. Yet there was also a formality in the sheer number of statues that created a mass sufficient to make an impression, possibly inviting viewers to run up the steps to the upper level for a view out over the entire lobby so as to assess the full impact of the action.

Frozen Grand Central created a rupture in the daily pedestrian flow of events by introducing something marvelous and unanticipated that prompted people to reflect, however fleetingly, on their own actions and their relative attentiveness to quotidian life. It encouraged a reconsideration of the flexibility of the social body to accommodate deviance, and the range of actions and events that it understands to be acceptable or not, and it demonstrated that such flexibility endures in spite of the tightened restrictions on one's movements resulting from the post-9/11 orientation toward terror. It also defied the anonymity of public space by creating a rubric in which individuals could potentially interact with strangers, forming a momentary social bond.

Exemplary of the ways in which flash mobs resist the commodification and anonymity of public space, the structure of *Frozen Grand Central* and that of other flash mobs has been appropriated by a variety of commercial institutions in order to promote their interests and products. For example, T-Mobile's take-over of the Liverpool Train Station in

2009 presented a collage of excerpts from different dance styles performed to well-known music ranging from the "Blue Danube" to "Do the Twist" by approximately 100 dancers.[8] The dancers performed in unison oriented toward a camera that documented the event from the second floor balcony. Subsequently posted to You-Tube, the film shows various passersby joining in to improvise to sections of the performance whose music was familiar, creating a kind of public celebration, a euphoric moment in an otherwise humdrum day.[9]

Although the dance abruptly interrupted pedestrian traffic flow and invited passersby to enjoy something unique, unanticipated, and delightful, much as in *Grand Central Station*, there exist subtle but crucial differences between the two events. First, because the dancers had previously rehearsed the routine they performed, their performance addressed the audience with far more formality, creating a clearly delineated stage space that contained the performance rather than a field of action through which passersby could wander. Also, unlike *Frozen Grand Central*, it was joyful and cute from the very beginning, thereby assuring viewers of its niceness. The dancers were clearly performing for the public rather than looking exactly like the public only frozen. Through their facial expressions and bodily address they asked passersby to watch and enjoy them.

The video of the event, posted to You-Tube and viewed by over 35 million people thus far, is titled the *T-Mobile Dance* and ends with the T-Mobile logo. There are no obvious connections between the dance and its sponsor, the smartphone company, beyond the intimation that T-Mobile similarly brings people together in a joyous way. Where previously, the public sector might have provided the opportunity to experience a free entertaining moment under the auspices of its dedication to providing enriching events for its citizens, now such events are accessed through the medium of advertisement. Furthermore, advertising itself no longer entails selling a product by demonstrating its virtues, but instead, consists simply in claiming a consumer's attention for a period of time. In the process the Liverpool Train Station becomes rebranded as a T-Mobile site, and the volunteers who learned and performed the dance as well as the passersby whose inventive responses make the video so entertaining have had their labor co-opted to promote the identity and renown of a corporation.[10]

Flash mobs are thus operating in multiple arenas that promote or contest the corporatization of public spaces. However, the distinctions between public and private and commercial and governmental are so blurred as to make the assessment of any given event quite complex. For example, a third example of flash mob usage comes from the performance conducted to promote the Governor's Awards for the Arts in York, Pennsylvania.[11] This event, taking place at an intersection in downtown York, featured a very diverse group of dancers, more so than the Liverpool performance, in terms of age, race, and training, all performing simple routines alongside one another while passersby cheered them on as if in support of a policy of broad inclusivity promoted by this governmental arts organization. Like T-Mobile, this public sector institution is advertising its values and commitments, yet in the name of a project, awards for artists, that generally receives very little public support. It is not merely the sponsor of the event that matters in terms of deciphering its political significance. The constituency performing, the organization of the choreography, and the narrative that the performance develops all play a role in constructing a mob's ideological impact.

PRANKS, MOBS, AND IMPROV

Todd does not consider what he does as within the category of the flash mob, although he admits that in the case of *Frozen Grand Central*, it is an accurate descriptor. He prefers the term "prank," and notes that he began his events two years prior to the self-announced beginning of the flash mob by Bill Wassik.[12] Like Wassik, however, he generally avoids commenting on the politics embedded in the events as I have outlined them above. He prefers to speak about "giving people a great story to tell,"[13] or providing a shared experience where an individual can laugh with others.[14] He also refers to pleasing people and giving them a chance to have fun:[15]

> Part of the message of Improv Everywhere is that there doesn't have to be a message. You can get together with others and stage creative projects in public places simply because it's fun. You don't need to be promoting a charity, cause or brand to come together and do something funny that makes others laugh or smile.

Todd continues by making a distinction between his pranks that are open to multiple interpretations and other more didactic performances with a single clear message:

> For our projects, having a message revealed at the end would ruin the moment. I want people to be walking through Grand Central, notice someone frozen in place in front of them, then notice that there are hundreds frozen all around them, and then briefly consider the possibility that time has stopped. If all of the frozen participants are wearing T-shirts that read, "Freeze for Global Warming," the moment is immediately ruined. The magic is gone.[16]

Not only is Todd proposing a distinction between events with messages and events without messages but he is also intimating the usefulness of performing useless acts shoulder to shoulder with others. Rather than focus on a specific issue or cause, Todd sees value in doing something that produces nothing other than an uncanny silliness.

A similar sense of collective fun-making is evident in choreographer Michael Gracey's assessment of a kick off party for Oprah Winfrey's 24th season. More than 20,000 people performed a dance choreographed to the Black Eyed Peas' "I Gotta Feeling," for an over-whelmingly large television audience along with a very surprised and thrilled Winfrey. About the event, Gracey commented that the interaction between the Black Eyed Peas and the crowd was what made the flash mob so extraordinary:

> There's something really special when you take an audience and instead of just being passive and watching, you invite them to participate. That's why it was so magical for both parties. Two groups of people came together to create something that neither of them could have done alone.[17]

Taking place in downtown Chicago, the full sequence of steps was posted well in advance online so that anyone could learn it, attend, and participate. Again, a simple set of instructions brought a massive number of strangers into a common enterprise, but this time with the purpose of celebrating Oprah. Were people that dedicated to Winfrey's work or were they merely enthralled with the possibility of all turning out to do something "fun" in unison?

Todd would also distinguish his approach from the kind of unison flash mob organized for Oprah based on the fact that a majority of his pranks contain a substantial amount of unplanned improvised interaction among all participants. Trained extensively in stand-up comedy and other improvised performance, Todd understands that improvisation does not imply a chaotic and un-orchestrated profusion of action, but instead a carefully blended negotiation between structure and discovery, and between the carefully planned and the unprecedented. Pranksters are given clear guidelines for how to act and interact, and the team makes a diligent effort to anticipate and prepare for every contingency. Like all good improvisers, they make use of already established material and kinds of responses along with well-learned principles for how to engage with the new.

In *Best Buy*, for example, eighty or more volunteers showed up to enter a Best Buy store sporting the same blue shirts and khaki pants that store workers wear. Advised by Todd to be helpful to customers when possible, the pranksters stood or wandered around in a very non-threatening manner. They engaged with customers, staff, and eventually managers and security guards, who became panicked at the large number of similarly clad pseudostaffers. In the dialogue documented online, a security officer asks Todd whether he is purchasing anything, to which he responds, "I'm waiting for my wife." Then, when told to leave because of what he is wearing, Todd repeats the command as a question "You mean you're throwing me out of the store because I'm wearing the same clothes you are?" thereby demonstrating the overreactive stance of the managers and the preposterousness of the event itself. Todd's demeanor and tone of voice are casual and unassuming, inviting the security officer to rethink the suddenly invented policy while also underscoring the discrepancy between the volunteers' gentle actions and the managerial response. His improvised dialogue with the officer takes place within well-conceived and practiced guidelines that establish his character.

Although Todd, like most other organizers of flash mobs, eschews any political significance within their actions, he does seem committed to the way that improvisation, when pursued as structured spontaneity, can function to encourage positive social interaction. He also admits that even if there are no messages in his work, there is a politics embodied in his work. He does not address the political potential within his absurd challenge of Best Buy's management, but he does admit to a politics of claiming one's right to free assembly in public:

> We are exercising our right to freely assemble and express ourselves in public space. We do not ask for permission for this expression; we just do it. New Yorkers are assaulted with outdoor public advertising, much of which is illegal, on every block. Our public space shouldn't be reserved for just paid advertiser messages. We as residents of the city should also have the right to express ourselves peacefully.[18]

For Todd, Improv Everywhere may tacitly assert a commentary, more than promote a message, about its right to occupy the streets, and take public space back from private control. But is there also a politics embedded in doing useless fun things?

THE VOLUNTEER BODY

One of the central and crucial features of Improv Everywhere's pranks and of flash mobs more generally is their reliance on volunteers, untrained bodies that simply show up to participate in the planned events. Unlike many varieties of corporeal cultivation today that strive for virtuosity, efficiency, or perfection, what I will call "the volunteer body" willingly donates its time and its labor. It has no desire to achieve an economy of motion or to profit from its work. Instead it disrupts economies by producing absurd excess, an excess that can sometimes reveal the underlying hegemonic organization of bodily motion.

For example, *Frozen Grand Central* made visible the inculcated efficiency of pedestrians' transit across the lobby and their preferred isolation one from another through contrast with the two hundred volunteers who showed up to freeze in place. A second example by Improv Everywhere, *Where's Rob*, likewise relied on volunteers to donate their ingenuity and physical energy, however in this prank they were unwitting participants in the performance.[19] For *Where's Rob?* an Improv Everywhere team bought tickets to a New York Knicks game at Madison Square Garden, and at half-time, one member of the team, Rob, leaves his seat to buy drinks and snacks from the vendors outside, returning to the stadium at a considerable distance from his seat. His fellow performers then begin to shout out his name, wave, and otherwise try to attract his attention so as to help him realize he is in the wrong section of the stadium. Rob's character is affable, but disoriented and none too bright, so he soon descends from that area of the stadium and emerges in another, even further removed from his original seat. His fellow performers become increasingly vocal, and begin to enlist others in attracting his attention. As Rob continues to look lost and unable to determine the location of his seat, more and more people begin to try to attract his attention and direct him toward the proper area. Some groups of bystanders invent chants, others hold up colorful T-shirts; others wave in unison, so that soon the entire section of the stadium in which Rob was originally sitting has been enlisted to alert Rob to the whereabouts of his seat. And even this concerted buzz of attention-getting choreographies begins to expand, so that eventually what seems like a full quarter of the stadium is involved in getting Rob back to his friends.

In this prank, bystanders spontaneously invented a variety of gestures, some individual, and some collective, in order to communicate with Rob. The gestures themselves travel, expanding as more people adopt them, morphing again as they join up with or otherwise interface with movements from other good-willed participants. The crowd incorporates song, chant, and props, creating a heterogeneous yet interrelated mélange of actions. The movements are not prescribed but instead created in order to suit a particular need at a given time. They decamp from the standard repertoire of vocal and physical actions performed at a game, and begin to circulate in a newly formed route of travel. Although they seek a response, they are not striving to win.

Those who conspire to help Rob, unknown to one another, are brought into connection with one another through their common desire to ameliorate the situation of an individual. They work collectively to improve social amiability. Their labor is unself-conscious and happily given to the project of recuperating Rob. They share a delight in contributing as both choreographers and performers with no motivation to economize or sell their actions. Additionally, their motions provide commentary on the game itself, since their gestures share basic features with the chants that would normally be deployed in cheering the team on. Rob, however, has proven a more enjoyable and fascinating project than the very game they paid money to watch.

Eventually, Rob is restored to his seat, only moments before the end of the game. As attendees move toward the exit, they stop to shake Rob's hand or pat him on the back, offering expressions of satisfaction and even joy at his safe return. As edited in the video, they seem both delighted with the diversion Rob provided and also relieved that he found his way back to his friends. As one attendee remarked, "You made my game." But how might that person feel watching himself on You-tube, a dupe who strategized and labored conscientiously to garner the attention of someone who was purposely ignoring him and only pretending to be in trouble?

FLASH MOBBING ETHICALLY

Where's Rob, along with countless other flash mob actions, raises questions concerning the ethical dimension of the encounters between those in the know and those who show up to participate and whose actions are subsequently documented online. In an era where privacy issues loom large in both pedestrian and online life, what responsibilities do Todd and other flash mob organizers have to those who, voluntarily or not, are swept up into the event? When Todd poses as an unknowing pedestrian in *Frozen Grand Central* and asks with seeming amazement "How long has this been happening?" what relationship with other legitimately unknowing passersby is he establishing?

Comparing flash mobs' engagement with the social to performances conducted by Augusto Boal, Muse argues that for Boal, participation in performance would liberate the "spect-actor," Boal's term for the new kind of audience member his events created, from societal restrictions and allow him to think and act for himself. Boal's practice of Invisible Theater sited the performance of highly scripted scenarios in nontheatrical spaces, where the public would witness and become engaged with the narrative being presented. Unlike Improv Everywhere's pranks that implement improvised interaction with spectators, Boal's theater crafted dialog so as to highlight issues of social injustice. Boal's spect-actors were also encouraged to suggest actions that might solve a social problem, whereas for participants in flash mobs, participation itself becomes its own reward (Muse, 19). As Todd argues, having a message would ruin the fun.

Boal worked in a historical moment and cultural location where socialist values were actively debated and sometimes promoted. If I open a discussion with my students at UCLA about Boal's actor posing as a workman who orders an expensive dinner at an elite restaurant in order to provoke a consideration of the relative worth of his labor as opposed to that of the other diners, the vast majority of those in my classroom respond in these terms: "If he didn't have the money he shouldn't have gone to the restaurant and ordered what he did." I interpret this response as indicative of the vastly diminished dialogue around the relative worth of different kinds of labor and the general acceptance of serious discrepancies in quality of life and access to public amenities for certain members in a class system which itself is unacknowledged. Perhaps Todd, sensing the inefficacy of an approach such as Boal's in New York City today, has determined to persist in shaking things up without debating the consequences.

Still, *Where's Rob?* garnered a significant amount of cooperation from participants who were assuming that Rob really was lost. Having elicited genuine concern and sympathy for the apparently disoriented sports fan, how might viewers feel if they learned that it was a hoax? Insofar as they might feel embarrassed or annoyed, *Where's Rob* tears at an already fragile social fabric, exacerbating the alienation and purposelessness that many urban dwellers feel about the possibility of functioning as a caring and compassionate public. Insofar as those participants might dismiss their gullibility in favor of the entertainment that Rob's cluelessness provided, it validates social tolerance while at the same time reminding participants that all is never as it appears.

Unlike the popular television show *Candid Camera*, where each hoax was revealed to the person "caught" on camera during the filming, Improv Everywhere's pranks are only revealed after the fact online. Perhaps this is why Todd was thrilled when the woman riding in the subway car filmed during the first *No Pants Subway Ride* in 2002 contacted him ten years later, having just been alerted to the fact that she was a major performer on their website. In preparation for the tenth anniversary of the ride, in which, over the years, increasing numbers of men and women have ridden the New York subway pants-less on a designated day and time, Improv Everywhere re-released the original footage, and the woman was identified by a friend who had seen it on the website. The woman, who was initially concerned and eventually bemused by the pants-less men who entered her subway car, was ten years later pleased to claim her renown as part of Improv Everywhere's online life.

The videos of performances by Improv Everywhere and other flash mobs that are uploaded onto You-tube and other sites focus both on the dancers and the viewers, and they typically include footage of unconventional or unpredictable responses to the performances by audience members. They also document the extent to which individuals deploy handheld devices such as smartphones as cameras to document their own version of the event, thereby reinforcing the connectivity between pedestrian and virtual realities. Everyone associated with the events can, insofar as they participate in Smartphone culture, upload their own version of what happened. In mobs that are more presentational such as the Liverpool Station performance, fewer ethical ambiguities seem to exist, since the sudden unison actions of a large number of people construct a clear distinction between performing and viewing, even as some passersby decide to join in. When they do choose to participate and their actions are subsequently displayed online, the fact that they acted knowingly in public mitigates against any claims to invasion of privacy.

A website such as Improv Everywhere's, well organized with arrestingly edited documents of most of the pieces, narrativizes all participants responses into clear and coherent interactions that develop over time. Everyone is having fun, and no one minds the interruption. Whereas T-Mobile's rebranding of Liverpool Station obfuscates its advertising campaign through an unambiguous presentation of fun dancing, Improv Everywhere masks over possible objections to the event through the careful placement of cameras and the subsequent editing of the footage. Each type of event avoids addressing some of its ideological impact, but in very different ways.

At the same time, Improv Everywhere's online documents generously share the strategic planning and schematics for each prank, providing a how-to kit of possible insurrections for anyone who would like to try one. Their website encourages others to contemplate ways in which to stage similar events in other cities, contexts, and environments. Todd even invites suggestions for future actions from those connected to his listserv around the world. Improv Everywhere does not guard their secret processes or remain silent about their techniques for implementation. Instead, they extend a generous invitation to come and play along, nurturing the inclinations of all would-be volunteers.

WHY NOT IMPROV EVERYWHERE?

When he doesn't call them pranks, Todd refers to Improv Everywhere events as "missions," whose volunteer participants are addressed as "agents." With this nomenclature Todd again debunks the seriousness of efforts to fight the war on terror or guard against corporate and national espionage. How could a mission consist in riding the subway pants-less? But that preposterousness is precisely what Todd is trying to achieve. Improv Everywhere's missions frequently test the limits of social tolerance for difference, and they reclaim public space for use by the public. Like other flash mobs, they invite passersby to experience something unusual and marvelous in their day and thereby to reflect on the nature and quality of their engagement with the pedestrian. They also defeat momentarily the alienation of urban pedestrian life and create a brief sense of connection or even community among all those in the environs of the event.

Despite their beguiling address and the opportunity they offer to reflect on public space, Muse argues that flash mobs construct a moment of connection that fails to sustain itself. He finds that the culture of narcissism and the consumption of spectacle are converging in the flash mob, such that community is achieved but only momentarily, followed by the unending opportunity to watch oneself online over and over again (Muse, 12). He is also concerned that the initial frisson that flash mobs offer when they first begin and transition from the pedestrian into the uncanny will soon become so familiar that all of us in the society of spectacle will become inured to their effects (Muse, 22). With the appropriation by corporations of the flash mob structure for the purposes of advertising and the privatization of public space, the impact of the flash mob becomes potentially even more diffuse and without effect. Since they offer no sustained opportunity for face-to-face contact but only the ability to post and share online, the mobs could be seen to present the illusion of community without any substantial engagement.

Still, large numbers of people show up to participate in these events, to volunteer their labor for the hell of it and for the possibility of forging some new kind of communal contact among otherwise alienated or disinterested parties. In so doing, they tacitly refuse to be efficient or otherwise fit into the economy of capitalism. Using what is at hand, and committing themselves fully to the action, they thwart the tendency, so rampant in today's live and media representations of dancing, to present a routine vocabulary of expressive gestures and virtuoso steps, all harnessed to promote a hyperbolic physicality in the service of spectacle.[20]

Or, seen from a different perspective, are they providing the labor and creativity for someone else's project? As Nicole Cohen argues in relationship to companies such as Facebook, the users of the product are also generating the content of the product. This is particularly evident in an event like *Where's Rob?* in which the spontaneously invented gestures and chants articulate an imaginative, new choreography, a choreography that subsequently entertains Improv Everywhere fans as they surf the website. Everyone had fun, but who profits in terms of cultural or financial capital? Or is this the right question to ask?

Bonni Rambatan has argued that the twentieth century was occupied with the problem of representation. As a result, discrimination and inequity consisted of an imbalance in degrees of and access to the means of production. Those critical of the distribution of power endeavored to expose the mechanisms that lie behind the means of production through tactics such as picketing or striking. In contrast, the twenty-first century has thus far been defined by presentation, with the problem of "presenting the right stuff" for all to see. In its first decade it has been defined by cynicism in which "scandals are always-already exposed" and "ideology already expects you to subvert it." Techniques such as urban hacking have emerged in response to the new focus on presentation, because as Rambatan points out: "In this century, with these new emergent hybrid spaces, resistance no longer means taking back the means of production, but *taking place as a means of production*." [emphasis in the original] (Rambatan, 48).[21]

If Rambatan has correctly assessed the epistemic shift that is underway, then having fun by participating in flash mobs takes on a whole new meaning. Participants in these events are showing up to perform as a means of production. Their useless actions not only debunk capitalist strategies of wealth acquisition and provide an antidote to efficient, productive work, but they also insist on their own productivity as something that has simply taken place. They "compete" with advertising campaigns that succeed by commanding consumers' attention, insisting on the value of performance, not in spite of its ephemerality but because of it.

Whatever the longevity and impact of flash mobs, we will not be able to assess the effects of these kinds of events if we fail to broaden our definitions of theater and dance. An analysis of the text or the movements will not suffice to deduce their significance. Instead, we must examine their auspices and location, their dramaturgy and choreography, and the resulting form of address through which they summon viewers into engagement with them.

NOTES

1. Brejzek refers to them as "temporary nodes of irritation into pedestrian and transport trajectories." Thea Brejzek, "From Social Network to Urban Intervention: On the Scenographies of Flash Mobs and Urban Swarms," *International Journal of Performance Arts and Digital Media* 6, no. 1 (2010): 110. She also sees them as designed to "halt the eternal mobility of the postmodern metropolis" (ibid., 117).

2. I do not mean to suggest that such forms of egalitarian exchange actually took place in these public spaces, but only that that possibility was cited as a prime motivation for their development.

3. For more perspective on the relationship between space, ideology, and art in public spaces, see Rosalyn Deutsche, *Evictions: Art and Spatial Politics* (Cambridge, MA: MIT Press), 1996. Deutsche examines the city's redevelopment policies in relation to various artistic initiatives designed to highlight the role of public art and its interactivity with issues of pressing social concern such as homelessness.

4. This seems to be particularly true in urban centers within the United States. Unlike Europe and Asia, where texting is far more common than talking on the phone, smartphone users in the United States converse frequently as they commute, shop, dine, and otherwise occupy public space.

5. Considerable anxiety and suspicion developed in the aftermath of September 11, 2001, as a consequence of the extensive national security apparatus that was constructed in the wake of the events of that day. In addition to more than 4,600 newly installed video cameras located in Manhattan alone, citizens were recruited to spy on one another through bus and subway billboard campaigns that urge residents to stay alert: "if you see something, say something." Subsequent New York Metropolitan Transit Authority campaigns

further stressed the necessity of individual participation to the security of the metropolis while warning potential terrorists that "there are 16 million eyes in the city. We're counting on all of them." For a full analysis of the surveillance campaign along with various artists' responses to it, see Sara Wolf, *Choreographing Citizenship in the Age of the IED*, PhD dissertation, University of California, Los Angeles, 2013. See also Shane Harris, *The Watchers: The Rise of America's Surveillance State* (New York: Penguin Press, 2010); David Lyon and Kevin D. Haggerty, "The Surveillance Legacies of 9/11: Recalling, Reflecting on, and Rethinking Surveillance in the Security Era," *Canadian Journal of Law and Society* 27, no. 3 (2012); Richard Maxwell, "Surveillance: Work, Myth, and Policy," *Social Text 83* (2005): 1–19; and Dana Priest and William M. Arkin. *Top Secret America: The Rise of the New American Security State* (New York: Little, Brown, 2011).

6. For more perspective on the repurposing of public space, see Jeffrey Hou, ed. *Insurgent Public Space: Guerilla Urbanism and the Remaking of Contemporary Cities* (New York and London: Routledge, 2010). An especially vivid example is covered in Caroline Chen's examination of middle-aged and elderly women in Beijing who meet regularly to perform "yangge," a dance form that they learned in northern China during the Cultural Revolution. See Caroline Chen, "Dancing in the Streets of Beijing: Improvised Uses within the Urban System," in *Insurgent Public Space: Guerilla Urbanism and the Remaking of Contemporary Cities*, edited by Jeffrey Hou (New York and London: Routledge, 2010), 21–35.

7. http://www.youtube.com/watch?v=jwMj3PJDxuo

8. http://www.youtube.com/watch?v=VQ3d3KigPQM

9. A similar example of appropriation of mobs for commercial interests took place in the Central Station of Antwerp, where a dance choreographed to "Do, Re Mi" was sponsored by the state television corporation, looking for a lead to play Maria in *The Sound of Music*. See http://www.youtube.com/watch?v=7EYAUazLI9k

10. It is unclear whether the dancers in the performance signed contracts with T-Mobile concerning their involvement, but it is highly unlikely that the passersby were contacted to give permission to circulate their performances online.

11. http://www.youtube.com/watch?v=P6VRFsSidIc&feature=autoplay&list=PLB77859F033 18602F&playnext=2

12. Charlie Todd, Answers about Improv Everywhere, Part 1," *New York Times*, January 15, 2010. For more on Wassik and the general relationship of flash mobs to the situationists and other forms of pranksterism, see John H. Muse, "Flash Mobs and the Diffusion of Audience," *Theater* 40, no. 3 (2010); and Brejzek, "From Social Networks to Urban Intervention."

13. Charlie Todd and Alex Scordelis, *Causing a Scene: Extraordinary Pranks in Ordinary Places with Improv Everywhere* (New York: HarperCollins, 2009), 12.

14. Charlie Todd, "Ted Talk," Ted.com, 2011, http://www.ted.com/talks/charlie_todd_the_ shared_experience_of_absurdity.html

15. For example, he explains in response to a question about why he should not use his resources to organize help for a soup kitchen, "Participation in Improv Everywhere events is just a way to have fun for a couple of hours on a weekend afternoon. While some people might choose to go to a sporting event, movie, or stay at home and type angry Internet comments, our participants choose to, say, shop in slow motion at a Home Depot with 200 other people. Whether or not that is 'stupid' is a matter of opinion, but it definitely doesn't preclude anyone from volunteering with a charitable organization the other 166 hours of the week." Todd, "Answers about Improv Everywhere, Part 2."

16. Todd, "Answers about Improv Everywhere, Part 3."
17. Michael Gracey, quoted at http://www.oprah.com/entertainment/Oprahs-Kickoff-Party-Flash-Mob-Dance#ixzz1ypZ878rw.
18. Todd, "Answers about Improv Everywhere, Part 3."
19. http://www.snotr.com/video/3468/Where_s_Rob.
20. I am thinking here of televised dance competitions such as *So You Think You Can Dance?*, *Dance Moms*, and *Dancing with the Stars*.
21. Rambatan adds, "What does it mean to have things "taking place?" Urban hacking is a "conscious effort to ask—through action or art, and as loudly as possible—such questions." Bonnie Rambatan, "Spandrel Evolution: Emergent Spaces for Resistance," In *Urban Hacking: Cultural Jamming Strategies in the Risky Spaces of Modernity*, edited by Gunther Friesinger, Johannes Grenzfurthner, and Thomas Ballhausen (Bielefeld, Germany: Transcript, 2010), 47.

BIBLIOGRAPHY

Brejzek, Thea. "From Social Network to Urban Intervention: On the Scenographies of Flash Mobs and Urban Swarms." *International Journal of Performance Arts and Digital Media* 6, no. 1 (2010): 109–122.

Chen, Caroline. "Dancing in the Streets of Beijing: Improvised Uses within the Urban System." In *Insurgent Public Space: Guerilla Urbanism and the Remaking of Contemporary Cities*, edited by Jeffrey Hou, 21–35. New York and London: Routledge, 2010.

Cohen, Nicole S. "The Valorization of Surveillance: Towards a Political Economy of Facebook." *Democratic Communiqué* 22, no. 1 (Spring 2008): 5–22.

Debord, Guy. *The Society of Spectacle*. Translated by Fredy Perlman and Jon Supak. Detroit: Black & Red, 1977.

De Certeau, Michel. *The Practice of Everyday Life*. Berkeley and Los Angeles: University of California Press, 1984.

Deutsche, Rosalyn. *Evictions: Art and Spatial Politics*. Cambridge, MA: MIT Press, 1998.

Friesinger, Gunther, Johannes Grenzfurthner, and Thomas Ballhausen, eds., *Urban Hacking: Cultural Jamming Strategies in the Risky Spaces of Modernity*. Bielefeld, Germany: Transcript, 2010.

Gore, Georgina. "Flash Mob Dance and the Territorialisation of Urban Movement." *Anthropological Notebooks* 16, no. 3 (2010): 125–31.

Harris, Shane. *The Watchers: The Rise of America's Surveillance State*. New York: Penguin Press, 2010.

Hou, Jeffrey, ed. *Insurgent Public Space: Guerrilla Urbanism and the Remaking of Contemporary Cities*. New York and London: Routledge, 2010.

Lefebvre, Henri. *The Production of Space*. Cambridge, MA: Blackwell, 1991.

Low, Setha, and Neil Smith, eds. *The Politics of Public Space*. New York: Routledge, 2006.

Lyon, David, and Kevin D. Haggerty. "The Surveillance Legacies of 9/11: Recalling, Reflecting on, and Rethinking Surveillance in the Security Era." *Canadian Journal of Law and Society* 27, no. 3 (2012): 291–300.

Marchbank, Thomas. "Intense Flows: Flashmobbing, Rush Capital and the Swarming of Space." *Philament* 4 (2004).

Maxwell, Richard. "Surveillance: Work, Myth, and Policy." *Social Text* 83 (2005): 1–19.

Muse, John H. "Flash Mobs and the Diffusion of Audience." *Theater* 40, no. 3 (2010): 8–23.

Priest, Dana, and William M. Arkin. *Top Secret America: The Rise of the New American Security State*. New York: Little, Brown, 2011.

Rambatan, Bonnie. "Spandrel Evolution: Emergent Spaces for Resistance." In *Urban Hacking: Cultural Jamming Strategies in the Risky Spaces of Modernity*, edited by Gunther Friesinger, Johannes Grenzfurthner, and Thomas Ballhausen, 45–49. Bielefeld, Germany: Transcript, 2010.

Rheingold, Howard. *Smart Mobs: The Next Social Revolution*. Cambridge, MA: Perseus, 2002.

Salter, Chris. *Entangled: Technology and the Transformation of Performance*. Cambridge, MA: MIT Press, 2010.

Stevens, Quentin. *The Ludic City: Exploring the Power of Public Spaces*. London: Routledge, 2007.

Todd, Charlie. "Answers about Improv Everywhere, Part 3," *New York Times*, January 15, 2010.

Todd, Charlie. "Ted Talk." Ted.com. 2011. http://www.ted.com/talks/charlie_todd_the_shared_experience_of_absurdity.html.

Walters, Ben. "Unamused at Abercrombie & Fitch." *Film Quarterly* (Summer 2008).

Todd, Charlie, and Alex Scordelis. *Causing a Scene: Extraordinary Pranks in Ordinary Places with Improv Everywhere*. New York: HarperCollins, 2009.

Wolf, Sara. *Choreographing Citizenship in the Age of the IED*. PhD dissertation. University of California, Los Angeles, 2013.

SECTION III

GENUS (PART 2)

CHAPTER 11

A THEATER OF BODILY PRESENCE

Pina Bausch and Tanztheater Wuppertal

ROYD CLIMENHAGA

> We shall need to reawaken our experience of the world as it appears to us insofar as we are in the world through our body, and insofar as we perceive the world with our body.[1]

PINA Bausch's *Café Müller* (1978) opens with a woman dressed in a white slip entering the dimly lit stage. She moves hesitantly along the wall, arms slightly extended in front of her, slowly moving past the scattering of café tables and chairs that cover the stage space. As she makes her way toward a revolving door at the back of the space, she runs into a chair, but after carefully negotiating her way around the obstacle, she continues on her journey. Another woman enters through the revolving door and skitters about the tables and chairs before simply exiting. A third woman, also in a white slip, enters through the revolving door and also carefully moves toward the center of what we now see in the growing light is a sea of tables and chairs filling the entirety of the café setting. With her eyes closed, she begins a slow gestural movement pattern, drawing her hand up across her cheek and down her breast and stomach. She looks to be mourning, lamenting the loss of a loved one, before she hurls herself across the space and toward the wall. A man enters and runs to clear her path, sending tables and chairs clattering across the floor, only to have to do it again as the woman flings herself in the other direction, oblivious to the chairs in her way and only narrowly averting danger as the man hurries to clear space for her every move.

The movements this woman performs fall roughly within our expected notion of what constitutes dance—sweeping arm movements, purposeful thrusts through space and gestural hand motions across her body as she pauses to go through her lamenting ritual before striking out into the space again—but we see those movement patterns within the context of what amounts to the theatrical scene that is created and the very real danger the dancer appears to be in as she risks her body in the dramatic action amid the chairs. We are forced to consider the scene from the compelling interaction of the real event that is taking place on stage and the possible interpretations of its metaphoric meaning, both of which take place through the dancer's body. We don't need to ask what the woman's actions mean, they do something, and the effect they have is built up from the felt response to the woman's roles as a character in the unfolding drama, as the performer of emotive qualities of movement, and the very real presence of the dancer in what is an increasingly dangerous situation. Bausch and Tanztheater Wuppertal were well on their way to reconfiguring dance expression in creating this piece in 1978, rigorously incorporating (making body) a theatrical placement in dramatic context, and coming out the other side to consider the relationship between the performer as represented presence and real person. Convenient boundaries between dance and theater are collapsed at the site of the performer's body.

THE REVELATION OF BODILY EXPERIENCE

In more conventional ideas of dance, the dancer's body acts as the carrier of a message, metaphorically addressing ideas or feelings by standing as a marker for them and explicating them through movement. For example, if a choreographer were given the task of creating a dance or section of a dance based on the idea of struggle, he would find specific movements that somehow captured this idea, whether built from a specific moment of struggle, a larger idea of struggle addressed metaphorically, or a combination of both. In all cases he would develop movement patterns, often derived from a set technique—be it ballet or any of various modern techniques—and the success of the piece would be dependent on the ability of the dancer to carry out these movement patterns and the degree to which these movements are able to affect an audience. In Bausch's tanztheater, however, the director simply provides an obstacle to be overcome, and the dancer's struggle to overcome this obstacle becomes the piece. In this case, each individual's struggle to overcome the obstacle is equally valid, whether done with the controlled movements of a trained dancer or the stumbling movements of a beginner. The moment created is necessarily bodily in its action, and it is inherently dramatic because there is no miming, there is only the obstacle that needs to be gotten past. Each approach is not, however, equally interesting or engaging, nor is any scenario. The piece becomes effective and expressive to the degree to which any developed moment of struggle fits into the larger context of the piece and metaphorically reverberates with other moments performed, and the force of the content is carried through commitment to the context. It is the context, and the moment of struggle's placement in that context, that is ultimately the means of expression here, even as that expression takes place solely through bodily engagement. The director or choreographer's craft becomes the selection and arrangement of these moments into a complex and evocative whole.

In *Café Müller*, the conflict with the space is certainly bodily in that we see the effects expressed in bodily terms, but it is constructed on different principles than the traditional dance piece. While the specific movements of the dancer are prescribed, the expressive content of the engaged presence of the dancer does not rely on an established or created movement vocabulary or the dancer's ability to carry out the movements prescribed, but, instead, depends on the bodily action placed within a larger dramatic structure. Beyond realigning the mode of development of a dance, this idea significantly alters the function of the dancer's body on stage, transferring its representational ground from that of an object expressing through developed movement to that of a subject involved in the unfolding of dramatic action.

Bausch's approach reveals this newly enlivened body's connection to the creation of the self and the world, and uses the idea of metaphor to expand and uncover the reality of the dancer's body on stage in all its aspects. Each dancer's body's real engagement with the world is recognized, and that engagement takes on a dual level. First, experience is developed into expressive images that are placed within a context that comments on the specific aspect of embodiment represented. Second, the staged experience simultaneously uses that context and representation to push beyond the surface of each dancer's involvement in specific situations to address the motivations and constructions of our involvements on a broader plane. The dancer, as body, transcends the role of an efficator of movement to reveal a connection to life and subjective placement in the world. That subjective presence, that person in short, can then engage in the larger thematic conceit. The dancers use their bodily involvement in the world to provide access to the idea or emotion being explored, giving the audience both the specificity of the image on stage to grasp and the freedom to make their own associations and interpretations. The content is expressed through the physical enactment of the dancer on stage and we connect to the idea of the performance through that visceral presence. We feel what is happening more than understand what it means on an intellectual level, but that feeling is placed in a context that provides the necessary tools to construct a viable meaning within the piece. The bodily form of expression directly gives rise to content.

Critics and dancers often meet arguments against dance for its anti-intellectualism with a defense of the human body in its ascendant form, where, for once, ideas are antithetical to the sensuous immediacy of the event. Dance becomes removed from life and ideas, only approaching that life through the intermediary of the dancer's body in motion, which stands as a sign to be interpreted. Dancers worked long and hard to achieve this autonomy of movement, but this concentration on movement values negates our bodily placement in the world and creates of the dancer's body an instrument for movement. As much as we might try to remove ourselves from our bodies to become detached, rational subjects, or, conversely, to lose ourselves in sensuous experience, it is through and with our bodies that we are placed in the world and through which we derive our experience of self. It is of and through sensuous experience that we maintain a thought process. Trying to remove sensuous experience from thought leaves us with a hollow, mechanical mind, which is unable to conceive of self and unable to incorporate that self into the creation of ideas. If we retreat into a purely sensuous consideration of dance, however, then our bodies are not aspects of our selves, not the means through which we experience the world, but are efficators of movement, similarly mechanical and removed things that, though lauded within the context of dance, remain separate from our selves as other.

This separation of body and self comes out of the dominant influence of Cartesianism. Descartes sought to take truth out of the abstract and develop it within each individual. In so doing, he elaborated on the concept of the soul as a distinct entity encased in our bodies and so led to a development of an individual self capable of managing and interpreting the world.[2] But Cartesianism hacks off its own structure of the self as an individual phenomena by taking that newly developed self outside of its body and situating it in an ethereal soul. This emphasis on the soul as independent from the body is never complete, however. As Francis Barker points out, "As the flesh is derealized, representation, which becomes at last representational, is separated from it and puts in train a mode of signification for which, to borrow a word from Derrida, the body has become 'supplementary.' Neither wholly present, nor wholly absent, the body is confined, ignored, exscribed from discourse, and yet remains at the edge of visibility, troubling the space from which it has been banished."[3]

Nietzsche begins the repair of this rent between the mind and reality by taking a detour via the body, which doesn't simply stand between experience and the world, but is the carrier of that experience and placement in that world at once. Each individual's engagement with the world is not simply the reading of information through the lens of the body, but is an act of interpretation that implies a subject not merely located in a body, but as body.[4]

Our bodies are never just objects that encase our selves as subjects, but are the very means by which we come into being as subjects through our engagement with the world. The distinction comes in defining subjective experience not as something that engages an abstract mind trapped in an objective body, but as corporeal (of and through a specific gendered and culturally impacted body).[5] Each individual subject creates existence based on her projection of herself into the world, by actively probing the perceptive field.

Pina Bausch implicitly addresses the active potential of the individual's body in the world in her works on stage and in so doing rewrites the essence of dance as organized movement and extends the boundaries of theater to include the reality of the performer's body in context. Bausch moves away from the formal concerns of a body that is arranged under the governing ideas of an established technique, even as she creates the sense of a cohesive physical style by working with dancers who mostly share a rigorous training in the Western balletic tradition. But Bausch begins her process with the individual expression of her dancers, who maintain their personal perspectives in surrounding an idea or group of ideas with various approaches to its representation. As Leonetta Bentivoglio states:

> The dancer is no longer simply a body to be used as artistic material and "regulated" in accordance with a set of technical rules (all the representatives of contemporary dance in the USA have searched for and found a distinct, individual technique). Pina Bausch's dancer is first and foremost, an individual; the protagonist in a theater that vies with reality: with human relationships, with hate and love, with the fear of death, with the desire for destruction, with the eternal longing for happiness and the importance of desire, with the secret illusion of a god and with the daily routine which is made up of frustrations and complexes, passions and obsessions.[6]

The emphasis on the individual is developed in bodily terms, where the expression is no longer filtered through an objective and more formal consideration of the body, but is considered from the dancer's body as the means by which subjectivity is determined. This change in the way the dancer's body expresses begins the transformation Bausch makes into something that might be considered a new form of presentation, outside of the formal concerns of ballet and postmodern dance of the time, and incorporating the move away from the illusionistic stage and collision with real presence put forth by Antonin Artaud and explored in the experimental theater of the day. German critic Norbert Servos points to this shift in bodily attitude: "The [dancer's] body is no longer a means to an end. It has become the subject of the performance. Something new has begun in the history of the dance: [Each dancer's] body is telling its own story."[7] The story of each dancer's body is developed in experiential terms, addressing the reality of lived experience and presenting it through intimate gestures and dramatic physical relationships, rather than the stories and characters of conventional theatrical expression (and theatricalized story ballets) or the formal reduction of the body to an expressive instrument in other forms of dance.

In Bausch's work, bodily experience is explored performatively, not just as the base of knowledge, but as knowledge itself. Knowledge *is* experience, not perception translated to the disembodied other of a Cartesian notion of the soul. This idea describes a connected self, one where mind and body are derived out of the same connection to experience. There is no split between mind and body, as maintained in Cartesianism, but a conjunction at the site of our bodies. The dancer's body's virtual presence on stage, or our placement through sensual awareness, constructs a form of knowing through dramatic action.[8]

This foregrounding of presence situates the development of my being, not only physically, but temporally as well. The here that my body describes brings with it the physical conditions of its location and the temporal conditions of its history and possible future.[9] Therefore, my current project of being is developed out of the specificity of my situation as well as my own history (both personal and as I am connected to a larger culture) and my hopes and fears for the future. This project of being is made real through my body and enacted with my body through expressive action. I am always in context, and I express my being through interaction within the context of my being. Bausch creates the performative context for being on stage and enlivens the process of becoming that we usually endow upon characters in traditional drama, but in Bausch's world we are forced to see the event in both its real terms and as an extension of the central metaphor that helps define the piece.

BODILY PRESENCE

Toward the end of *Kontakthof* (1978), a piece that exposes the often dehumanizing qualities of male/female relationships, a woman in a white dress and black shoes simply stands downstage center. She addresses the audience with her blank gaze and invites consideration. She provides no outward expression for us to receive. One man and another and another approach her and begin to caress her; rubbing her shoulder, stroking her cheek. But the woman remains passive. Gradually the men's gestures become more mechanical, moving from the warmth of a caress to the gentle prod of awakening to the investigative delving into a foreign object. The limp woman is now surrounded by the men, held up and shaken, her hair is smoothed, her face pinched, hand held up, all in a flurry of randomly repetitive motions.

The woman's passivity in what amounts to a tortuous situation forces me to try to invent a reason for her behavior based on my own ideas of abuse and acclimation, but the woman takes on, even through her passivity, the sheer fact of her situation. We are forced to consider the woman's presence wholly within the context of the piece rather than as reference to an outside world. The piece becomes not simply drama, where the characters are decided and play out their parts, but a drama of realization, where only through the process of involvement in the moment is the woman's presence, as the audience understands it, endowed with being. In the conventional drama, we construct being for a character based on the degree to which he reflects an interior reality, either realistic or fanciful, but in Bausch's case we are left with the actual conditions the woman encounters on stage. Despite the artifice of the situation, the woman goes through a very real event, and her presence on stage is determined by the parameters of the event. This moment is made real for the audience not through the ability of the woman to carry out the actions, or inaction, prescribed, but through her specific individual ordeal and our realization of her subjective presence as expressed in bodily terms. The moment only has power to the degree that we are able to see the woman as bodily subject enduring a real as well as a metaphoric trial, and Bausch has supplied a context that demands our attention to her subjectivity as expressed in bodily terms and extends that being to the larger metaphor of the piece, raising the moment above a simple voyeuristic glimpse at the subtlety of abuse.

Though we may hope for an existence for her beneath the surface of the situation, beyond the artifice of the act, we experience her existence as generated by the slow participation of the audience (in our silent witnessing of this abuse) and the other performers. Her character is built out of a stripping away and existence is present before us, the raw material out of which we are forced to create meaning. It is this very fight between her simply implied subjectivity and our attempts to create a role for this woman beyond the situation that gives the moment its peculiar poignancy. The woman's bodily expressed subjectivity frustrates any attempts we might make to extricate her from the situation. The long process of abuse is difficult to watch and places the audience in a complicit relationship to the event. But through our discomfort, the hope is for a moment of realization where we may uncover our own implicit involvement in cultural patterns.

Bausch has often been accused of glorifying violence, particularly against women. Arlene Croce famously described her as a "pornographer of pain,"[10] but we identify with the women who go through these ordeals and the feelings of helplessness that they project. The images exist as if in a dream where you are subjected to action and unable to react or respond, and it is that unrealized desire that truly reflects our experience and provides the potential to move toward meaningful change. As a man, I like to think of myself as outside of the cultural epidemic of violence against women. I believe I am a sympathetic voice who treats women with dignity and respect. And I am, but Bausch forces me to recognize and account for my role in a culture of oppression, and to continually remind myself of the need to remain alert to the subtlety of my actions. She won't let me off the hook, and she shouldn't. While some women react negatively to Bausch's depictions of violence (particularly in her earlier work), many more respond with feelings of empathy for the characters on Bausch's stage, characters built from the real experience of her dancers pushed to the root of the metaphor. This woman's real experience on stage embodies what Ann Daly refers to as the "unheard rage of women." "In Bausch's pieces, violence comes in bursts of dense repetition. These acts of violence are neither conventional, nor naturalistic, rather they exist on the plane of metaphor. They deal with the violation of women's bodies, but, more so, of women's autonomy."[11] In this image, the woman's body remains present in our awareness, calling on our ability to distinguish "the dancer from the dance"[12] and to acknowledge her as bodily subject, rather than disappearing into the reach toward something larger as it might in a more objective use of the dancer's body to signify abuse and repression. The woman's bodily presence acts as a constant implicit indictment against the men's actions.

The woman's situation renders her present, constructs a presence of her being as an empty vessel fulfilling the obligation of the context. This sense of placement, beyond the mere objectivity of the human form, is what Jean-Paul Sartre refers to as *facticity*: the ability to acknowledge bodily presence as it exists in the moment. But her being also moves beyond the situation to absorb the projections of others and the meaning of her condition. Her body absorbs being in this instance and her self is unbracketed, taken out of its projective context to allow a reevaluation, what Sartre calls *transcendence*: a movement beyond my current situation to other imaginings of myself and the world.[13] This aspect of our bodies, in which we move beyond our mere facticity, is created through our relation to desire. Within the figuration process lies a reaching toward something other. This aspiration toward an other relates to the attempt to make what we are becoming in some way our own, to control the process of creation that is continually directed at us and pulling away from us. To be is to be in process, reaching toward, always in an act of becoming and in an attempt to possess the illusive quality that is self.[14]

Bausch captures this constant state of striving for and the sadness that comes through the inability of the process to ever come to a grounded conclusion. For Sartre, this state exists as necessary alienation, we are continually outside of ourselves while simultaneously being ourselves, and it is this struggle of reunification that is the motivation for both life and art. By placing ourselves within a predetermined structure in the artistic process, we have a hope to move beyond the constant state of longing.

Rather than sculpting an objective body onto which a dramatic subjective persona is placed, tanztheater tends to work with this idea of the dancer as body-subject expressed through desire. On Bausch's stage, the dancer's body, through its movements and gestures, constantly states the action and potential of the subject as represented. In the example described above, the woman is rendered present, and in that presence stands both the facticity of the human form in its situation and the desire to transcend that situation as developed by others. The woman continually fights to become present, and it is this presence that reasserts itself in our consciousness as we create our perception of the event. The dancer's body transcends the facticity of its situation to become not the communicator of meaning, but that by which meaning becomes incarnate.

THE DANCER'S BODY AS OBJECT OR COMMODITY

We experience our bodies as dynamic systems of awareness, fluctuating between object and subject, facticity and transcendence, and a sense of the creation of the self and the performative construction of the world. Starting with an investigation of our bodies as dynamic totalities influences our consideration of individual aspects of the dancer's body. We can no longer simply bracket out our subjective tie to our bodies and view the dancer's body as pure object. Certainly, we experience the dancer's body objectively on Bausch's stage, but that objective status is always self-consciously developed out of a more complete picture of bodily experience, often set in metaphoric battle against our attempts to experience ourselves as bodily subjects. Bausch uses the objective consideration of the dancer's body embedded in prior models of dance to comment on the sense of self-alienation and hierarchical structure infused throughout our culture through the pervasive influence of Cartesian dualism. In this way, dance becomes a metaphor for systems of objectification and alienation.

In *Bandoneon* (1981), the dancers frequently tell stories of their past training in ballet, concentrating on moments of cruelty needed to achieve the unnatural weightlessness and grace of ballet. One woman brutally combs another's hair and forces her to smile despite the painful procedure. She explains that a dancer must always smile on stage and viciously dunks the other woman's head in a bucket of water whenever her smile wavers. A man tells how one ballet teacher used to hold a lit cigarette under his leg, forcing him to raise it higher and higher to prove that the unnatural extension is possible. One dancer sits with his legs apart and feet together while a woman stands on his knees to force his muscles to stretch. The other dancers come on stage and repeat this process, each pushing the other's body into this objective contortion.

The dancers show how ballet sacrifices our subjective connection to our bodies to achieve ethereal weightlessness. In ballet, the dancer's body has become other, a tool to use toward the desired end of grace and beauty and an obstacle to that goal. Beyond the explicit condemnation of ballet training, Bausch uses these images to address larger ideas of objectification and alienation. The dancers have all been through this process, and even as it objectively places them within the performative sphere, it also is the necessary training to be able to move within this sphere. The inherent contradiction stands in for the similarly complicated process of objectification in life. Servos explains: "Put on a pedestal in this way, the theater, or rather ballet, is revealed as a grotesque trial of strength, muscle-flaunting by champions while real needs and desires remain in the background. *Bandoneon* demonstrates that theater is like life. The dominant element in both is ruthless, suppressive competition."[15] Bausch does not didactically challenge the objectification of everyday life, she merely uncovers the processes by which we objectify and alienate ourselves, leaving the ethical implications unresolved.

But far from relishing in these often brutal moments on stage, as some critics have accused of Bausch, she hopes that we may see beyond the surface of the situation to the people underneath. The moments exist as the tension between the harsh reality of the stage and the desire to move beyond objectifying impulses toward real connection. As Bausch says:

> How can you make clear onstage the feelings if we don't see why there is suffering, or anger? I could just tell the audience, but I like them to feel it. Many things we do onstage are real: People run and smash themselves against walls, they fall, they get soaked in water and covered in soil. The contact between the public, it is real. If we experience that moment together in the theater—that realism—together, then that for me is hope. I am not a pessimist in that way. If we share feelings, there is something beautiful, and that gives us strength.[16]

Kontakthof investigates the performers presentation of self on stage as a defining moment, and the ethical implications of this reductionist thinking both for the theater and in our personal relationships. The piece begins with first one women and then gradually all the performers displaying themselves to the audience as if for sale. They offer themselves to the audience and to each other in preparation for the mating ritual to take place over the next three hours. This objective presentation of self has a simple power in alerting us to the objective selling of self inherent in the theatrical experience, but also calls attention to our insidious self-promotion and objectification in life and especially in the search for relationships.

Bausch is relentless in her exploration of the degree to which we objectify ourselves in our search for connection, and the ultimate futility of this objectification leading to anything more substantial than momentary attention. The images are developed out of and refer back to a theatrical metaphor, where the theater's reliance on presentation of the self is shown to be a metaphor for our daily attempts at connection through self-negating objective display.

Here, the dancer's bodies are displayed objectively as empty postures used either to lure a partner or as the material presented to the audience to satisfy their demands for entertainment. After the nearly three hours of *Kontakthof*, I left the theater with an uneasy feeling of participation in a ritual sacrifice, where, perhaps for the first time, I was made aware of the negation of self expected within the theatrical process. And yet, by taking to task the unquestioned objective depiction of dancer's bodies inherent in most dance, Bausch had created a space where the subject might emerge. Bausch counts on the audience needing to look past the dehumanizing aspects of self-presentation she displays to find the human element behind the theatricalized experience. She does not allow the audience to lose sight of reality through either technical virtuosity or the alluring completeness of a created world on stage. The dancers are certainly well trained, and we often get caught up in their ability to move in extremely accomplished ways, but the technique is usually undercut by a human moment that brings us back to earth and shows us the reality of the dancer's experience. The dancers do not re-present experience bodily, but begin the process whereby bodily experience is made present. This process, ultimately, is what renders the dancer's present as body-subjects, and what distinguishes tanztheater from more objectively driven forms of presentation found in conventional scenarios of dance or character driven work in the theater.

THE INCORPORATION OF GENDER

Judith Butler begins her essay on gender constitution with a discussion of phenomenological theory of acts. She describes how such thinkers as Edmund Husserl and Maurice Merleau-Ponty seek "to explain the mundane way in which social agents constitute social reality through language, gesture and all manner of symbolical social sign."[17] Butler uses this definition to support her claim that gender is just such a constructed mode of being that both draws from and contributes to social reality. She uses phenomenological concern with the lived body to place the gendered body in historical context and to place the subject that is that body as an actor in the process of gender constitution. Echoing Merleau-Ponty, she claims, "[o]ne is not simply a body, but, in some very key sense, one does one's body and, indeed, one does one's body differently from one's contemporaries and from one's embodied predecessors and successors as well."[18] She is careful at this point not to fall into the grammatical trap that places the self somewhere outside her body as an agent that acts on an abstracted body as other—that does it, as she says—but she stops short of claiming that it is that process of doing itself that develops what we might consider a subject. She does claim that "[d]iscrete genders are part of what 'humanizes' individuals within contemporary culture; indeed, those who fail to do their gender right are regularly punished."[19] It is often that act of "doing one's gender wrong" that Bausch employs to uncover the very process of gender constitution in contemporary society.

In *Palermo, Palermo*, Jan Minarik once again plays a rather brutal figure set apart from the rest of the ensemble. But after one episode at the downstage corner of the stage where he inhabits a small locker room and cooks a steak on an iron while watching a documentary about sharks, Minarik removes his suit and tie, applies lipstick, dons a feather boa, heels and a crown of cigarettes to become a grotesque version of the statue of liberty, holding aloft an apple with one lit birthday candle as the torch. Bausch takes the outward symbols of masculinity and femininity and deliberately subverts them for ironic effect. The effect is unsettling precisely because the episode exposes the degree to which our notion of gender is constructed in the first place, and the obvious cultural symbolism points to the way we adopt cultural signs and ultimately to the way we can reconfigure them.

Butler similarly argues that the point of recognizing the social construction of gender should be freeing, in that if gender roles are socially constructed, those roles can be changed, fully recognizing, however, the difficulty that such a change, however slight, implies. To make her point clear, she employs Simone de Beauvoir's famous catch phrase from *The Second Sex*, "one is not born, but, rather, becomes a woman," to explain the way gender is incorporated through performative action. Butler explains that to "be female is . . . a facticity which has no meaning, but to be a woman is to have become a woman, to compel the body to conform to an historical idea of 'woman,' to induce the body to become a cultural sign, to materialize oneself in obedience to an historically delimited possibility, and to do this in a sustained and repeated corporeal project."[20] Through often lengthy and repeated series of bodily postures and attitudes, Bausch uncovers the history of her performer's bodies as they exist not simply as males and females, but as men and women.

Kontakthof often returns to a series of gestures ranging from overtly feminine—patting the face as if applying makeup, thrusting the chest forward and rearranging a corset, and pursing the lips as if to apply lipstick—to gender neutral—brushing lint off of your clothing, and applauding quietly. These gestures are performed in unison by the entire ensemble in a delicate dance of body posturing. They both set the time and social strata within which the performance takes place—late 1940s to early 1950s German middle class—and lead the way into the exploration of gender roles that surround them. That the men also perform these gestures again points to the constructed nature of gender incorporation. We recognize that these actions are not simply ways for the women to identify the characters they play, but are the means by which we come to know them as feminine subjects, and we struggle to know the men as masculine despite the grace with which they adopt feminine gesture patterns. Bausch has placed our role as other in the constitution of subjectivity in question by forcing us to struggle with what we normally take for granted: the playing out of gender along prescribed models of bodily social behavior.

Butler identifies a similar process of enacting societal markers in the constitution of gender. As she says:

> gender is in no way a stable identity or locus of agency from which various acts proceed; rather, it is an identity tenuously constituted in time—an identity instituted through a stylized repetition of acts. Further, gender is instituted through the stylization of the body and, hence, must be understood as the mundane way in which bodily gestures, movements, and enactments of various kinds constitute the illusion of an abiding gendered self.[21]

This process once again incorporates both time and context in the revelation of the subject through bodily presence. The sense of the performer's body as a way to uncover our own construction of bodily behavior is specifically expressed through Bausch's exploration of gender, even as the larger process of bodily social inscription becomes a constant theme throughout Bausch's work.

THE DANCER'S BODY AS THE MAKING OF SELF AND CONNECTION TO THE WORLD

Bausch shows the dancer's body as self and in a constant state of becoming by recognizing the very context of theatrical presentation. As Inge Baxmann points out: "Dance theater is less a case of stories being told than experience being staged. The study of the relationship between lifestyle and body eliminates one basic requirement of classical dance aesthetics: the domination of the subject over her/his body."[22] In fact, the entire notion of a disembodied consciousness or intellect speaking through an objectified body is subverted from the start. By beginning with experience—always already a bodily phenomenon—rather than stories or movements into which the body is placed, Bausch invigorates the continual process of becoming a subject and places that developing subject within a meaningful metaphoric context.

Even Bausch's early story ballets (*Iphigenie on Tauris* [1973], *Orpheus and Eurydice* [1975], and especially *Bluebeard* [1977] and *He Takes Her by the Hand and Leads Her into the Castle, the Others Follow* [1978], which is based on Shakespeare's *MacBeth*) begin with the performer's experience of the story selected—both in its artistic form and in its reverberation within the culture—and develop from that point out. Similarly, Bausch's later pieces, developed from residencies at particular locales, work from the performers experience of that place, metaphorically placed within a larger context of human involvement. *Nur Du* (1996) came out of Bausch and her performers' experience of the American West, and despite many West Coast critics disappointment at not seeing themselves reflected in the piece, Bausch and the company effectively utilized what they found—feelings of isolation and desperate showcasing of arrogance and resiliency—to create a connection to an underlying feeling of self-removal and the need to be seen to demonstrate your own existence.

Palermo, Palermo (1989) begins with the performer's own experience of the town of Palermo and develops that experience metaphorically in the performer's body. Immediately after the astounding opening of the collapse of a cinder block wall that had completely filled the proscenium, Julie Shanahan runs on stage in a floral print dress. She looks a bit desperate. She draws an X on the floor with chalk and then one on her face. She does a short movement phrase from a standing position, using hand motions similar to sign language that rapidly pass over her body and face and then reach out to the audience. She appears to be trying to find a place for herself, and trying to find a way to communicate. She calls to someone, again with vague desperation, "Thomás, Thomás." A man enters and stands before her as if ready to provide whatever service might be needed. She says "hug me" and Thomás tries, but she stands still and then throws his arms away and repeats "hug me, hug me" to Thomás's failed efforts. Thomás does not appear surprised or frustrated by this event, merely compliant. A Dinah Washington song plays in the background, "Why Don't You Do Me Right, Like Other Men Do." Another man comes out and the trio go through a series of thwarted hugs, hand-holding, and hair touching. The woman quickly reaches a state of desperation and maintains her anguished tones.

On the woman's request, one man brings out a large piece of paper with something on it. The woman throws it up in the air and then lies down to let what we now see was dirt fall on her, as the paper flutters away. The woman appears to be so needy but will not allow any one to approach her. She will not be satisfied. It is as if this language she has to ask for things is not nearly adequate for what she needs and she is increasingly frustrated by the men's inability to provide her with anything beyond the surface of her requests. Her body, as usual in a Bausch piece, is the ground both for the desire and the dissatisfaction. She asks the men to get tomatoes and they come on with brown paper bags. She asks to be pelted and the men coolly oblige. The scene is funny, but she is in terror and the longer it goes on the more you have to give in to her terror rather than the humor of the moment. The scene is comic in a way, but the presence of her body is tragic and her body is where the battle is being fought. Ultimately, her bodily presence prevails as we recognize the assault this woman is enduring and her horror at the event. She is physically assaulted and her demands for control of the situation, her attempts to run the show, only leave her more vulnerable. Finally, beaten, she says "Take me off," and the men gingerly lead her off stage.

This section may have come from being foreigners in a strange city and being unable to speak the language, as Shanahan mentions, but it quickly moves beyond the specificity of that scenario to attack larger ideas of need and communication. As spectators, we are asked to connect with this representation of larger ideas and to account for them from our own ground of experience. And yet we cannot forget what we see this very specific woman go through on stage. Her experience has been incorporated into a series of physical metaphors that define her presence on stage while simultaneously referring us to our own experiences of frustrated communication. Her very real bodily presence is the base from which her character is developed, and it is a character that simultaneously recalls her personal experience and creates a staged presentation of the ground of her experience. The gesture is developed out of experience and recontextualized to give that experience value beyond the specific context of the event.

Body, Self, and Other

Bausch's change of context here, from one of the alienation of a tourist in a foreign land to one of the difficulty of defining oneself within an interpersonal (and specifically a male/ female) relationship, is both typical and telling. Bausch frequently places her performer's experience within a context of male/female relationships precisely because they show our attempts to define our selves through an encounter with the other. The male/female relationship expresses both conflict and the search for communion, and plays out those dynamics through the intimacy of love relationships. Other relationships occur on Bausch's stage—same-sex, teacher/pupil, parent/child, etc.—but it is her exploration of models of women's subjectivity set against a masculine oppressive force that are most resonant and receive the most attention. This encounter with the other is often viewed as the base of our subjectivity, the event through which we can begin the process of seeing ourselves within the context of our being. And this process takes place within an experiential framework, where experience is viewed as necessarily bodily.

Bausch's pieces show individual subjects arising out of bodily experience by placing that experience in conflict and connection with an other, as well as a specific developed context. The subject is represented in bodily terms as a constant presence, demanding to be noticed despite the objectifying conditions that dance usually entails, and reflecting our desire to exist beyond the objectifying conditions we find in life. This position of power is often developed out of the conflict of placing the dancer within an objectifying context to highlight the struggle toward subjective presence. The developed context demands a recognition of the dancer as bodily subject, and refuses to allow the body dancing to be subsumed by the dancing body.

Dominique Mercy struggles to exert his subjective presence in response to his being objectively positioned as a dancer based on his ballet experience when he is pressed into service in *Nelken* (1983). He is surrounded by his fellow dancers and forced to the front of the stage, screaming, "No, I have nothing to do, nothing to show. You do it. No, I have nothing to show," in a mixture of French, English, and German. He demands that the others leave him alone and throws them off. They retreat in uncomfortable silence, leaving him alone and trembling in the middle of the stage. He slowly begins to move off, when Anne Martin enters with a microphone and says to the audience "I simply wanted to say, its marvelous that you're all here this evening." Mercy begins clearing the stage and says "You want to see something? Well, I'll show you something. Get rid of those chairs," demanding that the others clear the stage. He moves to the rear of the stage and says, "What do you want to see? You want to see turns?" whereupon he does a series of *chaînés* turns across the carnation-strewn floor. Although he executes the fundamentals of ballet with more desperation than precision, the audience applauds. He continues to ask what the audience wants to see, and offers them a series of ballet moves, double *tours en l'air, grand jetés*, and *entrechat six*.

The audience responds to his desperate showcasing with awkward silence, until, finally, drenched in sweat and gasping he screams: "What else do you want to see? What else do I have to show you?" He begins to move off stage, utterly exhausted, and says, "I've had it, I'm tired." A man in a suit comes out, stops Mercy, and says, "Your passport, please." Mercy stands stunned, and the man moves away and says in passing "Put some proper clothes on."

This moment, perhaps more simply and straightforwardly than any other in Bausch's work, shows the dancer's struggle to maintain a sense of himself as subject amid the objectifying environment of ballet. For years these dancers were defined by their ability to accomplish certain tasks with grace and beauty. As their bodies begin to age they find themselves desperately in need of a new way to define themselves. The dancer's body exists objectively at this moment, a mechanism for carrying out a series of actions, but that objectivity is placed against a more all-encompassing struggle for subjectivity. Mercy searches for love (the overriding theme of *Nelken*) using the means with which he is most familiar, showcasing his physical talents in a desperate attempt to be considered present. The specific ground of exploration is this dancer's experience in ballet, but the performed moment metaphorically addresses our own struggles for identity beyond the markers that signal our existence. We have all felt, at one moment or another, that our existence has been reduced to the actions we have learned to produce, and the resumé or transcript that catalogs those accomplishments, or the driver's license or passport that defines us more succinctly than we desire.

In *Rite of Spring* (1975), Bausch reduces the ballet down to its most essential image. As she says; "'the most important thing to me was to understand what Stravinsky wanted. In *Rite of Spring*, there is nothing to add to what's already there. There is a young girl, the Chosen One, and that young girl dances, all by herself, until she dies.'"[23] The initial idea is pushed until even the structural grid that supports it, the foundational impetus for the work, takes on metaphoric value. Johannes Birringer suggests that in *Rite of Spring* "the ritual dance was constantly repeated—to the point of total exhaustion—as a central metaphor for the well-rehearsed behavior of men following the rules of society and selecting women as sacrificial victims, even as the women themselves envision and anticipate the selection."[24] We see the group author this woman's existence and her reaction both with and against this activity constitutes our perception of her as subject.

That subjectivity is expressed in bodily terms, even while the very ground of the action objectifies and metaphorically and literally stains the woman with the influence of a defining culture. Bausch calls on the reality of the stage setting to accentuate the drama as it is unveiled. As Norbert Servos says:

> Bausch's dance theater contains no simulation. The dancers have no need to act their growing exhaustion: it is genuine as they dance against the resistance of the ankle-deep earth. The energy demanded from the dancers is not disguised, it confronts the audience directly. No smiles mask the strain, it is made audible by the dancers' heavy breathing. The visceral sensuality which the actors create with this seemingly limitless physical exertion gives the story additional physical credibility, makes the sacrifice something one is exposed to at close quarters, a personal experience.[25]

The placement of the subject within an objective context and the subsequent struggle of the subject to emerge and become present in bodily terms takes place through an encounter with the other, both as he exists individually and as embodied within social inscriptions and cultural codes. The other, whether expressed individually or through a process of acculturation, provides the emerging subject with a scenario with which she might engage. The other provides the ground to develop subjectivity out of the context of being.

Michael Bowman and Della Pollack describe how Bausch creates a context where the subject might be realized not at the expense of the objective social depiction of the dancer's body, but because of it.[26] This process is apparent throughout Bausch's pieces, but takes on special relevance when the performers explicitly confront socially prescribed norms. Bausch's approach to this ground of bodily representation is developed through an attack on stereotypes in *Renate Emigrates* (1977). The piece explores the commodification of women in popular culture, among other things. One woman tries to give another a lesson in how to move attractively, but the lesson quickly degenerates from a commanding drill to a physical assault as one woman tries to manipulate the other into an ideal of beauty. The women allow themselves to be carried around like sacks, to be decorated, or to be examined as if they were goods to be purchased, the performed characters of the dancers both acquiesce and subtly stand in defiance to this commodification. They allow it to happen and do not fight back, but the confrontational and pained expression they project makes the audience aware and uncomfortable with their own implicit involvement in the objectifying practice.

Renate Emigrates shows us the means by which we all adhere to physical patterns of behavior. Emotional gestures like sighing, innocently raising the eyebrow, and kissing are taught as if at a dance class, but the learned gestures never quite match up in practice. Ultimately the women simply stand on the men's feet and allow themselves to be danced around the stage. "The men are able to determine the women's steps, to prevent them from standing 'on their own two feet.'"[27] The piece provides example after example of the degree to which our bodily presentation of our selves is determined by cultural codes, and the psychological and emotional ramifications of this cultural commodification. Bausch addresses the way we perceive ourselves and the way we define ourselves in connection with and response to a defining culture. That her exploration centers on gender identity, and particularly women's identity in a male-dominated world, merely reflects her own experience, and the power and relevance of her work indicates that those themes reverberate in the larger culture.

THE DANCER'S BODY IN THE WORLD AS A PERFORMATIVE CONSTRUCT

Bausch's innovation in tanztheater was to stop thinking of the dancer's body as a separate entity to be put through whatever developed technique was being employed and to start uncovering the history of the dancer's body as it is engaged in life, allowing the dancer's body "to tell its own story," as Servos claims. More than simply employing pedestrian movements drawn from life and made into yet another technique imposed on disparate bodies, Bausch begins a process whereby each dancer is allowed bodily presence as an expression of personal existence, and that personal existence is necessarily derived out of both personal and cultural placement in time and sensation. Indeed, Bausch shows that, although we are not always aware of our cultural placement as bodies in a social environment, aspects of our physical expression constantly affect our creation of self in situation.[28] She draws on her own experience, and that of her dancers, to approach our efforts at connection in love relationships and our confrontation with death. Each moment is an existential struggle to be in the face of conditions that pull us apart and eventually subsume us.

In addressing her work to these base conditions of humanity, Bausch reflects the priorities of her German dance predecessors Mary Wigman and Kurt Jooss. It is not the subject matter itself that renders Bausch's art distinct—all art has and continues to consider issues of love and death—it is the means by which Bausch confronts those ideas. Bausch does not use the dancer's body to represent eternal truths, but, instead, recognizes the place of our bodies in the continual expression of these truths. As Inge Baxmann points out, this leads away from a dance that considers the dancer's body as something that might be able to construct feeling through technical manipulation and toward a dance that "serves to use movement, gesture, rhythm and space in order to come to terms with present day forms of living."[29] Everyday experience is addressed in the way in which we inhabit it, as subjects derived from bodily experience. Bausch explores our bodily relation to everyday life, while simultaneously exposing the human element in our attempts to connect to art or myth.

In Bausch's art we turn to these larger structures in a desperate search for meaning in our lives, lives that continually demonstrate the emptiness of the roles in which we find ourselves enmeshed. Her pieces ask how we are connected to the behavioral patterns and the physical stereotypes to which we resort as a way to define ourselves through our tie to a community. The dancer's body is presented as a representative of our connection to the world, and it is a connection that, though it defines our individual subjectivity, constantly threatens to engulf us in a meaningless series of empty postures. Bausch captures this struggle to identify our selves out of the collection of cultural codes in which we find ourselves entangled, and succeeds in expressing something new in dance, the history of our bodies made manifest.

Dance has always concerned itself with the possibilities of physical expression, but never before had that expression been extended to include the way in which we define our selves through our bodily relationship to cultural codes. The dancer's body on stage is freed from the rules of a developed technique to represent each individual's physical connection to a world of his or her own creation. It is this connection that leads Servos to call Bausch's tanztheater a "theater of experience."[30] The pieces become more and more about each dancer's body as a representation of life, and they move beyond the dancer's specific engagement to metaphorically address our own bodily connections to life.

Baxmann relates this approach to the theatrical explorations of Robert Wilson, but with a significant difference. "An 'aesthetic of the senses' would be one possible definition of this practice, as long as aesthetic were understood as a specific type of behavior and perception, rather than an ideal or a concept. Dance theater can be understood as an 'archaeology of ways of life,' which not only delves into the significance of cultural structure in the body but at the same time seeks oppositional forces."[31] Unearthing these little moments of personal connection to cultural practice would take on an alien quality if placed within a more traditional dramatic structure. They would appear as things that happen to someone who is objectively other, with whom we may or may not identify. Bausch establishes a more vital link to these ideas and makes the confrontation with the past palpable in metaphoric terms, moving past the specifics of the world in which she and her performers are enmeshed to uncover problems of commodification and a loss of subjectivity to larger systems of power as we confront them in life.

This metaphoric approach is achieved in part by working with Brecht's model of the action performed as if in memory. Brecht says we are able to escape linear story line and enter into a more metonymic structure "if the actress were to play as though the woman had lived through an entire period and were now, out of her memory and her knowledge of what happens next, recalling those utterances of hers which were important at the time."[32] The moment played as memory naturally has a subjective slant in terms of what is chosen to stand for the whole; what is the important moment. It also leads to a lack of directed conflict in a linear narrative of events. The tension is in every moment and in the knowledge of the underlying idea that strings these moments together. But that conflict is never resolved in Bausch's pieces. We are left to fend for ourselves.

Brecht proposed this method as a way to engage life by holding elements out for a moment to give them special consideration. This is the base of the *Verfremdungs* effect, or making strange, to which Brecht refers; exploring something that you normally accept without question. Brecht hoped to provide an environment where the audience is free to reconsider traditional attitudes under a new moral rubric. Bausch holds moments of subjection and commodification up for consideration without applying a moral standard, however. In *Gebirge* (1984), for example, Jan Minarik portrays a horrific master of ceremonies, clad only in a red bathing suit, swimming goggles, a red bathing cap, and yellow rubber gloves, with a string tied around his head to flatten his nose. The stage is covered with dirt through which the performers often try to swim, to both grotesque and comic effect. A man tortures various women and gets them to say uncle, then chases them around the stage and screams that he wants to kill them while a Little Richard song plays. A man does dive rolls over a seated woman, putting her at real risk.

After this bout of frantic activity the performers all run off, leaving Minarik silently standing over Beatrice Libonati, who kneels with her back to the audience, making herself vulnerable. She pulls her dress up to her head, revealing her bare back. Minarik slashes at her with what we realize is lipstick in his hand, leaving a red streak down her back. After each lash with the lipstick, Minarik looks out to the audience for approval, waiting for someone to contradict, implying a kind of who's next? Libonati does a slow ritualistic movement, head down, dress pulled out. She has big red marks on her back, they look horribly painful. Minarik walks away in silence, and the woman continues her ritual. We are left to decipher the image on our own, with only the other images of sexual oppression that surround it and our sense of and outrage at sexual violence as it is enacted on the performer's bodies to use as guideposts for interpretation.

We are forced to attend to these images from the moments that surround them and from our own base of memories and conceptions, perhaps long since unquestioned. Bausch does not give us a way out of this questioning, does not provide a moral standard to be reached, but leaves the images for us each to confront individually. Bausch is not trying to convince us of anything, so there is no felt morality. Because none is imposed on you, you have to find it within yourself. This, ultimately, is the goal of Bausch's approach to representation, to demand of the audience an inner search for a way to approach the images she unearths, and, in part, confront the totalizing effect of dominating cultures. Bausch is uncompromising in her display of the way we are connected to the world. She shows a harsh world in harsh terms. Your own response is either one of shock because you have isolated yourself from this reality, or a feeling of connectedness in that you have struggled in this way too.

The connection to the world is played out in bodily terms. As Servos says, "The special quality of dance, the fact that it tells its story through the sensual presence of the bodies, now is given the chance to portray a reality that is defined by physical conventions."[33] These physical conventions are then given form through the subjective presence of the performer, often placing the personal creation of the body in conflict with its cultural creation by showing the roles that are created as self-consciously theatrical yet metaphorically personal. Moments are held out for special consideration, and yet they also reveal an underlayer of connections and assumptions that make up our experience, our bodily connection to life. As Servos continues: "The point of departure is authentic, subjective experience, which is also demanded of the audience. Passive reception is impossible. 'Theater of experience' mobilizes the affects and emotions because it deals with undivided energies. It does not pretend. It is."[34] The reality created is not held in an attempt to create something other, but in the physical and emotional truth of the moment as it is experienced. Rather than looking for a movement that might transport us, or a gesture that somehow captures authentic experience, tanztheater examines experience as it is lived in our daily connections to a larger culture and in our desperate search for connective meaning.

A THEATER OF BODILY PRESENCE

Conventional realist theater merges subject and character, and conventional dance practice merges subject and technique into one expanded object. Tanztheater, however, begins with a distinct subject that is then commented on and infiltrated into a dramatic process. This idea draws from and expands on Brecht's idea of *gestus*. In "On Gestic Music," Brecht defines "Gest" as follows: "Gest is not supposed to mean gesticulation: it is not a matter of explanatory or emphatic movements of the hands, but of overall attitudes. A language is gestic when it is grounded in a gest and conveys particular attitudes adopted by the speaker towards other men."[35] Gest is a form of metaphoric process, a performative construct for articulating certain feelings and social interactions, it provides the performer a means to behave a certain way and yet allows the possibility for conscious commentary on the behavior performed. In Bausch's case, the bodily action performed encompasses an idea or feeling and places that idea or feeling within a metaphoric context that both articulates it and opens it up to the possibility of interaction. The action as it is performed bodily is not a thing that is presented to an audience but is a starting point for a dialogue with an audience. The meaning developed through the action both comments on the situation as it is presented on stage and recalls our own individual situations in life, uncovering the base processes that motivate our own actions and behavior. We are given a way to see the modes of our own behavior as they are placed within a given staged context.

Rather than dissolving the subject into the part performed, Brecht called for, and I think tanztheater achieves, a distinct subject engaged in performative acts. Elizabeth Wright points out, however, that the difference between Bausch and Brecht is that Bausch's "actors show themselves; the split they enact between body and social role is experienced and enacted with their own bodies."[36] They still demonstrate, but it is a self-referential demonstration derived out of experience, and in this way recalls for us our own dealing with ourselves as bodies rather than taking us away into some idealized form of movement as other. The dancer's body becomes a performative construct within a social situation and shows the extent to which we all construct a persona out of our bodily engagement in context. We take the cues and conditions in which we are enmeshed, and through dramatic action, create a situation that stands for us individually. We create a distinct subjectivity out of the raw material of our bodies in situation, and that process of creation is necessarily performative.

The dancers on Bausch's stage continually express the plenitude of bodily presence, as the emergence of subjectivity and the entrance into a dialogue both with and in the world. Our bodies, as defined by society and as our connection to society, provide the ground from which content emanates. Bodily experience is the spring from which all else issues, showing Tanztheater's growth from and connection to dance, but dance reconfigured. Dance becomes the aesthetic articulation of the means by which we define our selves through our own embodiment, and necessarily moves toward the theatrical. But theater is now reenlivened with real presence made manifest through human bodies in time and space. Bausch is not the first to engage this type of presentation and expression, but she is the first to place that bodily presence at the center of her presentational praxis. Rather than for a constructed present, the performer is present, and that presence both creates and addresses our own sense of self intertwined with others. Our own connection to the world is shown as a bodily process, necessarily fractured, but what is important is not so much the gaps created between ourselves and others, but the persistence with which we try to bridge those gaps. We may be lonely in the world, but there is grace and hope in our attempts to achieve context.

NOTES

1. Merleau-Ponty, *The Primacy of Perception*, 239.
2. See in particular Descartes's "Description of the Human Body" and "Passions of the Soul" in *The Philosophical Writings of Descartes*, Vol. 1.
3. Barker, 63.

4. Eric Blondel places Nietzche's ideas on the body in the context of reigning ideas of Cartesian dualism in his *Nietzsche: The Body and Culture*.

5. Maurice Merleau-Ponty, drawing on the work of German phenomenologists before him, most effectively subverts this idea of Cartesian dualism in his description of experience as corporeal. In *Phenomenology of Perception* and *The Primacy of Perception*, he centers his discussion on the act of perception itself as our connection to the world through our corporeal involvement with it.

6. Bentivoglio, 28.

7. Servos, *Pina Bausch Wuppertal Dance Theater; or, The Art of Training a Goldfish*, 23.

8. See in particular Suzanne Langer's consideration of virtual presence through her exploration of dance in *Feeling and Form: A Theory of Art*, particularly "Virtual Powers," 169–87.

9. Heidegger describes this aspect of temporality as a condition of existence in his discussion of ecstasis in *Being and Time*.

10. Croce, 83.

11. Daly, 54.

12. In most conventional dance forms, it is the dance that communicates and the person dancing disappears into the process. This process of incorporation into the event is seen as an ideal to be worked toward, mirroring Yeats's famous depiction "How can we know the dancer from the dance?"

13. See Sartre's *Being and Nothingness*, in particular pp. 401–70.

14. Merleau-Ponty and Jacques Lacan both refer to this cultural construction of presence as the unconscious, and it exists in relation to the individual through a mediating influence. For Merleau-Ponty this specially charged mediating space is referred to as "flesh," while Lacan calls it "desire."

15. Servos, *Pina Bausch . . .*, 172.

16. Bausch, "Everyday a Discovery . . . ," 11A.

17. Butler, 519.

18. Ibid., 521.

19. Ibid., 522.

20. Ibid., 522.

21. Ibid., 519.

22. Baxmann, 56.

23. Qtd. in Finkel, 5.

24. Birringer, 92.

25. Servos, *Pina Bausch . . .*, 30

26. "For Bausch, the human body—whether dominant or submissive or resistant—can escape neither its social determination nor its objective materiality. Within the scope of Bausch's postmodern realism, hope lies not simply in the performative process itself but in the alternative power of the performed body: in finding the 'strength' to exert the signifying power of the body over and against—but without denying—its social insignia." Bowman and Pollock, 115.

27. Servos, *Pina Bausch . . .*, 80.

28. Inge Baxmann claims that "[t]hrough dance theater, an investigation of subjectivity is set in motion by way of the body, where everything from the genesis of expression through to the smallest ramification of so called 'private-intimate' desires is seen as being completely influenced by society" (56).

29. Ibid., 55.

30. "Pina Bausch's theater of experience takes dance as a form of communication initially based on physical expression, and modifies and extends it. Unencumbered by the aesthetic abstractions and strict rules of the *danse d'école*, subject matter and movements can be drawn from every day life. General physical constriction in all its manifestations increasingly becomes the theme. Dance is more directly related to reality. It provides us with the insight that the domination over people is not simply a matter of awareness and the balance of power, but also one of dominating the human body." Servos, *Pina Bausch . . .*, 96.

31. Baxmann, 56.

32. Brecht, 179.

33. Servos, *Pina Bausch . . .*, 21.

34. Ibid., 21.

35. Brecht, 104.

36. Wright, 119.

BIBLIOGRAPHY

Bakhtin, M. M. *Art and Answerability: Early Philosophical Essays by M. M. Bakhtin*. Edited by Michael Holquist and Vadim Liapunov. Translated by Vadim Liapunov. Supplement translated by Kenneth Brostrom. Austin: University of Texas Press, 1990.

———. *The Dialogic Imagination: Four Essays*. Edited by Michael Holquist. Translated by Caryl Emerson and Michael Holquist. Austin: University of Texas Press, 1981.

Banes, Sally, and André Lepecki, eds. *The Senses in Performance: Worlds of Performance*. New York and London: Routledge, 2007.

Bausch, Pina. "Everyday a Discovery . . . ." With Christopher Bowen. *Stage Bill, Cal Performances*. October 1999: 10C–11A.

———. "The Evolution of Pina Bausch." With Sylvie du Nussac. Reprinted from *Le Monde*. *World Press Review*, October 1989: 91.

———. "Gespräch mit Pina Bausch im Goethe-Institut Paris." Interview with Dr. Ros. Transcription by Susanne Marten. Goethe Institut Paris, 1994.

———. "Ich glaube nur, was ich gesehen habe." Interview with Ulrich Deuter, Andresas Wilink. *K. West*, October 2004: 5–10.

———. "I'm Still Inquisitive." With Jochen Schmidt. In *Pina Bausch Wuppertal Dance Theater; or, The Art of Training a Goldfish*. Cologne, W. Germany: Ballett-Bühnen-Verlag, 1984: 238–39.

———. " 'Man weiß gar nict, wo die Phantasie einen hintreibt': Ein Gespräch mit Pina Bausch gefürt von Jean-Mark Adolfe." In *Pina Bausch*, 25–39. Heidelberg: Editions Braus, 2007.

———. "My Pieces Grow from the Inside Out." With Jochen Schmidt. In *Pina Bausch Wuppertal Dance Theater; or, The Art of Training a Goldfish*, by Norbert Servos, 234–37. Cologne, W. Germany: Ballett-Bühnen-Verlag, 1984.

———. "Not How People Move but What Moves Them." With Jochen Schmidt. In *Pina Bausch Wuppertal Dance Theater; or, The Art of Training a Goldfish*, by Norbert Servos, 227–30. Cologne, W. Germany: Ballett-Bühnen-Verlag, 1984.

———. "Pina Bausch: An Interview by Jochen Schmidt." *Ballett International* 6, no. 2. (February 1983): 12–15.

———. "Pina Bausch über Lust." Interview with Eva-Elisabeth Fischer. *Süddeutsche Zeitung* 223, no. 25/26 (September 2004): 8–12.

————. "The Things We Discover for Ourselves Are the Most Important." With Jochen Schmidt. In *Pina Bausch Wuppertal Dance Theater; or, The Art of Training a Goldfish*, by Norbert Servos, 231–33. Cologne, W. Germany: Ballett-Bühnen-Verlag, 1984.

————. "'You Have to Keep Totally Alert, Sensitive, Receptive': Pina Bausch Talks with Norbert Servos." *Ballett International/Tanz Aktuell* (December 1995): 36–39.

Barker, Francis. *The Tremulous Private Body: Essays on Subjection*. New York: Methuen, 1984.

Baxmann, Inge. "Dance Theatre: Rebellion of the Body, Theatre of Images and an Inquiry into the Sense of the Senses." *Ballett International* 13, no. 10 (January 1990): 55–60.

Bentivoglio, Leonetta. "Dance of the Present, Art of the Future." *Ballett International* 8, no. 12 (December 1985): 24–28.

Birringer, Johannes. "Pina Bausch: Dancing across Borders." *TDR* (Spring 1986): 85–97.

Blondel, Eric. *Nietzsche: The Body and Culture: Philosophy as a Philological Genealogy*. Translated by Seán Hand. Stanford, CA: Stanford University Press, 1991.

Bowman, Michael, and Della Pollock. "'This Spectacular Body': Politics and Postmodernism in Pina Bausch's Tanztheater." *TPQ* 9, no. 2 (1989): 113–18.

Brecht, Bertolt. *Brecht on Theatre*. Translated by John Willett. New York: Hill and Wang, 1984.

Butler, Judith. "Performative Acts and Gender Constitution: An Essay in Phenomenology and Feminist Theory." *Theatre Journal* (December 1988): 519–531.

Climenhaga, Royd. *Pina Bausch: Performance Practitioner Series*. New York: Routledge, 2009.

————, ed. *The Pina Bausch Sourcebook: The Makings of Tanztheater*. New York: Routledge, 2012.

Cody, Gabrielle. "Woman, Man, Dog, Tree: Two Decades of Intimate and Monumental Bodies in Pina Bausch's Tanztheater." *TDR* (August 1999): 115–31.

Croce, Arlene. "Bad Smells." *New Yorker*, July 16, 1984: 81–84.

Daly, Ann, ed. "Tanztheater: The Thrill of the Lynch Mob or the Rage of Woman?" *TDR* (Spring 1986): 46–56.

Descartes, René. *The Philosophical Writings of Descartes*. Vol. 1. Translated by John Cottingham, Robert Stoothoff, and Dugold Murdoch. Cambridge, Cambridge University Press, 1985.

Finkel, Anita. "Gunsmoke." *New Dance Review* 4, no. 2. (October–December 1991): 3–10.

Fischer-Lichte, Erika. *The Transformative Power of Performance: A New Aesthetics*. Translated by Saskya Iris Jain. New York and London: Routledge, 2008.

Garner, Stanton B. Jr. *Bodied Spaces: Phenomenology and Performance in Contemporary Drama*. Ithaca and London: Cornell University Press, 1994.

Goldberg, Marianne. "Artifice and Authenticity: Gender Scenarios in Pina Bausch's Dance Theatre." *Women and Performance* 4, no. 2 (1989): 104–117.

Heidegger, Martin. *The Basic Problems of Phenomenology*. Translated by Albert Hofstadter. Bloomington: Indiana University Press, 1982.

————. *Being and Time*. Translated by John Macquarrie and Edward Robinson. New York: Harper, 1962.

Johnson, Mark. *The Body in the Mind: The Bodily Basis of Meaning, Imagination, and Reason*. Chicago: University of Chicago Press, 1987.

Kerkhoven, Marianne van. "Dance, Theatre, and Their Hazy Boundaries." *Ballett International* 16, no. 1 (1993): 11–15.

————. "Merging of All Boundaries: On the Autonomy of Dance." *Ballett International* 12, no. 1 (1989): 13–18.

————. "The Weight of Time." *Ballett International* 14, no. 2 (February 1991): 63–68.

Kirchman, Kay. "The Totality of the Body: An Essay on Pina Bausch's Aesthetic." *Ballett International/Tanz Aktuell* (May 1994): 37–43.

Klemola, Timo. "Dance and Embodiment." *Ballett International* 14, no. 1 (January 1991): 71–80.

———. "Frame, Look and Movement: The Phenomenology of Dance." *Ballett International* 14, no. 2 (February 1991): 13–14.

Kozel, Susan. "Bausch and Phenomenology." *Dance Now* 2, no. 4 (Winter 1993/94): 49–54.

Langer, Susanne. *Feeling and Form.* New York: Scribner's, 1953.

———. *Mind: An Essay on Human Feeling.* Abridged Edition. Baltimore: Johns Hopkins University Press, 1988.

———. *Philosophy in a New Key.* Cambridge: Harvard University Press, 1963.

Leder, Drew. *The Absent Body.* Chicago: University of Chicago Press, 1990.

Lehman, Hans-Thies. *Postdramatic Theatre.* Translated by Karen Jürs-Munby. New York and London: Routledge, 2006.

Lepecki, André, ed. *Dance: Documents of Contemporary Art.* London: Whitechapel Gallery, 2012.

———. ed. *Of the Presence of the Body: Essays on Dance and Performance Theory.* Middletown, CT: Wesleyan University Press, 2004.

———. "Skin, Body, and Presence in Contemporary European Choreography." *TDR* 43, no. 4 (Winter 1999): 129–40.

Levin, David Michael. *The Body's Recollection of Being.* New York: Routledge, 1985.

Madison, Gary Brent. *The Phenomenology of Merleau-Ponty: A Search for the Limits of Consciousness.* Athens: Ohio University Press, 1981.

Manning, Susan Allene. "An American Perspective on Tanztheater." *TDR* (Spring 1986): 57–79.

———. "Generation and Gender in West German Art Today." *Next Wave Festival Catalogue* (1985): 5–10.

Martin, Randy. *Performance as a Political Act: The Embodied Self.* New York: Bergin and Barvey, 1990.

Merleau-Ponty, Maurice. *Phenomenology of Perception.* Translated by Colin Smith. London: Routledge, 1962.

———. *The Primacy of Perception.* Evanston: Northwestern University Press, 1964.

Price, David W. "The Politics of the Body: Pina Bausch's Tanztheater." *Theater Journal* (October 1990): 322–31.

Sartre, Jean-Paul. *Being and Nothingness.* Translated by Hazel E. Barnes. New York: Quokka, 1956.

———. *Existentialism and Human Emotions.* Translated by Bernard Frechtman. Secaucus, NJ: Citadel Press, 1985.

———. *The Philosophy of Jean-Paul Sartre.* Edited by Robert Denoon Cumming. New York: Vintage, 1965.

Scarry, Elaine. *The Body in Pain: The Making and Unmaking of the World.* New York: Oxford University Press, 1985.

Schlicher, Susanne. *Tanztheater.* Reinbek bei Hamburg, Germany: Rowohlts, 1987.

———. "The West German Dance Theatre: Paths from the Twenties to the Present." *Choreography and Dance* 3, part 2 (1993): 25–43.

Schmidt, Jochen. "From Isadora to Pina: The Renewal of the Human Image in Dance." *Ballett International/Tanz Aktuell* (May 1994): 34–36.

———. "Preface." *Pina Bausch Wuppertal Dance Theater; or, The Art of Training a Goldfish,* by Norbert Servos, 13–16. Cologne, W. Germany: Ballett-Bühnen-Verlag, 1984..

———. "Pina Bausch and the New German Tanztheater: Movement from the Inside Out." *Festival des Nouvelle Danse, Montreal, Souvenir Program.* 1985: 59–65.

———. *Pina Bausch: Tanzen Gegen die Angst*. Munich, Germany: Econ Verlag, 1999.

———. "The Wuppertal Choreographer Pina Bausch—The Mother Courage of Modern Dance—Turns Fifty." *Ballett International* 13, no. 6–7 (June/July 1990): 40–43.

Servos, Norbert. "The Emancipation of Dance: Pina Bausch and the Wuppertal Dance Theater." Translated by Peter Harris and Pia Kleber. *Modern Drama* 22, no. 4 (1981): 435–47.

———. "In the Emotions Factory." *Ballett International* 8, no. 1 (January 1985): 6–12.

———. "On the Seduction of Angels." *Ballett International* 8, no. 12 (December 1985): 72–76.

———. *Pina Bausch Wuppertal Dance Theater; or, The Art of Training a Goldfish*. Cologne, W. G ermany: Ballett-Bühnen-Verlag, 1984.

Sheets-Johnston, Maxine. *Illuminating Dance: Philosophical Explorations*. London: Bucknell University Press, 1984.

———. "Phenomenology as a Way of Illuminating Dance." In *Illuminating Dance*, edited by Maxine Sheets-Johnstone. London: Bucknell University Press, 1984.

Sparshot, Francis. "The Dancing Body: Divisions on a Sartian Ground." In *Illuminating Dance*, edited by Maxine Sheets-Johnstone, 188–201. London: Bucknell University Press, 1984.

———. *Off the Ground: First Steps to a Philosophical Consideration of Dance*. Princeton: Princeton University Press, 1988.

Wehle, Philippa. "Pina Bausch's Tanztheater—A Place of Difficult Encounter." *Women and Performance* 1, no. 2 (Winter 1984): 25–36.

Weiss, Gail. *Body Images: Embodiment as Intercorporality*. New York and London: Routledge, 1999.

Winnacker, Susanne. "The Body as Art Work: Faithfullness in Dance." *Ballett International/ Tanz Aktuell* (November 2000): 18–23.

Wright, Elizabeth. *Postmodern Brecht: A Re-Presentation*. London: Routledge, 1989.

CHAPTER 12

....

THE TOTAL THEATER
AESTHETIC PARADIGM IN
AFRICAN THEATER

....

PRAISE ZENENGA

THE total theater aesthetic paradigm in African performance practices seeks to integrate theater, music, dance, and other creative artistic modes into its practices. African theater comprises distinct and varied practices, conventions, and aesthetic trends—all of which are as dynamic, diverse, and unique as the people who produce and consume them. This analysis focuses on specific creative trends that have come to be known as total theater. It argues that total theater is a complex, cross-disciplinary creative trend founded at the confluence of theater, dance, and music and it also incorporates various other performative and artistic practices in its creative processes and outcomes. In most African performance traditions and conventions, music, dance, drama, and other theatrical practices exist in a complex, complementary, and logical-dynamic system of performative expressions that are known as total theater.

This chapter is devoted to the theoretical perspectives of the distinct evolutionary history, aesthetics, patterns, and practices of total theater in Africa. It seeks to provide a descriptive and theoretical inquiry into the key characteristic features of total theater. What distinguishes African total theater from similar global practices is not only the people's unique historical experiences but also the perpetuation of a predominantly integrative aesthetic paradigm. Using examples drawn from both contemporary and classical African practices and productions, this chapter also explores the forces and conditions that shape and sustain total theater aesthetics and practices in various sociopolitical, historical, and geographical contexts. Thus, besides examining the ideological, philosophical, and aesthetic trends that have shaped total theater in Africa, this chapter analyzes the expectations, conventions, and traditions associated with the practice. While Western performance cultures tend to separate dance, speech, and music, mainstream contemporary African theater has always gravitated toward retaining the fundamental unity of movement, speech, song, poetry, gesture, games, and improvisation as the core essence of total theater.

The secondary goal of this chapter is to articulate a broader and more inclusive understanding of African theater consistent with the array of practices. Although "theater" is a European term with a specific meaning (Hutchison, 2004, 312), the African view regards theater as a broad practice and discipline that eludes narrow definition. Likewise, the African concept of total theater is not restricted to scripted drama alone, but is a broad and inclusive practice that incorporates drama, dance, and music. Kole Omotoso "suggests how notions of theater can be broadened to include engagements with intercultural syncretic performances" (cited in Hutchison, 2004, 312). The fact that "theater" translates into "game," "sport," "play," "ritual," "festival," "dance," "music," and "performance" in most African languages testifies to the breadth, depth, and complexity of the range of meanings and practices associated with the term. Part of the problem with such an inclusive and broad notion of total theater is that it leads to misinterpretation and disciplinary exclusion. In particular, some universalist approaches, which find it difficult to come to grips with this broad and complex performance practice, often deny African total theater its autonomy and what Sandra L. Richards calls the autodynamic quality of contemporary African drama (ibid., 168).

In the context of this discussion, the definition of Africa is based on the geographical and sociocultural parameters that include the entire continent (including North Africa). The general claims made about Africa are true to the same degree in all of Africa. Fragmenting Africa into North Africa and sub-Saharan Africa obscures the complex historical, cultural, and aesthetic interconnections and links that bind Africans of all shades, races, and creeds. Nowhere are these links so obvious as they are in the range of theatrical and performance practices as well as the many myths, rituals, ceremonies, and storytelling traditions among the continent's different cultures. For example, prominent Ghanaian scholar and playwright Mohammed Ben Abdallah conducted an ethnographic research trip to sites of ancient civilizations not only to establish concrete connections but also to ground his own practices and scholarship in the continent's cultural performative traditions. He describes this trip as an educational and spiritual odyssey beginning from the Great Lakes Region of Africa through the kingdoms of Nubia, Kush, Meroe, Ethiopia, and Axum to the Nile Valley and sites of ancient Egypt (Abdallah, 1359). Africa is a geographical, economic, political, and cultural entity with much more in common than is often imagined or stated. On the theatrical front, James M. Gibbs cites Abdallah's recent play *The Song of the Pharaoh* as clear evidence of the parallels, influences, and "links that exist between West Africa and Egypt" (1349–50). To ignore such historical and contemporary commercial political and social interactions or exchanges through sporting, trading, military, cultural, and religious activities within the African continent in any analysis is therefore erroneous. Consequently, total theater is inevitably a Pan-African concept insofar as its aesthetic experience relates not only to native Africans, but also to people of African heritage scattered throughout the world.

DEFINING (AND PRACTICING) TOTAL THEATER

Within the African context, Ghanaian scholar-artists Efua Sutherland (2012) and Mohammed Ben Abdallah (2012) were the first to theorize on the notion of total theater when they created the concept of *abibigromma* (Akan for African Plays) to define the modern African theater (as distinct from the European theaters of the colonial era) produced in the postindependence dispensation. In an effort to break away from the predominant colonial theatrical practices, Abdallah established a multidisciplinary theoretical aesthetic framework in the 1960s which laid the foundation of what he termed African total theater, referring to a modern integrated theater that incorporated music, dance, drama and story-telling. Wole Soyinka later adopted the *abibi* (black) concept in the title of his 1976 play *Ogun Abibiman* (The [Abibi] Black [man's] Nation) to encapsulate the Pan-African concept of the "Black World; that which pertains to, the matter, the affair of, Black peoples" (Soyinka, 23). For subjugated African and Diaspora communities, song, dance, and performance became alternative vehicles for sociopolitical and economic self-articulation. In these communities, creating a theatrical convention that brings together dance, theater, and music in a singular performance also functions to "resist Eurocentric dramatic theater practices which insist on their separation and purity" (Ravengai, 3). In African, Caribbean, and Black Diaspora communities, total theater gained currency after the attainment of political independence, and the practice represents a resurrection of the modes of artistic expression that were repressed, abolished, banned, and presumed dead under slavery, Jim Crow, colonialism, and apartheid.

African total theater is essentially a self-perpetuating system and integrative artistic concept in which hybrid blending of dance, theater, and music is very much a defining feature. It demands a multiagency approach in its practice and requires theater practitioners to apply their multiple skill-sets as they enter into creative collaboration with other artists. As a direct result of its inherently complex and integrative nature, the analysis and interpretation of total theater also require interdisciplinary approaches. African classics such as Mbongeni Ngema's *Asinamali* (1985), Mukotani Rugyendo's *The Contest* (1977), Ngugi wa Mirii and Ngugi wa Thiong'o's *I Will Marry When I Want* (1982), Okot p'Bitek's *Song of Lawino Song of Ocol* (1984), and Wole Soyinka's *Kongi's Harvest* (1971) and *The Lion and the Jewel* (1963) serve as examples of interdisciplinary theatrical productions that not only incorporate dance, theater, music, and poetry but also as touch on gender, history, culture, and politics of the cold war era. While African theatrical practices insist on upholding a unity of theater, song, and dance within a singular performance, academics often feel a need for hair-splitting in their interpretation and multilayer unpacking of these complex performance traditions. Mohammed Ben Abdallah identified this problem in the early 1960s and devoted his career to closing the void and addressing the discrepancies between practice and scholarship (1358–59). There has always been a significant and problematic discordance between African theatrical practice, audience reception, and academic interpretation. Arguments for the nonexistence of theater in Africa prior to colonization betray a lack of understanding and incapacity to unpack the continent's rich and complex performance cultures and traditions that have been in existence since time immemorial. Besides the inability to comprehend this ingenious amalgam of dance, music, and theater as a bonafide theater tradition in Africa, there also exist other ideological and political reasons for viewing African artistic productions as inferior. For example, definitions of drama which put primacy on the written text often fall short of addressing the African continent's more complex, diverse, ephemeral, and broad theatrical practices dependent on different kinds of texts. However one might argue that the primacy of the written text in Western drama developed in order to set itself apart from performance traditions that were/are body- and oral-based.

To date, the majority of African cultures place absolute primacy on the spoken text over the written text in their performance practices. The persistence of the oral text in contemporary African theatrical practices is a conscious aesthetic choice and not a hallmark of backwardness. Writing has been viewed as the mark of a superior civilization, and other societies have been judged, by this view, to be incapable of thinking critically and objectively, or having distance from ideas and emotions (Smith, 1999, 30). This tendency to equate writing with civilization smacks of ignorance and a monolithic outlook on African performance traditions. The fact that the key distinctions between theater and drama emphasize the written component implies that the fields of theater and drama have been defined in ways that exclude African people's ways of knowing and their performance techniques as well as their cultural and intellectual heritages and practices. The change from oral to written expressive modes which took place in most Western cultures in the late Middle Ages and shifted the primacy of the written text over the performed text and orally presented text, was not a global phenomenon. In African theatrical practices, the spoken word has remained the predominant and preferred mode over the written text. To equate the nonexistence of a written tradition to the absence of theater and drama in precolonial and contemporary Africa is to ignore the many established and intricate ways of thinking, knowing, doing, and problem-solving through theatrical expression, interpretation, and engagement. Examples include masquerades and puppetry, which are still very difficult to document through scripts but remain essential components of modern African theater. Similarly theater for development and theater for social change, which still constitute mainstream theater in most African countries, largely use music, dance, puppetry, gesture, and other nonverbal expressive modes mostly based on improvisation thus making it hard to freeze them in a written script. Scripts for such plays as *I Will Marry When I Want* and Ngugi wa Mirii and Ngugi wa Thiong'o's *Mother Sing for Me* (1978) were written as postproduction records and not sacrosanct scripts on which the performances were based.

Viewpoints that privilege written texts over texts that are spoken, danced, sung, or performed not only exclude the whole body of the African people's unwritten expressive cultures but also deny Africa's alternative knowledge systems and ways of knowing embedded in the continent's performing traditions. Dwight Conquergood laments how "scholarship is so skewed towards texts that even when researchers do attend to extralinguistic human action and embodied events they construe them as texts to be read" (2002, 147). This obsession with the written text not only promotes the supremacy of Western knowledge systems, but also "erases the vast realm of human knowledge and meaningful action that is unlettered" (ibid.). As Mark Fleishman argues, embodied practices that regard performance as a knowledge paradigm thrive on the continent's historical legacies and are particularly appropriate to African processes of oral and bodily transmission of knowledge through dance, storytelling, poetry, and song through communities and between communities (ibid., 116)— what Diana Taylor refers to as the "so-called ephemeral repertoire of embodied practice/ knowledge" (Taylor, 2003, 19). The organic unity of dance, theater, and song in total theater is one of the ways in which Africa's oral and performative cultures still persist across the continent, despite colonially imposed preferences for the written and the ravages of so-called modernity (Fleishman, 2009, 116).

Because total theater employs such a wide range of expressive artistic modes, it is often difficult to categorize African theater. Most scholars have struggled to classify African plays like Wole Soyinka's *Lion and the Jewel* (1974), Efua T. Sutherland's *The Marriage of Anansewa* (1975), Mukotami Rugyendo's *The Contest* (1977), Mbongeni Ngema's *"Asinamali!"* (1986), Ngugi wa Mirii and Ngugi wa Thiong'o's *I Will Marry When I Want* (1982), Femi Osofisan's *Esu and the Vagabond Minstrels* (1991), and Muhammed Ben Abdallah's *Verdict of the Cobra*

(2002) as dance dramas or just dramas with dance or musicals. The strong presence of dance and music in these plays and their translation into masterful narratives through kinesthetic, visual, and auditory modalities is what really sets them apart from conventional western musicals and dance dramas. In an interview, some British audiences who had watched a performance of the Kamiriithu Community Education and Cultural Centre's communally produced play *Mother Sing for Me* (1978) revealed the same dilemma in the following words:

> It all merged and, and really broke up what for us could have been long passages of dialogue we couldn't follow. For us the music gave the whole thing a sense of direction. I wouldn't say it was a musical in the western sense, but it was a dramatic experience that blended together words, music and dance. And the audience was of course very receptive. It was more than just a stage play. It was a total experience. (Bjorkman, 1989, 86)

The play was not a folk opera because it was not all song. Neither was it all drama nor all dance, but was a total amalgamation of the three expressive modes working together to fully convey a community's dynamic performance traditions and historical experiences.

Unlike Western theatrical practices in which music and dance only serve basic level technical support, they are viewed as a natural and integral component of total theater productions in Africa. As Daniel Avorgbedor testifies, "in African music and dance traditions, the visual plastic, tactile, olfactory, mime, gesture, and gesticulation, as well as a whole range of performance events, fall within the song-speech continuum but defy definition as 'song' or 'speech'" (2011, 1). This solid aesthetic unification is a key defining feature of African total theater; both audiences and practitioners have proudly held on to it for generations even in the face of slavery and colonialism that actively sought to eclipse or even subsume these traditional performance practices. In comparison, Western forms of total theater exemplified in the epic theater of Piscator and Brecht also deployed dance, theater, music, and various other artistic elements but mostly for aesthetic purposes. The *Oxford Companion to Theatre and Performance* locates the origins of Western total theater in twentieth century avant-garde experimental theater designed "to draw upon and exploit the totality of performative devices—music, dance, acting, scenography and the plastic arts, costume, masks, lighting, playhouse architecture, the configuration of the stage and auditorium, and spectator environment" (Kennedy). Although it is thought to have risen from Wagner's intention to produce a *Gesamtkunstwerk* or "total work of art," Artaud, Brecht, Piscator, Brook, and Schechner became the leading proponents of Western total theater, whose radical politics and audience participatory techniques parallel African total theater.

For most Africans, total theater not only represents their embodiment of the continent's living traditions, but is also a celebration and an expression of their undying culture. Effiong Johnson cites the continent's rich heritage and varied traditions of artistic expressive cultures as the wellspring of contemporary African performance practices, "particularly the total theater aesthetics where drama is shrouded with elements of dance, music, songs, acrobatics, crowds, masquerades, rituals, lores, magic" (Johnson, 2011, 110). The total theater concept thrives as a unifying aesthetic which takes into account every conceivable aspect of African expressive culture.

The common thread running through the continent's total theater practices is the strict adherence to a unified speech-song-dance aesthetic. Total theater not only increases engagement and enhances the dramatic content of art but also manifests culturally rooted logical emotional transitions through multiple auditory, visual, mental, and kinesthetic expressive modes. Whether friendly or contentious, theater, dance, and music are intricately connected and always working together to articulate the multiple levels of meaning and emotion. Since an inclusive aesthetic constitutes the bedrock of African theatrical practices, total theater does not necessarily adhere to any formulaic structure. Different artists, regions, and cultures constantly create and present a variety of new and exciting permutations of expressions designed to fulfill specific needs and functions.

FUNCTION (AND AESTHETICS) OF TOTAL THEATER

African theater practitioners have consistently adhered to a particular constellation of integrative aesthetic preferences and experiences so as to retain a distinctive pleasing and recognizable identity for their productions and also to meet audience expectations. For example, 75 percent of published African plays include music and dance scenes because audiences expect certain emotions to be expressed through song and movement in addition to the regular dialogue and speech. While ensuring instant recognition and a loyal following, the total theater tradition simultaneously serves to perpetuate an ideological and aesthetic autonomy that overtly and covertly defies centuries of colonial hegemony and cultural assimilation. In most African cultures, theater is viewed as a metadiscipline to be engaged and shared in its totality and not partitioned into splinter fields of drama, dance, and music. In other words, total theater is not just a simple mixture of theater, dance, and music, but is a much more complex amalgamation in which theater, dance, music, and other expressive art forms effectively engage, understand, and interact with each other to produce a unique practice. Within these contexts, there is strong interest in how these subdisciplines talk, merge with, incorporate, and enhance each other. In order to achieve certain aesthetic and artistic outcomes, theater, dance, and music occasionally challenge, collide, and contend as they go up against each other in spirited but friendly contests and alliances within a single production. The play *I Will Marry When I Want* serves as a classic example of an African play in which dialogue, speech, song, and dance compete fiercely to predominate in ways that create strong contrasts and harmonies while simultaneously complementing and reinforcing each other to provide the most complete and balanced aesthetic experience.

African cultures traditionally regard the theater or the performance space as a site where expressive forces co-exist and enhance each other. Total theater challenges the monolithic domination of the performance space by a singular mode of expression and embraces the notion of "artistic pluralism," which integrates the arts of dance, theater, and music into a unified, holistic aesthetic experience. Fusing each of their individual expressive aesthetic systems into one artistic synergy helps to provide a constant impetus for movement and change in total theater practices. Such artistic pluralism not only creates a fertile arena for experimentation and the development of newer and exciting forms but also challenges perspectives that view current trends of total theater as static and stuck in the Middle Ages, lacking the refinement and sophistication associated with contemporary Western theater.

Since dance, drama, and music express different levels of emotional intensity, total theater seeks to give audiences a holistic experience, understanding, and engagement with the performance. Its fundamental techniques engage all the audience's senses through movement and speech closely bound with music. The unity of speech, sound, and movement inevitably appeals to the sum total of the audience's senses. They constitute the much aspired for complete balance of mind, body, and spirit. In African total theater practices, movement is bound with music and speech in a much deeper and fundamental way. Thus, instead of serving mere technical and aesthetic functions, these various artistic modes are important constituent elements of the narrative and they work together to generate the play's overall meaning. For example, if music and dance are removed from *The Contest* and *Mother Sing for Me*, the plays will lose not only their inner essence but also their meaning. In other words, these three expressive modes are bound together in constellations of mutual obligation and dependence to effectively enhance each other. Thus, within the African worldview, the notion of theater oftentimes refers to a cohesive integration of cross-disciplinary expressive forms where theater, dance, and music do not exist in isolation but in a continuum that combines multiple performance modes into a unified whole. While adding to the total experience, this integrative dance, theater, and music expression not only heightens the dramatic effect, but also provides artists with a wider array of creative expressions.

Just as in many other global cultures, music and dance in African total theater are used to enhance atmosphere or create the mood for different parts of the narrative and also function to articulate the movements of dancers, give cues, and provide interludes or transitions. For example, besides serving as narratives within the main narrative (stories within the story) and working as important flashbacks to provide missing information, music and dance also function to bridge scenes in Abdallah's *The Verdict of the Cobra* (1972). Thus in addition to reinforcing content and amplifying themes, music and dance also serve many other functions, ranging from purely recreational and technical, to spiritual and aesthetic. Throughout history, total theater has generated high levels of audience engagement and aesthetic appeal, particularly for its indigenous African audiences traditionally attuned to integrated cohesive performance practices, where theater, dance, and music express varied, subtle, and deep emotional experiences.

In most African societies where speech, dance, and music carry the distinctive cultural freight of a people, total theater plays a vital role in passing down history, wisdom, lifestyles, spirituality, philosophy, social relations, customs, and cultural values from one generation to the next. For example in the classical Zimbabwean play *Mavambo/First Steps* (1986)—(an adaptation of Wilson Katiyo's novel *A Son of the Soil*), dance, music, mime, and storytelling complement each other to tell the history of colonial dispossession, resistance, and conquest. African total theater amounts to a holistic approach, which brings together theater, dance, and music to effectively express the sum total of ideas and emotions prevalent within a particular historical epoch. In Africa, the performer's body becomes the primary vehicle through which speech and the language of dance communicate meanings to the audience. Such practices treat the human body as the synergistic confluence where various expressive modes that include dance, music and theater, are brought together, actualized, and crystallized into a unified whole—known as total theater. Most importantly the performing body in African total theater plays a pivotal role not only as the transmitter of speech, music, and movement, but also as an embodiment of a people's history, culture, and memory.

Within the African context, the performing body "is often encoded by cultural practices, social and racial constructions, and gendered conditions of use and reception—all of which form layer upon layer of texts that convey certain meanings and power operations" (Loots, 1995, 53). Total theater emanates from a tradition of intangible texts and it strongly relies on oral texts, embodied texts, and memory texts that get translated into observable performance texts and often into written texts or audiovisual texts, as is the case with contemporary productions and practices. African total theater provides multiple avenues for cross-domain understanding; in resisting the separation of drama, dance, and music, it acknowledges the body as the primary repository and conduit of the sum total of the historical, political, and sociocultural experiences depicted. It rejects the separation of mind, body, and spirit apparent in most contemporary global practices. Total theater takes off from the premise that the body is a source of knowledge expressed variously through movement, speech, and song/sound. Within the African context, the human body is regarded as an archive due to its capacity to embody knowledge. Embodied knowledge does not just belong to traditional cultural practices but is a living tradition that is still highly regarded as one of the predominant and legitimate ways of knowing. Total theater provides unlimited space for the body to maximize and manifest all facets of its expressiveness in a singular performance. To this extent, it cannot be regarded as sheer entertainment but as an experiential and alternative way of knowing, as indicated earlier. This intellectual and kinesthetic understanding of the body transitioning across the holistic continuum of music, theater, and dance is an integral part of the African theatrical experience.

HISTORICAL EVOLUTION OF TOTAL THEATER

The historical evolution of African theater reveals a coherent and consistent unity of dance, theater, and music. From its origins in precolonial traditional rituals, games, dances, songs, and ceremonies to the more commercial traveling theaters, concert party theaters, protest or political theaters, and contemporary popular theaters and community-based theater practices, the unity of theater, dance, and song in African performance has persisted with astonishing cultural and aesthetic consistency. In today's complex multicultural world, aesthetic consistency in African theater not only helps to retain some core, defining theatrical principles but also functions to perpetuate the rich heritage of African performance traditions, thus making them easily identifiable and distinguishable from the other domineering global cultural practices that threaten to eclipse and subsume them. No matter how salient or inconspicuous it is, the intertwinement of theater, dance, and music is always a preeminent distinguishing aesthetic feature of African total theater. Today, different African aesthetic practices, which include, but are not limited to theater for development, theater for social change, community theater, and popular and people's theater, still incorporate a strong intertwinement of theater, dance, and music.

Universally, the historical origins of theater are intimately intertwined with the evolution of speech, movement, gesture, rituals, and myths as well as the capacity for *mimesis* (imitation) innate among mankind.[1] Within the African context, numerous studies increasingly cite evidence of ritual, magic, folklore, paintings, masks, sculptures and engravings in the prehistoric periods as the source of contemporary dramatic and performing arts. Most new African aesthetic trends originated, evolved, and spread from these earliest forms of prehistoric artistic expressions that have amalgamated to form the well-made plays we know today (see Abdallah, 2012, and Gibbs, 2012). The historical roots of total theater in Africa span several cultures, civilizations, and millennia. African total theater has managed to retain its traditional affinity and interaction with other modes of performance, in particular dance and music. Total theater consistently retains a strong unity of drama, dance, and music even amid the current globalization trends that have seen traditional expressive forms getting overshadowed, transformed, subsumed, and even replaced with entirely new practices. The principle of African theater's indivisibility is widely recognized. For example, most historical accounts of African theater from different regions point to ancient rituals, magic, and ceremonies as the source of contemporary theatrical practices.[2]

In 2004, Martin Banham edited a volume that attempts to provide the first critical panorama of African theater from the ancient and classical to the precolonial and colonial conquest as well as the present postcolonial dispensation. In almost all historical accounts examined in the volume, scholars agree that similar historical patterns exist in different African regions and cultures. There is obviously no formulaic way of describing or doing theater in Africa because of the continent's geographical scale as well as its demographic and cultural diversity. While there are so "many disconnections as there are connections," (Banham, 2004, xv), emphasis in this analysis is on common trends, conventions, and aesthetics. These dominant aesthetic paradigms have throughout history revealed fully consistent performance practices, which at the very least integrate fundamentals of movement, speech, theater, music, and many other modes of expression within a singular production. Additionally, most historical accounts point distinctively to an African theatrical practice that integrates dance, music, and theater in order to create and improvise unique performances.

Movement, speech, and music exist together as a unity to create the most fundamental common aesthetic pattern and key-defining feature of total theater practices in Africa and to some extent in the Diaspora. Traditionally, affinity interactions and engagements between theater, dance, and music have been studied separately in the twentieth-century academy. As Martin Banham argues:

> The roots of African theatre in ritual, seasonal rhythms, religion and communal communication are roots common to world theater, but whereas it may be argued that European Theater, for instance, is at so great a distance from its functional roots, as to be unaware of them, African theatre—even at the beginning of the twenty-first century—remains directly and immediately related to them. The contemporary literary playwright is likely to be drawing upon exactly the same performance imperative as the story-teller, or the masquerade, the performer is still the necessary chronicler of time and experience. (ibid. xvi)

These unique African-rooted performance traditions have continued to flourish as distinctive aesthetic features in contemporary total theater practices. Banham's analysis points to the evolution of distinct African theatrical trends. As the northern hemisphere moved towards a separation of drama and dance, the global south retained a unity of speech and movement.

Africa and most parts of the global south still share a belief in the idea of fusing various art forms, of incorporating dance, drama, and other expressive modes into a singular production. Within the African worldview, dance, theater, and music have never severed their historical ties with each other in the global south. Other viewpoints locate these shifts and changes in Western theater to as far back as the medieval era. "Dance in the West underwent a forced separation of drama and dance during the Middle Ages when the church split body from soul."[3] The separation of dance, drama, and music is also clearly reflected in the diverging and opposing methods of training emphasized in our contemporary stand-alone academic departments of dance, theater, and music. Although some African theater practitioners have also isolated the various expressive modes of performance, the continent's dominant informing aesthetics and practices have retained dance and music as integral components of theater. Even though the demands for a rigorous academic scrutiny and analysis may necessitate a separation of these disciplines, they should not always be positioned as antagonistic or perpetually divergent and detached from each other, but it is important to remind learners that historically, these disciplines are equally complementary and can engage each other in multiple and fascinating ways.

African theater, music, and dance have always existed in a fairly balanced give-and-take relationship. For example, it is not only theater that has an affinity for mutual cooperation, but African dance and music performances also actively incorporate theatrical elements. As Robert W. Nicholls observes in various traditional Nigerian dance performances, "A sense of pluralism is manifested . . . by the dynamic interaction of multiple elements. It is customary to integrate dance with other arts, with music, drama and oratory, as well as with various forms of visual displays such as masks, body paint and costumes" (44). In another separate observation he remarks, "At this time Ogirinye members take turns to honor the deceased by performing solo dances. The arrival of the Ogirinye masquerade is pure theater. He does not dance but simply runs at full speed through the meeting ground to the burial place" (48). This shows the extent to which the African performer fully exploits theater, dance, and music's capacity for mutual accommodation, mutual cooperation, and mutual reciprocity. The potential for these three artistic modes of expression to forge positive and mutually beneficial existences in various contexts should not be understated.

Total theater has a very long history dating as far back as the prehistoric era and generally continuing into the colonial period, when most African cultures made significant contacts with other cultures. When global cultures made contact with Africa and ushered in systems of slavery and colonialism during the mid-fifteenth century, Africans not only were subjected to atrocities but also were introduced to the separation of theater, dance, and music as well as cultures that prioritized writing as a method of record-keeping. In most parts of Africa, the deployment of multiple modes of cultural expression and performance was long established in the preliterate and precolonial indigenous theatrical traditions. The defining aesthetic in precolonial traveling theater and the colonial concert party theater traditions centered on the unity of theater, dance, and music, as illustrated in Kwame Braun's video documentary *Stage-Shakers! Ghana's Concert Party Theatre* (2001). Drawing boundaries between theater, dance, and music in most African performance traditions is not encouraged because it creates artificial schisms and bridges within a sacrosanct total theatrical practice that should never be separated. In cultural contexts where thoughts, emotions, acting, speech, and movement do not occur in isolation, separating the corresponding visual, oral, auditory, and kinesthetic modes of artistic expression is seen as leading to increased disequilibrium in mind, body, and spirit.

Although Erwin Friedrich, Maximilian Piscator, John Louis Barrault, Peter Brook, and Augusto Boal are often credited as the main scholars and practitioners of total theater in contemporary academic circles, the concept of total theater in African performance practices is not a recent development. Brook's concept of total theater refers to the impact a production has on audiences, while Piscator and Barrault respectively emphasize the extent to which performers evoke "whatever performance technique necessary" or "the whole range of their means of expression." While these prominent Western avant-garde directors, playwrights, and scholars have impacted and shaped performance practices in Africa and Asia, their own creative and scholarly endeavors have also consciously drawn from those same non-Western traditions.[4] Since Western and non-Western theatrical practices have historically influenced each other, it is important to emphasize that these interactions denote a two-way influence except in instances where parallel practices exist. Although Western notions of total theater parallel some key elements found in African total theater, they do not emphasize how the interaction of multiple texts and multiple modes of expression and performance reflects the sum total of the African historical experience.

In African total theater, the idea is not to subject audiences to a barrage of different artistic modes but to fulfill the dual task of preserving the indigenous expressive cultures and reflecting the African people's historical experiences. For example, the Kamiriithu Center in Kenya produced *Mother Sing for Me* with a clear objective:

> Bringing back the African theatre as it used to be (*before colonialism*). Dance and song were part of it. But the most distinguishing feature of the African theatre was its participatory aspect. The audience and the actors were one. There was no passive audience occasionally beaming self consciously at the peculiar, calculated mannerisms of an individual actor . . . The African theatre springs from people, as it were, and bounces back on them. It is a reflection of their accumulated experiences—an expression of themselves as a people with shared experiences. (Bjorkman, 1989, 58)

This example demonstrates that African audiences are a critical factor and vital stakeholders in the making of total theater. To a larger extent, the audience dictates and shapes the content, style, and aesthetics of African theater. Although African audiences are open to innovation and experimentation, they consistently demand a unity of dance, drama, and music, and playwrights, directors, and producers often comply to meet audience expectations. Thus while African audiences have generally been receptive to practices from other global practices, local works that lack a unity of dance, drama, and music are usually viewed as inadequate. A sense of audience expectation is critical for the African theater artist because audiences often feel shortchanged if they fail to experience sequential multiple expressive modes involving dance, music, and theater in a production.

In a way, total theater is not just an interaction of expressive forms but also involves sharing historical and cultural experiences as well as finding common ties that bind together people of African descent located around the globe. Thus, while acknowledging the complexity and dynamism of the African global community, it is also possible to speak of people of African descent scattered throughout the globe as sharing some unique historical, cultural, spiritual, artistic, scientific, and philosophical legacies dating back to the ancient times. This discussion argues that since Africans on the continent and in the Diaspora share common historical experiences, particularly those to do with their struggles against slavery, racism, colonialism, and neocolonialism, it follows that the cultural practices and artistic and performative expressions of these collective experiences constitute related and intertwined heritages that inevitably shape a common destiny defining them as one people. In the absence of a common language among African cultures, it is mostly through the universal language of music and dance that different communities establish common ties. Total theater provides the most comprehensive expressions and representations of Pan-African cross-cultural exchanges and engagements. Ideologically, total theater constitutes a vital body of antihegemonic and counterhegemonic discourses in most African and African

Diaspora political practices. From its origins in ancient rituals and magic, total theater constituted a liberating discourse for most African societies as they struggled against natural phenomena and other human beings, especially those representing forces of slavery, feudal monarchs, colonial and neocolonial intrusions, preindependence and postindependence dictatorships, and antidemocratic forces afflicting them throughout history.

CHALLENGES (AND TRAINING) OF TOTAL THEATER ARTISTS

Total theater challenges practitioners to integrate multiple distinct but complementary skill sets including but not limited to singing, dancing, and acting. In this practice, artists always strive to develop the tools and skills necessary to unify these multiple expressive modes into a coherent, aesthetic, or performative whole. African total theater challenges practitioners to depict experiences through a continuum of multiple expressive modes while at the same time adhering to a specific felt, thought, and emotional logic. The seamless connection of speech, dance, music, and song in total theater requires a multidisciplinary and multitalented artist who can easily transition and execute all the roles with equal skill. As variety artists, African total theater practitioners must be skilled at acting, dancing, and singing as well as many other areas like costume designing and instrument making and playing. Total theater artists in Africa are not just mechanical performers but also have a deep sense of social responsibility and responsiveness. In addition to their creative abilities, practitioners often demonstrate a commitment to social responsibility and making a difference in society. Artists always stay attuned to the political, economic, cultural, and ethical dynamics of their societies. Thus the total theater artist not only is accomplished in multiple areas and disciplines of the performing arts industry but also is a storyteller, historian, public intellectual, and political activist. Wole Soyinka and Ngugi wa Thiong'o are examples of well-known African academics, playwrights cum-political activists. Within the African context, total theater practitioners go through extensive formal and informal multilevel training in order to accomplish these numerous responsibilities.

In Africa and the world over, the modern academy still lacks programs that can accommodate the training needs of the total artist. College-level theater and performance studies units in Africa lack a comprehensive curriculum that can produce a complete artist who matches and fits into the continent's predominant performance practices that incorporate dance, theater, and music in almost equal measure. Enrolling either in a theater, dance, or music department in Africa does not equip students with the necessary skill-sets for a successful career in African total theater. For aspiring total theater artists, concentrating in just one discipline like music, dance, or speech and drama alone, amounts to only partial training and produces half-baked practitioners. To qualify as total theater artists, most African students often resort to postgraduate informal training to supplement their skills in the artistic, spiritual, and cultural realms through workshops, seminars, master classes, and total immersion experiences. For example, Ngugi wa Mirii, Ngugi wa Thiong'o, Kimani Gecau, and other academics from the University of Nairobi in Kenya (widely regarded as Africa's foremost playwrights and directors), have given wide-ranging accounts of how much they learned about their culture, history, dances, and songs from ordinary villagers during the production of the classical play *I Will Marry When I Want*. Experiences of these Kenyan intellectuals show that total theater requires not only a culturally competent practitioner but also a superartist fluent in all disciplines of speech, dance, music, culture, and history.

Total theater is inherently designed to develop broad and versatile creative abilities in artists. This means the actor/actress in total theater is at once a professional dancer, singer, musician, and designer, combining the finest craftsmanship and artistry in all the various fields. Within the African context, a master performer is one who executes the different artistic modes with equal or near perfect skill, passion, mastery, knowledge, and precision. Most importantly, from both the artistic and interpretive perspectives, total theater demands an equal mastery of the broad, general artistic and expressive modes that constitute the practice. In many African cultures, young performers are traditionally apprenticed to a famous master to acquire the necessary knowledge, values, skills, and understandings they will require throughout their artistic careers. This type of training has always been nonconventional, hands-on, and natural, allowing learners to develop personal strengths in their own unique ways, using methods of their preference at a pace they deem comfortable. This contrasts sharply with conventional training, whereby each trainee artist specializes in a specific discipline like dance, directing, acting, voice, speech, or instrument playing with emphasis on direct transfer of skill-sets and passing exams.

Popular theater demands multidisciplinary and well-rounded artists who are well versed in dance, music, and other aspects of theater. In most African societies, experiential training, especially in the field of performing arts, was and is still regarded as an integral part of one's personal growth and development. These nonconventional traditional African ways of experiential learning not taught in regular schools and colleges but dispensed informally through long-term internships involving participation and observation, allowed trainees to chart their own growth paths. The approaches required a personal commitment on the part of learners who dedicated and devoted a significant portion of their lives to learning the various trades in dance, theater, and music. Although theater, dance, and music are still treated as after-school or extracurricular activities in most African educational systems, the establishment of stand-alone theater and dance departments in some African universities complements the existing nonconventional training methods. The increased demand for certification to back one's skill-sets has seen many African performing artists abandon the age-old nonformal forms of training in favor of formal and quasi-formal training. Established artists and performing companies in Africa have developed training programs, institutes, or academies and also conduct regular workshops for up-coming artists to expand their skill-sets and meet the demands of contemporary governing bodies, accreditation organizations, agencies, and the general public.

CONCLUSION

African theater remains deeply rooted and firmly grounded in the past while marching ahead into the future, incorporating technologies of the digital era and sharing affinities with other twenty-first-century contemporary global practices. To a larger extent, total theater practices remain embedded in traditional expressive discourses of culture and performance that often include an amalgamation of dance, theater, and music. To date, total theater continues to appeal to audiences because it remains one of the most culturally attuned performance practices—one that not only is inclusive of multiple expressive modes but also consistently reflects the people's historical experiences. This performance practice is deeply rooted in traditional cultural practices and remains a source of connection between dance, music, and other expressive arts.

African total theater demands a well-rounded performer trained in dance, music, acting, and improvisation. It is based on a framework comprising multiple elements or expressive modes and requires a well-balanced performing body. To achieve the desired integrative aesthetic experience, these elements must be held in balance such that none is deficient. This means that in total theater, the actor/actress is simultaneously a master musician, master dancer, and master performer all in one body. In order to execute their multiple roles, African theater artists require an equally integrative and interdisciplinary training. It is therefore imperative for the African academy to design relevant curricula to match the practical, technological, and aesthetic requirements of these long-established total theater traditions and the ever-evolving performing arts industry.

Although African theater arises out of various geocultural, political, and historical circumstances, it cannot be viewed as a monolithic performance practice, despite some observable common aesthetic, structural, and ideological trends that make it identifiable as such. In particular, the unity of dance, drama, and music has consistently remained as the most dominant structural and aesthetic feature of African theater. In spite of parallel traditions that exist elsewhere, what sets African total theater apart from other global practices is not just the intricate dynamics that amalgamate its aesthetic, structural, and formal qualities but also the expression of historical marginalization, oppression, and resistance in many African and Diaspora communities.

While it has affinities with other global theatrical practices, African total theater should not be viewed as an imitation or appendage of Western theater. Such approaches deny the continent's art form its autonomous existence, development, and aesthetic choices. Also to suggest that contemporary African theater is equivalent to sixteenth-century Western theatrical practices that similarly treated dance, drama, and music as inseparable can be interpreted as promoting a political and ideological agenda that views African theatrical practices as perpetually inferior to Western theater. These perceptions reflect a failure to comprehend the dynamics of African theater's multidisciplinary, complex, and consistently multilayered nature. It amounts to a flawed understanding of the underlying cultural influences, aesthetic tastes, preferences, and values on which African theater is built and continues to thrive. In essence, African theater is as diverse as the cultures and practitioners that produce it. Besides total theater, African theatrical practices also comprise experimental trends and amalgamations that involve fusing together indigenous and global practices. Thus while not all African theater integrates dance, music, and drama and not all African theater is total theater, the predominant theatrical practices often incorporate multiple modes of performance in different combinations and dimensions.

Notes

1. Ancient philosophers Aristotle and Plato proffered the oldest and most widely held view on the nature of art. They developed the mimetic theory of art and characterized art as imitation, with Plato declaring in the *Poetics* that humankind is a mimetic animal.

2. The contributing practitioners and scholars to Martin Banham's edited volume *A History of Theatre in Africa* explore the key movements and stages in the history of modern African theater as well as the regions and cultures from which the various aesthetic trends and practices originate, evolve, and spread.

3. See "Dance East and West," http://www.easternartists.com/DANCE%205%20East%20 West.html (accessed September 15, 2012).

4. For example, following his famous encounter with Balinese theater at the Paris Exposition in 1931, French playwright and theoretician of the theater Antonin Artaud reveals how he admired Eastern theater because of its codified, highly ritualized, and precise physicality, which influenced him to create manifestos for a "Theater of Cruelty." Artaud wanted to position the audience at the center of action or what he calls "spectacle" in order to get them "engulfed and physically affected by it" as a way of forcing them to engage with the performance.

BIBLIOGRAPHY

Abdallah, B. Mohammed. "Bobokyikyi's Lament: Theater and the African Experience." In *Reclaiming the Human Sciences and Humanities through African Perspectives*, Vol. 2, edited by Kofi Anyidoho and Helen Lauer, 1357–76. Accra, Ghana: Sub-Saharan, 2012.

Artaud, Antonin. *The Theatre and Its Double*. Translated by Mary Caroline Richards. New York: Grove, 1958.

Avorgbedor, Daniel. "African Arts in Education: Theory and Practice." Foreword to *Music and Dance Traditions of Ghana: History Performance and Teaching*, by Paschal Yao Younge. Jefferson, NC: McFarland, 2011.

Banham, Martin, ed. *A History of Theatre in Africa*. Cambridge: Cambridge University Press, 2004.

Bjorkman, Ingrid. *"Mother Sing for Me": People's Theatre in Kenya*. London: Zed, 1989.

Braun, Kwame. *Stage-Shakers! Ghana's Concert Party Theatre*. Indianapolis and Bloomington: Indiana University Press, 2001.

Conquergood, Dwight. "Performance Studies: Interventions and Radical Research." *The Drama Review* 46, no. 2 (2002): 145–56.

Fleishman, Mark. "Knowing Performance: Performance as Knowledge Paradigm for Africa." *South African Theatre Journal*, 23, no. 1 (2009): 116–36.

Gibbs, James. "History of Theatre in Ghana." In *Reclaiming the Human Sciences and Humanities through African Perspectives*, Vol. 2, edited by Kofi Anyidoho and Helen Lauer, 1343–56. Accra, Ghana: Sub-Saharan, 2012.

Honko, Lauri. "Epics along the Silk Roads: Mental Text, Performance, and Written Codification." *Oral Tradition* 11, no. 1 (1996): 1–17.

Hutchison, Yvette. "South Africa." In *A History of Theatre in Africa*, edited by Banham Martin, 312–79. Cambridge: Cambridge University Press, 2004.

Johnson, Effiong. *Playwriting: The Fundamentals*. Bloomington: Indiana University Press, 2011.

Kennedy, Dennis. "Total Theatre." In *The Oxford Companion to Theatre and Performance*. Oxford: Oxford University Press, 2010. Accessed 15 September, 2012. http://www.oxfordreference.com.ezproxy1.library.arizona.edu/view/10 1093/acref/9780199574193.001.0001/ acref-9780199574193-e-3967.

Loots, Lliane. "Colonised Bodies: Overcoming Gender Constructions of Bodies in Dance and Movement Education in South Africa." *South African Theatre Journal* 9, no. 2 (1995): 51–59.

———. "The Body as History and Memory: A Gendered Reflection on the Choreographic 'Embodiment' of Creating on the Socially Constructed Text of the South African Body." *South African Theatre Journal* 24, no. 1 (2010): 105–24.

Nicholls, W. Robert. "African Dance: Transition and Continuity." In *African Dance: An Artistic, Historical and Philosophical Enquiry*, edited by Kariamu Welsh Asante. Trenton: Africa World Press, 2002.

Ravengai, Samuel. "The Political-Aesthetic Function of Song and Dance in Zimbabwean Theatre 1980–1996." *Muziki: Journal of Music Research in Africa* 10, no. 1 (2013): 1–18.

Richards, L. Sandra. "Wasn't Brecht an African Writer?: Parallels with Contemporary Nigerian Drama." In *Brecht in Asia and Africa: The Brecht Yearbook,* Vol. 14, edited by J. Fuegi and M. Silberman, 168–85. N.p.: International Brecht Society, 1989.

Smith, Tuhiwai Linda. *Decolonizing Methodologies: Research and Indigenous Peoples.* London: Zed Books, 1999.

Soyinka, Wole. *Ogun Abibiman.* London: Rex Coilings, 1976.

Sutherland T. Efua. "The Playwright's Opportunity: Our Children as Source in Producing Children's Drama." In *Reclaiming the Human Sciences and Humanities through African Perspectives*, Vol. 2, edited by Kofi Anyidoho and Helen Lauer, 1377–86. Accra, Ghana: Sub-Saharan, 2012.

Taylor, Diana. *The Archive and the Repertoire: Performing Cultural Memory in the Americas.* Durham, NC: Duke University Press, 2003.

CHAPTER 13

JEAN GASCON'S THEATRICALIST APPROACH TO MOLIÈRE AND SHAKESPEARE

JANE BALDWIN

IN reading Jennifer Homan's admirable history of dance, *Apollo's Angels*, which characterizes ballet as both a "science with demonstrable physical facts" and "an art full of emotions and feelings that come with music and movement,"[1] I was struck by the description's applicability to theater. What the description lacks, however, is any link between text and ballet, which, as this chapter will point out, does sometimes exist. My objective is to examine the relationship of theater and dance as seen in the use of the actor's body as an instrument to tell a story, express emotion, and define character in combination with text.

Its exemplar is the work of Canada's actor-director Jean Gascon (1921–1988),[2] who adopted and adapted Jacques Copeau's theory and practice, first in Quebec and later in English Canada, in his theatricalist movement-oriented productions. Gascon, an artist of eclectic taste, incorporated multifarious sources into his stagings. At various times, he used dance, cabaret, mime, vaudeville, a wide-ranging variety of musical genres, Brechtian practices, surrealism, opera, and commedia dell'arte. Metatheatricality, a recurrent motif in his productions, was often linked to corporeality. Gascon's visual and auditory approach was reinforced by his close working relationships with his designers and his composer Gabriel Charpentier.

Gascon was unique in Canada in having successfully crossed and merged its French and English theater worlds. The majority of his productions were staged at two of Canada's preeminent theatrical institutions: Montreal's Théâtre du Nouveau Monde, which he co-founded and directed for fifteen years, and the Stratford Shakespeare Festival, where he was the first Canadian artistic director, a post he held for seven years. As a director he was most reputed for his skills with spectacle and ritual in drama and his fast-paced, wildly imaginative farces, although he had successes with realistic plays. This chapter concentrates on several of his stagings of Molière and Shakespeare at Stratford to give a sense of his directorial ingenuity. During his career Gascon was the foremost exponent of Molière in North America, and the Stratford Festival was North America's leading theater devoted principally to Shakespeare. And, as mime scholar Annette Lust reminds us, the works of "Shakespeare and Molière integrated the physical with verbal expression."[3]

Gascon focused on building theater in Canada and wrote little. He kept articles that covered his professional life in France in the 1940s and 1950s, but few notes of his Montreal productions survive; a 1963 fire destroyed most records of the Théâtre du Nouveau Monde. The archives at the Stratford Festival contain reviews, some prompt scripts, pictures, a scattering of notes, and videos of his productions, starting in 1968. Despite their generally poor quality, the videos were a useful research tool. Stratford's collection of Gascon's reviews was singularly valuable, given that forty notices per production were the norm during his directorship, allowing a more complex view of his *mises en scène* than can usually be garnered from drama critics' writings.

Historical Context: Jacques Copeau and Movement Theater

In October of 1913, impassioned by his dream of the possibilities of theater, the drama critic Jacques Copeau opened his playhouse, the Vieux-Colombier, in Paris. His objective was to reinvigorate the theater and restore to it the centrality it had held in Ancient Greece, the Middle Ages, Renaissance England, and neoclassical France. Copeau's mission included the reform of the repertory, staging, theater architecture, set design, and, most importantly from the viewpoint of this chapter, actor training and its effect on performance style.

In preparation for the initial season, Copeau brought his new company to his country house for ten weeks of rigorous training. Although the training focused on text, physical exercise, under the direction of actor Roger Karl, was an important component, given that the troupe would perform Molière. Despite his literary rather than drama background, "Copeau obeyed an infallible instinct when he turned to the most plastic means at his disposal, the dimensions of human bodies, of human movement."[4]

The first year's programing included Shakespeare's *La Nuit des rois* (*Twelfth Night*) and three Molière productions, his comedy of manners *L'Avare* (*The Miser*), plus the one-act farces *L'Amour médecin* (*Doctor Cupid*) and *La Jalousie du Barbouillé* (*The Jealousy of the Barbouillé*). His dance-like approach to Molière's farce was approvingly noted.

> A scene became a set of actions or rather movements, obeying its rhythm and its own rules, like a dance when the performer leaves the barre . . . Through this bold and methodical return to farce, Copeau found the source of Molière's genius.[5]

Copeau employed similar farcical methods in his triumphant *Twelfth Night*. Romain Bouquet's Toby Belch was a fat, coarse, and jovial drunkard to Louis Jouvet's gangly Aguecheek, costumed and made up like a pasty-faced clown.[6] In the "gulling scene" (II, v), as described by Copeau, they "gamboled, grimaced, pricked up their ears, advanced, retreated, disappeared, cracked jokes, took a quick look, stifled a laugh"[7] as they relished Malvolio's reaction to their practical joke. Copeau's Malvolio was a "nervous, self-important, skipping little man, chatty rather than austere."[8]

In August 1914, three months after *Twelfth Night*'s début, Germany declared war on France. Most of the company's male actors were drafted and the playhouse requisitioned. Exempted because of a lung infection,[9] Copeau used the war years to plan his future theater school. In 1915, he went to Florence, and visited Gordon Craig, and Geneva, where he saw Émile Jaques-Dalcroze. Two years earlier, Craig had inaugurated his experimental School for the Art of the Theatre, which was no longer operative when Copeau arrived. Nevertheless, Copeau remained for two months trying to fathom Craig's championing of the über-marionette as a replacement for the actor. But, even as he argued for the über-marionette, Craig proposed an alternative technique for the living actor, consisting "for the main part of symbolical gesture."[10] Surely, this emphasis on the physical appealed to Copeau, who would integrate Craigian ideas into his attempt to generate a contemporary commedia dell'arte.[11] Émile Jaques-Dalcroze's eurhythmics presented a concrete approach to training performers through movement. Formulated to aid student musicians improve their rhythmic skills, his method synthesized sound, music, and body. The class's improvisational quality[12] liberated students and impressed Copeau.

Jacques Copeau formally launched the Vieux-Colombier School in 1921.[13] He and his reconstituted company had spent two seasons[14] performing in New York.[15] Although a difficult period (twenty-three shows in two seasons) for Copeau, it had long-term benefits for the school. He and actress Suzanne Bing structured the curriculum, which was partially based on improvisations derived from games, fables, and songs that she developed at Margaret Naumburg's Montessori-based Children's School in New York.[16] In Paris, Bing was in charge of the group of hand-picked students whose purpose was to take Copeau's reforms to their next level.[17] While they received an education akin to today's BFA theater programs, this section treats the physical aspect of their instruction. The mime careers of Vieux-Colombier students Étienne Decroux and Jean Dorcy are testaments to the centrality of the movement training.

In Bing's corporeal music, sound was explored through the body by means of rhythmic activities such as marching, stamping, tapping, and clapping.[18] Her theatre sense (*sens dramatique*) examined movement through improvisation, using theater games as the point of departure. The students progressed to characterization via physicality, drawing on fiction and plays, particularly Molière's.[19] In addition to comedic characters, they investigated Greek mythical figures in a first step toward tragedy. Here too, they began with the physical shape of the character, experimenting with specific walks, gestures, and behaviors.[20] They initiated mask work, where meaning must be expressed physically.

Copeau closed his theater and school in 1924 and led a small band of students, actors, and followers to Burgundy to establish a research center. The Copiaus, as they were known, devised collective creations, sometimes with Copeau, more often without, until he dissolved the group. In 1931, under the leadership of Michel Saint-Denis, Copeau's nephew and former right-hand man, they formed the Compagnie des Quinze, arguably the first professional company dedicated solely to collective creation since the days of the Italian commedia dell'arte.

Copeau's influence on French theater was pivotal. His disciples, direct and indirect, included the country's most notable directors, actors, and teachers of twentieth-century theater, all affected by his ideas on movement. They, in turn, introduced Copeau's practice abroad.

QUEBEC: ÉMILE LEGAULT AND LES COMPAGNONS DE SAINT LAURENT

Émile Legault, a priest infatuated with theater, was responsible for bringing Copeau's practice to Quebec in the late 1930s. While Quebec had no professional theater during the period, due in large part to the austere morality of its powerful Catholic Church,[21] drama was taught in its "collèges" or parochial high schools. A teacher at Montreal's Collège de Saint-Laurent, in 1937 Legault founded the Compagnons de saint Laurent [22] to perform religious plays. He soon discovered his inadequacies as a director and the poverty of his repertory.

A correspondence with the French dramatist, critic, Copeau adherent, and fervent Catholic Henri Ghéon led Legault to seven months of study in Paris.[23] Legault's Paris stay was devoted to exploring its art theater movement, which was divided into two streams, professional and amateur, both inspired by Copeau. Most noted on the professional side was the Cartel des Quatre, a loose association of directors composed of Louis Jouvet, Charles Dullin, Gaston Baty, and Georges Pitoëff, followers, but not absolute adherents, of Copeau's theatrical principles.

More important for Legault was Léon Chancerel's Catholic nonprofessional troupe, the Comédiens-Routiers,[24] whose rehearsals and classes Legault attended. Previously an assistant to Copeau, Chancerel taught theater games, mime, dance, song, improvisation, and ensemble building. Like Copeau, he delved into the commedia dell'arte, using it as a pedagogical tool with the aim of creating contemporary iconic characters.[25]

ENTER JEAN GASCON

Legault returned to Montreal in 1938 to adapt his new-found knowledge to the needs of the Compagnons de saint Laurent and to expand his repertory. Most of the prominent figures in Montreal's later transformation of the theater would pass through Legault's restructured company, among them Jean Gascon. Gascon, a medical student, had attained a reputation as an actor at the Collège de Sainte-Marie playing leading roles in French classical dramas. The qualities that would make Gascon's career as a character actor were present in raw form: an imposing presence, expressive body, splendid deep voice, charisma, imagination, and daring.[26]

Life as a Compagnon gave Gascon the chance to work on the craft of acting formally. During rehearsals Legault endeavored to inculcate Copeau and his disciples' techniques, emphasizing their acrobatic aspects, which were incorporated into the farces the company regularly performed. The internal aspects of characterization were ignored. Jean Gascon later described their acting "as demonstrating rather than being."[27] Following his début in 1941 in Henri Ghéon's *Le Noël sur la place* (Christmas in the Square), Gascon performed major roles: Noé (Noah) in André Obey's eponymous drama; Figaro in Beaumarchais's *Le Barbier de Séville*; Oedipus in Jean Cocteau's *Oedipe-Roi*; Lord Edgar in Jean Anouilh's comic *Le bal des voleurs* (*Thieves' Carnival*); Feste in a *La Nuit des rois*; Creon in Anouilh's *Antigone*. Although the programs did not identify the actors, due to Legault's belief in the importance of the ensemble, Gascon was conspicuous for his talent. Critic Claude

Gauvreau was not alone in his assessment of Gascon as "far and away the Compagnons' best actor."[28]

Gascon left the Compagnons to act with Ludmilla Pitoëff's Montreal company. From Georges Pitoëff's widow, a renowned Russian actress and director in France,[29] Gascon learned to develop the character's inner world.[30] In 1946, he rejected medicine for a French Government scholarship to train for the theater. He spent the next four and a half years in France studying acting, touring with Ludmilla Pitoëff's French troupe, playing leading roles with Brittany's Centre Dramatique de l'Ouest, and as a member of the Compagnie Grenier-Hussenot in Paris. Artistic directors Hubert Gignoux (Centre Dramatique de l'Ouest), Jean-Pierre Grenier, and Olivier Hussenot were former actors with Chancerel's Comédiens-Routiers, making them the second generation of Copeau followers. Among Gascon's most important roles in France was Harpagon in Molière's *L'Avare* (*The Miser*). Of the hundreds of productions he saw in France, Gascon was especially inspired by those of Jean-Louis Barrault, which synthesized mime and text.

GASCON AND THE THÉÂTRE DU NOUVEAU MONDE

It was not until Gascon's return to Montreal in the spring of 1951 that his career began as an actor-director. He co-founded the Théâtre du Nouveau Monde (TNM) and became its artistic director. His company was composed of Montreal's leading actors, well known because of their radio performances. They had prepared for Gascon's homecoming by meeting regularly over several years to hone their acting, voice, and movement skills.[31] Gascon planned to raise Quebec production standards to a professional level, create a drama school, and "awaken" his public to the "grand répertoire," which he defined as "the works of the great poets of the theatre."[32] Chief among them were Molière and Shakespeare.

For the French-speaking director, Molière is the challenge Shakespeare is to his/her Anglophone counterpart, with the difference that his language is closer to today's vernacular. Gascon made his directing début at the TNM's premiere with Molière's *L'Avare*, in which he played Harpagon. *L'Avare* was a hit in a long string of TNM hits. *Le Devoir* lavished praise on his staging, finding it "exceptional," "perfection," "pure theatre."[33] *La Patrie* concluded that Molière had never been better performed in Montreal.[34] Even Jean Béraud, Montreal's most rigorous critic, lauded the "meticulous staging, quality acting, and first class setting."[35] However, the reviews give little sense of the look of the show. The few production photographs help, but the best visual source is a brief documentary, *Côté cour . . . côté jardin*.[36] More a commentary on the difficulties and excitements of establishing a new theater company, it presents only short sections of the play, but these proffer a glimpse of the corporeal acting style Gascon was developing with the company. Théâtre du Nouveau Monde productions would be noted for their spontaneity, versatility, physicality, pacing, liveliness, intensity, and theatricality.

In one clip, Gascon stages a brief scene for two young lovers. Using his hands-on technique, he seats himself next to Valère (Jean-Louis Roux) to show Janine Sutto how to impart romantic warmth to Élise. He gazes into Valère's eyes and inhales deeply as his chest lifts in excitement. Gascon then turns away as a proper young lady might and raises first his downstage arm and then the other, bringing his hands together delicately and convincingly.

Other clips of the nonfarcical personages reveal similar flowing movements in what might be called the actors' choreographed performances. Denise Pelletier plays Frosine the matchmaker's coquettishness with grandiose self-assurance. She too is seated, her upper body erect. Although her gestures are similar to Janine Sutto's, they are more dance-like, varied, and used to charm and overwhelm. She tosses her head and laughs in a classical, even artificial manner, but one that is theatrically true. Production stills taken over the years establish that the company retained the stylized physical approach to characterization seen in L'Avare, including, when appropriate, the elegant pulled-up body.[37] Often, the actors are caught in movement, or on the point of moving, the line of their bodies telling the story.

When feasible, Gascon merged commedia dell'arte—as he understood and practiced it—into his *mises en scène*, beginning with L'Avare. His portrayal of Harpagon, as presented in the documentary,[38] was built on Pantalone, the miserly father of commedia. Gascon carried himself awkwardly, his head leaning forward, back hunched—a hump beneath his coat—knees often bent, crouching, his head twisted. Much of the time he paced back and forth as a means of controlling his underlings. In contrast to the rest of his elderly physique, Gascon's Harpagon, like the traditional Pantalone, moved his hands gracefully, "continuously gesticulating each thought."[39] At the same time, his white-face makeup departed from the colorful commedia image. Harpagon, clad in a simple, almost puritanical, shabby black coat and breeches and stringy white wig, projected expressiveness through his ghostly face almost as much as with his body. Gascon may have based this choice on his interpretation of Harpagon as a character as deserving of pity as mockery, despite his unlikability.[40] Devoid of a mask, Harpagon is more human and less farcical.

For the rest of Gascon's tenure, a Molière production was a yearly event at the TNM, with the exception of the 1961–62 and 1962–63 seasons, when he headed the newly created National Theatre School of Canada. Through Molière, Gascon and the company earned national and international stature. In January of 1955, the TNM received an invitation to perform at Paris's Festival International d'Art Dramatique. The TNM took the trio of Molière one acts—*Le Mariage forcé*, Gascon's first comédie-ballet; *Sganarelle*; and the *Jalousie du Barbouillé*—that had premiered to great success in Montreal. In selecting Molière, this almost unknown company from a country without a history of professional theater was declaring itself on a plane with France's classical troupes. Yet, Paris was as enthusiastic about *Three Farces* as Montreal had been. Critics and audiences were taken with the high-speed playing of Molière's farces interspersed with *lazzi* and comic dances. All the actors were acclaimed, but the evening belonged most to Guy Hoffmann, who played the stock character of Sganarelle in all three. As the documentary *Le Nouveau-Monde à Paris* illustrates,[41] Hoffmann's clever use of his physical attributes alone, "prominent eyes, wide mouth, bouncy rotund figure and fast footwork,"[42] could draw laughs.

Soon after, the TNM entered into the life of the Stratford Shakespeare Festival in a history-making experiment. Stratford, Ontario, first appeared on the theatrical map in 1953, when Tyrone Guthrie became the Festival's founding artistic director, mounting first-rate productions on its open stage. Three years later Michael Langham, a young British director about to replace Guthrie, came to see *Three Farces* in Montreal. Langham, intent on making his first production as artistic director speak to Canada, was considering Shakespeare's

Henry V with French-Canadian actors as the French court. Thrilled by the performance, Langham met with Gascon and the TNM administration to discuss his proposition. Perhaps because of the company's discomfort vis-à-vis English-Canada, Gascon stipulated that their acceptance hinged on Langham's booking *Three Farces* into Stratford. The Avon, Stratford's newly acquired proscenium theater, débuted with Molière.

Langham's legendary *Henry V*, starring a young Christopher Plummer, brought greater reputation to Gascon and the TNM. The presence of Canada's two major cultures onstage together was an extraordinary artistic and political experience for the critics, public, and actors. Numerous reviewers remarked on their differing techniques, often to the French-Canadians' advantage. Typical were Brooks Atkinson's comments: "The French scenes fairly crackle. Their incisive style . . . makes an illuminating contrast with the looser style of the English scenes."[43] The Canadian Arnold Edinborough applauded their "theatricality which most of the more phlegmatic English-Canadians lack."[44] The *New York Herald Tribune*'s Walter Kerr envisaged future exchanges leading to a new dramatic style.[45]

For Canadian audiences, the combination of French- and English-Canadian players enacting their traditional enmity and then coming together in harmony had an extraordinary immediacy. The history of *Henry V* was their history; old-world tensions having been carried into the new, where the French had again been vanquished in 1759 by the English on Quebec's Plains of Abraham, a symbolic battle for both sides.[46] For the actors, watching each other was instructive. Stratford actors had a disciplined approach, which translated into a "certainty of attack and sharpness of style"[47] appreciated by the TNM. Correspondingly, the Stratford players were bedazzled by the TNM's "free spirit of improvisation."[48] They delighted in a matinée of *Three Farces* for, like the public, they discovered that the troupe's antics and comic shtick rendered knowledge of French unnecessary.[49]

The greatest gain was Gascon's. Langham's admiration led to an invitation to direct *Othello* in the summer of 1959. *Othello* presented special challenges for Gascon, not least the complexities of the stage, which was for him "the world's most beautiful."[50] It had been the vision of Tyrone Guthrie, who combined the playing conditions of the English Renaissance outdoor playhouse with elements of the ancient Greek amphitheater.[51] The result was a permanent multilevel architectural setting that jettisoned the proscenium arch, made it impossible to use complex scenery, changed the actor/audience configuration, and made the stage hospitable to ritual. It was a pentagonal thrust platform with four steps leading down to a gutter that separated actors from audience. Upstage, a central balcony was supported by pillars with two smaller and higher balconies on either side, each with its own entrance. An area underneath the main balcony could serve as a "discovery space." Multiple entrances included two "tunnels" under the stage that allowed actors access to the front and sides of the platform, the theater aisles, and a trap.

As Gascon discovered, the stage requires actors to work harder physically at pulling focus. He noted: "The actor's body must be constantly present, as much an instrument as his voice."[52] Although the Stratford actors did not have the corporeal skills of the TNM company, Gascon infused movement into the production, painting vivid images with the actors' bodies. Entrances were flamboyant, particularly Othello's initial appearance, carried off "in the grand manner"[53] by Douglas Campbell. Douglas Rain's swaggering Iago prowled or lurked behind pillars like "a snake wrapping itself around a tree."[54] A local reviewer declared that the tricky Festival stage "had met a new master,"[55] an opinion shared by the *New York Times* critic, who noted it one of the Festival's "best productions," "the most engrossing *Othello* [he] had ever seen anywhere."[56]

National Theatre School of Canada/École Nationale de Théâtre du Canada

Theater makers throughout Canada had long felt the need for drama schools if the country were to develop a professional and "truly national" [57] theater. Using its staff as faculty, the TNM had operated a school from 1952 until 1956, when insufficient time and funds forced its closure. Although Quebec had instituted the still-functioning Conservatoire d'Art Dramatique in Montreal (1954) and its sister school in Quebec City (1958), Canada's amateur and professional theater sector advocated for a national school that would train both Anglophones and Francophones. The bilingual Michel Saint-Denis, former director of the London Theatre Studio, the Old Vic School, and the École Supérieure d'Art Dramatique in Strasbourg, France—all leading-edge schools inspired by the École du Vieux-Colombier—acted as curriculum advisor until Gascon assumed the directorship of the National Theatre School of Canada/École Nationale de Théâtre du Canada in 1960.

Gascon championed the school's mission to bring the French- and English-speaking cultures closer and build a uniquely Canadian theater that would incorporate the best of the two cultures' abilities and talents.[58] Working at the Shakespeare Festival had awakened his awareness of English-Canadian acting skills. In 1950s Stratford, largely due to Guthrie and Langham, acting was influenced by the prevailing British style, which meant technical discipline, close textual analysis, vocal virtuosity, and psychological character study. At the risk of overgeneralizing, the Stratford players tended to have a more intellectual approach than the more instinctive, extravagant TNM actors. Similar characteristics defined the students.

With the exception of speech and acting—both text-dependent—Francophone and Anglophone students took classes together. The innovativeness of the school, its utopian goals, and the opportunity to forge friendships that without bilingualism would not have come into being energized the student body. Actress Martha Henry recollects, "We thought we were creating a different kind of Canadian culture that amalgamated both points of view and did not destroy either one."[59] All agreed that the strengths of the English lay in their organizational abilities, doggedness, and determination to get it right; those of the French in their inventiveness, impetuousness, and emotionalism. While obviously these judgments are colored by stereotypes, there seemed to be a different approach to acting that, even if only behavioral, was remarked on by their teachers, who tried to exploit it. Jean Gascon envisaged the possibility of the school producing bilingual actors capable of playing Shakespeare, Molière, and the moderns in both English and French.[60]

After Gascon's departure in 1963, the sociological changes wrought by the 1960s' Quiet Revolution—Quebec's nationalist struggle to assert its identity—militated against bilingualism. Its detractors argued that "differences of temperament and background"[61] caused tensions that made teaching problematic. Bilingualism was replaced by colingualism, which denotes two related but separate theater programs, each based in its own way on the Saint-Denis/Gascon paradigm and sharing one building.

While colingualism put an end to the school's policy of cultural unification, it turned the Francophone section into a major player in the development of a Québécois theater. In 1968, Francophone students rebelled against a program that was grounded in French culture, rather than fostering Québéquois traditions. Matters reached a head when the third-year class resigned en masse. A year later, the ex-students took a key step in the evolution of Québécois theater when they developed Quebec's first collective creation, *Pot-TV*, 1969.[62] Ironically, the National Theatre School's Copeau-based training with its emphasis on movement and improvisation helped these students devise their first show. Collective creation would become a vital theatrical form in Quebec throughout the 1970s.

Over the next few years the Francophone section virtually became a training ground for collective creation and a laboratory for Québécois playwriting, commissioning plays by local dramatists for its public exercises. Embracing their new-found identity, the dramatists wrote in Joual, a Québécois dialect. The students, in turn, refused to learn to speak French with a Parisian accent, which had been the custom. These practices were (if somewhat excessive) a necessary stage in the creation of a "national," i.e., Québécois theater. Today, a glance at the catalog demonstrates how the Francophone section has moved closer to its original mandate, accepted broader training and an international as well as a Québécois repertory that it deems indispensable for the young actor. And Québécois theater has acquired international stature.

Stratford or the Théâtre du Nouveau Monde?

While continuing to direct the TNM, in 1963, Gascon became associate director, under Michael Langham, of the Stratford Festival, where he was tasked with broadening the repertory. In effect, the job functioned as a long audition for the artistic directorship during which Gascon mounted Shakespeare's *Comedy of Errors* (1963), an English translation of Molière's *Bourgeois gentilhomme* (1964), and three operas: Mozart's *The Marriage of Figaro* (1964); Bertolt Brecht and Kurt Weill's *The Rise and Fall of the City of Mahagonny* (1965); and Mozart's *Don Giovanni* (1966), the last three at the Avon. Also in 1966, he reworked his TNM production of *Dance of Death* in an English-language version for the Avon. Michael Langham was not alone in thinking it "one of the best performances in Stratford's history."[63]

For four years Gascon divided his time between the Festival and the TNM. His punishing schedule, directing (and occasionally acting) summers at Stratford, and acting and directing at the TNM during the year, with administrative responsibilities at both, became untenable. He opted for Stratford, whose Festival stage, costume and props department, and larger budget would allow him to continue developing his aesthetic without the financial constraints of the TNM. Gascon succeeded Langham as artistic director of the Stratford Festival in 1968 and remained for seven years.[64] He increased the number of plays per season, introduced French works, and engaged French-Canadian artists, certainly for their talent but also as a means of bridging the two national cultures. Significantly, under Gascon the Festival was known as the Stratford National Theatre.

Staging Shakespeare

Gascon loved Molière, but revered Shakespeare.[65] Despite his desire to excel with both, he was considered a master of Molière, whereas his reputation as a Shakespearean director was inconsistent. Conceivably, he was overawed by Shakespeare's place in the canon. While

Molière's preeminence as a playwright is unquestioned, it is limited to comedy. Although Gascon's appreciation of Shakespeare's poetry increased as his English skills improved, his chief interest was the characters, themes, styles, story, and inherent theatricality of the plays. Despite Gascon's proven success as a director of a variety of genres, Shakespeare's comedies and romances spoke to him more than the tragedies. Gascon came to Molière with "intense certitude about [the playwright] and his times,"[66] a confidence born of cultural immersion. Or in Gascon's words, "Molière was like a chum, part of the family."[67] As Canada's lone Francophone mounting Shakespeare in English professionally at the time, Gascon never overcame his anxiety when approaching the playwright's works, winning productions notwithstanding. [68] During his career Gascon mounted eight Shakespearean plays, six at Stratford: *Othello; Comedy of Errors; Merchant of Venice; Cymbeline; Taming of the Shrew*; and *Pericles*. While Stratford audiences usually found their strong visual and audio effects engrossing, for some Festival reviewers, his nontraditional stagings and seeming deemphasis of speech were displeasing.

Gascon and the Stratford players needed a period of adjustment to find a meeting place. Gascon's Montreal actors, although never a permanent company, worked together at the TNM, on television, and sometimes with other troupes. That Gascon customarily acted with them at the TNM added another dimension to their relationship. With few exceptions, he was respected for his talents—even loved—by his Montreal actors. Their closeness led to a deep awareness on Gascon's part of the actors' needs and abilities, and the actors' reciprocal understanding of Gascon's vision. A performance shorthand developed among them where a brief reference or gesture sufficed to resolve a question. This connection had to be built in Stratford, where a gulf existed between Gascon's style and the actors' previous experience. Gascon was accustomed to working faster and with a broader brush. During the early 1960s, his acquaintance with Shakespeare was still limited, as was his English. *The Comedy of Errors*, the second Shakespeare play he directed in English, tested both director and performers.

The Comedy of Errors

Essentially a one-joke play, *The Comedy of Errors* turns on a double case of mistaken identity involving two sets of twins bearing the same names—masters and slaves—who grew up in separate cities. It has two playing traditions: one an antic caper, the other exploring the work's darker side. Gascon leaned on the first option, and infused it with commedia dell'arte—a first at the Festival. Shakespearean scholars have long seen the commedia influence on this work. It can be found in its implausible hijinks and characters such as the two comic servants who evoke commedia's *zanni*, as well as the charlatan Dr. Pinch, who suggests Il Dottore. For Gascon, it was a pragmatic as well as an artistic decision, since commedia half masks resolved the problem of casting the identical twins. On another level, commedia's subversiveness, the ways in which it can reverse the social order, appealed to him. "The people's art against the official art,"[69] was how he characterized it.

Aware that some cast members would be unable to meet the demands of his commedia style, Gascon filled the production with gags, gimmicks, and business adapted to the actors' capabilities. Interestingly, he compensated for the actors' farcical shortcomings by going further with commedia than he had in Montreal. Gascon's direction actualized the doctrine that in the commedia, gesture and movement narrate the character's life.[70] It was a dicey experience for actors trained to prioritize language and look for emotion. Martha Henry (Luciana in the production) believes that Gascon was disappointed with their lack of vitality,[71] their inability to reach the level of speed that he demanded in farce. Over time, he adjusted his expectations and Stratford actors who continued to work on farce with him became less inhibited, more athletic, and more relaxed with its physical exigencies, although they never attained the panache of the TNM actors.

Several reviewers protested that the acting was subordinated to the directing.[72] Others felt that Gascon's "French tone" (meaning French-Canadian) enlivened a dull play with physical action.[73] He added a ribald chorus as commentators: five Punchinellos armed with slapsticks, who changed settings, functioned as props, provided sound effects, played instruments, danced, and mocked the goings-on.[74] He eliminated the tragic element by turning the Antopholi's father (Tony Van Bridge) into a recurrent figure of fun, who wandered the aisles, droning his lament to the accompaniment of a cello.[75]

With Montreal designers Robert Prévost and Mark Negin, Gascon created a metatheatrical world of dream and nightmare. A fairground booth framed the action, its carnival atmosphere emphasized by colored lights outlining the stage. Tables and mirrors were placed at entrances, where actors donned masks and wigs.[76] Painted backdrops designated the locales, and fantastical costumes represented no specific era. While Gascon was thrilled to have the technical riches of Stratford at his disposal, the spectacular production also camouflaged the actors' comedic deficiencies.

MOLIÈRE ON THE FESTIVAL STAGE

Gascon mounted his legendary 1968 *Tartuffe*[77] as his début production as artistic director of the Stratford Festival. Anticipating criticism and guided by his desire to offer the best of the French repertory to an Anglophone audience, he explained his choice: "Because *Tartuffe*'s stature, and the stature of Molière, demands inclusion in the Stratford National Theatre repertory."[78] He had a fine character actor in William Hutt and two strong actresses for the roles of Elmire (Martha Henry) and Dorine (Pat Galloway) and an excellent rhyming translation by Richard Wilbur. The actors' classically trained voices served the rhyme scheme. Their skills matched Gascon's vision for the production.

The rhythm and tone of Gascon's Stratford *Tartuffe* differed from his other Molière productions. He wanted to strip *Tartuffe* of all the theatrical clichés, especially the mannered acting style, "which cluster around . . . everything French in the seventeenth century."[79] With an eye to the turbulent times and his audience's unfamiliarity with the play, Gascon set it in 1830, the emergence of romanticism, "a moment of violence when youth turned its back on the establishment."[80] The struggle against authority and the older generation, a running theme in Gascon's productions, was certainly pertinent in 1968.

As in many of Molière's plays, an authoritarian father, driven by an obsession, plays havoc with the lives of his children and household. In *L'Avare*, the obsession is money; in *Le Malade imaginaire*, illness; and in *Tartuffe*, religion. Orgon (Douglas Rain) is a pious, tyrannical weakling who, on the one hand, struggles to maintain control as pater familias and, on the other, surrenders his common sense to a religious fraud, Tartuffe (William Hutt). Orgon plans to marry his unwilling daughter Mariane (Mia Anderson)—promised to a man she loves—to Tartuffe and makes the fraud his heir. Unknown to the family, Orgon gives Tartuffe the deed to the house. The play turns on the family's struggle to expose him to Orgon. Only Elmire, as Orgon's wife, but not his equal, has any influence on the nominal head of the family. But her success depends on her ability to unmask Tartuffe in Orgon's presence.

Gascon's unorthodox interpretation of Tartuffe's character shaped the other characterizations. Rather than a plotting, masterful monster, Gascon deemed him animalistic, impulsive, unintelligent—an inept con man. Every household member, except Orgon, sees through his ostentatious displays of religiosity, and it is Tartuffe who is duped by Elmire. Tartuffe's gaucherie contributed to Martha Henry's portrait of Elmire as self-confident, even playful. Gascon encouraged the very funny Pat Galloway to look for the maid Dorine's vulnerability rather than playing the character only for comedy. A more sensitive Dorine is united by bonds of affection to the family victims, and less the stock figure of the comic servant.

Orgon's motivation had long been a stumbling block for directors and scholars. Roger Planchon's 1962 production, whose Orgon was sexually attracted to Tartuffe—albeit unconsciously—influenced numerous directors. Gascon had a different reading. Quebec society, during Gascon's youth, had been dominated by the Church, which acted as the moral arbiter, in much the same way it had in seventeenth-century France. That Orgon could fall under the spell of a supposed religious zealot aroused Gascon's ire, but not his astonishment. He expounded Orgon's backstory: "Raised on the irrational prejudices of a blinkered, dehumanized Christianity, he brandishes bible and crucifix like instruments of vengeance which allow him to reassert his authority and convince himself of his manhood."[81] And for that he needs Tartuffe. It was not uncommon for aristocratic households to include a *directeur de conscience* or spiritual adviser,[82] whose prestige was akin to that of today's celebrities. As Orgon's *directeur de conscience*, Tartuffe raised the social status of this naïf and pretentious bourgeois. Orgon's relationship to Tartuffe was at times like that of a fan, and at others, that of a child who idolized his father. A representative photo shows a doleful Orgon seated and leaning against Tartuffe who consoles him.

Critic Walter Kerr astutely commented that it was "a seriously funny *Tartuffe* deriving its comedy from fierce concentration on what it is reasonable to expect of dimensional human beings."[83] And indeed, despite his well-earned reputation as a farceur, Gascon did not go for easy laughs. Gascon perceived the director's task as keeping *Tartuffe* balanced between dark comedy and farce.[84] His interests included humanizing the characters and giving the play social, political, and psychological weight. Nonetheless, low comedy marked the characters of Dorine, Madame Pernelle (Barbara Byrne), and to some extent, Orgon, but was most fully developed in Tartuffe.

Stratford's thrust platform aided Gascon in removing the encrustations of convention associated with the picture-frame stage. With a few props and set pieces, Robert Prévost created the impression of an upper-middle-class home. A huge rug was the principal playing area. Doorframes, curtains, chairs, and two tables completed the seventeenth-century parlor. The all-important table where Tartuffe is unmasked sat on an extension down left. A large bible set atop it symbolized the power of religion in the household. An outsize ceiling cross, flashing at the beginning of each act and fading as the lights came up, was the sole unrealistic component.[85] It hung over the family as both a threat—Tartuffe—and a blessing—the family saved in the end.

Gascon and Prévost swaddled Tartuffe, Orgon, and his mother, Madame Pernelle, in heavy dark, constricting, outdated clothing to emphasize the gap between them and the younger characters. In their breeches and simple white stocks (neck coverings) Tartuffe and Orgon could have stepped out of the seventeen hundreds, while Madame Pernelle in her head covering, long coat, gloves, and ruff was a Puritan caricature. In contrast, Mariane, her stepmother Elmire, and even the maid wore light colored, low-cut, puffy-sleeved, flattering empire-style dresses. Dorine's deep décolletage set up the handkerchief joke. The young men, Damis and Valere, were also fashionably dressed in 1830s-style high collars, trousers, and cut-away long-tailed coats.[86] More than a visual aid for the audience, the costumes helped define the actors' movement. Madame Pernelle, impeded by her enveloping garments, tottered around the stage leaning heavily on her cane.

Gabriel Charpentier created a score that alternated between a pastiche of animated nineteenth-century piano music, representative of the youthful characters, and baroque religious motifs scored for brass, obviously symbolic of Tartuffe, Orgon, and Madame Pernelle. At times, these two musical styles clashed with each other, a literal playing out of the generational conflict.

Dorine—often at the center of familial disputes—is in almost every scene of the first two acts, gossiping, defending, quarreling, and plotting. However, having bested Tartuffe in his long-awaited entrance in Act III, Dorine melts into the background, given little to say by Molière. French-trained Pat Galloway[87] was a strong Dorine, who "might have played everyone off the stage but for her skill in tuning her performance to the melody of the others."[88] Charming, pretty, playful, Galloway was more an older sister to Mariane than a domestic, thus making more sense of her interest in the girl's happiness. Her vociferous Dorine taunted Orgon, as she moved quickly in and out of his reach, mocking Tartuffe as husband-to-be for Mariane. In one of the production's more farcical moments, the furious Orgon swung at Dorine, missed, and hit a pillar.

This well-groomed, high-spirited Dorine, who complained about Tartuffe confiscating "our ribbons and colognes," was never seen carrying a broom or duster or involved in household tasks. Gascon made it clear that her sole function was to save Mariane's relationship with her fiancé Valere. In Act II, scene 3, she showed sympathy and affection toward Mariane when it would help the situation, lifting her up, for example, when the girl dropped to the floor sobbing after Orgon's ultimatum. But when timid Mariane refuses to defy Orgon, Dorine turned her back, threw her arms up in the air, and tried to leave in order to prod the girl into action. Mariane, in need of Dorine's strength, dragged her back, while threatening to die. On Dorine's line, "It won't be difficult to discover some plan of action," she seized Mariane and twirled her around as in a dance.

Dorine is most authoritative when she puts an end to an adolescent lovers' quarrel. Mariane and Valere (Leon Pownall), caught in a frustrating situation not of their own making, turn on each other as Dorine watched from upstage until she decided to take charge of the situation, and crossed down front. It became a chase scene with Dorine going after one, and then the other. Finally, taking Mariane by the hand, she slapped her bottom. Holding on to Mariane, Dorine struggled with Valere until she had the lovers clasping hands, all the while dispensing advice and warnings, before pushing them out separate doors to prevent their discovery by Orgon. Dorine has the ability to manipulate Mariane and Valere, but she has no real plan to resolve the situation. She counsels Mariane to humor her father and defer marriage to Tartuffe and tells Valere to obtain his friends' support. Her position in the household prevents her from wielding power.

Galloway's performance was energetic and speedy, as "she bustled about gossiping, plotting, insulting and most of all freely expressing her opinion to anyone who cares to listen."[89] She used expansive gestures except for rare moments when, pretending to be demure, she crossed her hands modestly in front of her body. Her exuberant rhythms contrasted with the other performers'. Hutt's beautifully outlined performance depended on exaggerated deliberation and gravity; Douglas Rain's Orgon alternated between bursts of rage against his family and blind adoration of his mentor, while Martha Henry was mistress of grace and dignity. Orgon and Elmire were played in a more realistic style.

The self-assured, but not-too-bright Tartuffe conducted himself as a luminary who expects special treatment. Hutt deliberately hyperbolized the role's play-acting features. As a fraud, Tartuffe must be an actor, but his talent is obviously limited inasmuch as his sanctity convinces only Orgon and Madame Pernelle. Hutt maintained a balancing act playing the hammy, uncontrolled Tartuffe while simultaneously giving a "magnificently controlled"[90] performance. His mask-like makeup—ashen face, heavy, elongated down-turned eyebrows, and gloomy expression—contributed to Hutt's portrait of the hypocrite, giving meaning to the question posed by Orgon's wiser brother: "Is not a face different from a mask?" He seldom stared directly at others, preferring to look heavenward or glance away. Hutt allowed Tartuffe two smiles, the first when he is on his knees to Elmire, hoping to make her his mistress, the second when he became Orgon's legatee.

Through his coldness and sometime brutality, Tartuffe conveyed danger while his clownesque physicality played up the farcical. Hutt frequently held his hands together piously, which contrasted with his "splayed legged"[91] wobble that made him look as if he had a constant erection. At times, his hands moved over his body "in erotic spasms";[92] at others, he bent over humbly. His gestures were narrow, close to the body, as if hiding something.

Gascon brought flamboyance to Tartuffe's first entrance by having him appear on the darkened balcony with his hair shirt and scourge, followed by his manservant Laurent, usually an offstage character. Tartuffe's self-flagellation prompted Dorine's laughter, goading him into exposing his sadistic lustfulness. As he uttered the famous "cover that bosom, girl" line, he placed his handkerchief over Dorine's breasts and squeezed viciously, looking away with scorn. Upon retrieving the handkerchief, he rubbed it with enjoyment as if still feeling her breasts.

Still more aroused in his first scene with Elmire, Tartuffe's brand of lechery reasserted itself. Martha Henry's poise was a match for Hutt's ardor. When he clutched her knee, she "raised her eyebrows elegantly"[93] and coolly put him down with the line, "What can your hand be doing there?" At the scene's end, he threw himself on his knees, begging pardon for his temerity. In the fourth act, where Elmire beats Tartuffe at his own game, Martha Henry played the vamp while her audience, Orgon, hid under the cloth-covered table. Confessing her love for Tartuffe, she circled her would-be seducer flirtatiously, moved downstage, and put her hand to her breast. Tartuffe, casting off his coat, hotly pursued. Gascon repeatedly brought them to the table and then away. Elmire teased Tartuffe; Orgon, motionless under the table, teased Elmire; and Gascon teased the audience. The scene was at once funny and fraught. At the crucial moment, Tartuffe grabbed Elmire, pushing her down onto the bible-covered table. She moved and Tartuffe grasped Orgon, who was hidden behind her, relieving the tension with low comedy.

Gascon ended the play as inventively as he began it. As the image of the ceiling cross faded away in the first scene, a light came up on Flipote (Jane Casson), Madame Pernelle's ill-treated servant, sitting on the front of the darkened stage chomping on a stick of celery, a funny, curious, and pathetic image. Flipote has no dialogue and exists only to underscore Madame Pernelle's despotic personality. In this production, by virtue of keeping her center stage throughout the rest of the scene as a frightened onlooker, Gascon gave her more significance as a member of the underclass.

As typical in neoclassical comedies, Molière's *Tartuffe* ends happily, the villain punished, order restored, and a marriage to follow. The omniscient off-stage king acts as the deus ex machina, ordering Tartuffe's arrest, the return of Orgon's property, and the restoration of his honor as a reward for Orgon's service to him. In Gascon's production, Orgon and his mother remained onstage, silent as the others rushed off joyfully to thank the king. This simple emendation transformed Orgon into an almost tragic figure who has recognized his beliefs were illusory.

Return to Shakespeare *Cymbeline*

By 1970, Gascon had developed a coterie of actors with strong movement and comedic skills. Among them were Leo Ciceri, Robin Gammel, Pat Galloway, Barry MacGregor, and Powys Thomas, who played principal roles in *Cymbeline*, Gascon's most noteworthy Shakespearean production.

Cymbeline is not only "the most overtly theatrical of Shakespeare's plays," according to Shakespeare scholar Roger Warren,"[94] but also a work of intriguing storytelling possibilities. For Gascon, "the greatest quality of Shakespeare's plays [was] that they are extraordinary raw material for stage productions."[95] And admittedly, *Cymbeline*'s material was completely raw in Canada, increasing its appeal for Gascon, who loved to astonish an audience. In Canada, it was an arcane work with a reputation for being second-rate Shakespeare. Some scholars regarded it as self-parody since Shakespeare seemingly mined his earlier plays for characters, situations, and plots. The tragedies, *Romeo and Juliet, Othello, King Lear, Macbeth*, and the cross-dressed comedies, *As You Like It, Twelfth Night*, and even *The Merchant of Venice*, all make an appearance, albeit in new guise.

Gascon thought of *Cymbeline* as an exploratory work for Shakespeare, writing in a new mode, having moved away from his tragedies with their psychologically based protagonists. With its implausible adventures, coincidences, disguises, potions, danger, reunions, supernatural intervention, and improbable happy ending, this play fulfills the characteristics of what we now conceptualize as romance. Its parodic elements strike us as metatheatrical, as they did Gascon. With collaborators, composer Gabriel Charpentier, designer Tanya Moiseiwitsch, and dramaturg Michael Bawtree, Gascon created a free-standing cosmos with its own rules and reality that exploited rather than disguised the play's magic. There was no attempt to deal with either the text or characters on a realistic level. Rather than striving for an illusion of reality, Gascon invited the audience to "share [the] process of playmaking,"[96] allowing the machinery of theater to show. And while Gascon may have read descriptions of previous productions, he did not "want to be bound by tradition."[97] This refusal gave him the license to handle in his own manner the play's knotty aspects, such as its anachronisms and lack of unity, liberating him to develop its comic elements to a greater extent than most directors choose.

Cymbeline contains three plots interconnected through Imogen (Maureen O'Brien), daughter of Cymbeline (Powys Thomas), the bumbling king of pre-Arthurian Britain, who is in thrall to his sorceress-queen (Pat Galloway). The Queen's goal is the kingship for Cloten (Robin Gammel), her churlish and lecherous son by a previous marriage. She manipulates Cymbeline into exiling his adopted son Posthumus (Kenneth Walsh) to Rome for having married Princess Imogen. There, Posthumus enters into a bet with Iachimo (Leo Ciceri) that Imogen will resist his seductive ploys. Iachimo fails to beguile the lovely princess, but persuades her to keep a trunk in her bedchamber. While Imogen sleeps, Iachimo emerges from the trunk, kisses her, notes a mole under her breast, and removes her bracelet, a present from Posthumus. In Gascon's version, he lowered her nightgown strap. Iachimo's "evidence" convinces Posthumus of Imogen's infidelity.

Enraged, Posthumus orders Imogen's murder. She escapes, masquerades as a boy, stumbles across her long-lost brothers dwelling in a cave with their kidnapper Belarius (Mervyn Blake), who they believe is their father. Cloten, attired as Posthumus, follows Imogen, determined to rape her and decapitate the real Posthumus. However, he is killed and beheaded offstage by Imogen's brother Guiderius (Leon Pownall). Imogen, ill, takes a potion and apparently dies. The brothers perform a funeral dirge, lay Cloten's body beside her, and depart. She awakes to discover the headless corpse that she mistakes for Posthumus.

Event tumbles over event. An invading Roman general (James Blendick) makes Imogen his page. Posthumus repents and is captured fighting for Britain. The brothers and Belarius rescue Cymbeline. In prison, Posthumus has a vision of his dead family and Jupiter (Barry MacGregor). The last scene consists of Shakespeare's most complicated dénouement as identities are disclosed, everyone is pardoned, returned to his/her rightful status, and the Queen's machinations revealed—two dozen revelations in all.

Gascon's slight textual revision became a coup de théâtre. Whereas in the script the Queen expires offstage (V, v), Gascon brought her on for a death scene. Her physician's lines describing her end became the Queen's. As she spoke the lines vituperatively, her hatred of the King and his retinue became a living thing. Gascon broke the tension of the charged moment with her slapstick demise, although Galloway played it seriously with "tongue in cheek."[98] She perished screaming, moaning, and twitching, her body dragged off by two serving women.

The play's anachronisms were boldly dealt with in the costuming. King Cymbeline's gray tunic, leather and fur-trimmed cloak, and medallion, conveyed an impression of first-century Britain. [99] The Queen—the emblematic wicked stepmother, complete with a raven perched on her shoulder[100]—sparkled in a tall crown and medieval gown whose sleek fit was strangely contemporary.[101] Iachimo, olive skinned with short black curly hair, neat beard, and moustache, was graceful in his opaque white shirt, a medallion round his neck, and elaborate flowing cloak—an Italian Renaissance aristocrat. He was given to languid poses and large gestures such as tossing his cloak aside in anger.

Almost all the actors were heavily made up; Imogen and Posthumus, exceptions. Posthumus's blonde hair, cut in a masculine version of Imogen's curly coiffure, pointed up the couple's resemblance. Imogen was given a "peaches and cream" complexion,[102] emblematic (in the West, at any rate) of innocence. Her flowered wreath and simple white clothing of no specific epoch at the beginning of the play added to this impression. Imogen's makeup and hair were unchanged in her masculine disguise. The effect rendered her father and husband's failure to recognize her that much funnier, but on a psychological level, it revealed their superficial knowledge of her.

Jupiter and the ghosts were masked in order to demarcate them as denizens of the spirit world. Cloten's makeup, like the Queen's, verged on travesty. Startlingly pale, he wore a bright red wig and crown.[103] This last subtly drew attention to his head, foreshadowing his bloody death.

The lost princes were barely covered by ragged animal skins. Their feet were wrapped in makeshift sandals; they carried knives in their breech cloths.[104] As befits "tanlings" whose lives were spent outdoors, their faces and bodies were bronze, distinguishing them from the members of the corrupt court, whose complexions were grayish or white. The actors were young, athletic, agile, and handsome. The Romans wore metal helmets and armor; the Britons, leather. Actors playing Romans were given accentuated noses, which made sense of Cloten's line:

> . . . and we will nothing pay
> For wearing our own noses. (III, i)

The music embodied the mélange of comedy and melodrama that Gascon worked for in *Cymbeline* as well as underlining its lyrical and idyllic moments. In consultation with Gascon, Gabriel Charpentier created the soundscape. They began by noting mood, atmosphere, and action[105]—a painstaking process where even the smallest potential sounds were explored. At several points *Cymbeline*'s text indicates the use of music. The first is "Hark, Hark the Lark" (II, iii), Cloten's unsuccessful attempt to woo Imogen with musicians and singers. Charpentier spoofed Schubert's romantic music to heighten Cloten's crudeness. During Posthumus's dream (V, v), "solemn music" presages the appearance of his spectral family. Imogen's funeral rites (IV, ii) offer the possibility of a song and, in fact, some productions introduce music here. At Stratford, the "song" was spoken—and beautifully, accompanied by formal gesture—in accordance with Guiderius's line: "I'll weep, and word it with thee." Charpentier added fanfares and marches to his score.

The play opened with surrealistic music that led the spectators into the fantastic. Charpentier made use of his preferred instruments: piano, harpsichord, harp, brass, and percussion. He composed a motif that elucidated each principal character as for example, pure harp sounds for Imogen, bell tones for the king Cymbeline, and an elegant harpsichord tune for the would-be seducer Iachimo. *Cymbeline*'s happy ending was given a cantata of twenty voices to express "the impression of heaven encircling the world."[106] The music echoed the production's penultimate image, in which the characters spread out in an enormous circle[107] and one by one came forth to divulge their identities and/or their part in the action with the utmost seriousness, evoking the laughter Gascon wanted. Charpentier's soundscape created visual effects like the creaking forest and birdsong heard as Imogen approached the cave of her long-lost brothers (III, vi) or the din of the battle scene between Romans and Britons (V, ii), where sounds conjured up an immense army, but in actuality, was metaphorized with few actors.

Gascon's production was praised for its clarity, a considerable accomplishment in this tangled tale. He played up *Cymbeline*'s comedy without parodying it, the melodrama without going overboard, the lyricism when appropriate. Performances were expansive and colorful. Leo Ciceri's intense Iachimo was purposely reminiscent of Iago. His movement was sinuous, particularly so in his Act I scenes with Imogen. He took command of the stage, circling round Imogen (I, vi) as he tried to raise her doubts about Posthumus, finally coming up close behind her both seductively and threateningly to whisper in her ear. His attempted seduction and Imogen's rejection played out as a dance as their two bodies drew closer and then separated. The dance motif was employed in Ciceri's other scenes as, for instance, when he "proved" Imogen's infidelity to Posthumus by referring to the andirons in her bedroom. On the words, "two winking Cupids of silver, each on one foot standing," Ciceri literalized the image, arrogantly raising his leg in an arabesque-like pose.

Robin Gammell's Cloten was a critic- and crowd-pleaser, though "it ran dangerously close to the edge of caricature,"[108] an edge where Gascon was comfortable. Gammell strictly interpreted the description of his character as a "clotpoll" (IV, ii.185) or blockhead. His jaw hung, his expression was sullen and vapid, except when roused to lust or rage. He derived humor out of the contrast between Cloten's posturing and his gawkiness. Ciceri and Gammell's performances captured the extremes of character that Gascon sought. Gammell's Cloten was the anti-Iachimo. In contrast to Iachimo, Cloten fumbled awkwardly with his cloak. Attempting gallantry, he knelt to Imogen, only to crawl after her on all fours when dismissed. Gascon emphasized their obverse qualities by occasionally duplicating their blocking. Gammell also circled the outside of the stage, but replaced Ciceri's grace with a lurching gait. This Cloten became perilously out of control after Imogen injures his self-regard. A production photo shows him (II, iii) advancing on her, his face contorted, body bent, arm and hand outstretched in threat as she dismisses him condescendingly.

Shakespeare aided Gascon in adding a jot of low comedy to Iachimo by placing him in a trunk, from which he pops up, a bit like a jack-in-a-box. Gascon and Ciceri added a low laugh. This clownesque entrance intensified Iachimo's menacing presence as he visually raped Imogen, who lay asleep, her head facing upstage, her arms outstretched, her body at an angle. He took up a taper, the better to enjoy her beauty.

Gascon handled the blocking dexterously and imaginatively. The *St. Catharines Standard* spoke for numerous reviewers: Gascon "has made as fine use of the multilevel stage as has ever been done."[109] An added playing area was created by a platform covering the steps down right. It was used for Imogen's bedroom, her "funeral rites," and Posthumus's jail cell. All three scenes are linked thematically through sleep and dreams.

Jupiter's entrance was the show's most spectacular moment. Barry MacGregor appeared on the balcony astride an enormous golden eagle,[110] wearing makeup inspired by an Inigo Jones design of Jove for a court masque. In a silver-gray mask, his body painted to match, MacGregor resembled a statue come to life. As the lights rose, Jupiter hurled lightning bolts while thunder rolled and smoke swirled.[111] His electronically amplified voice enunciated his divine stature even further. Taking this scene, whose extravagance is clear even on the page, to such extremes exemplifies Gascon's daring.

While the production was a critical success, the Festival reviewers' unfamiliarity with the play and its twentieth-century production history influenced their responses. Thus, Gascon was praised for having turned *Cymbeline*'s weaknesses into its strengths, for having taken an incoherent and disjointed work and made it into an extraordinary achievement. Others, however, having let go of their preconceptions, enjoyed a delightful discovery.

FIGURE 13.1 Barry MacGregor as Jupiter in the 1970 production of Cymbeline at the Stratford Festival. Photo by Douglas Spillane. Director: Jean Gascon. Designer: Tanya Moiseiwitsch.

Le Malade imaginaire

In 1974, Gascon brought Molière back to Stratford with the comédie-ballet *Le Malade imaginaire* (*Imaginary Invalid*), the last work written by the ailing playwright, who collapsed during its fourth performance and died within hours. A fantastical mélange of comic text, music, and dance devised by Molière, the comédie-ballet was a precursor to comic opera and musical comedy. Molière's general scheme was to interpolate dances that served or illustrated the text into the interludes. Until late in the twentieth century the comédie-ballet was dismissed as an inferior genre compared to Molière's more "serious" comedies such as *Tartuffe* and *Le Misanthrope*."[112] This production, staged at the end of Gascon's Stratford tenure, which reunited Pat Galloway and William Hutt, would be noteworthy if only as an example of Gascon's direction of a comédie-ballet, a genre seldom mounted then and, therefore, little understood. Fortunately for directors, actors, and scholars, the Stratford archives have a black and white video of the production.[113]

The Imaginary Invalid, a send-up of seventeenth-century quackery, had Hutt in the title role as Argan, the stingy, self-centered, infantile, fearful, and hypochondriacal father, who is obsessed by the state of his bowels. Argan has surrounded himself with a group of medical weirdoes who bilk him. In order to have live-in healthcare at no cost, he decides to marry his daughter Angelique (Pamela Brooks) to a doctor. Angelique, in love with another, turns to the maid Toinette (Pat Galloway), an older, cleverer version of Dorine, who puts everything right by means of a metatheatrical device, the comédie-ballet.

Gascon directed it with the extreme precision, attention to timing, and imaginative physicality that made his productions of French farce so very funny.[114] Classic commedia and vaudeville routines were scattered throughout. Although Argan spends most of the play in a chair, Hutt used his upper body to great effect. He slouched, twisted, leaned, grabbed, thrust out his hand in grandiloquent gestures, raised both arms to heaven, and pulled himself erect, etc. His health preoccupations were mirrored by visual metaphors. Hutt frequently lifted his robe, as when he warms his backside at the fire; Pat Galloway waved her bottom as she bounded round the stage. Gascon gave each member of Argan's male coterie an eccentric tic, gesture, walk, or prop, either singly or in combination.

Drollery reached its height in the finale or "burlesque ceremony," as Molière called it, in which comic text, dance, and music join together. Argan undergoes a counterfeit examination and is inducted into the medical profession, thereby becoming his own doctor. As the scene began, the platform darkened; ghostly figures in white danced across, miming warnings. Actors rushed about setting the stage, whispering in a feverish mood. Dance grew out of this "organized madness."[115] The actual ceremony began as a procession of doctors, surgeons, and apothecaries (nineteen in all) emerged holding skulls, bones, and pestles.[116] The leader (Nicholas Pennell) stood on a stool holding a scepter, and addressed the performers and audience in a mixture of Latin gibberish with Italianate endings and English. Three doctors stood on the balcony, peering down. Argan, cowed, sat on a low stool partially surrounded by five doctors in long-nosed zanni masks, white wigs, black pointed hats, and gowns that recalled both seventeenth-century medical garb and contemporary academic attire. Each one interrogated him, using different tones and rhythms. Some of the text was spoken, some chanted, some sung. Argan replied repeatedly, at first timidly, then quickly and confidently.

Enema donare
Postea bleedare
After that purgare.

After each section, the actors made percussive sounds using their feet, bottles, and pestles. A medical chorus chanted "bene, bene, bene, bene respondere."

Despite the hilarity, menace lurked beneath the scene, staged, according to one critic, "halfway between an auto da fe and a papal investiture."[117] Toinette, priestess of the rite, wearing a red robe and black mask, spun about holding up a chamber pot as if it were a sacred vessel to be blessed. Suddenly, she flipped it open and a recording of Handel's *Water Music* burst forth, while simultaneously an orchestra of doctors, surgeons, and apothecaries began to play the tools of their trade, seventeenth-century enemas (which looked like a "cross between a hypodermic needle and a caulking gun"),[118] saws, bones, and pestles, as if they were violins, cellos, horns, and percussion instruments. Their clicking and clacking remained in rhythm with Handel's music. A spinet and glass harmonica consisting of liquor bottles accompanied them. A new-born Argan conducted the chorus and orchestra rapturously.

AFTERWORD

Jean Gascon resigned from Stratford in 1974, leaving "the Festival and company with a deservedly high reputation."[119] During his tenure, Gascon laid the foundations for Stratford's future repertory in adding classics of different periods and cultures to Shakespeare's works, introducing modern plays, and through his operas and operettas—and perhaps his movement-driven productions—paving the way for the musicals that have become an indispensable part of the Festival's programming. His accomplishments included the addition of the Third Stage, a flexible 250-seat theater for experimental works, and the lengthening of the season. Although his attempt to bring English- and French-Canadian theater closer was not pursued by other directors, the continued production at Stratford of French and Québécois plays in translation owes a debt to Gascon.

He went back to Montreal expecting to resume his career as a Francophone actor and director. But Quebec had changed; separatism was in full force and Jean Gascon was viewed as a traitor. The theater was almost completely closed to him. In 1977, Gascon was appointed director of theater at the National Arts Centre in Ottawa, where he acted and directed in French and English. Funding cuts put an end to the NAC position in 1983. Gascon returned to Montreal, where he suffered a severe heart attack. His directing career languished until 1987, when he was invited to mount *My Fair Lady* for the 1988 season at Stratford. He had just completed the blocking when on April 6, 1988, he was stricken by another heart attack and taken to the hospital, where he died two weeks later. An ironic death for this devotee of Molière.

NOTES

1. Jennifer Homans, *Apollo's Angels: A History of Ballet* (New York: Random House, 2010), xv.
2. Unless otherwise indicated, all translations from the French are mine.

3. Annette Lust, *Bringing the Body to the Stage and Screen: Expressive Movement for Performers* (Lanham, MD: Scarecrow Press, 2011), 9.

4. Waldo Frank, *The Art of the Vieux-Colombier: A Contribution of France to the Contemporary Stage* (Paris: Éditions de la Nouvelle Revue Française, 1918), 50–51.

5. Jacques Copeau, *Registres III*, edited by Marie-Hélène Dasté and Suzanne Maistre Saint-Denis (Paris: Gallimard, 1979), 144.

6. Henri Bordeaux, *La Revue hebdomadaire*, June 12, 1914.

7. Jacques Copeau, *Souvenirs du Vieux-Colombier* (Paris: Nouvelle Éditions Latine, 1931), 40.

8. W. W. Lawrence, "*Twelfth Night* at the Vieux-Colombier," *The Nation*, 106, No. 2741, 1917, 72.

9. Jacques Copeau, *Registres IV*, edited by Marie-Hélène Dasté and Suzanne Maistre Saint-Denis (Paris: Gallimard, 1984), 19.

10. Edward Gordon Craig, *On the Art of the Theatre*, edited by Franc Chamberlain (London: Routledge, 2008), 30.

11. Jacques Copeau, *Les Registres du Vieux-Colombier V*, edited by Marie-Hélène Dasté and Suzanne Maistre Saint-Denis (Paris: Gallimard, 1993), 46.

12. Jacques Copeau, *Les Registres du Vieux-Colombier V*, edited by Marie-Hélène Dasté and Suzanne Maistre Saint-Denis (Paris: Gallimard, 1993), 302.

13. A trial version had operated the previous year.

14. The Company played two seasons. The first began in New York on November 1917 and ended in early April 1918, followed by a tour of approximately a week. The second season ran from October 1918 until April 7, 1919.

15. The War Ministry released his male actors.

16. Jacques Copeau, *Registres VI*, edited by Claude Sicard (Paris: Gallimard, 2000), 196–202.

17. The school had three divisions: one for the general public, a second for young professional actors, and the third, the special apprentice/acting student group. Although Bing was responsible for most of the hands-on work with the apprentices, Copeau appointed the writer Jules Romains administrative director of the school.

18. Copeau, *Registres VI*, 260.

19. Barbara Anne Kusler, "Jacques Copeau's Theatre School: L'École du Vieux-Colombier, 1920–1929," dissertation, University of Wisconsin, 1974, 118.

20. Ibid.

21. Professional theater was provided by the occasional French touring company as well as American and English companies for Quebec's Anglophones. Homegrown secular amateur groups were active as well.

22. Compagnons de saint Laurent rather than Saint-Laurent was Legault's preferred orthography.

23. Hélène Jasmin-Bélisle, *Le Père Émile Legault et ses Compagnons de saint Laurent* (Montréal: Leméac, 1986), 29.

24. Anne Caron, *Le Père Émile Legault et le théâtre au Québec* (Fides: Montréal, 1978), 59.

25. Maryline Romain, *Léon Chancerel: Un réformateur du théâtre français* (Lausanne: L'Âge d'Homme, 2005), 181.

26. Gabriel Gascon, Interview with author, March 18, 2004.

27. Jasmin-Bélisle, *Le Père Émile Legault*, 41.

28. Claude Gauvreau, "En causant avec Jean Gascon," *Le Haut-parleur*, August 4, 1951; Lucette Robert, "Portraits de Vedettes, Jean Gascon," *Photo Journal*, October 13, 1951.

29. Ludmilla Pitoëff spent the war years in North America.

30. Jean Gascon, *Propos et confidences*, Television interview, Jean Faucher, Producer, Radio-Canada, 1979; and Jean-Louis Roux, *Nous sommes tous des acteurs* (Montréal: Éditions Lescop, 1998), 129.
31. Gabriel Gascon, Interview.
32. Jean Gascon, Audio tape, Interviewed by Patrick McFadden, Undated.
33. Maurice Blain, *Le Devoir*, October 11, 1951.
34. Maurice Huot, *La Patrie*, October 10, 1951, 14.
35. Jean Béraud, *La Presse*, October 10, 1951.
36. Roger Blais, director, *Côté cour . . . côté jardin*, National Film Board of Canada, 1953.
37. See photos in Éloi de Grandmont, N. Hudon, and J.-L. Roux, eds., *Dix ans de théâtre au Nouveau Monde* (Montreal: Éditions Leméac, 1961).
38. Blais, *Côté cour . . . côté jardin*.
39. John Rudlin, *Commedia dell'Arte: An Actor's Handbook* (London: Routledge, 1994), 94.
40. Jean Béraud, *La Presse*, October 10, 1951.
41. "*Le Nouveau-Monde* à Paris," Bernard D'Aillencourt, director, Office National du Film, Canada,1955.
42. Lenore Crawford, *The Free Press*, July 3, 1956.
43. Brooks Atkinson, "Lively *Henry V*," *New York Times*, June 24, 1956.
44. Arnold Edinborough, "Consolidation in Stratford, Canada," *Shakespeare Quarterly* 7 (Autumn 1956): 404.
45. Walter Kerr, "*Henry V* Brought Back into Focus," *New York Herald Tribune*, June 24, 1956.
46. Although the actual war did not end until 1763, when the Treaty of Paris was signed, the dramatic battlefield deaths of the English General Wolfe and the French General Montcalm have given the battle mythic significance.
47. Atkinson, "Lively *Henry V*."
48. Christopher Plummer, *In Spite of Myself* (New York: Alfred A. Knopf, 2008), 200.
49. Bill Ross, "French-Canadian Players Delight Stratford Crowd," *Canadian Press*, July 3, 1956.
50. Jean Gascon, *Propos et confidences*.
51. While remaining to true to its origins, the stage underwent renovations in 1962 and 1975.
52. Berners A. W. Jackson, "The Shakespeare Festival: Stratford, Ontario, 1953–1977," *Shakespeare Quarterly* 29, no. 2, (Spring 1978), 181.
53. Sidney Johnson, "A Memorable *Othello*," *Montreal Star*, July 2, 1959.
54. Pierre Saucier, *La Presse*, July 2, 1959.
55. Joyce Goodman, *London Free Press*, July 2, 1959.
56. Brooks Atkinson, "Festival Triumphs in *Othello*," *New York Times*, July 2, 1959.
57. Betty Lee, *Love and Whiskey: The Story of the Dominion Drama Festival and the Early Years of Theatre in Canada* (Toronto: Simon and Pierre, 1973), 300.
58. Not until the 1990s were Canada's aboriginal peoples considered "a third national collectivity." See Kenneth McRoberts, *Canadian Journal of Political Science/Revue canadienne de science politique* 34, no. 4 (December 2001), 683–713. In 1974, James Butler founded a theater school in Toronto for Canada's aboriginal peoples, the Centre for Indigenous Theatre.
59. *The First Class at the NTS*, Theatre Museum, http://www.youtube.com/watch?v=8xrHSQI-Dps&list=PL78D9F9108B57FA66.
60. Herbert Whittaker, "A Dream Fulfilled, or Almost," in Jean-Louis Roux, M. Garneau, T. Hendry, eds., *L'École . . . The School* (Montreal: Éditions Internationales Stanké, 1985), 53.

61. "National Theatre School of Canada Brief Submitted to the Royal Commission on Bilingualism and Biculturalism," 1965.

62. Sylvain Schryburt, *De l'acteur vedette au théâtre de festival: Histoire des pratique scéniques montréalaises 1940–1980* (Montreal: Presses de l'Université de Montréal, 2011), 279.

63. Michael Langham, Interview with author, November 7, 2005.

64. Initially, Gascon was appointed executive artistic director and John Hirsch associate artistic director, an unhappy arrangement that lasted a year.

65. Marilyn Gascon, Interview with author, 2007.

66. Richard Wilbur, "A Letter from Richard Wilbur," in *The Stratford Scene 1958–1968*, edited by Peter Raby (Toronto: Clarke, Irwin, 1968), 195.

67. Jean Gascon, Interview with MacFadden.

68. Jean Gascon, *Propos et confidences*.

69. Herbert Whittaker, "Stratford Acquires the Pagan Touch," *Globe and Mail*, June 20, 1963.

70. Antonio Fava, *The Comic Mask in the Commedia Dell'arte* (Evanston, IL: Northwestern University Press, 2007).

71. Martha Henry, Theatre Museum, www.youtube.com/watch?v=IJAj2ig5D8E.

72. Disparagers included Nathan Cohen, *Toronto Star*, June 20, 1963; and Arnold Edinborough, *Vancouver Sun*, June 20, 1963.

73. *Buffalo News*, June 20, 1963.

74. Muriel Ready, "*Comedy of Errors* is Festival Treat," *Galt Reporter*, June 20, 1963.

75. Audrey Ashley, "Jean Gascon's *Comedy*—An Ancient *Hellzapoppin*," *Ottawa Citizen*, June 20, 1963.

76. Herbert Whittaker, "Inventive Director Shines with Minor Play," *Globe and Mail*, June 20, 1963.

77. Unless otherwise indicated, descriptions of *Tartuffe, Cymbeline*, and *The Imaginary Invalid* were drawn from the production DVDs at the Stratford Festival Archives.

78. Jean Gascon, "Director's Notes," in *Tartuffe* Program, 1968.

79. Jean Gascon, "Director's Notes," in *The Stratford Scene 1958–1968*, edited by Peter Raby (Toronto: Clarke, Irwin.), 1968, 192.

80. Jean Gascon, "Director's Notes," 192.

81. Jean Gascon, "Director's Notes," 193.

82. Emanuel S. Chill, "*Tartuffe*, Religion, and Courtly Culture," *French Historical Studies* 3, no. 2 (Autumn 1963), 171–73.

83. Walter Kerr, "The Supreme Work of Jean Gascon," *New York Times*, June 25, 1968.

84. Wilbur, "A Letter from Richard Wilbur," 194.

85. Frank Morriss, *Winnipeg Tribune*, July 12, 1968.

86. Jean Gascon, "Director's Notes," 192.

87. Pat Galloway trained first at the Royal Academy of Dramatic Art and then at the Conservatoire d'Art Dramatique in Paris.

88. Clive Barnes, "A Fine Figure of a Hypocrite, *New York Times*, June 13, 1968.

89. Audrey M. Ashley, *Tartuffe* Highly Entertaining Comedy," *Ottawa Citizen*, June 12, 1968.

90. Arnold Edinborough, *Canadian Saturday Night*, August 1968.

91. Terry Doran, "Actor Manages to Fulfill a Big Buildup as Tartuffe," *Buffalo Evening News*, June 12, 1968.

92. Kevin Kelly, "A Flawless Production of Molière's *Tartuffe*," *Boston Globe*, June 13, 1968.

93. Ashley, "*Tartuffe* Highly Entertaining Comedy."

94. Roger Warren, Introduction, *Cymbeline*, by William Shakespeare, edited by Roger Warren (Oxford University Press, 1998), 2.
95. Jean Gascon, "Director's Notes," *Cymbeline* Program, 1970.
96. Michael Bawtree, letter to Tanya Moiseiwitsch, December 15, 1969, Stratford Festival Archives.
97. Michael Bawtree, letter to Tanya Moiseiwitsch.
98. Nathan Cohen, "*Cymbeline* Unlikely to Kindle Interest," *Toronto Daily Star*, July 22, 1970.
99. Tanya Moiseiwitsch, *Cymbeline* Design Sketchbook, Stratford Festival Archives.
100. Berners W. Jackson, "This Is Shakespeare the Magician at His Miraculous Best," *Hamilton Spectator*, August 1, 1970.
101. Photo, Stratford Festival Archives.
102. Moiseiwitsch, *Cymbeline* Design Sketchbook.
103. Edgar Kloten, "*Cymbeline* Is for Now!" *West Hartford Times*, September 3, 1970.
104. Photos, Stratford Festival Archives.
105. Marilyn Gascon, Interview with author.
106. Lenore Crawford, "Musical Experiment with 22 Loudspeakers Success at Festival," *London Evening Free Press*," July 22, 1970.
107. Photo, Stratford Festival Archives.
108. Herbert Whittaker, "*Cymbeline* Filled with Delights," *Globe and Mail*, July 23, 1970.
109. E. H. Lampard, "*Cymbeline* Is Spectacular of Spectaculars," *St. Catharines Times*, July 22, 1970.
110. Photos, Stratford Festival Archives.
111. Kloten, "*Cymbeline* Is for Now!"
112. Stan Andersen, "Molière Misused across the Border," *Cleveland Press*, June 17, 1964.
113. Donald Brittain, director, *The Players*, National Film Board, 1974, a Technicolor documentary with several scenes from the production was also informative.
114. Martha Henry, e-mail to author.
115. Gabriel Charpentier, conversation with author.
116. Gabriel Charpentier's sound design notes.
117. Kevin Kelly, "Imaginary Invalid in Critical Condition at Stratford," *Boston Globe*, June 9, 1974.
118. Tony Mastroianni, "Crowd Says 'Ah' to Play at Stratford," *Cleveland Press*, June 4, 1974.
119. Dave Billington, *Montreal Gazette*, June 4, 1974.

BIBLIOGRAPHY

Attinger, Gustave. *L'Esprit de la commedia dell'arte dans le théâtre français*. Paris: Librairie Théâtrale, 1950.
Blais, Roger, director. *Côté cour . . . côté jardin*. National Film Board of Canada, 1953.
Bonner, Geraldine. "M. Copeau's Players." *New York Times*, March 17, 1918, 61.
Borgal, Clément. *Revue d'histoire litteraire de la France* No. 5/6 (September–December 1982): 735–43.
Brissenden, Alan. *Shakespeare and the Dance*. Atlantic Highlands, NJ: Humanities Press, 1981.
Brittain, Donald, director. *The Players*. National Film Board of Canada, 1974.
Caron, Anne. *Le Père Émile Legault et le théâtre au Québec*. Fides: Montréal, 1978.
Copeau, Jacques. *Souvenirs du Vieux-Colombier*. Paris: Nouvelles Éditions Latine, 1931.

——. *Le Théâtre populaire*. Paris: Presses Universitaires de France, 1942.

——. "Un Essai de rénovation dramatique." *Registres I. Appels*. Edited by Marie-Hélène Dasté and Suzanne Maistre Saint-Denis. Paris: Gallimard, 1974.

——. *Les Registres du Vieux-Colombier III*. Edited by Marie-Hélène Dasté and Suzanne Maistre Saint-Denis. Paris: Gallimard, 1979.

——. *Les Registres du Vieux-Colombier IV. America*. Edited by Marie-Hélène Dasté and Suzanne Maistre Saint-Denis. Paris: Gallimard, 1984.

——. *Les Registres du Vieux-Colombier V. 1919–1924*. Edited by Marie-Hélène Dasté and Suzanne Maistre Saint-Denis. Paris: Gallimard, 1993.

——. *Registres VI. L'École du Vieux-Colombier*. Edited by Claude Sicard. Paris: Gallimard, 2000.

Corbin, John. "Shakespeare's *Twelfth Night*." *New York Times*, February 25, 1919.

Defaux, Gérard. "The Comic at Its Limits." In *A New History of French Literature*, edited by Denis Hollier, 334–40. Cambridge: Harvard University Press, 1994.

Dock, Stephen Varick. *Costume and Fashion in the Plays of Jean-Baptiste Poquelin Molière: A Seventeenth-Century Perspective*. Geneva: Editions Slatkine, 1992.

Eerde, John van. "Le Bourgeois in New York." *French Revue* 29, no. 6 (May 1956): 472–76.

Eliot, Samuel A. "Le Théâtre du Vieux-Colombier." *Theatre Arts Magazine* 1 (November 16–August 17), 1918, 25–30.

Fava, Antonio. *The Comic Mask in the Commedia dell'arte*. Evanston, IL: Northwestern University Press, 2007.

Frank, Waldo. *The Art of the Vieux-Colombier: A Contribution of France to the Contemporary Stage*. Paris: Éditions de la Nouvelle Revue Française, 1918.

Gascon, Jean. "*Tartuffe*: Director's Notes." In *The Stratford Scene 1958–1968*, edited by Peter Raby, 192–205. Toronto: Clarke, Irwin, 1968.

——. *Cymbeline*. "Director's Notes." Program, 1970.

——. "Notes on *The Bourgeois Gentilhomme*." Unpublished Typescript.

——. *Propos et confidences*. Television interview. Jean Faucher, Producer. Radio-Canada, 1979.

Gauvreau, Claude. "En causant avec Jean Gascon." *Le Haut-parleur*, August 4, 1951.

Green, Martin, and J. Swan. *The Triumph of Pierrot: The Commedia dell'Arte and the Modern Imagination*. University Park: Pennsylvania University Press, 1993.

Hébert, Georges. *L'Éducation physique ou l'entraînement complet par la méthode naturelle*. Paris: Librairie Vuibert, 1913.

Hébert, Lorraine. "La Formation du comédien au Québec." In *Les Voies de la création théâtrale 9: La Formation du comédien*, edited by Anne-Marie Gourdon, 249–61. Paris: Éditions du Centre National de la Recherche Scientifique, 1981.

Homans, Jennifer. *Apollo's Angels: A History of Ballet*. New York: Random House, 2010.

Innes, Christopher. *Edward Gordon Craig: A Vision of the Theatre*. Amsterdam: Harwood Academic, 1998.

Jasmin-Bélisle, Hélène. *Le Père Émile Legault et ses compagnons de saint Laurent*. Montréal: Leméac, 1986.

Jouvet, Louis, Carol Volk, Erland Josephson, and Jennifer Forsberg. "How to Perform Molière." *Grand Street* no. 47 (Autumn 1993): 160–69.

Kusler, Barbara Anne. "Jacques Copeau's Theatre School: L'École du Vieux-Colombier 1920–1929." Dissertation. University of Wisconsin, 1974.

Lanson, Gustave. "Molière and Farce." Translated by Ruby Cohn. *Tulane Drama Review* 8, no. 2 (Winter 1963): 133–54.

Lust, Annette. *Bringing the Body to the Stage and Screen: Expressive Movement for Performers.* Lanham, MD: Scarecrow Press, 2011.

Mazouer, Charles. *Molière et ses comédies-ballets.* Paris: Klinckcksieck, 1993.

———. "Comédies-ballets." In *Cambridge Companion to Molière*, edited by David Bradby and A. Calder, 107–19. Cambridge: Cambridge University Press, 2006.

McBride, Robert. "A Neglected Key to Molière's Theatre." *Dance Research: The Journal of the Society for Dance Research* 2, no. 1 (Spring 1984). 3–18.

Molière. "Avertissement, *Les Fâcheux*." http://www.inlibroveritas.net/lire/oeuvre351.html.

Oliver, Richard A. "Molière's Contribution to the Lyric Stage." *Musical Quarterly* 33, no. 3 (July 1947): 350–64.

Powell, John S. "Musical Practices in the Theater of Molière. *Revue de Musicologie* 82, no. 1 (1996): 5–37.

———. "*Le Bourgeois gentilhomme:* Molière and Music." In *Cambridge Companion to Molière*, edited by David Bradby and A. Calder, 121–38. Cambridge: Cambridge University Press, 2006.

Roeder, Ralph. "Copeau, 1921." *Theatre Arts* 5, no. 1 (October 1921): 279–92.

Romain, Maryline. *Léon Chancerel: Un réformateur du théâtre français.* Lausanne: L'Âge d'Homme, 2005.

Roux, Jean-Louis. *Nous sommes tous des acteurs.* Montréal: Éditions Lescop, 1998.

Rudlin, John. *Commedia dell'Arte: An Actor's Handbook.* London: Routledge, 1994.

Ruffini, Franco. "Mime, the Actor, Action: The Way of Boxing." *Mime Journal* 20 (1995): 54–69.

Schryburt, Sylvain. *De l'acteur vedette au théâtre de festival: Histoire des pratiques Scéniques montréalaises 1940–1980.* Montréal: Presses de l'Université de Montréal, 2011.

Sorrell, Walter. "Shakespeare and the Dance." *Shakespeare Quarterly* 7 (1957): 367–94.

Tard, Louis-Martin. *Vingt ans de théâtre au Nouveau Monde.* Montréal: Éditions du Jour, 1971.

CHAPTER 14

··

DANCING DRAMA
Ancient Greek Theater in Modern Shoes and Shows

··

MARIANNE MCDONALD

DANCE was vitally important in ancient Greek drama and some modern adaptations. For the moderns, the focus will be on two practitioners who tried to change not only theater but also their societies: the American, Martha Graham (1894–1991), and Ariane Mnouchkine (b. 1939), who is Russian and French. Dance is the heartbeat of the drama, the drumbeat that adds to the understanding of the words. The dancers couple movements and gestures in a way that make the play a total experience. In my own performed translations, I could not imagine an effective presentation without this music and dance. These elements make up, in part, for the absence of masks in what was created originally for masked performance.

Modern adaptations depend less on music and dance, a disadvantage, unless they are in the hands of a master poet of stage language, like Eugene O'Neill (1888–1953). The pain of his mother's addiction, and his own alcoholism, inspired him to write both his *Mourning Becomes Electra* (1931), his three-play version of Aeschylus's *Oresteia* (458 BC), and *A Long Day's Journey into Night* (1956). He had mastered the music of language. His passion-inspired plays were comparable to Martha Graham's dance, and both were psychologically driven.

Both ancient drama and modern adaptations often depended on having a political thrust, which also would engage the audience's passion. Irish adaptations of Greek tragedy protested British occupation and its abuses, and Athol Fugard's adaptations, for example, *The Island* (1973), used an *Antigone* performed in prison to protest apartheid in South Africa, and theater like his led to its overthrow.[1] Fugard uses physical movement as protest, such as the repeated ritual at the beginning of that play to show the tedious tasks of men in prison. These political plays paralleled Mnouchkine's criticism of injustice in her *Les Atrides* (1990–93).

When dance was used in ancient Greek ritual, it was the earliest vehicle to try to influence those unknown forces that have power over man: nature and the gods. It was also one of the earliest ways for human beings to express joy and sorrow and all the other emotions. In performing Homer (c. 9th century BC) dance was an accompaniment to epic recitation (*Iliad*, XVIII, 603–6, *Odyssey*, IV, 17–19). Greek tragedy and comedy included danced poetry in the fifth-century BC yearly Greek dramatic festivals.[2] Greek tragedy was regarded in Athens as a way of educating its citizens.[3] Politics and passion informed the ancient plays and do so in many modern versions.

Masked movement in theater itself is a form of dance, and the choral sections made dance explicit. The word "chorus" is derived from the Greek word for dance (*chorós*). Greek tragedy's mask allowed the original three to four actors (all male) to play several roles, including women. Violence on stage was avoided, so it was rendered in dance, or some symbolic action initiated by the chorus, or through the words.

Much of the evidence for the choruses in fifth-century Greek drama is inexact and derived from mute sources such as vases, or later tracts.[4] Some speculate that the chorus originally had fifty members as suggested by numbers in the chorus, such as the fifty daughters of Danaus in Aeschylus's *Suppliants* (often thought to be an early play, but now evidence suggests it cannot have been earlier than 466 BC).[5] However most scholars now consider that number symbolic, and follow the ancient sources, which claim the original chorus in Greek tragedy was twelve and later expanded to fifteen. In Greek comedy it was twenty-four.

Lillian B. Lawler suggests that in Greek tragedy the chorus often danced in two rows that formed a rectangle,[6] but many plays suggest less formal arrangements, such as the bacchantes in Euripides's *Bacchae*. There was a chorus leader, and perhaps lines were delivered by that leader, or in unison. The chorus was the heart of the drama; the *chorêgos*, the main funder of ancient Greek tragedy in Athens, paid for the training and costuming of the chorus. Many thought that what the chorus enacted in their dance imitated the action described, but the details are unknown. No one can definitely claim what was authentic for the period in which Greek tragedy was first performed in Athens, although many draw analogies from modern dancing in Greece. The music was only fragmentary and speculative (e.g., in the *Orestes* a few notes were written over one passage).[7]

In Greek tragedy the chorus used hand gestures (*schemata*) that could, for instance, express fear, looking for something, or even warding something off (the *sime cheir* in which one bent back one's fingers).[8] Comparable gestures play a great role in Balinese dance, Noh drama, Kathakali, Beijing opera, and many Asian traditions. *Mudras* or hand gestures, augment the expression of *rasa* (human feelings and emotions), which leads to the *katharsis* of Greek tragedy evoked by its particular expressiveness, to say nothing of commedia dell'arte.

Fights are stylized in performance. Sometimes they were part of ritual. There were Greek dances that were meant not only to reveal the power of the warrior but also to ensure victory, such as the Pyrrhic dance, well described in Plato's *Laws* (7.815 A–B). Plato's *Laws* also describe the *emmeleia*, restrained dignified dances, used in tragedies, with songs that accompany words expressing emotions such as joy, or gratitude to the gods. These are the "peaceful" dances that contrast with the warlike ones.

Ancient Greek tragedies were followed by satyr plays that parodied elements in the tragedy. Both tragedy and this type of comedy had particular forms of dance, like the satyr dance, the *Sikinnis*, lively and sexually suggestive. The satyr dances and their choral reaction could make a potentially tragic scene comic. The dancing choruses in Aristophanes's comedies could be colorful and be part of the action (e.g., Frogs in *The Frogs*). Animals and personifications like clouds and islands appear in the choruses, another difference from Greek tragedy.

Martha Graham set a standard for the use of Greek theater in dance in America, establishing Modernism in dance as Diaghilev, the Ballets Russes, and Nijinsky (for instance, in the ballets of Stravinsky) did in Europe. She rebelled against her time in Denishawn, a school founded in Los Angeles in 1915 by Ruth St. Denis (1879–1968) and Ted Shawn (1891–1972), but at the same time she was influenced by their use of Greek costuming, emphasis on myths, and elements from various eastern cultures. Isadora Duncan (1877–1927) with her Greek-costumed "Isadorables" also blazed a path, but a very different one from the "Graham Crackers" as Graham's dancers were called because they cracked their joints and exploded into passionate fireworks.

Modern dance was shaped in America by women, mostly: Eva Palmer (1875–1952), besides St. Denis and Martha Graham, carried this on, but never in a stereotypical way. [9] She rebelled against the term "feminist," as did Ariane Mnouchkine, because they saw women as multifaceted, resisting classification.

Graham's early pieces were based on universal myths, which for her signified the basic drives in human beings that Freud had made popular and on which her father's psychiatric practice was based. She understood, as did her father and Freud, that movement betrayed a person's inner feelings. Graham wished to convey these psychological drives in her dance, so she used movement as expression and revelation of the inner self.

Graham turned seriously to dances based on Greek classics, partially inspired by Erick Hawkins, who studied classics at Harvard and joined her company.[10] Her pieces most obviously based on Greek drama and myth were *Tragic Patterns: Chorus for Supplicants, Chorus for Maenads, Chorus for Furies* (1933); *Cave of the Heart* (1946); *Errand into the Maze* (1947); *Night Journey* (1947); *Clytemnestra* (1958) (see figs. 14.2 and 14.3); *Alcestis* (1960); *Phaedra* (1962); *Circe* (1963); *Cortege of Eagles* (based on *Trojan Women* and *Hecuba*, 1967); *Flute of Pan* (1978); *Andromache's Lament* (1982); *Phaedra's Dream* (1983); and *Persephone* (1987). In 1931 she danced in a production of Sophocles's *Electra*, tracing the emotional storyline in dance. *Dionisiaques* (1932) was another early dance, dealing as Stravinsky did with the sacrifice of an individual for the community in his daring ballet *Rite of Spring* (1913), which led to riots in Paris. In 1984 Graham devised her own dance to Stravinsky's *Rite of Spring*.

Graham's *Lamentation* (1930, music by Zoltán Kodály) was a dance that well expressed the emotions of tragedy, and what was learned in it could apply to her dances based on tragic Greek myths. In a 1976 video, her *Lamentation* shows a woman alone, seated, and wrapped in what looks like a flowing Greek garment, a blue tubular jersey that envelops her, resembling as Graham put it, her own skin.[11] She moves underneath it like a trapped animal trying to get free, while expressing the agony of being trapped. She sobs. The end shows her still trapped inside, but fully covered; not even her head shows. She is a mound of shapeless sorrow. She created an American dance style that was an alternative to classical ballet and unique to her in its emotive expression. She stressed the pelvic contraction, which could be sexual, violent, or expressive of many fundamental emotions like grief, which is the distillation of Greek tragedy that this ballet illustrates. The pelvic contraction left the dancer doubled-up and sobbing. Being imprisoned in her jersey of grief is as constricting and liberating as the effect that tragedy has on the great heroes and heroines, besides the audience itself.

Cave of the Heart shows a Medea who sacrifices herself by killing her children to achieve her vengeance over her errant husband, Jason (danced by Erick Hawkins). The children are only suggested and do not appear: the struggles conveyed by her frenzied dance are those of a woman betrayed by a man.

Graham shows that Medea's vengeance is a corollary of jealousy, but Euripides showed it as much more complex (his Medea was out for honor and resembled a Greek hero, and murdering the children was the perfect vengeance).[12] Events in Graham's life also influenced

FIGURE 14.1 Martha Graham's *Cave of the Heart*. Medea (Martha Graham) faces betrayal by Jason (Erick Hawkins), with his new bride, Glauce (Yuriko Kikuchi). Photo by Carl Van Vechten, 1961. Library of Congress, Prints & Photographs Division, Carl Van Vechten Collection, [reproduction number, e.g., LC-USZ62-54231].

her choices, and her relationship with Hawkins, her student (from 1936), but soon her young lover (fifteen years younger than Graham), and finally husband (1948), who abandoned her when she didn't give him the dowry he expected: equality in her company and equal fame.

In *Cave of the Heart* (see fig. 14.1), Graham portrays the emotional deadliness of the wounded female.

She danced it originally with Hawkins as Jason. Her rival, playing the princess Glauce, was played by a young Japanese-American girl, Yuriko Kikuchi, who had been held in an internment camp. It was noted that Graham was one of the first to employ Asian Americans and African Americans in her company, long before the civil rights movement.[13] Not only was Graham color blind, but religion wasn't a factor; she was fiercely opposed to prejudice. She refused to dance, or have her company dance in Germany after a prestigious invitation that she received in 1935 from Dr. Joseph Goebbels to dance in the Olympic Games of 1936, that many would have accepted. She said: "It never entered my mind to say yes. How could I dance in Nazi Germany?"[14]

Besides this, her dance was a sexualized protest against the traditions, which frowned on dance. Graham's only requirements were talent and total devotion to her company. She demanded nothing less than total commitment for little pay.

Her dance was typically American and a defiant gesture against the sanitized versions of classical ballet, which was often racist. Two of the most American qualities were that her dance was also multicultural and assimilative. She chose composers like Barber, Hindemith, Copland, Della Joio, Hovhaness, Stravinsky, Menotti, and Halim El-Dabh, besides Louis Horst. Her musical choices avoided the emollient of tonal melody, and she opted instead for startling rhythms and jarring transitions, just as her dance made no concessions to the comfortable.

Isamu Noguchi designed the sets and costuming, which were appropriately suggestive. In the original performance of *Cave of the Heart*, Noguchi made a headdress of snakes for Graham that looked like a mass of coiled snakes, but the gown was of sharp gold wire, which also suggested the black widow in her web.[15] She tries to impale Jason in her embrace, but he escapes and Medea is left alone. At the end, after her sharp movements illustrate her vengeance, the wire web seems also to be her prison, from which she futilely tries to escape. Graham's make-up transformed her face into a mask, which was also appropriate for Greek drama.

In the 1976 video mentioned above, Takako Asakawa danced Medea's role with *kamikaze* intensity. Graham prefaces her dance by saying that when she performed this herself in Asia, she was described as an elephant gone mad (a powerful creature that will murder). The untamed mind as an elephant gone mad is a common concept in Buddhism. The Dalai Lama often quotes the *Bhavavivika*: "The crazy elephant of the mind behaving wildly is tied to the pillar of an object of observation with the rope of mindfulness. By degrees it is brought under control with the hook of wisdom." Graham also spoke of a woodblock picture she saw of a woman eating her own heart, called "Envy."

Graham's Medea dances to the jagged music of Samuel Barber. She is trapped, but utilizing what seems to be a cage of sharp branches. She is first seen crouching in front of it as if it were her web. She strikes her hip as if it were a gong sending her body into angry vibrations. She draws out a red ribbon flecked with silver from the center of her black garment covered by silver spirals like snakes, to match the ones in her hair/headdress. She mimes eating, swallowing, and vomiting the sparkling ribbon, which could represent her own heart or intestines, the price she will pay for the vengeance that she will exact from her upwardly mobile mate Jason, leaving her to marry another princess who could do more for him at this stage of his life. Medea kills her own sons by Jason with self-consuming cost. This Medea uses the ribbon as it is used in Kabuki to externalize her blood and inner organs; she puts it in her mouth as if to eat it, but she also binds herself with it. Graham will use it again in her *Night Journey*, where it becomes the umbilical cord that tied Jocasta to Oedipus, which will ultimately transform into the noose she uses to hang herself.[16] After an expressive dance, this Medea returns to her cage/web and lifts it so it looks like a deadly weapon as she advances on her prey: She is now totally the black widow at the center of her web of sharp branches that will stab Jason into a life that is a living death, forever impaled and stuck on Medea's web. Her last gesture is to look up to heaven, as if her cage/web will now transform into the dragon chariot that will carry her off to freedom in a new home offered her by the king of Athens in return for her curing him of his childlessness, an ironic sequel to child murder.

Medea has always been a play about vengeance, but also suggests the action of the "foreigner." Euripides's genius was to show that the "foreigner" in many cases is less barbaric than the "civilized" Greek. Jason may say he is looking out for the family economically by leaving Medea to marry the next local princess, but he shows the values of the accountant. Medea has the values of the heart. Of woman. A powerful woman. A woman of African descent has often been cast in this role: Hans Henny Jahnn's *Medea* (1926); Countee Cullen's *Medea* (1935); José Triana's *Medea in the Mirror* (1960); Robert Wilson's *Deafman Glance* (1970); Guy Butler's *Demea* (1990), a South African version in which *Medea* is a Tembu princess abandoned by Jason as a white trekker; John LaChiusa's *Marie Christine* (1999); J. Michael Walton's *Medea* (2002); my version, *Medea, Queen of Colchester* (2002), which shows Medea as a black male gay transvestite from South Africa who performs in Las Vegas; and my translation in 2007.[17]

My translation of *Medea* was performed as a stylized version in which at the moment that Medea needs to build up her courage to kill her children, Monique Gaffney, an African American actress, puts on African war makeup, white paint that turns her face into a mask. Then she dances a war dance filled with leaps and crouches in which she resembles the spider that the Medea in Graham's dance suggested in *Cave of the Heart*. Gaffney tapped into this tradition and her African pride to fight the white man who was abandoning her for a white princess. Gongs and drums playing in the background augment the rhythms of Medea's tortured body.

Graham's *Errand into the Maze* continues the theme of the power of women by her dancing the role of Theseus/Ariadne in confronting the Minotaur in its maze and killing it. Minos wanted to be king of Crete, so he asked Poseidon to send a bull from the sea, which he would sacrifice if his brothers competing for the rule would give him the throne. The bull was delivered to him and he won the throne, but he didn't sacrifice the bull. As punishment, Poseidon cursed Pasiphae, Minos's queen, with lust for the bull. From their union the Minotaur was born, half-bull and half-man. Daedalus was commissioned to build a maze for the Minotaur. Because Androgeus, Minos and Pasiphae's son, was unjustly slain by the Athenians after beating them in an athletic competition, seven sons and seven daughters were sent from Athens to the Minotaur as a sacrifice each year, but Theseus, the king's son slew the monster with Ariadne's help; she gave him a thread that he might uncoil when he entered so he could find his way out of the maze.

Ariadne's thread becomes Graham's sacred ribbon in her dance with the half-bull—a male dancer with horns and makeup to suggest a bull, which denoted "a creature of fear." Graham states her victory was to "express the conquering of fear in my life, fear of the unknown, fear of something now quite recognizable" (Freedman, 114). During her twelve years with Hawkins she found a love that she had never known, nor knew again. Fear of the unknown was apt. The bull, at least for the Greeks, was a very sexualized image.

Graham also said, "If I had to present one ballet to a child of six or eight . . . I would choose *Errand into the Maze*. This dance exemplifies, through the use of the rope on the floor and the object in the air, the strange place you are venturing into, something a child might understand. It is a conquering of fear—to find that one place onstage where the bird that makes you want to dance lives . . . It meant to me the passage through the unknown into life."[18] When she was in danger, as she was during a snowstorm as she flew from Abedon to Teheran in a small plane, she said: "I sat there and did *Errand* three times in my mind before we landed. And we did arrive safely in Teheran."[19]

The thread, as it did in the Medea dance, could suggest her entrails, or her heart, what she put at risk in her personal battle with the bull, the Minotaur, the unknown, love. The maze itself was an apt metaphor for the human subconscious. The monster in the maze was also the fear that all creators must face in challenging the unknown to achieve their goals. It is an apt analogy for what Graham herself achieved in her lifetime by conquering her own fears and overcoming her bouts with alcoholism because of her drive to escape the maze.

Night Journey was performed to music by William Schumann, and Isamu Noguchi once again provided his minimal powerful sets.[20] This dance version is a variation of Sophocles's play, simplified to recount the textless story from Jocasta's point of view. The ancient play began with Oedipus, king of Thebes, meeting with his populace to find solutions to the sickness that has descended on the city. Various clues are given that Oedipus must slowly piece together. It has been called the greatest detective story ever written: the search for one's identity. Oedipus will not give up until the solution destroys the world as he knew it. It shows the audience the tragedy and greatness of a man who courageously works out his destiny and solves his own riddle no matter what the cost to himself. In a sense it illustrates the danger of an analyst removing all the masks from a person's psyche, something that Freud warned against. The power of the unconscious could be overwhelming, and sometimes fatal to the person experiencing it.

Graham gives us Jocasta's story and how she deals with the deadly truth that she has married her son, the son she thought was exposed as a baby and died. She has borne him children. *Night Journey* refers to the day of discovery, and the night will be eternal darkness for her by her suicide. Her discovery was fatal for her. It cost Oedipus his eyes, which he stabbed with Jocasta's brooch to blind himself; he could not bear to see the world around him after his awful discovery. The original play shows Oedipus's courage in choosing to live, but Graham's dance version is no indictment of Jocasta. Graham's Jocasta is as heroic as Oedipus, as she chooses to die rather than live with her guilt and shame.

Graham's costume features a huge brooch on her head with a half moon at one end and a circle in the center of the half moon that it seems to be eating . . . the moon resembling the open jaws of a fish, but simplified. There is another large brooch holding her dress together, the deadly brooch that Oedipus uses to put out his eyes. She wears a scarf decorated with spiky flowers that could have come off a wall of a Cretan fresco. Her dress is black with circular patterns on the bottom.

The chorus is of women, contrary to the original that was of men, the elders of Thebes. Here it is nubile young women who dance Jocasta's emotions and are witnesses to her marriage and her death. They dressed in black with various coiling spirals suggesting snakes, or a rope. Their spiraling circles, like those on Jocasta's costume, also suggest the circular feminine. Zajko claims, "the sexual appetite of the queen is graphically represented by both Graham herself and the mimetic gestures of the female chorus. Graham emphasizes the active role of the woman in drawing the man into her body and so refocuses the sexual act around the image of incorporation rather than penetration. The chorus, who function throughout as a kind of collective externalization of Jocasta's memory and desire, shore up this image and Oedipus becomes an isolated male presence in a tidal current of contracting female corporeality."[21]

Oedipus wears skin-tight shorts that resemble a skimpy bathing suit, and a chest harness. Even his costume expresses his constricted sexualized fate. The trunks are decorated with coiling snakes, or possibly a long rope with its suggestive imagery.

Jocasta holds a rope at the beginning. Tiresias enters tapping a large staff, which he uses to stab his way across the stage; he wears a metal mask, which resembles a helmet beneath a metal wreath; His mask reminds us of his blindness. As he enters he seems also to be rowing across the stage, rather like Charon to escort Jocasta to the underworld. He takes the rope away from Jocasta. Her reverie begins.

In dance, Jocasta remembers how Oedipus, victorious after defeating the sphinx and saving the city, first approaches her. The chorus brings him in as their victorious hero. Their gestures toward each other show she welcomes him as her husband. Their gestures are explicit as Oedipus mounts her and strokes her breasts, then lower down on her body, executed suggestively but no actual touch occurs. It is the most erotic production I have ever seen of this phase of their relationship. In her autobiography Graham describes her "Invitation to their Intercourse" in the following terms:

> She has in her hands the branches that Oedipus had given her when he carried her from the bed onto her small stool where she became the queen. She drops into a wide split fall and puts one flower out tentatively toward him, sits back and crosses her knees, opening and closing, opening and closing. It is this that a dancer sometimes avoids, hesitating to realize that she is inviting him into the privacy of her body. He comes forward, takes his cloak, and puts it around her. He picks up the flower and the two proceed to the bed ... It is not only a movement, but rather a gesture of invitation for him to come between her legs.[22]

After they symbolically make love, Jocasta cradles and rocks Oedipus's head in a way that also suggests a mother-son relationship. This adds to the authenticity of the shocking revelation that Jocasta is, in fact, Oedipus's mother, which leads to their mutual destruction.

There were three terms for love in ancient Greek: *philia*, the love of relatives or friends; *eros*, erotic love; and *agape*, the altruistic love described in the New Testament. *Eros* was regarded as a disease, and usually was disastrous in Greek tragedy—Clytemnestra and Aegisthus in the *Oresteia, Medea, Oedipus Tyrannus, Hippolytus*, and the story of *Phaedra*—which is probably the reason that Graham chose to dance all of them. For the ancient Greeks, sex was regarded as a disease that interfered with one's life, and one tried to get over the disturbing effects of its passion as quickly as possible.[23] They prized reason instead. In *Clytemnestra*, Graham emphasizes the sexuality of the relationship of Clytemnestra and her son, who is commanded to kill her to avenge his father's murder at her hands.

The enacting of sexuality on stage was as foreign to ancient Greek tragedy as violence on stage, which was generally reported in a messenger speech. Dance restores the corporality. In *Phaedra*, the heroine is able to dance for Theseus the fictional rape she had so desired to consummate with Hippolytus. In *Night Journey*, Jocasta and the chorus carry a branch with green leaves to suggest the fertility of their union.[24]

A rope binds Jocasta and Oedipus over a bench designed by Noguchi; after he accepted his role as king and husband, Oedipus walks on this bench toward Jocasta. The bench, which resembles dinosaur bones and is punctuated by holes, functions as the marital bed and the throne. The rope defines the relationship of the couple. Tiresias returns, and his jerky movements communicate the curse he lays on them, rather like the admonishments of the minister in *Appalachian Spring* with his dire warnings to the newlyweds. But in this case Tiresias climbs over them on the bench, raises his leg and his staff, then lifts the rope that binds Jocasta and Oedipus together and they fall to the floor. Tiresias leaves. Oedipus takes

FIGURE 14.2 Martha Graham's *Clytemnestra*: Martha Graham as Clytemnestra and Bertram Ross as Orestes. Photo by Carl Van Vechten, 1961. Library of Congress, Prints & Photographs Division, Carl Van Vechten Collection, [reproduction number, e.g., LC-USZ62-54231].

up the rope and throws it to the ground as if he were rejecting the defiling relationship as revealed by Tiresias. He takes up Jocasta's brooch that fastens her robe and mimes stabbing out his eyes. He leaves. Jocasta rises, looks for her brooch, doesn't find it. She twists and her robe falls to the floor. Underneath, she is dressed in a white shift for death, a bride of death (the Japanese wore white when they committed hara-kiri). Jocasta takes up the rope, ties it around her neck and falls dead. Tiresias reenters and walks over Jocasta's body and past her diagonally. He and fate have won.

In the original, Jocasta's dead body is found by Oedipus, but in this dance, her death follows his leaving. Her intention to kill herself is turned into reality, as dance illustrates their dire history. It is a brilliant production and provides insight into the myth. Just as in Taymor's production of Stravinsky's *Oedipus Rex*, the woman is center stage, and the man to whom she gave birth is a puppet by comparison with this powerful Jocasta.

FIGURE 14.3 Martha Graham's *Clytemnestra*: Vengeance, even if ordered by Apollo, is difficult for a son who loves. Photo by Philippe Halsman, Magnum Photos.

Both versions reverse the Sophoclean tragedy, which shows instead a victory for Oedipus in the triumphant spirit of a man who refuses to give up. Music and dance, and the intention of the creators feminized their versions of this drama that concentrate on Jocasta. Graham shows Jocasta overshadowing Oedipus in dance, whereas Stravinsky's music and arias allow her to triumph over Oedipus in his opera.

In most of Graham's representations of the Greek tragic heroines, they are left suffering, just as Graham herself suffered so much in her life. But in both her case and the heroines she represented, this suffering was translated into impeccable art.

Another great interpreter of Greek tragedy in dance is Ariane Mnouchkine. She said she established Le Théâtre du Soleil to express truth in life: her sun heats up imagination ("*Le Théâtre du soleil exprime la verité dans la vie: le soleil rechauffe l'imagination*").[25] She says the heating of the imagination also comes from the body. She adds that in antiquity music was joined to theater, and she considers it essential for hers. Having learned from the suffering of her father as a Russian immigrant to France, and from the death of her grandparents at Auschwitz, her work conveys her political truths. She wants her theater to be a place where people get along, appreciate each other for their individuality, a place where no one oppresses another.

Like Graham, Mnouchkine uses dance as an interpretive tool in *Les Atrides*, her version of Aeschylus's *Oresteia*, prefaced by Euripides's *Iphigenia at Aulis* to help explain why

Clytemnestra does what she does.[26] Whereas Sophocles and Aeschylus show Agamemnon as a hero and justified in taking his daughter's life because it was ordered by the gods (although Aeschylus shows more ambiguity than Sophocles, who dealt with the theme in his *Electra*), Euripides shows Agamemnon as a power-hungry coward, cornered by corrupt priests. The validity of whether the command comes from the gods is questionable. What is not questionable is that Agamemnon will do anything not to lose at Troy.

Mnouchkine uses a larger-than-life alienating approach, which at the same time absorbs a person into her new complex point of view. As Adrian Kiernander said of Mnouchkine's work, "Her productions have at times even been compared with the theaters of classical Greece and of Shakespeare and his contemporaries, which are sometimes perceived as unifying their society by providing shared experiences which reach across class boundaries and by giving the social discourse a set of common reference points."[27] Dance is at the core of it. She uses elaborate white and black makeup emphasizing the features like a mask, a multicultural cast, and multicultural traditions. Kathakali with its makeup and dance is the major influence in *Les Atrides*, but other influences range from East to West via the Middle East: India, Japan, Armenia, Brazil, Spain, and elsewhere. Cassandra, "coming from the East," namely Troy, wears a white robe similar to a kimono, showing the most Asian influence. Like Graham, Mnouchkine eschews realism.

One main difference between her work and Graham's is that the latter transforms the ancient myths into just music and dance, whereas Mnouchkine adds text, and the music chosen is often the handmaiden to the text. The choral text is never sung or chanted by all of them, but clearly articulated usually by one, and usually between the dances so the words can be understood. Like Graham, her music is mostly percussive, preferring gongs and drums to violins, thereby serving the dance as well as the text.

Each chorus differs and conveys its own unique character. The Kathakali costumes are elaborate and swirl as the actors and dancers spin, as young girls in the *Iphigenia*. Their costumes are of light colors, gold with ornamental black, and cheery young headdresses. The old men in the *Agamemnon* have heavy black makeup with beards, turbans, and huge skirts that swirl as they turn (see fig. 14.5); red and gold dominates, heavier colors than for the young girls in the first play. In the *Choephoroi*, the women carry on the theme of red, gold, and black, but they begin to look like harpies, or other birds of prey (see fig. 14.4). In the *Eumenides*, three of the Furies resemble dangerous street-smart bag ladies, dressed in rags and wearing ashen makeup, with heaving black heightening their features. The rest are baboon-like dogs that both crouch and stand up menacingly. Special masks that add to their ferocity were constructed by Erhard Stiefel.

There is a progression, or regression here, from the promise of youth in the *Iphigenia* to a descent into the animal from the corruption of greed, lust for power, and oppressive violence enacted toward one's fellows by the actions of the adults in each play.

The dancing in all the plays but the last is well described by Kiernander:

> Usually during these sequences [dances with choreography] the choral members are arranged rank and file, and the dancing consists mainly of stamping, stepping, and kicking movements with the arms lifted and gesturing, and occasional leaps high in the air or whirling spins at moments of climax. In the *Eumenides* they are more static.[28]

Whereas Mnouchkine did not have the simplicity of the Noguchi set, she derived much of what she did in this drama from Graham. Both used the exoticism of the costume to evoke the period of ancient Greece. Graham, as noted above, performed her Clytemnestra in a bullfighting ring in Lisbon.

Both also had companies in which the actors were dedicated and wanted to work simply because of the reputation of the company and not for the salary. The work of Mnouchkine, however, was more political, whereas Graham's was more for the art of dance itself and the passions of human nature. Mnouchkine claimed the main issues in *Les Atrides* were about betrayal, namely how the play allegorizes the actions of the French Résistance during World War II. Betrayal was the name of the game, something to which Mnouchkine was particularly sensitive.

When not on tour, the performances took place at La Cartoucherie de Vincennes, a former armory on the outskirts of Paris and the company's home. There were no reserved seats (Madame was a dedicated enemy of elitism). As one entered the building one saw pits filled with large skirted figurines, which resembled the statues of the buried army to accompany in death the Chinese Emperor Qin Shi Huang (259 BC–210 BC) of China. But Mnouchkine's statues represented the dancers from the chorus who would take part in this modern enactment of an ancient tragedy; eventually there were three pits to accommodate the three choruses. The buried dead come to life through performance and drama just like the ancient tragedies themselves, resurrected on the modern stage. Mnouchkine's music was independently excellent, multicultural and eclectic like Graham's.

The main musicians and composers for *Les Atrides* showed again cultural collaboration: Jean-Jacques Lemêtre and Maria Serao. Two hundred forty instruments from forty-one different countries are used: the *derboukka* next to the clarinet. A sea of sound dominates from the moment one enters the building and throughout the performance. It is percussive, chromatic, and ranges from minimalist to folk as the keys from various cultures dissolve into each other. There are many Middle Eastern dances of triumph celebrating Iphigenia's marriage, Agamemnon's return, and in the *Choephoroi*, the slaying of the tyrants, and the final acquittal of Orestes in the *Eumenides*. There are other dances to celebrate Iphigenia's death and Clytemnestra's murder of Agamemnon and Cassandra, dances with Spanish and Indian overtones.

When the gods appear there is the sound of a whirring instrument, like the "bull-roarer," which would be fitting for a bullring. It also reminds one of the favorable winds, needed for victory at Troy, purchased by Agamemnon at the cost of his daughter's life.

The colors are striking, red, gold, black, and white. In the *Iphigenia*, Clytemnestra and Agamemnon are both in black, whereas Iphigenia the victim, is in white, which, as we said above, was the formal color for death in Japan, the color of Graham's Jocasta's gown when she will purge herself of guilt by suicide: shedding her black robe. In the dances, Agamemnon is regal, like a king; Achilles obsessed with himself, checking his appearance in a mirror that is part of an ornament dangling from his costume. Clytemnestra is shattered when Iphigenia's death is announced, and Achilles holds his hand over Clytemnestra's mouth to silence her.

The dance Iphigenia performs to convince her father to let her live is heart-rending and full of innocence and devotion as she finally, for his sake and Greece's, agrees to her own death. She believes in the ideals (defense, self-sacrifice) that she has been told but that only mask the true reasons for the war: power and wealth.

Clytemnestra, performed by the Brazilian Juliana Carneiro da Cunha conveys her suffering in the last scene through spasms of choked tears in the ultimate silence of agony. The dancing chorus members are giddy girls, all dressed in white. They came to Aulis for a

FIGURE 14.4 *Les Atrides* by Ariane Mnouchkine. In the *Choephori* (*Libation Bearers*), Clytemnestra (Juliana Carneiro da Cunha), celebrates with her chorus in, and dances her triumph in a bull ring: she slew the bull, her husband Agamemnon, to avenge her daughter, Iphigenia's death. Her blouse is still spattered with his blood. Photo by Martine Franck, Magnum Photos.

pretended marriage (the pretended excuse Agamemnon gave to Clytemnestra to bring their daughter to Aulis, when in fact she was to be sacrificed). White also seems to be the costume for the young. At the end of the *Iphigenia*, Clytemnestra is still, while the giddy girls dance around her, accepting the obviously false information given by a messenger that Iphigenia was saved at the last minute.

Just as Graham's dancers showed sexual ambiguity, so Mnouchkine's chorus fluidly assumed different roles. The chorus members are mainly dancers, and Catherine Schaub, the chorus leader, delivers their lines for them, resulting in clear enunciation for the audience to understand the text. The doubling of roles also adds commentary, besides blurring the sexual distinctions, and at times is humorous, since Abkarian (whom we remembered played Agamemnon and Orestes) also plays Cilissa, Orestes's nurse in the *Choephoroi*. She (he) speaks of the times when Orestes surprised her by wetting himself, another light moment in a very heavy drama.

The bullfighting ring is like a crucible for the action: there's a double gate for entrances at the back of the stage, and circular walls on which the actors climb freely.

There is another entrance from the back of the audience, who are seated on a frame of seats that resemble the ancient Greek theater in a skeletal form. The dead bodies are rolled in from this rear entrance, on Mnouchkine's equivalent of what the ancient Greeks used, the *ekkyklêma*. This way of entry is also comparable to the *hanamichi*, or the walkway in Kabuki over which some actors enter and exit, bisecting the audience.

It is certainly a way of making sure the audience is implicated, and no one leaves without *mains sales*.

The second in this tetralogy, *Les Atrides*, is the *Agamemnon* that began Aeschylus's trilogy. Mnouchkine biases the audience in Clytemnestra's favor by showing how she was deceived by Agamemnon. She also draws parallels that the audience is bound to notice. Iphigenia danced for Agamemnon, Cassandra also dances, and both are played by Nirupama Nityanandan, a young Indian dancer/actress. She brings gestures and dance from the Indian tradition of Kathakali. The dances and music flow freely with each performance and change according to inspiration.

Both Iphigenia and Cassandra are victims of Agamemnon, and Clytemnestra is bound to feel sympathy for Cassandra, who resembles her own young daughter (and both are played

FIGURE 14.5 *Les Atrides* by Ariane Mnouchkine. From the *Agamemnon*, chorus of old men, dressed in the Kathakali tradition. Simon Abkarian (Agamemnon) is in front. Photo by Martine Franck, Magnum Photos.

by the same actress). Both of these young women are princesses sacrificed to Agamemnon's lust for power. Clytemnestra caresses Cassandra as she caressed Iphigenia in the earlier play. Cassandra (another princess), daughter of Priam, king of Troy, is Agamemnon's concubine and war prize, sacrificed simply to his lust and pride. In the original, Clytemnestra views this girl as an insult to her, but in antiquity such prizes were usual. Nevertheless, in Greek tragedy, the men who bring concubines home usually end up dead, murdered by their wives. One thinks of Neoptolemus, who brought home as his trophy prisoner Andromache, who was married to Hector, the great hero of Troy. However, he was married to Menelaus's daughter, Hermione (Euripides's *Andromache*), who then had him killed. Heracles also brought home as his prisoner and prize a king's daughter, Iole. His wife Deianeira, was not amused (Sophocles's *Women of Trachis*). She killed him by sending him a love charm, a poisoned cloak, presumably to win his love back. These husbands, including Agamemnon, also entrust their concubines to their wives' care, which is hardly the tender response their husbands wanted.

However, Mnouchkine by her casting and dances draws parallels so that Clytemnestra shows sympathy for Cassandra as just another young girl victimized by Agamemnon, as she herself was when Agamemnon took her from her first husband and killed the baby she bore to another man.

This was revealed by Euripides in his play *Iphigenia at Aulis*, but not by Aeschylus in his *Agamemnon*. Mnouchkine has the sacrifice enacted before the audience in the *Iphigenia*. The cycle of vengeance is initiated. Iphigenia's sacrifice is symbolic of all young people sacrificed in wars. The old politicians declare war, but send out the young to fight it, and many young innocent victims fall as "collateral damage."

The watchman announces Agamemnon's victorious return with the Arabic high-pitched tongue trill or ululation (*zaghrata*). In the *Agamemnon*, Clytemnestra wears what looks like a bullfighting costume, with a white shirt-like blouse, black culottes to below the knee, soft black boots, and a sash: she has exchanged her feminine dress for a man's. The text calls her man-hearted, and her vengeance will match the violence that the men used on her daughter and to fight their war. Nevertheless she is a very feminine actress, contrary to many who have played this role, and this femininity adds to her effectiveness.

Clytemnestra expands her role as wife and mother to murderess, a generator of new signs, communicated well in her dance of triumph over Agamemnon, whom she kills like a bull in his arena where he thought he was safe: his own house. Cassandra's body is rolled out along with Agamemnon's; Clytemnestra dances a wild, impassioned dance of triumph to castanets and Spanish rhythms over the two bodies.

Faithful to the original play, she speaks of being watered by Agamemnon's blood like flowers in spring. This rite of spring was the sacrifice of the bull and celebration by the heifer, fertilized by a death when vengeance was her goal. Clytemnestra's lover, Aegisthus, appears dressed like a toreador, and he whirls in a few pirouettes, but through his boastful gestures reveals an essential weakness. Georges Bigot is smaller than Simon Abkarian who plays Agamemnon, and his size matches his character.

All these plays end with dogs barking. *Agamemnon* ends this way, showing the bitch triumphant. So ends also the *Choephoroi* to show that Orestes has descended to the animal level, just as his mother did. Both have lost their humanity by the end of the play, and one wonders if the dogs suggest that all who murder become animals. They will finally appear in the *Eumenides* as familiars of the Furies, who have been called hounds of Zeus. At the end of the *Agamemnon*, Aegisthus appears whining like Clytemnestra's puppy. The old men in the chorus conveyed their weakness by panting as they danced.

All of the plays also end with the actors and actresses dancing and clapping and the audience joins in with clapping, some rise and join in the expressive dance. But the dogs' barking is the final sound and seems to be part of the dance, with its wailing percussive animalistic ominous *basso ostinato*.

The duplication of roles throughout adds commentary to the enacted drama. Just as the same actress played Iphigenia and Cassandra, the two victims (she also plays Electra, not so innocent, but in her own way she is another victim), Abkarian plays Agamemnon and Orestes, the two murderers. Their identity underlines the repetitive cycle of violence.

Other details provide more commentary. In the *Choephoroi* the chorus resemble Furies, dressed in black and egging on Electra and Orestes to kill their mother. Their palms are painted red: *mains* not only *sales*, but bloody: they are also guilty. Like Cassandra's, Clytemnestra's corpse is rolled out before the audience, and her breasts are bared, showing the perversion of a thwarted motherhood.

Clytemnestra shows her breasts to Orestes when she tries to dissuade him from killing her, reminding him she gave birth to him. When her appeal fails, Orestes chases his mother around the bullring, and finally corners her to kill her. He then dances a frenzied dance of triumph that shows his incipient madness: His mother's Furies will drive him mad and chase him until the final trial in the *Eumenides*, where he is acquitted by the gods Athena and Apollo. According to mythology, Athena was born out of her father's head and thinks like a man the same as Clytemnestra did, and Da Cunha, who played Clytemnestra, also plays Athena. Orestes's dance over his mother challenges her repeatedly to rise again, so he can kill her again. Pylades, Orestes's friend, tries to help him remove Clytemnestra's body, but it seems to be enormously heavy . . . it weighs on them like guilt and madness: trying to remove it provides an additional grisly dance. Aegisthus's body also seemed to have enormous weight, and it seems nearly impossible to remove them: a palpable burden of murder.

One of the three main Furies in the *Eumenides* is played by Nirupama Nityandan, which is certainly important symbolically as she played both the guiltless victims Iphigenia and Cassandra; the other two are played by Catherine Schaub, the choral leader from the other plays, and Myrian Azancot, another chorus member. Da Cunha plays her own ghost as Clytemnestra, besides Athena as mentioned above. Apollo is played by Shahrokh Meshkin Ghalam.

This final play had subdued colors. Grays, blacks, and whites replace the red and gold of the victorious and fallen royalty. The Furies are dressed in gray rags; they seem exhausted; they wheeze in their sleep, and black blood seems to drip from their eyes; the young gods Apollo and Athena are lively and dressed in white and gold. The old gods ooze death, whereas the young ones seem bursting with life. Orestes appears in black, gold, and red: He still flaunts his bloodstains and his royalty. He is clearly on the side of the young gods, and they will protect him.

The priestess of Apollo's temple of Delphi enters at the beginning, escorted by men in black like the Japanese *kurogo* (they move the sets and help with costume changes and are conventionally accepted as invisible). She recounts her horror at seeing the Furies. Apollo, dressed in white and gold, and carrying a golden bow, tells Orestes to flee to the Parthenon, the shrine of Athena in Athens, and ask her for protection. The ghost of Clytemnestra enters from a vomitorium in the center of the audience, just as her body did in the earlier play.

She voices her complaints to unseen Furies about their inaction and then is dragged back to Hades by the black figures, who at this point could be considered slaves of hell (this of course puts Hell/Hades in the middle of audience).

Apollo chases the Furies out of his temple with his bow and arrows. The women here are presented not only as the avengers of wrongs but also as uncivilized beasts (the dog-ape followers), and male prejudice, which represents the female as barbaric and irrational, if not animalistic, contributed to keeping patriarchy strong in ancient Greece.[29] It is also a way of holding the colonized down (the Japanese were represented as grinning apes during World War II by the Americans; the English used genealogical tables to show the Irish as closer to the apes, to say nothing of how Africans have been represented by their oppressors). The Furies here are roaming illustrations of the id, even though they represent the super ego by enforcing punishments for blood crimes. In this, Mnouchkine replicates some of the basic concerns of human psychology as Graham did in her dances. Dance can represent the subconscious in drama best.

Athena protects Orestes in Athens, and the Furies can only roam on top of the walls of her temple. Orestes is tried in a court of law. The audience is enlisted to be the jury by Mnouchkine. Apollo argues absurdly that a woman is only the receptacle for the male seed (something supported by Aristotelian biology, *De Generatione animalium* IV.1.763 b.30), so Clytemnestra wasn't Orestes's mother whereas Agamemnon was his father, so he didn't commit matricide in avenging his father. The Furies argue that shedding blood demands the shedding of blood. The votes are even.

Athena breaks the tie by voting for Orestes (that she is played by the actress who played Clytemnestra provides ironic commentary by suggesting a type of coercion of the female in this miscarriage of justice). Orestes leaves, prancing his victory, and is escorted off as was Clytemnestra after killing Agamemnon. Athena pleads with the Furies, then sits like a Buddha; as one starts to attack her she turns and glares, and the Fury calms down, now transformed into one of the Eumenides, the kindly ones. As Athena embraces one of the Furies who accepts what is offered, we see once again Clytemnestra embracing Iphigenia, the avatars of the same actresses. The Furies dance their victory and defeat. They leave down the center of the audience as Orestes did, having accepted new honors, waving like Queen Elizabeth, and smiling ghoulishly. We know they will be back, just like the thoughts of the subconscious, the return of the repressed. One can exclude them from the city but not the human mind.

The dog baboons rush back onto the stage and begin to attack each other. The cast reenter dancing, and the audience applauds, but at the very end the beasts are left alone, menacingly, threatening the audience. Dance can convey both the godlike and the bestial. The audience continue clapping, but one could see how as the ape dogs at the end approach ferociously that their approbation turns to fear, sometimes the point of good drama: being able to look Medusa (one's own fears) in the face, without turning to stone.

Martha Graham used her plays to communicate her American heritage and her particular drive to be the leader of her field. She drove her devotees mercilessly to achieve the same heights that she did. She included all the races and sexual orientations. Perfection however, rather than politics, was her major thrust. But she had her honor.

Mnouchkine seeks the same perfection in her theater, and also drives her troupe to its limits. She runs her theater rather like a monastery, with strict schedules and no deviation from what "Madame" decides. She has a political conscience and always has the courage to deliver performances in countries where the message could have the troupe deported, imprisoned, or worse. She is a fearless defender of the underdog, and the way women are represented in *Les Atrides* shows how much Mnouchkine is against their oppression or abuse. She also shows clearly the disastrous cycle of vengeance following vengeance and the destructiveness of war that is endlessly repeated throughout history. The lessons seem never to be learned.

Her troupe is also inclusive of all the races, besides different sexual orientations. Both artists, Graham and Mnouchkine, reach the pinnacle of great art. Their messages touch the human heart, and dance keeps its beat.

Their dance drama has implicated and educated the audience. No one is immune to pain and guilt. By the use of music and dance in these plays the emotions of the audience are touched in a subliminal way that communicates to all the senses. The powerful dancers and directors that brought this about have not simply resurrected ancient drama but also shown that drama and theater live in our hearts and minds. They allow us to make informed choices rather than merely acquiesce, just as ancient Greek drama educated its citizens in the world's first democracy.

NOTES

1. McDonald and Walton, eds., 2002. "The Irish and Greek Tragedy," 37–86.
2. Pickard-Cambridge, 1991. See also David, 2007.
3. Christian Meier, 1993; and J. Peter Euben, ed., 1986.
4. Tyler Jo Smyth, "Reception or Deception? Approaching Greek Dance through Vase-Painting," in Macintosh, ed., 2010, 77–98.
5. See T. B. L. Webster, 1970.
6. Lillian B. Lawler, 1964, rpt. 1974.
7. M. L. West, 1992.
8. See Lucian, 1936, rpt. 2011, V:209–289. See also Yana Zarifi, "Chorus and Dance in the Ancient World," in McDonald and Walton, eds., 2007, 227–46.
9. Foley, 2012.
10. Russell Freedman, 1998, 111.
11. *Martha Graham Dance Company*, 1976.
12. "The *Medea* of Euripides," Knox, 1979, 295–322.
13. Freedman, 1998, 112.
14. Martha Graham, 1991, 151.
15. Gerald Newman and Eleanor Newman Layfield, 1998, 79–80.
16. Julie Taymor also used the image of the umbilical cord/red ribbon explicitly in her version of *Oedipus Rex*, danced by a master of butoh, Min Tanaka, and sung by an operatic virtuoso, Philip Langridge. Min Tanaka as Oedipus dances the moment he mates with Jocasta by falling on her body, as Oedipus falls on Graham as Jocasta in *Night Journey*. The singer Jocasta is played by Jessye Norman, and this casting shows the new strength of women in twentieth-century opera. Norman's Jocasta is a woman to be taken seriously. In her case, mother really knew best, and she and even the music overwhelm Oedipus. Oedipus is a frail equivalent to her, both lyrically and physically. In Taymor's version performed in Japan, there is more political commentary in the milling chorus at the beginning. They resemble the victims of Hiroshima and Nagasaki (the putative beginning of butoh to commemorate that tragedy, called the "dance of darkness"). Their bodies are contorted

and covered with ash that looks as if the flesh is peeling off of the dancers' bodies as they execute butoh figures. There is a huge carrion bird that flies overhead. This replicates the plague cited at the beginning of the Sophoclean play. "Stravinsky's *Oedipus Rex*: The King in a Trap," in McDonald, 2001, 133–57. Julie Taymor's version was made in Japan in 1992, Cami, Decca Music Group.

17. *"Medea è mobile*: The Many Faces of Medea in Opera," in Hall, Macintosh, and Taplin, eds., 2000. See also McDonald, 2013, 293–337.
18. Graham, 1991, 266–67.
19. Ibid., 267.
20. *Martha Graham in Performance, A Dancer's World*, filmed in 1957, Kultur; *Night Journey* in 1961; and *Appalachian Spring* in 1958. See also Vanda Zajko, "Martha Graham's *Night Journey*," in Macintosh, 2010, 344.
21. Vanda Zajko, "Martha Graham's Night Journey," in Macintosh, ed., 2010, 344.
22. Graham, 1991, 214–15.
23. McDonald, 1990.
24. This same device was used by Theodoros Terzopoulos in his production of Heiner Müller's *Verkommenes Ufer Medea Material Landschaft mit Argonauten*. He has Medea remember her union with Jason, and beat herself with a branch in her vaginal area. His actor's movements are tortured and twisted, based on his experience of firewalkers and mourners in Northern Thrace after their defeat in World War II. He also uses expressive movement to convey his text. He shows a world as destroyed by men and their materialism as Jason's drive destroyed Medea emotionally. See in McDonald, 1992a, "Theodoros Terzopoulos's Production of Heiner Müller's *Medeamaterial*: Myth as Matter," 147–69.
25. *The Adventure of the Théâtre du Soleil*, see Videos.
26. McDonald, 1992b, 1992c.
27. Kiernander, 1993, 6.
28. Kiernander,1993, 137. He also suggests this was indicative of the original fifth-century BC use of the chorus in Greek tragedy and cites John J. Winkler, "The Ephebes' Song: *Tragôidia* and *Polis*," 1990, 20–62.
29. Zeitlin, 1978, rpt. 1996, 341–74.

BIBLIOGRAPHY

David, A. P. *The Dance of the Muses: Choral Theory and Ancient Greek Poetics* Oxford: Oxford University Press, 2007.

Euben, J. Peter, ed. *Greek Tragedy and Political Theory*. Los Angeles: University of California Press, 1986.

Foley, Helene P. *Reimagining Greek Tragedy on the American Stage*. Sather Classical Lectures 70. Berkeley/Los Angeles/London: University of California Press, 2012.

Freedman Russell. *Martha Graham: A Dancer's Life*. New York: Clarion, 1998.

Graham, Martha. *Blood Memory: An Autobiography*. New York: Doubleday, 1991.

Hall, Edith, Fiona Macintosh, and Oliver Taplin, eds. *Medea in Performance 1500–2000*, Oxford: Legenda, 2000.

Kiernander, Adrian. *Ariane Mnouchkine and the Théâtre du Soleil*. Directors in Perspective. Cambridge: Cambridge University Press, 1993.

Knox, Bernard. *Word and Action: Essays on the Ancient Theatre*. Baltimore and London: Johns Hopkins University Press, 1979.

Lawler, Lillian B. *The Dance of the Ancient Greek Theatre.* Iowa City: University of Iowa Monograph, 1964; rpt. 1974.

Lucian. *On Dance.* Translated by A. M. Harmon. Loeb Classical Library. Cambridge, MA, and London: Harvard University Press, 1936; rpt. 2011.

Macintosh, Fiona, ed. *The Ancient Dancer in the Modern World.* Oxford: Oxford University Press, 2010.

McDonald, Marianne. "The Infected Hero: Love Ritualized as Disease in Sophocles's *Women of Trachis.*" In *Proceedings of the Sixth International Meeting on Ancient Greek Drama,* Delphi, Greece. Athens: European Cultural Centre of Delphi, 1990.

———. *Ancient Sun, Modern Light: Greek Drama on the Modern Stage.* New York: Columbia University Press, 1992a.

———. "The Atrocities of *Les Atrides*: Mnouchkine's Tragic Vision." *Theatre Forum* 1, no. 1 (1992b): 12–19.

———. "The Menace of Mnouchkine's *Eumenides*: Midnight Madness at Montpellier." *TheatreForum* 1, no. 2 (1992c): 11–17.

———. *Sing Sorrow: Classics, History, and Heroines in Opera.* Westport, CT, and London: Greenwood Press, 2001.

———. *The Craft of Athol Fugard: Space, Time, and Silence.* Los Angeles: Murasaki Books, 2012.

———. "*Medea, Queen of Colchester.*" In Kevin J. Wetmore Jr., *Black Medea: Adaptations for Modern Plays.* Amherst, New York: Cambria Press, 2013.

McDonald, Marianne, and J. Michael Walton, eds. *Amid Our Troubles: Irish Versions of Greek Tragedy.* London: Methuen, 2002.

———, eds. *The Cambridge Companion to Greek and Roman Theatre.* Cambridge: Cambridge University Press, 2007.

Meier, Christian. *The Political Art of Greek Tragedy.* Translated by Andrew Webber. Baltimore: Johns Hopkins University Press, 1993.

Newman, Gerald, and Eleanor Newman Layfield. *Martha Graham: Founder of Modern Dance.* New York: Grolier, 1998.

Pickard-Cambridge, Sir Arthur. *The Dramatic Festivals of Athens.* Oxford: Clarendon Press, 1953; rpt. 1991. 2nd ed. rev. with corrections by John Gould and D. M. Lewis, 1988.

Webster, T. B. L. *The Greek Chorus.* London: Methuen, 1970.

West, M. L. *Ancient Greek Music.* Oxford: Clarendon, 1992.

Wetmore, Kevin J. Jr. *Black Medea: Adaptations for Modern Plays.* Amherst, New York, Cambria Press, 2013.

Winkler, John J. "The Ephebes' Song: *Tragôidia* and *Polis.*" In *Nothing to Do with Dionysos? Athenian Drama in Its Social Context,* edited by John J. Winkler and Froma I. Zeitlin. Princeton: Princeton University Press, 1990.

Zarifi, Yana. "Chorus and Dance in the Ancient World." In *The Cambridge Companion to Greek and Roman Theatre,* edited by Marianne McDonald and J. Michael Walton, 227–46. Cambridge: Cambridge University Press, 2007.

Zeitlin, Froma I. "The Dynamics of Misogyny: Myth and Mythmaking in Aeschylus's *Oresteia.*" *Arethusa* 11 (1978): 149–84. Reprinted in her *Playing the Other: Gender and Society in Classical Greek Literature,* 87–119. Chicago and London: University of Chicago Press, 1996.

VIDEOS

Martha Graham in Performance, A Dancer's World. 1957, 1958, 1961 Kultur.

Martha Graham Dance Company. Nonesuch Dance Collection, Thirteen/WNET Nashville, Tennessee, 1976.

Mnouchkine, Ariane. *The Adventure of the Théâtre du Soleil.* Video by Catherine Vilpoux, Arte Editions, 2009.

Taymor, Julie. *Oedipus Rex.* Cami, Decca Music Group, 1992.

SECTION IV

HISTORIO-GRAPHICAL PRESENCE AND ABSENCE

CHAPTER 15

THE POST NATYAM COLLECTIVE

Innovating Indian Dance and Theater via Abhinaya and Multimedia

KETU H. KATRAK

The Post Natyam Collective creates contemporary approaches to South Asian dance ... These forms share a focus on rhythm, facial expression, hand gestures, and story-telling. We make these forms relevant to our contemporary realities by investigating them through scholarship, activism, and artistic innovation.

www.postnatyam.net[1]

A feminist postmodernism forces us to confront questions which otherwise remain unasked and that in engaging with them we also find our academic practice and our politics undergoing some degree of transformation and change. There is much to be said for opening discussion out, for taking risks with our ideas, for exercising our disciplines, taking them for a walk and exploring the points at which seem to reach a limit.

Angela Mcrobbie, *Postmodernism and Popular Culture*[2]

A deeply absorbing dance and theater world, with hybrid layering of movement and voice, script, and silence is created in The Post Natyam Collective's latest multimedia work, *SUNOH! Tell Me Sister* (hereafter *SUNOH!*), involving collaborations with visual artists, media designers, and musicians. *SUNOH!* recuperates the mostly erased history of South Asian courtesans, connoisseurs of the arts, connecting them politically and provocatively to contemporary South Asian women in domestic violence situations. The use of movement with theatrical script and multimedia evoke a postmodern fragmentation of time periods and spatial locations, imaginatively recreating female foremothers of Indian dance, namely, courtesans' past lives when they also provided sexual services to patrons, to contemporary realities of violence against women's bodies and minds. *SUNOH!* incorporates movement based on the Collective's varied training in Indian classical dance styles (bharatanatyam, kathak, kuchipudi) of portraying (*bhavas*) *rasas* (emotions) via *abhinaya* (gesture language to narrate stories and evoke emotions), along with their study of modern dance, ballet contact improvisation, theater, and yoga. The Collective originated in 2004 with founding members, Shyamala Moorty, Sandra Chatterjee, and Anjali Tata-Hudson. In 2007–08, Cynthia Ling Lee joined the Collective as a core member. Sangita Shresthova is their affiliated media choreographer.

Similar to several time and place zones co-existing in *SUNOH!* via the dancers' bodies on stage, live-video feed—where we see the same dancer in two locations simultaneously on stage—such creative juxtaposition of temporal and geographical locations is reflected in the Collective's transnational members who live in Kansas, Munich/New Delhi, and Long Beach, Santa Monica. They work collectively via a process where they take turns creating assignments, and working on them via movement and research, uploading work on video, and meeting virtually online. This process is delineated on their blog: www.postnatyam. blogspot.com. They bring the real and virtual together as seen in the opening of *SUNOH!*, when a visual image is projected on stage. This visual is a square, split four ways in "Cyber Chat," in which the four artists, each occupying one square, meet online and create choreography. This innovative method is rooted in negotiating space—physical space as well as giving space to each member's diverse training.[3]

The Collective is committed to scholarly research and a "border-crossing approach to contemporary South Asian performance," challenging the lines dividing "art-making and academic scholarship." Even as they connect to today's global reality, they remain attentive to "historical erasures and aesthetic constructs embedded within [South Asian] traditions" (www.postnatyam.net). *SUNOH!* excavates the courtesan tradition of the mid-eighteenth-century, when some of them were independently wealthy. In recent times, we find the sad reality of widows in parts of India who run away to become courtesans in order to escape cruel treatment by their families.[4] The use of the courtesan's body evokes other kinds of bodily abuse, such as domestic brutality endured by South Asian women who remain "good wives," upholding traditions that strangle them. Such a link across historical time and geographical space evokes Ernesto Laclau's notion of "radical incommensurability of different social groupings and divisions (age, sex, ethnicity, class, nationality) and takes as his starting point the unlikeness of their unity, outside the incidental, the unplanned, the contingent" (Mcrobbie, 6). Although the connections among courtesans and contemporary domestic abuse survivors evoke a solidarity, *SUNOH!'s* artists do not flatten out significant differences in the interest of asserting political alliance. In addition to courtesans' significant contributions to Indian art forms, especially the unique legacy of *abhinaya*, "we are interested," remarks Cynthia, "in the stories of the courtesans' lived realities and how these stories might explode the poetic surface of what we've learned as classical dancers."

Collective members also create solo work that may, at times, inspire and intersect with Collective projects. For instance, Shyamala Moorty's solo dance-cum-theater work, *Carrie's Web*, which represents the seamy realities of domestic violence in the South Asian American community in Los Angeles, partly inspired *SUNOH!* The latter was created jointly by the entire Collective in their multivocal, multiyear, long-distance process. Further, although *SUNOH!* was performed by US-based Collective members, the work emerged from the participation of all Collective members. The theme of domestic violence explored by Moorty quite incredibly with humor in *Carrie's Web* is developed further, layered, and given a

FIGURE 15.1 Post Natyam Collective: Cynthia Ling Lee (front), Shyamala Moorty (middle), Anjali Tata (back) in publicity photo for *SUNOH!* Photographer: Andrei Andreev.

different context in SUNOH! that invokes the courtesan tradition and draws parallels to the objectification of women's bodies in contemporary times.

In *Carrie's Web*, Moorty creates a "spider" character, Carrie, who is based on "the assertive, independent and headstrong main character," notes *India Post's* Melissa Acoba, "from Sex and the City, a popular cable TV show that catalyzed a more candid dialogues of women's issues and relationships."[5] Carrie comments on the human father's domestic violence on the mother and silencing her. Carrie is puzzled as to why humans, who are so much bigger than spiders, are afraid of them. "Why are they afraid of us little old things? Is that why I've seen the father human swatting and smashing the mother human?" Is he **afraid?**" (original emphasis). At another point, Carrie comments on the violence: "I would never let a man beat me up like that. In the spider world, if he acts up, we just eat him. Humans have so much to learn." This is taken up in *SUNOH!* when Cynthia, playing the courtesan, remarks that if a patron steps over a line of acceptable behavior, "he is thrown out of the *kotha*," i.e., the living space shared by a community of courtesans.

Carrie's Web theatrically explores the reality of human fear, where it comes from and how humans deals with it; why, at times, they express their fears via violence; and why, at other times, they are rendered silent (as the battered mother is). The staging, that divides the human and spider worlds, raises parallels between human fear of spiders and of violence versus Carrie mounting a resistance when she urges her compatriots "to take pride in (their) spider body." The spider body and the human body are both victims of violence who need to heal from their beaten down self-esteem, and reconnect with their bruised bodies and souls. Carrie's call to spiders "all over the house" to go on a hunger strike subtly voices how victims of violence must resist oppression and fight back.

FIGURE 15.2 Shyamala Moorty as "the spider" character in *Carrie's Web*. Photographer: Jen Cleary.

Moorty developed *Carrie's Web* when she was working in Los Angeles–based TeAda Theatre Works. TeAda received a grant to link performing artists to community health organizations whose leaders were interested in "how theatre/performance could enhance their work," noted Moorty to me in an interview. She was put in touch with an organization for Muslim women and youth in Los Angeles, called NISWA, that supports women survivors of domestic violence, although this social problem exists among South Asian Americans of different religions. Moorty worked with NISWA for nine months, meeting once a month in a library inside a mosque using yoga and performance-related exercises to elicit memory and encourage participants to speak about repressed violence experiences. Moorty created movement and script from oral testimony. She worked with theater director D'Lo, a Sri Lankan American transgendered artist whose skillful staging made this a successful show in TeAda Theater's "Healing Aloud" series. Along with the context of domestic

FIGURE 15.3 Shyamala Moorty depicting the *rasa* (emotion) of fear in *Carrie's Web*. Photographer: Jen Cleary.

violence, the two creative minds of Shyamala and D'Lo forged a work that powerfully "bears truths."

SUNOH! draws on information from a Los Angeles–based nonprofit community organization, South Asian Network's staff and support group for domestic violence survivors. Collective members not only integrate their training in Indian classical dance along with theatrical use of script and innovative staging but also undertake postmodern innovations of these dance styles. They bring their contemporary sensibilities to bear on their imaginative embodiment of significant aspects of Indian classical dance, such as *nrtta* (footwork in different rhythms) and especially the expression of (*bhavas*) *rasas* via *abhinaya*. In *Carrie's Web*, Moorty uses the integral linking of dance and theater in Indian aesthetics by intermingling the two, allowing one to flow into the other, or deliberately disjointing one from the other. Moorty reinvents *nrtta* as "inverted bharatanatyam" (*araimandi,*

FIGURE 15.4 Shyamala Moorty depicts the fear of spiders and parallels that to a domestic victim being assaulted. Photographer: Jen Cleary.

instead of open knees, turns inward with knees knocking as in fear, body collapsing when enduring physical or verbal blows in domestically violent situations); *abhinaya* evokes several of the *navarasas* (nine primary emotions—here, the primary emotion of fear leading to violence) with postmodern breaks in movement: *abhinaya* is interwoven with verbal storytelling and dialogue with imagined characters on stage. Moorty's syncretic interplay of *nrtta, abhinaya*, and words make the audience think in a Brechtian manner of social change. The overall style of *Carrie's Web* "defines categorization," notes Nirmala Nataraj in *India Currents*, who describes it "as postmodern dance, diaspora dance theatre or just a darn good show."[6]

The combining of dance and theater is a cornerstone of Indian aesthetics and philosophical traditions, hence, *natya* translated strictly as drama, integrally includes dance, music, gesture, dramaturgical elements, and the actor/dancer's expression of emotion (via the face, hand-gestures, i.e., *mudras*, and the entire body). These concepts were expounded initially in the ancient Indian treatise the *Natyasastra* (2nd to 5th centuries BCE).

Among the *Natyasastra*'s thirty-seven chapters there is a discussion of the qualities of ideal audience members called *rasikssa* or *sahrdaysas*, i.e., those who are knowledgeable and appreciative and who respond to a performance with open hearts. The very title of Post Natyam Collective's dance-theater piece, *SUNOH! Tell Me Sister* evokes connections among the performers and audience as in the word "sunoh," which translates as "listen," emphasizing the auditory as much as the visual, and "tell me" indicating verbal communication as well as other ways of "telling" via movement, music, and in our contemporary times via video images and other multimedia tools. The piece opens with audience involvement, a feature of contemporary performance art as well as the ancient *Natyasastra*, where the effects of *rasa* are transmuted from the performer to the audience members, who are active recipients. As spectators enter the auditorium to see *SUNOH!*, they receive note cards to write down stereotypes about themselves or what they may know about or may have experienced. These are collected and projected on screen—Oriental, exotic, curry, among others—making the audience into participants.[7]

RASA AND ABHINAYA IN THE NATYASASTRA

The theory of the *rasas* in the *Natyasastra* is a sophisticated psychophysical dramatic representation of emotions that are conveyed via multiple means, in particular, movement and dance along with theatrical acting accompanied by script or nonverbal gesture language and the entire body. *Rasa* is felt—bodily, mentally, and emotionally; however, because it is not seen in itself, it marks a departure from focusing mainly on what is seen in analyzing dance or drama. The symbiotic relationship between what the performer feels (*rasa*) and what the audience receives (also *rasa*) involves a psychologically sophisticated response. *Rasas* are conveyed partly via color and an emphasis on spectacle. The overall goal of *natya* is to create a kind of theatrical affect that at the end of a dramatic show infuses a sense of harmony in the audience.

Although *rasa* as such is not visible, the theatrical representation includes impact, effect, and affect that are all interwoven in the choices of the color in costume and makeup that influence the performers' and audiences' states of mind. When performance theorist Peggy Phelan asks, "what is the border between the visible and the invisible?" and when she probes further into "how our blindness to the opacity of the not-seen frames our experience of the visual," certain responses are conceivable via the theory of *rasa*.[8] *Rasa* is not seen and yet the emotional experience that it generates in actor and spectator enables us, to use Phelan's phrase, to "frame out experience of the visual" action transpiring on stage.

Apart from *rasa* as emotion, its meaning also includes a sensory taste in the mouth (sweet, salty, bitter) and, by implication, good or bad taste in art. Writers on Indian poetics are fond of explaining how *rasa* comes across to spectators via the analogy of a beverage, which, though made up of black pepper, candied sugar, camphor, and other ingredients, gives us a different taste from that of its individual ingredients.[9]

Rasa is conveyed via four types of *abhinaya*—*angika* (bodily, via movement and gesture), *vachika* (via speech and sound), *aharya* (via costuming, makeup, decoration—this may include multimedia uses in contemporary performances), and *sattvika* (via the dominant or prevalent feeling of a particular work of art). "The theory of *rasa*," remarks one of its major commentators, Kapila Vatsyayan, "is developed . . . by establishing a correspondence between the motor and sensory systems. The psychical manifests itself in the physical and the physical can evoke the psychical. The principles of tension and release are well understood."[10] Vatsyayan contends that the *Natyasastra* demonstrates "an amazing and staggering acquaintance with the body system, the anatomical structure (as well as) a psychosomatic system." This is evident in the chapters on *angika abhinaya*, where each joint of the body is examined. Above all, the *Natyasastra*'s foundational intermingling of movement and theater inspires creative work such as Moorty's *Carrie's Web*, and Post Natyam's *SUNOH!*

FRAGMENTING HISTORY

Along with several *rasas* conveyed via facial expression, especially the eyes; bodily movement/stance; and, in *SUNOH!*, theatrical voice, the juxtaposition of past and present times and spaces guides the work's trajectory. The Collective usefully fragments history, including multiple stories from various points of view in *SUNOH!* As Patricia Waugh remarks in *Postmodernism: A Reader*, "Postmodernism . . . still carries with it, wherever it goes, the idea of 'telling stories'. But the stories are now indistinguishable from what was once assumed to be knowledge: scientific 'truth', ethics, law, history."[11] *SUNOH!* represents the multiple layers—historical and ethical—of the courtesan's female sensuality in a nonlinear manner that highlights connections between these figures from the past to contemporary South Asian women's testimonies in domestic violence situations and other abuses where the female body is on the line (as well as autobiographical stories of grappling with the courtesan legacy and/or training Indianness through dance).

The courtesans' fractured and fragmented history demonstrates that theirs is not a single story; different points of view recall (or forget) segments of the past. Frederic Jameson's significant analysis of postmodern culture as the "logic of late capitalism" argues that in spite of trying to recover the past, there is "nothing new, only the old, the recycled, the second-hand," according to cultural studies scholar Angela Mcrobbie's analysis, "which can be reinserted into the world of the image and given meaning as simultaneously old and new." Mcrobbie continues, "This represents the death of the imagination, the death of politics and virtually the death of the social, and according to Jameson it is connected with different and more fragmented identities or subjectivities" (Mcrobbie, 3). However, even fragmented subjectivities do not indicate, argues Mcrobbie, and I agree, "the end of history, politics, or society." Mcrobbie calls for particular attention "to the assumptions which share social theory, the criteria which it uses and the pillars which support it. It means that we should also be alert to boundary-marking" (5).

In line with these contemporary notions of fragmented subjectivity and its implications for gender politics, the Post Natyam Collective's postmodern recuperation of history highlights their firmly political stance against bodily assaults on women, in the eighteenth century or today. Their approach effectively breaks a linear narrative line from past to present that is further reinforced by the overall work's fragmented structure; the segments of *SUNOH!* move between and among different time periods and spaces, drawing subtle and evocative links often left to the audience's imagination. In *Carrie's Web*, a similar fragmenting of time and space effectively conveys different points of view on the personal history of a South Asian family caught in domestic violence told dramatically though separately by two characters who occupy different parts of the house. Carrie, the spider, is supposedly in the recesses of the house though she takes center stage in her delightfully humorous high-heel-loving persona, and Artesia is a South Asian teenager (whose parents name her after "Little India" in Artesia, Los Angeles) whose private world unfolds in her bedroom on the Bluetooth (cell phone) with her close friend Monica. Artesia bemoans the fact that her parents live in a time warp, following fixed and old-fashioned notions of Indian tradition. Hence, they do not allow her to date, nor did they let her watch sex education videos in high school, and they will most likely arrange her marriage. Artesia's life is sexless even though she avidly watches and talks about the show *Sex in the City* with Monica on the phone. Tellingly, Artesia turns up the TV volume in her bedroom, Shyamala told me, to drown out the sounds of dishes breaking in another part of the house.

In *SUNOH!* the fragmentation of time and space moves between the history of courtesans and modern-day women in similar and different scenarios where the female body is on the line. This is represented, at times, via the past and present inhabiting the dancers' bodies simultaneously on stage, for instance, in one episode Cynthia, playing a courtesan in her inner chamber, sits behind a scrim, while Shyamala plays a contemporary dancer facing the hazily depicted courtesan figure in front of the scrim (backing the audience), and holding an imaginative dialogue with her, asking whether she feels "love" for her patrons. In this evocative recuperating of the courtesan's past and aligning it with the present, the Collective members take on the role of historians "ambling down the corridors of documentation," as Susan Leigh Foster puts it eloquently. In her excellent Introduction to *Choreographing History*, Foster delineates how the past rubs up against a present historian's attempts to excavate historical material:

> How to get at this skeleton of movement's meaning for any given past and place? . . . In their movements, past bodies also rubbed up against or moved alongside geological and architectural constructions, music, clothing, interior decorations . . . These partial records . . . document the encounter between bodies and some of the discursive and institutional frameworks that touched them, operated on and through them, in different ways . . . These documents never produce an isolable and integral single physical figure but instead stock an antiquarium storeroom with the sharded traces of bodily movement across the cultural landscape.[12]

Ann Cooper Albright's essay "Tracing the Past: Writing History through the Body" asks significant questions: "How do we trace the past? Reconfigure what is lost? Are traces always even visible? . . . Replac(ing) traces with tracing . . . incorporates the tactile, and thereby refuses the traditional separation of object from subject"[13] (101, 103). As Albright "reaches across time and space to touch (Loie) Fuller's dancing . . . (she) allow(s) (her) self, in turn, to be touched, for it is impossible to touch anything in a way that does not also implicate one's own body" (103). Albright quotes Walter Benjamin's words in *The Arcades Project*, namely, "To dwell means to leave traces."

The Collective's postmodern fragmentation of time in exploring history and the courtesan's past is enabled by their skillful use of multimedia visually and aurally, which embodies a coming together of the past and present. A virtual reality is created with multimedia tools that add layers to our limited knowledge of the past. As Sita Popat remarks in her book *Invisible Connections: Dance, Choreography and Internet Collaborations*:

> Internet and communications technologies offer dance and theatre new platforms for creating and performing work, with opportunities for remote interaction and collaboration on a scale never before imaginable . . . [There are] a range of technologies in the attempt to share devising experiences between choreographers, directors and performers in remote locations.[14]

Among the technological tools used in *SUNOH!*, a very moving video representation in a segment titled "Bitter Salt" (discussed below) evokes (without showing the figure but using sound and subtitles on the screen) a child bride from a past time (or sadly possible even in present time) and her unfortunate reality of becoming a widow and being "thrashed daily." The two artists playing mother and daughter follow this video. As the mother wraps the saree around the child, dressing her for her wedding, she enjoins her to be "obedient" to her in-laws. The audience receives this as deeply ironic because they have already seen the video and they know this child widow's unjust reality—although her husband dies in a flood, a natural disaster, she is blamed and beaten regularly by her in-laws. Post Natyam effectively brings past and present together in their representation via video followed by their embodiment of the widow's reality in their live human bodies.

Even as Post Natyam uses multimedia to recuperate the courtesan's figure from the past, they are also "touched" by this search in their own lives (experiences of sexual and cultural alienation within family, in relationships) and in the struggles of those around them such as battered women of the South Asian American community who shared their painful stories with Moorty enacted by her in *Carrie's Web* and by the Collective in *SUNOH!*

CREATIVE CHOREOGRAPHY WITH POSTMODERN USES OF *ABHINAYA* AND *RASA*

SUNOH!'s palimpsest of episodic vignettes tell women's stories via movement, music, and voice, relying on the performers' postmodern use of their training in Indian classical dance traditions of conveying emotions, the *navarasas*, the nine primary emotions—love, anger, laughter, fear, valor, disgust, sorrow, compassion, and peace—as delineated in the *Natyasastra*. These *rasas* with their attendant *vibhavas* (i.e., feelings related to the main rasa, such as anticipation and anxiety connected to romantic love) and their *anubhavas* (i.e., consequences, such as happy union or separation of lovers) are conveyed via *abhinaya*, nonverbal gesture language that uses *mudras* (codified hand gestures) and facial and bodily expression. The dancers worked in *SUNOH!* with two musical collaborators, Loren Nerell and Ravindra Deo, and multimedia designer Carole Kim. At times, the music was composed based on the choreographed movement, at other times, the dancers created video or movement to existing music and then had the musical composers create similar music. It was a back-and-forth process between the musicians themselves and the dancers. Along with the musical composition, there is live vocalization and text that layers with the movement in the piece. "Drafts of the soundscape" remarks musical collaborator Ravindra Deo, "did help organize the movement segments."[15]

SUNOH! begins with a preshow that is integrated into the main program. Two performers, Shyamala and Anjali, walk around the auditorium encouraging the audience to fill out their note cards with stereotypes that they have encountered in their lives. Many South Asian women shared how they had been stereotyped as "Oriental dolls," "exotic," or "mysterious," among other limiting concepts. These words are projected on a screen through live video feed by Cynthia. Sandra could not be present in the performances I saw; she made contributions via the Collective's method of creating choreography online. "Cyber Chat" follows, where the four Collective members appear together in a square image projected on the screen, split into four equal squares, each occupying one, and together virtually online, introducing the audience to their long-distance choreography making. We encounter them in different time zones—California-based member Cynthia appears sleepy, her head resting on a pile of books, and Shyamala has a cup of tea in her hand; Kansas-based Anjali (two hours ahead of California) and Munich-based Sandra (nine hours ahead of California) in their different time zones. The first sounds that we hear are the Indian classical dance syllables: tat, tat, ta, foundational and basic rhythms of the feet stamping the floor whether in bharatanatyam or in kathak. As they improvise *mudras* (hand-gestures) to the rhythm, they show each other different fabric and jewelry; Cynthia displays book titles such as *Abhinaya* among others, until we hear, "We lost Sandra." The screen goes blank.

The next segment projects the image of a beautiful courtesan wearing jewelry, traditionally dressed in long *gharara* (amply pleated skirt), fitting blouse with long sleeves, and *dupatta* (scarf covering the upper body). She is seated in the familiar style with one knee raised as if ready to do *abhinaya* with her torso, face, eyes, and arms. The image gradually fades, and we are in the present with Cynthia, Shyamala, and Anjali walking in stylized Indian dance manner, reciting dance syllables, their necks moving side to side in the familiar Indian dance movement though also conveying a parodic emphasis. Only Anjali, who plays the traditional dance guru, is dressed in a traditional sari; Cynthia has long pants and a princess crown on her head. Shyamala enters with a black top, without *dupatta*, and a bharatanatyam-dance sari (prestitched with the front pleats in place) from waist down, which she removes, revealing her shorts. Then she puts on long boots: all the wearing and removing of costumes and boots is done on stage in front of the audience as in performance art. Cynthia, then wearing a beret, and Shyamala in boots (both items create humor) move to kathak *bols* (syllables). As they perform, words are projected on the screen behind them: "Gross Guy vs. Oriental Doll," "Helpless Victim vs. Mail order bride." Cynthia then puts on an orange wig, raising audience laughter as she instructs Shyamala "to look more sexy than that" and giving her fake plastic breasts that keep sliding off! *Hasya rasa* (laughter) is evoked though Shyamala evokes a poignant compassion via her facial expression of fear and discomfort. Anjali plays the "Dominatrix Guru vs. Masochistic disciple," evoking power plays of some autocratic Indian gurus who do not welcome any questions or comments from their hapless students. There is much humor in the subtle critiques of teachers as well as gender stereotypes (such as in the practice of mail-order brides) in the larger society.

The words on the screen fade as the lights get shadowy and we glimpse Cynthia putting on a long, artificial braid—thick, and white—that reaches the floor. In this theatrical segment, she verbally narrates her autobiographical experience of going to India to study kathak—two different spaces are evoked as Cynthia in the present recreates that special past time in a

FIGURE 15.5 Cynthia Ling Lee, with a long, artificial braid, portrays a village woman. Photographer: Michael Burr.

different space. In postmodernism, the category of space, playing with it, simultaneously co-existing in two spaces (via the imagination) is played out. As Jameson remarks:

> It is at least empirically arguable that our daily life, our psychic experience, our cultural languages, are today dominated by categories of space rather than categories of time, as in the period of high modernism.[16]

Cynthia's everyday costume—very different from what is worn in a traditional Indian dance class—includes army fatigue pants, a long black top with a red trim around the shoulders and a red band at the waist. Here, the *aharya abhinaya* (costume and decoration as gestures conveying meaning) is distinctly contemporary even as it plays with color, combining black and red to evoke emotions of confusion and anger mixed with affection. She begins moving to the rhythms of the *tabla* and kathak syllables, stamping the floor, though without the traditional ankle bells. As the braid drops to the floor, her story begins. Her kathak teacher in India tells her: "You can't perform with short hair. You have to wear a wig." As Cynthia speaks, she moves the fabric (used for the braid) on the floor, makes a square with the cloth and then as she notes that she felt "so uncomfortable in her skin" as a Taiwanese American in India, it is as if she is trapped in that space. She faces the dilemma between really wanting to please her teacher, and not wanting to wear a fake braid. However, she convinces herself that the least she could do to fit in and "obey" her guru was to wear a wig without question or argument.

Another conflict arises as she learns about the *gopis* (milk-maids) "with long, black, lustrous hair who did not have a lot to do," and who "languorously" put a clay pitcher on their head and come to the banks of the river Ganges. "They dip the lip of the pitcher," narrates Cynthia in her poetic prose, as they linger. "Maybe he will come." They dream with *sringara rasa* (love) of Krishna playing his divine flute that makes them forget everything—their children and their household chores. Cynthia's words and gestures convey an amorous mellow mood. Krishna is the dark god, often represented in a deep blue color (this elicited laughter from audience members not familiar with this visual iconography). Cynthia then uses *abhinaya* to depict Krishna flirting and touching the *gopis*, whether they like this or not. She then undercuts these moves with her script and then wordlessly covers her crotch, her knees falling inward, indicating fear and discomfort. As she depicts the story via *abhinaya* and movement, she confides: "I found this confusing. Was I missing some spiritual meaning? Was the god sexually harassing the *gopis*?" Immediately, she censors herself, not to say anything critical as an outsider. She decides to keep quiet. "All I could say was: tat, tat, ta." The syllables recited with varying tone embody her discomfort in asking questions that she feels not at liberty to articulate for fear of offending her teacher and others. Her tangled consciousness is reflected in her feet getting caught in the fabric (the same fabric that had served earlier as the artificial braid) on the floor.

The segment moves on to the teacher, noting, "We're going to learn how to walk" with a pot on the head just like the *gopis*. Cynthia walks awkwardly (demonstrated for the audience as her feet caught in the fabric) until her teacher asks her what is wrong. Cynthia wanted so much to make her teacher happy but how could she explain her critique of the male/female roles played by the dominant Krishna and the submissive *gopis*? Cynthia's scripted words are, "sorry, I am having a hard time. I can't do it." Her teacher attributed her discomfort to the fact that Cynthia is "a modern girl. Always rushing, rushing, here and there. You see, Radha [Krishna's favorite] had lots of time." Cynthia notes that her teacher "got it partly, but the whole gender thing went over her head. I didn't want to break her heart, so I just smiled and I didn't say a word." This last line, "I didn't say a word" is highly significant in *SUNOH!* as it repeats in later segments—when the battered wife "didn't say a word" about her experience to anyone, and when a child is beaten and rendered silent.

Cynthia's thoughtful autobiographical piece, acted effectively with depth and humor, is followed by the phone ringing and the Collective members in another virtual meeting online, where they do *abhinaya* to dance syllables interspersed with lines: "that one," "the same problem," "Wait, it will get better," "No, will it ever get better? If you tell me sister, it'll be better." The hand gestures and fragmentary script somewhat ominously gesture to what is to come in the piece.

"The same problem" is enacted in the next section, where Shyamala through theatrical words and movement makes explicit links between courtesans and contemporary battered women. The same long piece of white fabric used as Cynthia's braid, and then as cloth on the floor, reappears as a leitmotif, a connecting thread through the vignettes of *SUNOH!*

FIGURE 15.6 Shyamala Moorty links contemporary domestic violence victims to sexual abuses endured by courtesans. Photographer: Michael Burr.

Shyamala, in jeans and a long black sleeveless *kurta* (long top), spreads the fabric on the floor and lies belly down, then rising up (as in yoga's cobra position), hits her body angrily as in *raudra rasa*, then falls flat on her belly. She recreates the story of a contemporary woman, Rasulanbai, a child widow who runs away from home to become a courtesan (narrated by Veena Talwar Olenburg). "When I heard her story," remarks Shyamala, repeating the beating gesture on her body as if evoking the widow being beaten, unfairly blamed for her husband's death, "I saw the connections between the courtesan and the working women who experience abuse, especially the story of Uma," who stayed with her abusive husband for thirty years. Movement and script are interspersed: "The problem is, all [that] people think about when they think about courtesans," she remarks, leaving the thought unfinished in words and letting gesture convey the meaning as her index finger moves from chest down to her crotch. This gesture of pointing to the crotch is more effective than words. Half-finished sentences float in the air, as Shyamala cannot get herself to articulate the stereotypes, the shame and humiliation) that considers courtesans as only sex providers. However, in recuperating and correcting these notions, Shyamala states assertively: "But courtesans are keepers of our dance tradition, they are independent people, revolutionaries. But . . . all people think about courtesans . . . and Uma and other survivors already feel so . . ." Again, leaving the sentence unfinished as she wraps the fabric around her is similar to Cynthia "not saying a word" to her teacher. Here too, the dance syllables take over and convey meaning without words: *tat, dhit tom num*, recited with increasing speed as Shyamala continues to hit her body. "I can't help but make the connection," she remarks, "but I'm not sure if I should. If I don't, I'm not interested in courtesans, or even Indian dance, unless I can make it mean something, make

FIGURE 15.7 Shyamala Moorty links contemporary domestic violence victims to sexual abuse endured by courtesans. Photographer: Michael Burr.

it relevant to the world I live in. Come sisters, what should we do?" Lights fade as she gathers the fabric close to her heart.

In the next segment of *SUNOH!* Shyamala portrays the battered woman Uma. The video projects three separate frames (like windows) on the stage screen, skillfully splitting the audience's focus. In the center, inside a beautifully ornate window with Mughal-style arches, sits a woman clad in white, with her back to the audience. The woman's figure is seen from behind a gauzy veil distancing her from the audience. The veil is also a resonant icon as in Islamic veiling, or as in the African American writer W. E. B. Du Bois's evocative notion of "double consciousness," where the racialized person is looking at him/herself "through the eyes of others" or "of seeing darkly as through a veil." We hear words spoken in terrified whispers, "silently crying inside, but nobody knows outside. Inside me, deep down in my heart."

Using live video-feed (i.e., video projected in real time) the face of the woman whose back is to the audience is projected in the frame on the right. Hence, we see the same dancer, Shyamala, with her back in the middle frame, and her expressive face in the right window. The split perspective also brings together the live body projected via a virtual face, as well as the past (back-story of the woman) and its present representation in real time. A woman's voice begins a voiceover in a whisper, somewhat fearful, as if narrating a terrifying event. Sure enough, the disjointed voiceover conveys a story of domestic violence: "One day, he was drunk. He came to me and said, 'tell me, how much do you love me? How much? How much?" The overlapping and jagged voice with the drunk aggressor repeating the words "how much" convey a fragmented consciousness of a battered woman who is forced to respond to her husband's insistent, somewhat sycophantic questions. This "face dance" done

FIGURE 15.8 Live video capture portrays the battered woman's face, played by Shyamala Moorty. Photographer: Andrei Andreev.

by Shyamala is based on Uma's actual testimony and her words, "all my tears, running, running" are recreated via the sound, "drip, drip" of bitter salty tears and Shyamala cups her hands and moves them to her mouth as in a drinking motion. She depicts Uma's hair being pulled and a contorted face at the aggression. She shakes her head as if to tell him to stop, or to say "no" she does not love him, until the shaking gets more intense, as if she is being battered, and the segment ends with her mouth wide open in a silent scream.

In this segment, "Uma's story," notes Shyamala, "was the driving force for the movement choices."[17] Cynthia remarks that the video and sound enable the audience to get a close-up view of *abhinaya* (expressive dance that is not seen close-up when done on a proscenium stage). Here, the *abhinaya*, though "spare," conveys an "intimacy," notes Cynthia, via the use of live video-feed that effectively gives a close-up of the courtesan's face in her salon. The subtleties of expressive dance via *abhinaya* are seen at close range in this contemporary rendition via technology recreating the reality of the past when the patron sat close to the courtesan.

Next, Cynthia sits at stage right and her hands respond to a *Ksetrayya padam*, where the images of the thorn, the banana leaf, and the butterfly are portrayed in explicit sexual imagery.[18] "As in the saying/about the thorn and the banana leaf,/it's always the leaf that gets torn." Cynthia also added and changed the original text of the *padam* to reflect Uma's story. Collective member Sandra Chatterjee comments that the goal here is to "translate through" the *padam*. And Sandra imagines as she noted in a feedback session, "a physical version performed simultaneous with Shyamala's silent cry ... overlapping, rather than really simultaneous."

FIGURE 15.9 Shyamala Moorty portrays the battered woman with her face covered, as if suffocating. Photographer: Andrei Andreev.

As Cynthia narrates the poem sitting downstage, we see Shyamala's face covered in fabric tightly pulling it, as if being battered and dragged. "Friend, you didn't say a word." Shyamala tugs at the fabric stretching her facial muscles and as if suffocating, trying to escape. "He had the nerve to ask for a hug. You were furious but protested gently." In the third square projected onto the screen, Anjali's hands, through *mudras*, depict the desperation that Uma feels, trying not to be held by the drunk husband with whiskey heavy on his breath, smiling and asking "how much do you love me?" Shyamala falls to the ground. "He made love to me. Same as always, I lay there unmoving." Then, she emerges from behind the scrim and pulls the fabric off her face, though it is knotted around her neck like the marital knot that has become a noose strangling her. She remains trapped in the fabric's folds as she was held down in the forced marital rape. She falls to the ground, gets up, and, leaving the fabric knotted around her neck, she carefully holds its two ends, fanning them out, and starts to move, tentatively at first and then with abandon as she circles the stage and smiles to herself. It is as if Uma has stepped outside the oppressive home environment where she is battered, and is discovering a world outside.

Uma makes the difficult choice of leaving the abusive home space after years of battering. Stepping outside the scenario that she knows well, however abusive, takes inordinate courage. Both the domestic realm and the new space allowing freedom, autonomy, and self-respect bring up issues of social justice. Here, I find geographer Edward Soja's critical analyses in his book *Seeking Spatial Justice* to be illuminating. Soja makes a persuasive case for the "'spatiality' of justice [as] an integral and formative component of justice itself, a vital part of how justice and injustice are socially constructed and evolve over time."[19] Soja's "idea that justice however it might be defined, has a consequential geography" is embodied, I contend, in Moorty's danced and theatrical representation of the injustice of domestic violence, where it unfolds, and how it is part of social processes and pressures on immigrant communities both in *Carrie's Web* and in "Uma's Story" in *SUNOH!* "An assertive and explanatory spatial perspective helps us make better theoretical and practical sense of how social justice is created, maintained, and brought into question as a target for democratic social action." Soja's "critical spatial perspective," enabling "spatial thinking," enables us to undertake progressive analyses of social formations such as immigrant families.

Apart from the depiction of Uma enduring domestic violence, another Collective member, Anjali depicts a different form of bodily abuse, namely, corporeal punishment. "When I was three," Anjali notes in a child-like voice, "I had the loudest voice"—different from the previous representations of women not being able to say a word. She wants to play with the fabric that Cynthia and Shyamala hold on the floor and move around, and Anjali notes that she liked "to push boundaries." As she enacts being hit, the space within the fabric's limits shrinks into a tight square, and as it gets smaller, Anjali is trapped in it. Then, at age seven, she notes that she had to have her tonsils out, and she is silenced. Her mouth opens and no voice emerges—now she too, like the women in previous segments, cannot say a word. She stamps her feet and opens her mouth wide, but no sound emerges. The theme of wordlessness and silence is reiterated in this experience of a contemporary woman.

A return to the present/past of courtesan's lives begins with Shyamala draping the fabric like a sari on Cynthia, playing a reluctant child bride. "*Beta* (child), be good, your in-laws, be good to them, obey them." The mother covers the child's head, and then pulls the long fabric from Cynthia's body to the other end of the stage, and on this white surface, we see video images. In this segment, the music, according to collaborator Loren Nerell is "an electro-acoustic piece, featuring field recordings, samples, processed and unprocessed acoustic instruments, and synthesizers."[20] Loren was "good at creating a sense of environment and space" remarks Cynthia, "through sound."[21]

Cynthia comments, "This haunting music combines with video and poetic text to evoke the story of Rasulanbai, a child widow from the 1960s who resisted her in-laws' abuse by escaping to become a courtesan. Rasulanbai's story was taken from (Veena) Oldenburg's fieldwork on the last remaining courtesan communities of Lucknow, India."[22] Rasulanbai's story inspires the segment "Ranri," which translates from Bengali as "courtesan" and "widow." One part of "Ranri" called "Bitter Salt" indicates the taste (*rasa*) of tears. Here, a child widow, though innocent, is blamed for her husband's death (as is common practice, although the death may have occurred from disease or natural disaster). Her grief is similar to the battered woman Uma's bitter, salty tears when she recalled "all [her] tears, running, running, running."

Our attention is on the video of "Bitter Salt," which begins with a hand making furrows in desert sand, evoking a sexual image as words are projected on the image: "50 acres of irrigated land" as if that is what the bride brings to her husband's home. Then the sand is wiped clean by the hand as if that bounty does not matter. "10 acres of wheat. 8 sacks of lentils." One finger starts to move forward like someone walking, as if the bride enters a new home. A shadow passes over. Next, the words projected are: "A flood, a death." The hand emerges from the depths of the sand and the words "a widow in white" are projected on the sand as we hear *tabla* sounds. The hand tries to hold the sand as if holding the sands of time passing, the death that is irreversible as is the heavy mantle that "a widow in white" will carry for the rest of her life. The next words convey the violence on her body: "Thrashed daily." The hand violently jerks the sand as if to escape the brutality.

Rasulanbai ran away to become a courtesan, depicting the historical reality of widows escaping in-laws' cruel treatment to become courtesans. Oldenburg's research documents that many *tawa'ifs* (courtesans) endured physical abuse before becoming courtesans and finding the courtesan profession more desirable than the violent homes that they left behind:

> The compelling circumstance that brought the majority of them to the various *tawa'if* house-holds in Lucknow was the misery they endured in either their natal or their conjugal homes. Four of these women were widowed in their early teens, two of whom hailed from the same district and had lost their husbands in a cholera epidemic; three were sold by their parents when famine conditions made feeding these girls impossible. Several were victims of physical abuse, two of whom were sisters who were regularly beaten by their alcoholic father for not obliging him by making themselves sexually available to the toddy seller. Three were known victims of rape and therefore deemed ineligible for marriage; two had left their ill-paid jobs as municipal sweeper women, because they were tired of 'collecting other people's dirt'; two were battered wives; one had left her husband because he had a mistress; and one admitted no particular hardship, only a love for singing and dancing that was not countenanced in her orthodox Brahmin home.[23]

"What would you have done?" asks Shyamala on stage, playing the contemporary dancer excavating this history as she backs the audience and faces an imagined Rasulanbai, played from behind the scrim by Cynthia. Shyamala asks: "Was is better?" (to be a courtesan than to live as a widow), to which Cynthia responds that it was "much better" being a courte-san. Cynthia plays the courtesan sitting behind the scrim and doing *abhinaya*—an impor-tant historical fact that courtesans *sat and entertained* their patrons with movement of the torso and alluring *abhinaya* with the face and eyes. In *SUNOH!* the courtesan is always seen through a scrim, never directly, as if evoking a hazy past that has to be imagined. The con-temporary dancer played by Shyamala imitates the courtesan's hand gestures and undulating torso—both reach out across time and space with their arms extended toward each other. Shyamala takes a reclining position as she observes Cynthia's subtle movements. As Cynthia "gives" as in passing down the legacy of the courtesan's *abhinaya* expression, Shyamala raises her cupped hands to her mouth as if drinking this in; a gesture that she had used previously to depict Uma's words, namely to "drink" her tears. The gesture connects the child-widow turned courtesan (as in Oldenberg's research) and the battered woman, both living in contemporary times.

Both Shyamala and Cynthia have distinctively different costumes in this scene—Shyamala as contemporary dancer wears a sleeveless tan-colored slip and shows a bare leg, whereas the courtesan is clad in proper modest fabric covering her body though without a *dupatta* across her torso or traditional jewelry adorning her face and body. The music evokes "older tradi-tions in Hindustani music," notes music composer Ravidra Deo, "more specifically those associated with the *kotha*" (where the courtesans lived and entertained their patrons).[24] "I set the *thumri*" continues Ravindra, "to *raag* Sohini, a *raag* that musicians know well but per-form less frequently; my understanding being due to its rank as a *raag* of ill repute."

Today's live dancer asks the imagined courtesan behind the scrim whether the patrons ever treated courtesans badly. The response is telling: "The *kotha* is a community, and if a client ever steps over the line, we kick him out." Further, the courtesan enlightens today's

FIGURE 15.10 Cynthia Ling Lee behind the scrim playing the courtesan and Shyamala Moorty in front as a contemporary dancer discussing the courtesan's history. Photographer: Michael Burr.

dancer with the comment that "dance is not about self-expression. Dance is about power. Having the ability—just with the glance of your eyes or the lift of an eyebrow—to make a man fall in love with you and pull out his pocketbook." Today's dancer is puzzled, because much of the poetry to which courtesans performed is about love and yearning. She asks, "do you feel real love or is that fake too?" The courtesan's response is revealing: "We have love. But love isn't for one's patron; love isn't for the public. Love? We keep that between ourselves." This brings in a potential queerness, leaving the possibilities open in terms of courtesans "keep(ing) the love between (themselves)" as in lesbian love relationships, or as in sisterly caring and looking out for one another in that female community where male patrons may take advantage—physically, mentally, and financially—of the women. The word "love" takes on many meanings, including the negative connotation of the abusive husband who insists on knowing how much his wife "loves" him.

SUNOH! ends with text projected onto the floor and on the bodies of the performers— stereotypes such as "powerful, sensual" on Shyamala's hips, fade out and fade in, as Shyamala interacts with the words projected on the floor. On the screen, a hand goes over the same words as if touching them and contending with them: "Oriental, loose woman." Then it is as if the words on the screen are wiped away; and Shyamala's hands erase those on the floor. She walks over and stamps on the words: "Servant of man," "helpless victim," "oppressed victim," "cheap prostitute," "STDs." Cynthia moves over to her and comforts her. The negative words continue: "Dancing toy," "man-hater." And finally, coming full circle, "Tell me, sister, what would you do?" appear both on the dancers' moving bodies as well as in steady print on another part of the screen. Shyamala and Cynthia take the fabric with them behind the screen, and both sit together in a gentle embrace backing the audience as lights fade to black.

Oldenberg's narrative of the widow's poignant testimony (that inspired *Ranri*), of finding refuge with a group of traveling entertainers provides an evocative conclusion to this discussion of *SUNOH!*:

> I wanted to run away but didn't know where I would go, except to the river to drown myself. Finally when an itinerant troupe of entertainers was encamped in our village I saw the performance and thought I would secretly apply to work for them, just do their housework or something. They agreed to shelter me after I told them my troubles and showed them the bruises on my body. They smuggled me out of that hell, gave me bit parts in their dramas, and finally brought me to the lap of Bibi Khanum [another *tawa'if* in Lucknow], and I have never looked back. I had no option but to run away. Tell me, sister, what would you have done in my place?

The question, "tell me sister, what would you have done?" brings us full circle to Post Natyam's masterful crafting of history, past and present, and of their skillful use of multimedia techniques, along with dance and theater to create artistic work across time and space. A commingling of dance, movement, theater, and multimedia provides an ideal avenue to convey the past and present, the courtesan's historical position and the modern woman's struggles against violence. The Collective takes the exploration of the body in postmodern directions—via unique uses of their Indian and western dance training as well as theatrical script, voice, and video—deconstructing the body, subverting the gaze from it, questioning stereotypes of femininity and restrictive social codes, and openly though subtly exploring female desire and pleasure. Their delving into the courtesan's legacy, bringing her to life in our twenty-first-century midst and usefully connecting how her body was used to today's battered women makes significant contributions to creative work in movement, theater, and multimedia.

The Collective's collaborative spirit and their conviction that the arts play a significant role in enabling people to open up and talk about their problems serve as a model for twenty-first-century art-makers. Post Natyam artists believe that art can lead to transformation and raise awareness of injustice. As in *Carrie's Web* (and prior to that, in Moorty's solo dance-cum-theater work *Rise*, dealing with communal violence in India with parallels to post-9/11 erosion of civil liberties in the United States), *SUNOH!* demonstrates unique combination of aesthetics and politics—artistic portrayal of domestic violence via historical connection with courtesan stories and subtle political engagement. Indeed Post Natyam's artistry communicates their activist ideas effectively to diverse audiences. Moorty's sentiment is resonant for the Collective as whole, namely that "the arts are about engaging with real people and their issues. A performance can be beautiful for beauty's sake, but [we are] not always inspired to merely create beautiful art. [We are] more driven to make work that can help the world" (*India Currents*, 36). As one survivor of domestic violence tells Shyamala: "Please accept my sincere praise . . . in handling such a strong and sensitive subject and for your efforts in instilling a sense of self in women." Like *Carrie's Web, SUNOH!* too in its successful intermingling of movement and theater inspires that special kind of healing that art can accomplish.

Notes

1. See also: http://postnatyam.blogspot.com.
2. Angela Mcrobbie, *Postmodernism and Popular Culture* (London and New York: Routledge, 1994), 2.
3. See Katrak, Ketu H., "The Post Natyam Collective: Negotiating Space in Making Contemporary Indian Dance," *Pulse: Asian Music and Dance* 110 (Autumn 2010), 9–11, for a fuller discussion of the Collective's process of choreographing online.
4. Veena Talwar Oldenburg, "Lifestyle as Resistance: The Case of the Courtesans of Lucknow, India," *Feminist Studies* 16, no. 2 (Summer 1990), 259–87. This essay is foundational in courtesan research from the past as well as contemporary interviews such as with widows who run away from cruel in-laws to become courtesans.
5. Melissa Acoba, "*Carrie's Web*," *India Post*, July 24, 2009.
6. Nirmala Nataraj, "A Post-Modern Artist: Shyamala Moorty Explores a Plurality of Dance," India *Currents* (August 2009): 34, 36.
7. I have seen two productions of *Sunoh! Tell me Sister*: one at the Miles Memorial Playhouse in Santa Monica, California on April 3, 2011, sponsored by Los Angeles based TeAda Theater Works, and one as part of the National Asian American Theatre Conference and Festival in Los Angeles, on June 24, 2011.
8. Peggy Phelan, "Performance, Live Culture, and Things of the Heart," *Journal of Visual Culture* 2, no. 3 (2003): 291–302, 293.
9. Sushil Kumar De, *History of Sanskrit Poetics*, 2nd ed. (Calcutta: Mukhopadhyay, 1960. First published in two volumes in 1923 and 1925), 203.
10. Kapila Vatsyayan, *Bharata: The Natyasastra* (New Delhi: Sahitya Akademi, 1996, repr. 2001), 19.
11. Patricia Waugh, *Postmodernism: A Reader* (London, New York, Melbourne, Sydney: Edward Arnold, 1992), 1.
12. Susan Leigh Foster, ed., *Choreographing History* (Bloomington: Indiana University Press, 1995).
13. Ann Cooper Albright, "Tracing the Past: Writing History through the Body," in *The Routledge Dance Studies Reader*, 2nd ed., edited by Alexandra Carter and Janet O'Shea (Oxford: Routledge, 1998), 101, 103.
14. Sita Popat, *Invisible Connections: Dance, Choreography and Internet Collaborations* (London and New York: Routledge, 2006).
15. E-mail correspondence, November 8, 2011.
16. Frederic Jameson, *Postmodernism; or, The Cultural Logic of Late Capitalism* (Durham, NC, and London: Duke University Press, 1991), 16.
17. E-mail correspondence, November 7, 2011.
18. The padam is taken from A. K. Ramanujan, Velcheru Narayana Rao, and David Schulman, eds. and trans., *When God Is a Customer* (Berkeley: University of California Press, 1994).
19. Edward Soja, *Seeking Spatial Justice* (Minneapolis and London: University of Minnesota Press, 2010), Introduction.
20. I am grateful to Cynthia for sending this to me in an e-mail, November 8, 2011.
21. Interview with Cynthia, November 7, 2011.
22. "Ranri" as courtesan and bride is according to Sumanta Bannerjee, *Dangerous Outcast: The Prostitute in 19th Century Bengal* (Calcutta: Seagull Books, 1998).
23. Ibid., n. 5.
24. E-mail correspondence, November 8, 2011.

Bibliography

Acoba, Melissa. "Carrie's Web." *India Post*, July 24, 2009.

Albright, Ann Cooper. "Tracing the Past: Writing History through the Body." In *Routledge Dance Studies Reader*, 2nd ed., edited by Alexandra Carter and Janet O'Shea, 101–10. Oxford: Routledge, 2010.

Bannerjee, Sumanta. *Dangerous Outcast: The Prostitute in 19th century Bengal*. Calcutta: Seagull Books, 1998.

De, Sushil Kumar. *History of Sanskrit Poetics*. 2nd ed. Calcutta: Mukhopadhyay, 1960. First published in two volumes in 1923 and 1925.

Foster, Susan Leigh, ed. *Choreographing History*. Bloomington: Indiana University Press, 1995.

Jameson, Frederic. *Postmodernism; or, The Cultural Logic of Late Capitalism*. Durham, NC, and London: Duke University Press, 1991.

Katrak, Ketu, H. "The Post Natyam Collective: Negotiating Space in Making Contemporary Indian Dance." *Pulse: Asian Music and Dance* 110 (Autumn 2010), 9–11.

Katrak, Ketu H. *Contemporary Indian Dance: New Creative Choreography in India and the Diaspora*. Basingstoke: Palgrave Macmillan, 2011.

Mcrobbie, Angela. *Postmodernism and Popular Culture*. London and New York: Routledge, 1994.

Nataraj, Nirmala. "A Post-Modern Artist: Shyamala Moorty Explores a Plurality of Dance." India *Currents* (August 2009): 34, 36.

Oldenburg, Veena Talwar. "Lifestyle as Resistance: The Case of the Courtesans of Lucknow, India." *Feminist Studies* 16, no. 2 (Summer 1990), 259–87.

Phelan, Peggy. "Performance, Live Culture, and Things of the Heart." *Journal of Visual Culture* 2, no. 3 (2003): 291–302.

Popat, Sita. *Invisible Connections: Dance, Choreography and Internet Collaborations*. London and New York: Routledge, 2006.

Post Natyam Collective. www.postnatyam.net.

The Post Natyam Collective. Blog. http://postnatyam.blogspot.com.

Ramanujan, A. K., Velcheru Narayana Rao, and David Dean Schulman, eds. and trans. *When God Is a Customer*. Berkeley: University of California Press, 1994.

Soja, Edward. *Seeking Spatial Justice*. Minneapolis and London: University of Minnesota Press, 2010.

Vatsyayan, Kapila. *Bharata, The Natyasastra*. New Delhi: Sahitya Akademi, 1996. Reprint, 2001.

Waugh, Patricia. *Postmodernism: A Reader*. London, New York, Melbourne, Sydney: Edward Arnold, 1992.

CHAPTER 16

··

PERSISTENT PAGANS
Dancing for Dionysos in the Year of Years

··

ODAI JOHNSON

TOPOS ARCHEOLOGY

··

In the ruins of a late Roman theater at Aphrodisias (Turkey), scratched on the wall of a corridor that leads between the back-stage rooms and the remains of the stage is a series of inscriptions that still reserve spaces for actors to store their props and costumes, their "*skeue*" or stuff, though the theater itself long ago crumbled.[1] One inscription, on the wall of Room 3, reads simply "τοπος αρχεολογων"—the topos or place of the archeologi. If there ever was an invitation for a shovel, this is it. "Dig here," it seems to say. But, like much of the past, even its invitations are beguiling. *Topos archeologon* refers, in this case, to a genre of mimes, the archeo-logi, who specialized in the "ancient" stories, that is, the classic Greek tragic myths, and the *topos* was nothing more than the literal backstage cupboard to store their props and masks. One might render it as "the old mime's space." There are similar inscriptions for the Homerist mimes, who presented combat scenes from Homer, as well as the more general category *mimologos*.[2] But the *topos archeologi* holds a particular fascination for me, serving as it does, as a linguistic portmanteau of our own making. I'm willing to take its double meaning at face value as an invitation to begin to dig for the place (literally, the topography) of the ancient stories lodged in the bodysites of dancers, their prohibition in the early Christian world as repositories of paganism, and their unspoken resistance.

"When the tragic poets were extinguished," wrote Libanius of the origins of the mimes of late antiquity, "one of the gods took pity on the lack of education of the populace and introduced instead the dance as a form of instruction for the masses in the deeds of the ancients. And now a goldsmith will converse not badly with someone from the schools about the houses of Priam and Laius."[3] Somewhere, perhaps late third or early fourth century of the Common Era, tragedy as a performance genre had disappeared, but the tragic stories continued in other genres, with and without words, stories that had been in circulation in the Greek world, now Roman world, soon to be Christian world, for nearly a millennia. The mimes, loved by Nero, expelled by Domitian, and the pantomimes danced what they could no longer recite, leaving their thousand-year-old stories household tales all across the Greek east and Roman provinces. Through traces of textual evidence, inscriptional and icono-graphic, on mosaics and in homilies, defenses, and critiques, the dancer's body remained a present and potent force for preserving the "ancient stories" (now pagan stories) even in its aphasia. Treatises on the art were penned by dancers (Pylades) and critics and defenders alike (Lucian, Aristides, Libanius, Choricius) all indirectly documented their skill; legisla-tion (the Codex Theodosius, discussed below) contained them when it could not suppress them, while the most famous of the mimes and pantomimes, like Pylades, Bathyllus of Alexandria, Vincentius of Timgad, or the unnamed dancer from Trier whose ivory plaque still remains, earned reputations that long outlived their glory on the stage.[4] And this quiet body of praise persists quite late into antiquity. Claudian, (c. 400), records the great applause a fine Hecuba or Niobe could still rouse, while Sidonius Apollinaris described the appeal of the popular fifth-century mimes Caramallus and Phabaton.[5] Choricus of Gaza does the same in the sixth century, for performances of Achilles, Hippolytus, and Phaedra; and of course the young Theodora practiced a craft without words in the theaters at Constantinople.[6]

The problem with this persistent tradition, however, began late in the fourth century of the Common Era, with a consolidation of Christian power that made all things associated with the pagan past illegal. The problem began with the Year of Years—that fulcrum of time that commenced with the battle of Frigidus in 394 CE, over which the culture of the Roman world tipped inexorably and permanently toward Christianity, and after which all expres-sions of the ancient art became tarnished with paganism. With the Christian victory of the eastern empire, Theodosius began a series of campaigns to purge the Roman world of its pagan practices in all their expressions. These policies were severe, devastatingly successful, and the wake of the destruction of paganism was wide and brutal, yet the policies to prohibit paganism was occasionally resisted. Dancers resisted.

THE YEAR OF YEARS

It was Augustine who recorded the pagan oracle circulating around the empire at the time (late fourth century), that after a year of years, that is, one year for each year, or 365 years) Christianity would come to an end.[7] It was a pagan fantasy, perhaps, but one bred of a very real fear of the growing consolidation of a Christian power over the empire. If one dated this *magnus agnus*, as Augustine did, from the crucifixion of 29 CE, 394 was the year that would usher in the return to paganism. The year 394 was portentous indeed. It saw the war of suc-cession, the revolt led by Eugenius in the west against Theodosius the Great in the east that promised to become, in Charles Hedrick's phrase, "the beginning of the pagan millennium." In the tradition of Christian historiographers, the war was a contest of ideologies: the pagans led by Eugenius and Flavianus marshalled under the statues of Jupiter and the banners of Hercules, while Theodosius bore the *chi-rho* of Constantine.[8] The two forces met at the river Frigidus, south of Milan. Day one went to the pagans. Ambrose, Bishop of Milan at the time, left the city while the troops mustered, intimating a Eugenius victory would mean a total persecution of the Christians.[9] But after sustaining heavy losses on the first day of the battle,

Theodosius prayed and providence interceded in the form of a severe dust storm that blew up the hill and advantage shifted to the Christian forces. Here is Rufinus's account:

> It may perhaps be hard for the pagans to believe what happened; for it was discovered that, after the prayer that the Emperor poured out to God, such a fierce wind arose as to turn the weapons of the enemy back on those who hurled them. When the wind persisted with great force and every missile launched by the enemy was foiled, their spirit gave way, or rather it was shattered by the divine power.[10]

Some 20,000 fell in the battle; the leaders of the revolt were executed (Eugenius) or self-impaled (Flavianus), and the victorious Theodosius consolidated his power in the eastern capital of Constantinople.

Christian writers, like Rufinus, Augustine, and Ambrose, refer to the revolt as a pagan assault on Christianity, a conception that found favor with a sizable bibliography of modern scholarship as well, who characterize it variously as "the last stand of paganism" (Bloch), "the last days of paganism" (Geffcken), or "the Clash of Gods" (Matthews).[11] With its failure, Theodosius pressed hard for the conversion of the surviving pagan elite—including the senatorial class—and Prudentius described the mass conversions that did indeed follow (*Contra Symmachus* I: 506–607). Subsidies to pagan priests and temples were withdrawn, and the decade that closed the fourth century and the opened the fifth saw the complete political triumph of Christianity at the full governmental level.[12] In the wake of that administrative consolidation also followed a wave of destruction targeting (silencing) pagan culture, a process that had been intermittent conflict for decades now galvanized into an abrupt offensive. Ritual by ritual, region by region, bishops, judges, prefects, monks, and mobs were deployed on a search and destroy mission: temples were razed and public and then private worship prohibited, as were funeral rites, sacrificing, soothsaying, oracles, festivals, and convivial gatherings on festal days; even the names of pagan gods were erased from monuments.[13] Statutes were toppled, altars dismantled, temples pulled down and reconsecrated. The wholesale destruction of pagan culture is recorded in many forms: Hagiographers serve up the destruction as a dish of some pride, like the account of Zacharias of Mytilene, whose narrative of the life of Severus is a running serial of burned books, smashed idols, and demolished temples; or Porphyrius's singular dedication to the destruction of eight temples in Gaza over a two-week period in May 402, or, more famously, the destruction of the great library at Alexandria.[14]

It is difficult to evoke the scale of the destruction. Orders were given, zealous "Philoponoi" ("the diligent") demolished altars, idols, temples, and statuary. Some of the destruction finds voicing, but little of the terror of a scorched-earth policy that could allow the brace of emperors, Honorius and Theodosius, to claim so completely of the pagans in 423: "we believe there no longer are any."[15]

Less poignant, but equally revealing, one may find in the Theodosian Code—the new canon that overhauled the legal corpus of Rome—the succinct authorizing of the violence that began early in the decade and continued with increasing aggression against the culture that looked to be the last pagan generation:

> Feb 391: prohibited public sacrifice, visiting or entering temples, and "revering images."
> Nov 392: prohibited private worship, adorning images, sacrificing.
> Dec 396: abolished privileges to priests of the "sacred mysteries"
> July 399: "If there should be any temples in the country districts, they shall be torn down without disturbance or tumult."
> August 399: disallowing "sacrifice or any accursed superstition."[16]

The pagan holocaust was a cataclysmic century, unmatched perhaps until the Spanish Conquista of Mexico eleven hundred years later. It was also an empire-wide *damnatio memoriae*, and left its mark as a memorial to the cancellation of a culture, the blotting out of pagan memory on the landscape. The silencing, suppression, and destruction, and the inscriptions of that destruction, were carried out exactly like a *damnatio*, not only to obliterate paganism but also to flag its obliteration. Like the broken torso of the Venus by the church of St. Matthias left standing for stone-throwers to assault, the obliteration of the pagan past was marked as a present spectacle.[17]

It is in the catastrophic aftermath of this year of years and the loss of classical culture that we must (finally) consider the theater and its mimes, among the great repositories of pagan antiquity that fell squarely in the thick of the culture now contraband to many of the most vocal Christians of the same generation. Christian polemics against the stage had a long history of invective. The central arguments of Tertullian and Novatian were constructed on the association of the stage and paganism (*"pompa diaboli"*), and as such no Christian should resort to the theaters.[18] Augustine, leaning on Varro for classical support, stated axiomatically that he and Varro both "found stage plays a part of the pagan religious rites," a conclusion John Chrysostom's career was spent in prosecuting.[19] Cyril of Jerusalem went so far as to describe the conversion to Christianity as a public renunciation of theater. For him, the initiates preparing for baptism, were to look to the west and declaim:

> I renounce you Satan, and all your works . . . and all his pomp. These are the Devil's pomps: a passion for the theatre, horse-races, hunting, and all other vain pursuits . . . do not indulge in the passion for the theatre, where actors put on indecent spectacles full of every kind of shameless obscenity, and effeminate men perform wild dances.[20]

Given the association with paganism, from Dionysos down, it should therefore not surprise us in the least that the theater would also be hard-targeted for erasure under the same sweeping antipagan campaign that characterized the Theodosian age and was so aggressively hoped for by the most vocal writers of that generation. Conversion to Christianity was also, to a great degree, a repudiation of the classical past, certainly classical culture, and that culture found its most persistent and public representation in the theaters. Mimes, telling still with their feet the ancient stories, would have been keenly aware that even while they danced their Dionysos, their Heracles, and Aphrodite, defaced statues and broken torsos of those same subjects—now criminalized—were landfill in the new postclassical world. There is every reason to assume the theaters would also be the quarry of paving stones for the new Christian order.[21]

But that is not what happened, not at all. The *damnatio* (memory sanction) levied against pagan culture, for all its damage to temples, libraries, rites, iconography, and festivals, met with enormous resistance in the theater; indeed, the theater seemed to be exempt from the purging of pagan memory for reasons that baffled the most strident voices of the age. Though the new initiates renounced it at time of conversion, and though Christian preachers and writers like John Chrysostom condemned it weekly, the theater resisted the spiritual colonization, unaffected by the pogrom on paganism, and continued so, a classical holdover, documentable for at least three more centuries, and quite likely longer still.[22] Rather than being silenced, the dancer's bodysite in the theater of late antiquity seemed to be the one place where pagan memory would not suffer erasure, where the "noise" of unspeakable paganism was inextinguishable and the long tradition of the "ancient stories" danced on, uninflected by the fires around them.

CONTAINMENT, RESISTANCE

If a picture representing an actor of pantomimes in humble costume . . . or a contemptible actor should be placed in public porticoes or those places in municipalities where our images are usually consecrated, such picture shall be immediately torn down . . . We do not, however, forbid that such pictures may be located at the entrances of the circus or in front of the stage of a theatre.

—*Codex Theodosius*, 15.7.12, June 394.

For centuries, as a testament to their popularity, images (pictures and statues) of celebrity mimes, past and present, were on public display. After the year of years, 394, however, they too were treated as enemies of the state. The edict passed on the representations of the actors was identical to that of any other traitor, with this exception: the images were not mutilated or made into landfill, but moved into the theater. Images, and the mimes they represented, were contained.

In the opening years of the fifth century, the legislation of the lives of the mimes found a heading in the revised Theodosiac Codes that sought to officially contain the profession. The *codex* was a decade in the compilation, codifying laws that would regulate every aspect of Roman life, including thirteen entries under the heading "*De Scaenicis*," regulating the lives of performers. They were prohibited from taking the sacrament, prohibited from leaving the profession, but protected against abduction (not out of concern for the welfare of the abducted but rather for depriving the state of its entertainment). Another provision allowed only the daughters of actors to perform on the stage, locking them into a generational serfdom. That their statues remained standing may alert us that the state had made its peace with the theater and that theater offered something even with its persistent paganism.

And so, locked into lives that were professionally permitted, socially "othered," they danced their ancient stories, their Agamemnon and Helen, Paris and Dionysos, Maenads and Medea, right through the fifth century and beyond, keeping alive a thousand-year tradition. Their detractors were legion—John Chysostom spent a career railing against the theater and the seductive pull of the mimes—and occasionally they found supporters (Libanius, for one), who left literary testimonials to the power of the mimes and pantomimes and the persistence of paganism that lived on in stories told through dance.

Beyond the literary record, one of the more moving evidentiary bodies is the mosaic record. Outside of Antioch, Chysostom's home pulpit, in the suburb of Daphne, a rich find of the remains of Roman villas are still decorated with mosaics of the same Greek myths that the mimes told, including several narratives of Dionysos and his history that remained on display in the new Christian world well into the sixth century. On borders and emblemata one still finds comic, tragic, and satyric masks inset into the pavement from Southern Turkey to Northern Africa. The mythic tales of Phaedra and Hippolytus, Aphrodite and Adonis, still adorn the floors in Madaba, where they were installed in the middle of the sixth century, and the postures reflect human bodies: that is, the mosaics reflect mimes dancing Hippolytus.

Many of the tales told in stone seem to be derived directly from the stage: Iphegenia in Aulis, Dionysos and Ariadne, several scenes of Phaedra and Hippolytus. On the ground, on the stones the war of the amazons played on, next to Odysseus and the Sirens, Dionysos and Heracles, Phaedra and Hippolytus, Dionysos and Satyrs, all dated from the first half of the sixth century.[23] In Beth Shean, on the floors of the Sigma, a semicircular plaza built early in the sixth century, we find represented in mosaic stones, allusions to Dionysos, the Muses, the Graces, and Aphrodite.[24]

In Ptolemais, North Africa, where Synesius of Cyrene resided, the theatricals were twice commanded to resume after the Eugenius disruption, in 396, and again most emphatically in 399: "We permit the theatrical arts to be practiced, lest, by excessive restriction thereof, sadness may be produced."[25] Ptolemais, in Cyrenaica, was an average Roman North African town, but it boasted two theaters and an odeon whose popularity continued right through the troubles. Further west, the theater of Mandaurs was restored at sizable expense in the years 399–400.[26] Across the empire—from Rome, where the contoriantes attest to the popularity of the mimes; to Constantinople, where John Chrysostom was impotent in his campaign against them; to Antioch (a city Julian satirized as having "more mimes than citizens"—*Misopogon* 342 b); to Syria, which exported the actors against whom the Bishop Jacob of Sarugh would still be composing homilies in the year 500; to Gaza, where two theaters were preserved well into the mid-sixth century (in spite of its conversion by Porphyrus) and Choricius (*Apologia Mimorum*) was still defending the mimes in the early sixth century; to the last prohibitions against tragic, comic, and satyr plays in 692, the theater of late antiquity not only survived the pagan purge but also in some centuries flourished, for several hundred years, in spite of its dense association with paganism, in spite of the most vocal antagonists of the age. In the sixth century Joshua the Stylite could still object to the pantomime as occasions where "heathen tales are sung," a sentiment shared by his contemporary Jacob of Serugh.[27]

Moreover, the mimes survived in ways other genres did not. For Macrobius, whose *Saturnalia* almost certainly dates to the same generation as the Theodosian Code (early fifth century), the pagan past was a past, not a dream of a revival. Alan Cameron has written of the work as a certain nostalgia, an imitation of a past tradition, already a thing of a prior generation.[28] The same could be said of Nonnos's *Dionysiaca* (early fifth c). But there is nothing nostalgic about the mimes in the theater. They lived still very much in a present, and for writers like Augustine, Chrysostom, Cassiodorus, Choricius, and Jacob of Serugh, their present remained very much a pagan present.

How much of the pagan past and practices were still in circulation after the year of years we will never know. Survival in certain capitals like Antioch and Constantinople lingered for decades, maybe a century or more, in curtailed, clandestine, or circumscribed forms. The point of such secret practices that Augustine speaks of is that they were secret. Purges against recusant pagans were still public news in 546, when a group of "illustrious and noble men, as well as a large group of grammarians, sophists, teachers and doctors" were denounced, tortured, and executed in Constantinople. Pope Gregory is still urging vigilance against pagans in 599, a practice particularly prevalent in the countryside.[29] But there was nothing clandestine about the theater, it remained a public and civic institution. Theodora certainly debuted in the sixth century with her notorious performances, and the theaters were still crowded at that point. The last preserved record of performance comes to us from 691/692, at the Council of Trullo, where prohibitions against celebrating Dionysos, against mimes using tragic, comic, and satyric masks are still being legislated, and those words are severe in their finality:

> CANON LXII.
>
> The so-called Calends, and what are called Bota and Brumalia [Bromios?], and the full assembly which takes place on the first of March, we wish to be abolished from the life of the faithful. And also the public dances of women, which may do much harm and mischief. Moreover we drive away from the life of Christians the dances given in the names of those falsely called gods by the Greeks whether of men or women, and which are performed after an ancient and un-Christian fashion; decreeing that no man from this time forth shall be dressed as a woman, nor any woman in the garb suitable to men. Nor shall he assume comic, satyric, or tragic masks; nor may men invoke the name of the execrable Bacchus when they squeeze out the wine in the presses; nor when pouring out wine into jars, practicing in ignorance and vanity the things which proceed from the deceit of insanity. Therefore those who in the future attempt any of these things which are written, having obtained a knowledge of them, if they be clerics we order them to be deposed, and if laymen to be cut off.[30]

And that, as they say, was finally that. It was the last active reference to the ancient practice of theater, and there at the close, the celebrants of Dionysos were still taking on the old masks in the same three ancient genres that Horace described, that Vitruvius prescribed designs for, that the Athenians judged twelve hundred years earlier, still dancing to the pressing of the wine in honor of a god long prohibited.[31] Under all the enforcements and prohibitions, the pogroms and purges, the memory of the cultic origins were still intact at its last suppression.

The traveling *archeologi* who left their inscriptions at Aphrodisias may still have lingered in circulation a while longer, criminalized, itinerant, cut-off from the church and the community that made the laws they lived by, but they may still have danced the old stories a while longer. I like to think so.

NOTES

1. For their "σκευη" or equipment, see Plutarch, Mor. *Gloria Athenesium*, 348 d. "Let them bring with them their equipment, their masks and altars, their stage machinery, their revolving changes of scenes, and the tripods that commemorate their victories."

2. The inscriptions from the third century CE (so posits Charlotte Roueché on internal evidence) on postscaenium rooms are cataloged in Charlotte Roueché, *Performers and Partisans at Aphrodisias in the Roman and Late Roman Periods* (London: Society for the Promotion of Roman Studies, 1993), I: i, 3 (17).

3. Libanius, *A Reply to Aristides on Behalf of Dancers*, Margaret Molloy, trans. In Margaret Molloy, *Libanius and the Dancers* (Hildesheim/New York: Olms-Weidmann, 1996), 173.

4. For tracing the evidentiary record of pantomime, we are all indebted to the fine collection edited by Edith Hall and Rosie Wyles, *New Directions in Ancient Pantomime* (Oxford: Oxford University Press, 2008). Pylades and Bathyllus, see Athenaeus, I:20.

5. Claudian, *Paneg. M. Theod.* 311–13; Sidonius Apollinaris, *Carm.* 23, 268–71.

6. Procobius, 9:6.

7. Augustine, *Civ. Die*, 18:53–54.

8. For the foundation of this pagan-Christian agon see Augustine, *Civ. Die*, 5:26, and Ambrose, *De Obitu Theodosius*, 10.

9. Ambrose, *Epistles*, 57.1.

10. Rufinus, HE XI. 33, quoted in Averil Cameron, *The Later Roman Empire* (Cambridge, Harvard University Press, 1993), 76. Other ancient accounts concur or retell the basic narrative: Socrates Scholasticus, *Historia Ecclesiasticus*, Book V, xxv; Theodoretus, *Ecclesiastical History*, Book V, xxiv.

11. See, for example, Arnaldo Momigliano, ed., *The Conflict between Paganism and Christianity in the Fourth Century* (Oxford: Oxford University Press, 1964); Pierre Chuvin, *Chronicle of the Last Pagans* (Cambridge, MA: Harvard University Press, 1990); Johannes Geffckin, *The Last Days of Greco-Roman Paganism*, trans. S. MacCormack. (New York: Elsevier North-Holland, 1978). To trouble the ideologic borders, see David Hunt, who lucidly begins the problem by stating, "Papers and books about Christianising the Roman Empire ought not to be encouraged." David Hunt, "Christianising the Roman Empire: The Evidence of the Code," in *The Theodosian Code*, edited by Jill Harries and Ian Wood (London: Gerald Duckworth, 1993), 143–58, 143.

12. Averil Cameron, 76. For a summary of the complexities of this process, see Ramsay MacMullen, *Christianizing the Roman Empire* (New Haven: Yale University Press, 1984).

13. See, Peter Stewart, "The Destruction of Statues in Late Antiquity," in *Constructing Identities in Late Antiquity*, edited by R. Miles (London: Routledge, 1999), 159–89; Charlotte Roueché, "Written Display in the Late Antiquity and Byzantine City," in *Proceedings of the 21st International Congress of Byzantine Studies*, edited by Elizabeth Jeffreys and Fiona Haarer (Aldershot, UK: Ashgate, 2006), 235–53, 247.

14. *The Life of Severus by Zachariah of Mytilene*, trans. Lena Ambjorn (Piscataway, NJ: Gorgias Press, 2008). Marcus the Deacon, *Life of Porphyrius*, trans. G. F. Hill (Oxford: Clarendon Press, 1913), 63–70.

15. *Codex Theodosius* (Cth), trans. Clyde Pharr (Nashville, TN: Vanderbilt University, 1944–1946), XVI, 10, 22; Pierre Chuvin, 78–79.

16. Cth 16.10.10; 16.10.12; 16.10.14; 16.10.16, 16.10.17. The suppression of pagan practices occupies its own section of the codex, 16.10.1–16.10. 25, Pharr trans.

17. Stewart, 175.

18. Tertullian, *De Spectaculis*, 1–4; Novatian, *De Spectaculis*. The argument is lucidly set forth by Richard Lim, "People as Power: Games, Munificence, and Contested Topography," in *The Transformations of Urbs Roma in Late Antiquity*, edited by W. V. Harris (Portsmouth, RI: Journal of Roman Archeology, 1999), 265–81, 267–68.

19. *Civ. Die.* 4:1, 3; also 2, 4, 2.

20. Cyril of Jerusalem, *Mystagogic Catecheses*, 1.4–8, in *Cyril of Jerusalem*, trans. Edward Yarnold (London: Routledge, 2000), 170–71.

21. There is an extensive bibliography on the mutilation of pagan statues. I have relied primarily on Frank Trombley, "Destruction of Pagan Statuary and Christianization," and Yoram Tsafrir, "The Classical Heritage in Late Antique Palestine," both in *The Sculptural Environment of the Roman Near East*, edited by Yaon Z. Eliav, Elise A. Friedland, and Sharon Herbert (Leuven and Dudley, MA: Peeters, 2008), 117–42, 143–64.

22. Christian attitudes toward the theater are thoroughly canvassed in C. C. Schnusenberg, *The Relationship between the Church and the Theatre Exemplified by Selected Writings of the Church Fathers and by Liturgical Texts until Amalarius of Maetz—775–852 AD* (Lanham, MD: University Press of America, 1988).

23. Rina Talgam, "The *Ekphrasis Eikonos* of Procopius of Gaza: The Depiction of Mythological Themes in Palestine and Arabia during the Fifth and Sixth Centuries," in *Christian*

Gaza in Late Antiquity, edited by Brouria Bitton-Ashkelony and Aryeh Kofsky (Leiden, Boston: Brill, 2004), 209–34, 219.

24. Y. Tsafrir, 138.

25. Cth, XV, 6.2

26. Frank Sear, *Roman Theatres, an Architectural Study* (Oxford: Oxford University Press, 2006), 282–83.

27. Charlotte Roueché, *Performers and Partisans at Aphrodisias in the Roman and Late Roman Periods* (London: Society for the Promotion of Roman Studies, 1993), 26; Jacob of Sarugh, see homilies 3–5, translated in *New Directions in Ancient Pantomime*, edited by Edith Hall and Rosie Wyles (Oxford: Oxford University Press, 2008), Appendix.

28. Charles Hendrick, Jr. *History and Silence: Purge and Rehabilitation of Memory in Late Antiquity* (Austin: University of Texas Press, 2000), 81.

29. John of Ephesus, *Ecclesiastical History* (fragment), in *Readings in Late Antiquity*, edited by Michael Maas (London: Routledge, 2000), 186; Jeffrey Richards, *Consul of God: The Life and Times of Gregory the Great* (London: Routledge, 1980), 235, 236.

30. From *The Seven Ecumenical Councils of the Undivided Church*, trans. H. R. Percival, in *Nicene and Post-Nicene Fathers*, 2nd ser., edited by P. Schaff and H. Wace, repr. (Grand Rapids, MI: Eerdmans, 1955), XIV, 356–408, 389.

31. Horace, *Ars Poetica* (*Epistles II:iii*); Vitruvius, 5.6.8–9.

CHAPTER 17

A WITCH IN THE MORRIS
Hobbyhorse Tricks and Early Modern Erotic Transformations

ERIKA T. LIN

In the conclusion to his excellent and comprehensive history of morris dancing from 1458 to 1750, John Forrest describes some of the challenges of studying dance in earlier periods.[1] The scarcity of primary records, combined with orthographic inconsistencies in manuscript sources and variant spellings in early published works, render nearly impossible the kinds of definitive claims possible when working in more recent eras. Because Forrest's central project is to trace the development of morris dance forms, the solutions he proposes to these methodological problems aim to isolate particular formal and contextual features so as to allow for comparison between individual records and enable quantitative analysis in the face of limited data.[2]

This tendency to study the formal, physical characteristics of early dance as distinct from their social meanings falls within a historiographic trajectory that is especially at issue when considering seemingly "theatrical" dance forms. Cecil Sharp, an early twentieth-century dance scholar whose writings and staged revivals strongly influenced subsequent studies of early English popular dance, famously distinguished between two types of dance. "Ceremonial" dances, he contended, were performed before audiences during holidays and festivals. They often involved spectacular costumes and were executed by an all-male elite. "Social" dances, by contrast, were a form of recreation in which both men and women engaged throughout the calendar year. Such dances, he argued, involved more basic choreography and did not require special dress.[3] Implicit in this taxonomy is the notion that some forms of dance are more similar to theater because they are enacted for the entertainment of spectators who are not themselves participants. Theater is here assumed to be set off from quotidian experience, and both ceremonial dance and dramatic performance are imagined first and foremost as *aesthetic* practices, in contradistinction to other forms of recreation.[4]

In this chapter, I work against the automatic aestheticization of dance and theater by examining how the performance dynamics of dance in the early modern playhouse functioned as a crucial mechanism for the production of cultural values and norms. In sixteenth- and seventeenth-century England, holidays were often celebrated with dancing, athletic combat, and other spectacles as well as paratheatrical role-playing, such as cross-dressing and the election of mock kings. In the professional theaters of Shakespeare and his contemporaries, these communal rituals came to function as commodified entertainments. If audiences at playhouses were themselves regular participants in amateur theatrical games, how did their familiarity with seasonal practices shape their experiences with commercial performance? And how did calendar customs enacted onstage, in turn, remake festivity outside the playhouses? In order to answer these questions, we must trace the interconnections between dance and theater not only as aesthetic practices but also as similar modes of communal observance.

This chapter explores one subset of these broader issues by analyzing the implications of festive performance for early modern gender and sexuality. I center my discussion on the morris dance episodes in *The Witch of Edmonton*, written by William Rowley, Thomas Dekker, and John Ford and first staged in 1621. The term "morris" encompassed a range of dance forms in early modern England. It typically involved performers with bells tied to their lower legs and scarves either held in their hands or sewn onto the shoulders of special morris coats. The dance's characteristically vigorous leaps were accentuated aurally by the sound of jingling bells and visually by the scarves set in motion via the performer's lively arm gestures. In some cases, the dance took a processional form, as in the colorful parades of London's annual Midsummer Watches and in the famous morris from London to Norwich by Will Kemp, the clown in Shakespeare's original company, the Lord Chamberlain's Men (Figure 17.1). In other instances, the morris involved either solo or partnered dancers weaving around each other in intricate patterns within a fixed area. Regardless of type, the morris may well have incorporated some mimetic activity, as it often featured characters from the Robin Hood legend, such as Maid Marian, as well as other stock figures, such as the fool and the "hobbyhorse," a cloth-covered frame resting on the hips of its human operator (distinctly unlike later children's toys that featured a horse's head on a stick).[5]

The spectacular aspects of the morris dance and its emphasis on role-playing suggest obvious parallels with scripted drama. Yet this happy coincidence begs the question of how both dance and theater are to be interpreted. Rather than taking for granted that these genres served first and foremost as aesthetic practices, this chapter considers their function as embodied discourses. In order to represent a dance taking place within the imaginary world of a play, actors had to actually dance in the real-life playhouse. This convergence of dramatic fiction and onstage action enables us to better understand how early modern performance qua performance functioned both inside and outside playhouses as part of the broader mechanisms through which social values and norms were (re)produced. In this chapter, I trace these processes by analyzing the impact of the morris dance on early modern theatrical spectators. Juxtaposing examples from the dramatic text with accounts from sixteenth- and seventeenth-century parish records, legal documents, and pamphlet literature, I argue that the morris episodes in *The Witch of Edmonton* are repeatedly associated with transgressive sexual practices that are transformed through the act of onstage performance into socially acceptable festive mirth. Not merely a physical form across which illicit desires are mapped, the morris becomes the means through which non-normative eroticisms are *re*mapped both within the fictional play and in the actual playhouse.

These transformations, I argue, take place on several interconnected levels of *The Witch of Edmonton*. In the main plot, marriage is imagined as merely utilitarian exchange; sex enables

FIGURE 17.1 Will Kemp, the clown in Shakespeare's original company, dancing the morris accompanied by pipe and tabor. He wears bells on his legs and scarves attached to the shoulders of his morris coat. Reproduced from William Kemp, *Kemps Nine Daies Wonder: Performed in a Daunce from London to Norwich*, edited by Alexander Dyce (London, 1840), xxvii, after title page of William Kemp, *Kemps nine daies vvonder Performed in a daunce from London to Norwich. Containing the pleasure, paines and kinde entertainment of William Kemp betweene London and that citty in his late morrice. Wherein is somewhat set downe worth note; to reprooue the slaunders spred of him: many things merry, nothing hurtfull. Written by himselfe to satisfie his friends* (London, 1600). With the assistance of Special Collections and Archives, George Mason University Libraries.

financial transfer and is segregated from festivity. The problematic union of Frank Thorney and Susan Carter figures the subsequent disintegration of the social order within the dramatic narrative—a breakdown that eventually culminates in murder and execution. The play juxtaposes this marriage plot against a subplot involving the persecution of the eponymous witch, her alliance with the devil in the form of a black dog, and the antics of the clown who plays the hobbyhorse in the morris dance. In contrast to the main plot, the subplot integrates sex with festive dancing, and it does so in three ways: by highlighting overlaps between cross-dressing practices in the morris and on the commercial stage, by foregrounding the hobbyhorse's relation to the transgression of erotic and theatrical categories, and by positioning the morris as embedded within sodomitical discourses that link devils and witches with anal play and bestiality. Even as it explores these illicit forms of eroticism, however, the play's performance dynamics repeatedly align the morris not so much with the perversion of sexual practices as with their *inversion*. Transgressive sexuality is repeatedly associated with festivity—and yet the festive morris is positioned as precisely that which spectators most want to see. Playgoers' viewing practices are thus imagined not simply as morally corrupt but as associated with communal parish celebrations in which the reversal of high and low was crucial to group identity—a kind of licensed licentiousness that was not merely tolerated but constitutive of social life.

Analyzing the social impact of performance as a presentational act during the crucial period when English professional theater became institutionalized suggests an alternative to epistemologies of theater and dance that grow out of more modern contexts. Spectatorship, I propose, was not merely the phenomenological glue binding together the two "artistic" genres of dance and theater but rather itself an embodied practice fully imbricated in the production of physical forms onstage. By examining the morris in *The Witch of Edmonton*, then, this chapter aims to reveal not only the sexual connotations of the dance when performed on the theatrical stage but also the mechanisms through which dance and theater in the commercial playhouses were productive of broader social formations and transformations. In leveraging the affective experiences of audience members, theater associated performance *both* with illicit desires *and* with traditional festivity. And this seeming contradiction between socially disruptive and conservative forces was precisely what opened up room for theater as a commercial institution—eventually remaking how performance itself was perceived.

MARRIAGE, MONEY, AND MATING

The main plot of *The Witch of Edmonton* centers around the bigamous marriage of Frank Thorney, who at the beginning of the play has already impregnated Winnifride, his master's maidservant, and secretly wedded her. For financial reasons, Frank decides nevertheless to go through with a marriage to Susan Carter that his father has arranged for him, since his fiancée's dowry is substantial, as is the inheritance he might lose should he refuse his father's wishes.[6] This main plot is connected to the morris dance subplot by several key threads. Most important of these is Dog, the physical incarnation of the devil, who drives Frank to murder Susan and who functions as the demonic familiar of the witch, Mother Sawyer. Less obvious perhaps but equally important are the sexual connotations that operate on both levels of the play with differing takes on the consequences of sin. In the main plot, fornication leads to murder and ruin. As Frank puts it in his final lines just before he is led off to execution, "Law should purge the guilt of blood and lust" (Sig. I3r; 5.3.140–41). In the subplot, by contrast, the lustful desire of the clown Cuddy Banks for Susan's sister, Katherine, results in amusing entertainment. As the devil Dog says, "I deluded thee for sport to laugh at" (Sig. H4r; 5.1.110). Whereas past scholars have been primarily concerned with the play's representation of the "guilt of blood and lust," the legal "purg[ation]" of such sins, and their relation to actual witchcraft trials, what interests me are the ways in which this nexus of concerns is not merely displaced *onto* but transformed *through* the morris dance.[7]

When Frank Thorney and Susan Carter first get engaged, the bride's father describes the upcoming wedding in terms that explicitly connect the idea of marriage to dance: "VVe'll e'en have an houshold Dinner; and let the Fiddlers go scrape. Let the Bride and Bridegroom dance at night together: no matter for the Guests" (Sig. C3r; 1.2.217–19). Here, sex on the wedding night—what in early modern terms was known as "dancing the shaking of the sheets" (a reference to a specific dance tune)[8]—is substituted for the customary practice of dancing at weddings. That this practice was generally observed can be seen in texts that take to task marriage celebrations held on the Sabbath, when dancing was prohibited. In the Consistory Court Act Book for 1634, a London baker charged with "entertaining [at] Company at a wedding in his house on sonday the 20th of April and daunsing" denies "that there was anie dauncing or anie rudenes."[9] The Puritan Nehemiah Wallington's commonplace book evinces similar sentiments when he describes a couple in the parish of Cripplegate, London, who married "vpon May day Last being the Lords day" and "spent all the afternoone in dauncing" and were therefore, according to Wallington, struck down by the plague.[10] These violations of official proscriptions against marriage dances on the Sabbath highlight the pervasiveness of this wedding custom. In *The Witch of Edmonton*, when Carter says, "let the Fiddlers go scrape," his decision to have only "an houshold Dinner" and no dancing for the guests goes against the general convention.

The lack of festive dancing in the main plot of the play is repeatedly linked to marriage as commercial exchange. In the engagement scene, Carter stresses that "Your Marriage-money shall be receiv'd before your VVedding-shooes can be pull'd on" (Sig. C3r; 1.2.224–25). The financial considerations, in other words, outstrip the celebration itself: marrying for money, as Frank does here with Susan, means that shoes—and the dances that require them—will take a backseat to the transactional nature of the event. There will be no music either at this wedding. Not only does Old Carter dispense with the "Fiddlers" who typically played dance music, but also he specifically substitutes sex for music when he says to his prospective son-in-law, "Take her to thee. Get me a brace of Boys at a burthen, *Frank*. The nursing shall not stand thee in a pennyworth of Milk. Reach her home and spare not" (Sig. C2v; 1.2.210–13). The term *burthen*, or *burden*, here refers overtly to pregnancy; as the *OED* notes, the phrase "at one burden" was used to mean "at one birth."[11] At the same time, however, the word "burden" was also used to refer to the "bass, 'undersong', or accompaniment" in music as well as to the "refrain or chorus of a song."[12] Moreover, "burthen" is precisely the word that Frank earlier uses when he first agrees to marry Susan: although he "finde[s] no disposition in me / To undergo the burthen of that care / That Marriage brings with it; Yet to secure / And settle the continuance of your [i.e., Old Thorney's] Credit, / I humbly yield to be directed by you" (Sig. C2r; 1.2.141–45). The wedding is here imagined in vulgar financial terms, and what should involve celebratory music and dancing is transformed into tedious "care." Marrying for money becomes merely mating—and music consequently goes missing.

CROSS-DRESSING, THE WITCH, AND MAID MARIAN

The failure of festivity in the union of Frank and Susan is directly juxtaposed against the morris episodes, which evoke the celebratory atmosphere absent at the wedding. Transposing dancing from the main plot to the subplot works against the standard moral valences: morris dancing, though demonized—quite literally, as we shall see, when Dog takes the place of the fiddler in the onstage dance—is ironically positioned by the play's performance dynamics as *more* legitimate than supposedly lawful matrimony. This contrast between the main plot

and subplot is foregrounded when the morris narrative is first introduced. Immediately following the engagement of Frank and Susan, we have Mother Sawyer's famous soliloquy on
why she is despised by her neighbors. This speech serves as an argument (in the early modern sense of the word)[13] to what promptly follows, when Old Banks throws invective at the
woman and then beats her just prior to the entrance of his son, Cuddy, and the other morris
dancers.

In this episode, the abuse heaped on the witch is specifically imagined in terms of music
and dance, and Mother Sawyer's body is presented as bent and broken—a discourse about
age that becomes significant in terms of gender difference, as I will discuss momentarily.
Here, the language strikingly connects the witchcraft narrative to the morris. The "blows
[that] have lam'd" (Sig. C3v; 2.1.32) Sawyer are described by Old Banks as making her "bones
rattle" (Sig. C3v; 2.1.22), a metaphor that ties together dancing, gaming, and violence.[14]
When the morris dancers enter immediately thereafter, Young Banks calls for "A new head
for the Tabor" (Sig. C3v; 2.1.37), juxtaposing the beating of the woman with the beating of
the "Tabor," or drum. These metaphorical echoes would have been enhanced in onstage
performance by the visual contrast between age and youth. Whereas the witch is "like a
Bow buckl'd and bent together" (Sig. C3r; 2.1.4), the morris dancers are quick and strong,
as is reinforced later in the play when Sir Arthur Clarington describes the dancers as "The
nimble-footed youth of *Edmonton*" (Sig. F2v; 3.4.2) and Sawgut, the fiddler, twice refers to
them as "Children" (Sig. F3r; 3.4.36, 37).[15] The physical differences between the witch and
the dancers are also underscored by the latter's reference to the obtaining of morris bells in
"*Crooked Lane*" (Sig. C3v; 2.1.39), an actual street in London as well as an echo of the language used in the play's source text, which describes the witch as "crooked and deformed,
euen bending together."[16] Moreover, the original quarto text, whose speech prefixes elsewhere refer to Cuddy as "Clown," throughout this scene dubs him "*Y. Bank.*"—that is,
"*Young* Banks" (Sig. C3v; 2.1.36.s.d.). As Randall McLeod has shown, such variations in the
textual apparatus may well have signaled thematic contrasts between age and youth marked
visually in performance.[17] In connecting the morris to the witch, the play positions dancing
and the demonic as parallel: both serve as spectacular entertainment even if—or perhaps
because—they are "crooked."

The contrast between age and youth is explicitly recast in the subsequent action as being
about gender inversion, a move imagined by the play as integrated with festive practice. That
this shift is particular to theater as a medium can be seen most clearly if we look toward a
printed text that describes (but does not enact) performance. In the popular pamphlet *Old
Meg of Hereford-shire*, morris dancing is repeatedly analogized to scripted drama. To take just
one of many examples, the anonymous work notes that "It was therefore now plotted, to lay
the Sceane in Age, to haue the old Comedie presented, Fathers to be the Actors, and beardlesse boyes the Spectators."[18] This emphasis on "beardlesse boyes" as "Spectators" figures a
humorous inversion of the usual roles: it is the young people who watch a group of elderly
morris dancers, not the other way around. Each of the performers is roughly a century old,
so that there are "*Twelue Morris-dancers in Hereford-shire, of twelue hundred yeares old*," as
the title page puts it. When *The Witch of Edmonton* was originally performed, however, such
a juxtaposition of different age groups may also have highlighted the issue of gender. Unlike
the "weyard" sisters in *Macbeth* and Falstaff disguised as the wise woman of Bradford in *The
Merry Wives of Windsor*,[19] Mother Sawyer is nowhere described as having a beard. Since
early modern drama typically includes humorous references to or wordplay on such stage

props whenever they *are* present, it seems likely that Sawyer's part was played by a boy. If the witch who was "buckl'd and bent together" (Sig. C3r; 2.1.4) was indeed played onstage by a beardless boy, then juxtaposing *differences* between Sawyer and the dancers would simultaneously draw attention to *similarities* between the performers who represent them: age and gender—two different kinds of disjunctions between actor and character—here converge. To link the witch and the morris via the contrast between youth and age highlights the *theatrical* witchcraft involved in effecting *gender*-crossing transformations.

This emphasis on transvestism is further underscored when the dancers discuss whether their morris bells should be of low, medium, or high pitch:

> *Enter Young* Banks, *and three or four more.*
>
> Y. BANK.   A new head for the Tabor, and silver tipping for the Pipe. Remember that, and forget not five lesh of new Bells.
>
> 1.   Double Bells: *Crooked Lane* ye shall have 'em straight in. *Crooked Lane:* double Bells all, if it be possible.
>
> Y. BANK.   Double Bells? double Coxcombs; Trebles: buy me Trebles, all Trebles: for our purpose is to be in the Altitudes.
>
> 2.   All Trebles? not a Mean?
>
> Y. BANK.   Not one: The Morrice is so cast, we'll have neither Mean nor Base in our company, Fellow *Rowland.*
>
> 3.   VVhat? nor a Counter?
>
> Y. BANK.   By no means, no hunting Counter; leave that to *Envile Chase*-Men: all Trebles, all in the Altitudes. (Sig. C3v; 2.1.36.s.d.–48)

On one level, the joke is about festive class inversion, with the base clowns ironically insisting that their "purpose is to be in the Altitudes" and that "we'll have neither Mean nor Base in our company." On another level, the episode refers to the sound of the changing voices of adolescent boys, which were understood in musical terms.[20] The word "Counter"—which the Third Dancer uses to refer to a countertenor, or the highest male singing voice—is here recast by the clown into a hunting metaphor, situating the morris as a game that involves good horsemanship and thus moving the scene toward the crucial issue of who will play the hobbyhorse.[21]

I will get to the hobbyhorse momentarily, but what I want to stress first is that this playing on musical pitch, while purportedly about the morris bells, also draws attention to cross-dressing customs associated with both morris dances and early modern theater. Cuddy Banks's first line mentions not only the tabor but also "silver tipping for the Pipe" (Sig. C3v; 2.1.37–38). The pipe was one of the morris dance's traditional musical instruments, but it was also another word for *penis.*[22] The word's relation to theatrical transvestism can perhaps best be seen in Shakespeare's *Twelfth Night*, when the cross-dressed Viola's voice is described as a "small pipe" that is "as the maidens organ, shrill, and sound" (TLN 283–84; 1.4.32–33).[23] Cuddy's reference thus works in tandem with the discussion of morris bells: both call attention to the gendering of actors in the commercial playhouse.

Moreover, theatrical transvestism is likened to cross-dressing customs in traditional festivity. In the morris dance, the part of Maid Marian was typically played by a boy. A 1589 Canterbury Quarter Sessions case, for example, refers to an amateur morris troupe with "mayd maryon being a boy in womans apparell."[24] The boy himself was "aged xii yers or theraboutes [examyned by] beyng dressed in womans apparell for mayd marryon without any breches with Breyded here."[25] Such cross-dressing customs were typical of festive role-playing in general, as can be seen in numerous court cases. One 1620 case from Bunbury, Cheshire, for instance, involved a "Richard Coddingtoun who was putt in womans apparell" with "a great trayne of rude people tumultuously gaddinge after him from thence to the Church hill to bringe a present of Cheryes to the sayd Elizabeth where shee sate as Ladye of the game readie to receive them."[26] These seasonal cross-dressing practices were associated with a kind of sexual excess that was itself understood as profoundly entertaining spectacle. A 1577 ecclesiastical court case from Elmstead, Kent, for instance, highlights Maid Marian's discursive links to promiscuity and prostitution. The defendants

> on sondaye before morninge prayer beinge mydsomer even ledd abowte the contrye a company of morres dauncers with their mayde marryon, representynge a whore, vsynge vngodly tryckes with their foles bable a comely sight I trowe for christyans to beholde, for ye which they were in many places well rewarded but at mr honywoodes of Elmested sharpely rebuked.[27]

As in the Cheshire case involving "a great trayne of rude people tumultuously gaddinge after" the cross-dressed revelers, the game of "mayde marryon, representynge a whore" was apparently quite popular with the crowds. His/her "vngodly tryckes" with the fool's bauble was "in many places well rewarded."[28] Transposing such acts onto the professional stage took advantage of the sexual connotations of festive cross-dressers and capitalized on the welcome generally afforded them.

That these erotic spectacles were a standard part of the festive repertoire is underscored by the fact that the reverse—imagining Maid Marian as chaste—is made fun of in *Old Meg of Hereford-shire*, which describes the eponymous elderly woman taking on this part. The pamphlet states that "a far more lamentable cause of sorow would it be, if Mayden-heades should stand so long vpon Wenches shoulders, as yours (Mother *Marget*) hath done vpon your owne, because if they did so, they would be seeded (like olde tough Turne-vps) and so not bee worth the cutting" (Sig. C3r). The reference to cutting in this passage is bound up with the convention that Maid Marian was typically played by a boy. The implication is that the old woman's stale maidenhead (here figured as if virginity were worn "vpon Wenches shoulders," like scarves attached to the shoulders of morris coats) is to be contrasted with the sexual desirability of the cross-dressed youth.[29] Moreover, the phrasing of the passage plays with reversals of high and low, of young boy and old woman, of maid and Maid Marian. Sex with an elderly virgin is compared to turnips because they are "Turne-vps"—that is, inverted, or "up-turned."[30] The removal of old maids' maidenheads (which reside in their lower parts) is imagined as cutting heads off of shoulders (their higher parts). This inversion is displaced and analogized onto the boys that actually played Maid Marians, since cutting off *their* lower "heades" evoked a different meaning entirely, one that played with a notion of castration as a kind of decapitation that is nevertheless festive, as in the case of the fool's coxcomb (where the fool wears his cock on his head).

In *The Witch of Edmonton*, the sexual valences of festive gender inversion were not only deployed to associate theatrical transvestism with holiday role-playing but also remapped specifically onto the figure of the witch. When the clown Cuddy inquires about which "part[s]" the dancers should include in their upcoming morris, he asks:

> [CLOW.]   . . . Have we e're a Witch in the Morice?
> 1.   No, no; no womans part, but Maid-marian, and the Hobby-horse.
> CLOW.   I'll have a Witch; I love a Witch.

1. Faith, VVitches themselves are so common now adays [*sic*], that the counterfeit will not be regarded. They say we have three or four in *Edmonton,* besides Mother *Sawyer.*
2. I would she would dance her part with us.
3. So would not I; for if she comes, the Devil and all comes along with her.
CLOW.   VVell, I'll have a Witch: I have lov'd a VVitch ever since I play'd at Cherry-pit. Leave me, and get my horse dress'd: give him Oats; but water him not till I come. VVhither do we foot it first?
2. To Sir *Arthur Clarington's* first, then whither thou wilt.
CLOW.   VVell, I'am content: but we must up to *Carter's,* the rich Yeoman. I must be seen on Hobby-horse there.
1. O, I smell him now: I'll lay my ears *Banks* is in love. (Sigs. E1r-E1v; 3.1.7–26)

Unlike Maid Marian and the hobbyhorse, the witch was not a traditional figure in the morris dance.[31] In referring to a witch in the morris as a "counterfeit," the characters in the dance are implicitly compared with those in the dramatic narrative proper, collapsing the semiotic distinction between performers who play witches and performers who play dancers who play witches. Moreover, by bemoaning that "VVitches themselves are so common now adays [*sic*]," the scene calls attention to real-life witchcraft trials, including the one that served as the basis for this play. Yet in highlighting this extratheatrical context, the line also simultaneously suggests what *is* available in the theater. Here you can see a clowning and a morris. A 1634 letter by Nathaniel Tomkyns about a "new comedie," *The Late Lancashire Witches*, at the Globe indicates that it was precisely these kinds of elements that were most appealing to spectators, for

> though there be not in it (to my vnderstanding) any poeticall Genius, or art, or language, or iudgement to state our tenet of witches (which I expected,) [or application to vertue] but full of ribaldrie and of things improbable and impossible; yet în respect of the newnesse of ye subiect (the witches being still visible and in prison here) and in regard it consisteth from the beginning to the ende of odd passages and fopperies to provoke laughter, and is mixed with diuers songs and dances, it passeth for a merrie and ex[c]ellent new play.[32]

Like the play that Tomkyns saw, *The Witch of Edmonton* took pains to go beyond the sensationalistic elements of actual witchcraft trials by including "fopperies to provoke laughter" and "diuers songs and dances."

That a witch play should be "full of ribaldrie"—like the sexual spectacles at early modern holiday revels—suggests cultural overlaps between the demonic and the festive that bear on the erotics of transvestite performance. In the scene about whether to have a witch in the morris, the play repeatedly refers to the act of cutting, recalling the description of Maid Marian in *Old Meg*. When Cuddy describes how lovers lament, "I have not seen my Love these seven yeers: there's a long cut" (Sig. E1v; 3.1.50), his allusion to the "long cut" (which editors gloss as "misfortune"[33]) echoes the language that follows when he tells the dancers, just prior to their exit, to "get *Poldavis,* the Barber's Boy for the Witch; because he can shew his Art better then another" (Sig. E1v; 3.1.60–61). In the list of "Actors Names" at the beginning of the quarto, this figure shows up as "*Poldavis,* a Barbers boy" (Sig. A2r), but aside from Cuddy's line he is never otherwise mentioned nor does he appear onstage. Although editors have speculated regarding his role in the morris dance in 3.4,[34] I would argue that this reference is significant not for the movement of a shadow character in the play but because it highlights the issue of gender performance. The barber's boy can play the witch because he is not a man: he has no beard and thus he need not be shaved.[35] Moreover, his status as a *barber*'s boy emphasizes the question of cutting: His "Art" is both his ability to cut and his artifice at playing the woman, or "cu(n)t." Indeed, whether he is himself "cut"—that is, castrated—is highlighted by the emphasis on barbering, since eunuchs were famously hairless and, as Dympna Callaghan argues, barber surgeons located near London playhouses also performed castrations.[36] Furthermore, the word *cut* was also associated, then as now, with dance: to "cut a caper" meant to scissor one's legs back and forth very quickly, a movement often used in the dance known as the *galliard*; and as the *OED* notes, *cut* in other similar phrases meant "To perform or execute (an action, gesture, or display of a grotesque, striking, or notable kind)," as we still see in our modern phrase "to cut a figure."[37] Poldavis, in other words, can play the witch *because* he "cuts."

By drawing attention to the "counterfeit[ing]" of the boy actor playing the witch, the play compares theatrical practices to the festive cross-dressing of Maid Marian. References to Poldavis and cutting make fun—quite literally—of this holiday transvestism, which is presented as ludicrous (that is, both ridiculous and playful *ludi*) even as the play celebrates that preposterousness (that is, it is fun *because* it is, quite literally, ass backward).[38] Like Cuddy, who has "lov'd a VVitch ever since I play'd at Cherry-pit,"[39] playgoers also "love a Witch." That "love" is here mapped onto theater's cross-dressing practices, and the experience of watching a play (and a morris in it) is sexualized through comparison to Cuddy's witch—i.e., Katherine Carter, who has "bewitch'd" (Sig. D2r; 2.1.217) him. Cuddy "must be seen on Hobby-horse" at the Carter residence because he is "in love." Desire here leads to dancing. The potential licentiousness of the commercial stage—precisely what opponents of the theater argued was a key element of its depravity—is here transformed into wholesome holiday mirth.

Hobbyhorses and Strange Postures

The morris may have no witch, but it does have a devil; and it has not only a horse but a dog. As we shall see, the playhouse audience's enjoyment of these figures and the dance is likened to (and collapsed into and across) enjoyment of the play as a whole and associated with increasingly transgressive forms of desire. That transgression is both erotic and specifically theatrical in the case of the hobbyhorse. In the scene I discussed earlier when the First Dancer declares that there is "no womans part, but Maid-marian, and the Hobby-horse," the syntax of his sentence introduces ambiguity about whether the morris hobbyhorse, too, is a woman's role. The joke is that the part was usually danced by a man, but in early modern usage the term *hobbyhorse* itself could also mean "a loose woman, prostitute."[40] To say that a woman played the hobbyhorse was tantamount to saying she was a whore. Discursive overlaps between whores and horses take on festive connotations when the villagers decide to burn Mother Sawyer's house. Old Banks accuses the "Jadish Witch, Mother *Sawyer*" (Sig. F3v; 4.1.4) of making ill his horse, "whose nose yesternight was as clean as any Man's here now coming from the Barbers" (Sig. F3v; 4.1.2–3). The line echoes earlier references to cutting in its mentions of barbers and "here," which was an early modern spelling for *hair* though also a possible homonym for the locational word *here*—especially amusing in this context given that "here" on stage were actors who wore "hairs," or wigs, to represent differences of age and gender. In addition, this line connects horses and hobbyhorses, as the term "jade" could mean both prostitute and horse. I will discuss this scene in more detail shortly, but for now, let me just underscore that Old Banks makes this overlap explicit when Sawyer comes to see why her house is on fire and he specifically insults her, saying "You hot VVhore, must we fetch you with fire in your tail?" (Sig. F4r; 4.1.24). In contrast to the main plot of *The Witch of Edmonton*, in which sex on the wedding night is imagined as an economic transaction, the subplot deploys overlaps between the witch and the hobbyhorse to transform commercial sex into theatrical entertainment.

This festive slippage between human and animal serves both as the pleasurable transgression of erotic categories and as the spectacular disruption of theatrical ones. In the episode when the morris dancers allocate their parts, the Second Dancer describes his lead role by referring to himself figuratively as a "Fore-horse" (Sig. C3v; 2.1.51) or "for gallant" (Sig. C3v; 2.1.52) in the morris team. His skill at dancing, he proudly states, derives from "an ancient Honor belonging to our house" (Sig. C3v; 2.1.51); his "Father's Stable," he declares, "is not unfurnish'd" (Sig. C3v; 2.1.52–53). In comparing himself to a horse, the Second Dancer here imagines himself as a kind of stallion or stud whose ancestors have passed along both sexual and dancing prowess. As the group moves on to decide who will play the part of the hobbyhorse, the dancers further conflate human performer with animal role:

> 3.   So much for the Fore-horse: but how for a good Hobby-horse?
> Y. *BANK.*   For a Hobby-horse? Let me see an Almanack. *Midsummer*-Moon, let me see ye. VVhen the Moon's in the full, then's wit in the wane. No more. Use your best skill. Your Morrice will suffer an Eclipse.
> 1.   An Eclipse?   Y. *BANK.*   A strange one.   2.   Strange?
> Y. *BANK.*   Yes, and most sudden. Remember the Fore gallant, and forget the Hobby-horse. The whole body of your Morrice will be darkned. There be of us. But 'tis no matter. Forget the Ho[b]by-horse. (Sig. C3v–C4r; 2.1.54–66)

Cuddy Banks's displeasure at being ignored by his fellows and his consequent sulky refusal to participate in the dance is condensed in the phrase "Forget the Ho[b]by-horse"—a reference to the early modern commonplace "the hobbyhorse is forgot."[41] The overlap between performer and role is further underscored by the fact that *hobby* was a common word for a small or middle-sized horse, and *cuddy* may have been a generic term for an ass.[42] This pun contributes to the sodomitical resonances of the situations in which the clown later finds himself, even as it foregrounds his desire not just to *play* the hobbyhorse but to *become* it. As in Tomkyn's account of *The Late Lancashire Witches* at the Globe, which mentions "the transforming of men and weomen into the shapes of seuerall creatures and especially of horses by putting an inchaunted bridle into ther mouths,"[43] the transformation of the fool into the hobbyhorse—a conflation of two separate morris dance roles—is precisely the kind of comic stage action that one might find in a witch play.

This foolish fusion of man and beast is repeatedly imagined as festive *con*fusion, a kind of mirthful madness that contributes to notions of the morris as a mad dance. Cuddy's unhappiness at the attention lavished on the Second Dancer as the foregallant in the morris becomes the occasion for a series of interlocking puns on this theme. When the clown says "For a Hobby-horse? Let me see an Almanack. *Midsummer*-Moon," his line draws attention to the dance's association with midsummer revels, and he plays on the proverbial notion of midsummer madness—or lunacy—for "then's wit in the wane."[44] This emphasis on madness is particularly appropriate for the clown, but what is striking is that the play later enacts the very trope that it here cites: madness, the almanac says, is a problem when the moon is full; if a morris without a hobbyhorse is like an eclipse, then a morris *with* a hobbyhorse is sheer lunacy. In recasting the literal darkness of a midsummer night without a moon as the figurative darkness of forgetting the hobbyhorse, these lines position the audience's enjoyment of the onstage morris later in the play as *participation* in the trope of festive inversion, whereby what is normally madness is transformed into mirth. This association with madness is further accentuated when Mother Sawyer enters. The First Dancer worries whether "our mirth be not cross'd" (Sig. C4r; 2.1.87–88), but he concludes that "The Divel cannot abide to be cross'd" (Sig. C4r; 2.1.94), and the dancers then "*Ex. in strange postur.*" (Sig. C4r; 2.1.98.s.d.). This stage direction is often viewed as a response to the witch;[45] I would argue, however, that it draws on the morris's association with lunacy. Cuddy's reference to the "strange" (Sig. C4r; 2.1.61) eclipse suggests the inappropriateness of a morris without a hobbyhorse—that is to say, its madness. The "strange" postures with which the dancers exit, I propose, suggest a visual allusion to the mad morris to come. As in *A Midsummer Night's Dream*, when Peter Quince cries "O monstrous. O strange" (TLN 918; 3.1.104) upon Bottom's first appearance wearing the ass's head, strangeness is also associated with the monstrous union of human and animal. Through embodied form, the dancers' exit associates the morris with the festive breakdown of such distinctions.

This transgression of categories works in tandem with the play's sexual valences. When Cuddy finally agrees, after much cajoling, to play the part of the hobbyhorse, he declares, "To shew I am not flint; but affable, as you say, very well stuft, a kinde of warm Dowe or Puff-paste, I relent, I connive, most affable *Jack*: let the Hobby-horse provide a strong back, he shall not want a belly when I am in 'em" (Sig. C4r; 2.1.82–85). The clown's comment draws on the trope of festive plenty to conflate playing the hobbyhorse with having a full stomach. Cuddy, who will be inside the hobbyhorse costume, fills out the role; he is thus like food in the horse's belly, and the hobbyhorse is, in this sense, "well stuft," just like Cuddy himself. However, the reference to the hobbyhorse requiring a "strong back" resonates with overlaps between horses and whores. If Cuddy is "in" the hobbyhorse in this sense, his exertions could potentially result in pregnancy, which would make the prostitute's belly "well stuft." The use of the pronoun "he" in the line "he shall not want a belly" seems at first to complicate the sexual connotations, but I would argue to the contrary that it is of a piece with the slippage we see throughout the passage between subject and object, human and animal, performer and role—and, as we shall see later, resonates with the play's sodomitical references. Cuddy is both the one who stuffs and the one who is himself "well stuft." He takes on all sexual roles. Playing the hobbyhorse is simultaneously sex with a whore, sex with a horse, and sex with a cuddy—or ass.[46]

The word *ass* in early modern usage, although usually referring to the equine, nevertheless evoked the human body part in its semiotic associations and phonemic overlaps, and it appears to have been used as early as 1613 in its more modern sense.[47] Like Bottom in *A Midsummer Night's Dream*, Cuddy is the clown figure whose liminal position between man and beast is explicitly sexualized. In Shakespeare's play, the fairy queen Titania "madly dote[s]" (TLN 548; 2.1.171) on the hybrid creature wearing the ass's head. As Richard Rambuss has shown, this representation of bestiality overlaps with the play's concern with anality in its many puns on Bottom and bottoms.[48] What is striking in both plays, though, is that it is not simply the character but also the actor who makes an ass of himself: the real-life player plays a character who aspires to be a player and who expresses, as both Bottom and

Cuddy do, not aversion but desire to take on the part of the beast of burden. The performer who wants the best role (or roles) in the show, who seeks to be the center of attention, is imagined as yearning for the equine. Watching the humiliation implicit in the downward movement from man to beast is imagined as both erotic and theatrical spectacle.

Yet however much this hybrid figure is shamed within the dramatic fiction—and I don't think he always is—in the actual playhouse he steals the show. His monstrous nature (to use period terms here) becomes an asset onstage, its theatricality inseparable from its function as pleasurable debasement. Rambuss has argued that anality in *A Midsummer Night's Dream* is seen as degrading, not ennobling, as was the case in certain other early modern contexts, such as those associated with military prowess.[49] I would argue that a similar set of associations pertains to Cuddy in *The Witch of Edmonton* but that, in both plays, hierarchies are inverted in the festive tradition so that sexually low *becomes* theatrically high. Rambuss has also speculated that Shakespeare's Bottom prefigures contemporary forms of "ponyplay" and "furry fandom," whereby participants dress up as animals to free themselves from the strictures of human behavior and to enjoy sexual acts, including those involving bondage, dominance/submission, and sadomasochism.[50] The morris subplot in *The Witch of Edmonton* draws on similar associations: as a manifestation of the early modern notion of "the world turned upside down," the license to take pleasure in transgressive sexuality is figured as integral to the playhouse experience.

DOG TRICKS, SODOMITICAL GAMES, AND THEATRICAL INSTRUMENTS

Just as the play folds the audience's enjoyment of the transvestite theater into the familiar mirth of Maid Marian and situates the sexual antics of the hobbyhorse as central to the spectacle playgoers have paid to see, its performance dynamics also complicate spectator attitudes toward even more transgressive erotic practices. Cuddy's desire for Katherine Carter and his desire to play the hobbyhorse both ultimately involve the intervention of the devil, and the clown's humiliation at the hands of (or should I say "paws of"?) Dog resonate with early modern notions of bestiality as a form of sodomy. The morris dance in *The Witch of Edmonton* is bound up with such sodomitical discourses. Yet in enabling Cuddy to quite literally make an ass of himself for the audience's sport, the play's performance dynamics transform anal sexuality into festive game—and situate theatrical spectators as complicit participants.

We can see this emphasis on bestiality and sodomy as mirthful sport in the episode when Mother Sawyer's house is set on fire and the Justice intervenes. Old Banks defends his actions as payback for being bewitched:

> O. BANK. So, Sir, ever since, having a Dun-Cow tied up in my Back-side, let me go thither, or but cast mine eye at her, and if I should be hang'd, I cannot chuse, though it be ten times in an hour, but run to the Cow, and taking up her tail, kiss (saving your Worship's Reverence) my Gow [*sic*] behinde; That the whole Town of *Edmonton* has been ready to be-piss themselves with laughing me to scorn.
>
> JUST. And this is long of her?
>
> O. BANK. VVho the Devil else? for is any man such an Ass, to be such a Baby, if he were not bewitch'd?

> SIR ART.   Nay, if she be a VVitch, and the harms she does end in such sports, she may scape
> burning.
> JUST.   Go, go; pray vex her not: she is a Subject, and you must not be Judges of the Law to
> strike her as you please.
> OMN.   No, no, we'll finde cudgel enough to strike her.
> O. BANK.   I, no lips to kiss but my Cows ——? (Sig. F4v; 4.1.53–68)

The witch is here described as instigating at Old Banks's expense what Sir Arthur refers to as
"sports." The "laughing" of all the townsfolk at watching Banks kissing his cow's "behinde"
makes him "an Ass." Moreover, that laughing is imagined as precisely that which will justify
clemency toward the witch. Playgoers who also laugh at Banks are imagined as being like
Sir Arthur and his neighbors. As with the morris, they are positioned as wanting to see such
sports. Moreover, in the scene's references to the townsmen's desire to "strike her," the beating elsewhere imagined as akin to dance and game is linked to bestial ass-play. Justice (and
the Justice) is subverted when perversion is refigured as festive *in*version, with "no lips to kiss
but my Cows ——."

Ass-play is likewise presented as one of Dog's entertaining tricks when the clown requires
the canine devil's help in obtaining Katherine Carter's love. Cuddy first seeks Mother
Sawyer's assistance in a scene that explicitly equates erotic desire with witchcraft: Katherine
has "bewitch'd" (Sig. D2r; 2.1.217) the clown, and he hopes the witch might "unwitch me,
or witch another with me for company" (Sig. D2r; 2.1.212–13). Drawing on extramission
notions of vision that imagine women's eyes as shooting Cupid's arrows into the hearts of
their admirers, Cuddy says, "I saw a little Devil flie out of her eye like a Burbolt, which sticks
at this hour up to the Feathers in my heart" (Sig. D2r; 2.1.219–20). The penetration imaginatively figured in these lines comes back to haunt him—quite literally—when Sawyer agrees
to his request. When the witch tells Cuddy to "turn to the West, and whatsoe'er thou hearest
or seest, stand silent, and be not afraid" (Sig. D2r; 2.1.234–36), the stage direction indicates
that she "*stamps*" and then Dog enters and "*fawns and leaps upon her*" (Sig. D2r; 2.1.236.s.d.).
The clown's response implies that he rotates his body onstage to face away from the witch
when Dog enters: "turn my face to the West? I said I should always have a back-friend of her;
and now it's out. And her little Devil should be hungry, come sneaking behinde me, like a
cowardly Catchpole, and clap his Talents on my Haunches" (Sig. D2r; 2.1.237–40). The "little
Devil" from Katherine's eye that penetrates Cuddy's heart is here transformed into the "little
Devil" who comes from "behinde" and grabs Cuddy's "Haunches." Indeed, Dog's physical
actions onstage are reinforced through verbal references to the devil as a "back-friend" (that
is, a false ally) as well as a "Catchpole" (that is, a bumbaliff, or debt collector who catches
one unexpectedly from the rear). The bawdy potential of this language is further accentuated through bodily form, since Cuddy is likely positioned onstage physically facing away
from the witch and Dog. Mother Sawyer's asides to the audience describe this gulling of the
clown as "sport" (Sig. D2r; 2.1.224) and as "a ball well bandied; now the set's half won" (Sig.
D2v; 2.1.269–70). Cuddy, for his part, declares, "I think she'll prove a VVitch in earnest" (Sig.
D2r; 2.1.228). Collapsing the line between fictional representation and onstage presentation,
both clown and witch transform heteroerotic tropes about Cupid's arrows into sodomitical
penetration. That such sexual practices are here associated with role-playing and sport likens
theatrical performance to a "little Devil"—morally wrong but very entertaining.

Indeed, Cuddy's desire for Katherine repeatedly slides into and across his desire for
the devil. It is the latter whom Cuddy repeatedly refers to as—and tries to convince to

become—a "ducking" dog, or water spaniel (3.1.73, 4.1.235–36, 5.1.158). Melissa Sanchez has suggested that the image of the spaniel is used to figure masochistic desire in *A Midsummer Night's Dream* and that Helena's reference to this breed in her pursuit of Demetrius "blurs the boundaries between masculinity and femininity, abjection and aggression."[51] In *The Witch of Edmonton*, that notion of a spaniel as both servile and sexual is not merely a verbal metaphor, as in Shakespeare, but embodied in the figure of the actor onstage and mapped onto same-sex (though not, it must be noted, same-species) relations. This performance condition renders the play potentially even more subversive than Shakespeare's in its representation of sexuality, especially since it ties transgressive desires and acts specifically to the spectacular dimension of theater as a medium. The performance dynamics embedded in the clown's anal-erotic connection to the devil are especially evident in the various names he uses to address Dog. When Cuddy asks for his name, the latter responds:

> DOG.   My Dame calls me *Tom*.
> CLOW.   'Tis well; and she may call me *Ass*: so there's an whole one betwixt us, *Tom-Ass*. She said, I should follow you, indeed. VVell, *Tom*, give me thy fist; we are Friends: you shall be mine Ingle: I love you; but I pray you let's have no more of these ducking devices.
> DOG.   Not, if you love me. Dogs love where they are beloved. Cherish me, and I'll do any thing [*sic*] for thee. (Sig. E2v; 3.1.115–22)

This exchange not only uses the trope of loving and being beloved of the devil—a discourse that informs the witch's relationship with her canine familiar as well—but also specifically figures Cuddy as if in sexual congress with Dog. Joining their names, the clown jokingly implies, makes them a single being with a single name—Thomas—and Cuddy himself will play the "*Ass*" in "*Tom-Ass*."[52] This anal reference is reinforced when the clown says that Dog shall serve as "mine Ingle"—i.e., a servant or catamite—a nickname that resonates with the ducking dog's associations with servitude and sexuality. And the term sticks: throughout the rest of the play, Cuddy refers repeatedly to the devil as his "ningle." Mario DiGangi has analyzed the (homo)erotics of early modern understandings of servitude and submission as integral to its converse: sexual mastery.[53] Here, Cuddy's relation with Dog has precisely this dual connotation. In his attempt to obtain Katherine, the clown did "follow you, indeed," both literally and metaphorically, and thus played the devil's "*Ass*." Dog will later serve as Cuddy's "ningle" in the morris, enabling the audience's entertainment. But the devil will have the last laugh when he reveals to the clown that he merely "deluded thee for sport to laugh at. / The VVench thou seek'st after, thou never spakest with, / But a Spirit in her form, habit and likeness. Ha, ha!" (Sig. H4r; 5.1.110–13). As Mary Bly has noted, the term "dog" was also a synonym for a male prostitute, and antitheatricalist John Rainoldes specifically accuses the theater of fostering such "dogs."[54] Being served by a dog and being sodomized by the devil both become "sport" for spectators "to laugh at."

In this context, then, Dog's crucial role in the onstage morris cannot be separated out from the erotics of playhouse performance and from the ways in which the dance situates spectators as willing confederates in demonic sexual games. After the devil tells Cuddy his name, the clown asks Dog to take part in the morris: "One thing I would request you, *Ningle*, as you have play'd the Knavish Cur with me a little, that you would mingle amongst our Morrice-Dancers in the morning. You can dance?" Dog responds, "Yes, yes, any thing: I'll be there, but unseen to any but thy self" (Sig. E2v; 3.1.135–38). The ningle

mingles, and yet he is to be invisible to all but Cuddy. When the dance is actually performed, however, the playhouse audience can well see Dog, who takes the place of the morris musician. In the engagement scene at the beginning of the play, Old Carter specifically
says "let the Fiddlers go scrape" (Sig. C3r; 1.2.218) when he declares that there will be no
dancing at the wedding. Yet *The Witch of Edmonton* specifically requires a fiddler named
Sawgut for the morris dance—and then stages the failure of his "Instrument" (Sig. F3r;
3.4.38, 43) at the crucial moment. The *OED* coyly alludes to the multiple sexual possibilities of the term when it notes that *instrument* could refer to "A part of the body having a
special function; an organ," as when Chaucer's Wife of Bath asks "Wher with sholde he
make his paiement If he ne vsed his sely instrument?" and declares that "In wyfhode I wol
vse myn Instrument As frely as my makere hath it sent."[55] When Sawgut describes how his
"Instrument has caught cold on the sudden" (Sig. F3r; 3.4.38), then, the fiddle's soundless-
ness links the spectacle of the onstage morris to sexual heat and lack thereof. This notion
is foregrounded by Cuddy's aside immediately after, when he refers to Dog using his favorite pet name: "My *Ningle's* knavery: black *Tom's* doing" (Sig. F3r; 3.4.39). The implication
seems to be that the devil has the power to pervert sexuality, to render impotent the musician's prowess. This supernatural cause is underscored when Sawgut insists, "I'll lay mine
Ear to my Instrument, that my poor Fiddle is bewitch'd" (Sig. F3r; 3.4.43–44). Communal
entertainment is only enabled when Cuddy commandeers the instrument and says "I'll
play and dance too" (Sig. F3r; 3.4.48–49), then hands it off to the devil with "*Ningle*, away
with it" (Sig. F3r; 3.4.49), and as the stage direction puts it, "*Dog plays the Morrice*" (Sig.
F3r; 3.4.50.s.d.). The devil in the form of Dog is precisely that which enables the dance,
and his critical function in this regard is heightened by the temporary musical and sexual
impotence also attributed to him.

This depiction of the devil as the musician for the morris resonates with a 1623 incident
described in the Archdeaconry of Chichester Register of Presentments that involved a fiddler (the aptly named "william witcher of Boxgrove") who, pied piper-like, would often lead
the youth astray. Witcher, it was charged, "causeth divers of other parishes sometimes 30 or
40 in a day to accompany him to yapton on ye sundayes" so that "many youth in yapton when
they should be in ye church . . . are then attending on him to daunce" while he is "all ye day
playing on his Instrument."[56] That the devil might be a fiddler was a narrative that also implicated the theater. One sermon, preached at Paul's Cross in London on May 10, 1579, is typical.
Its author, John Stockwood, warned against "idle loytering fidlars and minstrels, with whom
we are on the Lordes day as much troubled, as you are with Players. For they pipe away all our
audience in many places: so pleasaunt a thing is it to daunce after the Diuell."[57] Similarly, in
The Witch of Edmonton, the performance dynamics of the play situate the real-life audience's
enjoyment of the dance as being misled by the devil. That diversion (in both senses of the
term) is both theatrical and sexual: since Dog is the dance's musical consort, taking pleasure in the morris means consorting with the devil. Moreover, Dog is invisible—though not
inaudible—to the other characters within the fictional world of the play, yet actual playgoers
can see him as well as they can see the dance performance itself. Watching the onstage morris
is like playing with the devil's "Instrument." In doing so, spectators "take delight / In sins and
mischiefs" (Sig. E3r; 3.1.152–53), as Dog does with the clown and the morris.

When Cuddy pretends to be Dog himself, then, the play highlights the interpretive
quandaries of playhouse spectatorship by collapsing not only performer and role but also
devil and clown. Old Banks, who threatens to imprison Dog, is defied by his son, Cuddy,

who declares he will post bail for the beast. His father's imputations, the clown insists, are false:

> CLOW.   I say, Good-man Father-fool, it's a lye.
> OMN.   He's bewitch'd.
> CLOW.   A gross lye as big as my self [*sic*]. The Devil in St. *Dunstan's* will as soon drink with this poor Cur, as with any Temple-Bar-Laundress, that washes and wrings Lawyers.
> DOG.   Bough, wough, wough, wough.
> OMN.   O the Dog's here, the Dog's here.
> O. BANK.   It was the voice of a Dog.
> CLOW.   The voice of a Dog? if that voice were a Dog's, what voice had my Mother? so am I a Dog: bough, wough, wough: it was I that bark'd so, Father, to make Cocks-combs of these Clowns. (Sig. G3r; 4.1.243–53)

Cuddy, who has already played the hobbyhorse in the morris, who played the *ass* with Dog and together formed *Tom-ass*, here takes on the role of Dog himself. The "lye" is "as big as my self" because it *is* himself. Indeed, he calls attention to questions of parentage when he essentially calls his mother a bitch ("if that voice were a Dog's, what voice had my Mother?"). Moreover, in barking like a dog, Cuddy troubles the line between playing the clown and playing the devil. Dog is ultimately just an actor, and Cuddy could, if necessary, play that part himself. Audience members who must distinguish between the two are here instructed that there *is* no difference. This interpretive difficulty is mapped across the sexual valences that run throughout the play. When Cuddy explains why he pretends to be Dog, the clown describes his reason as "love," echoing the erotic language he earlier applied to Katherine and that the witch has throughout applied to the devil: "*Ningle*, you had like to have spoyl'd all with your Boughings. I was glad to put 'em off with one of my Dog-tricks, on a sudden, I am bewitch'd, little Cost-me-nought, to love thee—a Pox, that Morrice makes me spit in thy mouth" (Sig. G3r; 4.1.258–61). This action of spitting is described by editors Corbin and Sedge as "a gesture of affection which was believed to please dogs" (4.1.261n),[58] but it is also remarkably similar to kissing. Earlier in the same scene, Mother Sawyer tells Dog she has "yet / No blood to moysten these sweet lips of thine. / Stand on thy hind-legs up. Kiss me, my *Tommy*" (Sig. G1v; 4.1.155–57). Cuddy's affection takes a similar form. The morris has "bewitch'd" him, and he is in love with Dog. To the extent that playgoers agree, they, too, are imagined as having been taken in specifically by the devil's dance.

CONSTITUTIVE DELIGHTS

The early modern morris was often described as both devilish and lustful in ecclesiastical visitation articles and other texts against "unlawful" recreations on the Sabbath. Although *The Witch of Edmonton* might seem on the surface to reinforce such attitudes, what is striking about the play is that its performance dynamics work in the opposite direction, countering the moral censure implied in linking festivity to the devil. The broader cultural consequences of these dynamics can be seen in the dramatic narrative's structure. Outside the playhouse, marriage as an institution (at least ideally) worked in conjunction with festivity to produce and cement social formations. Within the world of the play, however, marriage decidedly fails. Frank's elopement with Winnifride does not legitimate their sexual union, and his wedding with Susan does not ensure their financial security. Rather, these acts initiate a chain of events that ultimately lead to murder and execution. Marriage, the play implies, cannot function either as erotic haven or as economic exchange. The juxtaposition of this main plot with the subplot advertises the centrality and importance of festivity in bridging this gap between sexual desire and commercial interest. Festivity is the glue that binds together the community and that undergirds social alliances, including marriage. The performance dynamics of the morris reinforce this view and might thus be seen as a powerfully conservative social force.

Yet in transposing the morris onto the commercial stage, the play also simultaneously manipulates audience allegiances in ways that render sexual relations more capacious. It situates playhouse entertainment as, on the one hand, a morally reprehensible sort of experience associated with illicit desires and, on the other, an essential element in community formation. Paying for performances involving dance and theater is like selling one's soul to the devil, and spectators' desire to see the morris dance is likened to transgressive sexuality. What one gets in return, however, is to "take delight / In sins and mischiefs, 'tis the Devil's right" (Sig. E3r; 3.1.152–53). This spiritually dubious delight may well have felt familiar to early modern playgoers, whose theatrical experiences regularly included morality plays that took the audience's spiritual fall as a critical component of both the dramatic narrative and the performance experience.[59] What theater historians often assume are dynamics applicable only to "medieval" drama here arise in connection with the seventeenth-century stage.

Moreover, this dramaturgical tradition enables a felt experience of festive community *even when* the material conditions and economic consequences of performance have changed. In this context, transgressive sexuality functions not just as licensed festive inversion in the Bakhtinian sense, but becomes incorporated *into* a more capacious understanding of the nature and functions of playing. Enacting reversals in hierarchy and role, commercial theater adopted and redeployed the sexual energies of holiday customs. Drawing on the weight and privilege of traditional festivity, it appropriated the erotic force of role-playing—rendering theater sexy and *thus* profitable. In so doing, the professional stage ensured the continued viability of performance as an integral part of social life. At the same time, linking theater to the erotics of festivity also reiterated the notion that seemingly subversive sexual desires were culturally central. That is, they were not merely tolerated but were in fact crucial to communal functioning. Just as festive inversion was *structurally constitutive* of early modern social formations, so, too, was professional theater as well as the forms of illicit eroticism and sexuality that it performed through embodied enactment.

This analysis of the consequences of early modern performance not only helps us make sense of the play's unusual attention to social marginalization (as we see in its depiction of the community's culpability in the witch's moral fall) but also has broader theoretical implications. Examining morris dancing in commercial theater enables us to see *how* performance does powerful work on multiple social and psychological planes through the production of shifting modes of audience identification. Whatever a spectator might think or say or do on a conscious level, the manipulation of audience reactions allows performance to leverage spectators' affective responses. Theater may have positioned the erotic charge of its own performances as devilish seduction on the surface so that *cognitively* its moral message lines up properly, but in linking theatrical *spectatorship* with transgressive sexuality, it played on and with the shifting emotional allegiances of audience members to reconfigure what counted as *affectively* acceptable. Performance, in this sense, might be viewed as "queer" less in its representation of same-sex desire than in its capacity to modulate the phenomenological experiences that constitute sexuality and that shape understandings of the erotic, to enable through bodily acts various amorphous sensations and affiliations that would be unintelligible or immediately disavowed in other contexts.

In exploring the sexual valences of the morris dance on stage, then, we can see how performance functions as *corporeal discourse*, (re)producing cultural attitudes, practices, and institutions through embodied form. This concept is at odds with dominant ideas about the social impact of theater and dance today. Contemporary stage performance is often assumed to be an aesthetic experience whose broader efficacy lies in the creative repurposing of art for progressive political ends. This "art as activism" mentality takes for granted the marginal status of these cultural forms even as it aims to spur social change through transformative audience experiences. In early modern England, however, there was a very thin line between an everyday kind of social activity, such as dancing at a wedding or in a neighboring parish, and a performance experience "set off" as a separate act onstage. The notion of performance as a conceptually distinct entity had to be produced. Its cultural space and purpose, its semiotic functions, its formal structures—all had to be defined and demarcated in particular ways to render intelligible a concept of performance as art. In the process of carving out this space, early modern commercial theater reshaped both festive practices and the social norms constituted through those practices. Performance was not simply a mode of artistic production that might be mobilized now and then for strategic political effects but an active and integrated cultural force, remaking social structures from the inside out. Because the efficacy of theater and dance grew out of their centrality to early modern life, playing did important cultural work. This work—the social and moral benefit of dallying with demons—meant that playing would continue long after "the play" was done. Or as Mother Sawyer puts it, "Come, let's home and play. Our black work ended, we'll make holiday" (Sig. G3r; 4.1.268–69).

NOTES

1. For their feedback on earlier versions of this essay, many thanks to Marissa Greenberg, Mario DiGangi, and Elisa Oh as well as to my generous hosts and interlocutors at the Folger Shakespeare Library, the University of Maryland, the Columbia University Early Modern Colloquium, and the Massachusetts Center for Interdisciplinary Renaissance Studies at the University of Massachusetts, Amherst.

2. John Forrest, *The History of Morris Dancing, 1458–1750* (Toronto: University of Toronto Press, 1999). On early morris, see also Michael Heaney, "Kingston to Kenilworth: Early Plebian Morris," *Folklore* 100 (1989): 88–104. On later morris, see Keith Chandler, *Ribbons, Bells, and Squeaking Fiddles: The Social History of Morris Dancing in the English South Midlands, 1660–1900* (Middlesex, UK: Hisarlik Press, 1993).

3. On Sharp's distinctions, see Theresa Buckland, "English Folk Dance Scholarship: A Review," in *Traditional Dance, Volume One: Proceedings of the Traditional Dance Conference held at Crewe and Alsager College of Higher Education, 28th March, 1981*, ed. Theresa Buckland (Crewe, UK: Crewe and Alsager College of Higher Education, 1982), 3–18. On historiographic issues related to the morris, see also Ronald Hutton, *The Stations of the Sun: A History of the Ritual Year in Britain* (Oxford: Oxford University Press, 1996), 262–76; and Claire Sponsler, "Writing the Unwritten: Morris Dance and Theatre History,"

in *Representing the Past: Essays in Performance Historiography*, ed. Charlotte Canning and Thomas Postlewait (Iowa City: University of Iowa Press, 2010), 84–113.

4. This conceptual distance between spectatorship and participation does not hold for early modern England. Given radically different ideas about the mechanics of vision and the social and moral consequences of viewing, watching a performance was, for them, itself a form of participation. See Erika T. Lin, *Shakespeare and the Materiality of Performance* (New York: Palgrave Macmillan, 2012), 107–33.

5. Hutton, *Stations of the Sun*, 92–93. On the hobbyhorse, see also E. C. Cawte, *Ritual Animal Disguise: A Historical and Geographical Study of Animal Disguise in the British Isles* (Cambridge, UK: D. S. Brewer for the Folklore Society, 1978).

6. As Old Thorney tells Frank, "If you marry / VVith wealthy *Carter's* Daughter, there's a Portion / VVill free my Land: all which I will instate / Upon the marriage to you. Otherwise, / I must be of necessity enforc'd / To make a present sale of all" (Sig. C1v; 1.2.130–35). Quotations from the play are drawn from William Rowley, Thomas Dekker, and John Ford, *The Witch of Edmonton* (London, 1658), with signature numbers from the original quarto followed by act, scene, and line numbers from Peter Corbin and Douglas Sedge, eds., *Three Jacobean Witchcraft Plays*, The Revels Plays Companion Library (Manchester: Manchester University Press, 1986). All quotations have been cross-checked also against Arthur F. Kinney, ed., *The Witch of Edmonton*, New Mermaids (London: A & C Black, 1998). Spelling and italics are retained exactly with the exception of the long *s*, which has been silently modernized, and tildes marking omitted letters, which have been lowered and italicized to accord with transcriptions of manuscript sources.

7. Previous scholarship on the play includes Todd Butler, "Swearing Justice in Henry Goodcole and *The Witch of Edmonton*," *SEL: Studies in English Literature, 1500–1900* 50 (2010): 127–45; Viviana Comensoli, "Witchcraft and Domestic Tragedy in *The Witch of Edmonton*," in *The Politics of Gender in Early Modern Europe*, ed. Jean R. Brink, Allison P. Coudert, and Maryanne C. Horowitz (Kirksville, MO: Sixteenth Century Journal Publications, 1989), 43–60; Anthony B. Dawson, "Witchcraft/Bigamy: Cultural Conflict in *The Witch of Edmonton*," *Renaissance Drama* 20 (1989): 77–98; Frances E. Dolan, *Dangerous Familiars: Representations of Domestic Crime in England, 1550–1700* (Ithaca, NY: Cornell University Press, 1994), 218–23; Michelle M. Dowd, "Desiring Subjects: Staging the Female Servant in Early Modern Tragedy," in *Working Subjects in Early Modern English Drama*, ed. Michelle M. Dowd and Natasha Korda (Farnham, UK: Ashgate, 2011), 131–43; Kirilka Stavreva, "Fighting Words: Witch-Speak in Late Elizabethan Docu-fiction," *Journal of Medieval and Early Modern Studies* 30 (2000): 309–38; and Holger Schott Syme, "(Mis)representing Justice on the Early Modern Stage," *Studies in Philology* 109 (2012): 63–85.

8. Corbin and Sedge, *Witch of Edmonton*, 1.2.218–19n; Kinney, *Witch of Edmonton*, 1.2.224n.

9. *Records of Early English Drama: Ecclesiastical London*, ed. Mary C. Erler (Toronto: University of Toronto Press, 2008), 215; brackets in original (marking cancellations in the manuscript text).

10. Ibid.

11. *Oxford English Dictionary (OED) Online*, 2nd ed. (1989), s.v. "burden | burthen, *n.*" (def. I4b), published online September 2012, http://www.oed.com/view/Entry/24885.

12. *OED Online*, 2nd ed., s.v. "burden | burthen, *n.*" (defs. IV9, IV10).

13. An *argument* was a brief summary of subsequent action in a play or a book.

14. On bones as dice, see *OED Online*, 2nd ed. (1989), s.v. "bone, *n.*" (def. I5a), published online September 2012, http://www.oed.com/view/Entry/21294. See also Thomas Dekker,

Lanthorne and candle-light. Or, The bell-mans second nights-walke In which he brings to light, a brood of more strange villanies than ener [sic] were till this yeare discouered (London, 1609): "*Cardes & Dice* (for the last Messe) are serued vp to the boord: they that are ful of coyne, *draw:* they that haue little, stand by & giue *ayme:* they *shuffle* and *cut* on one side: the bones *rattle* on the other" (Sig. E1r). On *rattle* as bodily movement with noise, see *OED Online*, 3rd ed. (2008), s.v. "rattle, *v.*1" (def. 5a), published online September 2012, http://www.oed.com/view/Entry/158558. For another example of bones rattling, dancing, and physical violence, see Peter Hausted, *The rivall friends A comoedie, as it was acted before the King and Queens Maiesties, when out of their princely favour they were pleased to visite their Vniversitie of Cambridge, upon the 19. day of March. 1631* (London, 1632): "either let your daughter daunce vvith vs, or I'le make your old bones rattle in your skin, I'le lead you a *Coranto* i'faith" (Sig. I4v).

15. See also a case recorded in the Archdeaconry of Chichester Detection Book for 1616/17 in which the defendant's "Children with divers other youthes of our parishe made them selues ready in a morrice daunce and a hobby horse, and a mayd marryan and went 4ᵒʳ myles to Cockeinge to daunce the morrice." *Records of Early English Drama: Sussex*, ed. Cameron Louis (Toronto: University of Toronto Press, 2000), 22. For examples of broader associations of morris dancing with youth, see the pamphlet *Old Meg of Hereford-shire* as well as the 1589 court case in Canterbury, Kent, both of which I discuss later on in this chapter.

16. Henry Goodcole, *The wonderfull discouerie of Elizabeth Savvyer a witch late of Edmonton, her conuiction and condemnation and death. Together with the relation of the Diuels accesse to her, and their conference together . . .* (London, 1621), Sig. A4v. In Goodcole's account of the actual witchcraft case, Sawyer's bent body is not a consequence of age but rather "happened but a little before her apprehension" and is thus suspected as one of the "markes," or signs, that she is a witch (ibid.).

17. Randall McLeod [Random Cloud, pseud.], "'The very names of the Persons': Editing and the Invention of Dramatick Character," in *Staging the Renaissance: Reinterpretations of Elizabethan and Jacobean Drama*, ed. David Scott Kastan and Peter Stallybrass (New York: Routledge, 1991), 88–96.

18. *Old Meg of Hereford-shire, for a Mayd-Marian: and Hereford towne for a Morris-daunce. Or Twelue Morris-dancers in Hereford-shire, of twelue hundred yeares old* (London, 1609), Sig. B1v.

19. On early modern references to bearded women and possible audience responses to bearded witches, see Brett D. Hirsch, "'What are these faces?': Interpreting Bearded Women in *Macbeth*," in *Renaissance Drama and Poetry in Context: Essays for Christopher Wortham*, ed. Andrew Lynch and Anne M. Scott (Newcastle-upon-Tyne, UK: Cambridge Scholars Press, 2008), 91–114.

20. Gina Bloom, *Voice in Motion: Staging Gender, Shaping Sound in Early Modern England* (Philadelphia: University of Pennsylvania Press, 2007), 21–65. Bloom argues convincingly that adult masculinity in early modern England was marked not simply by deeper pitch but also by vocal control. In this context, we might read the morris dancers' inconstancy in their choice of bells as reflective of the "squeaky" sounds of boy actors, whose voices frequently changed. Forrest suggests that the bells represent particular characters in the play, and he assigns each one to a specific dancer (*History of Morris Dancing*, 247).

21. Cf. also Cuddy's comment when he seeks out Mother Sawyer's help with Katherine: "I heard I know not the Devil what mumble in a scurvy base tone, like a Drum that had taken cold in the head the last Muster" (Sigs. D2r-D2v; 2.1.249–51)—a phrase that similarly ties

together low pitched sounds with social (and moral) baseness, that imagines voices in terms of musical instruments, and that connects the witch to the drum.

22. Eric Partridge, *Shakespeare's Bawdy* (1947; repr., London: Routledge, 1996), 160; Gordon Williams, *A Glossary of Shakespeare's Sexual Language* (London: Athlone Press, 1997), 236.

23. Quotations from Shakespeare's plays are taken from Charlton Hinman, ed., *The First Folio of Shakespeare* (New York: Norton, 1968) with through line numbers (TLN) followed by act, scene, and line numbers from G. Blakemore Evans et al., eds., *The Riverside Shakespeare*, 2nd ed. (Boston: Houghton Mifflin, 1997).

24. *Records of Early English Drama: Kent: Diocese of Canterbury*, ed. James M. Gibson, 3 vols. (London: The British Library; Toronto: University of Toronto Press, 2002), 1:222.

25. Ibid., 1:225; brackets in original (marking cancellations in the manuscript text). Forrest discusses this case in relation to the age of the participants, who, other than the boy, were all nineteen or twenty years old (*History of Morris Dancing*, 269).

26. *Records of Early English Drama: Cheshire (including Chester)*, ed. Elizabeth Baldwin, Lawrence M. Clopper, and David Mills, 2 vols. (London: The British Library; Toronto: University of Toronto Press, 2007), 1:32. The records for this case also include references to "Thomas Broocke & Thomas Manninge in womens apparell dansing like women after one Peacocke a fidler" and to two other men "in disguised apparell with naked swordes in theire handes daunsing with those that were in womens apparell, a great multitude of disordered and rude people gadding a longe after them" (ibid.). In the Quarter Sessions case from Canterbury, the amateur morris troupe was accused of unlawfully dancing on the Sabbath and feast days, but they were specifically involved in various May Games. The case dates their activities to May 10, 1589, and the boy Maid Marian testifies that he "hath gon in his womans atteyre sythens friday mornyng"—suggesting an extension of cross-dressing beyond a single dance performance (*Records of Early English Drama: Kent*, 1:222–25).

27. *Records of Early English Drama: Kent*, 2:535.

28. The Cheshire case also links seasonal festivities to sexual excess when it describes how "men and women promiscuously & lasiviously daunsed about Thomas Symme (as about a maypole) bearinge vpp the garland." *Records of Early English Drama: Cheshire (including Chester)*, 1:32.

29. On early modern notions of boys as erotic objects for both men and women, see Stephen Orgel, *Impersonations: The Performance of Gender in Shakespeare's England* (Cambridge: Cambridge University Press, 1996), 53–82.

30. See *OED Online*, 2nd ed. (1989), s.v. "turnip, *n*." (def. 3a), published online December 2012, http://www.oed.com/view/Entry/207708, which notes that the word can be used "In slang phrases, sometimes with pun on *turn-up*." The word *turn* was often used with bawdy potential (Partridge, *Shakespeare's Bawdy*, 207; Williams, *Glossary*, 316), and the *OED* also includes a 1612 quotation that implies the word *turn-up* could be used this way: "they are whores, harlots, trulls, baggages, bayards, turne-vps, curtesanes." *OED Online*, 2nd ed. (1989), s.v. "turn-up, *n. and adj.*" (def. 1), published online December 2012, http://www.oed.com/view/Entry/207732. The quotation refers to the speaker's dismay at embarking on a ship that includes female passengers. Benvenuto, *The passenger: of Benvenvto Italian, professour of his natiue tongue, for these nine yeeres in London. Diuided into two parts, containing seauen exquisite dialogues in Italian and English: the contents whereof you shall finde in the end of the booke . . .*, translated by Mr. King (London, 1612), Sig. Ss2r.

31. Kinney mentions in passing that Maid Marian was "originally queen of the witch's coven before becoming the companion of Robin Hood" (*Witch of Edmonton*, 3.1.8n) but includes no further citation, and I am not aware of any such references in primary sources.

32. *Records of Early English Drama: Somerset*, 2 vols., ed. James Stokes (Toronto: University of Toronto Press, 1996), 1:416; caret mark and half brackets in original. The latter indicates text written above the line in the manuscript. This letter was first transcribed with editorial remarks in Herbert Berry, "The Globe Bewitched and *El Hombre Fiel*," *Medieval and Renaissance Drama in England* 1 (1984): 211–30.

33. Corbin and Sedge, *Witch of Edmonton*, 3.1.50n; Kinney, *Witch of Edmonton*, 3.1.48n.

34. Etta Soiref Onat, ed., *The Witch of Edmonton: A Critical Edition* (New York: Garland, 1980), 334 [3.4.13.s.d.n].

35. On the beard as essential to early modern notions of manhood, see Will Fisher, *Materializing Gender in Early Modern English Literature and Culture* (Cambridge: Cambridge University Press, 2006), 83–128. See also Will Fisher, "The Erotics of Chin Chucking in Seventeenth-Century England," in *Sex before Sex: Figuring the Act in Early Modern England*, ed. James M. Bromley and Will Stockton (Minneapolis: University of Minnesota Press, 2013), 162n7, which mentions a ballad, "The St. James's Frolick" (c. 1683–1703), in which a barber chucks a woman's chin and then "straight away did trim her / far better than e're she had been." The act implicit in this moment connects chins and barbering to sexuality more broadly. Note that Fisher also states that erotic chin-chucking was in certain cases linked to supposedly "nonsexual" activities such as dancing and playing.

36. Dympna Callaghan, *Shakespeare without Women: Representing Gender and Race on the Renaissance Stage* (London: Routledge, 2000), 49–74. On this kind of cutting in relation to the shaving of beards, see Mark Albert Johnston, *Beard Fetish in Early Modern England: Sex, Gender, and Registers of Value* (Farnham, UK: Ashgate, 2011), 103–57. See also Williams, *Glossary*, 89, for the ways in which *cut* signifies "gelding" even while retaining a "Vaginal sense." The *OED* definition of *cut* as meaning "To castrate" dates back to 1465 and continues in use in this sense through the mid-nineteenth century. *OED Online*, 2nd ed. (1989), s.v. "cut, *v.*" (def. VII26a), published online December 2012, http://www.oed.com/view/Entry/46341. The early modern slippage between *cut* and *cunt* has been well documented (see Williams, *Glossary*, 87–88).

37. *OED Online*, 2nd ed., "cut, *v.*" (def. VI25). On cutting a caper, see Peter Walls, "Common Sixteenth-Century Dance Forms: Some Further Notes," *Early Music* 2 (1974): 164–65; and Toinot Arbeau [Jehan Tabourot], *Orchésographie* (Langres, 1588), trans. Mary Stewart Evans, ed. Julia Sutton (New York: Dover, 1967), 77.

38. As the *OED* notes, the term *preposterous* in the mid- to late seventeenth century meant, among other things, "Of an animal: having parts reversed in position, going tail first." *OED Online*, 2nd ed. (1989), s.v. "ludicrous, *adj.*," published online September 2012, http://www.oed.com/view/Entry/110945; *OED Online*, 3rd ed. (2007), s.v. "preposterous, *adj.*" (def. 1b), published online September 2012, http://www.oed.com/view/Entry/150508.

39. The phrase in this context may have had bawdy overtones. Corbin and Sedge note that "Cherry-pit" was "a children's game which consists in throwing cherry stones into a small pit or hole" (*Witch of Edmonton*, 3.1.19n). See also Kinney, *Witch of Edmonton*, 3.1.19n.

40. *OED Online*, 2nd ed. (1989), s.v. "hobby-horse, *n.*" (def. 3b), published online September 2012, http://www.oed.com/view/Entry/87463; Partridge, *Shakespeare's Bawdy*, 121;

Williams, *Glossary*, 158–59. See also Mary Ellen Lamb, *The Popular Culture of Shakespeare, Spenser and Jonson* (New York: Routledge, 2006), 66.

41. On this catch phrase and its implications for morris dance forms, see Forrest, *History of Morris Dancing*, 283. On the expression in Shakespeare's *Hamlet*, see Naomi Conn Liebler, *Shakespeare's Festive Tragedy: The Ritual Foundations of Genre* (London: Routledge, 1995), 177–82.

42. The earliest reference to the term *cuddy* as meaning "A donkey. (Also *cuddy ass.*)" is listed in the *OED* as 1714 with the figurative connotations of "A stupid fellow, an 'ass'" not until 1840. However, a similar meaning somewhat earlier seems likely, given that the related word *cudden*, meaning "A born fool, a dolt," is recorded by 1673. *OED Online*, 2nd ed. (1989), s.vv. "cuddy, *n*.3" (defs. 1a, 1b), "cudden, *n*." (def. 1), "hobby, *n*.1" (def. 1), published online March 2012, http://www.oed.com/view/Entry/45560, http://www.oed.com/view/Entry/45552, http://www.oed.com/view/Entry/87460.

43. *Records of Early English Drama: Somerset*, 1:416.

44. Moonshine, almanacs, and madness also figure prominently in Shakespeare's *A Midsummer Night's Dream*. On the calendar implications of this play, see David Wiles, *Shakespeare's Almanac: "A Midsummer Night's Dream," Marriage, and the Elizabethan Calendar* (Woodbridge, UK: D. S. Brewer, 1993).

45. Corbin and Sedge, *Witch of Edmonton*, 2.1.98.s.d.n; Kinney, *Witch of Edmonton*, 2.1.97.s.d.n; Onat, *Witch of Edmonton*, 305–6 [2.1.89n].

46. Note that when Cuddy initially refuses the part of the hobbyhorse, the First Dancer encourages him to "cast thy stuff" (Sig. C4r; 2.1.68–69)—that is, to dispense with his grudge. Cuddy is "well stuft" in that he is full of grudges, but that he then lets go of them means he is "affable." Indeed, the dancers specifically praise the clown as "Affable" (Sig. C4r; 2.1.81), a term he picks up on repeatedly in his subsequent line, when he refers to himself as "affable, as you say" (Sig. C4r; 2.1.82) and as "most affable Jack" (Sig. C4r; 2.1.84). According to the *OED*, the term *affable* may have been related to the verb *affy*, meaning "To promise or commit oneself formally to marry (a person)" or "To betroth (a person) *to* (also *unto, with*) another." The meaning is most understandable from a modern perspective if we think of the related word *affiance*. In both terms, ambiguity between the doers and receivers of the action, between the person being affied and the person affying someone else, is mapped onto and across conventional gender roles. Similarly, Cuddy is himself here situated in both the active and receptive positions, a fact underscored in the use of "he" in "he shall not want a belly." On a related fluidity and ambiguity in the use of pronouns in *A Midsummer Night's Dream*, see Richard Rambuss, "Shakespeare's Ass Play," in *Shakesqueer: A Queer Companion to the Complete Works of Shakespeare*, ed. Madhavi Menon (Durham, NC: Duke University Press, 2011), 236–37. *OED Online*, 3rd ed. (2012), s.vv. "affable, *adj*.," "affy, *v*." (def. 3, 4a), published online September 2012, http://www.oed.com/view/Entry/3302, http://www.oed.com/view/Entry/3566.

47. See Robert Anton, *Moriomachia* (London, 1613), Sig. A2v. I am grateful to Mario DiGangi for drawing my attention to this reference. On *ass* in early modern usage more generally, see Mario DiGangi, *The Homoerotics of Early Modern Drama* (Cambridge: Cambridge University Press, 1997), 64–65; Rambuss, "Shakespeare's Ass Play," 240–41.

48. Rambuss, "Shakespeare's Ass Play."

49. Ibid., 240.

50. Ibid., 239, 242–43.

51. Melissa E. Sanchez, "'Use Me But as Your Spaniel': Feminism, Queer Theory, and Early Modern Sexualities," *PMLA* 127 (2012): 505.

52. The moment recalls similar wordplay in Shakespeare's *Love's Labor's Lost*, when the pageant of the Nine Worthies goes awry around the representation of Judas Machabeus:

    BER. And thou wer't a Lion, we would do so.
    BOY. Therefore as he is, an Asse, let him go:
          And so adieu sweet *Iude*. Nay, why dost thou stay?
    DUM. For the latter end of his name.
    BER. For the *Asse* to the *Iude:* giue it him. *Iud-as* away.
    PED. This is not generous, not gentle, not humble. (TLN 2576–82; 5.2.624–29)

    The earlier confusion around whether the Judas here portrayed is Judas Iscariot is suggestive of possible wordplay emphasizing the "Asse" in "Iud-as" by linking his name to doubting Thomas's similar end syllable.

53. DiGangi, *Homoerotics*, 64–99.

54. Mary Bly, *Queer Virgins and Virgin Queans on the Early Modern Stage* (Oxford: Oxford University Press, 2000), 62.

55. *OED Online*, 2nd ed. (1989), s.v. "instrument, *n.*" (def. 4), published online December 2012, http://www.oed.com/view/Entry/97158; *Middle English Dictionary*, s.v. "instrument, *n.*" (def. 2a), last updated February 2006, http://quod.lib.umich.edu/cgi/m/mec/med-idx?type=id&id=MED23034.

56. *Records of Early English Drama: Sussex*, 181.

57. *Records of Early English Drama: Ecclesiastical London*, 263.

58. See also Kinney, *Witch of Edmonton*, 4.1.271n.

59. Though usually associated with earlier theater, morality drama in fact continued to be a popular genre well into the era of Shakespeare and his contemporaries. See Roslyn Lander Knutson, *The Repertory of Shakespeare's Company, 1594–1613* (Fayetteville: University of Arkansas Press, 1991), 42.

BIBLIOGRAPHY

Anton, Robert. *Moriomachia*. London, 1613.

Arbeau, Toinot [Jehan Tabourot]. *Orchésographie*. Edited by Julie Sutton. Translated by Mary Stewart Evans. Langres, 1588; New York: Dover, 1967.

Benvenuto. *The passenger: of Benvenvto Italian, professour of his natiue tongue, for these nine yeeres in London. Diuided into two parts, containing seauen exquisite dialogues in Italian and English: the contents whereof you shall finde in the end of the booke . . . .* Translated by Mr. King. London, 1612.

Berry, Herbert. "The Globe Bewitched and *El Hombre Fiel.*" *Medieval and Renaissance Drama in England* 1 (1984): 211–30.

Bloom, Gina. *Voice in Motion: Staging Gender, Shaping Sound in Early Modern England*. Philadelphia: University of Pennsylvania Press, 2007.

Bly, Mary. *Queer Virgins and Virgin Queans on the Early Modern Stage*. Oxford: Oxford University Press, 2000.

Buckland, Theresa. "English Folk Dance Scholarship: A Review." In *Traditional Dance, Volume One: Proceedings of the Traditional Dance Conference Held at Crewe and Alsager College of Higher Education, 28th March, 1981*, edited by Theresa Buckland, 3–18. Crewe, UK: Crewe and Alsager College of Higher Education, 1982.

Butler, Todd. "Swearing Justice in Henry Goodcole and *The Witch of Edmonton*." *SEL: Studies in English Literature, 1500–1900* 50 (2010): 127–45.

Callaghan, Dympna. *Shakespeare without Women: Representing Gender and Race on the Renaissance Stage*. London: Routledge, 2000.

Cawte, E. C. *Ritual Animal Disguise: A Historical and Geographical Study of Animal Disguise in the British Isles*. Cambridge, UK: D. S. Brewer for the Folklore Society, 1978.

Chandler, Keith. *Ribbons, Bells, and Squeaking Fiddles: The Social History of Morris Dancing in the English South Midlands, 1660–1900*. Middlesex, UK: Hisarlik Press, 1993.

Comensoli, Viviana. "Witchcraft and Domestic Tragedy in *The Witch of Edmonton*." In *The Politics of Gender in Early Modern Europe*, edited by Jean R. Brink, Allison P. Coudert, and Maryanne C. Horowitz, 43–60. Kirksville, MO: Sixteenth Century Journal Publications, 1989.

Corbin, Peter, and Douglas Sedge, eds. *Three Jacobean Witchcraft Plays*. The Revels Plays Companion Library. Manchester: Manchester University Press, 1986.

Dawson, Anthony B. "Witchcraft/Bigamy: Cultural Conflict in *The Witch of Edmonton*." *Renaissance Drama* 20 (1989): 77–98.

Dekker, Thomas. *Lanthorne and candle-light. Or, The bell-mans second nights-walke In which he brings to light, a brood of more strange villanies than ener [sic] were till this yeare discouered*. London, 1609.

DiGangi, Mario. *The Homoerotics of Early Modern Drama*. Cambridge: Cambridge University Press, 1997.

Dolan, Frances E. *Dangerous Familiars: Representations of Domestic Crime in England, 1550–1700*. Ithaca, NY: Cornell University Press, 1994.

Dowd, Michelle M. "Desiring Subjects: Staging the Female Servant in Early Modern Tragedy." In *Working Subjects in Early Modern English Drama*, edited by Michelle M. Dowd and Natasha Korda, 131–43. Farnham, UK: Ashgate, 2011.

Fisher, Will. *Materializing Gender in Early Modern English Literature and Culture*. Cambridge: Cambridge University Press, 2006.

———. "The Erotics of Chin Chucking in Seventeenth-Century England." In *Sex before Sex: Figuring the Act in Early Modern England*, edited by James M. Bromley and Will Stockton, 141–69. Minneapolis: University of Minnesota Press, 2013.

Forrest, John. *The History of Morris Dancing, 1458–1750*. Toronto: University of Toronto Press, 1999.

Goodcole, Henry. *The wonderfull discouerie of Elizabeth Savvyer a witch late of Edmonton, her conuiction and condemnation and death. Together with the relation of the Diuels accesse to her, and their conference together . . . .* London, 1621.

Hausted, Peter. *The rivall friends A comoedie, as it was acted before the King and Queens Maiesties, when out of their princely favour they were pleased to visite their Vniuersitie of Cambridge, upon the 19. day of March. 1631*. London, 1632.

Heaney, Michael. "Kingston to Kenilworth: Early Plebian Morris." *Folklore* 100 (1989): 88–104.

Hinman, Charlton, ed. *The First Folio of Shakespeare*. New York: Norton, 1968.

Hirsch, Brett D. "'What are these faces?': Interpreting Bearded Women in *Macbeth*." In *Renaissance Drama and Poetry in Context: Essays for Christopher Wortham*, edited by Andrew Lynch and Anne M. Scott, 91–114. Newcastle-upon-Tyne, UK: Cambridge Scholars Press, 2008.

Hutton, Ronald. *The Stations of the Sun: A History of the Ritual Year in Britain*. Oxford: Oxford University Press, 1996.

Johnston, Mark Albert. *Beard Fetish in Early Modern England: Sex, Gender, and Registers of Value*. Farnham, UK: Ashgate, 2011.

Kinney, Arthur F., ed. *The Witch of Edmonton*. New Mermaids. London: A & C Black, 1998.

Knutson, Roslyn Lander. *The Repertory of Shakespeare's Company, 1594–1613*. Fayetteville: University of Arkansas Press, 1991.

Lamb, Mary Ellen. *The Popular Culture of Shakespeare, Spenser and Jonson*. New York: Routledge, 2006.

Liebler, Naomi Conn. *Shakespeare's Festive Tragedy: The Ritual Foundations of Genre*. London: Routledge, 1995.

Lin, Erika T. *Shakespeare and the Materiality of Performance*. New York: Palgrave Macmillan, 2012.

McLeod, Randall [Random Cloud, pseud.]. "'The very names of the Persons': Editing and the Invention of Dramatick Character." In *Staging the Renaissance: Reinterpretations of Elizabethan and Jacobean Drama*, edited by David Scott Kastan and Peter Stallybrass, 88–96. New York: Routledge, 1991.

Old Meg of Hereford-shire, for a Mayd-Marian: and Hereford towne for a Morris-daunce. Or Twelue Morris-dancers in Hereford-shire, of twelue hundred yeares old. London, 1609.

Onat, Etta Soiref, ed. *The Witch of Edmonton: A Critical Edition*. New York: Garland, 1980.

Orgel, Stephen. *Impersonations: The Performance of Gender in Shakespeare's England*. Cambridge: Cambridge University Press, 1996.

Partridge, Eric. *Shakespeare's Bawdy*. 1947. Reprint, London: Routledge, 1996.

Rambuss, Richard. "Shakespeare's Ass Play." In *Shakesqueer: A Queer Companion to the Complete Works of Shakespeare*, edited by Madhavi Menon, 234–44. Durham, NC: Duke University Press, 2011.

Records of Early English Drama: Cheshire (including Chester). 2 vols. Edited by Elizabeth Baldwin, Lawrence M. Clopper, and David Mills. London: The British Library; Toronto: University of Toronto Press, 2007.

Records of Early English Drama: Ecclesiastical London. Edited by Mary C. Erler. Toronto: University of Toronto Press, 2008.

Records of Early English Drama: Kent: Diocese of Canterbury. 3 vols. Edited by James M. Gibson. London: The British Library; Toronto: University of Toronto Press, 2002.

Records of Early English Drama: Somerset. 2 vols. Edited by James Stokes. Toronto: University of Toronto Press, 1996.

Records of Early English Drama: Sussex. Edited by Cameron Louis. Toronto: University of Toronto Press, 2000.

Rowley, William, Thomas Dekker, and John Ford. *The Witch of Edmonton*. London, 1658.

Sanchez, Melissa E. "'Use Me But as Your Spaniel': Feminism, Queer Theory, and Early Modern Sexualities." *PMLA* 127 (2012): 493–511.

Sponsler, Claire. "Writing the Unwritten: Morris Dance and Theatre History." In *Representing the Past: Essays in Performance Historiography*, edited by Charlotte Canning and Thomas Postlewait, 84–113. Iowa City: University of Iowa Press, 2010.

Stavreva, Kirilka. "Fighting Words: Witch-Speak in Late Elizabethan Docu-fiction." *Journal of Medieval and Early Modern Studies* 30 (2000): 309–38.

Syme, Holger Schott. "(Mis)representing Justice on the Early Modern Stage." *Studies in Philology* 109 (2012): 63–85.

Walls, Peter. "Common Sixteenth-Century Dance Forms: Some Further Notes." *Early Music* 2 (1974): 164–65.

Wiles, David. *Shakespeare's Almanac: "A Midsummer Night's Dream," Marriage, and the Elizabethan Calendar*. Woodbridge, UK: D. S. Brewer, 1993.

Williams, Gordon. *A Glossary of Shakespeare's Sexual Language*. London: Athlone Press, 1997.

CHAPTER 18

DESIGNED BODIES

A Historiographical Study of Costume Design and Asian American Theater

ESTHER KIM LEE

In this chapter, I use the costume designer Willa Kim's career and designs as a case study to examine costume history in American theater and to situate her historiographically in the study of Asian American theater and performance. Willa Kim is, at once, Korean American, Asian American, woman, and an international artist who has designed for human bodies of all forms for over fifty years. A brief examination of her career unsettles how theater historians have understood race, representation, and body politics. The study of the body in performance has recently proliferated, and it is certainly necessary to move away from text-based study of performance toward an embodied one. However, it is critical to reexamine how the body is defined and assumed in performance history and historiography. The current assumptions about the body and how it should be understood as a theoretical concept is mostly performer based. Much attention is given to an actor's or a dancer's body, but little has been written about the costume that is usually inseparable from the performer onstage. A critical history of costume design and designers is particularly lacking. Costume designers must understand how performers act and move their bodies, and great designers can make the costume the most essential part of the body and the performance. Theater is inherently collaborative, and the visual language of the production should be documented and analyzed as rigorously as the scripted language or the performer's body in action. Using Willa Kim as a touchstone, I examine the absence and presence of costume design in theater and performance scholarship and argue for more integration of design studies in the discourse of the body and performance.

WILLA KIM: A CASE STUDY

Willa Kim (b. 1917) has had an extensive career as a costume designer in the United States for over fifty years, receiving numerous awards including two Tony Awards and two Emmy

Awards. Known for her perfectionism in the stage design community, she has revolutionized costume design and technology for theater, ballet, opera, commercials, fashion, and figure skating. Born in California in 1917, Willa Kim is the daughter of Korean immigrant parents: Soon-kwan Kim, an independence activist against Japanese colonial rule in Korea, and Nora Koh Kim, who immigrated to the United States in an arranged marriage. Her brother, Young-oak Kim, is a World War II hero who was the first Asian American to command a US combat battalion, and the Korean American Studies Center at the University of California, Riverside, is named after him. Willa Kim grew up in Los Angeles and studied art and fashion illustration. While working at Paramount Studios as a designer for cinema, she met artists and designers who influenced her to move to New York in 1945 and she became a costume designer. In 1955, she married the French American writer William Pène du Bois and settled down in New York City. Kim is credited with inventing customized painted costumes and with being a pioneer in using synthetic fabric—namely Lycra Spandex—on dancers. It was her technical innovation and artistic creativity that made her a highly successful costume designer. With a solid reputation and wide network, she has never lacked work during her long career. Willa Kim was also known for her social life in the world of dance and theater. For instance, a picture of Willa Kim is featured in the October 1971 issue of *McCall's* magazine in an article about three busy career women who also managed to "throw parties."[1] In the picture, Willa Kim is seating with a large spread of Korean food, including *kimchi, bulgogi*, and romaine lettuce in place of napa cabbage. She smiles at the camera wearing an outfit she designed: "ruffled shirt that was the prototype for a costume for one of the male dancers."[2] Kim has been widely recognized in the design community and the Asian American community, but her name has been virtually missing in the scholarship of both theater history and Asian American studies.

The only major work to document Willa Kim's work and career is *The Designs of Willa Kim*, written by Bobbi Owen. The book was published in 2005 by The USITT (United States Institute for Theatre Technology) as the inaugural volume in the USITT Monograph Series.[3] In introducing the volume, the series editor Del Unruh states, "This monograph on the career of Willa Kim is the first in what is projected to be an on-going series documenting the work of our best American theatrical designers."[4] The publication of the volume celebrates Kim as one of the best American theatrical designers, and featuring her first in the monograph series confirms her legendary status in American theater. However, with the exception of Owen's monograph, not much has been written about Willa Kim in academia. Designers in general have been consistently absent in theater and performance studies, and the USITT's monograph series is an important yet rare contribution to theater scholarship. Theater historians tend to focus on playwrights, actors, and directors in their research and teaching, and designers are studied only when they are part of major theater movements that feature other theater artists and theorists.[5]

Designers are absent not only in theater and performance studies but also in area studies. With her biography and stellar accomplishments, she would be expected to receive more attention in Asian American studies and women's studies. At the very least, she should be included in the study of Asian American theater. Willa Kim is currently the only Korean American and one of two Asian Americans in the American Theater Hall of Fame, which honors "those who have made outstanding contributions to the American Theater." The other Asian American artist in the Hall of Fame is Ming Cho Lee, the highly influential designer who is known as the "Dean" of American scenic design.[6] Other Asian American designers, such as Loy Arcenas and Myung Hee Cho, have worked in major productions and have received awards. A number of Asian American stage designers have consistently been active and successful in theater, opera, and ballet, but little attention has been paid to their careers and accomplishments outside of the design industry. Despite the highly successful Asian American designers, the narrative that has dominated Asian American theater history focuses on actors and playwrights, with some mention of directors and producers. I am guilty of perpetuating this narrative, and I have to admit that I did not learn about Willa Kim until the end of the research process for my book *A History of Asian American Theatre*. For the book, I relied on the network of Asian American theater artists for access to interviews and research materials, and none of the over seventy artists I spoke to mentioned Willa Kim. The only designer I interviewed for the book was Loy Arcenas, who was, at the time, turning his attention toward supporting new Filipino American playwrights. I learned about Willa Kim from the journalist and drama critic Terry Hong's article on Korean American theater in New York City.[7]

Most Asian American theater artists continue to have difficulty finding opportunities in mainstream theater (in which I include Broadway, Off-Broadway, and regional theater venues), and any success in those venues is seen as a major breakthrough. While there are many ways to define success in theater, Broadway productions and the Tony Award nominations are commonly considered an important measure of success in American theater. Using those measures, Willa Kim ranks at the top in Asian American theater. The only Asian American playwright to be produced on Broadway and receive a Tony Award is David Henry Hwang, and B. D. Wong is the only Asian American actor who has been nominated for and received a Tony Award. Willa Kim, in contrast, has received seven Tony Award nominations and was awarded two during her career (for *Sophisticated Ladies* in 1981 and *The Will Rogers Follies* in 1991). Moreover, she has received all of the major lifetime achievement awards a costume designer can possibly receive in the United States.[8] With the exception of Ming Cho Lee, there is no other Asian American theater artist who has achieved the scale of Kim's success in theater. With a career that spans from the 1940s to the early part of the twenty-first century, Willa Kim seems to occupy a different dimension in theater in comparison to other Asian American theater artists. Why, then, is she basically absent in Asian American studies and theater history? How should Willa Kim's career and accomplishments be explained in the context of Asian American theater? Why didn't the interviewees for my book mention Willa Kim, or why didn't it occur to me to ask about designers? Why was she absent in the narrative that my interviewees were collectively telling of Asian American theater?

Willa Kim was certainly in my scholarly blind spot, and this chapter is my attempt to explore how her presence requires epistemological shifting of the historiographical paradigm I have presumed and used as a theater historian. The essay is not a biographical study of Willa Kim nor does it provide formal analysis of her design work. Rather, her presence and absence in the narrative of current Asian American theater history are scrutinized to explain why costume history should be incorporated into the studies of theater, dance, and performance. In particular, focus is given to how the concept of the body is theorized in theater history and historiography and how design is absent in the theories of body in theater and performance. Moreover, Willa Kim and her career provide an opportunity to further question categories used in the study of Asian American theater and to understand how success is measured for minority theater artists in the United States.

Willa Kim is a versatile designer whose designs have ranged from everyday cloth-ing trends (such as bellbottom pants for a 1970s play) to fantastical creations (such as the octopus-inspired costume for Caliban in the ballet version of *The Tempest*).[9] On Broadway, she has designed straight plays, such as Eugene O'Neill's *Long Day's Journey into Night* (pro-duced in 1986), that required period clothing. Production photographs show actors wear-ing clothes true to the look of Connecticut in 1912 during which the play is set. But she is most recognized for her work in ballet, opera, and musicals that featured nonrealistic and conceptual costumes. Even with costumes specific to a period, Willa Kim's design has been described by critics as more than replica of known styles. The critic Robert Brustein best summarizes the general assessment of Kim's period costume design when he describes her costumes as "characterization in themselves."[10] Brustein does not explain what he means, and he writes only one sentence on costume design in his long review (which is typical of drama critics). It seems that for many critics and colleagues of Kim, what sets her apart from other designers is her ability to capture with her costumes what can be described as essential yet transcendental qualities of characters or the performers. Willa Kim's process has been described in equally mystical ways by her colleagues. Bobbi Owen's book includes many anecdotes of how Kim uses her instinct and how others find her process mysterious. Owen quotes Judy Adamson, a draper who has worked with Kim, as saying:

> No one quite understood why the position of those spots [on Kim's design] was so important until the costumes were together on stage in the musical number for which they were made, and suddenly their relative positions made sense. They were in exactly the right place on a group of dancers who were different heights.[11]

Owen credits Kim's "instinct" for having "a kind of 'perfect pitch' when it comes to color and shape": "Her instinct is uncanny—and unfailing."[12]

It is remarkable to see Willa Kim and her work discussed by her contemporaries in ways that describe her—and by extension her designs—as mystical and otherworldly. For exam-ple, the director and choreographer Tommy Tune describes her and her design as "really dreamy" and calls her "Girl of My Dreams":

> For years I had a recurring dream in which a beautiful woman floated past me in the clouds. She was veiled in gossamer. She paused mid-flight to whisper in my ear, "Shhhhhhh, IT'S A WILLA KIM" and floated on. For years I had this dream, then Willa Kim designed *The Will Rogers Follies* for me and then the dream mysteriously ceased! I guess it's because she became REAL. Willa Kim won the Tony for that show. She's really dreamy.[13]

The designer Tony Walton, in his Foreword to Owen's book, is equally profuse when he describes her as "a creature of limitless elegance and grace—who paints and draws like a dream and is relentless and entirely admirable perfectionist."[14] According to Bobbi Owen, Willa Kim's signature design elements have been "a whiff of period" and "a suggestion of a place."[15] The reoccurrence of the adjective "dreamy" and its synonyms in praise of Willa Kim raises the question, what does it mean? Does it connote the exotic or "oriental," terms that often get attached to artists of Asian descent? Given the overly poetic phrases attached to Willa Kim, it is more than probable that her ethnicity and gender contributed significantly to the support and opportunities she found during her career. As a designer, Willa Kim may have had an advantage in finding work in mainstream theater. Unlike Asian American actors, who are limited by their physiognomic traits, and playwrights, who are expected to write autobiographical stories, designers can often let their work speak for itself. Most likely, Kim encountered racism and sexism during the time and in the industry she worked, but her ethnicity probably did not have a devastatingly negative effect as it did for Asian American actors. In fact, she may have been readily accepted as a costume designer because of her ethnicity and gender.

I am not discrediting her unquestionable talent or effort, but I do speculate that her ethnicity and gender helped, rather than hurt, her career. It is likely that for many in the theater community, she was an immensely talented "oriental" woman who designed beautiful and "dreamy" costumes with her "instinct." Before analyzing Kim's place in theater history, it is critical to first contextualize Asian American theater in costume history. Willa Kim has been in the historiographical blind spot precisely because costume history has been absent in the constitution and documentation of Asian American theater. Artists who founded Asian American theater did so in opposition to the "oriental" conventions in acting and playwriting, but they did not directly address the conventions in costume design. Conversely, Asian American theater has been missing in costume history of the performing arts especially in the context of "oriental" conventions of theatrical costumes.

"ORIENTAL" CONVENTION IN COSTUME DESIGN HISTORY

I use the term "oriental" to echo the concept of orientalism famously articulated by Edward Said to define how the West has imagined and romanticized the East as exotic, mysterious, and weak. At the same time, "oriental" is an aesthetic style that describes a historically specific convention in theater. Since its beginning, American theater has been influenced by traditional European theater that used elaborate "oriental" settings, costumes, and makeup as theatrical conventions.[16] For centuries, fantasy and illusionism dominated European theater, and the exotic orient (however loosely it was defined) was a popular visual trope. Asian characters, or the stage oriental, appeared on the European stage since the beginning of European colonialism. In his article "The Global Parasol: Accessorizing the Four Corners of the World," Joseph Roach links seventeenth- and eighteenth-century European colonial curiosities and desires to visual representations of the world on maps and theatrical stages:

> On the stage and (cartographic) page at the beginning of the long eighteenth, the four corners of the world were represented synecdochically or metonymically in the form of selected costumes, sets, properties, and (where racial difference is concerned) makeup—hence the powerful symbolic importance that emanate from accessories. [. . .] To accessorize a costume is thus to furnish it with the supplementary but nonetheless crucial items that serve to identify or locate the wearer.[17]

According to Roach, London actors and actresses representing characters from exotic foreign lands wore accessories on their otherwise stock dresses "generally conventionalized within contemporary European norms." The accessories and decorations that signified foreignness included "the palm tree, the Chinese garden, the turban, the scimitar, the face made up in back, the feathered headdress, and especially the parasol."[18] Roach's example is one of many in the European theater tradition that influenced how the foreign, the other, and the "orient" were represented through costume onstage.

To cite another example, Voltaire's *Orphan of China* (1755; adapted into English by Arthur Murphy) was one of the first European plays to feature a Chinese character. The play opened in Philadelphia's Southwark Theatre in 1767 and presented the first stage image of a Chinese character to American spectators. According to James Moy, the actors playing Chinese characters wore "Middle Eastern dress in a vaguely 'Oriental' mode of representation."[19] Because the majority of the American spectators at the time had never seen a real Chinese person, the Middle Eastern ensemble of costumes would have been an image that most of them could accept as approximately oriental.

With the increase of the Asian (mostly Chinese) population in New York City in the late-nineteenth century, at least two different images of the "orient" emerged, and stage costumes and makeup corresponded with them. Images available from this period provide more concrete examples of oriental costumes and yellowface makeup. The costumes were not as vague and conflated as they were in the eighteenth century, but they were a combination of authenticity and fantasy. The first type was based on the perception of real Asian clothing, but onstage, certain features were accentuated for theatrical effect. In political cartoons, comedy theater, and minstrel shows, stereotypical images of Asians such as the Chinese coolies were caricatured. Actors playing the comic Asian character wore yellowface makeup, which consisted of pulling the eyes to create a slanted look and browning the skin. The performers playing Chinese coolies also wore the queue (braided plait of hair) worn by Chinese men loyal to the Qing Dynasty. Theatrical costumes based on Chinese laborers were intended to look clownish, and their overall appearances were popular topics for racist jokes.[20] Sean Metzger, in his study of the actor Charles Parsloe in the nineteenth-century American theater, categorizes the practice of yellowface as "conventional associations of signs and meanings that purportedly convey "Asian-ness."[21] Metzger explains the use of the queue as a signifier of Chineseness on the nineteenth-century American theater:

> This long braid appears more than any other signifier in various nineteenth-century visual portrayals of Chinese immigrants. Robes and blouses added to popular images of Chinese men; however, these outfits varied dramatically in cut and color. Actors on stage also used facial makeup, which may have included some simulation of epicanthic folds, but these cosmetic details would be lost to spectators in large performance spaces and were, at least in one case, perceived as inaccurate. By contrast, the queue could be seen from a distance. Moreover, its ubiquity in print media meant that it would have been easy for urban audiences to recognize it as a signifier of Chineseness.[22]

Metzger emphasizes that the entire ensemble of the costume became codified to represent Chineseness, and yellowface makeup was rarely practiced without orientalizing the rest of the body.

The second type of oriental costume catered to spectators of legitimate theaters as part of the *chinoiserie* and *japonaiserie* fads (popularity of art, decorations, and commodities from China or Japan respectively). It featured elaborate costumes and makeup created for theatrical performances, world fairs, or museums. Such images were partly based on actual performances and displays of Asian men and women who visited the United States and Europe to perform their cultures. For example, tours by Chinese opera troupes made particular impact on the perpetuation of the image in American theater. [23] Josephine Lee, in her book, *The Japan of Pure Invention: Gilbert and Sullivan's* The Mikado, demonstrates that the creation of the Japanese Village in Knightsbridge, London, in 1885 and the musical inspired the Victorian "craze" for anything Japanese in art, fashion, decor, crafts, songs, and gestures. The longevity of *The Mikado* in production into the twentieth century has contributed to the continual popularity of the Japanese kimono and items (such as the fan) on American and European stages.

In the first half of the twentieth century, the first type of oriental costume became less pervasive because the Chinese population decreased in size and assimilated.[24] However, the second type continued to dominate both the stage and the screen as the Far East increasingly became the dramatic setting of choice. Best exemplified by plays such as *Madame Butterfly* (1900) by David Belasco and *The Yellow Jacket* (1912) by Harry Benrimo and George G. Hazelton, plays, musicals, and operas of the early twentieth century often featured vague Eastern settings and elaborate costumes with yellowface makeup. Actors playing the characters were European Americans with very few exceptions. Major characters were almost always played by white actors in yellowface makeup. A few of the only notable exceptions were the Chinese American actress Anna May Wong, the Korean American actor Philip Ahn, and the Japanese actor Sessue Hayakawa, who played major roles, albeit mostly in films. The theatrical convention of elaborate oriental costume and yellowface makeup continued into the mid-twentieth century with popular musicals such as *The King and I* (1951), and the practice was readily borrowed by producers of film and television.

Audiences expected to see major Asian characters (both serious and comical) played by white actors whose made-up and dressed-up appearances signified something more theatrically "authentic" and "natural" than that of real Asians. In other words, they preferred to see the stage oriental, not the real Asian. For instance, when Japanese American actor Mako auditioned for the role of the Bandit in the American television version of the Japanese film *Rashomon* in the early 1960s, the casting director told him: "You gave a great reading, but as a real Japanese, you'd be too conspicuous. All of the other actors are white made up to look Japanese."[25] By the mid-twentieth century, the theatrical practice of yellowface makeup and elaborate oriental costumes on white actors had become an accepted and naturalized convention, and having a real Asian body on stage was simply too jarring.

THE FACES AND BODIES OF ASIAN AMERICAN THEATER

The yellowface makeup began to be challenged in the late 1950s in the United States, starting with the musical *Flower Drum Song* by Richard Rodgers and Oscar Hammerstein. Produced on Broadway in 1958, the musical featured a mostly Asian American cast and was set not in some far-away land but in San Francisco's Chinatown. For the first time, Asian American actors played Asian American roles in a major musical. The musical was the first Broadway show to open doors for Asian Americans in terms of both casting and storytelling. However, it was not completely free of the conventions of orientalization. Chinatown was exoticized, and a variety of oriental costumes—especially for female characters—were introduced. For instance, the character of Linda Lowe, a nightclub dancer, wore revealing versions of oriental clothing in dance sequences (such as in "Fan Tan Fanny," in which oriental-looking fans were part of the exotic and erotic wardrobe of the dancers).[26]

Many have criticized *Flower Drum Song* for perpetuating the model-minority myth of Asian Americans and for ignoring the realities of ghettoized Chinatowns. But in theater history, the musical is significant for featuring for the first time Asian American actors in major roles in American mainstream theater. The musical signaled the beginning of the end of yellowface, which reflected decades of racism and exclusion in American theater. As I have written in *A History of Asian American Theatre*, Asian American actors in the 1960s began to organize activist groups to protest the practice of yellowface on Broadway. In New York City, the members of Oriental Actors of America (OAA) specifically targeted shows that cast Asian characters with white actors. In the early 1970s, they filed a formal discrimination complaint with the New York State Division of Human Rights against the Repertory Theater of Lincoln Center. In the complaint, they contended that the Repertory's shows, *Good Woman of Setzuan* (a play by Bertolt Brecht), *Loverly Ladies, Kind Gentlemen* (a musical by John Patrick, Stan Freeman, and Franklin Underwood; based on the play *The Teahouse of the August Moon*), and *Narrow Road to Deep North* (a play by Edward Bond), had "Oriental themes and characters, which required preferential casting of Oriental actors."[27] They did not complain against the Asian themes and characters, which were mostly stereotypical. Rather, they focused their protest on casting. The message was clear: Asian characters had to be played by Asian or Asian American actors, and to do otherwise would be racism. They were protesting for the right to play oriental roles in oriental costumes. In other words, the oriental body would remain, but real Asian faces would replace the yellowface. With this focus on the face, the actors disregarded the fact that yellowface was inseparable from the rest of the body dressed in the oriental costume and decorated with oriental accessories. Yellowface was an established convention in Euro-American theater, and Asian American actors were simply stepping into it instead of supplanting it. To be fair, oriental roles were the only ones available to Asian American actors who wanted major roles in theater. Unlike African American actors, who found first acting opportunities in blackface minstrelsy, Asian American actors did not have to put yellowface makeup on their real faces, but the main signifier of the stage oriental was not the face but the costumed body.

Asian American actors demanded in the 1970s that they were the only ones who should be allowed to embody Asian and Asian American characters, including the archetype of the stage oriental. Their protests influenced the creation of Stephen Sondheim's musical *Pacific Overtures* (1976), which was the second Broadway show to feature an all–Asian American cast.[28] The musical is considered one of Sondheim's most daring experiments in casting, but it was also a way to test the effectiveness of having Asian American actors embody Asian characters created in the convention of stage orientalism. The director of the musical, Harold Prince, was fully aware of the recent protests by Asian American actors and decided to cast all roles (including white ones) with Asian American actors. And he made the distinction between Asian and Asian American actors and maintained that he would cast the show with Americans of Asian descent: "This is an American musical done *by* Americans playing Asian roles, and that's intentional."[29] Prince and Sondheim used the aesthetics of Japanese Kabuki theater to tell the story of Japanese-US relations. While the cast was Asian American, the story was not about their experiences: the set, costume, and makeup indicated a world far from the realities of their America. Florence Klotz's costume design included American uniforms with kimono sleeves, floor-length white hair, and others inspired by Kabuki theater. The makeup was also Kabuki inspired. Some actors painted their faces white and drew dark, high eyebrows, while others (especially those playing American characters) did not. In order to learn the techniques and styles of Japanese theater, Prince and Sondheim spent two weeks in Japan, "rushing around to all the Noh and Kabuki plays they could find."[30] This shallow knowledge of Japanese theater resulted in a visual stunning but essentially Western (more specifically, Sondheim) style of theater.

The decision to cast the show with Asian American actors made sense to Harold Prince precisely because the show was an "amalgam of Japanese and Western styles."[31] To him, Asian Americans actors embodied the transnational experiences articulated in the musical. However, most of the actors had no training in Kabuki theater or American Broadway musical theater. In fact, Prince acknowledged that he and the casting director Joanna Merlin had a difficult time finding Asian American male actors to fill all sixty-one parts.[32] Moreover, most critics and audiences did not appreciate the under-rehearsed performances by inexperienced actors; nor did they like the complex historical commentary delivered by the musical. (Having Commodore Matthew Perry dressed as the Kabuki "demon" didn't help either.) However, they unanimously appreciated the visual aspects of the show. For instance, *Pacific Overtures* was nominated for ten Tony Awards, including those for best musical, book, original score, actor (Mako), and director. Of the ten, it received two Tony Awards: for scenic design and costume design.

Yellowfaces were replaced with real Asian faces, but what made the most impact to the audiences of *Pacific Overtures* were oriental setting, costumes, and makeup. Because most of the cast lacked Broadway experience, they were not recognized for their artistry, and it was as if Asian American actors brought nothing more than their faces to the musical. Despite the emphasis on their cultural identity as Asian Americans, their life experiences were not reflected in the story of the musical. In short, their Asian American identities and subjectivities were buried behind elaborate oriental costumes and makeup.

By the end of the 1970s, the practice of yellowface began to disappear in American mainstream theater, and plays written by Asian Americans began to receive recognition. In 1988, David Henry Hwang became the first Asian American playwright to be produced on Broadway with his play *M. Butterfly*. Three other works by Hwang have been staged on Broadway: *Golden Child* (1998), a revised version of *Flower Drum Song* (2002), and *Chinglish* (2012). The first three works by Hwang were nominated for the Tony Award for excellence in writing: *M. Butterfly* and *Golden Child* for best play (*M. Butterfly* won the award) and *Flower Drum Song* for best book for a musical. The three works received other recognitions, but the only other award for which all three were nominated was costume design: Eiko Ishioka (*M. Butterfly*), Martin Pakledinaz (*Golden Child*), and Robert Longbottom (*Flower Drum Song*). Not incidentally, all three works feature elaborate traditional Chinese costumes.

Other shows with Asian themes that have done exceptionally well in the category of costume design in Tony Awards include: *The King and I* (winner in 1952); *Rashomon* (nominated in 1959); *The World of Suzie Wong* (nominated in 1959); *Lovely Ladies, Kind Gentlemen* (nominated in 1971); and the revival of *South Pacific* (winner in 2008). Is it a coincidence that most of the shows that featured Asian American performers in oriental costumes since the 1950s were nominated for the Tony Award for best costume? In twentieth-century America, theatrical shows set in Asia (or some variation of the "orient") have been consistently popular. Every time an Asian body has appeared on the Broadway stage, the oriental costume worn by the actor has received an unusual amount of attention. I argue that the connection between the Asian or Asian American actor and the oriental costume on Broadway has been not coincidental but essential. Moreover, such costumes have been popular not only because they provide visual pleasure to the audience with exotic spectacles. Rather, they are popular because the costumes reflect a long-standing convention necessary to make Asian-ness legible onstage on Broadway and in other mainstream venues. The practice of yellowface makeup has gradually disappeared because of Asian American actors' protest and because it no longer reflected the changing cultural values. However, oriental costumes have not been perceived as offensive as yellowface by both Asian American and mainstream theatergoers.

It can be argued that costumes are more neutral than yellowface makeup: The latter forcibly changes the look of the actor's face by distorting the eye to create the slanted look in order to represent the dominant culture's perception of the oriental. The face looks caricatured and artificial. Furthermore, browning the skin recalls blackface makeup, a practice with a well-known history now seen as categorically racist and appalling. In contrast, a costume can be an actual piece of clothing from Asia, or it can be celebrated for its beauty and tradition in an Asian culture (as in the kimono in Japan). But the fundamental purpose of the two as theatrical conventions is the same: both reflect the history that has privileged the white body in performance. White actors have had the free license to literally dress up and make up in any race as they wished and to interpret the racial character as they saw fit. Asian American actors in the 1960s and 1970s interpreted yellowface as a metonymy for the stage oriental embodied by white actors, and in many respects, it was so. But having Asian American actors embody oriental conventions does not mean that problematic representations have disappeared. Even with the yellowface gone, the costume has remained as the metonymy for the stage oriental that the audience is most familiar with and expects to see on Broadway. While protesting yellowface practice, Asian American theater artists embraced oriental costumes probably because clothing was seen as an innocuous way to market and consume Asian-ness in mainstream theater. By wearing the oriental costumes and embodying the conventionalized Asian-ness, Asian American performers finally had the opportunity to appear in major roles onstage.

ASIAN AMERICAN COSTUME DESIGNER

The founding ideals of Asian American theater were fundamentally political because its purpose was to oppose the accepted conventions of privileging white actors and Euro-American plays and to challenge the industry that excluded minority artists. At the same time, the convention of oriental costumes was not challenged by those who founded and led the Asian American theater movement. For example, when Mako began to lead the East West Players (the first Asian American theater company) in 1965, one of the first plays the company presented was *Rashomon* by Fay Kanin and Michael Kanin, a British play originally written for white actors in yellowface. How, then, should costume design and designers be included in the history of Asian American theater? Is costume design apolitical and open to interpretation by whoever uses it or views it? If so, does the costume designer have political agency? And what does it mean to call Willa Kim an Asian American costume designer?

Willa Kim's career as a costume designer began in the 1950s before the emergence of Asian American consciousness and Asian American theater as a movement. The dominant narrative of Asian American theater history is founded on the notion that Asian Americans and their stories need to be represented onstage and that Asian American theater artists deserve the same opportunities as any other theater artists in the country. Asian American theater, as a whole, was created because artists could not find opportunities in mainstream theater. "Asian American" as a panethnic category was used in order to make theater artists visible and to align Asian American theater artists with other artists of minority groups. The founding agenda for Asian American theater was, in a sense, the opposite of Willa Kim's trajectory as a designer. In the 1960s and the 1970s, Asian American theater was created as a way to critique the white-dominated mainstream theater, while Willa Kim was very much the insider of the very same mainstream theater.

Willa Kim may have been left out of the historical narrative of Asian American theater, but in reality, she has designed for productions of Asian American plays. She was the costume designer for the 1972 production of Frank Chin's *Chickencoop Chinaman* at the American Place Theatre, the first Asian American play produced in New York City. In 1981, she designed for the production of David Henry Hwang's *Family Devotions* at the Public Theater. Willa Kim has never worked with an Asian American theater company, and the productions are only two out of over 150 shows Willa Kim designed during her career. However, both *Chickencoop Chinaman* and *Family Devotions* are historically significant in that they were produced at the beginning of the careers of two of the most important Asian American playwrights. The fact that Willa Kim was involved in the production should not be an easily forgotten part of that history. More importantly, the two plays are representative of Asian American plays of the 1970s and 1980s, when the majority of Asian American writers wrote in the genre of realism. As Josephine Lee notes, theatrical realism can be used to denote "authenticity" and "realness" of representation, but it is also a political strategy against stage orientalism.[33] By showing "real" Asian American characters without exotic settings or costumes, their subjectivity as Americans can be made legible. For example, production photos of Frank Chin's *Chickencoop Chinaman* show the cast wearing outfits reflective of the 1972 fashion with wide pants and turtleneck sweaters. The images of the actor Randall Duk Kim wearing Willa Kim's costume in Frank Chin's first play signify one of the most important moments in Asian American theater history.[34] Had Willa Kim designed mostly for Asian American plays during her career, it would be easy to categorize her and even celebrate her as an Asian American costume designer, but the vast majority of her work has expanded well beyond Asian American theater.

It is difficult to include Kim in the narrative of Asian American theater because her range as a designer has exceeded expectations and transcended infrastructural categories of American theater. She has had a clear preference for nonrealistic works and found plays more challenging than ballets and operas. In an interview, she emphasizes that her work is best "when it's very imaginative and unrealistic."[35] Asian American theater, on the whole, is based heavily on realism in the politics of representation. Kim, on the other hand, prefers to move away from realism and focuses on innovation and technology of design. This meant that within her oeuvre, some of Kim's costumes could be described as "oriental" or even yellowface. In 1969, for instance, Willa Kim was asked to design for Gian Carlo Menotti's *Help! Help! The Globolinks* and Igor Stravinsky's *Le Rossignol* at the Santa Fe Opera Company. The former was a parable, and the set and costume design by Willa Kim was abstract, and the latter, the opera by Stravinsky, was a Hans Christian Andersen story set in ancient China.[36] Production photos show non-Asian performers in Kim's Asian-inspired costumes wearing makeup to look Asian. Bobbi Owen writes, "Willa Kim's Asian heritage, which has often been cited as underpinning her composed yet witty style, was clearly valued by Bliss Herbert [the director] for this production."[37] "Composed" and "witty" are not the usual descriptors for Asians, but Owen uses them to describe how Willa Kim's ethnic heritage was the source of her extraordinary creativity. Whether she was seen as a good designer because she was Asian or she played to the expectations of others by creating works that were oriental and exotic may never be answered in a satisfactory way, but the two possibilities seem to have coexisted and fed on each other. Ultimately, what remain as historical evidence are production photos that exhibit Willa Kim's versatility and range that include designs in the tradition of stage orientalism. And her colleagues and critics assumed and concluded that her art stemmed from her "Asian heritage."

In reviews and interviews with Willa Kim, very little is made of her Korean American background, and the narrative of her career lacks direct references to her ethnicity. When her Korean heritage is mentioned, it is done in a cultural sense (as in food) or in the context of her family (specifically her famous brother). Both Anna May Wong and Philip Ahn, who found mainstream success as actors in film before the Asian American Movement, have expressed difficulties caused by racism and stereotyping. Their biographies are fascinating because of the fame they achieved despite social barriers. Willa Kim's biographical narrative, on the other hand, lacks such race-based roadblocks, or at least, she seems to not care about them even if they did exist. In a 2004 interview in *American Theatre*, she is asked, "Were you from the first or second generation of Chinese Americans?" but she does not correct the interviewer. She answers, "I am second generation. I was born just outside of Santa Ana in Orange County, a Republican stronghold right now, unfortunately."[38] Kim takes the time to specify her preference for political party while not bothering to explain that she is actually Korean American.

The narrative that takes full account of her life and career would need to balance the celebratory acknowledgment of her undisputable success and the lack of political perspective that makes the reception of her success ambiguous. As a costume designer, Willa Kim has had the flexibility to work in a wide range of forms and genres of performance around the world, and the vast variety of work she has created makes it difficult to analyze her in the context of Asian American theater, which emphasizes dialogue-based realistic plays. Kim has worked in opera, ballet, Broadway musicals, plays, ice-skating, film, television, and even the Olympics. Kim was the designer of costumes for the dancers in the performance of Beethoven's *Ode to Joy* during the opening ceremonies for the XVIII Winter Olympic Games in Nagano, Japan, in 1998. Her work in international venues grew as her reputation as a top designer and innovator of design solidified.

Dance historian Yutian Wong explains in her study of the Japanese dancer Michio Ito that the trope of the "international artists" is often used to "deracialize" their identity:

> The desire to reclaim Ito is accomplished through the trope of internationality as a process of deracialization overlaid with the desire to domesticate his racial otherness. This desire both

distances Ito from the perceived limitations of race, ethnicity, or Japaneseness as a definitive qualifier of his artistic production, while assuming that the categories are in and of themselves limiting. The politics of whiteness, as that which remains invisibly central and absented from racial, ethnic, and national otherness, are never enunciated.[39]

A similar process of internationalization has taken place in creating a narrative of Willa Kim, and all sectors of the theater community have, for one reason or another, participated in deracializing her. For the mainstream design community, Willa Kim's ethnic background was mostly irrelevant because it was her work, not herself, that would be represented onstage. For Asian American theater artists, their focus has been to find opportunities for actors and playwrights and to remedy racist representations of Asian images onstage. In that framework, their political agenda had to precede aesthetic achievements, and it was often more urgent to tell Asian American stories onstage than to be concerned with innovations and creativity in design. With the trope of the international artist, Willa Kim's work can escape the scrutiny of political correctness and the paradigm that has dominated Asian American theater history. Even the costume designs that can be described as oriental can be categorized as art that transcends culture, race, and nation.

Toward a Historiography of Costume Design in Asian American Theater

Willa Kim presents a dilemma for scholars of Asian American theater. She is an Asian American artist whose successful career should be celebrated, and her design for plays by Frank Chin and David Henry Hwang should be recognized as important contributions. At the same time, her legacy as a designer has solidified as an artist of "Asian heritage" who has designed "dreamy" costumes with her "instinct." Moreover, she has designed many costumes that are unequivocally in the tradition of stage orientalism and convention of yellowface. Within the stipulation of what constitutes Asian American theater, she is too multifaceted and contradictory to impose any categorization. Without an appropriate category, Kim could not be made visible and comprehensible in theater scholarship. Perhaps Willa Kim has been in my blind spot because I had to narrow my historian's perspective in researching Asian American theater. The specificity of Asian American theater requires me to acquire a kind of myopic vision of history and to find historical truths in details. In order to study someone like Willa Kim, however, it would be necessary for historians to use hyperopic vision that can encompass all of the venues she worked in: theater, dance, opera, ice skating, the Olympics, and commercials. The convention of stage orientalism and yellowface may have been challenged and mostly eradicated in theater, but the tradition has continued in other variations in dance and opera. It would be even more critical to understand the innovations she made in costume and textile technology. Most theater historians simply do not have the critical vocabularies and knowledge to fully research and articulate design and designers. With my narrow focus, it is not surprising that I could not see and understand Willa Kim and her designs.

I have begun widening the historiographical focus with this chapter by providing a history of oriental conventions in costume design and describing the strategic choices made by founders of Asian American theater to fight against yellowface makeup while accepting oriental costumes. The separation of the face from the body was necessary for Asian American actors to find acting opportunities, but the meaning of the separation deserves further examination, particularly in the context of costume history and theories of body. Scholars who have written about the Asian American body onstage have not made clear what they mean by the body.[40] Often, when the Asian American body is discussed, it refers mainly to the face. Because of the specific history of yellowface and how it was instrumental in the creation of Asian American theater, the face has become the main trope of the body. Particularly, the Asian eyes have come to signify Asian-ness, as the yellowface makeup is defined primarily as the slanting of the eyes. While focusing on the face, scholars and artists have not paid as much attention to the body or the costume that give it meaning in performance. The body without the face does not have signification in Asian American theater history. In contrast, in African American theater, the color of the skin or the shapes of certain body parts have been central in the discourse of body politics and performance. In Asian American theater, a rich discussion of the Asian American body in its entirety has been absent, and with it, costume history and designers such as Willa Kim have been left out of its narrative.[41]

The inclusion of costume history and designers in the scholarship Asian American theater requires the broadening of definitions and contextualization. The historiographical shifting also needs the recentering of what is assumed to be most significant in Asian American theater history. If costume history were to function as the center of Asian American theater, Willa Kim's career would stand out as the representative success story, but more importantly, costume would be inseparable from how the body in performance is understood. Such shifting and recentering would align Asian American theater in history in ways that would make new interpretations possible. For instance, one of the first theatrical representations of Asian-ness was Afong Moy, who was called a "Chinese Lady," and in 1834 she and her "room" with Chinese items were put on display in a touring exhibition promoted by the Carne Brothers in New York City. After paying fifty cents, viewers could watch her walk on her bound feet and speak Chinese.[42] In advertisements and newspaper announcements, Afong Moy's bound feet are described as the most curious spectacle, but her elaborate costume is always highlighted as a noteworthy part of her performance. "She will be richly dressed in the Chinese costume," announces an advertisement in New York Times in the July 9, 1936, issue. Her costume covers most of her body with a long skirt and sleeves, and in her room, she looks like another form of decoration.[43]

In the discourse created around Afong Moy, her costume is essential to how her identity is described, and her body is inseparable from her costume and the exotic things that surround her. As Josephine Lee notes, commodity orientalism and decorative orientalism dominated how Asian-ness was introduced to Europe and the United States in the nineteenth century.[44] Afong Moy's body had little meaning without her costume and her "room." In stark contrast, African and African American women's bodies have attracted imperialistic attention when they were without clothing. From Saarjie "Sarah" Baartman (Venus Hottentot) to Josephine Baker, the naked skin and exposed body parts of the black female body have been fundamental to the discourse of blackness and primitivism. Anne Anlin Cheng makes an accurate observation in her comparison between Afong Moy and Baartman in her book Second Skin:

> That is, the primitive black woman is all about exposed nakedness, while the "Oriental" woman is all about the sartorial excess, the excessive covering and ornamentation that

supposedly symptomizes the East's overly developed, effeminized, corrupt, and declining civilization. [. . .] Where Baartman was stripped down for the white male gaze, the demure Moy was fully clothed and sat, herself ornament-like, among layers (tablecloths, draperies, paintings, panels, and so on) of Victorian fantasies of Chinese decorations.[45]

Cheng goes on to describe the Victorian fascination with fabric as a form of orientalism, but her discussion of Moy is only a few pages in a book entirely about Josephine Baker.

The comparison between the Asian body and the black body is fascinating, but what is startling to me as a theater historian is the vast lack of scholarly writing on Asian and Asian American bodies in comparison to the numerous books and articles written on the black body. Moreover, in African American performance history, there is an unyielding continuity in the history of the black body from Baartman to twenty-first-century performances. When it comes to the study of the body, the history of Asian American theater and performance is disjointed and full of epistemological gaps. I argue that focusing on costume history is one way to fill those gaps and to shift the historiographical paradigm of Asian American theater. There is much potential in examining how costumes have been as important as skin color and body shape in the performance of Asian-ness. By exploring such potential, Willa Kim's work in all of its complexities will be made truly meaningful in theater history and historiography.

Notes

1. Bobbi Owen, 35.
2. Owen, 6.
3. Since the publication of the book on Willa Kim, at least seven additional monographs on individual designers have been published by USITT. See http://www.usitt.org/store_category.asp?id=1 for a full list of the books.
4. Owen, 112.
5. For example, the lighting designer Adolphe Appia (1862–1928) is one of few designers included in theater history textbooks, but his work is made historically significant only in connection to Richard Wagner's opera.
6. The second monograph USITT published in its series is *The Designs of Ming Cho Lee*.
7. Terry Hong, 69. The articles focuses on contemporary Korean American actors and playwrights, and Willa Kim is mentioned as a pioneer Korean American theater artist.
8. To name only a few awards she has received: the Irene Sharaff Lifetime Achievement Award from Theatre Development Fund (New York) in 1999; Patricia Zipprodt Award for Innovative Costume Design from Fashion Institute of Technology (New York) in 2003; and the Distinguished Achievement in Costume Design from USITT in 2005. For a full list of all of the awards, see Owen, 91.
9. In 1980, Willa Kim designed the costumes for San Francisco Ballet's production of *The Tempest*, including the Caliban costume. She received her first Emmy Award for the broadcast of the ballet on PBS in 1981.
10. Owen, 65. Owen quotes Robert Brustein's review of *The Front Page* (written in 1928 by Ben Hecht and Charles MacArthur and produced on Broadway in 1986) in the magazine *New Republic*, in which he writes, "Jerome Dempsey as the rotund, orotund mayor, equipped (by the costume designer Willa Kim, whose period designs are characterization

in themselves) with tailcoat and fez, bouncing languorously about the stage like a huge beach ball on the surface of the pond." Robert Brustein, "Robert Brustein on Theater," *New Republic* (January 5, 1987): 25–27, 26.

11. Owen, 61.
12. Owen, 61.
13. Quoted on the back cover of Owen's book.
14. Owen, 7.
15. Owen, 11, 29, and 88.
16. In the rest of the essay, I use the term "oriental" without quotes, but I define it specifically to connote a theatrical convention with all of its historically complex ramifications.
17. Joseph Roach, 98.
18. Roach, 95.
19. James S. Moy, 9.
20. For examples of the jokes, see Robert G. Lee, *Orientals: Asian Americans in Popular Culture.*
21. Sean Metzger, 627.
22. Metzger, 635.
23. For studies on the reception of Chinese theater in America, see Daphne Lei, "The Production and Consumption of Chinese Theatre in Nineteenth-Century California" and chapter 4 in John Kuo Wei Tchen, *New York before Chinatown: Orientalism and the Shaping of American Culture: 1776–1882.*
24. The Chinese population decreased because of a series of anti-Chinese laws that were passed. The anti-Chinese sentiment reached its peak in the 1870s and 1880s and contributed to massacres and massive deportations. By the early twentieth century, new immigration virtually ceased, and those remaining in the states lived in ghettoized areas while their descendants increasing assimilated into the American culture.
25. Irvin Paik, 14.
26. These nightclub dance scenes were based on actual nightclubs in Chinatowns that reached the height of popularity in the 1930s and 1940s. Owners of the nightclubs, who were Chinese Americans, promoted the exoticization of Asian female performers to attract white patrons. Arthur Dong's documentary film *Forbidden City, USA* (1989) provides an accurate history of the nightclub and its influences and Asian American performers.
27. Margarita Rosa, A26. The OAA initially lost the case but won the appeal.
28. The musical tells the story of the "opening" of Japan to the West with the arrival of Commodore Matthew Perry of the US Navy in Tokyo Bay in 1853. The musical also makes commentaries on the exchanges between the two countries and ends with scenes set in modernized Japan of 1975.
29. Lillian Ross, 24–27.
30. "A New Musical Brings Japan to Broadway," 13.
31. Ibid.
32. In order to stay true to the Kabuki tradition, Harold Prince wanted to cast all roles, including the female ones, with male actors. But there were only a handful of Asian American male actors who could sing, dance, and act at the level of Broadway theater. Prince was adamant about his intention. When others tried to convince him to audition Puerto Rican actors "who look Oriental," he stayed committed to Asian American actors. One exception was Iaso Sato, an acclaimed Japanese actor. And there were three Asian American actresses in the cast: Kim Miyori, Diane Lam, and Susan Kikuchi.

33. For an extensive discussion on realism and Asian American spectatorship, see chapter 2 in Josephine Lee's *Performing Asian America: Race and Ethnicity on the Contemporary Stage*.
34. Production photos of Frank Chin's play can be seen in Frank Chin, *Chickencoop Chinaman/The Year of the Dragon: Two Plays*.
35. "Twenty Questions: Costume Designer Willa Kim," 128.
36. Images of the costume are reprinted on pages 32–33 in Bobbi Owen's book.
37. Owen, 33.
38. "Twenty Questions," 128.
39. Yutian Wong, 149.
40. I include myself in this group of scholars. For significant works that discuss representation of Asian American bodies onstage, see Dorinne Kondo's *About Face: Performing Race in Fashion and Theater*, Karen Shimakawa's *National Abjection: The Asian American Body Onstage*, and Josephine Lee's "Racial Actors, Liberal Myths." Other studies of the Asian American body address sexual and gender politics as exemplified by the anthology *Embodying Asian/American Sexualities*, edited by Gina Masequesmay and Sean Metzger.
41. One exception to this absence is Priya Srinivasan's *Sweating Saris: Indian Dance as Transnational Labor*, which examines the labor of Indian women dancers and the importance of their dancing bodies in *saris*.
42. James S. Moy discusses Afong Moy in his *Marginal Sights: Staging the Chinese in America*, 12.
43. The picture can be seen online at the National Women's History Museum website. http://www.nwhm.org/online-exhibits/chinese/4.html (accessed May 28, 2013).
44. See chapter one in Josephine Lee's *The Japan of Pure Invention*.
45. Anne Anlin Cheng, 151–52.

BIBLIOGRAPHY

"Twenty Questions: Costume Designer Willa Kim." *American Theatre*, January 2004.
"A New Musical Brings Japan to Broadway." *Cue*, January 10, 1976.
Cheng, Anne Anlin. *Second Skin: Josephine Baker and Modern* Surface. Oxford: Oxford University Press, 2011.
Chin, Frank. *Chickencoop Chinaman/The Year of the Dragon: Two Plays*. Seattle: University of Washington Press, 1981.
Hong, Terry. "Times Up: The Moment Is Now." *KoreAm Journal*, December 2003.
Kondo, Dorinne. *About Face: Performing Race in Fashion and Theater*. New York: Routledge, 1997.
Lei, Daphne. "The Production and Consumption of Chinese Theatre in Nineteenth-Century California." *Theatre Research International* 28, no. 3 (2003): 289–302.
Lee, Esther Kim. *A History of Asian American Theatre*. Cambridge: Cambridge University Press, 2006.
Lee, Josephine. *Performing Asian America: Race and Ethnicity on the Contemporary Stage*. Philadelphia: Temple University Press, 1998.
Lee, Josephine. "Racial Actors, Liberal Myths." *Xcp: Cross Cultural Poetics* 13 (2004): 88–110.
Lee, Josephine. *The Japan of Pure Invention: Gilbert and Sullivan's* The Mikado. Minneapolis: University of Minnesota Press, 2010.
Lee, Robert G. *Orientals: Asian Americans in Popular Culture*. Philadelphia: Temple University Press, 1999.

Masequesmay, Gina, and Sean Metzger, eds. *Embodying Asian/American Sexualities*. Lanham, MD: Lexington Books, 2009.

Metzger, Sean. "Charles Parsloe's Chinese Fetish: An Example of Yellowface Performance in Nineteenth-Century American Melodrama." *Theatre Journal* 56, no. 4 (December 2004): 627–51.

Moy, James S. *Marginal Sights: Staging the Chinese in America*. Iowa City: University of Iowa Press, 1993.

Owen, Bobbi. *The Designs of Willa Kim*. New York: United States Institute for Theatre Technologies, 2005.

Paik, Irvin. "The East West Players: The First Ten Years Are the Hardest." *Bridge: An Asian American Perspective* 5, no. 2 (1977).

Roach, Joseph. "The Global Parasol: Accessorizing the Four Corners of the World." In *The Global Eighteenth Century*, edited by Felicity A. Nussbaum, 93–106. Baltimore: Johns Hopkins University Press, 2003.

Rosa, Margarita. "Asian Actors Lost in a '73 'Miss Saigon' Case." *New York Times*, September 18, 1990.

Ross, Lillian. "Meetings." *New Yorker*, March 22, 1976.

Said, Edward. *Orientalism*. New York: Vintage Books, 1979.

Shimakawa, Karen. *National Abjection: The Asian American Body Onstage*. Durham, NC: Duke University Press, 2002.

Srinivasan, Priya. *Sweating Saris: Indian Dance as Transnational Labor*. Philadelphia: Temple University Press, 2011.

Wong, Yutian. "Artistic Utopias: Michio Ito and the International." In *Worlding Dance*, edited by Susan Leigh Foster, 144–62. New York City: Palgrave Macmillan, 2009.

Tchen, John Kuo Wei. *New York before Chinatown: Orientalism and the Shaping of American Culture: 1776–1882*. Baltimore: Johns Hopkins University Press, 1999.

Unruh, Delbert. *The Designs of Ming Cho Lee*. New York: United States Institute for Theatre Technologies, 2008.

CHAPTER 19

....

MOVING AMERICAN HISTORY
An Examination of Works by Ken Burns and Bill T. Jones

....

ANN DILS

> For "The Civil War," I began, essentially with my heart, to feel my way to a kind of truth for myself of how this material should be structured and presented.
>
> —Ken Burns

> [A]rt-making for me is participation in the world of ideas. What does it look like to see ideas struggle with each other?
>
> —Bill T. Jones

In this chapter, I investigate two prominent examples of American Civil War-era history delivered through publically accessible, theatrically rich means: film and dance. Ken Burns's "The Cause (1861)" is the opening installment of his 11-hour 1990 documentary film series, *The Civil War*. Bill T. Jones's 2009 *Fondly Do We Hope . . . Fervently Do We Pray* is an evening-length, multimedia performance project. "The Cause" details the opening year of the Civil War, its people and events and the national disagreements that led to war, through narration, expert commentary, period photographs and music, and new film of historic sites. *Fondly* is an examination of Abraham Lincoln as historical figure and continuing influence in public life. The work brings together ten dancers, an actor, and a small group of singers and musicians. Period texts are spoken, projected, and used as lyrics for new music. Video brings life to historic images.

I began rewatching Burns's *The Civil War* soon after seeing Jones's *Fondly* in live performance. Jones develops his work in two acts and an epilogue. He introduces individuals and issues then stages a civilized debate that breaks into churning chaos and a slow-motion war. Complicating this sequence are representational choices and a series of shared movement phrases whose meanings and development are subtle and invite further investigation. I turned to documentary film to better understand how history is delivered through theatrical means. As I repeatedly watched and analyzed "The Cause" and then *Fondly* on DVD, Burns's documentary provided a template through which I understood Jones's dance, which in turn prompted questions about the documentary. My first investigatory steps produced chronological descriptions that made theatrical strategies, among them structures, representations, and means of inspiring identification and empathy in viewers, clear. I have left a great deal of this description in the chapter, in part as an aid for those who might want to compare the works themselves, and in part to capture the nuances of each work and the differences between them. Next, I considered the central place of bodies in both works and their importance in fostering empathy and in posing questions. Lastly, I considered the impact of these strategies on the histories presented. Does theatricality thwart or provide and support a nuanced, reflexive historical experience? Both works serve as meditations on the poverty and potential of history, revealing how little some histories tell us and how rich encountering history can be in understanding our identities, aspirations, and ways of seeing.

World[s] of Ideas; Kind[s] of Truth

Burns and Jones are public artists and intellectuals whose perspectives and concerns speak to broad audiences. While live performance never reaches as many people as television and film, Burns's and Jones's works are high-profile productions. Forty million people watched *The Civil War* when it first aired on Public Broadcasting Service in 1990, and it garnered over forty major awards, stretching across film and television and academe. Among Burns's awards was the Gilder Lehrman Lincoln Prize for scholarly work on Lincoln or the Civil War. The series can still be watched on DVD and through online video services, and PBS hosts a website with images and teaching materials (http://www.pbs.org/civilwar/). *Fondly* was commissioned by the Ravinia Festival, a major performing arts presenting and educational venue near Chicago, to celebrate the anniversary of Lincoln's 100th birthday. Ravinia Pavilion holds 3,400 people, with another 15,000 possible seats on the lawn. *Fondly* has been shown numerous times since on tour. Its making is the subject of two PBS offerings, a 2009 installment of *Bill Moyers Journal* and a documentary, *Bill T. Jones: A Good Man*, part of the American Masters Series and shown in Fall 2011. While broadly known and appreciated, Burns and Jones are, perhaps, especially important to those of us who also grew up in mid- to late-twentieth-century America: Voices of our generation, they appeal to conflicting sentiments in our own histories.

American history, as Burns has remarked in interviews, is "a family story" (Walsh n.d.). In *The Civil War*, this is evident in Burns's attention to individual and regional experience, in poetic images that dignify everyday Americans, their histories, and cultural practices, and in a respectful even-handedness. While Burns denounces slavery in "The Cause," he attempts to relay the experiences and positions of Northerners and Southerners without obvious critique. Burns remarked in an interview with Joan Walsh,

> I think we have a hunger for national self-definition. And without a past, we deprive ourselves of the defining impressions of our being . . . The implication is that the airing out of history is a kind of medicine: Healing can take place. That's what I'm interested in: the healing power of history. (n.d.)

In watching "The Cause," it is clear that Burns sees history as national consciousness and the Civil War as a tragic event that made the United States, once a federation of disparate regions, into a mature nation, an American family. Burns may also see the Civil War as an extention of his personal history. Burns began and ended his World War II documentary, *The War*, with an unidentified image of his lieutenant father (Shister 2007). In making *The Civil War*, Burns may have found his respect and affection for the "greatest generation" co-mingling with his analysis of the motivations and actions of an earlier generation.

As he works in dance and multimedia to create beautifully structured mazes of images and ideas, Jones challenges audiences to explore moral positions and critique our histories and established social order. Jones's father and mother were sharecroppers who wept at the Civil Rights Act of 1964 and kept images of Lincoln, Kennedy, and Martin Luther King Jr. in their home. For Jones, history should be reclaimed and retold to empower contemporary people and inform their thinking. He makes clear that the debates of Lincoln's time, among them the extent to which individuals are free and the responsibilities of states and nations to protect their citizens, are contemporary questions as well. In a 2009 interview with Ariel Osterweis Scott, Jones describes his work with *Fondly* not as an exploration of Lincoln as historical figure but of Lincoln as touchstone in American life and means of interrogating individual beliefs:

> I was a bit shocked when I realized my young dancers had so little engagement with him, whereas he seemed to be huge in my life . . . Lincoln was the only white man I was allowed to love unconditionally . . . I want to find out what the dance- and theater-going audience thinks and feels, and I want to try to share something about the struggle between the 5-year-old [in me] who believed everything . . . with the 57-year-old who struggles to believe anything. Lincoln is going to be the petri dish for this struggle. (n.p.)

While I don't want to establish this contrast—Burns as a sentimental poet and Jones as a cultural critic—too firmly, these tendencies are clear from prelude and exposition to resolution.

"The Cause" opens to a cannon in silhouette against a sunset. Wind blows across the landscape, and actor Paul Roebling quotes physician and author Oliver Wendell Holmes: "We have shared the incommunicable experience of war. We have felt, we still feel, the passion of life to its top . . . In our youths, our hearts were touched with fire." Holmes's statement is the first of many nostalgia-tinged writings, some found in excerpts from soldiers' letters and from press coverage of Civil War reunions, that present war as romantic adventure and manly sacrifice. From the calm of a historic site at sunset, Burns invites audiences to contemplate Holmes's words and their several references, among them a war fought by idealistic youth, a young nation struggling for cohesion, and a group of filmmakers moved by their five years of making sense of historical materials and the lives and events they represent. It is also an invitation to the audience, calling viewers to share in these passions.

Burns doesn't position himself as a commentator, relaying his ideas directly, but allows the fabric of "The Cause," its layered images and sounds, to speak for him. The documentary takes on authority and veracity through the thousands of period images used and its many important voices. Historian David McCullough, then the host of PBS's *American Experience*, narrates "The Cause," and Burns presents the voices of actors such as Morgan Freeman and Jeremy Irons. Ideas about the war and its causes and outcomes are most obviously embedded in "The Cause" in the form of expert commentary. Near the end of his exposition, as Burns introduces his characters, historical and current, and arguments about the war, he juxtaposes interviews with scholars Barbara Fields, a Columbia profes-sor who has written a number of important social histories about the nineteenth-century South including *Free at Last: A Documentary History of Slavery, Freedom, and the Civil War* (1992), and Shelby Foote, the historian and novelist who wrote the three-volume *Civil War: A Narrative* (1958–1974). While much of Burns's *The Civil War* is about mil-itary history, Fields cautions us "not to think about soldiers and battlefields, but about humanity, human dignity, human freedom." Foote puts forward the view that the war was the "crossroads of our being" that defined American character in the twentieth century. Illustrating both statements, Burns scans the naked torso of a black man, and delivers Lincoln's words: "as a nation of free men we will live free or die by suicide." Fields and Foote return throughout "The Cause" and are joined by military historian Ed Bearss, who later discusses John Brown. After the Fields and Foote interviews, *The Civil War*'s theme music, "Ashokan Farewell" ends, signaling the end of the exposition: Burns has laid out his argument and introduced the players. Never far from war as heroic tale, Burns immedi-ately turns to newsreel clips of Civil War reunions that occurred into the 1930s and of the funeral of the final war veteran in 1959.

The epilogue of "The Cause," entitled "Honorable Manhood," is the most moving of Burns's statements of admiration for the Civil War soldier. Paul Roebling reads a letter by Sullivan Ballou, 2nd Rhode Island Volunteers, written to his wife in case he should be killed. Accompanying Ballou's letter are photographs of couples, the men in uniforms that suggest North and South, and various ranks: "My love for you is deathless . . . Yet my love of coun-try comes over me like a strong wind and bears me unresistibly on with all these chains to the battlefield." The camera moves slowly across a photograph to take viewers inside a tent. Focus comes to rest on a chair and then on a table next to it, helping the viewer imagine the setting in which the letter was written. The lens finally comes to rest on an image on the wall of the tent, by implication, a photograph:

> The memory of all the blissful moments I have enjoyed with you come crowding over me . . . And how hard it is for me to give them up and burn to ashes the hopes of future years when God willing we might still have lived and loved together and see our boys grown up to hon-orable manhood around us. If I do not return my dear Sarah never forget how much I loved you . . . Forgive my faults . . . I will always be with you.

A week later, Ballou was killed at Bull Run.

As *Fondly* begins, a cannon shot sounds through the dark auditorium. Clarissa Sinceno trav-els down an aisle holding a lamp and inviting audience and cast to move into the visual and aural spaces of the piece. Quoting "The Song of Solomon," she sings, "Arise, my love, my fair one and come away." Lights come up to reveal a stage divided into distinct areas. The central part of the stage is set apart through the use of a circular curtain. Later, the dancers open and close this space themselves by running sections of curtain around on overhead tracks. A giant moving silhouette of Lincoln walks across the space with top hat held behind him, and Shayla-Vie Jenkins follows, walking across the front of the space and into a small, circular satellite space marked out downstage left. These spaces indicate interrelated realms of Jones's "petri dish": The larger space is for mythic, often dreamy, enactments of received history; the smaller is the realm of personal experience and memory. They point, not just to our general understandings of Lincoln and his era but also to the ways we understand the past: partially available, partially understood narratives that are always encountered from our own vantage points and embroidered by our personal histories. The cannon volley is a warning shot: a confrontation is at hand.

Fondly contains period artifacts in the poetry of Walt Whitman and images of Abraham and Mary Todd Lincoln. Jones makes these animate through danced portrayals and video and by using them in new music. The veracity and authority in this work is in its ability to explain our own experiences of history and our relationship to Lincoln and his ideas. Brief biographies of individuals are danced in the downstage satellite space and relayed by the narrator. Antonio Brown dances a statement attached to Jones's biography, and this provides a set of questions to apply to other biographies: What is true here? Do these biographies capture individuals or types of people we think we know? Do the images, performances, and/or words ring true? Peter Chamberlin is a veteran of the wars in Iraq and Afghanistan. Jennifer Nugent is a woman just retired after working her whole life in a factory. LaMichael Leonard is introduced as a Bill T. Jones company member. Asli Bulbul dances as Mary Todd Lincoln. Each biography includes a reflection on feelings about wars, freedom, or the possibility of "great men."

Movement motifs reappear throughout the dance creating associations and contrasts that challenge the audience to question who and what we know. There is a romantic duet, a clinging social dance, between Paul Matteson and Asli Bulbul as Abraham and Mary Todd Lincoln that centralizes their young love and the birth of their four sons and reminds the audience that the Lincolns were sexual beings. Their dance is echoed in duets between LaMichael Leonard and Shayla-Vie Jenkins that come to stand for many un-namable romantic couples. While public fascination with the Lincoln marriage is still high, what knowledge do we have of other couples—of slaves who could not marry legally, couples who dealt with antimiscegenation laws, or with marriage as defined as a union between man and woman? While the 2012 *Lincoln* film reminded viewers of the relationship between Thaddeus Stevens, abolitionist and congressman, and Lydia Hamilton Smith, I am hard pressed to name another. These holes or indeterminacies point out gaps in knowledge and pose unanswerable questions.

Jones's epilogue does not resolve the work but takes the audience from the nineteenth century into the future. Dates speed by, projected on the circular curtain, as we hear bits of text from throughout the evening. Mary Todd Lincoln walks in funeral garb across a street in Times Square and snow falls. We next see her walking through a colonnade center stage as I-Ling Liu moves in the satellite space, performing a slow, delicate version of Shayla-Vie Jenkins's opening statement. The company lines up in back of Mary Todd Lincoln in a monumental pose of upraised arms, pointing to heaven, raised to swear an oath or to make a point. Jones leaves the audience with a biography of a woman a hundred years into the future. She still thinks about Lincoln and wants "to believe in great men and great women," but finds our actions difficult to comprehend. What will our descendants think of us? Of our handling of freedom and democracy? As she leaves, Lincoln, who has spent most of the work in a white suit, is now in the black and white suit we most identify him with as an historical figure. He, the narrator, and Mary Todd Lincoln appear in white squares, entrapped by the pages of existing histories.

Art-making: Materials Structured and Presented

Public historian Benjamin Filene has developed a discussion of current forms of public history that attract large numbers of participants or broad audiences that he terms "outsider histories." This is history practiced by filmmakers, television producers, genealogists, and reenactors working outside the academy and the usual spheres of public history such as museums and heritage sites (2012, 14).[1] Outsider histories may be the result of substantial and balanced research, but they differ from the defensible narratives of academic history or the measured, educational tone of most public history in their appeal to the emotions of contemporary people. By emphasizing individual voice, the familial and local, and "reexperiencing" the past, outsider histories encourage personal investment in an historical event or era.

While the three characteristics of outsider histories Filene outlines are employed extensively throughout Burns's and Jones's works, their means of helping viewers reexperience the past are especially important. One of the subtlest of these is their use of narrative arcs. While Burns's work is sectioned off in chronological or thematic units, viewers are propelled through his story by an underlying narrative arc: prelude, exposition, rising action, climax, falling action, and resolution or dénouement. As with feature films, this arc keeps viewers interested in an escalating problem and its resolution. Jones's work is presented in acts, and these divisions sit atop narratives and counternarratives delivered as movement phrases are presented and represented on varied bodies. This technique prompts us to ask whose narrative, whose story, is really told here? Lincoln's? That of many individuals and groups?

The narrative arcs that are so compelling in these works, and Burns's and Jones's use of bodies as points of identification and empathy call on our "cinesthetic bodies," which film theorist Christiane Voss describes as "synesthetic and pre-reflective, sensually emphatic reactions [that are] primary and meaning-founding ways of dealing with this medium" (Voss 2011, 144). Referring to the work of Vivian Sobchack, who first used the term "cinesthetic," Voss makes clear that the cinesthetic body joins the techniques of the film and the perceptions of onlookers in reciprocal relationship. It's not just that movement across the face of the photograph or the sweep of a narrative across time successfully mimics our experiences but that they organize multiple sensory, empathic, and, eventually, meaning-making responses that, in turn, become the film for the viewer. Too, as Deidre Sklar reminds us in her foundational 1991 "Five Premises for a Culturally Sensitive Approach to Dance," "the concrete and sensory, in other words, bodily aspects of social life provide the glue that holds world views and cosmologies, values and political convictions, together" (n.p.). The movement and bodily references within these works lead us to care about the histories and issues at hand. Viewers must ask themselves whether they've been coerced into loving versions of history they might otherwise question, or encouraged to consider bodily experiences as they critique their reactions to performances of history. In the following descriptions, I make clear how Burns and Jones handle these possibilities.

"THE CAUSE (1861)"

In the exposition, Burns begins with the Holmes quote and then introduces the places and people important to the war's first year and the techniques that will draw the audience into the story. He begins with anecdote: Wilmer McLean, a Virginia farmer, who "could rightfully say, 'the war began in my front yard and ended in my front parlor.'" McLean's farm at Manassas, Virginia, was the site of the First Battle of Bull Run, July 18, 1861. McLean moved his family south to Appomattox Court House, only to have the war end in his living room, where Robert E. Lee signed the terms of surrender, April 9, 1865. McLean's house is seen from one vantage point in a photograph, then Burns presents a closer view of men sitting in the weedy front yard. The audience assumes this is the Manassas home: Burns never labels his photographs nor refers directly to them in narration. Instead, he allows the viewer to range over them and make their own assumptions and associations. Another home is presented, recognizable as the structure that still stands at Appomattox Court House, and then viewers are drawn into a family group seated on the front steps.

The series title, *The Civil War*, appears, white letters with bold red underlining against stark black as the series' musical theme is heard for the first time. "Ashokan Farewell" is a waltz created by American folk musician and composer Jay Ungar in 1983. To Burns, Unger's sweet, plaintive music is "the equivalent of the tragedy and the purpose and the uplift and the loss that is the Civil War" (Burns quoted in Michaelson 1990). As the melody unfolds, devastated buildings, perhaps at Richmond, Virginia, appear. The camera pans across the image to mimic the experience of someone walking amid the buildings, head turned to survey the ruin. Burns shows the image of a soldier, and scans up from belt buckle and pistols to youthful face, followed by images of dead soldiers and a field of dead horses.

Burns's technique of enlivening historical images by moving camera lenses across them, simulating a walk through a landscape or movement toward people or objects, is so well known that software packages now contain a transition called "the Burns effect" (Wetta and Martin 2009). Burns accompanies images with sounds—crickets sing in the McLean's yard, a gentle wind passes—making them "come alive" (Burns quoted in Michaelson 1990). The viewer is additionally moved within the documentary by the music, which provides mood and unifies the materials, sweeping across images and sounds until Burns has completed explaining a bit of history or a structural unit of his film. Period pieces of music, among them "We Are Climbing Jacob's Ladder," "Battle Cry of Freedom," "Flag of Columbia," "All Quiet on the Potomac," and "Dixie," underscore regional character or support Burns's narrative.

Narrator McCullough's voice is layered in as "Ashokan Farewell" continues to wind its way across the photographs. Burns moves in on an image of a soldier warming his ungloved hands at a fire as snow falls, and McCullough provides an overview: "The Civil War impacted people from Florida to Vermont, from New Mexico to Tennessee; 600,000 men died; American homes and schools sheltered the dying; at Cold Harbor, northeast of Richmond, 7,000 Americans, mostly Union soldiers, fell in twenty minutes." Burns shows troops being moved by wagon and horseback and photograph after photograph of dead, disfigured soldiers along lanes and in orchards and fields that became battlefields. McCullough tells us, "They knew they were making history"; "It was the greatest adventure of their lives"; "It changed forever the lives of all who lived through it."

Burns makes sure that we pay attention to bodily experiences through vivid contrasts and illustrations. Portraits of fresh-faced soldiers are followed by images of field surgeons at work and stacks of severed body parts. Images of slaves balancing huge bales of cotton on their heads or working in fields are delivered with narration that describes short life spans, disease, and punishing work schedules. In an interview with Burns, published in *The Journal of Military History*, Roger Spiller remarks,

> I think the real signature of Ken's approach is the way he evokes individual experience as a way of epitomizing the larger historical subject. One of his favorite allusions . . . comes from a poem by William Blake, which speaks of seeing the universe through a grain of sand. All his films assume his very fine level of focus that gradually expands toward grander historical understanding. (2009, 1397)

Spiller refers to Burns's interest in biography and anecdote, but we should not miss the idea that part of "grander historical understanding" has to do with experiences of the body.

The major players of the war are introduced through photographs and descriptions. Burns never provides their names through narration or captions, a technique that calls for our participation. Layering North, then South, we see uniformed men and close-ups of serious men in spectacles: [U. S. Grant] "A lackluster clerk from Galena, Illinois, a failure in everything except marriage and war"; [Stonewall Jackson] "An eccentric and hypochondriac who rode into battle with one hand raised 'to keep,' he said, 'the blood balanced'"; [Joshua Lawrence Chamberlain] "A college professor from Maine who on a little hill in Pennsylvania ordered an unlikely textbook maneuver that saved the Union Army and quite possibly the Union itself." Then come the pictures and biographies of two ordinary soldier/diarists, one North [Elisha Hunt Rhodes], one South [Sam Watkins], who survived the war and whose experiences parallel each other. Throughout the series, Burns returns to all of these men, relying especially in Rhodes's and Watkins's diaries.

Finally, there are the elegantly turned out [Robert E. Lee] "courtly, unknowable aristocrat who disapproved of secession and slavery yet went on to defend them both at the head of one of the greatest armies of all time" and the powerful, somber-eyed visage of [Frederick Douglass] "The runaway boy who 'stole himself' from slavery, recruited two regiments of black soldiers" and helped transform the Civil War into "a struggle for the freedom of all Americans." The biographies close with a young, vigorous [Abraham Lincoln] "rough man from Illinois who would rise to be the greatest President the country has ever seen."

I leave the exposition suspicious of this noble story of nineteenth-century white manhood. Dead men? Dead horses? The only women visible sat on McLean's front porch, and Burns has presented no female voices. What befell the women who kept farms, businesses, and families together while the men were off at war? Later in "The Cause," diarist Mary Chestnut is introduced and we hear Barbara Fields, but this hardly balances the flood of male perspective. Southern historian Catherine Clinton, writing in *Ken Burns' The Civil War*, does a thorough analysis of the whole documentary series, finding almost no women mentioned at all. She offers her own revisions, including discussions of white and black women whose letters and diaries might have been used and women who fought in the Civil War whose images might have been included (Clinton 1996, 63–80). And there are many other troubling omissions. Aided by black and white photography, viewers can envision soldiers from many backgrounds in these images, but the only solid mention of soldiers who are not white occurs in the biography of Douglass. Too, Burns chooses to bring audiences into the twentieth century through Civil War reunions instead of reminders of reconstruction, Jim Crow laws, and the continuing struggle for freedoms in the civil rights and other social movements of the mid-twentieth century.

Burns deepens and complicates his Civil War story in a series of subsections in which the rising possibility of war is made clear. He pairs the sections to produce conflict and is careful to select resonant examples and images. "1861: The Cause," presents the United States as a peaceful nation where 31 million people live in small towns and on farms. We tour America through photographs, seeing, for example, an ironworks in Richmond, Virginia, where gun carriages and cannon are made for the US government and then an image of young men "who thought they would be friends forever" training to be military officers at West Point.

The next section, "All Night Forever," refutes this idyllic vision of America by discussing the lives of slaves and the economic realities of slavery. Burns uses color film to move along a river at sunset. Morgan Freeman's voice intones Frederick Douglass's words: "In thinking of America, I sometimes find myself admiring her bright blue sky—her grand old woods . . ., and star-crowned mountains. But my rapture is soon checked . . . When I remember that all is cursed with the infernal spirit of slaveholding." While the Holmes quote used in the prologue invited audiences to care about this film, the Douglass quote asks audiences to not get swept down this stream of sentiment, but to see this history from another set of concerns.

In "All Night Forever," Burns introduces "We are Climbing Jacob's Ladder," another song heard throughout the series, against images of slaves hoeing and carrying cotton on their heads. McCullough talks about life on Southern plantations: poor living conditions, short life spans due to heavy work and disease, marriages not protected by law. Burns presents new voices, including a rough recording of a former slave: "If I thought that I would ever be a slave again, I'd take a gun and end it all right away, because you are nothing but a dog." This plays against an image of a black man imprisoned by a spiked collar and then photographs of men with scarred backs and women and men with exposed breasts and buttocks. Although Burns doesn't label these, or any other images, they are well known. Made by Columbia, South Carolina, photographer J. T. Zealy, the images were taken at the behest of Louis Agassiz, a Harvard natural scientist, who studied the specificity of the races.[2] They are reminders of the complex of religious, social, and "scientific" beliefs that undergirded slavery. Fields tells the audience that "The Civil War was caused because of the establishment of the United States with slavery as part of our culture." Foote counters that Americans failed to do what he sees as our greatest national asset and cultural characteristic: compromise.

With only gentle contextual guidance in identifying what something is and why it's important, Burns prompts the viewer into several kinds of intertextual reading. We learn to piece together information by reading within the documentary: What does the repeated use of this image suggest? Why is Burns zooming into the image here? What are we meant to see, especially juxtaposed to this text? The viewer also moves out into memory, or out into research to secure that memory, noting where that image or voice, piece of music or text has been previously encountered and what it has meant in other contexts. This provides the viewer with several pleasures: recognizing the known, encountering the known in unexpected ways, and incorporating new information with the old. It also makes clear that this is one story that can be made of these images and that counternarratives are possible, including those developed by audience members in viewing the documentary.

Burns returns to discussion of blacks' efforts to create and maintain community and cultural expressions during slavery and he shows a painting of a nineteenth-century wedding and images of families outside dwellings. Here, Burns moves into large groups to reveal detail: these people may be a family; notice this young woman reading a book. McCullough reminds us that four million people, one out of every seven in the United States were slaves and that Eli Whitney's cotton engine revived slavery in the late 1800s. A sternwheeler's whistle sounds against an image of a boat headed out from the dock, packed solid with cotton bales.

Next, Burns moves the country toward war and "The Cause" toward climax in a series of countermoves. Abolitionists William Lloyd Garrison, Harriet Tubman, and Frederick Douglass are introduced in "Are We Free?" and Burns discusses violent backlash against abolition. "A House Divided" overviews Lincoln's rise as a political figure and his marriage to Mary Todd and presents economic and social concerns about the ending of slavery (as opposed to the moral ones previously presented). John Brown's raid on the federal arsenal at Harper's Ferry, an attempt to incite a slave rebellion, is developed in "The Meteor." Military historian Ed Bearss describes the importance of Brown in inciting the war, especially in turning Southern militias into viable military units. When Abraham Lincoln is elected president in 1860, Southerners believe the federal government can no longer represent them and become "Secessionists." South Carolina, called by a former congressman "too small for a republic; too large for an insane asylum," left the Union first, followed by Mississippi, Florida, Alabama, Georgia, Louisiana, Texas and later, Virginia, Arkansas, North Carolina, and Tennessee. The Confederacy chooses Mississippi senator Jefferson Davis as President as Lincoln, protected by sharpshooters lining Washington rooftops, is inaugurated.

Across these sections, Burns layers in new accents, creating the sense that the world is watching this war. Jeremy Irons gives voice to French political philosopher Alexis de Tocqueville's comments, from his 1835 *Democracy in America*, on the bustling industry in the American North versus malaise in the South. This is the first of several Europeans—English newspaper editors and French philosophers—whose words Irons presents. Burns has not presented diverse Americans—German Hutterites, Norwegian farmers, Irish Bowery Boys, or speakers of Spanish, African, or Native American languages. Perhaps Burns struggled with presenting this diversity without caricature.

Then, Burns heads into the major battles of the war, first presenting the war as boyish adventure, and then as harsh reality. "4:30 a.m. April 12, 1861" details the first battle of the war, the Southern artillery victory over Northern troops inside Fort Sumter, off the coast of South Carolina. In "Traitors and Patriots," Lincoln and Davis call for, and are inundated with, volunteers. Burns further introduces diarists Rhodes and Watkins, as well as filling out the ranks of generals on both sides: Grant and William Tecumseh Sherman; Lee and Nathan Bedford Forrest. Burns shows us colorful paintings of massing troops and, using diary and letter excerpts and photographs, the excitement of whole towns signing up to serve together and of young men being kissed by girls and getting new uniforms as they go off to war.

"Gun Men" presents troops arriving and training in Washington and "enjoying [them-selves] capitally," as they are photographed in mock sword fights and after being stuffed inside cannons. Burns focuses in on beautiful faces and on troops holding hands, perhaps as reminders of their innocence or a nod toward the women who served in both armies. Union handling of slaves escaping north is discussed. The army first returned them to plantations and then, as more and more appeared, used them as workers. Burns supplies a dramatic vision of Lincoln, first focusing on an outside image of the White House with an open window, and then moving into the window to dissolve that image into a photograph of

Lincoln sitting at a table. As the "Battle Hymn of the Republic" plays slowly, the narrator tells us that Lincoln ignored the Constitution in the early days of the war by declaring war himself instead of calling Congress into session, and sending troops to border states like Maryland to prevent secession.

Burns returns to the opening shot of a battlefield at sunset and prepares the climax to his narrative about the Civil War in its first year: the Battle of Bull Run/Manassas. When the Union army marches into Virginia, Confederate troops engage them in battle. Southern General Beauregard creates a headquarters in McLean's farmhouse. We again see the opening shot of the weedy lawn. Scanning across oil paintings of Virginia landscapes, Burns notes that Washingtonians drove out to see the battle with picnic baskets. Clouds moving over contemporary battlefield sites are shown through film, overlaid with ringing gunshots and marches. The South is victorious. The Union is stunned by its unprecedented 3,000 casualties, with the South sustaining about 1,750 more. Burns presents images of surgeons working on the wounded and then piles of amputated limbs. The spirited young men marching off to war are now dead or returning home without legs and arms. Burns presents a film of mist rising off water and newspaper coverage of the Union's embarrassment from newspapers around the world. "Ashokan Farewell" returns, this time played on a piano, as the familiar image of a cannon at sunset reappears.

To conclude his opening statement about the war, Burns checks in with Wilber McLean, who has now moved his family to Appomattox Court House. In "A Thousand Mile Front," General George McClellan takes command of the Union army with an elaborate plan to destroy the Confederacy, but does nothing; U. S. Grant is assigned to desk duty; William T. Sherman resigns and is close to suicide. The action recedes, and Burns delivers Sullivan Ballou's letter as epilogue and with it secures one of his central themes: the nobility of the Civil War soldier.

FONDLY DO WE HOPE . . . FERVENTLY DO WE PRAY

In an elegant, white sleeveless shirt and long, light gray skirt lined with yellow, Shayla-Vie Jenkins performs an opening solo that echoes the accompanying words, Walt Whitman's "Poem to the Body." Jenkins drops her head forward and rolls it to the side and the back to expose her neck as a young woman's recorded voice delivers Whitman's words "Head, neck, hair, ears, drop and tympan of the ears . . . ." Jenkins continues to celebrate the body, winding and turning back on herself, mixing lovely attitudes and ripples of the spine with concrete elaborations on Whitman's words: at "jaw hinges" Jenkins hinges at the knees, for example.

This prelude is important to understanding the work. Jenkins's solo and Whitman's words become counternarratives as they are reperformed and recontextualized over the evening. If an audience member can hold onto them and call them up for comparison to a new instantiation, they will understand the work in expanded ways. Performance scholar Randy Martin has written beautifully about "allegories of passing" in Jones's *Chapel/Chapter*:

> The dance points to the ways in which our ways of inscribing ourselves in history, in the social, might be reordered. Hence, this is one among the many allegories of passing—of moving through and beyond blockages and impossibilities, foreclosures and occlusions that clot the

old byways of assimilationist citizenship. Rather than offering a point-by-point refutation of the protocols by which race, class, and immigrant passing are constructed, the dance shifts the phenomenology of passing and its means of accomplishment from the inside from singularized sameness to a whole field of difference. (Martin 2008, 85)

This way of moving us through "blockages and impossibilities" leads to realizations about relationships between the dance's structures and the ways in which we understand history. Jenkins's solo (and there are others in the work, especially one connected to Jones's biography) create alternate through-lines in the piece, countering the central, well-known narratives about Lincoln and about a conflict between America's stated interest in liberty and its tolerance of slavery leading to war. If we follow Jenkins's solo, we find a history different from the prescribed version, one centered on personal, bodily experiences of women and of African Americans. The traditional stories of Lincoln as a great man and of conflict climaxing in war are thwarted by Jenkins's more episodic story about bodies that waver between transcending and being trapped by historical association.

Jenkins's solo is never paired with Whitman's words again, and the movement loses its references, seems more abstract, and signals back to Jenkins. It reminds us to pay attention to the body—to who is dancing and to their vulnerability, and to their possible relationship with Jenkins. This becomes clear when Jenkins's solo shows up performed by LaMichael Leonard in a section called "The Auction" and again at the end of the piece, performed by I-Ling Liu as a woman of the future. Who is presenting this movement, this "historical evidence," is important, but so is the viewer's vantage point. This match-and-interpret game calls audience members to self-assess, to catch ourselves in our biases and assumptions. Have I remembered correctly? Why am I making this association? Have I assumed too much?

The narrator, actor Jamyl Dobson in a nineteenth-century black frock coat and string tie, speaks to the audience, reciting Whitman's "Crossing Brooklyn Ferry": "I am with you, you men and women of a generation, or ever so many generations hence; I project myself—also I return—I am with you, and know how it is. Just as you feel . . . , so I felt." Presenting themselves one after the other or in pairs or trios in the satellite space, the dancers are clothed in dresses and suits that mix black and white into gray and are lined or accented with yellow or red. Their styles blur the nineteenth and twentieth centuries: frock coats or tailored suits for the men and sleek shifts or dresses that are nipped at the waist and full skirted for the women. The music also mixes past and present. Traditional songs are performed along with rock music made from biblical passages and the words of Lincoln and Whitman. The driving song accompanying this section has lyrics from Lincoln's Second Inaugural Address, "Every drop of blood drawn with the lash shall be paid by another drawn with the sword."

The dancers provide a fast-forward look at nineteenth-century social history as well as an introduction to movement we will see later. Antonio Brown dances an excerpt of a solo that will accompany a biography of Bill T. Jones. Jenkins returns to do a speedy version of her opening solo while pursued by Peter Chamberlin, a male aggressor. A romantic couple, Paul Matteson and Asli Bulbul, whom we identify as Abraham and Mary Todd Lincoln, dance together. Three men, Brown, Leonard, and Erick Montes, dive into each other and are flung apart. The music changes to quote the "Song of Solomon," "Arise My Love, My Fair One, and Come Away," and Jenkins returns in a love duet with Leonard.

I tried to remember a Bill T. Jones cast that is as international as this company, which includes dancers from Turkey, Mexico, and Taiwan as well as people from around the United

States. Should I pursue this? If I see some cast members, at least some of the time, as being and representing European Americans or African Americans, do I see other cast members as Taiwanese, Turkish, or Mexican Americans, at least part of the time? Performance studies scholar Danielle Goldman addresses this in "*Ghostcatching*: An Intersection of Technology, Labor, and Race." Quoting dance scholar André Lepecki, who sees an "ethics of transcultural performance," Goldman says:

> Claiming 'laziness in seeing' as dance viewers' primary pathology when faced with a body from another culture, Lepecki calls for a delicate partnering between audience and dancer. 'How can my audience body become a partner to those bodies dancing for me?' (Lepecki 2000, 13). Rather than brutally attempting to wipe out difference with an imagined formal purity, or remain content in a distanced relationship of 'respect' while reducing the other to his or her most obvious markers of alterity, Jones urges audiences to view the other doubly, with two sets of eyes, and meet the performer as a partner. (Goldman 2003/2004, 71–71)

Keeping track of one's willingness to pay attention to obvious identity markers can be revelatory. Even when the context, the Civil War, in this case, seems to call for it, why privilege one social identity over another? An obvious characteristic over one that is harder to see? Relationships between performer and performed become arbitrary or indeterminate when looked at this way.

Solos and duets flash by until the company takes a pose that recurs throughout the evening. It might be a reworking of John-Joseph Weerts's *Assassination of Marat*, but where Weerts's crowd gathers around the murdered revolutionary with upraised arms, ready to arrest the assassin, Jones's company looks at the prone figure with concern, reaching down as if to pull him from death. The narrator looks at the audience to more clearly introduce himself and to encourage careful observation and introspection: "So, we have started, and yes, we are a crowd up here. Who am I? I am one of a crowd . . . [M]y job is to say what they won't or can't say. My job is to introduce them if they won't or can't. My job is to see them if they can't see themselves and help you do the same . . . Tonight, we are who we are called and we are not who we are called." This ends the prologue, marked Act I: Introduction and Act I: The Crossing in the program.

The dancers then move into the exposition; the program lists this as Act I: Biographies. First is a biography of Bill T. Jones, voiced by narrator Dobson and danced by Antonio Brown in a series of impressive jumps, balances with the leg raised far up to the side, and turns. A projected silhouette of a dancing minstrel player appears here, as it does throughout the work when this solo is repeated, and Brown acknowledges it. "Will the circle be unbroken," from the American spiritual "Since I Laid My Burden Down," asks the audience to consider relationships among these men and their future, calling to mind Jones's often asked question: "Why can't I be free?" (Jones quoted in Goldman 2003/2004: 71) When will I no longer be locked into referential systems that make me "African American artist"? Jones next moves into the central space in an extended, storybook recitation of Lincoln's life. Paul Matteson dances this section as Dobson speaks, moving across a series of lighted rectangles on the floor that become pages of history. In a series of silky, winding moves, Lincoln grows up, marries, and fathers four boys. He is elected president and soon after, eleven states succeed from the Union. Matteson punctuates his movement with pauses and upraised forefingers: he must preserve the Union, preserve government "for the people, by the people," and issues the Emancipation Proclamation.

Matteson greets and dances with group members who also move into the satellite space and dance as the narrator speaks for them. Jones handles the representation of Mary Todd Lincoln, danced by Asli Bulbul, with sympathy. Often vilified for her excessive shopping and elitism, Mary Todd is shown as a martyr. Her solo includes the prone, head canted to one side pose familiar as the martyr's pose, but there are no supporters around to save or mourn for her. She must recover herself, masking her prostration by languidly running a hand across the floor. In between solos, company members dance together in groups of men and of women and in pairs in what looks like social dancing or the give and take of people meeting and parting. More poses are inserted into their movement. Sometimes a dancer crosses one leg over the other and rests his chin on his fist in a variant of Rodin's *The Thinker*. Other times, a dancer lays his hands on the heads of kneeling company members, reminiscent of many images of Jesus, points upward as if asking for a holy witness, or raises a hand as if being sworn into office or testifying in court. The crowd carries dancers aloft as celebrated heroes, and as fallen martyrs. Narrator Dobson returns to Whitman's "Brooklyn Crossing" (in the program, Act 1: Brooklyn Crossing): "What is it, then, between us? What is the count of the scores or hundreds of years between us? Whatever it is, it avails not—distance avails not, and place avails not."

Jones escalates the action at the end of Act I by pointing out the hypocrisy of American freedom in a country that allows slavery. Narrator Dobson delivers part of Lincoln's "Address at Sanitary Fair":

> The shepherd drives the wolf from the sheep's throat, for which the sheep thanks the shepherd as a liberator, while the wolf denounces him for the same act as the destroyer of liberty, especially as the sheep was a black one. Plainly the sheep and the wolf are not agreed upon a definition of the word liberty.

Jennifer Nugent dances "Lady Liberty," in a flowing toga with a wreath on her head. She is a reminder of the United States' investment in classical ideals and Greek-derived national symbols such as the Statue of Liberty and the Capitol Building's Lady Freedom and of another hypocrisy: that of woman used as a symbol of liberty in a country in which women could not vote. LaMichael Leonard joins Nugent, and they finish in the center of the stage, standing in the middle of four Greek columns. Lady Liberty blesses Leonard's head as he kneels. The following section is "The Auction." Dobson delivers Whitman's "Poem to the Body" but this time in the mode of slave auctioneer. Dancing Jenkins's opening solo and then the solo that went with Bill T. Jones's biography, once gem-like solos that displayed the skills of highly trained performers, Leonard is now the auctioned slave.

Company members bring stools out to the satellite space for Act 1: Debates/The Boil That Burst. For me, and although the war follows, this is the climax of the work. As the singer and dancers seated in the satellite space, narrate, the dancers engage in debates. They move with abstract movements—sharp angles of arms and legs, delicately maintained balances, sweeping gestures. The dancers do not act out the text, but move to its cadences, pauses, and emphases. The text distills debates that preceded the Civil War and introduces issues of our own day: the right to hold property versus the right of every person to be free; individual and states rights versus the responsibility of the federal government for the health and welfare of its people; whether governments are to be trusted; the responsibility of the government to protect individual freedom versus their need to protect citizens and secure national borders.

Gavels pound. Background voices anxiously buzz. A projection of the Capital dome crumbles. The assembled company repeats the solo that originally introduced Bill T. Jones (this is, perhaps, Jones pointing back at himself, at his own power as leader of this dance company) and the narrator states:

> We hold these truths to be self-evident, that all men are endowed by their Creator with certain unalienable Rights, . . . whenever any Form of Government becomes destructive of these ends, it is the Right of the People to alter or to abolish it, and to institute new Government.

The stage darkens. One lit column remains at the center and the company moves around it in violent spasms. We hear speeding trains and heavy guitar chords: "She is dangerous . . . see it in her eyes." A strobe effect sends shadows onto the back of the circular curtain. Never in unison, the company lurches rigidly around the central space, turning first to one person and then another in close combat. They topple the column. Now, the stage lightens and only Lincoln remains. He dances a contemplative solo in silence and reclines on the column, as we hear excerpts from Lincoln's Second Inaugural speech: "My countrymen, one and all . . . the government will not assail you. You can have no conflict without being yourselves the aggressors." A great wind rushes through, pushing projected clouds and the curtains are closed. "Another war came" appears on the curtains. Darkness.

In Act 2: The War, a train speeds in the darkness. Bits of opening solos and duets appear. Shayla-Vie Jenkins again encounters her tormentor and then her lover. Dobson and Matteson, the narrator and Lincoln, reappear carried on the shoulders of the company. Lincoln now has blood on his hands, as he wears red gloves. Whitman's "Poem to the Body" is read with references to contemporary tortures spliced in: "nose . . . water poured over the nose and mouth." The company comes slowly out of the parted curtains into the satellite space. As shells explode, they lift each other or roll on the ground in a dream sequence, bodies floating through the air: "Priceless blood reddens the ground" (an excerpt from Whitman's "The Wound Dresser"). [3] As epilogue, Jones moves into the future.

THEATRICALITY AND HISTORY

Burns's and Jones's works are theatrical, moving audience members along narrative arcs with music and dancing and re-presenting historical figures in compelling ways that trigger emotional responses. Both men's individual perspectives are evident in the materials and methods that make up these performances of history, and, for Jones, because he includes himself among the people represented by the cast. Too, they provide individuals with whom we can identify, through anecdote and by presenting the histories and views of everyday men and women, real and fictive. While both use theatrical means to bring the past alive and create emotional connection, they also create points of entry that allow viewers to realize their constructions of the past and create their own.

Both works depend on audiences seeing the work intertextually, moving within and outside the works to realize correspondences, especially through repeated images and gaps and indeterminacies caused when images and dancers are presented without identification or counter to historical expectation. While "The Cause" is a maddeningly white, male, middle-class introduction to the Civil War, Burns's indeterminate use of images and a para-doxical sense of separateness he builds about the past invite alternate understandings. Burns doesn't label images and uses them evocatively himself; they are grounds for imagination, not proof of an argument. In his study "Art, Perception, and Indeterminacy," in which he explores the impact of an indeterminate object on viewers' appreciation of and assignment of meaning to an image, Roger Pepperell notes that viewers slow down, take more account of the formal properties of the image, "while an intensive search for new hypotheses to fit the pictorial facts is undertaken" (2007). Further, he says that "we undergo a different kind of experience, one that is difficult, out of the ordinary, but perhaps more intense and compel-ling for being so." Burns's treatment of images is an invitation to explore, to reinvent through our own research and historical imaginations.

Historical images, combined with Burns's selection of text with formal and quaint or romantic language, creates a curio cabinet sense of the late nineteenth century. While I might argue that Americans are still dealing with the legacies of slavery or regret that gun control, immigration, and national security issues still have us arguing about the rights of individu-als and states verses national responsibilities, the late nineteenth century is a different world than our own. These people and events, ways of life and social constructions, are a unique milieu, one worthy of understanding on its own terms. While Burns's work has a great deal of legitimacy, he doesn't suggest his is an authoritative or definitive history of the late nine-teenth century. Instead, he provides a compelling model for, to return to the opening quote, "how this material should be structured and presented."

In Jones's *Fondly*, movement phrases are information that must be considered anew in different contexts, compelling audiences to regard bodies on display for their beauty and their value as labor, as they love and support each other and participate in debate and war. As we think about who is performing and when, we question whether history and its associa-tions must always enter into our seeing. These experiences ask viewers to take responsibility for how we understand things, not only by providing lightning-quick exercises in deciding "what if" or "what now," but in asking us which story, which arc, we want to follow within the work. Is this a work about Abraham Lincoln's legacy, or is it a story about our simultaneous inabilities to escape the past and to reinvent the future and ourselves? That depends on what we're paying attention to in the work. Are we tracking what happens to Shayla-Vie Jenkins's movement throughout the work? Do we see her as the progenitor of the evening? In depict-ing "ideas struggle[ing] with each other," Jones prompts our own perceptual and intellectual critiques.

Notes

1. There are lots of other terms that might be applied to Burns's and Jones's works. Jones referred to *Fondly* as "popular spectacle" in an interview in *Dance Magazine*.
2. See for example Brian Wallis, "Black Bodies, White Science: Louis Agassiz's Slave Daguerreotypes," *American Art* 9, no. 2 (Summer 1995): 38–61.
3. In an interview for *Dance Magazine*, Jones describes how the company generated this movement: "One early exercise was called the Maelstrom—this idea of a huge, frighten-ing, swirling action of nature, which I felt history was like, particularly the Civil War. I also felt that we are in an undeclared civil war now; as an individual I oftentimes feel buffeted

in it and lost. Now how do we choreograph this sense of something swirling, people fall-ing, supporting, carrying each other, and so on? We began to build meticulously using our knowledge of contact improvisation, of partnering, yet trying to create a very complex stage picture" (Jones quoted in Burke, 16).

BIBLIOGRAPHY

Burke, Siobhan. "Bill T. Jones: A Documentary Following the Choreographer Airs Nationwide." *Dance Magazine* (November 2011): 16.

Burns, Ken. "The Cause, 1861." *The Civil War* [documentary film series]. 1990. Accessed through Netflix, December 2012.

Clinton, Catherine. "Noble Women as Well." In *Ken Burns' The Civil War*. Edited by Robert Brent Toplin, 63–80. New York: Oxford University Press, 1996.

Filene, Benjamin. "Passionate Histories: 'Outsider' History-Makers and What They Teach Us." *The Public Historian* 34, no. 1 (Winter 2012): 11–33. Accessed December 31, 2012. http://www.jstor.org/stable/10.1525/tph.2012.34.1.11.

Goldman, Danielle. "Ghostcatching: An Intersection of Technology, Labor, and Race." *Dance Research Journal* 35, no. 2 and 36, no. 1 (Winter 2003 and Spring 2004): 68–87.

Jones, Bill T. *Fondly Do We Hope . . . Fervently Do We Pray* [DVD]. Dance and multimedia work filmed at Yerba Buena Center for the Arts, October 1, 2009.

Jones, Bill T. Interview by Michelle Dent and M. J. Thompson. New York University, March 20, 2002. In Danielle Goldman, "Ghostcatching: An Intersection of Technology, Labor, and Race," *Dance Research Journal* 35, no. 2 and 36, no. 1 (Winter 2003 and Spring 2004): 68–87.

Lepecki, André. "The Body in Difference." FAMA 1, no. 1 (2000): 6–13.

Lightman, Alan. "The Role of the Public Intellectual." MIT Communications Forum, 2000. Accessed December 31, 2012. http://web.mit.edu/comm-forum/papers/lightman.html.

Martin, Randy. "Allegories of Passing in Bill T. Jones." *Dance Research Journal* 40, no. 2 (2008): 74–87.

Michaelson, Judith. "A 'Civil War' for the Masses: Filmmaker Ken Burns Says His Five-night, 11-hour PBS Epic—Five Years in the Making—Is a Tale for Everyman." *Los Angeles Times*, July 22, 1990. Accessed December 31, 2012, http://articles.latimes.com/1990-07-22/entertainment/ca-1069_1_ken-burns/3.

Osterweis Scott, Ariel. "'That Unspeakable Somewhat': Bill T. Jones, Abraham Lincoln, and the Question of Iconicity." *In Dance* (May 2009). Accessed February 3, 2014. http://dancers-group.org/indance/archive/.

Shister, Gail. "Ken Burns' WWII tribute, "The War," Starts Sunday." *Philadelphia Inquirer*. September 21, 2007. Accessed February 3, 2014. http://seattletimes.com/html/televi-sion/2003894327_war21.html.

Sklar, Deidre, 1991. "Five Premises for a Culturally Sensitive Approach to Dance." *DCA (Dance Critics Association) News* (Summer). Available at http://acceleratedmotion.wesleyan.edu/primary_sources/texts/ecologiesofbeauty/five_premises.pdf.

Thelen, David. "The Moviemaker as Historian: Conversations with Ken Burns." *Journal of American History* 81, no. 3 (December 1994): 1031–50.

Voss, Christiane. "Film Experience and the Formation of Illusion: The Spectator as 'Surrogate Body of the Cinema.'" *SCMS (Society for Cinema and Media Studies)* 50, no. 4 (2011): 136–50.

Wallis, Brian. "Black Bodies, White Science: Louis Agassiz's Slave Daguerreotypes." *American Art* 9, no. 2 (Summer 1995): 38–61.

Walsh, Joan. "Good Eye: The Interview with Ken Burns." *KQED San Francisco Focus*. Reprinted at http://www.online-communicator.com/kenburns.html.

Wetta, Frank J., and Martin A. Novelli. "More Like a Painting—*The War*: A Ken Burns Film: An Interview with Roger Spiller." *Journal of Military History* 73, no. 4 (October 2009): 1397–405. Accessed December 31, 2012. https://libproxy.uncg.edu/login?url=http://search.proquest. com.libproxy.uncg.edu/docview/195640703?accountid=14604.

SECTION V

PLACE, SPACE, AND LANDSCAPE

CHAPTER 20

FROM LANDSCAPE TO CLIMATESCAPE IN CONTEMPORARY DANCE-THEATER

Meredith Monk, The Wooster Group, and The TEAM

AMY STRAHLER HOLZAPFEL

DURING recent decades, the term "landscape," traditionally the purview of geography and art history, forged inroads across a broad range of disciplines, from anthropology to media studies.[1] Often partnered with other paradigmatic "turns"—spatial and visual—of culture and art, landscape drew increased focus within dance and theater studies as well.[2] Critics of dance and theater examined the relationships of select performances to their sets, sites, architectures, environments, institutions, and habitats, hearkening back to Gertrude Stein's concept of "play as landscape."[3] In a 2004 essay published in *PAJ*, editor Bonnie Marranca went so far as to propose that "landscape in contemporary theatre seems to be the preferred definition of space for any series of discreet activities." [4]

I write intentionally in the past tense about landscape's defining role in contemporary dance and theater in order to demarcate a "landscape period" within performance criticism itself. There is little doubt, in other words, that landscape—as a methodological principle and critical terminology—has greatly impacted the aesthetic and cultural trajectories of contemporary dance and theater performance.[5] As I argue in this chapter, theater and dance, as discreet art forms, are often bridged through landscape. As we head deeper into the new millennium, however, it appears as though the most challenging aspect of our own time—human impact on global climate—has begun to shape the development and content of more recent forms of dance and theater. The critical model of landscape falls a bit short of capturing our rising anxiety about global climate catastrophe and our starring role in its production. The very word "land" feels oddly antiquated in comparison to "climate," which encompasses a sense of humans in relation to a larger, planetary spatiotemporal "scape." In the third part of this chapter, thus, I propose "climatescape"—an outgrowth of landscape—as a term that speaks to the formal organizations of more recent forms of dance-theater.

Throughout this chapter, I define landscape, in the broadest sense, as a medium between bodies and spaces.[6] Dance I consider as any form of stylized gesture, that is, "a movement of part of the body" performed "to express an idea or meaning."[7] For theater, I return to the foundational idea of a "seeing place," stemming from the Greek word *theatron*, to suggest an encounter that occurs between an audience and a performer within a designated space and time. I employ Claire Colebrook's approach to climate as "the milieu that that is necessary for our ongoing life, *and* as the fragile surface that holds us all together in one web of risked life."[8] Whereas landscape, I will argue, implies a bridging between figures and grounds, seers and seen (even as it gestures toward the collapse of such dichotomies), climatescape takes for granted that all bodies and spaces are already part of a much larger, interconnected, dynamic whole, one increasingly bent toward self-extinction. Conceptualized in such ways, landscape is a medium that forges connections between dance (gestures/body) and theater (places/times), whereas climatescape already accepts as a given the spatial/bodily basis of our communal existence and its deepening precariousness on our planet. Landscape, then, emphasizes space; climatescape stresses time.

To see ahead one must first look back. With this in mind, I begin this chapter by providing a brief overview of landscape's rise in art history and performance criticism. I then examine landscape's function and meaning within select multimediated works by two foundational postmodern American performance artist/collectives: Meredith Monk and The Wooster Group. Landscape in the dance-theater of these two artistic groups functions as a vehicle for expressing dynamic tensions and affiliations—archeological (Monk) and architectural (The Wooster Group)—between cultural embodiment and spatiotemporal practice. Landscape, I suggest, helps to activate the past in Monk's work and to conjure the present in the work of The Wooster Group. Climatescape, I argue, provides a new organizing principle for the dance and theater of the more recent experimental collective The TEAM (Theatre of the Emerging American Moment), whose work, though concerned with history, projects a utopian or dystopian future.

While I consider the work of Meredith Monk and The Wooster Group to be more associated with a landscape paradigm, and The TEAM to be moving toward a notion of climatescape, I nevertheless pose similar questions of all three artist collectives, including: How do they engage how space, place, geography, architecture, and community relate to the body? How do their renegotiations of body and/as space, corpus and/as environment, work to destabilize the still lingering opposition between figure and ground? In dance-theater works by Monk, The Wooster Group, and the TEAM, gestures and settings are contingent and relational rather than autonomous; embodied movements come from and dissolve back into spaces and social sites, and environments emerge, in turn, from bodies. Whether mediated through a conceptual frame of landscape or climatescape, borders between figures and grounds become fractured, mosaic, and permeable; dance becomes theater, theater dance.

LANDSCAPE AS "STEP"

"Landscape" is a historically evasive term. Originating in the sixteenth century as a painter's idiom meaning "picture depicting scenery or land," the word "landskip" (or *landtskip*) connotes an already refined space.[9] Landscape is disconnected from actual "land," in this sense, since the word underscores a visual framing process conducted by a viewer.[10] Though interest in framing the land through images began as early as the fifteenth century, it gave rise to the development of landscape as a dominant genre of visual art, a movement that reached its apex in Western painting during the mid-nineteenth century.[11] Landscape in art, thus, became a mode of privileging how we encounter and craft our environs. As Ernst Gombrich once stressed, landscape is never innocent.[12] The process of editing land into landscape involves the manipulation of space into a pattern, one that may be analyzed psychologically and symbolically. Gombrich's mid-twentieth-century acknowledgment of the "gaze" made implicit by landscape leads into the terrain of visual cultural studies: Even more compelling than the content of landscape may be its function as a *way of seeing*.[13]

In *Landscape and Memory*, Simon Schama reminds us that "Landscapes are culture before they are nature; constructs of the imagination projected onto wood, water, and rock."[14] Schama deepens the notion of the discrepancy between land and landscape by charting the mnemonic associations embedded within its iconic natural features, such as rocks, water, and trees. What child cannot recall a special tree she loved to climb, a favorite river, or a rocky ocean shore, or, as Meredith Monk investigates in *Quarry*, a vision of white clouds moving across a blank canvas of sky? For the visual theorist W. J. T. Mitchell, Schama's "depth-model" fails, however, to take into account the underlying ideological and power-based intent of landscape, as well: Far from a simple memory-retrieval aid, "one must register as well the sense in which landscape is all about forgetting, about getting away from the real in ways that may produce astonishing dislocations."[15] Whether as *memento* or escape-pod, landscape must be differentiated from "space" and "place," as Mitchell suggests:

> I think of *place* and *space* in the terms made familiar by Michel de Certeau: a place is a specific location; a *"space is a practiced place,"* a site activated by movements, actions, narratives, and signs. A landscape, then, turns site into a sight, place and space into a visual image.[16]

According to Mitchell, one way of defining landscape is, thus, as space that functions in excess of either providing mere ornamentation or acting as a setting for narrative events.[17] Landscape involves instead a refinement of place into a spatial object, a kind of theatricalization of place. Viewed as spatial objects—visual, sonic, or sculptural—landscapes do not exist independently of the *way we see* them, whether as art or culture, making us their sole arbiters and manufacturers.

No one understood this aspect of landscape better than the American writer, critic, and ex-patriot Gertrude Stein, who harbored a love for almost all things framed. Stein first coined the term "landscape play" to connote a type of theater that could exist free of the rigid, authoritative demands of a cathartic, linear-driven narrative, an idea explored by The Wooster Group in their mash-up of Stein's opera, *Dr. Faustus Lights the Lights*. Stein, who claimed to feel nervous about keeping track of the climactic shifts and turns of a traditional dramatic plot, wished to experience the theater instead as landscape, deriving a work's meaning based on her own encounter as a spectator with its compositional field. "I felt that if a play was exactly like a landscape," Stein admits, "then there would be no difficulty about the emotion of a person looking on at the play being behind or ahead of the play because the landscape doesn't have to make acquaintance."[18] Noting the emphasis given to freedom of point of view by the audience, Elinor Fuchs has suggested that "Stein uses landscape as a metaphor for a phenomenological spectatorship of theater, a settled-back scanning or noting, not necessarily of a natural scene, but of any pattern of language, gesture, and design *as if it were a natural scene*."[19] What drew Stein to landscape initially was not only its naturalness but also its relationality, its "being always *in relation*, the trees to the hills the hills to the fields the trees to each other any piece of it to any sky and then any detail to any other detail."[20] It was the "relations between things," particularly bodies and spaces, from which she constructed her own series of plays as landscapes.

Plays based on the relations between things may be another name for what Stein was getting at through the idea of landscape play.[21] How does landscape propose a way of persons and objects, humans and places, relating to one another and to the spatial world?, Stein would seem to be asking through her phraseology of landscape play. How do spaces (ceilings, skies, floors, walls, architecture), media (film, television, painting, photography), figures (bodies, gestures, sculptures, faces), things (props, objects, furniture), and grounds (environments, habitats, fields) relate to one another, whether purposefully or by chance? How might a story emerge by stringing together a series of compositional relations (crosses, migrations, transitions, transformations) between bodies and spaces rather than by weaving together a crisis, denouement, and scène à faire? What was at stake for Stein was a radical new experience of theatergoing, one that allowed for a dilation of interpretation toward an event rather than a narrowing-in of that same performance.

As a new and experimental form, Stein's landscape play greatly influenced the work of many postdramatic American theater artists, like Robert Wilson and Lee Breuer, as well as experimental choreographers, such as Merce Cunningham.[22] These artists were sympathetic to Stein's painterly concept for a performance that could operate free of overt sentimentality and dogmatic narrative, while emphasizing visual image over text. Yet, the relational aspect of Stein's landscape play strikes a meaningful chord when applied to the hybrid medium of dance-theater, as well. The very cross-pollination of the hyphenated term "dance-theater" gestures toward the intimate relations between bodies (dancers) and spaces (theaters), or, as it were, "plays on landscape." Emphasis on the relational networks and kinesthesia *between* and *across* cultures, countries, nationalities, and languages has grown in scholarship on performance, dance, and theater too. Joseph Roach hypothesizes kinesis as "the new mimesis," suggesting that,

> As the arts proliferate within the mediated and multicultural languages of transnational space, expressive movement is becoming a *lingua franca*, the basis of a newly experienced affective cognition and corporeal empathy. Mimesis, rooted in drama, imitates action; kinesis embodies it.[23]

Landscape calls attention not only to bodies and spaces but also to the potential migrations and passages of bodies *across* spaces, languages, national gulfs, histories, and even the transition itself from mimesis to kinesis, from the imitation of action to its more affective embodiment. In *Choreographing Empathy*, Susan Leigh Foster points out that the term "choreography" originally stemmed from the word "chorography," which arose in the sixteenth century in the subdiscipline of geography to connote the "the study of a region or landscape ... as a practice of mapping and also describing and analyzing a locale's terrain and its inhabitants."[24] Land, as Foster explains, "has been parsed and parceled using strategies very similar to those implemented for disciplining the body."[25] Yet, while it may have be the case that bodies and lands have always shared the experience of being marked and mapped by arbiters and authorities, it is equally possible that, through this communal history, they have also grown accustomed to one another in more empathic ways.

Landscape affectively mediates the relations between the body and space, dance and theater. It functions less as an artistic genre of expression, in this sense, than as a "potential space" or activating force *between* figures and grounds.[26] As Jean-Luc Nancy argues, "a landscape is always the suspension of a passage, and this passage occurs as a separation, an emptying out of the scene or of being: not even a passage from one point to another or from one moment to another, but the step [*le pas*] of the opening itself."[27] The "step" that is landscape is, in performance, constituted by the dancer or actor's embodied gesture or action, the early intention of forward, backward, upward, or downward movement in space. In performances by Meredith Monk and The Wooster Group, landscape, as *le pas*, names the possibility for connections to arise *between* bodies and spaces, *between* dance and theater.

MEREDITH MONK'S ARCHEOLOGICAL LANDSCAPE: ACTIVATING THE PAST

As a young artist starting out in New York in the late 1960s, Meredith Monk had already begun to formulate a type of choreography that would one day become her signature, as she puts it: "A primordial way of moving that was not based on the balletic or Western tradition but much more based on the body in its honesty."[28] Yet, she had not quite figured out how to incorporate what was at the time little more than great passion and talent for singing into her movement-based art, until she stumbled upon a revelation: "I could develop a vocabulary for my own voice in the same way that I had with my body. The voice could be gender, age, and landscape."[29] How a body or voice can be gendered or suggest a certain age is easy to imagine; but how precisely does the voice or body "become landscape" through a performance vocabulary?

Nearly all of Monk's dance-theater pieces gravitate toward or in some ways lend themselves to landscape. Through visionary performance and film pieces, such as *Vessel: An Opera Epic* (1971), *Education of the Girlchild* (1972/1973), *Quarry* (film 1975, opera 1976), *Ellis Island* (1981), *Book of Days* (1985), and *Atlas* (1991) as well as countless musical composition pieces and collaborations with artists such as Ping Chong, Lanny Harrison, and Robert Een, Monk has become herself a fixture in the culture of American experimental arts. Known for her pioneering site-specific performances, as well—such as *Juice: A Theatre Cantata in 3 Installments* (1969) and *Ascension Variations* (2009) for the Guggenheim Museum, and *American Archeology #1: Roosevelt Island* (1994)—Monk's hybrid performance works defy the familiar use of "setting" as background to story. In all of these works, in fact, both landscape and geography play a vital role. In *Ecologies of Theater*, Bonnie Marranca views a close connection between Monk and Gertrude Stein, in this sense: "Monk treats geography the way Stein, the guiding spirit of American avant-garde performance aesthetics, did: as a field of revelation."[30] Many of her works, as Monk herself describes, "thrive at the intersection of music and movement, image and object, light and sound in an effort to discover and weave together new modes of perception."[31] Monk views the voice, particularly, as both a method and instrument for "creating *landscapes of sound* that unearth feelings, energies, and memories for which there are no words."[32] Landscapes of movement, voice, vision, and sound—these are the orientation points that connect Monk's innovative form of dance-theater.

"In *Vessel*," says Monk, "I thought more of an overall gestalt. The scenic element, the mountain, came first, and I made the people fit into that, into this gigantic tapestry."[33] Likewise, she has suggested, "*Songs from the Hill* is another landscape, very much a nature piece, about day and night and the seasons going by. Pastoral, almost, but not related to greenery. It's more dry, almost a desert. It's about a person alone, not in a relationship, and there's a real sense of time going by. These scenic pieces have an autonomy of their own—you keep finding more layers."[34] The idea of "layers" and sediment is meaningful within Monk's dance-theater creations, as well. Many of her works engage the process of archeology and may be compared to "excavation sites," that is, buried landscapes unearthed by the artist.[35] Digging into land and into time is a process of simultaneously exhuming bodies and myths. Yet, what is found beneath the layers of sediment is not what one might expect; instead of grandiose designs, one finds shards and remnants of everyday lives, the stories of the powerless, the objects, gestures, and currency that make up our quotidian lives. Monk's theatrical landscapes build bridges between the small and the massive, between the daily habits and mundane customs of forgotten bodies and cultures, and the epic, historical spaces and narratives—the surface contexts—in which their untold stories are unearthed.

In one of her earliest works, *Quarry*, Monk produced a dance-theater-opera piece that sought to excavate the archeological landscape of World War II. Within *Quarry*, Monk herself performed as a young girl, envisioning a series of events, public and private, as they coalesce around her—a child in her bedroom, clouds passing, passersby on a street, a mother's voice projected by radio, a Nazi rally, and a concentration camp. As her audience, we cannot possibly distinguish between the events of history and those occurring in the interior dreamscape of a young girl. The personal journey of the artist as she digs into the sedimentary layers of World War II becomes as meaningful as the documentary newsreel showing clips of Hitler's troops invading Poland. In one interview, Monk says she views *Quarry*, subtitled an "Opera in Three Movements: Lullaby, March, and Requiem," in painterly terms, as well, seeing the elements of "landscape and human beings . . . as pretty integrated."[36] Yet, in another interview, she says that *Quarry*, is "not a landscape—it's about people."[37] To my mind, *Quarry* defies a purely formalist idea of landscape as the representation of an uninhabited space by merging the associations between figures and grounds. The work is dependent instead on a mode of "changing scales," as Sally Banes puts it, "a story of a child, widening to a story about a family, a people, a world."[38] This "telescopic" quality is what gives this piece, a journey of personal and communal consciousness of World War II, both its startling tenderness and its explosiveness. Monk creates a dance-theater mosaic containing patterns of memory, witnessed through the visions of an eight-year-old girl. *Quarry* is, in this sense, as much a *way of seeing* as it is a sight.

"It's my eyes, it's my eyes ... It's my ears, it's my ears ... It's my hands, it's my hands," cries the child, played in the original production at La Mama by Monk (see fig. 20.1). The child is a figural allegory of the illness that has beset a world where morals have disintegrated following one of the bloodiest periods in world history. When Monk finally does emerge from the bed, she runs to the windows and opens them so that light comes flooding in.

FIGURE 20.1 Meredith Monk in *Quarry*. Photo by Nat Tileston. Courtesy of Nat Tileston.

In a chanting, singsong melody that recalls the melodies of morning birds, Monk completes the portrait of this little girl as one full of innocence, suffering with the burdens of a brutal past. She lets the sunlight in, but cannot seem to get out of her pajamas and out of this room (see fig. 20.2). A mother figure now enters and whispers memories into the little girl's ears, showing her a photo book, provoking extreme anxiety in the child. How are we to deal with horrific events of the past? Where do we *place* our own bodies in relation to atrocities and to our ancestors? How do we both *see* and position our internal lives in relation to externalized, historiographical space and time?

In "Four Corners," on the stage floor appear characters in various everyday domestic scenes, almost *tranches de vie*, their stories unraveling side by side. In a square configuration around the bed are three women eating dinner, a gray-haired couple, a woman seated at a desk, and a couple from the Old Testament. We watch as the intimate details of their quotidian lives unfold for a few minutes. Though we don't know who they are, they are unbearably familiar; perhaps we see ourselves in them. Here, the telescope has widened to include a kind of disordered *tableau vivant*. This *tableau* is a tapestry full of the voices of many generations—archeological layers weaving a story from multiple perspectives. The audience's own "eye" is encouraged to wander, however, to take in each story separately, or all at once, as with Stein's creation of the "landscape play." This simultaneity of action is itself a key landscape component to Monk's dramaturgy, too, inciting

FIGURE 20.2 Meredith Monk in *Quarry*. Photo by Nat Tileston. Courtesy of Nat Tileston.

the audience members to form their own narratives by each creating her own pathway through the excavation site.[39]

The domestic *tableaux* break down as an entourage of Bunraku-constructed clouds enters the space, their shadows laying down a blanket across the theater's floor. The clouds are light and buoyant, moving across the space in natural speed, that is, in the speed of things occurring in nature. But they are also reminiscent of the rocks from a quarry, physical burdens of knowledge and consciousness filling the mind and space. Here, a metaphorical landscape—the "quarry"—takes on a vast range of symbolic and cultural interpretations. Accompanied by a rhythmic, repetitive chanting—a "vocal landscape"—sung by the chorus members, the clouds seem to speak as well as move. In Monk's dance-theater, image and sound resonate with more weight than any traditional dramatic storyline ever could. "I'm working like a filmmaker," says Monk in an interview with *TDR* from 1972, "I don't know why. That seems to be the way I think . . . I'm doing live movies, or that's what I think they are. And there are many more ambiances I would like to explore this way—like a mountainscape, or a desertscape, or water, a lake. I'm really interested in dealing with those things as theatrical materials. I'm not just dealing with theaters anymore."[40] Though Monk's theater speaks to a visual sensibility, it is important to stress that she gives equal weight to the musical score of her works, to dance, and to voice. Says Monk:

> For me, theater, in the broadest sense of the word is really a place where you can take storytelling, acting, visual images, movement and music, and put them into a form where these elements are not separated . . . All the elements of my work—the lighting, text, movement,

music, the image visual—are part of one mosaic which will hopefully form as full a perceptual, emotional, spiritual, kinetic entity as possible.[41]

Another sedimentary layer of World War II comes into view when a street scene emerges, complete with a man riding a bicycle, ringing his little bell. The bicyclist zips through this world; he captures our eye for a second, then he retreats into the darkness of off stage. Suddenly a barrage of tiny airplanes buzzes into the space. These miniature airplanes resemble the toys of little children. Isn't this, after all, how children see planes when they look up in the sky? Soon, the planes leave and we shrink back into the little girl's room, where Monk now dances in a kind of furious, chaotic state, as though expressing an unspeakable terror. Her choreography appears uncalculated and, yet, repetitive. She is like a wound-up doll who won't stop until her father enters and chases her around the bed and finally grabs her, putting her back to sleep. It's as if Monk's interior gestural body movements are channelings of the exterior landscape of war coalescing outside the bedroom. The spatial dichotomies of interior and exterior, and figure and ground, grow ever more obsolete as the world on stage begins to dig deeper into the mythic sediment of war—the archeological landscape of the quarry. Through the performative matrix of the quarry, theater (space) and dance (body) blend into one.

Monk's filmic technique comes into play, as well, as she positions the audience as a camera throughout the piece, spanning the tight La Mama space for both close-ups and far-away shots. Says Monk: "I'm trying to give the theatrical audience the kind of immediacy of environment that you can usually get only from film."[42] The camera moves back and forth between wide-shot angles, in which the whole space is used, and intimate gestures and movements of the little girl in her tiny room.[43] Monk also uses film as a spatial object—a landscape within a landscape—in *Quarry*. The 16-mm silent film component begins with a sculptural shot of a body, eyes closed, holding onto a wooden log, floating in water. As the camera pans out, more bodies are seen, heads and limbs and arms partially obscured. The bodies appear, at first, to be almost floating in mid-air, vertically. It is only when the camera pulls back farther that we understand them to be floating atop the dark, deep water of the pool of a quarry. In an interview with filmmaker Peter Greenaway, Monk recalls that while she had been teaching in Vermont at the time, she had visited an actual quarry, and she knew from that point that she wanted to shoot at this particular site. Throughout the film episodes occur, which muddle our ability, as spectators, to distinguish figures from their backgrounds. Monk chose to model the way she shot the film and its scale on Polish propaganda photographs showing workers in death quarries, carrying stones until they were literally worked to death. In an uncanny homage to such archival remnants, the camera encounters a massive pile of white rocks forming the steep sides of the quarry. The rocky landscape appears, at first, to be void of life; but ever so slowly, minute figures, dressed in white suits, are seen emerging from the colossal rubble of rocks. They begin to climb slowly over the stones such that we can barely make them out; in moments, they blend into the ground entirely. The archeological landscape of *Quarry* introduces a primordial choreography that renders bodies and their movements as indistinct from the contextual sites in which they are "dug up." Bodies become landscapes, the landscape embodied. Or rather landscapes, as bodies, bear the scars of historical practice.

The film sequence ends, and we snap back to the landscape of the actual stage space. This time, a frenzy of activity is taking place. Within the center is the little girl, surrounded by dancers performing in stylized, soldier-like movements. This is the "March" sequence. A group of people snake in through the space with arms hooked, clinging onto one another (see fig. 20.3).

Meanwhile a dictator appears. Throughout the scene, there are periods of both intense movement and absolute stillness. In the midst of the chaos, a simple, everyday gesture takes place: We see an old, gray-haired couple remove their hat and earrings and drop them on the floor. Suddenly, we catch a close-up that offers a reminder of victims entering camps, forced to relinquish personal articles before proceeding to their deaths. Though it is uncertain what it means precisely, this small physical moment embodies a flash of memory.[44]

The little girl is now shown a photo book again. Simultaneously, a man passes through the space with a wheelbarrow full of rocks. In a kind of chanting, moaning, and rhythmic lullaby—primordial landscape movement and vocal text—the girl expresses the pain, perhaps, of lugging these memories, these photos of a time she didn't know, these rocks from a quarry of the past. Jowitt writes that Monk "works as both archeologist and seer; wanting us to experience past and present simultaneously, she creates a poetic equivalent of a cross-section of soil strata."[45] Yet, we too become fellow mapmakers and "chorographers" in Monk's universe, on a journey back in time when we look in a different direction and chart our own understandings of past events.[46] *Quarry*, then, produces for its audience a unique landscape experience through sound and movement, dance and theater, one that is both a

FIGURE 20.3 Dancers in Meredith Monk's *Quarry*. Photo by Nat Tileston. Courtesy of Nat Tileston.

purgatorial chasm and a metaphorical digging-ground.[47] With *Quarry*, Monk ultimately gravitates toward landscape as an archeological medium that forges connections between figures and grounds.[48]

The Wooster Group's Architectural Landscape: Activating the Present

While Meredith Monk may feel at home operating in the mode of a landscape archeologist, Elizabeth LeCompte, director and co-founder of The Wooster Group, often envisions herself as a landscape architect. Why landscape? Why architecture? As she explains in an interview with the experimental playwright and director Richard Foreman,

> I want to organize space. I can't think unless I'm organizing space. Now obviously I've thought, 'Oh, I'll go outside.' I realize now, that's a big change. I'd no longer be an artist. I'd be someone organizing landscape.[49]

Yet, in many ways, organizing landscape is precisely what LeCompte does *inside* the theater too. The Wooster Group's iconic multimedia, tech-geeky practice of bric-a-brac assemblage as performance fashions an interior "landscape architecture," a way of orienting figures and grounds to create "relations between theatrical elements."[50] Landscape is, in fact, one of the principal modes binding the disparate architectural and spatial-temporal elements—sounds, music, dance, objects, video, film, acting—that make up their signature craft of intermedial performance.

How does landscape mediate the relation between bodies and spaces in works by The Wooster Group? Though almost all of their repertoire, stemming from as early as the late 1960s, speaks to the importance of the conceptual mode of landscape, their adaptation of Gertrude Stein's *Dr. Faustus Lights the Lights* (1938) represents one of the most obvious adaptations of Stein's own concept of "landscape play." Their production of *House/Lights* is a hybrid fusion of two scripts: the text of Stein's *Dr. Faustus* and footage from the B-Grade, sexploitation, "female dominant/submission" film *Olga's House of Shame* (1964), directed by Joseph Mawra. In her early notes for the production, dated January 5, 1996, LeCompte moves back and forth between sketches of the stage space and scribbles, writing: "Parts of Stein's plays adapted to Olga style (instead of bringing Olga to Stein, bring Stein to Olga)."[51] For the scenic design, LeCompte, from the beginning of the process, knew she wanted "many lamps with light-bulbs" and "ramps."[52]

In the production, two caged light bulbs placed at the end of two-foot rigid poles swing around from a horizontal grid that runs across the length of the stage. Two steel-studded ramps also run horizontally from either side of the stage, meeting in a crevasse in the middle, used to create "earthquake" and other effects. In the center of the space, the crack, is a live-action camera that feeds into a television screen, with microphones on either side and a stool upstage of it. All of these set pieces were themselves reassembled from other earlier sets whose components were just lying around the Performing Garage, making *House/Lights* a prime example of a foraged set, ultimately wrangled into its final form by scenic designer Jim Findlay.

FIGURE 20.4 The Wooster Group's *House/Lights*. Photo by Paula Court.

Stein's opera is a sound poem, of sorts, that attempts to represent the essence of Dr. Faustus. Though radical in its own time, the opera is structurally rather quaint when viewed from today, composed of three acts, which are each broken up by numerically sequenced scenes. Yet, the Wooster Group's approach to Stein's text highlights the earlier work's more experimental gestures: the split-subjectivity of its characters (one of whom is named Marguerite Ida and Helene Annabel), its simultaneity of narrative passages, and spoken stage directions, not to mention its classic Steinian repetitive and rhythmic language, the oddball, childlike roles of a speaking dog and a viper, as well as isolated song and "ballet" numbers that penetrate the scenes periodically. LeCompte was clearly drawn to Stein's project for its defiance of the traditional mimetic struggle to have action correspond with story and emotions. In Stein's "landscape play" form, the story is, simply, what's happening, *now*, a form of kinetic meditation. One is freed of trying to match feelings to actions. One may perceive in the present, and that is all and is enough.

Yet, for LeCompte, what's more interesting, it would appear, is the sheer difficulty of achieving a state of being in the present as either a spectator or actor. "Your emotion," as LeCompte writes in a notebook passage written on November 3, 1996, that begins, tellingly, with the heading "Landscape," "is either behind or ahead of the play at which you are looking (Stein). Performers watch video and react to moves—always a little behind the move OR anticipating the coming move."[53] The video movements, which the performers attempt to simulate live, are played on the screen downstage. Footage from the lowbrow, pop-culture iconography of *Olga's House of Shame* collides, overlaps, and bumps up against Stein's highbrow, modernist opera. The live performers mimic the action and gestures of the *Olga* video, reenacting the formal and structural vernacular of film by attempting to reproduce "close-ups" and "bleeds" and other such editing through the movements of their bodies up and down and throughout the stage space. In the merging of the low and high comes a kind of gestural-spatial architecture, a dance-theater performance, built on the collisions of these spatial and figural objects, texts and media, literary and erotic cultures, domestic and celestial motifs, dominant and submissive tones. Put together, these elements create the intricately assembled "landscape architecture" of *House/Lights*. As Jennifer Parker-Starbuck suggests, "The aesthetic of *House/Lights* is televisual, a sense that the screens produce the actions, shaping performers as object bodies within a larger landscape that is negotiated through its pieces, rather than an immersive 'whole.' "[54]

Symmetry, however, as both an architectural and thematic organizer, is important in *House/Lights* as well. *Olga's House of Shame* deals with the well-made story of a closet-lesbian dominatrix/sadist named Olga, a devil figure and madame, who ultimately brainwashes one of her prisoners, Elaine, into becoming her next protégé, just as Mephistopheles manipulates Faust, his own double, into signing a pact to go to hell. The power struggles between Faust and Mephisto and Olga and Elaine, "had a symmetry to it," explains Kate Valk.[55] Also, there was of interest the overarching symmetry of the famed relationship between Gertrude Stein and her lover, Alice B. Toklas, which mirrored the dynamics between LeCompte and the Wooster Group actresses, who, in the absence of male actors, self-admittedly formed a "girl-gang troupe" in the process of the show's creation. The directive of simultaneity, of two things happening at once—or, as LeCompte suggests, "two tracks humming next to each other"[56]—throughout the performance, makes it nearly impossible for the audience to be focused on a single story or moment or emotion occurring in any one place and time. Rather, as in Stein's idea of "landscape play," what one experiences is the relation between two or more things, vocal text and physical movement, and how they occur slightly "ahead or behind" one another.

Discussing how she used the structural device of film to "construct the physical score" of *House/Lights*, LeCompte suggests, "I thought of it a bit like when you're editing a Super 8 film. You see the film running through the machine and you watch the two frames go by. It was like that. You see the same action in the next frame—just a fraction of a second later . . . so it's never really synchronized but . . . just off."[57] This idea of "just off" synchronization became a rationale behind the use of an in-ear receiver device for Kate Valk, as well, performing as both Faust and Elaine. Throughout the performance, she "channels" spoken text from *Dr. Faustus* and *Olga* as it was being directly broadcast into her ear.

Says Valk, "It was the only way we could get Stein to feel more effervescent in the space and not purely dredged up by some memory."[58] It was also, more practically, a way to get Valk to become "in the moment with the material," and, as she puts it, "open enough, so that you can surprise yourself."[59] While the audience's experience of encountering the world of *House/Lights* is, thus, one of recognizing that they are always slightly out of sync with what's happening, the performers nevertheless strive for a more virtuosic enactment of being in the embodied present, vocally and physically. As a riff on Stein's "landscape play," *House/Lights* plays with the actor's striving to merge body and space, the blending of a figure into its spatial and temporal ground, so that there is no before or after, but only being in the present. Suggests Valk of her experience of wearing the in-ear device during performance: "It's interesting to watch somebody dealing with and channeling information, responding to stimulus as also negotiating the room, the whole room, with a kind of presence."[60] This idea of achieving "presence"—of things occurring simultaneously and in the moment—becomes

FIGURE 20.5 Kate Valk in The Wooster Group's *House/Lights*. Photo by Paula Court.

particularly meaningful in the show's choreographed sequences, during which little spoken text is performed.

Andre Lepecki has suggested that the appearance of dance in the Western cultural vernacular of the seventeenth century witnessed a "division of body and presence . . . the positing of an interval between one and the other that allows choreography to announce and enforce its project of regimentation and inscription of bodily movements."[61] This split between the body and presence, formulated on the visual schematic of a body positioned against the backdrop of an empty or "open field of absence," occurred in tandem with the rise of an aestheticized schism between figure and ground in Western painting.[62] Citing the work of Susan Leigh Foster, Lepecki considers how a body might then transcend or evade choreography's spatial distillation and regimentation of the moving body. In other words, How can choreography get around the historically charged power dynamic of figure and ground? The dance sequences in *House/Lights* consciously reveal the disciplinary codes that go into choreography itself, which is, at its basis, a process of regimenting moving bodies in an open architectural field. By juxtaposing "presence"—the embodied live actor—with the "open field of absence" inside the televisual monitor, The Wooster Group's performance challenges the stability not only of the figure but also of the ground.

Instead of representing something outside of itself, the dancing body, in *House/Lights*, to borrow the words of Lepecki, "smuggles its materiality into a charged presence that defies subjection."[63] Set to a fragmented soundscape by Hans Peter Kuhn, which includes not only his own orchestrations but also riffs from famous classical and popular music recordings (from Tchaikovsky's *Swan Lake* to Johnny Cash's "Ring of Fire"), the dances erupt in the space with energy, rawness, and eroticism. The production introduces early on, for example, a lengthy "Car-Ballet" sequence set to balletic classical music, in which Elaine desperately tries to run free of Olga and her criminal older brother, Nick. Valk mimics on stage the frantic actions of Elaine played for us on the downstage screen, as she first races in a car down a country road, runs through swampland, down thickly forested paths, and wades into a lake, where she's eventually trapped by Nick and Olga. The absurdity of staging a filmed chase-scene in a live theater is not lost on the audience; the sequence is comic, aided by the campiness of the film. As the filmed chase sequence veers into uncharted territory, the risers in the set move up and down, sending the entire world of the stage off-kilter. The electric lights flicker, and there is a sense of chaos and rupture, even though the actors are performing with the utmost athleticism and virtuosity in the attempt to dance the choreography of the film. Yet it is the material "presence" of the present choreographed body—Valk's uncanny attempt to represent the movements of an absent body in the film—that produces the most humorous (and nervous) reactions by the audience. What we find most unsettling is the schism in the architectural relation—the lack of symmetry, that is—between the present body and the absent space.

LeCompte provides emphasis on the materiality bodies of her actors through her costumes, as well, which gesture toward both the high-fashion silhouettes of Prada and the lumpiness of rag dolls. Into Valk's dress, a thirties throwback, is sewn a prosthesis, of sorts, that makes her body appear distorted and misshapen, but also more sexually alluring. Her bodice is at one point ripped at the breasts to reveal a lacy black bra beneath. LeCompte plays with the eroticism of dance in a sequence, in which Valk, as Elaine once more, performs the movements of a belly-dance scene from the film. She gyrates her pelvis and rotates her chest while Olga looks on. Later during the sequence, Valk is inverted, with her legs split open, while Roche, as Olga, buries her face into Elaine's crotch in homage to the kitsch aesthetics of lesbian porn. The erotic dancing body on the screen suddenly appears "absent" in comparison to Valk's "present" pulsating corpus, live with us in the space. This rift between the mediated absent versus present body is itself grounded in Stein's own poetic text, however, in which Marguerite Ida and Helena Annabel at one point professes, "and I I am not there I am here oh dear I am not there."[64] Indeed, Valk's portrait appears on the video screen now as a visually divided self—one Kate talking to another, or, Marguerite Ida addressing Helena Annabel? Where is the body of Marguerite Ida? Where is the body of Stein? Where is the body of Valk? Oh yes, they are all on TV *and* in the space simultaneously: they are all "not there" and "here" at once (see fig. 20.4). As a scenic quotation of the "wild wood everywhere" that Marguerite Ida and Helena Annabel now imagine she "sees" before her, a green-painted cardboard cutout of a tree enters the stage left space, representing the "landscape" of the Garden of Eden. Within this mythical wilderness, Marguerite Ida and Helena Annabel claims to have been stung by a serpent (see fig. 20.5).

The rest of the Stein text—the following two acts—concerns Marguerite Ida's attempt to locate the "Doctor" Faust, who she believes can cure her of her sting and prevent her from death. In *House/Lights*, several more "ballet" sequences now ensue, first among them a "Ballet of *Young Frankenstein*," set to the scene of the famed film in which Igor (Marty Feldman), aids the doctor (Gene Wilder) in awakening the monster. The summoning of Dr. Faustus apparently involves a trip to hell, a journey into a "turning ring of fire." Other dances are also set to more vaguely iconic film sequences: The "Grand Ballet of Lights" occurs in sync with a Busby Berkeley–style swim-ballet, in which Valk enacts underwater choreography. A final "Ballet," again set to classical composition, mirrors a scene from *Olga's House of Shame*, in which Olga "disciplines" her girls as if they were her workhorses, whipping them with a riding crop as they prance around a circle track, bridled to her long rope. The stage space at last erupts into a pseudo-Western film, with Valk, as Elaine/Marguerite Ida and Helena Annabel

FIGURE 20.6 Kate Valk with Serpent in The Wooster Group's *House/Lights*. Photo by Paula Court.

shooting off guns and Ari Fliakos cavorting around the space as a horse. Sound snippets of "Stayin' Alive" by the Bee Gees mix with classical music and the score of *Olga's House of Shame*. And suddenly it becomes clear that the landscape bridging the gap between the body and space, between figure and ground, and between dance and theater, is American cultural media detritus itself, from the highest form of modernist opera (Stein) to the lowest form of the B-grade mild-porn flic (Mawry).

House/Lights creates "landscape architecture" using American media refuse as its sculptural material. There is something profoundly nihilistic about the whole production as we hear the spoken text of Stein's opera—"What sin, how can I without a soul commit a sin"[65]—while watching Valk, as Elaine, now take the reins from Peyton, as Olga, becoming herself the "chorographer" of bodies. "*Now there were two of them*," runs the voice over from the film, "*Two vicious minds working as one. Set upon the destruction of all who stood in their way, by whatever means possible*."[66] Martin Puchner has suggested that, "the production is not grounded in representative space: it has no physical matrix, only the versions of the Faust story and the mediated space of film."[67] Space becomes "absence," in this sense, referring only to a mediated landscape—hearkening to the "white ground" of the seventeenth-century chorographer's book—into which the figural, live body is drawn by the disciplining forces of culture.

Architectural landscape in the Wooster Group's productions is never a stable entity, however, but rather a "step" between things—an intention, a passage, a going between. Nothing is ever in stasis—neither body nor space—despite its maniacally detailed compositionality. LeCompte admits, "I like to see things between the picture and the next picture. I like to make sure that nothing gets stuck, that is always changing. Even now, as I'm working with dance (*Poor Theatre* [2004]), I like to see how they get in and out of their moves, rather than the move itself."[68] Being in between things, thus—between motions, between genres, between media, between forms—is, it would seem, the ideal place for LeCompte and her performers to be. In their hybrid performance vernacular, "architectural landscape" becomes the passage that bridges dance with theater, vocal text with movement score, all the while making us more conscious of the present.

The TEAM's Climatescape: Activating the Future

On the one hand, landscape implies formal and cultural distance—spatial, cognitive, and emotional—toward an encountered space. On the other hand, landscape, as I've just emphasized, may imply the bridging or reaching toward interaction, even interdependency, between and across figures and grounds. Climatescape builds on this latter aspect of landscape, acknowledging the fragile interconnectedness and interdependency between bodies and spaces, figures and grounds. Climatescape is perhaps best theorized as a next "step" in landscape's own critical and conceptual development; rather than simply leaving landscape behind, climatescape builds on a landscape paradigm by theorizing the way we might frame ourselves as part of the global climate, not only of "land." Whereas landscape may turn a site into an image, climatescape frames in more apparent ways our temporal experience of oncoming catastrophic "change," one that we ourselves have set into motion. Climatescape reminds us that time (not only space) is being wasted. Climatescape marks our persistent bond as humans to what Claire Colebrook views as an "irreversible and destructive time,"[69] projecting forward to an era in which we will no longer exist as a species on the planet (a time now termed the post-Anthropocene era). Landscape shows us the enticing promise of a spatial frontier even as it critiques the imperialism of that same vision; climatescape shows us the projected dystopia built on the trash and ruins of that frontier. Yet, within the recognition of climate and ourselves as interdependent forces, there may arise a silver lining: a greater awareness of our commonness, our ties to each other as bodies that are already part of a complex, systemic whole. As The TEAM reveals in their performance of *Mission Drift*, the stakes of our awareness toward our temporal (not only spatial) existence as a species on the planet couldn't get any higher.

The very title of the collective, The TEAM (Theatre of the Emerging American Moment), gestures toward a temporally framed communal ideal: an "American Moment" that is always "emerging" but always just out of reach. Mythical sites of US geography—from New Orleans to Kansas to Las Vegas—constitute the already ruined landscape frontiers of their theatrical creations. There is a utopian spirit to their work, as well, as ensemble member Paz Pardo writes: "The TEAM focuses its exploration of utopia on emotional perfection . . . It is a space in which our experience can be fully shared with others, and which our destructive desires cannot shatter."[70] As a relational, affective medium of communal exchange between bodies and spaces, the TEAM's performance practice bridges the gulfs between past and future, dance and theater, and audience and performer.

The TEAM's works span roughly the past decade and include productions such as: *Give Up! Start Over! (In the darkest of times I look to Richard Nixon for hope)* (2005), a piece about "reality television and the search for authenticity in America";[71] *A Thousand Natural Shocks* (2006), focused on "a Hamlet panicked at the prospect of inheriting his father's country";[72] *Particularly in the Heartland* (2008), in which, as Carol Martin writes, "Kansas becomes an eternally-going-crazy landscape";[73] and *Architecting* (2009), which fuses history and the present by moving back and forth in time between "the U.S. Civil War, Reconstruction, post-Katrina New Orleans, a 1990s couple headed towards New Orleans for a Scarlett O'Hara pageant, and a meeting in contemporary Hollywood—all of which are portrayed onstage or on television monitors."[74] Throughout many of their works, all directed by co-founder Rachel Chavkin, "America" itself—as an eternally "potential space"—emerges as a fraught and fleeting tautology through dance, theater, original music, and video. Chavkin, writing about the intermedial and interdisciplinary aspects of their work has suggested that growing up in "an age in which multitasking and quick edits are the norm" has meant that "our work is dense because our minds are most focused when engaged on multiple levels simultaneously."[75] Each production is formed through a rigorous process of company collaboration through writing and composition, a model Chavkin has likened to an "intellectual board game" played by all members of the ensemble.[76] Yet, unlike the more ironic and visually composed postmodern design of The Wooster Group, the stories developed by The TEAM strive for more coherent, if messy, narrative emotional through-lines. Taking actual, historical events from US history and merging them with current and pressing concerns about life on the ground today, The TEAM considers each play to be "a history thesis—a chance to get another master's degree in some specific aspect of American history."[77] There is also a strong sense of being haunted by the past. As Chavkin suggests, "We are always telling a ghost story."[78]

What "America" has lost, gained, or is still haunted by through its national inheritance is a dominant trope in The TEAM's *Mission Drift* (2011), which examines the relentless pursuit of capital and commodity—manifest destiny—that drives the engine of US culture, identity, politics, and, ultimately, climate collapse. The work is a dance, musical, and theater piece informed by the tension between the conflicting desires of "going on a mission" versus "drifting." Within it, The TEAM examines how the history and mythology of the western frontier—and, more importantly, the gesture or "step" of forward movement that produced its unsustainable spatial practice—constitutes national character. Writes Chavkin, "The work is taking the form of a myth that unfolds like a bullet of narration and song, while examining American frontier mythology to determine whether the idea of freedom in this country is extricable from the freedom to make as much money as possible."[79] What happens, however, the production asks its audiences, when we become derailed from forward and linear-driven progress, from a single "drive"—whether in real life or in the narratives we construct to represent such journeys? What happens when the bodily step of journeying is put on pause? Using landscape as a medium for expressing the abusive and unsustainable relationship between bodies and spaces in late-stage, hyperindustrial capitalism, *Mission Drift* brings together stories from the past and present heritage of the frontier, colonial immigration and expansion, and the "Great Recession" and housing bubble collapse of 2008. The triangular spatial design moves between the colonies of New Amsterdam and New England and the apex of modern Las Vegas, a site resonant in the American mythic, cultural, and geographical vernacular. Yet, what is meant by "Las Vegas" is constantly changing. Over time, forward motion itself becomes suspect and even ceases to maintain meaning.

Stylistically, *Mission Drift* is part dance-theater and part rock-blues/gospel concert gig. It is a self-consciously cosmic drama. The piece begins with the entrance of a narrator and cosmic superstar, aptly named Miss Atomic, played by the immensely talented singer and composer Heather Christian, dressed in a gigantic rainbow-feathered headdress and white cape (typical Vegas show attire): "Before time there were two brothers. Mythic, beast brothers. Big scale. They slept between mountains with their legs in separate valleys. Their names were Love and Wrestling."[80] Love, we are told, carves massive continental forms in the Mojave out of rock, sandstone, and granite, "erecting elaborate countries that baked under the sun," whereas Wrestling, his brother, driven to destruction, "splits and tears and shakes the earth with belly flops," toppling all of Love's creations.[81] Taking over the story of the two brothers at this point is Joan, a recently laid-off casino waitress and native Las Vegas resident, who sips on a beer in the yard of her soon-to-be-foreclosed home. Wrestling, Joan informs us, curses the human race to experience never-ending "lust for improvement and development and expansion."[82] The rest of the play portrays the interweaving of two main narratives and their own restless pursuits: Joan's romantic relationship with a cowboy named Chris and the trans-Atlantic migration and colonization of America by two Dutch settlers, Joris and Catalina (see fig. 20.6).

The epic story of the Dutch settlers, who marry in 1624 before boarding the ship to the New World and reinvent themselves ceaselessly as they pillage the continent for its presumably bottomless booty, foregrounds a scathing critique of Western expansionism and greed. The music numbers in *Mission Drift* are powerful and explosive, often tapping into a collective, nationalistic nostalgia for an "America" that never even existed.

FIGURE 20.7 Libby King as Catalina, Ian Lassiter as Chris, and Brian Hastert as Joris, in The TEAM's *Mission Drift*. Photo by Ves Pitts.

The choreography of the show is richly iconic; gestures to the gyrating movement vocabulary of Elvis, the theatrical and grandiose expressions of Hollywood 1930s musicals, as well as snake-charming ritual dance and Gospel choir movements occur alongside less culturally traceable sequences (see fig. 20.7). Dancers often dance with objects—furniture and props—blending the material and illusionistic realities of the world on stage. A company-described "Lizard Ballet" occurs at one point, with various actors donning a mask of a Lizard.

Larger, group dance sequences, in which all members of the ensemble perform, are set to the rollicking, blues-inflected rock ballads of Miss Atomic, who belts out in a growling voice:

> Land you hard, hey
> Walk you west, ho
> Look you up, higher
> Look you loooooonger
> Jump the shark, hey
> Jump the frontier
> Back to land, ho
> We'll make millions here.[33]

The drive to possess land, name rivers, produce heirs, and take ownership is the very curse of lust placed on humans by the brothers Love and Wrestling—a drive as erotically charged as it is ethically bankrupt. "I want . . . I want. My own land," confesses Joris, "And I want to kill a buffalo," to which Catalina chimes in, "I want to have a thousand babies and I want to give each of them a piece of this land. I wanna do you on every acre of this continent."[84]

FIGURE 20.8 Amber Gray and Ensemble in The TEAM's *Mission Drift*. Photo by Ves Pitts.

In a perverse coopting of the Native American tradition of naming a member of a family after an association with the natural world, Joris renames Catalina "Eternal Frontier," and she rechristens him "Wealth of Nations." These are the very landscape-oriented ideals that the United States has forged itself upon, and which still haunt us today. Together, Catalina and Joris "dive into the wilderness," claiming the "virgin woods" of Pennsylvania, the coal of Virginia, a river in Montana, the gold and oil of "sunny California" all as their own. At each stop on their path of destruction and waste, Catalina and Joris die, only to be raised from the dead and transformed so as to continue on in the endless quest for capital. At last, however, exhaustion sets in with the closing of the frontier in the 1880s, and Catalina experiences her first loss of a child.

Progress halts. The world itself is stillborn. Miss Atomic sings a mournful chorus: "We walk, we walk we tire . . . We walk, we walk we tire . . . Release me. Release me. Release me."[85] But there is no release to be found. The stage is, rather, "*transformed from sand blasted forestry to Las Fucking Vegas.*"[86] As the new dystopian future now emerges, Miss Atomic soulfully sings a ballad to Vegas that casts it as a Lady Liberty, an Ellis Island arising as a mirage in the waterless desert of the southwest:

> Talk to me Vegas
> Sing me your strange song
> Bring me your tired your poor
> I am home to the weary and the wrong
> Do you feel luck?

FIGURE 20.9 Amber Gray in The TEAM's *Mission Drift*. Photo by Ves Pitts.

> I can be your oasis in the heat
> And I'm not your mama
> But I can be your sweet release.[87]

Set against this reprise, the exhaustive journey of Catalina and Joris continues on apace: they become nuclear bomb testers in the 1950s, tiger trainers in the 1980s, and real estate developers in the 1990s, breaking ground for the construction of The Ark, a new, gigantic casino set to replace the aging Frontier. The stories of the Dutch settlers and the present-day Joan at last collide when money grows tight and plans to construct The Ark fall through. The state of constantly being in motion, moving forward, comes to a paralyzing halt as the banks default on their loans and the economy takes a nosedive.

"Every story is a travel story—a spatial practice," suggests Michel de Certeau.[88] In *Mission Drift*, the journey that thematically drives the play serves as the fundamental defining feature of "American" cultural and national identity. But there is a metatheatrical and temporal awareness toward the journey, too: the theater becomes itself a metaphor not only for landscape but also for a ravaged, ruined climate, a dystopian space-time that is, in fact, always being activated in the present by the bodies that inhabit its metaphysical contours and dimensions and boundaries. A new climatescape on stage is birthed out of the trash and ruins of a ravaged landscape. Joan and Catalina at last meet in an abandoned Neon Bone yard, a "zombie gravesite of electric dinosaurs."[89] There is no more frontier to be conquered. Only nostalgia for a dream remains, eulogized by the neon signs of dead casinos: the

Desert Inn, the Stardust. The allegory of never-ending expansion and imperialism crumbles beneath Catalina's tired, aching feet as she herself, like Las Vegas, has become a ghost: "Catalina looks at her skin. She sees it is peeling back, like a lizard's. She sees that underneath it is dust. She sees that her canvas is tearing off her frame (see fig. 20.8)."[90] She has finally grown old, given up. She begins her last, long walk—this time, however, she turns around. She starts going back from where she came: east. In a culminating, final dance, the company blends together, bodies moving synchronously in space and time to the soulful gospel of Miss Atomic:

I am traveling, travelling, travelling
No one here remembers my song (Millleeeeeeooooonnnnnnssss)
My ghost is forgotten and so it be
Come swiftly
Come high
Come bury me
Throw desert over me
World turning over me.[91]

The TEAM's *Mission Drift* utilizes the theater as site to reveal how bodies are both bound to and conditioned by spatial and cultural practice. But, in so doing, the piece expands from the temporal and spatial boundaries of its own stage to affect its audience members at a deep, piercing level. As one critic wrote, *Mission Drift* did "exactly what I want the theatre to do to me: take me someplace I don't know how to get to on my own."[92] The TEAM's ability to produce a utopian, communal experience for its audiences suggests that, despite our egregious missteps as humans, we may still have the power to save ourselves.

In a darker sense, however, as a "climatescape play," the TEAM's *Mission Drift* ultimately forecasts a planet on which figure and ground cease to have meaning in any relational sense. This is because, whereas landscape makes us more aware of spaces in time, climatescape forces us to recognize the boundaries and endpoints of our own collective time in space. As Claire Colebrook suggests, the concept of "climate is not only … the surface or terrain upon which we find ourselves, but something that binds us to *this time* on the earth, with its own depletions and limits."[93] If the archeological landscape of Monk positions us as observant diggers of the past and the Wooster Group's architectural landscape casts us as skeptical builders of the present, the TEAM's climatescape initiates us, temporarily, as futurists, burying our past in the dust while barreling toward our catastrophic destiny. Landscape still makes us conscious of the ways figure and ground are always connected, indelibly marked by one another in both time and space. Climatescape foresees an era when the earth will no longer be inhabited by bodies, a moment when there will cease to be a figure to choreograph in relation to a ground.

NOTES

1. See, for example: Ingold, 2000, and Martin Lefebvre, ed., 2006.
2. For "spatial turn," see: Henri Lefebvre, 1991, and Michel de Certeau, 1984. For "visual turn," see: Jay, 2002.
3. Bonnie Marranca's "theatre of images," Elinor Fuchs's "death of character," and Hans-Thies Lehmann's "postdramatic" all describe a type of performance practice that, like Stein's

landscape play, resists a linear, cathartic narrative in favor of visual, sculptural, or sonic forms.

4. Marranca, "Landscapes of the 21st Century," 67 See also: Fuchs and Chaudhuri, eds., 2003; and Brater, 2006.

5. As Hans-Thies Lehmann observes, the formal qualities of landscape in theater may now be conventionally summarized as: "a *defocalization* and equal status for all parts, a renunciation of teleological time, and the dominance of 'atmosphere' above dramatic and narrative forms of progression" (*Post-Dramatic Theatre*, 63).

6. In so doing, I intentionally refer to W. J. T. Mitchell's definition of landscape as a "medium of exchange between the human and the natural, the self and the other" (*Landscape and Power*, 5).

7. "Gesture." *Oxford Dictionaries*. April 2010. http://oxforddictionaries.com/definition/english/gesture (accessed July 21, 2012).

8. Colebrook, "Framing the End," 55.

9. See Chaudhuri, "Land/Scape/Theory," 15.

10. Jean-Luc Nancy suggests that, "landscape begins with a notion, however vague or confused, of distancing" (*The Ground of the Image*, 53).

11. The rise of landscape as a genre in nineteenth-century painting is well established within art history. See Andrews, 1999.

12. See Gombrich, 1961.

13. See Berger, 1972.

14. Schama, *Landscape and Memory*, 61.

15. Mitchell, *Landscape and Power*, 262.

16. Mitchell, *Landscape and Power*, 265.

17. As Martin Lefebvre suggests, "in investigating landscape . . . one is considering an object that amounts to much more than the mere spatial background that necessarily accompanies the depiction of actions and events" (*Landscape and Film*, xii).

18. Stein, "Lectures in America," 263.

19. Fuchs, "Reading for Landscape," 44.

20. Stein, "Lectures in America," 264–65.

21. See: Fuchs, 1994.

22. See: Marranca, 1996; Robinson, 2003; Bowers, 2003; Copland, 2003; Profeta, 2005.

23. Roach, "Kinesis: The New Mimesis," 2.

24. Foster, *Choreographing Empathy*, 17.

25. Foster, *Choreographing Empathy*, 13.

26. See: Winnicott, 1971.

27. Nancy, *The Ground of the Image*, 61.

28. Monk, *Speaking about Dance*, 89.

29. Monk, *Speaking about Dance*, 89.

30. Marranca, *Ecologies of Theatre*, 231.

31. Text from Meredith Monk's website: www.meredithmonk.org (accessed July 18, 2012).

32. Monk's website (accessed July 18, 2012).

33. Jowitt, "Meredith Monk: Invocation/Evocation," 85.

34. Baker, "Landscapes and Telescopes," 68.

35. Monk explains how she viewed herself as an archeologist while making *Quarry*, digging up photographs from World War II within a filmed interview with Peter Greenaway. See: Jowitt, ed., 1991.

36. Jowitt, "Meredith Monk: Invocation/Evocation," 85.

37. Baker, "Landscapes and Telescopes," 68.

38. Banes, "Meredith Monk," 10.

39. Mark Berger has called Monk's theater one of "non-verbal collage with a narrative format. Elements of character and interpretation, heroes and heroines, plots and subplots, development and climax are all present, but kept in a state of flux: a metamorphic ordering of segmental parts that shift focus, disassemble and reassemble, spreading out in a multidimensional, musically organized *tableau*" ("Meredith Monk," 44).

40. McNamara, "The Scenography of Meredith Monk," 103.

41. Baker, "The New World for Old," 6.

42. Baker, "The New World for Old," 7.

43. Writes Sally Banes: "Meredith Monk's theater is a place of transmutation and transfiguration. Events occur, but their meanings shift and are wiped away; time and space become shattered and rearranged; objects shrink or become luminous and powerful. Inside the magically real universes that Monk creates within the borders of theatrical space, simple and familiar things accumulate into dense, resonant, fabulous images" ("Meredith Monk," 8).

44. "It's that way of distilling human behavior," writes Deborah Jowitt, "that gives such power to Monk's work" (*Meredith Monk*, 123).

45. Jowitt, *Meredith Monk*, 15.

46. For Rob Baker, "What Monk is uncovering in all her best works are glimpses of a vast tapestry, the scope of which can only be hinted at, whispered about" ("The New World for Old," 60).

47. For Signe Hammer, Monk operates in the "feminine" or "primitive mode," which is to "consider objects and events as one with their background" ("Against Alienation," 71). Sally Banes writes similarly that Monk "is interested in the dissolving of borders between public and private, interior and exterior events, the body and the universe, the individual and community" ("Meredith Monk," 14).

48. As Hammer writes of *Quarry*, "the piece, finally, is about connections. It helps give us back to ourselves" ("Against Alienation," 72).

49. Marranca, "The Wooster Group: A Dictionary of Ideas," 3.

50. Marranca, "Dictionary of Ideas," 4.

51. Quick, *The Wooster Group Workbook*, 168.

52. Quick, *The Wooster Group Workbook*, 168.

53. Quick, *The Wooster Group Workbook*, 170.

54. Parker-Starbuck, *Cyborg Theatre*, 111.

55. Quick, *The Wooster Group Workbook*, 214.

56. Quick, *The Wooster Group Workbook*, 217.

57. Quick, *The Wooster Group Workbook*, 215.

58. Quick, *The Wooster Group Workbook*, 216.

59. Quick, *The Wooster Group Workbook*, 217.

60. Quick, *The Wooster Group Workbook*, 216.

61. Lepecki, "Introduction: Presence and Body in Dance and Performance Theory," 3.

62. Lepecki, "Introduction," 3.

63. Lepecki, "Introduction," 6.

64. All references are taken from The Wooster Group's script for *House/Lights*, part of the materials included in the video-recording DVD *House/Lights*, 25.

65. The Wooster Group, Script for *House/Lights*, 56.
66. The Wooster Group Script for *House/Lights*, 56.
67. Puchner, "Drama and Performance," 301.
68. Quick, *The Wooster Group Workbook*, 215.
69. Colebrook, "Framing the End," 56.
70. Pardo, "*Mission Drift*: Remembering Utopia."
71. Martin, "What Did They Do to My Country," 102.
72. Martin, "What Did They Do to My Country," 104–5.
73. Martin, "What Did They Do to My Country," 105.
74. Martin, "What Did They Do to My Country," 101.
75. Chavkin, "Five Years and Change with the TEAM," 108.
76. Martin, "What Did They Do To My Country," 105.
77. Martin, "What Did They Do To My Country," 105.
78. Chavkin, "Five Years and Change with the TEAM," 108.
79. Chavkin, "Five Years and Change with The TEAM," 109.
80. All references are from the script of the TEAM's *Mission Drift*, unpublished and used by permission of the company: 1.
81. *Mission Drift*, 1.
82. *Mission Drift*, 2.
83. *Mission Drift*, 13.
84. *Mission Drift*, 28.
85. *Mission Drift*, 38–39.
86. *Mission Drift*, 41.
87. *Mission Drift*, 41.
88. de Certeau, *Practice of Everyday Life*, 115.
89. *Mission Drift*, 60.
90. *Mission Drift*, 66.
91. *Mission Drift*, 70.
92. Olmos, 2012.
93. Colebrook, "Framing the End," 55.

BIBLIOGRAPHY

Andrews, Malcolm. *Landscape and Western Art*. Oxford: Oxford University Press, 1999.
Baker, Rob. "Landscapes and Telescopes: A Personal Response to the Choreography of Meredith Monk." *Dance Magazine* (April 1976).
Baker, Rob. "The New World for Old: The Visionary Art of Meredith Monk." *American Theater* (October 1984): 4–34.
Banes, Sally. "Meredith Monk." *PAJ* 3, no. 1 (Spring/Summer 1978): 3–12.
Bear, Liza. "Meredith Monk: Invocation/Evocation, An Interview with Liza Bear." In *Meredith Monk*, edited by Deborah Jowitt, 79–93. Baltimore: John Hopkins University Press, 1997.
Berger, John. *Ways of Seeing*. New York: Penguin Books, 1972.
Berger, Mark. "Meredith Monk: An Introduction [by Angela Westwater] and A Metaphoric Theater." *Artforum* (May 1973): 57–63.
Bowers, Jane Palatini. "The Composition That All the World Can See: Gertrude Stein's Theatre Landscapes." In *Land/Scape/Theatre*, edited by Elinor Fuchs and Una Chaudhuri, 121–144.

Brater, Enoch. "Talk about Landscapes: What There Is to Recognize." *Modern Drama* 49, no. 4 (Winter 2006): 501–13.

Chaudhuri, Una. "Land/Scape/Theory." In *Land/Scape/Theater*, edited by Elinor Fuchs and Una Chaudhuri, 11–29.

Chavkin, Rachel. "Five Years and Change with the TEAM: Moving Fast Past the Apocalypse." *TDR: The Drama Review* 54, no. 4 (Winter 2010): 108–9.

Colebrook, Claire. "Framing the End of the Species: Images without Bodies." *Symploke* 21, no. 1–2 (2013): 55–67.

Copland, Roger. *Merce Cunningham: The Modernizing of Modern Dance*. New York: Psychology Press, 2003.

de Certeau, Michel. *The Practice of Everyday Life*. Translated by Steven Rendall. Berkeley: University of California Press, 1984.

Foster, Susan Leigh. *Choreographing Empathy: Kinesthesia in Performance*. London: Routledge, 2011.

Fuchs, Elinor. "Play as Landscape: Another Version of Pastoral." *Theater* 25, no. 1 (1994): 44–51.

Fuchs, Elinor. "Reading for Landscape: The Case of American Drama." In *Land/Scape/Theatre*, edited by Elinor Fuchs and Una Chaudhuri, 30–52.

Fuchs, Elinor, and Una Chaudhuri, eds. *Land/Scape/Theatre*. Ann Arbor: University of Michigan Press, 2003.

Gombrich, Ernst. *Art and Illusion: A Study in the Psychology of Pictorial Representation*. New York: Pantheon Books, 1961.

Hammer, Signe. "Against Alienation: A Postlinear Theatre Struggles to Connect." In *Meredith Monk*, edited by Deborah Jowitt, 68–72.

Ingold, Tim. *Perception of the Environment: Essays on Livelihood, Dwelling, and Skill*. London: Routledge, 2000.

Jay, Martin. "Cultural Relativism and the Visual Turn." *Journal of Visual Culture* 1, no. 3 (December 2002): 267–78.

Jowitt, Deborah, ed. *Meredith Monk [Art and Performance]*. New York: PAJ, 2011.

Lefebvre, Henri. *The Production of Space*. Translated by Donald Nicholson-Smith. Oxford: Wiley-Blackwell, 1991.

Lefebvre, Martin, ed. *Landscape and Film*. New York: Routledge, 2006.

Lehmann, Hans-Thies. *Post-Dramatic Theatre*. Translated by Karen Jürs-Munby. New York: Routledge, 2006.

Lepecki, Andre. "Introduction: Presence and Body in Dance and Performance Theory." In *Of the Presence of the Body: Essays on Dance and Performance Theory*, edited by Andre Lepecki, 1–12. Middletown, CT: Wesleyan University Press, 2004.

Marranca, Bonnie. *Ecologies of Theatre*. Baltimore: Johns Hopkins University Press, 1996.

Marranca, Bonnie. "Landscapes of the 21st Century: Towards a Universal Performance Language." *PAJ: A Journal of Performance and Art 76* 26, no. 1 (2004): 66–70.

Marranca, Bonnie. "The Wooster Group: A Dictionary of Ideas." *PAJ: A Journal of Performance and Art 74* 25, no. 2 (2003): 1–18.

Martin, Carol. "What Did They Do to My Country! An Interview with Rachel Chavkin." *TDR: The Drama Review* 54, no. 4 (Winter, 2010): 99–117.

McNamara, Brooks. "The Scenography of Meredith Monk." *TDR* 16, no. 1 (March 1972): 88–103.

Meredith Monk: Composer, Singer, Dancer, Filmmaker, Choreographer, Performance Artist. Produced by Revel Guest and directed by Peter Greenaway. New York: Mystic Fire Video, 1991.

Mitchell, W. J. T. "Imperial Landscape." In *Landscape and Power*, 2nd ed., edited by W. J. T. Mitchell, 5–34. Chicago: University of Chicago, 2002.

Monk, Meredith. "Meredith Monk." In *Speaking about Dance: Twelve Contemporary Choreographers on Their Craft*, edited by Joyce Morgenroth, 85–98. New York: Routledge, 2004.

Nancy, Jean-Luc. *The Ground of the Image*. Translated by Jeff Fort. New York: Fordham University Press, 2005.

Olmos, Matthew Paul. "*Mission Drift* by the TEAM, as part of P.S. 122's 2012 COIL Festival." *New York Theatre Review* (Wednesday, January 11, 2012).

Pardo, Paz. "*Mission Drift*: Remembering Utopia." Published May 5, 2011. A pamphlet distributed to audiences at a production of *Mission Drift* at The '62 Center for Dance and Theatre, Williams College.

Parker-Starbuck, Jennifer. *Cyborg Theatre: Corporeal/Technological Intersections in Multimedia Performance*. London: Palgrave Macmillan, 2011.

Profeta, Katherine. "The Geography of Inspiration." *PAJ* 27, no. 3 (2005): 23–28.

Puchner, Martin. "Drama and Performance: Towards a Theory of Adaptation." *Common Knowledge* 17, no. 2 (Spring 2011): 292–305.

Quick, Andrew, Ed. *The Wooster Group Workbook*. New York: Routledge, 2007.

Roach, Joseph. "Kinesis: The New Mimesis." *Theater* 40, no. 1 (2010): 1–3.

Robinson, Marc. "Robert Wilson, Nicolas Poussin, and *Lohengrin*." In *Land/Scape/Theatre*, edited by Elinor Fuchs and Una Chaudhuri, 159–88.

Schama, Simon. *Landscape and Memory*. New York: Vintage, 1996.

Stein, Gertrude. "Lectures in America." In *Gertrude Stein: Writings 1932–1946*, edited by Catharine Stimpson and Harriet Chessman, 191–336. New York: Library of America, 1998.

Winnicott, W. D. *Playing and Reality*. London: Tavistock, 1971.

The Wooster Group's script for *House/Lights*, part of the materials included in the video-recording DVD set *House/Lights*. New York: The Wooster Group, 2004: 25.

CHAPTER 21

COLONIAL THEATRICS IN CANADA

Managing Blackfoot Dance during Western Expansionism

LISA DOOLITTLE AND ANNE FLYNN

I never was a dancer and one day I was walking through the University . . . going to the library and I met a guy coming down the hallway and we were I guess about two or three of us and I was the only Native . . . and he stopped me and said, "Do you know anybody I can talk to about Native dancing and what not," and I looked at him and I said, "How come, why do you want to talk to this person?" He said, "We're going on a trip to New Mexico from New Mexico to Mexico itself to Belize and Guatemala and South America and back home. So we need a Native dancer to travel with us to perform those dances for these people." So I stood there and I said, a light came out and I said, "I'm a dancer. I want to go to this trip." . . . So I got to see those places. I don't dance. I never had danced so I was out there and to be honest, I was just out there having fun and I guess basically I was able to make the steps and do the right thing and stop at the right time and I had the energy. That was my only experience in dancing other than the Sundance. So, it was an uplifting thing and seeing people that probably don't know what I was doing because they talk Spanish and I was Blackfoot and English. Probably didn't know what I was doing and then I ended up getting a standing ovation and you get that extra adrenaline and that's how I saw those countries because I basically lied to the person that I was a dancer and I was a dancer.

—Pat Twigg, Kainai elder (laughing)[1]

WHEN author Lisa Doolittle met Pat Twigg recently (November 2012), and reminded him of this story, he spoke about how, while he had not trained to dance theatrically at all, when he danced, he could "feel the spirits coming down" as they had during his experience of the Sundance (▶). Further, he realized in retrospect that while performing the dancing Indian in these foreign lands he began to regain pride in his identity, an identity that he had previously hidden in shame.

On April 1, 2012, Calgary, Alberta, became the "Cultural Capital of Canada" for exactly twelve months, and the city proposed to celebrate itself in a variety of ways. The Calgary 2012 nonprofit organization that submitted the bid for the national competition highlighted that "2012 marks a pivotal year in Calgary's cultural history including the centennial anniversaries of some of the city's cultural cornerstones: Calgary Stampede, City of Calgary Recreation, Calgary Public Library and Theatre Junction Grand and Pumphouse Theatres."[2] Taken as whole, this list of hundred-year-old cultural institutions gives us a snapshot of some of the predominant ideas that were in circulation in 1912 regarding what constituted a modern urban center—the things that would help make Calgary look like other modern urban centers and an attractive place to live. These would have been the ideas of the colonial/imperial entrepreneurs investing in expanding markets and settler populations invested in recreating a largely British version of urban modernism, along with influences from the American west that allowed for some maverick maneuvers, such as the rodeo—a nostalgic restaging of the Wild West. Fast-forward one hundred years, and Calgary 2012 is operating within a postmodern, postcolonial, and explicitly multicultural milieu. One of the key activities taking place as a culminating event of the twelve-month cycle of staging cultural/artistic presentations and projects is a project called "Making Treaty 7," described as a theatrical reenactment of the historic signing of Treaty 7 in 1877, a negotiation that handed over Native occupied land and its resources to the federal government. Calgary 2012 is using its moment in the national spotlight to "to promote Calgary's cultural identity through and examination of the relevance of Treaty 7 to our past, present and future." The project description further states, "The purpose of Making Treaty 7 is to bring both the document, and the historic event, to life in a way that provides renewed understanding of our history, and our shared future."[3]

Many contemporary descendants of the original tribes who signed Treaty 7 have agreed to be partners on the project, scheduled to take up to three years to complete and then celebrated annually. The interest generated in this project indicates that Canadians continue to turn to theatrics as they process, and grapple with the consequences of, the colonial encounters of the nineteenth and twentieth centuries. Those egregious encounters have generational legacies that continue to negatively impact Native people today with no easy solutions to right the outcomes of the many misguided actions that occurred. Our efforts as dance scholars join forces with the international body of writing on colonialism and performance to offer an examination of the use of dance, theater, and spectacle as part of a complex set of maneuvers to negotiate identity and power. In the words of Kainai[4] teacher and filmmaker Narcisse Blood, "[W]e're commemorating Alberta's 100th anniversary, it's not even a blink of the eye for us but what has this 100 years taught us? What can we learn? That very question is one that needs to be looked at."[5] We hope to shed light on how dancing and the bodies of dancers figured in encounters between colonial and indigenous people during colonial settlement on the prairies. Stagings of the Native that occurred as part of touristic performances such as the Calgary Stampede and Banff Indian Days, theatricalized meetings between non-native and native dignitaries, and other public events constitute a convoluted, ongoing pageant where "solutions" to the "problem" of the persistent presence of indigenous peoples are imagined and embodied for public consumption and persuasion.

The story of settlement in Canada's west is most commonly told as an inevitable, natural evolution of unstoppable events, a narrative structure that tends to legitimize the disenfranchisement of aboriginal people. Working on this question, "what this one hundred years has taught us," we resist the chronology and present our analysis of western expansion, theatrics, and Blackfoot dance choreographically, in the form of themes and variations. We first reimagine received, imperial history as a script—a theatrical transposition that allows us to creatively foreground this story's grand themes rooted in Enlightenment philosophies and in European imaginaries. Yet how the master script—the global narrative of empire—played out locally was complicated by actual encounters with indigenous people, encounters that sparked creation of new variations on the grand themes.[6] Different imperial agencies operated with different sets of stage directions: make money; keep the peace; convert and save savage souls; acquire land; provide refuge from persecution in Europe, and buttress an already vast and powerful nation. We present descriptions and definitions of Blackfoot dance and western expansionism, tracing how expansion came to depend on eradication of the dancing while paradoxically repurposing and reinventing the dancing as theatrical memorialization. Finally, we map out specific versions of the imperial script in western Canada, using a variety of historical sources. Here, the Blackfoot exercised what agency they could in an oppressive context. The roles in which Blackfoot were cast did not represent indigenous perspectives. Yet, imperial theatrics afforded indigenous people a public platform where their embodied performances of traditions generated a whole series of effects. To "talk back" to the imperial script, we interpolate voices from a series of interviews (2005–07) we held with Blackfoot in Southern Alberta about their dancing and its role in their communities as they encountered the forces of western expansion. Their accounts of performed events over decades of interaction, including participation in theatricalizations of their own ceremonies, reveal cracks in the façade of the imperial epic, describing ways in which First Nations people accessed tools of theatricalization for their own purposes as they resiliently attempted to weather the onslaught of change.

Western Expansion, an Imperial Fantasy

CHARACTERS
Blackfoot people
Buffalo
Fur Trader
Imperial Dramaturg
John Locke
Imperial Scientist/Adventurers
Whisky Traders
Christian Missionaries
North West Mounted Police
Settlers
European and American Entrepreneurs/Industrialists
Tourists

THE ACTION of the play takes place in Blackfoot country, known to imperialists as the North West territories (now the Canadian provinces of Manitoba, Saskatchewan, and Alberta)

Prologue

A wide expanse, limitless horizons, vast grasslands, millions of buffalo, other animals. Dim light up reveals Blackfoot people, their dance movements synchronized with the rhythm of season changes marked by sublime lighting shifts and native flute and drum soundtrack, thick fog from hazer creates atmosphere of timelessness.

Act One—Expansion

Spotlight picks out entrance of a fur trader, with native guide exchanging goods with these dancers—pots and pans, needles and thread, guns and knives—for furs, exits with large pile of pelts.

Imperial Dramaturg:

Cut! Boring! We need inciting action, more suspense, we need a legitimation of our conquest of this territory . . .

Instead, Blackfoot perform a terrifying war dance, whoop like savages, attack innocent whites, scalp white men, rape white women, steal horses, fight furiously among themselves, create chaos.

Imperial Dramaturg:

Cut! Great theater! Great performances! But, that won't legitimize our conquest! We do all that same raping and pillaging stuff. No. We have to imagine a fundamental difference—like . . .

John Locke:

(Interrupts) . . . how about private property, you are only half a human if you do not own your own land. These Indians don't individually own any land, they just dance around on it.[7]

Imperial Dramaturg:

Ahhh, yes, so we can recast them as homeless and godless primitives, brilliant. Carry on.[8]

Offstage rumbling, a collage of eager and optimistic voices—the Anglo Saxon expansionists from Ontario—and various Sounds of Profit and Modernity—steam engines, whistles, printing presses, mechanical looms, farm implements, pianos. This is the moment of inciting action, the tip of a massive wedge driving westward from England through central Canada to the Western territories. An accelerating onslaught of events, entrances and exits, conflicts and conquests fill the stage.

Enter Imperial Adventurer/Scientists, nervously glancing at the Indians, checking out the dirt, the wind, the water; noting the lack of trees, they mutter, "will anything grow here so ranchers and farmers will come and make wealth for themselves and for us . . .?"

Thousands of Indians sicken and die as the Imperialists make contact in their travels across the stage. In a few brief moments, millions of Buffalo are massacred and they disappear, never to reenter. Thousands of Indians starve and die. Enter American Whisky Traders sneaking up from the American border. They set up renegade trading forts and poison Blackfoot with whisky-like concoctions. Enter the North West Mounted Police (NWMP). They clear the stage of Unscrupulous Whisky Traders. Tragic music ends on a major chord as Christian Missionaries enter. They set up missions, tame—I mean—convert the savages, create pockets of enforced order among the savagery and wreckage, tidying up the stage for Act Two.

Act Two—Settlement

A warm light, center stage, rises on an idyllic tableau of Blackfoot chiefs, Missionaries and agents of the British Empire signing Treaty Seven.

Voice-over proclaims triumphantly population growth statistics, new provinces, new trade routes.

Yet as more and more Imperialists arrive, Blackfoot remain, dancing. Imperialists gaze at them, fear evolves into visible irritation.

Stern voice-over proclaims the Indian Act, bans dancing, creates reserves, instigates forced attendance at residential schools.[9]

Blackfoot people rounded up into small enclosures far from center stage.

Triumphant fanfare. Enter a huge smoke-belching Canadian Pacific Rail Train, bulging with settlers, entrepreneurs, tourists. These newcomers spill out over the whole stage, staking out claims, homesteads, towns, ranches.

Act Three—The Disappearing Indian

Distant sound of mournful Indian flute and drum. Fog. A huge screen upstage fills with the indistinct image of proud warriors—the Blackfoot dancing. Mournful reprise of the prologue. All stop mid-action. Casting backward glances, a few imperialists wipe a nostalgic tear from their eye. All applaud, and turn their eyes to a distant point—the future. Curtain closes as bustling scene of progress recommences.

The script's major dramaturgical problem is that in order to accomplish imperial ambitions around resource extraction and settlement, the stage has to be cleared of the indigenous people. Scriptwriters and producers of empire—imperial and colonial governments, entrepreneurs, and fortune seekers—have to continuously reimagine the Indian characters, as they do not disappear on command. "If any single belief dominated the thinking about Canadian aboriginals during the last half of the nineteenth century, it was that they would not be around to see much of the twentieth. Some found the idea appalling; some found it regrettable; some found it desirable. But all were agreed that the Indian was doomed."[10] This is a crucial point for understanding the unfolding action. In the imperial imagination, the Indian must be continually transformed, to keep up with the changing vision of the colony, the dominion, and the Canadian Nation. In addition, imperial scriptwriters had to contend with the significance and power of the embodied culture—dancing and ceremony—they were disrupting.

WHAT IS BLACKFOOT DANCE?

Blackfoot dance is not, and was not, theatrical in the way that Europeans understood dancing. Dancing for the Blackfoot was an enactment of relationship, renewing through the action of opening sacred bundles, performing the associated songs, and dancing, the relationship to land, to ancestors, and to other beings with whom they shared their existence. "Intended to do something, to make something happen, (indigenous) acts were not metaphorical; they lacked the 'as if' quality of representation . . . Performers of the dancing offer a gift of human expenditure to divine forces rather than entertainment for an audience."[11] Imitation of animals was not an "as if"—a representation of the animal—it was creating and renewing a long-standing relationship with that being. As Inga Clendinnen suggests, reenactment in indigenous dance ceremony animated life-affirming forces, "render[ed] present by simulation."[12] These acts also served to transmit their knowledge, memories, and values from one generation to the next, thus simultaneously assuring their future at another, related, level. Many comments from the people we interviewed spoke of the centrality of dance as an embodiment of culture, and emphasized its resilient, continued existence.

> . . . why Kanai people still dance. You can go back a thousand years and still ask the same question of why. You know, it's just something that's been part of our life. Why do we breathe? Why do we speak? What do, it's sort of the same kind of question. It's always a part of life. Part of life of dancing is part of it. Part of singing of life is part of it. You know, it'll always be with us. It's like the stories and tales and legends are always going to be. We're always going to pass them down. So in respect of why we Kanai or Gana continue these dances and stuff like that, I guess it brings life. And to keep, I guess it kind of like protects you in a sort of speak, it protects you. It's like the warriors of one day used to go out on war parties and that and come and protect you, but that no longer exists anymore, so they preserved it in a way to continue this through dances, through songs. The only way that we can preserve it is to continue and keep the circle strong to protect us from any sickness or anything bad that comes to us.[13]
>
> [N]ow I'm mainly considered the grandfather to bundle holders. Because I've been involved . . . some are older than me but they just come back into it, and so I sit by the door and I remember my grandfather, and I call them my grandfather. Maybe not by blood, but my grandfathers . . . I remember the guy that used to sit there all the time, and the next one was my dad, and a few others since then. And now I'm asked to sit by the door, and I get the privilege of they always put up a chair for me, where I don't have to sit on the ground and I think back . . . and that's . . . that's about the best way I can tell you about that spiritual dance.[14]

Blackfoot elders' accounts reveal the power embedded in dancing, dancing which enacts their profound connection to the land and to their ancestors. Repeated performances of dancing embody a worldview that emphasizes reverence for the land, stewardship of the gifts from the creator, and connections across generations. This was the power that colonial arrivants had to erase, reimagine, and theatricalize in order to transplant a worldview of individualism, private property, and acquisitiveness.[15]

WHAT IS WESTERN EXPANSION?

During the settlement of the Canadian prairies in the nineteenth and twentieth centuries, the colonial government was forced into continuous negotiation with the indigenous populations of First Nations people in order to prepare the landscape for waves of mass arrivals of settler populations. Within and outside of these negotiations, colonist/imperialists did extraordinarily damaging things to indigenous people, their culture, and their land, acts that are incomprehensible (if no less damaging) until set in the context of the imperial imaginary. Ian McKay summarizes expansion as a voracious choreography of consumption and elimination: "One way of visualizing post-Confederation Canadian history is as the rise of a liberal empire centered in the Valley of the St. Lawrence, extending its geographical range and intensifying its ideological hold from 1876 to the present by digesting, rearranging, or eliminating alternative ways of ordering society and culture."[16] Contrast this image with the language used by Beverly Hungry Wolf, describing the colonial encounter from her people's perspective:

> You know, our people were a people that were taught to be kind, to be generous, and . . . and . . . the people that came and made treaties with us their whole world view was to get as much as they could, to use the land as much as they could, rearrange it, you know. The Native people lived in a world, where the world was alright, you know, it was . . . the people, you know, you had to teach them to be kind, because the creator had been really generous with us, the creator gave us everything that we needed to sustain our way of life.[17]

In Canada, the term "western expansionism" refers to a nation-building process promoted by "expansionists" that began in the mid-1800s when the Canadas (Quebec and Ontario) declared, based on government-funded "scientific" reports, that the land west of Ontario was, in short, inhabitable.[18] "For them, the years between 1857 and 1869 simply brought confirmation of the belief that Canada's route to greatness was through the opening and settlement of the North West."[19] While previous characterizations of the great plains and mountains popularized by the Hudson Bay Company's fur traders since the 1600s depicted the landscape as harsh, unfertile, and unwelcoming, expansionists, consisting of the commercial elite and politicians of central Canada, pushed for the government of Canada to explore "settling the West" as the key move in securing Canada's economic growth and national autonomy. By the 1850s expansionists worried about Canada's economic future as Ontario reached its capacity for agricultural development and began losing farmers to the US Midwest, and they saw the west as providing raw materials to support increased manufacturing and a potential population of consumers for these products. Expansionists had varying ideological agendas, but Doug Owram suggests that, "If the focus of the mission in the West changed over time it did possess one basic theme throughout. The Canadian sense of duty in the North West had as its initial determinant the sense of membership in the imperial community."[20] Moving west was simply the next logical step of securing access to land and natural resources for Britain.

Moving west meant that a cluster of actions had to happen all at once whose central aim was to attract new immigrants to Canada for the purpose of growth: negotiate deals with the indigenous inhabitants to acquire their land and its resources, build a railroad to transport settlers and supplies, establish government services such as law enforcement and education, and send in the missionaries to convert the indigenous population to Christianity, the religion of empire. It was a massive undertaking accomplished with unprecedented speed, and it transformed the landscape and the people. "The last half of the nineteenth century constituted a revolution for most of the native societies in the western interior, particularly those of the plains and parkland. None of the changes in the native way of life in the preceding two centuries could be compared to the extraordinary upheaval of this period, and, what is even more striking, nothing could compare with the speed of change."[21] In this avalanche of activity, it is not surprising that we find competing and conflicting agendas, loyalties, and management ideas pertaining to the number one issue that expansionists faced: what to do with the Natives who already occupied this land they wanted for themselves. For example, while the government was concerned with negotiating land treaties with them and bringing law and order to the region in order to advertise the west as a land of opportunity that was safe and open for business, the missionaries were concerned for the souls of the Natives, and the entrepreneurs were cooking up ways to develop a tourist economy in the west that featured domesticated Natives. In 1884, just one year before the completion of the Canadian Pacific Railway, the federal government was composing an amendment to the Indian Act that banned ceremonies, while entrepreneurs in Banff held the first Banff Indian Days to entertain tourists. This clear example of contradictory actions, one federal and one local, helps us grasp just how unsettled the settling of the west really was.

WHAT ARE THEATRICS?

By using "theatrics," we evoke both the term's performative/aesthetic and affective/emotional connotations; the transplantation of the real to the fictional as in staging a performance, and exaggeration and falsification, for example, of emotion as in an overly theatrical display in a temper tantrum. Performance studies theory has emphasized ephemerality as a major feature of theatrical and other kinds of performance—something which disappears. Indigenous dancing, on the other hand, by renewing and repeating performances in cyclical ways emphasizes ongoingness and long-standing relationship, which is antithetical to the Euro-colonial conception of performance as entertainment. "Theatrics" emphasizes the fundamental differences between indigenous dancing and the colonial "theatricalized" appropriation of it.[22] To enact strategies of assimilation, imperial players accompanied enforcement of policy through actual physical actions (for example, containment on reserves, abuse in residential schools), with performative tactics. Underpinning the tactic of theatricalizing the Native was both a total disregard for native cultural practices and the inkling that theatricalizing these practices, turning the sacred into entertainment, would sever the powerful link to land. For the Europeans, the persistence of indigenous memory embodied in cultural practices was exactly what needed to be annihilated for successful integration into modern Canada. Wiping out the embodied performance of identity and connection to place was central to a conquest that willed native cosmologies into extinction. So, European colonialists both banned and theatricalized indigenous dance. Banning the dancing, they recognized its centrality to indigenous existence and sought to replace it with farming, settling down, and praying. Turning enactment into acting, the sense of ancestral and natural/environmental connection into ephemeral entertainment, entrepreneurs theatricalized ceremony, and in the process, turned it into a profitable commodity. The Europeans appropriated acts of memory honoring the present and ensuring a future, transforming them into fleeting moments of entertainment with cash benefits for themselves. That the Blackfoot, like other indigenous peoples across North America, often participated willingly in imperial spectacles seems completely counterintuitive. Drawing on performance and dance studies theory, Foster explains:

Jacqueline Shea Murphy has detailed the extraordinary contradictions in the policies that would prohibit ceremonial dancing but allow commercial dancing, showing that these policies derived from the government's conception of dance as mere entertainment. Examining how and why Native dancers might nonetheless willingly participate in events such as Buffalo Bill Cody's Wild West Show, Shea Murphy argues that in their conception of dance its efficaciousness could be accomplished, regardless of the location, as long as the dancers dedicated themselves to it. Whereas the government officials dismissed dance as entertaining "representation," as a performance that conveyed no impact beyond a momentary diversion, Native dancers believed in their ability to enact the values called into by dancing every time they performed.[23]

The nature and effect of participation in performances is polysemic and multidimensional. The following analyses of theatricalized moments of encounter elucidate some of the many ways that dominance, agency, authenticity, and efficacy are contested in bodily performances as expansion meets indigeneity in Canada's west.

THEATRICAL IMAGES, BRUTAL REALITIES, BORROWED ETHOS

Various theatricalizations of benign Indian/colonial relationships co-existed with laws and policies that sought to orchestrate cultural genocide. Colonial government policy first made indigenous ceremonies and dances illegal by banning ceremonies[24] and later mandated attendance at residential schools, where the Christian emissaries who ran the schools forbade the speaking of indigenous languages and the practice of indigenous culture. Children were forcibly removed from their homes and families and often subjected to corporeal and psychological abuse.[25] Residential school policy would turn out to have by far the most devastating and long-term effect for the First Nations people. "Policy" is such a neutral sounding term, but its effects are anything but neutral. Adam Delaney's life story lets us glimpse how bad policy inflicts wounds on individual bodies and communal lives. The early part of Adam's life went like this: He was put into residential school at age three, when his father died. Thirteen years and five months later he emerged with a fourth grade level of education, and a hearing problem that he attributes to being slapped on the head so often. Was he a "bad" student? The school made sure he was not dancing, not learning his language, and not studying his own or anyone else's knowledge, because he was learning to work—milking cows, digging up root vegetables and putting them in the cellar, or cleaning, any menial work—doing slave labor from sun up to sun down, work that made sure that the school that imprisoned him could stay in business.[26]

While this sort of oppression was occurring, it is astonishing to hear Frank Weasel Head's story about how, in the 1930s, colonial agents used a theatricalized image of authentic native culture to advertise the very institutions that were attempting its eradication.

> In school I couldn't wear my feather or a beaded vest . . . . I'll tell a story of when I moved to school. I couldn't wear any of those, I couldn't bring, I couldn't paint my face, my grandmother couldn't paint me. But then there was going to be a story on the residential school. And the

principal had a buckskin outfit, hawked to him, I had to put it on, get on a horse and be photographed. And grandma had that newspaper clipping of that picture. I don't know whatever
happened to it but she had it framed. So you see why I hate it, I couldn't do that . . . . Yeah, so
it was all a lie, they didn't want us to do that, but to show . . . and then they make us do it. They
make us to do it . . . in some cases they forced us to do it.[27]

Beverly Hungry Wolf, whose generation was among the last group of students forced to
attend residential schools, describes the experience of moving between the school and her
traditional family context as "walking in two worlds." Her account displays the persistence
of the colonial fascination with indigenous culture. This fascination is acknowledged here as
ultimately helping to support the survival of native culture, as Hungry Wolf describes how
First Nations' worldviews were raided in support of counterculture ideologies that developed in the late twentieth century.

Well when I was a little girl I was learning to walk in two worlds, because at boarding school you
don't dare talk about uh stuff that happened at home in a traditional sense. When I was at home
it was like . . . my grandfathers, I came from really exciting people from my point of view . . .
the stories they would tell about the war trips they went on, the healing things that they saw,
and it was . . . you know . . . for me to reconcile those two and make them one, was . . . quite a
journey. Because when I was at residential school, of course we jived and did the twist and rock
and roll dance and, you know, there was an element of looking down at people that followed
the traditional way of life, and after I left school I went to college and there was this big change
happening in main stream society where all the rich people, their kids were turning into hip-
pies and they wanted to know the natural people, in the Americas. And that movement helped
our movement . . . it instilled "oh there's people really looking at our ways, they're finding our
ways exciting," and these are rich kids from all over the world are trying to find out how native
people lived.[28]

This nostalgic "hippy" view of indigenous culture is a more recent manifestation of the
place indigenous culture has held in the colonial imaginary as a kind of antimodernist tonic,
a back-to-the-land fantasy world that offered respite from the forces of twentieth-century
industrialization.

THEATRICAL ANTIMODERNISM

At the same time as assimilationist policies work to eliminate the cultural memory, the western expansionist entrepreneurs invented a new theatrical dance form: "Indian Dance." In
the invented Indian dance, indigenous dancers are cast as members of a disappearing culture, performing a no-longer-viable primeval communion with nature, performances
which serve as an antimodern tonic to the stresses of the progressive, industrial modern life.
One venue where one could experience this antimodern tonic was Banff Indian Days (see
fig. 21.1), a festival of Indian culture designed for tourists.

The construction of the Canadian Pacific Railway (CPR) ensured that the small town of
Banff, Alberta, nestled in the Rockies and Canada's first established National Park, and in
the heart of Stoney sacred lands, would become a center of tourism. The beginning of Banff
Indian Days is an emblematic story about indigenous dance and frontier entrepreneurship:

On June 1884, the Bow River flood washed out several miles of track and stranded guests at the Banff Springs Hotel. Tom Wilson, "Canada's foremost mountain man" who had worked for CPR and then provided independent guiding services for tourists, is credited with inventing Banff Indian Days . . . Realizing the fascination of tourists with Indians, Wilson suggested that the neighboring Stoneys be asked to participate in a series of contests for prizes to be put up by the CPR. He travelled to the Stoney reserve at Morley as the company's emissary and convinced the Indians of the benefits of his plan. A large contingent followed him to Banff, where the braves competed in horse races, bucking and roping competitions and traditional dancing while the women vied to outdo each other in horse packing and tepee [sic] pitching. The hotel guests were so taken with the performance that the CPR, with the assistance of local businessmen, sponsored Banff Indian Days as an annual event.[29]

It is also a story of the meshing of corporate and political interests. The CPR had always been an important factor in empire and nation building. When the government eventually granted the CPR authority to boost immigration they began using settlers as natural resources,[30] mining, importing, and exporting, which also enabled and required the "mining" and packaging of heritage like indigenous dancing.[31] These white men took charge of selling Canada via representations of nature and indigenous peoples, using "the paradoxical process by which the discourses of the nation require the remarginalization of some of its subjects even as they call for assimilation."[32]

The early years of the twentieth century saw other iterations of antimodern nostalgia—the creation of festivals like the Calgary Stampede that theatricalized the Wild West, the cowboy life, and the rodeo. At first the inclusion of Indians in the exhibitions that focused on theatricalizing the "Wild West"' was controversial. In 1909, in flagrant violation of the Indian Act, three hundred Stoney Indians paraded as part of the Dominion Day festival in Banff, and a few days later in Calgary close to six hundred attended the provincial exhibition. Methodist minister Reverend MacDougall disagreed with political officials who felt appearances like this sanctioned paganism, lascivious nudity, and indolence. MacDougall advocated Indian participation, arguing that dancing was part of religious practices and "ought to be tolerated in the spirit of religious liberty." The Indians paraded and were the hit of the festival and became a popular, regular, and still current feature of the Calgary exhibition.[33] Of course, the Blackfoot did not typically express their spirituality by parading through settler towns on horseback. McDougall was able to use his influence as a Christian authority to access tolerance of difference by appealing to people's sense of religion and godliness, which allowed the parade participation. If anything, this parading is an instance of the invention of a new kind of "dancing" of what had formerly been private and intrinsic to native communities, for both Indians and spectators. Parading in regalia, associated with membership in political and sacred societies, was likely not spiritual. Instead, parading became an emblem, of Indianness, and did not represent healing or other spiritual associations—for the participants—as claimed by McDougall. Here "theatrics"—parading down Calgary's main streets—framed tribes' local presence in several different ways. A parade's linear choreography embodies ideas of containment—spectators frame the participants, and of progress—it moves relentlessly forward. As choreographed by the settler organizers, the Stampede parade, that featured both arrivant and indigenous performers, imaginatively demonstrated how the nation-state may contain many identities marching under a single purposeful and preordained direction, organized in ways that implied hierarchies of leaders and followers. Yet the need for participation and witnesses

FIGURE 21.1 Dancing staged in front of CPR Hotel, Banff, during Indian Days. (NA-1241-567 Stoney Dancers at Banff Springs Hotel, Alberta. 1939. Glenbow Archives.)

make any large-scale performance—like festive parades—inherently open systems, unstable moments where many different agents influence their effects. When colonials met Indians in this parade, did they glimpse a "what-if" space, a choreography that both supported and destabilized power and authority? Did spectators interpret the Blackfoot presence as an embodiment of the domestication of the formerly wild Indians, just "actors" in a white-organized festival? First Nations parade participants likely felt a mixture of things; did they feel empowered by their imposing presence in this colonial/settler environment? Ongoing participation in Calgary Stampedes, including the parade, continued to give members of tribes across Alberta a rare opportunity to leave the isolation of their reserves to get together over a period of days every year. In the theatricalized spectacle of the parade, colonial processes of erasure, containment, and appropriation dance with indigenous strategies of protest and persistence.

Events like Indian Days and the Wild West exhibitions were of course not marketed as exercises in marginalization and assimilation. Advertising suggested instead that organizers' praiseworthy presentation of this exotic dancing conserved vestiges of a noble, yet vanishing civilization—in a trope anthropologists of that period now call "the salvage paradigm."[34] We can surely assume that as a kind of migrant worker, the native performers were not the main beneficiaries of the economic success of the festival, but there were other compelling motivations for participating. During the 1930s, Canadian natives remained heavily regulated, often confined on reserves and in abusive situations in ineffective residential schools, and impoverished by the very systems that purported to assist them toward "modernization." In this context, the festival setting brought members of different tribes together where embodied culture was enacted and acknowledged. The environments of touristic festival events continued to provide opportunities where Indians exercised agency.[35] How did the First Nations people themselves feel about these events? Beverly Hungry Wolf explains:

> Sometimes they would be [66:18] invited up to . . . ah . . . Banff, to perform, [and they'd say] Taakitawatato' kwa'kinnawa [We're gonna go play at the holy springs] And they would go and put up their camps and have dances for the tourists that came to the lodge but it was considered playing. And . . . they got paid.[36]

Because of its centrality to the colonial project there was no way of escaping the stereotypical Indian. So, many natives sometimes willingly theatricalized themselves to seize opportunities for cash and community togetherness. This nomadic and seasonal employment mirrored existing aboriginal conceptions of economic activity and survival. Yet primarily it was settler political and economic agendas that were served through the invention of Indian Days festivals and Indian participation in all evocations of the (formerly) Wild West, all of which were constructed to achieve two goals: bringing business to settler communities and performing the colonial ideals of Canada, including the assimilation/erasure of indigenous peoples.

THEATRICALIZING THE CANADIAN MOSAIC

Western expansionism slowed down significantly in the years before World War I, and Canada's internment of German and Ukrainian men in during that war highlighted and reinforced the control that Anglo-Saxon settlers had seized as the nation-builders of modern Canada. Carefully controlling immigration policy by creating lists of desirable newcomers, the Canadian government began a new phase of advertising the west as a land of growth and opportunity. The Canadian Pacific Railway continued to be a key partner in this project, and during the 1920s a series of luxury hotels were built in major centers across the country, a natural addition to the railroad itself and an architectural statement that modern Canada was here to stay. The CPR hired British writer Murray Gibbon as its publicity agent, a position he held for over three decades (1913–45), and gave him what appears to be carte blanche freedom to design and implement his own very colonial choreography of nationhood. Gibbon is credited with coining the term "Canadian Mosaic" in 1938, the beginnings of which can be traced to his creation of a series of folk dance, folk song, and handicraft festivals across the country between 1927 and 1931. One of these festivals was held in Calgary in 1930 and marks a shift from the staging of Indian Dance as a singular spectacle held in site-specific locations to the staging of Indian dance alongside a whole range of culturally specific dance forms representing distinct groups of immigrants in a theatrical setting. Gibbon begins staging Canadian multiculturalism fifty years before the legislation of the official Multiculturalism Act, selling tickets to new and old-time white settlers in order to promote the idea of "racial groups which are now being happily amalgamated into the Canadian nation."[37]

A perhaps astonishing act of imaginative inclusion, was the programming of British old-time dancers and First Nations dancers at a high tea performance prior to the opening night of the Calgary festival. On March 21, 1930, the Calgary Albertan published this review: "Dancing and music at the tea hour, and rows upon rows of rare, exotic and interesting exhibits attracted crowds of people to the Hotel Palliser all Thursday afternoon and evening for the Great West Festival. The first of the three day series of program teas took place in the main dining room of the hotel, opening at 4 o'clock, and here old English folk dancing done with conscious grace and measured tread contrasted strongly with the pure abandon and rousing joyousness of the native Indian dances."[38] After decades of government sanctioned bans on dancing among "Indians" beginning in the 1870s, it seems incredible that the displaced and disappearing "native Indians" were dancing on the same opening-day high tea program as the English "old-timers." Apparently no longer concerned with how dancing would prevent their assimilation into the new settler culture of white Christian farmers, was the government acquiescing to corporate interests, tightly bound as they were to the growing nation of Canada, who promoted the touristic value of the dancing "Indians?" The newspaper review continues,

> The men and women dressed in white danced the simple numbers of the country folk of England much as they were danced on the high days and holidays by a people of gentle yet imaginative minds. The dances are typical of the English people in their easy grace and conventionality. The Indians, on the other hand, danced with great exuberance, their vividly colored costumes suggesting something of the wild gaiety of the whole affair in the Rabbit dance, the Quadrille and the Breakdown, or the Duck Dance, and again in the Handkerchief dance which concluded the series, the spirit of fun and frolic which invested them seemed almost to be caught up by the audience. Wearing moccasins and bright costumes, their long black hair caught up into braids, the women were typical of their race. Reds and orange, black and red, orange and purple and a combination of blue, red and pink fashioned the dresses of the four women dancers, while the men wore vivid neckerchiefs to brighten their costumes. The Handkerchief dance was prettily done with continual toe dancing lasting for some time showing the strength as well as the grace these people possess.[39]

The sentiment in the review that commends the First Nation dancers on their "strength" and "grace" at performing the difficult toe dancing suggests that the reviewer has placed the First Nation dancers on a professional stage where they are evaluated for their technical accomplishments based on a European aesthetic of movement difficulty, such as "toe dancing." Such a pronouncement in a daily newspaper could be read as an indication of a shift in the relationship between settlers and First Nation Canadians, or it could simply be more of the same display tactics used by settlers for years to bring out the "Indians" on special occasions when it suited them. The demand for strong, national economic production was forcing Canadians to take a different view of First Nations' dancing than they held fifty years ago. In the late nineteenth and early twentieth century when Canada was actively recruiting only white European settlers, it had not been in the country's interest to display scary images of "Indians" dancing in wild abandon, so the government banned dancing. But fifty years later, now that the "Indians" had been "managed," on reserves and in residential schools, and amid the Great Depression, it was okay to sell "Indian" dances and handicrafts and to capitalize on their value as "folk." Within the capitalist frameworks of show business and tourism, rather than a colonial and nationalistic one of attracting white settlers, the "Indians" could now contribute the "pure abandon and rousing joyousness" needed to provide aesthetic balance in a variety-style live theatrical entertainment, while the English could take care of the "conscious grace."

The pairing of English and First Nation dancers created a balanced theatrical program, while at the same time displaying a new national identity of multiculturalism that included First Nation people and Europeans. Within this performance narrative, the "residue" of First Nation Canadians were now viewed alongside the British "old-timers," the French Canadians, and other European immigrant groups who possess long traditions of music, dance, and handicrafts that need to be preserved as folklore in the modern age. Dance allowed a list of formerly irreconcilable opposites to coexist in a staged representation and the practices of dancing, singing, and handicrafts could turn "Indians" into "folk," ascribing them collectively higher status than reserve or residential school residents because it put them on the same level as the European immigrants, temporarily. In the structural choreography of the Calgary festival, the "Indians" became one element of the "mosaic" with a need to make equal space for them on the stage and in public life. Including them in the imagined mosaic also paved the way for managing them in a similar manner to other new immigrants, transforming them from "savages" to "peasants." It might be argued that the inclusion of First Nation dancers in the festival could only have happened in a place like Calgary, the "last best west," which was far enough away from central Canada's dominant influence to allow for experimentation with a new script, and far enough away to not really matter.

THE LAST WORDS

The tactics of the colonial project of settlement in already occupied land during Canadian nation-building in the early decades of the twentieth century incorporated theatricalization of Blackfoot dance. The meeting up of radically different populations, with epistemologies and world-views that shared so little in common, and with one group arriving with a clear agenda to make themselves permanent residents, created uneven relations with inequitable outcomes that remain unresolved. The analysis shows a shifting and adaptive approach to these tactics from both the indigenous Blackfoot and the inheritors of the spoils of colonialism. As we write, indigenous peoples in Canada have entered the public arena in force with Chief Teresa Spence from the Attawapiskat reserve in northern Ontario undertaking a high-profile hunger strike to spark changes on apartheid-like impoverished northern reserves. Much of the current press continues to lump together diverse concerns, creating a colonial/native binary that, like previously noxious binaries, is completely counterproductive. Additional nationwide protests, against new omnibus parliamentary bills that are perceived to weaken environmental protections for all Canadians, but that especially weaken First Nations' ability to maintain stewardship of their lands, emerge out of a group called Idle No More, a group of friends who are not all First Nations, who wished to express concerns about the prime minister's environmental policies. The protesters also claim that the omnibus bills will allow government to renege on promises made in the historic treaty process. Pan-Indian round dances, on both gigantic and intimate scales, are the public face of these protests. The visual and audio theatrics that underscore the news stories—holding hands, circling solemnly in synchronization with a regular drumbeat—harken back to embodiments of traditional cultural performances, the inclusive social dances of the plains tribes. The protest performances, with indigenous (and a few nonindigenous) participants display and perform a unity that counters the divide between native and non-native Canadians, a unity which also evades the political bodies that represent First Nations people in Canada. The Calgary 2012 Making Treaty Seven project, involving both First Nations artists and elders and non–First Nations artists, launched in this politicized atmosphere, may, through public theatrical performance, and an accompanying public symposium, contribute to deeper understanding or continue to feed the polarization.

The through-line that we've constructed is of our own devising as we examine ways in which dancing and theatricalization figured in the relationships that occurred under western expansion in Canada. The Blackfoot elders and dancers we interviewed expressed diverse and sometimes conflicting points of view representing not only individual experiences but also gendered and generational perspectives. We began with Pat Twigg's story about how a casual invitation for him to dance theatrically surprisingly brought him back to his traditions. We leave the reader with excerpts from these interviews that reveal how the Blackfoot continue to revisit and to revise the script that imperial expansionism wrote, the last words so to speak.

Theresa Plume mourns the repercussions of the repression of traditional dance:

> Well, . . . First Nation people . . . like, well, just like when you're feeling bad, you know, or really good, like when you say you're in good spirits, hey. There's something inside you that make you feel that way. Like with me, when I started dancing, my friends, you know with the drum group, my husband. We all get up and we have lots of fun. Like say, I'm feeling a high, you know. Where there's laughter and closeness with the other people. So these are the things that you don't see anymore. And today I just see a lot of sadness. That's why I don't like going to the reserve too much.[40]

Karen Many Fingers defends her choice to participate in the neorevival of the forbidden piercing ceremonies of the sun dance and the participation of non-natives in such revivals:

> Well, you know, personally that's part of my teachings is, we can get so caught up in that politics that it takes away from being, who I need to be on this journey as a woman because there's a lot of negative stuff happening in our communities, you know in Lethbridge, on the reserve, everywhere and what I try to do, one of the teachings I got from ceremony was not to get caught up in all what people think.[41]

Narcisse Blood addresses intergenerational conflict about younger generations' perception of pow wow competitions' sacred aspects versus elders' wishes to preserve traditional sacred dance ceremonies:

> I have no problems with that (pow wow and commercialization) because you see the pride that these youngsters have, the validation that they get from being able to express themselves and how the families rally around them. We're very lucky, extremely lucky that we still have what

we have, but our people adapted. You see that's the problem with anthropologists, they've got us stuck in time somewhere that we didn't adapt to change.

A new word came up, "Storycide." It was a very deliberate effort to discredit those stories as just stories, you know and as we're talking about the storyteller to have the capacity, the ability to share and tell a story that you can just experience that you see it, it unfolds. When I was being brought up by my grandparents, the stories she told me, I experienced them, I saw the story . . . . All of that culminates in what I have said before and I have said that on other interviews. Is for me I am playing a very small and yet significant part of a continuum that goes so far back that it's so powerful that I don't know how many of my ancestors that did that. And so I say that expression, "History simultaneously occurs with the present." So when I dance in those ceremonies I am touching those, that aspect of my ancestors that I don't know how far back it goes, but it goes back a long, long way and that's my duty to do that and that is so wonderful, so beautiful words can't express that. So that's why I'm saying is when we do that, when you do the dance that's one aspect of the entire ceremony that is that connection. When we transfer, give me your hand. When we transfer anything we hold the person that's receiving the transfer and we go four times . . . . We have that unbroken hand holding of those ancestors. We're still holding on. So, dance is like that too.[42]

ACKNOWLEDGMENTS

The authors are grateful for the support from Canada's Social Sciences and Humanities Research Council Standard Research Grant, the University of Lethbridge University Scholars Grant; for research assistant and indigenous dance artist Troy Emery Twigg; and for all of the Blackfoot people who participated in various phases of the research. Thanks also to Kim Richards for her professional editing assistance.

NOTES

We have opted to work with several terms interchangeably in referring to First Nations peoples, including "native," "aboriginal," "indigenous," "First Nations" and "Indian." This is a gesture toward the fluidity of terms applied to Canada's first peoples through history, and as outsider voices considering a broad historical time frame, we are not in a position to decide between conflicting opinions of best terminology. Use of "colonial" is not meant to be historically specific (as in neocolonial, imperial, postcolonial) but rather generic, referring to authorities and processes that initiated and continue the occupation of formerly native-occupied territories of North America. To emphasize Canada's history as a settler colony (sharing historical similarity with Australia and New Zealand) we use "colonial/settler" to describe immigrants who remained in Canada.

1. Pat Twigg, "Pat Twigg's Interview on Dance with the Unique History of Blackfoot Dance July 17, 2005," interview by Lisa Doolittle and Troy Emery Twigg, *Blackfoot Digital Library*, July 17, 2005, http://blackfootdigitallibrary.com/en/asset/pat-twiggs-interview-dance-unique-history-blackfoot-dance-july-17-2005.

2. "Who We Are," Calgary 2012.com. http://calgary2012.com/who-we-are/organization (accessed November 16, 2012; site discontinued). Three of five of these "cultural

cornerstones" are theatrical in nature and represent a range of artistic aspirations and configurations: a tourist attraction whose content promotes the remembering and reproduction of the region's colonial and wild-west history; a sandstone proscenium theater in the European traditional style erected as a touring house to connect the city's inhabitants with an international perspective on the performing arts; and a locally produced and consumed community theater operation. The other two institutions (library and recreation) round out the picture with a focus on the intellectual and physical needs of the citizenry.

3. Project description by Michael Green (artistic director of Calgary 2012), personal correspondence, January 24, 2013. For further information on the Making Treaty 7 project see "Making Treaty 7," *The Making Treaty 7 Project*, http://www.makingtreaty7.com/.

4. The Blackfoot confederacy, or *Niitsitapi*, is made up of four nations who all speak a common language, the Blackfoot language. The nations include the Blackfoot, or *Siksikáwa*; the Peigan—*Aapátohsipikáni* or Northern Peigan, and *Aamsskáápipikani* or South Peigan; the Montana Blackfeet; and the *Káínaa*, or Blood Indians. They later allied with the unrelated Sarcee or Tsuu T'ina.

5. Narcisse Blood, "Narcisse Blood's Interview on the Unique History of Blackfoot Dance," interview by Lisa Doolittle and Troy Emery Twigg, *Blackfoot Digital Library*, July 14, 2005, http://blackfootdigitallibrary.com/en/asset/narcisse-bloods-interview-unique-history-blackfoot-dance.

6. Susan Leigh Foster maps these grand themes directly onto bodies as corporealities. She posits that the British established standards of comportment, ideals of discipline to be enacted at home, presumed as universal, and then "proliferated these standards and indexes of behavior to those foreign bodies it desired to govern" (177). "Exoticized as tantalizing excess, or ungovernable abandon, or dark, unknowable alterity, the foreign was treated as something to be managed or ministered to in an effort to salvage some aspect of its humanity" (178). See her book *Choreographing Empathy: Kinesthesia in Performance* (London: Routledge, 2011).

7. "In Locke's time, as European colonizers confronted the reality of Indigenous occupation of the lands they sought to exploit, they 'defined' Indigenous political entities in terms that denied their property rights in the lands *and*, in the same argument, they denied the legitimacy of the political entities themselves, in particular because of the Indigenous system of land tenure. The extent to which this obviously self-serving argument was consciously so is not important. The argument had the effect of rationalizing English appropriation of 'America.'" Frances Abele, "Belonging in the New World: Imperialism, Property and Citizenship," in *Insiders and Outsiders: Essays in Honour of Alan C. Cairns*, edited by Gerald Kernerman and Philip Resnick (Vancouver: University of British Columbia Press, 2005), 218. See also Ian McKay, *The Challenge of Modernity: A Reader on Post-Confederation Canada* (Toronto: McGraw-Hill Ryerson, 1992). McKay observes: "The liberal state has a limited job to do: to protect the rights of the individual. Of all the inalienable rights of individuals, the right to private property was central. Private property, no matter how acquired or on what scale, should take precedence as a value over other social goals" (xiii).

8. This draws extensively on art historian Daniel Francis's perspective: "The Indian began as a White man's mistake, and became a White man's fantasy. Through the prism of White hopes, fears and prejudices, indigenous Americans would be seen to have lost contact with reality and to have become "Indians"; that is, anything non-Natives wanted them to be . . . .

The image of the Other, the Indian, was integral to this process of [Canadian national] self-identification. The Other came to stand for everything the Euro-Canadian was not." Daniel Francis, *The Imaginary Indian: The Image of the Indian in Canadian Culture*, 2nd ed. (Vancouver: Arsenal Press, 2011), 21, 23–25.

9. "The 1857 Gradual Civilization Act was . . . based upon the assumption that the full civilization of the tribes could be achieved only when Indians were brought into contact with individualized property . . . For nearly one hundred years, the commonly held reserve lands were seen as obstacles to the members of the collectivity becoming full citizens of Canada . . . The Canadian state exercised extraordinary control over the lives of reserve members, limiting their mobility, ability to work, and perhaps most damagingly, their religious and traditional political practices." Abele, "Belonging in the New World," 217.

10. Francis, *The Imaginary Indian*, 38.

11. Diana Taylor, "Scenes of Cognition: Performance and Conquest," *Theatre Journal* 56, no. 3 (October 2004): 353–72, doi: 10.1353/tj.2004.0129, 367.

12. Inga Clendinnen, *The Aztecs: An Interpretation* (Cambridge: Cambridge University Press, 1991), 44, quoted in Taylor, "Scenes of Cognition," 367.

13. Raymond Manybears and Harrison Red Crow, "Raymond Many Bears and Harrison Red Crow 2005," interview by Lisa Doolittle and Troy Emery Twigg, *Blackfoot Digital Library*, http://blackfootdigitallibrary.com/en/asset/raymond-many-bears-and-harrison-red-crow-2005.

14. Frank Weasel Head, "Frank Weasel Head's Interview on Dance with the Unique History of Blackfoot Dance June 16, 2005," interview by Lisa Doolittle and Troy Emery Twigg, *Blackfoot Digital Library*, June 16, 2005, http://blackfootdigitallibrary.com/en/asset/frank-weasel-heads-interview-dance-unique-history-blackfoot-dance-june-16-2005.

15. See Diana Taylor: "The almanac, that shows the heavenly bodies in regular, endless motion, is the key to understanding the vital, mutually sustaining relationship of that which disappears and that which endures. The constant making and unmaking points to the active role of human beings in promoting the regenerative quality of the universe, of life, of performance—all in a constant state of reactivation. Through these reiterative acts, Amerindians made sense of the past and the present, even as they tried to secure their future. These acts also served to transmit their knowledge, memories, and values from one generation to the next, thus simultaneously assuring their future at another, related, level. For the Europeans, of course, the persistence of indigenous memory and cultural practices was exactly what needed to be annihilated. Performance-as-ephemeral was central to a conquest that willed native cosmologies into extinction." Taylor, "Scenes of Cognition," 368. See also Foster, describing European concepts of embodiment and how "[t]he (colonial) construction of corporeality enabled a certain view of the world . . . one that accompanied and to some extent facilitated British . . . projects of colonization." *Choreographing Empathy*, 175.

16. McKay, *The Challenge of Modernity*, xi–xii.

17. Beverly Hungry Wolf, "Beverly Hungry Wolf's Interview on Dance with the Unique History of Blackfoot Dance," interview by Lisa Doolittle and Troy Emery Twigg, *Blackfoot Digital Library*, July 11, 2005, http://blackfootdigitallibrary.com/en/asset/beverly-hungry-wolfs-interview-dance-unique-history-blackfoot-dance.

18. Canada changed dramatically during the last fifty years of the nineteenth century, and there is a considerable body of literature devoted to this expansionist period. See,

for example, Gerald Friesen, *The Canadian Prairies: A History* (Toronto: University of Toronto Press, 1987), 129–61; Howard Palmer and Tamara Palmer, *Alberta: A New History* (Edmonton: Hurtig, 1990), chapter 2, 29–49; Howard Palmer "Strangers and Stereotypes: The Rise of Nativism, 1880–1920." in *The Prairie West*, 2nd ed., edited by R. Douglas Francis and Howard Palmer (Edmonton: University of Alberta Press, 1992), chapter 16, 308–28.

19. Doug Owram. *Promise of Eden: The Canadian Expansionist Movement and the Idea of the West* (Toronto: University of Toronto Press, 1980), 78.

20. Owram, *Promise of Eden*, 125–26.

21. Gerald Friesen quoted in McKay, *The Challenge of Modernity*, 3.

22. See Foster's *Choreographing Empathy* for an extended exploration of how the combination of British colonial conceptions of empathy, choreography, and kinesthesia "were mobilized in part to rationalize operations of exclusion and othering" (11). She places her investigation of these terms into the context of Britain's discovery of the new world and subsequent colonial expansion, and poses the question of the power relations inherent between those who feel and those who feel for or with others. This perspective informs this chapter.

23. Foster, *Choreographing Empathy*, 161–62. This is the effect referred to by elder Pat Twigg in the opening citations.

24. Just eight years after the proclamation of the Indian Act in 1876, a section was added that expressly forbade the cultural practice known as potlatching, a give-away type of ceremony that included dancing. In 1894, the prohibition was extended to dances of the Plains Indians. Many amendments of various kinds ensued (many of which remained as part of policy until 1951) to variously contain amount of time spent dancing, control the spaces for dancing, and dictate the purposes and practices of the dance—the chest-piercing part of the sun dance ceremony was forbidden as a practice of torture, for example. Gatherings for the purpose of ceremonial dances were suspected of allowing political agitation. Administrative enthusiasts of the dance ban attempted to prohibit dancing at exhibitions, but it was a major tourist attraction and exhibition organizers ignored prohibitions. See E. Brian Titley, *A Narrow Vision: Duncan Campbell Scott and the Administration of Indian Affairs in Canada* (Vancouver: University of British Columbia Press, 1986), 165–67.

25. In 1932 only 100 students out of an enrolled 17,163 reached grade 6. John Sheridon Malloy, "A National Crime: The Canadian Government and the Residential School System 1879–1969," in *Diversity and First Nations Issues in Canada*, edited by John A. Roberts, Darion Boyington, and Shahe Kazarian (Toronto: Emond Montgomery, 2012), 47.

26. Adam Delaney, "Adam Delaney's Interview on the Blackfoot Dance: Selected Perspectives Project," interview by Lisa Doolittle and Troy Emery Twigg, *Blackfoot Digital Library*, July 11, 2005, http://blackfootdigitallibrary.com/en/asset/adam-delaneys-interview-blackfoot-dance-selected-perspectives-project.

27. Weasel Head, "Frank Weasel Head's Interview."

28. Hungry Wolf, "Beverly Hungry Wolf's Interview."

29. E. J. Hart, *The Selling of Canada: The CPR and the Beginning of Canadian Tourism* (Banff: Altitude, 1983), 59.

30. The Railway Agreement of 1925 allowed the nation's two train companies to recruit cheap labor under the guise of importing European agriculturalist immigrants. http://www.pier21.ca/research/immigration-history/railway-agreement-1925

31. "Alexander Begg's Emigration Department had launched its campaign to sell CPR lands in western Canada as early as 1881 with the distribution of the settlement guide *The Great Prairie Provinces of Manitoba and the Northwest Territories*. Soon afterward it began to distribute tens of thousands of maps, folders, and pamphlets in ten languages to agencies all over Britain and continental Europe. Coordinating its activities out of its London office, the department published ads regularly in 167 British and 147 continental journals and newspapers." Hart, *The Selling of Canada*, 22.

32. Ibid., 91.

33. Titley sets the context in which McDougall's defense took place: "Indian dances at exhibitions were thus opposed not just because they interfered with farming and had a demoralizing effect on participants and onlookers, but also because they fostered the wrong image of the Dominion (of Canada) abroad . . . Indian dancing suggested a raw frontier primitiveness that the country's image-makers wished to dispel." *A Narrow* Vision, 172–73. This early twentieth-century attitude contrasts sharply with the 1930s nostalgia for the vanishing Indian.

34. See Carol J. Williams, *Framing the West: Race, Gender and the Photographic Frontier in the Pacific Northwest* (Oxford: Oxford University Press, 2003), 81.

35. See the illuminating discussion of agency for Indian performers in shows like *Buffalo Bill's Wild West* in Jacqueline Shea Murphy, *The People Have Never Stopped Dancing: Native American Modern Dance Histories* (Minneapolis: University of Minnesota Press, 2007), 57–80. She argues that governments used the "theatrical disciplinary system" as part of ongoing strategies to contain and eliminate the power of Indian spiritual practices, which performed their connections to the land, yet these theatrical productions did not effectively contain Native American agency.

36. Hungry Wolf, "Beverly Hungry Wolf's Interview."

37. *Great West Canadian Folkdance, Folksong and Handicrafts Festival Program* (Canadian Pacific Railway Company, 1930), 2, Glenbow Museum Archives and Library Databases.

38. *Calgary Albertan*, 1930, 5.

39. Ibid.

40. Theresa Plume, "Theresa Plume May 31, 2005," interview by Lisa Doolittle and Troy Emery Twigg, *Blackfoot Digital Library*, May 31, 2005, http://blackfootdigitallibrary.com/en/asset/theresa-plume-may-31-2005.

41. Karen English, "Karen English August 22, 2005," interview by Lisa Doolittle and Troy Emery Twigg, *Blackfoot Digital Library*, August 22, 2005, *Blackfoot Digital Library*,

42. Blood, "Narcisse Blood's Interview."

BIBLIOGRAPHY

Abele, Frances. "Belonging in the New World: Imperialism, Property and Citizenship." In *Insiders and Outsiders: Essays in Honour of Alan C. Cairns*, edited by Gerald Kernerman and Philip Resnick. Vancouver: University of British Columbia Press, 2005.

Blood, Narcisse. "Narcisse Blood's Interview on the Unique History of Blackfoot Dance." Interview by Lisa Doolittle and Troy Emery Twigg. *Blackfoot Digital Library*, July 14, 2005. http://blackfootdigitallibrary.com/en/asset/narcisse-bloods-interview-unique-history-blackfoot-dance.

Delaney, Adam. "Adam Delaney's Interview on the Blackfoot Dance: Selected Perspectives Project." Interview by Lisa Doolittle and Troy Emery Twigg. *Blackfoot Digital Library*, July 11, 2005. http://blackfootdigitallibrary.com/en/asset/adam-delaneys-interview-blackfoot-dance-selected-perspectives-project.

Hungry Wolf, Beverly. "Beverly Hungry Wolf's Interview on Dance with the Unique History of Blackfoot Dance." Interview by Lisa Doolittle and Troy Emery Twigg. *Blackfoot Digital Library*, July 11, 2005. http://blackfootdigitallibrary.com/en/asset/beverly-hungry-wolfs-interview-dance-unique-history-blackfoot-dance.

Foster, Susan Leigh. *Choreographing Empathy: Kinesthesia in Performance*. London: Routledge, 2011.

Francis, Daniel. *The Imaginary Indian: The Image of the Indian in Canadian Culture*. 2nd ed. Vancouver: Arsenal Press, 2011.

Friesen, Gerald. *The Canadian Prairies: A History*. Toronto: University of Toronto Press, 1987.

Great West Canadian Folkdance, Folksong and Handicrafts Festival Program. N.p.: Canadian Pacific Railway Company, 1930. 2. Glenbow Museum Archives and Library Databases.

Hart, E. J. *The Selling of Canada: The CPR and the Beginning of Canadian Tourism*. Banff: Altitude, 1983.

Malloy, John Sheridon Malloy. "A National Crime: The Canadian Government and the Residential School System 1879–1969." In *Diversity and First Nations Issues in Canada*, edited by John A. Roberts, Darion Boyington, and Shahe Kazarian, 47. Toronto: Emond Montgomery, 2012.

Manybears, Raymond, and Harrison Red Crow. "Raymond Many Bears and Harrison Red Crow 2005." Interview by Lisa Doolittle and Troy Emery Twigg. *Blackfoot Digital Library*. http://blackfootdigitallibrary.com/en/asset/raymond-many-bears-and-harrison-red-crow-2005.

McKay, Ian. *The Challenge of Modernity: A Reader on Post-Confederation Canada*. Whitby: McGraw-Hill Ryerson, 1992.

Murphy, Jacqueline Shea. *The People Have Never Stopped Dancing: Native American Modern Dance Histories*. Minneapolis: University of Minnesota Press, 2007.

Owram, Doug. *Promise of Eden: The Canadian Expansionist Movement and the Idea of the West*. Toronto: University of Toronto Press, 1980.

Palmer, Howard. "Strangers and Stereotypes: The Rise of Nativism, 1880–1920." In *The Prairie West*, 2nd ed., edited by R. Douglas Francis and Howard Palmer, 308–28. Edmonton: University of Alberta Press, 1992.

Palmer, Howard, and Tamara Palmer. *Alberta: A New History*. Edmonton: Hurtig, 1990.

Plume, Theresa. "Theresa Plume May 31, 2005." Interview by Lisa Doolittle and Troy Emery Twigg. *Blackfoot Digital Library*, May 31, 2005. http://blackfootdigitallibrary. com/en/asset/theresa-plume-may-31-2005.

Taylor, Diana. "Scenes of Cognition: Performance and Conquest." *Theatre Journal* 56, no. 3 (October 2004): 353–72. doi: 10.1353/tj.2004.0129.

Titley, E. Brian. *A Narrow Vision: Duncan Campbell Scott and the Administration of Indian Affairs in Canada*. Vancouver: University of British Columbia Press, 1986.

Twigg, Pat. "Pat Twigg's Interview on Dance with the Unique History of Blackfoot Dance July 17, 2005." Interview by Lisa Doolittle and Troy Emery Twigg. *Blackfoot Digital Library*, July 17, 2005. http://blackfootdigitallibrary.com/en/asset/pat-twiggs-interview-dance-unique-history-blackfoot-dance-july-17-2005.

Weasel Head, Frank. "Frank Weasel Head's Interview on Dance with the Unique History of Blackfoot Dance June 16, 2005." Interview by Lisa Doolittle and Troy Emery Twigg. *Blackfoot Digital Library*. June 16, 2005. http://blackfootdigitallibrary.com/en/asset/frank-weasel-heads-interview-dance-unique-history-blackfoot-dance-june-16-2005.

Williams, Carol J. *Framing the West: Race, Gender and the Photographic Frontier in the Pacific Northwest*. Oxford, Oxford University Press, 2003.

"Who We Are." Calgary 2012.com. Accessed November 16, 2012. http://calgary2012.com/who-we-are/organization (site discontinued).

CHAPTER 22

....

A SLIP ON THE CABLES
Touristic Rituals and Landscape Performance in Yosemite National Park

....

SALLY ANN NESS

... bodily form does not simply express the social structure but also endows the self with particular capacities through which the subject comes to *enact* the world.

Saba Mahmood (anthropologist), *The Politics of Piety*[1]

Choreography is a way of thinking ... laying out the pieces, *organizing the trail*. Choreography is a way of seeing the world, the things that move against each other and then back into their own places.

Liz Lerman (choreographer), *Hiking the Horizontal*[2]

INTRODUCTION:
RITUAL THEORY AND TOURISTIC PERFORMANCE

Tourism today is a trillion-dollar industry mobilizing close to a billion travelers every year. The industry may not, at first glance, appear to share much in common with the performing arts of theater and dance. The actions and experiences of an ecotourist hiking on a path through some wilderness area may not on the surface bear any great resemblance to those of an actor performing on a cosmopolitan concert stage or a choreographer at work in a rehearsal studio. However, theorists of tourism have repeatedly found connections between the domains of tourism and the performing arts.[3] Conventionally recognized forms of theater and dance have often acquired the status of key tourist attractions. Even more basically, tourism can be observed as fundamentally theatrical and choreographic in its own right. As an enterprise, tourism always involves *staging* in some way, and this is as basic to its character and operation as it is to the performing arts. Tourism also depends on experiences of role-playing, not only as witnessed by tourists but as performed by them. Again, this is as central to tourism as it is to dance and theater. Whether they are acting like nobility, visiting castles on the Rhine, or impersonating great explorers in their adventures discovering new worlds, tourists are engaged in theatrical and choreographic processes that are comparable to those of more conventional kinds of performance, even if they are not exactly identical to them.[4]

Given these parallels, the study of tourism can shed light on what it means, very broadly speaking, to perform and on how it is that a person can become a performer, a role-player, and a staged being in the first place. It also can address the question of where, when, and how theatrical and choreographic kinds of performance can emerge and take form in the world at large—the world beyond the specialized subcultures of the performing arts. These lines of inquiry are best pursued, however, when the concept of performance is defined, not in terms of genres that do and don't exhibit it, but, rather, as a potential aspect of all action. In this regard, the concept of performance I espouse in this chapter aligns with that developed by sociolinguist Richard Bauman in his work on verbal art. It defines a broad spectrum of activity that exhibits both an emergent significance and an inherent capacity for appreciation, whether or not it is ever witnessed by any conventional audience.[5] In a nutshell, I look at performance as that aspect of action that makes it *lively*, so lively that it becomes attractive, engaging, and consequential when it might not otherwise be so. I observe tourists as caught up in acts of role-playing, staged for them by the industry, in which the characters they create and bring to life are none other than *themselves*, yet they are characters that can live and move and have their being most realistically only on the stages where they are enacted and made animate.

The correspondences between tourism and the performing arts of theater and dance may be attributed, at least in some measure, to the fact that the roots of all three appear to lie, however remotely, in ritual. It is not surprising, in this regard, that inquiry into the relation of the embodied performances of tourism and those of ritual has been one of the most productive theoretical foci motivating the study of tourism from anthropological orientations. Pioneers in tourism research pursuing this line of argument cast tourism as a "sacred journey," or as "secular ritual," to call attention to tourism's nonordinary, out-of-the-everyday, theatrical characteristics, and to its potential for producing transformative human experience. [6] Such characterizations have retained enduring value in tourism studies discourse.[7] Understanding both the enacted and the embodied aspects of tourism has to a significant degree been gained by investigating the ways in which it compares to ritual performance processes and functions.

It is my purpose in this essay to review and elaborate on the theory of tourism as secular ritual—specifically secular pilgrimage ritual. I seek to demonstrate in so doing how performance theory, when applied within an ecological framework of analysis, can produce a more accurate understanding of the capacity of touristic rituals in particular, and staged, embodied performances in general, to transform and create anew, certain cultural constructions (character roles in theatrical terms) that are typically understood to define subjective forms of individual identity. More important, however, such performances can also intervene in and reinitiate even more basic processes defining what it means to identify one's self as a living human being in the first place—as a playable figure, more broadly speaking, in the world at large. This more basic sense of personhood, or subjectivity, I argue, emerges in performances that stage the physical and energetic (in other words, *choreographic*) enactment of inhabiting a non-human-designed place or landscape. When such performances are understood ecologically, tourism's embodied rituals challenge not only the secular-religious and quotidian/extraordinary binaries that typically have been used to define them, but also the more general theories of culture and society in whose terms they, as well as the staged, embodied, role-animating enactments of the performing arts have been conceptualized as well.

THE DISCOURSE OF SECULAR RITUAL

One key feature of "secular ritual" tourism theory, particularly as articulated in pioneering anthropological analyses of tourism, has been that the relation between touristic and religious ritual processes is understood to be historically continuous, similar to the relation sometimes posited between conventional modern forms of theater and ancient Greek ritual. That is, touristic processes are understood as modern practices produced in relation to Western industrial forms of social organization that have replaced, or are in the process of replacing, religious rituals of older, premodern, traditional ways of life. Anthropologist Nelson Graburn, for example, in his seminal essay, "Tourism: the Sacred Journey," observes, "Vacations involving travel, i.e., tourism, since all 'proper' vacations involve travel, are the modern equivalent of secular societies to the annual lifelong sequences of festivals for more traditional God-fearing societies."[8] Touristic experience, although it evolved out of religious experience, was understood to be fundamentally different from it, as it existed in structural opposition to various formations of Western industrial labor.[9] Given this work/leisure structural dynamic, touristic practices were conceptualized as *secular* rituals. In Victor Turner's often-cited terms, they were identified as the staged "liminoid," counterparts[10] of premodern liminal religious ritual traditions.

The multidisciplinary evolution of secular ritual discourse over the last several decades has elaborated and qualified considerably this main argument, recognizing the diversity of what "modern society" can mean globally as it relates to various religious institutions and practices. However, what has remained continuous throughout this evolution has been an emphasis on the importance of tourism's experiential processes as they oppose or balance those of work and mundane life. Tourism theorists who have made more recent contributions to the discourse have generally written against research on tourism that characterizes its highly varied array of activities and pursuits as superficial, inauthentic, illusionary, or otherwise inferior with regard to their cultural and social meaningfulness.[11] While the discourse has continued to recognize tourism's secular foundations in a work/leisure binary, it has steadfastly rejected the line of reasoning that tourism's recreational or leisure social status renders it essentially profane and relatively trivial in experiential and cultural impact. On the contrary, following the line of argument established by Sally Falk Moore and Barbara Myerhoff in their edited volume, *Secular Ritual*,[12] proponents have demonstrated repeatedly that touristic experiences, in contrast to those of the workplace, or the home, or some other context of the everyday, have the capacity to transform the belief systems of their participants at fundamental levels, engaging vitally important, often otherwise unquestionable values that arouse profound emotions. They do this through a spectrum of performance processes whose staged and role-playing characters may be more or less evident, but which are generally integral to their transformative outcome. What enables the experiences of tourism to be taken seriously, in other words, what endows them with a cultural significance that is extraordinary, is their character as secular rituals.

The vacational identity of touristic practice, in this regard, has not been observed by proponents of secular ritual theory to render tourism's practices any less meaningful, powerful, or out-of-the-everyday. It simply renders them "secular"—neither prescribed nor ordained by the conventions of explicitly religious laws or doctrines. In this regard, Graburn associated touristic travel with the sacred phases of social life, only occasionally using scare quotes when employing the term "sacred" to characterize what it was that tourists valued most in their vacation experiences, and stressing that there was no absolute boundary between touristic and other forms of ritual life.[13] Throughout the history of secular ritual theory, what has connected the subjects of tourism and ritual is an understanding of tourism as belonging to the extraordinary, nonmundane times, places, and landscapes, of given social and/or cultural structural systems.

The understanding of tourism as secular ritual, in this regard, is itself based in a particular theory of social life, one in which human society is ordered by social institutions that define human experience and subjective identity according to their own interrelationships and the discourses they generate. Thus, as Graburn argues, tourist's choices in regard to the particular kind of experience or style of tourism practice they elect to pursue are governed by the cultural structure of the tourist's home society.[14] The extraordinary, often theatrical, character of tourist experience, likewise, is itself seen to be a consequence of the position in the larger cultural structure that is assigned to the touristic practice that endows it with such value. This touristic value holds its meaning in relation to those that the structure assigns to practices occurring in the relatively ordinary, utilitarian institutions of work or home. The activities, pursuits, and experiences of any tourist, in this regard, are seen to be a predictable outcome of his or her social identity and position within the larger sociocultural structure. Discourses and social roles defined in terms of class, occupation, race, gender, age, and ethnicity predispose tourists to seek out and experience along discursively prefigured lines, certain kinds of secular ritual.

Such a view of touristic rituals—and of cultural performances more generally—downplays the significance of the performance processes that constitute them. Ritual performance processes tend to be seen as the overdetermined expressions, albeit meaningful expressions, of the social structures that create their defining, attractive, and dramatic features. The staging of the performance and the roles played in ritual performance are basically reiterative in this regard, exhibiting little or no agentive character in and of themselves. While the performers in particular may be recognized as instrumental enactors, they are not, insofar as they are understood to be culturally constructed subjects, considered social *actors*, initiating consequential movements that might determine the course of the ritual action and the meaning it accrues. Likewise, the staging of the performance is considered a more or less mechanical execution of predetermined rules and conventions always already formulated in existing, well-established social and cultural discourses.

This social constructionist view of ritual practice recently has been challenged, however, by anthropologist and ritual theorist, Saba Mahmood. Mahmood's outstanding theoretical work on the relation of ritual, subjectivity, embodiment, and performance has gained widespread attention throughout the area of ritual studies in anthropology.[15] It is employed here as an exemplary point of departure for the present investigation of secular rituals occurring in Yosemite National Park. Mahmood argues against the constructionist view of ritual identified above, which she claims has dominated and continues to dominate anthropological analyses of ritual.[16] Employing and expanding on Judith Butler's performative theory of subject formation instead, Mahmood argues that ritual practices in general do not simply reinscribe nonpragmatic, "extraordinary" discursive symbolism onto passive human subjects. Rather, ritual practices provide a means by which participants can engage performatively, and thus agentively, in the mental-spiritual-physical constitution of their own subjectivity, their own sense of themselves as social and cultural individuals. Using as her case in point the practices of Muslim women involved in the mosque movement of Cairo, Egypt, Mahmood writes, "In this formulation ritual is not regarded as the theater in which a performed self enacts a script of social action; rather, the space of ritual is one among a number of sites where the self comes to acquire and give expression to its proper form."[17] It is this performative aspect of ritual that endows it with extraordinary meaning, rather than its theoretically extraordinary position in some larger social structure. Performance processes enacted by individual adherents of a ritual tradition may, in Mahmood's view, creatively enable the continuity of rituals as living, at times even spontaneously occurring, traditions.[18]

A Touristic Case in Point

As the following case of a touristic pilgrimage in Yosemite National Park will attempt to illustrate, what Mahmood has argued to be the case for traditional religious rituals can also be demonstrated for tourism's secular rituals as well. The practices that tourists engage in can be understood not simply as passive reenactments of already established social structures, identities, and discourses. Rather, they can be understood as the creative means by which subjects render themselves *who they are* as relatable, identifiable selves with respect to their given social and cultural worlds. Such a perspective yields deeper insight into both the societal and the subjective significance of touristic rituals. It illuminates how touristic practices, via their very performativity, create the conditions out of which extraordinary forms of ritual symbolism and of performance symbolism more broadly speaking, may be born.

However, the ethnographic description that substantiates this claim of tourism's performative significance also makes evident another. Once the performative dimensions of touristic ritual processes are observed in move-by-move detail, the discursively oriented theories of performance on which Mahmood's and Butler's analyses depend are also revealed to be inadequate to the task of conceptualizing the entirety of the subject-constituting, role-playing, and identity-defining processes that are occurring. Such discursive orientations invariably efface the very processes by which conventional symbolic formations and the roles they articulate emerge and are acted on via more basic formations and stages of performance production. These formations and stages relate to and incorporate place-specific, nonhuman aspects of performance into ritual and, eventually, into its social conventions of symbolic thought and enactment.

In the case of ecotouristic performance practice, it is the performative role of the destination landscape, in particular its nonhuman environmental features, in the staging and role-playing of touristic rituals that falls outside of an exclusively discursive analytical framework. In neglecting this, such theories fail to shed critical light on the kinds of meaning-making that render the term "secular" in relation to touristic rituals most problematic. They also fail to do full justice to the theatrical and choreographic role place can assume in the reinvention of self-world identifications as they occur in these kinds of touristic ritual processes.

The Half Dome Legendary Trail: A Self-testing Rite of Touristic Pilgrimage

Of all the embodied forms of touristic practice that might be exemplary of tourism's ritual performances, those that are constituted by elaborate forms of locomotion, such as hiking and climbing in wilderness landscapes, are in many ways the most outstanding and the most dramatically staged. Graburn identified these forms as "paralleling" religious rites of passage, in particular rites of pilgrimage. The qualities of nature, health, and wilderness, he noted, can effectively replace the conventional roles played by explicitly divine characters and, so, serve to inspire manifestations of wonder, awe, rapture, and reverence of an extraordinarily intense transformative character.[19]

Graburn classified touristic practices of this kind as "self-testing" in recognition of the arduous nature of the physical activity typically involved. Self-testing rituals, in the Western individualist discourses of modern tourism, he noted, served the social purpose of proving to the tourist/initiate his or her capacity to successfully make the life changes the rite of passage and its performance were designed to support and to symbolize.[20] The tourist performed the rite so as to enact a redefinition of his or her own individual character, in effect mastering a new role that would identify the tourist henceforth as a different kind of social being or player. Graburn's characterization of such forms of tourism as providing opportunities for self-testing rites of passage has maintained its currency in the tourism studies literature until the present time.[21]

This chapter reports on what might be, in the specific context of North American popular culture, the most renowned of all such self-testing ecotourism practices of the last century and a half: the hike to the summit of Half Dome in Yosemite National Park. After giving a brief synopsis of the classic Half Dome hiking ritual performance profile, the chapter will recount one performative moment that actually occurred on the crux of the Half Dome trail—a slip on the cables approaching Half Dome's summit. The episode illustrates one way in which the emergence of an original experience of individual self-definition and role-playing was staged ecologically via embodied performance in this particular visitor landscape, generating the seeds of a new self-world identification and a new embodiment of subjecthood.

The Half Dome Hike

A Yosemite "classic route,"[22] Half Dome is the sheerest cliff in North America. Its massive granite formation rises almost 5,000 feet above the floor of Yosemite Valley to an altitude of 8,842 feet, presenting a two-thousand-foot northwest face that is only seven degrees

FIGURE 22.1 Half Dome seen from the Yosemite Falls Trail, May 2011. Photo by Sally Ann Ness.

off absolute vertical (see fig. 22.1 and OWM Icon 22.1).[23] Its topographical structure embodies a monumental character that guidebooks to the park agree has become iconic of the park landscape.[24] This is evidenced in the logos of both the park's main concessionaire, Delaware North Companies, as well as its main service organization, the Yosemite Conservancy.[25] Both present images of Half Dome as their central iconic figure.

In Native American myth and religion, Half Dome, or *Tis-se-yak*, as it is named in the language of the Ahwahneechee people, has always been recognized as a sacred site. The name Tis-se-yak refers to a mythological character, a woman, who drank from the waters at the base of the dome, and who, as a consequence of a conflict with her husband, was turned into the stone constituting the dome. Her face is believed to be visible toward the top of the dome's northwest face, as are her tears.[26] The dome, however, is presented to park visitors, in both official and commercial discourse and imagery, in mainly secular terms. While the Tis-se-yak mythology is sometimes mentioned, Half Dome is generally characterized as a place affording spectacular views of the Valley from its summit, as well as providing a

OWM 22.1 North face of Half Dome, or Tis-se-yak, seen from Glacier Point, July 2005. Tis-se-yak's face appears within the darker regions of the north face. Photo by Erich Reck.

scenic wonder in its own right. It is this non–Native American, secular ecotouristic characterization that is generally understood to motivate Half Dome's touristic self-testing rite of
pilgrimage.

The hike from Yosemite Valley's floor to the summit of Half Dome is around 16 miles
round trip and involves an elevation gain of 4,842 feet.[27] It can only be done between late
May and early October, when snow is least likely to be present. The hike is, by all published
English language accounts "strenuous." Guidebooks recommend allowing 9 to 14 hours for
the hike, if it is attempted in a single day.[28] An overnight strategy, which divides the hike into
two unequal sections, is also a popular alternative—a 4.4-mile hike into the Little Yosemite
Valley campground on the first day, gaining 2,100 feet, leaving the remainder of the ascent
and all of the descent for the following day.

The popularity of the Half Dome trail cannot be overstated, as far as American ecotourism and the internationally diverse visitor population it attracts is concerned. While the
Yosemite landscape affords innumerably various kinds of hiking, and while it is certainly
hiked and experienced in almost inconceivably many ways by its diverse visitor population,
the Half Dome trail, in its contemporary manifestation, nonetheless attracts and engages a
kind of "outdoors"-loving tourist that is archetypal of the contemporary American National
Park visitor subject identity. As veteran hiking guide and American wilderness expert
Suzanne Swedo states in one of her several Yosemite guidebooks, "Half Dome is the symbol
of Yosemite: its summit the goal of just about everybody who has ever donned a pair of hiking boots."[29] While the Half Dome trail is not the trail that every Yosemite visitor hikes—in
fact only a minority of them actually do—it is the trail that epitomizes what the hiker role,
as an admirable visitor character type, is all about. It is the hiking performance to which all
other Yosemite hiking experiences, among many others, may be compared and by which
they may be judged, in terms of their virtuosity and the self-testing ritual they are capable of
staging and enacting.

In its most heavily trafficked recent years, the count of hikers on the summit of Half
Dome during peak season rose to over 1,300 a day. A series of accidents and other problems related to overuse, however, compelled the National Park Service to institute a permit system in 2010. Since that time the daily number of hikers reaching the summit has
decreased to around 400. The ongoing popularity of the hike is indicated both by the fact
that the National Park Service has resorted to a lottery system to issue permits to the large
number of applicants and also by the severity of the penalty for hikers attempting to summit
without a permit. Fines of up to $5,000 as well as a jail sentence of up to six months may be
imposed.[30] The popularity of the hike is also indicated by the large array of consumer goods,
including T-shirts, coffee mugs, and water bottles, that are sold in the Valley's shops. These
sport the phrase, "I made it to the top!," and most have an image of Half Dome emblazoned
somewhere on them as well. Sales of these items number in the thousands each year. They
are a significant source of income for the park's primary concessionaire, Delaware North
Corporation.

The route of the Half Dome hike, as developed and maintained by the National Park
Service, divides into six, clearly defined stages. Each endows the summit pilgrimage with a
socially distinct and place-specific opportunity for enactment of the self-testing character
role. Collectively, they produce a structured ritual complex that has the capability to instill
a deep and enduring appreciation of the grandeur and sublime beauty that are claimed to
be inherent in the park landscape and to afford tourists the opportunity to play the role of

the heroic wilderness explorer to its ecological hilt. Actual visitor experiences of the Half Dome hike are, of course, as diverse as the visitor population that attempts it. However, the way in which the trail is constructed and managed, the self-selected specificity of the hiking population, and the distinctive givens of the nonhuman features of the environment all combine to define as well a performance profile of sorts that sets a standard against which actual individual pilgrimages may be interpreted. How closely visitors approximate in their own experience this general profile varies greatly, of course. However, since it is the profile that best symbolizes and defines the ritual's staging and role-playing capacities, it is this classic hiking experience that I summarize below.

The first stage of the ritual complex is a steep, wide .8-mile asphalt path that leads through oak and pine forest, gaining around 500 feet in elevation to arrive at a bridge over the Merced River (see fig. 22.2). Here, the most easily accessible view of one of the park's "crown jewel" waterfalls, Vernal Fall, can be obtained (see OWM Icon 22.2).[31] This initial section is designed and maintained so as to be used by the entire spectrum of Yosemite's international array of tourists: honeymooners of all shapes and sizes, families with children in strollers, ninety-something great-grandmothers, heavily racked-up climbers off to tackle a "big wall," as well as experienced backpackers heading out for weeks on the Pacific Crest Trail.[32] At the bridge that is its end, visitors stop to rest, use bathrooms and water fountains available there, and take pictures. It is the first station of a longer pilgrimage for summiters, but the ultimate reward for many other visitors. The Vernal Fall Bridge stages a kind of gateway, in this regard, by which Half Dome summiters may leave and reenter a relatively diverse social world compared to that in which they are immersed while hiking. They typically arrive at this bridge at the beginning of the day, at first light or even before, being among the first to reach it. When they return, they will pass over it in the early evening when it is far more heavily trafficked. This affords them a chance to compare and contrast the role they have played while hiking in relation to those they can now observe being enacted by other visitors.

Across the bridge, the second stage of the Half Dome hike will bring hikers to the top of first Vernal and then Nevada Falls, over a distance of approximately 3 miles, and an elevation gain of nearly 1,400 feet (see fig.22.3). This section can be accomplished by one of two standard trails. One route, called the Mist Trail, brings hikers up beside both falls, affording close-up views of both. It is very heavily trafficked and its large stone steps are often slippery from the fall's spray. It is popular with summiters on a single-day schedule (not carrying heavy packs) and also with those who may never be able to hike the trail again, as it is a "legendary trail" (in National Park Service discourse) of extraordinary scenic value in and of itself. The other alternative is to continue on a slightly longer, less steep trail that arrives at the top of Nevada Fall by traversing an eastern corner of Yosemite Valley's southern wall. In either case, this second stage of the hike affords hikers their first experience of prolonged ascent. Coats, hats, and gloves, typically are taken off and stowed away as hikers move from "warmed-up" to "second winded" in their physical condition. Snack breaks are often taken, as pictures of the falls are shot. The ending point of this stage is marked by another bridge also built over the Merced River, now at a higher elevation (see OWM Icon 22.3).

This second stage of the route is still accessible to a wide variety of visitors. However, strollers are no longer evident, and both toddlers and elderly visitors become few and far between. Specialized, "technical" outdoor gear now appears as the norm rather than the exception. There are still many hikers typically observable at this stage who are obviously out for nothing more than a fun morning, or an easy afternoon's outing. However, the trailhead has now

FIGURE 22.2 Vernal Fall Bridge, June 2012, taken at around 8 a.m., at the beginning of an overnight trip to the summit of Half Dome. Photo by Sally Ann Ness.

OWM 22.2 View of Vernal Fall from the Vernal Fall Bridge, April 2009. Photo by Sally Ann Ness.

been left thousands of feet and several hours behind. Spectacular views have been appreciated, and the physical being of the hiker following the route has been palpably altered by the ascent landscape. An experience of playing a role that is now changing one's own character in relation to the landscape is now perceivable not only via intentional processes, but also on relatively involuntary registers of breath patterning, digestion, and body temperature regulation. Summiters may be more or less attentive to these changing indicators, but they are in evidence and occurring, regardless.

The third stage of the hike is designed so as to afford something of an intermission in the ritual progression. It is a short, flat mile-long walk through a wooded area paralleling the Merced River to the Little Yosemite Valley Campground, the halfway point of the ascent to the summit (see OWM Icon 22.4). This stage allows summiters the opportunity to progress along the trail with relative effortlessness, if they so choose (effort investment tends to vary at this stage, depending on how urgently hikers may be intending to approach the summit). In any case, this stage provides many places where a longer rest or lunch may be taken. The sense of relative ease that emerges on this section of the trail can serve to build confidence in

FIGURE 22.3 Second stage view of Nevada Fall, June 2012. Photo by Sally Ann Ness.

OWM 22.3 Second station bridge at the top of Nevada Fall, June 2012. Photo by Robert Finch II.

OWM 22.4 Little Yosemite Valley Campground, June 2012. Photo by Sally Ann Ness.

summiters who are making their first ascent and, so, embodying this role for the first time. The stage ends at a ranger station/campground area, where hikers have their last opportunity to use facilities before summiting. For those on a two-day schedule, this station serves as the end of the first main backpacking phase and the place to set up camp for the night.

The final half of the trail to the summit of Half Dome is designed so as to move visitors through three distinct stages: a relatively long trek up to the Valley rim, an exposed climb up several hundred steps on a monumental feature named the Subdome, and a final 400-foot ascent up cables and planks of Half Dome's eastern surface. Each stage is constructed in a manner that affords increasingly intense experiences of having ventured into an awe-inspiring, celestial landscape, one where organic life forms (humans included) do not naturally belong.

The trek to the rim is in some ways the most demanding stage of the entire Half Dome trail's self-testing pilgrimage. It is a grueling 3-mile stretch, gaining around 1,800 feet in altitude, moving through terrain that affords no breathtaking views, no riverine pleasures, and no inviting resting places. The way ahead is never discernable for more than 50 to 100 yards at a stretch. Relentlessly steep, dusty, and dry, it seems designed to torment rather than to inspire. Summiters who choose to follow it and maintain their previous pace will generally have to "dig deep" at this stage. Those with less experience or stamina may start to lose resolve and turn back. The role of the summiter is defined here as one that requires a depth of commitment, perseverance, and strength if it is to be well played.

The social character of the Half Dome trail transforms markedly during this fourth stage. Social boundaries typically (though not universally) maintained during earlier phases begin to dissolve in the experience of adversity and the more intense forms of suffering now occurring. Hikers who may have competitively passed unknown neighbors on the trail without recognition lower down at this stage may start to ask strangers descending from higher points for information about the distance left to go to the summit, the conditions of the trail, or the weather forecast. Joking behavior, which is abundantly observable at earlier stages, here becomes considerably more rare. Facial expressions may harden into masks of determination and resolve, or become openly baleful and appealing of support from any quarter; breathing patterns can become easily audible and uncontrolled; limps and other abnormalities of gait now may be painfully obvious, to observers as well as to those experiencing them. Hikers in this stage are often observed resting at spots on the trail that do not seem particularly accommodating, sometimes blocking the route partially or entirely to others. They may often be observed taking off their shoes and getting out bandages from first aid kits to deal with minor cuts, scrapes, and blisters. The summiter population at this stage also becomes noticeably more homogeneous in certain performance-oriented respects. All but those actually capable of enacting a "strenuous" experience have generally disappeared. A younger and predominantly male majority is now evident in the population. Its gear on average can be observed to meet a higher technical standard.

This fourth stage of the hike is designed so that it ends with a great reward. Summiters are led to reach a point on the southeastern rim of Yosemite Valley where they have their first sight of the top of Half Dome since they began (see OWM Icon 22.5). They may also enjoy a panoramic view of the mountains to the northeast of the Valley and of the Valley floor, now several thousand feet below. For the first time since the top of Nevada Fall, they are afforded a global sense of orientation in the landscape that is magnificent in scale. For the first time, they can see exactly how their journey leads to its end. The sense of exhilaration occurring at this ending station can be dramatic. Hikers may enact for the first time at this point on the trail the sensing and expression of a kind of triumphal quality that those who chose to play the role of summiter typically seek to embody and perform.

While it has no restrooms or other facilities, this fourth station, with its pine trees and exposed granite surfaces, also affords a sense of haven to summiters, who may tarry here with an extra snack while contemplating the stages still left to undertake in their hike. It is

OWM 22.5 View from the end of the fourth stage of the final stages of the ascent over the Subdome to the summit of Half Dome, June 2012. Photo by Sally Ann Ness.

▶

OWM 22.6 View from the top of the Subdome, June 2012. Photo by Sally Ann Ness.

▶

OWM 22.7 View of the Sierra Nevada from the top of Subdome, June 12. Photo by Sally Ann Ness.

the last place where summiters are immersed in a predominantly organic landscape. From this station on, as they can see, the trail's environment consists of mainly granite and sky.

The fifth stage of the hike, the Subdome, traverses a series of tight, highly exposed switchbacks hewn into a rounded shoulder of rock beside the main dome of Half Dome. While it lasts less than half a mile, this stage gains around 700 feet and is one of the steepest sections of the trail. The risk of injury increases at this stage. What has until this point been merely strenuous activity now takes on the character of danger. The large rocky steps are strewn with gravel. A fall down them carries very serious, even fatal consequences. Wind conditions become readily apparent and can now affect balance. Signs of organic habitats become minimal. An experienced guide once commented to me that at this stage of the route hikers often start to feel the ill effects of the altitude change very strongly. Toward the top of the Subdome, the trail disappears completely—a fact that may intensify the sense that one is no longer in a landscape inhabited or controlled in any ordinary sense by human beings. Hikers must find their own individual way over the granite by attending to piled stone cairns.

At the top of the Subdome, summiters arrive in a top-of-the-world environment greeted by panoramic views all around (see OWM Icons 22.6 and 22.7). The only obstacle blocking a 360-degree panorama is the main dome itself. It now looms at relatively close range, remaining a formidable feature even as the details of its surface become more easily visible.

The final stage of the hike takes place on the main dome's surface itself. Summiters ascend it with the aid of cables that are run through metal poles drilled into the granite face and wooden planks nailed into the surface at around five-foot intervals (see fig.22.4). While the cables can be climbed in less than half an hour if conditions are optimal, summiters sometimes have had to spend as long as an hour and a half or more progressing along them when they are crowded.

The incline of the rock face during this final stage is never more than around 45 degrees. However, it is steep enough that guidebooks describe it as "scary,"[33] and adrenaline-producing.[34] This stage of the hike can carry as much, if not more, nervous intensity when summiters are descending as it does when they are ascending. On the way down, they must look downward at least momentarily to find their footing. In so doing, they are compelled to register their exposed position on the dome. While it may not be as dangerous as it can look and feel, this final stage of the Half Dome hike is, in fact, life threatening. Losing one's hold at any point can result in a fatal free fall down the dome's ledge-less sides.

The final station of the hike, the all-but-lifeless, trail-less summit of Half Dome itself, is a relatively large area of around 13 square acres in size. Slabs of granite afford places to sit and take photos at varying distances from the face. Some of the favorite spots for photo opportunities are right at the edge of the face. Visitors are not allowed to camp overnight on the

FIGURE 22.4 Cables of the final stage of the Half Dome hike, June 12. Photo by Sally Ann Ness.

summit, so the main activities they may be observed to engage in at this stage are eating and drinking snacks and taking pictures.

The summit stage completes the ascent of the Half Dome hike. At this point, the role of summiter is fully embodied and the new identity of the performer is considered to have been fully enacted and mastered. However, the performance of the hike is by no means complete, as the stages now must be performed in reverse so as to return the summiters to the larger social and cultural world they left behind on the hike. With the exception of the retreat down the cables, the descent back down to the Valley floor is constructed as a straightforward process that presents no new challenges. Descending can be a long, painful ordeal, however. The repetitive strain on knee and ankle joints is greater on the way down than it is ascending. Fatigue becomes an increasingly significant factor. The propensity to slip and fall on the gravel-strewn trail is much greater. The return to the trailhead can also be a period of self-testing, in this regard, adding significantly to the character definition embodied in the summiter role. In many cases, the most trying, self-testing times experienced on the hike are, in fact, experienced on the way down.

When they reach the trail's end on the Valley floor, summiters typically head directly for one of the Valley's showers, swimming pools, or for a swim in the Merced River. Washing activity, followed by eating a meal is usually the first active practice of reincorporation back into the social context left behind on the hike. From this point onward, summiters will typically encounter increasing numbers of friends, family, and other familiar and unfamiliar characters, who will witness and celebrate the role they have played, the test they have passed, and the new identity they have embodied by having "made it to the top" of the Half Dome trail.

THE HALF DOME HIKE AS THE ENACTMENT OF ECOLOGICAL ROLE-PLAYING

The pilgrimage quality of the Half Dome trail's performance profile should be readily apparent from the description above. Regardless of variations in hiking style and experience, the summit is obtained only via a journey that meets contemporary definitions of the term "epic." It is a journey that is at every stage carefully choreographed by conventions of practice—prescribed steps, many of them literally carved in stone. Moreover, the route has been undertaken by countless multitudes, a fact that imparts to individual hikers, even the most intentionally deviant, a sense that they are anonymously influenced by rules of action formulated by others in long-established traditions of practice. Though individual and collective styles of hiking may vary substantially, there is no achieving the journey's end without exceptional effort, even for the most experienced and well-trained athletes. The performative effect of expending this effort, in this particular environment, in this particular way, endows the hike with dramatic experiential qualities for all who seek to embody its summiter character role.

Viewed from the theoretical perspective Mahmood articulates, the Half Dome performance profile appears as a kind of "spiritual exercise"[35] in a landscape where natural phenomena are endowed with ultimate meaning. Through the assiduous practice of hiking, the

Half Dome pilgrim directs his or her own process of subject enactment. He or she coordinates outward behaviors—innumerable weight shifts, gazes, rests, etc.—with conventional notions of what it takes to be an admirable summiter. In this way, the summiting visitor cultivates the habits of a particular kind of righteous self—a role-player energetically attuned to the landscape and fit to explore its various stages, even its most challenging monumental features.

Summiting Half Dome is, in this regard, a way of achieving something very much like touristic piety. Mahmood identifies piety in religious terms as resulting from "imagining the immensity of God's power and [a practitioner's] own insignificance," while at the same time performing an experience of being "close to God."[36] An analogous imagination, the imagination of being close to nature at one summit of its immensity and power, can be acquired similarly on Half Dome. By putting one's self through the activities of each stage of its route, the summiter pilgrim performs the embodiment of a new closeness to nature and its incredible powers. The hike, in this theoretical regard, can be witnessed as a series of acts that enable participants to define and produce themselves performatively as pious ecotouristic visitors.

Mahmood's theoretical perspective thus illuminates the Half Dome hike's character as a performative rite of pilgrimage. However, it does nothing to trouble the claim that the hike should be considered an example of *secular* pilgrimage. "Nature," the governing concept of this pilgrimage, as it is articulated in the discourses of the National Park Service, as well as the conservation sciences that authorize them, and the commercial Yosemite tourism industry that capitalizes on them, is a quintessentially secular concept. In its scientific aspect, the concept is defined and functions within a modernist atheistic discourse, around which the mainstreams of the natural sciences worldwide currently orient themselves. With regard to its aesthetic aspect, the concept is rooted in a nineteenth-century European discourse of sublimity that initially, traditionally, and continuously endows the features of the Yosemite landscape with a certain kind of romantic beauty.[37] While this sublime beauty is conceived as having spiritual overtones and allusions, the discourse constructs these as fundamentally mysterious in character. It is a sublimity that does not subscribe overtly to the tenets of any particular religious faith, text, or creed, nor is it ordained by any as a sanctified expression of one or several of them.[38]

In sum, while the concept of nature, as it informs the Yosemite landscape, may be seen as situated within a Western cultural-historical context that contains Judeo-Christian religious orders, the relations between those orders, their theologies, their conventions of practice, and the symbolic conventions that determine the admiration and appreciation of nature in Yosemite remain indirect and ambiguous at best. Visitors engaged in performing the appreciation of, and the embodied relating to, what they understand to be Yosemite's natural environment, on Half Dome's trail and elsewhere, are indeed nothing other than pilgrims of a liminoid, secular variety. The selves they seek to test, transform, and reinhabit through the more dramatic stages of the hike may be ethical, virtuous, and extraordinarily meaningful. However, they are not, in fact, pious. They remain bound by the forms of secular symbolism that produce them, symbolism that is itself the product of social institutions governed by worldly, irreligious, interests and forces.

This might well seem to be the end of the story, then, regarding the ritual, theatrical, and embodied significance of ecotouristic hiking practices in Yosemite National Park. Certainly, it is the end of the story regarding their *conventional* significance. It is the end of the story of their discursively predetermined significance. However, it is only one part of the story of their full *performative* significance and, so, only the beginning of the story of their dramatic and embodied significance. It omits a key dimension of performance occurring in these self-testing rites: the story of their *ecological* significance. This is the story that recognizes the distinctly nonhuman stages of the hike as agentive figures—as animated theaters of meaning-making—figures with performative capabilities undetermined by anything discursive in design. It is only by including this part of the ritual's performance profile that the entire story emerges of how subjecthood in general and cultural character roles and identities in particular can be created and transformed in ways that are not, strictly speaking, secular. This story lies in performative relations of vitality connecting nonhuman landscape features to embodied organismic forms of human being and acting. Such connections define creatively and place-specifically basic forms and figures of both human and superhuman being. They prefigure influentially, in this respect, human subjectivity, the designs of human symbolism, and various forms and figures of cultural performance and role-playing.

A Slip on the Cables: Ecological Performativity

To substantiate the claim above, it is necessary only to recount in detail an incident that exposes in high relief the ecological dimensions of performativity in touristic rituals that invariably go missing in discursively framed analyses. Such an incident occurred during a hike I undertook on the Half Dome trail on June 24, 2012. The incident was constituted by a slip that happened between two planks nailed to the surface of Half Dome, on one of the steeper intervals of the final plank/cable stage of the route, around midway up the main dome. At that time that the slip happened, I was doing my utmost to perform a role that conformed exactly to the choreographic conventions articulated for this stage of the hike. I was attempting to impersonate the actions demonstrated by a commercially trained guide that I was following up the face at the time. However, while the slip was in process, the performativity of the act acquired a fundamentally different, ecologically staged, character. When it did, my secular pilgrim identity was disabled. I lost my agentive, subject-constructing capacity. "I," the culturally and socially defined, English-language-speaking, modern-dance-trained, ethnographer-actor, in the performance of that moment, lost control of my organismic self. My life form became immersed in a new ecologically defined character, an emergent *persona*, a "presubject" in a landscape now exhibiting superhuman powers of agency, influence, staging, and performativity. "I," quite literally speaking, was possessed.

To recount the details of the incident, I had been standing on one leg around 100 feet up off the base of the cables just before it happened. I was second in a line of eleven hikers that included myself, two guides, and eight other summiters. Three of these secular pilgrims, the ones directly behind me, were university students I had brought along with me. We were all participating in an enactment of the two-day performance profile, an overnight excursion advertised as "Half Dome: Make It to the Top." I was balancing on one of the wooden planks with the wind gusting strongly from my left over the face of the dome. My foot was turned lengthwise along the plank, only the left half of it able to find purchase on the wood. My arms were down at my sides, each hand loosely enfolding a cable. Even with the wind blowing, I was not holding onto the cables. I merely had my hands encircling them, ready to grab them if need be.

This pose was how we rested between movements up the cables. The strategy was to relax as completely as possible, and, then, to climb on up onto one and then another plank in an unbroken pattern of exertion. Every two planks, we would rest until a normal breathing rhythm reestablished itself. Then, it was again up two more planks to rest.

This two-plank/rest movement patterning had come as a complete surprise to me. It was initiated by the guide in front of me without explanation. He seemed to be improvising its design himself in response to unusual wind conditions occurring on that day. I greatly appreciated his role modeling. It produced a pacing in my efforts that I might not otherwise have had. Left on my own, I would have tried to climb further without resting, exhausting my strength and probably panicking far below the summit. As it was, I felt secure about what I thought was going to happen next. I had the breath and the strength to reach up as high as I could with both arms, grab firmly onto the cables, plant my left foot on some bulge, crack, lip, ledge, or bump in the granite face—whatever looked like it would give the best purchase—and hoist myself up so as to step again with my right foot onto the relative safety of the next wooden plank, repeating everything then again to reach the plank after that. That was my role, and I was vitally invested in performing it.

I was rested, now, breathing normally. My muscles were signaling no fatigue. The actions to be performed were familiar. I was set to push onward in what seemed like an endless series of stepping/hoisting patterns that were inching us upward toward the distant summit. I was only waiting for a sign from above to begin.

It must be noted for the purposes at hand that, even before I slipped, I was not enjoying the astounding view of the Sierra that my position on the main dome afforded me. My slip wasn't due to wandering attention or some other leisure-associated lapse. In my commitment to the cables discipline, I had directed all my mental energy to the guide above me. It was a "monkey see; monkey do" relationship. When he reached, I reached. When he shifted, I shifted. When he rested, I rested. How he stood, so I stood. How he breathed, I breathed. I intended nothing other than to move as his double. I had even felt annoyance with myself rise up whenever I realized I was deviating from his example in the slightest—failing to release fully my grip on the cables, for example, or balancing only on the ball of my foot, instead of on its entire surface. The guide had climbed these cables many times without mishap, and I trusted his experience. He was, in a sense, my performative ticket to safety on the summit. I was replaying his role to the nth degree.

This practice of following the leader, which invested me more and more deeply into a secular discipline of touristic pilgrimage, was also my way of tuning out the environmental situation I found myself to be in—high up on the dome, unprotected, lacking any cable climbing expertise. It was my way of pushing out competing discursive formations and their associated cultural identities: thoughts about my child, who still needed her mother to be alive for a few more years, and thoughts about the National Park Service, who had engineered this particular accident-waiting-to-happen, not only to me but to the students with me and all the others who had trusted their judgment. However, my powers of concentration were not absolute. There were sensations being registered involuntarily by parts of my organism that were not governed by either will or discursive faculties. These were apprehending, in their own way, the wind, the light, the temperature, the wood, the rock, and the gravity of the scene. They were assessing them as they affected my weight center, my eyes, the skin on my face, my hair, my throat as I breathed, and the entirety of my skeletomuscular system. Nonetheless, despite all of these persistently influential organismic relational processes, I was doing my best to concentrate only on the guide.

At this stage of the hike, a feeling on the order of chagrin had been building up inside of me as well. Had I known how dangerous this last stage was actually going to be, had I known how steep a 45-degree incline actually was, had I known how slick and smooth the granite would be, I would not have undertaken this stage in the "free solo" manner I was doing—that is to say, without being roped in and led by a professional climber.[39] That thought had formed itself clearly despite all efforts to focus elsewhere much earlier on. I could not escape it. It emerged out of the embodied doing of the cable ascent itself, with all of the experiential similarities its performance established to other climbs I had embodied in Yosemite Valley. Unfortunately, in this case, I had trusted the guidebooks, with their "everybody does it" talk. I had trusted the park service, which I thought would never allow the public to get up on anything this dangerous totally unprepared and unprotected. I had attributed the previous falls I'd heard about off the cables to be the result of exceptionally substandard visitor conduct and overcrowding, the latter of which at least we had avoided by reaching the base of this stage well ahead of the main influx of hikers, at around 8:00 in the morning. Now, too late, it was clear that I had been wrong in my estimations. Negative feelings accompanied these fragmented, momentary reflections, intensely negative feelings. I was deeply certain, however, that my best chance for avoiding a catastrophe lay in committing myself to simply cloning the guide's movements. So, I focused on this process. I formed myself into the character choreographed by the guide's actions down to the smallest detail. I acted in this stage of the hike exactly as I would have done had the guide been a dance artist and I a student in his master class.

When he moved again, I was on my way up as well. He reached, and I reached. He stepped, and I stepped. Then, he hoisted, and I slipped. I was with him, one hundred percent, until that moment. Then, in less than a heartbeat, I was completely on my own. For about a heartbeat, or perhaps a little less, I was alone on the rock. My weight was centered on a foot that was sliding freely out of my control down along the polished surface of the granite. There had been no bump, no crack, no ledge, no anything to place it onto or into at this particular interval. I had had to simply set it on the steep granite slope and hope for the best. The best, however, had not happened. The foothold had failed. My hands weren't grabbing the cables at that moment either. They had been sliding upward over and along them seeking a higher hold. I felt the whole of myself giving way, sinking into the gravitational field that I had been resisting successfully until that moment.

When the slip occurred, everything went negative in a flash of awareness. The unintended was happening. I had no foothold, and I had no handhold either. I was in an uncontrolled descent. At this instant, my entire universe consisted of the rock, myself, and gravity. We were locked in a rapidly changing set of relations of force and tension that carried my survival in the balance.

Thoughts, now racing, focused first on my hiking shoe, as it was sliding smoothly over the granite. I cursed wordlessly at the absence of my climbing shoes. I'd left them at the campground, deciding they were probably not worth the trouble of bringing along. None of the other hikers had brought theirs. The climbing shoes, however, were relatively flexible and their soles gave far better traction. "I could have done this, no problem, in climbing shoes," I had told myself lower down. I wondered why the guidebooks had not suggested this, why the supposedly safety-conscious park service information had made no mention of it. Only the wearing of gloves had been suggested. I felt something on the order of hatred lighting up the pathways of my nervous system as these thoughts occurred.

However, even as this inner discourse was beginning to unfold, several other things happened simultaneously. My hands both grabbed firmly and held onto the cables that they had been sliding along. Initiating all at once from my torso, arms, legs, and head, I found myself making a slight hop off of the rock, shifting my center of gravity slightly down and inward toward the face. My left leg contracted quickly and, then, just as quickly, replanted its foot on a different part of the face. The leg bore down this time at a different angle than before, so that more force was sent through a larger area of the ball of the foot, and pressure was sent upward into the granite. The kinetic energy approximated that produced by a doctor's office "knee-jerk" reflex test: it went from the top of the thigh, through the knee to the back of the calf-ankle-heel, moving forward under the arch of the foot, driving the bottom of the ball into the rock. The foot smacked against the granite, punching into the stone like the clapper on a bell rung sharply, and stuck there. My right leg contracted and rose up to serve as a second support beside the left.

All of these acts took place so quickly that, in about the time it would have taken to snap my fingers, I had stopped losing ground and regained a stable position on the rock. The time that elapsed wasn't even long enough for me to fall noticeably behind the guide's tempo. In a twinkling, as it were, I was back in sync with him. The thoughts above had no more than begun to form. The entire slip/plant episode constituted only a minor glitch in the group's patterning of ascent. It was over literally before I could give it a second thought, or even a single, fully blown, first one.

Short as the interval was, however, it had a lasting impact on my experience of summiting and on the process of subject definition and enactment in which I had been invested. The movements that had happened to me, although they were never again to be repeated, proved unforgettable. On one level, this was simply a consequence of the fact that their existential stakes had been relatively high. An unabated downward slide at this height would more than likely have proved lethal. The performativity of the slip/plant sequence was of the same caliber as a sacred act, in this regard, given the difference between life and death that it had entailed. The planting move literally had proven to be my salvation. The intensity of the lesson learned from this episode in relation to my understanding of what it could mean to be a human subject on Half Dome was exponentially greater than it had been with actions that had not been so dangerous. The performance hammered home the truth about the awful power of nature over human life in this environment more forcefully than had any other action performed along the way.

However, the performativity of the episode was also different in relation to the agency that now choreographed the hiker subject identity formerly underway in the ritual "exercise." In this regard, the slip/plant episode illuminates the ecological performativity hidden within the enactments of the conventional hiking performance profile. The human character being defined and produced as this accidental moment unfolded was no longer acquiring its identity by means of a culturally constituted subject's intentional performance. It was no longer conforming to the character role that the park discourse and its conventions of summiting had designed to be enacted. It was failing utterly to embody those established codes of conduct. In this unintended moment, that subject was now learning who it *actively* was as a living figure in a performance staged by nonhuman environmental factors. It was learning what its basic character as a motile figure in this particular landscape was, outside the limits of conduct defined by the park discourse. The cultural subject, the "me" that had been in charge, was now being taught a formative lesson in a deeply immersed way on this final hiking stage.

In this performance, in other words, the hiker pilgrim became a being whose subject-hood was no longer fully self-determined. It became now an ecologically liminal charac-ter. Its cultural "I" was caught up in potentially life-altering actions of which the landscape was more or less in charge. "My" actions were no longer my own. They were not being per-formed under my intentional direction or command—by the I that, until this moment, had believed itself to be conducting the ascent. That subject was busy elsewhere, generating an inner discourse about hiking shoes, trying unsuccessfully to perform virtuous movements, and repressing undesirable emotions. Even had that I not been so occupied, it could not have conceived of performing the actions that in fact were being performed by its bodily members in this emergency episode. The slip/plant movements and their coordination were well beyond that I's capability. The midair actions, in particular, were definitely not in its movement repertoire. In this regard, the performance was experienced by the hiking me, the intending subject, as shockingly unintentional, yet nonetheless intensely personal. They registered as something on the order of miraculous. They were "mine" but also emphatically not mine. They were, in Schechner's theatrical terms, "not-not-mine."[40] "I," the character role-under-construction, was now being defined restoratively, experiencing the definition of its own bodily members through the dynamic forces at play in the landscape.

Mahmood's performative theory of subjectivity might attempt to characterize this state of affairs as a moment when a "spontaneous" expression of ritual virtuosity manifested itself.[41] Such expressions, in her perspective, occur regularly when the self-directed work of a devoted ritual practitioner occasionally produces a more or less automatic response to a given situation that conforms nonetheless to what conventions of thought and action might expect for an unforeseen situation or event. Ritual performances, in this regard, are theo-rized as working to produce subjects who learn to enact their character roles so well that, even when caught by surprise, they still manage to conform piously to the expectations of their religion.

While a similar kind of automatic reenacting might also have manifested on the Half Dome hike, this was not the case with the slip/plant performance process. Its movements were anything but well rehearsed. They were not the echoes of previously ingrained habits of practice. They were memorable precisely for the ways in which they did *not* conform to the capabilities and acquired patternings of the human subject who found herself embody-ing them. The prior history of intentional, discursively oriented subject enactment that had been underway was not called on in this moment. The episode's embodied character fell outside that history. It constituted part of what Mahmood's and Butler's theories would cast as the unspeakable, unknowable, and subjectively nonsignifying, repressed aspect of the human experience of the hike. Yet, the slip/plant performance bore none of these qualities. It was emphatically expressive, significant, and memorable. It contributed substantially and even representably to the overall enactment and definition of the summiter identity being cultivated.

It would be more accurate to say, in this regard, that the slip/plant movements on the Half Dome hike were generated, performed, designed, staged, enacted, and registered not by the individual human subject of this hiking process, nor by any exclusively human discursive formations or conventions, but, rather, by an environmental-organismic *assemblage*, to use a term set forth by Bruno Latour in his conceptualization of actor-network-theory.[42] That is, it was co-produced by an assemblage in which agency, energy, and even significance were distributed among several elements of the environment. The gravitational field, most obviously, took command of the performance initially, motivating and giving form to the slip as it occurred. The surface character of the rock, and the sole of the hiking shoe, also played active roles in this slipping movement process, defining the character of the pathway that was pursued. The slip's nonhuman environmentally assembled performativity changed the nature of the hiker's being immediately, integrating it into a set of circumstances that were atypical of those normally (and normatively) sought out in summiting exercises. A liminal being emerged, a "slipper" figure, acutely attuned to the dynamics of the environment. The culturally designed, summiter "I" was consumed, absorbed, and transformed by this gravitationally governed, vitally moving integration. Previous subjective intentions became relatively meaningless and insignificant. All that mattered—all that *signified*—to this slipping assemblage was the force of gravity, the incline and slickness of the rock, and the smoothness of the hiking shoe. "I," the agentive subject—the hiker, the mom, the anthropology professor, the performing actor—dissolved instantaneously into relations of greater force and power, a passive figment carried along in the assemblage.

Then, in the response of the planting movement, my slipping organism again became active in this performance process as well. My organism reacted in a way that subjective thought did not govern, producing a life-saving movement that no discursive formation had prefigured. My organism interacted, not randomly, not brainlessly, but adaptively and creatively. Its engagement was born out of environmental intelligence that had been growing as it had lived through the previous stages of practice taking place. My organism initiated a move, responding to a blink-of-an-eye subjective error, and, in so doing, became a player in this otherwise nonhuman process. It became the figure initiating and coordinating a viable "Plan B" to the hiking pilgrim's failed "Plan A." It was this pre(post)subjective, liminal figure that choreographed and performed a salvational act, in a state of what might best be characterized as ecological, not subjective, grace.

One might say, in regard to this intelligent relating of land, gravity, and being, that an organism and a landscape had a meeting of the minds, halfway up on the side of Half Dome. Better, perhaps, would be to say that they had a new exchange of material information in a relationship that had been ongoing for quite some time. From that exchange, a new sustaining capability of the organism in this topographical context emerged. A new means of standing under the given environmental circumstances was embodied. From that, a new conceptualizable understanding and a new character definition based on it began to take place and form in the being as well. The organism's reaction and the life lesson that its performance embodied, in essence changed "me." The remembering, recognizing, conceptualizing subject, "I," had now lived through a new relation of vitality, a role whose playing had gone bone deep. The role expressed its intelligence in "my" nervous system. "I" was now a living feature of the landscape in a new way. My consciousness had itself imaged something of its superhuman powers, my organism had existed as a symptom of its integrative agency.

In the wake of this episode, as the hike continued, the cultural "I" had to adjust itself to these realities. A different kind of enactment, a different sort of play, had intervened informatively in the conventional pilgrimage practice that had been in process. The summiter role-playing exercise now became the partial outgrowth not only of discourse but also of the landscape's propensity to stage its own version of an action sequence as well. "Nature," in this regard, both the concept and its material referents, would never mean the same thing to me, or mean it in the same way, again. Our relationship had been altered and recalibrated ecologically by the consequences of the slip/plant performance process.

CONCLUSION

The slip/plant episode described above is meant in part to illustrate how misleading the discursively generated label "secular" can be when applied to embodied ecotouristic rituals such as the Half Dome hike exemplifies. When life-saving or life-taking consequences are immediately forthcoming in such landscape-immersed performance processes, the idea of secularity seems both inadequate and overly elaborate as a characterization of the incidents unfolding. The concept obscures the presence and agency of the superhuman ecological factors that assemble, become incarnate, and participate definitively in the enactment of the character role that is embodied. It ignores the part that nonhuman factors play in the transformations the tourist identity undergoes at existential levels of awareness and play. And it fails to bring out the incipient status of the creative processes at work in emergent ecological performances and the relatively early stages of character definition and signification they enact. The ecological dimensions of performativity inherent in the Half Dome hiking performance profile, in this regard, might better be identified as staging a kind of "protoreligious" ritual process rather than a secular one. Their enactments serve to bring about kinds of understanding and awareness out of which collective, social, and cultural conventions and discourses of religious practice and identity might potentially be seen to evolve, even while they are not themselves religious in nature.

However, the touristic enactments occurring on Half Dome also clearly refute the idea that such protoreligious creative processes would necessarily have to follow an evolutionary path toward religious kinds of cultural performance. Half Dome's thriving secular discourses and conventions provide ample evidence that self-testing acts of pilgrimage, even those in which human subjecthood is transformed and reinvented from the existential grounds of its being on up, can serve to generate and evolve unambiguously secular conventions of identity enactment as well as religious ones. What seems forthcoming from this examination of the performance profile of Half Dome summiting, in this regard, is that ecotouristic landscape rituals, particularly in their most transformative dimensions, are as likely to lead in secular directions as they are in religious ones. Such performances might also conceivably lead in fundamentally new social and cultural directions as well.

In their incipient relations of vitality, embodied touristic landscape performances stage protean forms of self-enactment. They produce place-specific manifestations of subjecthood and ecologically assembled identifications of organismically human being and living. In this regard, the touristic story of the pilgrimage up Half Dome must remain, in social and cultural terms, a continually emerging, ever-unfinishable one. It is an open-ended story, not only because the performance processes of human role-playing are a fundamentally creative phenomenon, but because the vital forces of the Yosemite landscape are constantly creative in character as well. They constitute dynamic stages for the genesis and definition of new kinds of roles and actors, via events whose experience and understanding may serve to transform established conventions and discourses. Their involvement in self-testing rites of touristic passage suggests how the kinds of experience out of which more conventional artistic traditions of performance emerge and evolve may also precede as well as follow discursive constructions of subjects, identities, and selves.

The Half Dome hiking ritual demonstrates, in this final regard, that there is much more to the performing life of a tourist and to ecotouristic forms of performativity, than conventional human symbolism and its social and cultural discourses can explain or determine. The processes of touristic subject identity enactment require relatively inclusive, ecological theoretical frameworks, if their most basic, vital, and creative characters of meaning-making and self/role definition are to be fully understood. So, too, do the processes of other kinds of role playing, particularly those entailing analogously staged embodied performances in environments that exhibit nonhuman features of design and character. A wide variety dance and theater performances and performers, might, in this regard, be productively reexamined along similar lines as well. While their stages and roles may be crafted to a greater extent by products and interests shaped by cultural and social discourses, they, too, in at least some respects are immersed in realities that go beyond them. To the extent that they are, they, too, have ecological dimensions, engagements, influences, and consequences.

NOTES

Grateful acknowledgement is given to Channing J. Carson, Ernesto "Susto" Carlos, and Robert Finch II, whose support during the field research related to this essay proved vital to its successful completion. Thanks are also due to Nadine George-Graves, for her insightful editorial comments and suggestions.

1. Saba Mahmood, *Politics of Piety: The Islamic Revival and the Feminist Subject*, 2nd ed. (Princeton: Princeton University Press, 2012 [2005]; emphasis added), 139.
2. Liz Lerman, *Hiking the Horizontal: Field Notes from a Choreographer* (Middletown, CT: Wesleyan University Press, 2011), 282, emphasis added.
3. The work of Edward M. Bruner and Barbara Kirshenblatt-Gimblett has been particularly effective in this regard. See, Bruner and Kirshenblatt-Gimblett's seminal article "Maasai on the Lawn: Tourist Realism in East Africa," *Cultural Anthropology* 9 (1994): 435–70. The notion of the "domain" employed here is intended as a reference to Lerman's idea of "transdomain" research (*Hiking the Horizontal*, 203–4).
4. Dean MacCannell's work on the "staged authenticity" of tourism and its general character as a spectacle has been particularly illuminating in this regard. See MacCannell, *The Tourist: A New Theory of the Leisure Class* (Berkeley: University of California Press, 1973) and "Remarks on the Commodification of Cultures," in *Hosts and Guests Revisited: Tourism Issues of the 21st Century*, edited by Valene Smith and M. Brent (New York: Cognizant Communication Corporation, 2001), 380–90.
5. See Richard Bauman's classic text, *Verbal Art as Performance* (Prospect, IL: Waveland Heights, 1977).
6. See, for example, Nelson H. Graburn, "Tourism: The Sacred Journey," in *Hosts and Guests: The Anthropology of Tourism*, edited by Valene Smith (Philadelphia: University of Pennsylvania Press, 1977), 17–31; MacCannell, *The Tourist*; Victor Turner, "Liminal to Liminoid, in Play, Flow and Ritual: An Essay in Comparative Symbology," *Rice University Studies* 60 (1974): 53–92; and Sally Falk Moore and Barbara Myerhoff,

"Introduction: Secular Ritual: Forms and Meanings," in *Secular Ritual*, edited by S. F. Moore and B. Myerhoff (Amsterdam: Van Gorcum, 1977), 3–24.

7. For example, Nelson Graburn's most recent revision of his essay, "Tourism: the Sacred Journey," is titled "Secular Ritual: A General Theory of Tourism," in *Tourists and Tourism: A Reader*, edited by Sharon B. Gmelch (Long Grove, IL: Waveland Press, 2010), 25–36. The contemporary value of Graburn's argument is indicated by its placement in the text as the first essay after Gmelch's introduction. Examples of contemporary work contributing to the tourism/ritual discourse include Ellen Badone and Sharon R. Roseman, *Intersecting Journeys: The Anthropology of Pilgrimage and Tourism* (Urbana: University of Illinois Press, 2004); Dallen J. Timothy and Daniel H. Olsen eds., *Tourism, Religion, and Spiritual Journeys* (London: Routledge, 2006); R. Zachary Finney, Robert Orwig, and Deborah Spake, "Lotus-Eaters, Pilgrims, Seekers, and Accidental Tourists: How Different Travelers Consume the Sacred and the Profane," *Services Marketing Quarterly* 30, no. 2, (2009): 148–73; Banu Gokariksel, "Beyond the Officially Sacred: Religion, Secularism, and the Body in the Production of Subjectivity," *Social and Cultural Geography* 10, no. 6, (2009): 657–74; Veronica della Dora, "Taking Sacred Space out of Place: From Mount Sinai to Mount Getty through Travelling Icons," *Mobilities* 4, no. 2 (2009): 225–48; and Doron Bar and Kobi Cohen-Hattab, "A New Kind of Pilgrimage: The Modern Tourist Pilgrim of Nineteenth Century–Twentieth Century Palestine," *Middle Eastern Studies* 39, no. 2 (2003): 131–48.

8. Graburn, "Sacred Journey," 25.

9. See also MacCannell on tourism as "modern ritual" in *The Tourist*, 13.

10. Victor Turner's liminoid/liminal distinction is elaborated in, "Liminal to Liminoid," 53–92. See also his "Variations on a Theme of Liminality," in *Secular Ritual*, 24–41.

11. Edward Bruner has argued that this negative view of tourism is related to French postmodernism and its concept of the *simulacrum*. See Edward Bruner, "Abraham Lincoln as Authentic Reproduction: A Critique of Postmodernism," *American Anthropologist* 96 (1994): 397–415.

12. Moore and Myerhoff, "Introduction," 19–24.

13. Graburn, "Sacred Journey," 33.

14. Graburn, "The Anthropology of Tourism," *Annals of Tourism Research* 10 (1983): 9–33, 23.

15. Mahmood, *Politics of Piety*.

16. *Politics of Piety*, 127–31. Mahmood cites Catherine Bell, *Ritual Theory, Ritual Practice* (New York: Oxford University Press, 1992), and Talal Asad, *Genealogies of Religion: Discipline and Reasons of Power in Christianity and Islam* (Baltimore, MD: Johns Hopkins University Press, 1993), in this regard.

17. Mahmood, *Politics of Piety*, 131.

18. Mahmood, *Politics of Piety*, 129.

19. Graburn "Anthropology of Tourism," 9.

20. Graburn "Anthropology of Tourism," 12–16.

21. See, for example, Sharpley and Sundaram's recent characterization of the tourism-as-pilgrimage literature in "Tourism: A Sacred Journey? The Case of Ashram Tourism, India," *International Journal of Tourism Research* 7 (2005): 161–72. See also Valene Smith, "Introduction: The Quest in the Guest," *Annals of Tourism Research* 19 (1992): 1–17, and M. Brown, *The Spiritual Tourist* (London: Bloomsbury, 1998).

22. Steven Medley, *The Complete Guidebook to Yosemite National Park* (El Portal, CA: The Yosemite Association, 2002), 33.

23. *The Rough Guide to Yosemite National Park* (London: Penguin Books, 2002), 26–27; Stacey Wells, *Frommer's Yosemite and Sequoia/Kings Canyon National Parks* (New York: MacMillan, 1998), 144.

24. *Rough Guide*, 26, 100; Medley, *Complete Guidebook*, 39. Suzanne Swedo, *Hiking Yosemite National Park: A Guide to 59 of the Parks Greatest Adventures* (Guilford, CT: FalconGuides, 2011), 50.

25. To view the Delaware North Companies' Yosemite logo, visit: http://www.yosemitepark.com/?ic_campid=4&ic_pkw=GH_Ahwahnee_Fall_Pref_Email-Sept11. The logo is used as a link to the Yosemite reservations website. The Yosemite Conservancy logo may be viewed at: http://www.yosemiteconservancy.org.

26. The Tis-se-yak myth is summarized in *Rough Guide*, 27, and in Peter Browning, *Yosemite Place Names: The Historic Background of Geographic Names in Yosemite National Park*, 2nd ed. (Lafayette, CA: Great West Books, 2005).

27. Swedo, *Hiking Yosemite,* 50. Swedo has produced guides for Yosemite, for the Hawaiian Islands, and for wilderness survival.

28. Medley, *Complete Guidebook*, 33; *Rough Guide*, 100; Wells, *Frommer's*, 50.

29. Swedo, *Hiking Yosemite*, 50.

30. Information on the Half Dome permit system can be found at the National Park Service website: http://www.nps.gov/yose/planyourvisit/hdfaq.htm.

31. The phrase "crown jewel" is from Mike Osborne, *Granite, Water, and Light: The Waterfalls of Yosemite Valley* (Berkeley, CA: Heyday Books, 2009), 55–84.

32. The Pacific Crest Trail runs from the Mexican to the Canadian border a distance of 2,650 miles. It was established by Congress in 1968 as a National Scenic Trail and is another example of a classic American ecotouristic pilgrimage. The Pacific Crest Trail runs through Yosemite National Park and can be reached from Yosemite Valley via the John Muir Trail.

33. Swedo, *Hiking Yosemite*, 50.

34. Medley, *Complete Guide*, 33.

35. Mahmood cites Pierre Hadot in relation to this phrase, *Politics of Piety*, 122.

36. *Politics of Piety*, 130, 122.

37. This beauty is represented most influentially in the more poetically inclined writings of John Muir; in the paintings of Carleton Watkins, Albert Bierstadt, Thomas Hill, and William Keith; and (arguably) in the photographs of Ansel Adams.

38. For discussions of this Yosemite-specific romantic discourse, see William Deverell, "Niagara Magnified: Finding Emerson, Muir, and Adams in Yosemite," and Kate Ogden, "California as Kingdom Come," both in *Yosemite: Art of an American Icon*, edited by Amy Scott (Berkeley: University of California Press, 2006), 9–22, 23–54.

39. "Free solo" in climbing jargon refers to climbing without using any protection—no ropes securing the climber to the rock. See Alexander Huber and Heinz Zak, *Yosemite: Half a Century of Dynamic Rock Climbing* (London: Baton Wicks, 2002), 174. It is generally considered to be an ethically transgressive style of climbing, as it incurs unnecessary and excessive risk to the climber. It is also generally admired when it is performed successfully.

40. Richard Schechner, *Between Theatre and Anthropology* (Philadelphia: University of Pennsylvania Press, 1985), 112.

41. *Politics of Piety*, 129.

42. See Bruno Latour, *Reassembling the Social: An Introduction to Actor-Network-Theory* (Oxford: Oxford University Press, 2005).

BIBLIOGRAPHY

Asad, Talal. *Genealogies of Religion: Discipline and Reasons of Power in Christianity and Islam.* Baltimore, MD: Johns Hopkins University Press, 1993.

Badone, Ellen, and Sharon R. Roseman. *Intersecting Journeys: The Anthropology of Pilgrimage and Tourism.* Urbana: University of Illinois Press, 2004.

Bar, Doron, and Kobi Cohen-Hattab. "A New Kind of Pilgrimage: The Modern Tourist Pilgrim of Nineteenth Century-Twentieth Century Palestine." *Middle Eastern Studies* 39, no. 2 (2003): 131–48.

Bauman, Richard. *Verbal Art as Performance.* Prospect, IL: Waveland Heights, 1977.

Bell, Catherine. *Ritual Theory, Ritual Practice.* New York: Oxford University Press, 1992.

Brown, M. *The Spiritual Tourist.* London: Bloomsburg, 1998.

Browning, Peter. *Yosemite Place Names: The Historic Background of Geographic Names in Yosemite National Park.* 2nd ed. Lafayette, CA: Great West Books, 2005.

Bruner, Edward. "Abraham Lincoln as Authentic Reproduction: A Critique of Postmodernism." *American Anthropologist*, 96 (1994): 397–415.

Bruner, Edward M., and Barbara Kirshenblatt-Gimblett. "Maasai on the Lawn: Tourist Realism in East Africa." *Cultural Anthropology* 9 (1994): 435–70.

Deverell, William. " 'Niagra Magnified': Finding Emerson, Muir, and Adams in Yosemite." In *Yosemite; Art of an American Icon*, edited by Amy Scott, 9–22. Los Angeles: Autry National Center in association with University of California Press, 2006.

Dora, Vernoica Della. "Taking Sacred Space out of Place: From Mount Sinai to Mount Getty through Travelling Icons." *Mobilities* 4, no. 2 (2009): 225–48.

Finney, R. Zachary, Robert Orwig, and Deborah Spake. "Lotus-Eaters, Pilgrims, Seekers, and Accidental Tourists: How Different Travelers Consume the Sacred and the Profane." *Services Marketing Quarterly* 30, no. 2 (2009): 148–73.

Gokariksel, Banu. "Beyond the Officially Sacred: Religion, Secularism, and the Body in the Production of Subjectivity." *Social and Cultural Geography* 10, no. 6 (2009): 657–74.

Graburn, Nelson H. "Tourism: the Sacred Journey." In *Hosts and Guests: The Anthropology of Tourism*, edited by Valene Smith, 17–31. Philadelphia University of Pennsylvania Press, 1977.

Huber, Alexander, and Heinz Zak. *Yosemite; Half a Century of Dynamic Rock Climbing.* London: Baton Wicks, 2002.

Latour, Bruno. *Reassembling the Social; an Introduction to Actor-Network-Theory.* Oxford, UK: Oxford University Press, 2005.

Lerman, Liz. *Hiking the Horizontal: Field notes from a Choreographer.* Middletown, CT: Wesleyan University Press, 2011.

MacCannell, Dean. *Tourist: A New Theory of the Leisure Class.* Berkeley: University of California Press, 1999 (1976).

MacCannell, Dean. "Remarks on the Commodification of Cultures." In *Hosts and Guests Revisited: Tourism Issues of the 21st Century*, edited by Valene Smith and M. Brent, 380–90. New York: Cognizant Communication Corporation, 2001.

Mahmood, Saba. *Politics of Piety: The Islamic Revival and the Feminist Subject.* 2nd ed. Princeton: Princeton University Press, 2012 (2005).

Medley, Steven. *The Complete Guidebook to Yosemite National Park.* El Portal, CA: The Yosemite Association, 2002.

Moore, Sally Folk, and Barbara Myerhoff. "Introduction: Secular Ritual: Forms and Meanings." In *Secular Ritual*, edited by S. F. Moore and B. Myerhoff. Amsterdam: Van Gorcum, 1977.

Ogden, Kate N. "California as Kingdom Come." In *Yosemite; Art of an American Icon*, 23–53. Los Angeles: Autry National Center in association with University of California Press, 2006.

Osborne, Mike. *Granite, Water, and Light: the Waterfalls of Yosemite Valley*. Berkeley, CA: Heyday Books.

Schechner, Richard. *Between Theater and Anthropology*. Philadelphia: University of Pennsylvania Press, 1985.

Sharpley, Richard, and Priya Sundaram. "Tourism: A Sacred Journey? The Case of Ashram Tourism, India." *International Journal of Tourism Research* 7 (2005): 161–72.

Smith, Valene. "Introduction: The Quest in the Guest." *Annals of Tourism Research* 19 (1992): 1–17.

Swedo, Suzanne. *Hiking Yosemite National Park: A Guide to 59 of the Parks Greatest Adventures*. Guilford, CT: FalconGuides, 2011.

Timothy, Dallen J., and Daniel H. Olsen, eds. *Tourism, Religion, and Spiritual Journeys*. London: Routledge, 2006.

Turner, Victor. "Liminal to Liminoid, in Play, Flow and Ritual: An Essay in Comparative Symbology." *Rice University Studies* 60, no. 3 (1974): 53–92.

Wells, Stacey. *Frommer's Yosemite and Sequoia/Kings Canyon National Parks*. New York: MacMillan, 1998.

....

CHAPTER 23

ORIENTATIONS AS MATERIALIZATIONS

The Love Art Laboratory's Eco-Sexual Blue Wedding to the Sea

....

MICHAEL J. MORRIS

INTRODUCTION

....

I first encountered the work of the Love Art Laboratory (2005–2011) when I was an undergraduate dance major living in Jackson, Mississippi. I do not recall how I first came to the online archive of their work, only that I visited their site constantly. On difficult days, I would navigate to the homepage where I would be greeted by voices repeating over and over, "*We* love you! We *love* you! We *LOVE* you! We love you!"[1] I would peruse the site, re-viewing each of their projects, each one so vibrant and colorful, each one seeming to be so full of loving and living and community. The project impressed me, not only because it enacted and gave visibility to big, bright, beautiful queer love—of which there was a dearth in Jackson, Mississippi—but because it operated as a positivity. Although the project is framed as a collaborative "response to the violence of war, the anti-gay marriage movement, and our prevailing culture of greed," it does so by "doing projects that explore, generate, and celebrate love."[2] Each year, these artists staged elaborate performance art weddings, each one themed around a specific chakra and the color associated with that chakra.[3] I remember feeling deep, twenty-something-year-old rage in the face of the politics to which the Love Art Laboratory (LAL) was responding, but from the LAL—Annie M. Sprinkle and Elizabeth M. Stephens—I began to learn a form of response that channeled rage into something other than conflict, violence, or even protest. Instead, Sprinkle and Stephens were *making something*: they were making a life of love together, they were making art that performed that love in ostentatiously public ways, and they were making that art with other people, creating collaborative communities around and through the work that they made together. The project responded to war, hate, and greed by becoming performative proponents of a different kind of world rather than responding as antagonists against the world in which we were living.

By the time I went to graduate school, I had become obsessed with one particular facet of the LAL project. True to their Fluxus roots, the LAL project seemed to be a dynamic integration of art and life. Sprinkle and Stephens lived out their love in and through their art; their art was about their love, but it was not merely a representation of their life together. As performance, it was a way in which they enacted their life together and love for one another. This integration of life and art, as well as the kind of life that this art enacted—a life that was all about love, a love that was persistent, marrying one another again and again and again, a love that was oriented toward inclusivity and bringing more people together into creative endeavors and the formation of community, rather than being oriented toward the exclusivity of a unilateral exchange between only two bodies—was something that I wanted to understand, and undoubtedly something that I wanted for myself as an art maker.

In 2009, I secured a small grant to travel to San Francisco to meet Sprinkle and Stephens, to interview them about their work, and to see a new exhibit their work entitled "SEXECOLOGY: Making Love with the Earth, Sky + Sea," on display at Femina Potens Gallery.[4] The exhibit included ephemera from their *Green Wedding Four* (2008) and their *Blue Weddings* (2009), photographs by Sprinkle and Stephens, a series of "ecosexual" collages that they made in collaboration with Camille Norton, Adam Harms, and Tessa Wills, and a video that documented Sprinkle and Stephens's "ecosexual coming out" narratives titled *When I Knew . . .* (2009). The first day I went to the exhibit, I felt my interests in the work beginning to expand. I had come to San Francisco on a kind of research pilgrimage, to try to understand how Sprinkle and Stephens created work through which they lived their love, but as I spent time with the work in this exhibit, I was seduced by other possibilities being opened by the LAL. *Sexecology. Ecosexuality.* These were the themes of the exhibit, and had become central to the LAL project since 2008.

Beginning in 2008 with *Green Wedding Four*, Sprinkle and Stephens declared themselves "ecosexual" and began to make ecological vows in addition to annually reiterating their love and commitment to one another through their weddings.[5] In 2008, they made their vows to take the Earth as their lover in Santa Cruz, California. They made similar vows in the year that followed, marrying the Sky in Oxford, England, and the Sea in Venice, Italy (2009). "Ecosexuality" was bigger than the integration of life and art that I had come to San Francisco seeking. In these ecosexual artworks—the ephemera from the weddings as well as the collages and photographs—I still saw the enactment of inclusive love and the formation of communities through collaborative arts practice, but there was more: this work turned toward the material world—a world that might be called "nature," a world of organic and inorganic, nonhuman and human matter—in ways that refigured both the position of the human and the nature of "nature" toward which these bodies turned. The performances of ecosexuality in the work of the LAL engaged the material world—the Earth, the Sky, and the Sea—not as passive or inert "natural resources" for human use or as an "environment" in which human action takes place; rather, these performances figured erotic entanglements with a material world of which we are always already a part, a material world that includes of a spectrum of nonhuman and human participants that together enact the materialization of that world.

Since the time of that exhibit, the LAL—a seven-year project inspired by Linda Montana's *14 Years of Living Art*—has come to a close. Sprinkle and Stephens have continued to stage ecosexual weddings and adjacent projects for the duration of the LAL: They married the Moon in Los Angeles, California, and the Appalachian Mountains in Athens, Ohio (2010);

the Snow in Ottawa, Canada; the Rocks in Barcelona, Spain; and Coal in Gijon, Spain (2011). Their final LAL wedding project was *The White Wedding to the Sun: Pleasuring the Planetary Clitoris* in San Francisco, California, in December 2011. Additionally, they have led Ecosexual Walking Tours all over the world; premiered and toured a stage work entitled *Dirty Sexecology: 25 Ways to Make Love to the Earth*; have become actively involved in the fight against mountain top removal in the Appalachian Mountains, activism that includes the filming and producing of a film entitled *Goodbye Gauley Mountain—An Ecosexual Love Story* (2013); organized multiple EcoSex Symposiums in both the United States and abroad that brought together artists, scholars, and activists to discuss the development of ecosexuality in a range of cultural arenas; offered free Sidewalk Ecosex Education Clinics; and have continued to tour, teach, lecture, and exhibit their work with sexecology and ecosexuality around the world.[6] Having completed their seven-year LAL project, Sprinkle and Stephens have devoted their focus to the ongoing development of "sexecology," their term for a field of research "exploring the places where sexology and ecology intersect in our culture—in art, theory, practice and activism."[7]

In this chapter, I will discuss ways in which the performance of ecosexuality in the work of the LAL suggests ontologies of both performance and the material world that consider performances as materializing phenomena in which material entities—such as "the human" and "the environment"—do not merely interact, but are intra-actively produced. I will focus my articulation of these themes through an analysis of the *Eco-Sexual Blue Wedding to the Sea* (2009), although I believe that this "ecosexual intervention" is accomplished in Sprinkle and Stephens's work more generally, and that each project and performance offers a different inflection to ecosexuality and how we might understand its elaboration.[8]

MATTER PARTICIPATING IN PERFORMANCE

> We welcome you all, humans and animals, bio and trans, men and women, transgender bodies, mutants and survivors. You've been invited by Annie Sprinkle and Beth Stephens to celebrate the blue year of their love and together, forming a liquid community in order to marry the Sea.[9]

This passage is taken from the homily offered by Beatriz Preciado as part of the Love Art Laboratory's *Eco-Sexual Blue Wedding to the Sea* in Venice, Italy, in 2009.[10] The *Blue Wedding to the Sea* is one installment in the seven-year LAL project and is intended as a "symbolic gesture" aiming to "instill hope, to be an antidote to fear, and act as a call to action."[11] Specifically, this wedding is between the artist-brides Sprinkle and Stephens and the Sea, a gesture of "loving the Sea erotically" and being taken deep inside their "primordial selves."[12] The artist-brides extend an invitation to the community of artists, performers, scholars, educators, activists, sex workers, and supporters who gather to participate in this event to also take vows to "love and protect Sea" along with them, acknowledging that "our bodies are made largely of water so in fact we are the Sea."[13] The wedding takes place at the Fear Society Pavilion (Arsenale Novissimo, Tese di San Cristoforo, Tesa 92) during the 53rd Venice Biennale International Art Exhibit. For several hours, participants gather at the edge of the waters of the Laguna Veneta to perform with and for one another before processing through the city, eventually starting their vows in an open air café and

FIGURE 23.1 Participants in the Love Art Laboratory's *Eco-Sexual Blue Wedding to the Sea* at the Fear Society Pavilion, Venice, Italy. Photo by Gigi Gatewood, used with permission from Elizabeth Stephens and Annie Sprinkle.

completing them on a flight of stairs leading down into the water near the Grand Canal at Arsenale.[14]

This wedding ceremony includes a diverse range of performers and disciplines (Figure 23.1).[15] The ceremony begins with a procession from the interior of the Fear Society Pavilion out to the water's edge. The performers and participants form a rough circle where the stone of the city meets the sea, sitting and standing alongside one another, facing toward the central space where performances will take place. Throughout the ceremony, off to one side, Natalie Loveless kneels in front of a bucket of water, gradually and carefully wrapping her head tightly in clear filament, disfiguring her face. Beatriz Preciado, the "Anti-Priest," leads the assembly in a chant written by Linda Montano (Figure 23.2). Carol Queen offers a pagan invocation, calling the quarters in each of the cardinal directions. Lian Amaris and Sadie Lune, dressed in metallic blue Lycra mermaid costumes, roll on the ground with one another, removing objects from zippered pockets at their crotch and sucking a double-headed dildo. Sarah Stolar and Jeff Medinas—performing as "Starlight" and "Neptune"—contribute a hoop and staff partnered "wave dance." There is a group meditation in which participants are asked to contemplatively caress erogenous parts of their body. There are several pieces in which clothes are removed, and several readings including poetry, storytelling, and spoken word. Tim Stüttgen performs a piece he refers to as "the final castration" that involves being wrapped in tin foil and smeared with whipped cream, and ends with the artist flinging himself into the canal, resurfacing having removed the dildo he had been sporting. Lady Monster performs a burlesque dance, spinning and twirling seductively before the gathered participant-spectators. Diana Pornoterrorista, covered in blue body paint, pulls a scarf out

FIGURE 23.2 Beatriz Preciado leads the assembly in a chant written by Linda Montano at the Love Art Laboratory's *Eco-Sexual Blue Wedding to the Sea*. Photo by Gigi Gatewood, used with permission from Elizabeth Stephens and Annie Sprinkle.

of her vagina and performs a blue anal fountain on a platform in the center of those gathered for the ceremony, with assistance from Beatriz Preciado. There is a scene of butch-femme seduction that finishes with strands of blue beads being hooked into the skin of one performer's back. Finally, wailing, Loveless dunks her bound head into a bucket of deep violet water. She proceeds to cut herself free of the filament that she had wrapped meticulously throughout the ceremony. Her face bears deep marks from the twine.[16] Each of these performances enacts a series of intra-actions between human and nonhuman materials, in ways that are far too numerous to describe.[17] While each of these various acts deserves its own analysis, what I would like to emphasize is that this event is distinctly collaborative and interdisciplinary, comprising a diverse range of actions that are motivated by participation in this event and particularly enabled by the interdependency—or, to use a term that will become more significant below, *intra-activity*—of this particular collaborative community. In addition to the performers and participants in the wedding ceremony itself, Sprinkle and Stephens consistently recognize the community of collaborators that contribute to the production of the LAL weddings, including costume designers, makeup artists, wedding planners, graphic designers, Web designers, photographers, videographers, caterers, funding bodies, exhibition spaces, producers, spiritual advisors, and so on. Whether in conversation, in archival materials, or in exhibitions, these weddings are never presented as only the work of Annie Sprinkle and Elizabeth Stephens, nor are Sprinkle and Stephens situated at the center of the work. Rather, credit for the work is distributed across the whole community of participants, displacing any clear, singular, lead artists, and emphasizing the collaborative nature of these projects. I would like to suggest that these collaborative interdisciplinary endeavors do not merely bring together a collection of preexisting art works and artists that are curated into these events, like a variety show that leaves the participants and their contributions unchanged. Rather, the operation of these LAL performances—of which the *Blue Wedding to the Sea* is only one to which attention might be given—is such that the collaborative endeavor produces both a community of action as well as its constituent parts. To be clear, I am suggesting that the performers and performances that constitute the *Blue Wedding to the Sea* do not preexist the event as such, but rather come to exist as they do in and through the particular material-discursive arrangements enacted as this ceremony.[18]

In order to articulate this claim, I will suggest that this performance is a material-discursive apparatus, a phenomenon comprised of ontologically inseparable intra-acting participants that include both nonhuman and human actants.[19] This apparatus relies on particular material supports that function as participants in the intra-active production of the ceremony. It involves spatial and ideological orientations through which ecosexual subjects and communities of action are produced, orientations that do not merely arrange preexisting subjects and communities toward or within a preexisting material world, but are themselves the intra-active production of such worlds, communities, and subjects. The orientations and relations that constitute this apparatus and through which its constituent actants emerge are accomplished in part through the redeployment of the wedding performative, specifically the wedding performative as it has been entangled in the material-discursive history of Venice and the Sea.

My understanding and description of the *Blue Wedding to the Sea* in these terms has been made possible by the significant influence of several theorists. Most notably, Karen Barad's articulation of *agential realism* and *posthumanist performativity* in her diffractive reading between science studies and performative approaches in critical social theories has provided new materialist epistemological, ontological, and ethical understandings of how the world comes to *matter*. Drawing primarily from the work of quantum physicist Niels Bohr, Barad articulates a relational ontology that takes *phenomena* to be the primary ontological unit rather than preexisting independent objects. She writes:

> [T]he primary ontological unit is not independent objects with inherent boundaries and properties but rather *phenomena*. In my agential realist elaboration, phenomena do not merely mark the epistemological inseparability of observer and observed, or the results of measurements; rather, *phenomena are the ontological inseparability/entanglement of intra-acting "agencies."* That is, phenomena are ontologically primitive relations—relations without preexisting relata. The notion of *intra-action* (in contrast to the usual "interaction," which presumes the prior existence of independent entities or relata) represents a profound conceptual shift. It is through specific agential intra-actions that the boundaries and properties of the components of phenomena become determinate and that particular concepts (that is, particular material articulations of the world) become meaningful.[20]

Barad's agential realist account of phenomena as the fundamental unit of ontology enacts a significant intervention in how we understand and represent the ongoing materialization of the world. The world is not simply an iterative interaction between subjects and objects, between the activities of human culture and passive nature as a resource; rather, these relata or agencies are themselves produced through their intra-activity. Barad writes that "intra-action" is a neologism intended to signify "*the mutual constitution of entangled agencies.*"[21] I will not summarize here the detailed account of specific experimental proce-dures within quantum physics and technoscience that Barad uses to provide empirical evi-dence of this relational ontology that takes phenomena as the fundamental unit through which intra-active relata become differentially produced; rather, I refer to Barad's work as a useful framework and vocabulary through which to account for the performative roles of both the nonhuman and the human, the material and the discursive, in performance, in ways that figure these actants as mutually constitutive rather than preexisting.

Two other terms that Barad elaborates are useful to this discussion: *performative* and *apparatus.* Of performativity, Barad writes:

> *Performative* approaches call into question representationalism's claim that there are repre-sentations, on the one hand, and ontologically separate entities awaiting representation, on the other, and focus inquiry on the practices or performances of representing, as well as the productive effects of those practices and the conditions for their efficacy. A performative understanding of scientific practices, for example, takes account of the fact that knowing does not come from standing at a distance and representing but rather from *a direct mate-rial engagement with the world.* Importantly, what is at issue is precisely the nature of these enactments. Not any arbitrary conception of doings or performances qualifies as perfor-mative. And humans are not the only ones engaged in performative enactments (which are not the same as theatrical performances). A performative account makes an abrupt break from representationalism that requires a rethinking of the nature of a host of fundamental notions such as being, identity, matter, discourse, causality, dynamics, and agency, to name a few.[22]

For Barad, "performative" is not co-extensive with "performance," but is instead concerned with the productive effects of practices of knowledge and representation. A performative account is concerned with the material engagements with the world—engagements that are themselves intra-active phenomena—through which the world is not merely measured and represented, but is iteratively produced through specific reconfigurations enacted through specific material-discursive arrangements, or "apparatuses." Barad defines appara-tuses as *"specific material configurations, or rather, dynamic (re)configurations of the world through which bodies are intra-actively materialized."*[23] They are "the practices of matter-ing through which intelligibility and materiality are constituted," or *"material-discursive practices—causal intra-actions through which matter is iteratively and differentially articu-lated, reconfiguring the material discursive field of possibilities and impossibilities in the ongo-ing dynamics of intra-activity that is agency."*[24] In this sense, apparatuses are practices or performances through which materialization is enacted. They are choreographies that do not merely organize but also produce the relations through which agential bodies—both nonhu-man and human—emerge. Although Barad suggests that such performative enactments are not the same as theatrical performances, neither can performances in the theatrical sense be excluded from this ontological framework. Rather, theatrical performances—which I take to include those performances germane to the disciplines of theater, dance, performance art, and so on—are themselves material-discursive practices, entanglements of a spectrum of actants that are intra-actively produced through the particular arrangements of the given apparatus. If we are to take "discursive practices" to be "specific material (re)configurings of the world through which the determination of boundaries, properties, and meanings is differentially enacted,"[25] it would be short-sighted to suggest that these theatrical disci-plines do not deploy material-discursive apparatuses. In examining our disciplines/events of performance—whether dance, theater, or performance art, let alone the endless list of events that are not the domain of theater-proper but might be considered nonetheless theatrical, such as public protests, athletic events, beauty pageants, political campaigns, funerals, military spectacles, and so on—our concern must be to consider not *whether* such events materialize the world through agential intra-actions but *how* these material-discursive practices produce boundaries, properties, meanings, and possibilities through differential becomings. How does each of these disciplines produce particular relations through which its constituent relata emerge? For instance, how do the practices associated with a particular dance technique or choreography shape what a body is and what it can do?[26] What objects—props, sets, costumes, puppets, pointe shoes, theaters, etc.—are produced in and through their use within a particular performance discipline? How are roles such as "spectator" and "performer" materialized as bodies through the particular relational activities ascribed to each role within situated settings? In short, how might matter come to matter differently if we *were* to consider dance, theater, performance art, and so on, as apparatuses through which relations and relata come to materialize? Departing from Barad, I consider the *Blue Wedding to the Sea* to function as such an apparatus, a set of material-discursive practices constituting a phenomenon of intra-active performers—including both human and nonhuman participants—through which those performers are differentially produced.

What then are the particularities of this apparatus? What are its material-discursive practices? And who or what are the intra-active performers produced in and through this apparatus? I will suggest that the *Eco-Sexual Blue Wedding to the Sea* is primarily an apparatus of *orientation*, a turning toward objects that enact the differential production of ecosexual subjects and the material world—here, the Sea—toward which they turn. These practices of orientation are accomplished through actions—collective *intra-actions* of performers, spectators, and the material supports for those acts—that produce a community of action which includes the Sea at Venice itself as a participant.

Sara Ahmed usefully expands the discourse on sexuality in ways that assist in this articulation of ecosexuality when she attends to sexuality as it is figured as an *orientation*. She writes of orientation, "Orientations involve directions toward objects that affect what we do, and how we inhabit space. We move toward and away from objects depending on how we are moved by them."[27] Orientations, then, are not merely about object choice; to turn toward an object produces a direction, a way of moving and taking action.[28] If we consider such an orientation to then produce or enact a particular material arrangement, it follows that to become oriented is an intra-activity through which both the oriented subject and the object toward which the subject turns are produced. This is consistent with Ahmed's discussion of objects. She writes, "The object is not reducible to the commodity, even when it is bought and sold: indeed, the object is not reducible to itself, which means it does not 'have' an 'itself' that is apart from its contact with others. The actions performed on the object (as well as with the object) shape the object. The object in turn affects what we do."[29] Orientations for Ahmed are directions for actions, and those actions shape the object toward which one orients; in turn, the affected object—notably here produced through the intra-action of orientation—affects what we do, reconfiguring the action that we take or can take, and in doing so, participating in the production of the orientation itself as well as the body that becomes through that orientation. If we take orientation to be an apparatus for intra-activity that differentially produces objects and subjects, we can here also see how this apparatus is an ongoing (re)configuration in which both objects and subjects participate. The turn toward the object produces an orientation from which the desiring subject emerges, bringing the subject into proximity with the object, and enabling particular actions (or intra-actions) to take place. The object is itself shaped and produced through these intra-actions—how it is engaged or handled or used—and in its (re)materialization, the object enables different possibilities and impossibilities, participating agentially in what actions [can] take place and thus how the world unfolds in and through the intra-actions made possible.

Within the *Blue Wedding to the Sea*, bodies turn toward the Sea, taking the Sea as the object toward which they orient. They gather together on the banks of the Venetian *lagune*, their orientation bringing them into proximity to the Sea toward which they turn. These bodies gather from all over the world—the United States, Canada, South America, Italy, Greece, Germany, Switzerland, Spain, and England, among others—drawn together to the waters of Venice by their orientation, an orientation pronounced "ecosexual" in the name of the event itself. Following Ahmed and Barad, the Sea—and the city built on and around it—must here be considered to be participating in this gathering, the object that enables particular intra-actions within the apparatus of this event. What is the effect of this gathering? What does it matter that these bodies—including the bodies of Sea and of Venice—are brought together by this ecosexual orientation? Ahmed writes:

> To direct one's gaze and attention toward the other, as an object of desire, is not indifferent, neutral, or casual: we can redescribe "towardness" as energetic. In being directed toward others, one acts, or is committed to specific actions, which point toward the future. When bodies share an object of desire, one could say they have an "affinity" or they are going in "the same direction." Furthermore, the affinity of such bodies involves identification: in being directed *toward* a shared object, as a direction that is repeated over time, they are also oriented *around* a shared object.[30]

The shared orientation of bodies turning toward the Sea produces both a gathering *on* the banks of Venice, where stone meets water, and also a gathering *around* this shared object. A collective is formed through this gathering on and around a shared object, a collective that does not preexist the gathering but is produced as an effect of this apparatus. In this sense, while the orientation toward the Sea produces subjects turning toward an object with which they take action, it also brings bodies together around a shared orientation toward this object, enabling a diversity of actions that are performed with and for one another. Bodies do not merely turn toward the Sea, but they turn toward the Sea *together*.

Judith Butler addresses the necessity of collectivity for political action and the production of public space in her lecture "Bodies in Alliance and the Politics of the Street," presented in Venice as part of "The State of Things" lecture series sponsored by the Office for Contemporary Art Norway in conjunction with the 54th Venice Biennale—two years after the LAL married the Sea during the 53rd Venice Biennale. She argues that "for politics to take place, the body must appear," a space of appearance that is always established through sociality, a being for the other in forms of appearance for which we cannot individually give an account. She goes on to say:

> No one body establishes the space of appearance, but this action, this performative exercise happens only "between" bodies, in a space that constitutes the gap between my own body and another's. In this way, my body does not act alone, when it acts politically. Indeed, the action emerged from the "between."[31]

Butler figures the gathering of bodies together as a necessary condition for political action. The *Blue Wedding to the Sea* takes this condition as an organizational practice within the event. In addition to bodies turning toward the Sea and the production of a community of action around this shared orientation, bodies also turn *toward one another*, performing with and for one another in turn. The unfolding of the performance over time does not maintain a stable unilateral orientation of spectators toward performers; rather, the performers are the spectators for one another in turn, distributing the "center" of the community in a shifting, mobile direction of attention. In some cases, the spectators are recruited as participants in the performances, creating a situation reminiscent of Augusto Boal's *Theater of the Oppressed*, in which the community as a whole is active, performing with and for itself as a whole.[32] The space of appearance that Butler suggests is a necessary condition for political action emerges in the *Blue Wedding* again and again amid the shifting positions of performers and spectators as bodies appear with and for one another.

Significantly, within this same talk in which Butler claims collectivity and plurality as a necessary condition for political action, she includes the material environment as a participant in the action that takes place. In her discussion of political protests such as those taking place in North Africa and the Middle East in 2011, she states, "the square and the street are not only the material supports for action, but they themselves are part of any theory of public and corporeal action that we might propose. Human action depends upon all sorts of supports-—it is always supported action."[33] For Butler, this material support is not only a stage for action, but the material environment is configured as a part of the action. "So when we think about what it means to assemble in a crowd . . . we see some way that bodies in their plurality lay claim to the public, find and produce the public through seizing and reconfiguring the matter of material environments; at the same time, those material environments are part of the action, and they themselves act when they become the support for action."[34] While it seems as if Butler's account of material agency continues to rely on human action as the means through which the agency of material environments becomes articulate—primarily as a support for human action—this inclusion of material environments as participants in political action and the production of publics is a significant step in developing ontologies of performance that take account of the role of nonhuman material actants with which we intra-act in our various disciplines.

Jane Bennett, in her development of a *vital materialism*, pursues a politics that engages intentionally with the vibrancy and liveliness of matter itself. She writes:

> How would political responses to public problems change were we to take seriously the vitality of (nonhuman) bodies? By "vitality," I mean the capacity of things—edibles, commodities, storms, metals—not only to impede or block the will and designs of humans but also to act as quasi agents or forces with trajectories, propensities, or tendencies of their own. My aspiration is to articulate a vibrant materiality that runs alongside and inside humans to see how analyses of political events might change if we gave the force of things more due.[35]

She goes on to suggest that there is an ethics to how we imagine matter. She suspects that "the image of dead or thoroughly instrumentalized matter feeds human hubris and our earth-destroying fantasies of conquest and consumption."[36] Her book pursues a range of places at which we might consider the agency of materiality, in ways that displace agency as primarily a human property and distribute it across a field of nonhuman and human actants, and that take the "ontologically heterogeneous 'public' coalescing around a problem" as the appropriate unit for analysis in any democratic theory.[37] Following Butler and Bennett, it becomes useful to consider the ways in which the *Blue Wedding to the Sea*, which is figured explicitly within the "Artists' Statement" and the Anti-Priest Beatriz Preciado's homily as a political act, operates as an "ontologically heterogeneous public" comprised of human and nonhuman material-discursive actants across which agency is distributed. How does the "material environment" (as Butler refers to it) participate in the action of the performance, in ways that are entangled with but not reducible to human action?

Before addressing this question, it is necessary to recall that the collective action of these nonhuman and human actants *produces* the differential components of that collective. Within Ahmed's terms of orientation, and Butler and Bennett's discussions of gathering and collectives and publics, it might be easy to default to a perspective of preexisting individual entities that are then arranged through the apparatuses of group action and shared orientations. However, we must continue to recall that Barad's agential realist contribution to this analysis is that the *relata do not precede the relation*; the apparatus enacts practices that configure phenomena as states of relation from which differential terms such as object and subject, or material environment and human, emerge. We must then do more than inquire after how the city of Venice and the Sea on which it is built participate in the action of this performance; we must consider how they are *produced* through participation in this intra-action and, in turn, how the human participants emerge simultaneously through this intra-activity.

How does the Sea participate in this action, which is to ask, in what ways is the Sea performatively constituted through its iterative intra-active participation in the performance of the *Blue Wedding to the Sea*? The Sea operates in a range of material-discursive becomings. The materiality of the waters flowing around and through Venice cannot be disentangled from the discursive productions through which they have come to matter, discursive productions including but not limited to the LAL wedding ceremony; likewise, such discursive productions cannot be disentangled from the material constraints, supports, and consequences through which they become enacted. Discourse is never merely ideological, but always relies on material apparatuses for its articulations, articulations that themselves participate in the (re)configuration of material possibilities and impossibilities, the ongoing materialization of the world and how it matters. Within the *Blue Wedding*, the Sea—specifically, the Venetian *lagune* of the Adriatic—flows alongside the banks of the city, waters and stone that are here given by way of an ancient history of materialization, centuries of nonhuman and human intra-action engaged in commerce, politics, religion, society, and culture.[38] The city itself might be considered the materializing effect of human intra-actions with these waters of the north Adriatic Sea, a materialization that reconfigures both "the human" and "the Sea" in the differential production of what becomes possible and impossible due to its iterative becoming. The *Blue Wedding* is one such possibility enabled by the long history of formative intra-action between the city of Venice and the Sea. The materiality of the Sea has functioned for centuries as a material condition for the city; in turn, the materiality of the city functions as a necessary condition and support for this performance, which in turn conditions the possibility for particular orientations and groupings of bodies. The city and the Sea do not only provide the support for these human actions, as if such actions and actants preexist the apparatus of the performance in which they take place; rather, such actions are already intra-actions *with* the city and the Sea, and the performance itself participates in the history of material-discursive production through which "the human," the city, and the Sea are entangled.

In order to offer a more thorough account for the material-discursive entanglement between human actants and the Sea, it is necessary to turn attention toward another way in which this performance operates performatively. Here, I will consider how the *Blue Wedding to the Sea* functions as an "illocutionary performative" in the sense described by J. L. Austin and taken up by Butler.[39] Austin described the "illocutionary performative speech act" as that which accomplishes what it says in the moment of the saying. Its efficacy relies on a "total speech situation"; specifically, it relies on the correct ritualized circumstances for the invocation to be authorized to accomplish what it says. Butler writes, "The illocutionary speech act performs its deed *at the moment* of the utterance, and yet to the extent that the moment is ritualized, it is never merely a single moment. The 'moment' in ritual is a condensed historicity: it exceeds itself in past and future directions, an effect of prior and future invocations that constitute and escape the instance of the utterance."[40] She goes on to write:

> If a performative provisionally succeeds (and I will suggest that "success" is always and only provisional), then it is not because an intention successfully governs the action of speech, but only because that action echoes prior actions, and *accumulates the force of authority through the repetition or citation of a prior and authoritative set of practices.* It is not simply that the speech act takes place *within* a practice, but that the act is itself a ritualized practice. What this means, then, is that a performative "works" to the extent that it *draws on and covers over* the constitutive conventions by which it is mobilized. In this sense, no term or statement can function performatively without the accumulating and dissimulating historicity of force.[41]

It is significant to note that Austin discusses marriage, specifically the accomplishment of marriage through the performative of the wedding ceremony and its speech acts, as one such illocutionary speech act, and that this is a performative that gets taken up and redeployed queerly and subversively in the LAL project. However, it is not only the wedding performative in the general sense that is enacted in the *Blue Wedding to the Sea*. In the section that follows, I recount the specific performative history of marrying the Sea in Venice.

The Performative Marriage of Venice and the Sea

> Why marry the Sea in Venice? During the Renaissance, the Doge (chief magistrate) decreed that, "Venice must marry the sea as a man marries a woman and thus become her Lord." So each year the Doge would go out on a boat and drop a ring into the water. But can people really Lord over the Sea? What is perfectly clear is that people have the power to destroy her, and are rapidly doing so. We will follow the tradition of marrying the Sea in Venice—as two women who have moved beyond the dominant-male and submissive-female dynamic, as seductive eco-sexual artists, and as global citizens who care deeply about the welfare of our planet.[42]

This passage, taken from Sprinkle and Stephen's "Artists' Statement" for the *Blue Wedding to the Sea*, clearly situates their project within a performative history of ritual weddings between Venice and the Sea. However, the story is even more complex than the version summarized for the LAL's "Artists' Statement," and it is a complexity that deserves closer examination in order to fully appreciate the performativity of this event.

It is true that for centuries Venice has held an annual "Sensa festival" in conjunction with the celebration of Ascension Day in which the Sea has been blessed and wed. In this ritual, the Doge sails out to where the Venetian lagoon opens onto the Adriatic, and drops his gold ring into the Sea, declaring, "We espouse thee, O sea, as a sign of true and perpetual dominion."[43] However, the origins of this tradition do not lead back to a magisterial decree. Rather, this marriage between Venice and the Sea was arranged by none other than the pope of the Catholic Church, Pope Alexander III.

In 1177, Doge Sebastian Ziani played a significant role in securing peace during a conflict between Pope Alexander III and the Holy Roman Emperor, Frederick Barbarossa. As an expression of his gratitude for Ziani's assistance, Alexander issued a series of symbolic gifts—or *trionfi*—to Ziani and Venice, the final gift being a golden ring and the right to marry the Sea. Giving the ring to Ziani, Alexander declared, "Take this, O Ziani, which you and your successors will use each year to marry the sea, so that posterity knows that the lordship of the sea is yours, held by you as an ancient possession and by right of conquest, and that the sea was placed under your dominion, as a wife is to a husband."[44] The pope went on to assure that the ceremony would "protect sailors and consecrate the waves as a cemetery for those lost at sea."[45] It is significant that this was a marriage that was not only blessed but was initiated by the Catholic pope. In our contemporary historical moment, in which ongoing debates about the right to marry and have marriage recognized is so often populated with claims from the religious right that marriage is exclusively defined as a union between one man and one woman—verbiage that has even been adopted into federal law within the United States of America[46]—it is significant that in 1177 the pope of the Catholic Church orchestrated a marriage between a man and an environmental entity. In this convoluted debate, the church's endorsement of what we might retrospectively consider to be an ecosexual union certainly goes disavowed, and while the role of the pope was not made explicit in the LAL's "Artist's Statement" or in the wedding ceremony itself, the *Blue Wedding to the Sea*, through its participation in this performative history, brings attention to the rupture that this history enacts within the historical definition of marriage as practiced by the Catholic church.

In addition to the intervention that this history and its redeployment makes in the discourse of marriage today, it also brings attention to centuries of material-discursive production through which Venice and the Sea have been intra-actively constituted, specifically through the deployment of "marriage" as an apparatus that has configured and reconfigured the materiality of Venice and the Sea in a differentiating production of each in and through their intra-action. I will go into more detail below as to the particular ways in which marriage functions as a performative apparatus in the configuring of Venice and the Sea—both historically and in the *Blue Wedding to the Sea*—but first I want to address this condition more generally. In considering how this site where Venice meets the Sea has come to matter—and by "matter," I follow Barad in signaling both its *materialization* and its *meanings*, which are fully entangled with one another—the apparatuses deployed must be considered. How this site has been made meaningful has been enacted materially and has material consequences. The materiality of the site has been and continues to be a participant in the apparatus through which it comes to matter. And it is through the meaningful intra-actions between human and nonhuman actants that both become differentially produced, enabling some possibilities while foreclosing others. How we turn toward the world is an apparatus through which both the world and those who turn are produced, as discussed above.[47] Ahmed reminds us that our orientations shape the contours of the world by affecting and enacting states of relation and proximity between bodies; "orientations shape not only how we inhabit space, but how we apprehend this world of shared inhabitance, as well as 'who' or 'what' we direct our energy and attention toward."[48] It is significant that the joint human and nonhuman enterprise of Venice choreographed its orientation toward the Sea as an act of marriage; this ritualized gesture ascribes meaning to the positions of "the human" and the Sea, drawing on the performative force of the wedding to achieve that meaningfulness. While this chapter is not intended as an exhaustive account of the mattering of Venice, which would involve detailed analyses of the political, economic, religious, and ecological situation of this site, what I hope to bring attention to is that the apparatuses that are used to produce these actants and their qualities in their differential specificity are not only accomplished materially—through the direct physical engagement between the Doges of Venice, through the ritualized choreographies of sailing onto and dropping a ring into the waters of the Venetian lagoons, for instance—but also produces an orientation that enables further materializing possibilities and impossibilities. Venice was built and maintained and defended and mythologized all through direct intra-active engagement with the Sea, engagement that was significantly configured through the material-discursive apparatus of marriage. This cannot be viewed as merely incidental. Barad writes:

> Recall that apparatuses are themselves phenomena—the result of intra-actions of material-discursive practices—and the enfolding of phenomena into subsequent iterations of particular practices (which may be traded and mutated across space, time, and subcultures, in the iterative reconfiguring of spacetimemattter itself) constitutes important shifts in the nature of the intra-actions that result in the production of new phenomena, and so on. Which shifts occur matter for epistemological as well as ontological reasons: a different material-discursive apparatus of bodily production materializes a different configuration of the world, not merely a different description of a fixed and independent reality.[49]

The apparatuses through which bodies are configured and produced *matter*. For Venice to turn toward the Sea in a different way would be to shift the apparatus and to thus materialize both Venice—itself already a complex collective of human and nonhuman material relations—and the Sea differently. This should emphasize both the significance of marriage as an apparatus in the history of material-discursive intra-action between Venice and the Sea and the significance of the ways in which the LAL redeploys and reconfigures this apparatus in the *Blue Wedding*.

This marriage between the city of Venice and the Sea was itself performative in that it relied on the particular ritual conventions of marriage within the period and culture of Venice at that time. Edward Muir records:

> The marriage of the sea was so richly symbolic precisely because it imitated a universal and socially meaningful contractual relationship. In Venetian law the husband was the *padrone* of his wife: his authority was considered to be the most ancient, preceding the authority of fathers over children, masters over servants, and princes over subjects; and it was supported by the divine law of the Bible and the civil law of Rome. Scripture, by saying a wife should be a companion, not a slave, in theory moderated the harshness of the Roman civil law, which included the precept that the husband, in consultation with his wife's relatives, had full power to punish his spouse for adultery or libertine acts. The Roman wife, on the other hand, had no rights against a husband even if his adultery could be proven. Whatever moderation there was

under Christianity, the supreme position of the male remained. Venetian women owned their dowries as their share of their natal patrimony, but husbands could legally invest their wives' dowries as they saw fit.[50]

To configure the Sea into the role of the wife and Venice into the role of the husband was to produce these positions differentially within an ancient authoritarian and gendered arrangement. The Sea was not merely produced as feminine, but as a wife, the subjugation of which produced Venice as not only masculine, but as husband and lord. These roles are complex, especially for the Sea. In one sense, to figure the Sea as a wife is to figure the material world as sexual subject, and in doing so to produce the Sea as other than so much passive, inert, dull matter; it would seem to figure the Sea as more than simply a natural resource. However, following Muir, if we examine the conventional understanding of marriage in Venice during the Renaissance, wives were to husbands little more than resources over which they maintained near-total authority. To figure the Sea as a wife during this time, then, was to enact the complex operation of imbuing the Sea with a form of "wifely" subjectivity, and in doing so to also enlist the Sea in the proliferation and reiteration of a discursive production of the wife as a compromised subject, a subject position already reduced to that of a material resource. This is a condition addressed by many ecofeminist writers and philosophers—in more or less tenable arguments; such writers attest to cultural histories in which the denigrated positions of both women and nature within hierarchical dualisms are aligned to constitute mutually reinforcing systems of oppression of those who come to inhabit such terms.[51] As stated above, the particularities of this arrangement enable particular meaningful materializing possibilities. To figure the Sea as a compromised sexual subject, herself little more than a natural resource to be possessed and managed, is to suspend an ethical orientation that recognizes the constitutive entanglement between "the human" and the Sea. In order to be possessed and dominated, the Sea must be dissimilar from its "lord." The constitutive history in which the formation of Venice itself relies intra-actively on the Sea must be disavowed in order to consolidate Venice as a fully independent masculine subject.[52] In the reconfiguration of the wedding performative in the *Blue Wedding to the Sea*, this entanglement becomes fully avowed, producing a different orientation toward the Sea, different positions and properties for intra-active actants, and thus different possibilities and impossibilities for action.

In the homily for the *Blue Wedding*, Preciado states:

> To marry the Sea today, in 2009, is to embrace a sick being. The Sea we are going to marry is, as we ourselves are, polluted, sick, but alive and historically charged. During the last two hundred years the human species has contributed to poisoning the water, killing fish and water mammals, threatening the health of the Sea and therefore putting at risk the survival of the planet. For this, we come here today, to Venice, a city made of water, to ask the Sea for forgiveness. We are here to give our love back to the Sea . . . The anxiety to be immune comes from the fear of the other. From the fear of not to be and not to have in common. The other is here seen as a threat to the community. An immune community is a community of Fear. As we marry the sick Sea today, let us get rid of fear of the other, fear of queerness, fear of sickness, fear of ugliness, fear of the grotesque, fear of the virus, fear of death. As we marry the sick Sea today, let us remember to construct community on 'the social and biological vulnerability of the body' rather than on immunity and fear of the other . . . To get married to the water means to abandon identity and nationality and to become a liquid community able to permeate different soils and to cross political and moral frontiers without fear.[53]

The Sea that is configured in the LAL's *Blue Wedding* is not the same Sea that was configured in the weddings between the Sea and the Venetian Doges. This reconfiguration of the apparatus necessarily produces the internally intra-active participants differently. It is an orientation that enacts a different material-discursive relation, and that relation produces different relata. Gone is the language of "lordship," "possession," and "dominion," and although the Sea is taken as a wife, it is not figured as a discrete natural resource for consumption and management. Rather, the Sea is figured as "sick" and "polluted," as we ourselves are sick and polluted. Here the wedding takes on explicit ethical dimensions. The Sea is characterized as sick, and Preciado—speaking as "we," presumably the "we" of the human species—takes responsibility for this sickness, a pollution and sickness in which we also take part, through which both we and the Sea have been intra-actively produced. It is not enough to state that human action has polluted the Sea, as if such actions were accomplished by preexisting human actants, and as if the Sea itself was a passive material "surface" that received the marks of our actions. Rather, the Sea itself—as polluted and sick—is produced through the intra-actions accomplished with human collaborators, who are themselves produced through this history of pollution. The Sea participates in the sickness, carrying toxicity in its waves, its liquid properties complicit in its polluted production. In turn, the human is not immune from this sickness. The polluted world that we have produced is a world of which we are a part; it is not merely a sickness of our environment, but also a sickness that reconfigures the possibilities of what it means to be human. It is a sickness affects our own health and wellness, participating in the cellular materialization of our bodies, as well as the practices deployed in maintaining and regulating our bodies as a part of—or toward becoming apart from—a sick world. It is a sickness that affects what actions become available and unavailable to us, what places become hospitable or inhospitable, what spaces become accessible or inaccessible, and how life and livability become managed in the face of such sickness. Preciado emphasizes the planet as a system of living relations, and the threat to the Sea as a threat to the survival of such relations. This testimony to the precarity of the planet, and the implication of our own vulnerability within such precarity, should not be taken as a reduction of responsibility; rather, it is a distribution of agency that increases the range and reach of our entangled responsibility. It is an assertion that our ethical responsibility is toward the life and livability of the planet as a network of intra-related lives, and that our own lives are produced, sustained, and threatened within such relations.

It is especially relevant that Preciado characterizes this community and the ethical responsibilities that it demands within immune system discourses. The very notion of immunity, itself a highly theorized field of discourse,[54] is often predicated on a mythology of a boundary that is not to be permeated, on keeping the inside in, the outside out, and the clear distinction between the two prohibiting any possibility of contamination. This model of immunity has been deployed within a range of discourses, including but not limited to body politics of gender, sexuality and race, environmental management, cultural studies, and war and nationalism. In each of these settings, there is a representation of a bounded ontology, a body or being that must be preserved by maintaining a clear exclusion of that which it is not. What could be more terrifying to a subject whose ontology is predicated on boundaries, exclusion, and fear of the other than to recognize that one's existence is already given over to a world of others, that one's constitution and survival depends on a relation in which both the subject and the other are internal and undone?[55] There is no possibility of ontological immunity if we take intra-active phenomena as the fundamental unit of ontology; "I" am already of "you," and "you" are already of "me." As Haraway has asserted, "The relationship is the smallest possible unit of analysis."[56] Recall that in their "Artists' Statement," Sprinkle and Stephens remind us that "our bodies are made largely of water so in fact we are the Sea."[57] "We" are already of the Sea and the Sea is fully entangled in the formation of "we." To attempt to conceive of any "we" otherwise would be to deny something of the conditions of our formation and survival. "It is futile to seek a pure nature unpolluted by humanity, and it is foolish to define the self as something purely human."[58]

The performative operation of the *Blue Wedding* is not only accomplished through language; the richly diverse spectrum of bodies and physical performances that constitute the event do considerable labor toward the production of bodies that affirm their own relationality and vulnerability. The variety of acts performed offer a demonstration of what a body can do—what a body can become—further physicalizing much of what is affirmed through the language in and around the wedding. As I review the documentation of the wedding, I ask what it is that bodies become through this *Eco-Sexual Blue Wedding to the Sea*—a "becoming" that is accomplished through "doing." Here bodies gather and process through the streets and stand and sit together, supported by the stone promenades of an ancient city, itself the sedimentation of political, economic, and religious human/stone/Sea intra-activity. Bodies face one another, appear for one another, and witness one another, and in doing so are given over to one another. Bodies become extended into other materials, modified by a range of prosthetics: strap-on dildos, breastplates, blue Viking helmets with rabbit ears, metallic false eyelashes. They become painted and glittered, wrapped in blue silk and lycra and velvet and foil, adorned with wigs and ribbons and jewelry and pasties. These are bodies open to amelioration. Bodies handle swinging, circling hoops and staves, articulating roundly through skeletal joints and creating new joints where hands adroitly grasp these objects. The movements of these bodies reveal their capacities: they twist and twirl, gyrate and undulate, dancing with and for one another's pleasure; they roll and crawl along the gravelly ground, shining blue mermaids writhing against one another in public displays of affection. Bodies sweat and glisten where flesh meets the thick dewy humidity of Venice, and fan themselves and squint their eyes in the bright light of summer sun. Bodies squirt blue anal fountains out onto the stone and submerge themselves into shimmering body of the Laguna Veneta. Bodies are bound in filament, and when the filament is cut loose, the flesh is mangled, retaining deep marks where bindings have been pressed into their surfaces. Bodies pierce and become pierced, puncturing flesh with hooks and affirming both their vulnerability and penetrability. Act after act, more and more qualities and capacities of bodies are performed, and through such performances, bodies are thus produced as the materialization of so many qualities, the actualization of so many potentialities. The assertion of ourselves as given over to a world of others, as precarious and permeable in our relations—to one another, to objects, to environments, to histories, and so on—is not merely rhetorical or discursive; it has been material all along, physicalized through how these bodies do their own becomings.

The formation of community also figures explicitly in Preciado's reconfiguration of the wedding performative in her homily. Preciado says that "to get married to the water means to abandon identity and nationality and to become a liquid community able to permeate different soils and to cross political and moral frontiers without fear." In marrying the Sea, of which we have already been figured as a part, we are also marrying ourselves, a metonymic slide that reinforces this wedding not as a unilateral engagement between two brides and the Sea, but as a formation of a community of action, a community that turns toward one another and the Sea. Here, to turn toward the Sea is also to turn toward one another, a turn that is literalized in the choreography of the wedding ceremony, in which participants face one another in the round and perform for one another in turn. This recalls and expounds Ahmed's claim that communities or groups form *around* shared objects of desire. For Ahmed, the object toward which a community turns is internal to the community, a condition of its emergence in its specificity. She writes, "Groups are formed through their shared orientation toward an object . . . In a way, 'what' is faced by a collective is also what brings it into existence. As such, the object 'in front' of the 'we' might be better described as 'behind' it, as what allows the 'we' to emerge."[59] In this turn toward the Sea, the condition for emergence takes on further material implications. The water of the Sea is literally internal to the formation of our bodies, a participant in the "*particularly rich and complex* collection of materials"[60] from which we are formed. The community that gathered together for the *Blue Wedding to the Sea* turns toward one another through the cycle of performance and spectatorship, and also turns toward one another/themselves in their orientation toward the Sea, with which we are always already productively entangled.

These are the differences produced through the LAL's reconfiguration of the wedding to the Sea: the Sea is not produced as a resource to be possessed and dominated but as a vibrant materiality of which we are a part, produced through a history of intra-active engagement. The Sea is not figured as separate or separated from ourselves but as flowing in and through our bodies and our communities. We are not figured as bounded and discrete, but as ourselves open to pollution, penetration, and prosthesis. The Sea is figured as sick, and it is a sickness in which we are a part, attesting to the pervasive vulnerability of material intra-activity through which we and the Sea are produced. This attention to the vulnerability that conditions our relations with the Sea in Preciado's homily foregrounds the ethical project of the *Blue Wedding to the Sea*. We are entangled with the Sea, and it is an entanglement that iteratively produces the material world through our ongoing intra-actions. Venice and the Sea have emerged from a history of performative intra-active engagements, and the LAL—along with all those who join them—participate in this performative history in ways that (re)configure ourselves and the Sea differently. This act might be considered emblematic of our ethical responsibility to the ongoing materialization of the world. As Barad writes, "The point is not merely that there is a web of causal relations that we are implicated in and that there are consequences to our actions. We are a much more intimate part of the universe than any such statement implies . . . Our (intra)actions matter—each one reconfigures the world in its becoming—and yet they never leave us; they are sedimented into our becoming, they become us. And yet even in our becoming there is no 'I' separate from the intra-active becoming of the world."[61]

Conclusions

Preciado's homily concludes, "As we marry the sick Sea today, let us be bound by a love bigger than human love, reaching non-human animals, the elements and the earth. As we marry the Sea today, let us make love to water, have non-human sex with the elements. As we marry the Sea today, we invite you to open your mouth, your hands, your vaginas, urethras and anuses to non-human love."[62] Preciado's words articulate an ecosexuality that brings me back to and reconfigures what initially drew me to the LAL: an art that enacts a life that is all about love, a love that is persistent, marrying one another again and again and again, a love oriented toward inclusivity and bringing more bodies together into creative endeavors and the formation of community. This ecosexual love turns toward a rich spectrum of nonhuman and human bodies, enabling intimate encounters and intra-activities through which our bodies become reconfigured, reoriented, and produced anew. In *Blue Wedding to the Sea*, Sprinkle, Stephens, Preciado, and all those gathered together—which includes the material environments with which they take action—turn toward and open to one other, moving across borders of identity, and embracing the other as already internal to the self. This orientation invests vulnerability with eroticism, reconsiders sites of impingement as sites of potential pleasure, and emphasizes that ethical responsibility can be more than the preservation of life through prohibition: our ethical responsibility/responsivity must also include a recognition of our ongoing intra-active materialization through our engagement with the world of which we are a part, our participation in the apparatuses through which such intra-active engagements become enacted, and our capacity to reconfigure such apparatuses in ways that produce new possibilities for the materialization of the world.

Within fields of performing arts such as dance, theater, performance art, and other adjacent and overlapping disciplines, our responsibility is to consider how the work that we create functions materially and discursively as apparatuses through which we engage intra-actively with the world.[63] In what ways do we orient or turn toward the world? How is the world produced through how we turn toward it, and how are we also produced through such turns? What are the communities and collectives established through shared objects toward which we orient, and where are the spaces of appearance and political action enabled through such gatherings? What is brought into reach and into contact through our actions, and what is made more remote or out of reach? What possibilities and impossibilities are enabled through such intra-actions? If we consider the work that we do to enact phenomena in which we participate in the materialization of the world through particular apparatuses, how are those phenomena picked up and enfolded into other apparatuses through which the world becomes? Ultimately, these questions lead us to ethical considerations for the work that we produce. We can no longer operate as if the world is composed of preexisting individual entities and inert matter, and that our work merely organizes or represents such independently existing bodies. To do so would be to deny our role in producing the ways in which the world comes to matter. We need to consider our work as sites of agential participation in which we have the opportunity to enact the world differently, reconfiguring what becomes possible through how the world is enabled to intra-act. We need to begin to consider how our work does not merely enact the intentions of preexisting subjects, but rather performs material-discursive practices through which we ourselves and the world of which we are a part come to matter.

NOTES

1. "Love Art Laboratory" Homepage, Love Art Lab (Annie Sprinkle and Elizabeth Stephens), 2007, http://loveartlab.org/index.php.
2. Ibid.

3. Chakras are energy centers in the body taxonomized in yogic philosophy. See Anodea Judith, *Wheels of Life: A User's Guide to the Chakra System* (Woodbury, MN: Llewellyn, 2006).

4. "Blue Year Gallery Installation," Love Art Lab (Annie Sprinkle and Elizabeth Stephens), 2007, http://loveartlab.org/gallery-installations.php?year_id=5.

5. For a more detailed account of Sprinkle and Stephens's declaration of ecosexuality, see "Ecosex Manifesto," Elizabeth Stephens and Annie Sprinkle, http://sexecology.org/ research-writing/ecosex-manifesto/; "Ecosex Herstories | sexecology.org," Stephens and Sprinkle, http://sexecology.org/research-writing/ecosex-herstories/; and *The Journal of EcoSex Research* 1, no. 1, http://sexecology.org/research-writing/the-journal-of-ecosex-research/.

6. In addition to my scholarly interest in the LAL's work, I participated in *The Purple Wedding to the Appalachian Mountains* in 2010, *The White Wedding to the Sun* in 2011, and the EcoSex Symposium II in 2011.

7. "Short Bios | sexecology.org," Elizabeth Stephens and Annie Sprinkle, http://sexecology. org/about-us/short-bios/.

8. To be clear, I believe the framework of "ecosexuality" to be a field of diverse potentialities that become articulated differently in different situations, contexts, and sites. The LAL and the *Blue Wedding to the Sea* comprise a series of nodes at which ecosexuality becomes articulated, but I believe its potential as a framework exists at innumerable sites at which sex and sexuality become entangled with "ecology," "nature," the "environment," and the material world more generally.

9. "Beatriz Preciado's Homily," Love Art Laboratory (Annie Sprinkle and Elizabeth Stephens), http://loveartlab.org/slideshow.php?year_id=5&cat_id=126.

10. For the most part, I will refer to the *Blue Wedding to the Sea* in the present tense, gesturing toward how it might be inhabited as a figuration of ecosexual orientation, and also toward its continuing digital "performance" through the LAL website archive.

11. "Artists' Statement: Eco-Sexual Blue Wedding to the Sea," Love Art Laboratory (Annie Sprinkle and Elizabeth Stephens), http://www.loveartlab.net/PDF/statement_blu09_final.pdf.

12. Ibid.

13. Ibid.

14. Michelle Tea, "The Fifth Wedding: A Dispatch from a Three-Way Marriage at the 2009 Venice Biennale between a Porn-Star-Turned-Performance-Artist, her Chakra-Savvy Partner, and the Ocean," *The Believer* (November/December 2009): 15–20.

15. For documentation of the event, visit "Ecosexual Blue Wedding to the Sea," Love Art Laboratory (Annie Sprinkle and Elizabeth Stephens), http://loveartlab.org/slideshow. php?year_id=5&cat_id=121.

16. My account of the wedding ceremony is reconstructed from the wedding program, http://www.loveartlab.net/PDF/VeniceProgramDesign.pdf; *Blue: A Documentary about "Eco-Sexual Blue Wedding to the Sea" by Annie Sprinkle and Beth Stephens*, by Francesca Fini, http://loveartlab.org/slideshow.php?year_id=5&cat_id=123; and Tea, "The Fifth Wedding." In accounting for this event as an intra-active phenomenon of material-discursive arrangements, it is significant to note that this chapter, itself a partici- pant in the material-discursive life of this event, is reliant on digitally archived materials, the technoeconomic relations of Internet access, and the mediating devices/practices of film and journalism. This account is not a representation of a preexisting independent event; rather, it is the production of an event—the event of this chapter—in which the *Blue*

Wedding to the Sea and its documentation are constituent parts that are themselves reconfigured and produced anew in and through the phenomenon of this account.

17. Costumes, themselves material participants in these performances, play a big role in the *Blue Wedding*. Michelle Tea recounts: "Everyone is wearing blue, and the overall look is very Burning Man—costumes and body paint, rhinestones and glitter, ribbons, tulle, sequins, chiffon, lots of tattoos, and some scarification markings keloiding across arms and collarbones. There are Venetian masks, fake flowers, and paper fans fluttering in the humidity." Tea, "The Fifth Wedding," 17.

18. By "material-discursive," I mean to signal the entanglement of discursive practices—the social, cultural, linguistic, and disciplinary conventions that condition the materialization of bodies and worlds—with the material conditions through which such discursive practices are accomplished. I use this term in order to resist a reductionism that figures matter as the passive surface on which discourse acts, or matter as fully determinate. Rather, material-discursive apparatuses and actants are operations of the agencies of both matter and discourse, which are never disentangleable from one another. Karen Barad writes, "In my agential realist account, *discursive practices are specific material (re)configurings of the world through which the determination of boundaries, properties, and meanings is differentially enacted.* That is, *discursive practices are ongoing agential intra-actions of the world* through which specific determinacies (along with complementary indeterminacies) are enacted within the phenomena produced." *Meeting the Universe Halfway: Quantum Physics and the Entanglement of Matter and Meaning* (Durham: Duke University Press, 2007), 148–49 (italics original).

19. The term "actant" is Bruno Latour's, and has been picked up by various scholars of science studies and adjacent inquiries into the nature of matter. Jane Bennett writes, "*Actant,* recall, is Bruno Latour's term for a source of action; an actant can be human or not, or, most likely, a combination of both. Latour defines it as 'something that acts or to which activity is granted by others. It implies no special motivation of human individual actors, nor of human in general.' An actant is neither an object nor a subject but an 'intervener,' akin to the Deleuzian 'quasi-causal operator.' An operator is that which, by virtue of its particular location in an assemblage and the fortuity of being in the right place at the right time, makes the difference, makes things happen, becomes the decisive force catalyzing an event." *Vibrant Matter: Towards a Political Ecology of Things* (Durham: Duke University Press, 2010), 9.

20. Barad, *Meeting the Universe Halfway*, 139 (italics original).

21. Ibid., 33 (italics original).

22. Ibid., 49 (italics original).

23. Ibid., 170 (italics original).

24. Ibid. (italics original).

25. Ibid., 148.

26. For more analysis on the relation of activity, agency, and the body, see Carrie Noland, *Agency and Embodiment: Performing Gestures/Producing Cultures* (Cambridge, MA: Harvard University Press, 2009).

27. Sara Ahmed, *Queer Phenomenology: Orientations, Objects, Others* (Durham, NC: Duke University Press, 2006), 28.

28. Here, Ahmed suggests that such orientations affect how we inhabit space; however, this configuration produces space as a preexisting container for action. Within Barad's agential realist account, the agential intra-actions of phenomena do not merely unfold in time and space but are the iterative reconfigurations/production of space, time, and matter. See Barad, *Meeting the Universe Halfway*, 140–42.

29. Ahmed, *Queer Phenomenology*, 43.

30. Ibid., 120 (italics original).

31. Judith Butler, "Bodies in Alliance and the Politics of the Street" (lecture at The State of Things lecture series, sponsored by the Office for Contemporary Art Norway, Venice, September 7, 2011), http://www.eipcp.net/transversal/1011/butler/en.

32. Augusto Boal, *Theater of the Oppressed* (London: Pluto Press, 1979).

33. Butler, "Bodies in Alliance and the Politics of the Street."

34. Ibid.

35. Bennett, *Vibrant Matter*, viii.

36. Ibid., ix.

37. Ibid., 108.

38. For a detailed account of the formation of Venice on the waters of the Adriatic, see Francis Cotterell Hodgson, *The Early History of Venice: From the Foundation to the Conquest of Constantinople A.D. 1204* (London: George Allen, 1901).

39. J. L. Austin, *How to Do Things with Words* (Cambridge, MA: Harvard University Press, 1962); Judith Butler, *Excitable Speech: A Politics of the Performative* (New York: Routledge, 1997).

40. Butler, *Excitable Speech*, 3 (italics original).

41. Ibid., 51 (italics original).

42. "Artists' Statement: Eco-Sexual Blue Wedding to the Sea," Love Art Lab (Annie Sprinkle and Elizabeth Stephens), http://www.loveartlab.net/PDF/statement_blu09_final.pdf.

43. For a detailed account of the full traditional ceremony of marrying the Sea, including what could be considered the choreography of the event, see Edward Muir, *Civic Ritual in Renaissance Venice* (Princeton: Princeton University Press, 1981), 119–23.

44. Muir, *Civic Ritual in Renaissance Venice*, 124.

45. Ibid.

46. See the Defense of Marriage Act, adopted January 3, 1996, amending Chapter 115 of title 28, United States Code, to "define and protect the institution of marriage," http://www.gpo.gov/fdsys/pkg/BILLS-104hr3396enr/pdf/BILLS-104hr3396enr.pdf.

47. There can be no doubt concerning the very real ways in which human activity has profoundly influenced the ways in which the Sea has materialized. While my focus here is on the specific role of the wedding performative in the materialization of Venice and the Sea, we might also consider how the effects of global warming and the exploitation of underground water resources have contributed to rising sea levels and the sinking of the city of Venice. See John Keahey, *Venice against the Sea: A City Beseiged* (New York: St. Martin's Press, 2002), and Peter D. Ward, *The Flooded Earth: Our Future in a World without Ice Caps* (New York: Basic Books, 2010).

48. Ahmed, *Queer Phenomenology*, 3.

49. Barad, *Meeting the Universe Halfway*, 389–90.

50. Muir, *Civic Ritual in Renaissance Venice*, 125.

51. For a critical genealogy of such ecofeminist positions, see Catriona Sandilands, *The Good-Natured Feminist: Ecofeminism and the Quest for Democracy* (Minneapolis: University of Minnesota Press, 1999), and Val Plumwood, "Ecofeminism: An Overview and Discussion of Positions and Arguments," *Australasian Journal of Philosophy* 64 (June 1986).

52. Here it might be useful to consider Butler's critical account on the melancholia of gender formation alongside the production of a feminized Sea and a masculinized Venice. See Judith Butler, *Gender Trouble: Feminism and the Subversion of Gender* (New York: Routledge, 1990).

53. "Beatriz Preciado's Homily," Love Art Laboratory (Annie Sprinkle and Elizabeth Stephens), http://loveartlab.org/slideshow.php?year_id=5&cat_id=126.

54. To name a few relevant texts from a range of disciplinary positions: Donna Haraway, "The Biopolitics of Postmodern Bodies: Constitutions of Self in Immune System Discourse," in *Simians, Cyborgs, and Women: The Reinvention of Nature* (New York: Routledge, 1991); Emily Martin, *Flexible Bodies: Tracking Immunity in American Culture from the Days of Polio to the Age of AIDS* (Boston: Beacon Press, 1994); Catriona Sandilands, "Eco Homo: Queering the Ecological Body Politic," in *Environmental Philosophy as Social Philosophy*, edited by Cheryl Hughes and Andrew Light (Charlottesville: Philosophy Documentation Center, 2004); Barbara Browning, *Infectious Rhythm: Metaphors of Contagion and the Spread of African Culture* (New York: Routledge, 1998); David Gere, *How to Make Dances in an Epidemic: Tracking Choreography in the Age of AIDS* (Madison: University of Wisconsin Press, 2004).

55. For a seminal analysis of ideologies and practices through which unified, bounded subjects are produced through the defense against pollution, see Mary Douglas, *Purity and Danger: An Analysis of Concepts of Pollution and Taboo* (New York: Routledge, 1966).

56. Donna J. Haraway, "Cyborgs to Companion Species: Reconfiguring Kinship in Technoscience," in *The Haraway Reader* (New York: Routledge, 2004), 315.

57. "Artists' Statement: Eco-Sexual Blue Wedding to the Sea," Love Art Laboratory (Annie Sprinkle and Elizabeth Stephens), http://www.loveartlab.net/PDF/statement_blu09_final.pdf.

58. Bennett, *Vibrant Matter*, 116.

59. Ahmed, *Queer Phenomenology*, 119.

60. Bennett, *Vibrant Matter*, 11 (italics original).

61. Barad, *Meeting the Universe Halfway*, 394.

62. "Beatriz Preciado's Homily," Love Art Laboratory (Annie Sprinkle and Elizabeth Stephens), http://loveartlab.org/slideshow.php?year_id=5&cat_id=126.

63. For other discussions of the engagement between the performing arts and the material/natural world, see Wendy Arons and Theresa May, eds., *Readings in Performance and Ecology* (New York Palgrave Macmillan, 2012); Gabriella Giannachi and Nigel Stewart, eds., *Performing Nature: Explorations in Ecology and the Arts* (Oxford: Peter Lang, 2005); and Bronislaw Szerszynski, Wallace Heim, and Claire Waterton, eds., *Nature Performed: Environment, Culture, and Performance* (Oxford: Blackwell, 2003).

BIBLIOGRAPHY

Ahmed, Sara. *Queer Phenomenology: Orientations, Objects, Others.* Durham, NC: Duke University Press, 2006.

Arons, Wendy, and Theresa May, eds. *Readings in Performance and Ecology.* New York: Palgrave Macmillan, 2012.

Austin, J. L. *How to Do Things with Words.* Cambridge, MA: Harvard University Press, 1962.

Barad, Karen. *Meeting the Universe Halfway: Quantum Physics and the Entanglement of Matter and Meaning.* Durham, NC: Duke University Press, 2007.

Bennett, Jane. *Vibrant Matter: Towards a Political Ecology of Things.* Durham, NC: Duke University Press, 2010.

Boal, Augusto. *Theater of the Oppressed.* London: Pluto Press, 1979.

Browning, Barbara. *Infectious Rhythm: Metaphors of Contagion and the Spread of African Culture.* New York: Routledge, 1998.

Butler, Judith. "Bodies in Alliance and the Politics of the Street." Lecture presented at The State of Things lecture series, sponsored by the Office for Contemporary Art Norway, Venice, September 7, 2011. http://www.eipcp.net/transversal/1011/butler/en.

———. *Excitable Speech: A Politics of the Performative.* New York: Routledge, 1997.

———. *Gender Trouble: Feminism and the Subversion of Gender.* New York: Routledge, 1990.

Douglas, Mary. *Purity and Danger: An Analysis of Concepts of Pollution and Taboo.* New York: Routledge, 1966.

Gere, David. *How to Make Dances in an Epidemic: Tracking Choreography in the Age of AIDS.* Madison: University of Wisconsin Press, 2004.

Giannachi, Gabriella, and Nigel Stewart, eds. *Performing Nature: Explorations in Ecology and the Arts.* Oxford: Peter Lang, 2005.

Haraway, Donna. "The Biopolitics of Postmodern Bodies: Constitutions of Self in Immune System Discourse." In *Simians, Cyborgs, and Women: The Reinvention of Nature*, 203–30. New York: Routledge, 1991.

———. "Cyborgs to Companion Species: Reconfiguring Kinship in Technoscience." In *The Haraway Reader*, 295–320. New York: Routledge, 2004.

Hodgson, Francis Cotterell. *The Early History of Venice: From the Foundation to the Conquest of Constantinople A.D. 1204.* London: George Allen, 1901.

Judith, Anodea. *Wheels of Life: A User's Guide to the Chakra System.* Woodbury, MN: Llewellyn, 2006.

Keahey, John. *Venice against the Sea: A City Beseiged.* New York: St. Martin's Press, 2002.

"Love Art Laboratory" Homepage. Love Art Lab (Annie Sprinkle and Elizabeth Stephens). 2007. http://loveartlab.org/index.php.

Martin, Emily. *Flexible Bodies: Tracking Immunity in American Culture from the Days of Polio to the Age of AIDS.* Boston: Beacon Press, 1994.

Muir, Edward. *Civic Ritual in Renaissance Venice.* Princeton: Princeton University Press, 1981.

Noland, Carrie. *Agency and Embodiment: Performing Gestures/Producing Cultures.* Cambridge, MA: Harvard University Press, 2009.

Plumwood, Val. "Ecofeminism: An Overview and Discussion of Positions and Arguments." *Australasian Journal of Philosophy* 64 (June 1986): 120–38.

Sandilands, Catriona. "Eco homo: Queering the ecological body politic." In *Environmental Philosophy as Social Philosophy*, edited by Cheryl Hughes and Andrew Light, 17–39. Charlottesville: Philosophy Documentation Center, 2004.

———. *The Good-Natured Feminist: Ecofeminism and the Quest for Democracy.* Minneapolis: University of Minnesota Press, 1999.

"SexEcology.org | Elizabeth Stephens and Annie Sprinkle." Elizabeth Stephens and Annie Sprinkle. Accessed June 13, 2014. http://sexecology.org/.

Szerszynski, Bronislaw, Wallace Heim, and Claire Waterton, eds. *Nature Performed: Environment, Culture, and Performance.* Oxford: Blackwell, 2003.

Tea, Michelle. "The Fifth Wedding: A Dispatch from a Three-way Marriage at the 2009 Venice Biennale between a Porn-Star-Turned-Performance-Artist, Her Chakra-Savvy Partner, and the Ocean." *The Believer* (November/December 2009): 15–20.

Ward, Peter D. *The Flooded Earth: Our Future in a World without Ice Caps.* New York: Basic Books, 2010.

AFFECT, SOMATICS, AND COGNITION

CHAPTER 24

SOCIAL SOMATICS AND COMMUNITY PERFORMANCE
Touching Presence in Public

PETRA KUPPERS

IN this chapter, I revisit one of the foundations of much performance practice: an attention to the embodied engagement that shapes how we appear on stage and in public, how we train ourselves to become more than sign holders, more than transmitters of language. As somatic explorers, we enter three-dimensionally into an encounter. Explore with me the potential of focusing on this dynamic as a different way of understanding political arguments in the public sphere.

To do so, become aware of your bodymind as you are reading this—surely an unusual request in academic writing, but one that respects the particular research trajectory I am sharing. My argument is not only articulated in the words, but hopefully is also encoded in the rhythms of the essay, in the sound of words, and in the juxtapositions between themes and media.

There are four different sections here: one to introduce the concepts I am working with; one that speaks about an Australian dance theater performance; one that witnesses moving in a participatory performance in Oakland, California; and, lastly, an argument in the form of a video, creating its own rhythms and soundspaces. In each section, my writerly audience address changes.

For now, breathe. Become aware of the feeling of the keyboard beneath your fingertips or the feel of the paper of this book. Adjust how you sit, and feel gravity flowing through you, anchoring you as you give your attention to the argument developing in these words, to their sound and their rhythm.

SOMATICS

The study of "the somatic" has different contours in dance studies. Somatics allowed a way out of the anti-intellectual accusations that embroiled dance studies and still shape its psychological stance. "What a body knows"—this Spinozian phrase might seem like an obvious statement to a lot of people who have undergone any kind of conscious bodily training. But for a while, it was a taboo phrase, one that signaled inadequate socialization in critical theory. Over the past fifteen years or so, these issues have slowly been laid to rest, from two different directions.

The first direction comes from dance's engagement with critical theory. Dance studies discovered critical theory's always already existing critical bodily and sensorial heritage. Particular moments in this reencounter centered on a rethinking of Walter Benjamin and early twentieth-century work on the city and the flaneur; on de Certeau's corrective to Foucault (1984), explicating the workings of power on the level of daily habitus; and on Deleuzianguattarian work in its vitalist lineage and its exploration of energetic shifts (particularly influential to many dance practitioners is *A Thousand Plateaus* [1980] 2004, see, for instance, Lepecki and Jenn 2009).

A second line of connection emerged from rethinking the work of anthropologists like Mauss (1935) and Csordas (1993) and phenomenologists like Merleau-Ponty [1947] (2007), a rethinking that helped rehabilitate an intense and specific thick description of bodily sensation and allowed for connections between these sensations and the coming to personhood, subjectivity, identity, and the social.

Outside of critical theory, the study of somatics, developing out of training in embodiment, slowly transformed the dance world itself and influenced the writing on movement and bodily experience. Martha Eddy (2009) charts many influences and practitioners in the field, from Rudolf Laban, Moshe Feldenkrais, and Ida Rolf to Anna Halprin, Joan Skinner, and Bonnie Bainbridge Cohen. This way of charting somatics out of anti-industrialist, pro-personal-empowerment movement practices shaped Thomas Hanna's (1989) naming of the field as "somatics."

When I read Eddy's essay with my performance studies students, what resonates most clearly with them is the argument that somatic education is a pathway to taking responsibility for one's self, in the absence of hard truths, in experimentation and playful process. And we also acknowledge that the written word alone, before our experiences of actually engaging in exercise work, observing each other breathe, is only part of our exploration. This is not knowledge only to be gained from reading *about* somatics but knowledge that becomes available when embodiment becomes a form of reading practice, informs attention to sounds and signs, a visceral close reading.

Embodied labors of attention: that is one of my working definitions of the somatic field.

SOMATICS IN THE COMMUNITY STUDIO

Somatics are the foundation for much that cultural workers and community dancers do in their everyday work life. If you are a performance artist working with communities, you most likely engage in one of three things in your daily or weekly sessions: you use somatic work to calm, focus, and develop bodyminds, you listen to and tell (body)stories, and you shape what you build on in these ways through dramaturgical choices.

The somatic work is foundational here: you can only listen if you breathe in peace and have space in yourself for yourself and for others. You can only tell your story or move your body if you have a provisional or momentary sense of stability, in yourself. You need to have a sense of ownership in order to be free with yourself. You need a point of anchorage, for instance, but not only, in your diaphragm, to speak. Expression emerges from somatics. Which is why to me, somatics, and the honoring of breath, space, embodiment, are so vital to a political aesthetics of access.

A lot of my initial experimentation with somatic practices emerged from my early work in community performance. I was working with mental health system survivors, and I thought that my training in Brecht and Boal would guide me well. My plans included dramatic sketches, creating embodied tableaux about power dynamics in mental health settings and the workings of stigma. But when I started my sessions, I quickly found that the basic foundation for dramatic work was not a given. As our warm-up, my participants joined me in centering ourselves, standing upright, swaying back and forth, and from side to side. This is a very ordinary exercise in much theatrical work: a self-centering, a grounding, sensing one's self in space (try it: stand up for a bit. Sway. Find your center. Then read on).

In my sessions, my collaborators fell over. They had to step out to catch themselves as they toppled over. I was mystified: I could never quite get to the later levels, to what I deemed to be the actual work, as the basis was not a given. It took me a while to work it out: my collaborators had an impaired ownership of their own body. Most of them had been institutionalized against their will at some point in their lives. Many had been homeless, and moved from space to space. Some had been imprisoned. Many had depot medication inserted under their skin, leaching chemicals into their bloodstream.

In order to do political work, we breathed. We used somatic methods to take back and improvise around our damaged bodyminds, invaded, incarcerated, beaten, and medicated (for a full account of this process, see Kuppers 2003). This is the basis of my understanding of the politics of somatics, making more space for more bodies, damaged and invaded, sharing breath, in public, enlarging which bodyminds get to take up space and stance in our shared world.

Many of us are denied the basics of what somatic modalities foster in us: freedom of expression. Freedom of breath. Touch. Lovingkindness. A nonexclusive, nonjudgmental focus on what is, and how it can be easier. Being not seen as a human being denies us. Our perspectives, our intensities, our pleasures denied denies us. What it means to be human is so much more than having a voice in the sense of being able to put forward a rational, discourse-driven, individual, self-dependent agenda. I cite Erin Manning, who approaches the issues of how bodies know, and how they become politically active, through a somatic lens:

> The body senses in layers, in textures, in rhythms and juxtapositions that defy strict organization into a semiotic system. (Erin Manning 2007, xiv)

Manning does not think in this statement about disability aesthetics, but I do: Sensing in layers, in textures, in rhythms, not in the units that linguistic discourse offers us, is to me the core experience of moving with fellow disabled people. Dispersed centers, interdependence, multiple sites of engagement, nonverbal concentration, joy at the site of encounter—these are moments that blossom in the performances I discuss in these pages. In the next section of this essay, I show how a perspective on somatic presence in a theatrical framework can shift the stakes of what political actions can be.

FIGURES 24.1–24.6 *GAWK*, by Rollercoaster Theatre. Photography: Petra Kuppers.

FIGURES 24.1–24.6 (*Continued.*)

FIGURES 24.1–24.6 (*Continued.*)

SENSING IN PUBLIC: ROLLERCOASTER THEATRE

This section focuses on the Melbourne performance of *GAWK*, by Rollercoaster Theatre. Rollercoaster Theatre is a group formed out of graduates of the Certificate in Live Production, Theatre and Events (ignition theater training). This course is a vocational theater training course for people with a broad range of disabilities and learning needs, and the majority of students in this course have developmental or cognitive differences.

The *GAWK* performance took place on Federation Square, a postmodern deconstructed, architecturally kinky, weird civic center site in Melbourne. It is a place designed for commotion and mixing, and many performances take place there and insert artful behaviors into the habits of the city.

In this site, Rollercoaster Theatre set up three high scaffolds for a promenade performance event, and they also used a giant animatronic screen to show a video they had created.

I could try to capture this performance in a number of critical theory frames: I could talk about how the group inverts the flaneur, turning the gaze around, highlighting their own status as objects of the gaze, or how the actors become starees who use sophisticated techniques to deflect or deal with being the object of stares. There are many ways in which the performers shield themselves; they wear fat suits, beehives, bishop's miters, huge hair, and even cheese wedges. All is armor, all is white, reflecting rays back out. I could make quite a lot of that, could offer citations and readings that would develop this analysis of the show as a political statement about the public sphere.

Or I could focus on one particular narrative offered in the show. Naomi Chainey, general manager of Grit Media, an Australia-based disability media content provider, wrote a review of the show, and I will cite the most relevant paragraphs here:

> The imagery was stark with six over-lit performers shrouded in white sheets and heavily coiffed costumes lined up across the stage. Movement was minimal—the occasional reveals of large open eyes painted on the performer's palms which "stared" at the crowd making up the majority of the actual performance—the figures effectively dehumanized, as the piece delved viscerally into the issues of perception. Through use of repetition, sound bites, music, animation and photography (effectively displayed on the overhead screen) the piece portrayed an intense loneliness that gradually built to a crescendo as the performance went on. Voices crying "stop looking at me!" and "can anybody see me?" were, I thought, particularly powerful, as was the repeated image of the eye painted on the hand. (2008)

But neither flaneur/public sphere imaginings nor this review's focus on sadness does quite grasp my experience that day, in Melbourne. "The body senses in layers": My main experience was not involved with a measured assessment of the political aesthetic strategies employed by the group. Instead, my experience was one of particulate impressions, of multiple attentions gliding over my body, including sadness, including thoughts of flanerie, but also including the feeling of the palm of my hand, the desire to paint, and thoughts on clothing. I felt quite directly the sadness of reaching out and being denied, of what it might feel like to be excluded, and of not being seen, of not being seen as human. But watching the show, I kept rescuing myself, by focusing on how much fun it must have been to construct this or that costume. How much time and attention was involved in putting on this makeup. On creating the images on the hands, or painting the images that make up the video.

I kept looking for glances between the performers, assuring me of a community of people in tune with each other. But all were performing very well, their focus outward, not on themselves but wholly engaged in playing the particular script they had chosen. The performances were fairly static, as all performers where fixed in place behind their desks. This, of course, while looking somewhat restrictive to me, also allowed real focus. Looking, reaching out with eyes and hands, receiving and giving attention: that was the script that seemed to be going on.

The Intensity of Process Play

The Ignition course uses interesting ways to train its students:

> The methods used by the teachers engage multiple learning styles and abilities, taking into account that many students do not read and some do not use spoken language as their main form of communication. For example, the theory subjects introduce important Australian plays by using images and videos to create their historical and geographical contexts and by workshopping segments of the plays themselves. (Hutchinson 2005, 14)

I imagine that Rollercoaster Theatre built on these ways of presenting knowledge by slipping into roles, tasting history and theory through embodied doing. What I saw that day in Melbourne reminded me of that process, playing bits of various pieces and roles: I can easily imagine that the performers chose a particular costume because of a sensual affinity with a particular hairdo, for instance. The local paper saw things in a similar way, as they report,

> Stanley, of Seddon, thought he looked quite sexy in his costume and he was not intimidated at the thought of sitting high on a platform. (O'Doherty 2008)

They asked Stanley for his opinion on his role, and printed it, without reference to his particular impairment or by making it inspirational.

I have read in the write-ups of the show that the idea of the eyes on the hands came from a Dr. Who episode. Again, I can imagine that in their rehearsal space, at the Footscray Senior Citizens Centre in Melbourne, Rollercoaster Theatre slipped into Dr. Who characters, got fully into painting eyes on their hands, and played with all their hearts at seeing through their hands: playing with touch and sensation, feeling heat and cold on their skin, all these somatic exercises that are part of a cultural worker's vocabulary.

At this point, I draw a parallel with Anna Hickey-Moody, an Australian researcher who co-directed a show for Restless Dance, a dance company of people with developmental disabilities. She writes in an intriguing way about a particular moment in her show, a man lighting a candle. She uses a Deleuzian framework of affect to address the intensities involved in the repeated lighting of the candle as an embodied act of wishing:

> His embodied memory of the way that the "candle lighting" happens is an extension of his personal style. Weeks of working ... have cultivated the corporeal affect of "the wish" and have instilled a method for lighting the candles in his blood, flesh and bones. (Hickey-Moody 2009)

Not irony and analysis, but intensity and specificity, embodied in blood, flesh, and bone: that seems to me at stake here, in the *GAWK* performance, too. As a witnessing critic, I reach toward a different vocabulary, as Anna Hickey-Moody does:

> The question is no longer about ability and disability but is about sense, affect and relation. (Hickey-Moody 2009)

DESIROUS READINGS

Messages fragment and shift kaleidoscopically. To use a unifying perspective like the flaneur or the single message "it's sad to be excluded" feels to me to be too restrictive and too normate. A focus on somatic practices can help me toward understanding a different time and space flow, one less concerned with the semiotics of political agendas, and instead with the pulsing of life—even life denied life by many eugenic techniques, by the kind of technologies that lead to so many disabled people, in particular people with Down Syndrome, being killed before birth. I have to work within hope, cruising utopia (to cite Jose Muñoz's resonant phrase): desirously finding openings for pleasure and connection. This is reparative criticism, to cite Eve Kosofsky Sedgwick's (2003) call to engage in critical practices that move toward productive engagement and toward the world we want to live in.

If I witness in a somatically flavored way, paying attention to the textures, rhythms, and echoes in my bodymind, I can bodysurf on this Australian show, and in the realm of counterpublics. My desirous reading tries to be both sensitive to and ameliorative of the public images of disability. Michael Warner writes,

> Counterpublics are, by definition, formed by their conflict with the norms and contexts of their cultural environment, and this context of domination inevitably entails distortion. Mass publics and counterpublics, in other words, are both damaged forms of publicness, just as gender and sexuality are, in this culture, damaged forms of privacy. (2002, 63)

How can we refigure the damaged, stigmatized identities of disabled people toward a new public, one that is aware of the processes of damage and can be open, elastic, and plastic enough to widen our sense of who can come to voice, presence, or agency in public?

In reading my way through the performance and its critical embedment, the spoken and unspoken, the known and the unknown, I want to open up the concept of "distortion" and "damage" and place here instead Gerard Vizenor's concept of survivance. Native American scholar and writer Vizenor writes in *Bearheart: The Heirship Chronicles* about a surreal encounter with "cripples," and about the survival techniques they use to live—imaginative self-imaging enables public presence and vitality.

I quote from Joseph Coulombe, who cites Vizenor—and I leave the language of my allies here in place. Sometimes, in order to move forward, I need to be open to language patterns beyond my own, and that might, today, include "deformed" or "handicapped."

> when they [the heroes of the book] come across a large group of physically deformed people, some of whom lost their faces or legs due to industrial toxins, the pilgrims [and the readers] receive a lesson in the use of the imagination to combat debilitating situations. Some of the "cripples" dress as moths, some wear special masks; all envision their lives as whole, so each

is whole in his or her own way. They cope creatively with their handicaps: "Their incomplete bodies lived whole through phantoms and tchibai dreams." (Vizenor 1990, 145; Coulombe 2011, 82/83)

There are many books in which literary cripples become the heartful center, the carriers of life lessons to be learned. Vizenor's work is not that flat. His cripples end up devouring one of the pilgrims, pulling her limb from limb in an orgiastic ceremony. These tchibai dream creatures are more Bakhtinian carnivalesques than plucky survivors. They are excessive, transgressive, voracious. Vizenor calls all fixed, static belief systems "terminal creeds." In this universe of postcolonial indigenous collage, movement, engagement, even eating (and being eaten) is life.

By taking my critical field here not just from queer and brown performance studies, but also from Native American criticism, I can enlarge the field of allies, and I can look for the moths, for those of us who find ways of entering imaginatively into the public sphere, armored with play against the stares and the stories. In the case of this performance, I cannot really speak about what Muñoz has called disidentificatory moves: That's not really what I think is going on, a conscious play on the stereotypes out there. Vizenor's emphasis on dreams give me a different purchase for thinking through the political agency of people with cognitive differences. Moth dreams, gossamer desires, weaving images out of what finds a hold in one's bodymind.

And so my argument moves me toward somatics as a way of witnessing and participating in life unfolding. I move toward an attention to what Shannon Jackson has called the support structures of participatory art: the kind of training, the kind of architectures, the kind of durational interventions that make the labor of touch experiential.

FLOCKING ATTENTION: DANDELION DANCETHEATER

My second example is set in Oakland, California, a traditionally less affluent neighbor to San Francisco. Here, in front of the Civic Center, at the center of political decision making, at the place where, at that very moment, heavy budget cuts eviscerated the welfare net of US social policy, Eric Kupers from Dandelion Dancetheater directed *WonderSlow* one sunny day in Summer 2011.

My writing here offers to take you right into my audiencing experience. I am using a different technique in presenting this show: I do not offer much information about the background to the show, but I use writing to enter the experience of being there, my somatic/poetic witnessing of what happened to me, that day as my bodymind sensed, in layers, in temporal shifts.

At the center of the amphitheater, performers engaged in day-long flocking. It is here I entered the participatory performance: Instructions to the audience were clearly marked and easily readable, and verbal instructions were also available. So I wheeled with my wheelchair into the middle of the stage in front of the Oakland Civic Center, in full view of the politicians' entry doors, and aligned myself with the person already there, a woman also using a powerchair.

FIGURES 24.7–24.8 *WonderSlow*, by Dandelion Dance Theater. Photography: Luiza Silva.

As you enter a flocking score, the world changes: Attention hones itself down. My perception both broadened and tightened at the same time, as my limbs entered a zone of multiplied attention, responding to the fine small movements the front dancer was transmitting through her back, her arm resting on her powerchair joystick, the sway of her head. Bodily translation becomes meditation. My focus is not with translating her movements into my different body but to feel myself entering into the energy lines that emerge from her limbs and torso. The sun is shining down. We are dressed in white (I had just borrowed a white tank top from the company box, and had donned a white wig which mercifully shielded my scalp). It is warm, and getting hotter. My blood rises to the surface of my bare limbs, slathered in sun screen. I move, my movements not determined by my core, but by the fine sun lines that weave in the flock. Others enter: a bi-pedal dancer, another one. As the frontal orientation changes, I at times find myself the leader, and there is a minute shift as the golden lines change tension, and I swing myself into the movements that come most deliciously to me: arm sways, rounded limbs extending into space, stretching my sitting body. Movements from core to extremity, spirals around my spine. Cat stretches and circles. There is no desire to stay at the front, though: the spirals naturally draw me into a different frontality, I move sideways, and another dancer takes over the flock. There are moments of tuning in: waiting, watchfully with eyes all over my body to respond to the smallest twitch of the one in front. There is the relaxation as the front dancer moves into familiar gesture, allowing me to swing freely with the gravity that extends between the earth and my movement memory of opening and closing, advancing, retreating, sways and contractions.

I dance for a long time, caught in the pause of attention. Time flows around me. Our dance is slow, magnetic, not concerned with building energetic arcs or narrative structures: It is a meditation of connection, carving time pockets in the congealing heat of the early summer day.

I return in the evening, ready to immerse myself again in the flow of *WonderSlow*, the meditative flocking procedures that enlarge my skin, that shoot out lines of connection, that anchor me so beautifully different in the en passant flow of a workday in the center of Oakland.

In the evening, though, my experience was different. The sun had moved: no longer was my body suffused by the strong heat, my vision attenuated by the golden glare. What felt like molasses and hammock days lounging in my limbs had become the crispness of the Bay Area's evenings: a touch of cold always in the air, my muscles on the edge of contraction, tensing back against the wind. I dressed warmer, and reentered the amphitheater, joining this time not one dancer, or three, but a whole crowd, flocking together.

This evening flocking was much quicker, and demanded a different attention from me. Instead of joining another chair user, I was now the only chair user in a flock of bi-pedals (although some visibly disabled bi-pedals). The mechanics of the dance had changed through this: the flock turned quickly, and a lot of step work with traveling patterns made it impossible to pick up the fine lines of energy, of losing myself in the attention to another's body translating itself into my own movement. I was always a step behind: if I extended my arms, and joined the upper body wave that moved through the flock, I could not control my joystick and retreat the five steps the bi-pedals took, becoming a static obstacle in their migratory path. If I followed with my joystick the weft of feet moving forward, sideways and back, my body felt left out and unintrigued, longing for the stretching arcs and whole-body engagements. I left the stage, and joined other wheelchair users at the bottom of the plaza, the lower level, and there we watched the flock for an hour or two: feet up on stone, a fulcrum of movement rather than the radiating arms of it. Again, my attention shifted, and I left behind my longing for the sun-drenched languor of liminal control the afternoon's flocking had afforded me.

Instead, I entered a new phase of audiencing, of being woven into the giant dial that *WonderSlow* became, transforming again. There was a space for me here, too, even if not as part of the flocking crowd, at that moment. I now was a still point at the center of a radial action. Around the edges of the plaza, dancers moved very slowly, engaging in a walking meditation that had them beat a quiet gong every few steps, circumambulating the plaza in an hour-long duration. I also became aware of the metronomes at my back—many small apparati ticking away time, a tiny Greek chorus to the day's action, kept in motion through the tending of audience participants.

I took in much more detail: the white umbrellas that wafted with the cooling winds across the plaza, wheeling and shifting, a ballet of natural forces just as delicate as the energy lines I had so reveled in just hours before when I was being moved/moving myself.

Over the day's action, sounds drifted, an orchestra of voices and various instruments, droning and drowning, drifting and patterning. There were gongs and song driven by breath, audibly panting and gyrating with the exit and entry of air into lungs. There were folk elements, a fiddling violin and a banjo, ballade-ing to unintelligible words, stretching out in time, singing on the edge of exhaustion.

Breath. Movement. Wind. Passers-by. The blank windows of City Hall. Time ticking. The patterns on the Plaza. People. Wigs. Order and Multiplicity.

In my witnessing words here, time has slowed to a pace where I can feel my attention broadening and lensing, where there is space for words to appear as I remember the intensities of "being there." This is to me a somatics of audiencing, invited by dance performance modes that stress not only duration but also meaningful participation. Joseph Beuys speaks of the Social Sculpture:

> Let's talk of a system that transforms all the social organisms into a work of art, in which the entire process of work is included ... something in which the principle of production and consumption takes on a form of quality. (reprinted in Bishop 2006, 104)

Art practice can help to transform toward a gaze and a broader sensorium that becomes aesthetic, and that encompasses City Hall as much as the woman in her powerchair in her majestic, smooth, turning circle. The way the city unfolds around us, in Oakland and in Melbourne, shifts as my attention is honed and revisioned. "I" produce and "I" consume, artfully, changing gears, finding space in the density of the city. The everyday of the flaneur, the city dweller, the politician, the shopper, the homeless person, the person in the mass, the person experiencing herself in singularity, all these everydays can hinge, can pivot when challenged at the level of somatic engagement. They can change when you end up experiencing yourself as a small but complete whole, to use Vizenor's phrase. These projects invite this axial pivot, the social sculpture, the unfolding of aesthetic spacetime, to offer a new perspective on shared humanity in public, on a trajectory toward repairing damaged publics. They invite the interconnectedness of things as living works of art, as cultural productions, open to improvisatory interventions.

EPILOGUE: MEMORIALS OF LIFE

We visited Berlin invited by a group of Butoh artists
who were interested in disability
We thought about doing an action at the Holocaust Memorial

I felt the tension of all war and the inhuman acts of war
I am Jewish
My partner is German
This black stone row after row
Gives me no peace
I don't comprehend it
I am speechless
We needed a new sculpture
A memorial of life
An accessible place of commemoration and assembly
A practice of peace
May I touch you?
May I touch you?
Thank you for coming.
Thank you being here.
Go through the gate
Please lie down, if you are comfortable with this
And place your head on this person's belly, the soft part
Go to the left
Breathe
Relax
Give your weight to the person beneath you
Feel the small movements of life
Listen to the sounds our bodies make
See what emerges
You go to the right
May I touch you?
May I touch you?
Feel the wave of breath running through this braid of humanity.
May I touch you?

Remember. (read by Neil Marcus and Petra Kuppers,
transcript of video poem)

To close, I offer a meditation on many of the themes woven into this essay. My voice shifts again: This time, you can hear its timbre, its accent, its locatedness directly, as a video supplants the text, and as I move from witnessing critic into the artist position.

As you will see, the videopoem, a form of documentation of a participatory action, has few easily identifiable disabled bodies in it, but that's a function of documentation practices and participatory performance ethics. The Olimpias, the performance research collective I lead, ran this event many times, on three different continents, with Holocaust survivors, with disability culture activists whose different bodyminds meant we had dogs in the braid with us, with transgender activists, with people with cognitive differences. We ran this with Australian Aboriginal activists, with people from the Butoh archive in Tokyo a few weeks after the devastation of the Tsunami, with people who remembered the division of Pakistan and India while lying with us.

Since the action is participatory, and since it is very hard to share what it is like before one does it, it proved ethically impossible to assume informed consent to video or photographs. So no documentation exists of most of these events. The only event we did record took place as part of a three-day Somatics, Movement, and Writing symposium (University of Michigan, 2011), where all participants had read a reading pack before assembling, and had engaged with the ethical issues at the heart of the action in multiple ways.

As you watch the video, chart how you feel. Chart if your breathing changes, if your body posture moves from reading a screen or book to the more laid back reception many of us associate with TV watching. Listen to the sounds of the studio, to my voice, to the bell that rings out in the video. What is the effect of all this on you? What is added, what is given up when the text fragments, when video echoes a live event inaccessible to you? What distances and connections offer themselves in different media?

FIGURE 24.9 Journey to the Holocaust Memorial in Berlin. Performance Documentation. The Olimpias, directors: Petra Kuppers and Neil Marcus. http://www.outubeom/watch?v=RMoZASfTvao

The title is all participants/audiences know before they come to this participatory action. *Journey to the Holocaust Memorial in Berlin*—a weighty and long title—sets up its own contract with an audience. All positions, apart from the "facilitator" position (me) and "the judge" (Neil Marcus), are sourced in a few short minutes from attending audience members as we get going. The only space shaping is the projection of the two Holocaust Memorial photos on some flat surface in the studio or community hall where we are meeting. All other spatial delineations happen through the changing geometries of the moving bodies and the lines they make as they begin to overlap and assemble. We offer minimal verbal introduction: we just run the score, and we see what people take from it, what content they bring to their movement experiences.

A sharing circle, often long and elaborate, followed each performance—and the sharing circle is not part of the videopoem or recorded anywhere. In the sharing circle, people spoke, danced, or sang about what memories came up, what emerged from ages and experiences of empire, colonialism, eugenics and division, atrocity and healing. Participants shared personal memories, cultural memories, somatic experiences, dreams, trance images, and intellectual engagements. Some participants saw ghosts, some stacks of the dead, some fell asleep lulled by the rhythm of communal breath. Some wondered about issues of permission and obedience, saw the tension between the simple structure and the care of the judge's gaze and my voice. I have decided not to write down any of the many stories that have been told in the sharing circle: You, watching this videopoem in the flow of what you are reading here, will have your own response, and enough imagination to trace echoes of the lyrical and expressive material people shared afterward through words, dance, and song.

POST-READING SCORE: WITNESSING YOURSELF

An essay on the politics of somatic engagement does not lend itself to a summary. "The body senses in layers": Somatic practices foreground personal experience, the assemblage of images, sensations, narrative and movement in one's own sensorium. So this closing is yours: as you trace through the layers offered here, through the sensations of words, rhythms, images, and video, through your breath and your heartbeat, what do you conclude?

BIBLIOGRAPHY

Bishop, Claire, ed. *Participation: Whitechapel Documents of Contemporary Art*. London and Cambridge: MIT Press, 2006.

Chainey, Naomi. Review of GAWK. *Gritmedia* website, unpaginated. 2008. Accessed December 2012. http://www.ritmediargu/enews/enews_november_2008df.

Coulombe, Joseph. *Reading Native American Literature*. London and New York: Routledge, 2011.

Csordas, T. J. "Somatic Modes of Attention." *Cultural Anthropology* 8, no. 2 (1993): 135–56.

de Certeau, Michel. *The Practice of Everyday Life*. Translated by Steven Rendall. Berkeley: University of California Press, 1984.

Deleuze, Gilles, and Félix Guattari. *A Thousand Plateaus*. London and New York: Continuum, 2004 (1980).

Eddy, Martha. "A Brief History of Somatic Practices and Dance: Historical Development of the Field of Somatic Education and Its Relationship to Dance." *Journal of Dance and Somatic Practices* 1, no. 1 (2009): 5–27.

Hanna, Thomas. *Somatics*. Reading, MA: Addison-Wesley, 1989.

Hickey-Moody, Anna. "Little War Machines: Posthuman Pedagogy and Its Media." *Journal of Literary and Cultural Disability Studies* 1, no. 3 (2009): 273–80.

Hutchinson, Mary. *Making the Journey: Arts and Disability in Australia*. Walsh Bay: Arts Access Australia, 2005.

Jackson, Shannon. *Social Works: Supporting Arts, Performing Publics*. New York: Routledge, 2011.

Kuppers, Petra. *Disability and Contemporary Performance: Bodies on Edge*. London and New York: Routledge, 2003.

Lepecki, André, and Jenn Joy, eds. *Planes of Composition: Dance, Theory, and the Global*. London: Seagull, 2009.

Manning, Erin. *Politics of Touch: Sense, Movement, Sovereignty*. Minneapolis: University of Minnesota Press, 2007.

Mauss, Marcel. "Techniques of the Body." In *Beyond the Body Proper: Reading the Anthropology of Material Life*, edited by M. M. Lock and J. Farquhar, 50–68. Durham, NC: Duke University Press, 1935.

Merleau-Ponty, Maurice. *The Phenomenology of Perception*. Translated by Colin Smith. London: Routledge, 2005 (1947).

Muñoz, Jose Esteban. *Cruising Utopia: The Then and There of Queer Futurity*. New York: New York University Press, 2009.

———. *Disidentifications: Queers of Color and the Performance of Politics*. Minneapolis: University of Minnesota Press, 1999.

O'Doherty, Fiona. "Have a Gawk at This." *Wyndham Leader*, November 18, 2008. Accessed April 2013. http://wyndham-leaderhereiliveomu/lifestyle/story/have-a-gawk-at-this/.

Sedgwick, Eve Kosofsky. *Touching Feeling: Affect, Pedagogy, Performativity*. Durham, NC: Duke University Press, 2003.

Vizenor, Gerald. *Bearheart: The Heirship Chronicles*. Minneapolis: University of Minnesota Press, 1990.

Warner, Michael. *Publics and Counterpublics*. Cambridge, MA: Zone Books, 2002.

CHAPTER 25

BODIED FORTH

A Cognitive Scientific Approach to Performance Analysis

AMY COOK

ACT ONE: ENTER LAUGHING

WATCHING the recorded broadcast of *Lay Me Down Easy*, I laugh with the live audience when Anna Deavere Smith, as white male bull rider Brent Williams described the pain he should have felt, but didn't, when the doctors stuck the rods up his nose to straighten the break. I laugh when Smith, as Texas Governor Ann Richards quoting Governor "Ma" Ferguson says, "If the English language is good enough for Jesus Christ, it's good enough for every body." Laughing, I wonder: at whom am I laughing and with whom am I laughing? What perspective must I take on this quote to find it funny? I am curious about our laughter: What is communicated from spectator to spectator when we laugh in this moment? I love being in an audience that is laughing together; I love the communal shake and release that comes with laughing and I love getting the joke.

ACT TWO: START SQUIRMING

I was not the only one that flinched and squirmed in my seat when he plunged the knife into the horse's head. I felt, saw, and heard many involuntary reactions to the killing that night as I sat safely in the Lincoln Center Theater, watching *War Horse*. Not only was my body never in danger, of course, neither was there a horse. The character was a puppet, made of wire and netting and manipulated by three visible men. The audience knew the horse had died when the puppeteers extricated themselves from the shell and left the stage. I did not believe that a horse died, and yet that might have been the most powerful staging of death that I've ever experienced.

ACT THREE: MAKING SENSE

Jetlagged and delirious, I enter the warehouse space on the Thames in London to see dream-thinkspeak's *The Rest Is Silence* and am told that we won't be able to leave for an hour and a half, so if I have to pee, I should do it first. When I demur, I am led into a big, empty room with what seems like large square screens or darkened windows on all sides. The room fills as the "curtain" time approaches. Directed by Tristam Sharps, *The Rest Is Silence* is a slightly deconstructed *Hamlet*. The scenes take place—overlapping, crunching, and stretching time and space—in the windows surrounding the space in which the audience walks around freely. Sometimes there are two scenes happening on opposite sides of the big room, so you can walk over and watch Hamlet wait in the conference room or listen to Laertes give parting advice to Ophelia. The audience moves and flows from wall to wall, conducting its own way through the play, bumping into each other, spreading out, closing in, ebbing and flowing like a murder of crows.

PROLOGUE

When an audience shares a physical reaction, there is generally a coherence of interpretation; it is funny or aversive at a particular moment and for a particular reason. I want to argue that cognitive science can be deployed to produce a richer and more rigorous analysis in order to improve the sophistication of our understandings of performance events and how they operate and also to improve our ability to create performance events that evoke a particular experience. I want to understand how a room full of individual spectators can become a singular audience, laughing and responding as one. As Ellen Spolsky puts it, "Literature and art are part of the arsenal of tools that can change understanding, and these changes or reinterpretations may then mediate conflicts in ways that make cultural life more tolerable or more satisfying—maybe even more pleasant."[1] Spolsky applies cognitive science to reimagine a historical moment in light of the minds/bodies that found a particular work of art compelling. Looking back on the art of the Renaissance, Spolsky sees evidence of what Andy Clark calls "representationally hungry" problems, that demand "feeding with a large amount of representation."[2] What I want to explore is this: Can we see evidence of this cognitive hunger in the theater around us? I'm interested in the degree to which the live theatrical event shapes perspective—for the two hours' traffic on the stage and beyond. Research in the arts and humanities traditionally relies on "reading" of works; while I'm not ready to abandon this strategy, I think the "reading" metaphor privileges a conception of disembodied reception.[3] Most of my work has focused on the potential of cognitive linguistics to push, challenge, and reimagine our understanding of poetry onstage, particularly Shakespeare's. Lately I've been thinking about how contemporary performance is staging category shifts, particularly related to ideas of the self. What I'm seeing onstage is a staging of embodied and distributed cognition.

The history of studying audience responses is a long one, but the intervention made possible through cognitive science is recent. "Cognitive science" is a large and developing field and as such it contains disagreements and contested areas. For example, the relationships between the body and the mind, the brain and language, and the mind and its environment are still understood differently by different scientists. Interdisciplinary travels, I believe, must take care to understand these differences and avoid cherry-picking experiments or theories in a vacuum. That being said, I aim to mount an argument about the impact of theater based on the research in cognitive science that proves the most coherent and productive to my goals. To that end, I have found theories of embodied cognition and the cognitive linguistic theory of conceptual integration (or blending) to be extraordinarily useful tools for attending to the complexities of our understanding of the composition of meaning during any performative event. I am not alone: from literature to music and theater, scholars have been integrating the sciences into their understanding of the arts and humanities, and while the topography of the field is tremendously exciting and varied, I will skip an exhaustive literature review as well as the theoretical heavy-lifting that I think needs to go at this point of a chapter. [4] I want to stick close to the experiences that guide my interest and my analysis, allowing them to prompt whatever move to the science is most useful.

Enter Laughing

Laughing in an audience, with an audience, is a great way to feel connected; laughing together, for this moment at least, we all must see things the same way. Certainly there are times when spectators find different things funny about something, but for the most part, it is funny from *one* perspective and if you are laughing, you have found that perspective. Our laughter is a physical reaction indicative of an internal composition of meaning. So when Smith, as the bull rider, talks about his "high tolerance for pain," I am seeing it partially *through* her eyes, not just *in* her eyes. I must view his ridiculous ability to withstand pain from the perspective of Smith, the interviewer and performer. Getting the joke requires seeing her travel, dispersing her mental states, taking on different perspectives. Watching an Anna Deavere Smith play, I travel with the author, with the performer, and with the characters and compose meaning at the site where they all come together. What I understand when I laugh, when I shake with the other audience members, when I share their perspective, is that what I usually think of as an "individual" fails to encompass the network of selves being performed.

Anna Deavere Smith performs documentary or "verbatim" theater pieces based on interviews she collects on a given subject. She performs all the "characters" (the "subjects" of her interviews) with few costumes and in bare feet. She does not become these people—we never forget that it is her up there and not the Reverend Al Sharpton, for example—but she reproduces them, their vocal tics, and pauses, in a kind of embodied echo. Smith's acting method repeats, precisely, the sounds and movements of her subject. She does not "become" them psychologically, she in-corporates them physically. The sound of the packet of sugar against the saucer is as much a part of the interview—the enacted meaning of the event—as what is being said. By foregrounding her body—her gendered and raced body—but also by surrendering it to the sounds and tics of her subject, she is staging the interaction *on* and *with* her own body. In that singular body the audience sees the interviewer, the interviewee, and the audience: it is not a one-woman show, it's a network of organisms, vibrantly coming to life onstage.

Smith has said: "My grandfather told me that if you say a word often enough, it becomes you." And so she is finding her way from her Self to the Other through the words of the others. She goes on to say: "I can learn to know who somebody is, not from what they tell me, but from how they tell me."[5] This is unlike the kind of symptomatic reading of text of method acting wherein the lines are analyzed for subtext, for what the character feels but is not saying.[6] As Charles Lyons and James Lyons note, "Both Freudian psychology and method acting interpret the surface of speech and gesture as material to be interpreted, to be analyzed and translated. The literal speech and action of a character become secondary, important only as points of access to the real substance of the figure."[7] Method acting, in this way, reflects an older model of how the brain works: as a kind of algorithmic processing center—enter the given circumstances to the "function" of the character's internal psychology and output behavior. Watching traditional psychological realism, then, reinforces this idea: We are watching to see an internal function—what caused that stutter? Why is he so mad at women?—an idea of a magical inside, rather than a cognitive network.

Smith insists:

> It's not psychological realism. I don't want to own the character and endow the character with my own experience. It's the opposite of that. What has to exist in order to try to allow the other to be is separation between the actor's self and the other. What I'm ultimately interested in is the struggle. The struggle that the speaker has when he or she speaks to me, the struggle that he or she has to sift through language to come through.[8]

We might say that Smith engages in deep surface reading, wherein the richness of *how* things are said is presented as containing all the information necessary. Smith honors the salience of "superficial" utterances by attending to the music of the stutters and expressive tics. Her line memorization has been called "a mental martial art";[9] she repeats the line from the recording of the interview with actors she hires to drill her until the utterance matches—not word for word but uh for uh. She works to duplicate the "organic poetry" she heard, not read. She has said, "I think if I'm working well, what people really admire is the effort I'm making to try to leave myself and be someone else."[10] This is, I think, what made the audience and me laugh: the Sisyphean effort to present—and the failure to represent—a white male bull rider from Idaho who doesn't need pain killers when having his nose straightened.

She has called acting "the *travel* of the self to the other"—not a becoming of the other or a channeling of the other but a movement between the two.[11] Her language is instructive here because to take her seriously requires a reconceiving of self and other. When I think of myself, I think of the thing I do all my traveling in, not something I can travel from. But Smith uses language and acting to imagine and theatricalize just this travel. In discussing her approach to the character of Leonard Jeffries in *Fires in the Mirror*, she told Martin:

> The point is simply to repeat it until I begin to feel it and what I begin to feel is his song and that helps me remember more about his body. For example, I remembered he sat up but it wasn't until well into rehearsal that my body began to remember, not me, my body began to remember. He had a way of lifting his soft palate or something. I can't see it because it's happening inside. But the way it played itself out in early performances is that I would yawn, you know, 'cause he yawned at a sort of inappropriate moment [yawns]. I've realized now what is

going on. My body begins to do the things that he probably must do inside while he's speaking. I begin to feel that I'm becoming more like him.[12]

Traveling, perhaps, through the contagion of the yawn. Smith divests herself from her body here, suggesting that there is a body that can remember separate from her. But in this link between her body and his—the sitting up, the lifting of his soft palate—is the portrayal of character. An actor interested in duplicating a kind of internal psychology might read the yawn, the sitting up, for what it *indicated*, as a symptom of internal, subtextual information. Smith duplicates the yawn and finds the palate. There is no judgment or narrative, just a struggle to travel from one body to the other, leaving behind her "self"—and staging an alternative to self—in the process. Most articles on Smith or her work talk about its postmodernity, the way in which the bricolage of voices, the performativity of self, speaks to the theoretical concerns of the 1990s. Certainly documentary theater challenges a presumption of a historical truth, and Smith's performances across race and gender lines do illuminate the way the characters are "playing" their parts for Smith, the interviewer who is playing her part for them. But Smith stages a shifting epistemology not just of history but of self, a self disindividuated from the body and environment. This is where I make sense of my laughing, where I understand why I love shaking with the audience when Smith is funny. Because I can see and feel what embodied cognition might mean.

Cognitive linguistics argues for the "experiential realism" of embodied, metaphoric thinking against the "objectivism" of the traditional view.[13] Key to this understanding of how we think are the following points: (1) categories are based on prototypes and not objectively assessed shared properties; (2) meaning is embodied; (3) metaphors exist in thought and language; (4) meaning is not literal or transcendental. Metaphor structures both language and thought, there is no literal meaning that receives primary attention, and all cognition and language is embodied. We project information about our experience in our bodies onto more abstract concepts in order to understand the more abstract in terms of the concrete and physical. Thus, my experience seeing something is used both to talk about and to understand my experience knowing something. I can say, "I see your point" even though there is nothing to see; intellection is understood via access to the visual system. This is incredibly creative, efficient, and powerful; we may not always notice the projections and connections at work to make something meaningful. The connection made between security, love, and the physical experience of warmth as an infant, for example, structures our understanding of positive experiences or people as warm and negative ones as cold.[14]

This is in part because cognition is not what happens in the brain based on inputs from the senses producing a thought or intention as an output. Thinking is embodied, embedded, and distributed in the environment. It is not an individual act but a networked process. Embodiment here is not the same as expressing an idea with the body or integrating a "fully present" body into a performance. Theater artists and scholars rarely put up a fight when told that thinking is embodied. We talk about "the wisdom in the body," "getting out of our heads," "letting your body remember," "don't think, just do," etc. It can be tempting, then, to assume that embodied cognition is simply the scientists getting money for what we have always known, but it is important see the radical shift and the game-changing possibilities of a redefining and relocating of cognition. In articulating how his conception of "meaning" is profoundly embodied, Mark Johnson gives the example of "doubt:" *The meaning of doubt is precisely this bodily experience of holding back assent and feeling a blockage of the free flow of experience toward new thoughts, feelings, and experiences.*"[15] Doubt is not in the mind based on the body, it *is* the body's reaction. Part of the challenge is that our language about thinking and feeling returns us to a conception of the two as separate—even when we yoke them together ("embodied mind" or "mind/body") we are conceiving of two things that need connection, rather than a dynamic organism that is fundamentally inseparable.

Perhaps part of the confusion comes from the different kinds of things we say we "know." I know when the person I am talking to is sad. I know when something bad is about to happen onstage. I know chair. The first involves emotions and empathy and a clear need to feel into the knowledge referred to—few would argue that thinking about another person's emotional state could be solely logical. The second is a dynamic cognition that folds past, present, and future together. The third, though, is referential—a chair is a chair—and less obviously embodied, but understanding *how* we understand chair is one thing scientists have not been able to teach a robot to do. This is referred to as the binding or symbol-grounding problem: How do we perceive the chair as a whole and as separate from what surrounds it? How does it acquire a unity in our minds? Any theory that suggests there are representations in our heads of real things out in the world must deal with how they come together. How does a physical thing connect to a nonphysical thing? A nonrepresentational theory of cognition sees that a chair has no meaning independent of what we do to or with it. According to Alva Noë, "we ought to reject the idea—widespread in both philosophy and science—that perception is a process *in the brain* whereby the perceptual system constructs an *internal representation* of the world. [. . .] What perception is, however, is not a process in the brain, but a kind of skillful activity on the part of the animal as a whole."[16] Cognition is what happens when I sit in the chair.

The meaning of the thing is the actions afforded by it. In other words, as Michael Anderson notes:

> "chair" is not a concept definable in terms of a set of objective features, but denotes a certain kind of thing for sitting. Thus is it possible for someone to ask, presenting a tree stump in a favorite part of the woods, "Do you like my reading chair?" and be understood. An agent who has grounded the concept "chair" can *see* that the stump is a thing for sitting, and is therefore (despite the dearth of objective similarities to the barcalounger in the living room, and despite also being a tree stump) a chair.[17]

If one had to refer to an internal definition of chair as thing for sitting it would not allow the listener to see immediately the stump as chair; she "must know what sitting *is* and be able to systematically relate that knowledge to the perceived scene, and thereby see what things (even if non-standardly) afford sitting. [. . .] grounding 'chair', that is to say, involves a very specific set of physical skills and experiences."[18] Research has shown that visual perception of an object includes the action afforded by those objects.[19] In the forest we see the chair in the stump immediately—it requires no more imagination or creativity than seeing an Eames as a chair. In daily and extra-daily life the agent navigates the world not receiving what things are but rather what things *could be*. Our perception of possibilities allows us to both visually and imaginatively see the world as a stream of *could be*.

If I imagine a creature with a similar physical makeup—legs, arms, torso, eyes, etc.—but without that ability to assign "chair" to environmental objects on which he sits, every encounter with the environment for him is a first time, a set of perceptions that afford actions—pull hand away from hot thing, rest on that smooth thing. Then this creature evolves a kind of cognitive lasso, around which he can group elements in his environ-ment that afford similar actions: All these things I must run from, all these things I can rest on. Now he has categories and objects in his environment, not just perceptions in his environment. As he goes along, he will add to and change his categories; instead of just a category for things to run from, he might have "large animals with teeth" and "fire." Teaching babies to talk is teaching them to categorize: "where's the doggy? What sound does the doggy make?" Language allows babies to give words to categories and thus to manage them.

In his door-stopping and discipline-shifting book *Women, Fire, and Dangerous Things*, George Lakoff outlines the ways in which a new understanding of categories shapes how cognitive linguists think about the brain and language. Lakoff takes his title from a study of an Australian aboriginal language. In Dyirbal, all objects are classified in one of four ways, but the four classifications are not immediately obvious. For example, the first includes men and most animals, as well as some spears and storms, whereas the second includes women, bandicoots, most birds, the hairy mary grub, and things connected with water and fire. What Lakoff argues, extending the work of the anthropologist who conduced the fieldwork, is that the objects are grouped based on "the domain-of-experience principle: If there is a basic domain of experience associated with A, then it is natural for entities in that domain to be in the same category as A."[20] Accounting for the most striking of the aberrant cases (the hairy mary grub, for example, should be in group I, as it is an insect, but is in group II) is the "myth-and-belief principle" which privileges the myth or belief about a thing over what we would see as its "objective" taxonomy. The hairy mary grub, then is classified with the sun in group two because its sting feels like a sunburn. For Lakoff, the extraordinary contribution of this anthropological study is the way in which categories are experientially created; what from our perspective looks fantastical (grouping women, fire, and hairy mary grubs), "is from the perspective of the people doing the classifying a relatively regular and principled way to classify things."[21] What we lasso into our rope depends on where we stand and what we need.

Andy Clark argues that giving names and categories to experiences or actions in our envi-ronment provides a linguistic scaffolding that shapes and builds our minds and more and more advanced tools with which to build our minds. The first block in the linguistic struc-ture is labeling, and Clark points to a study about a chimp trained to understand numerals. Despite this understanding of numbers, when the chimp was shown two plates of treats (one with more than the other) and asked to point to the one her friend should get, she would point to the bigger one, even though it gave her fewer treats. When, however, they labeled the plates with the number of treats on them, she was able to choose the smaller number to give to her friend, leaving herself the greater plate of treats. Tagging, the researchers hypothe-size, allows her to override the complicated information about lots of treats into information tagged and assessed, the effect of which "is to reduce the descriptive complexity of the scene" and make thinking about the choice possible.[22] Clark extends this to sentences and ideas, arguing that once we make an idea into a written thought, it can be seen and manipulated. We can see this with personification—a set of culturally valued traits can be given a name "virtue" and then given a female shape "Virtue" so that we can think about her, it, or them.[23] We could extend this to stories, allegories, and performances: We stage an idea to interact with it. As embodied and embedded cognitive agents, for something to be thought about it must be an "it," so we make "objects" out of "airy nothing."

Indeed, Lakoff and Mark Turner point to the conversation about the language created by madmen and poets between Theseus and Hippolyta. Theseus rejects the "antique fables" in the "seething brains" of lovers and madmen who "apprehend more than cool reason ever comprehends" (5.1.3–6). "And as imagination bodies forth/The forms of things unknown, the poet's pen/Turns them to shapes and gives to airy nothing/A local habitation and a name" (5.1.14–17).[24] Lakoff and Turner argue that this is a "position reminiscent of a literal meaning theorist, arguing that poets are like lovers and madmen: they are fanciful and therefore misperceive the truth."[25] Hippolyta, for Lakoff and Turner, is right to see that such stories both perceive and create a kind of stable "truth" from which to operate:

> But all the story of the night told over,
> And all their minds transfigur'd so together,
> More witnesseth than fancy's images,
> And grows to something of great constancy;
> But howsoever, strange and admirable. (5.1.23–7)

It is through poetic imagining that we make manifest what we can then play with, change, reinvent. As Clark insists,

> For . . . as soon as we formulate a thought in words or on paper, it becomes an object for both ourselves and for others. As an object, it is the kind of thing we can have thoughts about. In creating the object, we need have no thoughts about thoughts, but once it is there, the opportunity immediately exists to attend to it as an object in its own right. The process of linguistic formulation thus creates the stable attendable structure to which subsequent thinkings can attach.[26]

This, in turn, allows us to manipulate and alter the structures we have created to facilitate different and better action or success in our environment. Embodied cognition locates thinking in the whole organism, as inseparable from the actions of that organism, and using language to create worlds within which to manipulate and imagine new things to encounter.

Smith's performed interviews generally include a reference to Smith, the interviewer, whose racial/ideological identity the interviewees are often trying to assess. It is not clear to them whether she is black, white, or Jewish, and she includes these confusions in the text of her plays. In *Fires in the Mirror*, Anonymous Black Girl #1 asks, "You black?" Sharpton excludes her from the white people who have misconceptions about his hair, and a Lubavitcher woman hints that perhaps Smith knows the rules of the Sabbath. In performance, though, she also needs me, the spectator/scholar who, hailed by her text as "you," takes on the role of the interviewer. I am then cast as the racially ambiguous Smith; I must travel between my self and another. In this performance, I can see/feel/hear/know/experience the radical paradigm and the game-changing possibilities of a redefining and relocating of cognition. Because I am in this travel with her.

The story is not located in an Aristotelian plot, it is dispersed across networks—the network that connects ideas about hair, say, to the events of Crown Heights. The literary event is the telling of the story, and it requires her racial identity as it requires her bare feet. The "characters" are not people stand-ins, essences temporarily housed in the body of an actor. It is a person staging for us the nodal points of character, of self, of other. The agency is systemic, the action is perception.

ACT TWO: START SQUIRMING

In his review of *War Horse*, Ralf Remshardt notices, as I did, the audience's reaction to the "pain experienced" by the inanimate objects: "When the horses were seen to suffer—there was a chilling scene in which they got caught in barbed wire—the audience suffered audibly as well."[27] This was certainly my experience also, but it brings up a funny question: Why would people pay so much money to suffer? Why do audiences enjoy watching aversive stimuli? From *Oedipus* to *Titus Andronicus* to *Pillowman* and *War Horse*, people have come together to watch people pretend to be in pain. Like the laugh, I follow my body's physical reaction for clues: What do I do when the knife goes into the horse's head? I squirm. I don't sit forward and smile and I don't look at my watch. The squirm is a body adjustment that engages proprioception to avoid the temporary feeling of boundary extension. I squirm and I return.

Am I empathizing with the horse? Most theories of narrative empathy or emotion suggest that we believe the fictional world is real and therefore feel real emotions toward an unreal event.[28] I do not think that a spectator could believe that there were real horses onstage being hurt. I believe that the response is both greater and lesser than the one suggested by Coleridge's "willing suspension of disbelief." In her essay on empathy and watching differently abled dancers, Wanda Strukus argues that "the experience of watching performers with different physical abilities can contribute to changing our perceptions about physical difference . . . I am suggesting that there is a fundamental, automatic, kinesthetic way of experiencing or trying to experience similarity and difference, and our understanding of such foundational processes can be valuable in changing our perceptions."[29] In *Choreographing Empathy: Kinesthesia in Performance*, Susan Leigh Foster points out that kinesthesia is a "central component of modernism," but she criticizes the term "kinesthetic empathy": "The fact that the experience of empathy needs to be qualified with the adjective 'kinesthetic' belies the pervasive assumption that emotional and physical experiences are separate."[30] Her genealogy helpfully points out the political uses to which "kinesthesia" and "empathy" have been put: "Sympathy/empathy served to establish the grounds on which one human being could be seen as differing from another. It also helped to rationalize how and why they could relate to one another as they did, exercising forms of political and social control, punishment and torture, and enslavement."[31] As a model of connection between self and other, the crucial problem, it seems, is that it connects two things by presuming they are separate. Maybe this dyadic relationship is the wrong way to model what's going on.

Fritz Breithaupt posits that empathy involves side-taking in a three-person dynamic. He argues that empathy must be studied not within a two-person scene but in a more complicated social scene: "Most theories thus portray empathy as a particularly close observation in a two-person scene that also takes into account the intentions and emotions of the other person . . . it seems that this focus on observation within a two-person model may be too narrow for the most social animal."[32] His three-person model of empathy posits that because empathy is generally stronger when we perceive causality—this pain was caused by that person or event—it "results from taking sides in a three-person scene."[33] As I have said elsewhere, though, this suggests a cause-and-effect chain that suggests linearity: First I take sides with the horse and then I feel something with him when he is hurt. The squirm complicates this for me because I do not need to adjust my body to take a side or feel with the horse.

The squirm here, the contagiousness of the aversive stimuli, does not equal a movement or gesture to avoid the blow, as if I temporarily fear it is happening to me. I do not protect my own head from the knife. Nor do I stand up and stop the player from hurting the horse—as passionately as I may react to what is happening onstage, I do not take action to stop it. I also don't take action to make sure none of my friends have to go through this: Indeed, I tell them all they have to experience this precious torture.

What is at stake is not just the unquestioned importance of "believability" in the theater, it is fundamentally how we perceive and react to the bodies and the stories around us. We are always in relation to others, and understanding that, perceiving those locations of permeability in our self, is part of why we return again and again to the theater to shriek, laugh, lean forward, flinch, and squirm. Jill Bennett, in her book on visual art, describes the squirm as a "recoil,"

> a moment of regrouping the self, it is also the condition of continued participation, the sensation that works with and against the deeper-level response, which on its own is unbearable. The squirm lets us feel the image, but also maintain a tension between self and image . . . . The recoil, as described above, is not a retreat but a way of negotiating the felt impact of the image . . . Such micro-bodily responses enable us to locate ourselves in relation to the image . . . By sustaining sensation, we confirm our sense of the ontological status of the image and inure ourselves to its effects—effects that are, nevertheless, felt.[34]

Jody Lyneé Madeira sees this as salient for challenging legal models that take relationality as the ground from which assessments should be made, rather than the insistence on the individual:

> The squirm sensation is relational; it is a recognition of the other and her perspective, of different orientations and attitudes, and the impact of these differences upon relationships. Its experience encompasses the unnerving sensation of vulnerability. If we look closely at ourselves when we feel this sensation, we find that the smooth, free-standing narrative edifices of our self-identity are revealed as rough and ready concrete walls riddled with pock marks and cracks.[35]

To understand my reaction to the knifed puppet, I question, again, the assumption of individuality. As with Smith's performances, to feel with this puppet suggests that my ability to feel pain and experience life is far more expansive than the boundary of my body. Squirming, like laughing, returns me to my borders while reminding me how fluid and flexible they can be.

To have negotiable boundaries means that we are, as Theseus might say, "bodied forth" and that the whole of us is understood experientially; it is me up and until I am aware of the seat or puppet that is the not-me. The boundaries must be perceived but they can be shifted. Clark notes that while there are those who believe humans are "merely embodied" (there is a body with senses that engage the world in order to take actions decided on through reason) and others who believe we are "basically embodied" (our bodies are resources that can be "actively exploited allowing for increasingly fluent forms of action selection and control")[36] he argues (with others) that humans are "profoundly embodied," that is, "agents whose boundaries and components are forever negotiable and for whom body, sensing, thinking, and reasoning are all woven flexibly and repeatedly from the accommodating weave of situated, intentional action."[37] Research on primates has found neurons that respond both to sensation from a particular body region and to information coming from the visual field surrounding that body region. Experimenters noticed that while Japanese macaques used a rake to reach for food, the neurons that respond to visual information surrounding the hand began to respond to visual information surrounding the rake "as if the rake was part of the arm and forearm."[38] If a rake can come to be experienced—at least in some discreet cells—as part of "me," then what about my character's cane? Or the "monstrous little voice" I put on to become my character? What would it mean to rethink theatrical performance from the per- spective of embodied cognition? Onstage, when every body is both an actor and a character, where is the cognitive agent?

If embodied cognition locates thinking in the whole organism, as inseparable from the actions of that organism, embedded or extended cognition argues that cognition uses the environment. The prop table organizes what is needed by the actor so that between scenes the actor does not need to look at the table, remember what he needs for the next scene and search for it. The stage manager marks the paper on the table so that the prop goes in the same place every night—often tracing the edge so the hammer goes where the hammer silhouette is. This allows us to "travel information light," using prompts in our environment to guide our actions in the moment. We can take advantage of this—as the stage manager does—and alter our environment to support the offloading of cognitive tasks, which David Kirsh and Paul Maglio call "epistemic action" as opposed to "pragmatic actions" which make an envi- ronmental change because it is desirable in and of itself, not because of what it affords.[39] We create tight feedback loops between our actions and the world it is acting on and with in order to operate quickly and efficiently. Extended cognition sees these "coupled systems" as cognitive in their own right, taking the mind beyond the body. In this view, thinking is what happens between agents and their environmental tools, coupling seemingly discreet units in a system that extends what and where we imagine the "mind." If our environment becomes part of the cognitive act, I am only as smart as the system that surrounds me.

Imagining Shakespeare's Globe as an environmental tool used by the players to facilitate the heavy cognitive task of performing five to six different plays per week, Evelyn Tribble argues that the players and environment of the Globe can be thought of as a system that cre- ates and perpetuates cognition. Her book, *Cognition in the Globe: Attention and Memory in Shakespeare's Theatre*, is an excellent example of the potential for cross-disciplinary work: she applies the paradigm shift coming out of the sciences about how cognition works to one of history's most amazing cognitive events—Shakespeare's plays—and weaves a story impossi- ble without both fields lending their best insight to the mystery at hand.[40] Seeking to answer the question of how playwrights and players came together and, in such a short time and night after night, put on a play for a demanding audience, Tribble looks for an answer *not* in the individuals, but in the system. As Tribble importantly points out: distributed does not mean parceled out, it means spread over. If the cognitive environment of a theater includes its constitutive elements—the audience, the props, the plots backstage, the verse structure of the poetry, the conventions of staging, the girl selling oranges to the groundlings—it is not just individual cognition that needs to be questioned but our investment in the idea of individuals.

Sitting there, feeling for the horse surrounded by audience members similarly "audibly suffering" with the horse, I try to understand what might be the cognitive work being done in this system, the space of the theater in this moment. What about *War Horse* has made it so popular and influential? Getting to and from Lincoln Center I witnessed (if ignored) many instances of suffering that I did not experience as profoundly as the puppet death, so clearly it is not the suffering (let alone "believable" suffering) that pulls us in. Those who saw it with me that night said that we felt for the horse because it was so life-like and that is reviewer Remshardt's experience as well: "As in Bunraku, once the illusion is established, they appear as real as if they were the animal itself."[41] I disagree. It was not that I believed that the horse was alive; it was that I saw a network of forces engaged in bringing life *to* the horse. This is what moved me: Three puppeteers worked together, breathed together, to lend their life to an inanimate object and I was capable of seeing life where there was none. Basil Jones explains the magic of the puppets in a Ted Talk this way: "Puppets always have to try to be alive. It's their kind of, ur-story, onstage, that desperation to live." Adrian Kohler then added, "Yeah, it's basically a dead object as you can see, but it only lives because you make it. An actor struggles to die onstage, and a puppet has to struggle to live and in a way that's a metaphor for life."[42] The puppets in *War Horse* are staging this alternate conception of life and individuality for me: We are not precious as individuals with life, life is something spread out over the system, something that requires effort, labor, to generate and perceive. It is not a given and it is not isolated in the bounds of my body.

ACT THREE: MAKING SENSE

Standing in the big space before *The Rest Is Silence* begins, I notice the other spectators—there's a tall man with a clearly academic air about him and some clusters of youngsters. I can feel the audience react when the room goes dark—somehow there's a different tension to the breathing because we are not carefully placed in protective seats. We are standing, free floating, and the darkness calls for a kind of renegotiation of our collective agreement—that weak and tacit agreement humans have when they enter the collective arena that none of us will misbehave or call too much attention to ourselves. Somehow, standing untethered to a seat, I'm aware of just how shaky my belief in this agreement is. But then a film projection starts against one wall of screens and the combination of the light and the joint attention assuages my fear of rampant individualism in a small space.

We are watching a man walk through an orchard; he's about the same size as we are, so the perspective is familiar—it's like he's just over there, walking. Then a huge head lifts up from the bottom of the screen and our perspective changes. The man's face looks similar to the man we saw walking, but blood is pouring out of his ears. He is King Hamlet and the walking man is Claudius. Lights change and one of the screens on an opposite wall becomes clear and we are able to see into a play-space; it's like a large department store window or TV screen with live content. We watch a man start from sleep and get out of bed, naked. It's Claudius. There's a woman next to him. He goes into the adjoining room and the lights go on in that cubicle. It is his bathroom and the sink is attached to the glass wall facing us. Claudius begins his first speech, as if practicing for a press conference to come. He looks into his "mirror" and out at us; we are his reflection. He looks down into the sink, after splashing his face with water, and the image of his face being splashed with water is projected onto the screen in the ceiling. Our perspective has changed again. We can see up through the sink and the running water, seeing him from below. Shifting my weight while watching, I am made aware of our watching—how we are staged in relation to the action, invited to move, and taught to see.

FIGURE 25.1 *TheRest Is Silence*: press conference (1.2 in *Hamlet*). Photograph by Jim Stephenson.

Practicing his speech, he can only get to the third or fourth line before he has to start again, as if he just can't maintain belief in his own performance:

Though yet of Hamlet our dear brother's death The memory be green, and that it us befitted To bear our hearts in grief, and our whole kingdom To be contracted in one brow of woe

He keeps trying, and failing, to get further than this. Another wall of rooms opens up and it is Polonius setting up for the press conference to come. Scenes begin to happen on top of each other and we often watch the set up or rehearsal of a scene to come—Ophelia practicing what she's going to say to Hamlet about those remembrances of his or Rosencrantz and Guildenstern practicing how to sound believably casual to Hamlet. In order to make sense of this, we have to call on our knowledge of the play, or at least an understanding of performance and rehearsal and pretense. What we are seeing now was rehearsed for us, just as what Hamlet will see in a few minutes will be Ophelia's attempt to sound calm as she returns his letters. It may not seem like a repetition to him at the time, but we know it is. Throughout the play, the audience is given perspectives that highlight our perspective and call attention to the multiple perspectives at work in the play. Our bodies stage this as well, since we must move them to change our perspective.

Norman Holland's analysis of cognition in the theater is that we suspend disbelief because our frontal cortex, responsible for making plans and managing movement, is deactivated as we sit there, so we can believe what is happening is real because it isn't tested.[43] I have disagreed with this account elsewhere for other reasons, but this type of production actively engages our bodies.[44] I have to move to keep my legs from getting tired, to see around that tall man, to go look at the new room that just opened up. I am involved and engaged in choosing the perspective from which I watch this performance.

At one point, the rooms along that wall change into three identical versions of Hamlet's bedroom, which previously had occupied the central room. We watch Gertrude, Claudius, and Rosencrantz and Guildenstern each enter one of the rooms, searching for something. Claudius and Gertrude both find similar versions of a journal in which they begin to read the "to be or not to be" speech. We have previously seen Hamlet tear this piece of paper out of his journal and deliver it to Ophelia in her room, which she now begins to read as well. Rosencrantz and Guildenstern, however, only find small torn up pieces of that paper, which they attempt to put together into a coherent text, to comical results ("to sweat under a bear is a desire consummately to be wished"). This project they continue later—partially as a competition between them for who can make the most sense out of the series of words and phrases that they found—on board the boat to England. We laugh as we hear them try to make sense of this famous speech—laugh because we know it and laugh because we also have been trying to put together Hamlet's meaning for many many years. We watch them in the room that was the original sitting room and is now made to look like the back of boat, come up with various versions of the famous speech as we also hear Hamlet read the letter explaining how he sends them to their death. The central room is then a screen wherein we see a film of the two characters on an actual boat, sail into the distance, trying to make sense and make each other laugh as they sail to their death. There is no confusion; the audience does not think: wait, how are they all reading the same document? How are they all in the same room at the same time? Past and future and near and far are all compressed in this storytelling device, and the spectator accesses all this information to make sense.

When I leave, I feel good. Buzzing. I'm reminded of Jonathan Haidt's argument that humans are 90 percent chimp and 10 percent bee.[45] What he means by this is that we are "groupish;" we come together to create structures, to work together, to form teams and then that group can, at times, come to mean more than our individual self.[46] Bees, of course, are related; humans come together with strangers. Paul Seabright points out the evolutionary oddity of this collaboration: "[N]owhere else in nature do unrelated members of the same species—genetic rivals incited by instinct and history to fight on another—cooperate on projects of such complexity and requiring such a high degree of mutual trust as human beings do."[47] A tremendous amount was gained when humans started treating strangers as honorary friends, but one problem becomes how to handle freeloaders, how to ensure the values and rules of the system are maintained. This is also the question at the base of moral psychology: How do I know, standing in that dark room, untethered to a seat, that the other spectators will behave morally? What does it even mean to recognize an action as immoral? For Haidt, people make moral decisions emotionally and then reason them out post hoc. Bertrand Malle argues that our moral reasoning operates fairly rationally: We assess whether a negative event has happened, then whether or not someone caused it, then whether that person could have stopped it.[48] Crucial to the moral psychology literature is how we manage the attribution of blame and punishment in order to maintain social balance. Peter DeScioli and Robert Kurzban argue that morality is a way of managing bystander reactions so as not to escalate disputes—if there is some predictability to which "side" is more "moral" then you can trust that enough other bystanders will choose that side as well and the dispute can be contained.[49] How we think about morality, how we judge, how we assess blame, how we locate a morally opprobrious event all depend on how you think about agent, action, and intention.[50]

In 1967 Philippa Foot set out a series of thought experiments in an essay called "The Problem of Abortion and the Doctrine of Double Effect." The most influential of these thought-experiments was what came to be called the "Trolley Problem;" the driver of a runaway tram can only steer the train from one track to another. On one track there are five people and on the other there is one. The doctrine of double effect, according to Foot, is "based on a distinction between what a man foresees as a result of his voluntary action and what, in the strict sense, he intends."[51] The driver of the tram does not intend to kill the one man; it is a consequence of not killing the other five. Judith Jarvis Thomson extended the trolley problem to include a bystander, one who could stop the train by throwing a large man off a bridge to his death or by pulling a lever that would divert the train to the track with only one person.[52] Foot's conclusion is that there is a key distinction between "what we *do* (equated with direct intention) and what we allow (thought of as obliquely intended)."[53] Thus, the trolley driver (or the bystander) is not morally culpable for the death of the man on the tracks—though most of us feel it is more wrong to throw the man on the tracks than to pull a lever. While some researchers focus on the victim (there was a morally questionable event because harm has occurred), others focus on the agent (there was a morally questionable event because this person violated this norm). All of them struggle with questions of intention, cause, and effect.

Going to the theater, of course, is all about watching the ballet of intention, cause, and effect. Usually visible in the story or characters—Claudius wants to be King, Hamlet causes Polonius's death without intending it, Ophelia's madness and suicide is the effect of Polonius's death—it is present even in postdramatic performances, dance, ritual, performance art.

We watch agents do things, causing things, and we imagine this was intended. This is how we organize the world around us, into intentional agents taking actions, causing effects. This may be a very useful way of understanding the world, but that does not mean it is always accurate. Even if Hamlet can't see it, *Hamlet* stages this very confusion about whether or not there can be a simple relationship between cause and effect. In 1955, long before any of the cognitive science research referred to here, N. R. Hanson wrote an essay challenging our assumption that effects have causes and link up in clean causal chains. As Hanson points out: "I hear that John is indisposed and ask 'Why?' [. . .] But on any ordinary Tuesday morning I would not ask after the cause of John's moderate good health."[54] The attempt to find a cause is motivated by the assessment of something as an effect: "[T]he main reason for referring to the cause of X at all is to explain X. Of course, there are as many causes of X as there are explanations of X."[55] Hanson points out that X will be explained differently depending on your perspective, on what you imagine you know about X, etc. He argues:

> But the things we refer to as "causes" and "effects" are theory-impregnated from beginning to end. They are not just simple, tangible links in the chain of sense experience . . . Causes *are* connected to effects. But this is because our theories connect them, and not because the world is held together by a kind of cosmic glue. The world *may* be so held together, but that is irrelevant for understanding the nature of causal explanation. The very notions of *the cause* X and *the effect* Y are intelligible only against a comprehensive theory of some sort—one which puts an at least provisional guarantee on inferences from X to Y. It is this logical guarantee that distinguishes a truly causal sequence from a mere coincidence.[56]

How we decide that there is an event, what the boundaries are, and what the question is will change our cause-and-effect chain.

The problem, it seems to me, is that our reliance on causal chains is too comfortable—how delightful if a chaotic tragedy could be understood as a series of billiard balls striking one another and thus I could stop one and avoid the promised end—but it isn't this way. Our systems are dynamic and always in flux and that which counts as an event, or an agent for that matter, is only visible post hoc—which renders it shaky ground on which to carry too much empirical weight. Flowing through the audience space, composing the story of *Hamlet* from the compressed and extended and overlapping scenes, I experience this dispersion of cause, effect, agents, and intention; I get plugged into the network of beings that are making up this cognitive event. *Hamlet* happens in the spectators' movement, in the rehearsal and performance of found text, in the shifting of perspectives, and in the redesignation of space. I am part of this enacted meaning but it is not *within* me. I have tried to make sense of what distributed cognition means, tried to explain it to students. In this moment, it is clear.

Epilogue

Theater allows society a place to stage and reimagine categories like self, life, and death, during moments when they are placed into flux. The last fifty years have greatly complicated our ability to understand the "event" that is life or death. Dolly the sheep, Terry Sciavo, *Roe v. Wade*, and Snowflake Babies are just some examples of how we are being asked to reimagine the boundaries between dead and alive, self and other. The psychological realism of Arthur Miller or Tennessee Williams, a dramaturgy of the internal causes that motivate the individual, is giving way to a theater shifting our perspective from the "insides" of characters (wherein one finds their history or "backstory") to the networks that connect us, that make us enact the event together. If I can feel for a puppet, or laugh at the collision of three characters in one body, or make sense of a story only held together by the centripetal force of the audience that it surrounds, then perhaps thinking and feeling is more complicated than I originally thought. Perhaps what it means to mean, what it means to be, are different from what I imagined. Theater is helping us stage this category shift. If modernity is equated with individuality, than perhaps, as Bruno Latour insists, we never have been modern.[57] We emerge in the power to come together and bring something to life; we emerge in the network.

ACKNOWLEDGMENTS

This research was supported in part by a travel grant from Indiana University's College of Arts and Humanities Institute. I also received valuable support through the IU Institute for Advanced Study's Remak Seminar on "Moral Reasoning in Context" (2012–2013) and invaluable intellectual engagement from the members of that group: John Kruschke, Fritz Breithaupt, Colin Allen, Jody Madeira, Andrew Weaver, Torrin M. Liddell, and Samuel Zorowitz.

NOTES

1. Spolsky, "Making 'Quite Anew': Brain Modularity and Creativity," in *Introduction to Cognitive Cultural Studies*, edited by Lisa Zunshine (Baltimore, MD: Johns Hopkins University Press, 2010), 91–92.
2. Spolsky, 93.
3. For a similar argument, see Bruce McConachie, *Engaging Audiences: A Cognitive Approach to Spectating in the Theatre* (New York: Palgrave Macmillan, 2008), 3.
4. For more of a review, and an application of conceptual blending theory to *Hamlet*, see Cook, *Shakespearean Neuroplay: Reinvigorating the Study of Dramatic Texts and Performance through Cognitive Science* (New York: Palgrave Macmillan, 2010). For work on acting and the sciences, see Rhonda Blair, *The Actor, Image, and Action: Acting and Cognitive Neuroscience* (New York: Routledge, 2008), and John Lutterbie, *Toward a General Theory of Acting* (New York: Palgrave Macmillan, 2011). On audience reception, see Bruce McConachie, *Engaging Audiences: A Cognitive Approach to Spectating in the Theatre* (New York: Palgrave Macmillan, 2008), and Naomi Rokotnitz, *Trusting Performance: A Cognitive Approach to Embodiment in Drama* (New York: Palgrave Macmillan, 2011). For integrations with literature generally, see: Lisa Zunshine, *Strange Concepts and the Stories They Make Possible* (Baltimore: Johns Hopkins University Press, 2008); Mary Thomas Crane, *Shakespeare's Brain: Reading with Cognitive Theory* (Princeton: Princeton University Press, 2001); Barbara Dancygier, *The Language of Stories* (Cambridge, UK: Cambridge University Press, 2012); Ellen Spolsky, *Word vs Image: Cognitive Hunger in Shakespeare's England* (Basingstoke: Palgrave Macmillan,

2007); and Patrick Colm Hogan, *Cognitive Science, Literature, and the Arts: A Guide for Humanists* (New York: Routledge, 2003).

5. Carol Martin and Anna Deavere Smith, "Anna Deavere Smith: The Word Becomes You. An Interview," *TDR* 37, no. 4 (1993): 51.

6. On symptomatic versus surface reading, see Stephen Best and Sharon Marcus, "Surface Reading: An Introduction," *Representations* 108 (Fall 2009): 1–21.

7. Charles R. Lyons and James C. Lyons, "Anna Deavere Smith: Perspectives on Her Performance within the Context of Critical Theory," *Journal of Dramatic Theory and Criticism* 9, no. 1 (1994): 47.

8. Martin and Smith, "Anna Deavere Smith: The Word Becomes You," 56.

9. Susan Dominus, "Can Anna Deavere Smith's One-Woman Play about Health Care Bring Other Voices to the Debate?" *The New York Times Magazine*, October 4, 2009 (accessed December 28, 2011).

10. Ibid.

11. Quoted in Attilio Favorini, "Fires in the Mirror: Crown Heights, Brooklyn, and other Identities," City Theatre, Pittsburgh, Pennsylvania (theater reviews) *Theatre Journal* 48, no. 1 (March 1996): 105.

12. Martin and Smith, "Anna Deavere Smith: The Word Becomes You," 57.

13. For more on this divide, see Cook, *Shakespearean Neuroplay* (2010), and for a detailed history, see George Lakoff, *Women, Fire, and Dangerous Things: What Categories Reveal about the Mind* (Chicago: University of Chicago Press, 1987).

14. And, in fact, you can "prime" a metaphoric association through accessing the physical system. Researchers at Yale found that subjects could have their assessments of people or things manipulated by tactile experiences. See Joshua M. Ackerman, Christopher C. Nocera, and John A. Bargh, "Incidental Haptic Sensations Influence Social Judgments and Decisions" *Science* 328, no. 5987 (2010): 1712–14.

15. Mark Johnson, *The Meaning of the Body: Aesthetics of Human Understanding* (Chicago: University of Chicago Press, 2007), 53–54 (italics in original).

16. Alva Noë, *Action in Perception* (Cambridge, MA, and London: MIT Press, 2004), 2.

17. Michael L. Anderson, "Embodied Cognition: A Field Guide," *Artificial Intelligence* 149 (2003): 101–2.

18. Anderson, "Embodied Cognition: A Field Guide," 102.

19. For a terrific book on this and other studies from within cognitive science, see Benjamin Bergen, *Louder Than Words: The New Science of How the Mind Makes Meaning* (New York: Basic Books, 2012).

20. Lakoff, *Women, Fire, and Dangerous Things*, 93.

21. Lakoff, *Women, Fire, and Dangerous Things*, 95.

22. Andy Clark, *Supersizing the Mind: Embodiment, Action, and Cognitive Extension* (New York: Oxford University Press, 2008), 46.

23. For an analysis of the conceptual integration network involved in Hamlet's "mirror held up to nature," including a discussion of the personification of Virtue at work in the text, see Cook, *Shakespearean Neuroplay* (2010).

24. From *The Riverside Shakespeare*, 2nd ed. (Boston: Houghton Mifflin Company, 1997).

25. George Lakoff and Mark Turner, *More Than Cool Reason: A Field Guide to Poetic Metaphor* (Chicago: University of Chicago Press, 1989), 216.

26. Clark, *Supersizing the Mind*, 58–59.

27. Remshardt, Ralf. "Warhorse, and: Stovepipe (review)," *Theatre Journal* 62, no. 2 (May 2010): 273.

28. For more on emotion and empathy in the theater, see Cook, "For Hecuba or for Hamlet: Rethinking Emotion and Empathy in the Theatre," *Journal of Dramatic Theory and Criticism* 25, no. 2 (Spring 2011). See also Suzanne Keen, "A Theory of Narrative Empathy," *Narrative* 14, no. 3 (October 2006): 207–36. Bruce McConachie also critiques Coleridge's "willing suspension of disbelief" in *Engaging Audiences: A Cognitive Approach to Spectating in the Theatre* (New York: Palgrave Macmillan, 2008).

29. Strukus, Wanda. "Mining the Gap: Physically Integrated Performance and Kinesthetic Empathy" *Journal of Dramatic Theory and Criticism* (Spring 2011): 91.

30. Foster, Susan Leigh. *Choreographing Empathy: Kinesthesia in Performance* (New York: Routledge, 2011), 8, 10.

31. Foster, 129.

32. Breithaupt, "A Three-Person Model of Empathy," *Emotion Review* 4, no. 1 (January 2012). He goes on to suggest not only that we must study empathy in social scenes but also that perhaps social scenes are impossible without empathy.

33. Breithaupt, 15.

34. Jill Bennett, *Empathic Vision: Affect, Trauma, and Contemporary Art* (Stanford, CA: Stanford University Press, 2005) 43.

35. Jody Lyneé Madeira, "A Change of Heart: Towards a Relational Model of Reproductive Decision-Making," unpublished manuscript, 24.

36. Clark, *Supersizing the Mind*, 42.

37. Clark, *Supersizing the Mind*, 43.

38. A. Maravita and A. Iriki, "Tools for the Body (Schema)," *Trends in Cognitive Sciences* 8, no. 2 (2004), cited in Clark, 38.

39. David Kirsch and Paul Maglio, "On Distinguishing Epistemic from Pragmatic Action" *Cognitive Science* 18 (1994): 513–49.

40. Evelyn B. Tribble, *Cognition in the Globe: Attention and Memory in Shakespeare's Theatre* (New York: Palgrave Macmillan, 2011).

41. Remshardt, 273.

42. "Handspring Puppet Co.: The Genius Puppetry Behind *War Horse*." TED.com. Posted March 2011. http://www.ted.com/talks/handpring_puppet_co_the_genius_puppetry_behind_war_horse (accessed June 2011).

43. Holland, Norman, "The Willing Suspension of Disbelief: A Neuro-Psychoanalytic View," *PsyArt: A Hyperlink Journal for the Psychological Study of the Arts* (article 020919): 4, 6. http://www.clas.ufl.edu/ipsa/journal/2003_holland06.shtml (accessed February 4, 2005).

44. See Cook, "Staging Nothing: *Hamlet* and Cognitive Science," *SubStance* 35, no. 2 (2006): 83–99.

45. Haidt, Jonathan. *The Righteous Mind: Why Good People Are Divided by Politics and Religion* (New York: Pantheon, 2012), 190.

46. Later that same week I hear about Robert Shaughnessy's work on entrainment and wonder if starting my week abroad with theater decreased my jet lag.

47. Seabright, Paul. *The Company of Strangers: A Natural History of Economic Life* (Princeton: Princeton University Press, 2004), 2. I am grateful to Mark Turner for pointing me to this book.

48. See, for example, Steve Guglielmo, Bertrand Malle, and Andrew Monroe, "Moral, Cognitive, and Social: The Nature of Blame," in *Social Thinking and Interpersonal Behavior*, edited by J. Forgas, K. Fiedler, and C. Sedikides (Philadelphia, PA: Psychology Press, 2012), 311–29.

49. Peter DeScioli, and Robert Kurzban, "A Solution to the Mysteries of Morality," *Psychological Bulletin*, July 2, 2012, 1–20.

50. For the role of narrative formation in moral choice, see Fritz Breithaupt, Kevin M. Gardner, John K. Kruschke, Torrin M. Liddell, and Samuel Zorowitz (2013), "The Disappearance of Moral Choice in Serially Reproduced Narratives," in *2013 Workshop on Computational Models of Narrative*, edited by Mark A. Finlayson Bernhard Fisseni, Benedikt Löwe, and Jan Christoph Meister (Saarbrücken: Dagstuhl, 2013), 37–44.

51. Philippa Foot, "The Problem of Abortion and the Doctrine of Double Effect," *Oxford Review* 5 (1967): 5–6.

52. Judith Jarvis Thomson, "A Defense of Abortion," *Philosophy and Public Affairs* 1, no. 1 (1971): 47–66.

53. Foot, 10.

54. N. R. Hanson, "Causal Chains," *Mind*, n.s. 64, no. 255 (1955): 309.

55. Hanson, 293.

56. Hanson, 294, 304.

57. Bruno Latour, *We Have Never Been Modern* (Cambridge, MA: Harvard University Press, 1993).

BIBLIOGRAPHY

Ackerman, Joshua M., Christopher C. Nocera, and John A. Bargh. "Incidental Haptic Sensations Influence Social Judgments and Decisions." *Science* 328, no. 5987, (2010): 1712–14.

Anderson, Michael L. "Embodied Cognition: A Field Guide." *Artificial Intelligence* 149 (2003): 91–130.

Bennett, Jill. *Empathic Vision: Affect, Trauma, and Contemporary Art*. Stanford, CA: Stanford University Press, 2005.

Bergen, Benjamin. *Louder Than Words: The New Science of How the Mind Makes Meaning*. New York: Basic Books, 2012.

Best, Stephen, and Sharon Marcus. "Surface Reading: An Introduction." *Representations* 108 (Fall 2009): 1–21.

Blair, Rhonda. *The Actor, Image, and Action: Acting and Cognitive Neuroscience*. New York: Routledge, 2008.

Breithaupt, Fritz. "A Three-Person Model of Empathy." *Emotion Review* 4, no. 1 (2012): 84–91.

Clark, Andy. *Supersizing the Mind: Embodiment, Action, and Cognitive Extension*. New York: Oxford University Press, 2008.

Cook, Amy. "For Hecuba or for Hamlet: Rethinking Emotion and Empathy in the Theatre." *Journal of Dramatic Theory and Criticism* 25, no. 2 (Spring 2011): 71–87.

———. *Shakespearean Neuroplay: Reinvigorating the Study of Dramatic Texts and Performance through Cognitive Science*. New York: Palgrave Macmillan, 2010.

———. "Staging Nothing: *Hamlet* and Cognitive Science." *SubStance* 35, no. 2 (2006): 83–99.

Crane, Mary Thomas. *Shakespeare's Brain: Reading with Cognitive Theory*. Princeton: Princeton University Press, 2001.

Dancygier, Barbara. *The Language of Stories*. Cambridge, UK: Cambridge University Press, 2012.

DeScioli, Peter, and Robert Kurzban. "A Solution to the Mysteries of Morality." *Psychological Bulletin*, July 2, 2012, 1–20.

Dominus, Susan. "Can Anna Deavere Smith's One-Woman Play about Health Care Bring Other Voices to the Debate?" *New York Times Magazine*, October 4, 2009.

Favorini, Attilio. "Fires in the Mirror: Crown Heights, Brooklyn, and Other Identities." City Theatre, Pittsburgh, Pennsylvania (theater reviews). *Theatre Journal* 48, no. 1 (March 1996): 105.

Foot, Philippa. "The Problem of Abortion and the Doctrine of Double Effect." *Oxford Review* 5 (1967): 5–15.

Foster, Susan Leigh. *Choreographing Empathy: Kinesthesia in Performance*. New York: Routledge, 2011.

Haidt, Jonathan. *The Righteous Mind: Why Good People Are Divided by Politics and Religion*. New York: Pantheon, 2012.

Hanson, N. R. "Causal Chains." *Mind* n.s. 64, 255 (1955): 289–311.

Hogan, Patrick Colm. *Cognitive Science, Literature, and the Arts: A Guide for Humanists*. New York: Routledge, 2003.

Holland, Norman. "The Willing Suspension of Disbelief: A Neuro-Psychoanalytic View." *PsyArt: A Hyperlink Journal for the Psychological Study of the Arts* (article 020919): 4, 6. Accessed February 4, 2005. http://www.clas.ufl.edu/ipsa/journal/2003_holland06.shtml.

Johnson, Mark. *The Meaning of the Body: Aesthetics of Human Understanding*. Chicago: University of Chicago Press, 2007.

Keen, Suzanne. "A Theory of Narrative Empathy." *Narrative* 14, no. 3 (October 2006): 207–36.

Kirsch, David, and Paul Maglio. "On Distinguishing Epistemic from Pragmatic Action." *Cognitive Science* 18 (1994): 513–49.

Lakoff, George. *Women, Fire, and Dangerous Things: What Categories Reveal about the Mind*. Chicago: University of Chicago Press, 1987.

Lakoff, George, and Mark Turner. *More Than Cool Reason: A Field Guide to Poetic Metaphor*. Chicago: University of Chicago Press, 1989.

Latour, Bruno. *We Have Never Been Modern*. Cambridge, MA: Harvard University Press, 1993.

Lutterbie, John. *Toward a General Theory of Acting*. New York: Palgrave Macmillan, 2011.

Lyons, Charles R., and James C. Lyons. "Anna Deavere Smith: Perspectives on Her Performance within the Context of Critical Theory." *Journal of Dramatic Theory and Criticism* 9, no. 1 (1994): 43–66.

Madeira, Jody Lyneé. "A Change of Heart: Towards a Relational Model of Reproductive Decision-Making." Unpublished manuscript.

Malle, Bertrand, Steve Guglielmo, and Andrew Monroe. "Moral, Cognitive, and Social: The Nature of Blame." In *Social Thinking and Interpersonal Behavior*, edited by J. Forgas, K. Fiedler, and C. Sedikides, 311–29. Philadelphia, PA: Psychology Press, 2012.

Maravita, A., and A. Iriki. "Tools for the Body (Schema)" *Trends in Cognitive Sciences* 8, no. 2 (2004): 79–86.

Martin, Carol, and Anna Deavere Smith. "Anna Deavere Smith: The Word Becomes You. An Interview." *TDR* 37, no. 4 (1993): 45–62.

McConachie, Bruce. *Engaging Audiences: A Cognitive Approach to Spectating in the Theatre*. New York: Palgrave Macmillan, 2008.

Noë, Alva. *Action in Perception*. Cambridge, MA, and London: MIT Press, 2004.

Remshardt, Ralf. "Warhorse, and: Stovepipe (review)." *Theatre Journal* 62, no. 2 (May 2010): 273.

Rokotnitz, Naomi. *Trusting Performance: A Cognitive Approach to Embodiment in Drama*. New York: Palgrave Macmillan, 2011.

Spolsky, Ellen. "Making 'Quite Anew': Brain Modularity and Creativity." In *Introduction to Cognitive Cultural Studies*, edited by Lisa Zunshine, 84–102. Baltimore, MD: Johns Hopkins University Press, 2010.

Spolsky, Ellen. *Word vs Image: Cognitive Hunger in Shakespeare's England*. Basingstoke: Palgrave Macmillan, 2007.

Thomson, Judith Jarvis. "A Defense of Abortion." *Philosophy and Public Affairs* 1, no. 1 (1971): 47–66.

Seabright, Paul. *The Company of Strangers: A Natural History of Economic Life*. Princeton: Princeton University Press, 2004.

Shakespeare, William. *A Midsummer Night's Dream*. In *The Riverside Shakespeare*. 2nd ed. Boston: Houghton Mifflin Company, 1997.

Strukus, Wanda. "Mining the Gap: Physically Integrated Performance and Kinesthetic Empathy." *Journal of Dramatic Theory and Criticism* (Spring 2011): 89–105.

Tribble, Evelyn B. *Cognition in the Globe: Attention and Memory in Shakespeare's Theatre*. New York: Palgrave Macmillan, 2011.

Zunshine, Lisa. *Strange Concepts and the Stories They Make Possible*. Baltimore: Johns Hopkins University Press, 2008.

CHAPTER 26

IMAGES OF LOVE AND POWER
Butoh, Bausch, and Streb

SONDRA HORTON FRALEIGH

> Power without love is reckless and abusive, and love without power is sentimental and anemic.
>
> —Martin Luther King Jr.

THIS chapter covers three topics at the boundary of dance and theater, (1) the façade, as deliberately assumed behavior in dance and theater; (2) love and power in butoh, Pina Bausch, and Elizabeth Streb; (3) embodied imagery in dance theater.

Relationships of love and power, as they appear in dance theater, draw on questions of consciousness and human will. I pursue these relationships philosophically in terms of the aesthetics of the artists explored. All of them have challenged conventional paradigms of theater. Butoh remains the main topic, as I explain this art and contrast it with the work of Bausch and Streb. Bausch's tanztheater swims in a stream of expressionist theater related to butoh, but her work draws up gender clashes and the social body, while butoh bonds with nature and sinks toward disappearance. The natural or elemental world plays a different role in Bausch, as can be seen through the inclusion of leaves, sod, animals, flowers, and water in her sets. Bausch and butoh are both rooted in surrealist methods that utilize subconscious life, dream imagery, and the irrational absurd, but with highly contrasting aesthetic results, as we will pursue. Streb provides a keen contrast to both butoh and Bausch, being objectively cast in the physical nature of the human body and its capabilities in relation to laws of nature, such as gravity. She strives to ride the wave of difficult tasks such as flying. Butoh and Bausch are decidedly subjective, while Streb is a study in objective awareness.

We consider these forms of dance theater separately, and also look at ways in which they compare and contrast. I ask how imagery is embodied in each of these, and more specifically how their aesthetic images function in terms of love and power. When I identify butoh as a specific form of dance theater, I capitalize the first letter; otherwise it flows into the text without capitals, as any other genre of dance would, such as modern dance or ballet. Japanese names are written with the last name first, in keeping with convention.

THE FACADE

Butoh morphology addresses the audience in ways that Western cultures of embodiment do not. Butoh had its genesis in Japan through Hijikata Tatsumi's dances of protest after World War II. He resisted America's incursion into Japan, politically and aesthetically, while also thumbing his nose at elements of his own culture. Rustic Japan was in danger of being subsumed by Western rationalism at the onset of the information age. Hijikata's works looked behind production and progress, expressing a chthonic and native spirituality. As Hijikata's put it often and succinctly: "I come from the mud."

Many people were shocked by Hijikata's *Forbidden Colors* (1959), the dance that initiated butoh. Some saw bestiality and sodomy represented, at least by the time the dance had been reinvented in several publications and audience versions. This dance placed Hijikata squarely in the contentious era of sixties and seventies Japan, the same era that defined postmodern dance in America. Hijikata was just beginning to explore the surrealist tactics that would finally define much of his work and the legacy of butoh. Soon after that came the initial experiments of Bausch and Streb. Morphology and collage would supersede concerns for content in butoh, where content morphed toward "nothingness," the theme of Hijikata's final workshop. Meaning would not be the intentional outcome, but rather, *experience*, as Hijikata eventually made explicit in the title of his first concert, DANCE EXPERIENCE (written in English). One might easily argue that *experience*, rather than meaning, is also at the core of Bausch and Streb. For Bausch, this takes on aspects of the emotional body, and for Streb, physical powers and the courage to overcome, at least to be fully alive in the moment of action.

Metamorphosis and cultural protest are just part of the story of butoh. From its beginnings, its disruption of tradition and boundaries had cross-cultural imagery and potential, now being increasingly realized. Since its founding in the mid-twentieth century through the surrealist genius of Tatsumi Hijikata and the passionate, gentle dances of Ohno Kazuo and his son Yoshito, butoh has spread its curious alchemy around the globe. I experience it as a form of dance and theater that connects liberally to the unconscious. Because it does not ignore pain, it can also be healing. Butoh often acknowledges pain, pays attention to it, and does not deny it, as is typically the case in dance.[1] In his recent teaching, Ohno Yoshito transforms pain and suffering through the realization of emptiness in dance, leaning toward Zen.[2] Even so, butoh is not a simple acknowledgment of pain and suffering, nor does it focus on spiritual practice; rather, it courts theatrical façade. This conjures its transformative power. We can dance our pain and connect to the pain of others, refracting it consciously in butoh processes and performances, depending on how the dance is framed. One might argue that butoh, Bausch, and Streb each take a perspective on pain, as we take up toward the end, after we look at each of these arts separately.

Gesamtkunstwerk

As a form of dance that is intensely theatrical, butoh uses all of the arts, allowing them to co-exist in performance. It has evolved as a form of dance theater that can be highly architectural. In its less formal manifestations, it is performed extemporaneously in nature and environmentally. In its varied and often raw performances, it presents unique opportunities to examine crossovers between dance and theater, proffering an Eastern ethos both imagistic and morphic.

In this article, I will show how butoh, Bausch, and Streb like other forms of dance and theater present deliberately assumed behavior, and in the best sense, a façade, not a false appearance but a distinctive architecture of expression. I discuss these three as forms of dance theater because they are all based in dance, but each in its own way produces complexly structured visual and visceral theater. None of them depend on text, even as Bausch sometimes includes spoken phrases and laughter, and all of them are architectural in the way their parts link and function throughout the whole. The closely designed works of butoh, Bausch, and Streb are not singular lyrics, but vertical arrangements of many overlapping parts that change in myriad directions and timings.

All of the arts combine in the forms of dance theater we examine here, but not with an eye toward purity of each element in proximity as in the Wagnerian *Gesamtkunstwerk*. I avoid this German term with its totalizing connotations when speaking about the butoh aesthetic, because butoh even when it is highly produced is seldom grandiose or total. Bausch and Streb can also produce works on spectacular scales, but they do not impose grandeur, as we will see, neither are they examples of pure art. In fulfilling space, Sankai Juku Dance Theater with its large-scale sets and props and its profuse lighting effects is probably the best example of highly architected butoh.

Hijikata is often referred to as the architect of butoh, because of his use of material objects in collage imagery for motivating movement and also in his structured choreography. Ohno contrasted Hijikata's systematic, surreal, and imagistic choreography with an improvisational and poetic style. Sankai Juku, Hijikata, and Ohno represent three styles of butoh that can satisfy theatrical space, but they are not examples of total theater. Art historian Juliet Koss follows a theoretical model that sees modernism itself as understood through *Gesamtkunstwerk*, or total work of art. She attends to such theories of modern spectatorship as estrangement, abstraction, and empathy and argues for *Gesamtkunstwerk* as a concept central to modernism.[3] Beyond theoretical and historical elaborations of modernism, ideas behind *Gesamtkunstwerk* have become nebulous.

In contrast to those well-knit operas of Wagner, which gave meaning to "total work of art," butoh explores the underside of life, the margins, not the center. Bausch also explores the marginal as taken-for-granted repetitions in social life, which creep into the social fabric. She doesn't seem interested in grand narratives, more in overlooked or hidden motives, while Streb subverts our understanding of totality in dance through engaging machinery, not for effects in the background of the stage but at the forefront, and not hiding the difficulty of movement. Her dances don't look easy, because they are not easy.

Images of Nature and Culture

We have already noticed that all of the artists we examine approach nature in a different way. Some butoh works focus on natural processes of decay and are performed in rural environments, like those in the stale, moldy sheds of Broellin, an old castle in the country-side just beyond Berlin, Germany.[4] Butoh is not a modern movement, but rather emerged against modernism as a Japanese postmodern art, not commensurate with the pedes-trian American postmodern. Butoh's way into the postmodern aesthetic was closer to the eclectic postmodern of architecture, mixing elements from various historical periods and moving across cultures. Bausch explores human happenings and dramas in terms of habit and social constructions, often subverting these to make them more apparent, while Streb challenges assumptions about physical nature, human movement, and courage.

From the beginning until now, various cultures co-exist in butoh; it draws on Eastern and Western music and costumes, and uses the creative impulse toward originality that Ohno and Hijikata encountered in studying German Expressionism. This was the modern dance form that entered into Japan through Eguchi Takaya and other Japanese teachers who had studied in the West beginning in the first half of the twentieth century.[5] Because of the perceived potency of modern dance, it was dubbed "poison dance" in Japan. In his speech for the JADE international dance conference in Tokyo in 1990, Japanese dance scholar and

PHOTO 26.1 Atsushi Takenouchi dancing to heal the earth in Valle De La Luna, Bolivia. Photographer: Hiroko Komiya © 2009.

⊙

VIDEO 26.1 Atsushi Takenouchi in *Bu*. Film from Dance on Camera Festival in New York City, 2013. Film by Michel Tabet. Film courtesy of Atsushi Takenouchi.

critic Gungi Masakatsu, in a cryptic and facetious tone, called Hijikata and Ohno "failed Western dancers, expelled from Japan, and then rediscovered."[6] Butoh's eclectic genealogy connects it to the West, but its Japanese ethnicity is apparent whenever the kimono appears, or the performer's knees bend softly to lower the body's center of gravity, and the movement slows to a meditative, ceremonial crawl.

The powdered white phantoms of Japan, typically associated with white-powdered bodies in traditional butoh, are just one of its many contemporary appearances. Butoh is a form of dance theater, but it also exists as an idea with unfinished edges, and its several varieties are still evolving. We might even see it as a unique genre with different styles. As an idea, butoh carries the meaning of "ancient dance." For contemporary butohist Takenouchi Atsushi, this is the dance that is already happening inside the body.[7] Takenouchi travels to the four corners of the globe, performing in the environment to heal the earth in endangered places, or on "killing grounds" where large masses of people have died (Photo 26.1).

Ohno set the example for this when he danced at Auschwitz from his feeling for the stones there. Takenouchi and Ohno's environmental dances attest butoh's elasticity as a genre (Video 26.1).

They spiritualize love without apology, and their power is not politically coercive. Takenouchi has been filmed and photographed dancing in the environment, not for show but as a way to grieve war and earth's endangerment, and to connect with others through a sense of place (Photos 26.2–26.4).

Streb and Bausch have also danced to capture environments, Bausch's "City Dances" are a good example of this, and Streb's large-scale sets are made for outdoor performances.

Deliberately Assumed Behavior

Performance is learned. It is constructed, assumed, and fabricated behavior. Dance and theater performance have this in common, but the fabrications are not lies, and the assumed behavior is a very valuable façade. It provides a way to test beliefs and performative abilities, to look into and beyond the problems and pleasures of the everyday. The stage is the stage because it offers the opportunity for performers to assume behavior outside of cultural and personal norms, and to test those norms. Performance requires tests of nerve and will, bodily tests if you will, involving endurance, speed, and balance, but also tests of inventiveness and imagination. We see this clearly in Streb's works, as I will show. Performance tests human actions and possible fictions. The audience participates in the tests vicariously. Audiences test their fears, attractions, habits, and politics in the safety of the performer's façade, as conjured tests of emotional life and human fears in the works of Bausch. Theater is full of play, because in some sense it is not real, but made up. Nevertheless it is real as theater.

PHOTOS 26.2–26.4 Three photographs of Takenouchi dancing in the environment in *Bu*, Houdan, France. Photographer, George Karam © 2012. Photograph courtesy of Atsushi Takenouchi.

PHOTOS 26.2–26.4 *(Continued.)*

LOVE AND POWER IN BUTOH, BAUSCH, AND STREB

> Butoh should reject any notion of symbolism, message, or formalism, and only express its energy and freedom. It is not art that I aspire to, but love.
>
> —Nakajima Natsu, female founder of butoh

Butoh, Bausch, and Streb each give us unique portals into questions of power and the will, expanding on what it means to achieve a purpose, and they each unsettle romantic definitions of love. Or maybe they give us windows into a gritty romance of practical ideals that connect power and love to the eros of mud and dirt, on one hand, and evanescence, or fleeting reality, on the other. Nakajima Natsu, quoted above, provides an example of the latter, especially through *Niwa* (The Garden, 1985), the work she toured internationally for several years. Her performances introduced butoh to Western audiences, including this author, and her teaching influenced dancers, actors, and directors in Europe, as well as North and South America. Ohno Kazuo, who was one of her mentors, also toured extensively. The spiritual butoh styles of Ohno and Nakajima were among the first seen in the West. Hijikata, Nakajima's other mentor, never left Japan.

Hijikata gives us an earthier, rough view of spirit. His Ankoku Butoh ("darkness dance"), like the dance theater of Bausch, and Streb is edgy and not afraid of grunge. They all seem to realize what Peter Brook writes about "rough" theater, that it can be socially liberating.[8] The gruff singing of Louis Armstrong, for instance, satisfies a human taste for roughness. Perfection, it seems, can be boring. Pure electronic imitations of acoustic instruments were originally unsatisfying to the musical ear. Electronic music needed that slightly discordant edge that humanizes art. In butoh this includes actually handling dirt, smearing mud on the face and body, as Takenouchi Atsushi often does in his contemporary butoh for imperiled environments. Bausch's stages full of sod, as in *Rite of Spring* (1975), her "getting down" into nitty-gritty emotional life, would be part of her grunge. In Streb, strife manifests in sweat and risk, in thudding falls from testy heights, and in shattering noise, as when she hurls herself through plate glass (Photo 26.5).

Facets of love and power appear in all of these artists. Rapprochement of these interpersonal values is not simple, but therein lies the art.

We learn through the opening quotation from Martin Luther King Jr. that love is ineffective without power, and power can fall into brute roughness without love. Love, we might recognize, is expressed in various forms, erotically in sex and the drive to create; through *filia* or friendship; and as *agape*, devotion to the welfare of others. I believe that King was speaking to the issue of social fairness and human interconnections. Rollo May writes thematically in *Love and Will* that the *experience* of love is a blending of kinds. Love gives power to the will, and it also tempers it. A phenomenologist would say that until love and power are embodied in action, they only exist as concepts. Artists give form (embodiments) to love and power. In dance, these are kinesthetic forms that we also recognize as dance images, discerned through the larger gestalt of the work. Dance images exist in movement and in context, in other words. They embody feelings and ideas and are the keys to meaning through interpretation.

The risky theater of Elizabeth Streb hones physical strength and speed in movement, in contrast to the slowness often seen in butoh. We cannot mistake uses of power in Streb, but

PHOTO 26.5 Elizabeth Streb in *Breakthrough*. Photograph courtesy of Elizabeth Streb.

"where is the love"? I believe it can be found, as we see later. After three extensive interviews with her, and being an audience for her work over the years, I have observed how thoroughly she researches physical matter. She explores movement scientifically like a physicist, presenting her findings in highly theatrical contexts with an emphasis on power through stunts and psychophysical tests. Her circus-like work is rough, but more in terms of risky tasks, extreme physicality, spoken instructions on stage, and sometimes "dissing" illusion through direct rapport with the audience. Some might not classify her work as dance or theater. I do (Video 26.2).

VIDEO 26.2 Elizabeth Streb, *Human Eye,* 2013. Video courtesy of Elizabeth Streb.

Butoh's power is not so overtly physical as that of Streb and not as laden with sexual politics as that of Bausch. Love (as sentience) and power (as often diffused) have a symbiotic relationship in butoh, one that associates humans with animals and plants, and flows from a meditative and morphic presence, as we examine further. Sexuality in butoh is sometimes diffused in gender bending, or for some it might be heightened in the imaginative transfer. Sexuality in Bausch is often overt, with movement both emotionally painful and salacious, and also playful. Sexuality in Streb is not overt; rather sex and gender are mollified in equality. Regarding such matters of interpretation, we look briefly into philosophies of will and representation below, especially as these involve love and power.

Power and Will

> Love and will are interpersonal experiences, which bring to bear power to influence others significantly and to be influenced by them.
>
> Rollo May, *Love and Will*

In his statement above, May articulates a definition of love and will that links to power.[9] He sees that love and will are both ways of relating to others and affecting or being affected by them. Power involves will. Love, we sometimes think, just happens. Is it possible that love and power both are highly textured matters of the will? I submit that they are, that they both involve choice, and will is much larger in human life than simple control. Will is not commensurate with willfulness. Control and grace both reside in matters of will, as do love and power. Mahatma Gandhi and Martin Luther King Jr. provided examples of nonviolent uses of power toward social change, demonstrating how will can be urgent without being coercive. Bifurcated views of the world conceive love and power as opposed. When we split these qualities in experience, somatically—we lose the will to act with a moral purpose. This is why more recent readings of Western philosophy question the ideal of aggressive upward momentum.[10]

We also understand through May's definition that love and will are *experiences*. As such they are embodied. Love is sometimes called an emotion as well as an experience. Power is a dynamic potential of the will. Thus we can speak of "willpower." It points toward our ability to act, to love, or even hate. Power is a neutral concept until it is realized in action, shaped and formed by the will. In dance and theater, we observe uses of will and manifestations of power through embodied performance as poured through imagination. Embodiment itself is an ongoing dynamic as understood in phenomenology, a process that is never complete or solid. As ongoing, embodiment proffers acts made visible, tangible, and audible. Such acts can be tested and expanded, as Streb does. As fragile, embodiment also tenders corporeal ephemerality. Butoh in some of its expressions gives us a vision of fragility. All of the arts give us consciously directed ways of constructing and reflecting embodiment, and as such, they give us windows into uses of the will. The processes of embodiment involve development of the will, the subject that has engrossed philosophy from Kant through Schopenhauer to Nietzsche, moving into the twentieth century with Heidegger and later Foucault.

Foucault's study of the history of sexuality posited the problem of "docile bodies," or we could say that he elucidated the somatic problem of blind obedience. His interest is in studying regulatory power over bodies.[11] The study of the will, and thus human agency, is the study of embodiment and the emergence of self. Paul Ricoeur in his study of voluntary and involuntary movement taught that *the will becomes the form of the body*. Humans are creating bodily life performatively through the arts, as also in everyday actions through habitual uses of the will. Aesthetic innovation is part of this creation.

A cumulative purpose of creative arts is the expansion of options for thinking and acting beyond habitual uses of the will. How do people get past themselves, in other words? In their experiments, the arts present opportunities for personal and cultural renewal by playing with edges and boundaries, disrupting habit and cultural constructions. The artists we are considering here have all challenged cultural and aesthetic norms, which doesn't mean they have embraced the view that innovation and originality in themselves bring improvement.

Among philosophies of art and will, one would need to cite Arthur Schopenhauer's study of nonrational will and rejection of rationalistic conceptions of the world, his concern for the meaning of life, life as suffering, and his theories of art and music. Schopenhauer's works *On Vision and Colors* (1816), *The World as Will and Representation* (1818), and *On The Will in Nature* (1836)[12] foreground the twentieth century vision of butoh, still evolving, that the world is going nowhere—lest we forget that butoh rejected the idea of continual progress and was antimodern as it turned back the clock to celebrate instinctual forces.

Schopenhauer encouraged the gaze beyond one's own limited horizon. His theories set the stage for the arrival of surrealism and psychoanalysis, the latter finally exploring the unconscious mind, or the "collective unconscious," as Carl Jung called it in his psychology. Both of these visionaries studied nonrational elements of Eastern thought, and they have relevance for butoh's East/West border crossings because they urge expositions of the arts beyond the conscious mind. Butoh and Busch, in their attempts to exhume the unconscious, circumvent upwardly ascendant forms of art and, alongside this, deflate the romance of genius. Schopenhauer, himself on the precipice of a romantic age, holds that everyone has genius; this is what allows humans to understand a phenomenon as complicated as art. He also sees that those who study and practice the ways of art develop their native genius further. He uses "will" as a familiar designation that can be signified by other words such as "wanting," "desire," "effort," and "urging." To this we add, the will to do, to accomplish, to create, and to love. Schopenhauer's philosophy, strongly influenced by Buddhist thought, holds that all nature, including man, is the expression of the *will to life*.

Butoh moves into life with its disturbances and flaws, sometimes disappearing into life/death/life, while Bausch moves in spite of life or because of it and Streb wants to be in the flow of life's possibilities. In the following sections, we develop the unique characteristics of Butoh, Streb, and Bausch, as we also pursue issues of love and power. Eventually we develop more comparisons in terms of imagery.

Butoh

Nonrational Will in Butoh

The sometimes foolish, often crazy, and hauntingly ridiculous façades of butoh can be celebrated in part through Eastern doctrines of emptiness and darkness. Hijikata's unique invention, Ankoku Butoh, is "darkness dance." As it has scattered around the world and developed globally, butoh has changed, as any art needs to if it is to survive, but in its core, it continues to cultivate a limitless gaze into nature and the unconscious, one that is open to interpretation.

The darkness of butoh is not Jungian, even if it does admit shadows. Rather it is more Buddhist and meditative, washing the conscious mind of its rational clutter. In Zen Buddhism, the irrational mind can erupt suddenly and unpredictably, prompting grief and laughter at once, and silly answers to Zen questions are just as good as profound ones. Butoh is not all slow-smoothness; it is also gritty and holds sudden surprises, as contemporary butohist Endo Tadashi teaches in his workshops.[13]

Hijikata's project influenced decades of butoh and was beyond dance and theater. He was political and presented a personal ethnology of suffering that could nevertheless be universalized: "Tohoku is everywhere," he often said, speaking of his birthplace. He expressed power in his protest of the West's incursion into Japan and ambiguities of love through tuning back toward his Japanese roots while "slashing space" (his expression), reaching as far back as the early Kabuki before its popular vulgarity was cleaned up for Western audiences. His dance eventually made use of both Western and Eastern sources, critiquing both. Hijikata said that his dancers were terrorists in protest of rationalism, materialism, and production.[14] Through his appreciation of French novelist and dramatist Jean Genet, he embraced the antirational methods of European surrealism, using the West, but for his own purposes. More shockingly in his day, he used Japanese nativism in postmodern pastiche. From a much more Western perspective, Pina Bausch also challenged rationalism, as we will pursue in our fuller discussion of Bausch.

Excavating Love and Power in Butoh

Much of theater and dance has been an effort to define love, this elusive glue of relationship or tenor of feeling, whether we think of narrative manifestations or sense the presence of love in abstract or natural forms. I discern love, for instance, in the soul-searching morphology of butoh, but seldom as narrative. In this dance genre, love does not seek its fulfillment in the other, but in connecting to the natural world and the unconscious. By the same token, butoh crops up in city landscapes. Min Tanaka liked to be photographed in costumes or nearly naked against steel girders at construction sites; and butoh, ever difficult to pin down, has favored the city as much as rural landscapes. Its malleability is part of its power. Its morphing states connect to change as a principle of life. I sense a love of natural processes in butoh, even in its acceptance of life/death/life cycles. On the other hand, butoh in its craft shows a consummate love of theater.

Love in butoh is not polarized, not passionate, not pure and porcelain, nor is it laden with desire and loss, rather it can be found in junk and mud, embracing beauty in messy places of rejection. Brotherly, nonsexual love wouldn't describe this kind of love. It surpasses familiar human terrain, finding satisfaction in spirit, not in human connectivity. It casts an eye beyond, looking into dark forgotten corners, and respecting death. "I carry all the dead with me," is how Ohno Kazuo set the stage for butoh's occupation with matters beyond self-interest and transient passions. Love can appear unexpectedly in moments of butoh's slow time, blossoming through an unprotected face. Unlike much Western theater and dance, butoh eschews narrative to favor the cauldron of flow and change, which I sometimes think of as its alchemy.

Ohno Kazuo liked to say that there is enough ugliness in life. His favorite form of life was flowers—and in a leap of faith, he taught dancers and actors how to become stones. He didn't consciously employ ugliness. Rather his butoh, like that of many, took spiritual development seriously. But even in its muddy and ugly faces, and also when it courts falling edges of movement and tipping over, love in butoh is distilled spiritually, carried as transformative potential. Yoshito Ohno in his butoh teaches the transformative potential of love through pain. "Every step is pain," he teaches in his workshops, as students transform in the cauldron of the body, softly, slowly stepping toward compassion.

Butoh continues to fascinate me partly through its inclusion of dissonance and pain as aesthetic values, parts of life not to be pushed away. Is ugliness bad and beauty good? Not in butoh. They simply are. We as audiences and performers have a chance to appreciate both. Critics do not have the last word, but we at least hope that they have studied the art they are writing about, and can lend an informed account. Butoh offers unique challenges and experiences in the cycle between the artist, the performer, the audience, and the critic. Its framework is not Western, even when it appears in Western theaters. It is an East/West art, with East coming first. Its boundary is permeable and alchemical, and its use of will is not toward overcoming. It does not "up" the technical "ante," but rather appreciates the body in decline, admitting illness and weakness. *It engages grace as an aspect of will.* For instance, "the twisting power" of the face, seen in a lot of butoh, might be interpreted as an intentional exploration of ugliness or absurdity, but in its morphing state the face is not used for strangeness but for its transformative potential, akin to the transformative potential of pain. At some point grace will arrive. Some surprising contour of the face will appear out of nowhere, glowing like silk, glanced in passing.

Sankai Juku Dance Theater

The theatrical sweep of butoh spans a spectrum of presentations, from the understated dances of Min Tanaka, such as *Tree IV* installation (Tokyo, 1990), with a simple box frame set and plain costumes, to the awe inspiring set designs of Sankai Juku, made to display slate white, powdered bodies against light reflecting, pounded metallic surfaces. *Shijima* (*The Darkness Calms Down in Space*, 1988) features a dancer standing high in vertical space on a transparent ledge, appearing in the air, while dancers below move like morphing calligraphy, their arms in constant process of discovery. The five-man butoh company, Sankai Juku, first became famous for its hanging tricks, dangling from tall buildings on ropes, reminding one of a risky Elizabeth Streb stunt. On main stage theaters throughout the world, draped skirts rim the slim male hips of Sanki Juku's performers, or they wear just a thong.

Amagatzu Ushio is the company's director. His choreography over the years has included the contemporary music of Yoichiro Yoshikawa and Yas-Kas, architectural visual art, costume design, and compelling dance, a spectacle for the eye and spirit, and an unmistakable example of Butoh as dance theater. Amagatsu's abstract images flow cleanly in space, with space given light and shadow and sometimes-falling sand as a reminder of butoh's shifting essence. Personal features of the performers are diminished, so we watch the morphing scene as we might a mysterious landscape.

Love in Leprosy: Hijikata's Summer Storm

Tsuchi kara umareta (I come from the mud).

Hijikata Tatsumi

Most butoh can trace its ancestry back to Hijikata Tatsumi, including that of Amagatsu. We go behind his highly sophisticated work to take a brief look at Hijikata's *Summer Storm*, a rustic form of dance theater with complexly designed choreography and costumes. Hijikata's dance company performed this work in 1973 at the University of Kyoto. As part of his full-length dance concert, he performed *Leprosy*, his last solo dance in public. This solo is a small but poignant section of *Summer Storm*, Hijikata's indictment of war and prayer for peace. It is not easy to describe the aesthetic power of *Leprosy*, except to say something about Hijikata's inclination toward his rural roots, the vulnerability of old people and cripples, and that he never forgot crying infants confined in rice baskets in the fields of Tohoku while their parents worked. Hijikata's legs can barely hold him in *Leprosy*, and yet they do, somehow. His light and slightly contracted way of walking became a signature movement that defined an era of butoh.

Cautiously, he wobbles to the outside edges of his feet. The whole of his dance is understated, more inwardly cast than projected toward the audience. Wordlessly, he asks the audience to come into a condition of pain and isolation. It is not what I expected, having seen more flamboyant examples of Hijikata, such as *Rebellion of the Body* (1968) caught in part on film and in many photographs (Photo 26.6).

His dance, *Leprosy*, is not a demonstration or imitation of suffering, rather does it empty out and let the wobbly body be. The whole of *Summer Storm* is on film,[15] but even at this remove, it breaks one's heart. Here love is shown through affliction, and the power to transcend is not heroic, but a gift of time. Hijikata's dance evokes several fears in me, common ones, like fear of rejection, of the dark unknown, and of losing control. With submission, he embodies illness and deformity, loneliness and estrangement (Photos 26.7 and 26.8).

PHOTO 26.6 Hijikata in *Rebellion of the Body* (1968), Photographer, Tadao Nakatani. Photograph courtesy of Hijikata Tatsumi Archives in Tokyo.

In other parts of *Summer Storm*, we hear the names of famous places and battles of World War II layered over the music and the dance. Butoh as dance theater is first realized in Hijikata's choreography. In *Summer Storm*, the arts come together in poetic fragments, carefully crafted group dance, and costumes that range from medieval masks and headdresses to near nudity. Hijikata himself wears a simple female shift in *Leprosy*, dirty and hanging, much like that of Pina Bausch in *Café Muller*. The shift covers them both plainly, signaling futility in Bausch and surrender in Hijikata.

As a genre, butoh grew internationally, heuristically, involving experiences of risk, change, and discovery. Experientially, the butoh body morphs; it changes through several states in the course of one performance, even in one phrase, and seldom as a consequence of narrative. If *dance expression* typified the modern dance of the twentieth century, *dance experience*

PHOTOS 26.7–26.8 Hijikata in another work on disease, *A History of Smallpox* (1972). Two photographs on *Smallpox* by Tadao Nakatani. Photograph courtesy of Hijikata Tatsumi Archives in Tokyo.

is at the core of butoh, and its experiential spectrum is vast. Love is everywhere expressed in butoh, love of spirit, love of nature, and love of theater. Butoh melts desire and gives power a rest, or situates power inside of love. In my recent extended study of butoh, I call it "soul work." This is how I understand the advent of butoh and its task.[16] Consider how Yoshito Ohno speaks about the kind of love inspired by his father's dances: "Kazuo's warmth and tenderness are not those of flesh and blood. The form of love he epitomizes pierces the public's heart."[17]

ELIZABETH STREB

Anthropologist of the Stunt: Love and Power in Elizabeth Streb

> I love New York.
>
> —Elizabeth Streb

Postmodern dance took a turn away from narrative in its early phases, as it exacted tests of the dance medium. What would result from its task-related explorations of carrying mattresses and people, of saying "No to spectacle," as Yvonne Rainer put it in her famous manifesto? If we look at more recent manifestations in the developments of dance, we might see that *difficult moves*, the more the better, fuel the inheritors of the American postmodern. We could pick a few central driving images for contemporary dance today, but none more prominent than tests of movement and the body itself. Exacting tests of the body in the physically demanding work of Elizabeth Streb exemplify crossing points between dance, theater, and daredevil spectacle (Photo 26.9).

The work of Elizabeth Streb's dance theater exudes toughness and physical power, and it also probes the imagination. Her work gives us images of physical prowess and true grit. I see Streb in high contrast to butoh, since the latter becomes ever subtler, soft and slow in its movements, not always, but often. For example, *Shin* is a guiding concept for Ohno Yoshito, which he takes to an extreme of slowness in his metaphysical teaching, including classes on "the courage of not starting," echoed in his work *Kuu* (Emptiness, 2007).

Akin to action movies, Streb's dances start and finish with displays of physical power and imagination. Perhaps they wait on emptiness, but not visibly. Yet, they are slow where they need to be, as in a smooth wrapping duet, winding and unwinding around a center axis with dancers harnessed on wires moving beautifully aslant in *Orbit*, scene two of a recent work, *Streb VS Gravity* (Video 26.3).

Streb's clockwork dancers pack a wallop, tempting fate and risking broken bones when performing *Human Fountain*, the last scene of *Kiss the Air* (2010), also performed at the World Financial Center Plaza in New York in July 2011. In *Human Fountain*, based on the Bellagio Fountain in Las Vegas, dancers fly horizontally and fall in overlapping ensemble from a three-tiered 30-foot platform to land like planks on thick mats. It is clearly obvious that the intent of her work is toward risk and beauty, not harm (Photos 26.10–26.12).

Violence is the intent to do harm, and this is nowhere evident in Streb's action plans. She has developed a troupe of able gymnast-dancers who perform in theaters, arts festivals, and

PHOTO 26.9 Elizabeth Streb's daredevil dancers skydive from 30 feet, landing on mats, in *Human Fountain*. Photograph of *Human Fountain* at the Park Avenue Armory in December 2011. Photographer, Antoine Douaihy © 2011, Tom Caravaglia Studio, used by permission of Antoine Douaihy.

VIDEO 26.3 *Streb VS Gravity*. Photograph courtesy of Elizabeth Streb.

sports stadiums around the world, crossing the aesthetics of dance with the thrill of sports contests. The contest is not between dancers, however; it lies within the dance itself, testing human tendencies toward inertia, honing fine points of balance and dangerous feats of falling, pitting muscle and momentum against obstacles. Streb wants to press the "yes" button. What once couldn't be done, now can. *Give us an S for Streb!*

She has even been able to dispense with the proscenium stage through the invention of a box truss. This custom-designed apparatus fits in a shipping container that can be unpacked and assembled in a Las Vegas casino as easily as in New York, where her works have shown in such diverse locales as Grand Central Terminal, Central Park, and the Joyce Theater. Streb favors theater as spectacle, even in outdoor spaces: on the beach in Miami; at the mall in Washington, DC; and at the Minneapolis Metrodome during a Minnesota Twins vs. New York Yankees double header. Her work *Lookup!*, in which harnessed dancers performed off a 40-foot wall, was featured at the Brooklyn Bridge Anchorage. STREB, the dancers and the show, have been seen on both popular and prestige stages (Video 26.4).

If risk, contest, and danger guide Streb's work, stories also seem to abound, but not the literal kind. They connect her to the narrative aspects of dance theater. Streb's nonfiction

PHOTOS 26.10–26.12 Three images of *Human Fountain* (2011) by Elizabeth Streb. Photograph by Antoine Douaihy, Tom Caravaglia Studio. Photograph courtesy of Elizabeth Streb.

PHOTOS 26.10–26.12 (Continued.)

VIDEO 26.4 Samples of Streb's work—*Spatial Rift*, 2010. Video courtesy Elizabeth Streb.

dance *Tied* is a short story of two people tied together. Might this be as in marriage, "tying the knot"? *Tied* is a relentless theatrical dance of tugs and hard bumps, pulling, and tearing. There is no easing into it. The performers thud together, then move here and there harmlessly, jerking each other's chains. This is not a pleasant story, but it is a logical one for Streb to showcase because it deals with an enormous stunt—the spectacle of living tied together.

Stunt, I believe, is a central image or metaphor for Streb's work. Her dances show difficult escapes, for instance, as from a glass coffin in *Squirm*, or frantic moments enforced in small spaces as in *Little Ease*. This is Streb's signature work, choreographed when she was a dance major at the State University of New York at Brockport, where I once taught, but after she had graduated. We met there when she returned to perform a solo concert in 1975. This was my first acquaintance with Elizabeth Streb and her work—curiously objective and provocative. It was then that I saw *Little Ease* and her ball and hoop pieces. She had just begun to identify her works with the title *Ringside*, and was already intrigued with circus and game-playing structures.

The difficulties of navigating the physical contours of love can be found in Streb. Love as dedication and care can also be found in Streb's relentless pursuit of excellence in split-second timing of movement, staging it extravagantly. Her dances are objective studies in architecture, physics, and gravity's pull, while their physic commitment is to stories of strength and nerve (Photo 26.13).

Above all, Streb loves and studies the physical word, as she told me in an interview in 2002. Twelve years earlier she also used the word "love": "I love to ride the wave of a movement," she told me in 1980. Tempting cliché, Streb says, "I love New York, especially the drive, high energy, and hectic pace."

Timespace and Stunts

Both avant-garde and pop, Streb, the action hero, honed a street formula for her venue first performed in 2002, *STREB GO! ACTION HEROES*. I was fortunate to see this early version at the Joyce Theater in New York. Some critics have called her works antidance, and her works have been seen as circus acts and sports. She calls them dance, and so do I. Dancers, she holds, especially trained in her physical technique, are the only performers who have the ability to execute her work. And there is no faking the dance. Either you can scale a wall and drop flat from twenty feet, or you can't. A good athlete could do this, with special training, but could they capture the performative qualities Streb wants? She says it takes dancers.

Why a plank dance based on slapstick in *STREB GO*? "The stick in slap stick can kill you," the voice-over says just before the *Plank* dance. Why the bilevel of *Bilevel* and the Millar sheets in *Heavy Metal*? These titles set the scene for what Streb calls "Wild Acts and Movement Moments" in her program heading. At the opening of the show an announcement is made: "Please feel free to make as much noise as you want to." Streb calls it a "show" because of its informality. I call it a show because of its popular appeal and because something is being shown. The body is being shown and celebrated as it is tested through fantastic

PHOTO 26.13 Wall Run from Streb's FORCES (2012), Photograph by Elyssa Goodman, 2012. Photograph courtesy of Elizabeth Streb.

stunts that each scene stylizes and every setting equips. Ultimately technology enters the scene, or more aptly sets it, as in *Slide Strip*, a section toward the end of *STREB GO* that introduces the dancers by name as they slide across a metallic accelerator strip. The dancers slide on knees, on shoulders, tumbling over, and yes, even on their feet.

Why the *Cannonball Drop* into three big buckets of water at the stage apron? The audience in the front rows is instructed to put on the protective wraps given them if they are concerned about getting wet. Most decline happily, waiting for the fall. To emphasize the time it takes falling bodies to land, Streb comes out on stage in her black horn-rimmed glasses and leather boxy suit, cartoon-like, and drops one red feather. There is a hush and lull in the excitement, as we watch it waft lightly on the air to barely settle. Then the dancers begin to fall, to climb and fall, and to jump from heights most would never dare.

Streb told me that she does not fully apprehend her attraction to a feat until she has tried it, or more completely exposed its physics. No matter how meticulously conceived her tactics and renderings of aerobatics, she also achieves a feeling for heightened existence in the moment of movement here and now. If she has a weakness, it lies in her full-court press of physical elements. Shadings have a hard time in such bold games, and there is a tendency to overreach, but isn't this rather the point? The truth lies not in the test, but in how the test is met. A dance from last year will tell its truth as well as a recent one. Aided by material affordances and equipment, Streb's dances focus our attention on the mettle of the body in motion. This is her inimitable *forte* (Photos 26.14–26.16).

PHOTOS 26.14–26.16 FORCES (2010) by Elizabeth Streb: Photo 26.14 "Whizzing Gizmo" by Sue Weisler; Photos 26.15 and 26.16 "Fly" by Elyssa Goodman. Photographs courtesy of Elizabeth Streb.

PHOTOS 26.14–26.16 (*Continued.*)

Emergent Time, Streb's Power

"Movement is governed by gravity and emergent time," Streb says. She works to find what she calls "the inherent time" of a movement, just how much time a particular movement takes. "Space, Body Time: This equation always holds," she told me in an interview (2002).

All of her works derive from this absorptive scrutiny. Unlike many choreographic stylists, Streb's terse, burstive pieces do not go off in different directions but, rather, converge through the attempt to pierce reality. Temperamentally, her dances are not wildly liberal as in much avant-garde experiment. There is in fact almost a conservative approach to the tasks of the mover. Not just anything will do, and there is absolutely nothing to trim from the finished product. The dance is strictly choreographed, even though it does not live in musical time. Emergent time can be captured after the real time of a particular movement is known. How much time does it take in the trampoline dance, *Up and Down*, to build enough momentum for horizontal layouts in the air, and how would this be different from a gymnastic performance? Flying, perching, bouncing, and partnering each other, Streb's dancers move in duets, trios, and quartets. Formalist structures sustain body rhythms and timings that only dancers who work in ensemble can perform.

This might be synchronized swimming in the air, more than gym tricks. The formal patterns please the eye, and the energy of the performers has been tested in light of their own movement. As though this were not enough, the time of the movement is communal as well, fulfilled intuitively through group action. The trampoline becomes a launch for the dance not the reason for it, and the bilevel platforms—one above trampoline level and one on the floor—provide unique landing pads, not always for the feet.

Dancers fling themselves into action and fall bravely, assembling every cell to absorb the ground. At the end, they trudge. Walking on the tramp is also a dancer's ploy. In gymnastics the comedic task of walking on the tramp would not enter into the performance per se.

Anthropologist of the Stunt

One curious form of human behavior is stunts. *Streb loves stunts.* Aside from being stunted in our growth, playing tricks on others is one form of stunt that most of us have experienced as children or adolescents. Pulling pranks is part of growing up that some of us never get over. Children like to see how the ordinary course of things can be subverted—or turned upside down—as in Streb's dances. But her works are not pranks; they are studies of human nature in bodily action. Stunts bear a relationship to pranks, but they come from another place in the psyche. *Stunts are incredible acts.*

"What are movers capable of," Streb seems to ask, as she excavates the heroes of stunts. How can we dance a stunt, and why would we want to do this? Streb has consciously looked into the lives and works of stunt masters: Evel Knievel, who jumped incredible distances on his motorcycle, Harry Houdini, the incomparable escape artist, and Annie Taylor, braving a plunge over Niagara Falls, are her prototypes.

What's in a stunt? A stunt is a deed on one hand, maybe a melodramatic dastardly deed (Never pull that stunt again!), but a stunt can also be a spectacle. Streb is an anthropologist of the stunt in the latter sense. Amazing, fabulous, brilliant, fantastic, extravagant, magnificent—these are the immodest goals of stunt artists. Streb has broken ground in turning stunts into spectacular dances for main stage theaters and outdoor environments. Give us an S!

An elementary school friend who saw a STREB performance recently reminded her of a stunt she pulled when she was still just Elizabeth and in the third grade, how she managed to turn away all the school buses one windy day in Rochester, New York. Elizabeth had arrived at school early. When the buses came, she told the drivers that school was closed because it was too windy. And they believed her. School was closed for the day. She became affectionately known as the "too windy girl."

PINA BAUSCH

Back to the Future: Love and Power in Bausch

Love as distorted by passion, competition, and even hate, can be found in the work of Pina Bausch, just consider her work *Bluebeard* (1977). Ugliness and absurdity infuse the profuse imagery in this, one of Bausch's prominent early dance theater works. I saw *Bluebeard* in New York in the early 1980s. Its style represents a strain of dance theater that began with Bausch and continued through her more complex designs for dance theater like *Kontakthof* (1978). These and later works became icons of dance theater with complicated set designs that filled the stage with sod, water, and sometimes flowers. Her works are not narratives, yet they are full of short stories and characters that gesture more than they speak (Photo 26.17).

The new expressionist dance works of Susanne Linke, also German, followed. In both of these artists, the intensity of Mary Wigman's German Expressionism resonated historically; her massive dance theater works and solo concerts were recalled, but not imitated, in the postmodern expressionism of Bausch and Linke.

Café Muller (1978) is dance theater, but much simpler than Bausch's epics and also more personal as a statement of grief and struggle. Bausch sometimes danced this work herself. The plain shift and hollow eyes of *Café Muller* signal resignation, a passing theme in later more tense and sculpted works. I saw Bausch often the 1980s in New York, Toronto, and Montreal, when her troupe traveled widely, and her work was considered by many in America to be violent and antiwoman. Several of my feminist associates who were involved in the postmodern movement in America were conscientious objectors of Bausch. But I liked her work and still do. I had tired of the neutral and pedestrian postmodern, and thought that American feminism needed time to catch up with Bausch. If her work is not didactically feminist, it does have the interest of women at stake. The question might be whether she exposes violence toward women, indeed the escalating violence between the sexes, or exploits the problem. The answer, to my mind, would not be definitive. It depends on how one reads or receives her work. I receive it as existentially insolvable, or as Merleau-Ponty puts it well, "I know myself only in my ambiguity."

Bluebeard takes place between a nameless and almost faceless He and She. Anna Kisselgoff remarked in her review of the work that Bausch's characters become universal in their

PHOTO 26.17 Pina Bausch's *Nur Du*. Photographer: Ursula Kaufmann © 2011. Photograph courtesy Ursula Kaufmann.

anonymity.[18] *Bluebeard*, while based on the Bela Bartok opera *Bluebeard's Castel*, is not an opera but takes its cue from the secretive character of Bluebeard who has already killed three wives and is courting a new one, when she discovers a floor awash in blood. Bausch doesn't replicate the script, rather she conjures movement metaphors, or images if you will, for psychological impasse and entrapment. In the first image, a nameless She thrashes along a leaf-strewn floor, propelling herself nightmarishly on her back with her head flipping uncontrollably. Before long He throws himself down on top of her, and she heaves his dead weight around, still slogging along the floor. How many women can identify with the emotional weight of carrying an impossible load, or being trapped in a loveless castle? The load might be self-imposed, and maybe the woman in the dance or the real-life woman needs to find the courage to get out from underneath? Bausch, never didactic, isn't going to solve the problem, but she does display it. The search for love and solace laces through her work, but she doesn't pretend to know how to find these. She leaves us stranded between desire and hope, needing to find our own way.

Circle Images in *Rite of Spring*

One of the unforgettable images in Bausch's *Rite of Spring* (1975) is geometric and visual. She uses circles to mythic advantage in her choreography of Stravinsky's music. Circles show up in many forms, knotted, in small groups, and binding the company together as one tribe. Symbolically, circles represent continuity, thus also seasonal renewal. Bausch uses the circle to link people in community and ritual return. She also anthropomorphizes ritual in the distressing figure of virgin sacrifice, extending the image dramatically. Why does the return of spring require a virgin sacrifice? Is it because Stravinsky included this narrative in his score? But this is in any case not a necessary interpretation, as Molissa Fenley showed in her *State of Darkness* (1988) to the same music, dancing bare-breasted into the night, challenging her powers of endurance. Bausch powerfully distills the mythical feminine connection to nature through the image of blood, as the virgin's blood covered scarf is passed among the women. As an image, it is literal.

Bausch became more complex in her later works, but first became known as a great choreographer, and not simply a dramaturg, through her *Rite of Spring*. Choreographies of angst in passionate torques, falls, and repetitions began to define her dance style, with arms flung out, then wrapping in, only to reach out again. Flinging, wrapping, and reaching are signature images for Bausch, but not the only ones. As a dramaturg, she staged haunting, often absurd, spectacles of emotional life. In his film *PINA*, released in 2012, Wim Wenders captures the visceral and visually stunning work of Bausch in 3D, filming her legendary dancer-actors on stage—sliding down large, craggy wet rocks, falling, splashing, flailing, and leaping through rain and water. The men have bare chests and wear black pants; the women wear simple flowing, diaphanous dresses, also signature Bausch. Wenders's film follows the dancers into the surrounding city of Wuppertal, which for thirty-five years was the home of *Pina Bausch Tanztheater*.

As of this writing in June of 2012, the *New York Times* reports that this summer's London Olympics will present Pina Bausch's city pieces: ten works based on residencies all over the world, performed by her company. The cost of bringing twenty performances of ten works, decathlons in themselves, often over three hours long, and the seventy-three-member

Wuppertal Tanz Theater to London is $2.8 million dollars, unheard of for a dance season anywhere.[19] Bausch's works have extended well beyond the dance world, into photography and movies, and now Olympian art. Dogs, mice, chickens, sheep, and white doves must be hired in London for Bausch's *World Cities*, works of love that share a wish for wellness, while exposing fears and obsessions, human hopes, and memories, not personally cast, but globally.

IMAGE AND IMAGINATION

We identify easily with visual images, such as the use of circles in *Rite of Spring* we just mentioned, but images are not confined to the visual, especially in the arts. Image is a broad concept and the semantic root of imagination. The use of imagination, as well as its extension, is primary in all of the arts. It enters into dance and theater in intriguing ways. We exercise imagination in creative arts processes from several standpoints: that of the author, the performer, and the audience. A phenomenologist would say *images are embodied, and as such they are experiential*, that they are perceptual and stem from the senses. In dance, they manifest kinesthetically in movement, because movement (and stillness) is the medium of dance.

Dance images are seldom literal, except when they are gestural, as in a shrug or a nod. Dance images are abstract, because they are movement inventions, and they are concrete because they are embodied. The finished dance is composed, a façade in the best sense. It is composed of movement images, sometimes called dance images, or phrases and larger gestalts of movement resulting from choreography and improvisation. The circle in Bausch's *Rite of Spring* is a geometric and spatial image embodied in movement and in context of dance. Movement images stimulate imagination and interpretation. *Images* validate our ability to sense and more broadly experience, or somehow conjure, what does not appear literally before us. Suddenly magic is possible. As in Bausch's *Rite*, community, time, and space are one, and the power of love and sacrifice is held in the circle of life.

Image as Sense Impression and Interpretation

In *The World and Will and Representation*, Schopenhauer used the word "representation" (*Vorstellung*) to signify the mental idea or image of any object that is experienced. Images represent, and in so doing mediate between, experience and meaning in art. Broadly, and as artifacts, *images are method-dependent products of human creativity*, phenomena that cross over all of the arts in different ways. Dance and theater images often flow directly from sense impressions and kinesthesia, the feelings produced by movement. Images can be visual, as we have said, but for theater and dance, *moving images* are primary. Theater and dance can exist without words but not without embodied movements and stillness.

Images are associative by nature. They are sensate connective links that bridge between creative, performative, and receptive spaces. The creative position of the author begins the interactive cycle of art. In the case of dance and theater, the choices of the choreographer or the playwright are distilled in images: visual, aural, and kinetic. These have a somatic basis in bodily feeling. Suffice it to say that we can identify them when they appear, and we say,

"So that's what this is about." Then the image is no longer abstract, it has meaning through interpretation.

Aesthetic (Artfully Sensate) Uses of Imagery

Bausch exploits the use of imagery that we easily associate with historical and lived circumstances, particularly distilled in emotional uses of movement and gesture. She also uses narrative imagery, as we have seen in *Bluebeard*. Hijikata created collage images from poetry, architecture, and art from various historical periods and cultures, and he let them grate against one another in postmodern fashion. His imagery protested modernization. "I will no longer be cheated by a bad check called democracy," is how Hijikata put it.[20] He demonstrated this by morphing through images of decay and disease, and through the antirational approach of surrealism. Bausch also became known as a master of surrealist tactics. Her dances don't make sense; rather they grow out of the senses, especially taste, touch, and kinesthesia. Streb, I have said, creates an objective awareness toward tasks and difficult movement, but is she really less subjective than the other two examples? If Jean Paul Sartre is right, we cannot escape our subjectivity; it is ever present in the living body. Streb hones "break through" images of transformative subjectivity. She arrives there by means of objective experiments in daring.

In a very different way, images of transformation also guide butoh. Consciousness morphs for the butoh performer through the use of transformative/poetic visualization, music from every genre, and a broad use of theatricality including eclectic costuming. One of the many morphic techniques instituted by Hijikata is "Hidden Arms," arms in constant discovery of themselves, itching, twitching, and in flow. We could even call this a guiding image, and it is just one concrete example, while others like "Ash Pillar," are much more elusive. Waguri Yukio, possibly the best butoh technician in the style of Hijikata, explained Hijikata's image of Ash Pillar to me as an illusive pillar, something "ashen and frozen" at once, like Hiroshima, a place in the mind, with a wind coming like a knife to cut the Ash Pillar, making it fall in an instant.[21] I had the impression that he might have other equally evocative ways of explaining this diaphanous, cutting, and falling image.

Ashikawa in her butoh workshops says that you may not get the exact image in the mind of the choreographer and dancer, but you cannot mistake the image-making process.[22] Images in butoh morph through states. In a workshop I took with Ashikawa that was based on Hijikata's teaching, we morphed through stinking fish, shaking, walking on a razor blade, smoke carrying our hair back on a river, and incense rising from the feet. This doesn't make sense, and it isn't supposed to. It did elicit very evocative movement and lent an aura of mystery to our dances. I liked the image of a peacock in high heels moving on a diagonal and looking away from the line of movement. The turning away from the movement gave me an oblique, rather than direct, feeling. It seemed a relief to look away.

I have used the movement dichotomy of the absurd peacock image in various ways in my own work, not as I actually learned it, but letting it morph liberally. From Yoshioka Yumiko, I learned how to image my body as a "water bag," sloshing the contents around in fascinating ways. This was a new image to me in the beginning, as I was used to Western dance techniques that focus on how to move adroitly, fast, with rhythm and extended limbs—how to fall, leap, run, and turn on a dime. Contemporary technique classes in America are usually about perfecting movement, even if there is an occasional image to assist the dancer, such as, "fall like water."

Comparing Butoh and Bausch: Embodied Images of Love and Power

The kinesthetic image of being pinned down in hopeless desperation can be witnessed in *Mourning* (2007), a butoh work by Eiko and Koma, which I saw in New York in 2007. This is also a dance of an unidentified He and She as in Bausch's *Bluebeard*, their rooting and restless shapes moving close to the ground, rustling in leaves and branches strewn on the stage floor. The man kills the woman in both dances, but accidentally in *Mourning*, not out of anger or possessive jealousy as in *Bluebeard*. Initially disconnected, the dancers find one another but are unable to bond. The dance, continually inching in radial directions, is about our mistreatment of the earth and so our bodies. Its dirty elegance shows a deep longing for contact, but without the power to merge. Here love seeks power, unsuccessfully. As their fur rubs together, the partners try to stand up using a tree as a prop. He falls down gripping her. She flops, rolls, and lies still, as he backs up into her open legs, asexually.

In both of these floor dances, *Bluebeard* and *Mourning*, the partners can't seem to find the power to stand up; they are exploring love and power from the ground and dissociating them for different reasons. Bausch shows emotional violence as the problem. The butoh of Eiko and Koma explores the problem of nature in ruins, our creature likeness and kinship with earth and animals. As partners in the dance of nature, Eiko and Koma seek the pleasure and solace of love, but without the animal power to find it. This work may well be seen as an example of "the emaciated body," or "the weak body," that Hijikata initiated as a butoh dynamic, the opposite of realized perfection in dance, and more able to show decay, disease, and inertia.

Sensing Pain: Dropping the Façade

The audience completes the image-making process as they experience and interpret the dance, and in this process they tend to take the images apart in what might be seen as a process of discovery. They try to get to the bottom of the work, to decipher its possible meanings, as any good phenomenologist would, and they respect intuited knowledge in the process. They dissemble and deconstruct the façade or the assumed behavior, to find out what is behind it. Butoh, Bausch, and Streb all court pain in their works—and as intrinsic to love and power. In butoh pain is admitted, worked with, and not distanced. Pain is swallowed, spiritually, often poetically, as emptiness dawns. In Bausch, pain is the shadow that allows the light to manifest. Bausch develops images of painful love, lack of love, lack of power, and yet also the power of wrapping and reaching, falling down rocks and leaping through rain. Streb most certainly courts pain, facing danger physically, and moving past it. Pain and power comingle in demanding escapes in love with flying, and falling from scary heights.

Taking apart images is seldom a rational process of the mind, we do it automatically, as we make sense of what we experience and eventually say something about it or show it in another form, a poem, a narrative, a description, a diagram, or for the critic, a review and critique. When we ask what a work means, or how we experience it, we are interpreting. What is more kinesthetically instinctual in the beginning now becomes conscious, cognitive knowledge derived from psychic (felt) states.

Culture also plays a role in how we experience and understand art. We understand the phenomena of theater according to our already constituted perceptual conditioning, and according to our experience. Aspects of my understanding of butoh come from my experience in meditation and my study of Japanese history and World War II. I find consonance between butoh and Noh theater, the slow time, for instance, and the meditative qualities of both. So I appreciate the slow time of butoh. By the same token, I like the speed of Streb. I am after all American! I spent a year studying with Mary Wigman in Germany in 1965, so I have a special affinity for German Expressionism and its postmodern revival through Pina Bausch. This is part of the culture of dance that has become a part of me. It is defined by the times I have lived through and the art I have enjoyed.

Thirty years after seeing Bausch's *Rite of Spring* I can visualize it as I like. It is a vague state that I'm describing, an idle hope, even unrealistic, that the façade will drop even more, as the truth of its emotional pain continues to evolve for me. I critique its double standard in a typical sacrifice (rape) of the virgin. There could be other ways to display puberty rites, and Bausch has shown these, but never literally. For this, I need my imagination. This would be the beauty underlying all theater, its power to show us ways toward a better life through the exercise of imagination. The show is the façade; the showing is more.

Notes

1. For an extensive account of the history and globalization of butoh, see Sondra Fraleigh, *Butoh: Metamorphic Dance and Global Alchemy* (Urbana: University of Illinois Press, 2010). For metamorphosis of pain in butoh, see the section, "Shifting the Pain Body," 49–50.

2. Weiss, Michael, "Realizing Emptiness through Dance—Ways of Transmission of the Japanese Butoh Dance of Yoshito Ohno," Unpublished Postdoctoral Paper, University of Vienna.

3. Koss, Juliet, *Modernism after Wagner* (University of Minnesota Press, 2008).

4. For accounts of butoh at Broellin, see Fraleigh (2010), chapters 10 and 11, 149–60.

5. Fraleigh (2010), 21–23.

6. Fraleigh (2010), 93–95.

7. The meaning of butoh as "ancient dance," was discussed at the "Symposium on the Origins and Legacy of Butoh," with symposium speakers Iishi Tatsuro, Waguri Yukio, and Sondra Fraleigh, New York Butoh Festival, November 12, 2007. Waguri and Takenouchi, who both knew Hijikata well, helped clarify this definition. Butoh also means, "dance step," and Ankoku Butoh is "darkness dance."

8. Peter Brook, *The Open Space* (New York: Simon and Schuster, Touchstone Edition, 1968), 68.

9. Rollo May, *Love and Will* (New York: Norton, 1969), 276.

10. For several views on this, see *Why We Are Not Nietzscheans*, edited by Luc Ferry and Alain Renaut, trans. Robert de Loaiza (Chicago: University of Chicago Press, 1997).

11. Michel Foucault, *The History of Sexuality*, vol. 1, trans. Robert Hurley (New York: Pantheon Books, 1978), 152–55.

12. For a translation of his enduring philosophy of representation, see Arthur Schopenhauer, *The World as Will and Representation*, vols. 1 and 2, trans. E. F. J. Payne (New York: Dover, 1969).

13. Tadashi teaches this element of surprise, as I experienced at his workshop at the Daiwa International Butoh Festival in London, Jackson's Lane Theater, October 1, 2005.

14. Hijikata Tatsumi, "To Prison" (*Keimushoe, 1961*), in "Hijikata Tatsumi: The Words of Butoh," trans. Jacqueline S. Ruyak and Kurihara Nanako, *The Drama Review* 44, no. 1 (Spring 2000): 43–48.

15. Ari Misao filmed the 1973 Kyoto performance of *Summer Storm*, and it sat in a can for thirty years until he finally made it into a movie and available in DVD format in 2003. I saw the film and spoke with Misao in 2005. My full account of *Summer Storm* is in *Butoh: Metamorphic Dance and Global Alchemy* (2010). See Part 2, chapter 1, "One Thousand Days of Sunshine and Peace," 80–90.

16. Fraleigh (2010), 13–15, 44–45.

17. Kazuo Ohno and Yoshito Ohno, *Kazuo Ohno's World: From Without and Within*, trans. John Barrett (Middletown, CT: Wesleyan University Press, 2004), 125–26.

18. Anna Kisselgoff, "Dance: A 'Bluebeard' by Pina Bausch Troupe," *New York Times*, June 13, 1984.

19. Roslyn Sulcas, "A Twirl around the Globe," Dance Section, Arts & Leisure, *New York Times*, June 3, 2012, 1, 8.

20. Hijikata Tatsumi, "To Prison," 43.

21. Conversation with Waguri, "Symposium on the Origins and Legacy of Butoh," symposium speakers Iishi Tatsuro, Waguri Yukio, and Sondra Fraleigh, New York Butoh Festival, November 12, 2007.

22. Fraleigh, *Dancing into Darkness: Butoh, Zen, and Japan* (Pittsburgh: University of Pittsburgh Press, 1999), 142.

CHAPTER 27

THOUGHTS ON THE DISCURSIVE IMAGERY OF ROBERT LEPAGE'S THEATER

DARCEY CALLISON

FOLLOWING an evening of theater created by Robert Lepage, I often hear comments suggesting that his use of technology and his spectacle are fantastic but that his dramatic narratives are weak, which points out that Lepage is not building on a tradition that privileges narrative as the intellectual content of theater. Therefore, if he is not working with the intellectual potential of narrative that many people expect when attending theater, what makes his theater so intellectually compelling? After attending a Lepage production, I'm often energized by what I see as the discursive elements of his staging; I see ideas that speak to me through his use of imagery, technology, and spectacle.

This chapter reflects on the content found in Lepage's images, the technology used to devise his imagery, and the resulting spectacle's discursive subject matter. My contention is that Lepage's theater is compelling because it speaks to audiences living in visual cultures dominated by the suggestions, both conscious and subconsciously produced within the imagery of popular culture, ranging from advertising, Hollywood movies, to mobile devices. Of course, audiences today still expect to find intellectual content in the text that characters speak and in the narratives so familiar in Hollywood films and classical theater. Therefore, comments such as, "Lepage's dramatic narratives are weak" speak to expectations of audiences who are familiar with television, film, and select aspects of the Internet. These are entertainment values that almost never challenge how we know what we know. Still, this is not to argue that Lepage's spoken text and dramatic scenes are not important and recognizable elements in his theater, but when a certain character is the primary focus in one scene and then never seen again, one realizes that narrative, character, and spoken text are not Lepage's primary focus.

THOUGHTS ON IMAGE AS JUXTAPOSITION

There are always a number of provocative images in Robert Lepage's productions, and many of them speak to our need to find meaning and place in a world of ever-expanding global communications. In his nine-hour production *Lipsynch* (2009) [⏵] he builds dramatic events around his characters' local/personal experiences in order to explore how incidental comments, chance meetings, unexpected catastrophes, and other seemingly isolated events impact the characters' immediate choices and their lives. The image that made me realize something other than narrative was the primary focus in *Lipsynch* happened the moment an actress appeared to walk on top of an airplane. The set, for this scene, was the interior of a commercial plane, with small windows located on a back wall that curved over rows of passenger seats. Inside the plane, actors appeared to be going about their normal business as a young woman unnoticeably and quietly dies. After her death, inside the plane, the actress appears on top of the set and slowly walks the length of the plane/set as if she were a child balancing on the edge of a sidewalk, and the moment she appeared on top of the plane there were audible sounds from the audience. It was an exciting moment, as our belief in the world of the stage suddenly, almost violently, shifted. The image of her walking on the plane, juxtaposed against the ordinary events inside the plane and not her death, made the everydayness of passengers' lives appear extraordinary. Who was this spirit on top of the plane? Was she an angel or a forgotten, unnoticed soul? It seems impossible that the passengers inside the plane would be unaffected by what the audience viewed as a death transformed.

In the remaining eight hours of *Lipsynch*, the effects and traces of this unnoticed transformation are explored in the lives of the characters who may or may not have noticed a woman die. This remarkable image was in the first act I witnessed, but audiences were allowed to begin viewing *Lipsynch* at different intervals in this nine-hour production. Like viewing work in an art gallery, each scene was a complete statement that could be viewed in any order. It is hard to know how I might have interpreted the same image if it had been located in the middle of the production or in the final act. Still, however one chooses to interpret the image, it brought Lepage's theater into philosophical discourse and is an example of theater director Anne Bogart's contention that new theater is not interested in psychology but in creating juxtapositions that inspire audiences to find motivations and connections for themselves (9). The creation of juxtaposition is at the heart of Lepage's use of imagery and is often the catalyst for his theater's intellectual impact.

THOUGHTS ON POWER

Although the scenes in *Lipsynch* are a series of local/personal events, the dramatic scope is international; his characters speak different languages, and scenes take place in different global locations. The scenography for these many locations is created with Lepage's inventive use of theater technology which, in many of his productions, is omnipresent and takes on a life of its own, a personality that becomes an all-encompassing character/presence framing everything happening on stage—a "Big Brother" that produces the visual environment for each scene and transitions the audience from one location to the next. It is an ever-present unseen force that shapes and is shaped by the events on stage. Whereas certain human characters in *Lipsynch* dominate one scene and are never seen again, Lepage's technology is always present, witnessing and working as a memory, as context, as social environment(s) helping the audience trace the history of the evening's many events.

This framing of personal/local dramatic events with the ever-present character of technology suggests a power relationship between personal and external (hegemonic) forces that the characters are not aware of. This juxtaposition of the personal/local and the unseen forces of Lepage's ever-present scenography may be interpreted as a visual representation of Foucault's observation that power functions invisibly within a weblike system of relationships that impact the personal and the global and creates the conditions for both. Having viewed several of Lepage's recent productions, I would argue that his productions reveal this Foucauldian observation; that power resides in the personal but that the personal is informed by the scenography's system(s) of framing, spacing, and transitioning. This use of scenography produces invisible, hegemonic-like spaces for the dramatic events to unfold but are theatrically visible for audiences who are willing to view the character/scenography relationship as real, impactful, vital, and unavoidable.

Lepage's evenings of theater inspire these kinds of intellectual reflections, philosophical questions, possible interpretations, and visual inquiries into our relationship(s) with a world/scenography of ever-changing discourses. To emphasize these theatrical relationships, Lepage makes visible the inner workings of his visually complex staged world created specifically for each new production. For example, in *Lipsynch*, the theater world is made up of moving set pieces that the audience witnesses fitting together like a puzzle. In *Blue Dragon*, everything happens within the confines of a small apartment that functions like a Pandora's box and constantly transforms to reveal the inner world(s) of the characters' memories, desires, fears, and choices. On a grand scale, Lepage's enormously complex, fully moving construction of twenty-four large planks rotating around a central axis, which he devised as living scenography for his 2012 Metropolitan Opera production of *Wagner's Ring Cycle*, [▶] creates the mythological world of the opera with the current science of machines and computer-generated designs.

THOUGHTS ON DISCURSIVE DISTINCTIONS

The term "discursive" has been used by many scholars interested in the process of producing knowledge and who argue that knowledge is not primarily about "the facts" but is fluid, ever changing, and often understood only fleetingly. In very simple terms, this thinking can be traced back to Socrates and his argument that knowledge or truth is found in the dialogue that ensues between citizens. Today the work of Foucault and Derrida have brought the idea of discourse into the twenty-first century and suggest that everything we interact with is a form of discourse, from the clothes we wear to the images we hang in our homes. Both our relationship to what we assume we know and what we struggle to understand are categorized through a framing discourse that objectifies both the objects and the individuals involved in the discourse. This happens automatically in order to create meaning and to locate ourselves in each new situation or event. Therefore, when I suggest that Lepage creates discursive images as theater, I am building on the work of scholars such as Roland Barthes, who regarded the production of photographic imagery as a primary outcome of modernity and whose writing on the history, production, and content of the photograph continues to inform our understanding of how visual culture, memory, history, and meaning is suggested by the chemical components of a photograph. The "suggestion" of a meaning is at the heart of Barthes's critique of and fascination for photography that, like Lepage's theater, is a lie that reveals the truth.

The use of technology to produce imagery, or the lies that Barthes is so fascinated with, is not new to contemporary theater, as one needs only recall the elaborate stage machinery used in Louis XIV's baroque spectacles in the late 1600s to know that Lepage is building on a rich history of theater scenography. However, today the use of scenography is enhanced with ever-new computerized effects, digital technologies, and machinery that allow theater artists to build a seamless series of illusions that flow before our eyes. This seamless transformation of theatrical images may have a closer relationship to film and to Barthes's critique of photography than to theater history.

There are, of course, differences between Lepage's manufactured imagery and the production of images in the theater of the past. For example, in Lepage's productions, the means of creating the theatrical image is often revealed as part of the dramatic content of the scenography and included in the audience's experience. Traditionally, the priority has been to view what happens on stage as real and for audiences to suspend their disbelief in order to accept the make-believe world on stage. Therefore, in order to help audiences suspend their disbelief when watching Louis XIV descend—deus-ex-machina—from the clouds, the machinery needed to float the Sun King to earth was hidden from the audience's view behind pretend clouds and artificial angels. In Lepage's theater, the machinery needed to create his illusions is usually revealed as part of the information audiences take on. This references insights from Barthes's *Camera Lucida* that the process of production is what's being communicated to viewers who imagine they are seeing a real/truthful moment. Basically, Barthes argued that early photographic images were constructed, framed, and produced by a photographer and these images are not the real events but interpretations of events/moments/characters that viewers imagine are real. Several years after a photograph has been taken, the image may be viewed by anyone, but what they are viewing is paper, chemicals, and lighting produced in order to be reproduced as a moment that was, in reality, constructed. Therefore, the challenge when viewing a photograph—similar to the challenge of viewing theater—is to see what is not being shown, what remains invisible in order to manufacture the illusion of the real. Barthes could have been reflecting on Lepage's theater when he wrote the following:

> Technically, Photography [theater-of-image] is at the intersection of two quite distinct procedures; one of the chemical order: the action of light on certain substances; the other the physical order; the formation of the image through an optical device. (10)

For Lepage, the optical device is his scenography, which produces both the environment for his characters and a continuum of images that flow past an audience. This continuum of images functions like an art gallery that allows the audience the autonomy to view, interpret, and find connections unique to their personality and social/cultural experiences. For example, as mentioned earlier, Lepage's nine-hour production of *Lipsynch* invites audiences to begin watching the production at different points in the nine hours. It was possible to watch the entire nine hours in one day, or view the first half one day and the other half on another day. The order of events, the narrative, is not as important as the many relationships Lepage's images suggest, in whichever order they are viewed. For my own purposes, it has helped to view Lepage's *Lipsynch* as a mosaic of images and events that is similar to what communications scholar Marshall McLuhan used for his book *The Guttenberg Galaxy* and defended when he wrote, "The Gutenberg Galaxy develops a mosaic field approach to its problems. Such a mosaic image of numerous data and quotations in evidence offers the only practical means of revealing causal operations in history"(i). Using McLuhan's mosaic method as a lens to view Lepage's theater supports Socrates's contention that truth is found in the discourse between citizens/audiences and not in the order that dramatic events are disseminated or the specific events

being communicated. Also, when viewing Lepage's mosaic, it helps to remember Barthes's suggestion that, to fully appreciate photography, the viewer must understand how the photograph
was produced. As it is with photographs, so it is with the theater and the visual world we live in;
meaning is more often than not found in means of production. In turn, this is the same observation Marshall McLuhan argued for in *Understanding Media: The Extensions of Man*, when he
wrote, "the medium is the message." In the end, both Barthes's and McLuhan's insights help us
understand the importance of viewing the materiality of producing an image as an outcome of
its meaning and in turn, of Lepage's theatrical discourse (16).

A second discursive distinction that applies to Lepage's theater is found in his creative
process. Lepage does not possess an absolute authority that has traditionally been given to
directors. Today, Lepage is regarded as a theater artist and collaborator who is as involved in
designing, inventing, and creating new technologies as he is facilitating, developing, writing,
and directing the dramatic through-line. One could easily argue that theater has always been
a collaboration among designers, actors, directors, et cetera; however, that Lepage may act
in one of his productions, write the script in another, and design the scenography for both,
suggests that his creative process builds on a methodology of collaboration that replaces the
director's point of view as the primary authority. Although Lepage is clearly the author of his
work, the creative process he engages in is reflective of the creative discourse that this chapter
argues is the heart of his theater. Even the audience becomes part of this collaborative process,
as he introduces a new work in phases and one evening's performance may be very different from the next. Developing his work in front of an audience helps Lepage's collaborators
understand the audience's reactions to or interpretations of the events on stage, which in turn
allows for a fuller understanding of what is being communicated. In the past, Lepage has been
criticized for presenting works-in-progress, but I would argue that just because one evening
is different from the next does not mean the work is not fully realized. There are many ways
to tell the same story, many ways to reveal and to visualize a theatrical event. The possibilities
for transitioning from one scene to the next are many, and each transition carries a means
of production that produces its own meaning and frames theatrical events differently. Early
audiences of Lepage's work are simply viewing one possibility and entering a collaborative discourse that informs Lepage's understanding of the choices he is making as the primary author.

A final distinction that informs Lepage's work from theater of the past is that today's audiences
come to the theater already inundated with images in every aspect of their lives. As never before,
it seems, audiences bring to their theater experience a heightened sophistication from living
in a visual world that, in turn, informs their understanding and interpretation of the images in
Lepage's theater. Like photography and film, the manufacturing and the focus on images as theater is an outcome of modernity that emerged as one of the primary signifiers for contemporary
theater, as Hans-Thies Lehmann outlines in his influential book *Postdramatic Theatre*:

> Theatre is catching up on an aesthetic development that other art forms went through earlier.
> It's no coincidence that concepts which originated in visual arts, music or literature can now
> be use to characterize postdramatic theatre. It was only under the influence of reproductive
> media like photography and film that theatre became conscious of its specificity. Important
> theatre practitioners often have a background in visual arts. (94)

That Lepage's theater builds on the visual culture dominating most everyone's lives on the
Internet, in fashion, on television, in movies, and through advertisements, should not be
surprising. Theater is often a reflection of the world, and when that world is dominated by

the image, it can be argued it is theater's role to reflect that domination. However, the images Lepage produces not only reflect the visual world his audience comes from, but challenges them to view his images—and by extension all images—as part of a larger discourse. With this in mind, there is one image in *Lipsynch* that is particularly poignant and resonates, for me, as philosophical discourse. To produce this image, the stage crew, working in full view of the audience, carried on several flat two-dimensional props attached to long thin poles with strong support bases. After the crew set these odd shapes in exact spots and at precise angles on the stage, the shapes seemingly floated above the floor in the space between the audience and the set. When a front camera projected these floating shapes onto a screen they came together as silhouettes of a table, a chair and other recognizable pieces of furniture. Exposing the material means of producing this illusion was fun for the audience to witness, but the illusion of the furniture on the screen was completed dramatically when actors entered the frame camera to interact with odd shapes as if they were actual pieces of furniture. It was a magic-like theatrical effect for the audience who could simultaneously see the oddly shaped cutouts floating in the air, the stands the shapes rested on, the cameras that project the shapes onto a screen to create the illusion of furniture, the live actors interacting with the shapes on stage, and the projected actors interacting with furniture on the screen. This inventive layered illusion is, for me, an obvious reference to Plato's cave metaphor that suggests we, like the characters in Lepage's production, are hypnotized by a view of reality that is nothing more than shadowy shapes projected on the wall of a cave. More challengingly, Plato suggests that we firmly believe, as the screen actors did, that the furniture is real and we are unable to recognize that we are chained like slaves to our unquestioning conviction that what we see is real. Over and over again, incidental events and chance happenings change the characters' lives in *Lipsynch*, but the conditions, the materiality or the theatrical world Lepage invents, is obviously constructed, like the shadows projected on the wall of a cave. Building on Plato's metaphor and on the dramatic construction of Lepage's postdramatic theater, it is not a great leap to speculate that many political and faith-based energies may be devoted to defending the ideologies of shadows. Is this what Lepage was suggesting when he produced this cave-like illusion for his characters to believe in? What are we viewing when we watch a theatrical event, if not a construction? What is real for the characters and what is real for the audience? How might theater encourage audiences to turn around, to metaphorically leave the cave and to seriously consider that our most assured convictions of reality might be shadows?

THOUGHTS ON IMAGE AND MODERNITY

Although my interpretation of Lepage's shadows makes sense to me, it is tempered by Canadian scholar Marshall McLuhan's adage that "A point of view can be a dangerous luxury when substituted for insight and understanding" (*Media* 216). For McLuhan, advertisement was the signature art form of the twentieth century, and he was among the first scholars to warn us that the explicit and implicit codes within ad images were encoding ideologies that served industrialists and not the individual. McLuhan's warning that images are both seductive and misleading substitutes for knowledge seems particularly significant for those of us interested in understanding how Lepage's theater communicates. It is helpful to think of Lepage's images as one voice of a discourse that allows each member of the audience to engage as an independent thinker. However, we know from the work of McLuhan and other communication scholars that we are not independent thinkers. In reality, we are culturally, socially, and historically conditioned to think, see, and interpret within the cultural, social, and historical limitations of our specific location, era, and historical moment.

Still, I would argue that Lepage's theater challenges McLuhan's warning and our cultural conditioning with the use of two interrelated intellectual elements throughout his productions. First, Lepage's theater emphasizes the image-based literacy that McLuhan argued was the new dominant force shaping modernity. Lepage does this, in part, by refusing to privilege narratives that easily seduce audiences into identifying with certain characters and desiring endings that confirm how the world occurs to them. Second, Lepage reveals the theatrical equipment used to produce the images in his theater, so the magic of theater is removed and replaced with the magic of the imagination, suspended disbelief, or pretend. By making audiences constantly aware that his pictures, locations, or effects are manufactured, he is also making them aware that their suspended disbelief in his theater is an agreement—a theatrically constructed agreement. These two elements work together and allow the audience to know intuitively and/or analytically that his theater is an assemblage of beautiful, inviting lies. For example, once audiences are fully engaged with a dramatic happening on stage, the scenery changes; what was a table becomes a bed or the location immediately shifts to the other side of the world, or the actor appears as a different character. These theatrical effects and dramatic changes require the audience to reconfigure any attachment they might have formed in one scene for something different in the next, and these constant changes remind audiences that in Lepage's theater nothing is real and even one's emotional attachments are constructed.

In many ways, this interpretation of Lepage's theater addresses Brecht's call for audiences to attend theater as if they were at a sporting event. Wanting audiences to be involved with the events being staged, Brecht also wanted audiences to notice they were involved and to notice the choices they were making when they agreed or disagreed with the action on stage. To make this happen, Brecht suggested that directors remind audiences they were watching a theatrical event and help them remember that theater was not real but an interpretation of something in the world. Although I have never seen a Lepage audience stand up to cheer or boo as Brecht imaged, it is impossible to be in his audience and not notice how easily and successfully one's imagination is being seduced while simultaneously reminding us that we're watching a theatrical production. McLuhan was concerned that images too easily seduce. Brecht wanted theater artists to expose the seduction of theater, and Lepage brings both these concerns to the fore by emphasizing the construction/machinery of each dramatic/seductive event created in his productions as imagery.

THOUGHTS ON POSTMODERN DANCE AND LEPAGE

So far, this chapter has suggested that aspects of Lepage's theater can be linked to the history of photography as an outcome of modernity, that it can be linked to Brecht's ambitions for the modern theater and to McLuhan's warning that images are infused with ideologies. Also, the chapter has suggested that Lepage's use of scenography can be traced to Louis XIV's Baroque spectacles and that his use of ever-present technology can be viewed through the lens of Foucault's argument that power structures are invisible and ever present. However, it is hard to imagine Lepage's theater without the contributions of postmodern choreographers like Yvonne Rainer and Trish Brown, who helped audiences accept that unfamiliar relationships might be interesting and that meaning did not have to be obvious.

Establishing his career in Montreal of the 1980s, Lepage was part of a zeitgeist of creative initiatives that produced such remarkable Montreal choreographers as Édward Lock, Ginette Laurin, and Marie Chouinard. Many Montreal dance artists from this era studied in New York City and brought back artistic questions and ambitions rooted in the surge of postmodern activities that dominated alternative and/or new-dance practices in New York in the late 1970s and 1980s. Exploring such questions as "Who can dance?" and "When is someone dancing?," postmodern choreographers challenged the accepted theater and music hierarchies that privileged narrative, character, and music visualization. Working with many of the same issues already explored in this chapter (image/environment), postmodern choreographers were interested in the body of the dancer as a site of invention in and of itself. Creating, producing, and performing activities that were previously assumed to be untheatrical and unworthy as choreographic content, these dance artists challenged audiences' expectations and asked their audiences to consider how else meaning might be produced on stage. Like Lepage today, postmodern choreographers explored their questions in collaboration with composers, writers, directors, and film and visual artists. Also, postmodern choreographers researched how physical activities and media might belong together on stage and, in doing so, they introduced abstraction as a means of interacting with and interpreting space both internally (physical) and externally (environment). Presenting audiences with unrecognizable gestures, new relationships between media and the body and between pedestrian dancers and interactive audiences, these dance artists' contributions are now, often, taken for granted. However, I am convinced their intellectual ideas and progressive choreography helped lay the foundation for the bold, unexpected juxtapositions that Lepage theater uses to build events and content.

Postmodern dance artists built on the important contributions of choreographer Merce Cunningham's chance procedures and his artistic relationship with avant-guard composer John Cage. Challenging what was considered performance, postmodern dance artists included everyday movement and performed in unusual spaces as part of their choreographic research, which challenged the status quo and helped us see space and the body within the same continuum of expression that now dominates Lepage's theater. As dance scholar Sally Banes suggests in her 1981 article "Democracy's Body: Judson Dance Theatre and Its Legacy," postmodern dance artists challenged the assumed hierarchies of the arts, the body, and space:

> Perhaps the most important legacy of Judson Dance Theater for post-modern dance was the attitude that anything might be looked at as dance, if its maker presented it as a dance. Not only the activities of the dancer, but also those of a visual artist, a musician, or a filmmaker might be thought of as choreography, might be re-examined in light of choreographic conventions simply because they were framed as a dance. [. . .] Another aspect of Judson legacy for post-modern dance, again one with a peculiarly American neo-romantic tone, was the exploration of space. And again, the issue was both practical and aesthetic. (104–6)

The continuum of expression suggested in Banes's quote is at the heart of Lepage's productions. To understand the historical traces from postmodern dance to Lepage, what follows is a short analysis of Yvonne Rainer's *Trio A* (*The Mind Is a Muscle, Part I*) (1965) [⏺] and Trish Brown *Man Walking Down the Side of a Building* (1970) [⏺] Both these choreographies are historically significant for their contribution to postmodern aesthetic and are representative of the continuum of choreographic intelligences referenced in Banes's quote and present in Lepage work as a theater director.[1]

Viewing the identity of each body part in Rainer's solo *Trio A*, one begins to understand that the body, in itself, is the site of numerous collaborations; between elbow and knee, between head and floor, and between space and gravity. Choreographing the functional identity of each body part, Rainer guides us beyond the need to move organically or "naturally" and past our assumption that gestures are inherently infused with physiological truths, character, or social narratives. In her pedestrian, noninterpretive performance, she emphasizes the fact that only one possible gesture has been choreographed and the connections among gestures appear random or unimportant. This separation of the performer from the performance allows us to see the body as a blank canvas; a blank canvas that was possible to understand and move beyond the societal narratives that infuse our body's gendered and social identities and beyond our assumption that the body is the sole producer of meaning.[2]

Viewing images of Brown's dancer walk down the wall of a building, one sees the body challenging/resisting gravity and working in union with the technology of pulleys and ropes that are holding the dancer in place. And one sees the dancer's body in an immediate relationship with an inanimate object that works as the dancer's physical support/partner in this site-specific duet between body and wall.[3]

The impact of these two iconic choreographies is vast, as they helped locate the body as the primary site of collaboration, in and of itself, and to see the body is one element in the complex visual experience of theater. These two choreographies helped us understand that any physical sequence has an inherent meaning, even when that meaning is outside our immediate understanding; meaning always exists. Although the body was the primary focus of both these choreographers, the body was no longer privileged as the sole producer of meaning. Each gesture/any gesture, contributed to the production of meaning, and walls, chairs, floors, films, gravity, and technologies could also be manipulated, infused with content, and choreographed.[4] One has only to go online (YouTube) and view promotional previews for Lepage's Metropolitan Opera production of Wagner's *Ring Cycle* in order to see how he has built on the material of these two iconic choreographies to choreograph and create meaning with everything on stage; scenography, sound, projections, the bodies, and the spaces he manufactures. The means for Lepage to use the body as a theatrical site that configures and reconfigures its meaning as an element of scenography, as personality, as movement, as a outcome of space, as space, and, when necessary, as character is a direct outcome of the postmodern dance/theater.

These choreographic traces in Lepage's work are endless, and one could continue to search through choreographic history and find many connections, such as the use of spectacle and artistic collaboration in Diaghilev's *Les Ballets Russes*. However, I hope it is now clear that use of images, juxtaposition, scenography, and relationships between media and the body in Lepage's theater build on the rich and complex histories of choreographic practices that are all too often taken for granted and/or forgotten.

FINAL THOUGHTS

As I conclude this article, it is important to emphasize that Lepage works with live theater as a medium of communication and that live theater produces unique meanings. When attending

Lepage's production of *The Blue Dragon*, I was sold a graphic comic book that told the story we were about to see on stage. Returning to this article's opening statement, audiences often leave Lepage's theater feeling that his narratives are lacking; however, I would argue the graphic comic book emphasizes narrative and is a poor substitute for the live performance.

As a print medium, graphic comic books interpret dramatic events as a series of still images. However, any effects and information that Lepage's projections and technology have on audiences is completely missing from the comic book. Although I enjoy reading comic books, their particular limitation became clear for me when I discovered that *The Blue Dragon*'s main choreographic sequence is missing from the comic book. In the live performance, a choreographic sequence is used to signify the lead actor's journey into the countryside of China; the actor rides a bike on stage and a scrim is lifted, revealing a female dancer in a uniform from the Cultural Revolution, standing in a low arabesque and holding a rifle.

PHOTO 27.1 *The Blue Dragon*'s graphic comic-book cover written by Robert LePage and Marie Michaud, with illustrations by Fred Jourdain. Toronto: House of Anansi Press, 2011.

PHOTO 27.2 Tai Wei Foo: actress/dancer in *The Blue Dragon*. When the scrim is lifted, a female dancer is revealed wearing the uniform from the Cultural Revolution.

The aggressive shapes of the balletic choreography that followed reminded me of the lead character in the revolutionary ballet *The White Haired Girl*, which I was lucky enough to see when it toured in 1977. *The Blue Dragon*'s short, impactful choreography not only tells us the character is riding his bike in the country but also reminds us of China's turbulent and troubling cultural revolution and its aggressive use of ballet as propaganda. It is a physically impactful choreography that reveals a dynamic history completely missing from the graphic comic book. This one example emphasizes that although Lepage's theater focuses on images, his theater is not only about the image. His theater and the images he produces are interactive, live representations of a global world that is filled with interactions, histories, memories, and unexpected connections. His theater is about how a simple bike ride into the county is infused with memories and histories that are both present and invisible; relationships that are best communicated with live theater.

In the mid-1990s, while on tour in Toronto, Lepage took part in an audience outreach event in which he was asked, "Why do people attend theater?" To answer this question, Lepage compared attending theater to the popularity of working out at a gym and the pleasure of engaging our muscles in vigorous activity in order to stay in shape. Building on this metaphor, Lepage suggested audiences attend theater as a workout for the body's largest muscle, the brain. Audiences like to think, they long for it, and the possibility of engaging their mental capacities, thinking new thoughts and seeing what they thought they understood differently is something people enjoy. The pleasure of thinking, Lepage suggested, is the primary reason people want to attend theater. This reasoning seems to motivate Lepage's work, and it emphasizes the impact of his discursive imagery—to create theater that assumes audiences enjoy the challenge

PHOTO 27.3 With Assistance of the Touring Office of The Canada Council Shanghai Ballet of the People's Republic of China Canadian Tour May 5–June 1, 1977 This tour is part of an official cultural exhange programme between the People's Republic of China and the Canadian Department of External Affairs. (beside photo) Hsi-erh lives a new life now. Taking up the gun she joins the Eighth Route Army.

of seeing new ideas, engaging in intellectual discourses, thinking differently, and devising their own thoughts.

NOTES

1. There is a rich canon of postmodern choreographs to select from but, these are popular examples and easily accessible on YouTube for anyone who might be interested.
2. Yvonne Rainer's performance of *Trio A* (The Mind is a Muscle, Part I) can be viewed on YouTube.
3. A reconstruction of Trish Brown's "Man Walking Down the Side of a Building" can be viewed on YouTube.
4. These contributions are integral to Lepage's theater and are now commonly used by many postmodern theater directors. Traces to postmodern dance in postmodern theater has been minimized or often forgotten. But, when looking at the work of theater artists such as Lepage, Robert Wilson, Anne Bogart, and, to a certain extent, The Wooster Group, to

mention only four, it's clear they owe much of their success and aesthetic integrity to the questions, research, and choreography of postmodern dance artists. Although this particular insight could be the subject of another article, in this chapter I want to emphasize that the contributions of postmodern dance artists opened the door for Lepage to build his ideas. To view images from Robert Lepage's theater you can visit his company's website: *Ex Machina*—http://lacaserne.net/index2.php/.

BIBLIOGRAPHY

Barthes, Roland. *Camera Lucida: Reflections on Photography*. Translated by R. Howard. New York: Hill and Wang, 1980.

Brecht, Bertolt. *Brecht on Theatre: The Development of an Aesthetic*. Edited and Translated by John Willett. New York: Hill and Wang, 1992. First published 1964.

Brown, Trisha. "Man Walking Down the Side of a Building." Accessed June 9, 2009. www.youtube.com/watch?v=MpGsEOR9dbo.

"'Das Rheingold' at the Met." nytimes.com/video. Accessed September 28, 2010. www.youtube.com/watch?v=TDUUJzlma74.

Dundjerović, Aleksandar Saša. *Robert Lepage: Routledge Performance Practitioners*. New York, London: Routledge, 2009.

Lehmann, Hans-Thies. *Postdramatic Theatre*. Translated by K. Jürs-Munby. New York, London: Routledge, 2006.

LePage, Robert, and Marie Michaud. *The Blue Dragon* (Graphic comic-book). Toronto, House of Anansi Press, 2011.

"Lipsynch by Robert Lepage (Ex Machina)." Accessed December 24, 2014. https://www.youtube.com/watch?v=ChdeR--QIbw.

McLuhan, Marshall. *The Gutenburg Galaxy: The Making of Typographic Man*. Toronto: University of Toronto Press, 1997. First edition 1962.

McLuhan, Marshall. *Understanding Media: The Extensions of Man*. Corte Madera, CA: Gingko Press, 2003. First edition 1964.

Rainer, Yvonne." *Trio A*. Accessed December 24, 2014. https://www.youtube.com/watch?v=qZwj1NMEE-8.

SECTION VII

UNRULY BODIES

CHAPTER 28

··

A SLENDER PIVOT
Empathy, Public Space, and the
Choreographic Imperative

··

PATRICK ANDERSON

THIS chapter[1] takes a somewhat circuitous route in its attempt to combine a consideration of public space with a critique of what Frank Wilderson has termed the "ruse of empathy," through the practice of what I am calling the choreographic imperative. I begin with a series of court cases resulting from the arrest of a woman who organized a series of "silent dances" at the Thomas Jefferson Memorial in Washington, DC, and consider how dance and choreography are conceived, constructed, and constrained by the two federal courts presiding over the cases. I use these cases to propose that what goes by the name of public space is structured in part by what I call a choreographic imperative, and turn to the practice of "Stop & Frisk" policing protocols in New York City not as an analogue of the Jefferson Memorial cases, but rather as an indication of how that imperative is profoundly racialized in its enactment.

This writing emerges from a broader, critical study of empathy in contemporary aesthetic practice and political discourse. I do not here dwell on the affective register of empathy's resonance; indeed, this writing is part of a multipronged attempt to materialize the empathic and thus to detach our understanding of empathy from a strictly (and strictly contemporary) focus on emotional experience—or rather, on *assumed* emotional experience derived from imagined proximity, similarity, and/or analogy. To that end, I focus here on embodied experience and embodied practice rather than on what goes by the name of emotion. Although I spend little time considering it explicitly here, empathy "itself" flares up in the details of the enactments I consider, as the banal drive to extrapolate from contextual specificities to universalist values ("freedom," "justice"), as the colonial urge to analogize those specificities and erase their differential effects, and sometimes (if we are lucky) as an ethical crisis offering us the opportunity to challenge those urges and drives.

Just before midnight on April 12, 2008, a group of eighteen people gathered at the Thomas Jefferson Memorial in Washington, DC, ostensibly to celebrate Jefferson's 265th birthday. Playing music through their individual headphones, those gathered danced silently and alone. Within minutes, organizer Mary Brooke Oberwetter had been restrained, silenced, and arrested for "interfering with an agency function." Three days later, she was also retroactively cited for "demonstrating without a permit."

Neither citation was fully prosecuted; but shortly after her arrest, Oberwetter filed a federal lawsuit against the park officials citing violations of her first and fourth amendment rights. The case drew widespread attention both domestically and internationally, and became a *cause célèbre* for Libertarian (and libertarian-leaning Republican) groups in particular. Concerned by what they viewed as a blatant infringement on the individual's free exercise of physical movement in public space—figured as that most beloved and misunderstood term, "freedom"—such groups began to proclaim what more or less came down to an inalienable right to dance. Oberwetter's case makes this claim explicit: "expressive dancing is protected by the First Amendment, and therefore Officer Hilliard's suppression of that activity is unconstitutional" (Oberwetter 1: 1). Bolstered by a groundswell of "common-sense" rage at the thought that US government officials could restrain the gestural life of individual bodies, Oberwetter's suit asked the courts for injunctive, declarative, and monetary relief from the head of park security at the memorial and, by proxy, the Secretary of the Department of the Interior (1).

The specific grounds for Oberwetter's claim pivoted on her insistence that movement can be "expressive," qualifying its protection under not only the Fourth Amendment but also the First. In other words, by asking the courts to intervene on her behalf, Oberwetter argued that the constitutional protection against unwarranted "seizure"—read here as the immobilization of the individual body—combined with the constitutional protection against the suppression of "speech" and "assembly" to protect the expressivity of the moving body. That is, Oberwetter claimed that when properly understood as a communicative act, dance is a constitutionally protected civil right.

The DC district court was not sympathetic to this claim, and dismissed the case in 2010. The terms of that dismissal rested on two central arguments. First, regulations governing the use of such memorials prohibit "demonstrations and special events" without first obtaining a permit (or, when the event in question includes "fewer than twenty-six individuals," satisfying all the requirements of a permit even if one has not been obtained); at four designated sites (the Washington Monument, the Lincoln Memorial, the Jefferson Monument, and the Vietnam War Memorial), the park service is barred from issuing permits at all. On this argument, the court ruled that in arresting Oberwetter, the park official in question acted in accordance with his duties and thus had not violated her constitutional rights. Curiously—and without much in the way of exposition—the court cites in its decision a provision explaining the outright embargo of demonstrations at these particular historical sites: in addition to "protecting legitimate security and park value interests," the ban is intended to "[maintain] an atmosphere of calm, tranquility, and reverence in [their] vicinity." The implication here—later made explicit—is that expressive movement actively and inherently disrupts the strict public composure of peaceful veneration: presumably silent, presumably still.

But in addition to citing the technical regulations for park gatherings—and in order to expound on this latter declaration—the district court also mused on the nature of dance as enacted by Oberwetter's event. As part of her case, Oberwetter cites the official park regulations:

> The term "demonstration" includes demonstrations, picketing, speechmaking, marching, holding vigils or religious services and all other like forms of conduct which involve the communication or expression of views or grievances, engaged in by one or more persons, the conduct of which has the effect, intent or propensity to draw a crowd or onlookers. This term does not include casual park use by visitors or tourists which does not have an intent or propensity to attract a crowd or onlookers. (11)

Contradicting her earlier claims about dance as inherent expression, Oberwetter here distinguished her movement from the regulatory definition of "demonstration" in part because she did not intend explicitly to "communicat[e]" a "view," and in part because she did not expect to "draw a crowd or onlookers." The court quickly dispensed with this argument, but not before parsing its intricacies:

> The Court finds it no stretch to conclude that such activity would pique the curiosity of a passer-by. It certainly is foreseeable to expect visitors to stop and observe a group of expressive dancers at a national memorial. But Oberwetter argues that the Court cannot stop its analysis here—the mere fact that conduct may have the effect or propensity of drawing a crowd is insufficient by itself for that conduct to fall within [the class of prohibited activities]. Rather, in her view, the challenged conduct must also be sufficiently similar to the activities listed. [. . .] She contends that her expressive dancing is unlike [the regulations'] enumerated activities because although they "typically involve loud vocalization, acting together as a tight-knit body of people and conveying a uniform message," her conduct "was meant to celebrate the individualist spirit for which Jefferson is known." But the enumerated activities encompass a spectrum, from the boisterousness of picketing or speechmaking to the quiet solicitude of a vigil. The common thread is that all of the listed activities "have as their primary purpose the communication or expression of views or grievances." Oberwetter's celebration of Jefferson's individual spirit is one example of such an activity. The Court need not parse whether Oberwetter's conduct falls closer to picketing or to a vigil; that it is "roughly similar" to such conduct is sufficient to bring it within [the regulations'] definition of "demonstration." (12–13)

This lengthy citation from the court's decision is helpful in tracking one legislative figuring of dance as a social practice that can be regulated by the state, particularly in sites designated as public. In the logic of the decision, dance inherently embodies—and, most pressingly, *enacts*—the communication of a "view or grievance." As such, dance operates and gains traction as socially significant in part through its power to signify—and thus to convey and transmit meanings beyond its physical gestures. Too, the court figures dance inherently as a *social* practice; in its very occurrence, dance invites not only an audience, but also "curiosity" in the minds of passers-by. As such (and here again) dance operates and gains traction as socially significant as what Louis Althusser might call its interpellative force, a notion to which I will return in a moment. On the formal qualities of dance, the court remains silent except to include it within a "spectrum" of "roughly similar" activities, though the terms of that similarity are never spelled out in their particulars. A later appeals court crudely extended the conceptual boundaries of this "spectrum": "expressive dancing might not draw an audience when nobody is around. But the conduct is nonetheless prohibited because it stands out as a type of performance, creating its own center of attention and distracting from the atmosphere of solemn commemoration that the Regulations are designed to preserve" (Oberwetter 2: 7). To the question "what genre is this that includes vigils, demonstrations, speechmaking, and now dance?" the field of performance studies has arisen in response, a development of which the courts seem entirely unaware but on which the court's decision seems simultaneously reliant.[2]

If in dismissing Oberwetter's complaint the court was unwilling to engage in anything beyond the most rudimentary form of performance analysis, it showed no such modesty in attending to the political geographies of expressive practice. Turning to the site of the Jefferson Memorial, the court began by considering the architectural specifics of the memorial's buildings and grounds. After noting that the territorial site was chosen "for its aesthetic and architectural significance," the court describes:

> The Memorial is a circular, open-air structure topped by a domed roof. It is surrounded on all sides by a series of Ionic columns, and its interior is again ringed with a series of Ionic columns. To enter the Memorial, visitors must climb forty steps, rising from ground level to a portico. These steps are accessible only by means of a public path that runs along the Tidal Basin, and a public path that runs through West Potomac Park. After ascending the steps, visitors must travel through the portico to enter the Memorial's interior chamber. This portico provides the only method of accessing the Memorial's interior chamber. When entering the chamber, visitors pass a sign requesting "Quiet Respect Please." (4)

These details—and the brief narrative description of pedestrians' options for entering the structure—become relevant when, after dismissing Oberwetter's claims on the grounds of free expression, the court turns to distinguish between "three types of public property" and the applicability of First Amendment claims to each. These types include the "traditional public forum" and the "designated public forum," wherein the First Amendment is (presumably) carefully protected, and the "nonpublic forum," which is "not by tradition or designation a forum for public communication" (14 fn. 5). Careful to cite its precedent cases, the court makes clear that expression can be limited depending on a particular site's designation, and finds its way to its ultimate goal—justifying the park service's prohibition on dancing—by way of a careful consideration of sidewalks, to which I will return in a moment.

After Oberwetter's case was dismissed by the circuit court—and again by the federal appeals court in 2011—the cause was adopted by libertarian folk hero Adam Kokesh, a decorated Marine and member of Iraq Veterans Against the War (IVAW). In response to the appeals court's decision to affirm the lower court's dismissal of Oberwetter's complaint, Kokesh organized a dance protest at the Jefferson Memorial on May 28, 2011. In a video posted to Kokesh's YouTube channel (imprinted with a logo reading "Adam vs. The Man"), shaky footage shows two uniformed park officers approaching a group of people milling about around the Memorial ("Adam Kokesh Body Slammed"). In a brief exchange, one officer affably informs the group that no dancing is allowed. "What is dancing?" one participant demands; "what if you're out of time when you're making movements with your body?" The camera turns to a man and a woman, rocking back and forth while locked in an embrace. Two park officers approach them, saying "stop," and then pull them apart and handcuff them. The camera begins to pan more quickly, focusing on Kokesh, who has begun to circulate while performing what can only be described (with apologies to experts in the genre) as a loose kind of jig. "I wanna dance in America, sir," he retorts to an officer who has approached him.

The action begins to accelerate: a crowd has begun to gather, photographing the scene, as two white men link arms and move together, suddenly pulled apart and forced to the ground. "Stop resisting," an officer shouts. "I have a bad shoulder," one of the men responds.

The camera turns; Kokesh is being held with one arm behind his back. He raises the other, stepping forward in a vaguely rhythmic motion as the officer shouts, "this is your last warning." In a rush, Kokesh is lifted into the air, slammed to the ground, and restrained in a choke-hold as he is handcuffed. The Monument is closed by the officers, and the video loops to replay its opening scenes.

The scene of Kokesh's dance is no doubt disturbing, and the video is effective in rousing an imprecise indignation at what seems, at first blush, to be an outright assault on the "free" movement of individual and collective bodies. These scenes rhyme visually and ideologically with other sites of police violence as enacted in ostensibly public spaces in recent years (though it is worth asking if, as the video's title claims, "police brutality" is really the operative term here[3]). Invoking the sentiment that public space—especially in a national capital—should be available for all forms of free expression, the video intends to evoke outrage in its viewers on the realization (or panic) that they, too, might face restrictions on their ability to speak (or dance, or otherwise express) their minds.

I am obviously relying here on a reductive assumption about the affective influence I imagine the video's makers to intend. But I am curious about the implied reading of dance as a *form* of expression denied to those at Oberwetter's and Kokesh's events, a figuring that understands state power (as practiced by park officials and, later, the courts) as regulating and restricting access to that form, but also as defining its appropriate contents. In other words, state power is here exercised as a *choreographic* function, delineating which movements constitute dance (and by such constitution can be prohibited). Consider, for example, the questions posed by one of Kokesh's participants: "What is dance? What if you're out of time when you're making movements with your body?" If the first query is a fairly pedestrian invocation of genre trouble, the second operates on a more intensely disciplinary register, interrogating the (rhythmic and metrical) terms by which dance comes to be dance at all: "if I move to an inconsistent beat," he seems to ask, "would you recognize and regulate my movement as dancing?"

To reframe this latter question: how might we understand these events, and the disciplinary effects they eventuated, not strictly as a prohibition on dance, but rather as the state's choreography of public (and nonpublic) space? It might be useful briefly to consider how choreographer Ann Carlson, for example, might approach the scene. For a performance at Stanford University in spring 2010 called *Still Life with Decoy*, Carlson staged dance performances in two separate buildings separated by a wide swath of Stanford's campus—one in Roble courtyard, the other in Memorial Auditorium ("MemAud" in the local vernacular). After watching the piece in Roble, audience members were instructed to walk across campus to MemAud; to help them find their way, Carlson had choreographed "breadcrumbs"—minor *tableaux vivants*—along the way. In an essay co-authored with Jill Dolan and published in *Theatre Survey*, M. G. Renu Cappelli remembers:

> Carlson thus built into her performance a fifteen-minute walk across campus that mimicked travel between two disciplinary homes [dance and theatre]. To find their way between the venues, audience members were instructed to follow a trail of "breadcrumbs" in the form of immobile bodies, or at least *approximations* of immobility that cued and framed the movements of the audience as well as other passersby on campus. This is where our students made their debut: they became the "breadcrumbs" by striking poses and holding them—completely still—for the duration of the audience's transit (this took about thirty-five minutes). Reproducing a bike accident, a backpack spilling open, a cramming session in the shade of

a tree, and daring steps into the cold water of ornamental fountains, the students chose poses that recalled their daily experiences on campus, frozen in midaction; and the audience members found their way from studio to auditorium by spotting each successive 'still' body in turn. (Cappelli and Dolan 107)

In choreographing stillness as a form of expressive movement, Carlson enacts a disciplinary force on her audience: Cappelli remembers the function of the posed "breadcrumbs" as a kind of choreographed interdisciplinarity, understood as a series of directives to move audience members from one disciplinary site (in Roble, a dance studio) to another (MemAud, in the Drama department, used for theatrical events).

I gesture to Carlson's use of immobility—and its elegant rendering through Cappelli's narrative—to suggest that the regulatory wrangling over dance at the Jefferson Memorial, and the arrests of Oberwetter and Kokesh, might be understood not simply as the *proscription* of expressive movement, but more precisely as the *prescription* of a certain type of dance—still "reflection"—in the interest of promoting "Quiet Respect Please." That this choreographic imperative should be policed at the site of a monument immortalizing Thomas Jefferson, perhaps the most oft-claimed "forefather" of neoliberal individualism and self-interest above common good, only intensifies its seemingly paradoxical effects.

My use of the choreographic imperative as a model for what I will, for the moment, reference as *biopolitics* is not an entirely original one. Among many other scholars, Susan Foster has extended our understanding of choreography to include enactments of the "everyday" alongside exceptional cases of staged performance. She writes:

> Proposing a dialectical tension between choreography and performance, I [have] emphasized the ways that choreography presents a structuring of deep and enduring cultural values that replicates similar sets of values elaborated in other cultural practices whereas performance emphasizes the idiosyncratic interpretation of those values. Not a permanent, structural engagement with representation, but rather a slowly changing constellation of representational conventions, choreography, more than any performance, is what resonates with other systems of representation that together constitute the cultural moment within which all bodies circulate. (Foster 5)

For Foster, choreography—the design of a system of movement—distinguishes itself from a given performance of dance in its attachment to and production of cultural and political values. More than just a vocabulary, more than representational form, choreography indicates, makes legible, and enacts a cultural *force*; in this, choreography is a disciplinary function that can itself register in reproductive or interventional modes: "choreography can productively be conceptualized as a theorization of identity—corporeal, individual, and social [and as the] setting forth of what the body is and can be" (6).

I would add to Foster's important and provocative claims that choreography can "set forth" not only what a "body is and can be," but also what a *subject* is and can be, and indeed how that subject comes to be a *subject* at all. Turning for a moment to one of the twentieth century's most influential origin stories for the production of subjectivity—Louis Althusser's notion of interpellation—we might be surprised to find that choreography has been a critical component of subject formation all along. Althusser's narrative of interpellation's "hailing" function—by which individuals "become concrete subjects"—takes place on a public street:

Ideology "acts" or "functions" in such a way that it "recruits" subjects among the individuals (it recruits them all), or "transforms" the individuals into subjects (it transforms them all) by that very precise operation which I have called *interpellation* or hailing, and which can be imagined along the lines of the most commonplace everyday police (or other) hailing: "Hey, you there!"

Assuming that the theoretical scene I have imagined takes place in the street, the hailed individual will turn round. By this mere one-hundred-and-eighty-degree physical conversion, he becomes a *subject*. Why? Because he has recognized that the hail was "really" addressed to him, and that "it was *really him*" who was hailed (and not someone else). Experience shows that the practical telecommunication of hailings is such that they hardly ever miss their man: verbal call or whistle, the one hailed always recognizes that it is really him who is being hailed. And yet it is a strange phenomenon, and one which cannot be explained solely by "guilt feelings", despite the large numbers who "have something on their consciences." (Althusser 174)

This passage has been taken up in an enormously broad range of scholarly work on subjectivity, the vast majority of which has used its pivotal scene to consider what Judith Butler has famously called the "psychic life of power": the manner in which ideology becomes incorporated into subjects' sense of themselves, and thus becomes (quite literally) "internalized" (Butler).

Far fewer thinkers have considered the *material* and *corporeal* conditions in which ideology functions for Althusser. The "hailing" so central to his claim takes place, after all, within the domain of public space: a city street. More urgently for the scope of the present essay, the manner in which the individual in Althusser's story "becomes a subject" fundamentally involves a "mere one-hundred-and-eighty-degree physical conversion." That is, Althusser cites a *corporeal turn*—a half-pirouette—as the site and the scene of becoming-subject to the call of the cop. I would like to mark this invocation of movement (and its summoning in and by the police) as what I have been calling the choreographic imperative.

Lest readers think I am using what may seem like an irrelevant narrative detail simply to further a point, let me use this moment to transition to a scene far more dispersed (and far more dire) than the Jefferson Memorial; and let me ask: how might the choreographic imperative be understood in its fuller interpellative function, particularly when the bodies toward which it is aimed are not white dancers who have chosen to move (in celebration of the "individualist spirit" of Thomas Jefferson) at the site of a memorial, but Black and Brown pedestrians on a public street? It is worth beginning—given Althusser's decision to situate his subject within public space—with a brief return to the court documents dismissing Mary Brooke Oberwetter's complaint, if only to recall the court's crucial distinction between public and nonpublic forums. In stipulating that dance could be prohibited even when considered as expressive conduct, the court took note of the architectural and geographic specificity of the memorial and its surrounding area, in part because its decision cited as precedent a previous case in which political expression on the sidewalks surround the Vietnam War Memorial was deemed protected by the First Amendment.

In concluding that the sidewalks were a public forum, the court focused on the fact that (1) the sidewalks were physically indistinguishable from ordinary sidewalks "used for the full gamut of urban walking"; (2) the sidewalks "are used by thousands of pedestrians every year, including not only the Memorial visitors, but also people going to other places"; and (3) the record did not indicate the sidewalks at issue had a specialized use. (Oberwetter 1: 14–15)

The court used this juridical delineation—the use of sidewalks in everyday life and the demarcation that sidewalks provide—as an indication of precisely the kind of space that the Jefferson Memorial is *not*. Because the memorial is indicated as a distinct space from those "used for the full gamut of urban walking," it is a site in which free expression can be limited and indeed prohibited.

But as Althusser's narrative makes clear, and perhaps precisely *because* they are situated as "public," sidewalks are sites on which intense disciplinary practices are enacted and policed. Bertolt Brecht understood this, and cited the "street scene" as the idealized origin story for his development of a documentary mode of performance that would not simply "represent" but also would effect change on the world with which it is engaged. More harrowingly—and more delicately conscious of the uneven structures of the social that define public space—Frantz Fanon narrativizes such public encounters as the site of profound dislocation from the possibility of agency, of subjectivity, indeed of any kind of participatory social presence:

> Sealed into that crushing objecthood, I turned beseechingly to others. Their attention was a liberation, running over my body suddenly abraded into nonbeing, endowing me once more with an agility that I had thought lost, and by taking me out of the world, restoring me to it. But just as I reached the other side, I stumbled, and the movements, the attitudes, the glances of the other fixed me there, in the sense in which a chemical solution is fixed by a dye. I was indignant; I demanded an explanation. Nothing happened. I burst apart. Now the fragments have been put together again by another self. (Fanon 109)

Fanon's citation of this public encounter enacts a repetition of—to put it far too simply—the radical disenfranchisement from social subjectivity that he experiences as constitutive of Blackness; his recitation embodies and accentuates what Frank Wilderson has called the "menacing and unbearable" pressure for many Black social theorists to articulate subjective presence (indeed, subjective *possibility*) within a social structure ontologically founded on Blackness-as-social death.[4] For Fanon, the impact of this impossibility resonates on a register as material as it is affective, as somatic as it is psychic: "I progress by crawling," he finally proclaims (Fanon 116).

To extrapolate out from Fanon's scene, what the Courts identify as being unimpeachably "public" as the city street—which is in turn protected as a site for "free expression" *for some*—is, for Fanon, structured by and within the repetition of an anti-Blackness as old and as relentless as the *social* through which it runs.

That is, in the late twentieth and early twenty-first centuries, "the movements, the attitudes, the glances of the other fix[ing him] there" recalled by Fanon have been constitutive not only of informal "everyday" encounters, but indeed of explicit public policy. We might go so far as to say that at the same time that anti-Blackness—or what Saidiya Hartman terms the "afterlife of slavery"—has infused the fuzzy, indiscrete frame of mundane sociality, it has also founded and defined the very structure of the social through which the "everyday" can be said to have been lived, felt, and valued at all. Perhaps the most notorious—but also, perhaps, the most banal—archetype of this structuring, the infamous "Stop, Question, and Frisk" policy practiced by the New York Police Department (NYPD) explicitly enacts what I above term the choreographic imperative while implicitly (but no less pressingly) reenacting the systems of racialized violence that underpin that imperative. First instituted by the NYPD in 1971, Stop & Frisk endows police officers with the ability—we might even say a *mandate*—to interrogate and, in many cases, to search pedestrians on public streets who may or may not be engaged in any activity deemed illegal.

As in many other municipal jurisdictions, the NYPD's Stop & Frisk policies were developed in the months and years following the US Supreme Court's decision in *Terry v. Ohio* (1968) that Fourth Amendment rights against unwarranted search and seizure are *not* violated if a cop has a "reasonable suspicion" that a person has just committed, is committing, or might be about-to-commit, a crime. Although the original case on which the *Terry* decision was based involved three men charged with carrying concealed weapons and observed planning what seemed to the officers involved to be a "stick-up," in the five decades since that original scene Stop & Frisk has become, in many districts and neighborhoods, a pedestrian and ubiquitous structuring of public space along distinctly racialized lines. In a 2010 exposé on Brownsville, Brooklyn, for example, the *New York Times* found that officers routinely "stop and question people who merely enter the public housing project buildings without a key; they ask for identification from, and run warrant checks on, young people halted for riding bicycles on the sidewalk" (Rivera et al.). The article notes that of the 52,000 Stop & Frisk encounters in this community of 14,000 people, fewer than 9 percent were initiated because someone "fit the description" of someone *particular* being sought; for the plurality of these stops, cops listed either "furtive movements" or "other" as justification (Ibid.). "Fitting a description," of course, describes precisely the implementation of Stop & Frisk in its recent manufacture, if more broadly than the authors of the *Times* article imply: As numerous studies of the data have unambiguously demonstrated, the practice is immensely disproportionate—the very archetype of dis-proportion!—in its racializing function. As just one example: In 2011 alone in Park Slope, Brooklyn, where 24 percent of the population is Black and/or Latino/a, fully 79 percent of all "Stop & Frisk" encounters involved pedestrians who identified as Black and/or Latino/a (New York Civil Liberties Union). With these data in mind, "fitting a description" takes on more dire, more structural, and more direly structured nuance. And with these data in mind, "Stop & Frisk" appears more manifestly involved not just in a practice that *happens to occur* in public space, but rather as a choreography of interactive social movement that has *produced* (and is actively producing) a particular kind of public space.

We must simultaneously attend to the particulars of that choreography: the collapsed temporality of Stop & Frisk, for example, positions "seized" subjects within a deliberately arbitrary "moment" of criminality, a moment that expands infinitely so as to abandon the possibility of any other possible moments. Recall the single explicitly named demand of Stop & Frisk: a cop must imagine that the "suspect" has just committed, is committing, or might be about-to-commit, a crime. In this temporal schema, it is precisely the temporal that falls away; the stopped-and-frisked are always already suspect, always already potentially criminal. And within this time that is no time—or rather, this time that is infinitely timeless, collapsing any notion of past (becoming), present (being), future (will-have-been-ness) into itself—the body of the seized becomes the locus for—the object of—the state's tightly regimented and intensely racialized structuring of the social.

Since 2011, several videos documenting and demonstrating the NYPD's use of Stop & Frisk have been posted online, garnering a strong groundswell of public criticism of the practice (leading to the announcement in 2013 that the policy had been deemed unconstitutional). As a genre of public discourse, these videos perhaps necessarily jump scale in their representation of both the personal experience of, and the systemic problems with, Stop & Frisk: they include both personal narratives about interactions between young Black and Brown men on the street and the cops who have accosted them, and structural data about the number of stops in specific neighborhoods. As a form of public argument, the films are immensely effective especially in connecting the personal and the systemic, and in demonstrating how the practice operates in both corporeal and social modes. One film in particular, called "The Hunted and the Hated" and posted widely on social media websites, narrates the experiences of a young mixed-race man named Alvin who is stopped almost daily (and often several times in a single day) by cops in Harlem (Schneider and Tuttle). Alvin documented one such encounter with his mobile phone, thus producing one of the only known audio recordings of a full Stop & Frisk interaction.

The stop is harrowing; Alvin is accosted by the cops, who demand to know why he walks "suspiciously" (looking over his shoulder when he becomes aware that the police are following him). They threaten to punch him in the face and to break his arm when he asks why he has been stopped and why they say they will arrest him if he does not silently submit; they explicitly claim that he has been stopped because he is a "mutt." And, unexceptionally, a physical struggle ensues as they wrench his arms behind his back, shove him down a hill, and then force him up against a wall. "I feel like they were trying to make me resist, or fight back," Alvin describes before demonstrating for the camera precisely how the cops had moved his arms and legs, forcing him into compliance. This portion of the video seems almost rote, so unconsciously does Alvin move into the position of arrest: his arms above his head, then his hands linked behind his neck, then twisted into handcuff position behind his back. As we watch his quick, precise movements, it becomes clear that we are watching a particular mode of public movement—a choreographic design—demanded of Black and Brown men on the street and enforced by a policy profoundly rooted in uneven structural violence. What the video reveals is the manner in which, with Stop & Frisk, public space becomes produced in part through a choreographic function that positions Black and Brown pedestrians as always already criminal, and as "good subjects" (to use Althusser's phrase) only insofar as they submit corporeally to that figuring.

Too, the racialized logic of Stop & Frisk policies in cities across the United States seriously complicates a key concern underlying the Jefferson Memorial dancers' argument that their "free expression" was constrained by the park officers who arrested them. Oberwetter's and Kokesh's claims, founded on a common indignation masked as political complaint, understand movement and its relationship to "freedom" in universalist terms detached from the racialized structures of belonging that enable them to make such claims at all. That is, when imagined simply in terms of broad corporeal and expressive "freedom"—unaffected by the everyday political economy of differential social positioning—the "right to dance" *seems* to take on resilient significance, vibrating with the intensity of a claim "we" can "all" get behind. With a studied appraisal of Stop & Frisk in mind, the concern's terrain shifts to consider which bodies and subjects are enabled, in the first place, to demand such a right to dance, and which bodies and subjects are so challenged in their ability to exist at all in public space, so that dance is not even a question. We might ask how choreographic imperatives affect not only who is permitted to dance, and where, but also who is permitted to *be*, and where, and how space generally marked as public becomes defined as much by those who are absent as it is by those who are there.

By way of closing, I would like to turn, finally, to an experiment with these notions staged at my home institution—the University of California, San Diego (UCSD)—in June 2010.

During spring quarter of that year, I convened a gathering of undergraduate students interested in exploring how what was then going by the name of a "budget crisis" manifested its impact in uneven ways across the social demographics of the UCSD campus and the California public more broadly. For our seminar, called "Performing Crisis," the students pursued archival research on the history of "crises" on our campus; considered the local use of public art (especially in UCSD's excellent Stuart Collection) to stage community and commemoration; and collectively produced two large-scale projects intended to "publish" the results of their research. The first of these projects was a 60-foot mural covering an interior wall in the department of Communication tracing a history of crisis in the UC system; it included the formation of each campus, shifts in admissions policies to include women, radical activist histories on each campus, the development and passage of the California Master Plan for Higher Education, and recent happenings (including not only the "budget crisis," but also a series of racist, sexist, and homophobic events) at UCSD. The mural was designed to reflect both historical representations of these and other historical moments and to invite design "input" from passers-by (on a relatively bare section of the wall covered in chalkboard paint).

Inspired by Fanon's rethinking of public space and social subjectivity, the students planned the second project as a public performance on the UCSD campus during the final week of the quarter. Having completed ethnographic interviews with a wide range of faculty, staff, students, and alumnae/i, the students selected portions of text from those conversations to be chalked repetitively across the expansive Library Walk, at the center of campus. Also having studied a selection of performances staged by artists in public space, the students devised a writerly performance similar to the crawl pieces created by US-based artist William Pope. L. For two hours on a hot spring day, the students crawled from the end of Library Walk to the base of the Geisel Library, silently using chalk to inscribing the broad path with the narratives they had collected. The collective crawl stretched across the berth of the walk, interrupting the everyday thoroughfare and those who crossed it; and as crowds began to gather, the affective momentum of the performance slowly built as the crawlers (quite literally) inched along.[5]

On the same day as the Crawl, members of UCSD's Muslim Students Association (MSA) and Students for Justice in Palestine (SJP) groups had built a large installation as part of the annual Justice in Palestine Week. The installation included a series of stages and booths, as well as a mock Israeli checkpoint and a wall on which were posted the names, biographical details, and photographs of people slayed by the Israeli military in its ongoing occupation of Palestinian land. The installation was particularly large during that year's events, and had drawn especially charged crowds of students, faculty members, and others from the local community. Students involved in the crawl performance had not known the exact size or location of the MSA/SJP installation; nor had they realized that their extended crawl would cross the invisible constructed "border" of the mock checkpoint and would take them past the memorial Israeli Apartheid Wall. As the crawlers approached the area, tension built: students from the MSA and SJP began to move quickly, asking onlookers what was happening; and the sizable crowd grew larger as viewers began to suspect a conflict may be brewing. Several groups of students began backtracking along Library Walk, reading backward through the narratives chalked onto the path. A dozen or so people with cameras began to record the scene; a group of representatives from the nearby Chancellor's Complex huddled nervously alongside the walk, talking frantically on their mobile phones and rubbing their heads; and the crawling students murmured inaudibly among themselves.

At the threshold of the mock border, the group of crawlers suddenly shifted the content of their scrawl. Having arrived at a kind of impromptu consensus, the students began to write "Free Palestine" and "Access for All" across the walk. As their text changed, so too did the mood of the crowds: The MSA and SJP began cheering loudly, playing music, dancing, and bringing the sweating crawlers bottles of water. A collective sigh seemed to escape from the various institutional officers standing around—the campus police and especially the Chancellor's representatives. The crawlers continued until, finally, they reached the base of the library. They stood; a chosen leader wrote Fanon's "I progress by crawling" across the walk, and the group silently linked arms and walked back across campus to the Communication department building where they had begun, cheered by the several hundred onlookers who had stopped to see.

We experienced (and later discussed) that mock border, and the crescendo of the moment when the crawlers encountered it, as a model for what we might call the precipice of empathy's promise: a crisis-in-the-making occasioned by the embodied enactment of a relatively simple gesture: a crawl. At that border, the crawl's proposition—to disrupt the banal choreography of Library Walk by spectacularizing the banal crisis in access to higher education—was sharpened by an unforeseen encounter with another set of political claims. And in that fleeting moment of crossing, an exceptional coalition was formed, however briefly, to redefine a space ostensibly defined as "public" but unevenly accessible. When, early the next morning, the university dispatched high-powered water trucks to wash away the chalk narratives—obliterating any physical evidence that the crawl had ever happened—all that remained was the still-pulsing memory of an encounter in which, if only for an instant, the promise of "public space" shone through.

Notes

1. I borrow the phrase "a slender pivot" (and its choreographic undertone) from Peggy Phelan's *Mourning Sex*, 25.
2. My quick (and snide) comment here is troubled by a later comment within the decision potentially excluding "a history professor giving a lecture in the Monument" from its interpretation of barred "demonstrations," suggesting that the courts are perhaps even more in need of performance scholars' assistance than I might have originally imagined. See the original district court opinion (2010), 18.
3. As Dylan Rodriguez notes, " 'police brutality' has become a vastly misused term. While the phrase intends to communicate a sharp criticism of state power that has presumably violated its own self-defined laws and regulations, it is often used to refer to violent police practices that are utterly, ritually *sanctioned by law*" ("De-provincializing Police Violence: On the Recent Events at UC Davis").
4. I borrow the notion of "Social Death" from Orlando Patterson's *Slavery and Social Death*.
5. See "Chalk Walk" for video of the performance.

BIBLIOGRAPHY

"Adam Kokesh Body Slammed, Choked; Police Brutality at Jefferson Memorial." YouTube. Accessed November 10, 2011. http://www.youtube.com/watch?v=8jUU3yCy3uI.

Althusser, Louis. *Lenin and Philosophy and Other Essays*. New York: Monthly Review Press. 1971.

Butler, Judith. *The Psychic Life of Power*. Stanford, CA: Stanford University Press, 1997.

Cappelli, M. G. Renu, and Jill Dolan. "The Greater Good." *Theatre Survey* 52, no. 1 (2011): 105–13.

"Chalk Walk." YouTube. Accessed December 1, 2012. http://www.youtube.com/watch?v=4HKICl3Ie7I.

Fanon, Frantz. *Black Skin, White Masks*. New York: Grove Press, 1994.

Foster, Susan. *Choreographing Empathy*. New York: Routledge. 2011.

New York Civil Liberties Union. "Stop and Frisk Facts." Accessed December 1, 2012. http://www.nyclu.org/node/1598.

Oberwetter v. Hilliard and Salazar. US District Court for the District of Columbia, civil action no. 09-0588 (JDB). 2010.

Oberwetter v. Hilliard and Salazar. US Court of Appeals for the District of Columbia, civil action no. 10-5078. 2011.

Patterson, Orlando. *Slavery and Social Death*. Cambridge, MA: Harvard University Press, 1982.

Phelan, Peggy. *Mourning Sex: Performing Public Memories*. New York: Routledge, 1997.

Rivera, Ray, Al Roberts, and Janet Roberts. "A Few Blocks, 4 Years, 52,000 Police Stops." *New York Times*. Accessed July 11, 2010. http://www.nytimes.com/2010/07/12/nyregion/12frisk.html.

Rodriguez, Dylan. "De-provincializing Police Violence: On the Recent Events at UC Davis." *Reclaim UC*. December 9, 2011. Accessed December 1, 2012. http://reclaimuc.blogspot.com/2011/12/de-provincializing-police-violence-on.html.

Schneider, Erin, and Ross Tuttle. "Stopped and Frisked: 'For Being a F***ing Mutt.'" *The Nation*. Accessed December 1, 2012. http://www.thenation.com/article/170413/stopped-and-frisked-being-fking-mutt-video.

CHAPTER 29

··

CONJURING MAGIC AS SURVIVAL

Hip-Hop Theater and Dance

··

HALIFU OSUMARE

> Icon defines itself in act south of the Sahara. Things done, sculpture and dress, combine with things happening, music and dance. A fundamental principle is made manifest: action is a superior mode of thought.
>
> Robert Farris Thompson, *African Art in Motion*, 1974

THOMPSON's wisdom that I use as epigraph to begin this meditation says it all: In Africa, artifice and corporeality interact to manifest magic that the West calls art. Effective enactment necessitates a kind of conjuring; to truly perform is to enter heightened thought. I saw this kind of magical conjuring in Togo in 1976, when a Ewe man at an annual festival performed a dance specifically to show his metaphysical powers, exiting the outdoor arena with his two assistants carrying him on two large banana leaves his full weight, which the soft leafy surface miraculously fully supported. I also saw similar "magic" in a Ghanaian hiplife theatrical show in 2008 at Accra's International Conference Centre when a contemporary pop musician mesmerized his youthful fans by taking them back in time: He entered the proscenium stage hoisted overhead on an Akan palanquin in full Ashanti *kente* cloth regalia, only to descend, strip to his regular cloths and perform his award winning hip-hop song in regular rotation on Ghanaian pop radio. Both "African" performances, thirty-two years apart, fused artifact and physicality that enabled their audience to transcend the immediate present. Both examples of performance allowed their audience to enter a realm of thought that facilitated lucid examination of their human subjectivity.

Hip-hop culture is the latest manifestation of a long continuum of Africanist performance based in this particular multidisciplinary approach to enacting subjectivity, where the boundaries are blurred between sound, movement, oratory, and even visual props. One uses whatever is at one's disposal to create conjured magic that manifests a "superior mode of thought." The fact that this Africanist aesthetic philosophy is based on performance, process, and the doing, as opposed to the written word—*logos*—is important. Life's clarity of articulation is determined not by recorded rational thought, but rather by corporeal improvised enactment within the structure of inherited traditions. With this performative approach, high thought, then, is manifested in its actual embodiment: The Malian *jeli* or griot historian commits his/her stories to memory and *performs* hundreds of years of history; the Ashanti *fontomfrom* dancer adeptly re-enacts centuries of war battles with his well-placed kicks and semiotic improvised hand gestures within the sonic power of the accompanying complex polyrhythms; the Trinidadian calypsonian bard spontaneously composes his scathing social commentary to guitar and *cuatro* melodies that exactly capture the wrongdoings of the corrupt politician; while the "dope" rap emcee incarnates, along with her hype-man, the right combination of body-rocking rhythm and double-entendre lyrics that create the mind-body link that only hip-hop can. This is the philosophical, process-oriented performance continuum of which hip-hop is a part.

From the above, one can discern that "performance" is an appropriate term for much of modern-contemporary black theatricality. The tradition of Africanist performance is implicitly interdisciplinary, where *embodiment* of the word and music is central, and conversely where learned and improvised oratory brings into being embodied sound. Even when considering literary dramatic plays, a *conjuring* performance tradition continually insinuates itself. Soyica Colbert captures this multidisciplinary nature of black theater in *The African American Theatrical Body* (2011):

> I argue for the centrality of the African American literary tradition of black performance traditions expressed in cakewalking, preaching, hustling, migrating, rituals (e.g., dancing the juba and making blood sacrifice), and singing of blues and gospel. These performance traditions create the performative ground of African American literary texts.[1]

Indeed, Zora Neale Hurston's *Color Struck* (1926) and August Wilson's *Joe Turner's Come and Gone* (1984) are prime examples of this Africanist conjured magic of performance embedded within scripted plays, with their use of minstrelsy-era cakewalk and ring shout/juba respectively.[2] Yet, it is not the American Broadway musical tradition to which I draw attention; rather, I explore a unique, less direct approach to the admixture of spoken scripted text, music, and dance. Indeed, this particular multidisciplinary perspective of Africanist performance is where the elements merge to become *ritual* that blurs the sacred and secular and, in turn, obscures the lines between theater and dance.

Ntozake Shange's choreopoem embodies this Africanist performance approach best in the transitional 1970s with *For Colored Girls Who Have Considered Suicide/When the Rainbow Is Enuf* (1976).[3] In one scene, the Lady in Purple and the Lady in Blue, for example, create a dual-medium image of the character of Sechita, a contemporary woman who indiscriminately sleeps with different men as she dreams of New Orleans Creole mistresses who are her historical precursors. The Lady in Purple seductively renders the poetic lines, as the Lady in Blue visualizes the spoken words in a ritual dance that blends seamlessly with the text. Shange's *choreopoem* became a counterculture manifesto of '70s theatrical conjure magic (i.e., "a laying on of hands") that spoke of the sorrows and joys of the black woman struggling for liberation on many levels. Evolving out of the long tradition of word-movement-sound performance, the choreopoem forged a "new" take on an old methodology, as the precursor to spoken word and slam poetry of the 2000s.

I examine the intersections between contemporary hip-hop dance and theater from this theoretical perspective to explore its effects on the aesthetic, existential, and socio-political realms of human expression. To accomplish this, I first interrogate hip-hop culture's transformation into multidisciplinary dramatic theater, particularly through major New York companies, such as Danny Hoch's Hip-Hop Theater Festival and The Hip-Hop Shakespeare Company, as well as solo artists like Rha Goddess and Will Power. I then move to hip-hop dance theater and its myriad experimental amalgamation of movement, music, and text and its long trajectory out of African dance performance. I do this particularly with Philadelphia's Rennie Harris Puremovement dance company and his articulate bridging of the "democracy" of the b-boy street circle and the proscenium stage's formal choreography. The chapter demonstrates how, through hip-hop culture's *conjuring magic as survival*, the theatrical stage has been reinvigorated as a social movement.

Hip-Hop Theater as Performance Mashup

Because the youth subculture is implicitly interdisciplinary in artistic approach, hip-hop theater is lodged within this Africanist performance continuum. For example, many hip-hop theater artists and emcees (rappers) started as graf writers (graffiti artists) or b-boys/b-girls (breakdancers). Hip-Hop's four primary elements of b-boying, rap, deejaying, and graf art, along with the added fifth element of beat boxing, as well as what some call the sixth as knowledge, created a holistic approach that reflects its Africanist roots. The majority of today's hip-hop theater artists began with grassroots street artists. Actor-playwright Danny Hock, founder of New York's Hip-Hop Theater Festival (HHTF), for example, started as a graf writer; while solo theater artist Will Power began as a neighborhood emcee. Their career trajectories are predicated on hip-hop's requirement: a connection to the grass-roots arts movement that started in poor neighborhoods like South Bronx, Harlem, North Philadelphia, and Southside Chicago as well as East Oakland and South Central Los Angeles, California.

However, due to rap music's multibillion dollar commercialization, "street cred" as a seminal tenet of hip-hop over time has become a hackneyed, overused concept. Yet, originally the notion of street credibility kept hip-hop culture bearers linked to its "making-something-outta-nothing" neighborhood origins. In lieu of constructed identities and excessive branding of personas in the Internet age, today's street cred has become a manipulated marketing ploy with little meaning. At the second decade of the twenty-first century, given the lack of originality forced on hip-hop artists ironically by their own global commercial success, many are now turning to various forms of theater to make fresh, and more meaningful, artistic statements. Some are transitioning to the legitimate theatrical stage from the high-powered sonic and visual power of hip-hop street culture, and in the process new counterhegemonic theatrical challenges are being produced against racism, classism, sexism, and homophobia in the United States and other countries.

Although many hip-hop icons have become Hollywood film "raptors," such as Ice-T, Ice Cube, Will Smith, Queen Latifah, Mos Def, and even 50 Cent, other hip-hoppers have transitioned to the theatrical stage; they have thereby kept the six elements of hip-hop in tandem, allowing for a new innovative vibrancy that actually gives the entire culture new life. Original hip-hop musical scores, innovative choreographed b-boying, popping, and locking dance styles, visually stunning graffiti scenery, and well-crafted scripts using rhymed raps and spoken word all constitute much of today's hip-hop theater. But, Danny Hoch reveals that "the consistent challenge has been to define not what hip-hop means as culture, but what hip-hop means as art—in fact, to make the case that hip-hop *is* art."[4] This is the essential work of hip-hop theater artists today: to translate the implicit aesthetic theatricality and often scathing social critiques of their street art to the proscenium stage. Commercialization separated and created hierarchy among hip-hop's elements, essentially dividing the culture in order to conquer it for profit (rap is now the signature element, with the uninitiated assuming it is solely synonymous with hip-hop). Hip-hop theater repositions the culture's elements into an aesthetic dialogue that reinvigorates the culture by keeping it intact for future survival.

New York's Hip-Hop Theater Festival (HHTF) is a good place to start a vertical dive into hip-hop theater as a genre. Founded by Danny Hoch in 2000, HHTF has over a decade of stabilized institutional development. The overall mission of the Festival is "to elevate Hip-Hop Theater into a widely recognized genre by empowering artists to develop new works and build coalitions with artists and institutions around the world."[5] HHTF maintains a staff of six in Brooklyn under Hoch's guiding definition of hip-hop theater that is crucial to the mission and its subsequent programming over the last decade: "Hip-Hop theatre must fit into the realm of theatrical performance, and it must be by, about and for the hip-hop generation, participants in hip-hop, or both."[6]

At the heart of Hoch's definition is his recognition of the post–Civil Rights, post-soul generation of youths who have made a strong impact on American culture. The concept of the hip-hop generation has been explored by several hip-hop scholars, such as Kitwana Bakari, who wrote *The Hip-Hop Generation: Young Blacks and the Crisis in African-American Culture* (2002). Bakari's take on the hip-hop generation, as one implicitly involved within African American cultural politics, obviously echoes the music videos we see on MTV, VH-1, and BET: young African Americans, mostly male and often originating from the ghetto margins, as synonymous with the youth culture. But this image of hip-hop as solely the purview of street-wise blacks, particularly since the commercialization of rap music, belies the culture's multicultural origins in the South Bronx. As I wrote in *The Africanist Aesthetic in Global Hip-Hop* (2007) about Robert Farris Thompson's seminal historical analysis,

> Thompson reminds us that contrary to the idea of a monolithic black American culture in North America, the Bronx in the 1970s, as it does today, represented the "black Atlantic." Jamaicans, Puerto Ricans, Barbadians, Cubans, and North American blacks represented five distinct African-derived cultures that, although discretely different, all had music and dance diffusive factors that crossed-referenced each other as African diasporic expressive culture.[7]

But Hoch's emphasis on the hip-hip generation is even broader than the varied African diasporic blacks living in the Bronx during hip-hop's inception. As a white native New Yorker who came of age during the very beginning of hip-hop's commercialization, he has a stake in recognizing the Latino, poor white, and even Asian influences in hip-hop's origins: "The notion that hip-hop is solely an African-American art form is erroneous, and this becomes clear when we really examine its aesthetics. It is certainly part of the African continuum, and if it were not for African-Americans there would be no hip-hop, but hip-hop would not exist if it were not for the polycultural social construct of New York City in the 1970s."[8] This multiracial vision of the hip-hop generation has a direct effect on hip-hop theater. Hoch notes that

The clamor for more hip-hop theatre on the legitimate stage is not unlike the cry of theatre artists of color during and after the Civil Rights Movement. But few hip-hop theatre pieces fit into a solely African-American slot, or an Asian-American or Latino one. This is because the face of the Hip-Hop generation is considerably more diverse. And this is a good thing, because Hip-Hop shouldn't fit into a tokenized "slot", and certainly not one that narrows its scope.[9]

As hip-hop became national, and indeed global, not only did it carry the "polycultural" nature of '70s Bronx, but also cultures as far flung as India, Japan, South Africa, and Ghana. Many of the top US rap artists are doing collaborations with hip-hop artists in Asia, Africa, and South America. Youth cultures from all over the world constitute what is now called the Global Hip-Hop Nation (GHHN).[10] For example, in 2006 theater educator Daniel Banks took his Hip Hop Theatre Initiative to Ghana and South Africa to invigorate and learn from the artists committed to working on social change through hip-hop. Working with artists at Ghana's National Theatre in Accra and students at the University of Ghana, as well as inhabitants of the Buduburam Refugee Camp in Ghana's Central Region, Banks used hip-hop theater to "foreground young people and model youth empowerment" to deal with some of African youths' issues.[11] From the global cosmopolitan reality of today's hip-hop, lodged in its elements' Africanist aesthetic parameters, many hip-hop cultural manifestations emerged with educational opportunities that continue to promote this rebellious in-your-face youth culture.

Hip-hop, therefore, straddles the sociopolitical exigencies of African American culture in the United States *and* a global cosmopolitan youth movement with its own "connective marginalities."[12] From this complex perspective, hip-hop is, perhaps, the first American pop culture phenomenon to navigate such a complex subaltern cultural space. Hoch quips about hip-hop's racial/cultural dilemma for the theater: "It's a bad thing because theatres don't seem to have a category of this work, and therefore don't now what to do with it. That's okay, they'll catch on soon enough."

The HHTF has produced some vibrantly provocative theater works that showcase artistic innovation while representing the cultural complexity of hip-hop. One such play was *Rhyme Deferred* by Hip-Hop Theatre Junction, which thematically explores the story of two emcees who are brothers, while two deejays improvised a live score to innovative hip-hop choreography. Another show was one that the Tortuga Project brought from Albuquerque called *Five Elements of Change*, where the creators' methodology echoed the thematic script: Aztec dance and Brazilian capoiera mingled with b-boying and rap to illuminate hip-hop's relationship to indigenous culture and sustainable farming. Many hip-hop theater works blur the lines between dance and theater, as was the case with Philadelphia's Olive Dance Theatre's work *tOy/bOx* that creates minimalist statements from traditional b-boy movements. The HHTF has also produced Philadelphia's Rennie Harris Puremovement, the "godfather" of hip-hop dance theater, whom I explore extensively below.

The HHTF has grown in stature to present international theater companies. They have presented Jonzi D, formerly of London's Breakin' Convention, who combines b-boying and scripted text to make creative testimonials about black hip-hop London youth, American pop cultural hegemony, and British police brutality. In his work *Lyrikal Fearta* he breakdances on an American flag on the ground, only to rise and point a fake gun at the audience. This irreverent piece has been presented at London's premiere dance theater venue, Saddler Wells. Hip-hop theater has indeed made its transition from the streets to legitimate theater.

The Festival has also included the 2013 Alpert Award Winner in Theatre, Eisa Davis, who is the niece of famed political activist Angela Davis. Her original plays have earned distinguished awards, while her *Bulrusher* was a finalist for the Pulitzer Prize in Drama. Davis' *Angela's Mixtape* was produced at HHTF and was named a best of 2009 by *The New Yorker* magazine. As Hoch says about this work, "*Angela's Mixtape* is literally a hip-hop generation musical and theatrical mixtape of weaved together scenes and memories of the playwright's childhood growing up as Angela Davis's niece." Davis's *Umkovu* "is a conventional play about people struggling with the conflation of violence and commerce within the Hip-Hop music industry."[13] It takes the hip-hop generation to truly explore the intricacies of their subculture in which they came of age, and theater is providing a creative means to make important statements about our hip-hop times. In the process hip-hop is advancing theater itself to encompass a new age-group cohort with innovative sensibilities and approaches.

Hoch, himself, has been very prolific in creating his own artistic statements in hip-hop theater. Although he has appeared as an actor in several mainstream Hollywood movies, such as *We Own the Night* (2007), as well as the limited-released 1999 film *Whiteboyz* (directed by Marc Levin and written by and starring Hoch), he is best known for his one-man shows.

> My own work ranges from monologues dealing with hip-hop commercialization and the prison industrial complex in *Jails, Hospitals & Hip-Hop*; to the explorations of polycultural hip-hop in *Some People*; to a standard two-act play, *Till the Break of Dawn*, about a group of

FIGURE 29.1 Eisa Davis and Linda Powell in *Angela's Mixtape*. Photo by Jim Baldassare.

idealistic hip-hop generation teachers and activists who go on a trip and learn how to live with some difficult contradictions.[14]

In his solo shows, Hoch is on a mission to illuminate "real" hip-hop culture, as opposed to what Viacom, Madison Avenue, and EMI-Universal and Sony have created and profited from. In one of his performance pieces, he says,

> "There is not a culture in the world that you can buy off the shelf in a store called Tower Records. Hip-hop is not wearing diamond earrings; diamond earrings that were mined by African children of war. Hip-hop is not wearing clothes sewn by Honduran, Haitian, Dominican children of war either; you are not hip-hop if the clothes on your back cost more than the monthly salaries of the people that made your clothes, motherfuckers,"
> Then he reaches down and looks at the pants he is wearing, and says,
> "Oh, shit!"[15]

Here Hoch points to the root capitalist contradiction that hip-hop has made crystal clear: How do those producing a culture founded in poor people's reality not become hypocrites as their expressive culture is commodified into "the ghettocentric hood" as the multibillion dollar global hip-hop industry? Does capitalism make frauds out of us all? How do we continue the communal caring at the basis of indigenous cultures while individualistic neoliberal corporatization becomes the foundation of our reality? How do today's expressive youths continue to "conjure magic" in this era of late capitalism? These are among the crucial questions that hip-hop theater explicitly investigates, exposing the contradictions of the hip-hop generation within America's and the world's twenty-first-century context. Hoch takes his theater work seriously, while simultaneously conducting important *political* work: he is a senior fellow at the Vera List Center for Art and Politics, and sits on the board of Theatre Communications Group in the United States. His HHTF therefore becomes the artistic arm of the larger cultural politics of the culture wars. After all, the goal of the HHTF is not only "to invigorate theater through hip-hop aesthetics," but to also "ignite dialogue and social change through performance art."

But of course the hip-hop theater movement is larger than the HHTF, with several other arts institutions and a plethora of solo performance artists. The Hip Hop Shakespeare Company (THSC), founded by 20-something Akala (Kingslee James Daley) in 2008, is a music theater production company with a live band. Dedicated to exploring the intersections of artistic similarities between rap's and Shakespeare's use of "rhythm, metaphor, lyricism, and poetry," the company has given workshops and performances in London and Mumbai.[16] Full Circle Productions, initiated in 1992 by Puerto Rican dance artists Gabriel "Kwikstep" Dionisio and his wife Ana "Rockafella" Garcia, produce scripted and danced theatrical productions as well as major neighborhood events for youths. The company has also appeared in television documentaries and Hollywood films.

With hip-hop culture's ubiquitous presence in American culture, mainstream experimental theater companies have embraced the youth aesthetic. HERE, a New York City theater company co-founded by Artistic Director Kristin Marting, is an example of a theater devoted to unconventional multidisciplinary work. During Fall 2012, HERE theater joined with the HHTF in association with Collective Consciousness Theatre to premiere *How to Break*, "a new play fueled by human beat-boxing, breaking, popping and locking, linguistic flow and multimedia graffiti art." What is interesting about *How to Break* is that it was a script emerging out of writer Aaron Jafferis's work in the 2010 and 2011 Oregon Shakespeare Festival Mixing Text project. Mainstream theater companies, such as The Old Globe, The Public Theater, and Sundance Theatre Lab, have all produced other hip-hop inflected plays by Jafferis, such as *Shakespeare: The Remix* and *No Lie*. The *New York Times* theater critic Bruce Weber realized in the early 2000s that

> [f]orging the rebellious and original spirit of an aggressive new cultural movement with a respect for performance skills and training, hip-hop theater is gaining momentum. It's sill on the fringe of the stage universe, but there are signs (for example, the rapper Mos Def's starring in "Topdog/Underdog" on Broadway) that the very force of a culture ever more influenced by youth and diversity is beginning to turn the battleship of American mainstream theater.[17]

Over the last decade, since this New York theater establishment assessment, traditional theaters have recognized not only hip-hop's obvious cultural influence but also the new artistic prospects offered by the youth culture in order to stay contemporary. Traditional theaters have initiated various projects to utilize hip-hop's aesthetic possibilities to speak to twenty-first-century sociocultural issues.

Yet, solo artists are the mainstay of the hip-hop theater movement. One such artist is Marc Bamuthi Joseph, an African American born in New York City who moved to Oakland, California. He is a National Poetry Slam champion, has appeared on Russell Simmons's HBO Def Poetry, and has performed internationally in Cuba, Venezuela, Panama, Columbia, Europe, and Africa. His second play, *Scourge*, developed from his artist-in-residence time at the Yerba Buena Center for the Arts in San Francisco, represents the plight of Haiti in the postcolonial New World. Rha Goddess is an African American female hip-hop artist and playwright best known for coining the now ubiquitous hip-hop term, "floetry," representing the unique poetic flow of hip-hop rhyming and spoken word. She has collaborated with foundational hip-hop artists such as Afrika Bambaataa's Zulu Nation and Chuck D of Public Enemy. Her play *Low* had its debut in 2006 at the annual Actors Theatre of Louisville, an internationally known new works festival.

Will Powers has become a stronghold of the hip-hop theater movement as an actor, rapper, playwright, and spoken-word artist with international awards and acclaim. His solo performances have become tours-de-forces that cover critical topics of race, culture, HIV, violence, intergenerational communication, and the celebration of life itself. Through total theater, Power combines movement, storytelling, rhyming, and music that he himself composes. His one-man shows include *The Gathering, Flow*, and *The Upper Room*. One of his masterpieces, *The Seven*, is an adaptation of the Greek tragedy *Seven Against Thebes*, and has become a standard in hip-hop theater with its successful run Off-Broadway at New York Theater Workshop. Continuing his exploration of Western theater's relationship to hip-hop, in July 2012 Power released a video and soundtrack of Shakespeare's "The Isle Is Full of Noises" speech by Caliban from *The Tempest*. What Power calls his "Tempest"/Hip Hop Mashup" for the Royal Shakespeare Company's online myShakespeare project explores the basis of the hip-hop aesthetic: sampling past music, dance, styles, and now scripted plays into new syntheses, creating a contemporary "mashup" that converges into a new artistic statements. As Grandmaster Caz, one of the original Bronx founders of hip-hop, has prophetically said, "Hip-hop didn't invent anything; hip-hop re-invented everything." Hip-hop theater becomes a new medium of this cultural adage.

HIP-HOP DANCE AS POSTMODERN THEATER

Although I have been exploring hip-hop dance as a part of hip-hop theater, the myriad movement forms that have emerged from hip-hop culture since its inception in the mid-1970s can be extricated from scripted dramatic plays and performance art. In fact, hip-hop dance theater has formed its own wing of hip-hop theater on the proscenium stage, as well as taken its place in the world of theatrical dance. Even though this genre is often presented within theater seasons like the annual HHTF, hip-hop dance is most naturally lodged within the international dance world. With the myriad experimentations since the '60s in dance theater that often includes spoken text, theater and dance have increasingly overlapped, and new terms, such as "performance art," emerged to delineate various experimentations with movement, music, and text. What follows is an exploration of hip-hop dance theater that emphasizes movement as the primary medium of storytelling.

Before elucidating the main artists in this genre, it is necessary to examine dance as one of the primary elements of hip-hop culture, usually the first to be adopted in the culture's internationalization. As I have said elsewhere, at the foundation of the Africanist aesthetic is the power of the Word, or *nommo*, what Brenda Dixon Gottschild calls the "verbal movement" that forms the subjunctive mood. The interchangeable dynamics of movement and sound co-join to form the first principle of an aesthetic that is not merely product but indeed about *process*, always in motion, always becoming. *Nommo* is an African principle that emphasizes the changing now, the improvisatory self.[18] I conceptualize hip-hop dance as a cultural extension of the Africanist dance continuum: from traditional West African dance through American tap and early jazz dance to the 1970s street corner b-boy competitions. B-boying/b-girling is embodied text just as rap music is oral poetry. Dance in hip-hop culture, as a part of the African diaspora, can be likened aesthetically to a Séné-Gambian village *bantaba* circle, where a *griot*, or oral historian, sings the genealogical lineage of the people, along with symbolic gestures and often-spontaneous dance by the people that serve to focus the expressive energy of the entire event. Hip-hop translated this creative community circle into the *cipher* that hip-hop scholar Imani Perry defines as "a conceptual space in which heightened consciousness exists . . . a privileged outlaw space."[19] Given this *bantaba/cipher* tradition, it becomes imperative for today's hip-hop choreographers to make each of their dance works collaborations between them and their dancers, if not their audience, through their engagement with this improvisatory tradition.

The best of hip-hop choreography, as composed dances that make intact artistic nonverbal statements, become eloquent articulations of both direct text and subtle subtext nuances through the body. In hip-hop culture, choreography, or even improvisation as spontaneous movement composition, become nonverbal narratives that indicate, identify, imagine, and subvert. This text-like aspect of hip-hop dance was made lucid early on in the culture's development by Sally Banes's description of the potential of the *freeze* in b-boying:

> Another important set of motifs in the freeze section was the exploration of body states in a subjunctive mode—things not as they are, but as they might be—comparing and contrasting youthful male vitality with its range of opposites: women, animals (dogs, horses, mules) babies, old age, injury and illness . . . and death.[20]

Innovative freezes and the stop-on-a-dime syncopated breaks in the fast-paced rhythmic phrasing become a part of the masterful b-boy or b-girl's solo.

Although b-boying/b-girling is often considered the original hip-hop dance form at the inchoate neighborhood level, Katrina Hazzard-Donald has identified three phases of hip-hop dance's evolution, all of which are often a part of staged hip-hop dance theater.

> Hip-Hop dance can be characterized in three stages: waack, breakdancing, and rap dance. Waack dancing appears about 1972. Dance moves such as locking (later known on the East Coast as pop-locking), the robot, and the spank, along with splits and rapidly revolving spins combined with unexpected freezes, were part of the waack's outrageous style. Here the fusion of theatrical expectation and outrageous showmanship occurs that would mark later hip hop styles known as breakdancing.[21]

It becomes apparent from this description of hip-hop dance's evolution that previous moves, styles, and approaches to improvised dance composition, associated with breaking as the signature hip-hop style, was already implicit in the previous more upright style that she calls waack, and others have called "The Good Foot" from the influence of James Brown's 1972 hit funk song, "Get on the Good Foot." It must be noted that early waack dancing was the purview of African Americans, while breaking became primarily associated with New York Puerto Ricans, again alluding to the multicultural nature of hip-hop's early development.

However, most of today's casual hip-hop audience is most familiar with Hazzard-Donald's third stage of hip-hop dance: rap dance. Media-projected rap dance is the hip-hop choreography seen on ubiquitous rap music videos and music award shows that range from well-choreographed combinations using elements of waack, breaking, and popularized commercial stage dance to the controversial booty-popping viewed on late night X-rated MTV hip-hop stations.

> The third stage of hip-hop dance, which I will label rap dance, developed as a response to the popularity and athletic requirements of breaking. Combining aspects of both breaking and waack, it is influenced and cross-fertilized by a less athletic form of popular dance, house dancing, which uses much of the traditional African American vocabulary.[22]

By the late '90s and early 2000s this third stage of hip-hop dance splintered off not only into commercial video and dance studio styles, including hip-hop dance video games like HipHop DX, but also into new derivative street styles, which included aspects of the previous two stages of breaking and waack. Resulting street forms such as *krumping* in South Central Los Angeles, *turfing* in Oakland, and *jerking* in Los Angeles, the latter of which was inspired by the New Boyz's 2009 rap song called "You're a Jerk," all furthered the Africanist dance continuum. The commercial end of rap dancing, following rap music's commodification, also combined elements of what Hazzard-Donald calls the "traditional African American vocabulary," but it necessarily also incorporated the exigencies of commercial television and film with its overemphasis on sex and violence. However, all three stages borrow from the Africanist dance continuum that becomes the foundation of what hip-hop choreographers have at their disposal to construct innovative and often poignant theatrical statements about the human condition.

Hip-hop staged concert dance exists within several genres: (1) international hip-hop dance competitions (World Hip Hop Dance Championships); (2) staged history of hip-hop dance (Rennie Harris's Illadelph Legends of Hip-Hop Festival); (3) community studio-oriented hip-hop dance companies (Culture Shock Dance Troupe National Network, L.A.'s We Break Dance Company); (4) hip-hop dance in commercial television shows and staged musicals (BET Hip-Hop Awards); and (5) hip-hop-inspired choreography by artistic directors of contemporary concert dance companies. It is this latter category on which I focus the remainder of this chapter.

The burgeoning of contemporary hip-hop dance companies by theater-focused artistic directors is an outgrowth of the globalization of hip-hop culture through Hollywood films such as *Beat Street* and *Breaking 2: Electric Boogaloo* in the early '80s. For example, San Francisco's SoulForce Dance Company, founded by choreographer/producer Micaya in 2001, fuses traditional hip-hop dance styles with other dance genres and theatrical formats. Philadelphia's Olive Dance Theater, founded in 2002 by Jamie Merwin and Raphael Xavier, has a distinctive African American "flava," with their mission to validate African American vernacular dance and indigenous American hip-hop. London's hip-hop dance companies, such as Avant Garde Dance Company, Impact Dance, Scope Dance Theatre, and the aforementioned Jonzi D Projects, often blur the lines between dance and theater with mixed media as they experiment with the boundaries between the two.

One of the dance world's oldest and most recognized and acclaimed international-touring dance companies, based solely in the hip-hop dance genre, is Philadelphia's Rennie Harris Puremovement. Harris was able to transform a dance form meant as virtuosic spectacle into an often delicate and subtle, pared down, concert-oriented movement vocabulary that explores the human condition. His oeuvre is based in his thorough entrenchment in hip-hop dance's street origins. Lorenzo "Rennie" Harris founded Rennie Harris Puremovement (RHPM) in 1992, after he established himself in his North Philadelphia community as a stepper, performing a precision style of rhythmic unison dancing made famous by African American fraternities and sororities. He is well versed in many styles of the black-Latino vernacular dance that falls under the large rubric we call hip-hop dance: popping, locking, electric boogie, house, and b-boying/b-girling. From street stepping he graduated to the Scanner Boys as a b-boy, where his tags or names became Disco ("because I was always dancing"), and PSK or Prince Scare Krow (because of his penchant for the popping and electric boogie styles of hip-hop dance), as well as the one that really stuck, "Prince of the Ghetto."

Harris was discovered by the larger mainstream world when the Smithsonian Institution's Folklife Center came mining for American folk culture in his Philadelphia community in the late seventies. At age 14 he began teaching hip-hop dance for the Smithsonian, which had recently discovered the new phenomenon of hip-hop culture around the same time the first rap song, Sugar Hill Gang's "Rapper's Delight," was broadcast nationally. Harris was, therefore, one of the first hip-hop dancers to be legitimized by a preeminent US cultural institution. Having established himself as a precocious authority on street dancing in his teens, Harris went on to teach workshops at UCLA (where he is currently a part-time lecturer), Columbia College, and Bates College. He also has credits within the world of rap, having toured with famous old-school rappers like Run-DMC, The Fat Boys, and Kurtis Blow. Although he worked for a while in commercial music videos, he quickly realized that he wanted more creative freedom to offer an alternative to hip-hop's commercial side.

Today, he brings these dynamic styles to the concert stage in powerful statements that have mesmerized audiences throughout the world. Notably, he has won three Bessies (New York Dance Performance Award) for his choreography, and has received choreographic commissions by many well-established companies like the Alvin Ailey American Dance Theater.

FIGURE 29.2 Rennie Harris. Photo by Rose Iekenbaum. Used by permission from Rennie Harris Puremovement.

He has simultaneously become one of the leading spokespersons for the positive and creative aspects of hip-hop culture. As popular dance scholar Sally Sommer recognizes, "Since Harris has survived into his forties he has taken the mantle of elder statesman, historian, teacher, and defender of hip hop's best values. Harris experienced guns and death, and he is tired of the hip hop that glorifies violence."[23] Harris has definitely earned the right to be hip-hop culture's moral conscious and to "represent," in the hip-hop sense, its regenerative and evolutionary side.

What Harris has uniquely succeeded in accomplishing is the shattering of the high art (read ballet and modern dance) and low art (read popular street dance) paradigm in a definitive style that challenges our notions of modernism in dance. "I like to manipulate time, where now, past, and future are at the same time."[24] Harris crafts his dances to play with the time signature of movement, attempting to dance outside of time into an eternal space. In the process, he unintentionally contested the concert dance world in a fundamental way by establishing the first American concert dance company to solely utilize the vibrancy, virtuosity, and showmanship of hip-hop dance as its foundation, employing street dance to probe the human psyche, as well as to make poignant personal, cultural, and even epochal statements.

It is precisely the *informality* of street dance manipulated by a creative artist that can challenge the status quo of modern, ballet, and modern jazz dance as the only legitimate

FIGURE 29.3 Rennie Harris Puremovement Dancers in *Something to Do with Love.* Photo by Christopher Duggan. Used by permission from Rennie Harris Puremovement.

concert forms capable of compelling choreographic content. Harris explains: "Urban dance is not formal. It's an experience. It's social. That's what allows it to denounce what tends to control."[25] Indeed, Harris has taken the experience of street dance, in all its unceremonious improvisational, at-the-moment creation, and transformed it into poignant choreography that is on the cutting edge of today's dance and theater worlds. In order to reproduce the spontaneity and in-group rules, Harris cannot always control the b-boy circles that he inserts into his choreography. Although he attempts to retain the structure and social process of good b-boy form, his choreographic works become a give and take between choreographic structure and the at-the-moment creation by the dancers. This becomes a part of Harris's version of conjuring magic.

> Because it's on the stage, people think community does not exist. My dancers will change my choreography [to fit their needs at the moment], sometimes to the point that I don't even recognize it. We have actually had b-boys come up on stage from the audience and represent.[26]

In his form of dance, Harris must be ready for anything. The "democracy" of the b-boy circle demonstrates how individualism of dance style works with what Robert Farris Thompson calls the "looking smart" aspect of improvisation that creates the necessary communal social context within the Africanist aesthetic.[27] In the end, it is the collective energy of the circle to which each individual has contributed that is evaluated as a successful performance. The socializing process promoted by this communal aesthetic becomes salutary for typically staid concert dance audiences. This in itself is another revolution in theater, because each time a new medium breaks the fourth wall of the proscenium stage and performer-to-performer and performer-audience improvisations occur, infinite possibilities emerge.

Since the inception of Rennie Harris Puremovement, Harris has created many acclaimed choreographic works; however, for the sake of space, I will illuminate only two: his solo *Endangered Species* (1994) and his evening-length epic work *Facing Mekka* (2003). Harris's tour-de-force solo, *Endangered Species*, which he himself performed, ostensibly established the artistic direction of hip-hop dance as a concert form. As Harris emphasized, "I'm not interested in entertaining anymore. I have personal issues to deal with, and I have to deal with how they affect me."[28] The centrality of Harris's personal issues as an impetus for his choreography became clear in *Endangered Species*, his first attempt at inserting his personal life as a black male, growing up in a Philadelphia ghetto into his developing artistic corpus. The work begins with a sole black male figure entering a smoke-filled center stage spotlight, using a slow mime-like electric boogie run that turns in the four sacred directions. It is as if he is both blessing the stage for the story that is about to unfold *and* simultaneously running for his life, all in slow motion. He wears black pants and a long-sleeved sweatshirt, while sporting dread locks that drape his anguished face. The entire effect transports one outside of physical time.

The solo male figure in *Endangered Species* becomes every (black) man with a particular family story to tell. The prerecorded textual soundscape becomes crucial to the statement that Harris makes as he breaks down his story: "Two of my brothers are hustlers, AKA gangsters," Harris's own recorded voice begins. The text of the soundtrack includes the violence against his lesbian sister by one of his brothers. "Maybe he thought he could beat it out of her." Harris reveals the violence from which he comes, from which many of us emerge onto life's stage: "It sounds crazy, but maybe we're all guilty . . . I didn't have a choice. I had to adapt . . . My identity was lost. It was taken from me. As a kid I wanted to be white. I guess that was because of that European concept." As the recorded text positions this black everyman into a specific story—a particular family in a particular urban ghetto—ambiguity, fear, and despair ripples through his body with the hip-hop popping dance techniques of the "snake" and "ticking," allowing us to literally see his anguish in the adeptly executed isolations of his muscles.

Cornel West has been particularly articulate about black male angst within the realities of urban ghetto life. In delineating the taxonomy of sociological urban problems of unemployment, poor housing, unequal education, gang violence, and the like, West examines the existential *personal* in relation to these sociological indices: "[P]eople, especially degraded and oppressed people, are hungry for identity, meaning, and self-worth."[29] This is exactly the story Harris's *Endangered Species* is attempting to tell: "My identity was lost. It was taken from me." The soundtrack continues: "If I'm for my race, does that make me a racist? I don't hate anyone, so I guess I'm not a racist. Racism! That's a funny word. Yet that is what America was built on." Racism and its insidious effects, particularly on the black male, is what he is trying to exorcize through the probing of his body and soul.

West gives us further reflection on the complexity surrounding the victimization process in black urban ghettos:

> Although black people have never been simply victims, wallowing in self-pity and begging for white giveaways, they have been—and are—victimized. Therefore, to call on black people to be agents makes sense only if we also examine the dynamics of this victimization

against which their agency will, in part, be exercised. What is particularly naïve and peculiarly vicious about the conservative behavioral outlook is that it tends to deny the lingering effect of black history—a history inseparable from though not reducible to victimization.[30]

Harris allows us an up-close and personal view of one black male victim in this US history, exercising his personal agency against it through dance theater. In *Endangered Species* form and content are made poignantly inseparable through Harris's well-crafted aesthetic.

Facing Mekka, Harris's 2003 mammoth evening-length theatrical undertaking, premiered at Pennsylvania's Lafayette College. This multimedia work followed the premiere and world tour in 2000 of his first evening-length work, the critically acclaimed dance-theater work *Rome and Jewels* as a reenvisioning of Shakespeare's classic *Romeo and Juliet*. A press kit explanation of *Facing Mekka* reads, "Interested in the human commonalities found in the marriage of movement and music from different cultures, Harris aims to show the common ground among people/cultures." The dance theater piece was unlike any of his previous works in its global multicultural ambitions. Musically, the herculean work is a vivid aural cacophony of hip-hop deejaying, prerecorded soundtrack, and East Indian *tabla* music. The video collage backdrop by digital artist Tobin Rothlein serves as a visual *bricolage* of world cultures and events, from brutal images of the civil rights movement and World War II to scenes of Islamic pilgrimages to the holy city of Mekka. In today's cosmopolitan global era, contemporary choreographers are engulfed in a fusion of cultures and styles that reflect the United States as a center of world culture. Harris's *Facing Mekka* is a vertical dive into to this cultural fusion through the human body and spirit via the African diaspora.

Although the work is based in hip-hop dance, b-boying, and popping, the robot movement styles are broken down into their essential movement phrasings and contrasted with traditional African dance as well as the Japanese butoh aesthetic. The internal muscular work of butoh connects with the skillful muscular isolations of popping, forming a parallel movement exploration to reveal deep cross-cultural connections through the body. As Suzanne Carbonneau analyzes, "for Harris, extending hip hop means expanding the possibilities for the form to achieve meaning, depth, and significance, rather than to simply increase its physical thrills and acrobatics."[31] In *Facing Mekka* one views the minute changes in movement from a West African stomp or jump with a graceful throw of the arm, to a sensual Caribbean hip movement, to a familiar skillful power move of a b-boy, to the slow, meditative gestures of his female dancers, all in the service of probing the potential of the human spirit. To confront the self, Harris uses a multicultural approach to forge potent human linkages that reveal universality itself. In the process he becomes a movement philosopher who articulately demonstrates hip-hop dance to be as poignant as any movement form in the exploration of the human condition. "Action is a superior mode of thought," and Harris conjures magic through the skilled construction of embodied beliefs that probe the meaning of human survival, and thereby adds a new dimension to the notion of postmodernism in dance.

CONCLUSIONS

Hip-hop theater and dance are powerful contemporary performance methods continuing the Africanist tradition of conjuring magic that expands what it means to be human. Hip-hop culture's commercialization and globalization does not only mean its cynical profitable manipulation by multinational "fat cats"; it also means the increased creativity of youths who use theater and dance to tell their personal stories, providing new fuel to art for social change. The best of today's hip-hop theater and dance companies use their mashup media to continue exposing extant inequalities and an insidious neoliberal corporatization that invades every aspect of our contemporary lives. Many of these hip-hop artists focus our attention on issues of systemic social inequities, as well as on the contradictions embedded in individualistic materialism as a result of the corporatization of hip-hop.

The conjured magic of hip-hop performing arts extends a long tradition of the Africanist performance continuum that creates and centralizes performative community. It simultaneously creates a "polycultural" focus, to borrow Hoch's term, which represents hip-hop's origins and internationalization. As Imani Perry analyzes, "taking issue with [hip-hop as black] essentialism should not occur at the risk of failing to understand politics or cultural frameworks."[32] Indeed, I have reinforced that "Hip-hop culture has grown out of both the black cultural lineage in the United States and the dialogue of African diaspora cultures in the Americas,"[33] and I would add the poor white youths who were/are a part of those sociocultural environments. White hip-hop theater artists like Danny Hoch emphasize hip-hop's multicultural origins while interrogating the construction of blackness and whiteness in the new hip-hop convolutions of America's historical racializing project. Hip-hop youth culture, like black culture in general, has always recognized skill (hence white rapper Eminem's undisputed reign in rap music). Having emphasized hip-hop's inclusiveness, Perry also warns us that along with the multiculturalism and hybridity of hip-hop it continues to "exist within black American political and cultural frameworks,"[34] which is so eloquently articulated by artists like Rennie Harris. And in today's shrinking globe with social media and instant communication, *perception* is central.

The social movement that I have explored in this chapter, which is composed of hip-hop theater and dance companies and festivals that either function within a community context or use their original community as their foundational launching pad, has influenced the commercial arena as well. For example Starz Entertainment, one of television's powerful cable conglomerates, is scheduled to premiere a new series called *Turf*, a drama about the birth of hip-hop from the violence of gang life in the 1970s Bronx. Starz is also developed an hour-long drama with 50 Cent as star and executive producer called *Power*. The grassroots movement that continues with community-oriented staged productions fuel the multimillion dollar potential of televised commercial hip-hop drama.

It can be stated with certainty that hip-hop theater has become a social movement. This movement is also reinforced by newly published texts that document the power of hip-hop theater, such as Daniel Banks's 2011 anthology *Say Word! Voices from Hip Hop Theater*. The hip-hop theater movement, ostensibly initiated at the beginning of the twenty-first century, challenged "the contemporary theater [that had] abdicated its role in addressing contemporary life, turning a blind eye to emerging generations of artists with new and different stories to tell and a new and different way of telling them."[35] Over the first decade of the new century mainstream theater has slowly infused hip-hop sensibilities into experimental parts of its annual seasons. The same has been true of dance: The commercial end of hip-hop dance, as it has become a staple in dance studios nationally and internationally, has crept into traditional choreography of major dance makers; while hip-hop dance companies, like Rennie Harris Puremovement, have wedged their way into international dance touring rosters. And when the two genres merge in various theatrical mash-ups, one experiences the revitalization of the word and the body as one, as the soul of *nommo*—as the essence of conjuring magic. But one can argue that mainstream theater and dance had no choice, for hip-hop culture that reflects today's youths, having wedged its way into every aspect of our contemporary lives, is here to stay.

NOTES

1. Sonica Diggs Colbert, *The African American Theatrical Body: Reception, Performance, and the Stage* (Cambridge, UK: Cambridge University Press, 2011), 11–12.

2. In Wilson's stage directions to *Joe Turner's Come and Gone*, the ritual kitchen scene is instructed to be a "juba," a secular tap dancing style that grew out of southern "patting juba," which repositioned rhythm in the feet and body slapping after the official banning of the African drum in the mid-eighteenth century. However, the ritual that must evolve in the scene is a sacred "ring shout" that historically precedes the juba, and as an American Christianized reinvention of a traditional counterclockwise spiritual African ring dance. I choreographed this scene for San Francisco's American Conservatory Theatre in the early 1990s. See, for example, Samuel A Floyd, *The Power of Black Music: Interpreting Its History from Africa to the United States* (New York: Oxford University Press, 1995), for a penetrating investigation of the American ring shout in the context of its African precursor.

3. *For Colored Girls* was originally performed on Broadway in 1976 at the Booth Theatre. The original Broadway Lady in Purple was performed by Rise Collins and the Lady in Blue by Laurie Carlos. The book was published in 1977 (New York: Bantam Books). I personally worked with Ntozake Shange as a dancer/choreographer during 1973–1975, when she was living in the San Francisco–Oakland Bay Area and developing the poems and the concept of the choreopoem in local poetry readings, all of which eventually became the famous play. She studied dance with me and acknowledges such in the Acknowledgments of the book.

4. Danny Hoch, "Toward a Hip-Hop Aesthetic: Manifesto for the Hip-Hop Arts Movement," September 14, 2005, Archived from the original October 2, 2011, http://www.dannyhoch.com/pdf/TowardsAHip-HopAesthetic.pdf (accessed December 22, 2012).

5. "About the Hip-Hop Theater Festival Online," http://www.hhtf.org/ (accessed December 22, 2012).

6. Danny Hoch, "Toward a Hip-Hop Aesthetic," 5.

7. Halifu Osumare, *The Africanist Aesthetic in Global Hip-Hop: Power Moves* (New York: Palgrave Macmillan, 2007), 30, paraphrasing Robert Farris Thompson, "Hip Hop 101," in *Droppin' Science: Critical Essays on Rap Music and Hip Hop Culture*, edited by William Eric Perkins (Philadelphia: Temple University Press, 1996), 214–15.

8. Hoch, "Toward a Hip-Hop Aesthetic," 2.

9. Ibid., 6.

10. For good explications of the GHHN see H. Samy Alim, Awad Ibrahim, and Alastair Pennycook, eds., *Global Linguistic Flows: Hip-Hop Cultures, Youth Identities and the Politics of Language* (New York: Routledge, 2009), and Halifu Osumare, *The Hiplife in Ghana: West African Indigenization of Hip-Hop* (New York: Palgrave Macmillan, 2012).

11. Daniel Banks, "Youth Leading Youth: Hip-Hop and Hiplife Theatre in Ghana and South Africa," in *Acting Together: Performance and the Creative Transformation of Conflict*, Vol. 2, edited by Cynthia E. Cohen, Roberto Gutiérrez Varea, and Polly O. Walker (Oakland, CA: New Village Press, 2011), 56.

12. See chapter 2, "Beat Streets in the Global Hood: Hip-Hop's Connective Marginalities," in Osumare, *The Africanist Aesthetic in Global Hip-Hop*, 61–104, for a complete investigation of my term "connective marginalities" as extant global inequalities that hip-hop illuminates.

13. Hoch, "Toward a Hip-Hop Aesthetic," 6.

14. Ibid.

15. "Danny Hoch: Hip Hop Theatre," Hemispheric Institute Encuentro, http://hemisphericinstitute.org/hemi/en/enc07-performances/item/950-enc07-danny-hoch (accessed December 23, 2012).

16. Zaira Arslan, "The Bard of Hip-Hop," *The Indian Express*, November 3, 2012, http://www.indianexpress.com/news/the-bard-of-hip-hop/1026072 (accessed December 24, 2012).

17. Bruce Weber, "Critics Notebook; Hip-Hop's Distinct Voice Is Reshaping Theater," *New York Times*, June 25, 2002.

18. Osumare, *The Africanist Aesthetic in Global Hip-Hop*, 31. See Brenda Dixon Gottschild, *Digging the Africanist Presence in American Performance: Dance and Other Contexts* (Westport, CT: Greenwood Press, 1996), Chapter 2: "The First Premises of an Africanist Aesthetic," for a more in depth study of *nommo* and the Africanist aesthetic in general.

19. Imani Perry, *Prophets of the Hood: Politics and Poetics in Hip Hop* (Durham, NC: Duke University Press, 2004), 107.

20. Sally Banes, "Breaking," in *Fresh Hip Hop Don't Stop*, edited by Nelson George (New York: Random House, 1985), 97. For one of the most complete theoretical texts on the language-like semantic features of dance, see Judith Lynne Hanna, *To Dance Is Human: A Theory of Nonverbal Communication*, 2nd ed. (Chicago: University of Chicago Press), 1987.

21. Katrina Hazzard-Donald, "Dance in Hip Hop Culture," in Perkins, ed., *Droppin' Science*, 225.

22. Ibid., 227.

23. Sally Sommer, "Prophets in Pumas: When Hip Hop Broke Out," *Dance Magazine*, July 2004, 31.

24. Rennie Harris, Interview by author. Ann Arbor, Michigan, January 11, 2002.

25. Ibid.

26. Rennie Harris, Interview by author. Tallahassee, Florida, March 4, 2005.

27. Robert Farris Thompson first explicated specific aesthetic principles of African-based performance in his "ten canons of fine" form and his "aesthetic of the cool" in *African Art in Motion* (1974).

28. Rennie Harris, "Dance and the Community," (Plenary Session), Congress on Research in Dance Annual Conference, Tallahassee, FL, March 4, 2005.

29. Cornel West, "Nihilism in Black America," *Black Popular Culture*, edited by Gina Dent (Seattle: Bay Press, 1992, 1983), 38.
30. Ibid., 39.
31. Suzanne Carbonneau, "Facing Out, Facing In: Facing Mekka," http://www/puremoevment.net/rhpub.html (accessed May 3, 2004 and currently unavailable).
32. Perry, *Prophets of the Hood*, 10.
33. Osumare, *The Africanist Aesthetic in Global Hip-Hop*, 24.
34. Perry, *Prophets of the Hood*, 10.
35. Weber, "Critics Notebook," 1.

BIBLIOGRAPHY

Alim, H. Samy, Awad Ibrahim, and Alastair Pennycook, eds. *Global Linguistic Flows: Hip-Hop Cultures, Youth Identities and the Politics of Language*. New York: Routledge, 2009.

Arslan, Zaira. "The Bard of Hip-Hop." *The Indian Express*. Accessed November 3, 2012. http://www.indianexpress.com/news/the-bard-of-hip-hop/1026072.

Banes, Sally. "Breaking." In *Fresh Hip Hop Don't Stop*, edited by Nelson George. New York: Random House, 1985.

Banks, Daniel, ed. *Say Word! Voices from Hip Hop Theater*. Ann Arbor: University of Michigan Press, 2011.

———. "Youth Leading Youth: Hip-Hop and Hiplife Theatre in Ghana and South Africa." In *Acting Together: Performance and the Creative Transformation of Conflict*, Vol. 2, edited by Cynthia E. Cohen, Roberto Gutiérrez Varea, and Polly O. Walker, 43–72. Oakland, CA: New Village Press, 2011.

Carbonneau, Suzanne. "Facing Out, Facing In: Facing Mekka." Accessed May 3, 2004. http://www/puremovement.net/rhpub.html.

Colbert, Sonica Diggs. *The African American Theatrical Body: Reception, Performance, and the Stage*. Cambridge, UK: Cambridge University Press, 2011.

Floyd, Samuel A. *The Power of Black Music: Interpreting Its History from Africa to the United States*. New York: Oxford University Press, 1995.

Hanna, Judith Lynne. *To Dance Is Human: A Theory of Nonverbal Communication*. 2nd ed. Chicago: University of Chicago Press, 1987.

Harris, Rennie. "Dance and the Community" (Plenary Session). Congress on Research in Dance Annual Conference, Tallahassee, FL, March 4, 2005.

Hazzard-Donald, Katrina. "Dance in Hip Hop Culture." In *Droppin' Science: Critical Essays on Rap Music and Hip Hop Culture*, edited by William Eric Perkins, 220–37. Philadelphia: Temple University Press, 1996.

Hoch, Danny. "Toward a Hip-Hop Aesthetic: Manifesto for the Hip-Hop Arts Movement." Accessed September 14, 2005. http://www.dannyhoch.com/pdf/TowardsAHip-HopAesthetic.pdf.

Osumare, Halifu. *The Africanist Aesthetic in Global Hip-Hop: Power Moves*. New York: Palgrave Macmillan, 2007.

———. *The Hiplife in Ghana: West African Indigenization of Hip-Hop*. New York: Palgrave Macmillan, 2012.

Perry, Imani. *Prophets of the Hood: Politics and Poetics in Hip Hop*. Durham, NC: Duke University Press, 2004.

Shange, Notzake. *For Colored Girls Who Have Considered Suicide When the Rainbow Is Enuf: A Choreopoem*. New York: Bantam Book, 1977.

Sommer, Sally. "Prophets in Pumas: When Hip Hop Broke Out." *Dance Magazine*, July 2004, 31–32.

Thompson, Robert Farris. *African Art in Motion*. Los Angeles, CA: University of California, Press, 1974.

———. "Hip Hop 101." In *Droppin' Science: Critical Essays on Rap Music and Hip Hop Culture*, edited by William Eric Perkins, 211–19. Philadelphia: Temple University Press, 1996.

Weber, Bruce. "Critics Notebook; Hip-Hop's Distinct Voice Is Reshaping Theater." *New York Times*, June 25, 2002.

West, Cornel. "Nihilism in Black America." In *Black Popular Culture*, edited by Gina Dent, 37–47. Seattle: Bay Press, 1992.

CHAPTER 30

NOTORIOUS JEFFREY HUDSON

The 'Court Wonder' of the Caroline Masques (1626–1640)

THOMAS POSTLEWAIT

INTRODUCTION

ON February 22, 1631,[1] Jeffrey Hudson performed in *Chloridia*, a court masque sponsored by Queen Henrietta Maria, who played the role of Chloris, the goddess of the flowers. Written by Ben Jonson and designed by Inigo Jones, the masque was staged at the Banqueting House in Whitehall (also designed by Jones). According to Jonson's stage directions, Hudson paraded forward during the antimasque "richly apparelled, as a PRINCE of HELL, attended by six INFERNAL SPIRITS." He "first danceth alone," and then the infernal Spirits danced with him.[2] His performance, which captured the comic, adversarial spirit of the antimasque, charmed the court audience. And most importantly it pleased the Queen, who was responsible for his participation in this and several other masques during the reign of Charles I.

So who was Jeffrey (or Geoffrey) Hudson?[3] Not surprisingly, many of the documents on Hudson pertain to his activities and adventures beyond the stage. Those adventures, often dangerous, involved a mission to France for the Queen, his capture and subsequent release by Flemish pirates in the English Channel, military battle during the Civil War, a daring escape from England with the Queen in 1644, a deadly duel on horseback in France that resulted in his forced separation from the exiled Queen, his capture by Barbary Corsairs, slavery in north Africa for several years, his subsequent return to England during the Restoration, his possible involvement in the Popish plot during the reign of Charles II, and his imprisonment for suspected treason. These events, often harrowing, would seem to overshadow Hudson's fifteen years as a performer, yet his court life served as the initial catalyst for these other events. It is crucial, therefore, to understand how and why these often life-threatening adventures are linked to the court milieu in which he emerged and flourished as a dancer, despite his humble origins.

Between 1626 and 1640 Hudson performed regularly in the court masques, entertaining the exclusive court spectators, including ambassadors from Spain, France, Venice, Morocco, and the Savoy. Several playwrights, including Jonson, Aurelian Townshend, and William Davenant, wrote roles for him in order to feature his specific skills as a dancer and comic character. Davenant also wrote a mock-epic poem, *Jeffereidos; or, the Captivitie of Jefferey* (1630), about Hudson and the Channel pirates. His performances were distinguished by the visual codes of his costumes, his antic disposition, and the burlesque dance routines. Despite the limitations of the short antimasque sketches, he became one of the most famous performers in the Caroline masques.

Although Hudson's roles were usually confined within the antimasques, he sometimes participated in scenes with the aristocratic and royal performers. For example, in his first court role in 1626 at Somerset House, the Queen's residence, he took part in a farcical scene with three members of the Privy Council, including the Duke of Buckingham. And in his last role at Whitehall in 1640 he initially performed a dance in the antimasque, then joined the King and Queen at center stage for the concluding spectacle. This final scene, which proved to be "the swan song of the Caroline court,"[4] offers a significant clue to Hudson's unique place in the calibrated social world of the court.

What, then, do we know about Hudson? The documentation on his performances is piecemeal, but we can identify a number of his roles, costumes, characters, and dramatic actions. Besides the texts for the masques, which identify Hudson in several cases, the sources also indicate that he was tutored by Barthélemy de Montagut, who served as the dancing master for not only Buckingham but also the Queen and King. Montagut trained Hudson in many of the popular dances of the era.[5]

In addition, a substantial visual record of drawings, engravings, and paintings exists on Hudson, who was portrayed by John Droeshout, Daniel Mytens, George Glover, and Anthony Van Dyck. Two, perhaps three, of Inigo Jones's drawings represent Hudson in a masque costume. In two paintings, one by Mytens and one partially credited to him, Hudson is a secondary figure in portraits that feature the King and Queen. Mytens also painted a full-length portrait of Hudson in 1630 that was commissioned for Charles I. Then in 1633 Van Dyck painted an impressive portrait of the Queen and Hudson. Although these paintings, unlike Jones's drawings, do not portray Hudson in stage costume, they are still suggestive of the social order and values that the masques reproduced on stage. The clothes, poses, and spatial arrangements of people in these portraits display some of the same visual codes of social identity and rank that operated in the masques.

Hudson is portrayed more often than any other performer from the Elizabethan, Jacobean, and Caroline eras. Indeed, we have close to a dozen depictions of him. By contrast, only about two dozen images in total have survived of all other players from the 1580s to the 1640s. Scholars have identified portraits of William Kemp, Edward Alleyn, Richard Tarlton, John Lowin, Robert Armin, Richard Perkins, and Thomas Greene.[6] In addition, we apparently have single representations of Richard Burbage, Nathan Field, John Green, Will Sly, and Tom Bonds, though there is disagreement on the identity of some of these portraits.[7] In most cases we have only one image of each of these players.

Given the scope of extant sources, both verbal and visual, on Hudson, he should be a familiar figure in our scholarship on early modern performers. And yet he has been ignored by almost all theater and dance scholars. For example, in the seven volumes of *The Jacobean and Caroline Stage*, which covers all aspects of London theater from 1603 to 1660, G. E.

Bentley catalogs in great detail the documentary evidence on several hundred performers.[8] He identifies the most obscure players, including those on the provincial circuits. Even a Spanish player, John Nararro, receives a separate entry on the basis of a single record of payment in 1635. And stretching his procedures beyond expectation, Bentley provides a place for Thomas Barnes, who "was not a player at all, but a carpenter."[9] But Hudson does not receive an entry. He does get mentioned, however, in a brief, tangential aside in the section on "Plays and Playwrights." Here, as part of the description of Jonson's *Chloridia*, Bentley notes that "the notorious Geoffrey Hudson" appeared in the antimasque.[10] Why does a "notorious" performer not warrant an entry in the "Players" section?

Since the appearance of Bentley's seven volumes (1941–1968), well over a dozen significant books on court performances have been published by historians who specialize in drama, theater, dance, or music. The scholarship is quite commendable, and often excellent; but Hudson remains out of sight, even though his name appears in the published texts of the masques by Jonson and Davenant. A few scholars, echoing Bentley, mention Hudson's entry in *Chloridia*.[11] Two scholars note in passing the mock-epic poem by Davenant.[12] And the van Dyke painting receives attention from a few scholars.[13] But basically scholars have nothing to say about Hudson's performances. Why? Why have we compiled information on hundreds of other performers, yet ignored Hudson?[14] This question is at the heart of my study.

If no documentation existed on Hudson, his absence from our theater and dance scholarship would be understandable. But he was famous—or at least "notorious"—in his own time. Both the poet John Taylor and the dramatist Thomas Heywood wrote tributes to Hudson.[15] During the Restoration two short biographical portraits of Hudson were published, one by Thomas Fuller, the other, after Hudson's death, by James Wright.[16] Wright's profile, which was published in 1684, appeared soon after Hudson's death in London. A century later, Horace Walpole offered a biographical sketch on Hudson in his account of Daniel Mytens's paintings. From Walpole's perspective Hudson was "a considerable part of the entertainment of the court."[17] Then in the nineteenth century Hudson served as a character in Sir Walter Scott's historical novel, *Peveril of the Peak* (1822).[18] More recently, Hudson received an entry in both the *Dictionary of National Biography* (1885–1901) and the revised *Oxford Dictionary of National Biography* (2004).[19] At least anecdotally, Hudson has warranted attention across several centuries.

There are, however, some anomalies about Hudson that contribute to our disregard. He was not a professional player but instead an "amateur" who performed in the masques for fifteen years. Also, he began his career as a child actor. No doubt these factors have contributed to his invisibility in our scholarship. There is, however, another factor that has been paramount. Beyond the anomalies, we have ignored Hudson for a definitive reason, and it has nothing to do with his invisibility or our blindness.

The fundamental issue is not Hudson's invisibility, but the specific nature of his visibility. A sad irony has shaped our scholarly perception of Hudson. We have turned away from him because we can see and identify him without difficulty. But *what* we see has been determined by *how* we see, and that *how* reveals a striking case of willful avoidance or dismissal. A bias cuts across and directs our angle of perception. For most of us the first—and often the only—relevant thing about Hudson was his physical size. Jeffrey Hudson was a dwarf.[20]

For this reason, more than any other factor, Hudson lacks a place in our histories of the Caroline masque. He fits, all too neatly, within the confining—and often dismissive—category of "the Queen's dwarf." Nothing more needs to be said. This categorical anomaly, far more than the other factors, has been the determining cause in our scholarly disregard. Of course, we reject the idea that we have been prejudicial in our scholarship.[21] And yet, despite our modern understanding, our perception of "the Queen's dwarf" reveals a striking case of tendentiousness, if not outright bias. Without intending to, we have still displaced Hudson to the far margins of our scholarly inquiry.

In order to rectify at least some part of our historical disregard, I want to take the measure of Jeffrey Hudson and his place in the Caroline masques. No doubt the designation of "the Queen's dwarf" has hindered our scholarship; but instead of trying to evade or dance around the designation, I want to embrace it because the relationship between the Queen and Hudson was central to Hudson's accomplishments.

Hudson's participation in the court society was far more complex than the identification of "the Queen's dwarf" usually implies. For the Queen, he was a close and dear companion for two decades. Their mutual regard and friendship contributed directly to Hudson's performances in the masques. Because of her support he became an accomplished dancer and comic performer. My aim, therefore, is to claim a place for Hudson in theater and dance history and to challenge the historical predilections (if not prejudgments) that have confined Hudson within the "embodied" categories of dwarf, freak, amateur, and child performer. I do not wish to claim that Hudson was a major comic actor of the era, but I do want to insist that he made unique contributions to the aims and methods of the Caroline masques. Convivial, witty, and talented, he was a popular and vital performer. I therefore invite us to consider not only the accomplishments of Jeffrey Hudson but also the historiographical aspects of this case, which reveals some basic problems with how we designate and construct the evidential record in theater and dance history. Although there are some gaps in the documentary record on Hudson, especially after he and the Queen fled England together in 1644 during the Civil War, it is possible to provide a basic assessment of his performances and activities during the reign of Charles I (1625–1649).[22]

JEFFREY HUDSON: THE RECORD

Jeffrey Hudson was born on June 14, 1619, at Oakham, Rutland. He was not deformed; instead, he was a wholly proportional dwarf.[23] His mother, Lucy Royce, and father, John Hudson, were both of normal stature, as were the rest of their children. John Hudson, a butcher, served as the overseer of bulls at Burley on the Hill, the country estate of the Duke of Buckingham. In the autumn of 1626 the Duchess, Katherine Villiers, suggested to the parents of young Jeffrey that he could have a place at Burley, with fine clothes and servants to care for him. Whatever their preferences, the parents acceded to the offer. Young Jeffrey—all eighteen inches of him—moved into the Burley estate. A few weeks later the Duke, who was the most powerful man in Britain, excepting the King, conceived his own plan for Hudson, a plan tied to a grand entertainment he was preparing. Within days of having acquired young Jeffrey, Buckingham was rehearsing him for a royal debut.

On November 5, 1626, the plan became clear when Buckingham presented a banquet and masque at York House, his palatial London residence. The guests of honor were Charles I, the Queen, and the ambassadors from France and Venice. This banquet was part of Buckingham's campaign to regain the good will of the Queen, whose marriage to Charles had undergone a series of crises during its first year. Quite appropriately, the Queen held Buckingham responsible for several of the problems that had occurred since she left Paris the previous year. The sixteen-year-old Queen had learned a hard lesson: The Duke guided Charles in both public and private affairs.

The marriage of Henrietta Maria to Charles had taken place in Paris on May 1, 1625, in a proxy ceremony held at the west door of the cathedral of Notre Dame.[24] Two weeks later, Buckingham arrived in Paris to escort the new Queen and her several hundred retainers to Dover, where she first met Charles on June 12. Upon reaching London, Henrietta Maria and her household staff, which included over two dozen Catholic priests, took up residence at Somerset House.[25] But a year later, in accord with the King's wishes, Buckingham removed most of the Queen's French retinue from Somerset House, including many of the Catholic priests. They were sent back to France.[26] The decision enraged Henrietta Maria, who, as a French-speaking Catholic in a Protestant country, felt isolated and mistreated. Despite her tantrums and hunger strike, neither the King nor Buckingham relented.[27]

Three months later the Duke offered his grand entertainment at York House. By honoring the King and Queen he hoped to overcome the months of discord. He knew that she loved theater, for she had already staged and acted in a French pastoral, Sieur de Racan's *Les Bergeries, or L'Arténice,* which was performed at Somerset House in February 1626. For this performance, which she and her French ladies had rehearsed for several months, the Queen had asked Inigo Jones to build a proscenium stage, with perspective scenery in the French style.[28] With this production in mind, Buckingham decided to stage an entertainment that would appeal to the Queen and her French heritage.

The Duke's entertainment, entitled *The Discords of Christianity,* featured an elaborate scenic pageant. A key scene represented the sea that divided England from France. Above the sea, "sitting on a throne among the gods," was the lifelike appearance of Marie de Medici, the mother of Henrietta Maria.[29] The "French queen mother" beckoned the royalty of England and France (as well as the Duke and Duchess of Savoy and the Elector and Electress of Palatine) to set aside their political and religious differences. In her appeal, she urged them to put "an end to the discords of Christiandom."[30] From Buckingham's perspective, the masque, besides making a public petition to the national leaders to unite against Spain, expressed a private entreaty to Henrietta Maria to resolve her disagreements with the King and his government.

This personal message, which appealed to the emotional ties between mother and daughter, was complemented by the Duke's special plan for Jeffrey Hudson. Buckingham sought to appeal to the young Queen's kindhearted feelings. During the evening's festivities, which included a grand banquet, a very large "bulwark pie" was carried to the table of the King and Queen who were seated on a raised dais. Hidden inside the pie was young Jeffrey, who was seven years old and less than twenty inches in height. Dressed in a military costume of body armor, Little Jeffrey emerged out of the pie as the crust was rolled back. Stepping onto the table, he proceeded to parade in a spirited march that apparently incorporated dance steps taught him by Barthélemy de Montagut, the dance master for Buckingham and choreographer for the evening's masque.[31] The Queen was captivated by the cute little soldier. Taking note of the Queen's enjoyment, Buckingham stepped forward as a man of goodwill and offered Hudson to her as a gift.[32] When Henrietta Maria accepted the gift, the Duke's stratagem was a complete success; his power over the Queen and King had reached its zenith.

After the masque and banquet had concluded in the early morning hours, young Jeffrey left York House hand in hand with the Queen. They exited through the Duke's gardens and gate to the river dock. Mounting the Royal Barge, they then sailed together down the Thames to Somerset House, where Hudson was to become not just a fascinating new member of the Queen's reduced staff but one of her closest companions for the next two decades.[33] (The fate of Buckingham was far less promising; less than two years later, on August 23, 1628, he would be murdered by a deranged army officer.)

Hudson's arrival at Somerset House changed his life. He was provided with the clothes and education of a gentleman.[34] The Court granted him a monthly allowance and also allotted to him a French servant, Jerome Gregoire, who attended to Hudson for close to two decades.[35] Hudson learned French, which facilitated his close relationship with the Queen (who took several years to learn English), and he participated regularly in the Catholic services that the Queen maintained throughout her reign. Hudson was taught court etiquette, including the manly skills of fencing, shooting, riding a pony, and dancing. All of these talents would contribute to his many court activities. But his skill with a pistol and the religious education would have dire consequences later in Hudson's life.

Two weeks after his move to Somerset House, Hudson performed a comic role in a masque entitled *Gargantua and Gargamella*.[36] Presented on November 16, 1626, in celebration of the Queen's birthday,[37] the production also honored the French ambassador François de Bassompierre. Sponsored by the Queen, and supported as well by Buckingham, the masque, which is lost, was loosely derived from Rabelais's *Gargantua and Pantagruel*.[38] In preparation for the performance, Sir John Tunstall and six assistants worked for eighteen days, making ready the Presence Chamber and other rooms in Somerset House.[39] To muffle the sound of the dancers, green cotton cloth was spread and tacked across the dance floor and the elevated stage.[40]

The masque featured a scene in which the three tutors attempt to educate the unlearned Gargantua. Three members of the Privy Council played the tutors: Buckingham, the Earl of Holland, and Sir George Goring. In the role of a fencing master, the Duke was able to display his fencing and dance skills, for as Barbara Ravelhofer reports he "knew a multiplicity of dance styles, among them the latest French and Spanish fashions."[41] The role of Gargantua was played by William Evans, the 7', 6" giant who served as the "Porter of the backstairs" at Somerset House. At one point in the lesson, as Buckingham danced about, flashing his foil at the frustrated Gargantua, Evans reached into a large pocket of his costume and drew out Jeffery Hudson.[42] Hudson and Evans, dwarf and giant, then quickly transformed the fencing lesson into farcical combat, with Hudson likely using his toy sword to fence with the Duke. The contrast in size between Evans and Hudson evoked the popular stories of the adventures of Gargantua, the giant, and Tom Thumb, the midget. Indeed, the text and tone for the masque scene may well have been influenced by Richard Johnson's *History of Tom Thumb*, which was published in London in 1621. In this book, Johnson presented a series of contests between the slow-witted giant and the clever midget.[43]

The Venetian ambassador praised the Duke's dancing, which he termed "very elegant."[44] But others in attendance disapproved of members of the government participating in a farcical scene. One court observer complained about Buckingham's role as a fencing tutor: "His grace took a shape ... which many thought too histrionical to become him."[45] Unlike most masques that usually kept the noble and royal participants separated from the comic characters of the antimasque episodes, *Gargantua and Gargamella* collapsed together the two worlds, to the discomfort apparently of some observers.

Whatever the mixed judgments on the Duke, the performances of Hudson and Evans pleased the Queen and many others. Over the following decades anecdotes about Hudson being pulled out of Evans's pocket spread widely. Even two centuries later the farcical episode was served up in a prison scene in Sir Walter Scott's novel *Peveril of the Peak* (1822). At one point the prison turnkey reminds the character of "Sir" Geoffrey Hudson that "Master Evans . . . carried you about in his pocket, as all the world has heard tell."[46] This episode was one of many that contributed to the "notorious" reputation of Jeffrey Hudson.

Within court society Jeffrey quickly attained his unique status as the Queen's dwarf. He became a close companion, accompanying her on various occasions to London events. In 1627, for example, they visited Whitehall for a bullbaiting entertainment which was possibly arranged by Buckingham and carried out by Hudson's father, the keeper of bulls. In the same year, as a surviving letter reveals, Hudson had a dangerous adventure at Somerset House: "Little Geffry, the Queen's dwarfe fell last day out of the window . . . The Queene took it soe heavily that she attyred not her selfe that day."[47] The social engagements for the day were all canceled as the Queen worried over the injury to her young charge.

Henrietta Maria, who was only ten years older than Hudson, quickly became attached to him. Though he could not replace the many French servants who had been sent back to France, Hudson proved to be a compensatory replacement. The young Queen and the precocious Jeffrey bonded emotionally. In part this bond depended on a shared experience. Both the Queen and Hudson had been forced from their original homes at a young age; in this they were mere tokens of transfer in the agendas of powerful people. Initially, in the late 1620s they were outsiders in the world of the English court. In 1629, after the birth and early death of the Queen's first child, Hudson, wearing his new black mourning suit, stayed with her in Tunbridge Wells during her convalescence. In some ways, he served as both a companion and surrogate child for the Queen during the four years before the birth of her son Charles in 1630. And even after the Queen had other children, and her marriage blossomed into a strong love affair, Hudson remained a constant companion of the Queen during the 1630s and early 1640s.

Throughout this period Hudson participated in the daily court life, often serving in his capacity as an official member of the Queen's retinue. In 1630, for instance, he was selected to be a member of a royal delegation to France. Their primary task was to bring back for the Queen a midwife, nurses, and ten Capuchin friars. Also in the delegation was the French dance master Jacques Cordier dit Bocan (c. 1580–1653), with whom Hudson trained during this period. Although the French court had its own dwarves, Hudson was displayed in the Paris court and salons, entertaining everyone with his masterful dance skills. Bocan was already a dance celebrity in Paris; Hudson, in his own capacity as a performer, became one, receiving gifts from Marie de Medici and ladies of the court.[48] The purpose of placing him in the royal delegation proved to be a great success.

Upon the return to England the ship, which sailed from Calais on March 18, was overtaken by Flemish pirates from Dunkirk. The master of the English ship, four women including the French midwife Madame Peronne, and Hudson were taken as prisoners, but Bocan and the Capuchin friars were released, apparently less valuable than a midwife and a dwarf. When Henrietta Maria was informed, she became distraught over the fate of Hudson and the midwife. A court observer noted that the abduction caused the Queen and her party to be "more upset . . . than if they had lost a fleet."[49] A week after the abduction, however, the Governor of Calais successfully negotiated the release of the prisoners, though the pirates kept the treasures of the delegation, especially the jewels worth £2500 that Marie de Medici had sent to her daughter by way of Hudson. With the crisis resolved, the full delegation, including Hudson and the midwife, sailed safely for England.[50] Two months later, in May 1630, Madame Peronne successfully performed the delivery of the Queen's first son (the future Charles II).

Hudson's adventures at sea and his safe return provided the occasion for two artistic representations of him, one a painting, the other a poem. A month after the birth of Charles the queen commissioned Daniel Mytens to paint a portrait of Hudson. A warrant on June 24, 1630, authorized the payment of £40 to the painter, a considerable sum. In this painting, which is 84 by 59 inches, young Jeffrey is the exclusive figure, staring ahead confidently, as if inviting the future. The painting, which today hangs in Hampton Court, was sent to St. James's Palace as a gift for the King.[51]

A less ennobling representation of Hudson appeared in Davenant's mock-epic poem, *Jeffereidos; or, The Captivitie of Jeffrey*, which offers a satire of Hudson's adventures with the pirates. Written and published quickly in 1630, the poem in rhyming couplets represents "puissant Jeff'ry" as "a second Tamberlaine" (Canto I 38, 43). In the culminating scene of the poem, "Jeff'ry the bold" (II 67) draws his sword—by now a familiar emblem of Hudson—for battle with a barnyard turkey. He sheds the turkey's feathers by the "fury of the blow" (II 76). But when the turkey assaults him, he faints, and has to be rescued by the midwife.[52] The poem sold well that summer and autumn, enhancing Hudson's notoriety.

A few months later Hudson played the role of the "Prince of Hell" in *Chloridia: Rites to Chloris and Her Nymphs*. The dance master Barthélemy de Montagut was probably the choreographer, though he was not named on the title page, as were Ben Jonson and Inigo Jones.[53] The masque was staged on February 22, 1631, in the Banqueting Hall at Whitehall. The Queen played the role of Cloris, the goddess of spring, and the ladies of the court played the fourteen nymphs.[54] As he had done five years earlier for the Queen's French pastoral *Les Bergeries, or L'Arténice*, Jones created a proscenium stage, with a drawn curtain and movable scenery.[55] Thanks to the Queen's insistence and Jones's substantial talents, French staging methods were finding their way into the English theater.

The masque begins in a pastoral setting: "The curtain being drawn up, the scene is discovered, consisting of pleasant hills planted with young trees, and all the lower banks adorned with flowers" (ll. 15–16).[56] After the spectators "had enough fed their eyes with the delights of the scene" (21), a cloud parts to reveal the character of Zephyrus, "a plump boy" (22), who calls forth in the first song the characters of Spring and Fountains. The setting is idyllic, but trouble has developed because Cupid is offended that the gods have excluded him from their guild. Spring announces the crisis:

> Whereat the boy, in fury fell,
> With all his speed is gone to hell,
> There to excite and stir up Jealousy,
> To make a party 'gainst the gods,
> And set heaven, earth, and hell at odds—(82–86)

The character named Fountains fears that Cupid will "raise a chaos of calamity" (87). Then, after a dance by the fourteen nymphs, an abrupt scene change occurs as the underground opens for the antimasque in hell.

Hudson's arrival on stage is announced during the third entry of the antimasque: "The Queen's Dwarf, richly apparelled, as a PRINCE of HELL attended by six INFERNAL SPIRITS. After his solo dance, the spirits join him, "all expressing their joy, for Cupid's coming among them" (131–33). Hudson was arrayed in a costume of white, crimson, and green that Jones had designed.[57] Although Jonson does not identify the types of dances that were presented in this scene, Hudson's role allowed him sufficient opportunity for the burlesque spirit of the antimasque, including the comic possibility of reproducing some of the dance steps, gestures, and postures that the court ladies presented in their roles as nymphs. He was well trained by Montagut, Jacques Cordier dit Bocan, and other French dance masters, such as Jehan de la Motte, who were employed by Henrietta Maria.[58] Hudson participated in a court society that was dedicated to learning various styles of dance, including the coranto, the farandole, the galliard, the pavane, the round, and the sarabande. These dances, emblematic of what Barbara Ravelhofer calls the "proto-*danse noble* aesthetics,"[59] were regular features of the Caroline masques. They were performed by the noble performers, then burlesqued on occasion by the antimasque performers. Both the masque proper and the antimasque required accomplished dancers.

Besides the role of the Prince of Hell, Hudson may also have taken on the major role of Postilion, the "DWARF-POST from hell" (92), whose entry launches the antimasque. Although Jonson did not identify the performer of this role, Karen Britland states confidently that "Henrietta Maria's servant . . . performed a large and histrionic part in *Chloridia* as a Dwarfe-Post from Hell."[60] To support this assertion, Britland observes that Hudson "was then about twelve years old and was evidently thought capable of delivering a long and complicated prose speech."[61] It is tempting to assign this additional role to Hudson, but can this hypothesis be supported?[62]

The most apparent evidence, of course, is the basic fact that the role of the Dwarf-Post requires a dwarf. There were other dwarves at court, and a few of them may have occasionally participated in minor roles in court entertainments, but Hudson is the only one who acted consistently. And he is the only dwarf identified as a performer.[63] But who could have assigned this additional role to him? The two most likely people were the Queen and Inigo Jones. Either separately or working together the two of them were capable of making the decision. Because *Chloridia* was sponsored and supervised by the Queen, she could have made a unilateral decision. Ever since her arrival at court, Henrietta Maria had asserted full control over the productions that she sponsored, organized, and performed in. She was quite capable and determined in her responsibilities. Indeed, the evidence for the productions illustrates her total commitment to details large and small—from casting to final approval on the style and color of the costumes.

As for Jones, he served as the primary designer and supervisor of the masque spectacles. In consultation with the Queen, he made decisions on almost all aspects of the productions. Aware of Jeffrey's recent adventure with the North Sea pirates, which Davenant's poem had made notorious, Jones may have decided that the time was right to give Hudson the extra role. By 1631, Hudson was much more than a mere novelty item for court entertainment. Britland is surely correct that he was "evidently . . . capable of delivering" the Dwarf-Post role.

Unfortunately, we lack direct evidence for these conjectures. There is, however, a tempting piece of circumstantial evidence provided by Inigo Jones: his costume drawing of the Dwarf-Post. Did he have Hudson in mind when he made this drawing? It seems to portray Hudson, right down to his ever-present sword, but we need to keep in mind that Jones copied the figure of the dwarf from a drawing by Jacques Callot that appears in his *Varie Figure Gobbi di Iacopo Callot* (1616).[64] Jones reproduces the details of the face, body, hat, costume, and sword in Callot's drawing. Consequently, even if the drawing represents the hat and costume that the performer of the Dwarf-Post wore, we cannot claim that this image represents Hudson—at least not exclusively. There are, though, two other features of the drawing that Jones did not derived from Callot. He also provides the image of the "curtal" (a horse with a docked tail) that the Dwarf-Post rides. Jonson calls for "a curtal, with cloven feet" (93), yet Jones, ignoring the proper traits of a horse, replaces the cloven feet with large claw feet. Likewise, in a separate costume drawing he gave claw feet to the two lackeys who attend the Dwarf-Post in the scene.[65] Why claw feet, which are quite inappropriate? We cannot prove that Jones had Hudson in mind when he made these drawings. But if the dwarf performer wore claw feet, as the drawing implies, the image may well have evoked for spectators Hudson's infamous battle with the turkey in Davenant's poem (published a few months earlier). Dancing in large claw feet, Postilion and his lackeys must have been comic figures, like Jeffrey in the poem.

Of course, the drawing does not prove that Hudson portrayed the Dwarf-Post, even though the role seems to be tailor-made for him. It opens with the entry of Postilion (i.e., the rider of the left or sinister horse),[66] who is "riding on a curtal" and accompanied by "two lackeys" (92–3). The lackeys dance, then Postilion, alights from his curtal. "Hold my stirrup, my one lackey; and look to my curtal, the other. Walk him well, sirrah, while I expatiate myself here in the report of my office" (95–96). The giant William Evans possibly played the role of one of the lackeys. If so, a burlesque scene between Hudson and Evans would have had popular appeal, especially for those court people who recalled their performances in *Gargangua and Gargamella*. The giant and the midget were already yoked as comic figures.

Early in his news report Postilion makes reference to the responsibility of the gate keeper at the Banquet Hall, a duty Evans performed on several occasions between 1626 and the early 1630s.[67] A turnstile controlled the entry of spectators into the masque. As the imposing guard who blocked or "held ope the passage" (119), Evans admitted only those people who were invited and had tickets. With such diligence in mind, Postilion delivers a lament:

> Had hell-gates been kept with half that strictness as the entry here has been tonight, Pluto would have had but a cold court and Proserpine a thin presence, though both have a vast territory. We had such a stir to get in, I and my curtal and my two lackeys all ventured through the eye of a Spanish needle, we had never come in else, and that was by the favour of one of the guard who . . . held ope the passage" (113–19).

If Evans was "one of the guard" (118) that evening, the joke would have been obvious to everyone present; and if he was also on stage, spectators would appreciate Postilion's extended complaint (which makes most sense if Jonson wrote the passage with Evans in mind).

In his speech, which serves as a news report from Hell, Postilion announces that the realm of Pluto and Proserpine offers "perpetual holiday" for its denizens, including Ixion, who "is loosed from his wheel and turned dancer" (101, 104–5). Ixion "does nothing but cut caprioles, fetch friscals, and leads lavoltas with the Lamiae" (105–6). Though spectators apparently had to imagine the Lamiae [vampires] who dance lavoltas with Ixion, Postilion likely demonstrated some of the dance steps of caprioles as he delivered his lines. The speech then concludes with more dancing: "For joy of which I will return to myself, mount my bidet [pony] in a dance, and curvet [frisk about] upon my curtal" (123–24).

These various clues and conjectures raise the possibility that Hudson played both roles. If so, a quick change of costume would have been required during scene two, which featured a dance by Cupid, Jealousy, Disdain, Fear, and Dissimulation. But if Hudson took on both roles, why did Jonson identify the "Queen's dwarf" for scene three, but not for the opening scene one? Perhaps the additional assignment was made after Jonson wrote the text; perhaps even as late as the rehearsal period. But neither the quarto edition of *Chloridia* (1631), published at the time of the production, nor the folio (1640) identifies the player of the Dwarf-Post. The naming of the Queen's dwarf appears only in scene three. So we are left with uncertainty. Even if we are inclined to credit the internal evidence and circumstantial argument, the proposition that Hudson portrayed Postilion remains a matter of *possibility*, not *probability*. The conjecture cannot be proved or disproved without some solid evidence.[68]

Whatever the extent of Hudson's involvement in *Chloridia*, he obviously had obtained a regular place in the court masques. And he continued to perform throughout the 1630s, at court and perhaps elsewhere. For example, when the King and Queen went on summer progresses into the countryside, Hudson joined them, and indeed had his separate carriage for the visits. In July 1634, for example, the royal progress traveled to the estate of William Cavendish, the first Earl of Newcastle.[69] There, on July 30, Jonson's last masque, *Love's Welcome at Bolsover*, was performed.[70] Besides featuring Jonson's infamous attack on Inigo Jones, delivered by the character of Colonel Vitrivius, this masque presents two "Loves" (two Cupid characters) who are named Eros and Anteros. Jonson identifies Eros with the Queen and Anteros with the King. Although the text of the masque does not name the performers, Hudson may have played Eros, the "lesser" or smaller of the two "elf" characters.[71] Eros and Anteros banter, and at one point Eros says, "I was a dwarf, an urchin, I confess,/Till you were present" (107–9). After their banter, the two dance in celebration of the love that unites the King and Queen.

The following year *Florimène*, a French pastoral, was staged by the Queen and her ladies on December 21, 1635, in the Great Hall at Whitehall that John Webb designed. Aurelian Townshend provided the text, Inigo Jones the stage design. Only a fragment of this pastoral has survived, including "A Pigmees Speech," which served as an epilogue that may have been delivered by Hudson:

> If I should tell yee whence I come,
> Some I should please, and anger some,
> But by my Stature, yet may see,
> Not much above a Ladies knee;
> Sometimes, they lay me in their lappes,
> And give me kisses, sometimes Clappes;
> And then I talke, and so doe They:
> But there's an end, and come away;
> Lords take your Ladies by the hands,
> Let yours be Questions, Theirs Commands,
> Bee not so nice! you'l meet anon!
> When Lights are out, and people gone:
> The Night is shorter now than I;
> Loose it not all, too mannerly;
> Rest would doe well, If ye can get it;
> Beshrew their fingers would permit it,
> Until the Morning Clocke strike Ten;
> Speake out like Clerks, and cry Amen.[72]

The speech captures the playful and confident spirit that Hudson had attained at court by the 1630s.

Indeed, by 1636 Hudson's fame had spread beyond the court. He was featured in several publications, including John Taylor's poem *The Old, Old, Very Old Man*, which honored Thomas Parr, who was supposedly a hundred and fifty-one years old. Besides describing Parr, the poem also celebrated William Evans and Hudson. The three of them were honored as "the oldest, the greatest, and the least" in the King's kingdom.[73] In concert with Taylor's poem, George Glover published a broadside print of the tallest, the smallest, and the oldest men of their time. In this representation Hudson has his ever-present sword and the feathered hat that he apparently wore on public occasions. Joining the celebration of Parr, Evans, and Hudson, Thomas Heywood then contributed the *Three Wonders of the Age*.[74] Of Hudson he writes: "And for him, he is one of the prettiest, neatest, and well-proportioned small men that ever Nature bred, or was ever seene, or heard of beyond the memory of man, for his fine behaviour and witty discourse."[75]

Also in 1636 an anonymous little book appeared in honor of Hudson. It was entitled *The New-Yeeres Gift: Presented at Court, from the Lady Parvula to the Lord Minimus (commonly called Little Jefferie), Her Majesties servant, with a Letter as it was penned in short-hand wherein is proved Little Things are better than Great. Written by Microphilus*.[76] Although the identity of the author is open to question, the little book was most likely written by Heywood. In the second edition from 1638 a portrait of Hudson is provided by John Droeshout, who is best known for his engraving of Shakespeare in the First Folio. Below the portrait, an epigram celebrates Hudson: "Gaze on with wonder, and discerne in me, The abstract of the world's Epitome." The word "epitome" means not just an abstract or short statement but to cut short, an abridgement. Like Taylor's poem and Heywood's *Three Wonders of the Age*, the little book by Microphilus serves as another register of Hudson fame.

To be expected, Hudson continued to appear in the court masques, including the last two major spectacles by Jones. On February 6, 1638, Davenant's *Luminalia, the Festivall of Light* was staged in the new Masquing House. For this Shrove Tuesday entertainment the Queen asked Jones to create a "high and hearty invention" of "Scenes, strange apparitions, Songs, Musick and dancing of severall kinds."[77] The elaborate scene changes, taking place within the proscenium arch, shifted from settings of Night, then Sleep, and then Light.

The primary performers were the Queen and the ladies of the court. In addition, over a dozen gentlemen of the nobility participated with Hudson in the antimasque, which presented the inhabitants of a city of Sleep, with "strange apparitions." During this antimasque, the text reports the entrance of "Five Fayries of which Master Jeffrey Hudson, the Queenes Majesties dwarfe, presented [the character of] Piecrocall, a principall Captaine under King Auberon."[78] Hudson and the "attendants of Night" present a series of strange images and shapes brought forth by Sleep. Then, with the appearance of the morning star, the final scene commences, revealing the Queen, dressed as an Amazon in a military costume. Representing the glorious sun that chases away darkness, she proudly shone her blessings on the assembled audience. The masque thus revealed "the unanimous and magnificent virtues of the King and Queen's majesties' making this happy island a pattern to all nations, as Greece was amongst the ancients."[79] Unfortunately, because of the battles between the Court and Parliament, the Queen's sunshine did not reach beyond the walls of the Masquing House. And her military costume seemed to express the defiant political tone of Charles's government.

Two years later, on January 21 and February 18, 1640, Hudson performed in the last court masque, *Salmacida Spolia*, also written by Davenant and staged by Jones in the Masquing House, with music by Lewis Richard. If anything, this idealistic masque was even grander in its scenic wonders than *Luminalia*. The Queen's mother, Marie de Medici, was the guest of honor. Several Catholic ladies appeared in the masque. Hudson appeared in the antimasque as a "little Swiss who playd the wag" (ll. 282–84)[80] with two of his countrymen. Attired in a military costume, including a tiny helmet and a breastplate, he represented a Swiss Guard. He engaged in a farcical dance, "while Mr. Cottrell, master of ceremonies, and Sir Henry Newton, gentleman of the privy chamber, pretended to sleep."[81]

With the conclusion of the antimasque, a mountaintop scene was revealed. After a song that blessed the Queen Mother, the scene revealed the King on his "Throne of Honour (345)." Surrounded by his lords, he reigned from a "seat of gold." Hudson joined this spectacle, having attained a central and concluding place in the masque proper. After a choral song in praise of the King who reconciles "quarreling winds" (367), the Queen and her ladies descended on a large cloud. Then, after another choral song, the King and Queen, followed by the Court gentlemen and ladies, entered the lower floor and danced. No doubt Hudson participated in the celebratory dance with the lords and ladies. Following the scenic appearance of a "great city" (463) and the heavenly spheres, the masque concluded by praising an adored royal couple, "Loved even by those who should your justice fear" (482).

But Charles and Henrietta Maria, who had lost touch with the nation, were not loved. Soon the Scottish War turned into a Civil War. Hudson, who was twenty-one years old in 1640, remained loyal to the King and Queen. Although the Queen apologized to Parliament in 1641, her statement was too late and conceded too little. In January 1642 the full Court, including Hudson, abandoned London as the country divided into two warring camps. A month later Hudson traveled with the Queen to Holland as she tried to acquire arms for Charles's army.[82] After a series of negotiations with the Dutch, they returned a year later with some soldiers and guns, but again too late and too little.

For a few months the Queen and Hudson join Charles at Oxford, where the semblance of court life had been reestablished. But in April 1644 Henrietta Maria parted for the last time from Charles. She left Oxford, fleeing south with the aim of escaping to France. Hudson, now her "Captain of Horse," joined her. Pregnant and very sick, she reached Exeter, where she gave birth to a daughter on June 16.[83] Two weeks later, leaving her daughter in the care of a trusted supporter, the Queen journeyed to Falmouth in disguise, hiding out along the road while enemy troops searched for her. Supposedly, a reward of fifty-thousand crowns was announced for her capture. Her health was dire and her pain was severe, but the Queen and her party, including Hudson, made the perilous escape to France in a Dutch ship, breaching the naval blockage of the Parliamentary fleet, which chased her most of the way across the Channel.[84] Within a few days they arrived in Paris, staying in royal rooms at the Louvre.

For eighteen years, from 1626 to 1644, Hudson and the Queen were the closest of companions and dear friends, but that relationship soon came to a terrible end. After the brief stay in Paris, the Queen and her party shifted to Nevers and the castle of the Dukes of Bourbon so that she could regain her health. Several of the young Cavaliers who had escaped from England had joined the Queen's party. Some of them enjoyed teasing Hudson. Having felt insulted by the bantering of Charles Crofts, Hudson challenged him to a pistol duel. Crofts first arrived with a water squib, and squirted Jeffrey. Further insulted, Hudson demanded a duel with pistols on horses. With one shot, while they rode toward one another, Hudson fired a bullet into the head of Crofts, who died on the spot.[85] After consulting the French government, the Queen decided that Hudson would not be punished, for no law forbade dueling, but she also decided that he had to be sent into exile as punishment.[86]

A few months later, once again at sea (but we don't know where), Hudson was captured by Barbary pirates and sold into slavery in North Africa, where he remained a prisoner for years, doing hard labor apparently. He disappeared from the historical records until after 1660, when Charles II had taken the throne in England. After finally gaining his freedom, Hudson returned to England, perhaps redeemed from slavery with the help of the Queen, who divided her time between France and England during the 1660s, until her death in April 1669.

For mysterious reasons, Hudson had grown to three feet, nine inches in height during his exile—perhaps because of a change in diet in North Africa, or because of the labor, as James Wright reports.[87] We lack information on Hudson's last years in London, except for evidence that the son of George Villiers, the Duke of Buckingham, and some other Royalists provide pensions for Hudson, who lived in the countryside during his years back in England. In 1678 or 1679, however, after Hudson had moved to London, he was accused of joining a Popish plot. He was imprisoned at the Gate house.[88] Despite the suspicions about his Catholic loyalties, Hudson was protected, at least partially, by the King. We have records of further payments to Hudson from Charles II in 1680 and 1682.[89] This charity and protection may have offset the charges of treason against the aged Hudson, who died a Catholic, circa 1682, shortly after his release from prison.

CONCLUSION

As I hope my brief narrative reveals, the dismissive category of the "Queen's dwarf" has seriously hindered our scholarship on Jeffrey Hudson. Of course, the designation is a necessary starting place for investigating Hudson's life and achievements, but he attained a unique status as the Queen's dwarf. Despite his physical identity, he became an accomplished comic performer and dancer who entertained and charmed court society. As was the case for many masque performers, he was an amateur, not a professional, player. He began as a child actor, which allowed him the liberty to display himself. Yet his accomplishment expanded as he aged; he was capable of much more than being just a cute and adorable dwarf. His talents—along with the abiding support of the Queen—allowed him not merely to survive but to conquer court society. And because of the mutual admiration, love, and loyalty that existed between the Queen and Hudson, he became an epitome, not just an anomaly, of the world of Caroline masque and political society. His career and life, so closely yoked to Henrietta Maria, warrants our study, our understanding, and our admiration.

NOTES

1. I identify events and dates by the Julian or Old Style calendar that was used in England during this period, but I start the year on January 1, not March 25.
2. Knowles, *Chloridia*, Vol. 6, 370.

3. Hudson's first name appears in several variations in the documents including Jeffrey, Jeffry, Geoffrey, Geoffrie, or Geffry.

4. Bentley, *The Jacobean and Caroline Stage*, III, 214.

5. For an excellent study of court dance and the choreographers, see Ravelhofer, *The Early Stuart Masque: Dance, Costume, and Music*.

6. See R. A. Stokes, *Illustrations of the English Stage 1580–1642*.

7. On the questionable portraits of Burbage, Field, Sly, and Bonds, see Cooper, *Searching for Shakespeare*, 133–36. On the suspect image of Edward Alleyn, see Postlewait, "Eyewitnesses to History: Visual Evidence for Theatre in Early Modern England," 575–606.

8. See the section on "Players" in Bentley's *The Jacobean and Caroline Stage* II, 343–629.

9. Bentley, *The Jacobean and Caroline Stage*, II, 358.

10. Bentley, *The Jacobean and Caroline Stage*, IV, 638; Herford, Simpson, and Simpson, *Ben Jonson: Works*, VII, 755.

11. Walls, *Music in the English Courtly Masque 1604–1640*; Tomlinson, *Women on Stage in Stuart Drama*; Britland, *Drama at the Courts of Queen Henrietta*.

12. Ravelhofer, *The Early Stuart Masque*; Bailey, *Staging the Old Faith*.

13. For example, Britland, *Drama at the Courts of Queen Henrietta*, and Knowles, " 'Can ye not tell a man from a marmoset?' "

14. Barbara Ravelhofer is an exception to the general disregard. She describes Hudson as "a rare comic talent," and mentions him, however briefly, on four occasions: She names four masques in which he performed, quotes from a letter about events that contributed to Davenant's poem, describes the costume he wore in *Chloridia*, and notes that in the 1650s his costumes were displayed in a cabinet of curiosities (or "rarities"). See *The Early Stuart Masque*, 62, 74, 148, 159. In addition, James Knowles, who edited *Chloridia* for *The Cambridge Edition of the Works of Ben Jonson*, edited by David Bevington, Martin Butler, and Ian Donaldson (2012), provides a supplementary footnote that complements Ravelhofer's identification of four masques. He also names *Florimène*, and he places "Hudson and four dwarves" in a work that he identifies as *The Rabelaisian Masque* (Bevington, Butler, and Donaldson, eds., *The Cambridge Edition of the Works of Ben Jonson*, Vol. 6, 368, note for line 92 in *Chloridia*).

15. Taylor, *The Old, Old, Very Old Man*; Heywood, *Three Wonders of the Age*.

16. Fuller, *History of the Worthies of England*; Wright, *The History and Antiquities of the County of Rutland*.

17. Walpole, *Anecdotes of Painting in England, with some Account of the Principal Artists*.

18. Scott, *Peveril of the Peak*. Three chapters, set within a prison, feature the character of "Geoffrey Hudson." Scott identifies Hudson as "Sir" Geoffrey Hudson, but there is no evidence that he was knighted.

19. Stephen and Lee, *Dictionary of National Biography*; Goldman, Matthew, and Harrison, *Oxford Dictionary of National Biography*. To be expected, miscellaneous anecdotes about his adventures off the stage displace information about his onstage career.

20. Even the word "dwarf" may make us feel uncomfortable; nonetheless, I insist on using the word because its denotations and connotations are central to the historical issues I am examining in this chapter. We cannot deny the basic fact that the Renaissance courts of Europe treated dwarves as objects of curiosity. Their status was often precarious, even when they were allowed some comic and satiric liberty as court fools or jesters. But we also know that in many cases dwarves became active participants in court society. And some dwarves, like Hudson, attained a special status within the court society.

21. Although previous ages defined and treated dwarves as freaks or as objects of amusement, we disapprove today of such prejudicial attitudes and categories.

22. For the details on Hudson's life, see the biography by Nick Page, *Lord Minimus*.

23. By medical definition, he was a "*hypopituitaristic* dwarf," suffering from a problem with the pituitary gland that regulates the growth hormone.

24. Because Charles was not a Catholic, the ceremony could not take place within the cathedral. The pope's letter of dispensation required Henrietta Maria to remain a faithful Catholic and to raise her children as Catholics. The marriage negotiations also required Charles to provide a Catholic chapel for Henrietta Maria in her new household.

25. Somerset House had been the residence of Anne of Denmark, the Queen of King James I and mother of Charles. The name was officially changed in 1617 to Denmark House, but many people continued to identify the residence as Somerset House. And many subsequent documents used the older name, as Martin Butler notes in his valuable "Calendar of Masques and Entertainments, 1603–1641." See Butler's *The Stuart Court Masque and Political Culture*, 359. I follow his lead.

26. The Queen's household was cut to less than a dozen people, and one priest, but four months later the staff was enlarged by several servants, twelve priests, and a bishop. On the early years of the marriage, see Bone, *Henrietta Maria, Queen of the Cavaliers*, 39–72. Also see Carlton, *Charles*, 64–90, and Plowden, *Henrietta Maria*, chapters 1–3.

27. Hamilton, *Henrietta Maria*, 76–80.

28. Hamilton, *Henrietta Maria*, 72–73, and also, Orrell, *The Theatres of Inigo Jones and John Webb*, 81–84. This proscenium stage was likely the first to be built in England. Inigo Jones was beginning to use movable scenery in his Jacobean masques; this pastoral helped to complete his introduction of continental staging practices into the English court performances.

29. Henrietta Maria's father, Henry IV, was assassinated when she was only six months old. I use the standard English spelling for the name of the queen mother, but of course in Italian her name was Maria de' Medici and her French name was Marie de Médicis.

30. For two primary sources, see Bentley, *The Jacobean and Caroline Stage*, VII, 62. The ambassadors of France and Venice provided reports on this lost entertainment. Their comments are summarized by Bone, *Henrietta Maria*, 61–62. The poet is unknown; Inigo Jones apparently provided the scenic spectacle. See also Butler, *The Stuart Court Masque and Political Culture*, 276, 278–79; Ravelhofer, *The Early Stuart Masque*, 55–56; Hamilton, *Henrietta Maria*, 98. Hamilton and Ravelhofer mistakenly collapse together these two entertainments: *The Discords of Christianity* and *Gargantua and Gargamella*.

31. During November, Buckingham was also rehearsing another masque, *Gargantua and Gargamella*, in which Hudson would dance. And the Duchess at this time was training her young daughter, Mary, in Spanish and French popular dances, including the *sarabande*, which was quite popular. It seems likely that Hudson, who had moved into Burley on the Hill, participated in the dance lessons. See Ravelhofer, *The Early Stuart Masque*, 18–19, 53–61, 64–67.

32. This anecdote about Hudson is reported in both Fuller's *The Worthies of England* and Wright's *The History and Antiquities of the County of Rutland*.

33. On river traffic from York House to Somerset House, see Page, 44–48.

34. In her research on the Queen's household accounts, located in "the National Archive (LR 5/64)," Caroline Hibbard discovered an extensive yearly record on the outlays for Hudson: "Gilbert Morrett, tailor for the boys and for Jeffrey, provided one suit after

another for the dwarf. In 1628 there was 'an ashcolor barracan suite and cloak with sleeves for Mr. Jeffrey', as well as a 'black mourning suite of Flanders aye and a long cloak', a green taffeta suit and a blue satin suit, and the next year scarlet hose 'to wear under his armour.' For Mayday 1629, there would be a new cloak, doublet, suit and waistcoat at a coat of £6 for the material alone. Dipping into the bills in the following decade we find masking suits, riding suits, 'a suit for Jeffrey, for a comedy' and a 'morning suit'. The hats (some with feathers, some beaver hats with silver bands), the boots and shoes, the points, gloves, and embroidered handkerchiefs, the satin stockings and the linen are all detailed in the bills. The standard order of silk hose for Jeffrey was twelve pair in every quarter. Grynder the upholsterer provided a bed for him with a 'round French canopy', and Cordell the cabinetmaker made cases for his looking-glass and his combs." Caroline Hibbard, " 'By Our Direction and for Our Use': The Queen's Patronage of Artists and Artisans Seen through Her Household Accounts," in Griffey, *Henrietta Maria*, 115–38/131–32.

35. Gregoire, who identified himself as Jeremy Griggory, was paid by the Queen, but Hudson took over the payment when he became an adult.

36. The dates and sources for the two masques in November 1626, *The Discords of Christianity* and *Gargantua and Gargamella*, are "difficult to disentangle," as Orgel and Strong point out (*Inigo Jones*, I, 389). See Orgel and Strong, *Inigo Jones: The Theatre of the Stuart Court*, 376. Orgel and Strong as well as W. R. Streitberger confuse the dates and identities of these masques. See Streitberger "Jacobean and Caroline Revels Accounts, 1603–1642," *Malone Society Collections*, XIII, 96.

37. The Old Style or Julian calendar was ten days behind the New Style or Gregorian calendar; this discrepancy explains why the Queen's birthday was celebrated in London on the sixteenth of November instead of the twenty-sixth, the date of her birth according to the Gregorian calendar.

38. Birch, *The Court and Times of Charles I*, Vol. I, 180. Perhaps Henrietta Maria suggested *Gargantua and Pantagruel* as the source for the masque.

39. Cook and Wilson, "Dramatic Records in the Declared Accounts of the Treasurer of the Chamber, 1558–1642," 123). See also Bentley, *The Jacobean and Caroline Stage*, VII, 62.

40. The use of green cloth as a floor covering became common for Caroline masques. See Walls, *Music in the English Courtly Masque 1604–1640*, 315; Astington, *English Court Theatre*, 86.

41. Ravelhofer, *The Early Stuart Masque*, 107. On the dance masters connected with the Duke of Buckingham, Henrietta Maria, and Charles I, see also Howard, *The Politics of Courtly Dancing in Early Modern England*.

42. Evidence for the costume can be found in the Public Records Office for Christmas 1627: "a suite and Cloke for Ieffry the Dwarfe" and "a suit for the Great Porter" William Evans. This scene with Evans and Hudson was described by Thomas Fuller in his account of Evans in *The Worthies of England* (1952), 401. See also Orgel and Strong, *Inigo Jones*, I, 389.

43. On Gargantua and Tom Thumb, see Prescott, *Imagining Rabelais in Renaissance England*, 28–32.

44. *Calendar of State Papers Venetian 1626–1628*, xx, 32: letter by Pietro Contarinie, Venetian ambassador, on November 27, 1626. Reprinted in Raverhofer, *The Early Stuart Masque*, 56.

45. Butler, *The Stuart Court Masque and Political Culture*, 370, note 42: "The details of the subject [of the masque's plot action] are in a letter of 3 December 1626, printed by T. Birch, *Court and Times of Charles I*, 2 vols. (1848) I, 180." The letter was sent to Joseph Mead.

46. Sir Walter Scott, *Peveril of the Peak*, ed. Alison Lumsden (2007): 352.

47. Page, *Lord Minimus*, 60. The letter is in the *Calendar of State Papers Domestic, Charles I, 1627–1628*, 222.

48. On Bocan, see Ravelhofer, *The Early Stuart Masque*, 61–62.

49. The source is a manuscript of Attorney General Sir John Bakes; it is located in the Bodleian Library. Quoted by Carlton, *Charles I, The Personal Monarch*, 136.

50. Birch, *The Court and Times of Charles I*, II, 59–70.

51. For details see catalog #135 in Millar, *The Tudor-Stuart and Early Georgian Pictures in the Collection of Her Majesty the Queen*.

52. Davenant, *The Shorter Poems, and Songs from the Plays and Masques*, ed. A. M. Gibbs: 37–43, for the poem; 363–65, for Gibbs's notes.

53. Supporting evidence on Monagut's likely role as dance instructor can be found in the Public Records Office (E403/2191; LR5/64). See Ravelhofer, *The Early Stuart Masque*, 57.

54. The published quarto of *Chloridia* identifies each of the court ladies. They are also named in volume one of *The Cambridge Edition of the Works of Ben Jonson*.

55. The text describes the arch and curtain: "The ornament which went about the scene was composed of foliage, or leaves, heighten with gold, and interwoven with all sorts of flowers, and naked children playing and climbing among the branches; and in the midst, a great garland of flowers in which was written CHLORIDIA" (Bevington, Butler, and Donaldson, eds., *The Cambridge Edition of the Works of Ben Jonson*, 365, ll. 11–14).

56. Bevington, David, Martin Butler, and Ian Donaldson, eds., *The Cambridge Edition of the Works of Ben Jonson*, VI, 366. Subsequent quotations are from this Cambridge edition. James Knowles served as editor for *Chloridia*, the text of which is based on the 1631 quarto rather than the 1640 folio.

57. The record for the "masquing suit" appears in Public Records Office LR5/64. See Ravelhofer, *The Early Stuart Masque*, 159.

58. "Experienced teachers such as Jeremy Herne, Thomas Giles, Bocan, Montagut, or Sebastaian Lapierre ensured a high performance quality." Ravelhofer, *The Early Stuart Masque*, 75.

59. Ravelhofer, *The Early Stuart Masque*, 63.

60. Britland, *Drama at the Courts of Queen Henrietta Maria*, 97. Apparently James Knowles, the Cambridge editor of *Chloridia*, also places Hudson in the role of the Dwarf-Post. In his footnote for this character, Knowles states that dwarves appeared in Caroline masques; he then describes Hudson and the masques in which he appeared between 1627 and 1640 (VI, 368).

61. Britland, *Drama at the Courts of Queen Henrietta Maria*, 97. Unfortunately, her passive construction fails to identify who "thought" that Hudson was "capable" of the Dwarf-Post role.

62. The lack of identification by Jonson is not surprising, because he seldom names any of the performers in his antimasques. Hudson is the only person identified in the eight entries of the antimasque of *Chloridia*.

63. The King's dwarf, Richard Gibson, was a talented drawer. In later life he became a successful miniaturist, providing portraits of many people, including Oliver Cromwell. Another dwarf at court was Anne Shepherd. When Gibson and Shepherd married, a special ceremony was arranged by Charles and Henrietta Maria, who served *in loco parentis* for their dwarfs. See Page, *Lord Minimus*, 55–57.

64. Jones reversed the figure, with minor alternations. In Callot's drawing from 1616 the figure is turned toward the right side of the page; in Jones's drawing from 1630 the figure is turned

toward the left. Orgel and Strong, *Inigo Jones*, II, 434. As Orgel and Strong note, Jones used this character again in *Salmacida Spolia* in 1640. Inigo Jones's drawing of the Dwarf-Post and his curtal is entitled "Dutch Post". Newspapers and "Dutch posts" provided news from the continent, as James Knowles observes in his footnote for the entry on the Dwarf-Post in *The Cambridge Edition of the Works of Ben Jonson*, VI: 368.

65. Both the "Dutch-Post" and "Lackeys" drawings by Jones (or his assistants) are reproduced in the *The Cambridge Edition of the Works of Ben Jonson*, VI, 353–54.

66. The word "Postilion" also means the person who rides the left-side horse of the two leaders for a four-horse carriage.

67. On turnstiles, Butler, *The Stuart Court Masque*, 384, note 34: "Turnstiles first appeared at Buckingham's York House masque [*The Discords of Christianity*] in November 1626, at which (said the French ambassador) 'on y entroit par un tour, comme aux monastéres sans aucune confusion' (F. de Bassompierre, *Journal de ma vie* (Paris, 1870–7), III.274)." Although Butler apparently misses the gate-keeping reference in Postilion's speech, he catalogs the continuing use of turnstiles in performances of *Coelum Britannicum* (1634), *Triumph of Peace* (1634), *The Triumphs of the Prince d'Amour* (1636), and *Britannia Triumphans* (1638). Clearly, gate-keeping was standard practice for Caroline masques.

68. If Hudson did not play the Dwarf-Post, who then did? If a professional player took the role, we are still faced with a mystery. Was there a dwarf among the acting companies in 1631?

69. A year earlier, on May 21, 1633, the royal progress had also visited the Earl's estate, where *The King's Entertainment at Welbeck*, also written by Jonson, was performed.

70. As Bentley reports, for this entertainment "the King and Queen and court stayed at Welbeck but were entertained at Bolsover, the Earl's nearby estate." See *Jacobean and Caroline Stage*, VII, 93.

71. Knowles, ed., *The Cambridge Edition of the Works of Ben Jonson*, VI 692, l. 72. This masque is also known as *The King and Queen's Entertainment at Bolsover*.

72. See Orgel, "*Florimène* and the Ante-Masques." In Schoenbaum and Dessen, *Renaissance Drama, New Series*, 135–54. Also see Townshend's *The Masques and Poems* in Brown, ed., *The Masques and Poems*.

73. Page, *Lord Minimus*, 98.

74. For a description of Taylor's poem and Heywood's book, both published in 1636 in London, see Page, *Lord Minimus*, 97–101, 250.

75. Page notes, "Heywood's text confirms what we learn about Jeffrey from Taylor's poem: that he was known, not only for his stature, but for his behaviour. That he was witty and funny and charming." *Lord Minimus*, 101.

76. Two copies of *The New Yeare's Gift* are held by the British Library (London, 1636, 1638). For commentary on the likely author, see Page, *Lord Minimus*, 101–106, 198–99.

77. Queen's message reproduced in Nicoll, *Stuart Masques and the Renaissance Stage*, 116.

78. Orgel and Strong, *Inigo Jones*, II, 707.

79. Orgel and Strong, *Inigo Jones*, II, 706.

80. Orgel and Strong, *Inigo Jones*, II, 732.

81. Page, *Lord Minimus*, 128.

82. In one of her letters Henrietta Maria reports that in 1642, when she and Jeffrey Hudson had come to attain arms for Charles I during the Civil War, the Dutch ambassador in The Hague assumed that Hudson, who was twenty-three years old, was Prince Charles, the

twelve-year-old son of the King and Queen. He kissed Hudson's hand. See Green, *Letters of Queen Henrietta Maria, Including Her Private Correspondence with Charles the First*, 62.

83. A few weeks after the Queen left Exeter, the King arrived. Taking up his new daughter, he named her Henrietta, in honor of her mother. On the Queen's flight, see Bone, *Henrietta Maria*, 170–74, and Hamilton, *Henrietta Maria*, 209–12; also see Oman, *Henrietta Maria*.

84. Besides the *Letters of Queen Henrietta Maria* (1857), see Birch, *The Court and Times of Charles I*.

85. On the duel, see Green, *Letters of Queen Henrietta Maria*, 260; also see Page, *Lord Minimus*, 170–79.

86. Because Crofts's brother was a member of the Queen's party, she felt honor-bound to punish Hudson in some capacity.

87. Wright, *The History and Antiquities of the County of Rutland*, note 2, page 105. Page, *Lord Minimus*, 237–39.

88. This imprisonment and the topic of the Popish plot served as the basis for the scenes representing Hudson in Sir Walter Scott's novel, *Peveril of the Peak*.

89. Akerman, *Moneys Received and Paid for Secret Service of Charles II and James II*, 14, 28.

BIBLIOGRAPHY

Akerman, J. Y., ed. *Moneys Received and Paid for Secret Service of Charles II and James II*. London: Camden Society, 1851.

Astington, John. *English Court Theatre 1558–1642*. Cambridge: Cambridge University Press, 1999.

Bailey, Rebecca A. *Staging the Old Faith: Queen Henrietta Maria and the Theatre of Caroline England, 1625–1642*. Manchester: Manchester University Press, 2009.

de Bassompierre, F. *Journal de ma vie*. Paris, 1870–7.

Bentley, G. E. *The Jacobean and Caroline Stage*. 7 vols. Oxford: Clarendon Press, 1941–1968.

Bevington, David, Martin Butler, and Ian Donaldson, eds. *The Cambridge Edition of the Works of Ben Jonson*. 7 vols. Cambridge: Cambridge University Press, 2012.

Birch, Thomas. *The Court and Times of Charles I*. 2 vols. London: H. Colburn, 1848.

Bone, Quentin. *Henrietta Maria, Queen of the Cavaliers*. Urbana: University of Illinois Press, 1972.

Britland, Karen. *Drama at the Courts of Queen Henrietta Maria*. Cambridge: Cambridge University Press, 2006.

Brown, C. C., ed. *The Masques and Poems of Aurelian Townshend*. Reading: Whiteknights, 1983.

Butler, Martin. *The Stuart Court Masque and Political Culture*. Cambridge: Cambridge University Press, 2008.

Calendar of State Papers, Domestic Series, of the Reign of Charles I, 1625–1649, edited by John Bruce, W. D. Hamilton, and Mrs. S. C. Lomos. 23 vols. London: HMSO, 1858–1897.

Carlton, Charles. *Charles I: The Personal Monarch*. London: Routledge and Kegan Paul, 1983.

Cook, D., and F. P. Wilson, eds. "Dramatic Records in the Declared Accounts of the Treasurer of the Chamber, 1558–1642." In *Malone Society Collections*, Vol. 6. Oxford: Oxford University Press, 1961/1962.

Cooper, Tarnya. *Searching for Shakespeare*. New Haven, CT: Yale University Press, 2006.

Davenant, William. *The Shorter Poems, and Songs from the Plays and Masques*, edited by A. M. Gibbs. Oxford: Clarendon Press, 1972.

Fuller, Thomas. *History of the Worthies of England*, edited by John Freeman. London: George Allen & Unwin, 1952. Originally published in 1662.

Goldman, Lawrence, Colin Matthew, and Brian Harrison, eds. *Oxford Dictionary of National Biography*. 60 vols. Oxford: Oxford University Press, 2004. Available online at www.oxforddnb.com.

Green, Mary Anne Everett, ed. *Letters of Queen Henrietta Maria, Including Her Private Correspondence with Charles the First*. London: R. Bentley, 1857.

Griffey, Erin, ed. *Henrietta Maria: Piety, Politics, and Patronage*. Aldershot: Ashgate, 2008.

Hamilton, Elizabeth. *Henrietta Maria*. New York: Coward, McCann and Geoghegan, 1976.

Herford, C. H., Percy Simpson, and Evelyn Mary Spearing Simpson. *Ben Jonson: Works*. 11 vols. Oxford: Oxford University Press, 1925–1952.

Hibbard, Caroline. "'By Our Direction and For Our Use': The Queen's Patronage of Artists and Artisans seen through Her Household Accounts." In *Henrietta Maria: Piety, Politics, and Patronage*, edited by Erin Griffey, 115–38. Aldershot: Ashgate, 2008.

Howard, Skiles. *The Politics of Courtly Dancing in Early Modern England*. Amherst: University of Massachusetts Press, 1998.

Knowles, James. "'Can ye not tell a man from a marmoset?': Apes and Others on the Early Modern Stage." In *Renaissance Beasts: Of Animals, Humans, and Other Wonderful Creatures*, edited by Erica Fudge, 138–64. Urbana: University of Illinois Press, 2004.

Knowles, James. *Chloridia*. In *The Cambridge Edition of the Works of Ben Jonson*, 7 vols., edited by David Bevington, Martin Butler, and Ian Donaldson. Cambridge: Cambridge University Press, 2012.

Millar, Oliver. *The Tudor-Stuart and Early Georgian Pictures in the Collection of Her Majesty the Queen*. 2 vols. London: Phaidon Press, 1963.

Nicoll, Allardyce. *Stuart Masques and the Renaissance Stage*. New York: Harcourt, Brace, 1928.

Oman, Carola. *Henrietta Maria*. London: White Lion, 1936.

Orgel, Stephen, and Roy Strong. *Inigo Jones: The Theatre of the Stuart Court*. 2 vols. London: Sotheby Parke Bernet; Berkeley: University of California Press, 1973.

Orrell, John. *The Theatres of Inigo Jones and John Webb*. Cambridge: Cambridge University Press, 1985.

Page, Nick. *Lord Minimus: The Extraordinary Life of Britain's Smallest Man*. New York: St. Martin's Press, 2002; London: Harper Collins, 2001.

Plowden, Alison. *Henrietta Maria: Charles I's Indomitable Queen*. Stroud: Sutton, 2001.

Postlewait, Thomas. "Eyewitnesses to History: Visual Evidence for Theatre in Early Modern England." In *The Oxford Handbook of Early Modern Theatre*, edited by Richard Dutton. Oxford: Oxford University Press, 2009.

Prescott, Anne Lake. *Imagining Rabelais in Renaissance England*. New Haven, CT: Yale University Press, 1998.

Ravelhofer, Barbara. *The Early Stuart Masque: Dance, Costume, and Music*. Oxford: Oxford University Press, 2006.

Schoenbaum, Samuel, and Alan C. Dessen, eds. *Renaissance Drama, New Series IV: Essays Principally on the Playhouses and Staging*. Evanston: Northwestern University Press, 1971.

Scott, Sir Walter. *Peveril of the Peak*. London: Hurst Robinson, 1822.

Scott, Sir Walter, *Peveril of the Peak*. Edited by Alison Lumsden. Edinburgh: Edinburgh University Press, 2007.

Stephen, Leslie, and Sir Sidney Lazarus Lee. *Dictionary of National Biography*. 63 vols. London: Smith, Elder, 1885–1901.

Streitberger, W. R., ed. "Jacobean and Caroline Revels Accounts, 1603–1642." In *Malone Society Collections*, Vol. 13. Oxford: Oxford University Press, 1986.

Stokes, R. A. *Illustrations of the English Stage 1580–1642*. Stanford, CA: Stanford University Press, 1985.

Taylor, John. *The Old, Old, Very Old Man*. London, 1636.

Thomas Heywood. *Three Wonders of the Age*. London, 1636.

Tomlinson, Sophie. *Women on Stage in Stuart Drama*. Cambridge: Cambridge University Press, 2005.

Walls, Peter. *Music in the English Courtly Masque 1604–1640*. Oxford: Clarendon Press, 1996.

Walpole, Horace. *Anecdotes of Painting in England, with Some Account of the Principal Artists; and Incidental Notes on Other Arts*. 3 vols. Additions by James Dallaway; revised by Ralph Nicholson Wornum; catalogue of engravers by George Vertue. London: Chatto and Windus, 1876. London: John Major, 1826–1828. Originally published London: John Majors, 1826–1828.

Wright, James. *The History and Antiquities of the County of Rutland*. London, 1684.

CHAPTER 31

"WHAT DO WOMEN WANT, MY GOD, WHAT DO THEY WANT?"
Mimesis, Fantasy, and Female Sexuality in
Ann Liv Young's Michael

KRISTA K. MIRANDA

"AIN'T no sunshine when she's gone." Dressed in identical black shirts, shorts, derby hats, and white heels, Ann Liv Young and Liz Santoro, contrapposto at their respective mic stands, suck helium from black balloons, layering their now cartoon-like voices over the vocals of Bill Withers. "It's not warm when she's away." Inhaling more helium between the lines, Young and Santoro push lyrics from their lungs with the exaggerated projection of a bad junior-high school play. There is no sense of nuance, no effort at moderation. Their voices mimic each other's, drowning out Withers'. "And she's always gone too long." Michael Guerrero, Young's real-life partner and stand-in for a third performer, Emily Wexler, occasionally sings along and toils with the sound and set while onstage. *Solo* requires three people.[1]

There are no wings, no backdrop. The upstage wall is covered in mirrors. *Solo* is composed of multiple bodies, repeated, both in the flesh and reflected behind them. Once the balloons deflate the performers pause. Rewind. Young plays the song from the beginning. They start again, differently, this time exhaling into the latex to reinflate the balloons. Making, remaking, until Young shouts, "Stop! Go!" Young sits on Santoro's lap as they sing/scream "Chain Gang" a capella while Santoro plays the triangle around Young's waist. As is customary in Young's work, the women get naked. They remove everything except for their white heels to dance on and with the chairs staged perpendicular to each other. Their movements are aggressive, unapologetic. After admonishing Guerrero for his ineptitude during a somewhat incoherent skit about hurricanes, suicide bombing, and a plane crash, Young puts her script aside: "Let's try again." The section repeats twice, each time with small differences in execution or content. *Solo* then evolves into a series of trio sing-a-longs with Guerrero on the guitar, including an original piece about a woman Young dated in college with the refrain: "Sex with a guy still isn't as good as sex with a woman." Young interrupts: "Stop: That was offensive." The rest of the performance involves dancing on chairs, inflating balloons, choreography performed to Young's militaristic cuing, a tantrum, both women shooting Guerrero with fake guns, a rhythmic gymnastic-like routine with a ribbon executed by Santoro, then both women pouring chocolate syrup on themselves and each other. Their pale, white skin browns throughout the course of the performance, exemplifying Young's emphasis on skin color and its mutability as recurring themes throughout her work.

Solo: "a thing done by one person unaccompanied, in particular."[2] This chapter, and Ann Liv Young's *Michael*, is not about *Solo* (2006). And yet, it always is. By beginning a brief account of one performance to introduce another, I intend to lay the groundwork for an analysis of *Michael* by signaling (1) the major themes in her oeuvre—the anatomizing exposure of the performers' bodies on stage, the accentuation of the pallor of the skin, the verbal and performed narratives of violence and sexuality, the multiplicity and cloning via both the layering of the performers' voices over popular music, the often militaristic choreographic synchronicity, the repetition(s) with a difference, the senselessness of the works themselves, and the hyperbolized, amped up execution of it all; and (2) this chapter's primary concern: the harried, messy nature of subject formation, particularly in terms of gender, sex, sexuality, and race. *Solo*/solo is not an act of autonomous personhood performed in isolation, but has context, is a group piece, a relational project. To be solo is to be unstable, unfixed, to be multiple. To dance from one subject position to another.

The following analysis of Ann Liv Young's *Michael* will attend to the slippery and mimetic nature of subject formation—strikingly performed by *Solo*—specifically in terms of the depiction of female sexuality in the context of the (seemingly unremarked) racialized family cell via Young's unsettling engagement with the uncanny. By depicting a recognizable domestic environment, *Michael* elicits the possibility for identification between the audience and the performers through a doubling of "real life" in the space of the theater. Young then cranks up the volume of the aesthetic and exoticizes the familiar through hyperbolization by performing *Michael* with, in Luce Irigaray's terms, "an excess that exceeds common sense."[3] *Michael* exploits the mimetic character of the piece by skewing the "real" into the "hyper-real," providing the conditions for experiencing the "[u]ncomfortable, uneasy, [and] dismal" sensation characteristic of the uncanny—what Sigmund Freud calls "that class of the frightening which leads back to what is known of old and long familiar."[4] Through the lens of the uneasy effect of the uncanny on the audience in conjunction with Freud's discussion of the beating fantasy, this analysis will explore the implications of Young's "hyper-real" aesthetic and use of mimesis by examining *Michael*'s chaotic presentation of the "primal scene" as both home to and catalyst for the development of (what I will argue is an inherently racialized) female sexuality. The final turn of this chapter will employ elaborations on Michel Foucault's analysis of the sexualization of the family cell[5] to expose how the inter-articulations of race, gender, and sexuality are intrinsic to the formation of an intelligible, embodied—and in this case, female—subject.

Upon descending the stairs that lead to Dance Theater Workshop's[6] main stage, one is immediately confronted by a life-sized diorama of a kitschy living room, complete with seventies-inspired floral wallpaper. A vintage refrigerator looms stage right. A skinny door and window flank the upstage wall. A boudoir picture of *Michael*'s female performers hangs above a Victorian-style, off-white couch. In front of the couch is a white, drop-leaf coffee table with performer Jana Panconesi curled on top in the fetal position. Her bare back and white cotton underwear face the audience while she breathes, her ribs fanning wide with each inhalation. I stare at the tag that shows through her thin underwear, her hair falling over the side of the coffee table. I'm not sure if I should stop talking. She adjusts herself a few times, moves an elbow to rest it on her side. Shifts a foot. There are neither wings nor curtains. Walking into the theater I feel simultaneously like a voyeur of and performer in the production of *Michael*. One of the last people to take her seat, front row center, is a woman who will turn out to be somewhat "in" the piece by acting as an in-view stage director, shouting out cues. Wearing stark white pants, a white tank top, and a white vest, she is Ann Liv Young. Set, audience, and performer(s) exposed, the performance has already begun.[7]

When Eminem's "Crazy in Love" resounds, there is an immediate explosion of colorless light that persists for several seconds, momentarily blinding me to everything but whiteness. It takes a few moments for my eyes to adjust to the scene. The dancer on the coffee table is the spitting image of Young with her identical long, straight, brown hair, similar build, and facial features. They could have been sisters. Twins. Panconesi begins her frenetic, fast-paced dance by flailing around the set with seemingly unchoreographed spontaneity. She whips her hair, grinds into the coffee table, rolls around on the stage with unrelenting high energy (ignoring the pink cast on her ankle and the bloody bandage on her knee that falls off mid-performance). Young stands, mic in hand, rapping along with/on top of Eminem. It takes a while for me to notice Todd Duerkenson, who I assume plays the role of "Michael," materialize behind the window, watching, masturbating, and eventually, ejaculating. During the second chorus, Panconesi walks to the refrigerator and opens it while three more women, identically dressed solely in white underwear, appear from behind the couch to dance around/on top of the set with the same manic, libidinal energy as Panconesi. Their tit shaking, pelvic gyrating, furniture humping, self-caressing varies in speed and vigor, reminiscent of pre-, during-, and postcoital waves of intensity. Notably, the "dirtiness" of Young's choreographic chaos plays out against, and therefore besmirches, the excessively "pure" white set. The performance proceeds as a breathless collage of monologues, skits, musical numbers, and theatrical dance interludes. It *might* be erotic—the bare breasts and stripper-like movements initiated from the pelvis suggest *something* like tantalization—but more than anything else I can articulate, it is chaotic, too much to take in all at once. I don't know where to look. I don't know what I am looking at. I cannot stop looking.

While the decor presents a domestic space—the aesthetic partially inspired by Young's mother's home[8]—the details, on closer inspection, push what seems "real" and familiar toward the "hyper-real"[9]: the refrigerator is filled with an absurd number of Coca-Cola cans; the naked bodies, covered in cuts and bruises, are lit with harsh, unforgiving lights that strip their skin of pigment so they appear "hyper" white, which both mirrors the aesthetic of the set and accentuates what seems to be the entire cast's obvious and hyperbolized "whiteness"; dangling high from the rafters is Emily Wexler, clothed in a pasty, papier-mâché-looking dress, swinging on a tire that is also painted white. One performer says it best: "I swear to god, every time I come over here it gets weirder and weirder."

What unfolds before me triggers . . . something. I'm not sure if it is the glare of the bright lights, the volume of the music, or the content of the performance—although I'm certain any notion of Young's "perversity" is not the problem. This scene is recognizable, close to home, and not at all. Freud describes the *Unheimlich*, or the uncanny, as the confrontation with what is normally "[c]oncealed, kept from sight, so that others do not get to know of or about it."[10] He explains: "'*heimlich*' exhibits one which is identical with its opposite '*unheimlich*' . . . '*heimlich*' is not unambiguous, but belongs to two sets of ideas, which, without being contradictory, are yet very different: on the one hand it means what is familiar and agreeable, and on the other, what is concealed and kept out of sight."[11] Freud makes sense of this complex,

FIGURE 31.1 Jana Panconesi and Todd Duerkenson in Ann Liv Young's *Michael*, performed at The Kitchen in New York City, 2005. Photo courtesy of Jason Akira Somma.

noncontradictory coupling of a quality with its opposite by associating the uncanny with the phenomenon of the "double." This unsettling sensation of uncanniness occurs "from the fact of the 'double' being a creation dating back to a very early mental stage, long since surmounted."[12] Upon its return, the double "has become a thing of terror," for it evokes the familiar and unfamiliar at once.[13] One is confronted by a sense of unease created by the friction of these seemingly incongruent worlds of familiar and strange butting up against each other. Sitting in DTW I am not simply a passive spectator of yet another downtown New York performance. I am implicated. I am worked on, chafing from the incongruent sensation of the *unheimlich* and *heimlich* at once.

Ann Liv Young, born in 1981 in North Carolina and a graduate of Hollins College, has been creating performance work since the early 2000s. She is one of the youngest artists to present at prestigious venues in New York City and Europe, such as P.S.1 Contemporary Art Center, Dance Theater Workshop, Brooklyn Museum, The Kitchen, Laban Centre London, Impulstanz, Springdance, and Theatre de la Bastille, among others. An experimental dance-theater artist who has garnered much attention, both positive and negative, in the past decade, Young is widely considered controversial and "obscene," a classification often leveled at both her persona and the work itself. Given the context of Ann Liv Young's oeuvre as part of an avant-garde arts scene in New York City, which dates back to the mid-twentieth century with performance artists like Carolee Schneemann and Karen Finley, I find such accusations of impropriety particularly perplexing. This chapter proposes that the feeling of dread induced by the phenomenon of the uncanny—and not simply the (infamous) "pornographic" character of Young's work—provides a possible explanation for why audience members of a diverse demographic regarding age, race, gender, and sexuality, often leave in the middle of her performances.

Michael's juxtaposition of the quotidian with the "hyper-real" exploits and blurs the audience/performer divide, for the effects of this domestic tableau invite the spectators to identify with the familial scene—simply because it is a familial scene—and further incorporates the audience into *Michael*. The bodies that compose the audience are drawn into the performance space, thereby reconfiguring the assumed binary between performer and spectator. During the first "skit" instigated by Young's empathic "Go!," three performers sit side by side on the couch and speak to each other while looking directly at the audience:

LIZ SANTORO: What's the matter with her? [Referring to Panconesi, who stands behind the couch, fixated on the tableau of the women on the wall.]

RENÉE ARCHIBALD: The real question is, what's the matter with you?

TOSHA TILLMAN: No, the real question is, what are we doing tonight and I don't know what to cook.

SANTORO: No, the real question is, who am I going to lay, and what am I wearing to do it?

ARCHIBALD: You are a complete ignoramus. You completely change every conversation around so that you're the topic of convo. I just want you to realize that I, and maybe they don't, but I notice it and it's not that appealing.

PANCONESI RETORTS, LOOKING DIRECTLY AT SANTORO: As a matter of fact, it's not flattering at all, and you have baby weight, and you're not as pretty as you used to be when you were lighter.

ARCHIBALD: Don't say that. It's not nice.

TILLMAN: It's true though. And isn't the truth always nice? Ok ladies, enough hubble bubble. Let's talk about our plan of who's going to cook what.

PANCONESI: I have an idea. Let's kill someone tonight. I know you think that I'm crazy, but I'm ready. I feel I can do it. And I wouldn't leave a trace.

TILLMAN: I'm in.

FIGURE 31.2 Renée Archibald, Jana Panconesi, Liz Santoro, and Tosha Tillman in *Michael*. Photo courtesy of Jason Akira Somma.

They speak *to* each other but *at* us with dialogue delivered so loud and rapid-fire, with very little space between sentences and speakers, that it is hard to catch what is being said.[14] After more talk of sex, murder, various versions of incest, and a break to do what looks like lines of cocaine, Duerkenson finally enters and eventually joins the conversation. In unison, Santoro and Archibald address the audience directly:

SANTORO AND ARCHIBALD: What do you guys think we should do? Do you think we should continue living? Do you think we should continue doing the same old same old? Well we won't. And you can't make us. So heh.

DUERKENSON [also speaking directly to us]:   Are you guys tired of this show already? Are you guys tired of watching other people have fun? Does this show make you think of bad performance art, or dance, or theater, or physical theater? Well I've got news for you, this is art, and art is life. Did you know that my dad is a dance critic? Did you know that my mother is a painter? . . . My dad is sitting in the middle row. Yes that's the one, the one with the toupee. Sorry Dad, I just wanted everyone to know that was you. And that's my mother in the corner with the easel. My dad is writing about this show. Or is he? He probably has his porno hidden in front of his legal pad. Just kidding. My father loves my mother. I bet you guys didn't know that I'm married and that I'm deeply in love. That's right, it's possible to be in love.

Notably, *Michael* is self-conscious about itself as a performance with an audience by first questioning whether *Michael* is simply "bad performance art" and then supposedly pointing out the performer's family in the risers, which effectively places the boundaries of the performance proper into crisis, infusing the entire space of the theater with the potentiality of being part of *Michael*'s domestic scene. While the dialogue suggests there is a specific Father and a specific Mother in the seats of DTW, this is likely just a projection, a familial subject position directed at any one of us, or no one at all. This interpellative approach of openly addressing the audience provokes a meditation on both the conditions of possibility that induce the experience of uncanniness, and what, exactly, is revealed and called into question by this affective phenomenon.

Perhaps the most obvious coupling of the familiar with the strange involves Young's superimposition of the peep show trope on top of a domestic milieu. Although the set is the replication of "home," what Young presents in this space is anything but comforting domesticity. As *Michael* begins with Panconesi's self-absorbed dancing in her underwear, I feel like a voyeur catching glimpses of what is not meant to be seen, as if I were peeking through a keyhole to spy on a teenaged girl singing into her hairbrush while she unabashedly parades, half-naked, in front of her mirror. Panconesi uses the entire space of the set, traveling across the stage in what looks like spontaneous, improvised movement that is both highly libidinal and exceedingly violent. It is self-indulgence via the body at its finest, or most disturbing—celebratory and tantrum-like at once. Simultaneously, Duerkenson, standing behind the window, does his own share of peeping at a scene that, as it unravels throughout the performance, evades narrative coherence.[15]

As the performance unfolds, Duerkenson is incorporated into the domestic sphere as a lover, a libidinous slave, and later, a fraternal partner. His initial entrance is an interruption, a bang on the door that takes time, and an argument among the women, to be answered. After they put the "cocaine" away, Panconesi opens the door, sees Duerkenson—wearing white pants, a sullied white jacket with a pink shirt and tie—and says, "Ladies, would you make some room for the gentleman?" They reply in unison: "We're not moving for him." Panconesi asks Duerkenson to excuse her for a moment, closes the door, screams at the other women to get off the couch, and threatens Santoro that if she doesn't get off the couch she'll "tell everyone you sucked your granddad off for five bucks. Come in!" The rest of the women disappear behind the couch as Duerkenson enters and shoves Panconesi while yelling, "I love you!" Panconesi orders him to "Sit down. Don't push me like that." They have a quarrel over why she's dating someone else. When she joins him on the couch she pours a can of soda over his head, defiling his skin and costume with the sticky brown liquid. During her lecture about how long it's been since they broke up, and how many people they've each fucked, she straddles him while he gropes her. She brags about being the best lay that he'll never have again, her thighs clamped around his, her bare breasts brushing up against his chest. He tries to speak but she roughly covers his mouth and tells him that when she's done talking he needs to undress while she "films his dick with [her] webcam." She does not film his dick with a webcam. Instead, she asks him to hold the can of Coke and if he'd like some gum, quickly shoving a piece in his mouth. "Now for my favorite part," she announces, pulling red ribbon from the crevices of the couch: "Ladies, I'm tying this thing [his now exposed penis] to the couch." The women come out from behind the couch with more red ribbon and chant: "We are hot, we are heavy, we are into each other. We're gonna make it gonna make it gonna make love tonight." This chant repeats while they all tie one end of their ribbon to his penis and the other to the couch. This chaos of libido and aggression—the shifts from lust to violence, from domination to submission—reads like a simultaneous projection of a variety of fantasies (of the audience members as well as the performers).

Aside from the flickering between love, lust, and violence, Duerkenson's initial inclusion in the living room ignites a profound transformation for the rest of the characters—from

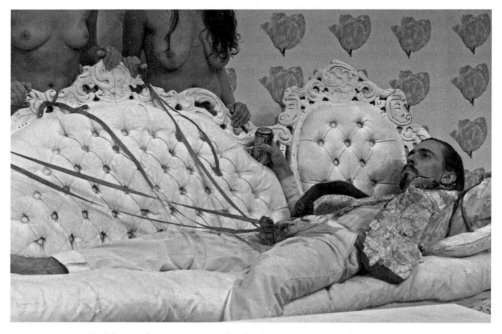

FIGURE 31.3 Todd Duerkenson in *Michael*. Photo courtesy of Jason Akira Somma.

this point on the performers begin shifting from one subject position to another. After Duerkenson's speech to the audience mentioned earlier regarding his parents and about being in love, performers Santoro and Archibald respond while Archibald looks directly at Duerkenson and Santoro stares at the audience. At first it seems that both women have feelings for him. Archibald gasps, looks at Duerkenson and says, "I didn't know any of that stuff about you." Santoro exclaims, "I knew all of that stuff. I knew everything. From the toupee, to [the . . .] wildflowers from the garden. We dated for three years. He has the most beautiful hands." Eventually they begin to overlap. In unison, Archibald and Santoro say, "He's the only guy I've never cheated on." Duerkenson takes note, "This is over-whelming" and asks himself how to handle having two women interested in him at the same time. However, the thoughts, feelings and histories involving these three perform-ers increasingly fold in on each other. The women sing their dialogue as one, narrating an elaborate story about seeing him talk to a lady while she/they bit her/their lip(s), drawing blood: "Oh my god, he's screaming my name . . . We're going to go out, have a beer, oysters, have sex-ual[16] intercourse. It will be ok, not that good." They overlap, mimetic, pull apart momentarily to express potentially individual thoughts, only to replicate each other again. They become each other.

While sex, gender, and sexuality are the explicit concerns in this particular scene, and much of the performance in terms of the dialogue, *Michael*'s hyper white aesthetic and per-formance of mimicry implicitly point to an underlying theme of quite present, yet unre-marked, racialization. In *Location of Culture*, Homi Bhabha explains how the discordant push/pull of ambivalence is central to discourses on mimicry[17]—which speaks to Freud's theory of the uncanny—for "mimicry emerges as the representation of a difference that is itself a process of disavowal."[18] Mimicry is not a neutral strategy of metonymic presence, or simple choreographic synchronization that one may expect in the context of dance-theater, but, according to Bhabha, is an authoritative technique in colonial discourse.[19] Colonial mimicry, then, is a strategy to create a "recognizable Other, *as a subject of a dif-ference that is almost the same but not quite.*"[20] This *not quite* (not quite identical, not quite white), the excess (the piercingly bright lights and cranked up acoustics), the slippages that create such repetitions with a difference, are what make mimicry particularly dangerous regarding unseating the Original—the taken for granted norm of (white) race and (hetero) sexuality. I will expand on how Young's tropes of identicalness and hyper whiteness disrupt the "natural order of things" regarding subject formation throughout the course of this chapter.

Shortly after this particular skit, Archibald and Santoro break from mimicry as Duerkenson and Santoro disappear behind the couch. Archibald talks to the audience about house sitting, takes off her underwear, puts it in her mouth, then on her head, and dances on the coffee table with 80s jazzercise-like choreography. She grabs her foot to extend her leg *a la second*, as if warming up during ballet barre, then shifts into a quick, hunched over running in place/donkey kick sequence that evolves into body rolls and shimmies with jazz hands— her movements reminiscent of the iconic dance movie, *Flashdance*. Duerkenson pops up from behind the couch, also fully naked, and dances in circles, galloping around the coffee table while keeping one hand on Archibald's waist. This is not "dance" dance per se, nor does it have the aggressive, frenetic character of the opening number. Duerkenson is amusingly awkward, orbiting Archibald like a giddy twelve-year-old. A naked Santoro appears from behind the couch and shoves Archibald off the table and takes her place for a solo. She begins with a series of dizzying spins with her arms extended while Duerkenson and Archibald roll around on the floor groping each other. Santoro performs a somewhat juvenile (yet not easily executed) acrobatic sequence consisting of a headstand with leg straddle on the coffee table, a perfect split with "victory V" arms onto the floor, finishing with a cartwheel—recognizable movements that have been practiced and repeated again and again by many a young dancer and gymnast. Eventually Duerkenson leaves and the two women dance a *pas de deux*, alternately partnering and mirroring each other with Young, now on stage, barking orders to ensure their synchronicity. After shimmying in unison Santoro assists Archibald in a technically impressive *arabesque* and *dévelopé* into a *rond de jambe* that repeats itself. When the chorus of A-ha's "Take on Me" begins, the women break into a series of horizontal and vertical punches, accompanied by Duerkenson who has returned from offstage, before collapsing into laughter on the couch.

Freud's "'A Child Is Being Beaten': Contribution to the Understanding of the Origin of Sexual Perversions" facilitates an analysis of this perpetual substitution of subject positions as the performers slip from one character and relationship to another through *Michael*'s dialogue and choreography. Freud discusses how the beating fantasy, a "primary trait of perversion" that arises in early childhood,[21] has three phases, of which only the first and third are conscious: "In the first two fantasies the child being beaten is always someone else, in the middle phase it is only ever the patient . . . [T]here is the additional fact that girls change sex between the second and third phase, fantasizing themselves into boys."[22] The story, from the point of view of the one fantasizing, evolves from "The father is beating the child," to "I am being beaten by my father," to "I am probably watching" as a father substitute beats

FIGURE 31.4 Renée Archibald in *Michael*. Photo courtesy of Jason Akira Somma.

many children.[23] Much like the way this psychic scenario destabilizes the subject positions of witness and participant, *Michael* undermines the notion that the embodied subject is stable through a series of displacements performed throughout what, I argue, can be read as an enactment of Freud's beating fantasy.

The series of substitutions performed by all of the characters in the fantasy *regardless* of gender specificity is particularly striking. The position of the subject in the third phase, "I am probably watching," parallels the spectatorship of the DTW audience members. As mere witnesses, we too are implicated and interpellated into the mise-en-scène: the fantasy, at least in this moment, is shared by us all. As spectators *of* and *in* *Michael*, we too slip from one subject position to another, a process that potentially scrambles our own gender specificity. I am an audience member. I am Duerkenson's character. I am an unacknowledged observer. I am Duerkenson again. Does this mean I am "Michael"? Perhaps I am—or at least am sitting next to—Duerkenson's character's "Father" or "Mother." By implicating the audience in *Michael's* libidinous beating fantasy, Young evokes an uncanny sensation by presenting "something repressed which *recurs*."[24] Since only the first and third phases of the beating fantasy are conscious, according to Freud, what does it mean to witness, consciously, all three phases in a nonteleological performance context? Freud argues that the unconscious, what is repressed, is that "part of [man's archaic] legacy that must always be left behind in the case of progress toward later phases of development."[25] In other words, something that "must" be left behind is stirred. Unearthed. Something is triggered. There is nothing passive about this version of witnessing. I am worked on. Worked over. The rest of this analysis will explore the psychic scars of this libidinous legacy as well as the performative effects of materializing, on stage, what Freud deems must be left behind in his narrative of sexual maturation.

In a review titled "Young and Loveless," Alexandra Beller's assessment of *Michael* betrays, I believe, a displaced hostility directed not at a performance that fails by whatever standard she applies to experimental dance-theater,[26] but toward Young's archeology of the unconscious and resulting destabilization of normative associations with sex, love, family, and the (female) body.[27] Beller's review in "Offoffoff" indicts *Michael* as an "unadulterated spew of venom . . . [where] nakedness is no longer vulnerable, love is not anyone's ideal, sex is not an act of communication, and relationships offer no moral support through the darkness of life."[28] Beller is particularly offended by the way the "performers inure us to the meaning of the body: not only to its taboos, but also to its beauty. In fact, the naked body becomes ugly, . . . a vehicle for meanness and little else."[29] None of this is untrue. By critiquing *Michael* for its "sociopathic," "nihilistic," "aggressively unselfconscious" tendencies, as well as Young's disassociation of the erotically invested body from its normative significations, Beller exposes what, exactly, this doubling characteristic of the uncanny exploits. Freud explains that the uncanny involves the subject's uncomfortable identification with someone else, causing a "doubling, dividing and interchanging of the self."[30] This identification is engendered, most obviously, by the domestic elements of *Michael* described above. While this doubling proceeds through repetition, it is a repetition with a difference, whereby the familiar is rendered strange—the domestic scene is the backdrop for the materialization of both conscious and unconscious beating fantasies—both *heimlich* and *unheimlich* at once.

I am not convinced that nihilism and vulgarity alone are what repel dancer/choreographer Beller, for I am familiar with her own often violently passionate work. (I've seen Beller choke on a fake blowjob to a speech by George W. Bush and breastfeed the American flag.) Instead, I argue that it is the disengagement of familiar tropes from their expected meanings that apparently shakes Beller, who is not alone in her harsh critique of Young's work, to her core. The repetition with a difference performed by *Michael* paints the body and home space, with which we are encouraged to identify, in an unsettling shade. In "Hello Dolly Well Hello Dolly: The Double and Its Theater," Rebecca Schneider, building on Bhabha, discusses what is so troubling about such encounters with repetition and doubling in terms of what she identifies as a "Western Cultural distrust of mimesis."[31] This distrust of mimesis, Schneider explains, reveals a "fear [that] concerns the threatening potential of the seeming Second (the double, the theatrical, the rib) to unseat the prerogatives of the First."[32] Consequently, we are profoundly disturbed by the revelation that what we deem to be "natural" and self-evident, what we call the Original, is also a product of culture and is therefore no longer sacred.[33] Although uncanniness results from a *failure* of mimesis in the sense that *Michael*'s doubling portrays repetition with a difference, I would argue that Schneider's theory of the displacement of the Original—the Western (gender-, hetero-, and racial-) normative associations connected to the home, the family, and the body, articulated in Beller's review—still applies.

In other words, this doubling, the unsettling repetition with a difference that engenders an uncanny sensation, nevertheless exposes the Original for all of its social construction. Young commingles the "real" with the "hyper-real," displacing the Original—the stable, intelligibly sexed, racialized, and gendered body—from its self-evident status in a number of ways: she cranks up the volume of her domestic aesthetics both literally and figuratively; she hyperbolizes the seemingly obvious racial classification through the blanket of white that spreads across the bodies and set of *Michael*; she destabilizes any notion of fixed subjectivity as the characters continue to overlap by acting as one person with shared histories and relationships before pulling apart again; and she interpellates the audience (through projection and identification) into the mise-en-scène. What I call Young's hyperbolization of the "real" into the "hyper-real," where the familiar is evoked then perverted, relies on the performance's employment of doubling and mimesis. The unsettling, uncanny performative effects that *Michael* has on the audience speak to Schneider's description of how this "hyper" aesthetic acts to destabilize the pure, the Original, the "white," in other words, the normatively raced, sexed, and gendered body: on "close inspection it is precisely the heteronormative tenet that femininity and masculinity are fully distinct from each other that is instantly threatened by the clone."[34] It is the clone's attempt *and* failure to be perfectly identical to the Original, for it has undergone a mutation through a hyperbolization that exoticizes the familiar, that undermines the tenets of gendered and racialized heteronormativity, articulated by Schneider and dramatized by *Michael*.

Freud explains that the beating fantasy is simply a manifestation of the Oedipus complex; like the well-known "inferiority" that accompanies the castration complex for boys and penis envy for girls, the beating fantasy reflects "the scars that remain once the process is completed."[35] For the purpose of this examination, I will disregard my own rejection of the veracity of the Oedipal Complex[36] to focus on the performative force of the *notion* of the castration complex, what I believe to be the most relevant and persistent aspect of this theoretical scenario regarding subject formation.[37] Beller's horror at Young's disassociation of the body, specifically the naked, female body, from its cultural meanings also speaks to the narcissistic scar left behind by the castration complex, for Beller's critique, which comes from a self-professed feminist perspective, still assumes the naked (and, I add, white) female body to be a site of vulnerability and idealized love.

The horror evoked by disembodied or decontextualized body parts is an uncanniness that develops because of its resemblance to the castration complex.[38] In his account of the "Wolf Man," Freud offers a number of affective phenomena engendered by the child's first witnessing of parental intercourse: the comprehension of the scene as an expression of a sado-masochistic dynamic between the parents (which I liken to the love-hate dynamic performed by Panconesi and Duerkenson); an interpretation of the goings on as anal coitus (there are numerous allusions to anal sex in *Michael*'s dialogue); and, most importantly for this analysis, an opportunity for libidinal excitation while, upon viewing the mother's female genitalia, provoking anxiety about the child's own castration (Duerkenson's penis is tormented upon his inclusion in the domestic milieu).[39] Putting Freud, Schneider, Young, and Beller into conversation with one another strengthens the notion that *one* of the Originals threatened by *Michael* is the female form of the Oedipal complex. According to Freud, the female form of the Oedipal complex results in penis envy, supposedly set into motion by the child's witnessing of a primal scene of heterosexual union, exposing the expected outcome in the narrative of sexual difference, among other (heteronormative) things. This process, the viewing of the primal scene in conjunction with one of its possible effects, the castration complex, is chiefly responsible for "the development leading to womanhood."[40] Therefore, the performative force of *Michael* is its challenge to the efficacy of this supposedly formative coupling. By putting the primal scene and its developmental effects into question, I argue that the very viewing of/participation in *Michael*—presented as a series of chaotic dance interludes and often incoherent skits—can potentially interfere with the "culturally proper" rendition of female sexuality and performance of gender (in an often unremarked racial context).

One notable moment of doubling in *Michael* not yet discussed is the double witnessing that occurs within the first ten minutes of the performance: we, the audience, watch Duerkenson masturbate while witnessing a messier, nonheteronormative, and tacitly but aesthetically articulated racialized primal scene. Instead of Mom and Dad getting it on in the theater of the family bedroom, we watch Duerkenson watch the women (whom we also watch) grind on the couch, molest the refrigerator, gyrate, thrust, flail, grab at themselves and each other, roll around wrapped up in each others' naked bodies, eat their own underwear, and talk about boyfriends, incest, and murder. This is not the picture of "proper" pubescence I'm sure Mom and Dad (and Freud) had in mind. In his discussion of the girl's development into sexual maturity, Freud explains, in contrast with the love characteristic of womanhood, "[c]hildren's love is boundless, it demands exclusivity, it is not satisfied with scraps."[41] This type of love from which we've all (supposedly) obediently, yet painfully developed, according to Freud, is without a specific goal, is insatiable, inevitably leaving us doomed to abide with an acute sense of longing and hostility.[42] Such chaotic, aimless love characteristic of childhood is strikingly played out by *Michael* during the first sequence of the performance alone. Throughout the second half of Eminem's "Crazy in Love," the stage and everything it contains becomes increasingly sexualized: one dancer is on all fours on the coffee table rhythmically gyrating faster and faster; another humps the couch in an impressive, extremely open-legged straddle; another rubs her ass up and down the fridge. *Everything* is fuckable. No particular body, no object, holds the attention of each performer for very long—they keep circulating, finding something new to grind on. Consequently, the "something familiar" that precedes the uncanny sensation experienced in the seats of DTW is the messy love of childhood sexuality that has been dutifully repressed.[43]

FIGURE 31.5 Renée Archibald, Jana Panconesi, Liz Santoro, and Tosha Tillman in *Michael*. Photo courtesy of Jason Akira Somma.

Freud's extended examination of female sexuality reveals that the girl's road to sexual maturity is more extensive and more treacherous than the boy's, and therefore, more vulnerable to perversion. Since the Oedipus complex in women is "not destroyed by the influence of castration, but rather created by it,"[44] the evolution from one phase of development to another requires added disavowals and conversions, which includes the transfer of the girl's affection from her mother to her father. It is perhaps not surprising, according to Freud's logic, that "all too often indeed the female doesn't overcome it at all."[45] Freud presents "normal" female sexual maturity as only one of three possible outcomes. Upon the discovery of her "organic inferiority," the girl, as an effect of the castration complex, will either (1) give up on sex altogether; (2) have a masculinity complex; or (3) become a "normal" (heterosexual, appropriately gendered) woman.[46] By portraying female sexuality among the chaos of polymorphous perversity, "taboo" renditions of intimacy (lesbian and incestuous love), while presenting the pride of the clitoris (the naked acrobatic routines on the coffee table display a variety of confident vulvas), Young's *Michael* not only strays from a developmental narrative that delivers the girl into "normal" womanhood, but also allows for performances of gender and sexuality, drenched in the assumed racial neutrality of whiteness, that evade Freud's triad altogether.

While I am tempted to employ Ann Liv Young's *Michael* to flesh out a new primal scene theory sated with girl on girl action and clit envy, which would result in a wholly different account of female sexuality, I hesitate to be so prescriptive by simply replacing one model of sexual development with another (even if my model is decidedly queer and positively aimless). In fact, it is the messiness and meaninglessness, which so offended Beller, that I find particularly productive. *Michael* effectively theatricizes a primal scene provoked by the cultural mandate to move away from this aimless, supposedly immature love, into a heteronormative mode of sexuality that secures the roles of mother, father, wife, husband, daughter, and son firmly into place. One of the most perplexing moments in the piece—this is quite a competition—involves the monologue from Wexler hanging from the tire above the set. Apparently, this is not an unusual practice, for upon her detection one of the performers says, "Oh my god, look, she's at it again." She asks for the audience to pray for her, she yells, apologizes, then says she's "just fucked up from head to toe" because she's still in love with her ex-boyfriend. Wexler tells a sad, twisted story about love and loss before confessing, "I've been lying to you this whole time. I've never even had a boyfriend." She then narrates strange, violent tales of her parents and sister, about feeling guilty for "hurting things" like toads and putting them in her family members' beds. She stops herself, changes gears: "It's morbid. Let's talk about sex," but then admits she's never had sex, unless you count her uncle molesting her, before trailing back into a story about her fictitious ex-boyfriend. Is it all a complete fabrication: the sex, the love, the boyfriend, the incest? There is no developmental narrative to trust in this family cell. Nothing is reliable when it comes to *Michael*.

Had the performance provided another model with which to replace the phallocratic order Freud describes, and, in a sense, prescribes, wouldn't Young have simply replaced one normalizing system with another? In Luce Irigaray's revision of Joan Riviere's "Womanliness as Masquerade," she argues that instead of providing a new model that accounts for sexual difference, or a new primal scene, one must disrupt the old phallocratic order altogether.[47] This means destroying the *discursive mechanism* that perpetuates the truth-effects of femininity

FIGURE 31.6 Renée Archibald, Jana Panconesi, and Liz Santoro in *Michael*. Photo courtesy of Jason Akira Somma.

and sexual differentiation as opposed to just toppling the model by other means. By deliberately taking on the task, or mask, of "the feminine" through mimicry (repetition and mimesis), one impedes subordination through political appropriation because female sexuality is only defined in reference to the masculine. Irigaray then emphasizes one of the functions that Freud, or more specifically, the discourse of psychoanalysis, performs—the attempt to investigate female sexuality as merely an "actual state of affairs," which Freud accepts as a norm, without accounting for the historical circumstances that foster these understandings and presentations of gender. By emphasizing this taken-for-granted state of affairs of female sexuality, performances like *Michael* jam up the theoretical machinery through repetition and mimesis beyond the bounds of common sense. Returning to Schneider's discussion of the performativity of cloning and the double, we can see how *Michael*'s play with repetition threatens the social order of gender- and heteronormativity (and racial "normativity" through the assumed neutrality of whiteness, which will be discussed below). Since "the original" of gender performativity "*becomes* itself through [a] repetition" that is disavowed, repetition then usurps the naturalized status of the original: "Thus the copy will re-place the original even as it founds an original, backward, as having come first."[48] By hyperbolizing female sexuality through mimesis, Young's work makes a mockery of the masquerade that is femininity as presented through a phallocratic discourse that accounts for sexual difference. As a repetition of a repetition, an imitation of mimesis, this performance of female sexuality through a restaging of the primal scene challenges what is often thought to be "the 'natural order' of things."[49]

As noted earlier, providing an alternative model of female sexuality would, among other things, replace one essentializing discourse with another. However, discussing the repetitive performance of "womanliness" in terms of gender and sexuality alone—devoid of a consideration of racial formation—would provide a myopic analysis that carries out its own version of essentialism. By examining Young's aesthetic choices that frame the performance of female sexuality in *Michael*, I'll attempt to elucidate the broader context within which this domestic story is told. Upon first reflection, when considering race in relation to *Michael*, all I could see was white, an effect that eventually led me to reconsider the ways in which I was blinded by the excess of whiteness and examine the performativity of the infectious pallor of the couch, fridge, baseboards, and crown molding. How can this blanket of whiteness, which spreads across the stage and the bodies of the performers, be understood not as neutrality, but as a seemingly "unmarked" factor that holds this (familial) picture together? Schneider describes the "uncanny properties of repetition" as "history brought back, again, across the body on stage, or across the body as stage."[50] What other histories might this whiteness blind us to as we witness Young's portrayal of sexual maturation? Painfully lit by a glaring sea of white, gel-less lights, the performers' skin is increasingly battered by the performance throughout the night—the friction of body against body, body against object, materializes on their flesh. White turns to a welted red on a shoulder, a thigh, across the side of a back. The off-white marley floor, dirty and scuff-marked, mirrors the bodies of the dancers. This background of white, accentuated by the pasty textures layered on the couch and the costume of the dangling performer, provides a stark backdrop that sets the details of a "hyper-real" domesticity—which conjures the (Western) image of the family, and in this case, "family" is defaulted as a white family—and its role in the primal scene and sexual development into relief. Clearly, this conceptualization of the universalized family is by no means neutral. Therefore, anyone who does not identify as white is left out of this particular narrative of subject formation.

Before further elaborating on the significance of the interarticulation of sexuality and race, I turn to Michel Foucault to illuminate the centrality of the family cell regarding sexuality in an alternate version of the psychoanalytic primal scene. Foucault's analysis of the family in *Abnormal* provides insight into how the very matrices of power that enforce the policing of childhood in turn infuse the family with an abundance of sexuality. At the center of the construction of this family cell—what Foucault refers to as "the universal secret shared by everyone but disclosed to no one"[51]—is the masturbating child. In an effort to deny the existence of infantile sexuality, someone else must be to blame for this apparent epidemic of autoeroticism.[52] The fault, therefore, must lie with the parents or childcare workers.[53] In order to purge the household of the monster of the masturbating child, surveillance regarding childcare is increased with permanent attention paid to the child's body.[54] As a result of this unrelenting gaze—a phenomenon of rigorous witnessing amplified in the context of performance[55]—the family cell is further sexualized. *Michael* certainly speaks to this Foucauldian primal scene: We watch the figure of the child/lover masturbating in the wings as he witnesses a hypersexualized family (of women) grope one another while telling tales of incest as a matter of fact.

The significance of the centrality and content/context of the family cell is articulated in Frantz Fanon's well-known discussion of how psychoanalysis—a discourse that both describes a state of affairs and produces its own truth-effects in the process[56]—studies allegedly universal social phenomena within the context of the family. The family cell and its dynamics stand in for the nation in general, thereby erasing the cultural and racial specifics of the family in particular.[57] What results from this erasure is the assumption of a "neutral" background, where "neutral" is simply a place-holder for "white." The "family cell,"

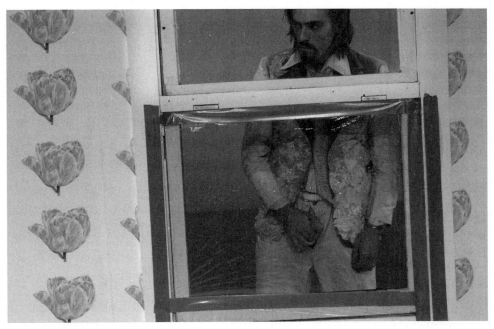

FIGURE 31.7 Todd Duerkenson in *Michael*. Photo courtesy of Jason Akira Somma.

universalized in discourses of sexuality as racially neutral, is, therefore, a decidedly white nuclear family. Race and sexuality, then, must be understood as entities that come together to create their own intersectional logics. One axis of analysis (sex, gender, and/or race) is dependent on the discursive effects of the other.

Freud's story of sexuality performed within the theater of the family, where the parents' bedroom takes center stage, can therefore be read as a progress narrative on two levels. Most obviously, sexual maturity, according to Freud, is developmental. Anyone who strays from this progress narrative—homosexuals, primitives—is infantilized and pathologized to some degree, described as either being fixated on one stage or another or having regressed to an earlier phase. The progress narrative that tends to go unnoticed is the racial one embedded within this story of sexuality, for the savage, who is both hypersexualized and racialized, is, in the words of David Eng, "securely positioned as temporally other" to the "civilized," modern (European) man.[58] Normative sexuality, then, finds its footing on (unremarked) white ground.

Work like Ann Liv Young's *Michael* not only jams the discursive mechanism that delineates a phallocratic model of female sexuality through mimesis, but it also exposes the unmarked factors that hold this picture together by literally, painfully, blinding us with whiteness. *Michael* also provides the audience with yet another transformative opportunity to subvert the developmental narrative of sexuality that psychoanalysis purports to describe, but actually proscribes. Freud explains that one's sexual development through the Oedipus complex, with its periods of latency, dictates "the fate reserved for human beings ... of having to begin their sexual lives twice—first, like all other creatures, from early childhood and then, after a long break, again during puberty."[59] Ann Liv Young's *Michael* allows us to begin again ... again. Granted, many who see Young's work do not quite get the joke. They either perceive the mimicry of the female masquerade as yet another instance of objectification, or simply dismiss the work as pornographic smut. However, I believe *Michael*'s nonnarrative structure, along with the excess of execution that tips the balance of any coherent understanding of what, exactly, Young is getting at, should cue the audience into the nonrepresentational logic of her work. Although *Michael* literally places the (Freudian/Foucauldian) primal scene(s) center stage, Young refuses to offer a coherent judgment or alternative to normative formulations of love, sex, gender, the family, and the body.

By superimposing one (presumably developmental) phase on top of another, performing libidinal histories buried in the unconscious, and presenting it all with an excess that exceeds common sense, *Michael* succeeds in creating a space that undermines notions of socially intelligible subjecthood by centralizing sex, gender, sexuality, and race. *Michael* encourages the audience to identify with the performers through Young's presentations of a familiar domestic environment—a potentially collective identification made possible by its replication of popular cultural representations of a white, heterofamilial "norm"—then distorts these details past the point that allows for identification. It is this failure of mimesis, the repetition with a twisted difference, that triggers the experience of uncanniness—for, the audience does not leave with normative significations of the body, the family, or the home intact—causing some to write scathing reviews and others to escape the theater in horror.

But does this performance of *Michael*, of an inherently, yet not always notably, raced female sexuality actually come to a definitive endpoint? The finale is an a capella version of "Somewhere Over the Rainbow" with the entire cast posed in a naked, strangely sweet tableau considering the aggressive, messy, violent character of what came before it. And yet, after the last note they all scream "fuck you" at the audience and leave the stage without a "proper" bow, the performers not acknowledging the audience as they exit the stage. Where does this leave us? What do we make of what we just saw? In the almost decade since I first viewed this work, I've loved it, hated it, loved it again, and analyzed its meanings in a variety of often-conflicting ways. That, I believe, is what makes *Michael* so painfully, powerfully, incoherently effective.

Notes

1. *Solo*, choreographed by Ann Liv Young, Berlin, Germany, 2006. My analysis for this performance, which I did not see in person, is referenced from a DVD supplied by the artist.
2. "Define Solo," Oxford Dictionaries, http://oxforddictionaries.com/definition/american_english/solo?region=us&q=solo (accessed July 10, 2012).
3. Luce Irigaray, "The Power of Discourse," in *This Sex Which Is Not One*, translated by Catherine Porter (New York: Cornell University Press, 1985), 78.
4. The former definition of the "uncanny" is one among many included in Freud's essay and refers to the English translation of the German *Unheimlich*. Sigmund Freud, "The 'Uncanny,'" in *The Standard Edition of the Complete Psychological Works of Sigmund Freud, Volume XVII (1917–1919): An Infantile Neurosis and Other Works*, translated by James Strachey (London: The Hogarth Press, 1971), 220, 221.
5. Family "cell" is Michel Foucault's term for the family unit.
6. Dance Theater Workshop (DTW), established in 1965, is a center for contemporary dance and performance located in Chelsea, Manhattan.
7. *Michael*, choreographed by Ann Liv Young, performed at Dance Theater Workshop, New York City, October 2005. All references to *Michael* are derived from my live viewing of the performance in 2005 and a DVD provided by Ann Liv Young.
8. Young revealed this source of inspiration in an interview with Dance Theater Workshop's Cathy Edwards, included in the press kit for Ann Liv Young's *Michael*.
9. By "hyper-real," I specifically refer to Young's aesthetic: the "natural," unglamorized or unbeautified presentation of bodies and objects hyperbolizes what is deemed to be untouched-up "reality" by accentuating the "raw" elements (such as the dancers' skin) with lighting, costuming, and staging techniques.
10. Freud, "The 'Uncanny,'" 200, 223.
11. Ibid., 224–25.
12. Ibid., 236.
13. Ibid.
14. The transcription's punctuation, or lack thereof, is intended to imitate the dialogue's execution.
15. Because of this lack of narrative coherence, and the structure of my argument, I take the liberty to describe this piece somewhat out of order.
16. "Sex-ual" is written as such because the performers make a notable pause after the first syllable.
17. Homi Bhabha, *Location of Culture* (New York: Routledge, 1994), 225.
18. Ibid., 122.
19. Ibid., 129.
20. Ibid., 122, original emphasis.

21. Sigmund Freud, "'A Child Is Being Beaten': Contribution to the Understanding of the Origin of Sexual Perversions," in *The Psychology of Love*, translated by Shaun Whiteside (New York: Penguin Books, 2007), 283.

22. Ibid., 297.

23. Ibid., 287.

24. Freud, "The 'Uncanny,'" 241.

25. Freud, "A Child Is Being Beaten," 304.

26. Although I must concede that perhaps it does.

27. Beller's review does not address race.

28. Alexandra Beller, "Young and Loveless," review of *Michael*, by Ann Liv Young, Offoffoff, November 4, 2005, http://www.offoffoff.com/dance/2005/michael.php.

29. Ibid.

30. Freud, "The 'Uncanny,'" 234.

31. Rebecca Schneider, "Hello Dolly Well Hello Dolly: The Double and Its Theater," in *Psychoanalysis and Performance*, edited by Patrick Campbell and Adrian Kear (New York: Routledge, 2001), 96.

32. Ibid., 96.

33. Ibid., 97.

34. Ibid., 98.

35. Freud, "A Child Is Being Beaten," 295.

36. For Freud, in short, the Oedipus Complex is the developmental desire (from the young male subject position) to kill the father and sleep with the mother.

37. Unfortunately, it is out of the scope of this project to describe how the oeuvre of Ann Liv Young effectively undermines the validity of the Oedipus Complex altogether, but it must be noted that while a theory proposing a castration complex is, I argue, unsound at best, its perpetuation in popular and social discourse must be attended to, for it has very real effects on social life.

38. Freud, "The 'Uncanny,'" 244.

39. Sigmund Freud, "The Dream and the Primal Scene," in *Three Case Histories: The "Wolf Man," The "Rat Man," and The Psychotic Doctor Schreber* (New York: Simon & Schuster, 1996), 186–204.

40. Sigmund Freud, "Female Sexuality," in *The Psychology of Love*, translated by Shaun Whiteside (New York: Penguin Books, 2006), 314.

41. Ibid., 315.

42. Ibid.

43. Freud, "The 'Uncanny,'" 247.

44. Freud, "Female Sexuality," 314.

45. Ibid.

46. Ibid., 315.

47. Irigaray, 68.

48. Schneider, 103.

49. Ibid., 97.

50. Schneider, 103.

51. Michel Foucault, "22 January 1976" in *Abnormal: Lectures at the Collège de France*, translated by Graham Burchell (New York: Picador, 1999), 59.

52. Foucault, "5 March 1975" in *Abnormal*, 243.

53. Ibid., 244.

54. Ibid., 245.
55. Here I am referring to "conventional" performances that have an audience.
56. Frantz Fanon, *Black Skin, White Masks*, translated by Richard Philcox (New York: Grove Press, 2008), 120.
57. Ibid., 121.
58. Psychic regression, then, is racially coded as well, for the "primitive" is infantilized in terms of the development and organization of the ego. David L. Eng, *Racial Castration: Managing Masculinity in Asian America* (Durham, NC: Duke University Press, 2001), 7.
59. Freud, "A Child Is Being Beaten," 295.

BIBLIOGRAPHY

Beller, Alexandra. "Young and Loveless." Review of *Michael*, by Ann Liv Young. Offoffoff. November 4, 2005. http://www.offoffoff.com/dance/2005/michael.php.

Bhabha, Homi. *Location of Culture*. New York: Routledge, 1994.

Eng, David L. *Racial Castration: Managing Masculinity in Asian America*. Durham, NC: Duke University Press, 2001.

Fanon, Frantz. *Black Skin, White Masks*. Translated by Richard Philcox. New York: Grove Press, 2008.

Foucault, Michel. *Abnormal: Lectures at the Collège de France*. Translated by Graham Burchell. New York: Picador, 1999.

Freud, Sigmund. "'A Child Is Being Beaten': Contribution to the Understanding of the Origin of Sexual Perversions." In *The Psychology of Love*. Translated by Shaun Whiteside. New York: Penguin Books, 2007.

———. "The Dream and the Primal Scene." In *Three Case Histories: The "Wolf Man," The "Rat Man," and The Psychotic Doctor Schreber*. New York: Simon & Schuster, 1996.

———. "The Ego and the Id." In *Beyond the Pleasure Principle and Other Writings*. Translated by John Reddick. New York: Penguin Books, 2003.

———. "Female Sexuality." In *The Psychology of Love*. Translated by Shaun Whiteside. New York: Penguin Books, 2006.

———. "The 'Uncanny.'" In *The Standard Edition of the Complete Works of Sigmund Freud, Volume XVII (1917–1919): An Infantile Neurosis and Other Works*. Translated by James Strachey, 218–56. London: The Hogarth Press, 1971.

Irigaray, Luce. "The Power of Discourse." In *This Sex Which Is Not One*. Translated by Catherine Porter. New York: Cornell University Press, 1985.

Schneider, Rebecca. "Hello Dolly Well Hello Dolly: The Double and Its Theater." In *Psychoanalysis and Performance*. Edited by Patrick Campbell and Adrian Kear. New York: Routledge, 2001.

Young, Ann Liv. *Michael*. Performed at Dance Theater Workshop, New York City. October 2005.

———. *Solo*. Berlin, Germany. 2006. DVD.

SECTION VIII

BIOPOLITICS

CHAPTER 32

DANCE YOUR OPERA, MIME YOUR WORDS

(Mis)translate the Chinese Body on the International Stage

DAPHNE P. LEI

SINCE the late nineteenth century, "Oriental" bodies in performance have been familiar sights for the international gaze: Michio Ito in Yeats's "Noh" plays, the "Nautch" dancers in St. Denis's "American" modern dance, Chinese actors in the Gold Rush–era San Francisco Chinatown, just to name a few.[1] These odd Oriental bodies stood out, either alone or among others, and created a peculiar spectacle that subsequently generated a type of powerful performative discourse as the world moved into the modern era. Seeing, critiquing, imitating, and reinventing these alien bodies have become a form of surrogate performance for the original performance. Very often, it is the strange Oriental bodies, or the kinesthetic or visual imitation of the Oriental bodies, instead of the sounds they make or the stories they tell, that carve out a space for Oriental performances on the world stage.[2] I argue that it was the *spatial and visual existence*, which might be bargained with the sacrifice of temporal and aural co-existence, that actually gave the rise of Asian performances on the world stage; unfortunately, as technoglobalism pushes performing culture into a largely visual-based consumption, muted Oriental bodies become almost the sole representative of Asian performances from the global perspective.

This chapter will focus on the Chinese dancing bodies in the context of Chinese opera on the international stage. The mistranslating of Chinese bodies has played an important role in recreating and disseminating the art; I will even further argue that the misread body, instead of the misheard voice of Chinese performers, is the only way that Chinese opera could secure a space on the world stage in the first place. The misreading of Chinese opera was not only an invention by the arrogance and ignorance of European Enlightenment, or by a distortion under the Victorian anthropological gaze, but also by a desire to posit the Chinese ethnicity against the Western norm, the Chinese dancing body against Western dramatic body, and Chinese antiquity against Western modernity. Eugenio Barba uses traditional Indian dance terms to illustrate the differences between behavior in daily life (*lokadharmi*) and dance behavior (*natyadharmi*); the stylized movements based on daily life that constitute the extra-daily theatrical behavior. While Western realism-based theater does not distinguish daily and extra-daily behaviors clearly, traditional Asian theaters almost always do.[3] Extra-daily technique should be applied to artistic genre, not race or ethnicity. However, I would argue that Chinese bodies are almost inevitably translated as Oriental dancing bodies (the non-norm, extra-daily bodies) in performance, no matter if it is in dance, opera, or realistic drama. That Chinese bodies always exist in the form of extra-daily dancing bodies in the context of Chinese opera has become the "racial common sense" on the world stage.[4]

The desire to read Oriental performing bodies as dancing bodies corresponds to the notion of eternal equation of culture, ethnicity, and dance. In the specific case of Chinese opera, the dancing body of the actor is highlighted but singing and story are ignored; the performer does not create new meaning from the text she utters because her dancing body *is* the Chinese culture that has not changed since antiquity. Her body has to be seen as an extra-daily body to represent her culture and to be disassociated with contemporary life and meaning. This common notion is seen in many writings about traditional non-Western dance in the West, as Susan Leigh Foster points out in the introduction to *Worlding Dance*: From musicologist Curt Sachs (1930s) to anthropologist Alan Lomax to sociologist Pierre Bourdieu (1960s), ethnicity, dance, and culture seem to be locked in a rather stable situation, which in general assumes that an ethnic dancing body channels or expresses the more or less unchanging culture.[5] Since the culture does not change, the dance does not need new interpretation.

This concept—that the Orient is both aged and ageless—is itself a very old concept. Voltaire made a comment two centuries ago: "The Chinese, like the other Asiatics, have stopt at the first elements of Poetry, Eloquence, Physicks, Astronomy, Painting, known by them so long before us. They begun all things so much sooner than all other people, never afterwards to make any progress in them."[6] My study in *yueju* (Cantonese opera) in the nineteenth-century San Francisco Chinatown reveals many instances where critics conflated Chinese theater, ethnicity, and culture in their negative writings. Moreover, while geographically present, Chinese opera suffered from a sort of temporal disjunction, or what Johannes Fabian calls "denial of coevalness," because Chinese opera was always compared with Elizabethan theater or attached to such adjectives as "old" or "ancient."[7] In other words, the physical co-existence of Chinese opera with Western theaters on the world stage depends on temporal absence in the contemporary scene.

In the age of multiculturalism and globalization, an age of multiplicity and speed, it is the continuation of this type of misreading that secures a comfortable niche for traditional Chinese opera on the world stage today. Orientalized dance spectacle of the past is the stereotypical role that Chinese opera needs to play in order to be cast for the world theater. This small performance space is built by generations of performers—Oriental and Orientalized—and its rules reinforced by performative discourse from the West and mimicked by self-Orientalized gestures from Chinese.

This chapter will address dance as the golden rule of performing Chinese for the past two centuries. The notion of Chinese dance is broadly defined because it is wildly imagined: from exquisite dance movements and spectacular acrobatics in traditional Chinese opera, to badly mimicked gestures that faintly suggest Oriental flavor; in any case, they are considered as derived from Chinese opera, the symbol of authentic Chineseness. I will first introduce the visual, aural, and kinesthetic elements in Chinese opera and its connection with Chinese classical dance. Then I will discuss the early encounters between Chinese opera and the West, both in the nineteenth-century San Francisco Chinatown and in the early twentieth-century China as an effort of Chinese modernity, and analyze how the Oriental bodies upstage music in opera performances for Western audience. Such misuse of Chinese opera (the general emphasis on the dancing body instead of voice) is adopted in intercultural theater performances as the symbol of East and in Asian American theater as the racial common sense to signify homeland. Finally, following the global trend of misreading Chinese opera, performances by Chinese today also adopt this similar method to secure their entry ticket to the world stage.

CHINESE OPERA AESTHETICS AND CHINESE CLASSICAL DANCE: A HISTORICAL OVERVIEW

"Chinese opera" is an erroneous Western naming of traditional Chinese theatrical performances: Since singing/music is the basis of theater (*xi*), there was no nonoperatic "drama" in premodern Chinese performance;[8] furthermore, "Chinese" indicates a unified national identity, whereas most of these forms are locally distinctive. However, for the sake of international perspective in this article, I use the familiar term "Chinese opera" instead of Chinese music drama, Chinese musical, or *xiqu*. Therefore, "Chinese opera" here refers to a general understanding (or misunderstanding) in the West of traditional Chinese performances involving large proportion of singing and dancing, regardless of linguistic and musical traditions or local references.[9]

Chinese opera performers speak of the four skills that they have to master: singing (*chang*), speaking (*nian*), acting (*zuo*), and fighting (*da*). However, the distinctions between categories are often blurred; for instance, the stylized speaking and recitation contain strong musical quality, and acting is a combination of stylized movement and dancing. The choreographed fighting punctuated by percussion is definitely a form of dance. While the text is mostly conveyed through singing and speaking, codified gestures and movements also "speak" part of the text. It is indeed the organic synthesis of the four that truly give the full life of the art.

Nevertheless, the categorization indicates a sense of hierarchy in Chinese training and aesthetics. Although all players have to go through basic training containing all four skills, singing is regarded the highest art among all. "Only those who don't have a voice need to fight" is a common attitude placing voice over physicality in the Chinese opera circle. Music and singing are essential in Chinese opera in many ways: A "play" in Chinese opera can be regarded as a compilation of songs; regional music determines local opera genres (Cantonese opera vs. Sichuan opera); aural appreciation is much more important than visual appreciation. "Listening to theater" (*tingxi*) and "singing theater" (*changxi*) are how Chinese traditionally refer to "going to theater" and "acting in theater."[10] Eager to sing along, opera fans have been learning the songs from early songbooks to vinyls to karaoke. As a matter of fact, the survival of *yueju* (Cantonese opera) in the late twentieth century, especially in diaspora, had a close connection with karaoke singing.[11]

Dance as a form of ritual or entertainment certainly existed in antiquity. Some early dances were also dramatic, such as "Big Mask" (*damian*). Possibly of the Uyghur (non-Han Chinese) origin, this masked dance was associated with the dramatized combat of Lord Lanling (541–573) and often considered one of the earliest forms of Chinese theater,[12] even as an inspiration for the painted face (*jing*) tradition in Chinese opera.[13] The Lanling masked dance went out of fashion in China but reached Japan, probably via Korean peninsula, and survived over a millennium. The "Lord Lanling" (*Langling wang*) dance, known in its Japanese pronunciation as the dance of "Ranryou-ou," is now recognized as part of the classical Japanese court dance tradition, *bugaku*.

In the 1950s, the famous *jingju* (Beijing opera) actor Li Shaochun (1919–1975) learned the Lanling dance in Japan and brought it back to China. The revival of a lost ancient Chinese art brought a nationalistic boost that the new Chinese nation desperately needed.[14] The term "Lanling" became a synonym for theater; Langling Ensemble (*Lanling jufang*), under the banner of Taiwan's first experimental theater, modeled on the Western little theater and avant-garde theater, with physicality, experimental spirit, and ensemble creative energy as the focus, was named with the old term.

The first systematic and institutional way of studying dance probably should be dated during the Sui (589–618) and Tang (618–907) dynasties. The Pear Garden (*liyuan*), established by the Emperor Xuanzong (r. 712–756) to train court musicians and dancers, could be considered the first academy for classical music and dance in China. This was also a period of multiculturalism: Many artistic concepts and forms as well as religious thoughts were imported from Central Asia and India. With exotic and diverse origins, music, dance, and theater gradually "Sinicized" throughout history and became the classical traditions.

Today, when we speak of traditional Chinese dance, the diverse forms can be generally divided into three categories: classical dance, folk dance, and ethnic dance; while the first two are for the Han majority, separated by their social status, the last one indicates its connection with ethnic minorities. While folk and ethnic dances continued to develop at the margin, classical dance was incorporated into theater and seemed to have lost its status as an independent discipline, as various theatrical forms (*zaju, nanxi, chuanqi*, and regional drama later) became more established through the Song (960–1279) to Qing (1644–1911) dynasties. Dance historian Wang Kefen states, dance "served" theater, for enriching the dramatic theme, characters, and plot.[15] Although pure dance is sometimes part of a play, dance is usually *not* considered an independent element in Chinese opera in premodern times. It is part of the requirement for acting and movement; in other words, all actors are dancers. As a matter of fact, when contemporary scholars attempt to reconstruct a history of Chinese classical dance, they had to trace the roots in various existing Chinese operas.

VISUALIZING A CHINESE MODERNITY: A DOUBLE WESTERNIZATION PROCESS

From the mid-nineteenth century to the mid-twentieth century, through intercultural encounters, Chinese opera experienced a series of reforms, which I see mainly as the result of voluntary westernization as both a survival tactic in diaspora and as an effort for Chinese modernity at home. Other than the obvious modernization in theater technology and in dramatic themes, there is also a deliberate separation between "drama" and "opera" and a general shift from aural to visual emphasis in Chinese opera.

While China was being forced to open itself due to the arrival of Western imperial power in the mid-nineteenth century, *yueju* (Cantonese opera), a regional operatic form from southern China, bravely crossed the Pacific to join in the Gold Rush in California. 1852 marked the first documented Chinese opera performance in the New World and soon this art form became part of the "local" attractions of San Francisco in the nineteenth century.[16] The international sojourners, opportunists, and tourists of this new metropolitan frequented Chinese theaters and offered their not-so-subtle ethnocentric comments. The comments fall into the pattern of admiring the spectacle (beautiful costume, extraordinary movement, and the femininity of the Oriental bodies) but ridiculing the singing, speaking, and music.

Comments on costume generally express amazement: "[T]he Celestial actors ... will appear in an array of semi-barbarian splendor never seen outside of the walls of Pekin [*sic*],"[17] and their dresses are made of "a profusion of satin, silk and painted cotton stuffs, and are covered with tinsel, outlandish ornaments and barbaric display."[18]

Furthermore, a lot of attention is paid to the peculiarity of the Chinese body, either on their extraordinary movement—"juggling and feats of dexterity"[19] and "feats of skill, vaulting, tumbling,"[20] or on the feminine features—"almond-shaped eyes,"[21] "fine, long tapering fingers,"[22] and "The Beautiful Little-Footed Lady! The only one ever on public exhibition."[23]

The writing on singing and dialogue is very different:

> The dialogue being of course unintelligible, the American portion of the audience had to enjoy themselves in imagining what was going on, and in admiring the stage properties and the costumes of the numerous performers, some of which were really splendid.[24]

Music and singing are satirized as,

> The wailings of a thousand love-lorn cats, the screams, gobblings, brayings, and barkings of as many peacocks, turkeys, donkeys, and dogs—the "ear-piercing" noises of hundreds of botching cork-cutter, knife-grinders, file-makers, and the like—would not make a more discordant and agonizing concert than these Chinese musical performers ... Heaven has ordered it, no doubt, for wise purposes, that the windy chaos is pleasant to the auricular nerves of the natives.[25]

The clear distinction between sight and sound of Chinese opera, the enjoyable dancing body but intolerable singing has gone beyond artistic critique or even cultural confusion. Comprehension of the Chinese language should not be a problem, as translation, either on "theater hand-bills" or through interpreters, was not uncommon during those performances.[26] Is Western ocularcentrism, then, the real obstacle for appreciating Chinese aurally? From the Renaissance obsession with perspectives, Michel Foucault's panopticon, and Guy Debord's society of spectacle to Martin Jay's scopic regimes, it is hard to refute there exists an undeniable zest for seeing in the Western tradition.[27] However, the detailed and vivid descriptions of the music and singing suggest that the Chinese sound actually attracts great attention and inspires critical discourse among Western audience. It is the negative auricularcentricism, the overemphasis on the negative aspects of Chinese sound, not the positive ocularcentrism that carries out the critical racial judgment here. The description of Chinese sound—that the animal sounds are appealing only to "the auricular nerves of the natives"[28]—points to a racial hierarchy associated with biological differences, which forms the basis of this type of discursive entertainment: Admiring the spectacle and satirizing the unintelligible text and unbearable music seem more amusing than theatergoing itself.

The Oriental body was often seen as existing in extremity—it was either noticed through super masculine martial arts, or through a display of ultimate femininity. Theatrical convention of the period had male actors play female characters most of the time, and this knowledge was not unknown to American or European playgoers. However, the conflation between players and characters, and between stage femininity and the gender of players, demonstrates a typical voyeuristic gaze toward the ethnic other during that time. The comments on the "ladies" (with a wink) can be seen as the origin of effeminization of Asian American men in the United States, another "racial common sense." Chinese opera in the nineteenth-century United States gradually became another Barnum-esque wonder, represented by the spectacular or freakish dancing bodies.

At home back in China, the shift from aural to visual emphasis was not a result of ethnocentric gaze but a strategic voluntary westernization, or, as we can imagine, a deliberate way to "catch up" with time to create an illusion of modernity and democracy. Joshua Goldstein writes about the spatial change for *jingju* (Beijing opera) performance at the turn of the twentieth century, when China moved from the imperial dynasty to a republican nation-state. The teahouse, the traditional commercial performance venue for *jingju* with table seating, functioned as a social space and marketplace besides performance space. The audience ate and chatted while listening to the opera and only turned to stage when something really caught their attention. However, such teahouses were gradually replaced by Western-style playhouses as the major performance venue for *jingju* during the early republican era. Theaters now had proscenium stages and auditorium seating as well as modern lighting with spotlights and the capability to dim the house.[29] The architectural innovation points to a number of shifts: from an imperial dynasty to a modern nation-state, from separate seating of clear social hierarchy to seating of apparent democracy, from an interactive player-audience relationship to a one-direction controlled gaze for the audience. The noisy, interactive crowd was silenced and made civilized in the modern architecture.

The introduction of Western style theater, spoken drama (*huaju*) by students who studied in Japan, also had an impact on the modernization of Chinese drama.[30] Spoken drama, also named "civilized drama" (*wenmingxi*), which often focuses on social issues and contemporary themes and has modern settings and performance styles (colloquial dialogue instead of verse singing), further frames traditional operas as old-fashioned and even backward (as noncivilized drama). In order to appear civilized and modern, traditional operas also went through a lot of innovations, such as adopting modern costumes and contemporary themes. Mei Lanfang, for instance, was instrumental in modernizing *jingju* and making it much more visually appealing with new costume and set design and with his emphasis on dance. As a matter of fact, dance, rather than drama (opera), was his way to attract Western audiences. In 1915, Mei rechoreographed an old play *Chang E Flying to the Moon* (*Chang'e benyue*) with an added pure dance number. His friends commented: "Now we have something to show foreigners!" Later he created/choreographed a number of dance-dramas, such as *Heavenly Maidens Scattering Flowers* (*Tiannü sanhua*) and *Hegemon Kings Says Farewell to His Queen* (*Bawang bieji*), famous pieces his fans would later remember him with.[31] These pieces, along with *Drunken Princess* (*Guifei zuijiu*) and other dance pieces, presented Chinese opera as a visually astounding, elite form of national art during his US tour in 1930.

From the Gold Rush San Francisco to the early twentieth-century Beijing and New York, the Oriental body, in dancing or acrobatics, has come to the forefront in Chinese opera, as a result of westernization and modernization, whether involuntary or not. Although I do not deny the world trend of moving toward a more visually based culture because of the innovations in media in the twentieth century, I believe in the case of Chinese opera, the concept of "being accepted by the West" and "catching up with the Western time," a process of double westernization, played a crucial role in the visualization of the art.

THE INTERCULTURAL FORMULA: LOGO WESTERN + DANCING ORIENTAL

No one can trace the origin of "when East meets West" in performance, but performance created as a result of a conscious East/West encounter probably started in the 1960s or 1970s. I have written elsewhere about hegemonic intercultural theater (HIT), the classic form of intercultural theater from the West, which usually combines "First World capital and brain power with Third World raw material and labor, and Western classical texts with Eastern performance traditions."[32] Ariane Mnouchkine's *Les Astride* (kathakali) and Richard Schechner's *Oresteia* (*jingju*) are examples of such intercultural theater. In this part of the chapter, instead of analyzing power imbalance in the intercultural bargaining or collaboration, I mainly focus on the foregrounding of the Oriental dancing bodies in intercultural performances.

First of all, historically, there seemed to be a strong obsession to play Chinese, to be in the imagined Chinese body, even at the early intercultural theatrical encounters. I am not addressing racial satires such as Mark Twain and Bret Hart's *Ah Sin* (1876) or Henry Grimm's *Chinese Must Go* (1879), which could be seen as a direct response to the immigration labor issues in the nineteenth-century United States. I am interested in the history of the portrayal of Chinese with the apparent sincerity and seriousness, from early "Chinese" plays such as *The First Born* (1897) by Francis Powers and *The Yellow Jacket* (1912) by George C. Hazelton and Harry J. Benrimo, to the most recent controversial production of a new translation of the Chinese classic *The Orphan of Zhao* (2012) by the Royal Shakespeare Company.[33] Many Chinese characters were created, but their bodies were usurped and replaced by Orientalized bodies. These Chinese characters were written with certain loftiness and distance; in other words, they were not daily bodies in Chinese costume, but extra-daily bodies with imagined Chinese opera stylization.

The Yellow Jacket was first produced in New York, but soon this novel play became a European sensation, enjoying great success from London to Vienna to Moscow.[34] The major innovation is what Erika Fisher-Lichte calls "the rules of the game," the prescribed ways of being Chinese, which consist of specific instruction of imagined Chinese gestures and movement.[35] The major "Chinese" invention is the Property Man, who is made as a stage character with both his extra-daily behavior (such as striking a gong) but also daily behavior (such as "enters indifferently" and "smokes pipe" while moving props).[36] In traditional Chinese opera, both stagehands and musicians are not in costume; the musicians are on stage, either in the back or on the side, and stagehands enter and exit as their jobs dictate, without trying to steal the show. The audience understands the convention to distinguish dramatic action from nondramatic action within the stage perimeter, so a property man's "entering indifferently" is never supposed to be confused with the drama proper. The significance of *The Yellow Jacket* is the meticulous prescription of daily behavior as extra-daily behavior, because to present Chinese authenticity is to deny Chinese the possibility of being "natural" and "normal," which means nontheatrical. The overtheatricalization of the nontheatrical is itself an Orientalist gesture that was dominant in the early twentieth century. Overtheatricalized Oriental body, like ethnic dance, is part of the racial common sense.

The trend of playing Chinese physically but not vocally continued throughout the twentieth century. Orientalized costume and makeup and dance-like movements, both largely based on imagined Chinese opera stylization, offer a satisfying experience for actors to *be* Chinese; however, while Western actors painstakingly learned to be Chinese visually, they did not make the slightest attempt to be Chinese vocally, that is, to speak or sing Chinese opera, despite the fact that they are almost always under the impression that they are performing Chinese opera. To be Chinese is to play Chinese opera without singing opera! Why is playing Chinese vocally so unimaginable while playing Chinese visually can be enjoyable? Is logocentrism, the dominance of text, which Artaud abhors, the main force preventing Western actors from imagining playing Chinese vocally because of the sense of superiority? Or, is the challenging vocal technique in Chinese opera simply beyond the realm of possibility in the Western imagination? The male impersonator's falsetto voice is often considered ridiculous. However, difficult vocal training is not unique in Chinese culture, as Western opera, itself a distinctive genre with long history, requires very arduous training. One can even argue that the classical tradition of castrato in the West makes Chinese opera vocal training appear easy. When it comes to training in Chinese opera, the emphasis is always on the intense or even sadistic physical training.[37] It is the fear, a type of Orientalist version of xenophobia that wants to confine the potentially threatening foreign ethnicity to something harmless, frivolous, child-like, yet ancient and beautiful "dance." Even when Chinese ethnicity and culture are deliberately included to create a new synthesized form of theater, they are inevitably presented in dance-like movements and in costumed spectacles. Chinese have moved out of Chinatown, but their art is confined in the Orientalized reservation. The model minority syndrome, that Asian Americans are viewed as successful but complacent today, has had a very long history and part of that history can be traced directly to performance.

As intercultural theater became a distinctive genre since the late twentieth century, many intercultural theater productions involve "real" Chinese opera bodies, such as Richard Schechner's *Oresteia* (1995), a collaboration with Taiwan's established intercultural group Contemporary Legend Theater (CLT), and Peter Sellars's *The Peony Pavilion* (1998), starring Hua Wenyi, renowned *kunqu* (Kun opera) diva. In both productions, the maestros did not intervene much with the actors' artistic expressions. Their operatic performances were "left alone" more or less in their own style; in other words, their traditional performances were "quoted" or "juxtaposed" with other performance styles, instead of being altered to fit in the directors' intercultural schema. Nevertheless, it is clear that their dancing bodies are much more valued than their singing voice; it is the visual memory of their dance that becomes part of the archives of world intercultural theater.

For *Oresteia,* both Wu Hsing-kuo (Agamemnon) and Wei Hai-Ming (Clytemnestra) are powerful *jingju* (Beijing opera) actors; even the chorus (with minor *jingju* actors) delivered a very professional performance. The stylization of the parts linked to the original story

Oresteia correspond with the innovative *jingju* style that Contemporary Legend had been using for a decade. Schechner's intercultural contribution, as I see it, is his signature environmental theater approach to set the production outdoors (a park in downtown Taipei) and his postmodern framing—with Athena as a game show hostess, the added satire serves as commentaries on contemporary Taiwanese society. Most criticism centers on the added satire, because this is what deviates most from CLT's previous performances: how it makes a travesty of both *jingju* and Greek tragedy,[38] or how it misinterprets and disrespects certain serious issues in Taiwan.[39] However, I believe, in Schechner's mind, it is the visual elements that made the whole experiment worthwhile and memorable.[40]

Peter Sellars's ambitious avant-garde production *The Peony Pavilion* starred Hua Wenyi, the *kunqu* artist of the stature of national treasure.[41] It is a production of multiplicity and hybridity, mixing artistic genres, media, and storylines; this is what Sellars calls "much too much!"[42] Among cacophonies and chaos of Western opera, ballet, multimedia projections and American realistic acting is the pure, largely uncontaminated Chinese opera scenes performed by Hua Wenyi. She demonstrated the most exquisite fan dance and elegant movements and beautiful opera voice, all without traditional makeup and costume. She wore a silky pantsuit with natural makeup, appearing as a middle-aged woman reminiscing the beautiful opera past instead of a sixteen-year-old maiden pining for love.

Unfortunately, her quiet singing was almost drowned out by the bombardment of Western operatic singing, and her elegant dancing blurred by the blinding neon lights, and multiple moving projections and perhaps did not leave much impression for the Western audience. However, even though her music presence was short, her dancing body lingered. She was asked to move along with the ballet dancer Michael Schumacher around the stage for a long time after her own brief scene. She appeared uncomfortable, her movement a little random and awkward. She was first stripped of her traditional costume and makeup and now her codified movement. She appeared naked, and a little out of place.

Hua had expressed her discomfort with wearing the modern suit, which lacked the flowy elegance that a loose-fitting robe and water sleeves can provide. The water sleeves are not just pretty decoration; they function as the extended limbs for specialized dance movements for specific role types. Without the water sleeves, her dance appeared ruthlessly severed and her character betrayed. When asked the reason for discarding the traditional robe, Sellars answered: I want to see her legs![43] The seemingly crass answer might have been a joke, but it also reveals the Western directors' philistine vision for Chinese opera and the desire to uncover the enigmatic Oriental body. While connoisseur audience members read the flowy costume and cumbersome headdress as part of the dance movement and characterization, Western directors like Sellars and Schechner need to present the X-rayed (and X-rated) Oriental dancing bodies in order to express the essential Chineseness.

SELF-ORIENTALIZED DANCING BODIES ON THE ASIAN (NORTH) AMERICAN STAGE

Upstage SONG, who appears as a beautiful woman in traditional Chinese garb, dances a traditional piece from the Peking opera, surrounded by percussive clatter of Chinese music.

> *Then, slowly, lights and sound cross-fade; the Chinese opera music dissolves into a Western opera, the "Love Duet" from Puccini's* Madame Butterfly, SONG *continues dancing, now to the Western accompaniment. Though her movements are the same, the difference in music now gives them a balletic quality.*[44]

Probably the most memorable character from the Asian American canon is presented as a "fake" beautiful Chinese opera diva. *M. Butterfly*, the first Asian American play on Broadway and the most anthologized Asian American play, has been serving as a token both for the Asian American theater community and for multiculturalism and diversity in theater education. The central character Song, the female impersonator both in Chinese opera and in life, as well as drag diva in Western opera, epitomizes the ultimate Oriental stereotype in gender, ethnicity, culture, and art. *M. Butterfly* successfully uses Oriental stereotypes to deconstruct stereotypes while reinforcing certain stereotypes related to Chinese opera and culture.[45]

Hwang is conscious of his invented Asianness. Growing up in southern California, Hwang learns to create an Asia from senior Asian American writers like Maxine Hong Kingston and Frank Chin. From his early plays *FOB* (1979) and *The Dance and the Railroad* (1981), to the Tony Award–winning *M. Butterfly* (1988), Chinese opera has been used as a stable image to remind his audience of the Asian home, which can only be authenticated on Asian American stage.

The lesser known *The Dance and the Railroad*, which dramatizes two Chinese railroad workers in the 1860s, is a short play that typifies the hyphenated state of Asian-American. Asia(n) and America(n) are respectively represented by the older Lone and the younger Ma, as well as by the dance (Chinese opera) and the railroad (the transcontinental railroad). Ma, the naïve young railroad worker, is attracted by Lone's opera performance and hopes to learn from him. Note that John Lone, the Hong Kong–born, *jingju* trained, and Hollywood-bound actor played Lone and choreographed the first production. Throughout the play, playing Gwan Gung, a historical heroic figure who has a distinctive theatrical persona, has been presented as the goal for reaching the perfection of Chinese opera. Martial art movement instead of opera singing or stylized speaking, is what the railroad workers, the imagined founders of Asian America, see as the symbol for home, and what American audience as the synonym for the Far East. Even though Chinese opera is a clear reference here, the play is choreographed more like a martial dance. Below are some examples:

> *A Mountaintop.* LONE *is practicing opera steps. He swings his pigtail around like a fan.*
> *Silence.* LONE *pulls out a gong.* MA *gets into position.* LONE *hits the gong. They do the following in a mock-Chinese-opera style.*
> MA *bows to* LONE. *Gongs. They pick up fighting sticks and do a water-crossing dance.*
> LONE *and* MA *begin a second battle dance. This one ends with them working the battle sticks together.* LONE *breaks away, does a warrior strut.*[46]

As a matter of fact, such stick fights accompanied by a gong first premiered in Hwang's *FOB*, a play he wrote as a Stanford undergraduate student. The play takes place in the backroom of a Chinese restaurant. The FOB (fresh off boat) Steve and the ABC (American-born Chinese) Dale are vying for the attention of Grace, a 1.5-generation Asian American[47]—they perform a stick combat and verbal fight, while Grace strikes two pots. Later she also embodies Fa Mu Lan (Hua Mulan), the legendary woman warrior, joining in the martial dance. Asianness, Americanness, and Asian Americanness are discussed and represented and misrepresented through the martial art/dance movements in the bodies of Gwan Gung or Fa

Mu Lan. Steve, who possesses the most Asianness among the three, eventually wins the fight with the "opera" dance.[48]

Both these early plays present Chinese opera with masculine martial art movement but without opera makeup or costume; these Bruce Lee–inspired plays reflect the immaturity of the playwright as well as of the genre itself. *M. Butterfly*, a much higher artistic achievement, plays with a different concept in using Chinese opera to represent gendered Asianness. While masculinity seems to be presented with open honesty, femininity is always mysterious; the faked Chinese opera is so alluringly feminine and deceiving that it can even dupe the French diplomat Gallimard. With traditional costume and makeup, the femininity of the Chinese dancing body is heightened but also obscured. The Oriental dancing body is presented as a riddle both for Gallimard and for American audience—how is Butterfly faked, as Chinese, as woman, as Chinese opera diva? The success of *M. Butterfly* is both a blessing and a curse: It has pushed Asian American theater to the mainstream but also stabilized the misrepresentation of Chinese opera as Orientalized dancing bodies. It is difficult for later Asian American plays to escape the spell of Chinese opera dancing bodies.

Chay Yew's *Red*, similar to *M. Butterfly*, has Chinese opera actors as central characters. Sonia Pickford, an Amy Tan–like popular Asian American writer returns to China, encounters her former self, and relives her family and historical trauma. Like *The Yellow Jacket*, this play is written with a prescribed Chinese opera dramaturgy: The stage is bare, with only a few chairs that can be used as different furniture or set pieces. Stagehands remain on stage to hand out appropriate props or move chairs or to function as extra bodies in the play. *"Fluidity between scene is key. Musical transitions can be used."*[49]

A major part of the story deals with how Master Hua, a renowned *jingju* artist trains his daughter Ling, who in turn "struggles" him during the Cultural Revolution after she has become a red guard. However, Chinese opera, once again, is presented as mainly visual elements. The Asian American actors, despite their ethnicity, have clear signs of Western realistic actor's training tradition in their physicality. The free-spirited Asian American bodies are thinly veiled with their limited opera movement training. As Master Hua scolds his young daughter for her awkwardness in a training session: "Look! Look at you! You walk like a duck!"[50] I imagine the Asian American actors sense an equal uneasiness when imitating stylized Chinese opera movement, which, if not executed meticulously, is considered ugly. However, I find their ethnic affinity accentuates their ethnic drag: While faking Chinese with Orientalized stylization by Western actors is not a pleasant sight, such faking within ethnic proximity (East Asian American playing Chinese) appears even more absurd. The problem of Asian yellowface points to an essential problem of American institutionalized multiculturalism.

Patrice Pavis, in theorizing acting in intercultural theater, writes that actors "simultaneously reveal the culture of the community where they have trained and where they live, and the bodily technique they have acquired."[51] This is a fair assessment for any intercultural acting; however, the problem here is the ethnic *proximity*. As I have discussed so far, in the long history of playing Chinese in the West, Chinese opera is imagined as a sign that automatically signifies Asian authenticity, even if it is only a gesture vaguely suggested or badly executed. It is the intention of the sign, not the quality of the sign that matters. The Anglo actors in *The Yellow Jacket* can play Chinese with minimal Chinese opera gestures because their ethnic distance ensures their acting is *artistically representing* Chinese but not *realistically presenting* Chinese, whereas Asian American actors are often viewed under a very different lens. In a country like the United States, where multiculturalism is promoted but not fully understood at the institutional level, there is a general conflation among race, ethnicity, and culture; as a result, Asian American theater is seen as a product born out of this type of rainbow-colored blessing: separate but equal. Asian American actors are not allowed to *play* Asian because they are *being* Asian; their art disappears because their individual bodies are erased under the yellowface. Problems arise: What if the Oriental flavor is badly mimicked by Asian American actors? While Western actors' bad imitation might be seen as a drag or camp performance, Asian American actors' bad Asian impersonation would be measured on a paradoxical scale: It is unforgivable, on one hand, because Asian American actors should be able to do it *naturally*; on the other hand, their shortcomings have to be forgiven because the multicultural America respects every color of the ethnic rainbow. What else can Asian American actors do if they are not allowed to play white and cannot play Asians artistically? The actors are not to blame because no matter how long the rehearsal period is, it can never compete with ten years of rigorous training in opera school, and the "culture of the community where they have trained and where they live" will shine through their recently acquired Chineseness. The audience is also not to blame because the multicultural America definitely consists of some Chinese opera connoisseurs who can easily detect a badly executed sign of Chineseness. The real problem lies in the culture, which leads playwrights and directors to believe that faking Chinese opera *visually* as a theatrical trope is dramaturgically possible and theatrically convincing, even in the multicultural society in the twenty-first century. Chinese opera/dance, unfortunately, is caught in the multicultural dilemma and is often used as a lazy stage device to legitimize bad ethnic faking.

North of the border, Asian Canadian playwright Marty Chan wrote *The Forbidden Phoenix*, with music by Robert Walsh,[52] "a hybrid of Chinese Opera and North American Theater, using martial arts, music, costumes, and magic to convey a mythical story with historical relevance."[53] This play tells a story of the Chinese legendary character Monkey King, but with Asian Canadian immigration history, the "bachelor men" as the background. This new production, generally following the Western tradition of playing Chinese, adopted both American and Chinese performing cultures but instead of finding a balanced fusion, these two elements were very separated. In other words, *The Forbidden Phoenix*, with a mixed-race cast, looked Chinese but sounded American.[54]

William Lau, who is on the board of the Canada Council for the Arts, served as the mentor for the Peking opera–based movements because of his training in Chinese classical dance and opera.[55] It is very clear from the beginning that visuality is where Chineseness lies: "They need to have the look of Chinese opera," stated William Lau. In terms of casting, it was also generally agreed that "skills were far more important than an Asian heritage, particularly since the performers would be wearing extensive Peking Opera style makeup" and "iconically recognizable costumes from Peking opera." Adrian Young, who "used 'the Jackie Chan' type of kung fu and wushu," designed the choreography of "a martial art that favours showiness and acrobatics."[56]

The bachelor men were Chinese immigrants in Canada in the late 1800s, who mainly came to work in the railroad construction. Having to leave their families behind in order to seek better lives, the bachelor men share a similar story of nostalgia, adventure, and discrimination with other immigrants. However, Chan claims that he wants to tell the story "from a Chinese viewpoint," so the combination of Monkey King and bachelor men, Peking opera façade and mixed-race cast, Chinese look and musical sound are all his ways of authenticating *himself* as Chinese. Chinese opera, once again, is reduced to a form of Orientalized dance spectacle in order to contribute to the process of incorporating Chineseness into Canadian multiculturalism.

The examples above show that for three decades, when multiculturalism has become part of the theatrical trope in the Americas, Asian (North) American theater has created a distinctive image for itself: It is an American story with visual Asia, which is represented in the Orientalized dance, extracted from imagined Chinese opera. I have expressed frustration in Asian American theater's incessant and formulaic use of Chinese opera to represent "home." The unimaginative ways of using Chinese opera dancing bodies is one of the symptoms that show the fatigue of this genre.[57] Whether it is a Bruce Lee/Jackie Chan type of kung fu mimicking or tapered-finger *M. Butterfly* type of femininity embodying, the Chineseness exists in Orientalized dancing bodies. During the long immigration and acculturation process, Chinese opera has been muted; it is now an art with colors and quasi-dance movements, and it is this erroneous concept that symbolizes the ultimate Chineseness, for Chinese and for non-Chinese.

This muting process is not just an old concept but an idea that continues to be promoted through institutionalized multiculturalism. *The Forbidden Phoenix*, for instance, other than appealing to the general public, was also designed as an educational piece. The study guide compiled by Karen Gilodo and Christina Sangalli is to help school children (third grade and up) understand "why people leave their homelands, how the state of the earth affects our communities, and identify the sacrifices we make and that have been made for the sake of our families." It provides articles written by the playwright, composer, an immigration lawyer, and others. It also contains a glossary that defines "less developed countries" as "Africa, Asia (except Japan), Latin America and the Caribbean, and Oceania (except Australia and New Zealand)" and "more developed countries" as "Europe (including all of Russia), the United States, Canada, Australia, New Zealand, and Japan." The guided activities include suggested discussion topics on immigration and other matters and a physical activity "mask and movement," with a chart showing symbolized colors in Chinese opera "mask" (such as red for loyalty and white for cunningness).[58] Note that "mask" is a common misconception regarding Chinese opera practice in the West: The painted face (*jing*) characters do not wear masks; their theatricality is heightened by the colorful makeup connected with exaggerated facial movements, along with their sonorous voice and grand postures.

The misconception of Chinese opera mask epitomizes the misconception of embodying Chineseness: Ethnicity and culture are mask-like objects, easy to put on and take off, because underneath the mask everyone shares the common, ethnic-free humanity! From the study guide for school children, the separation between Western logocentrism and Asian visuality is clearly presented; moreover, in the act of promoting a nationalistic multiculturalism, Monkey King is appropriated as a symbol of Canadian (universal) immigrants, and his Chineseness is reduced to imagined Chinese colors and dances. The reduction and muting process of Chinese opera goes on to the next generation.

MULTIPLE WESTERNIZATION AND SELF-ORIENTALIZATION AS SELF-REPRESENTATION

As discussed earlier, I see the visualization of Chinese opera with the result of placing dance over singing roughly a century ago as a double westernization and modernization process. Asian American theater, as part of the contemporary American theater, generally follows the realistic style in portraying Asian Americans; however, when it is necessary to symbolize Asianness, Chinese opera is often adopted as a familiar trope, as we have seen from *FOB* to *The Forbidden Phoenix*.

How then, does Chinese opera present itself on the world stage today? In the age of globalization, when technology often acts as a filter or censorship for selecting performances, how does Chinese opera survive such scrutiny? As downloading speed increases, audience's patience decreases every day, so how does the slow and archaic Chinese opera compete with other performing arts? With such accelerated decline, when will Chinese opera be completely dead and erased from the global theater history?

In 2004, in the low tide of Chinese opera rose the miracle *kunqu, The Peony Pavilion: The Young Lovers' Edition*. It is a very successful transnational joint-venture, combining actors from China and capital and brain power from the Chinese peripheries (Taiwan, Hong Kong, California). From its premiere in Taipei in 2004 to 2014, this young lovers' *Peony* has enjoyed enthusiastic reception and favorable reviews for over two hundred performances in many parts of the world.[59] The production is lavishly but elegantly done, with every aspect of the performance carefully planned and exquisitely executed. The singing and dancing follow the traditional *Peony* stylization; however, it is designed with modern staging sensibility in mind, with minimalist set and stylistic and effective lighting and sound effect (which is produced by a live orchestra)—the fresh approach is unprecedented in the history of Chinese opera.

Visual aesthetics is the highest priority of the play. In the producer Pai Hsien-yung's mind, the story of *Peony* is about young lovers, so the play has to take a youth approach: by young actors and for young people. Understanding the YouTube generation's gravitation toward visual pleasure instead of aural enjoyment, he focuses on enhancing visual beauty for the production. Other than the gorgeous handmade silk costumes and stylistic lighting, the young actors are chosen mainly for their physical beauty, not their voice. Traditionally, these difficult roles are performed by seasoned actors, so Pai had the young actors go through a boot camp style of actor training by reputable masters to minimize criticism about the actors' qualifications. With the help of portable microphones, the leading actress can use a kind of ethereal voice instead of solid operatic voice to express her longing and sorrow; the weakness in her voice is minimized because the audience focuses on her exquisite eye movement, blushing smile, and elegant dance. Numerous photography exhibits and coffee table books and souvenirs of the young lovers' *Peony* further help visualize the performance.

The emphasis on the visual beauty, for the transnational audience, is placed on the dancing bodies. There is a large dance number for the flower spirits, who are young women beautifully clad in embroidered skirts that expand like butterfly wings. As they move and turn, each flower spirit is like a blooming flower continuing to form wonderful kaleidoscopic patterns. Pai paid special attention to the flower spirit dance for the California tour; he commented on some small dance imperfection in front of the cast after one rehearsal: "Don't think Americans don't understand Chinese opera. They do! They can see everything clearly."[60] This is not so different from Mei Lanfang's friends' comment on his new dance as "something for foreigners." It is interesting to see such similar assumptions across space and time: it seems almost unimaginable for the Chinese opera circle to expect non-Chinese to understand the intricacy of the opera singing, but dancing as a universal art can be appreciated by all. Whether it is a Chinese version of the racial common sense of the non-Chinese or a hard lesson learned in the multiple encounters with the West since the nineteenth century, one thing is certain: To play the international card well is to have a beautiful dance number.

While Westerners are unwilling to "appreciate" Chinese opera singing, Chinese have no confidence in promoting opera music in the international arena. Chinese dance seems to become the happy middle place where two forms of racial common sense can meet. The universality of the Oriental dancing body also expresses itself in martial movements. In each day of the three-day performance, a short martial scene is inserted, partly as a way to "wake up" the audience after long singing, partly because of the belief in the Western audience's preference for spectacle. These scenes are tangential to the main plot, but provide lavishing spectacle of colorful costumes and magnificent tumbling and fighting, as well as a change of tempo for the lengthy Chinese opera performance. From the long melodic singing and slow dancing come the exciting acrobatic splendor; the "wow" effect is clearly audible in the auditorium.

A recent production by Taiwan's Contemporary Legend Theater *When Jingju Meets Rock & Roll* (*Shuihu 108 Zhongyitang*; premiered in Hong Kong in 2011) relies much more on the visual effects that appeal to youth sensibility. Basing the work on the classical novel *The Water Margin* (*shuihuzhuan*), contemporary writer Zhang Dachun wrote the script and popular singer composer Zhou Huajian wrote the music. Fourteen young *jingju* actors (age 17 to 22) were cast to provide a grand acrobatic spectacle. The production is a combination of musical, rock concert, and *jingju*; furthermore, the traditional *jingju* aesthetics seemed to be replaced by manga-inspired characterization. Contemporary Legend, founded in 1986 by the *jingjui* actor Wu Hsing-Kuo (the Agamemnon in Schechner's *Oresteia*), is experimental and intercultural in nature but also plays an important role in preserving and promoting traditional *jingju* in Taiwan. However, from the inaugurating performance *Kingdom of Desire* (a *jingju*-stylized *Macbeth*, 1986), the company has continuously reduced singing and increased "dancing" in their productions.[61] *When Jingju Meets Rock & Roll* contains traditional operatic singing, but parts of the play also stages large number of *jingju* actors dancing to rock & roll music, with a choreography that resembles musicals but is spiced with *jingju* acrobatics, something that is not so different from *The Forbidden Phoenix*.

While both *When Jingju Meets Rock & Roll* and *The Forbidden Phoenix* are largely for the local audience, some ambitious Chinese opera performances continue to dance toward the world stage. A large-scale *jingju* production *Red Cliff* (*chibi*) premiered in the National Theatre in Beijing in 2008. This "large scale innovative *jingju* epic" was a synthesis performance of renowned traditional *jingju* performers Yu Kuizhi, Li Hongtu, Li Shengsu, and others; high-tech stage craft (ship fire, arrow shooting, flag flying); large-number dance and acrobatic spectacles; and traditional and symphonic music. It is described as a production that is "expensively produced,"[62] "high tech," and has a "movie-like opening"[63] and "innovative visual presentation and dance beauty."[64] It is not surprising to know that the director Zhang Jigang, the president of the Song and Dance Troupe of the People's Liberation Army General Political Department, was also the assistant director of the 2008 Beijing Olympics Open Ceremony, a grand "Oriental" spectacle.

As a matter of fact, one can see this new *jingju* production as the aftermath of the Beijing Olympics, and part of the whole movement of "Brand China." In 2009, the concept of "Brand China" was launched by Brand China Industry Union (BCIU), soon after the Olympics. It is a desire to promote a new image of Chinese brands with quality and high standards to "win China respect on the global stage."[65] Naturally, Brand China is not for Chinese customers; it is an upgraded repackaging of "made in China" with a new logo and slogan, for foreign consumption. *Red Cliff* joined in the brand making: in 2009 it was broadcast in Times

Square on eight giant screens, and a smaller version of the production toured a number of European cities in 2012.[66] This sensational, astounding performance with dance, acrobatics, and special effects was enthusiastically received with wild applause and exclamation. The most amazing opera singing by the traditional stars seems to have been forgotten.

The logo for "Brand China" is made up of four teardrop-shaped brush strokes in red and black, on the white background. It recalls the Olympic logo, but also heavily resembles a Chinese painted face in an abstract way. It is explained as "an abstract Peking opera mask" and "the shape of a dancer."[67] Once again, China is not only presented through Chinese opera to the world stage, it is also deliberately misrepresented as "mask" and "dance," familiar images to the West, this time by the Chinese themselves. Chinese opera keeps dancing in colorful costumes and masks, mutely miming erroneous signs of Chineseness, well into the twenty-first century. Perhaps it is the dance that will extend the life of the art to the next century.

Thomas Faist uses awkward dance partners to describe the relationship between diaspora and transnationalism, two somewhat overlapping but distinctive disciplines.[68] If dance is often seen as not threatening and universally pleasing, and is considered the safest way to test out the international market, do Chinese dancing bodies have to dance alone? Who are their dance partners, awkward or not? Are other "oral and intangible heritage of humanity" types of traditional performing arts automatically turned into Orientalized solo dances under the global gaze? Perhaps insisting on cultivating a global auricular taste for Chinese opera endangers the already precarious existence of the art. Perhaps, if the "dancers" of Chinese opera are permitted to utter a sound, the global audiences will try to listen.

NOTES

1. For studies on these topics, see, for instance, on Michio Ito, Yutian Y. Wong's "Artistic Utopias: Michio Ito and the Trope of the International," in *Worlding Dance*, edited by Susan Leigh Foster (New York: Palgrave Macmillan, 2009), 144–62; on the Nautch dancers, Priya Srinivasan's "The Bodies beneath the Smoke or What's behind the Cigarette Poster: Unearthing Kinesthetic Connections in American Dance History," *Discourse in Dance* 4, no. 1 (2007): 7–47, and on Chinese actors in the nineteenth century, Daphne P. Lei's "Chinese Theatre and Eternal Frontier in Nineteenth-Century California," in *Operatic China: Staging Chinese Identity across the Pacific* (New York: Palgrave Macmillan, 2006), 25–85.

2. Words like "Oriental," "East," and "Asian" in this article are always used in the international or intercultural context. "Oriental," a loaded term after the introduction of Saidian *Orientalism*, here generally refers to the invented, othered, imagined East by the West. "Asian" and "East," on the other hand, are not totally neutral terms either, as the demographics of Asians in any Western country depend on the immigration policy in any given time. Temporality always plays an important role in defining these terms. Another way to conceptualize these terms is to consider the binarism in which these terms are often situated. For instance, East is the "non-West" in the East-West binary, or as the "non-first-world" in the "West and the Rest" binary.

3. Eugenio Barba, "Introduction: Theatre Anthropology," in Eugenio Barba and Nicola Savarese's *A Dictionary of Theatre Anthropology: The Secret Art of the Performer* (New York: Routledge, 1991), 8–12.

4. Michael Omi and Howard Winant write about race as a social construct in the United States: The hegemonic way of categorization, identification, and theorization of race, through popular systems such as education, media, religion, and folk wisdom, has formed a sort of racial "common sense." The refusal of such racial common sense is an important step to understand racism. See "Racial Formation," in *Racial Formation in the United States: From the 1960s to the 1990s* (New York and London: Routledge, 1994), 53–76.

5. Susan Leigh Foster, "Worlding Dance—An Introduction," in Foster (2009), 1–13.

6. Voltaire, "To the Lord Marshal Duke of Richelieu, Peer of France, First Gentleman of the KING'S Chamber, Commandant in *Languedoc*, one of the FORTY of the Academy," in *The Orphan of China: A Tragedy* (London: R. Baldwin, 1756), ix–xv. Translator is unknown. This is Voltaire's letter to Richelieu for his adaptation of the fourteenth-century Chinese classic *The Orphan of Zhao* (Chinese title, *Zhaoshi gu'er*; French title, *L'Orphelin de la Chine*; English title, *The Orphan of China*). *L'Orphelin de la Chine* appeared in 1755.

7. Lei (2006), 25–85. Johannes Fabian writes about "denial of coevalness" as "a persistent and systematic tendency to place the referent(s) of anthropology in a Time other than the present of the producer of anthropological discourse," in *Time and the Other: How Anthropology Makes Its Object* (New York: Columbia University Press, 1983), 31.

8. Naturally, dialogue-based skits, pure dance, and pure singing existed as separate performance genres since ancient times, but the traditional concept of orthodox drama/ theater/*xi* always includes operatic singing.

9. For the theorization of the naming of "Chinese opera," see Lei (2006), 8–11.

10. Elizabeth Wichmann, *Listening to Theatre: The Aural Dimension of Beijing Opera* (Honolulu: University of Hawaii Press, 1991), 1.

11. Casey Man Kong Lum has written about the connection between karaoke practice and Cantonese opera in diaspora. *In Search of a Voice: Karaoke and the Construction of Identity in Chinese America* (New Jersey: Erlbaum, 1996), 34–53.

12. Big Mask's Uyghur connections are tenuous; on the other hand, it is equally difficult to prove on the basis of available historical documents that it is a pure Han Chinese form. For research on the origins of the art, see Ren Bantang, *Tang Performances* (*Tang xinong*) (Taipei: Hanjing, 1985), 106–9. Lord Lanling's dance is recorded in a number of documents from the Tang dynasty, such as *The Conservatory Records* (*Jiaofang ji*) by Cui Lingqin (fl. 749).

13. Jiao Xun, *On Drama* (*Jushuo*) (Taipei: Taiwan Shangwu, 1974), 2.

14. In 1949, The People's Republic of China was established by the Communist Party in mainland China, while the original government of the Republic of China, KMT (the Nationalist Party) moved to Taiwan. The revival of Lanling in the 1950s was a perfect opportunity to legitimize the new communist government as the real China.

15. Wang Kefen, *The History of Dance Development of China* (*Zhongguo wudao fazhan shi*) (Taipei: Nantian, 1991; originally published in China, 1989), 363–64.

16. See *Alta California*, October 16, 1852, for the advertisement. The performance was on October 18, 1852. For the experiences of Cantonese opera in the New World (the nineteenth-century San Francisco Chinatown), see Lei (2006), 25–85.

17. *Alta California*, May 10, 1860.

18. *Daily Evening Bulletin*, December 6, 1856.

19. J. D. Borthwick, *Three Years in California (1851–54)* (Edinburgh and London: William Blackwood, 1857), 76–77.

20. *Alta California*, October 20, 1852.

21. *Alta California*, December 14, 1856.

22. *San Francisco Chronicle*, April 24, 1856.

23. An advertisement in *Figaro* (February 26, 1873)

24. *Alta California*, October 20, 1852.

25. Frank Soulé et al. *Annals of San Francisco* (Berkeley: Berkeley Hills Books, 1999), 382.

26. *Alta California*, May 14, 1860.

27. Michel Foucault, *Discipline and Punish* (New York: Pantheon, 1977); Guy Debord, *Society of the Spectacle* (New York: Zone Books, 1995); Martin Jay, *Downcast Eyes: The Denigration of Vision in Twentieth-Century French Thought* (Berkeley: University of California Press, 1994).

28. Soulé et al., 382.

29. Joshua Goldstein, "From Teahouse to Playhouse," in *Drama Kings: Players and Publics in the Re-creation of Peking Opera 1870–1937* (Berkeley: University of California Press, 2007), 55–88.

30. Japan, the first country in Asia that adopted voluntary westernization as a way of modernization, was a popular destination for Chinese intellectuals since the late nineteenth century. *Shinpa* (modernized kabuki) and *Shingeki* (modern theater) were inspirational for Chinese intellectuals and artists. The first spoken drama performances were the students' translation of *Camille* and *Uncle Tom's Cabin* in 1907, Japan; they were fundraising performances for flood victims in China. For more information, see Daphne P. Lei, "Local, National, and International Performance of Barbarians at the Turn of the Twentieth Century," in Lei (2006), 87–132.

31. Qi Rushan, *The Journal of Mei Lanfang's US Tour (Mei Lanfang youmei ji)* (Shenyang, PRC: Liaoning jiaoyu chubanshe, 2005), 5–6. This book documents detailed planning of the tour as well as the repertoire and reception of the tour. This was an ambitious tour, a first in history. Mei visited several cities (San Francisco; Los Angeles; Chicago; Washington, DC; New York; and Honolulu) in about half a year and met with celebrities such as Douglas Fairbanks and Charlie Chaplin.

32. Daphne P. Lei, "Interruption, Intervention, Interculturalism: Robert Wilson's HIT Productions in Taiwan," *Theatre Journal* 63, no. 4 (December 2011): 571–86. This is in a special issue on the subject of "rethinking intercultural performance."

33. *Ah Sin, Chinese Must Go, The First Born*, and *The Yellow Jacket* are all written by non-Chinese writers and for non-Chinese actors. All four plays can be found in *The Chinese Other: 1850–1925: An Anthology of Plays*, edited by Dave Williams (Lanham, MD: University Press of America, 1977). *Orphan of Zhao (Zhaoshi gu'er)*, by the Royal Shakespeare Company, on the other hand, is a new adaptation by James Fenton of the Chinese classic by Ji Junxiang from the Yuan dynasty. The controversy of *Orphan* is centered on its casting: Among seventeen cast members, only three actors of East Asian descent (two as puppeteers to manipulate a dog and one as a maid) were employed to play Chinese. A later "American" production of the same adaptation, with a cast of largely Asian actors, was performed in San Francisco and in La Jolla in 2014. See Daphne Lei, "Orphan à la *Crouching Tiger*." *Contemporary Theatre Review* 24:4 (2014). http://www.contemporarytheatrereview. org/2014/orphan-a-la-crouching-tiger/.

34. Min Tian, *The Poetics of Difference and Displacement: Twentieth-Century Chinese-Western Intercultural Theatre* (Hong Kong: Hong Kong University Press, 2008), 27–30.

35. Erika Fisher-Lichte, "What Are the Rules of the Game? Some Remarks on *The Yellow Jacket*," in *The Show and the Gaze of Theatre: A European Perspective* (Iowa City: University of Iowa Press, 1997), 73–90.

36. Williams (1997), 223, 272.

37. Such physical training is portrayed in Chen Kaige's award-winning film *Farewell My Concubine* (1993) and in Chey Yew's *Red* (see discussion below).

38. Min Tian (2008), 210–11.

39. Liu Jihui, "New Pantheon in Taipei: *Oresteia* in Da'an Forest Park" (http://www.srcs.nctu.edu.tw/joyceliu/mworks/mw-taiwantheatre/Oresteia.htm).

40. In a talk at the University of California, Irvine, 2004, Schechner played the video of the production and drew everyone's attention to Wu Hsing-kuo's body, at the moment before he (as Agamemnon) stepped on the carpet. Wu suspended his leg in midair for a long time and created wonderful dramatic tension. Although it generally embodied the flavor of *jingju*, Agamemnon's costume shows bear legs, a nonconventional approach. It is the suspended bare foot that was the focus for both the park audience and the video audience.

41. Peter Sellars's production is based on Cyril Birch's translation of *Mudanting*, with Tan Dun's music. It was premiered in Vienna in 1997 and then performed in Berkeley in 1998. I was involved in early stages in 1996 and 1997, serving as interpreter for a few occasions, and the discussion below is based on the 1998 Berkeley production and the panel discussion I attended the next day.

42. Steven Paul, "A Review of the *Peony Pavilion*," *Chinese and Japanese Newsletter*, Valparaiso University (May 1999).

43. These are the conversations at and after the panel discussions at the University of California, Berkeley, the day after the US premier at the Zellerbach Theatre in 1998.

44. David Henry Hwang, *M. Butterfly*, in *Modern and Contemporary Drama*, edited by Miriam Gilbert, Carl H. Klaus, and Bradford S. Field Jr. (New York: St. Martin's Press, 1994), 814. Discussion in this section covers both the United States and Canada. "Asian American" is the US term referring to immigrants and descendants from Asia, while "Asian Canadian" is the Canadian equivalent; therefore I use "North American" to refer to these two countries of the Americas.

45. Such as the discussion in Josephine Lee's "The Seduction of Stereotype," in *Performing Asian America: Race and Ethnicity on the Contemporary Stage* (Philadelphia: Temple University Press, 1998), 89–120.

46. David Henry Hwang, *The Dance and the Railroad*, in *David Henry Hwang FOB and Other Plays* (York: Penguin Group, 1990), 51–86. The stage directions are based on the two productions in 1981, both directed by John Lone.

47. The term "1.5 generation" refers to those who immigrated to the United States as children.

48. Hwang (1990), 3–50.

49. These stage directions are based on the 2001 production at the East West Players, directed by Chay Yew himself. Chey Yew, *Red*, in *Hyphenated Americans: Four Plays by Chay Yew* (New York: Grove Press, 2002), 5. I took my Asian American theater class to see this production and arranged a postshow discussion with the actors.

50. Ibid, 44.

51. Patrice Pavis, *The Intercultural Performance Reader* (New York: Routledge, 1996), 3.

52. Marty Chan, Derek Mah, and Robert Walsh, *Forbidden Phoenix* (Toronto: Playwrights Canada Press, 2010). The production analyzed here is from 2009.

53. This description is from Marty Chan's own website. See http://www.martychan.com/theatre.html. Here Chinese opera means *jingju* and North American theater is American musicals.

54. The production discussed below is the 2009 World Premier at the Citadel Theatre, directed by Ron Jenkins. It was presented by Loraine Kimsa Theatre for Young People as a production for children

55. Peking is another way to Romanize Beijing. I use "Peking opera" instead of Beijing opera in the context of *Forbidden Phoenix* because of the Canadian convention.

56. Heather Fitzsimmons Frey, "Intercultural Bodies: *The Forbidden Phoenix* and *ANIME* in Edmonton," *Canadian Theatre Review* 139 (Summer 2009): 43–49.

57. Daphne P. Lei, "Homeland under Attack: Looking for a New Theatrical Paradigm for Asian Americas." In *Asian Canadian Theatre: New Essays on Canadian Theatre*, vol. 1, edited by Nina Lee Aquino and Ric Knowles (Toronto: Playwrights Canada, 2011), 33–48.

58. The study guide is available at http://www.citadeltheatre.com/pdf/SGuide_Phoenix_08. pdf.

59. The full version of the Young Lovers' Edition consists of a three-day program (about three hours per day). It is sometimes reduced to a one-day program during the tours. For a comprehensive analysis of the California tour, see Daphne P. Lei, "The Blossom of the Transnational Peony: Performing Alternative China in California," in *Alternative Chinese Opera on the Age of Globalization: Performing Zero* (New York and London: Palgrave Macmillan, 2011), 98–141.

60. At the rehearsal in the Barclay Theatre, Irvine, California (September 21, 2006).

61. After the twentieth-anniversary performance of *The Kingdom of Desire*, Wu told me the major difference between the original and the new productions was the reduction of singing (Taipei, 2006).

62. Yang Furong, "Sold-Out *Jingju Red Cliff* Still Loses Money: High Ticket Price for Audience, Low Pay for Actors," http://hk.huaxia.com/zhwh/ycxx/3052549.html.

63. Tang Xuewei, "Movie-like Opening: *Jingju Red Cliff* Premiered with High Tech," http://news.xinhuanet.com/tech/2008-12/23/content_10545287.htm.

64. Qi He, "*Jingju* Epic *Red Cliff* Will Arrive Shanghai Theatre Soon," http://enjoy.eastday.com/e/20121105/u1a6971694.html.

65. Brand China, "Brand China's Blog International," http://brandcnbciu.wordpress.com/2010/04/19/an-introduction-of-brand-china-industry-union/

66. For discussion on the Times Square broadcasting, see Megan Evans, "'Brand China' on the World Stage: Jingju, the Olympics, and Globalization," *TDR* 56, no. 2 (Summer 2012), 113–30.

67. Brand China, "Brand China's Blog International."

68. Thomas Faist, "Diaspora and Transnationalism: What Kind of Dance Partners?" in *Diaspora and Transnationalism: Concepts, Theories and Methods*, edited by Rainer Bauböck and Thomas Faist (Amsterdam: Amsterdam University Press, 2010), 10–34.

BIBLIOGRAPHY

General Works

Barba, Eugenio. "Introduction: Theatre Anthropology." In *A Dictionary of Theatre Anthropology: The Secret Art of the Performer*, by Eugenio Barba and Nicola Savarese, 8–12. New York: Routledge, 1991.

Borthwick, J. D. *Three Years in California (1851–54)*. Edinburgh and London: William Blackwood, 1857.

Brand China. "Brand China's Blog International." http://brandcnbciu.wordpress.com/2010/04/19/an-introduction-of-brand-china-industry-union/.

Chan, Marty, Derek Mah, and Robert Walsh, *Forbidden Phoenix*. Toronto: Playwrights Canada Press, 2010.

Chan, Marty. "The Forbidden Phoenix." http://www.martychan.com/theatre.html.

Debord, Guy. *Society of the Spectacle*. New York: Zone Books, 1995.

Evans, Megan. "'Brand China' on the World Stage: Jingju, the Olympics, and Globalization," *TDR* 56, no. 2 (Summer 2012), 113–30.

Fabian, Johannes. *Time and the Other: How Anthropology Makes Its Object*. New York: Columbia University Press, 1983.

Faist, Thomas. "Diaspora and Transnationalism: What Kind of Dance Partners?" In *Diaspora and Transnationalism: Concepts, Theories and Methods*, edited by Rainer Bauböck and Thomas Faist, 10–34 Amsterdam: Amsterdam University Press, 2010.

Fisher-Lichte, Erika. "What Are the Rules of the Game? Some Remarks on *The Yellow Jacket*." In *The Show and the Gaze of Theatre: A European Perspective*, 73–90. Iowa City: University of Iowa Press, 1997.

Foster, Susan Leigh. "Worlding Dance—An Introduction." In *Worlding Dance*, edited by Susan Leigh Foster, 1–13. New York: Palgrave Macmillan, 2009.

Foucault, Michel. *Discipline and Punish*. New York: Pantheon, 1977.

Frey, Heather Fitzsimmons. "Intercultural Bodies: *The Forbidden Phoenix* and *ANIME* in Edmonton." *Canadian Theatre Review* 139 (Summer 2009): 43–49.

Furong, Yang. "Sold-Out *Jingju Red Cliff* Still Loses Money: High Ticket Price for Audience, Low Pay for Actors." http://hk.huaxia.com/zhwh/ycxx/3052549.html.

Gilodo, Karen, Thom Vernon, and Jan Borkowski. "The Forbidden Phoenix Study Guide." http://www.citadeltheatre.com/pdf/SGuide_Phoenix_08.pdf.

Goldstein, Joshua. *Drama Kings: Players and Publics in the Re-creation of Peking Opera 1870–1937*. Berkeley: University of California Press, 2007.

He Qi. "*Jingju* Epic *Red Cliff* Will Arrive Shanghai Theatre Soon." http://enjoy.eastday.com/e/20121105/u1a6971694.html.

Hwang, David Henry. *The Dance and the Railroad*. In *FOB and Other Plays*. New York: Penguin Group, 1990.

———. *M. Butterfly*. In *Modern and Contemporary Drama*, edited by Miriam Gilbert, Carl H. Klaus, and Bradford S. Field, Jr. New York: St. Martin's Press, 1994.

Jay, Martin. *Downcast Eyes: The Denigration of Vision in Twentieth-Century French Thought*. Berkeley: University of California Press, 1994.

Jiao Xun. *On Drama (Jushuo)*. Taipei: Taiwan Shangwu, 1974.

Liu Jihui. "New Pantheon in Taipei: *Oresteia* in Da'an Forest Park." http://www.srcs.nctu.edu.tw/joyceliu/mworks/mw-taiwantheatre/Oresteia.htm.

Lee, Josephine. "The Seduction of Stereotype." In *Performing Asian America: Race and Ethnicity on the Contemporary Stage*, 89–120. Philadelphia: Temple University Press, 1998.

Lei, Daphne P. *Alternative Chinese Opera on the Age of Globalization: Performing Zero*. New York and London: Palgrave Macmillan, 2011.

———. "Homeland under Attack: Looking for a New Theatrical Paradigm for Asian Americas." In *Asian Canadian Theatre: New Essays on Canadian Theatre*, vol. 1, edited by Nina Lee Aquino and Ric Knowles, 33–48. Toronto: Playwrights Canada, 2011.

———. "Interruption, Intervention, Interculturalism: Robert Wilson's HIT Productions in Taiwan." *Theatre Journal* 63, no. 4 (December 2011): 571–86.

———. *Operatic China: Staging Chinese Identity across the Pacific*. New York: Palgrave Macmillan, 2006.

Lum, Casey Man Kong. *In Search of a Voice: Karaoke and the Construction of Identity in Chinese America*. Mahwah, NJ: Erlbaum, 1996.

Omi, Michael, and Howard Winant. *Racial Formation in the United States: From the 1960s to the 1990s*. New York and London: Routledge, 1994.

Paul, Steven. "A Review of the Peony Pavilion." *Chinese and Japanese Newsletter*. Valparaiso University. May 1999.

Pavis, Patrice. *The Intercultural Performance Reader*. New York: Routledge, 1996.

Qi Rushan. *The Journal of Mei Lanfang's US Tour (Mei Lanfang youmei ji)*. Shenyang, PRC: Liaoning jiaoyu chubanshe, 2005.

Ren Bantang. *Tang Performances (Tang xinong)*. Taipei: Hanjing, 1985.

Soulé, Frank, et al. *Annals of San Francisco*. Berkeley: Berkeley Hills Books, 1999.

Srinivasan, Priya. "The Bodies beneath the Smoke or What's behind the Cigarette Poster: Unearthing Kinesthetic Connections in American Dance History." *Discourse in Dance* 4, no. 1 (2007): 7–47.

Tang Xuewei. "Movie-like Opening: *Jingju Red Cliff* Premiers with High-tech." http://news.xinhuanet.com/tech/2008-12/23/content_10545287.htm.

Tian, Min. *The Poetics of Difference and Displacement: Twentieth-Century Chinese-Western Intercultural Theatre*. Hong Kong: Hong Kong University Press, 2008.

Voltaire. "To the Lord Marshal Duke of Richelieu, Peer of France, First Gentleman of the KING'S Chamber, Commandant in *Languedoc*, one of the FORTY of the Academy." In *The Orphan of China: A Tragedy*, ix–xv. London: R. Baldwin, 1756.

Wang Kefen. *The History of Dance Development of China (Zhongguo wudao fazhan shi)*. Taipei: Nantian, 1991. Originally published in China, 1989.

Wichmann, Elizabeth. *Listening to Theatre: The Aural Dimension of Beijing Opera*. Honolulu: University of Hawaii Press, 1991.

Williams, Dave, ed. *The Chinese Other: 1850–1925: An Anthology of Plays*. Lanham, MD: University Press of America, 1977.

Wong, Yutian Y. "Artistic Utopias: Michio Ito and the Trope of the International." In *Worlding Dance*, edited by Susan Leigh Foster, 144–62. New York: Palgrave Macmillan, 2009.

Yew, Chey. Red. In *Hyphenated Americans: Four Plays by Chay Yew*. New York: Grove Press, 2002.

Nineteenth-century Newspapers

Alta California, December 14, 1856.

Alta California, May 10, 1860.

Alta California, May 14, 1860.

Alta California, October 16, 1852.

Alta California, October 20, 1852.

Daily Evening Bulletin, December 6, 1856.

Figaro. February 26, 1873.

San Francisco Chronicle, April 24, 1856.

CHAPTER 33

EL GÜEGÜENCE, POST-SANDINISTA NICARAGUA, AND THE RESISTANT POLITICS OF DANCING

E. J. WESTLAKE

WHEN Irene López began her career staging the folkloric dances of southwest Nicaragua in the capital of Managua, she was met with harsh criticism by the traditional dancers of the region. "She came to rip off the true folklore," Flavio Gamboa told T. M. Scruggs in a 1998 article in the *Latin American Music Review*, "she created a representation in her own style and [says] 'this is a traditional performance from Monimbó'" (16). Similar accusations were leveled at her when she first staged the national dance drama *El Güegüence*[1] in 2003 as the Ministry of Culture was in the process of applying to UNESCO to grant it the status of intangible heritage. Her staging of the piece altered the national dance drama *El Güegüence*, embellishing certain parts of the story and inserting extra folk dances. She titled her work *El Gran pícaro* in an attempt to avoid the misconception that she was staging the "original," but no matter, the new creation irritated the dancers in Diriamba, the birthplace of the dance tradition, yet Irene López considers herself to be a guardian of that tradition.

By the same token, groups all over Nicaragua have taken up the dance drama with its unlikely cultural hero to comment on the political situation in the twenty-first century, to explore the performance of Nicaraguan identity, and to practice a certain level of resistance to the status quo. While some see the title character Güegüence as the corrupt politician, tricking imperialist powers for his own enrichment, others see Güegüence as a representative of the oppressed. The wildly different interpretations of the national treasure spin from the politics of the dance as either a unique cultural expression or one that represents a broader idea of a people, either the indigenous who created the dance during colonial times or the nation of people who have adopted it. Is *El Güegüence* a unique heritage, or does it apply to the whole of the nation? Is it a form to be preserved, or invented tradition? Is dance a form of reiteration, or a form of resistance? It is through the bodily practice of *El Güegüence* that I wish to explore a chain of erasures, highlights, and reanimations that make up the lived culture of postrevolutionary Nicaragua.

Folk dance fulfills a particular function in the creation of communal memory. As Theresa Buckland notes in her article on dance and authenticity, dance has "a particular propensity to foreground cultural memory as embodied practice by virtue of its predominantly somatic modes of transmission." In other words, movement acts as a dynamic repository for collective knowledge. She continues, "Indeed in traditional forms of danced display, it could be argued that longevity of human memory is publicly enacted, demonstrating the ethereality of human existence and the continuity of human experience, as successive generations re-present the dancing" (1). The community history and identity live through the animated body. But in the case of *El Güegüence*, a dance many feel is a contested tradition with a contested set of significations, the memory is fractured and ruptured in ways that produce a unique and dynamic discourse.

In this chapter, I focus on the creation of *El Gran pícaro* by Irene López as collective memory and as an act of *restored* tradition. Such a restoration is an invention meant to stand in for the original as faithfully as the inventor can imagine, by which I mean that it is faithful to the idea of the tradition, as a reimagining of what the experience of participating in the tradition must have meant in the lives of the people engaged in it in the past. I will also examine the redeployment of *El Güegüence* by groups who have embraced the figure and the act of dancing the masked drama as an expression of the subaltern, the marginalized, and the closeted minority identities within the context of the national culture, specifically Grupo Relajo, with their playful workshops built around the popular story. Ultimately, *El Güegüence* represents an artifact of the erasure of dance, and by extension, the indigenous body. Both López and Grupo Relajo, through their staging, reanimate the body of the mummified indigenous Other and create a vehicle for the body to move in resistance to such erasure.

Background

The history of the development of *El Güegüence* is very complicated and has been the subject of much speculation. The commonly held version is that indigenous people of southwestern Nicaragua began performing the drama during colonial times. Its blend of Nahuatl and Spanish is unique among Latin American dramatic texts and is the source of most of the word play that gives the title character the upper hand over the colonial governor. In the piece, the traveling merchant Güegüence and his two sons are called before the greedy governor to pay taxes. Through the clever use of the mixed language and through feigned deafness, Güegüence tricks the governor. Güegüence shows him goods stolen from the governor's own home to convince the governor he is wealthy. This in turn convinces the governor that he should marry his daughter to one of Güegüence's sons. Güegüence, however, is a despicable character: a liar, a thief, a womanizer, and a child molester. But he is celebrated as a clever mestizo who stands up to colonial authority.

A Nicaraguan linguist, Juan Eligio de la Rocha, transcribed the text of the play twice in the nineteenth century. Those copies were in the hands of his brother Jesús after Juan died. A German linguist and explorer, Karl Hermann Berendt, was studying the languages of the region and was particularly interested in collecting any remaining fragments of the Mangue language. Although it contains no Mangue words, the play was performed by the Mangue people, and Berendt may have been interested in the text for that reason.

Berendt was allowed to examine de la Rocha's copies, so the story goes, and made one interpolated version of his own. He met anthropologist Daniel Brinton in the United States and sold his documents to him to house at Brinton's home institution, the University of Pennsylvania. His handwritten copy is still in the collection in Philadelphia. Brinton published Berendt's copy along with what he called his "loose paraphrase" in his 1883 edition of the Library of Aboriginal Literature. The text came to the attention of Nicaraguan intelligentsia through Brinton's publication. It is important to note that Berendt did not see the dance being performed, nor did he copy any description. This is true of an alternate copy obtained some years later by Walter Lehmann from a different location. Only what scholars believe is the text was preserved through these artifacts.

The text came to the attention of Nicaraguan intelligentsia through Brinton's publication and through the writings of the Cuban José Martí, who encountered the text when he lived in the United States. Rubén Darío, the Nicaragua national poet, commented on the elegance of the blended language in 1897. Pablo Antonio Cuadra, the head of the literary avant-garde movement of the 1920s and 1930s and staunch advocate of establishing a national theater, referred to the piece as the first mestizo drama and praised the character's unique ability to subvert oppression. The play was then translated into Spanish using Brinton's publication. It was initially translated from Brinton's English-language "loose paraphrase," before Nicaraguan linguistic scholars made translations directly from Berendt's copy of the Nahuatl blend. While these translations capture some of the cultural references and humor better than Brinton's text, it was not until Carlos Mántica translated the work and footnoted the places where there was potential double-meaning that there was a copy that was close to communicating the original text.

The Sandinistas, the revolutionary government of the 1980s, emphasized grassroots theater and native culture. This ignited a movement to rediscover tradition obliterated by colonization and continued imperialist oppression, making Güegüence a popular figure. By the 1990s, the drive to have *El Güegüence* classified as intangible heritage by UNESCO was on. The designation was obtained in 2005.

The growing enthusiasm throughout the twentieth century spurred new interest in the work, and people began to migrate in earnest to Diriamba every year to see the performance at the festival of St. Sebastian.

El Gran pícaro

At a rehearsal of Irene López's *El Gran pícaro*, her young students shift restlessly at the edges of the stage of the school, waiting for their turn to go on. López's version of *El Güegüence* takes place at the market, and the story is told by characters created by López—the market gossips. The story provides a framework to showcase several of the folk dances that were popular in Nicaragua in colonial times.

This is not the same performance one sees in Diriamba each January. The folk dance that precedes the procession on St. Sebastian's Day is a simple set of steps involving "machos"

FIGURE 33.1 *El Güegüence* as it is performed in Diriamba before the procession at the Fiesta de San Sebastián. The human characters are surrounded by the mules or *machos*. Photograph by E. J. Westlake.

(mules) that perform a circle dance around the characters of the dance drama (see fig. 33.1). The governor and his deputy, Güegüence, and his two sons, dance with Suche-Malinche and the other women of the court. The regular group in Diriamba range in age from grade-school–age children to experienced dancers in their forties and fifties (such as the man who dances the part of the lead Macho, see fig. 33.2).

All of the dancers carry chischils, an indigenous rattle that is flicked upward to create sound, but only the men are masked. The dramatic part of the dance drama is not usually performed. However, I did see part of the drama performed by the regular group and a visiting company in 2008. The players wore microphones (which occasionally cut out) while reciting the hybrid Spanish-Nahuatl text, and the dance was interspersed at times designated in the text. The text was abandoned, however, as the performers ran out of time before the main procession was to begin.

The dance is performed while several other folk dances are performed around the square. I have seen Toro Huaco (see fig. 33.3), Moros Y Cristianos, El Viejo y La Vieja, El Gigante, Baile de Las Húngaras, and various local Inditas accompanied by the marimba. I have seen older people join in and dance an Indita while the marimba is playing (see, for example, fig. 33.4).

El Güegüence makes up only a fraction of the preprocession dance activity. Folkloric dance groups will make up part of the entertainment in the evenings, including more elaborate versions of *El Güegüence*. In particular, Ronald Abud Vivas, director of the Ballet

FIGURE 33.2 The lead macho with the treasure box and the chischil. Photograph by E. J. Westlake.

Folklórico Nicaraguense, has brought his version to the Diriamba fiesta, but Abud is a native of Diriamba, and his project was one of preserving the original dance steps.

In the version choreographed by López, the text is in Spanish instead of the hybrid language. López uses the story as a framework to showcase several of the folk dances with folk music that were popular in Nicaragua in colonial times to augment the original steps. The characters are not masked. Certain interpretations of the text are clearly stated in López's version through the use of characters who gossip at the market. As López's gossips tell the spectators:

> An important element of every festival market [. . .] is gossip, talk. [. . .] In every village it is used to announce, denounce and mock the system that represents the ruler of the time [. . .] so then there are the gossips, those who deal throughout the play [. . .] with charlatanism, lies,

FIGURE 33.3 Another dance performed at the fiesta, Toro Huaco. Photograph by E. J. Westlake.

> and mischief [. . .] they announce, denounce and report to Güegüense and all the market [. . .] what happens in the governor's house. (5)

The dialogue of the gossips makes no secret of the idea that the play is about political corruption. The gossips introduce the first scene by noting that it is the governor's own corruption that has caused the poverty of his government. They also provide transitions, offering explanations to the characters that help to advance the action.

López states that she uses the gossiping merchants specifically to clarify what the original text means. "When the governor attempts to tax the merchants, they gossip, those who hang out in the market: It is there where there is plenty of gossip, hot gossip; how is it that Güegüence heard about everything that happened in the Cabildo Real [seat of colonial government]? So I suggest that it was through the merchant's gossip" (personal interview). When the governor attempts to tax the merchants, his collectors discover that Indians are poor and that he isn't going to get much out of them. But they inform the governor that Güegüence is in town and has plenty of money from his travels through Mexico and Guatemala. After a gossip dance, the merchants see Güegüence coming through the market with his sons. The gossips warn him about the tax and tell him to prepare himself: "HA, HA HA, Güegüense, get ready. They're coming to beat you black and blue for being such a show off, talking about what you have: a huge treasure, chests of gold and silver, and a lot of fine things. You'll have to pay taxes on that pile of rags you've got!" (5).

FIGURE 33.4 An older couple dances the steps of the local Indita. Photograph by E. J. Westlake.

López also adds a number of folk dances to the performance that are not found in the Diriamba performance. The scene where the governor and the deputy mourn the fact that they lack fine furnishings is accompanied by a devil character and a vulture, who dance with Death, a character danced by López's daughter. The governor and the deputy, with their arms on each other's shoulders, perform the "Dance of Poverty": they step side to side, then lean back to sigh over their misfortune while the gossips scold them. Not only does the dance introduce folk dance figures from other dances, but the three figures further the story in that they represent a death of the soul through greed. Death appears later when the performers explain that gold and greed are a major theme in the drama. One woman remarks on this while moving Death, who wears a gold-colored costume, around her.

Numerous other dances are featured, including a dance of the police, here acting as tax collectors, and a dance of the gypsies. López places these dances in the logical context of the performance. The police go to the market to collect taxes for the governor and his court to continue their extravagant lifestyle. They move through the market crowd with their hands extended while merchants shake their heads and indicate that they have nothing to give them. The police move in a line shaking the chischil and occasionally twirl with their hands to their foreheads in despair.

When the characters introduce Güegüence, López uses the opportunity to introduce a dance of the mule being pulled by an old woman. The performers explain that *El Güegüence* and *Macho Ratón* (dance of mules) were combined into one. They demonstrate the dance of the old women and the mules. The dance "El Viejo y La Vieja" (the old man and old woman) are typical folk dances during patron saint festivals. They walk rapidly to show unsteadiness, and the mask has a small cigar sticking out of the mouths of both characters. When I saw this dance in 2012, men danced the roles of the old women as well as the roles of the old men.

The performers also note that merchants like Güegüence would encounter a variety of people, including "húngaras" or "gitanas." Indeed, Roma culture surfaces in highly stylized, albeit stereotypical, ways in folk dance and literature in Central America.[2] In *El Gran pícaro*, the gypsies are "Traveling in their carts, looking for work, acting in troupes, throwing caution to the wind, and dancing with their costumes and tambourines" (9). Güegüence and his sons don caps and sashes and perform a dance he calls "the Walloon," a series of steps performed with his hands held behind his back, while bare-bellied girls dance in their bare feet while playing tambourines against their hips and above their heads. On the raised stage in the back, three women play tambourines as well until one stops to peer into a crystal ball in order to tell the fortunes of the men.

López also uses the dance to study important points of the Güegüence story. In the dramatic text we have from Berendt, Güegüence reminisces about his youth, referring to it as the "time of blue thread." Many scholars have analyzed what this means. Les Field, in his comprehensive study of artisans of Carazo, brings together the range of commentary on the mysterious reference, including Jorge Eduardo Arellano's contention that it refers to a bygone indigenous practice of dying cloth with the ink from a certain shellfish. López, in her years of study of the material related to the text, created a dance of girls with blue fabric draped on their shoulders. The girls begin by sitting on the stage, one end of the fabric in each hand, opening one wing of the fabric, and then the other, then both. Then they do this while kneeling, and then they stand and move with the opening and closing of the fabric.

After Güegüence seals the deal to marry his son Don Forsico to the governor's daughter, everyone drinks a toast and the final dance begins with music that "slurs" up the scale and with wide, sweeping motions of drunkards raising a glass. The men shake the chischils by their mouths as they lean back. The women dance behind them with their fans. Then in a finale, the most familiar music of *El Güegüence* begins and everyone does the familiar back and forth step, moving side to side as they shake the chischil first by the hip and then up in one flip.

After the rehearsal, I interview López for a while. I buy her children's book on folk dance and she gives me the DVD of the full performance of *El Gran pícaro*. The interview ends as I run out of tape. My friend Rubén Reyes, who has taken folk dance lessons with López, is along to help me with some of the language, Nicaragua's special dialect, which drops the "s" sound almost completely. I am turning off my camera as Rubén leans forward and says to her: "You know, it's interesting that you call yourself the Guardian of Folklore. But you are taking such liberties with *El Güegüence*, embellishing a lot, adding dances and changing the dialogue. How is that part of your program of protecting folklore?" It is the question I was afraid to ask.

Flavio Gamboa's quote in Scruggs's article reflects a larger issue, that of cultural appropriation. As Scruggs notes, while the sharing of culture can create connections between diverse people, a power differential exists when something is taken from the margins and deployed in the center:

> When appropriation occurs, these forms leave the control of smaller, more bounded communities and are reproduced in larger power centers. In this process, these important expressive resources, what Bourdieu insightfully calls forms of cultural capital (1984), become charged

with a symbolic power to represent larger social constructs. Often social actors at the centers of power go further, drawing upon these forms in attempts to forge emblems that represent the totality of a nation-state, recasting the music and dance as a national symbol.

López was not raised in Carazo. She did not see folk dance of the region until returning to Nicaragua after attending high school in the United States. In fact, she recently confessed that she didn't enjoy her first encounter with folk dance because, as she said: "it was all very foreign" (Salazar ¶7). Some would accuse López of appropriating folk dance, but altering it and then presenting it as a national form. These alterations have consequences, not just for the dance, but for the music that accompanies the dancers.

I struggle to get another tape in my camera and turn it on again. López smiles and shakes her head: "The work *El Güegüence* is not folklore because it does not participate in the dynamic of folklore. I dare say, . . . the dance *El Güegüence*, that is this moment performed in the procession of Diriamba, . . . involves little of the dance, involves just a few people dressed in the masks of the machos and the others in those of the Spaniards, practically walking . . . Normally, one scene in a performance would involve three, four dances, right? But this one doesn't present them, and it is dead folklore. The piece I've made is just a work of art, we can make art of it, a work of art. But I don't say nor did I set out to do the original folklore" (personal interview). Generally, López's piece has been met with good reviews by the mainstream press. Stories in the Managua newspapers, *El Nuevo Diario* and *La Prensa* have been overwhelmingly positive. She is careful to explain that this is not *El Güegüence*. She explains that this is her own version. As she reported to Scruggs in his article on Marimba, she has "liberated the expressive form from the restrictions of its localized reproduction through a reconceptualization of the dance as malleable source material for artistic creation" (17). She reiterates this in her children's book, *Indias, Inditas, Negras Y Gitanas: Los bailes de marimba en el Pacífico Nicaragüense*, when she writes:

> The guardians of tradition are those who are charged in one way or another of keeping folklore alive and dynamic, and that the transformation or evolution of it never causes it to lose its identity. They are responsible for transmitting practice, from one generation to another, the values of the cultural legacy and, together with their communities, developing, selecting, accepting or discarding those elements that do not interest them. [. . .]
> If the guardians of tradition die or leave for other countries then the folklore disappears, is no longer dynamic, the tradition is not passed onwards and then is used only for information or for cultural or educational art projects.

López recognizes that daily practice may change and that folk dance is a dynamic and changing form as the life of the community changes. But the loss of daily practice makes folk dance a frozen and dead form. *El Güegüence* is a special case because a break in the regular practice of the dance creates a vacuum of information about the dance drama's original mise-en-scène.

López maintains that too much was lost of the music and the actual dance of *El Güegüence* to stage the original. The movement was lost in favor of the text. López is merely filling in the blanks and making something that is no longer a living tradition live again for the modern audience. She bases her concept on careful research and balances the work in terms of art, scholarship, and tradition. I believe this makes her both interpreter and guardian, restoring something to what it might have been as lived tradition.

White nineteenth-century ethnographers excluded the dance in their documentation for several reasons. On one hand, documenting the actual movement proved impossible to them. While we can debate the efficacy of capturing movement through later systems of notation, dance could never actually be captured, as even repeat performances by the same dancers will be different every time. It is however, relatively certain that Berendt, Brinton, and Lehmann never witnessed the dance itself and probably did not find descriptions of it in their work. Brinton, the ethnographer chiefly responsible for interpreting the gathered information (Berendt and Lehmann were mere fieldworkers) making *El Güegüence* available in print, never set foot in Nicaragua during the course of his career. In the introduction to his 1883 "loose paraphrase," he reports that anthropologist Earl Flint told him that the dance was no longer performed anywhere at all because of the expense involved for the patron (xli). Whether the practice had ceased or paused or not is up for debate. But his belief that the practice was extinct would have made any vague interest in witnessing the movement moot.

However, and even more importantly, ethnographers of the time did not value the recording of the physical movement of performance. Generally, the project of anthropology as a discipline involved cataloging and analyzing of the various people of the world in an effort to support evidence of human evolution and establish a racial hierarchy. Brinton, specifically, focused on the people of the Americas, people he never met. The first part of his career involved writing *Races and Peoples*,[3] a catalog of every race according to physical measurements, full of racist speculations about what each physical characteristic meant in terms of racial inferiority. In keeping with his training as a physician, Brinton ostensibly freezes the body of the Indian, keeping it mummified as a biological specimen, dissected, measured, and labeled.

Brinton's career took him from the body to the text; his later work of linguistic anthropology, *The American Race* (1891), was to catalog all of the languages of the Americas to show that the "Indian" was actually descended from Europeans and not from Asians as was commonly believed, thus placing them slightly higher in his racial hierarchy. To press *El Güegüence* into his service, he erases the body of the Indian altogether, and allows the Other only to speak. López attempts, then, with her staging of *El Gran pícaro*, a resurrection of sorts, freeing the body to move, and to have space beyond the repetitive and rigid confines of the Diriamba festival, where *El Güegüence* survives as a frozen and precious artifact. She succeeds I believe, because she pulls it into the realm of lived practice, transformed, yes, but her call to transmit the embodied folk lore to the next generation reanimates the public body.

Grupo Relajo

Not surprisingly, the nationalist project of reviving the dance drama emphasizes both the authenticity of the form and the universality. Darío, Cuadra, Alan Bolt, and the organizers of the festival emphasize the originality, specifically the Nicaraguan-ness of the piece. It is interesting, too, that *El Güegüence* receives more nationalist attention than the "purely" indigenous drama, fitting the trope that Nicaragua is a mestizo nation and that its mixed European and indigenous heritage is to be celebrated above all else. In this sense, the drive is universalist, that Güegüence represents every Nicaraguan, flattening the cultural and historical diversity of the nation into one identity. For this reason, attempts to resist such flattening, to explore both the supposed authenticity of the piece and the diversity of its subject, generate a discourse directly connected to the current political crisis in the country.

The members of Grupo Relajo use the dance drama to interrogate the idea that the trickster Güegüence represents all Nicaraguans and to generate a resistant discourse. The use of different bodies to stand in for the Indian of the festival represents a different kind of resurrection. In 2008, I traveled to a retreat run by Puntos de Encuentro, an organization with services for gays and lesbians and people with HIV/AIDS. The group also provides advocacy for women, minorities, people with disabilities, and youth as they attempt to raise awareness about domestic violence, racism, homophobia, and sexism.

From the center of Estelí, I walk east up the road that leads to the Miraflor Reserve and then turn off toward a conference center a couple of miles from the town. When I arrive at the "camp" outside of Estelí for Relajo, the "Latin American Network for Play," the facilitators hand out masks to the participants of the workshop. The participants represent Nicaraguans from across the spectrum of the services offered by Puntos. The masks are of the human characters in the *El Güegüence* dance. The facilitators instruct participants to wear them for the duration of the first part of the workshop. They divide participants into two lines and teach them a basic step from the dance drama. Facing each other, the dancers hold the chischil and move in the back and forth step, looking down when moving back, the dancers shake the chischil by the hip on that side, then as they step forward, they look up and shake the chischil up and ahead of their bodies. They play a CD of traditional music associated with *El Güegüence*, the same music used by López in *El Gran pícaro*.

The facilitators of Relajo take many of their cues from Paolo Freire and Augusto Boal, encouraging the participants to explore ways to creatively resolve conflict in the story and, at the same time, to explore issues in their own lives. In the next phase of the workshop, they instruct them to dance *at* each other after a nonverbal confrontation between two workshop leaders, Mercedes Gonzalez and Andrea Calvi. The two show their line how to dance in a way that expresses disdain for and superiority over the people in the other line, a sort of physical playing the dozens, and then the group would dance it together. The leaders then encourage participants to come up with a dance and lead their lines in vanquishing the other. At this workshop, moves involved sometimes trotting up to the other line, tapping the participants in the other line on the head or the rear with the chischil, bending over and waving their rears at the other line, tossing the head and the chischil flippantly, or a pronounced stabbing motion toward the others with the chischil or with a quick side motion of the hip.

Eventually, the third leader, Félix Román, enters as Relajo's version of Güegüence, however he wears a mask of one of the machos, or mules, instead of the old man. Relajo's Güegüence is a "hybrid half animal, half man" (Gonzalez, personal correspondence), perhaps in reference to the Caliban of Fernández Retamar and the Latin American hybridized identity. Román incites everyone to dance together, the dance becoming something that unites and liberates the participants. The dance is the same step they taught participants at the beginning, the back and forth step while shaking the chischil low and then high. At this point, Calvi acts as the Governor Tastuanes and demands that the music be stopped: "Silence! Silence! Hold the chischils! And keep those masks on! Don't take them off!" Gonzalez explains to him that this is just a game: "a game between police and criminals, conquerors and vanquished, men and women, winners and losers, revolutionaries and counterrevolutionaries." Román intervenes and asks: "And who here is a revolutionary? Where are the counterrevolutionaries? Where are the imperialists and anti-imperialists? Who is a friend? Who is an enemy? Who are those on one side and who are on the other?" Calvi takes this to the participants: "And you? What side are you on? I am tired of being on a side! And I don't want 'your side.'" The leaders ask if there is a way to be that doesn't involve sides, if there is a new way of thinking. They set up the participants in opposing lines again and set up a series of dichotomies: "Go to this side if you are a Sandinista. Go to this side if you identify as gay or lesbian. Go to this side if you are unemployed. Go to this side if you have been abused." The list continues as participants continually shift sides, moving back and forth, physicalizing the movement along a continuum of identities, its own dance about our shifting selves.

Güegüence gets them to dance to celebrate the idea that love might be the answer to their problem. Calvi, as the governor, stops them again and complains that the dancing is too disruptive and has to stop. Güegüence tells the dancers that maybe they can continue dancing if they dance more quietly and slowly. The governor complains that it is still too much noise and disorder. He commands: "I don't want anyone to move in this place. Quiet! This is how I want to see everyone, calm and silent." The governor turns his back, and Güegüence convinces everyone to dance anyway, although even more quietly and slowly. The dancers swing back and forth slowly and gently, and they barely shake the chischil. The governor turns around and everyone freezes. However, the governor commands that anyone caught moving should be arrested, and Gonzalez, as the police chief, obliges. This happens several times until a large percentage of the dancers are "in jail." Finally, Güegüence leads the participants in an aggressive dance to liberate both the jailed and the jailer. Eventually, the governor joins them as well, removing the governor's mask and turning on the chair he had occupied as the source of oppressive power. He asks: "And now who is going to occupy the chair? We will do the same to him."

Movement, throughout the workshop, is synonymous with liberation, individual expression, and personal and collective power. The people dance even when it is forbidden. The governor forbids dance, while Güegüence inspires it. Together they create a disruption that state power cannot contain. Eventually, the impulse to wipe out the physicality of dance leads to a state that is so repressive, every single person is imprisoned, which leaves no one to govern. The action of dancing liberates the governor from himself and removes him to face the chair of authority. Dance is about connecting with one's own body while discovering the bodies of others. It is playful, campy, dangerous, and revealing. The mask also has both oppressive and subversive potential.

The workshop continues with a series of movement and character games. At one point, they move to music—in pairs, one person waves a ribbon and that person's partner attempts to move like the ribbon. When the music stops, they freeze. Based on their position when they freeze, they are to come up with a persona and introduce themselves to each other, exploring the connection between movement and the performance of identity. They tell each other where they live, what they do, and how they feel at that moment. Late in the workshop, they dance to slow music, removing their masks, but placing their hands in front of their faces "like a fan." They move their hands, eventually revealing more and more of their faces. The leaders continually ask the participants: "Who is Güegüence? Is he the mask or the person behind the mask?" They play with the idea of the Nicaraguans as Güegüence: "Are they the feudal lords that make pacts and seek to dominate everyone for their own benefit?"

When Nicaraguans talk about pacts, they are referring to "The Pact" that was made between the current president, Sandinista leader Daniel Ortega, and disgraced former president and Liberal Party member Arnoldo Alemán. Alemán has often been likened to

Güegüence for embezzling millions of dollars from the government. But Ortega has been particularly vexing for many people who supported him in the 1980s. While he continues to market himself as someone who fights for the subaltern, he continues to consolidate power. He married into one of the wealthiest families in Nicaragua and claims to have found God, reversing many of the positions he held on women's rights and reproductive health. Ortega struck a power-sharing deal that kept Alemán out of prison. If any politician has been wearing a mask, it is Ortega.

The facilitators continue: "Or is Güegüence he that has at one time used the mask in order to avoid being persecuted and destroyed and now desires and demands the freedom to, without the mask, denounce the situation without fear and open the way to the joint construction of a more just, equal, and integrated society?" They urge the participants to empower themselves: "We the 'Güegüences' can decide: do we show our face? Or do we continue to allow for the 'false Güegüences' that use us while they hide behind the masks of the pact, the power, religion, and politics?"

The mask of the Güegüence hides the politician, but also hides the individual. The individual has the option of going along with the masquerade or speaking against it. The use of *El Güegüence* as a jumping-off place is interesting to me, especially in light of Mercedes Gonzalez's strong feelings about how the piece has been used. She told me after the workshop that she resents the idea that the character and the dance have been held up as a representation of all of Nicaragua: "Sectors of the dominant culture have been able to sell us the idea that 'we are all Güegüenses,' but in reality this figure represents a specific sector of the Pacific (Carazo). And the image that they offer us is the same that is reduced to the musical heritage, or dance drama, or the product of 'the joker and trickster going against authority,'" (e-mail correspondence). She feels that framing the story in this way causes other aspects of the story to be lost, that attention isn't paid to the women of the story, who are unmasked and silent, or to the age of Güegüence and his position in indigenous culture as a respected elder rather than a scoundrel, or to the status of one son as legitimate and the other as not. And what of the myriad identities in Nicaraguan culture beyond just the mestizo of the southwest? What does *El Güegüence* mean to other indigenous groups, to people of African heritage, to gays and lesbians? Erick Blandón echoes this sentiment in his book *Barroco descalzo* when he decries the attempt to make the trickster stand for the typical Nicaraguan:

> [S]ome go along with attributing to the figure the characteristics of what would be "the Nicaraguan identity": mestizo or Indian, revolutionary or fool, of great ethical values or simply an opportunist . . . it is part of an imaginary homogeneity by means of all the Nicaraguans, including the mestizos and Spanish-speaking people of Nahau ancestry, who would be Catholic, heterosexual and male . . . while no reference is made to any kind of differentiation of classes, to the Caribbean Africans, to the homosexuals, and the women. (130)

Is there a place for the subaltern in the discourse that is *El Güegüence*? Relajo explores the appropriation of the Güegüence figure while interrogating it, creating a space for all Nicaraguans to explore their myriad identities.

The workshop in Estelí became a parade the following day, making visible the diverse bodies of Nicaragua: gay men and lesbians, transgendered people, women, people with HIV and AIDS, indigenous people, people of African descent, and people with disabilities moved through the streets. The parade culminated in performances in the square, where the participants attempted to engage the audience. At first, the audience was reluctant, perhaps because the parade participants were considered outsiders of the dominant culture. During the performance of the Güegüence workshop, participants put audience members in jail after the governor ordered them all to stop dancing and freeze, signaling that oppression doesn't discriminate, that the arresting of the body of the Other reveals in that moment the instability of the boundaries of otherness. With an arbitrary exercise of power, the question arises: What is the norm and who can claim to possess the body that falls within that category? Putting audience members "in jail," however, liberated them to participate and folded them into the narrative of oppression and liberation. They were then "free" to participate (and many did) in the dance of revelation, where participants hide themselves behind their hands until they unmask themselves.

The frozen and arrested body of the dancer in Relajo's exercise has much in common with the dead and dissected body of Brinton's Indian. Dance, then, by itself becomes a revolutionary act, breathing life into the dead folklore of *El Güegüence* and calling attention to the heterogeneity of bodies that resist categorization and slip away from the ethnographic structure of meaning and power. To use the reverse of Pierre Nora's model of lived memory (*milieux de mémoire*) crystallizing into official sites of memory (*lieux de mémoire*), the embodiment of the dance drama reverses museumification: The lived bodily experience, in all its multiple forms, resists being mummified and keeps on dancing.

NOTES

1. Roughly pronounced Gway-gwen-say or Gweh-gwen-say. It is also sometimes spelled with an "s," as it is in López's text, in place of the "c."
2. I am thinking here of Guatemalan writer Miguel Ángel Asturias's play *Soluna* (1955), where gypsies tell the protagonist Mauro that time will run backward.
3. Although he didn't publish this until 1890, it was based on lectures he gave throughout his career.

BIBLIOGRAPHY

Blandón, Erick. *Barroco descalzo: Colonialidad, sexualidad, género y raza en la construcción de la hegemonía cultural en Nicaragua.* Managua: URACCAN, 2003.

Brinton, Daniel G. *The American Race: A Linguistic Classification and Ethnographic Description of the Native Tribes of North and South America.* New York: Hodges, 1891.

Brinton, Daniel, ed. trans. *The Güegüence; A Comedy Ballet in the Nahuatl-Spanish Dialect of Nicaragua.* Philadelphia: Brinton, 1883. Library of Aboriginal American Literature, no. 3. Reprint, New York: AMS Press, 1969.

Brinton, Daniel. *Races and Peoples: Lectures on the Science of Ethnography.* New York: Hodges, 1890.

Buckland, Theresa J. "Dance, Authenticity and Cultural Memory: The Politics of Embodiment." *Yearbook for Traditional Music* 33 (2001): 1–16.

Gonzalez, Mercedes. Personal correspondence. February 27, 2008.

López, Irene. *El Gran pícaro.* Rehearsal, June 7, 2008.

López, Irene. *El Gran pícaro: Una recreación basada en la historia de "El Güegüese."* Miami: Mántica Waid, 2005.

López, Irene. Personal interview. June 7, 2008.

Mántica Abaunza, Carlos. *El Cüecüence o El gran sinvergüeza: Obra maestra de la picaresca indoamerica.* Managua: Academia Nicaragüence de la Lengua, 2001.

Nora, Pierre. "Between Memory and History: Les Lieux de Mémoire." *Representations* 26 (Spring 1989): 7–25.

Scruggs, T. M. "Cultural Capital, Appropriate Transformations, and Transfer by Appropriation in Western Nicaragua: 'El baile de la marimba.'" *Latin American Music Review/Revista de Música Latinoamericana* 19, no. 1 (Spring–Summer 1998): 1–30.

CHAPTER 34

FROM *SOBERAO* TO STAGE
Afro–Puerto Rican Bomba *and the Speaking Body*

JADE Y. POWER SOTOMAYOR

THE *bomba* dancer enters the *soberao*, moving fluidly across the space, her feet stepping in time to mark the downbeat played by the drums, the *buleadores*.[1] The lead singer calls and the chorus responds. She is surrounded by sound. The dancer nods her head, tilts the upper body, bowing slightly in deference to the lead drummer, making eye contact and signaling the beginning of a conversation that is about to take place. She punches the elbow, *brap*, snaps the skirt quickly with a flick of the wrist, *tun-tun*, drags the foot three times, *tun-brap, tun-brap, tun-brap*, and then waits, suspending the sound, deciding how many measures she will let pass before closing the phrase on the downbeat, choosing her next move as the lead drummer hunches over the barrel drum, also waiting, watching attentively to see what sound she will ask for next, what rhythm she will dictate to the drum, which part of her body will speak next: shoulders, hips, foot, elbows. The singing continues, the *buleadores* marching at a steady tempo. The dancer executes a few more steps, the lead drum sounding a crescendo of slaps. She likes the way her dance has been aurally reflected back to her, enjoys the rhythm she has created, knowing she has been heard, seen and understood. Someone in the crowd, in the chorus, or sitting at the drums yells out "¡*habla!*"[2] She has spoken. She continues to dance, to speak in faster, shorter phrases until she is almost breathless, yet still fully composed. She has finished. Having executed her last *piquete*,[3] she closes with a bow to the drums, thanking and respecting not only the one who plays the lead drum, but the drum itself and the history it represents. With an inclination of the head, the drummer also acknowledges and thanks the dancer for speaking with and through the drum (See fig. 34.1).

Bomba music and dance was first created by enslaved Africans and their descendants in the sugarcane plantations of Puerto Rico as early as the sixteenth century. A product of the encounter between Africa, Europe, and the Americas, this tradition of singing, dancing, and percussion is one of many syncretic African diasporic forms that fan out through the Americas. A word whose origins may come from the Kikongo (Bantu) word *ngomba*, used to describe "an event where drums are played," or similarly the Akan (Ashanti) usage of *bombaa* to denote "drum," *bomba* is today used to refer to this embodied music-making as

FIGURE 34.1 Grupo Aguacero—Oakland, June 2011.

Photographer: Edwin Monclova.

both practice and performance, instrumentation and dancing.[4] What began on the plantation as a form of expression, resistance, and, ultimately, survival, *bomba* was developed into a thriving cultural practice in dialogue with the free blacks, mulattoes, and working-class white Puerto Ricans who together created what Angel Quintero Rivera refers to as the world of the "counter-plantation."[5] Additionally, the forced migration of slaves across the Caribbean, particularly following the Haitian revolution, brought Puerto Ricans of both the plantation and the "counter-plantation" into direct contact with distinct, but similarly derived, drum-song-dance traditions. The resultant amalgamation is evidenced by the many French creole lyrics in traditional *bomba* songs as well as in the parallels between the names used to describe the instruments across the Caribbean, and to some extent in the movement vocabularies themselves.[6] Driven underground in the early twentieth century by a climate of musical racism, *bomba* was later celebrated and "re-vived" through folkloricized stage performances in second half of the twentieth century. Since the mid-1990s, however, there has been an off-stage resurgence of the tradition not only on the island but also among Puerto Ricans living in the United States, as both Puerto Ricans and others practice *bomba* with varied attention to preservation and innovation and to cultural, racial, and regional identities. In other words, *bomba* has shifted from being marginally practiced by the families whose embodied knowledge was directly responsible for its long-term survival in what Diana Taylor refers to as the "repertoire," to something which a much broader population claims as their own, celebrating and reclaiming a collectively erased history through the body.[7]

In this chapter I examine *bomba* as both practice and performance, outlining the dynamic tensions that exist between theatricalized representations of the form (the stage) and performative enactments of community (the *soberao*). While I underscore the ways that *bomba* is fundamentally different in these two spaces, I am also interested in how "the stage" draws on improvisational dance as practiced in the *soberao*, just as the twenty-first-century *soberao* is also fueled by the visibility and cultural capital acquired through staged enactments of *bomba*. Ultimately, the survival and continued salience of *bomba* relies on this constitutive process. I demonstrate how the marked differences between these two representational modes are primarily understood in terms of how the body constructs narratives of race and nation in both of these spaces. Engaging history as a static, knowable object, folkloricized staged presentations of *bomba* explicitly frame this tradition as "telling the story" of African slaves in Puerto Rico, re-presenting history and thereby situating blackness in Puerto Rico's past. On the other hand, in using this practice as a contemporary mode of individual expression, *bomba* performed in the community space of the twenty-first-century *soberao* celebrates the survival of this Afro–Puerto Rican cultural product/practice, and, by extension black-identified Puerto Ricans themselves. Thus, performances of *bomba* in each of these spaces, provide a window into the multiple power dynamics surrounding issues of authenticity, commodification, innovation, the circulation of this embodied practice as a source of pleasure and employment and finally, of bomba as a signifier for racial and political subalternity.

Instead of framing the stage and the *soberao* (and by extension theater and dance) through a model of erasure, where one lens/framing replaces/dominates the other, I am interested in the transparencies contained in each. In other words, how the *soberao* is ghosted on the stage and when and how ghosts of theatricalized *bomba* appear in the *soberao*; how dance and theater are each other's ghosts and how dance and theater are each other's presence? As I outline below, I am invested in the racial, national, and gendered politics articulated in each of these spaces but I am also wary of suggesting that "real" *bomba* dance is disappeared on the stage or that the *soberao* does not also explore ideas of narration and impersonation fundamental to understandings of theater. Instead, I argue that close examination of the particular conventions of *bomba* dance as an improvised, embodied music-making enables an understanding of how both of these performance modes (*soberao*/stage, dance/theater) fundamentally rely on what I call the "speaking body." I employ the "speaking body," to describe the use of signifying gestures and embodied "speech-acts" that construct and intervene in the discourses of race, nation, and individual subjectivity historically created through the logocentrism of the island's lettered elite. As such, the "speaking body" is the central element that makes *bomba* effective in enacting an embodied response to antiblack racism and discourses of belonging as well as enabling the genre's recent popularity. Simultaneously, thinking about the ways that notions of speaking, narrating, and representing rely on moving bodies demonstrates the permeability of entrenched disciplinary distinctions that construct theater as narrative and dance as aesthetic expression.

It is in fact the persistent presence of the speaking body in *bomba*, throughout centuries of practice and performance, in a variety of contexts and settings, that marks this genre not only as a powerful site for articulating an oppositional narrative of belonging, but also that allows for twenty-first-century *bomba* to serve a communal and societal *function* that echoes its origins. Scholars writing about *bomba*'s origins have described the way that it was used as a vehicle for building community among slaves of multiple ancestries and native languages. As such, it was part of a circum-Atlantic, transethnic and transnational language that was used not only to plan insurrections[8] but also as a way to create what Sara Johnson refers to as a "diasporic literacy" [9] that presented a challenge to a particular language ideology that created a hierarchy between literate and nonliterate peoples. Thus, the speaking body, I argue, serves as a form of corporeal literacy that, despite efforts to create and re-present *bomba* through discourses produced through the hierarchy of logocentric literacy, inherently resists such attempts.

This performance ethnography, based on fieldwork and interviews conducted between 2009 and 2012, is also informed by my own experience as a *bomba* dancer and practitioner. My work as a participant observer in *bomba* communities both on the island and in the diaspora since 2004 not only provides me with insight into the multiple dynamics and "unofficial" conversations that surround this practice but also gives me the embodied knowledge that comes only from the experience of dancing. Finally, while I identify as a Diasporican,[10] I do not identify as Afro–Puerto Rican,[11] therefore my knowledge of *bomba* is not informed by this embodied experience. Nonetheless, this research is informed by the ways that *bomba* has been an important force in helping me examine my own corporeal negotiations of *puertorriqueñidad*,[12] *Latinidad*, and community belonging.

STAGING *BOMBA*

Historically, *bomba* was practiced in the space of the *soberao*. *Soberao* is the word used to describe the circle created around the area in front of the drums where *bomba* dancers dance. The drummers, lead singer, and chorus, along with spectators, together trace the circumference of the circle. In this way, the spectators, as opposed to being in a proscenium stage relationship to the performers, surround the *soberao*, and actually help to create and shape the circle around the open area for the dancers. Individuals moved to dance emerge from the crowd, or from behind any of the drums. In this way, the *soberao* is similar to the "cipher" in which breakdancing and other Afro-diasporic dances take place; the playing/dancing space, one that is constituted through a community understanding of the protocols (see fig. 34.2).

The creation of the *soberao* is ultimately a claiming of territory and an articulation of existence/presence for the bodies that enter it. It also enacts community exchange that challenges clear distinctions between spectator and performer relationships even as it demarcates the performative space. The word itself has interesting etymological origins. In Castilian Spanish, "*soberado*" [13] refers to a space that is architecturally not habitable, or useless. In Puerto Rico, the current usage of "*soberao*" derives from the word used to describe the shared dirt floor space in a hut dwelling, and has come to be used interchangeably with the *taíno* word "*batey*" which describes an interior patio space. In a discussion about African influences on Puerto Rican architecture, Arleen Pabón writes about this as a private-public space over which homeowners took much pride, signaling that "the *soberao* proves you have a space of your own (even if you are an *arrimao* and the land belongs to another person), that you possess your very own dwelling locus."[14] Today, the *soberao* represents precisely this claiming of space, a simultaneous distancing from the "outside world" and a gathering of creative and communal energies. Thus the space is both protected and open, private and public, and it is into the sanctity of the *soberao* that the dancers enter.

These origins are useful in thinking about both the twenty-first-century *soberao* and what I am calling here the prefolkloric *soberao*.[15] Recent interviews with *bomba* elders in

FIGURE 34.2 Open *bombazo* in the *batey* of the Ayala family—Loíza, Puerto Rico, 2009
Photographer: Edwin Monclova.

Puerto Rico conducted by Jorge Emmanuelli Nater and Melanie Maldonado-Emmanuelli have provided evidence for the fact that *bomba* was practiced not only in the privacy of individual homes but also at dance events that were used commercially to attract clientele to local bars and businesses serving black and mulatto communities throughout the early and mid-twentieth century.[16] Even so, given the conventions of the form, these public performances of *bomba* continued to make use of and rely on the *soberao*. In the current climate of resurgent interest in *bomba*, contemporary *bombera/os* are increasingly reclaiming the simultaneously public/private, community/commercial space of the *soberao* and foregrounding its fundamental importance in framing their practice. This move marks a stated response to the circulation of *bomba* as folkloric product that became synonymous with the genre in the second half of the twentieth century.

Prior to the 1990s, for the vast majority of Puerto Ricans, it was more likely that they would have experienced *bomba* as part of a staged spectacle at a cultural event intended to promote Puerto Rican culture, not through participation in a *soberao*. In 1955, Luis Muñoz Marín—the island's first elected governor—created the Institute of Puerto Rican Culture (ICP). Its stated mission according to its founding director, Ricardo Alegría, was to "counteract decades of harmful influences, which at times were openly contradictory to our local values, with an effort to promote those values."[17] Among the "harmful influences" cited by Alegría and other prominent proindependence intellectuals of that time was the racism (which as part of an anti-imperialist discourse has often been framed as being imported from the United States) that was in part responsible for driving black cultural practices such as *bomba* underground.[18] According to the island's lettered elite responsible for scripting *bomba* into a narrative of Puerto Rican national identity,[19] the work of the ICP then, was to rescue, preserve, and celebrate these "autochthonous" traditions through education and increased visibility of their practice.[20] Thus, through this process *bomba* becomes a symbol of cultural differentiation in the midst of US imperialism, at the same time that it is interpreted, framed, and valued through a discourse that is fundamentally understood through writings about the nation. The "speaking" enacted by the *bomba*-dancing body and the horizontal relationships necessitated by the *soberao* are inserted into a model of belonging structured through systems of meaning-making that inscribe a hierarchy where linguistic capital trumps embodiment. Even so, as I describe below, despite the ICP's success in folklorizing this practice, *bomba* and the "speaking body" ultimately supersede this interpretation, as evidenced through the continued existence of the *soberao*.

Although *bomba* rhythms had already been incorporated into the popular music of the time,[21] the ICP sought to ensure the survival of *bomba* as folk tradition. Thus, in order to accomplish the task of adequately commodifying and presenting the form for the above stated purposes, the ICP courted two important *bomba* patriarchs, Don Rafael Cepeda and Don Castor Ayala. With the sponsorship of the ICP these two figures formed folkloric dance groups composed mostly of members of their respective families and immediate communities. From the late 1950s to the 1990s, between Ballet Folklórico de la Familia Cepeda and Ballet Folklórico de los Hermanos Ayala, *bomba* could be seen by tourists and locals in hotels, in films, on television, and at many government-sponsored cultural events, something that prior to this institutional intervention would have been considered inappropriate and vulgar for such public spaces. Always appearing in "traditional" dress, which consisted of late-nineteenth-century "Sunday-best" domestic servant attire for the women, and white *guayaberas*,[22] red handkerchiefs, and straw hats for the men, these dancers and musicians transformed the *soberao* into a proscenium stage performance, a theatricalized representation of a bucolic Puerto Rican past. Furthermore, ICP-sponsored groups have historically been held to specific standards in terms of their instrumentation, costuming, and thematic content, which ultimately leads to an institutional sanctioning of "authenticity" that translates to material concerns in terms of being hired for performances.[23] Thus, although the ICP can be commended for addressing musical racism and creating a level of visibility and appreciation not previously enjoyed by *bombera/os* on the island, this institutional support not only marks the move from the *soberao* to the stage, and the subsequent changes to the form that this implies, but also reframes the discourse of black *puertorriqueñidad* in highly problematic ways that reify essentialist ideas about blackness and black Puerto Ricans.

The folkloric staging of *bomba*, an Afro–Puerto Rican tradition, and certainly part of a larger Afro-Caribbean tradition, enacts the complicated relationship between discourses of blackness and *puertorriqueñidad* that persist in Puerto Rico and in the diaspora. The celebration of *bomba* and other Afro–Puerto Rican traditions by institutions like the ICP (and by extension, other "cultural organizations" in the diaspora) as signifiers of the island's black heritage, effectively constructs *puertorriqueñidad* as essentially nonblack. While the inclusion of *bomba* in these events gives credence to the narrative of a *mestizo/o-mulata/o* Puerto Rican identity, it is presented as a novelty to be consumed and possessed, with blackness discursively relegated to the margins. Indeed, this discourse is so powerful that, despite different racial identifications, Puerto Ricans of all backgrounds are to varying degrees consumers of this commodified blackness. In other words, honoring black heritage can result in not only a reification of the objectifying and essentializing attitudes about black Puerto

Ricans but also the construction of blackness itself. Isar P. Godreau reminds us of this deeply troubling relationship when she writes that "this inclusion and celebration of blackness is not distinct but instead compliments ideologies of *blanqueamiento*[24] because it is rooted in the same ideological principles that distance blackness, geographically and temporally, from the imagined margins of the nation."[25] Godreau then goes on to say, "this distancing has the effect of locating the phenotypic and cultural signs of blackness 'somewhere else,' and in premodern times of idealizing black people as happy and rhythmic tradition bearers who still inhabit supposedly homogenous and harmonious communities."[26] Therefore, just as the performance and celebration of *bomba* music and dance holds great potential for the articulation of a politics of antiracism in terms of creating public visibility of black heritage in Puerto Rico, such acts can often fail to recognize the contemporary lived experiences of the descendants of African slaves on the island. Or, equally disappointing, these performances produce overly simplified understandings of an essential blackness and whiteness, without asking how these constructions operate in relationship to larger structures of power.

Melanie Maldonado provides another example of this dynamic in her article "*Bomba Trigueña*: Diluted Culture and (loss of) Female Agency in AfroPuerto Rican Music and Dance Performance," where she writes about her decision to never again wear the typical folkloric dress codified by the ICP after overhearing someone say that she looked "just like Aunt Jemima." I concur with Maldonado's conclusion that *bomba* is effectively whitened, that is, emptied of its relevance to contemporary Afro–Puerto Rican experience, when female dancers, dressed in costumes that resemble slave-women and mammy stereotypes, perform *bomba* in spaces that celebrate *puertorriqueñidad* through this folkloric trope.[27] The practice of *bomba*, and by consequence the historical conditions of the plantation and counter-plantation worlds from which this tradition emerged, is thus excised from contemporary life and presented instead as an object of the past. The use of the mammy trope works simultaneously to make signifiers of blackness hypervisible while black bodies are rendered invisible. Finally, this "whitening" takes place in the name of shaping an all-inclusive narrative of Puerto Rican identity, of which blackness is only one small, largely symbolic, not material, component.

Bomba's circulation as folkloric product is only one of countless instances across cultures and throughout history where blackness is disembodied and affectively appropriated as a signifier for the nostalgic remembering of the premodern, uninhibited body. Much like the primitivist movement of the artists of the early twentieth-century avant-garde, that celebrated blackness and African cultural aesthetics as symbols for rejecting the strictures of modernity, relocating their own liberatory aesthetic in the always already distant past associated with black bodies,[28] the celebration of black traditions within narratives of Puerto Rican folklore has further entrenched the frozen linear temporality of contemporary black experience. Furthermore, by locating the black body as the *object* of premodern experience, as is the case when *bomba* is celebrated on the folkloric stage, this Cartesian distancing between mind and body precludes any possibility of addressing black cultural production as a site for subject formation, open to shifts in practice, location, and approach.

Thus, as *bomba* moves from the prefolkloric *soberao* to the folkloric stage, spectators are separated from the performers not only spatially, but also temporally through the period costumes, effectively distancing *bomba* from the immediate lives of the Puerto Ricans viewing the performance. The dancers and musicians are converted to signifiers representing an aesthetic practice that is explicitly marked "Puerto Rican" and "Afro–Puerto Rican," yet a practice that exists, as Godreau reminds us, "somewhere else." For spectators *and* performers alike, *bomba* in this setting becomes the past reenacted, staged as an object to be admired, examined, and yes, respected, but as some*thing* that resides outside the Self. Staged as narratives of national identity, these performances feature black Puerto Ricans as protagonists, but in such a way that extends neither to the overall discourse of *puertorriqueñidad* nor to the politics of representation on the island. Audience members who look to these performers as somehow reflective of their own history and identity, even as they are able to revel in the pleasures of the spectacle they are witnessing, may find it more difficult to incorporate this idealized, utopic presentation of Self into their ontological experience of the Self. In addition to the problematic discourse that already surrounds the celebration and essentializing of black cultural practices in this context, the embodied relationships and theatrical elements that frame such a performance work to further entrench difference.

Furthermore, in its move from the *soberao* to the stage, *bomba* practice changes not only in its reformulation of spectator/performer relationship but also in terms of the embodied protocols for executing the dance. As I will discuss in more detail below, contemporary *bomba* practice in the twenty-first-century *soberao* has been largely influenced by the conventions that came about through staged performances of *bomba* and in this way is fed by the work of/on the stage. Previously, the *soberao* was a space where couples of men and women would dance together, facing each other while marking the basic foot pattern to the drum's downbeat, usually consisting of a step-together-step movement or a simple swaying and stepping from side-to-side much like a chorus member, or back-up singer would do while standing behind the microphone. Couples would move through the *soberao* doing this and whoever was closest to the lead drum would mark a few *piquetes* while their partner maintained the basic tempo-marking step.[29] Additionally, as the dancers were standing in such proximity to the drum, often in a more crowded space, both men and women executed *piquetes* with smaller steps, closer to the body and thus less visible to someone standing at a distance. Therefore, two major changes take place when the dancer moves from the *soberao* to the stage: The dance is executed by one single dancer though they may enter the stage as a couple, and the dancer engages in more dramatic, expressive *piquetes* in an effort to be visible to the spatially distanced audience and, ultimately, more entertaining.

In the most recent staging of *bomba* in the twenty-first-century *soberao*, musicians and dancers have incorporated elements of theatricalized *bomba* into a defolkloricized performance that is focused on individual expression, communal catharsis, aesthetic exploration, and the celebration and embodiment of black cultural practice. By placing *bomba* in the *soberao*, the theatricalized re-presentations of blackness are potentially deessentialized. Performances become more about *doing* than *showing*, about producing an active embodied conversation through the bodies of the dancer and drummer, and thus less about showing blackness as a role to be donned. Certainly, the twenty-first-century *soberao* is often created in public performance spaces, from night-clubs to town plazas. However, the performative elements, in large part enabled by the theatricalization of the form, have shifted to reflect the performance of individual identity instead of the performance of a racialized trope or caricature. Thus, *bomba* as performance, in the *soberao* or on the stage, is simultaneously a *doing* and a *thing done*. This process/product dual nature of performance that Elin Diamond has famously described is made especially evident in looking at *bomba* as practice and performance.[30]

The twenty-first-century *soberao* has the potential to articulate an altogether different set of relationships than that framed by the folkloric stage, particularly in considering the important way in which diasporic performances and practices of *bomba* complicate discourses of belonging (race, nation). Because of the horizontal relationships necessitated by the structure of the *soberao* and by the genre itself, the twenty-first-century *soberao* offers a critical site for articulating and building communities of belonging through a variety of affinities and contingencies. *Bombera* and scholar Raquel Z. Rivera, writing about the *bomba* scene in New York, notably an important site for the development of the twenty-first-century *soberao*, addresses the value of using this practice, not as a way to deessentialize blackness as premodern, but rather to deessentialize *bomba* as Puerto Rican.[31] In denationalizing the rhetoric surrounding *bomba*, it is instead privileged as the product of a circum-Atlantic circulation of embodied practices, and thus lends itself to examining the deterritorialized contemporary experiences of the descendants of *bomba*'s original practitioners. In other words, *bomba* in this context creates a sense of belonging that directly reflects the material realities of *bombera/os*, realities that are most often influenced by proximity and shared community with other racialized subjects in the United States. For instance, in Rivera's example she argues that Diasporicans in New York often feel culturally and experientially closer to African Americans and other Francophone and Anglophone blacks than to other groups. As such, *bomba* can be valued not as a signifier of *puertorriqueñidad* but rather as an embodied practice that connects Puerto Ricans to their own black heritage[32] and to this experience as it is shared by other members of the African diaspora.[33] Alternatively, Puerto Ricans living in California practice *bomba* in a context where they often experience proximity, shared resources, and collaboration with Chicana/os and Central Americans. In this way, *bomba*, while it remains a signifier for island heritage and culture, is also denationalized and used as the site for articulating shared histories of African slavery, colonization, and contemporary experiences of subalternity. As such, *bomba* becomes a live(d) contemporary practice that actively engages, at the same time that it deconstructs multiple trajectories of identification, including both race and nation. Undeniably, accomplishing such a task necessitates the space of the *soberao*.

While I have intentionally been highlighting the tensions that exist between the *soberao* and the folkloric stage, I am interested in thinking about these performances beyond the binaries of traditional/contemporary and retention/adaptation that often frame discussions of African diasporic dance. More importantly, I am interested in how juxtaposing *bomba* performances in the *soberao* and on the stage reveals the slipperiness between distinctions of dance and theater. In both of these spaces, the dancer's body speaks and performatively enacts identity through an improvised, expressive solo in a public space. Thus the speaking body, fundamental to both theater and dance, is simultaneously rhetorical and representational, aesthetic and political, ultimately challenging not only "disciplined" understandings of performance but also the hegemony of identity as a logocentric construct. Even though its etymological roots lie in the words "to see," theater is often imagined to be a form invested in words, text, and narrative. Conversely, dance is often framed as a visual practice, not privileged as having a rhetorical impact. However, using the speaking body of the *bomba* dancer as a lens to understand what the dancer is *saying* in the *soberao* and also what the dancer *doing* in a theatrical space subsequently reveals the constructedness of this theater/dance divide. Therefore, even as I have demonstrated that different presentational framings for these embodied performances result in distinct embodied discourses, ultimately *bomba* also reveals the way theater and dance share a dependence on a speaking body.

The Speaking Body

Much of the discourse surrounding *bomba* practice and performance has historically focused on questions of racial and national identity. Recently however, practitioners and scholars alike have begun excavating the *bomba* repertoire as a way to map musical evolutions, geographic movement of *bombera/os* within the island and throughout the Caribbean, and the work of important historical figures noted for their virtuosity as *bombera/os* and/or their role in the preservation and dissemination of the tradition.[34] Although the mechanics of the dancer/drummer relationship are used to describe the form, these accounts pay less attention to embodiment itself and the role of the body in navigating these ideas. Furthermore, much of the extant scholarship about *bomba* has focused on the genre as practiced on the island. The fact that *bomba* is an important tool for community building and expression among the Puerto Rican diaspora in the United States still comes as a surprise to many in Puerto Ricans. In what follows, I describe the mechanics of *bomba* dance as a corporeal speaking, an essentially "pedestrian" movement practice that is generative in confirming and asserting identity in a variety of trajectories, but particularly in regard to race and gender. By looking specifically at examples of how diasporic *bombera/os* use the twenty-first-century *soberao* as a way to enact identity, individually and communally, I aim to further underscore the porous nature of the disciplinary distinction between "theater" and "dance." In doing so, I am examining a number of interlocutory relationships: theater/dance, *soberao*/stage, island/diaspora, call/response, dancer/drummer, practice/performance, quotidian/virtuosic, all examples of the call and response inherent in *bomba*'s structure and practice.

Indeed, the interlocution between theater and dance is further troubled when we think of *bomba* as additionally blurring lines between "music" and "dance." Though the focus of this essay is on dancing bodies, as discussed below, *bomba* is an experience that is incomplete, and in fact inoperative, when one of the elements of song, drums, or dance is missing. The fact that the dancer's body is a central musical element further underscores the inability to extricate the various performative elements. This becomes important when considering how *bomba* is commodified for performance, or even as a consumable product in the space of a workshop. In performances of *bomba* in the diaspora, different event producers will demonstrate varying levels of interest in highlighting the musical *or* the dance aspects of the performance, indicating as much by lack of sound equipment or lack of enough space for the dancers. Alternately, in the performance settings where *bomba* is valued as a "cultural art," or at community *bombazos* or *toques de bomba*[35], there tends to be less categorical "disciplining" of the different elements into "music" or "dance."

Although the embodied speaking present in *bomba* dance is unique, particularly in regard to its "pedestrian" nature (a term I will describe below), it is one of various genres of music/dance that employ movement practices in asserting an identity and creating a community of belonging. For instance, scholars have documented extensively the important function of *salsa* dance in diasporic communities of Puerto Ricans who, due to what is often a lack of access to other signifiers of cultural affiliation such as language, are able to use *salsa* to corpo-really articulate said affiliation.[36] Priscilla Renta writes the following:

> Puerto Ricans and other Latina/os living in the US often employ salsa dance performances (along with language and music) to construct and affirm individual and collective sense of cultural identity . . . For Latina/os the need to affirm cultural identity grows in part out of their diaspora experience, which brings with it the pressure of assimilating and of being subsumed and homogenized by Euro-American culture that dominates US mainstream society.[37]

Novelist Mayra Santos Febres writes about her own discovery of the liberatory potentials of salsa as "a participatory musical genre" that "resists binarisms of audience/artists, performers/consumers, founder/follower, subject/object," privileging both "continuity and rupture, order and hazard, sequence and simultaneity."[38] While I argue that *bomba* fundamentally differs from salsa music and dance practices not only because of the relationship between the dancer and the musicians but also because of the distinct ways in which they both circulate in popular culture, these parallels are nonetheless useful in thinking about how the dancing body works to script identity affiliation. Furthermore, as Santos Febres invokes an unraveling of binarisms in her description of *salsa*, she similarly signals the productive potential of the *soberao* to do the same. In both of these "participatory musical genres," dance is valued as a product viewed and consumed by spectators, but also, and perhaps more importantly, a process experienced by the dancer.

One of the main distinguishing features in *bomba* dance practice is what I call the "pedestrian" nature of the dance itself. While there are extremely skilled and detail-oriented *bomba* dancers, and truly understanding the intricacies of the drum/dance relationship takes many years, it is not a form that requires specific physical training, making the dance more accessible to a broader population. So, not only does the *soberao* as a space, and *bomba* as a form, enable performative participation in cultural meaning-making but also the dance vocabulary itself is key in creating a broader sense of access and ownership. This meaning-making is not limited by physical talent, and, especially significant among Diasporicans who may or may not speak Spanish, is not conscribed by linguistic ability. Though many of the *bombera/os* with Puerto Rican heritage interviewed for this project are in fact Spanish-English bilingual, a number of them rely primarily on English. While this can present an issue in learning the lyrics for the responses to the lead singer (the *coro*, or chorus), dancing requires an altogether different set of skills and experience level, predicated on rhythmic facility more than physical virtuosity. Learning to dance *bomba* has come to provide many Diasporicans with a space to not only be with other Puerto Ricans but to *be* Puerto Rican, a *puertorriqueñidad* that is here fundamentally constituted, not with blackness as a melting pot ingredient, but rather *as* blackness.[39] Ultimately, in making this embodied claim, these Diasporican *bombera/os* are simultaneously responding to the experience of being marked Other in the United States and actively performing resistance to assimilation.

Because many of the moves used in *bomba* dance appear pedestrian in their execution, individuals watching a performance or a *bombazo* are often inspired to try it out themselves. For instance, Puerto Ricans in California,[40] who may or may not have contact with Puerto Rican communities elsewhere, or who may or may not have established relationships with contemporary island culture, are moved to actively use their bodies to performatively invoke Puerto Ricanness. Whether because of an imagined idea of how this identity is constructed, or in response to the material reality of being racialized as Ethnic Other/Puerto Rican in the United States without an adequate narrative of cultural belonging, entering the *soberao* to "speak" *bomba*, marks entry into an "imagined community."[41] Sounding the drum with bodily signification as simple as a foot stomp, singing the chorus of the call-and-response song, an encounter with *bomba* in the diaspora, for the first or hundredth time, is simultaneously an act of "speaking Puerto Rican," "speaking black," "speaking Latina/o," "speaking subalternity," and "speaking community." Because *bomba* can be figured as a corporeal rhetoric in a different way than performances like *salsa* dancing, much like speaking in the unique cadence of Puerto Rican Spanish, *bomba* dance is a unique speech-act that for many instantiates this cultural and racial belonging.

As a fundamentally "pedestrian," and quotidian dance, the meaning-making potential of *bomba* is often framed through the metaphor of speaking. Dancers are told not to go dance in the *soberao* unless they "have something to say;" the act of entering the space in front of the drums, called the *paseo*,[42] is figured as the moment to say "Hello, how are you? This is who I am." The dance phrases should be separated with "punctuation," "periods, commas, and exclamation points," otherwise they become unintelligible. Clarity and precision will distinguish a "good dancer." While attention is paid to visual elements such as elegance, posture, and style, the dance is privileged as a musical form; the sound it calls forth from the drum is equally important, if not more so, and thus the laudatory "*habla*" when something sounds good. Halbert Barton writes:

> *Bomba* drum improvisations and the dance movements that correspond to them are noted for having a speechlike quality—novice *bomba* dancers must not only internalize a movement vocabulary, with commonly used words, phrases, and punctuation marks, but also a grammar by which a sequence of movement combinations can make sense. To perform adequately, then, according to the standards of the *bomba* community, *bomba* dancers, and the *subidor* who gives sound to their movements, must learn to "speak" in a free-flowing way that is not stilted or repetitive, as in an ordinary verbal conversation.[43]

The ability to make the drum sound through movement, to become audible through visually interpreted actions, marks the exchange between the dancer and the *subidor*[44] (lead drummer) as exceptionally important in distinguishing the physical act of playing an instrument, in this case a drum, from the physical act of dancing *bomba*. Unlike embodied instrumentation where lungs, fingers, arms, and legs work to produce sound on and through an object, and verbal expressions where the diaphragm, the lips, teeth, and tongue push and shape air to create rhythm and tone, *bomba* dance movements arrive aurally only through communication with the drummer. There are conventions for how to mark certain moves, which the dancer learns to use strategically (movements with two hands are marked with both hands slapping the drum, foot taps are marked with a high pitched open-tone, hip movements are interpreted through a syncopated rumbling sound, etc). However, while certainly the dancer controls the frequency and speed of hits, it is the drummer who ultimately decides how the dance will sound and is responsible for interpreting the dance with *golpes*, or hits, that happen in near simultaneity. In this way, the *bomba* dance, indeed much like speaking, is as much about legibility and conversational exchange as it is about self-expression.

While performances of *bomba*, whether on the folkloric stage or in the *soberao*, both rely on this conversation between drummer and dancer, the *soberao* privileges the process, as opposed to the product, of this exchange. Although some stage performances use choreographies where the *subidor* marks rehearsed steps executed by a group of dancers moving in unison, they almost always include improvised solo dancing. At times however, the presentational style of stage *bomba* may place more importance on dance aesthetics and the musical complexity of the drum than on the synchronicity of the two. The *soberao* on the other hand enables a focus on the music-making aspect of the dance relying on a deep sense of communication between the dancer and the *subidor*. Although clearly the dancer leads in initiating a musical sequence, it is imperative that they not be making music "to the beat of their own drum" but rather enters the *soberao* using a basic step that follows the rhythm that is being played and held by the other drums, the *buleadores*. Part of upholding the dance end of the conversation is to place the *piquetes* in the time dictated by the rhythm of the *buleadores*. The dancer, as an important musical element, should not "*jalar el tiempo*," or pull the overall tempo of the song, though certainly, as a dance builds in intensity, the lead singer who plays the maraca and controls the tempo, is sometimes moved to also accelerate the song.

The conversation between the *subidor* and the dancer, much like an oral conversation, will quickly become incomprehensible if the *piquetes* are danced out of time. Skilled dancers use the *contratiempo*, or upbeat, in order to create more musically complex phrases, fully aware of the tensions they playfully create and break as they play rhythmically by placing steps to be marked on the two and the four (the upbeats) instead of the one and the three (downbeats).[45] However, steps placed without awareness of this rhythmic dynamic result in cacophonous slaps from the *subidor*. In fact, while some *subidores* will "fix" the sound of *piquetes* thrown off the repetitive downbeat pattern so that they do not ruin the overall dynamic of the music, the convention, especially in the space of the *soberao*, is for the lead drummer to interpret the dancer's moves *exactly* as the dancer executes them, thus reflecting back to the dancer the relative effectiveness of the dance. In other words, in the *soberao*, a *subidor* is much less likely to "fix" the sound of a dancer's *piquete* than in a staged performance, where the dance may be more scripted, fulfilling aesthetic requirements as opposed to expressive actions and engaged communication. In part this convention exists as a way to emphasize the fact that it is the dancer creating the rhythmic patterns and should therefore be held responsible for creating intelligible, or interpretable, phrases. The moment a dancer hears their dance aurally interpreted differently than how they intended it to sound, they must rethink the clarity of their movements and question whether the communication with the lead drummer is locked in.[46] In other words, while the dancer can experience personal satisfaction and empowerment in dancing a solo, it is accomplished only as the result of cooperation and clear embodied communication. Meaningful participation in the *soberao*, then, actually privileges *making* and *doing* something, as opposed to *showing* or *representing*. The dancer's speaking body reimagines narrative at the same time that it resists being read as an aesthetic object, pushing against conventions of *both* dance and theater even as it also employs elements of both.

The initial entrance of the dancer to the *soberao* through a *paseo*, which is not marked by the *primo* player, gives the lead drummer a chance to solo or to underscore the more fluid, less percussive moves of the dancer with broader interpretive strokes. This is the time for the dancer and the drummer to come into the space together, frame the conversation that is about to take place. The *paseo* resembles a stylized walk in which the dancer steps in time to the downbeat, using the arms to create shapes; opening them wide, placing one or both hands on the hip, playing with opposition by bringing one arm in front of the body while the other curves around toward the back. The dancer moves across the open floor space as if to mark the territory, playing with directionality, and distance covered in each step, completing the *paseo* with a salute to the drummer, an inclined head, or a bow that bends slightly at the waist, maintaining an almost erect posture. Eye contact is made and the first *piquete* is executed, after which point the improvisation continues. While some *bombera/os* have figured this relationship as a "challenge" to the drummer on the part of the dancer, a *reto* (drummers will play the *primo* with relative amounts of enthusiasm depending on their conception of the dancer's skill level and general attitude), if the challenge is taken too far, if the dancer throws *piquetes* that are too fast, complicated, or unclear, the central defining principle of *bomba* as genre ceases to exist.[47] Thus, here we can again see how *bomba* as product depends on the process through which it is enacted.

Because the *subidor* is attempting to mark the dancer's moves with as much simultaneity as possible, clarity and control is paramount in together completing the act of signification. In this way, a simple *piquete* is valued more than a series of movements that may *look* good, but do not land aurally. Firmness, or *firmeza*, one of the three "cardinal rules" of *bomba*[48] is also crucial in having clear *piquetes*, because the strength and decided precision behind completing the move enables the *subidor* to anticipate when a move is initiated and thus when it will be punctuated. The "challenge" or the "trick" can come in faking an anticipated *piquete*, by initiating a move, and unexpectedly suspending the closure, waiting to complete it. An example of this would be when the dancer lifts the hand to the shoulder as if about to draw a sharp line from the shoulder to the space out in front of the chest, the conclusion of which would be marked with a loud slap. Instead, the dancer either keeps the hand at the shoulder, forcing the *subidor* to catch themself from playing that which was expected. Or alternately, the dancer throws the *piquete* with the other hand, which may have previously been in a relaxed position on the hip with no indication that it was about to move. This dynamic is gradually developed throughout the improvised solo, interspersed with clear, strongly marked phrases. Typically the level of rhythmic intensity builds gradually until the *piquetes* are no longer interrupted by dramatic pauses or the traveling *paseo* that marks the basic step, and the movements have become faster and sharper. The dancer determines the end of the exchange with a closing salute.

Clearly, the space of the *soberao* offers an opportunity for individual empowerment through an embodied speaking that while certainly present in stage performances, is often compromised there. One of the ways that the *soberao* as a community-centered space offers this potential is in framing the performing female body as a subject. Though *bomba* dance is widely appreciated and practiced by both men and women, and while it is difficult to make empirical claims regarding gender participation in *bomba* practice, I argue that *bomba* offers a unique opportunity for female dancers who challenge gendered expectations for social behavior in making the drum speak through their dancing bodies. This sense of empowerment and accomplishment, while also achieved by playing drums, is distinct when it takes place through the moving, dancing body, precisely because of the way the dance operates in relationship to discursive power. As Jane Desmond writes, "formal or informal instruction, quotidian or 'dance' movement, the parameters of acceptable/intelligible movement within specific contexts are highly controlled, produced, in a Foucauldian sense by specific discursive practices and productive limitations."[49] Thus, in activating the drum through the speaking body the dancer is intelligible in an altogether different discursive register. By using visual signification (executing dance movements) to create audible patterns (hearing the specific dance choices reflected in the sound of the drums), the visual object of the female dancing body becomes an active subject through her own embodied movement choices and the communicative force of the drum. Additionally, the act of throwing the skirt with forceful, repetitive, but precise flicks enacts a kind of controlled violence that causes the drums to sound louder at the same time that the heart rate of the dancer increases, releasing endorphins and adrenaline that cause physical excitement, creating a sense of physical release. Thus, the dancer enacts her subjectivity on physiological and phenomenological levels as she feels the effects of her dance moving through her body at the same time that she is made aware through other sensory perception of this dance having created a visible/audible effect in the surrounding community/audience/spectators. However, *bomba* practitioners from earlier generations provide insightful perspectives on the evolving history of women's expressive *piquetes* by reminding us that women were not permitted such assertive public displays in their dance. Instead, they used to dance by making very small, subtle *piquetes* (a shoulder shrug, small flick of the skirt) to which the *subidor* would have to be paying very close attention.[50] Thus, the style and force of the *piquetes* executed by women are directly parallel to the gendered behavior dictated by the particular historical and social contexts in which they are living. Therefore, when thinking about the female subjectivity achieved through the solo improvisation of today's *bomba* dancers, it is important to keep in mind that demonstrating this degree of physical dominance in the *soberao* inevitably engages, and perhaps even calls into question, the expected norms for gendered comportment in public spaces.

As *bomba* practice has continued to develop since the turn of the century, stronger and more forceful *piquetes* have become the norm for female dancers both on the stage and in the *soberao*.[51] In fact, the requirements of stage dancing may arguably have encouraged the development of more dramatic movements legible to an audience placed at a distance from the dancer. Nonetheless, when performed as spectacle as opposed to as a self-expression framed by community understanding of the practice and its protocols, the acts of signification create different results. Strong *piquetes* for women may consist of any of the following moves: Using great force, the arms throw the skirt, beginning with the hands together, in front of the chest area, and ends with the arms openly extended, elbows slightly bent, muscles flexed, the skirt tensed and taut as an indication of the active work of the arms pulling against each other. Done quickly, this move can create the sensation of breaking through something, or tearing apart something that is bound. This final open pose is struck and held with *elegancia*, shoulders back, head high, even if slightly inclined forward at the waist. The move may be repeated, in double-time or triple time, building intensity, or may serve as a punctuating end to a series of other moves. Another example is the shoulder shrug. With hands in fists, wrists straight, not bent, and thus creating an image of strength, knuckles placed on the hips, and elbows out to the side, the dancer lifts her shoulders up toward her ears and decidedly drops them, not passively letting them fall, but actively pushing them down to mark the *piquete*. She may lift the shoulders, and drop them again in a repeated series of shrugs, where the up and down motions are distinguished by the decided physical emphasis on the downward movement which is accented by the drum. She may also lift the shoulders and suspend the forthcoming *piquete* while the *subidor* plays a drum roll in anticipation of the dropping shoulders that will eventually break the building suspense, providing a cathartic sensation of relief and satisfaction. During both the shoulder shrug and another move that consists of elbow hits, it is common for the dancer to start creating tension by moving across the *soberao*, emphasizing the distance between the drummers and herself, whether several yards or a couple of feet, and gradually approaching the lead drummer as she builds in intensity. As she pulls her shoulders up and the drum rolls, waiting for her to drop them, she averts her gaze by turning her head away from the drum, as if to signal that she could be there all day. Her apparent relaxed and unhurried stance contrasted with the pending completion of the phrase creates a sensation of control, power, and agency. The decision is hers when the slap will finally come.

Although many female dancers who perform in the *soberao* choose to wear the full skirt that has become the principal visual signifier for *bomba* dance, women in diaspora and on the island are increasingly choosing to dance without the skirt. Sometimes the skirt is substituted with a scarf, or at times the dancers simply use their arms to make *figuras*, or shapes, as the men do. This allows for more of a focus on elaborate footwork, further expanding expressive possibilities without the gendered costume requirements.[52] In distancing the dance from the signifiers of the folkloric stage, these women are able to activate *bomba* as a way to explore and deconstruct gendered behavior, thereby also challenging discourses of race and nation that rely on the aesthetic of the female body. By focusing on the feet and arms of the dancer, instead of the skirt, not only is physical strength privileged, but the entire focus of the dance is shifted to the dancer's body. One of the strongest and simplest usages of the feet, whether wearing a skirt or not, comes with the foot stomp. The dancer raises her foot by lifting the whole leg as a unit, as if a puppet string attached to the slightly bent knee were being pulled, while maintaining the posture in the upper body, and then forcefully dropping the foot. Or, while holding the rest of the body in a pose in which the arms are engaged in a *figura* and the upper body is appropriately *elegante*, the foot is kicked back, like a horse stomping a fly, hinging at the knee, and quickly brought down with the sole of the foot landing soundly on the ground. While the foot may be making a sound as it hits the ground, the sound on the drum amplifies this gesture to a much louder degree. The foot stomp can take place at the same time as a shoulder shrug, elbow hit, or skirt breaking open, either increasing the force of any one of these individual moves, or serving as a connector between them. The foot stomp is interspersed with slides, toe taps, shuffles, and foot crossing in a forward and backward direction in order to create a varied rhythmic pattern. Footwork can be done while wearing a skirt, but requires a lifting of the skirt, which not only makes the sequence limited in duration but makes it difficult to use the arms to make *figuras*.

In highlighting *bomba*'s speaking body as a means for empowering women and destabilizing categories of gender I wish to be clear that this is undoubtedly a practice that men also find empowering and one that may offer a space for challenging dominant narratives of masculinity.[53] *Bombero* and founder of the Los Angeles–based group *Atabey*, José Rodríguez, describes his experience of dancing in the following way:

> When I dance, its funny because I could be smiling when I'm dancing, but in my own mind I am very serious, and I feel very serious about what I am doing, it almost feels like, I can't even describe it, there is this energy that kind of pulls me, and I end up doing these movements and it's like *my* time, where like every movement is some kind of attitude that I am giving, but not because I like hate somebody or am pissed off that day. I could be totally happy but I love the feeling of getting to be aggressive and assertive in my movement, especially when the drum is following you and marking everything you do, it's like you lose yourself, or I lose myself on the dance floor.[54]

In addition to underscoring the cathartic effect of the dance on the dancer, it bears noting that this "aggressive" and "assertive" quality described by Rodríguez, has not always been available to women when they dance. Furthermore, in locating the suspension of his individual identity ("myself") in the space of "the dance floor," Rodríguez signals two important functions of the *soberao*. First, even as he is empowered through personal expression, the individual is always actively interacting with the drum, and thus is collectively part of something outside of himself. Thus individualism, while key in underscoring the power of the speaking body, is secondary to the communal effort that enables this experience, the shared conversation of which the speaking body is a part. Second, by using the frame of "the dance floor" as the *soberao*, he demonstrates how this space values the dance as an exploration of identity, rather than as an aesthetic product.

Just as the *soberao* provides a space for the body to speak and engage individual empowerment, it also facilitates an embodied speaking that productively engages and challenges hegemonic discourses of race and nation. By leaving the space of the folkloric stage, resisting codification in terms of costume and privileging creative practice, Afro–Puerto Ricanness is collectively celebrated through the experience of the moving body, not through the image of a stereotype. The dancing body in the *soberao* articulates the survival of this tradition, of black-identified Puerto Ricans, the collective ownership of this history, reclaimed from institutional control. Nonetheless, it is imperative to critically address the way that using *bomba*, a racialized practice, as a vehicle for individual empowerment may inadvertently result in the equation of corporeal blackness with embodied freedom. Marking *bomba* as a black cultural product *and* as a practice enabling individual empowerment should not rhetorically link these two functions.

One way of challenging this problematic association is to think about how *bomba* uses what Robert Farris Thompson calls the "aesthetics of cool," juxtaposing both "hot" and "cool" elements of movement and performance. As opposed to relying on dance elements that are primarily considered "hot," liberating, and empowering, *bomba*'s use of "cool" as an expressive register not only shows the nuance required in executing these seemingly simple movements but also destabilizes connections between blackness and corporeal force and strength. First written about in Thompson's 1974 book *African Art in Motion*, the "cool aesthetic," is described as an attitude that "combines composure with vitality."[55] Thompson identifies "cool" as an African cultural value, stemming from spiritual beliefs central to African aesthetic practices and later influential in the African diaspora. Although certainly European cultures have their own version of "cool," Thompson and subsequent scholars argue that it tends to be more about self-control in the face of stress, or even cold-bloodedness, and less about the pleasure found in the "juxtaposition of detachment with intensity"[56] or "hot" with "cool." Brenda Dixon Gottschild in her book *Digging the Africanist Presence* writes the following:

> The aloofness, *sangfroid*, and detachment of some styles of European academic dance are one kind of cool, but they represent a completely different principle from the Africanist cool. The European attitude suggests centeredness, control, linearity, directness; the Africanist mode suggests asymmetricality (that plays with falling off center), looseness (implying flexibility and vitality), and indirectness of approach. "Hot," its opposite, is the indispensable compliment of the Africanist cool . . . It is the embracing of these opposites, in being and playing the paradoxes, from inside out and outside in, and in their high-affect juxtaposition, that the aesthetic of cool exists.[57]

The cool aesthetic of *bomba* can be seen in the way in which the torso shifts quickly from erectness in a vertical axis to breaking at the hip and leaning forward and to the side, even if ever so slightly (asymmetricality). It can be seen in the way that the dancer approaching the drummer looks toward the drummers and then away as if to indicate that though the dance is becoming intense, she is relaxed and unperturbed (indirectness). The looseness necessary for the wrists and hands to make the skirt flow delicately as they forcefully throw their arms to land in a taut and tensed *figura* demonstrates flexibility combined with strength and vitality. Expressing preference for the "hot" elements of *bomba* dance, hip-shaking, foot pattering, shoulder shimmying, without taking into account how these work in concert with, and are in fact framed by, the cool elements of control and precision, undermines the complexity at play in *bomba* dance and reveals essentializing attitudes about blackness and movement. The notion of cool is further underscored by the belief expressed by some *bombera/os* that dancers should not break a sweat. The composure, or the *elegancia*, of the dancer is viewed as a performance of pride. This reference to pride and coolness goes one step further in destabilizing notions of uncontrolled physical "freedom" as somehow attached to black bodies. Lack of excess physical exertion (no sweat), while similar to European coolness in that, in appearing to be carefree, the person downplays and disguises this effort, is not in fact an imitation of the European approach of disdain and detachment. Rather it is a performance that purposefully highlights *bomba*'s interlocutory nature; the tensions and contrasts created between the drums, dance, and song, between the performer and the spectator, between speaking and listening. Ultimately, the speaking body's vacillation between hot and cool elements emphasizes the way that *bomba* dance relies on individual artistry and expressiveness and even as it is also pedestrian and communitarian.

CONCLUSION

The speaking body inherent to *bomba* has allowed for the continuance of this form as a tool for articulating an embodied counternarrative to discourses of belonging imposed by the logocentrism of the lettered elite. Even as I have pointed to the problematic discourses produced through the folklorization of *bomba* and the essentializing lenses of race and nation subsequently applied to the form, the folkloric stage nonetheless works to inform the twenty-first-century *soberao*. Not only is the twenty-first-century *soberao* influenced by the heightened expressiveness permitted in this theatrical space but also the cultural capital acquired through the prestige afforded by the folkloric stage has also effectively regenerated a popular interest in *bomba*, indeed ensuring its public visibility in the twenty-first-century *soberao*. The folkloric stage did not replace the *soberao*, nor did the twenty-first-century *soberao* entirely eclipse the folkloric stage. I have instead demonstrated how they work in a dynamic dialogue with each other. While certainly the *soberao* persisted throughout the period of folklorization alongside performances of staged *bomba*, the popularization of the twenty-first-century *soberao* both on the island and in the diaspora is in large part indebted to the work of the families who created a "respectable" image for *bomba* and its practitioners. Yet simultaneously, even as the *bomba* practiced today is in dialogue with the representational framing of the stage, the twenty-first-century *soberao* is responsible for the exponential increase in the number of *bomba* practitioners and promises to be the primary site for ensuring its continuation for generations to come. As such, the potential of the speaking body in *bomba* proves to be uncontainable, slippery, and impossible to fully harness by dominant representational discourses. While the original purpose of the folkloric stage was to "clean up" *bomba*'s vulgar image, simultaneously also controlling its potential as a threatening and subversive practice, the renewed interest in the twenty-first-century *soberao* in fact reveals quite the opposite effect. Despite attempts to appropriate the genre in the service of a whitened narrative of belonging and framing *bomba* as a primarily aesthetic practice, the folklorization of the form effectively reinvigorated *bomba* of the *soberao* by lending it legitimacy. Finally, in a similar way, I have shown how the twenty-first-century *soberao* allows *bombera/os* in the diaspora to effectively mark Diasporican subalternity in a way that resists both the hegemonic narrative of the melting pot and the commodification and circulation of the form as a depoliticized multicultural product. Diasporic *soberaos* reflect communities of belonging shaped through the various experiences and intimacies of life as immigrants and/or racialized/ethnic Other. The speaking body thus ensures not just *bomba*'s continued existence, its inherent resistance to appropriation and commodification, but also its original function.

The singularity of *bomba* as an embodied music-making that necessitates community exchange and collective creative expression allows for a unique opportunity to examine and juxtapose the constitutive elements of dance and theater. As a form that is valued both as practice and performance, unquestionably framed as dance *and* as theatrical event, as culture and as cultural product, *bomba* facilitates an understanding of the inadequacy of these disciplinary distinctions. Because of the particular conventions of the form, both the stage and the *soberao* require a speaking body. By looking at *bomba* dance as pedestrian, foregrounding the quotidian nature of this embodied practice, activated as theatrical only through individual "speaking," I have shown how this is a dance form that cannot exist as pure movement. Conversely, theatricalized representations of *bomba* fundamentally rely on meaning-making produced by moving bodies.

Bomba practice and performance will inevitably continue to evolve and shift in both of these spaces. In the process it will accommodate new narratives of identity and belonging, new geographies and bodies. Traditionalists would argue that the *bomba* of today is an altogether different form than that practiced half a century ago. Today's *bombera/os* will undoubtedly feel the same way as we watch new generations develop their purpose and style, writing original songs and experimenting with rhythms and movements. Ultimately though, whether framed as dance *or* theater, performed in the *soberao* or on the stage, as long as there is a speaking body involved, an individual subjectivity enacted through communal exchange, through shared knowledge of history, culture, and above all, struggle and survival, *bomba* as I define it, will continue to exist.

Notes

1. *Soberao* is a cipher, or circular playing space around which drummers, singers, and spectators gather while the center is used for dancing. *Buleadores* are the drums that all play the same rhythm, marking the basic pattern while the lead drum marks the dancer's movements.
2. "Speak."
3. Movements that the dancer asks the drummer to mark.

4. Álvarez Luis Manuel Rivera and Ángel G. Quintero, "Bambulaé Sea Allá: La Bomba Y La Plena, Compendio Histórico-Social," http://www.tradicionmusical.com/noticias.html (accessed January 18, 2013).

5. Quintero Rivera identifies the counter-plantation as a group of subalterns that operated beneath the radar of the surveillance and controlling forces of the plantation society, often forming maroon communities. Quintero Rivera describes the dialectic of the plantation/counter-plantation as a dynamic tension between these two worlds.

6. Very similar genres appear across the Caribbean: *tumba francesa* in eastern Cuba, *tumba* in Haiti and Curacao, *gwo-ka* in Guadaloupe, *bele* in Martinique, *palos* in the Dominican Republic, and *bamboula* in Lousiana and St. Croix.

7. Diana Taylor, *The Archive and the Repertoire* (Durham, NC: Duke University Press, 2003).

8. From Archivo General de Puerto Rico. Fondo de los Gobernadores, Caja 59. Negociado de Seguridad Pública. Carta de Santiago de Cardona, 4 de julio de 1823. Cited in Guillermo A. Baralt, *Esclavos Rebeldes: Conspiraciones Y Sublevaciones De Esclavos En Puerto Rico (1795–1873)*, 1st ed. (Río Piedras, PR: Ediciones Huracán, 1982): 44.

9. Sara Johnson, *The Fear of the French Negroes* (Berkeley: University of California Press, 2012), 161–72.

10. Puerto Ricans living in the diaspora (typically the United States). This term was coined by Nuyorican poet Mariposa (María Teresa Fernández) in her 1997 poem "Ode to the Diasporican."

11. Because of the history of racial mixing in Puerto Rico, racial identification among Puerto Ricans is a complex matter that differs greatly from the process of racial formation in the United States. While many, if not most, Puerto Ricans have African ancestry, "Afro–Puerto Rican" has been used as a term of self-identification by those that experience antiblack racism within either a US or a Puerto Rican context.

12. Puerto Ricanness.

13. Colloquial Puerto Rican Spanish tends to shorten the syllables at the end of words, thus turning *soberado* into *soberao*.

14. Arlene Pabón, "*Por la Encendida Calle Antillana*: African Impact on Puerto Rican Domestic Architecture," in *Places of Cultural Memory: African Reflections on the American Landscape*. National Parks Survey Conference Proceedings (Washington, DC: National Center for Cultural Resources, 2003), 140.

15. In distinguishing the "prefolkloric" *soberao* from the twenty-first-century *soberao* it should be clear that the use of the *soberao* persisted throughout the period during which *bomba* was most publicly consumed as a folkloric product. *Bomba* of the *soberao* always existed alongside stage *bomba*, however, what I call the twenty-first-century *soberao* uses the conventions of the "prefolkloric" *soberao* but is nonetheless influenced by given transformations of the form that have taken place through stage performances of *bomba*.

16. "Entrevista con 'Don Chato' Guayama, PR 2008. Hermanos Emmanuelli Náter & PROPA," August 24, 2011, video clip, YouTube, http://www.youtube.com/watch?v=PXE2hyiJTS4&feature=youtube (accessed January 2, 2013).

17. Ricardo E. Alegría, *El Instituto de Cultura Puertorriqueña 1955–1973: 18 años contribuyendo a fortalecer nuestra conciencia nacional* (San Juan, PR: Instituto de Cultura Puertorriqueña, 1978).

18. See, for example, Tomás Blanco's *El prejuicio racial en Puerto Rico* (San Juan: Editorial Biblioteca de Autores Puertorriqueños, 1948).

19. For a discussion on the power of written discourse in the historical formation of Latin American societies see Angel Rama's *The Lettered City* (Durham, NC: Duke University Press, 1996).

20. See Tomás Blanco's essay "Elogio de 'la plena,'" *Revista del Ateneo Puertorriqueño* 1 (1935): 97–106.

21. Musicians such as Rafael Cortijo and Ismael Rivera were instrumental in incorporating the rhythmic elements and songs of traditional *plenas* and *bombas* into the popular music of the 1950s.

22. Dress shirts commonly worn in the Caribbean.

23. Arlene Dávila, *Sponsored Identities: Cultural Politics in Puerto Rico* (Philadelphia: Temple University Press, 1997), 75–79.

24. Whitening.

25. Isar P. Godreau, "San Antón for TV: Gender Performances of Puerto Rican Black Folklore," *e-misférica* 5, no. 2 (2008), http://hemisphericinstitute.org/hemi/en/e-misferica-52/godreau.

26. Ibid.

27. Melanie A. Maldonado, "*Bomba Trigueña*: Diluted Culture and (Loss of) Female Agency in AfroPuerto Rican Music and Dance Performance," in *Caribbean without Borders*, edited by Dorsia Smith, Raquel Puig, and Ileana Cotés Santiago (Newcastle upon Tyne, UK: Cambridge Scholars, 2008), 95–117.

28. Rebecca Schneider, *The Explicit Body in Performance* (New York: Routledge, 1997), 126–52.

29. Victor Vélez, Public Lecture, Oakland, CA, September 22, 2012.

30. Elin Diamond, *Performance and Cultural Politics* (London and New York: Routledge, 1996), 2.

31. Raquel Z. Rivera, "New York Bomba: Puerto Ricans, Dominicans, and a Bridge Called Haiti," *Rhythms of the Afro-Atlantic World*, edited by Mamadou Diouf and Ifeoma Kiddoe Nwankwo (Ann Arbor: University of Michigan Press, 2010), 178–99.

32. While elsewhere Rivera does acknowledge the importance of skin color in terms of access to privilege, her argument here has less to do with looking black than with blackness as culture.

33. Rivera, 190.

34. An example of this can be seen in Jerry Ferrao's 2012 documentary *Los Ayeres de la Bomba*.

35. A *bombazo* is a community dance. The term comes from a movement in the late 1990s initiated by José E. Emmanuelli to remove *bomba* from folkloric discourse by making it accessible to youth and other interested participants. Today, the term *toque de bomba*, or *bomba* jam, is also used to describe such an event.

36. For another discussion about *salsa* dance practices in non–Puerto Rican communities see Cindy Garcia's *Salsa Crossings: Dancing Latinidad in Los Angeles* (Durham, NC: Duke University Press, 2013).

37. Priscilla Renta, "Salsa Dance Performance: Latina/o History in Motions," in *Technofuturos: Critical Interventions in Latina/o Studies*, edited by Nancy Raquel Mirabal and Agustin Láo Montes (Lanham, MD: Lexington Books, 2007), 270–71.

38. Mayra Santos Febres, "Salsa as Translocation," in *Everynight Life: Culture and Dance in Latin/o America*, edited by Celeste Fraser Delgado and José Esteban Muñoz (Durham, NC: Duke University Press, 1997), 176–77.

39. For more on the black foundations of Puerto Ricans and Puerto Rican culture see Arlene Torres's essay "La gran familia puertorriqueña 'ej prieta de beldá,'" in *Blackness in Latin America and the Caribbean: Social Dynamics and Cultural Transformations* (Bloomington,

IN: Indiana University Press, 1998). Also see Jose Luis Gonzalez's *El país de cuatro pisos* (Río Piedras, Puerto Rico: Ediciones Huracán, 1989).

40. While I have conducted some fieldwork in Puerto Rico, Chicago, and New York, most of my research has taken place in California *bomba* communities.

41. I argue that the communities forged through these processes are not just imagined in the Andersonian sense of collectively imagining nations of disparate peoples through shared narratives and ideologies, but that they are also actualized, in a performative sense, through the everyday acts of embodied speaking particular to *bomba* practice and performance. As Benedict Anderson reminds us in his influential study *Imagined Communities*, for as much as imaginings of nation are constructed they are also, in fact, "real." Furthermore, in thinking about the central role of print capitalism and the "fixing of print languages" (45) in creating an imagined community, counter-languages and alternatives to hegemonic linguistic practices (such as the embodied speaking I refer to here) are useful sites for understanding other modalities through which "community" is imagined and enacted.

42. Loosely understood as a "promenade" as way of introduction. During the *paseo* the dancer does not ask for *piquetes*, for the lead drum to mark their steps.

43. Halbert Barton, "A Challenge for Puerto Rican Music: How to Build a *soberao* for *bomba*," *Centro* 16, no. 1 (2004): 82.

44. I have left the word in its masculine form, even though there are increasingly more female drummers. However, the number of lead female drummers who play the *primo*, the higher pitched lead drum, are still relatively few. In such cases, the term *subidora* is sometimes used. The literal translation of *subidor* means "the one who raises it up."

45. This applies to most 4/4 rhythms but will be different for other rhythms such as the *yubá*, which has a 6/8 *clave*.

46. It should be clear that different *subidores* have unique styles of interpreting *piquetes* and skill levels in doing so. However, in order to be respected enough to even play this lead drum, it is expected that the *subidor* will first have years of experience developing rhythmic facility with the other instruments (*buleadores, maraca*, and *cua*).

47. Alamo-Pastrana, 586.

48. *Figura, firmeza, elegancia*, or, making a figure, firmness, and elegance.

49. Jane Desmond, "Embodying Difference," in *Everynight Life: Culture and Dance in Latin/o America*, edited by Celeste Fraser Delgado and José Esteban Muñoz (Durham, NC: Duke University Press, 1997), 37.

50. Victor Vélez.

51. Although I am discussing here particularly expressive *piquetes*, it should also be clear that there are different conventions for different rhythms. For instance, the *piquetes* used to dance to a *cuembe* rhythm are going to have a softer quality because of the *cuembe* cadence than those used for the *yubá* rhythm. Although the steps may be the same, the quality of the execution will vary.

52. Additionally, queer and gender queer identified *bombera/os* will now, in some spaces, dance "as men" or "as women" using given movement vocabulary or dress to mark these differences.

53. Alamo-Pastrana, 586–90.

54. Jose Rodriquez, Interviewed by the author, San Diego, CA, September 27, 2011.

55. Robert Farris Thompson, *African Art in Motion* (Berkeley: University of California Press, 1979), 43.

56. Brenda Dixon Gottschild, *Digging the Africanist Presence in American Performance.* (Westport, CT: Greenwood Press, 1996), 13.
57. Ibid., 17.

BIBLIOGRAPHY

Alamo-Pastrana, Carlos. "*Con el eco de los barriles*: Race, Gender and the *Bomba* Imaginary in Puerto Rico." *Social Identities* 16, no. 5 (2009): 573–600.

Barton, Halbert. "A Challenge for Puerto Rican Music: How to Build a *soberao* for *bomba*." *Centro* 16, no. 1 (2004): 69–89.

Butler, Judith. *Bodies That Matter.* New York: Routledge, 1993.

Dávila, Arlene. *Sponsored Identities: Cultural Politics in Puerto Rico.* Philadelphia: Temple University Press, 1997.

Desmond, Jane. "Embodying Difference." In *Everynight Life: Culture and Dance in Latin/o America*, edited by Celeste Fraser Delgado and José Esteban Muñoz, 33–64. Durham, NC: Duke University Press, 1997.

Diamond, Elin. *Performance and Cultural Politics.* London and New York: Routledge, 1996.

Godreau, Isar P. "San Antón for TV: Gender Performances of Puerto Rican Black Folklore." *e-misférica* 5, no. 2 (2008). http://hemisphericinstitute.org/hemi/en/e-misferica-52/godreau.

Gottschild, Brenda Dixon. *Digging the Africanist Presence in American Performance.* Westport, CT: Greenwood Press, 1996.

Maldonado, Melanie A. "*Bomba Trigueña*: Diluted Culture and (Loss of) Female Agency in AfroPuerto Rican Music and Dance Performance." In *Caribbean without Borders*, edited by Dorsia Smith, Raquel Puig, and Ileana Cotés Santiago, 95–117. Newcastle upon Tyne, UK: Cambridge Scholars, 2008.

Pabón, Arleen. "*Por la Encendida Calle Antillana*: African Impact on Puerto Rican Domestic Architecture." In *Places of Cultural Memory: African Reflections on the American Landscape*, 139–44. National Parks Survey Conference Proceedings. Washington, DC: National Center for Cultural Resources, 2003.

Renta, Priscilla. "Salsa Dance Performance: Latina/o History in Motions." In *Technofuturos: Critical Interventions in Latina/o Studies*, edited by Nancy Raquel Mirabal and Agustin Láo Montes, 269–294. Lanham, MD: Lexington Books, 2007.

Rivera, Raquel Z. "New York Bomba: Puerto Ricans, Dominicans, and a Bridge Called Haiti." In *Rhythms of the Afro-Atlantic World*, edited by Mamadou Diouf and Ifeoma Kiddoe Nwankwo, 178–99. Ann Arbor: University of Michigan Press, 2010.

Santos Febres, Mayra. "Salsa as Translocation." In *Everynight Life: Culture and Dance in Latin/o America*, edited by Celeste Fraser Delgado and José Esteban Muñoz, 175–88. Durham, NC: Duke University Press, 1997.

Schneider, Rebecca. *The Explicit Body in Performance.* New York: Routledge, 1997.

Taylor, Diana. *The Archive and the Repertoire.* Durham, NC: Duke University Press, 2003.

Thompson, Robert Farris. *African Art in Motion.* Berkeley: University of California Press, 1979.

CHAPTER 35

LINDY HOP, COMMUNITY, AND THE ISOLATION OF APPROPRIATION

WILLIAM GIVEN

DRAWING inspiration from the Charleston and the Breakaway in the 1920s, Lindy Hop, in its most recognizable form, began emerging on the dance floor of the Savoy Ballroom in Harlem in 1935. Owned by Moe Paddon, a white Jewish gangster, the Savoy Ballroom was unique for its time, for whereas it was common practice for dance clubs to be designated as "whites only," or at best to have a single night set aside during the week for African Americans to come dance, the Savoy was integrated from its inception in 1926. It was here that the Lindy Hop was born. As primarily a challenge dance, with couples entering a jam circle to show-case their interpretation of the various steps to cheering onlookers for a few bars of music before being displaced by the next pair of dancers, Lindy Hop extended past being solely a partner dance and instead became more reflective of a communal experience. On the dance floor, individuals from across the community, and from varying professions and socioeco-nomic strata, could gather together in order to share in an experience of revelry that was based in equality and commonality on the dance floor. This dance floor became a subculture in itself, a place where communication that transcended racial and social boundaries could take place through movement. When Frankie Manning completed the first aerial with his partner Frieda Washington at the Savoy in 1935, flipping her over his back, the element of the Lindy Hop that allowed it to be distinguished from its deeply rooted to the ground predeces-sors was in place, and other regular dancers at the Savoy began to develop their own air steps. This quickly established the Lindy Hop as an exciting theatrical experience, one that was reliant not just on the dancers who were performing but on an audience as well, and soon large crowds were being drawn from outside of Harlem into the club. The dance was then further reinterpreted from being based primarily on a participatory structure, with everyone taking a turn in the jam circle despite their varying levels of ability, into a performative spec-tacle, with a clear delineation between the audience and the dancer.

  To capitalize on the popularity of the Savoy dancers, black entrepreneur Herbert "Whitey" White organized a troupe of regulars from the club, named "Whitey's Lindy Hoppers," to travel around and perform at various social events in New York City. Their increasing popularity led the troupe to appear on Broadway, beginning with a run of six shows of *Black Rhythm* in December 1936, and then most notably in eighty-five performances of *The Hot Mikado* with Bill Robinson at the Broadhurst Theatre in 1939, as well as in films including *A Day at the Races* with the Marx Brothers in 1937. I will be arguing though that this disconnection from the jam circle, and the subsequent appropriation of this black dance form by white audiences who viewed only the disembodied theatrical spectacle of the exciting air steps outside of their original contexts, transformed the meaning of the dance from being one that had an inclusivity of community at its central core into something that now had a liminal space that created a distance between observer and participant. Ultimately, this reappropriated the cultural capital of the dance into a mere commodity that was openly traded until it eventually became a reconstituted, but albeit veiled, form of minstrelsy that was reflective of pervious incarnations of blackface performance on the minstrel stage and whose aim was the disempowerment of the African American artist. Just as George-Graves finds with ragtime dance in the decades preceding the development of the Lindy Hop, the cultural appropriation of a dance is not just problematic because of the mixing of the cultures, but rather, it is the "subsequent disenfranchisement, exploitative commercialization, and disavowal of African American culture by hegemonic forces"[1] that need to be addressed. This becomes most readily apparent when in 1943, just eight short years after Lindy Hop first began to emerge, *Life* magazine featured a cover photo on the August 23 issue titled "Lindy Hop" with two young dancers, both white, rigidly posed and grounded, smiling together with no one surrounding them and thus firmly representing the dilution of the dance's original meaning, and further leading to the establishment of a homogenized catchall term of "swing dancing" that included both the African American dances that were being appropriated and the white European and American social dances such as the Balboa that were also popular at the time. While Lindy Hop was an African American dance, swing dancing became the presumed safe and marketable moniker to attach to the movement for white audiences.

While there is much debate as to where the name of "Lindy Hop" first originated, most variations center on a remark made by black dancer George "Shorty" Snowden at a dance contest at New York's Manhattan Casino in 1928. After performing a Breakaway, Snowden was asked by Fox Movietone News, "What are you doing with your feet?" and Snowden replied simply, "The Lindy."[2] While in the vernacular of the time "lindy" was slang for "girl," and "hop" was slang for "dance," the white reporter instantly associated Snowden's response as one that was celebrating the white aviator Charles Lindbergh who had successfully crossed the Atlantic on his solo nonstop flight from New York to Paris the previous year. The dance first began to appear though in its original form, where the dancers remained grounded to the dance floor, and without any aerial steps, in the clubs in Harlem in the late 1920s.[3] The Lindy Hop was an amalgamation of various dances, although it primarily combined elements from the Charleston, the Collegiate, and the Breakaway. Having first appeared in the 1923 Broadway musical, *Runnin' Wild* that featured an all-black cast, the Charleston had been quickly appropriated by white audiences and by the end of the 1920s was at the height of its popularity. The dance helped to define the predominantly white flapper culture as it moved from the dance floors and began to permeate popular culture, appearing in countless books and movies, and although the Charleston had made stars out of performers such as Josephine Baker and Joan Crawford, it is important to note that the African American performer Baker was only able to find her fame across the Atlantic in France, whereas the white actress Crawford was able to do so in the States. The Charleston was a departure from traditional European ballroom forms such as the waltz and the foxtrot, which relied primarily on having the dancers remain in contact with one another throughout the entirety of the dance. The Charleston though could be performed individually or with a partner, and even when it was done with another person, the two dancers would generally remain separated. Both the Collegiate and the Breakaway were joined partner dances, and while the Collegiate focused on rigid upper bodies with fast moving footwork, the Breakaway would allow for one of the dancers to "break" free of the traditional ballroom frame in order to "swing out." Frankie Manning recalls: "As I've mentioned before, at that point, they were still doing the breakaway. You only separated a little from your partner, but it was this release that gave the dancers the opportunity to improvise on the footwork."[4] This improvisation was key to the development of the Lindy Hop, as it afforded the dancers to break free from the constraints of the rigid confines of traditional ballroom dances in order to experiment and infuse the dance with elements of their own individual personalities. It was within this improvisation though that the Lindy Hop became a theatrical performance piece as well as a dance. By not relying on a set of prescribed choreographed movements, the dancers were thus free to respond to the spectators, so the feedback of the audience became vitally important to the development of steps that were increasingly more difficult as well as equally more spectacular and would thus draw a more emphatic response from the audience. Lindy Hop was about the performance, but the performance was one that was not set and instead remained in a fluid conversation with spectators. This created a dance that was rooted in dualities; it was at equal times a partner dance as well as one that allowed for each individual performer to shine, while at the same time it was a dance that was based in other previous forms but was focused primarily on the reinterpretation of those dances in order to create a new theatrical expressive embodiment of the self through emotion that was further fueled by spectators' responses.

While some could regard art forms such as Lindy Hop, jazz, and the blues, as ones that are uniquely American, and primarily grounded within the specific geographical centers from which they originated, doing so becomes another form of ethnocentric appropriation that does not take into account the varying cultural influences that work in concert with one another to shape the art form. As Katrina Hazzard-Gordon finds with her study of the jook joints in America in the early part of the twentieth century, "Dances in the jooks included the Charleston, the shimmy, the snake hips, the funky butt, the twist, the slow drag, the buzzard lope, the black bottom, the itch, the fish tail, and the grind. Most of these trace back to Africa and can be observed there today (as well as in African and African-American communities around the world)."[5] Thus, the Lindy Hop reflected not only the dancehall experience, where it would be performed in the center of a crowded circle of onlookers, with couples taking their turns to enter the circle in order to show off the new dance steps they had learned, or to respond to an unspoken challenge from the dancers who had just left the circle before them, but likewise was at the same time imbued with the dances that came before it that were danced in the American jooks as well as with the African challenge dances such as the juba. This challenge dance aspect created a competitive community, and the Lindy Hop was just as much about the social aspects of the dance as it was the dance steps being performed. It was a dance that was indicative of the societal composition of Harlem at the time. It was a dance that was allowed to morph rapidly because its contributors were all approaching it from a base in tradition, yet were still consistently testing out and incorporating those steps that may or may not have worked on the dance floor each night based on the response of the crowd. It was in this way that the Lindy Hop became a theatrical expression of a dance tradition, and even though for many the Lindy Hop is synonymous with the jitterbug, and the two terms are used interchangeably, I believe they are distinctively separate, for the jitterbug is primarily a white ghosting of a black dance. Described by John Martin in the *New York Times*, "The white jitterbug is oftener than not uncouth to look at, though he may be having a wonderful time and dancing skillfully, but his Negro original is quite another matter. His movements are never so exaggerated that they lack control, and there is an unmistakable dignity about his most violent figures."[6] While this could, of course, be viewed as a white dance critic attempting to legitimize an African American form rooted in a tradition that he is himself unfamiliar with, the key elements are the implications that the jitterbug was a dance that was out of control, whereas the Lindy Hop was indeed a theatrical performance, one that Martin attests that "of all the ballroom dancing these prying eyes have seen, this is unquestionably the finest; but let the white man attempt it at his peril."[7] So while the jitterbug was an oftentimes seemingly frenetic free for all with no inherent structure, as evidenced in a filmed number that was cut from *The Wizard of Oz* in 1939, where the white Dorothy and her traveling companions are bewitched to dance a dance they do not know to the point of exhaustion, the Lindy Hop was being developed based on its own traditional roots and its theatrical impact on an audience.

To develop the dance, the Lindy Hoppers would see a step another dancer performed and then go home and try to not only learn it but also improve on it and make the step something uniquely their own. While the dancers themselves could most often easily identify which step was developed by which dancer, and generally when and where it was first performed, since the dance was theatrical in presentation, that is, put on display for a paying audience and not merely being done socially, this allowed for the appropriation to initially take place, because although moves could be attributed to the collective of Whitey's Lindy Hoppers, the law at the time did not allow for the dancers to retain ownership over the steps and combinations they were inventing, as the copyrighting of choreographed works did not come into effect until the 1976 Copyright Act in the United States. Even for early cases that did question this practice, most notably as Anthea Kraut finds with Alberta Hunter, who claimed to have copyrighted the Black Bottom dance in the 1920s, "asserting collective authorship in this climate was not enough; a work had to be individually authored to qualify as intellectual property. Even unsubstantiated, Hunter's copyright claim should thus be seen as a weapon against and check on white hegemony in the theatrical marketplace."[8] The Lindy Hop was completely rooted in this form of collective authorship since it was an open communal theatrical event. Numerous styles existing outside of just the Charleston, Collegiate, and Breakaway all came together to create the Lindy Hop, but while Joel Dinerstein argues that, "Unlike the Charleston, however, the lindy had no immediate southern antecedents. It was not derived from the African tradition of animal dances, nor did it contain the flat-footed shuffle of blues dances and the 'slow drag.' Without these features, the lindy calls attention to itself as something new in the black vernacular,"[9] I would unequivocally disagree. Though I feel that it is indeed of paramount importance that the Lindy Hop is considered to be the first African American form of dance created in the north, the relevance here is not due to the fact that it was created by disavowing traditional derivatives of African dance but rather that it was shaped by the closely packed energy of the city itself, where a plethora of individuals could join together to create something that was whole-heartedly their own. The Lindy

Hop did carry these traditional forms embedded within it simply because it was created by the performers on the dance floor who each brought to it myriad personal experiences that developed a pastiche of a cultural archive.

The epicenter for the development of the Lindy Hop was at the Savoy Ballroom[10] in Harlem, where the group that would later be known as Whitey's Lindy Hoppers[11] was born, and where the best Lindy Hoppers could be found at the northeast corner of the dance floor continuously developing the dance to the delight of eager spectators. Unlike the other main Harlem landmark, the Cotton Club,[12] where African American patrons were not allowed in to dance to the music being performed by African American artists, the interracial dance floor of the Savoy helped contribute to the semiotical language of the Lindy Hop that was developing, but it also started to shift the focus of the dance dramatically. Originally, as Manning notes, "it wasn't like we were putting on a performance or dancing for applause. One couple would start dancing, and a crowd would form around them. Then another guy standing on the side would say, 'I can cut that,' swing his chick out, and do his little bit. Then someone else would come out, and you had a jam. It was always impromptu."[13] This impromptu nature of the performance is a critical element in understanding how the Lindy Hop functioned, for it allowed for a fluid interplay between spectator and performer, where a two-way conversation was established and which allowed the performer to respond accordingly to the input from the audience without being trapped within a structured regiment of steps. In this manner, both spectator and performer become active in the creation of a dance, which cannot be repeated, because the dance is never the same and instead relies primarily on the unspoken conversation taking place between each dancer and the audience. As more white spectators began to come to the Savoy to observe the African American dancers who were starting to generate buzz about their exciting new dance though, the cultural capital of the inclusiveness of the collective identity of the community of the dance floor began to be fragmented into a distinctive audience and performer binary, and the dynamic interplay between individual contributors began to be usurped by the conversation thus taking place with that audience. So although the focus was initially not about the performative aspect of the dance but rather the communal nature of the experience, the transition of the dance into the theatrical helped, in turn, shape the dance, as moves that were ultimately incorporated into the Lindy Hop became those that drew the biggest reactions from the audience, whereas those moves that did not were quickly abandoned.

The performer, caught up in the moment of the dance, then exists simultaneously as both an individual and as a member of a collective; the performer is an embodiment of his own cultural knowledge that he expresses on the dance floor during the Lindy Hop. He is the product of the other dancers he has watched the night before, or the minute before, who had taken their place in the circle, and he is engaged in multiple and simultaneous semiotical conversations involving his partner, the other dancers forming the dance circle, and the audience of spectators on the periphery of that circle. This becomes indicative of Guy Debord's understanding of time in the Hegelian sense, where he states that time is "the *necessary* alienation, the environment where the subject realizes himself by losing himself, where he becomes other in order to become truly himself."[14] So in, what was originally dubbed "The Corner," and would later be known as "The Cat's Corner," the spot where the best dancers congregated at the Savoy Ballroom, the Lindy Hopper was negotiating a very nuanced balance between being an individual performer, and being a member of competing communities: the multilayered community of dancers at the club comprising the elite members of Whitey's Lindy Hoppers and those dancers who aspired to dance in The Corner, as well as the community of the nondancing spectators who simply watched the dancing for its entertainment value. More importantly though, these dancers were also taking part in a form of time that exists outside of Debord's alienation model and were instead being directly linked through the historicity of the traditions the Lindy Hop was created from. As the subject loses himself, he or she does not cease to exist, but rather becomes part of a collective tradition. Time is actually conflated here and is no longer linear, so that the Lindy Hopper is simultaneously a dancer in Harlem in the 1930s, a dancer in the southern jooks of the turn of the last century, one who danced as a form of performative resistance or as a means to communicate during slavery in the nineteenth century, and a dancer on the African continent itself. Through the Lindy Hoppers performance, this lineage was thus being displayed theatrically.

When the dance is mimetically reproduced though, such as happened when white spectators viewed the Lindy Hop as nothing more than a series of steps or tricks to be copied at home, it becomes devoid of the lineage that is engrained in the performances of the Savoy dancers. This creates a space where "defining individual expression in the context of working closely with another person (i.e., thus revealing its true jazz character) enabled the Lindy Hop to make such a dramatic impact. Black dancing bodies became 'hep' and respectfully imitated."[15] So while the theatrical performance of the dance did make a dramatic impact on those who observed it, enough so that audience members went home and tried to do the steps on their own, essentially the black body becomes erased from the performance. Individual spectators who watched on the periphery ultimately may not understand the community of the Lindy Hop, or the cultural traditions it reflects, traditions that span both geography and temporality. Thus when they begin to appropriate what they see, not to then share with their fellow dancers in the circle the following evening as the dancers at the Savoy were doing, but instead to disseminate that observed knowledge into their respective white cultures as an augmented form, the dance is essentially stripped of the meaning that it holds when found on the dance floor from which it originated and from within the Lindy circle itself.

When extending the community of the Lindy Hop circle outward, though, in order to also encompass what was happening both socially and culturally within Harlem at the time as well, and because social dancing was quickly becoming an American pastime, new layers of meaning become imposed onto the dance. In a post–stock market crash society, Americans began using social dances in order to "reclaim the human body as a site of joy and *human power*, of athletic and aesthetic display."[16] While dance has of course always been a vehicle to release emotion, in Dinerstein's example it is now also imbued with the angst that could be associated with a rapidly advancing technological society, where mass production of the automobile[17] and methods of communication had drastically changed American society at the time. The integrated dance floor of the Savoy could thus become a safe space, a place where African American dancers could go for an evening and express themselves through movement and be seemingly free of the racism that they were facing outside of the club. It was a place where theatricality led to popularity as more people came to Harlem to witness the stars of the dance floor. But the dance floor of the Savoy was not an idyllic utopian idealization, for the Lindy Hoppers could still effectively be Othered, as the dance floor did not belong to them but rather to a white businessman, who allowed them to dance because of the revenue that was being generated by the white clientele who were now traveling uptown. Although the Lindy Hoppers were not the ones in control at the Savoy, it was still a space where joy could indeed be celebrated, where fierce competition could push the boundaries of performance, and where the dancers could reinvent themselves night after night within the confines of the imagined community of the dance floor.[18] The problem was that this imagined community oftentimes was not reflective of the world outside of the dance club. As Norma Miller, one of the original members of Whitey's Lindy Hoppers found, the integrated Savoy Ballroom and the multiracial community that was created on the dance floor were not indicative of the racial tensions that were occurring in the world outside the doors to the club. As she recalls, "The victory at the Harvest Moon Ball put Whitey on top as far as Lindy Hop dancing was concerned, but rumors were flying, and supposedly they were coming out of the mayor's office. Action was being taken to keep the (white) downtown money from flowing uptown to Harlem. White businessmen had been unhappy about Harlem being New York's playground for quite some time, and the dissatisfaction was increasing."[19] So while the integrated dance floor of the Savoy Ballroom did allow for the creation of a space that was truly about camaraderie, competition, and the expression of joy, it did so within the protection of a vacuum that was still based on a model of white hegemonic power, creating an underlying racial tension within the club itself.

While this imagined community was allowed to flourish within the Savoy Ballroom, it was when it began to be taken outside of the club that it began to be diluted by its intersection with those other communities who, like Miller asserts, were actively trying to disband what the Savoy Ballroom represented in a racially divisive society. This was solely because the Lindy Hoppers were now no longer seen as a community comprising numerous individual identities but rather as simply a collective identity with a singular homogenized purpose. So whereas "like the jazz band and the basketball team, the Lindy synthesized collective and individual creativity, providing opportunity for both in a single form,"[20] when the individual creativity is eliminated from the gaze of the public, the artistic statement begins to be diluted as well, for the collective of the spectatorial audience will search for the quickest and easily reductive meaning of what they are witnessing in order to process it and move on to the next item. Even in large theatrical productions, different audience members are drawn to different individual characters, or different individual stories, for it allows the spectators into the piece as they try to decipher the messages being conveyed as it relates to them specifically on a personal level. If however, the large-scale production is focused on something like an artistic display of choreography being executed with precision en masse, it operates as more of a spectacle, something that the spectator witnesses but does not find access into. This notion of the spectacle necessitates a further examination of Debord and his belief that "culture is the locus of the search for lost unity. In this search for unity, culture as a separate sphere is obliged to negate itself."[21] Here, the spectator, no matter what his or her race or cultural background, is actively searching for this lost unity, and creates it by viewing a group of individual performers like Whitey's Lindy Hoppers into a collective entity, devoid of individualizations, and ascribes to them an interpretation of meaning based on superficiality. In doing so though, the very meaning that constituted the original message being transmitted by the performers becomes obscured and diluted to the point of negation. Ultimately, this begins to establish both the performer and the audience as separate entities and begins to widen the liminal space between the two groups, transforming the inclusiveness of the Lindy as viewed on the Savoy Ballroom dance floor into more of a performative spectacle.

The liminal space that is being created then between the performer and the audience is a direct result of this shift to a collective identity and ultimately serves to create a new semiotic message that is based on a reinterpreted construct that thus serves to undermine the original performances of the dance by Whitey's Lindy Hoppers. This becomes best evidenced in looking at the *Life* magazine photos of Lindy Hop that appeared in the December 28, 1936, issue. In a full page photo, two Lindy Hoppers, Leon James and Willamae Ricker, appear in midturn, their backs to one another with a caption that reads: "These Harlem Negroes are dancing Harlem's favorite dance with a native gusto and grace that no white couple can hope to duplicate. The Lindy Hop is a combination of fox-trotting, truckin', the Suzie-Q and adagio dancing. The expert Lindy Hoppers whose dancing is shown on these two pages are now an errand boy and a laundress. Soon they may be on Broadway."[22] From the onset, the two dancers are unnamed, thus stripping away any individuality and instead grouping them together into the constructed collective of "Harlem Negroes." The words utilized in this short caption are designed to establish the liminal space between performer and spectator by immediately creating a binary. James and Ricker are said to dance with a "native gusto" that "no white couple can hope to duplicate," creating the impression of primitivity by the invocation of "native" but also subliminally asserting that the dance is something that is natural and not the result of exceptional talent and countless hours of practicing. The dances mentioned as inspiration are a hodgepodge of various social dances that were in vogue at the time but that really held no influence on the creation of the Lindy Hop, illustrating the disconnect occurring when an outside audience begins to try to interpret the semiotics of the Lindy Hop as nothing more than a detached observer, without joining in to learn the dance or to learn the stories of those who are in fact dancing. Further, although they are described as being "expert Lindy Hoppers," they are also immediately designated as being an "errand boy" and a "laundress." While these terms are designed to relegate the two dancers to a specific class for the readers of *Life*, the language utilized also alludes to an underlying an inherent form of racism at play, as "boy" becomes a problematic term in itself, since James was 23 years old at the time the photo was taken.

When James and Ricker were featured once again in the August 23, 1943, issue of *Life*, they are now both named, but the corresponding text still speaks to the class designations that were continuing to be imposed on the Lindy Hoppers, and there is also a distinctively racial divide being executed that further widens the liminal space between the performer and the spectator. Nine pages are devoted to the Lindy Hop, and *Life* describes the dance this way: "In its early days the Lindy flourished only in the lower strata of society. Negroes were its creators and principal exponents, and Arthur Murray would no more have taught the Lindy Hop than Rachmaninoff would have given lessons in boogie-woogie. But with the renascence of swing the Lindy climbed the social scale."[23] Having been removed from the Harlem dance floors from which it originated, the Lindy Hop is now being measured purely against the parameters of a white society. By stating that the dance is not something that the white ballroom instructor Arthur Murray[24] would have taught (though ironically that was the place where I first learned the dance while studying there in the late 1980s and early 1990s), there is an underhanded commentary that is designed to undermine the credibility, and in turn, the authenticity of the dance itself by suggesting that since the Lindy Hop did not have its roots in the classical European ballroom traditions, it was therefore a lower form of art. Also, by further extending this critique on the form to state that the thought of Murray teaching a predominantly African American dance is akin to the white Rachmaninoff teaching a style of piano made famous by African American artists such as Pinetop Smith[25] in the 1920s (and later appropriated by myriad white big band acts that helped define the swing genre), there is the further implication being made that the original form is only a first step toward the art being refined by white artists. The dance is not allowed to exist on its own, but rather the desire is felt to measure it against disparate forms of white entertainment. Lindy Hop has nothing to do with the styles Murray was teaching just as Rachmaninoff and Smith were each developing completely different forms of art. Trying to group the various elements together into a single cohesive progression serves to weaken the influence of African American artists as a white hegemonic power structure attempts to graft elements from its own cultural artistic production onto the dance in order to lay claim to it.

By splitting the dance into very distinctively separate units of spectator and audience, and by widening the liminal space between these elements by falsely ascribing to it roots in white American and European dance traditions, and without giving credence to the African American dances that actually did inspire the Lindy Hop, it essentially attempts to legitimize dances such as the Foxtrot while simultaneously disavowing the importance of dances such as the Black Bottom in a form of revisionistic erasure. By attempting then to measure the dance's merits by these standards, the very form of the dance begins to change. The first thing that begins to be stripped from the dance is the call and response nature of its original form. The Lindy Hop is an unspoken semiotical conversation that is taking place between the participants and the observers. As dancers enter the circle, they are responding to the feedback from the spectators. If the crowd likes the dancers' moves within the improvised jam circle, then the dancers will remain in the center of that circle dancing for a few bars of music more. If however, the crowd does not respond positively, the dancers will quickly clear out of the circle in order to make room for the next pair. There is a give and take relationship occurring, where the audience pushes the dancers to continuously improve and where the dancers themselves are striving as well to please the crowd. Locating this very precise moment of interchange within the jam circle then creates a instance where "from the place of the 'meanwhile', where cultural homogeneity and democratic anonymity articulate the national community, there emerges a more instantaneous and subaltern voice of the people, minority discourses that speak betwixt and between times and places."[26] The cultural homogeneity of the dance floor within the clubs in Harlem constitute then the national community, whereas Anderson's imagined community becomes indicative not of the everyday interaction with others, as Bhabha is referring to with his discussion of nation, but of the community that exists in the dancers' minds as they are tied to past cultural traditions. The subaltern voice then becomes that of the plethora of semiotical conversations taking place between dancer/dancer and dancer/spectator, but when this voice is thus removed as the dance becomes more theatrical, and is supplanted with another outside discourse, the dance begins to transform from community to spectacle.

This becomes most apparent when looking at how the very physical structure of the dance begins to be augmented as well, for once it is taken out of the ballroom, the jam circle is uncoiled and is flattened out in order to fit the parameters of a traditional Western theatrical viewing experience, where the performers and the audience exist on parallel planes to one another. For a dance that was designed to be performed, as well as viewed, within the circle, this transition to the linear only gives a portion then of the semiotical conversation taking place as spectators are only permitted to see a singular element of the dance from a carefully constructed and choreographed viewing angle. In amateur home movie footage from the 1939 World's Fair held in New York, the Savoy exhibit is seen with Lindy Hoppers performing with a band under a banner that reads "Savoy: World's Greatest Colored Dancers."[27] The dancers perform on an elevated platform, and though the audience is not visible in the clip, there is a small railing to designate the performative space and to create a strong delineation between the dancers and the spectators. The stage is up against a large wall to the exhibit, so the traditional proscenium theater aesthetic is invoked and the audience has been removed from the conversation taking place. While of course there can still exist a call and response between audience and performer even when the two are framed in a linear motif as opposed to one that is circular, it is a much different experience now. Lindy Hoppers are not surrounded by the vocalization and the energy of the crowd, a crowd that they have to be very cognizant of so as not to kick or collide with exuberant onlookers who may get too close to the action as is the case in the jam circle, but now the Lindy Hoppers exist only as performers, as they are not allowed to move between various roles effortlessly as is the case in the true Lindy form. Just as the dancers' identities were simultaneously individual and communal, so too were they originally defined as being both performer and spectator during the improvisation of the dance. When the dance morphs though into merely a performative theatrical spectacle, the participatory nature of it becomes lost and the dancers are no longer able to assume both roles as spectator and performer.

This nuanced shift in the roles that is being reinforced once this flattening of the form occurs instills the audience with a greater sense of power through its gaze thus firmly transitioning the Lindy Hop over into the realm of spectacle by completely stripping its participatory nature from it. Even though the Savoy Ballroom was being hailed by some as "a community institution and the most important public space in Harlem; it was famous for its interracial clientele and its egalitarian treatment, and was a symbol of social equality,"[28] this also meant that the club, in large part due to the growing popularity of the Lindy Hoppers, soon became a must-visit destination for Harlem locals, New Yorkers traveling uptown, celebrities, and tourists alike. As the dance progressed into spectacle then, the layering of the audience's gaze began to increase as well. Tourists, who came to see the Lindy Hoppers, were also trying to catch a glimpse of their favorite movie or stage stars, while locals were observing the influx of tourists and how that was changing the environment of the club itself as well as the surrounding neighborhood. Thus, the audience's gaze became fractured, and even though the Lindy Hoppers may have been the main draw to visit the ballroom in the first place, they now only existed as another form of spectacle for the tourists coming in droves to the Savoy Ballroom. As was remarked in an article from 1929: "To Americans, the Negro is not a human being, but a concept,"[29] an objectification of the African American performer occurs here where they are not only dehumanized, but also relegated to existing outside of the national community of "Americans." No longer are the individualized dancers performing as part of a participatory community, nor are they even the collective identity of Whitey's Lindy Hoppers, but now they are mere spectacle producing objectless art for the cultural tourists who view the dancers in the same manner as they do the 50-foot by 250-foot burnished maple dance floor of the Savoy Ballroom itself. Here, "the resistance to psychic and socioeconomic violence emerges not from a resistance to recognizing any object, but from the inversion of the ways in which the subject/object relationship is traditionally racialized, both in the realm of the arts and in everyday social experience."[30] The African American Lindy Hoppers on the dance floor are indeed being recognized as objects by a white audience, but once that same audience begins representing them as nothing more than an objectified spectacle, the Lindy Hoppers now become a performative concept, and this makes it easier for the appropriation of the dance outside of the club to occur. The subject/object relationship is one that is based on continuous struggles for power, so by first relegating a subject to the role of object, and then subsequently interpreting that object as only spectacle, something that may be dazzling in its artistry is assumed to have no deeper substantive meaning; a struggle for power ensues.

As the Lindy Hop grew in popularity in its flattened performances outside of the ballroom, a shift occurs when it is thus brought back into its original environment, for if audiences outside of the Harlem clubs were exposed to the dance in its linear, proscenium theater exhibited form, and if the form is then re-presented in its circular form on the Savoy dance floor, where the new demographic visiting the club now has a fractured gaze, then the semiotics of the dance can no longer be interpreted correctly. This form of cultural tourism thus generates a palpable tension as the spectatorial gaze begins to relegate the performers to merely a background element that an audience member could choose to look at or not. Langston Hughes remarks on this phenomenon in his autobiography *The Big Sea*, where he states that "nor did ordinary Negroes like the growing influx of whites toward Harlem after sundown, flooding the little cabarets and bars where formerly only colored people laughed and sang, and where now the strangers were given the best ringside tables to sit and stare at the Negro customers—like amusing animals in a zoo."[31] Two elements of Hughes's comments become key to unpack here, for not only is he alluding to the spectacle of the scene as existing simply for the amusement of the white spectators but also he is illustrating that those spectators' gaze is now centered not necessarily on the performers, dancers, or musicians inside the bars and cabarets, but is instead focused on the customers themselves. Thus, within the framework of the cultural tourism occurring in Harlem in the late 1920s and early 1930s, there is the suggestion being made that there is no differentiation between the African American performer and the African American customer; both are being conflated into an objectified concept that white audiences are thereby trying to decipher through a spectatorial gaze.

As this codified message is being interpreted by the cultural tourists of Harlem through a lens of their own individualized and differing backgrounds, and as the Lindy Hop is transplanted from outside of the environment of the dance clubs and put into the national spotlight in America, there becomes the desire to lay claim to it in order to possess it once it has become objectified. Just as was seen in the examples of those outside of the world of the Harlem dance clubs who attempted to quickly attribute it to any number of European based ballroom dances, now too was Lindy being approached as part of a national heritage. In the August 23, 1943, issue of *Life* magazine, the interior photo spread of the Lindy Hop is titled "The Lindy Hop: A True National Folk Dance Has Been Born in U.S.A."[32] in large letters above a photo of two white teenagers, Kaye Popp and Stanley Castron, dancing.[33] After five pages of photos of Popp and Castron demonstrating different steps, the unnamed members of Whitey's Lindy Hoppers who were featured in the 1938 issue of *Life* previously examined, James and Ricker, appear once again with text that reads:

> In entering new realms of creative invention, it [the Lindy Hop] is following the evolutionary cycle of all dances since the beginning of recorded time: first the rhythmic, primitive folk dance, sprung from the spontaneous responses of humble people to musical inspiration; then the social dance, popular with all classes and defined by fixed and basic patterns; and final the classic form, far removed from proletarian origins and ornamented with complex flowery figures attainable only by those who spend years in their practice. The Lindy Hop is now in the second phase.[34]

In this statement, the racially motivated appropriation of the dance becomes evident as the original Lindy Hoppers at the Savoy ballroom, as represented by James and Ricker, are equated with the "first phase" of the dance, that of being a "primitive folk dance" of "humble people," while Popp and Castron now lay claim to the perceived second phase of the dance. Here, the objectification and appropriation of the dance creates something that is now perceivably accessible to all classes and that has been reduced to "fixed and basic patterns" that individuals can seemingly learn from merely imitating the pictures that *Life* includes in the article.

This belief, that a dance that was primarily based in improvisation and in impromptu conversations, both spoken and semiotical, between the dancers and the spectators, can quickly be mastered through mimesis alone, brings the Lindy Hop even closer to its complete commoditization. This is further evidenced in the photos in the same issue of James and Ricker demonstrating "air steps," where one of the photograph's captions reads: "Borrowing from ballet repertoire, Leon James executes a pirouette [*sic*]."[35] Unfortunately, it appears that in the two photograph sequence James is in actuality doing a high kick-turn that would have come from the Charleston and not from classical ballet. Positioning the dance though as one that draws its influence from classical forms of dance is a very deliberate move to make the commoditized form of the Lindy Hop more accessible to the readers of *Life* magazine, for it would thus instill it with a false cultural connection to understanding the codified message of the dance. This is reinforced in the "Shine Steps" section where a caption to a photo of Popp and Castron demonstrating one of the foundational moves of the Lindy Hop, the swing-out, states: "Fast swing-outs can be just as graceful as ballet pirouets [*sic*] when they are properly performed."[36] In this attempt to legitimize the dance in order to make it more marketable, and therefore increase its commodified value, the language that *Life* chooses is loaded. First, it is asserting that the Lindy Hop is striving in its form to be like classical ballet. Second, it is stating that classical ballet is the standard by which to measure how successful one is in performing basic Lindy steps. Including the phrase "properly performed" under the photo of the two white dancers is also another subtly veiled indicator of the racial divide and appropriation that is occurring as the Lindy Hop is becoming more spectacularized. In this example, Lindy Hop has become nothing more than a commoditized version of its authentic form.

The commodification of the Lindy Hop becomes its ultimate downfall then, as the semiotical message that was originally encoded within the dance, a message that is tied to a rich cultural tradition and history, becomes blanched and reconstituted for paying audiences. Whitey's Lindy Hoppers began to dance outside of the clubs in Harlem as their popularity made them an in demand act to make appearances dancing at trendy socialite parties in New York. This increased their exposure and eventually led to them appearing in the Broadway shows *Black Rhythm*[37] in 1936 and *The Hot Mikado*[38] in 1939 as well as in feature films such as the Marx Brothers' vehicle, *A Day at the Races* in 1937, (see fig. 35.1).

As Josephine Lee finds in her examination of the various interpretations of the Gilbert & Sullivan musical *The Mikado*: "The addition of such favorite acts as the Lindy Dancers from the Savoy Ballroom in Harlem further reinforced that the fantastic sets and costumes of *The Hot Mikado* did not reference Japan but the more familiar nightclubs of Harlem. Thus *The Hot Mikado* openly evoked how African American musicians and dancers became 'hot' racial commodities for white consumers."[39] Just as Hughes had remarked about how the tourists would sit and gawk at the African American customers, now those audiences are

FIGURE 35.1 Whitey and the eight members of Whitey's Lindy Hoppers who appeared in *A Day at the Races* in California, early 1937. *Left to right*: Herbert "Whitey" White, Willamae Ricker, Snookie Beasley, Ella Gibson, George Greenidge, Dot Miller, Johnny Innis, Norma Miller, Leon James. Photograph courtesy of Chazz Young.

able to do so from the comfort and familiarity of Broadway theaters, without ever needing to travel uptown to the actual Harlem clubs. The cultural tourists were simply having the "culture" brought to them in a prepackaged form as the Lindy Hop was removed from its own environment. The form was changed, the venue had changed, and the buying consumer that constituted the new form of spectator had changed as well. Theatergoers at shows like *The Hot Mikado* were not necessarily interested in deciphering the meaning of the underlying historicity and traditions of the dances they were witnessing, they were simply reveling in the spectacle of it all in a show that was built entirely on the appropriation and reinterpretation of a culture through racialized role-playing.

What becomes even more interesting with Lee's statement above though is that , just as it was with the remark by Hughes in his autobiography, the dancers now are no longer even viewed as performers. Lee's assertion of them as "hot racial commodities for white consumers" is absolutely correct in its assessment, but it also follows her claim about the "fantastic sets and costumes" of *The Hot Mikado* referencing Harlem more than they do Japan. The dancers become merely set dressing used simply to invoke a specific setting and atmosphere for the musical. They are not actors and actresses a director is working with to convey character and emotion in order to drive the story forward, but instead they are objectified and exist on the same level as the set pieces and the costumes; they are placed on the stage and moved around as scenery. Even when the dancers then return to the Savoy Ballroom, their presence has changed as well, since: "While sustaining the reputation of the Savoy by their dominance of New York City's major dance contest—the Harvest Moon Ball—and through their resultant performances in newsreels, feature films, stage shows, and touring productions throughout the United States, they still masqueraded as social dancers at the Savoy in front of visiting celebrities and bussed-in tourists."[40] The new role of commodified spectacle now usurps the original role of the Lindy Hoppers, that of social dancers, and they, unfortunately, find themselves performing in a venue that is not the same as when they left it. The "authentic" atmosphere and the environment that shows like *The Hot Mikado* tried so desperately to capture with their fantastic sets and costumes become in actuality a ghosting of that which may have been true at one point but that in reality no longer exists. Even outside of the Broadway stages then, the Savoy Ballroom itself, with its bussed-in audiences clamoring to see what the buzz is about in Harlem, is dealing primarily in the marketing of its chief commodity, the dancers who are masquerading as themselves.

The semiotics of the conversation have now changed as what once began as primarily an African American dance in an integrated club in Harlem in the 1920s has instead become one about drawing in larger crowds, and thus generating more revenue for the clubs, giving the audience ultimately more influence in the conversation. No longer is there the equality found in the unspoken conversation when the performer and the spectator exist as one, but now the performer begins to shape his dancing in order to speak directly to the crowd, and this shifts the focus of the Lindy Hop into a level of needing to be much more spectacular in its execution.

This drive eventually manifested itself in the development of the air step, which now has become one of the quintessential, and most easily identifiable, elements of the Lindy Hop, (see fig. 35.2). Two of the original members of Whitey's Lindy Hoppers, Frankie Manning and his partner Frieda Washington, worked for weeks to develop a new step that would impress the crowds at a 1935 contest at the Savoy Ballroom. Dancing to music by Chick Webb and his orchestra, Manning and Washington got into a dance position where they stood back to back, and after interlocking their arms, Manning flipped Washington in a summersault over his head. The "over-the-back" was the first air step in the Lindy Hop, and as Manning recalls: "When Frieda landed, for one second, it seemed like everyone in the audience caught their breath. Their mouths opened, but no sound came out. It was as if people weren't sure they had really seen what they'd seen, like they were trying to figure out what we had just done. They were awestruck."[41] While on the dance floors in the clubs in Harlem the spectacularization of the Lindy Hop was being fueled by the audiences who wanted to see even more from the dancers, taking the Lindy Hop in new directions that had previously been unimaginable, a much different dynamic was occurring when the audience was positioned to have the power in the conversation taking place between the performers and the spectators in the seats of the Broadway houses.

Whereas in the Harlem clubs the audience's influence was centered on pushing the dancers to extend past the limits of perceived ability and to develop even more complex and spectacular dance steps, the dancers began to lose their performative power as the dance began being regarded as a spectacle by the white audiences, and even more dramatically, when the semiotical conversation took place outside of the ballrooms. Lee notes that "*The Swing Mikado* and *Hot Mikado* were clearly employed in the service of racial uplift, using

FIGURE 35.2 Whyte's Hopping Maniacs performing with "Le Cotton Club de New York" at the Moulin Rouge in Paris, summer 1937. *Left to right*: Naomi Waller and Frankie Manning, Lucille Middleton and Jerome Williams, Mildred Cruse and Billy Williams. Photograph credited to Studio C. Bracken. Photograph courtesy of Chazz Young.

the performances of Japanese as a way of proving that African Americans perform musical classics in ways that demonstrated their talents and rendered their skin color moot. On the other hand, these productions made use of rather than challenged racial clichés about African Americans, casting them as primitive and sexualized."[42] It is remiss to posit that the dancers' skin color was rendered moot, instead, as has been seen, it was an objectified and exoticized commodity that became a form of cultural capital the Broadway audiences were trading in. Asserting that these shows could lead to a form of racial uplift is illustrative of the fact that white audiences were attempting to establish a power dynamic in the performances that simply was not present when the same dances were performed at dance clubs like the Savoy Ballroom, for the term "racial uplift" itself is already assuming a relationship of power where one group strives for elevation in the eyes of another. So while in shows like *The Swing Mikado* and *Hot Mikado* audiences were valuing the performances in relationship to a perceived Broadway standard of performance, at the Savoy, the dancers were not seeking any form of validation from the white audiences, so the play for power instead came from the audiences attributing the Lindy Hop representationally as simply spectacle. Just as would later be found in the text that accompanied the photos of Popp and Castron in the *Life* article in 1943, which stated how the exciting new steps of the Lindy Hop "spread across the land, invading colleges and dance schools, the Lindy Hop gained respectability as a truly national dance,"[43] the attempt to control and to disseminate the Lindy Hop was in essence a way to establish a control and powered dominance over the originators of the dance themselves. While the Lindy Hoppers at the Savoy were possessive of the power of the dance through its cultural traditions, there was an attempt made to systemically erase these roots as the dance was presented on the Broadway stage, and later in colleges and dance schools, in order to finally appropriate it and deem the Lindy Hop to be a truly "national," meaning white American, dance.

This appropriation, reconstitution, and re-presentation of the Lindy Hop by the primarily white audiences ultimately becomes a veiled form of minstrelsy designed to render the black performative body invisible. Within the first two pages of the *Life* magazine article, the claim that the Lindy Hop is a dance that is quintessentially American, and not one that is representative of the Harlem clubs it came from, is alluded to on five different occasions, including the assertion that, "Today, after 16 years of evolution and accretion, the Lindy Hop has become America's national dance."[44] The cover for this issue of *Life* features a full black and white image of Popp and Castron that is completely posed. The two white teenagers are in a static and rigid frame, simply mimicking a Lindy Hop position instead of engaged in the performance of it. Gone are the vitality and the emotion of the performance of the Lindy Hop. It is no longer about joy. It is no longer about challenging a rival. There is no improvisation, or feeling, but only rigid mimesis. In reality, when *Life* refers to the "sixteen years of evolution and accretion," it is referring to the grafting of the white face of youth onto the Lindy Hop in order to theoretically legitimize it to an American consumer base. This is the first step to the minstrelization of the Lindy Hop, for it ultimately has the same effect as was found in the early days of the dance when presenting it simply "as an anonymous, novelty response to Lindbergh's flight, rather than an aesthetic expression of evolving African American consciousness in Harlem, in effect obscured its true identity."[45] Making the dance a novelty, and something that was mainstream and safe enough for white teenagers to do on the cover of a national magazine, did not merely obscure the true identity of the dance, it imposed a brand new identity onto it.

Although Popp and Castron were most certainly accomplished dancers for their age, appearing in a Broadway musical at the time, by simply mimicking the Lindy Hop, they are becoming in essence minstrel performers, sans blackface, who have observed a form of artistic expression, discarded any of the original meaning that was imbued within it, and reconstituted it as a superficial mode of entertainment with new sets of cultural markers attached to it. This is not done as a form of the reverential, but is instead done to culturally erase that which came before by eliminating the key elements that made the dance unique in the first place, such as the improvisation of it and the importance of the interplay with the spectators forming the jam circle. As *Life* suggests: "It is true that as recently as three years ago a jitterbug was anyone who bounced, wiggled and jumped in time to hot music without any particular knowledge of what he was doing. But the accomplished jitterbug of the present day does the Lindy Hop, a dance still in a phase of transition and growth, but whose basic steps have crystallized into recognizable patterns."[46] Here, there is the distinction being made between the old, or those who were simply wiggling and jumping around without any "particular knowledge," and the new, or those who have been able to decipher, contain, and deconstruct the dance into a didactic form. Unfortunately though, as is made abundantly clear in the captioning for a photo of Popp and Castron demonstrating a shine step, where it states: "the tip is an open step which faintly resembles the old-fashioned cakewalk,"[47] that the "new" is being represented by the likes of the white Popp and Castron, while the "old-fashioned" are the African American dancers, and the dances such as the Cakewalk, that held cultural relevance to them.

Once the mimetic appropriation of the dance is permitted to usurp the real emotional content of the Lindy Hop, and once the cultural traditions that helped shape the dance become obscured or lost, the dance exists merely as spectacle. Hughes saw this occurring even in the air steps of the original Whitey's Lindy Hoppers on the Harlem dance floors where he stated: "The lindy-hoppers at the Savoy even began to practise [*sic*] acrobatic routines, and to do absurd things for the entertainment of the whites, that probably never would have entered their heads to attempt merely for their own effortless amusement. Some of the lindy-hoppers had cards printed with their names on them and became dance professors teaching the tourists. Then Harlem nights became show nights for the Nordics."[48] The dance had become a commoditized spectacle, and the cultural capital was being traded freely in order to make a quick buck. The danger in this taking place though is that the white patrons who were visiting the actual dance floors of Harlem, as opposed to merely being exposed to the dance on the silver screen or at the theaters of Broadway, could begin to believe that they were a part of the dance's shared history. This allows for a revisionist approach to the history of the dance to occur, as *Life* indicated in the opening sentence to its article on Lindy Hop that: "Although the Lindy Hop did not receive a name until 1927, elements of it were visible as early as 1924, in the Broadway and Harlem 'mooch' and 'sugar.' "[49] Here, by referring to an early pre-1910 variant of the Texas Tommy swing dance, the Mooch and Sugar is given a hybridized origin of belonging to both Broadway and Harlem and the foundation is being laid for it to be said that the Lindy Hop, as a later incarnation of swing, similarly must have been developed from miscegenated origins. This, coupled with the incessant need to delineate the dance's origins as being classically European, serves to obscure not just the racial identity of the dancers themselves but also the communally shared history of the dance as well.

Ultimately then, in the *Life* cover photo of Popp and Castron, they are not in the circle, but exist only as themselves on display as the newly adopted surrogate identity of Lindy Hop. The community has been disbanded and has now been replaced with the smiling face of a white American society in 1943. The Charleston, the Collegiate, and the Breakaway have been relegated to more of a minor influence on the development of the dance in order for the revisionist history of it being a cultural byproduct of Broadway experimenting with its uptown Harlem neighbors to be adopted. The photo section in *Life* with Popp and Castron demonstrating steps states: "The Lindy Hop picked up where the Charleston left off,"[50] thus asserting that the Lindy Hop is a simple passing fad like the Charleston that was the craze of the 1920s, but without acknowledging the cultural roots of either. This distancing is deliberate, for as Dinerstein argues, "The Charleston's spirited syncopation and irregular rhythmic accents helped create a symbiotic relationship between musicians and dancers that owed more to West African dance aesthetics than to court, ballroom, or peasant dancing."[51] By obscuring the individualized identities of the dancers as well as the history of Lindy Hop itself, which includes roots in West African dance, the effects of the minstrelization of the dance become most apparent, for the efforts made by the white individuals who appropriate and repackage the dance for their own needs, whether done out of reverence or out of a maliciously deliberate attempt to steal the form of artistic expression through a mimetic representation of it that is devoid of historical traditions, serve to render the African American performative body as invisible within the very dance they in fact created.

In the end, the Lindy Hop in its originating form was about becoming part of a much larger tradition that tied the African American performers to a lineage encompassing dancers in the jooks of the south, dancers on the plantations, and dancers from their home countries. It was about adding their own voices and interpretations into a conversation with their ancestors. It was a way for working-class individuals to escape to the clubs in Harlem in the 1920s and 1930s and to bond together in a common experience. It was a dance that was about the competitiveness of camaraderie just as much as it was about pushing the limits of artistic expression to continuously grow and evolve as artists. It was a space where the performer and the spectator were one in the same and where the semiotical conversation that was taken place was bidirectional. While it was a place where a young group of African American dancers could gain fame within New York for a brief moment, it was also a place where white hegemonic power quickly appropriated the dance and branded it as a national folk dance, forever changing its meaning while also attempting to rewrite the dance's history in a subtly veiled form of minstrelsy. While the original Lindy Hoppers all went their separate ways and seemingly disappeared from the performative arena,[52] some were reunited again with the swing revival craze that hit America in the 1990s. Individuals such as Frankie Manning and Norma Miller, two of the original members of Whitey's Lindy Hoppers, were soon in demand once again to teach a new generation how to Lindy Hop at swing clinics and events around the world. While it would be easy to view this modern incarnation of the Lindy Hop from a colorblind perspective, and to think that the swing revival craze was done purely out of reverence for the past masters, the underlying driving force of the movement must still be examined with just as much scrutiny as is done when questioning what was happening to the dance in the early 1940s. With white artists such as The Brian Setzer Orchestra, Big Bad Voodoo Daddy, and the Cherry Poppin' Daddies at the forefront of the 1990s swing culture, and with companies such as Gap capitalizing off of a 1998 commercial[53] featuring predominantly white dancers (in fact all of those who enter the now reconstituted jam circle in the spot are white), wearing khakis and Lindy Hopping to Louis Prima's "Jump Jive and Wail," one must not shy away from asking the question once again if what is being marketed is in fact a form of modern-day minstrelsy.

Notes

1. Nadine George-Graves, "'Just Like Being at the Zoo': Primitivity and Ragtime Dance," in *Ballroom, Boogie, Shimmy Sham, Shake: A Social and Popular Dance Reader*, ed. Julie Malnig (Urbana: University of Illinois Press, 2009), 63.
2. Marshall Stearns and Jean Stearns, *Jazz Dance: The Story of American Vernacular Dance* (New York: Da Capo Press, 1994), 315–16.
3. In the novel *Parties: Scenes from Contemporary New York Life* (1930), author Carl Van Vechten describes seeing the Lindy Hop performed at the Manhattan Casino in 1928. The first recorded images of the Lindy Hop were in the Paramount short film *After Sebden* in 1929, where George "Shorty" Snowden dances with a partner and two other couples.
4. Frankie Manning and Cynthia R. Millman, *Frankie Manning: Ambassador of Lindy Hop* (Philadelphia: Temple University Press, 2007), 79.

5. Katrina Hazzard-Gordon. *Jookin': The Rise of Social Dance Formations in African-American Culture* (Philadelphia: Temple University Press, 1990), 83.

6. Martin, John, "The Dance: Social Style—Looking at Ballroom in Some of Its Aspects—Events of the Week," *New York Times*, January 10, 1943.

7. Ibid.

8. Anthea Kraut, "Race-ing Choreographic Copyright," in *Worlding Dance*, ed. Susan Leigh Foster (New York: Palgrave Macmillan, 2009), 84.

9. Joel Dinerstein, *Swinging the Machine: Modernity, Technology, and African American Culture between World Wars* (Amherst: University of Massachusetts Press, 2003), 254.

10. The Savoy Ballroom opened on March 12, 1926, and occupied a full city block between 140th and 141st Streets on Lenox Avenue. It closed on July 10, 1958.

11. Whitey's Lindy Hoppers were an elite group of dancers formed at the Savoy Ballroom by Herbert "Whitey" White. The group would perform at social events throughout New York, in films, and on Broadway. In 1935, they performed to a sold-out crowd at Madison Square Garden during the first annual Harvest Moon Ball.

12. The Cotton Club was opened in 1923 by the mobster Owney Madden and was located at 142nd Street and Lenox Avenue. It closed in 1940.

13. Manning and Millman, *Frankie Manning*, 78.

14. Guy Debord, *Society of the Spectacle* (Detroit: Black & Red, 1983), 161. Original emphasis.

15. Karen Hubbard and Terry Monaghan, "Social Dancing at the Savoy," in *Ballroom, Boogie, Shimmy, Sham, Shake: A Social and Popular Dance Reader*, ed. Julie Malnig (Chicago: University of Illinois Press, 2009), 133.

16. Dinerstein, *Swinging the Machine*, 253.

17. For example, the Ford Model A had increased from just over 4,000 production units in 1927 to over 1.7 million in 1929.

18. Benedict Anderson coined the phrase "imagined communities" in his work on nationalism, *Imagined Communities: Reflections on the Origin and Spread of Nationalism*. I argue that an imagined community was indeed being created in the microcosm of the Lindy circles at the Savoy Ballroom in the 1930s.

19. Norma Miller and Evette Jensen, *Swingin' at the Savoy: The Memoir of a Jazz Dancer* (Philadelphia: Temple University Press, 1996), 83.

20. Gena Caponi-Taberi, *Jump for Joy: Jazz, Basketball and Black Culture in 1930s America* (Amherst: University of Massachusetts Press, 2008), 52.

21. Debord, *Society of the Spectacle*, 180.

22. "Lindy Hoppers," *Life*, December 28, 1936, 30–31.

23. "Floor Steps," *Life*, August 23, 1943, 96.

24. Arthur Murray (1895–1991) was an American ballroom dance instructor who became famous for selling cutout footprints via mail order for students to learn how to dance before beginning his dance studio franchise in 1925 that still operates to this day.

25. Clarence "Pine Top" Smith (1904–1929) was an American pianist from Alabama who had a hit with the boogie-woogie song "Pinetop's Boogie Woogie" in 1929.

26. Homi K. Bhabha, *The Location of Culture* (London: Routledge Classics, 1994), 227.

27. "Lindy Hop at the New York World's Fair 1939," *Prelinger Archives*, September 23, 2009, YouTube video, http://youtu.be/T9zb7KGWXvc.

28. Dinerstein, *Swing the Machine*, 263.

29. George Chester Morse, "The Fictitious Negro," *The Outlook and Independent*, August 21, 1929, 648.

30. Brandi Wilkins Catanese, "'How Do I Rent a Negro?' Racialized Subjectivity and Digital Performance Art," *Theatre Journal* 57, no. 4 (December 2005): 704. While Catanese focuses her argument on a digital performance piece by the artist damali ayo, I am asserting that dance performance similarly creates an objectless art, and in the case of the African American Lindy Hoppers, they are similarly being objectified.

31. Langston Hughes, *The Big Sea: An Autobiography* (New York: Thunder's Mouth Press, 1991), 225.

32. "The Lindy Hop: A True National Folk Dance Has Been Born in U.S.A.," *Life*, August 23, 1943, 95.

33. Kaye Popp and Stanley Castron were seventeen years old at the time of the photo and appeared in the Broadway musical *Something for the Boys*, which starred Ethel Merman and ran from January 7, 1943–January 8, 1944 at the Alvin Theatre.

34. "Air Steps," *Life*, August 23, 1943, 100.

35. "Air Steps," *Life*, August 23, 1943, 102.

36. "Shine Steps," *Life*, August 23, 1943, 98.

37. *Black Rhythm* ran for only six performances from December 19, 1936, to December 24, 1936, at the Comedy Theatre.

38. *The Hot Mikado* was the reinterpretation of Gilbert & Sullivan's *The Mikado* that added a swing element to the show. *The Hot Mikado* ran from March 23, 1939, to June 3, 1939, at the Broadhurst Theatre. The show was appearing on Broadway at the same time as the similarly framed *The Swing Mikado* that ran from March 1, 1939, to May 20, 1939 at the New Yorker Theatre and then the 44th Street Theatre.

39. Josephine Lee, *The Japan of Pure Invention: Gilbert & Sullivan's* The Mikado (Minneapolis: University of Minnesota Press, 2010), 103.

40. Hubbard and Monaghan, "Social Dancing at the Savoy," 129.

41. Manning and Millman, *Frankie Manning*, 100.

42. Lee, *The Japan of Pure Invention*, 101.

43. "Floor Steps," *Life*, August 23, 1943, 96.

44. "The Lindy Hop: A True National Folk Dance Has Been Born in the U.S.A.," 95.

45. Hubbard and Monaghan, "Social Dancing at the Savoy," 131.

46. "The Lindy Hop," *Life* 23 August 1943, 95.

47. "Shine Steps," 98.

48. Hughes, *The Big Sea*, 226.

49. "Floor Steps," 96.

50. "Floor Steps," 96.

51. Dinerstein, *Swinging the Machine*, 254.

52. The group disbanded during World War II, as many of the male members were drafted. While members such as Al Minns and Leon James created a small novelty dance act and regularly performed, they did not achieve the level of notoriety they had with Whitey's Lindy Hoppers. After the war, Manning had a small dance troupe as well before he ultimately began his career with the US Postal Service.

53. "Khaki Swing," directed by Matthew Ralston, *Gap*, 1998. Along with the 1996 film *Swingers*, directed by Doug Liman, Ralston's commercial for Gap was regarded as being one of the penultimate factors in swing gaining national recognition once again in the 1990s. The commercial was voted the number one commercial by the *LA Times* and *TV Guide*.

BIBLIOGRAPHY

"Air Steps." *Life*, August 23, 1943, 100.

Anderson, Benedict. *Imagined Communities: Reflections on the Origin and Spread of Nationalism*. London: Verson, 2006.

Bhabha, Homi K. *The Location of Culture*. London: Routledge Classics, 1994.

Caponi-Taberi, Gena. *Jump for Joy: Jazz, Basketball and Black Culture in 1930s America*. Amherst: University of Massachusetts Press, 2008.

Debord, Guy. *Society of the Spectacle*. Detroit: Black & Red, 1983.

Dinerstein, Joel. *Swinging the Machine: Modernity, Technology, and African American Culture between World Wars*. Amherst: University of Massachusetts Press, 2003.

"Floor Steps." *Life*, August 23, 1943, 96.

George-Graves, Nadine. "'Just Like Being at the Zoo': Primitivity and Ragtime Dance." In *Ballroom, Boogie, Shimmy, Sham, Shake: A Social and Popular Dance Reader*, edited by Julie Malnig, 55–71. Chicago: University of Illinois Press, 2009.

Hazzard-Gordon, Katrina. *Jookin': The Rise of Social Dance Formations in African-American Culture*. Philadelphia: Temple University Press, 1990.

Hubbard, Karen, and Terry Monaghan. "Social Dancing at the Savoy." In *Ballroom, Boogie, Shimmy, Sham, Shake: A Social and Popular Dance Reader*, edited by Julie Malnig, 126–45. Chicago: University of Illinois Press, 2009.

Hughes, Langston. *The Big Sea: An Autobiography*. New York: Thunder's Mouth Press, 1991.

"Khaki Swing." Directed by Matthew Ralston. Gap, 1998. Commercial.

Kraut, Anthea. "Race-ing Choreographic Copyright." In *Worlding Dance*, edited by Susan Leigh Foster, 76–97. New York: Palgrave Macmillan, 2009.

Lee, Josephine. *The Japan of Pure Invention: Gilbert & Sullivan's* The Mikado. Minneapolis: University of Minnesota Press, 2010.

"The Lindy Hop: A True National Folk Dance Has Been Born in the U.S.A." *Life*, August 23, 1943, 95.

"Lindy Hop at the New York World's Fair 1939." *Prelinger Archives*. September 23, 2009. http://youtu.be/T9zb7KGWXvc.

"Lindy Hoppers." *Life*, December 28, 1936, 30–31.

Manning, Frankie, and Cynthia R. Millman. *Frankie Manning: Ambassador of Lindy Hop*. Philadelphia: Temple University Press, 2007.

Martin, John. "The Dance: Social Style—Looking at Ballroom in Some of Its Aspects—Events of the Week." *New York Times*, January 10, 1943.

Miller, Norma, and Evette Jensen. *Swingin' at the Savoy: The Memoir of a Jazz Dancer*. Philadelphia: Temple University Press, 1996.

Morse, George Chester. "The Fictitious Negro." *The Outlook and Independent*, August 21, 1929.

"Shine Steps." *Life*, August 23, 1943, 98.

Stearns, Marshall, and Jean Stearns. *Jazz Dance: The Story of American Vernacular Dance*. New York: Da Capo Press, 1994.

Van Vechten, Carl. *Parties: Scenes from Contemporary New York Life*. New York: Bard, 1977.

Wilkins Catanese, Brandi. "'How Do I Rent a Negro?' Racialized Subjectivity and Digital Performance Art." *Theatre Journal* 57, no. 4 (December 2005): 699–714.

SECTION IX

NATIONAL SCALES AND MASS MOVEMENTS

CHAPTER 36

RUSSIAN MASS SPECTACLE AND THE BOLSHEVIK REGIME

SANDY PETERSON

ON November 7, 1920, in Petrograd,[1] over 100,000 spectators gathered in Uritsky Square (formerly Palace Square) to witness one of the largest and most complex open-air mass spectacles in Russia on record, titled *The Storming of the Winter Palace* (*TSOTWP*). More than eight thousand individuals participated in the event, including members of Proletkult clubs, ballet dancers, circus artists, members of the Red Army Theatre Workshop, soldiers (some of whom had participated in the actual "storming" of the Winter Palace), workers, and members of the Bolshevik Party. There were five assistant directors, three directors (Nikolai Petrov, Aleksandr Kugel, and Iurii Annenkov—Annenkov was also the set designer), and one lead director—Nikolai Evreinov. This particular production was the culmination of a series of mass spectacles, all of which dramatized, in various ways, the October Revolution. The purpose of such spectacles was multifaceted: they marked significant political, national, and international anniversaries; they were celebrations of the revolutionary spirit; and, most importantly, they created a narrative that gave the Bolshevik Regime a distinct moment of origin, which then rapidly became mythologized.

These open-air mass spectacles, especially those in 1920, were studies in a kind of "total event," or "total theater," as they used at least one element of nearly all existing art forms in Russia at the time: ballet, choreography, "unpolished realism," avant-garde design, circus and commedia artistry, and music. Even though they were all performed live, they increasingly used techniques from film. Russian filmmakers, in turn, were influenced by these live spectacles. For example, Sergei Eisenstein's film *October* (commissioned for the Revolution's anniversary in 1927) was directly influenced by *TSOTWP*. The drive to create a new kind of Soviet theater also included an attempt to rethink the audience-actor relationship, as many important artists of the time, including Evreinov, sought to dissolve the distinction between the two. Although the scale and subject matter of these spectacles are unique to this particular time period, mass spectacles developed from a long history of pageantry and festivals, and although they rapidly declined after *TSOTWP*, their effect on the masses and the Bolshevik Regime was long-lasting. Mass spectacles were clearly important to Soviet leaders, as the peak season for mass spectacles—1920—coincided with the civil war, which had been raging since 1917.

This essay will situate the 1920 Russian open-air mass spectacles in their political and historical contexts, demonstrating how mass spectacles functioned and for what purpose they were performed. I will begin with a discussion of the relationship between earlier forms of mass celebration (including parades, pageants, and festivals), the desire of revolutionary artists to create a new theater (developed largely through the work of the Proletkult), and the mass spectacles of 1920. Using, at least in part, earlier forms of celebration allowed the Bolshevik Regime to begin creating a revolutionary narrative grounded in both the present and the past. Public celebrations and spectacles created a community with a shared past and shared future, and the mass spectacles of 1920 were especially important in determining what parts of the past would be highlighted so that the present, and the future, would seem part of one grand narrative. The most significant historical moment dramatized by these mass spectacles was the taking of the Winter Palace on October 25, 1917, which, through these performances, became the moment of origin for the Bolshevik Regime. As such, I will dedicate a large portion of this essay to a discussion of Evreinov's *TSOTWP*, carefully analyzing the various elements that made this mass spectacle the largest, most complex, and politically most important mass spectacle of its time.

The mass spectacles of 1920 do have a genealogy, born both from the previously existing festivals and celebrations of the region and from the desire on the part of revolutionary artists (and political figures) to develop a uniquely "soviet" theater. To be clear, throughout this essay, I will use the term "soviet" theater to indicate a new kind of theater, done for and by the people but not yet controlled by the state (although it may be funded by the state). Furthermore, there is an important difference between "revolutionary" artists and Bolshevik leaders and political figures. During the time frame discussed in this essay (post–October Revolution and primarily 1920), revolutionary artists like Evreinov shared a common cause with Bolshevik leaders—both were interested in experimenting with and creating this new soviet theater. This is not to say, however, that all revolutionary artists were or ever became members of the Bolshevik Party. Indeed, several artists involved in *TSOTWP*—including Evreinov—later emigrated from the Soviet Union. This distinction between revolutionary artists and Bolshevik leaders is important, as the years following this time period found an ever-increasing control of theater by the state. As such, it is helpful to remember that while these mass spectacles absolutely served the Bolshevik Party, they were also an attempt on the part of revolutionary artists to completely reimagine the relationship between theater and the masses. Both the Bolshevik leaders and revolutionary artists benefited, albeit in different ways, from their collaboration.

Returning to the genealogy of Russian mass spectacles, there were numerous popular culture festivals, liturgical rites, and tsarist ceremonies in nineteenth-century Russia. For example, the autocratic tradition of festivals created a regular means of communication between the rulers and their subjects, reinforcing the power dynamics of this political system while simultaneously celebrating them. James von Geldern describes the many celebrations during the reign of Nicholas II, including the two hundredth anniversary of the founding of St. Petersburg (1903), the fiftieth anniversary of the defense of Sebastopol (1906), the one hundredth anniversary of the Battle of Borodino (1912), and the most important—the tercentenary of the Romanov dynasty (1913).[2] Such anniversary celebrations often included fireworks, carnivals, and ceremonial proceedings. These autocratic festivals, however, were a reminder of the power the autocracy wielded, as such celebrations were always state sponsored, and demonstrations not sponsored by the state were prohibited.

With the February Revolution,[3] the autocratic tradition of anniversaries and celebrations would be replaced. The obvious problem for the revolutionaries was how exactly to replace them. One solution was to celebrate holidays associated with socialism, like May Day and the Third International. May Day festivals had previously been suppressed, but were now supported by the Provisional Government. May Day festivals after the October Revolution continued to be significant holidays. In fact, in 1917 the revolutionaries abandoned their Gregorian calendar so that they could celebrate May Day with the rest of the world.[4] However, the celebration of these international holidays needed to be supplemented with holidays that would celebrate a uniquely Bolshevik identity. In his introduction to *The Invention of Tradition*, Eric Hobsbawm argues that "'Invented tradition' is taken to mean a set of practices, normally governed by overtly or tacitly accepted rules and of a ritual or symbolic nature, which seek to inculcate certain values and norms of behavior by repletion, which automatically implies continuity with the past. In fact, where possible, they normally attempt to establish continuity with a suitable historic past."[5] He also argues that the invention of traditions occurs most frequently when "a rapid transformation of society weakens or destroys the social patterns for which 'old' traditions had been designed."[6] Although the subject matter of *The Invention of Tradition* does not include a discussion of the Russian Revolution, this notion of invented tradition is certainly applicable to both the Provisional Government and the Bolsheviks, as both political bodies attempted to deal with the destruction of "old" traditions while attempting to create some sense of historic continuity. As such, the "suitable historic past" adopted by the Bolshevik Regime was, not surprisingly, a revolutionary one. For example, in the 1920 mass spectacle *The Mystery of Freed Labor*, a series of revolutions are presented: First is the slave revolt of Spartacus (73 BC), second is the revolt of the Cossack leader Stenka Razin (1670), and third is the 1917 October Revolution.[7] The Russian revolutionaries are, in this historic and symbolic narrative, the natural inheritors of the revolutionary spirit.

Thus, mass festivals that celebrated the revolutionary spirit also began to create a historic narrative, the culmination of which is the October Revolution. Before a deeper discussion of this narrative as it was presented in mass spectacles, I would like to briefly explain which individuals and organizations were partly responsible for the theoretical foundation of these spectacles. Just as it was necessary to replace the autocratic tradition of anniversaries and festivals, so too was it necessary to replace prerevolutionary theater. Two organizations simultaneously devoted to the creation of this new theater were the People's Commissariat of Enlightenment, headed by Anatoly Lunacharsky, and the Proletkult (acronym for Proletarian Cultural and Educational Organization). Both organizations, concerned primarily with "culture," had divisions dedicated entirely to theatrical production. Neither organization was beholden to the other, although there were some (including Lenin) who sought to subordinate the Proletkult to the People's Commissariat of Enlightenment, which I will discuss shortly.

During the height of the Proletkult movement (1920), there were around 400,000 members of the organization, led by Alexander Bogdanov, Planton Kerzhentsev, and Valerian Pletnev.[8] The Proletkult movement is mostly responsible for the enormous increase in amateur theater in Russia during the Civil War, and the movement embraced two different kinds of theater—agit plays (later club plays) and mass spectacles. In 1918 Kerzhentsev wrote a book titled *Creative Theatre*, arguably his most important work, in which he outlines both the purposes and methods of revolutionary theater. He argued that the old theater must be abolished—everything associated with prerevolutionary Russia, including theater practices, must be replaced. Since theater had been performed indoors, by professionals and was an activity reserved for the elite, it made sense to Kerzhentsev to embrace outdoor theater for the masses, which was performed by amateurs. Kerzhentsev was greatly influenced by Romain Rolland's *The People's Theatre*, a study of mass spectacles that had been translated into Russian in 1916. In it, Rolland outlines several points:

> The poet should select historical subjects that are already well-known so that exposition can be condensed . . . Everything must be done on a large scale—vast, festively arranged pictures, marches, sacrifices, battles, dances, pantomimes. All of these scenes and occurrences should flow quickly if in terms of the sense of the presentation they are only of secondary importance . . . All poetic parts of the presentations and those involving song should be simple, imbued with a single feeling . . . In this type of theatre it is necessary to simplify the action, to broaden the dialogue, using fewer words, fewer gestures but greater expressiveness . . . Strong dramatic contrasts will be exploited . . . Heavy use will be made of light and shadow . . . The vast size of these theatres will permit separate episodes to be presented simultaneously.[9]

Although not all of these ideas were successfully incorporated into the mass spectacles of the time, they are all present in *TSOTWP*. Of Rolland's suggestions, the last was the most difficult to achieve.

Funding for the Proletkult became increasingly problematic. According to Lynn Mally, "Despite the military insecurity of the new regime, its political instability, and the rapid economic disintegration caused by the revolution and Civil War, the Proletkult's leaders wanted the state to place considerable resources at their disposal."[10] Lunacharsky for the most part believed that the Proletkult should maintain as much independence as possible, but was at odds with Lenin, who wanted all new theater forms aligned with and subordinated to the state. The Proletkult took quite seriously the privileged position of the proletariat, so much so that they believed the Soviet government "could not operate as a single-minded advocate for the proletariat because it had to consider the needs of other classes," and so their grand desideratum was to be completely independent of the government, but at the same time to remain completely funded by them.[11] Lunacharsky and Lenin also had slightly different ideas about theater and culture in general and how they could, or should, function. Lenin and his supporters believed that "political power must precede culture building," whereas Bogdanov and the Proletkult "considered proletarian culture the prerequisite of a worker state."[12] As a result, the state leaders were approaching art from a "what can it do for us" point of view, whereas the Proletkult leaders were, according to Lenin, failing to see the big picture. However, Proletkult leaders believed the picture would only come into focus once a true proletariat culture was created, hence their emphasis on new amateur theater.

In addition to their contrasting views on the relationship between politics and culture, Lenin and Lunacharsky privileged different aesthetics. This difference is perhaps best captured in Richard Stites's comparison of the 1918 May Day celebration in Petrograd with the 1918 October Revolution anniversary celebration in Moscow.[13] Lunacharsky (and many major artists of the time) had stayed in Petrograd, while Lenin was at the Kremlin in Moscow. Stites describes the Petrograd celebration as having a "religious and carnival quality," where artists turned the city into "a cartoon, a Pleasure Island, a Castle in Spain, and a Land of Cockaigne."[14] Moscow's (quite solemn) celebration exhibited much more planning and control by Bolshevik leaders, complete with a double sacred center—the Kremlin and Lenin. All processions led to the Kremlin, and Lenin of course was celebrated as the living center of the celebration (having recently survived an assassination attempt likely aided in the framing of Lenin as a hero).[15] Again, the contrast between artistic and state control is present, and one must also take into account the ongoing tension between the two cities, as leaders of each felt their city was the "true" capital; however, the significant revelation of these aesthetic differences further explains why mass spectacle was a frequent form of celebration in Petrograd rather than Moscow. Mass spectacles were "massive" but also for and about "the masses." The protagonists of such spectacles were always "the people"—Lenin was not the living center of the mass spectacles of Petrograd. Furthermore, Petrograd had, at the time, more people to stage such spectacles, as thousands of soldiers were stationed in Petrograd (which was closer to the war front than Moscow) during the civil war.[16]

The desire to replace prerevolutionary theater led to the creation of many different kinds of performance, one of which privileged spectacle and movement above all other stage elements. There is an obvious marriage between these two elements—hundreds of bodies performing intricate choreography is, in itself, a spectacle. Of the many reasons the Bolsheviks produced mass spectacles, it is worth briefly discussing one more: representation of society. This is accomplished through mass spectacles in two ways. First, many of the performers were Russian workers, soldiers, and sailors—groups that the Bolshevik Party owed its success to in 1917.[17] Not surprisingly, these performers were usually performing themselves, in that the mass spectacles featured "the masses" as primarily composed of workers, soldiers, and sailors. Second, the aesthetic appeal of hundreds or thousands of bodies moving in a tightly choreographed performance shares similarities with the aesthetic appeal of communism. For example, in *The ABC of Communism*, written in 1919 by Nikolai Bukharin and Evgenii Preobrazhensky, the description of a communist society mirrors the choreography of a mass spectacle like *TSOTWP*:

> [F]rom childhood onwards, all will have been accustomed to social labour, and since all will understand that this work is necessary and that life goes easier when everything is done according to a pre-arranged plan and when the social order is like a well-ordered machine, all will work in accordance with the indications of the statistical bureaux. There will be no need for special ministers of State, for police or prisons, for laws and decrees—nothing of the sort. Just as in an orchestra all the performers watch the conductor's baton and act accordingly, so here all will consult the statistical reports and will direct their work accordingly.[18]

Not all mass spectacles were "well-ordered" machines, but *TSOTWP* certainly was. This description of a future communist society, while frightening to some, captures a particular aesthetic that is largely matched by the choreography of mass spectacles, especially *TSOTWP*. That the Bolsheviks could (with the help of revolutionary artists), in a relatively small amount of time, conduct eight thousand performers in a well-timed and tightly choreographed spectacle, which itself advertised the possibilities of a large, urban, well-organized industrial society, was a demonstration of what a Bolshevik-led future would be. The aesthetic appeal of communism was dramatized through the prearranged, well-ordered choreography of the masses.

Before I move forward in my analysis of Russian mass spectacles, I would like to clarify the difference between agit plays as produced by the Proletkult movement and the mass spectacle of *TSOTWP*. The amateur theaters that sprouted up all over Russia during the civil war did not have much in the way of resources to begin with. Still, those that participated in these amateur theaters were driven by a passion to "defend Soviet power and protect the Revolution."[19] As such, they almost always included Bolshevik propaganda. The amateur theater was produced and performed by the Red Army, and by worker and agricultural theater clubs. According to Rudnitsky, "The plays themselves were deliberately composed as reason and pretext for a rally and were hastily written for propaganda purposes. From this derives the expression 'agit-plays,' popular in these years. The agit plays could not boast of artistic perfection, but substituted a directness of political aim."[20] Agit plays were usually book-ended by speeches and rallies, and the waving of placards as well as the shouting of slogans were a common occurrence. The focus of these plays was always the proletariat, and they could be produced for relatively little money. Leach notes that the agit plays "sometimes took the form of a simple 'slice of life,' probably framed by a Prologue or Epilogue (or both) explaining the message, but more often the playlets treated—or deformed—reality for political purposes, perhaps through melodramatic action . . . or through distorted décor or acting styles."[21] Mally argues in her book *Revolutionary Acts: Amateur Theatre and the Soviet State, 1917–1938*, that club plays (Proletkult plays usually performed in found spaces) are direct descendants of agit plays. They differ in that club plays added complex characters and included a single and unified plot—basically, club plays transitioned from agitation drama to agitation-propaganda drama, the propaganda component being a more complex message.[22] The term "agit-prop theater" that we use today comes from this marriage of agitation and propaganda in the Proletkult theater clubs.

Mass spectacles, on the other hand, were so big and cost so much to produce that they were always scheduled on a holiday or anniversary, such as the anniversary of the October Revolution. Because of the size of these spectacles and the events they celebrated, the stories told were on a grand, even epic scale; as such, they were less about the proletariat and more about "the people." Furthermore, "There is a strong sense in the performances of a new mythology being created to enable the community to understand and celebrate its new identity, just as the mystery play explicated and celebrated the identity of the Christian community."[23] This "new mythology" is a point that I will unpack later in the chapter, as the shaping and celebrating of a specifically Bolshevik narrative is exactly what I think *TSOTWP* accomplished. However, both mass spectacles and agit plays share the open-air locale and the purpose of being performed for the masses. Also, there was certainly a propagandist element to the mass spectacles: to create a new mythology/identity, the state first needed to establish a value system that would influence the thoughts and thereby behavior of the people—thus the first step of this process includes the justification of their own (brand new) position of power. As von Geldern notes, "the Bolsheviks invested valuable resources in festivals for the purpose of indoctrinating the population with new ideas and legitimizing the October Revolution."[24] This moment of indoctrination and legitimizing the October Revolution is where I would like to pause, as this is at the heart of what mass spectacles attempted to do, and where they were most successful. To create a framework for this moment, I will turn to Benedict Anderson's work on imagined communities.

Anderson's book on the subject investigates a number of topics under the umbrella heading of "nationalism," one of which is the origins of nationalism.[25] While this chapter is not about the creation of the Bolshevik state, the mass spectacle was a part of a larger attempt to clarify who was in charge and why, which is why Anderson's theories are useful to a point. The first idea of Anderson's that I will employ is that of time. Anderson argues that during the Enlightenment "a fundamental change was taking place in modes of apprehending the

world, which, more than anything else, made it possible to 'think' the nation."[26] This fundamental change was the idea that individuals *simultaneously* exist through calendrical time.[27]
Even though one individual of an imagined community doesn't know the thousands of others members, that person knows that everyone is progressing through time simultaneously.
This seems especially important in a nation the size of Russia, as multiple ethnic groups
were brought under the rule of the Bolsheviks. For Anderson, there are two connections
between time and nationalism. The first is the sense of calendrical time passing—he uses
the example of a date on the top of a newspaper—to indicate the "steady onward clocking
of homogeneous, empty time."[28] He also points out that in a newspaper, the front page story
changes—and that even though the story may change from event A to event B, we know
that event A still exists, as a kind of character, even though it is no longer on the front page.
The second link to simultaneous time is simultaneous consumption. Again using a newspaper as an example (here, Anderson refers to a newspaper as an extreme form of a book),
the relationship between the popularity of the newspaper and the market means that great
quantities of people are reading the same thing at the same time. More importantly, these
individuals are aware that, even though they do not know and cannot see everyone reading
the paper, they can imagine them doing so—at the same time.

Peter Kenez has done in-depth research on the importance of Bolshevik newspapers and
the importance of the press in the creation of the new Soviet regime.[29] However, I would
argue that theater was as important as the printed word, because about 80 percent of the
Russian population was illiterate.[30] As Spencer Golub notes, "Until the period between 1861
... and 1917 ... Russian popular culture was more dependent on oral traditions than on
'common literacy.'"[31] Even Kenez consents that due to the civil war, the Bolsheviks were
unable to teach literacy to the peasants as they would have liked—they simply didn't have
the resources at the time.[32] Faced with a huge illiterate population, spread over thousands of
miles and coming from sometimes radically different ethnic and linguistic backgrounds, the
Bolsheviks out of necessity had to be creative to stay in power. As noted by Kenez, "The Civil
War was a time of desperate struggle, a time when the survival of the regime was repeatedly in question. In these circumstances, the Bolsheviks were forced to make extraordinary
efforts and to try new and unconventional methods."[33] These methods included resetting
bell towers to play songs associated with the Revolution like the *Internationale*; placing monuments of important revolutionary figures around the city; and staging speeches and political theater in the streets—to create a "talking city."[34] Of course, an additional method was to
employ mass spectacles to help communicate their political agenda to the masses—to claim
victory after the Revolution and glorify that victory in order to solidify the new regime. In
this venue literacy was not important—in fact, one did not even need to speak Russian to
understand what was happening during these spectacles (a point to which I will return).

To address Anderson's first argument about the simultaneous onward marching of time,
some individuals could read the daily/weekly/monthly press (when they had access to it) and
those who could read could share with those who could not. However, as von Geldern points
out, "Social, economic, and political life were shaken to the core; still, everyone remembered
the holidays."[35] Despite the civil war, festivals (both religious and secular) remained a part
of Russian life, so much so that the argument could be made they marked the simultaneous
passage of time in the same way a monthly newspaper would have for European countries.
To address Anderson's second argument about simultaneous consumption requires pointing out that festivals could be celebrated in both rural and urban communities at the same

time, and the heyday of mass spectacles reached upward of 100,000 spectators per spectacle. In this way, festivals (and mass spectacles) could reach the illiterate Russian people in a manner comparable to a newspaper. Festivals helped people mark the passing of time and gave them a sense of community.

Another point made by Anderson that helps illuminate the purpose behind mass spectacles is that no matter how recently a ruling party has come into power, it is necessary for them to create a unified history so that they can begin to see a unified future: "If nation-states are widely conceded to be 'new' and 'historical,' the nations to which they give political expression always loom out of an immemorial past, and, still more important, glide into a limitless future."[36] What is fascinating about the Bolsheviks' attempt to create an immemorial past is that their past was practically still present. The Bolsheviks did not have a long history they could look back on or even appropriate. Therefore they needed to create the sense of history even though the October Revolution was still so fresh in everyone's minds. Von Geldern argues, quite rightly, that the most successful tool used by the Bolsheviks for creating an immemorial past in order to see the limitless future was mass spectacle: "The urge to dramatize the Revolution . . . inspired a new mythology of revolution that was enacted in the mass spectacles. Each spectacle presented a new understanding of the revolutionary past, which suggested new needs in the present and new paths into the future."[37] Through the mass spectacle, the Bolsheviks, along with revolutionary artists and the Russian masses, tried to create a narrative or a lens through which to view the past as well as the future. Mass spectacles were new, but they were not so different from other festivals celebrated on a regular basis in Tsarist Russia. Indeed, Frederick Corney speculates that a spectator of *TSOTWP* might have been reminded of the 1913 Romanov tercentenary celebrations, as both enacted, albeit in radically different ways, a drama of power.[38] Furthermore, because of the Bolsheviks' ideological distrust of past hierarchical power structures, they had to negotiate a very precarious transition into power themselves. Von Geldern argues, "Festivals countered this tendency by shaping the past into a myth of destiny"—associating with progressive moments in history, the Bolsheviks created a hierarchy of events, at the top of which sat the October Revolution.[39]

Given this context, it makes sense that the Bolshevik regime would invest so much time and money into such enormous theatrical events. Investing in mass spectacle was equivalent to investing in newsprint journalism and the like. This is not to say, however, that theatrical events like mass spectacles had even remotely similar infrastructures as something like a weekly newspaper. As I have discussed in this chapter, there was no clear sense of a singular "authorial" control when it came to mass spectacles—it was more a marriage of convenience between Bolshevik leaders and revolutionary artists. The revolutionary artists who worked on these spectacles did not answer to an editor. In this sense, mass spectacles were the opposite of newsprint—they were collectively written and directed. Additionally, because they were performed live and on such a grand scale, there were often mishaps. It is also important to note that not every mass spectacle created was part of a larger narrative like *TSOTWP*. Mass spectacles marked holidays like May Day and anniversaries like the October Revolution, and while they were always celebrations of the revolutionary spirit, it was not until 1920 that mass spectacles began to create a narrative that could be used by the Bolshevik Regime. This is due largely to the fact that open-air mass spectacles up to this point were more like demonstrations than theatrical events.[40] In other words, as mass spectacles developed over the course of 1918–1920, they increasingly transitioned from a demonstration-driven framework to a dramatic framework. Along with *TSOTWP*, which was the most successful mass spectacle in terms of production and narration (because of its dynamic dramatic structure), two other mass spectacles produced in 1920 can also be read as earlier attempts—rough drafts, perhaps—to create a narrative that would place the October Revolution, and the Bolshevik Regime, at the apex of history.

The Mystery of Freed Labor (directed by three individuals, including Annenkov and Kugel, who later assisted in the direction of *TSOTWP*) was performed on May Day 1920, and *In Favor of a World Commune* (Petrov assisted in the direction of this spectacle, and he too would assist with the direction of *TSOTWP*) was performed on July 19, 1920 in honor of the second congress of the Third International.[41] Both spectacles were performed on the site of the former Stock Exchange in Petrograd. Although neither spectacle matched *TSOTWP* in size (35,000 people watched *Mystery*, and around 70,000 people witnessed *Commune*),[42] the dramatic structure of both spectacles situated the October Revolution as the natural inheritor of previously attempted revolutions. As has already been mentioned in this chapter, *Mystery* included three movements: the slave revolt under Spartacus, the peasant uprising under Razin, and the October Revolution. *Commune* depicted the Russian Commune as the realization of what the Paris Commune had hoped to become, demonstrating how Russian workers, complete with a new consciousness, established the Third International, which paved the way for the "World Commune."[43] Although neither of these spectacles depicts the storming of the Winter Palace, they both are structured so that the climax of the spectacle is a "storming" of some kind. The many steps leading up to the former Stock Exchange allow for a visually dynamic "storming," as revolutionaries in both spectacles charge up the steps, defeat their enemy, and proclaim victory. Because "storming" is a collective action, these spectacles emphasize the strength of the masses over individuality.

I refer to *Mystery* and *Commune* as prototypes of *TSOTWP* for two reasons: first, the dramatic structure and narrative strategies employed in both are similar to *TSOTWP*, and second, many of the mishaps and technical problems that occurred in these two spectacles were worked out by the staging of *TSOTWP*. For example, all three of the directors of *Mystery* participated in the spectacle as actors as well, which meant that no one was actually directing, or what today is more commonly known as stage managing, the spectacle. However, in *Commune*, one director decided to oversee the spectacle as a whole, while four others assisted. Also in *Commune*, the directors divided the participants into twenty-five groups, each with a leader.[44] This military style of organization and directing was particularly successful and was used by the directors of *TSOTWP*. In addition to a better organized method for controlling the participants (there were four thousand performers), *Commune* used the whole square of the former Stock Exchange. *Mystery* had been performed in what could be considered proscenium staging—there were three platforms built around the stairs of the Stock Exchange, but the front of the building was the only playing area. *Commune*, on the other hand, expanded the playing space, including two bridges across the Neva River, minesweepers that were anchored nearby, and the St. Peter and St. Paul Fortress.[45]

This staging placed the audience in the middle of the action, further blurring the line between performers and spectators. However, expanding the playing area added a significant complication to the staging of *Commune*, as it was difficult to direct the audience exactly where to look. For example, the performance was supposed to begin with an explosion, coming from the St. Peter and St. Paul Fortress. When the explosion failed (the gunpowder had gotten damp during the night) Petrov called the minesweepers on the Neva and asked them to deliver a salvo. They did so—unfortunately, the direction of the explosion caused the audience to turn toward the Neva (directly opposite the Stock Exchange where the action was taking place), and it was only after the lights from the ships blinded the audience that they turned toward the building.[46] The expanded playing area also made it difficult to move fluidly from one scene to the next. As discussed earlier, a key element to the successful staging of mass spectacles as outlined by Rolland includes moving swiftly from one episode to the next (*Commune* had 110 episodes). *Commune* was, to use von Geldern's words, "plagued by dead time," as the spectacle was six hours long and transitions between episodes were less than fluid.[47]

These problems were overcome with *TSOTWP*. In fact, *TSOTWP* was an aesthetically successful production because most of the directors who worked on it had learned valuable lessons via *Mystery* and *Commune*. But *TSOTWP* also had a much tighter script. The previous mass spectacles had focused on a series of movements, the last of which was always the October Revolution; *TSOTWP* was itself entirely devoted to dramatizing a brief amount of time before the Winter Palace was taken and the storming of the Palace itself. This spectacle was done on such a grand scale and with such dramatic flair that the actual storming of the Winter Palace pales in comparison.

In numerous histories of the Russian Revolution, the actual "storming"—and it really was more of a "taking" than a "storming"—receives little attention. This is so because the Bolsheviks had won even before the armed seizure of Petrograd was launched, as the soldiers of the capital had agreed to follow the orders of the Soviet's Military-Revolutionary Committee (or MRC, which was controlled by the Bolsheviks and their allies).[48] The actual seizure of the city, as described by Sheila Fitzpatrick, began on October 24, when the forces of the MRC began to occupy telegraph offices and railway stations, set up roadblocks, and surround the Winter Palace, where the Provisional Government was in session.[49] By the next afternoon, the Bolshevik coup was entirely accomplished, with the exception of the taking of the Winter Palace. Fitzpatrick's description of the taking is particularly insightful:

> The Palace fell late in the evening, in a rather confused assault against a dwindling body of defenders. It was a less heroic occasion than later Soviet accounts suggest: the battleship *Aurora*, moored opposite the Palace in the River Neva, did not fire a single live shot, and the occupying forces let Kerensky slip out a side entrance and successfully flee the city by car. It was also slightly unsatisfactory in terms of political drama, since the Congress of Soviets—having delayed its first session for some hours, on Bolshevik insistence—finally began proceedings before the Palace fell, thus frustrating the Bolsheviks' wish to make a dramatic opening announcement.[50]

Other historians agree with Fitzpatrick's statements. Ronald Suny describes the Winter Palace as "defended only by the Women's Battalion of Death and a few teenage cadets."[51] Marc Ferro, who describes the process of the taking of the Winter Palace in great detail, recounts the disorder among the attackers. For example, he notes that the warning shot (a blank salvo, not a live shot) from the *Aurora* was delayed. It was to have been delivered at 7:10 p.m., but because the searchlight at the St. Peter and St. Paul Fortress, which was supposed to give the signal to the *Aurora* to fire, was burned out, the warning shot was delayed until 9:40 p.m. The two men sent to fix the searchlight got lost, as there was heavy fog.[52]

I share these descriptions because they all contribute to an overall picture of the taking of the Winter Palace. Nowhere in these historical accounts is there a dramatic, well-organized "storming." The seizure of the city was already assured, the Winter Palace was not well defended, Kerensky (leader of the Provisional Government) had fled, and even the drama of a warning shot from the *Aurora* was delayed to the point that a warning shot became void of purpose. The taking of the Winter Palace was entirely anticlimactic. The Bolsheviks were even denied the dramatic moment of announcing the taking of the Palace, as the Congress of Soviets had already declared them the victors. Because the taking of Petrograd and the Winter Palace was done fluidly with few casualties, the Bolsheviks were denied the creation, or even the dramatic announcement, of a moment of origin.

Yet the Bolsheviks needed a moment of origin. They had no storming of the Bastille, no signing of a Declaration of Independence. Without a moment of origin, there is no Bolshevik mythology; with no Bolshevik mythology, there is no claim to power, as the claim to the symbolic center of Russia demands a myth of origin—a singular myth that allows the transition from the moment when history began to the unfolding of the future.[53] Here is the main reason for staging *TSOTWP*. The Bolsheviks may have missed out on the opportunity to create a moment of origin, but they could certainly stage a mass spectacle on such a scale that no one would remember the real taking of the Winter Palace. Instead, Soviet history would remember the events as dramatized in the mass spectacle. The commemoration of the taking of the Winter Palace, then, was less of a reenactment and more of a re-presentation. As Paul Connerton argues in *How Societies Remember*, the performance of commemorative ceremonies allows for the transfiguration of historical events into unchangeable myths.[54] To demonstrate how a mass spectacle made it possible for the Bolshevik regime to create a myth out of their very recent history, I will work through *TSOTWP*, which was staged on the third anniversary of the October Revolution and was sponsored by the political administration of the Petrograd Military District.[55]

Several English-language descriptions of the spectacle exist.[56] As mentioned in the introduction of this chapter, there were over 8,000 participants and over 100,000 spectators that attended this event in Petrograd. The chief director was Nikolai Evreinov, and there was a 500-person orchestra directed by Hugo Varlikh for the event. The set was designed by Iurii Annenkov (see fig. 36.1). Just as in *Commune*, the participants were divided into small groups, and each group had a leader. The leaders rehearsed in the evenings for three weeks prior to the spectacle, and participants under each leader were told by their leader what to do. During the performance, Evreinov communicated with his assistant directors through the use of a field telephone, light signals, and motorcycle couriers. Amazingly, the only technical difficulty during the performance happened when Evreinov lost the telephone connection with the battleship *Aurora*, and it continued to fire until a motorcycle courier arrived and told them to stop.[57]

As shown in figures 36.2 and 36.3, *The Storming of the Winter Palace* was actually staged in front of the Winter Palace, and the staging area was divided into three triangulated parts, with the spectators situated in the middle. As with the staging of *Commune*, the spectators of *TSOTWP* were surrounded on all sides by various staging areas, including the streets leading to the square, and the Neva, where the *Aurora* was anchored exactly where she had been in 1917. The performance began exactly at 10 p.m. with a single gunshot. It is worth underlining the importance of this particular mass spectacle being staged in the exact historical geographic location. Staging a spectacle in a theater automatically removes the audience at least one step from historical dramas, and thus it was especially effective for the Bolsheviks to recreate their moment of victory (again, not a historically

FIGURE 36.1 Annekov's design of *TSOTWP* (reprinted with permission from MIT Press).

dramatic moment) in the exact locale—it helped create a sense of "truth" for the audience and made it easier for them to believe that what they were seeing was what had actually happened.

Opposite the Winter Palace, in front of the general staff buildings, two platforms were built: the Red platform on the left side and the White platform on the right (see figures 36.4 and 36.5).[58] A different assistant directed the action on each platform, and a bridge connected the two platforms. Having one side of the staging area associated with the Bolsheviks and the other side their enemy created a clear visual narrative of us vs. them. As Deák notes, "the idea of two opposing platforms connected by a bridge came from the Red Army Theatre Workshop. The principle was to put into direct opposition two conflicting views or ideologies."[59] This simplified staging also eliminates any potential confusion as to whose side the audience should take.

Opposing acting styles were also used to create a visual difference between the two platforms:

> The style of the left platform was basically that of heroic drama, with large gestures and exaggerated postures, especially in the movement of the crowd. But elements of agit-prop theatre, the shouting of slogans, and certain formal divisions of the crowd balanced the heroic

FIGURE 36.2 Ariel view of the Winter Palace (reprinted with permission from MIT Press).

approach. The style of the right platform was that of buffoonery with elements of variety the-atre and circus.[60]

Thus, it would not have mattered to the audience if they could hear or even under-stand the dialogue—even the acting styles were so over-the-top they indicated which side was heroic. Like dance, mass spectacle relies on the combination of music, cos-tumes, scenic design, and movement to convey its message, instead of dialogue. The overall visual of both the costumes and the set was a combination of the real and the exaggerated. The costumes of the Red performers were realistically drab for both the workers and the soldiers. The costumes of the White performers, however, were exag-gerated and frivolous. For example, bankers wore gold and silver top hats and gigantic carnations on their lapels. Behind the Red and White platforms were flats, slanted at sharp angles. The flats behind the White platform were pink and light brown, while the flats behind the Red platform were brick red, an intended indication of factory works complete with smokestacks. The Winter Palace, however, remained free of constructed set pieces.[61] Despite the exaggerated costumes, angular flats, and buffoonery, the spectacle was very life-like, primarily because the final action sequence took place in front of and inside the actual Winter Palace.

The dramatic structure of the spectacle was fairly simple. Beginning with a single gun-shot, lights and music rise on the White platform. The Provisional Government is decid-ing to continue the war against Germany.[62] Then the lights illuminate the Red platform, where proletarians are staggering home, tired, and soldiers are wearily reforming ranks. The music is quiet and tentative. Then searchlights are used again to transition to the White platform. It was the use of these searchlights that enabled this spectacle to overcome all the dead time that plagued *Commune*. This back-and-forth action continued for several

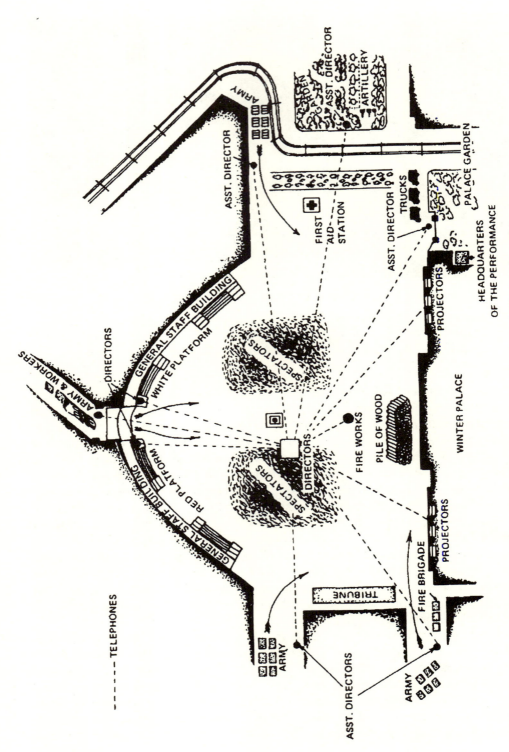

FIGURE 36.3 The general plan for *TSOTWP* (reprinted with permission from MIT Press).

FIGURE 36.4 The "white" platform (reprinted with permission from MIT Press).

FIGURE 36.5 The "red" platform (reprinted with permission from MIT Press).

episodes. Gradually, the action on the White platform became chaotic, while the action on the Red platform became more confident and organized. For example, in one scene, Kerensky makes a speech while being loudly applauded, and aristocrats bring large gifts (sacks of money with the '$' sign printed on them—the size of the sacks matched the size of the potbellies of the aristocrats, as shown in fig. 36.6). In the next Red scene, meetings and

FIGURE 36.6 The Bourgeoisie (reprinted with permission from MIT Press).

agitations begin to occur. Gradually the Reds become impassioned and ready to fight. This arc from being downtrodden to emboldened can be seen visually through the bodies of the actors.

Similarly, the arc from control to chaos is visually demonstrated through the performers. For example, as the character Kerensky continues to desperately orate, his ministerial bench begins to jerk in unison. This row of actors, sitting on a bench, jerk sharply to the left, then to the right, etc., the movement gradually increasing in pace until the entire ministerial bench crashes to the ground. As the White platform descends into chaos, Kerensky and his ministers dash to their motor cars, and are rushed from the White platform to the actual Winter Palace, across the square. This transition is significant, as the action up to this point had been entirely on the platforms built in front of the general staff buildings. However, when Kerensky and his ministers flee to the Winter Palace, they step, to use von Geldern's words, into "real space."[63] As performers storm the Winter Palace, various windows of the Palace are lit, and the audience can see the shadows of the performers engaging in various fights. This was a particularly ingenious use of the Winter Palace on Evreinov's part, as the Palace itself became a kind of character in the drama. This unique use of lighting also gave the spectacle a cinematic feel—both the quick transitions from White to Red platform and the lighting of interior scenes in the Palace allowed Evreinov to direct the audience's attention in a way that was usually reserved for film. In fact, it was this brilliant use of lighting that reduced *TSOTWP* to an hour-and-a-half performance.[64] During the climax of the spectacle, the Red Army marches on the steps of the Winter Palace, singing the *Internationale*. The guns of the battleship *Aurora* fire, and machine guns continue to fire in the streets.[65] Kerensky flees the Palace, dressed as a woman;[66] a rocket is fired, everything goes quiet, and then, softly at first, the performers begin to sing the *Internationale*. Eventually, even the spectators join in the singing.

The performance was very tightly choreographed. Spatial relationships were another visual indicator for the audience as to whom they should support, and each director created careful patterns of movement. For example: "A line of people climbs the broad steps diagonally from the bottom corner to the opposite top corner, the Red soldiers enter confidently through the archway in a curving line, a vast troop marches in in greatcoats and puttees, their sloped rifles like a forest of leaning needles."[67] At other times, one group is energetically running up stairs while another is wearily marching down—there are choreographed attacks and charges—even the entrances and exits were carefully planned, as the production used real horses, vehicles, and motorcycles.

The mass spectacles of this time were championed as examples of collaboration. Even though Evreinov was the lead director, *TSOTWP* was genuinely dependent on a very distinct organization, right down to the individual leaders of each small group. Likewise, the performers often moved and acted as one body, one collective actor. The result of this mass acting and tight choreography was to "provide 'the masses' with the notion that they were not an inchoate mob."[68] In contrast to the collective performer of the Red platform was the individual character of Kerensky—the only individual character in the entire production. Even Kerensky, however, was at times played by a team of performers. For example, at one point twenty-five ballet dancers, all playing Kerensky, enter the White platform and read a speech three times in a row.[69] The repetition of speech and gesture (like the ministerial bench jerking from left to right) occurred frequently throughout the performance. The actor playing Kerensky maintained the same type of acting style as the rest of the Whites, and according to all accounts was highly comedic.

Along with the visual staging of the opposing platforms and the distinct acting styles, music helped to underline the fight and eventual victory of the Reds. The performance begins with the orchestra playing Henry Litolphe's *Robespierre Overture*.[70] As the action starts, the *Marseillaise* (anthem of the Whites) is playing strongly, and then the *Internationale* (anthem of the Reds) plays, quietly and hesitantly. Close to the moment of attack, the *Marseillaise* is heard playing out of tune. As the battle begins, the *Internationale* is heard quite strongly.[71] To indicate victory, the actual Winter Palace is suddenly illuminated, shots are fired from the *Aurora* warship and there is much gunfire for a few minutes, then "A rocket goes up and everything becomes instantly quiet: Victory. A chorus of 40,000 voices sings the 'International.'"[72] Of course, how many audience members joined in the singing of the anthem can never be known, but the visual/aural image is a powerful one. Indeed, Huntley Carter notes "Anyone who witnessed an heroic spectacle of this kind—exhibiting as its salient features a Government being overthrown, the mingled shouts of men slaying and being slain, a great divided crowd returning through mimic warfare to the savage state, yet striking for liberation as each side conceives it—cannot fail to be impressed no matter what his politics may be."[73] Note how drastically Carter's description of the spectacle differs from the historical taking of the Winter Palace as described above.

After *TSOTWP*, the production of mass spectacles declined.[74] The form faded away in part because it was so costly (especially during a wartime economy). In fact, Evreinov was only given a fox fur coat in compensation for his work, and his eight assistant directors were each given a dozen eggs and a half-pound of tobacco.[75] Additionally, state leaders' trust of many of the revolutionary artists that produced these spectacles dwindled as the state began to exert more control over artistic endeavors. Once the civil war ended in 1921, there were no longer large numbers of troops and mobilized artists available in Petrograd.[76] However, the influence of these mass spectacles, especially *TSOTWP*, was long-lasting. This particular mass spectacle "fixed the final, irreducible center of the Revolution,"[77] declaring for a national and international audience that the Bolshevik Regime had arrived, and announcing the storming of the Winter Palace as its grand entrance. The importance of this declaration would gradually shape the cultural memories of both the mass spectacle and the historical taking of the Winter Palace. Corney notes that by the mid-1920s, the spectacle was couched entirely in Bolshevik terms . . . no longer were there Red and White platforms and participants—now there was the Kerensky regime, and Bolshevism.[78]

Although *TSOTWP* was performed only once, its impact was significant for the Bolsheviks. The revolutionary artists' job was finished when the spectacle was finished; however the Bolsheviks' job was just beginning. Re-creating the storming of the Winter Palace gave the Bolsheviks their moment of origin. As such, it really did not matter that only 100,000 people in Petrograd saw the spectacle. Sergei Eisenstein would go on to make the film *October*, which was directly inspired by *TSOTWP*, and its audience would be much greater. The Bolsheviks would have their coherent historical narrative, situating their regime as the natural inheritor of the revolution. The series of mass spectacles in 1920 "constituted a fanciful text that wove cultural, psychological, and historical episodes and dramas far removed in time and space from October 1917 into a mythic textbook."[79] The power of combining storytelling and personal experience was greater than any newspaper could convey. It was much more effective to "remember" (i.e., mythologize) the storming of the Winter Palace as it was re-created by Evreinov. In addition, mass spectacles like *TSOTWP* helped to solidify certain elements of revolutionary theater, particularly the blurring of spatial distance between action and audience and the marriage of conventional and spectacular elements used in an emblematic setting.[80]

Though much more can be said about the theatrical elements of *TSOTWP*, the actual geographic locale, use of opposing platforms, competing acting styles, tightly controlled choreography, and use of music are a clear indication of the (successful) attempt to create a political, national, and cultural narrative. Revolutionary artists and Bolshevik leaders worked together and were inspired and aided by the Proletkult: "[T]he mass spectacles convinced many theatre workers that they could contribute to the building of the new society through their profession."[81] Many hands helped to shape *TSOTWP*, considered the most successful mass spectacle not only because of its size and complexity, but also because of its role in creating the moment of origin for the Bolshevik Regime. Mass spectacles of the 1920s were but one faction of the new soviet theater, where the stage was "an alter on which is sacrificed the old social evil in order to purge the community of unrighteousness that they may enter upon a new epoch animated by the new spirit."[82] Though void of traditional religious symbolism, this new alter was revered in its own right by revolutionary artists and Bolshevik Party members.

Notes

1. Formerly called St. Petersburg, the Russian capital's name was changed in 1914 to Petrograd because Russia was at war with Germany, and St. Petersburg was considered too

"German." This city was later renamed Leningrad. After the communists fell from power in 1989, the city reverted back to its original name.

2. von Geldern, *Bolshevik Festivals*, 16–17.

3. In February 1917, Tsar Nicholas II was forced to abdicate and the Romanov dynasty was replaced by a provisional government headed by Aleksandr Kerensky.

4. Hobsbawm, *Nations and Nationalism*, 285.

5. Hobsbawm, *Invention of Tradition*, 1.

6. Ibid., 4.

7. Deák, *Russian Mass Spectacles*, 9.

8. Rudnitsky, *Russian and Soviet Theatre*, 45.

9. Golub, *Evreinov*, 193–94.

10. Mally, *Culture of the Future*, xviii.

11. Ibid., xx.

12. von Geldern, *Mass Culture*, xiv.

13. See pages 83–97 of Stites, *Revolutionary Dreams*, for a detailed description of both celebrations.

14. Stites, *Revolutionary Dreams*, 85.

15. Ibid., 92.

16. Ibid., 96.

17. Fitzpatrick, *The Russian Revolution*, 72.

18. Bukharin and Preobrazhensky, *The ABC of Communism*, 118.

19. Rudnitsky, *Russian and Soviet Theatre*, 46.

20. Ibid., 46.

21. Leach, *Revolutionary Theatre*, 37.

22. Mally, *Revolutionary Acts*, 90–91.

23. Leach, *Revolutionary Theatre*, 42–43.

24. von Geldern, *Bolshevik Festivals*, 10.

25. While for Marxists nationalism is a form of false consciousness, and the Bolsheviks still hoped for an international revolution, Lenin especially understood that nationalism "had to be accommodated if it were not to become a threat" (Fitzpatrick, *The Russian Revolution*, 69).

26. Anderson, *Imagined Communities*, 22.

27. In his book *How Societies Remember*, Paul Connerton also makes a persuasive case for the importance of calendrically observed ceremonies to historical narratives and mythicization, necessary for any claim to legitimacy.

28. Anderson, *Imagined Communities*, 33.

29. See his book *The Birth of the Propaganda State*, especially pages 21–49.

30. Rudnitsky, *Russian and Soviet Theatre*, 41.

31. Golub, *The Recurrence of Fate*, 8.

32. Kenez, *Birth of the Propaganda State*, 11–12.

33. Ibid., 15.

34. Stites, *Revolutionary Dreams*, 87–92.

35. von Geldern, *Bolshevik Festivals*, 2.

36. Anderson, *Imagined Communities*, 11–12.

37. von Geldern, *Bolshevik Festivals*, 11.

38. Corney, *Telling October*, 203.

39. von Geldern, *Bolshevik Festivals*, 12.

40. For example, on March 12, 1919, the Red Army Theatre Workshop (an organization dedicated to open-air street performances) staged *The Red Year*, using placards and rather crude costumes and makeup, the overall style of which was a mixture of parade and demonstration—what Leach refers to as "poster style" (Leach, *Revolutionary Theatre*, 42).

41. For a detailed description of the plots, scenic designs, and acting styles of these two mass spectacles, see František Deák's essay *Russian Mass Spectacles* and James von Geldern's book *Bolshevik Festivals, 1917–1920*, Chapter 6.

42. Corney, *Telling October*, 74.

43. Ibid., 75.

44. Deák, *Russian Mass Spectacle*, 13.

45. Ibid., 11.

46. Ibid., 14.

47. von Geldern, *Bolshevik Festivals*, 193.

48. Suny, *The Soviet Experiment*, 64.

49. Fitzpatrick, *The Russian Revolution*, 63.

50. Ibid., 64.

51. Suny, *The Soviet Experiment*, 65.

52. Ferro, *October 1917*, 254.

53. von Geldern, *Bolshevik Festivals*, 199.

54. Connerton, *How Societies Remember*, 41–43.

55. von Geldern, *Bolshevik Festivals*, 200.

56. See Deák, 15–22; Corney, 75–82; von Geldern, 199–207; Leach, 46–50; Golub, 196–200; Carter, 143–149; Stites, 96–97.

57. I cannot help but point out the irony that the only mishap in the mass spectacle was that the signal to the *Aurora* to stop firing failed, whereas in the actual taking of the Winter Palace, the *Aurora* did not get the signal to fire its warning shot until an hour and a half after it should have.

58. The color red has traditionally been associated with revolution, hence the term "Red October." The Provisional Government, and later the counterrevolutionaries of the civil war, were known as the "Whites."

59. Deák, *Russian Mass Spectacles*, 20.

60. Ibid., 20.

61. Golub, *Evreinov*, 198–99.

62. Russia was allied with France and England during World War I. After the February Revolution, which overthrew Tsar Nicholas II, the Provisional Government decided to continue fighting the unpopular war. Numerous battlefield defeats created extreme unrest throughout the country and contributed to the Bolshevik seizure of power.

63. von Geldern, *Bolshevik Festivals*, 206.

64. Ibid., 205.

65. To prevent widespread panic, the press had widely published that there would be gunfire, sirens, and movements of armed soldiers associated with the performance (Corney, *Telling October*, 81).

66. Though not the purpose of this chapter, I think a gender analysis of the production, particularly in light of the rumor that Kerensky fled the Palace in women's clothing, would be illuminating. The literal feminization of Kerensky is perhaps a function of the creation of the new Soviet man.

67. Leach, *Revolutionary Theatre*, 48.

68. Corney, *Telling October*, 77.
69. Golub, *Evreinov*, 199.
70. Stites, *Revolutionary Dreams*, 96.
71. Leach, *Revolutionary Theatre*, 47.
72. Deák, *Russian Mass Spectacles*, 19.
73. Carter, *The New Spirit*, 148.
74. This is not to say, however, that their influence was not felt elsewhere. For example, American communists produced a mass spectacle in January of 1928 at Madison Square Garden for the Lenin Memorial Celebration. This spectacle included a reenactment of the Russian Revolution with 1,000 participants and 20,000 spectators (Hohman, *Russian Culture and Theatrical Performance in America*, 106).
75. Leach, *Revolutionary Theatre*, 49.
76. Stites, *Revolutionary Dreams*, 96.
77. von Geldern, *Bolshevik Festivals*, 206.
78. Corney, *Telling October*, 246.
79. Stites, *Revolutionary Dreams*, 97.
80. Leach, *Revolutionary Theatre*, 50.
81. Ibid., 50.
82. Carter, *The New Spirit*, 17.

BIBLIOGRAPHY

Anderson, Benedict. *Imagined Communities: Reflections on the Origin and Spread of Nationalism*. London and New York: Verso, 2006.

Bukharin, Nikolai, and Evgenii Preobrazhensky. *The ABC of Communism*. Translated by E. Paul and C. Paul. London: Penguin Books, 1969.

Carter, Huntley. *The New Spirit in the Russian Theatre 1917–1928*. New York: Arno Press and The New York Times, 1970.

Connerton, Paul. *How Societies Remember*. Cambridge: Cambridge University Press, 1989.

Corney, Frederick C. *Telling October: Memory and the Making of the Bolshevik Revolution*. Ithaca, NY, and London: Cornell University Press, 2004.

Deák, František. "Russian Mass Spectacles." *The Drama Review: TDR* 19, no. 2 (1975): 7–22.

Ferro, Marc. *October 1917: A Social History of the Russian Revolution*. Translated by Norman Stone. London: Routledge & Kegan Paul, 1980.

Fitzpatrick, Shelia. *The Russian Revolution*. 3rd ed. Oxford and New York: Oxford University Press, 2008.

Golub, Spencer. *The Recurrence of Fate: Theatre and Memory in Twentieth-Century Russia*. Iowa City: University of Iowa Press, 1994.

———. *Evreinov: The Theatre of Paradox and Transformation*. Ann Arbor: University of Michigan Research Press, 1984.

Hobsbawm, E. J. *Nations and Nationalism since 1780: Programme, Myth, Reality*. Cambridge: Cambridge University Press, 1990.

———. Introduction to *The Invention of Tradition*, edited by Eric Hobsbawm and Terence Ranger, 1–14. Cambridge: Cambridge University Press, 1983.

Hohman, Valleri J. *Russian Culture and Theatrical Performance in America, 1891–1933*. New York: Palgrave Macmillan, 2011.

Kenez, Peter. *The Birth of the Propaganda State: Soviet Methods of Mass Mobilization 1917–1929.* Cambridge: Cambridge University Press, 1985.

Leach, Robert. *Revolutionary Theatre.* London and New York: Routledge, 1994.

Mally, Lynn. *Culture of the Future: The Proletkult Movement in Revolutionary Russia.* Berkeley and Los Angeles, University of California Press, 1990.

———. *Revolutionary Acts: Amateur Theatre and the Soviet State, 1917–1938.* Ithaca, NY, and London: Cornell University Press, 2000.

Rudnitsky, Konstantin. *Russian and Soviet Theatre 1905–1932.* Translated by Roxane Permar. New York: Abrams, 1988.

Stites, Richard. *Revolutionary Dreams: Utopian Vision and Experimental Life in the Russian Revolution.* New York and Oxford: Oxford University Press, 1989.

Suny, Ronald Grigor. *The Soviet Experiment: Russia, the USSR, and the Successor States.* New York and Oxford: Oxford University Press, 2011.

Von Geldern, James. *Bolshevik Festivals, 1917–1920.* Berkeley and Los Angeles: University of California Press, 1993.

———. Introduction to *Mass Culture in Soviet Russia,* edited by James von Geldern and Richard Stites, xi–xxvii. Bloomington and Indianapolis: Indiana University Press, 1995.

CHAPTER 37

MOVEMENT CHOIRS AND THE NAZI OLYMPICS

MARIE C. PERCY

RUDOLF von Laban, the father of modern dance, made an undeniably important contribution to our ability to describe and understand movement. He left us a collection of concepts and ideas: a system of language that describes movement through experience, observation, and analysis. Laban's work has been applied to creative pursuits, primarily dance and theater, as well as more functional applications such as physical therapy and increasing productivity and efficiency. He is particularly well known for his development of the movement choir: a dance form that allowed for personal expression within a choreographed form containing massive numbers of professional or amateur dancers.

Laban was working in Germany in 1933 when the Nazis came into power, and in 1937 he escaped from Germany to England. He felt a great sense of horror, sadness, and regret about his time working for the Reich Chamber of Culture (RCoC). However the time he spent working for the RCoC is a fascinating intersection of events in history for several reasons. Within this historical moment one of the twentieth century's most influential theorists on human movement and massive movement choirs briefly came in contact with one of the twentieth century's most brutal users of mass movement to support a political agenda. Within this meeting there is an opportunity to compare two very different approaches to the performative body en masse in terms of political and cultural implications and power. On one side we have Laban, a movement theorist who, through observation and movement choirs, sought to understand and reach to the heart and soul of man within his community. On the other side, we have the Nazi regime, a political machine led by a single force bent on control of a populace and acquisition of power.

This chapter will examine that historical moment. It will discuss Rudolf von Laban's relationship with the Third Reich in the light of the political trends that created the RCoC, and examine the historical and political context under which Laban's association with the Third Reich was terminated. It will then look at the performed body aesthetic of both parties in an effort to explain why the prevailing performative body culture supported the regime's goals at the 1936 Berlin Olympics, while Laban's movement choir was censored that same summer. A look at this complex pattern of cultural and political context surrounding two different

FIGURE 37.1 Rudolf Laban with some of his space symbols.

forms of mass performance will illuminate the relationship between power, body culture, and performance as seen in Laban's work and the Nazi pageantry of the 1936 Olympics.

THE HISTORY

This section presents Laban's relationship with the Third Reich. It displays Laban's artistic works and projects in juxtaposition to the Third Reich's political development and seizure of power in order to reveal how these two titans of mass movement collided in history.

In 1933 Germany was in a state of political turmoil. Tensions between the Communists and the Nazis often erupted into street violence. Hitler was sworn in as chancellor on January 30, 1933, and within six months had seized power and built the political machinery necessary to support his dictatorship.

In that same year Laban was working as the ballet master of the Berlin State Opera. On February 6, the Ballet Opera House was ordered to reduce the number of children in its school (Preston-Dunlop 173). On March 3 the RCoC was formed, and Joseph Goebbels was appointed its head. Division VI, of which dance was subsection 3, was concerned with monitoring and controlling all performance-related cultural activities (Kant 78–81). Racial cleansing became possible by Hitler's ruling on April 7, 1933, on "The Reformation of the

Professional Civil Service" (Doerr 155). It was at this time that artists like Bertolt Brecht, Max Reinhardt, and others fled the country. On May 10, 1933 members of the Nazi Party burned books by "undesirable" authors in a massive bonfire in front of Berlin University near the Opera House where Laban worked. During the year Laban revived his "Bayreuth staging of *Tannhäuser* Bacchanale" (Koegler 31). On July 7, 1933, he took steps to ensure that non-Aryan children were removed from the children's ballet classes (Doerr 159). Over the summer Laban went to Warsaw to judge the International Dance Competition; in September he staged a lavish performance of *Carmen*, and during December he went on a small lecture tour in Germany (Doerr 175-77).

During 1933, Mary Wigman met with her teachers to discuss how they could best adjust their teaching methods to emphasize the German qualities in their work. During the Fall, Kurt Jooss, who had refused to fire the Jewish dancers in his company, fled to England with his company in the guise of an impromptu tour. Twenty-three of Laban's performing students and several of his faculty fled the country and eventually joined Jooss at Dartington Hall.

The year 1934 saw the vise grip of Hitler's control tighten substantially. Hitler appointed himself Führer and had any political figures shot whom he feared were gaining too much power. In this year Germany saw the beginning of an economic recovery.

In 1934, Laban continued his work at the Berlin State Opera until his contract ran out on August 31. A farewell matinee was held in his honor on July 1, and both Hitler and Goebbels attended. It is at this point in history that Otto von Keudell, an employee of the RCoC assigned to deal with special issues in theater and dance, emerged as Laban's benefactor and liaison to the RCoC. In a July memo, von Keudell suggested that the best way to showcase German dance to the world was through festival performances. Laban was appointed the man for the job (Karina Kant 104). On September 1, Laban signed a contract with the Nazi regime wherein he was appointed the leader of the professional dance association that was taken over by the ministry. This effectively put Laban in charge as the director of movement and dance.

Laban's first major project was to organize the regime's first German Dance Festival, which was held from December 9 to December 16, 1934. It featured very little ballet; it focused primarily on the newly appropriated German modern dance. The festival was successful, and it was followed by a tour to ten German cities.

Laban's appointment also put him in charge of The Dance Theater, an institution created to centralize German dance as well as provide jobs and training for dancers. During the last few months of 1934, Laban began to make plans for the future unification of all German Dance. He met with Mary Wigman, Lizzie Maudrick, and Dorothee Günther to create standardizations of dance instruction. Their plans included a subsection of The Dance Theater, The Master Workshops, which would function as an educational branch. They also began creating a standardized test that dancers would be required to take upon completion of their studies at The Master Workshop. This test, once established, would be required for any dancer who wished to work professionally in Germany (Karina Kant 111–13).

In 1935, the Nazi machine began to pick up momentum. New laws and prohibitions were continually being put into effect. Jews were no longer allowed in sport facilities, and a law prohibited Aryans and Jews from marrying. On August 1, 1935, Decree Number 48 put into effect the regulations for the Conduct of Examinations in dance; in order to dance professionally a dancer must pass the test Laban had conceived the year before (Karina Kant 119).

Hitler's grand schemes were being put into effect beginning with the annexation of the Saarland (Koegler 41).

During March of this year, Laban and his team of supporters attended a meeting in which three major events were planned for the German dance community; for each of these events Laban would serve as artistic director. Germany would host an international dance competition. A second dance festival was planned as a follow up to the 1934 dance festival, and a new open-air theater, the Dietrich Eckart Theater, would be built and opened by a performance choreographed by Laban (Preston-Dunlop 191). Laban's plans didn't stop with these events. During this year he also suggested that the "Reich League for Group Dance" be established in order to gain political recognition for dance (Doerr 162). Not many of these plans came to fruition in 1935, although the wheels were set in motion.

In the summer of 1935, The Dance Theater hosted a summer workshop in Rangsdorf as a precursor to the opening of The Master Workshop. Laban ran the camp. He taught and choreographed choric dances, and current professional dancers presented new pieces. This workshop focused on how German modern dance could support or reflect Nazi policies and the German National aesthetic. Goebbels visited the camp and wrote in a memo "Laban does his job well" (Preston-Dunlop 192). This workshop fed directly into the 1935 Dance Festival, which took place November 3–10, 1935. Many of the pieces at the festival had been choreographed or workshopped at the summer camp. This year, the festival featured a balance of the new German modern dance and the old theatrical ballet.

In 1935, Laban had also begun choreographic plans for *Of the Warm Wind and the New Joy*. This piece was to be his crowning achievement. He intended to present it at the opening of the Dietrich Eckart Theater, and Von Keudell and the RCoC approved his plans (Karina Kant 119).

The year 1936 was the year of the Berlin Olympics. The more offensive facets of the Third Reich were toned down as the city prepared to dazzle the world (Koegler 45). While Germany was focused on preparations for the Olympics, German troops occupied the Rhineland, and the groundwork was laid for the occupation of Austria and the Sudetenland.

For the dance community, January through May was focused on preparing for the main events and debuts of the summer. On May 1, 1936, Laban was named the director of the newly created Master Academy for Dance, which was the actualization of Laban's dream for Master Workshops. Laban directed another summer workshop in June that was supported by the Reich League for Group Dance and had the official title "Reich League Week of Choral Dance." The German Dance Festival was enlarged and moved from the fall to July 15–30; it became the International Dance Competition. Laban served as a judge on the committee and gave awards to all contestants.

In a single day, June 20, Laban's fall from the graces of the ministry began with the final dress performance of his masterpiece *Of the Warm Wind and the New Joy* in the newly built Dietrich Eckart Theater. The piece employed more than one thousand dancers from all over Germany. It was an impressive piece in scale and content. Unfortunately, both Hitler and Joseph Goebbels were at the dress rehearsal, and they reacted negatively. They forbade its performance at the opening of the Dietrich Eckart Theater, and the pageantry and rallies for the rest of the summer and the 1936 Berlin Olympics were choreographed and organized by others.

Laban's position in German Dance swiftly deteriorated. His close friend and sponsor, Otto von Keudell, had been removed from his position in the ministry in June. Rolf Cunz, who was much less sympathetic to Laban, replaced him. At the beginning of August, Laban submitted his plans for the coming year, most of which Cunz denied, and then he left Berlin due to severe intestinal ulcers. Laban kept in contact with Cunz through a series of letters, and he and his doctors hoped that he would be able to return to work by October. However, when his ill health continued, Laban admitted that he would not be able to continue with his directorial responsibilities. He turned these over to Cunz, requesting that he be kept on in an advisory capacity. They negotiated a new contract, wherein Laban would stay on as an advisor to the Ministry for Dance until the spring of 1937 with a much smaller salary.

While Laban was ill he was investigated first by the police and then by the Gestapo. He was asked to provide verification of his Aryan decent. During the investigations he admitted to having been a Freemason in the order OTO (Ordo Templi Orientis) as a Grand Master from 1917 to 1918. This put Laban in danger in Germany. In 1937, he left Germany on an invitation from the Ministry for Foreign Affairs to attend the Science and Arts Congress in Paris (Preston-Dunlop 202). While in Paris, he was shocked and hurt to hear of the smear campaign that was being run against him in Germany. False accusations of homosexuality barred his return to the country. Desperately ill and penniless, he traveled to Dartington Hall, where he stayed and worked for the rest of his life.

WORKING TOGETHER

The above story provides an overview of what happened in this historical intersection between Laban and the Third Reich. The story ends with a transition from collaboration to sudden acrimonious divorce. One moment Laban is doing his work without upsetting Goebbels, and the next moment he is leaving the country while his good name is being ruined behind him. This sudden shift occurred when it became clear that their working relationship was not founded on a clear and unified aesthetic vision. It was political convenience. Their collaboration was formed by some key political factors that contributed to the ease with which Laban became an employee of the RCoC. This section will take a look at these factors.

The first factor is related to the formation of the RCoC. In the early 1900s artists in Germany had begun to recognize that occupational associations and groups could be useful in championing the cause of the artist to legislators. Consequently there was a preexisting constellation of artistic groups and associations already in place when the Nazis came into power. Instead of the Regime wasting effort by creating a whole new structural framework to govern the arts, it appropriated the preexisting associations and pulled them all together under the umbrella of the RCoC.

This was facilitated by the dominant ideas among artistic professionals that can best be described as neocorporatist:

> Neo-corporatism represented a non-Marxist alternative to a failing liberal social and economic order. It envisaged a society divided into self-regulating estates each composed of members of the same profession or occupation. The estates would establish qualifications for professional practice and safeguard market monopolies for their own members. Such regulatory powers would be constitutionally and legally recognized. (Steinweis 17)

When Goebbels put the RCoC together he exploited this idea. He took the individual preexisting associations and legally recognized them under the umbrella of their Chamber within the RCoC. The Nazis were feeding directly into the popular opinion of the time, and this notion of free professional self-administration under the protective, guiding hand of the state resonated nicely even in non-Nazi artistic circles.

As a result, the Chambers operated relatively freely in 1934 and 1935, which was the time during which most of Laban's projects under the regime were happening. Much of Laban's actions unifying and codifying dance and creating a test to create a standard for professional dancers fit directly into the prevalent neocorporatist mode of thinking.

How the RCoC was created feeds directly into how the chain of command for financial and artistic decisions worked. Otto von Keudell operated as Laban's patron and benefactor. He helped to finance Laban's projects and championed his causes to the regime. Goebbels, whom history has identified as the mastermind behind the propaganda machine created in Nazi Germany, had some direct contact with Laban and his work, but von Keudell functioned as the primary go-between. What was understood between Laban and Goebbels was the overall cultural goal for dance in Germany. Laban was instructed to codify and define the dance and physical life of the German volk. Initially Laban and Goebbels thought they were working toward the same aesthetic goal, an expression of the volk, which facilitated their working relationship. The eventual dissolution of their working relationship was in large part caused by a disagreement about the identity of the German volk. Through observation of the movement he saw in life around him Laban was analyzing and expressing the complex cultural identity of a people, while Goebbels was interested in manifesting Nazi political beliefs through mass movement.

The relatively easy political transition, riddled with the seeds that would later end the working relationship, was not the only reason Laban stayed. Lilian Karina was one of the dancers who left Germany when Hitler came to power. In her book *Hitler's Dancers* she described the state of the dance community at that time. There were essentially two factions in the dance world: the traditional ballet dancers and the new modern dancers. These two factions of dance were fighting for dominance and support from the government. Laban was the leader and progenitor of the modern dance community. His appointment as the ballet master at the Berlin Opera House in 1930 was a victory for the modern dancers; however, it was not well received by the ballet community, because he immediately did away with the star system. As an employee of the state when Hitler came to power in 1933, he became by default an employee of the new Nazi regime. In the context of the struggle between the dance factions, it's not difficult to understand why Laban wanted to hold onto his position. Additionally, when the Nazi regime appointed him the director of the Dance Division of the RCoC, it meant that the regime was supporting modern dance as an outgrowth of what it meant to be German solely because it existed in opposition to the foreign French ballet. This support was an appropriation of work that had existed independent of the regime previously, and in fact Laban and his work did not originate in Germany at all. Laban was born in Bratislava, Austro-Hungary, and didn't become a German citizen until November 5, 1935.

Laban's position as ballet master at the Berlin State Opera, and then as a leader in dance in the RCoC, provided him with a steady source of income, a stability that is rare even among great artists. His work was receiving the kind of financial support from the regime that most artists can only dream of. Combined with the ease with which the RCoC was created and the freedom with which it operated, the buffer of von Keudell in the chain of command, and the financial support for modern dance over ballet, it is not difficult to see why Laban accepted the support of the Nazi regime despite the glaring differences in their actual goals and aesthetics, which become more obvious when looking at the reasons why Laban was forced to flee.

BREAKING APART

Within the sudden dissolution of this seemingly mutually beneficial relationship, we find the cultural and political gap between Laban's aesthetic and the Nazi mindset. The inciting incident was when Laban had his most ambitious project, *Of the Warm Wind and the New Joy*, shut down. The censoring of such a momentous piece of work indicated that the message of this mass performance was not in line with the Nazi aesthetic and goals, and it marked the fracturing of this initially symbiotic relationship. The seeds for this sudden rupture in the working relationship were sewn during the development of the RCoC in its early years and culminated in the artistic censoring of *Of the Warm Wind and the New Joy*.

Before looking directly at the aesthetics of the piece, let's examine the political atmosphere that caused Laban's work to be viewed in a more critical light. In the mid-thirties the Nazi regime became more radical, and Goebbels felt that the freedom he had granted the Chambers within the RCoC, with their neocorporatist ideas, had been abused. What had been created out of convenience became disadvantageous for Goebbels. Toward the end of 1935 Goebbels began rearranging the RCoC and purging it of anyone who caused waves. Goebbels had disagreements with many of the heads of the Chambers, and they were replaced. The reorganization of the Theater Chamber, of which dance was a subsection, started in September 1935. While there is not any direct evidence that censoring Laban and forcing him out of his position at the RCoC happened because of this reorganizational trend, it is possible that Goebbels had already planned to oust Laban as part of the purge he was conducting among the leaders of the different chambers. *Of the Warm Wind and the New Joy* was a good excuse to do it. While Goebbels's exact intentions are difficult to ascertain, this censoring act can be viewed as part of this political trend.

As a part of the restructuring of the RCoC in early June 1936, Otto von Keudell was removed from his position and replaced by Rolf Cunz, who was not at all sympathetic toward Laban. This drastically affected the amount of support and approval Laban's ideas received, and it was another political event that likely had some affect on the censoring of his piece and his dismissal.

At the same time that the RCoC was being restructured, Goebbels was continuing to structure the aesthetics of the nation. Laban was pursuing the expression of the German volk, and indeed humanity, as he had come to understand it during the inception of the völkisch movement in the Weimar Republic. He was working on a physical language that was expressive of the inner workings of individuals in relationship to their cultural history, their land, and their community. Through dance festivals and workshops he sought to create a joyous sense of a community celebration within the movement choirs. These movement choirs would have had a varied and expressive use of space and effort. He used explorations of the pathways the body could take through its own personal space, its Kinesphere, and Effort, the quality with which an action is done, to create work that was abstract and dynamic and pulled inspiration directly from the wide variety of movement he observed and analyzed in life around him. The legacy he left to practitioners of his work today—his unique ability to analyze movement, describe it, and turn it into art—made him perfectly positioned to create work that truly reflected the movements and lives of the people around him.

At the same time, Goebbels and the Nazi regime were developing their own understanding of what it meant physically to be German under the new political paradigm. The Nazis appropriated the term "volk," and redefined it so that it encompassed anti-Semitism, racial adoration, and a political unification of the German people. Unlike the variety that was inspired by the world Laban saw around him, the physical presence of the Nazi volk stamped out individuality in favor of rigid, strong, and directly focused ranks. Their aesthetic was one of militaristic-like control. In this context variety and individualistic expressions of humanity were frowned on. This idea is antithetical to the philosophy behind Laban's work.

This created a gap between how the term "volk" was originally used and how it developed under the Nazi appropriation. The evolution of the term meant that while both Laban and Goebbels agreed they were working toward the ultimate expression of the unified German volk, they had drastically different ideas of what that meant physically. Both Laban and the Nazis collaborated in pursuit of a physical expression of the volk, but while Laban used it in a cultural context based on his observations, the Nazis' goal was pure political power.

These political machinations set the scene for the revelation of the aesthetic gap between Laban's art and the Third Reich, which was shortly followed by Laban's dismissal. This aesthetic gap will now be explored in depth by looking at *Of the Warm Wind and the New Joy* in comparison to the main cultural public event of the same summer, the 1936 Berlin Olympics.

OF THE WARM WIND AND THE NEW JOY

Moving away from the shifting political tides in which *Of the Warm Wind and the New Joy* is situated, here is a closer look at what this piece was and what it said. It is difficult to get an exact image of what this masterpiece must have looked like because it was only performed for an audience once at the final dress rehearsal before it was censored. The description of the piece and the ideals within it are based on Laban's own words and the reflections of other scholars.

Of the Warm Wind and the New Joy was performed by one thousand dancers, forty-one movement choirs from twenty-seven different cities, with the help of kinetograms, movement notation developed by Laban. They all came together to perform a final dress rehearsal on June 20, 1936, in the Dietrich Eckart Theater, which was built specifically for the Olympics.

The piece emphasized a German movement toward unity by telling the story of Germany from the crushing defeat at the end of World War I through to the 1936 present. The piece worked in four cycles: struggle, reflection, joy, and consecration. It highlighted the German struggle to survive, beginning with choirs of defeated soldiers and mourning women, moving into a slow section representing reflection on the previous struggle. Then fanfares came in with *Germany Awake!* uniting people in a single community. This section moved quickly, denoting work, progress, and the joy of creating a new state. Finally the group joined together in prayer, forming a large Germanic Sunwheel, and swinging into joyous circles that united the stage space and the audience (Kew 81).

FIGURE 37.2 The Dietrich Eckart Theater in 1939. (Attributed to Bundesarchiv, B 145 Bild-P019137/Frankl, A./CC-BY-SA)

Laban was concerned with capturing and expressing the inner essence of the German people. His choreography was greatly influenced by German völkisch thought, from Nietzsche's *The Birth of Tragedy*, that the German cultural heritage could be reawakened by a return to a Dionysian spirit. This Dionysian spirit placed emphasis on the expression and embodiment of the inner reality of man. Laban, in an attempt to represent the German volk, tried to capture the cultural state of the people, to depict their recent journey and who they became because of it through a festive movement celebration. The original Greek choral dance was held to honor and worship Dionysus, but without the deity to worship, the object of worship in Laban's choreography became unclear. Breda Prilipp attended a rehearsal and wrote, "The face of these dances is not directed outwards, but inwards," and so the object of worship and focus became the performer in a Dionysian self-expression within a community of similar individuals (Kew 75–79).

What Laban created was a piece expressive of the German experience, wherein both the performers and the German audience shared in a common experience because they shared in a common past. Laban viewed this to be completely in line with völkisch ideology, precisely the verbiage under which he had been hired. His piece was performed by Germans, celebrating the German volk, and for a German audience.

Of the Warm Wind and the New Joy had a strong focus on the individual within the community, and the most compelling evidence for this is the speech Laban himself gave before the final dress rehearsal performance.

> It is on this road that we seek the purpose of our individual and communal lives . . . Our groups and our gatherings illustrate above all a harmonious community and healthy individuals . . . Just as we do not want to be the slaves of our economic, technical, and social organizations, so little can we declare ourselves ready to sacrifice our inner and outer freedom and to waste our time with meaningless dogmas. (Doerr 168)

Many individuals from all over Germany came together to perform this piece, and it takes many individuals coming together to create a community. Within this speech Laban reveals that the choreographic choices he made for this piece were considered from both sides of this relationship, the individual and the community. The individual expressions of struggle and loss fed into the rebuilding of a stronger community, individuals helping each other to create something that is stronger because they each brought their own personal strengths and strife to the table. Likewise once the community was formed it aided in the individual overcoming their personal struggle. The piece emphasizes the person and the group coming together. Individual and community related to each other in a dynamic and fluid relationship without sacrificing the expression of either within this piece.

THE 1936 BERLIN OLYMPICS

The main cultural event of the summer in Germany was the 1936 Berlin Summer Olympics. Goebbels's efforts to bring the RCoC under tighter control led directly into the '36 Olympics. They became a stage on which to showcase the prevailing body culture that supported militaristic National Socialism to the rest of the world. The performances were created to support the propagandistic goals of the state on a global stage. In contrast to *Of the Warm Wind and the New Joy*, the pageantry at the Berlin Olympics clearly embodied the volk as a force united with no room for individual expression.

Leading up to the 1936 Olympics, the world was wary of Germany. Despite the regime's attempts to keep its burgeoning racial crimes a secret, the world was torn between disbelief and disgust at the stories of racial discrimination leaking out of Germany. The Olympics provided the regime with a golden opportunity for propaganda that functioned on a global level with the opportunity to change the world's opinion. The RCoC, which was becoming a solid team of propaganda experts, and the coordinated efforts of thousands of Germans created a mask that portrayed the Third Reich as strong, prosperous, beautiful, the rightful athletic heirs of the Olympics, and unified under Hitler. Carefully woven into this peaceful façade was Goebbels's invisible propaganda that supported militaristic National Socialism. The whole of the Olympics was a nationwide performance, wherein even the German spectators became active performers and participants for the global audience. This made every German citizen a performer, knowingly or not, and the citizens of the world became the audience.

The Nazis wanted the nation to appear completely and happily unified, the German volk acting as one. The individual only existed to support the whole and follow Hitler. A fundamental part of the creation of this cultural image was building the gigantic Olympic Stadium where the track and field events were held and the adjoining parade ground, the May Field, which could hold 250,000 people. These colossal structures set the stage within which hundreds of thousands could gather and display their unity.

FIGURE 37.3 Aerial view of the Olympic stadium, Berlin 1936. (Attributed to Bundesarchiv, Bild 183-R82532/CC-BY-SA)

FIGURE 37.4 Olympic statuary erected in the style of Ancient Greece, Berlin 1936.

The architectural design and decoration of these buildings was carefully planned to contribute to the manufactured image of strength and supremacy. Part of that image was the purposeful creation of an historical link between the Germans and the ancient Greeks. The Germans were portrayed as the descendants and rightful heirs of the physical prowess and splendor of the ancient Greeks. In keeping with this theme, the grounds and architecture were decorated with statues and reliefs that depicted the Aryan Man with huge muscles and athletic prowess, heroic and awe-inspiring. Thus the stage for the Olympics was set in new buildings that demonstrated the nation's ability to build monumental structures, larger than any Olympics facilities yet seen, wherein the people could unite as the rightful heirs of the Greek Olympics.

The opening montage of Leni Riefenstahl's film about the 1936 Berlin games, *Olympia*, evidences the same theme: the Germans inheriting the athletic prowess and dominance of the Greeks. The film opens with shots of ancient Greek statuaries and ruins. The comparison of German to Greek is made in a dramatic shot where a statue of a Grecian discus thrower transforms into a living physically fit Aryan discus thrower who, clothed only in a loincloth, hurls the discus with excellent form.

VIDEO 37.1 The opening sequence of *Olympia* directed by Leni Riefenstahl. The discus thrower transforms from statue to man at 5:30.

VIDEO 37.2 In this section of *Olympia*, depicting the opening ceremonies, the crowd can be seen giving the Nazi salute with total solidarity in response to other countries performing the Olympic salute, Hitler's speech opening the games, and the torch bearer.

They further emphasized their claim as the rightful heirs of the Olympics by being the first nation to implement a running of the torch from Greece to Berlin, bearing the sacred flame of their claimed ancestors to preside over the Olympics.

It was important that the nation appear unified on a global stage, and the Nazi "Heil Hitler" salute was the perfect physical manifestation of the nation's solidarity. It made a large impact on those foreigners who witnessed the games. It was simple to execute and joined thousands of people together showing their support and allegiance to Hitler and the National Socialist völkisch ideals of racial solidarity. This gesture was extremely effective as a physicalization of a political identity for several reasons. It was something that could be easily learned and executed spontaneously together within a large crowd, creating a sense of belonging and unity. From there the gesture could be taken outside of the group and performed individually, and every individual performance of the gesture pointed directly back to the experience of unity and belonging. Much like when Catholics make the sign of the cross, the gesture becomes a way of branding oneself physically as belonging to a population that thinks and believes the same way. It allows an individual to identify with a group and exclude others with a wave of the hand. It runs deeper than a verbal identifier because gestures can be read across the language divide. It turns the world into a binary set of populations, us and them, in or out. During the Olympic Opening Ceremonies the crowd had myriad opportunities to give the salute. The German crowd roared its approval when other nations gave the Olympic salute because it is easily confused for the Nazi salute. The German audience responded with an uproar of applause and a unified "Heil" to the young blond-haired, blue-eyed, athletic youth who carried the flame into the arena, and they "Heiled" again when Hitler arrived in army uniform. It was particularly effective because it could spontaneously unite huge audiences. Everyone could simultaneously speak and be heard with their physical voice, and it effectively transformed a passive spectator into an active participant. This very simple performative action became an outward symbol of a nation, given strength through unity.

For the Nazis, being physically powerful and athletic was inextricably tied to military strength. As a result of this, many of their massed performances and rituals involved thousands of Sturmabteilung (SA) men and Hitler youth. The framework for these spectacles was militaristic, including uniforms, exacting formations, and synchronization. However the actual activities performed weren't necessarily militaristic. For example 28,000 young people participated in a youth festival. It wasn't the festivities that belied the militaristic leanings, but rather the strict way they lined up rank and file while waiting to participate that framed the celebration with a militaristic underpinning. The rule of the day was synchronicity, impressive feats of organization, and athleticism. While the ceremonies were not overtly militaristic in nature they still showcased to the world a powerful regimented youth who could perform a variety of athletic and gymnastic feats. Peace, friendship, and hospitality were emphasized, despite the militaristic framework of the pageantry. The National Socialist propaganda within the ceremonies was primarily visible in the framework and structure of the events, rather than in the actual content of the events.

All of these measures coalesced to make the Reich appear to be a strong, unified, and healthy nation descended from the quintessential ancient athlete, the Greek Olympian. The Berlin that tourists visited didn't coincide with the brutally racist Berlin from the stories of escapees, and even though many foreign dignitaries were not fooled by the sumptuous parties thrown for them by Goebbels, the smoke screen created by these efforts was enough to keep the world audience guessing about the Nazis' true intentions.

OLYMPIC YOUTH VERSUS OF THE WARM WIND AND THE NEW JOY

Of the Warm Wind and the New Joy didn't fit into the massed body movement aesthetic of unified power that the Third Reich was creating during the summer of 1936. However the movement choir *Olympic Youth* did. Direct comparison between the two will reveal further differences between the Nazi use of mass movement for power and Laban's culturally expressive mass movement choir.

Olympic Youth was able to achieve what Laban had not: a massive movement choir spectacle that supported the invisible propaganda in the 1936 Berlin Olympics. It was ten times as large as Laban's piece, featuring ten thousand performers. It featured the traditional Olympic symbols of international unity: the Olympic rings, the Olympic torch, the parade of flags, and the Olympic bell. The opening section, *Children at Play*, featured thirty-four hundred children. Together they formed the Olympic Flag, and then broke up into two groups by boys and girls. The boys formed the Olympic rings in the center of the field while the girls lined the outside of the field, using half a hoop each to assist in creating the correct spatial formation. The next section, *Maidenly Grace*, featured a group of twenty-three hundred older girls, who all sat in circles on the outside of the field looking inward to Gret Palucca, who danced a waltz. After watching Palucca they then performed an athletic dance together with clubs, hoops, and balls. The following section featured twenty-three hundred older boys in *Youth at Play and in a Serious Mood*. Once again the girls moved to the outside of the arena, passively performing circle dances, while the boys took center stage to set up camp and perform exercises often practiced by the Hitler Youth. The girls stayed quiescent as the boys moved the piece forward from the exercises into a mock battle, which then included sixty men and became the next section, *Heroic Struggle and Death Lament*. After this the women became more active, following Mary Wigman, in a dance lamentation for the dead, and here Hitler emerges as a male figurehead and object of deference from his position watching because no male leaders are left on the field alive. The final scene, *Olympic Hymn*, culminated in a spectacular light display around the edge of the stadium (Manning 196).

The performers within every section of the piece were divided into two groups: the group with strength and agency, primarily the boys and men, and the group of performers who acted as the onstage audience following and supporting the strong leaders. At times there was only one leader in the performance (Gret Palucca, Mary Wigman, or Hitler himself from the stands) with the rest of the performers being observers and followers. Whether there was one leader or a strong group of leaders, the focus of the performance always pointed toward the division between leader and followers. This created a performance that appeared to be focused on unity, but in reality was divided into active and passive, strong and weak, leader and followers. By setting Hitler up as an unspoken leading figure within the performance, these ritualistic movement choirs did not focus on the volk as a self-governing unit like *Of the Warm Wind and the New Joy* did in its Dionysian expression of unity. Instead there was an Apollonian tone with a clear focus of respect pointed at Hitler and the ideal male warrior and subservient woman. One only has to look at footage of any of the Nazi rallies to see this concept clearly illustrated in the huge crowds of Germans energetically supporting Hitler. This artistic framework reinforced the social framework seen in the Third Reich, whereas *Of the Warm Wind and the New Joy* did not. The different ways large groups of people were dealt with spatially and structurally within the choreographic pieces was part of the gap that made one suitable for the invisible propaganda of the 1936 Berlin Olympics and the other an objectionable banned piece.

As previously discussed, one of the problems with *Of the Warm Wind and the New Joy* was the lack of any single central figure of worship and adoration. The central figure of worship was the unified experience of the volk. Because *Olympic Youth* was able to capture the highly regarded division between leader and followers within the Third Reich, the problem of whom the piece exalted was no longer an issue. The object of celebration was clearly the strong, male, Aryan warrior and Hitler himself.

While both pieces deal with war, the chronological story the two pieces tell reveals another key reason for *Olympic Youth*'s success. *Of the Warm Wind and the New Joy* told the story of the defeated German nation finding a unified identity and reclaiming their strength and joy through the power of individuals coming together to form a community. *Olympic Youth* also deals with defeat, but it depicts war as a natural outgrowth of the process of growing up into a man, and the joyous celebration in the end is not one of the unity and harmony of a people but rather a flashy show of the power of German engineering in the form of a jaw-dropping light show.

Just as was seen in the other festivities of the day, it was not necessarily the content of the performances, movement choirs, celebrations, and pageants that proved revelatory of the Nazi ideals. In fact the content of these performances often included the symbols and themes of international cooperation and harmony commonly associated with the Olympic Games and peace, as seen in *Olympic Youth*. Rather it was within the structure of these pieces that the invisible propaganda can be detected, and the inherent structure of *Of the Warm Wind and the New Joy* was antithetical to the societal structure that was being created.

THE AESTHETICS OF ART AND POWER

This historical moment is a fascinating intersection between an artist who used massive groups of people as his medium for cultural expression, and a government that used massive groups of people to create and display political power. There are subtle yet vital differences in the aesthetics and intended effects of these performances of masses of bodies. This historical example will now be used to extrapolate broader statements about people moving together to make art, versus people moving together to make power.

The intentional facing of these two types of performances is opposite. Here facing refers to the overall direction of focus and energy of the movers within the performance. This can include, but is not limited to, where they are literally facing in space. *Of the Warm Wind and the New Joy*, and perhaps other massive artistic endeavors, looks inward and seeks to express something that has been observed within the human experience. At the end of Laban's movement choir the performers are in huge rings that include the audience, focusing inward toward the rest of the group. The piece faces inward. *Olympic Youth*, the Nazi Heil, and the strict militaristic-like formations within the Olympic pageantry all face outward toward the source of power. *Olympic Youth* used circles, but they were always circles with a single center of focus in the middle, a leader. The Heil spokes from the individual outward as a sign of respect and recognition of another individual who has the same political facing as the performer; perhaps most obvious, the ranks of people all facing the same way gives power to whatever their united focus is bent on. Perhaps within *Of the Warm Wind and the New Joy* the source of power is internal, springing from the individuals looking at each other within the community. In either case the facing of the movement dictates where the seat of power lies.

All of the massed movement described in this article is celebratory in nature. The more people come together the more reverence, power, and joy is brought to whatever the community is honoring. The key difference here is that Laban's artistic endeavor celebrated itself, the people who performed in it, and the cultural context that gave birth to it. As suggested by Kew, it was a Dionysian celebration of self, while the Nazi manifestations of massed movement were a more Apollonian honoring of a leader and a politics of power. The art celebrates itself while the propaganda celebrates its message.

The relationship of the individual to its community is also different in these two aesthetics. Within the Nazi political performances an individual only stands out if they are a powerful leader figure. The rest of the individuals must disappear in favor of the rigid rank. Even in greeting, or physically speaking in a crowd, the Heil doesn't acknowledge one's individuality; it brands one as a member of and supporter of the group. It does not speak to the individual's uniqueness, but says, "I am one of us, not one of them." Laban's work came out of observation. One cannot avoid individuality and uniqueness when observing the world, and from these observations patterns begin to emerge. It is these patterns that all of his analytical work practiced today is based on, and from this analysis the individual experience, indeed the human experience, can be expressed through a higher and more general artistic statement. Here the individual experience is brought to and creates the patterns within the community. Once again the expressive artistic mass speaks to the human experience while the political mass expression speaks to a division of people and amassing of power.

All of the differences in structure and content between *Of the Warm Wind and the New Joy* and *Olympic Youth* within the Olympic context described above are based on two fundamental differences in the ideology behind the choreography. The difference lies in the source of the inspiration for the work and who the intended audience is. As was described when detailing *Of the Warm Wind and the New Joy*, Laban created the piece by observing the movement around him and the German people's journey. He took those observations and created a movement choir that would speak to the same people he was depicting. *Olympic Youth* sprung from a political ideology that emphasized the division between a community and its leader with the intention of impressing a global audience. Laban created a work that was of a people and for that people, while *Olympic Youth* was from a political ideology and for the world audience. This simple, yet subtle, difference accounts for the different sizes between the performances, the divergent symbols, the unique structures, and ultimately the inclusion or exclusion from performance that summer.

CONCLUSION

This chapter has looked at a highly charged moment in history with a lens that included cultural, political, and artistic concerns. These three things combine to create a complicated snapshot of how power and body culture interplay to create performance. By looking at Rudolf Laban's narrative in relationship to the RCoC, understanding how the relationship worked, why it terminated, and why his aesthetic did not fit with the Nazi aesthetic, several themes emerge regarding the interplay of political power, body culture, and performance arise. Reflected within performance and politics varying ways in which the individual can exist and be viewed in relationship to the group emerge. Laban's own historical narrative demonstrates this. His struggle to achieve notoriety for modern dance over the traditional ballet within the dance community, his struggle as an individual to create dance that was reflective of the whole volk experience, and his struggle to work within the shifting political currents around him all coalesce to form a narrative about an individual in relationship to the whole circumstance. This theme was also a key factor in determining the suitability of a performance piece with the Third Reich where the individual must disappear in favor of the group while in support of the leader. The idea of the part versus the whole is a key theme in Laban movement studies today.

Another key theme to this chain of events is the difference between a performance that is reflective of a culture versus one that is reflective of a political idea or social structure. This becomes a question of identity within performance. Are a people defined by their politics, their history, their commonalities, or the way they move and express themselves? How is this reflected within performance? The Nazis used large-scale performance to redefine the identity of a people by conflating their cultural and political identity within ritual, rallies, and performance. This theme greatly contributed to Laban's fall from grace with the RCoC because he created movement choirs that were reflective of a cultural identity without capturing a political identity.

Within massive performances, what the performance is about and whom the performance is for are important questions whether the movement is choreographed or spontaneous simultaneous action. In this chapter, this question draws a large line between the two aesthetics of mass performance considered. Laban's work was about a people and for that people, the subject and the audience were one, and it ended in inclusive circles that extended out into the audience to signify that there was no gap between the performance and the spectator. The entirety of the Berlin Olympics was a performance that divided Germany from the world along a political line, making Germans and Nazism the subject of the performance and the world at large the audience.

It is the hope of the author that these themes of identity in performance, relationships between power, culture, and performance, and the influence that the moving body can have on our understanding of the world continue to be asked and discussed across disciplinary borders within our continued historical musings and our current artistic expressions.

NOTE

This research was part of an MFA Thesis at Virginia Commonwealth University. Marie C. Percy, *The Universality of Laban Movement Analysis*, Thesis, Virginia Commonwealth University, 2012, https://digarchive.library.vcu.edu/bitstream/handle/10156/3857/Boyette_Marie_MFA.pdf?sequence=1.

BIBLIOGRAPHY

Bradley, Karen K. *Rudolf Laban*. New York: Routledge, 2008.

Döerr, Evelyn. *Rudolf Laban: The Dancer of the Crystal*. New York: Scarecrow, 2007.

Fischer-Lichte, Erika. *Theatre, Sacrifice, Ritual: Exploring Forms of Political Theatre*. London: Routledge, 2005.

Hart-Davis, Duff. *Hitler's Games: The 1936 Olympics*. New York: Harper & Row, 1986.

"Herr Joseph Goebbels Propaganda Minister." YouTube. May 7, 2008. Accessed October 17, 2009. http://www.youtube.com/watch?v=w2uCMpE5faI.

Hodgson, John. *Mastering Movement the Life and Work of Rudolf Laban*. New York: Routledge, 2001.

"Joseph Goebbels Cultural Speech." YouTube. October 18, 2007. Accessed October 17, 2009. http://www.youtube.com/watch?v=Dv9yHe6gdes.

Karina, Lilian, and Marion Kant. *Hitler's Dancers German Modern Dance and the Third Reich*. New York: Berghahn Books, 2004.

Kew, Carol. "From Weimar Movement Choir to Nazi Community Dance: The Rise and Fall of Rudolf Laban's "Festkultur." *Dance Research: The Journal of the Society for Dance Research* 17, no. 2 (1999): 73–96.

Koegler, Horst. *In the Shadow of the Swastika: Dance in Germany, 1927–1936*. New York: Dance Perspective Foundation, 1974.

Laban, Rudolf. *A Life for Dance*. New York: Theatre Art Books, 1975.

Large, David Clay. *Nazi Games: The Olympics of 1936*. New York: Norton, 2007.

Manning, Susan. *Ecstasy and the Demon: Feminism and Nationalism in the Dances of Mary Wigman*. Berkeley: University of California, 1993.

Mosse, George L. *The Nationalization of the Masses: Political Symbolism and Mass Movements in Germany from the Napoleonic Wars through the Third Reich*. New York: Fertig, 1975.

Olympia. Directed by Leni Riefenstahl. 1938. DVD.

"Olympic Games 1936." YouTube. April–May 2008. Accessed October 17, 2009. http://www.youtube.com/watch?v=p18MHAjdglo&feature=related.

Partsch-Bergsohn, Isa, and Harold Bergsohn. *The Makers of Modern Dance in Germany Rudolf Laban, Mary Wigman, Kurt Jooss*. Boston: Princeton Book Company, 2002.

Preston-Dunlop, Valerie Monthland. *Rudolf Laban: An Extraordinary Life.* London: Dance Books, 1998.

Steinweis, Alan. *Art, Ideology and Economics in Nazi Germany: The Reich Chambers of Music, Theater, and the Visual Arts.* Chapel Hill: University of North Carolina, 1993.

Strobl, Gerwin. *The Swastika and the Stage German Theatre and Society, 1933–1945.* Cambridge: Cambridge University Press, 2007.

"The Opening Ceremony of the 1936 Olympics." YouTube. Accessed February 2013. http://www.youtube.com/watch?v=_s_K3-FEwQA.

Vertinsky, Patricia. "Movement Practices and Fascist Infections: From Dance under the Swastika to Movement Education in the British Primary School." In *Physical Culture, Power, and the Body*, 25–51. London and New York: Routledge Taylor and Francis Group, 2007.

CHAPTER 38

....

TALCHUM
An Embodied Inquiry

....

J. L. MURDOCH

DEEP in the center of Korea, a man in traditional attire entered the temporary stage set under large shade trees beside the river and spoke for about five minutes in Korean. It was still early in my formal Korean language training, but I understood enough to know that he gave a history of Hahoe Talchum (pronounced ha-hwey tal-choom), and the preservation efforts that are taking place through the Hahoe Mask Dance-Drama Preservation Society and the Andong Mask Museum. After he left the stage the band, with instruments consisting of four types of traditional drums (the hourglass-shaped *Changgo*, the gong-like *Ching*, the brassy *Kkaenggwari*, the *Jeolgo*, a barrel drum) and a clarinet-like *T'aep'yongso*, entered in procession and circled the stage in a tighter and tighter pattern.

As the musicians circled, another performer entered with a masked character standing on his shoulders and waving her long sleeves back and forth in flowing arcs over her head. She was the impersonation of the goddess specific to Hahoe, who is invoked to cleanse the playing space before every performance. Her status as deity requires that she not touch the ground.

Once the goddess was taken off the stage two *Chuji* (lions) danced and fought together. Unlike the lions in other dance traditions that are made up of two or more actors under a length of fabric that give the impression of a four-legged beast, these lions were each represented by one individual standing upright and covered in a burlap fabric. These masks were significantly different from any other mask in the Hahoe tradition or any other in Korea, and were not worn on the actor's heads. Instead, the actors held the flat-billed masks in their hands and over their heads. The female "won," and their simulated sexual relations in the space were considered to further cleanse the area and symbolize a bountiful harvest throughout the coming year.

From here the performance took on a series of plots, vaguely joined together by the presence of *Ch'oraengi*, a meddler who related directly to the audience and provided the majority of the satire throughout. The next six scenes included a butcher attempting to slaughter a stubborn bull, an old widow who complained of her difficult life and collected monetary contributions from the audience, a depraved monk seducing a bar maid, a fool laughing at the upper class while weeping at his own circumstances, a nobleman and scholar fighting over the attention of a young woman, and a group dance where the behavior of the nobleman and scholar build to the extreme and all of the previous characters enter to witness and comment on their actions. At its conclusion, the cast circled the stage one last time and then took off their masks as the audience clapped politely for a moment before then quickly dispersing into the traditional village nearby. I was nearly euphoric. After three years of inquiry and extensive travel, I had finally seen my first Talchum performance.

Talchum, the masked folk dance drama, has been hailed as a popular as well as therapeutic form of entertainment in historic Korea. It has been characterized by bawdy plot lines, improvised dance steps, and interaction between characters, along with biting satire of oppressive elements of society. In a festival atmosphere that strengthened community ties, it emphasized audience participation allowing villagers an opportunity to vent frustrations without fear of retaliation. Talchum, like other traditional performance and cultural forms, was nearly lost during the Japanese occupation in the first half of the twentieth century. Since the early 1960s, however, practitioners and historians have, through the Intangible Cultural Heritage initiative, identified thirteen regional practices of Talchum and have built thriving tourist and educational programs designed to celebrate, preserve, and perpetuate the form. These efforts have largely remained performed on the Korean peninsula and written in the Korean language. Accessing information on Talchum is difficult in the extreme for a foreigner without the financial means to travel to Seoul or the Korean countryside. Additionally, scripts were written in antiquated Korean well before the influence of other

FIGURE 38.1 The *Yangban* and Scholar argue over the bull testicles being sold by the Butcher while *Halmi* (far left) and *Ch'oraengi* look on. (Photo by J. L. Murdoch).

languages and industrialization. This makes the writings difficult for many Koreans to understand and more so for those for whom Korean is a second or further language.

These challenges to discovering more about Talchum highlighted the need for primary research on the Korean peninsula. A Fulbright fellowship allowed me to conduct extensive field work in South Korea from August of 2008 through October of 2009. During this time I traveled throughout the country observing performances and participating in training sessions. As part of these travels, I was able to view eleven of the thirteen currently preserved forms of Talchum, train in five forms, and conduct multiple interviews.

Early in this process it became clear that there is a mutual desire for the exchange of information and appreciation of Talchum. Practitioners throughout Korea generously gave of their time and expertise with the request that I assist them in attracting Western attention toward their cherished folk dance-drama. Scholars representing theater departments in Australia, Canada, England, South Africa, and the United States have all expressed the desire to include information on Korean performance forms in their syllabi, their frustration at the extreme lack of information available in English, and their anticipation of published or presented material that they could incorporate into their classrooms. The language barrier, however, as well as a lack of connections between practitioners and educators was keeping this masked dance drama from becoming known in English-speaking communities.

My original proposal for study in Korea put a significant emphasis on written materials that I intended to search for at length. Before leaving, though, a trusted advisor who had conducted extensive fieldwork throughout Japan, China, Vietnam, and Indonesia, as well as other countries, recommended that I reconsider the textual approach and, instead, prioritize the voices of the practitioners that I would meet (Clark, 2008). With this in mind, I chose to engage physically with the form and to consider how those bodily interactions and the conversations that those interactions generated affected my understanding of Talchum and the culture by which it was created. At outdoor performances I wrestled my way through the crowd and struggled to hold my position in order to see the action. I regularly left those events with deep bruises to show for my efforts, several times I also bled. In training sessions I performed the same movements for hours at a time under the scrutiny of a region's master teacher or the instructor he assigned in order for my muscles to instinctively remember the order and precision of the dance steps. During that time, stories of the history of the style and links to regional priorities and rituals were shared. For example, the central region of Korea was primarily an agricultural section of the country, and the *Yangju* style of Talchum reflects elements of daily life within a farming town. All of the movements are firmly rooted to the ground, little if any jumping is done, and one foot is always connected with the earth. Each series of steps mirrors human and animal interaction, such as a cat circling a hen, the opening of ceremonial doors, and the exaggerated strut of a nobleman. By participating in this manner, I minimized my reliance on textual transmission of the form and emphasized what I learned through what Diana Taylor would term the "embodiment" of the Talchum experience (Taylor, 2003). In this chapter, I unpack embodied experiences of training and performances specific to Hahoe and Bongsan Talchum as entrée into this dynamic and engaging Korean folk form. Hahoe Talchum is arguably the most commonly known form across the country and within the expatriate community, and Bongsan Talchum is generally considered the most popular form among Koreans.

My training in Hahoe Talchum was my first experience in learning the actual movements of the dance-drama. At the time I took my first class, I had only seen one performance of any type of Talchum, the event detailed at the beginning of this chapter. I had met my instructor, Shin Jun-ha, through the curator of the Andong Mask Museum at the Andong Mask Festival in the fall of 2008. Once the fall festival season concluded, we made arrangements for me to travel to Andong for two long weekends of instruction in January 2009.

My original approach to Talchum was through the discipline of theater, not dance. However, I did have a strong martial arts background (I hold a third-degree black belt in Okinawan karate) that assisted in my understanding of the training hours, physical demands, and many of the movements within the dances. The approach to learning and performing the sequences resonated with my earlier training. For example, a lecture on the possible ways that Bongsan Talchum could have been a form of military or self-defense training held particular interest for me and the encouragement to "see" several movements in advance of the phase I was currently completing was identical to instructions given when I was learning kata.

The first day was completely lecture and conversation. Shin Jun-ha outlined the history and mythology behind the tradition and patiently answered a host of questions. He also brought out the masks used in performance and allowed me to photograph and study each one in detail.

The second day began the physical training. He explained that Hahoe Talchum has two core or foundational dances that all performers must know before they are allowed to begin learning any of the character dances. Kuguri was the first in the sequence, made up of smaller, slower movements. Chajin mori was the second of the pair and had larger, faster movements. After I had learned the first two sequences, he would then teach each of the character-specific series of movements one by one.

As I learned each step, Shin Jun-ha demonstrated the movement and then played the drum while I practiced. The first sequence functioned almost as a warm-up. The tempo moved rather languidly, and the footwork felt much like simply walking at a relaxed pace. Most of the work was in the shoulders. In fact, the gesture is so common throughout the Korean expressive experience that it is known as the shoulder dance. Quite a bit of time was spent in learning to raise my shoulders evenly to a specific height—not too high, not exaggerated, but relaxed and natural—and then letting them drop casually so that the motion flowed out across my extended arms, dipped through my elbows and then fluttered passed my fingertips.

As we shifted into the second sequence, the tempo picked up significantly. I became winded much more easily, and the footwork became complicated enough that I began stumbling. If I didn't complete a gesture correctly he was quick to use his hands to shape my arms, legs, hips, shoulders, or back in the way that they should move, which assisted in overcoming the language complexities and getting the movement into my body correctly.

Across the two intense weekends that I spent in Andong learning Hahoe Talchum, I was able to experience each character's dance. This was important because, as Shin Jun-ha stated, character is communicated through the choreography, not through dialogue or any other manner. Improvisation is seen in the personal variations with which performers inflect the dance steps far more than ever reflected in verbal repartee.

I returned to Hahoe in August of 2009 to experience a regular Saturday and Sunday performance offered during the tourist season each weekend between March and November. The hours of training in January as well as similar experiences with several other forms of Talchum during the intervening months provided a deeper understanding of what was happening throughout the event. These summer performances are held in the more formal *madang* built within the last thirty years on the outskirts of the village rather than on the raised and painted stage floor between the trees near the river where the first performance I observed the October before had been held.

Most styles of Talchum have some form of private rehearsal space, but practitioners must rent a *madang* for public performances. Hahoe, however, is one of the few styles that has its own performance space. The circular shape mimics the way in which the audience would have historically surrounded the performers in a field or within the marketplace (Shin and Suk, 2009), but the raised concrete steps of the contemporary *madang* not only provides the audience with a seating area providing better sightlines, but also act as a physical boundary keeping the audience neatly separated from the acting space. This particular *madang* has a thatched roof circling the audience's seats and open to the elements at the center in a way that seems reminiscent of Shakespeare's Globe theater in London.

Just before the space was officially opened for the public, a musical recording of both traditional and modern instruments playing old and new rhythms began playing over the sound system. The space filled quickly with audience members from the surrounding village area until soon the aisles were crowded to capacity and there was no room to exit the venue without stepping on someone. A group of women in their forties and fifties sat next to me and had brought an extra seat cushion to ease the discomfort of the concrete seats. To get my attention, the woman next to me swatted my arm brusquely with the cushion and then smiled broadly to offer it to me. The performance was delayed for several minutes in order to create as much space as possible for all who wanted to take in the event. Community leaders in traditional clothing assisted in moving those already seated so close together that we felt wedged tightly shoulder to shoulder. Performers and technicians, all in traditional apparel, wandered from the training space to the back stage area in full view of the gathering audience carrying masks, drums, and props without apparent concern of being seen. Once the performance began, I recognized each section as I had seen it the autumn before, including the verbal introduction from a member of the troupe. Since I had learned the meaning of the masks and moved in the steps of the characters from Shin Jun-ha the previous winter, the next hour became a completely different experience from that of the festival performance by the river.

The first character on stage wears the mask of a young woman and is carried in on the shoulders of another actor. The face of the woman has three red circles, one on each cheek and one at the center of her forehead. The hair is black and appears to be coiled shortly on one side with a much longer loop down the opposite side of the face. Compared to the rest of the masks, the hair gives this mask a square appearance rather than the rounded look of each of the other masks. Looking more closely at the details of the mask reveals two particularly interesting elements. The mouth is painted onto the mask, as there is no opening through which the actor can speak. This is one of the ways in which the young woman's place in society is indicated. For centuries, the understanding was that a new bride would move into the home of her husband with his extended family. For the first three years she was little more than a servant as she learned the ways of her new home. It was not until years later that she would come to have any voice in her daily life. Because of this, the young woman's character does not have any lines. Hence, the mask has no need of an opening for the mouth or an articulated jaw, as the others have.

A further indication of the young woman's social status is in the eyes of the mask. One eye opening is angled upward, which gives the actor a clear view of his or her surroundings. The other eye, though, is more slit-like and angled, as if a Venetian blind tilted toward the ground. This positioning makes it more difficult for the actor/actress to see clearly from this opening. The variation in angles and size of openings in the eyes represents the advice given to a young bride before entering the home of her new husband and his family: Keep one eye on the details of the household that are your responsibility and the other eye half shut (Shin, 2009). The reason that the young woman's mask is worn to represent the goddess has to do with the origin myth of Hahoe Talchum. The local spirits asked a young, engaged man to purify and sequester himself in the wooded mountains nearby in order to carve a set of masks. These masks were to then be used in performances to entertain the spirits, but no one in the village was to know about them or his assignment until he had completed his task. He left for the mountains immediately and began his work. His fiancé, worried about his well-being and curious about his abrupt departure, searched the mountains for him for 100 days. When she found the small house where he was working, she gently made a hole in the rice paper wall and peered in to watch him. As soon as she saw the young man he began bleeding heavily from the nose and mouth and fell dead. The mask he was working on at the time was never finished and is represented by the one mask of the Hahoe set that has no articulated jaw. The young woman was grief-stricken and died quickly after the death of her fiancé, without ever having married. For this reason, the legend says, the spirits chose the young woman's mask as their representative image (Shin, 2009).

The second scene is also ritualistic in nature and involves two mythical lions. During my training in January, Shin Jun-ha stated that the lions that perform a cleansing and fertility dance are observed by Chorengi, a figure that Westerners would understand as a clown character that challenges hypocrisy, comments on the status quo, and insists that the audience confront difficult social and moral issues all from a humorous and relatively carefree perspective. Chorengi later returns to interact with several other characters and is discovered to be the servant of the local nobleman in the penultimate scene.

The next scene features an old woman whom the audience only knows as *Halmi*, an abbreviation of the Korean word for grandmother. This is also the only scene with an actual set piece. Members of the troupe carry out a wooden loom and set it up in the center of the *madang* before *Halmi* arrives. It is made of a very basic frame with a bench seat and what look like large foot pedals at the opposite end of the seat. To some extent it works, or at least has moving sections that *Halmi* manipulates. She sings a lengthy solo about the bitter circumstances that have made her life so difficult. According to Shin Jun-ha, her husband died three days after they were married and she was required to live out the rest of her life basically as a slave in her in-laws' home. They did not provide well for her, and she was forced to work very hard. Her top is always very short, revealing her back and stomach, to represent her threadbare rags.

Halmi's mask has numerous lines (or wrinkles) in it and her right eyeball is disfigured. The center of it appears to be gouged out as a tracing of the flow of the many tears that she has cried during her lifetime. She leaves the loom and circulates around the edge of the stage collecting money from the audience. She assures the crowd that she will sing pleasing songs to the spirits on behalf of anyone who gives her alms which will, in turn, bring them good fortune, so people are quick to give what they can (Chung, October 15, 2010). Children in particular rush to the stage to hand over the bills and coins that their parents gave them, and those who get overlooked seem deeply disappointed. Her dance steps involve being bent at a nearly 90-degree angle and swinging her hips from side to side stopping occasionally to pound her back where the pain is. One hand is generally behind her back, and the other swings wide to assist in balance. The actor uses a gourd to collect the money and bows gratefully with each donation made.

The Butcher is one of the most popular characters with the audience and his scene is one of the longest pieces in the performance (aside from *Halmi*'s, which runs long because of the collection of money). The butcher enters alone carrying a straw basket and a large mallet. He circles the *madang* a time or two, speaking directly to audience members that he singles out in the crowd. His costume is all white, and he wears a straw hat. His mask has an articulated jaw that fits flush with the actor's chin and moves as he speaks. This gives the mask an uncanny impression of actually saying the words that are being spoken by the actor. The nose on the mask is its largest feature, and the middle of the mask's forehead has an egg-sized knot between the eyebrows. Both the nose and the knot symbolize the Butcher's questionable character earned through his "murderous" method of earning a living. His dance steps include several skipping steps, knees high, and one large, circular swing of the mallet past his ankle and up to rest on his shoulder.

As the scene picked up momentum, a stubborn bull, made up of two men under a length of fabric, joined the Butcher in the *madang*. The bull circled the crowd in the same way that *Halmi* and the Butcher had, but this time, instead of collecting money, it lifted its back leg and sprayed the audience with water contained in a plastic bladder underneath the costume. Quite surprised at first, the crowd became increasingly excited by the bull's attention and many shifted position in order to be in the line of spray as it made its way past them. The butcher intended to kill the bull, but it refused to go quietly. There was a bit of a skirmish as the bull charged the butcher several times and the butcher responded as if he were a matador. At last the bull was still enough that the butcher could kill it, using his mallet to strike the bull twice on the head. The bull fell over dramatically and the crowd responded audibly with sounds of dismay at its death. The butcher then sang and talked to the audience again as he cut out the bull's testicles. He told the audience that he should be able to get good money for them and circled the crowd attempting to "sell" them to one of the onlookers before he made his way off stage.

In the next scene, Bune, a local tavern owner, is seduced by a depraved monk. Since she was a business woman, in contrast to the young bride who has no mouth opening, no lines, and no agency within the script or even her improvisational choices, Bune could and did speak for herself to a certain extent. Her mask reflects this with a very small opening for the mouth. Bune did not actually speak in the scene (the opening was not enough to allow for lines to be heard through it) but the symbolism remained. She had mincing steps, and her arm motions were performed fairly close to her body. She crossed somewhat slowly to each side of the stage to check to be sure that she was alone and had privacy before crouching down on stage, holding her skirt out wide as if urinating. She did this close to where the stubborn bull had recently "died" so there was something of a wet patch (from the prop bladder) on the *madang* which assisted in the effect the actor was attempting to create. As she crouched there, the Depraved Monk came on stage and behaved as though he was hiding behind nearby bushes in order to spy on her. After she got up and moved to the other side of the stage, the Monk danced over to where she had just been, gathered the sand where she urinated into his hands, and sniffed deeply. This was exciting to him and he rushed over to

Bune and attempted to seduce her. Culturally, she was required to refuse him at first, but she was ultimately helpless against him, even if she wanted to say a firm no. As she gave in to him Chorengi, the clown figure, came in and caught them, so the Monk put Bune on his back and carried her out while Chorengi followed, mocking the Monk for his hypocrisy.

Shin Jun-ha referred to one of the most popular scenes in all of the Talchum forms as the "idiot" scene. In it was featured a character with some form of physical and mental handicap and difficulty speaking. In Hahoe Talchum, the character's name was Imae. He moved slowly and with a heavy limp, which caused him to fall several times while on stage. His left arm was bent in a permanent 90-degree angle at the elbow and frozen to his side and chest. His speech was heavily slurred, but the audience did not seem to have any trouble understanding him. Understanding is made easier by the fact that Imae's mask is the only one without the lower portion of its face. (This was the mask reported by legend to be left incomplete because the original carver was struck dead by the angry gods as he was in the process of making it). Imae was the servant of the Scholar, and Chorengi was the servant of the *Yangban*. Together they mocked their masters to the encouragement of the crowd. In each scene I watched, even when Imae was being performed as a repertoire piece by an individual performer independent of the larger Talchum performance structure, the masked actor would find a Korean audience member to bring on stage, and then ask that person to find a foreigner to join the two of them on stage as well. Together the three (or four, if Chorengi was still in the stage area) would dance with varying degrees of success. The audience generally seemed entertained at the foreigner's efforts to follow Imae's dance movements, and the foreigner was usually a good sport about participating in the fun. From what I could gather, this was one way of nodding to the festival atmosphere of historical performances. Stopping the performance in order to encourage the entire audience to dance would have made continuing the performance an impossibility, so a representative few were allowed to dance vicariously for the many.

Next, the *Yangban* and Scholar came on stage together, arguing about who is the better between them and should, therefore, receive the additional respect from the other man. They tried to outdo each other in regard to their accomplishments, resorting to designations that have never existed. For example, they made up advanced degrees, such as a "superdoctorate." Each topic saw them inflating their arrogance even further in excessively ridiculous ways. Chorengi, who was still in the *madang* from participating in the scene with Imae, was revealed to be the *Yangban*'s servant. When he saw the *Yangban* and Scholar approaching, he began a running commentary aimed at the audience. He spoke to his master in double entendres that the audience understood but that confused or even flattered the *Yangban*, which then added to the audience's amusement.

The Scholar walked with stooped shoulders, and his mask was pinched and angular. His eyes were prominent within the mask because he spent so much time huddled over his reading. The *Yangban* walked slowly, hips first, because a nobleman never hurried, regardless of how late he might have been or the urgency of the meeting he was going to attend. He had a wide gait and held his elbows out from his body and his shoulders bent back from his hips. He carried a fan that he moved slowly back and forth, and spoke in a large, bold manner that supported the relaxed and arrogant physicality. Both characters wore similar, almost identical, outer garments, one in pale blue, the other in pale yellow. The masks were also similar, especially from a distance. So similar, in fact, that before the preservation initiative in the 1960s there was disagreement as to which one was actually the *Yangban* (Ch'oe, 1979).

The mask now known as the *Yangban* has broader features, less prominent eyes, and a softer eyebrow ridge than the Scholar's mask. All of these distinctions are echoed in the physical carriage and dance steps of the actor/dancer.

While none of the scenes built on previous scenarios, the final act included all of the characters that were introduced throughout the performance and the level of farce included gave the impression of building toward a climactic moment. The Butcher came back on stage as if walking through the same part of town where the *Yangban* and Scholar were engaged in heated debate. When the Butcher saw the *Yangban* and Scholar, he tried to sell them the testicles that he had removed from the stubborn bull at the beginning of the performance. At first, neither man was interested and both found the offer repulsive. But, when the Butcher changed his sales tactic and told them that eating the genitals would make the eater virile, both men began fighting over which one deserved to have such a noble item. Each made his case for why he was more deserving, and then the two began to struggle physically in a tug-of-war with the desired object between them. As they fought, *Halmi* also joined the group and watched the dramatics. The fight ended with the testicles slipping from the grasp of both men and flying toward the edge of the stage while both stumbled and fell backward to the ground. *Halmi* picked up the testicles and commented about never having seen such an outrageous fight over something so common and useless as bull genitalia. This further supported the hints from earlier in the scene that the Butcher was simply using the suggestion of an aphrodisiac as a sales tactic and not because there was any truth, perceived or otherwise, in the suggested usage.

The performance ended much as it began. The cast circled the stage using their unique dance steps and then recessed off stage only to return again a moment or two later in order to mingle with the audience. The performers lingered for some time, having their pictures taken with various groups and allowing children to wear their character's masks. As the crowd thinned, the performers made their way off stage again. This mingling with the audience was another way of referencing the historical community party that took place after the performance far into the night. At this party residents made offerings to appease the regional god and offered food and drink to the spirits of ancestors who had passed on. After the spirits and ancestors had been "fed," everyone in attendance then had plenty to eat and drink and caroused together for the rest of the evening.

This performance is largely representative of the current performances of Talchum throughout the peninsula. Events are generally hosted during important holidays such as Lunar New Year as well as during summer and the fall festival season when tourists are most abundant. Performances have a heavy educational component for the benefit of foreigners as well as urban residents disconnected from farming communities and traditions. These educational elements are required of all forms of performance that have been designated Intangible Cultural Properties in order to maintain both their status and their governmental funding.[1] This funding allows the vast number of performances to be free and open to the public.

In February of 2009, a few weeks after my training in Hahoe Talchum, I saw my next performance. My excitement at having arrived early enough at the Namsan Traditional Village in order to get a good seat for the celebratory Lunar New Year performance of Bongsan Talchum was tempered by the fact that I then had to wait another hour in the frigid February temperatures for the performance to begin. The crowd filled in around me quickly, often stepping on me and tripping over my tripod. I clung to my video camera and tried to take up as little space as possible but that didn't save me from bruises on my feet and scratches on my hands.

A raised stage had been erected in front of a wooden pavilion for special events during the New Year celebrations. As with the Hahoe performance, a costumed but unmasked member of the troupe gave a brief introduction. Instead of a processional of musicians to begin the performance, though, the musicians filed onto the left of the stage unceremoniously and casually settled themselves as the introduction was being given. The performance was structured in brief vignettes in the same way as the Hahoe performance, but the characters, costumes, and storylines were distinctly different.

The performance began with four identically dressed individuals in plain white masks, piqued white hats, and white robes with red and blue tunics. Together they danced a slow, elegant series of motions that were repeated four times, each toward a different compass direction. Their size suggested that they were female, but absolutely no section of their bodies was visible under their costumes. I took them at the time to be shamans cleansing the space in much the same way that the representation of the goddess functioned at the beginning of the Hahoe performance.

The next scene was the dance of the eight monks, one of the most frequently performed and photographed within Bongsan Talchum. One at a time, a series of eight monks in red masks with tissue paper tassels around the outside edges and wearing brightly colored, silken and intricately embroidered jackets and sashes made their way on stage and chased off the previous monk. Each one said a few brief words and then danced the same movements as the previous monks had. After the eighth monk took his turn on stage, the first seven monks returned to join him in a corporate dance that filled the stage with flashing colors and swirling ribbon-like sleeves as the performers leapt, crouched, and spun their way around the platform.

The next scene appeared to be a monk supposedly in prayer who was distracted by the presence of a young woman. The monk wore darkly colored, rough-appearing garments and a straw hat over his black mask with white spots across it. The black mask seemed unusual in contrast to the previous eight monks in their finery. The young woman wore a brightly colored and embroidered traditional dress, a plain white mask similar to the four in the first scene, and a black wig with a small circular hat that gave the impression of a crown. She spurned the monk's attention at first but gradually gave in to him. Suddenly a rogue monk in a red mask similar to the other monks but with a much higher forehead interrupted the two dancers. The young monk fought the old monk three times before the old monk gave up and left the stage.

The young monk turned his attention to the young woman. She again resisted but quickly changed her mind when the monk brought out a lengthy string of coins from his money belt.[2] The two danced together until the woman began to evidence signs of pain. She continued her solo dance of agony which became clear was representative of giving birth. A small doll dropped from beneath her billowing costume and she hastily exited from the stage.

Alone now on stage, the young monk considered the doll skeptically at first but then became more comfortable with it as he picked it up, spoke to it, and eventually cradled it. Early in his interaction with the baby, the monk spoke directly to the audience, but his focus shifted to the child until they were sitting together on the stage floor and he was talking directly to the doll.

When his conversation ended and he carried the doll off stage, a performer carrying a whip and dressed in the same mask and colorfully embroidered costume as the monks in the first dramatic scene escorted a lion onto the stage. The lion was created with two performers under a length of fabric much like the stubborn bull in the Hahoe performance. The lion's "fur" was white with a wide dark yellow, almost gold, colored stripe down the length of its back. The face of the lion was a large, circular mask with enormous eyes accentuated by what appeared to be two oversized jingle bells. The bells caught the light and accentuated the rhythmic steps of the performers as they created the movement of the beast. The mask was large enough to be held with two hands by the dancer under the front section of the fabric. This performer used sweeping gestures that reached far over his head, dipped down to his feet, and swayed from side to side, all to give the impression of a lively and unruly creature that had yet to succumb to the taming efforts of the monk that accompanied it. In the final moment of the scene the front performer climbed onto the shoulders of the back performer to give the impression of the lion standing and walking on its hind legs—a bit of spectacle received with impressed "oohs" and "aahs" as well as a generous round of applause from the audience.

My next experience with a Bongsan Talchum performance was in May 2009. In April and May of that year, I was invited to participate in a Bongsan Talchum class taught by Professor Choi Chang-ju at the Korea National University of Arts. The lecture and narrative elements that accompanied the physical training combined to create a richer understanding of the performance I was about to see.

According to Professor Choi (and confirmed by numerous others across my experience in Korea) Bongsan Talchum is considered the most popular style of Talchum among Koreans. Indeed, it is not uncommon to see the brightly colored and tasseled masks along with the vibrant and intricately embroidered costumes on performers captured in midjump on publicity photos within glossy promotional materials for a wide variety of cultural events and locations. Originally developed in the northern regions of the Korean peninsula, the thriving preservation society in Seoul maintains this performative national heritage through training and public performances. Currently, performances of varying lengths, generally up to an hour long, are held around the city, most often during Lunar New Year, Chusok (a harvest festival and the most important holiday of the year), and at other celebrations throughout the year.

Bongsan Talchum, like all of the other preserved forms of Talchum, is structured in a series of scenes reflecting traditional life in the Korean countryside. Some of the characters reappear in more than one scene, but the individual vignettes are self-contained and do not combine to create a cohesive narrative arc as do Pansori, a traditional operatic form, and other storytelling traditions. Between scenes, live musicians play traditional instruments and, at times during the dramatic action, will also speak with the actors. Several of the scenes can be played in any order, but the performances consistently begin with four young shamans blessing the space and end with an old woman's funeral rites after she dies in a confrontation with her husband and his mistress. Between these framing scenes eight monks dance individually and then together as a group, a depraved monk attempts to seduce a young woman but is thwarted by a younger prodigal monk, the prodigal monk fathers a baby that is born on stage and then he pensively converses with his newborn son, several corrupt noblemen are mocked by their servant, and a lion tamer attempts to wrangle a spirited lion.

FIGURE 38.2 The Lion standing on its hind legs at the end of the performance. (Photo by J. L. Murdoch).

The costumes and masks of this form are rich in color and detail. Many of the costumes have bold, multicolored stripes, and the fabrics have a shine to them in any light. Quite a few also include elongated sleeves that performers attach to their wrists, extending the enormous arm movements and creating a fluttering, ribbon-like appearance, particularly in the dance of the eight monks. The masks, as in other forms of Talchum, show the inner qualities of their characters in the number of creases on the forehead, the shape and size of the nose, and the shape of the mouth. Characters considered to be normal will have two or three wrinkles on their forehead, a proportionately sized and straight-shaped nose, and/or a complete mouth. Depraved, prodigal, or morally deficient characters are represented by ten or twelve wrinkles, an oversized and/or twisted nose, and/or a mouth with a cleft palate, jagged teeth, or an alignment angular to the rest of the facial features. None of the masks have articulated jaws, as the Hahoe masks do, and they are made of heavy paper rather than carved from wood, as the Hahoe masks are. Historically, the performers would burn the masks after the all-night performance in order to release any of the invited regional spirits that may have entered the masks (Bongsan Training Sessions, 2009).

I had seen the hour-long presentation as well as several scenes performed independently at festivals or openings to events, so I had an understanding of the masks specific to Bongsan Talchum and the major characters and plotlines. I had taken pictures of the performances as well as captured video but, while recording those performances, my attention was more focused on gathering material that I could observe and evaluate in more detail at a later time. Participating in Professor Choi's class, though, gave me the opportunity to dwell with the dance, characters, and rhythms on a more sustained basis. As we worked our way through several series of movements I began to connect the patterns that I was jumping and swaying through to the performances that I had already seen. These flashes of insight began to change the way I perceived the characters that I was dancing. Their motivations became clearer and the actual plotlines took on a more vibrant meaning for me. What I had originally thought were white-masked shamans cleansing the space in a manner similar to the function and presence of the goddess in the Hahoe performance were actually young female Buddhist monks and they weren't simply moving through the same gestures but communicating with and relying on each other throughout the sequence in order to create the appropriate effect. The red-faced monks weren't angry with each other but elbowing for attention in a selfish and somewhat childish manner. Each one had his own sense of pleasure at his given circumstances and wanted to celebrate within the group because of those circumstances.

The classes I attended lasted a minimum of three hours each, and often we would train between four and six hours in a given day. Bongsan Talchum is known for its large, sweeping, energetic movements, which some say originated from a need to keep warm in the northern regions of the peninsula. Another suggestion that was brought up a number of times by various professors, instructors, and students was that this particular form was perhaps also used as a self-defense mechanism. Several arm movements near the head seemed to rush past the face and torso and push away from the body in a manner that could easily be read as protective.

The class was structured quite differently from the time I had spent in Andong. Instead of learning a core set of movements and then character dances, we were taught two specific dances: the energetic dance of the eight monks and the slow, deliberate cleansing dance of four young female shamans that opens every performance. The majority of the six-week class was spent on the dance of the eight monks with only one four-hour session spent on the cleansing dance.

When I received the invitation to the first-year conservatory class, I had anticipated watching for an afternoon as the students did their work. To my surprise, I was handed long white sleeve extensions to put over my wrists, was introduced to the group, and was then instructed to take the floor with everyone. The first series of footsteps were fairly easy to grasp, and I was pleased to see that I was keeping up with the group well. My work in Andong had been in private so I was less concerned about making a fool of myself there. Here in a classroom full of young people, though, I felt a very strong pressure to prove myself worthy of the invitation that had brought me.

Things started to go wrong when we added the arm movements to the freshly learned footsteps. The arm gestures were to send the sleeve extensions into specific arcing patterns that generally felt to work at cross-purposes with the accompanying kick or leap. Initially I felt that I was at least getting the ribbon-like sleeves to float gracefully above my head but, after a full hour of repetition I was simply lurching across the floor, the ribbons flailing erratically around my head and in the faces of those on all four sides of me.

I was motivated to practice throughout the next week by the fear of public humiliation. To my delight, though, the next series of movements in the dance seemed to flow, and I connected with them with much more ease that any other series. I happily skipped in the group circle swishing my sleeves back and forth over my head, leaped with both feet off the floor and landed in such a crouched position that my hips touched my ankles. Immediately from that crouched position I leaped back into the air and spun backward, leading with my left shoulder, reaching with my left hand, and arching my back until, airborne, by body stretched out fully and arced above the floor and then returned to solid ground first with my left foot followed by my right foot, which instantaneously began the pattern all over again.

During week five we put all of the pieces of the dance of the eight monks together into the full performance. We divided into groups of eight and were each assigned a number within our group. I was Monk 4, safely nestled in the middle of the pack, where I could participate most fully without being a liability. After performing in groups we were singled out to perform the entire dance on our own.

The final day in class and the day before the annual Bongsan Talchum performance at the National Theatre, we learned the shamanistic cleansing dance that opened each Bongsan event. At first it was a bit of a relief from the high jumps and deep crouching movements of the dance of the eight monks. We slid our feet along the floor and stretched our arms out toward each other. Instead of dancing in circles and trying to avoid crashing into each other as we had in the earlier classes, we lined up in two groups facing each other and wove our reaching and swaying back and forth among each other. We had to concentrate on sliding and reaching slowly, gracefully, and in unison as though we were manipulating enormous swaths of fabric hanging from our extended arms. The more we repeated extending the right side of our bodies and then slowly dragging the left side to meet the right in its progress the deeper into the lunges and stretches we were instructed to go. It wasn't long before our muscles began to shake and the fluidity that we were attempting to achieve was compromised. I was still concerned about making a fool of myself, but my classmates (while still quite willing to laugh at me when compelled to) continued to be helpful and accepting of my efforts and participation.

The strongest evidence of the way in which participating in the physical training gave me clearer access to the form, though, was in attending a required performance of Bongsan Talchum at one of the National Theatre venues several weeks into the course. This three-hour annual event was immediately different from any other Talchum performance that I have seen. First, it was a paid event and all others that I attended were free and open to the public. Second, I was unable to document the performance through video and still images because an official recording was being made for sale at a later date. This allowed me the luxury of taking notes throughout the performance instead of focusing on achieving quality technological documentation. This difference in activity during the event as well as the fact that I was attending with classmates that I knew instead of alone or with an interpreter allowed me to feel more of an active audience member. Third, the *madang* was an enclosed, atmosphere-controlled location, unlike the vast majority of performances, which are commonly held outside in a park pavilion. As the performance was about to begin, all of the doors were closed so that all outside noises were buffered and electronically controlled shades lowered over the windows so that lighting effects directed the attention of the audience throughout.

A processional traditionally begins each Talchum performance, and this particular parade circled the *madang* twice instead of the single round made in other locations. Each performer in the company circled the *madang* in his or her costume and waved happily to the audience. Several interacted directly with specific individuals in the crowd via handshakes, waves, and brief comments. After the processional concluded, four monks with red masks carried four young shamans on their backs and called out the opening lines to the performance before leaving the stage. The four shamans proceeded to perform a very slow, graceful series of moves to cleanse the *madang* and invite the local deities to observe or participate in the afternoon's celebration. I had just studied this particular dance sequence the day before and my response to it on this day was quite different than it had been at any of the other times I had audienced it. What previously had held the least amount of interest for me was suddenly full of meaning. As I watched I remembered stepping through the very same movements and recalled the discomfort that I'd felt attempting to keep my balance and focus while moving so slowly and the surprising amount of fatigue that followed from what originally seemed like such a simple part of the overall performance.

The next scene was an individual dance that I rarely saw again. The Prodigal Monk threw himself on the ground center-stage and methodologically lifted his hips off the ground, then one leg at a time before flipping over onto his stomach and writhing as though in pain. Even though I never learned this particular scene, because of the work I'd recently done with the slow-moving shaman dance, I was more aware of the technical skill that went into this new, even slower performance.

The next scene involved a series of monks dancing individually in the *madang*. This group of monks were all drunk and all violating their religious vows by leaving the monastery, indulging in forbidden behaviors such as drinking, participating in sexual relationships, and using prayer journeys throughout the country for personal entertainment. At the transitions from one dancer to the next, the incoming dancer would hit the dancer currently within the space with a peach tree branch. The wood of a peach tree is said to keep away all spirits, good or bad, so the monks were actually using a talisman to chase off their fellow clerics. The conclusion to the set of scenes involves all eight monks returning to the stage and dancing together in one of the most easily recognized dances of all Talchum, the dance of the eight monks.

The first performer took quite a bit of time talking to the audience and dancing through the core steps. Each subsequent monk spoke a few less lines and danced a little faster through the core. Within these individual dances, the performers seemed to have had the autonomy to improvise movements, as is common in Talchum and across folk performances. I recognized the basic steps and several of their variations as a theme throughout the many iterations presented, but there were a few that I had not seen before. One monk used larger, more flashy arm movements, another positioned his chest more prominently than any of the others, yet another used hopping steps on both feet and alternating on individual feet, a fourth used strong and somewhat "quirky" arm movements. The fact that I was able to differentiate among the monks and identify their choreography was exciting and satisfying in a way that surprised me.

As the performance continued I recognized the steps that I had been learning in class. This recognition allowed me to feel more a part of the performance, as audience members often know, move to, and call out lines within each scenario. My former illiteracy of these important elements excluded me from experiencing the events in ways that were similar to the rest of the audience, regardless of whether they tolerated my presence or even made the effort to make me feel comfortable and welcome with gifts of food or a cushion to sit on. The recognition also assisted in building a base of awareness that grew with each subsequent observation of Talchum performances in general. I now had a physical repertoire that I could identify, compare, and contrast as I moved through each other form throughout the next year. Further, I understood the rhythms that I was hearing from the musicians and the pattern of the chants being called out by the audience. Several of the audience members were classmates, and I enjoyed watching the way that they engaged in the call-and-response elements. Most of the other performances that I attended were on my own, so it was a new experience for me to enjoy this event as a member of a community, however peripheral that membership might have been.

The next scene involved a young woman and a monk. The first time I watched this performance I understood the scene to be a depraved monk seducing a young woman that he comes upon in his travels. However, after discussing the video with Chung Moon-sik, he explained that the monk was actually devout (Chung, October 29, 2010). In fact, the monk's black mask with white dots indicated that he had been sitting in the sun meditating so long that his skin tone had deepened dramatically and he had been sitting so still that flies had crawled across his face and defecated without his awareness.

However, the monk had a friend who had never been married because of his poor behavior. This friend, *Ch'wibari*, was jealous of the devout monk and set out to tarnish the monk's credibility. Everything that the rogue used to tempt the monk was ineffective until he introduced a young woman dressed in her finest and seen to be at her most beautiful. The monk relinquished his vows and began a romance with the young woman, making the rogue jealous. In an infrequently performed scene-within-a-scene, a peddler interrupts the threesome as he walks across the *madang* on his way to the next town. As the monk attempts to buy shoes from him, a little monkey, generally played by a young child, hops from the peddler's basket and climbs up the young woman's back. This parenthetical scene is most often cut from the longer program during the more common one-hour tourist performance. Once the peddler leaves, *Ch'wibari* reenters and instigates a fight between himself and the monk. The two men use choreographed movement involving the monk's walking stick and *Ch'wibari*'s peach tree branches to fight three times. The first two times the monk gets the better of *Ch'wibari*. Frustrated, the rogue uses an incantation to request aid from a dark spirit. During the third fight the influence of the dark spirit is noticed not by physical presence, but in the way that the monk is unable to defeat *Ch'wibari* again, which causes the monk to runs away in shame.

Ch'wibari offers the young woman a large amount of money to leave the monk and become his bride. She accepts the money and the proposal, but after she has *Ch'wibari*'s child, she runs away from her responsibilities and leaves the baby with his father. The rogue then carries on a humorous conversation with his son and vows to become more responsible.

Ch'wibari's actions caused the monk to break his vows, which is a serious offense and cannot be overlooked. Because of this, *Ch'wibari* must be punished, and the spirits send a lion to eat him. *Ch'wibari* dashes off stage as the lion enters with a different monk, who is committed to assisting the lion in carrying out its divine mission. This monk attempts to tame the lion so that it can fulfill its duties appropriately and efficiently. The dramatic and entertaining dance performed by two men under a length of furry costume and an enormous mask ends with the "lion" standing on its hind legs. This requires one man climbing onto the shoulders of the other man while both remain under the costume. This scene consistently garners the most positive audience response of any of the other scenes, which is likely why it concludes most hour-long versions of the performance. The tamer leads the lion off stage, presumably in pursuit of *Ch'wibari*, and in the abbreviated version, upon their exit a Western-style curtain call begins, where all of the performers gather in a straight line across the stage and take a bow. In the full-length performance, the next scene simply begins with the entrance of the next set of performers.

Bongsan Talchum is one of a number of forms that include at least one scene consisting of a variously sized group of noblemen who stand in a circle and pontificate. Very little action happens while the men are attempting to convince all of the other men in the group that they are the most noble among them. Each costume is exquisite in color and detailing, but each mask is deformed in obvious and often grotesque ways, such as phallic noses, misshapen mouths, hairy growths, and pox marks. These satirical masks symbolize the moral corruption hiding under the *Yangban*'s fancy clothing and comfortable lifestyle. The *Yangban*'s greed and cruelty are brought to light and put on display for the common people to judge, mock, and jeer (Suk, 2009).

In the lengthy final scene an old woman makes her way onto the stage. She and her husband have been separated for ten years since a battle took place within their village and they both ran in opposite directions in order to save their lives. (The Korean peninsula was frequently invaded by armies making their way through the country on their way to or from China, Japan, or the greater Pacific region, so stories of families separated by armed conflict abound in traditional performances.) During those ten years, the old woman has been searching endlessly and in a painfully meticulous manner, turning over every pebble, climbing trees, and looking under each leaf on each branch for evidence of her husband. She travels the entire country and moves systematically southward. At the same time, her husband is conducting a half-hearted search for his wife. In a moment unique to Bongsan Talchum, the band leader takes on the role of a barkeeper and, from his position with the other instrumentalists, asks the old man a series of questions. The old man's answers reveal that he is not truly interested in reuniting with his wife. For instance, the old man leaves a vague description of her so that if the barkeeper actually meets his wife, he would find it impossible to identify her. The band leader suggests that the old man call the old woman's name and, perhaps, she would answer him. The old man does so, but in a soft tone that barely carries off the stage. Eventually the old man and old woman find each other and enjoy their reunion until the old man's mistress arrives. The old woman is quite angry and instigates a physical fight. In an effort to get the old woman to leave his mistress alone, he hits her over the head with his fan and accidentally kills her. He grieves loudly and superficially, and his mistress quickly persuades him to leave the old woman where she is and to run away with her.

Another old man comes upon the old woman's body and recognizes her from her search for her husband. He assumes that she ran into thieves on the road and died at their hands. He feels compelled to find a shaman to aid the old woman's soul in transitioning to the afterworld. He leaves the stage briefly and returns with a shaman who has agreed to perform a ceremony that will aid the old woman's spirit in transitioning to the afterworld. The old man helps the shaman set up a small altar and then the shaman jumps and spins her way through the ceremony, ending the performance.

In a performance that included commentary that I audienced several weeks later (Bongsan Talchum), Jin Ok-sub, director of the Korea Cultural Heritage Foundation in Seoul, stated that this scene is often misinterpreted as tragic instead of being seen as a happy ending. In a personal interview, I asked Director Jin how this scene could be considered "*haehak*" (satisfactory or happy conclusion). His response was that there is humor within the conversation between the old woman and the mistress but that the true positive conclusion comes in the performance of the ritual for the old woman's death. In this ritual, reconciliation between the old woman, her husband, and his concubine is sought which brings the performance to a satisfactory, even happy ending (2010).

Engaging physically in Talchum assisted me throughout my time in Korea to develop a deeper understanding of the masked dance-drama as well as the Korean culture. Participating in training and then observing the annual professional performance of the full Bongsan Talchum repertoire was extremely beneficial in heightening my ability to recognize dance steps, identify themes throughout the performance, and place movements of particular importance in each scene. Sitting in the frigid morning air during the Lunar New Year was rewarding in that I had successfully navigated the city, located the performance, and taken video and still images despite the jostling crowd, but there was no emotional connection. I had a general idea of what was going on because of the physical nature of the form and some of the earlier reading I had done, but otherwise I was unable to access anything more meaningful or enjoyable. The afternoon at the National Theatre, though, my body moved in my chair with the rhythm of the music and I cheered on the performers with my classmates as cued by my training. Afterward, instead of packing up quickly and hiking to the nearest public transportation stop, I lingered and mingled with the crowd, met several performers, and socialized with my class. I experienced similar connections and meaningful exchanges with Hahoe and other styles' practitioners as well. Making an effort to learn the repertoire instead of simply reading or observing the archive had transformed my entire experience with Talchum and allowed me a glimpse of the community behind the masks.

NOTES

1. An enormous amount of time and effort has been spent in developing preservation methods and programs in Korea in order to ensure against the loss of history and culture during times of war and civil unrest. The choices made in regard to preservation methodology have become a topic of contention among scholars and practitioners, which quickly makes itself apparent in any inquiry of depth into the history of the form. For example, some who are supported by the government's patronage feel that the financial assistance is too meager for the amount of training, performing, and paperwork that is required of them. Others feel that the system is too easily manipulated by those who are more interested in personal gain. Even more have foundational concerns about the actual material thought to be preserved. Is anything more than a historical reference being preserved? Or does even that reference fall short and, instead, has something new been created instead of something precious being preserved?

2. Historically, Korean money was primarily in coin form. Each denomination coin had a square hole in the middle through which a string was run and tied for ease of carrying on a belt or to keep tidy in a larger traveling bag. Images of these coins abound in traditional and tourist shops throughout the country.

BIBLIOGRAPHY

Bongsan Talchum. Korea Cultural Heritage Foundation, Seoul. April 15, 2009.

Bongsan Training Sessions. Korea National University of the Arts, Seoul. March–April, 2009.

Ch'oe, Sun-U. "The Masks of Korea: The Case of Hahoe Mask." *Korea Journal* 19, no. 4 (April 1979): 45–50.

Chung, Moon-sik. Personal conversation. October 15, 2010.

Chung, Moon-sik. Personal conversation. October 29, 2010.

Clark, Bradford. Personal conversation. July 18, 2008.

Jin, Ok-sub. Personal interview. November 15, 2010.

Shin, Jun-ha. Personal conversation. January 12, 2009.

Suk, Jong Kwan. Personal Conversation. July 17, 2009.

Taylor, Diana. *The Archive and the Repertoire: Performing Cultural Memory in the Americas.* Durham, NC: Duke University Press, 2003.

CHAPTER 39

....

CIRCUS ECHOES
Dancing the Human-Equine Relationship
under the Millennial Big Top

....

KIM MARRA

In its last New York appearance to date (1998–99), the globe-trotting French equestrian dance-theater troupe Zingaro performed *Eclipse* under a round big top specially erected in Battery Park City and redolent with the earthy smells of horses working.[1] Playing on the show's black and white yin-yang patterning to particularly striking effect, two sequences inversely mirrored each other to set up a culminating synthesis enacted by the company's founder and principal performer, Clément Marty, who goes by the single name Bartabas.[2] In the first sequence, a diaphanously white-robed and fully hooded and masked dancer twirled à la Loie Fuller to the rising tempo of live Korean pansori music in the center of a pristine white sand circle roughly twenty-five feet in diameter. Long rods swathed in yards of fabric extended from the dancer's arms to make huge wings that fluttered sensuously like giant labial flower petals in a mobile Georgia O'Keefe painting. A glistening white stallion with flowing mane and tail galloped "at liberty" (sans rope, bridle, saddle, or rider) on the ring of dark tanbark footing encircling the white sand, gaining speed with the dancer but traveling in the opposite direction, to create an exhilarating vortex of human and equine motion. (See Figure 39.1.)

Above the music, we in the audience could hear the horse's pounding hooves and his breath pumping through the bellows of his lungs as his body stretched and contracted with each powerful stride. We could feel the air move and the ground tremble up through the scaffold seating as the force of a thousand pounds of beautifully conditioned athleticism charged past. He tossed his majestic head, returned our looks with fiery eye, and awed us with massive muscles surging under his satiny coat. As the dancer slowed, so did he, and when the dancer collapsed into an immobile heap of fabric in the circle's center, the horse turned and walked in to nuzzle the white folds until a flash of orange carrot peeked through. After he took his reward gently in his velvet lips, a lithe black female dancer gracefully unfolded herself from the white fabric and led him from the stage. The second sequence inverted these elements so that a black stallion and black robed figure spun the vortex in opposite directions, and a white female dancer emerged from folds of black fabric at the end.

FIGURE 39.1 The white vortex sequence in *Eclipse*. Still shot from *Eclipse* [videorecording], originally produced as a motion picture in 1998, published in DVD 2004.

Bartabas synthesized this human and equine mobility in the conjoined figures of centaur and Pegasus. Bestriding one of his famed longtime mounts, Vinaigre, a feisty grey-turned-white Lusitanian stallion, and wearing a shimmering black robe with his arms manipulating long wings as the female dancers had done, he executed a series of high level dressage ("horse ballet" or "horse dancing") moves. With his winged arms extended upward and his torso undulating side to side, he kept the horse's hind legs still while prompting him to march in place with his front legs and swerve his shoulders and neck back and forth with the wing movement. (See Figure 39.2.) He then urged Vinaigre forward, first into a Spanish walk, where each leg lifts high off the ground and reaches forward in extended movement, and then into a slow canter (a collected three-beat gallop) through a series of figure eights complete with flying lead changes (skipping motions where the horse changes the legs that lead the canter stride) and pirouettes (where the horse pivots 360 degrees on the hind legs while maintaining the canter) while he waved the wings like a bird in flight. These moves would be difficult enough to execute with the rider's hands on the reins, but Bartabas rode handless with the reins attached like an umbilical cord to a buckle at his waist. He directed Vinaigre entirely with his lower body; the horse's legs became his legs, and the two species melded into one dancer.

Producing an oeuvre of such works built around Bartabas's virtuosic equestrianism over three decades, Théâtre Equestre Zingaro has inspired other large touring equestrian performance companies, such as Cavalia, Cheval-Theatre, and Apassionata, all of which fuse circus with dance and theater to varying degrees and feature multicultural casts and a stable of exotic horse breeds.[3] These shows center on humans' relationship with horses and magnify the embodied presence and power of live performance by combining diverse human and equine bodies in dazzling feats of kinetic display. That human-animal connection and massive embodiedness gain special appeal in a millennial age when increasingly disembodied,

FIGURE 39.2 Bartabas on Vinaigre in *Eclipse* as winged Centaur/Pegasus. Still shot from *Eclipse* [videorecording], originally produced as a motion picture in 1998, published in DVD 2004.

denatured entertainment forms permeate the global marketplace. In contrast to the forced dominance/submission paradigms of traditional animal training evident in circus history, leading members of these equestrian companies are aligned with "ethological" or "natural" horsemanship (NH), which claims a deeper understanding of equine psychology and fosters a more harmonious and egalitarian relationship across species. While its roots extend back into Classical times, NH has flourished with the millennial need to reconnect with the natural world, and its spread has fueled the popularity of these performance troupes that practice it in various versions. Théâtre Equestre Zingaro's Bartabas may not use popular NH terminology, but his methods derive from some of the movement's leading European forebears. He is widely recognized as a consummate horseman able to achieve surpassing communication with his animals on the ground as well as in the saddle. Among directors of current large touring equestrian performance companies, he is also the most self-consciously artistic in his use of these methods, and his work is regarded most seriously in the worlds of dance and theater as well as spectacular entertainment. Bartabas places himself in the company of Peter Brook, Ariane Mnouchkine, and Pina Bausch.[4] In recognition of Théâtre Equestre Zingaro's cultural status, the French Ministry of Culture's theater department, not its circus department, sponsors Zingaro productions.[5]

Significantly, Bartabas disavows not only traditional circus but also classical dressage, even as echoes of both traditions resound powerfully in his work. From the French verb *dresser*, "to train," dressage was developed through Renaissance military exercises for optimum maneuverability of horses on the battlefield and elaborate equestrian displays of royal grandeur. It consists of a rigorous program of suppling and conditioning exercises to develop the horse's athleticism and responsiveness to the rider so the pair can execute lateral as well as forward movement through the various gaits. At the highest levels, it also involves controlled prancing, pivoting, rearing, leaping, and kicking. Dressage became a staple of circus bills in the late eighteenth and nineteenth centuries as former army officers, following Philip Astley (1742–1814), who is considered the founder of the modern circus, turned their equestrian skills into profitable entertainment. "With classical dressage," Bartabas asserts, "horses are taught more mechanically to do something very specific. They are under what I call permanent control. That's exactly the opposite of what I try to do . . . My aim is to bring out the personality of the horse as you might with people, to let the horses express themselves."[6] Bartabas teaches the horse moves from the classical dressage repertoire but in exceptionally individualized ways, exceeding the abilities of most other trainers in how he plumbs the particular animal's temperament and needs and allows for spontaneous energies and responses that cross the bounds of tradition. A more free-flowing art than classical dressage, his equestrianism is keyed to horse and rider's shared feelings in the moment rather than the formal exigencies of to-the-letter military precision.

This cultivation of individual equine expression is not an end in itself, however; it is a means of using the horse as a vehicle for expressing his own artistic vision. The circus not only bears a history of animal cruelty but also limits that artistic pursuit. "The circus," Bartabas says, "is always a series of acts, the lion tamer, the trapeze artist, the juggler. What holds them together is the show. But with Zingaro, it is the horse. I'm not interested in showing how well we handle horses. That's our job. I am only interested in saying things with the horses. With a horse, one can say as much as a dancer does through his body or a musician through his instrument."[7] Eschewing harsher training methods to express himself through horses, Bartabas nonetheless freely acknowledges that with equine partners "We are always moving back and forth in a dominated-dominant relationship; that way we are complicit with each other."[8] I wish to explore the flows of power that circulate through this equestrian art—along lines of gender, sexuality, race, and ethnicity as well as species and breed. What is he saying as a white European male director/choreographer when he swaps a black for a white female dancer for the same artistic reasons as swapping a black horse for a white one? How do horses compound or complicate such unabashed imperialistic exchanges and deployments of Pan-Asian stereotypes as those woven through a show like *Eclipse*? In the heat of training, rehearsal, and performance, how do the physical intensities and power dynamics of working with horses' bodies and personalities inform the work with human performers and vice-versa?

I bring my own embodied knowledge as a rider as well as my scholarly expertise as a theater historian to this investigation. Before I became a full-time academic, I pursued a serious competitive career in the cavalry-derived sport of three-day eventing, or equestrian triathalon (dressage, cross-country jumping, and stadium jumping), and I still ride for pleasure. Although the dressage in the three-day event is not as elevated as that practiced by *haute-école* (high-school) dressage specialists, I have some corporeal understanding of the moves Bartabas uses even as he pushes beyond the discipline's stricter limitations. From working with a number of riding teachers, including for several years with an Olympic veteran coach, I have also experienced the intensity of advanced equestrian pedagogy. The "circus echoes" of this essay's title mean not only those of the circus as a performance genre but also, and more fundamentally, echoes of *circus* as in "circle" and the incessant movement round and around the arena, the primary site of equestrian training, the incubus of what Bartabas calls complicity, where human and horse undertake a physically and mentally exacting and inherently dangerous dance of give and take. The human learns to give in order to get more from the horse, and the horse learns to give its all in response to human desires. The two species entwine in a form of sustained, mobile, rhythmic bodily contact in which the familiarity with each other's bodies exceeds what two humans, even two longtime human dance partners and lovers, would tolerate from one another.

Although this dance is enacted today primarily in coterie recreational circles of sport, art, and entertainment, in eras past its enactment has reverberated with enormous socio-economic and cultural consequences. Today's equestrian recreation re-creates to varying degrees how humans have derived power and mobility from horses and how horses have contributed to human efforts in ways that often go unremarked in historiography.[9] With high cultural aspirations and concerted invocations of history in practicing an age-old art, Bartabas and Théâtre Equestre Zingaro offer an extraordinarily revealing re-creation of the civilization-forging relationship between these two species. If the standard imperialist paradigm involves white Christian European heterosexual males conquering and enslaving bestialized, feminized, and racialized Others for power and self-definition, Bartabas's riding at once recapitulates and exacerbates these dynamics. To bestride a horse like Vinaigre, whose Lusitanian breed was originally derived from crossing native Iberian with Barb horses from Muslim North Africa to optimize war maneuverability, is, literally and figuratively, to bestride the Orient. In the exquisite equestrianism Bartabas practices, dominance comes, paradoxically, through an extreme degree of submission to this Other—that is, in the giving to in order to get more from the horse. The intercorporeal melding Bartabas achieves in the saddle, an ideal of NH approaches, counters older, often rougher models of horsemanship based on Cartesian dualism, which positioned the human male rider as the controlling mind and the horse as the obedient body, eliding the corporeal interconnectedness of the two species. The fully acknowledged and ardently pursued intimate physicality of Bartabas's riding thus highlights and intensifies the risk, inherent in the imperial encounter, of losing himself in the Other. Bartabas negotiates that risk through artistic mastery and autocratic self-positioning as a theatrical impresario. In so doing, he helps us imagine how horsemanship, in times when horses were an economic and military necessity, could increase the dialectical tension between conquering autonomous selfhood and self-dissolution through imperial contact that has driven the historical construction of white masculinity, and how what happened on horseback could inform what happened not only on roads and battlefields but also in bedrooms, offices, and backstage. These dynamics, whose cultural politics resound well beyond the horse and performing arts worlds, become most visible through an examination of the Zingaro lifestyle, training, and riding methods that produce both the individual dances of Bartabas's oeuvre and the larger historical human/equine dance.

LIVING AND WORSHIPPING THROUGH HORSES

The opening epigraph of the film of Théâtre Equestre Zingaro's inaugural production, *Cabaret Equestre*, captures the company's life/art ethos: "Its caravans, music and horses give it the appearance of a circus but here, the show is a ritual, the music a calling, and the love of horses a religion."[10] This first of several commercially produced French films Bartabas has made of his work, all with accompanying interviews explaining his aims and methods, is especially revealing. It was shot in 1990 at the company's home base in Fort d'Aubervilliers,

France, where three permutations of the live show of *Cabaret Equestre* had been running since 1984. Bartabas is credited with the conception, scenography, and *mise en scène* of the film. He intercuts sequences of the performance with scenes from the company's rehearsals and daily life in their stables and trailer camp around the theater. These scenes are admittedly staged for the camera and must be read as such, but they nevertheless offer a significant glimpse into the on- and offstage workings of the company. As Bartabas asserts, "Zingaro is not just a show, it is a way of life."[11] That lifestyle is seminal. "The true inspiration of the show is our daily work here. The theme is just a pretext."[12] So Bartabas told the *New York Times*' Alan Riding in an interview in Fort d'Aubervilliers about *Eclipse* in advance of the New York run.

Worship of horses for Théâtre Equestre Zingaro requires dwelling as much as possible in a romanticized nineteenth-century era when equestrianism still reigned over animal acts in the circus and horsepower still superseded mechanical power in the wider socioeconomic arena. The name Zingaro—"gypsy" in Spanish and Italian—is itself antiquarian in its reference to wandering, horse-loving nineteenth-century tribes. On the Fort d'Aubervilliers site, originally established in the 1840s as a military outpost of Paris, about fifty "gypsies" live in parked caravans and small wooden houses near the stables and what stands for the equine religion's cathedral: a 900-seat octagonal wooden performance pavilion containing the circular arena that was built on the model of Astley's first Parisian theater (1783).[13] Although Aubervilliers is a modern city of 75,000 with highly trafficked two-lane avenues bordering the fort, inside the high fence and gate of the wooded company compound, the lifestyle built around horses is antitechnological, that is, against technologies that would distance humans from the natural world and bodily sensation. Caravan living reflects Bartabas's devotion to embodied experience: "It's not because I can't afford a house," he explains. "Everything starts with the body. I can't imagine not feeling cold or heat." He laughs derisively at "people leading artistic revolutions on stage and going back to apartments on the Champs-Elysees."[14] Most importantly, he asserts, "If I live in a trailer, it's to live next to the horses."[15] Living close to the elements keeps the two species experientially closer together. For Bartabas, "Time spent with a horse is never time wasted; it's fundamental, it's the soul. One mustn't let oneself be caught in the dissipations and dispersals that characterize our flawed lives at this century's end. One mustn't give in to comfort."[16]

Bartabas pushes these themes even further in another film, *Mazeppa* (1993), which was made shortly after *Cabaret Equestre*, and which, although ostensibly fictional, offers additional insight into his vision. He not only provided the original idea, screenplay, and direction, but much of the film was shot on location at his training center in Fort d'Aubervilliers, France, used human and equine members of his company, and co-starred himself in the role of Romantic Era circus impresario Antonio Franconi (1738–1836). Because the film is set in the pre-Industrial era where Bartabas prefers to dwell, the historical characters and setting intriguingly allow for more overt expressions of the same philosophy and practices that are discernible in Théâtre Zingaro's real-life contemporary work. The aversion to technology manifests itself most obviously in Bartabas/Franconi's dread at having to submit to the installation of a semaphore telegraph machine on top of his circus pavilion because it is the highest structure in town. The machine groans and creaks ominously throughout the film as its unseen operator in the cupola below pulls its cabled timber arms into coded positions to transmit signals. It reaches into the sky like a weirdly articulated church cross, but stands opposite to the equine religion practiced on the temple's earthen circle below.

This semaphore system, devised by Claude Chappe during the French Revolution, was the first practical telecommunications system of the Industrial Age, precursor to the electronic media that would help render the horse and the embodied labor surrounding its use obsolete and give humans presumptively greater autonomous power over nature and Others. Thus the building itself as dressed for the film encapsulates the dialectical tensions between body and mind, nature and technology, and self-dissolution and control that Bartabas enacts with his company of human and equine members.

If the horse is a religion at Théâtre Equestre Zingaro, Bartabas presides over the company as its impresarial high priest, gathering human and equine followers and dictating rituals of daily life as well as performance. Company members join at his behest with the understanding that their commitment cannot just be for a short-term visit; they must immerse themselves fully with him in an "adventure of life." The austerity of accommodations (the caravans are antiquated models devoid of the luxury conveniences of today's motor coaches) becomes a test of their devotion to his vision. Ties of socioeconomic necessity also bind. Some longtime company members report having arrived at the Zingaro gate as paupers to whom Bartabas gave a livelihood and a home. The trade-off: "all live there as in a tribe with an uncontested leader . . . . One adapts, or one leaves."[17]

Bartabas freely attests that he chooses his people as he chooses his horses, following his instinct, "au coup de coeur," according to qualities that captivate or fascinate him.[18] The company bills itself as "a tribe roaming through cultural traditions" in part because of the diverse backgrounds of the equine and human members to whom its leader is drawn.[19] As David Williams learned in a visit, "Initially attracted by a face, en eye, a coat, a rhythm, a quality of attention, an aberrant behavioural energy, he works with horses of many different kinds: Andalusians, Lusitanians, Hackney ponies, Anglo-Arab crosses, Percherons, Friesians, Akhal-Tekes," all types infused with Eastern blood, the latter purely so (from Turkmenistan in Central Asia), and refined through selective breeding.[20] Like some of the human members of the troupe, the horses are often outcasts, with troubled histories, injuries, and behavior problems that need to be dealt with. Bartabas insists that his company members "are not puppets who have been chosen by somebody who had the idea to do this, so I must find the man or the horse who is capable of doing that movement—No . . . These people have very different rhythms and personalities, but then because they are here, through the work or even simply their presence, they give you ideas for tableaux for moments, or they just give you the idea themselves. And the horses, it's the same thing."[21] The particularities of what the humans and horses bring—different looks, colors, and physical capacities; different musical traditions, dances, and languages—all comprise his artistic material, there for his using, regardless of species, to create works for which he claims sole authorial credit. Typically, he wraps these diverse bodies with a skim coat of a single cultural tradition that he appropriates for the overarching visual and aural motifs of a given show, such as Indian Rajasthan for *Chimère*, Korean Pansori for *Eclipse*, or Tibetan for *Loungta*. Human company members are given no more cause to object to occlusions, elisions, or manipulations of their specific heritages than are equines. Drawing on scant research, he makes these shows mostly from his imagination—"I travel in my head," he says—pursuing his exoticizing and objectifying fascinations with individuals of both species, exerting mind over Orientalized matter as a director while absorbing the Orient through his body as a rider.[22]

Cross-species communal living facilitates bodily familiarities integral to Bartabas's artistic process. He organizes rituals of daily life inside the Zingaro compound around horse care and training. Given that company members live close to the elements with few modern conveniences, human ablutions are often juxtaposed with equine caretaking and pursued with some of the same liberties taken with and by the horses. In the behind-the-scenes sequences of the *Cabaret Equestre* film, grooms feed and water horses in the stable while a mother, Bartabas's wife, feeds their children breakfast in their caravan. Standing outdoors in the sunlight, two hairy men take turns washing each other's backs, much as a groom washes a horse in another scene. Stalls are mucked out in the stable after a night of horses relieving themselves. A bathrobed man steps outside his caravan and pees with little regard for privacy or care about proximity to what is presumably a shared living and eating space.

Such rustic, private-made-public acts endemic to the company lifestyle can put women in particularly compromising positions. Bartabas's young son climbs up on a stack of trunks to peek through a caravan window at the company's premiere female circus equestrienne, Eva Schakmundes, taking a bath. Turning her naked breast to the camera, she reaches for the inevitable exotic accoutrement, a snake conveniently coiled on a table next to the tub, and holds it up playfully to scare the boy away. The boy next appears examining a model of the Zingaro arena, suggesting he might be following in his father's footsteps. Directed by Bartabas, the camera treats viewers to an adult version of the boy's voyeurism in the cabaret performance as it follows the back seam of Schakmundes's fishnet-stockinged legs over her shapely buttocks flexing during her tumbling routine atop a white Percheron stallion. Private intrusions shape public acts.

As a trainer and rider orchestrating these performances, Bartabas assumes the position of "Le Maître," "The Master." This is how company members address his alter-ego Franconi in the fictional *Mazeppa* film, and articles on the Zingaro company website along with more critical journalistic accounts use the appellation for the real-life Bartabas as well.[23] The title refers not only to his titular authority as head of the company, but also to his supreme mastery of equestrian art, a mastery gained by learning the horse's nature and needs and giving himself over to them. In critic Alan Riding's phrase, he is "the company's guru-like artistic director" whom people follow because they believe him to possess special gifts with equines.[24] As Franconi tells his pupil, the painter Theodore Géricault, while the two watch the eponymous Zingaro, Bartabas's glorious black Friesian stallion descended from medieval chargers, sitting on his haunches alone in the arena like a king surveying his domain, "You ask who is my master? Where I get this finesse, this lightness, this severity? This sensation which troubles you? He [Zingaro] is my master. I confided my soul to his limbs. They say I am of another species, that I have supernatural powers, but all I want is to understand him."[25]

Bartabas carries that mystique to the extent of Franconi wearing a smooth horse hide mask over his whole head, like a quasi-equine version of the Phantom of the Opera, to cover up a disfiguring facial injury incurred in battle. (See Figure 39.3.) For Bartabas in real life, the disfiguring injury happened not to his face but to his legs at age seventeen when they were crushed in a motorcycle accident.[26] A shot in *Mazeppa* of Franconi walking away from the camera in form fitting breeches and tall boots reveals the crookedness in The Master's legs and the unevenness of his gait. This physical disfigurement intensifies his bond with horses who can so miraculously compensate for and exceed what the human body lacks. A scene in his retrospective film *Galop Arrière* (2010), a compendium of selections from his live productions, actually shows him in a wheel chair in the center of the arena and then cuts immediately to a curtain rising to reveal the prancing legs of a horse. The shot continues up the horse's body to show the figure of Bartabas in the saddle, "confiding [his] soul to

FIGURE 39.3 Bartabas as the masked Franconi with Miguel Bosé as Géricault. Still shot from Bartabas's film *Mazeppa* (1993), published in DVD 2005.

his [horse's] limbs." Given that he primarily performs on stallions, generally considered to be more powerful, expressive, and fiery than mares or geldings (neutered males), he also arrogates to himself their physical and sexual prowess.[27] With and through his equine partners, this broken man becomes a sublime and charismatic dancer and autocratic trainer and director.

INTERSPECIES PERFORMANCE PEDAGOGY

Through his extraordinary bond with horses, Bartabas has mastered to a profound degree those aspects of equine nature that NH practitioners contend make horses eminently trainable. According to Robert M. Miller, DVM, and Rick Lamb, "[d]ominance means leadership" and, as prey and herd animals, horses "seek and need leadership" for survival. "In horses alone of all domestic animals, the dominance hierarchy is established by the leader controlling the movements of its peers." Natural horsemanship teaches humans to become surrogate leaders who cause or inhibit equine movement. "Done correctly, the horse will soon recognize our authority and signal with its body language, 'Okay, you are in charge. I accept your leadership. I feel safest when I am with my leader. I *want* to be with you."[28] This is the key to how learning to "speak horse," or, in essence, to "become horse" by absorbing and giving in to its nature, leads to greater dominance. Horses evolved to be exceptionally responsive to stimuli so they can detect and flee from danger: they see monocularly out of both eyes independently and have near 180-degree peripheral vision front to back on each side; they also have superior night vision and highly developed senses of smell and hearing; their skin is so sensitive they can feel a fly land anywhere on their hair-covered bodies; their quick-twitch muscles are among the most highly developed in the animal kingdom; and, among land mammals, only the cheetah can run faster. These attributes mean they can respond to the slightest cue from their leader, whether their leader is standing on the ground or riding on their back. They will also trust their leader to reassure and thereby desensitize them to stimuli posited as nonthreatening, which is how they learn to tolerate gunfire, traffic, parades, circus clatter, etc. Natural horsemanship practitioners learn to sense and exploit these equine capacities and channel them to human purpose.[29]

The archetypal training scenario involves the trainer working the horse around him in a circle and gradually drawing the animal in closer, both physically and in terms of intimacy of communication and understanding. This pattern recurs through Bartabas's choreography, as in the vortex sequences in *Eclipse*. These emanate from the foundational work in *Cabaret Equestre* at his home theater, where his mastery of the horse's sensitivity and capacity for trust and desensitization became so advanced that he was able to entice the horse to perform savagery while he himself feigned blustering brutishness as a wild animal tamer. He works Zingaro around the circle, yelling, running, leaping, spitting, and cracking a whip, when the horse is actually responding to the subtler angles and movements of his leader's body. The whip, which never touches the horse, seems to have the primary effect, but Zingaro takes more direction from the smaller stick in his master's other hand, the so-called carrot stick in NH parlance, that Bartabas uses to lead the horse around him. Never taking his eyes off Bartabas, the horse knows exactly when to run, pivot, stand with his front hooves on the circle's edge, and bare his impressive teeth to mock bite. He lies down on cue and waits for the signal to sit up on his haunches and let Bartabas sit against his front legs. The Master draws Zingaro's huge head and neck around him while clownishly proffering treats. (See Figure 39.4.) A more serious version of that equine embrace with the horse's massively rippling, satiny ebony body encircling Bartabas's huddled slender white form has become an iconic tableau painted on the exterior wall of the Théâtre Zingaro in Fort d'Aubervilliers and on the cover of Bartabas's retrospective DVD *Galop Arrière*. (See Figure 39.5.) It beautifully emblematizes the paradox of dominance through submission: Zingaro crouches "on top," yet Bartabas remains in control of the encounter, issuing commands and dispensing rewards; the mightily well endowed stallion is in the more feminine and, as his breeding most literally indicates, Orientalized position.[30] Nevertheless, given the horse's size and fundamental unpredictability, Bartabas places himself at considerable risk to attain this intimacy and strike such a vulnerable, sensual, even homoerotically suggestive pose, a tantalizing but only seeming inversion of commanding equestrianism from the saddle.

Dynamics of this human/equine complicity provocatively inform interhuman and cross-racial relations in the film *Mazeppa*. The film turns on the triangulated relationship among Bartabas/Franconi, the Romantic painter Theodore Géricault, played by the youthful and handsome white French cinema star Miguel Bosé, and Franconi's premiere circus equestrienne and mistress, the exotic Alexandrine, played by the same Eva Schakmundes of *Cabaret Equestre*, who was a featured performer in Théâtre Equestre Zingaro for ten years. From the opening moments, we see Géricault desperate to understand horses, to get inside them and

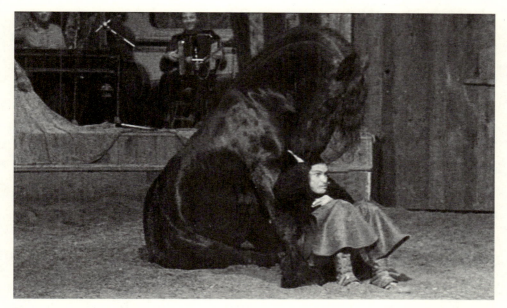

FIGURE 39.4 Bartabas and Zingaro in *Cabaret Equestre*. Still shot from *Cabaret Equestre* [videorecording], originally filmed in 1990, published in DVD in 2004.

FIGURE 39.5 Bartabas being interviewed on the steps outside his theater in Fort D'Aubervilliers, France, with the exterior wall painting of Zingaro wrapped around him. Still shot from "Entretien avec Bartabas" accompanying the film *Galop Arrière: Un Film de Bartabas*, MK2 Editions. 2010.

them inside him, even drinking their blood in an abattoir, so he can capture them more fully in his painting. To deepen his education, he seeks out Franconi, who invites him into the circus. At a company banquet in the arena, he is introduced to Bartabas/Franconi's imperial world order. A motley crew of subservient, culturally diverse company members in "savage" gypsy makeup tears into cooked flesh around a large table. The Master presides with his dark, sultry, Orientalized mistress beside him and his white, blue-eyed, light-haired European wife Mouste (played by Bartabas's actual wife, Brigitte Marty) seated stoically at the opposite end of the banquet. In this preindustrial, prefeminist setting, the Master adopts an air of total entitlement. He can consort with a favorite exotic human female performer just as he can ride a favorite fancy horse while expecting his wife and other company members to sit by like secondary mounts waiting attentively in their stalls for their master's attention.

During postprandial conversation, the disfigured veteran behind the mask cautions his handsome young pupil: "Your need to be seen will keep you from seeing . . . You canter for pleasure to charm the girls who see you, that's all. For me to understand a horse is to flow into the slowness of its soul." Bartabas/Franconi presents dressage not just as a form of showing off and courting but as a mode of lovemaking, underscoring the more deeply embodied and profoundly sexualized as well as gendered aspects of the riding he practices: "Imagine lusting heatedly after someone only to realize you missed out on the pleasure. Speed won't get you anywhere, slowness will." He offers to show Géricault "the secret of the canter," which, he contends, is the most difficult to manage of the horse's three basic gaits. As Bartabas/Franconi demonstrates dressage moves on Vinaigre and another Lusitanian stallion, Quixote, while Géricault struggles to sculpt a horse with clay on a pedestal in the center of the arena, The Master continues in a voice-over:

> Free your lover from your embrace. Study her. Learn from her … learn why you want her … learn to be generous. Want only what she wants. It's the same on horseback. I don't impose. I propose. In short, we make love [*En somme, nous fornicons*] passionately. Be excessive but respect your horse's wants. Question your mentors but never your horse. Force your hand to be patient. Let your horse teach you how. Be humble.

Employing this lovemaking analogy, Bartabas/Franconi effectively equates the woman with the horse and makes masculinity about gaining dominance over both through submission: Accede to their wants to learn their natures and then use that knowledge to manipulate them. This assumes that the woman, like the horse, will want to accept the man as her leader as a matter of instinct so that he can guide by soft and subtle proposition rather than forced imposition of his will.

Gaining this control requires an intensely embodied, receptive connection to the Other. Bartabas/Franconi's art of horsemanship is all about feel, which is notoriously difficult to acquire and teach. In one riding lesson scene, an impatient, imperious Master yells down from his office window to a bumbling pupil working a horse in the arena below: "Feel it, for God's sake!" The desired sensations between horse and rider are inarticulable and constantly shifting; they must be coordinated through intimate bodily familiarity gained through years of partnership, hard work, and mutual sweat. Ultimately, the Master's lessons about feel and embodied artistry are lost on Géricault, who pursues fame and immortality in the realm of looking, being seen, and practicing visual art, as he tries to capture in painting and sculpture that which Bartabas/Franconi knows cannot be fixed. For The Master, visual art is both more superficial and dangerously limiting; indeed, the calls of vanity and attempts at fixity distract from true experience and ultimately kill the living relation and the object of desire. Géricault desperately wants The Master's knowledge of horses but also needs to keep his subjects at a distance to paint them. He complains to his teacher, "You are suffocating me in their flesh. It's less important to work a horse's muscles than to sculpt them." Unable to acquire the necessary feel of his partner, he fails to know either the woman or the horse sufficiently and thereby gain the dominance that would support his own masculine sense of selfhood. Instead, he unwittingly loses himself through his encounters with the Other in Bartabas/ Franconi's circus imperium.

The trouble begins when Géricault and Alexandrine fall prey to looking at each other with mutual admiration of their physical beauty while she holds her performance partner, a gleaming beefy white Percheron stallion, on a lead for a blacksmith to shoe him, and Géricault tries to paint the scene. Pressing her chest sensuously against the underside of the horse's neck and passing her head and long black tresses through the horse's long white mane, she performs a visual merger of woman and horse that starts to confuse Géricault about his object of desire and hence about his own sexual, gender, and race/species identity. (See Figure 39.6.) Mocking laughter from the surrounding company members led by an androgynous clown and a male transvestite dancer signals that this will not be the easy, ego-affirming dalliance to which the Romantic Lothario painter is accustomed. The merger of woman and horse continues as he follows her deeper into the underground stable and she kisses him while they fondle a foal.

Aware of his mistress pupil's transgressive desire, Bartabas/Franconi disciplines her in the arena of equestrian pedagogy where he simultaneously trains human and equine bodies. He puts her on a steed he is schooling in the capriole, a *haute-école* dance maneuver

FIGURE 39.6 Eva Schakmundes as Alexandrine merging with her white Percheron stallion while Géricault tries to paint the scene in the film *Mazeppa*. Still shot from Bartabas's film *Mazeppa* (1993), published in DVD in 2005.

originally devised for warfare, in which the animal, on command, leaps high in the air and kicks out violently with its hind legs. After barking out the instructions so familiar to riding students, "Head up! Heels down!" he cracks a long whip to cue the horse. Each of the several times he makes the pair repeat the exercise, Alexandrine's torso and head snap punishingly backward with the force of her mount's thrust, and she comes down painfully askew on the saddle's protruding pommel with her crotch. The rigor of the session is directed more at the woman than her mount; the horse must bear the brunt of the Master's feelings toward his mistress.

For his part, Géricault, seeking to appease The Master, tries to discipline his own loins by having his legs stretched excruciatingly around a barrel in a crude and masochistic attempt to deepen and improve his seat for horseback riding. His effort proves futile, and The Master dismisses him. He retreats into visual art, filling his studio with frenzied efforts to capture horses' movement on canvas. Having failed in the equestrian art of feel, he struggles as their surging, muscular bodies overrun his mind and hands. In a deeply disturbing sequence, he sets up his easel in a stable where numerous children with Down syndrome sit on stacks of straw bales to watch an equine breeding session conducted by burly male handlers. While one man subdues the mare with a device called a twitch that grasps her upper lip in a twist of rope, another prepares her for the mating by pushing his lubricated fist into her vagina to elicit a spurt of liquid. He signals for the approach of the stallion, a massive grey Percheron draught horse like the one Alexandrine merged with in the earlier blacksmith scene. Nickering and squealing with excitement, the stallion first sniffs the mare fiercely and then lifts his giant front end to mount her with surprising gentleness, nuzzling her and laying his heavy head and neck over her back and side. As the children squirm and giggle trying to make sense of what they are seeing and feeling, so does Géricault seem confused; his eyes widen madly, and his body sweats and trembles with apparent uncertainty about what parts of the mating arouse him.

Although the character Franconi's orchestration is not explicitly apparent in this scene, Bartabas's directorial manipulations raise provocative questions of voyeurism and exploitation as well as domination. In "de la piste a l'ecran" ("from arena to screen"), the interview with Bartabas included on the published DVD version of the film, the director expresses his desire to bring greater visibility to the "heavy horses" of France, most notably the two-ton Percherons bred for agricultural and military labor and meat at the national stud farms (Les Haras Nationaux). This scene appears to have been shot in one of the stud farms' cavernous historic brick barns. Bartabas's camera zooms in on equine labor and meat as he shoots from the ground looking through the mare's legs to capture the huge genitals of the approaching stallion and then takes close-ups of the copulation from multiple angles. A shot from the stallion's rear shows his enormously powerful buttocks contracting rhythmically with the strain of penetration and ejaculation. The sound of the animal's heavy breathing further registers his hard effort. In the interview, Bartabas remarks on how the stallion manager's pride and the horse's putative willingness to repeat this act served the filming process: "I said to myself after each mating I will need to wait fifteen minutes so they can start the thing again. But they said no, it's good, five minutes is enough, I know him well, he's already done it twelve times consecutively. They really took pleasure, they were proud that their horse could mate a mare like that."[31] Masculine identification with the horse's sexual prowess informs the exploitive history of using these animals for human endeavors, which Bartabas's filmmaking compounds. Making the children with Down syndrome complicit in the scene's voyeurism adds even more troubling layers to the exploitation. They are not credited in the film, nor are they referred to in the interview, and public documentation of how they became involved remains elusive. At the very least their presence indicates the extreme limits to which Bartabas goes to make an artistic point about Géricault's self-dissolution.

Bartabas goes to more directorial extremes in his alter-ego Franconi's machinations to emasculate Géricault as an artist and a romantic rival. In a sadistically manipulative gesture of "want[ing] only what she wants," The Master concedes to Alexandrine's wish for him to commission Géricault to paint her portrait. He pointedly asks this of the painter unmasked, indicating that he needs Géricault to help him make her feel beautiful in a way that he with his horribly disfigured face cannot. He knows this will be a perilous challenge, if not an impossible test of loyalty. As Mouste narrates in a voice-over "To push his student to his utmost limits, that's what counted for him. But did he doubt that the void into which he had cast Géricault would cast all peace from the painter's soul?" When Alexandrine poses for him, Géricault can see and sketch only horses. Frantic sounds of horses mating fill his ears. He turns from the canvas and his model in despair. The voice-over continues: "They hoped to finish their task by helping each other. The Master was the first to realize they would hurt each other. He did nothing to stop them." Alexandrine tries to console Géricault, which leads to lovemaking in the stable, their bodies upright, horse-like. The camera highlights the cross-species analogy by closing in on the painter's thrusting naked buttocks as it did on those of the mighty Percheron stallion in the earlier breeding scene. The Master confronts the two lovers naked on their knees like Adam and Eve caught before an angry God in the Garden. Not only did his mistress succumb to the charms of a younger, undeformed man, she did so trying to help that man achieve success in the realm of visual art because she seeks the stardom of beauty. She has betrayed both her Master and his equestrian art of feel.

Bartabas/Franconi dances an even crueler revenge on horseback. Amid a raging thunderstorm with the Semaphore on the rooftop creaking its weirdly articulated arms against a lightning-lit sky, he rides Vinaigre handless indoors on the circular floor below. The pair perform many of the same moves they would later do in the Pegasus/Centaur sequence in *Eclipse*, including the high-stepping Spanish walk and weaving movements and pirouettes at the canter, but working into a faster tempo to convey fiercer emotions. As horse and rider dance inside, Géricault, barefoot in a smock, walks all over his canvases stretched out over the cobblestones in the pouring rain while gazing upward, hailing the creaking Semaphore, and laughing madly. Linking the paintings below with the machine above, the scene captures his insanity over his art and desire for widespread fame. It also portends a scary future when flesh-to-flesh contact diminishes, and disembodied images that travel via telecommunications media immune to the elements hold more sway over modern reality. This commentary registers in Bartabas/Franconi's choreography as the film intercuts indoor and outdoor scenes. Rather than the flowing Pegasus wings he would undulate in *Eclipse*, his arms in this dance, whirling in shirt sleeves, enact more rapid and angular movements that mimic the Semaphore arms above. He mocks the airy signals with his upper limbs while connecting with the horse so efficaciously through his seat, loins, and legs. The choreography begins with his arms alternately bending sharply from the elbow toward and away from his head, like the Semaphore's two indicator arms rotating into coded positions at their respective ends of the larger crossbeam. As his hands pass in front of his face, he uses flattened palms deliberately to cover and uncover his eyes in an apparent "I told you so" about the perils of looking and not seeing, which he attributes to vanity and the superficial images and telecommunications that propitiate it.

A distraught Alexandrine watches Bartabas/Franconi and Vinaigre through a window from an outdoor upper balcony of the arena. With the driving rain streaming down her imploring face, she pounds on the glass begging for The Master to let her back in. The more she begs, the fiercer his ride on Vinaigre becomes. Clip 39.1 shows him spurring the horse faster through pirouettes that change direction and then driving the horse forward with his legs while his seat and weight hold him back. These contraindications are used to get the horse's hind legs under him to increase power and impulsion. Especially in a hot-tempered horse like Vinaigre, they can also cause agitation, which Bartabas exploits to express the high emotion of the scene. Vinaigre starts hopping back and forth from back to front legs, building up momentum, until he lifts his front legs off the ground and jumps only from his back legs, an impressive *haute-école* move called a *courbette*. Alexandrine watches as The Master brings Vinaigre to a halt in the center of the circle and sits impassively in the saddle, utterly impervious to her pleas, while the sweating horse breathes heavily underneath him. The camera pans the horse from the bottom up, lingering over his large genitals (penis completely retracted into the sheath), heaving belly, and flaring nostrils to register the rider's masculine mastery and victory over the desire that had made him vulnerable to an exotic woman's vanity. Realizing her pleas are futile, Alexandrine withdraws from the window and climbs to the roof peak, where she reaches for the Semaphore, perhaps vainly to signal for help. Bartabas/Franconi resolutely holds his impassive pose atop his panting steed, even as Géricault's mad cackle shifts into a prolonged scream of horror watching Alexandrine hang by her hands from the Semaphore's seesawing crossbeam and then let go, plummeting several stories to her death. When she crashes, Géricault sees not her form but an agonizing close-up on a white horse coming down in slow motion with the side of its head and neck taking the final impact as it hits the ground.

Mazeppa's cross-species, cross-racial power dynamics of gender and sexuality torque inversely in Géricault's final scene for which the film is named. In the original drama of *Mazeppa*, based on the poem by Byron and played across theatrical and circus stages in England, France, and the United States throughout the nineteenth century, a handsome, well-born Ukranian page adept on horseback is punished for consorting with an older count's exotic young wife ("She had the Asiatic eye") by being tied naked belly up and backward on an untamed steed and sent galloping into the wilderness.[32] Along with the obvious danger and painfulness of being tied down to an untethered live animal with one's limbs wrenched backward, the punishment consists in the emasculating humiliation for a conquering white male equestrian of that pridefully horse-powered Romantic era to be put on the horse against his will in such an utterly powerless position. The historical Géricault famously painted the moment when the horse, a beautifully muscled coppery Arabian on his 1823 canvas, launches himself up a river bank with the naked Mazeppa still lashed supine to his back but revived by the water and flexing his strong thighs and chiseled

CLIP 39.1 Bartabas as Franconi dancing his revenge on Vinaigre in the film *Mazeppa* (1993), published in DVD in 2005.

CLIP 39.2 Scene of the Mazeppata: Géricault (Miguel Bosé) tied to the galloping horse on the treadmill in Bartabas's film *Mazeppa* (1993), published in DVD in 2005.

abdomen to suggest the sensual, if not erotic, possibilities of the power inversion.[33] On late nineteenth-century circus and melodramatic stages, the "wild ride" was enacted at least partly on a treadmill backed by a moving panorama and other theatrical effects.[34] Bartabas's film uses some of that stage machinery in a sequence framed as the delirious nightmare of a sickly and insane Géricault; the once dashing white Lothario is now spectacularly dehumanized and emasculated.

The sequence begins with Géricault sweating abed in his studio hallucinating images of horse-torturing paraphernalia, such as a strangling carriage harness, castration shears, and even the twitch rope around the mare's upper lip as though he were the one about to be bred. His own subjectivity has totally collapsed into his confusion of equine and human objects of desire. He laments to his Moroccan-clad black servant, "I am using myself," meaning, among other connotations, he must put himself in the scene in order to paint, which is how he is about to paint Mazeppa. Drunken revelers push a horse up multiple flights of stone steps to him in the studio—not exactly Byron's "fiery steed," but a coarser spotted Appaloosa more like those tolerant veterans of the sawdust circus arenas who gamely endured these human follies. When the horse balks at ascending the last flight, the reveler heave-ho-ing with his shoulder against the animal's haunches gooses him in the anus with a wine bottle for extra motivation, a portent of the penetration haunting the painter's imaginings. As the horse is tied to a treadmill already set up in the studio, other revelers strip Géricault and lift him by ropes strung through pulleys on the ceiling out of bed and onto the horse, securing him belly up and backward in the Mazeppa position. The treadmill cranks up to speed, the horse obligingly moves into a gallop, the revelers whoop, the black servant laughs hysterically at his master. Clip 39.2 shows the painter's grimaces of pain turning almost to smiles of homoerotic ecstasy in bondage as he arches over the horse's back, and its massively muscular hindquarters bump against his own with each powerful stride. In his delirium, Géricault sees the curtains parting to reveal the "wild ride" in progress as though he is performing at Franconi's circus. Prominently seated in the audience applauding this humiliation is the masked Master, mistress Alexandrine and wife Mouste on either side, surrounded by his gypsy troupe, like a Roman emperor with his retinue in his royal box at the Colosseum. (See Figures 39.7 and 39.8.) Mouste comments on Géricault's position in a voice-over: "It's not the body of a rider, it's a mane of twisted muscles. A clandestine act of love between man and animal."

Corporeal Intimacies of Equestrian Dancing

In diametrical contrast to this powerless, emasculating Mazeppa pose, Bartabas/Franconi brandishes his signature equestrian dance, the famed *galop arrière* or "backward canter." With this move, his embodied equestrian art of feel reaches its zenith. It is the most difficult and most complicated of *haute-école* exercises, according to its self-professed originator, the

FIGURE 39.7 Bartabas as Franconi flanked like a Roman Emperor by Alexandrine (Eva Schakmundes) and Mouste (Brigitte Marty) and surrounded by his company members applauding Géricault tied to the galloping horse in *Mazeppa*. Still shot from Bartabas's film *Mazeppa* (1993), published in DVD in 2005.

FIGURE 39.8 Miguel Bosé as Géricault lashed to the galloping horse on a treadmill in Franconi's Theater for the pleasure of The Master and his retinue. Still shot from Bartabas's film *Mazeppa* (1993), published in DVD in 2005.

renowned English-born French riding master James Fillis (1834–1913), whose teachings and writings have influenced generations of dressage riders. Bartabas claims to be only the second rider since Fillis to have achieved it. He did so with his equine partner Quixote, whom he calls "Quichotte," a sumptuously athletic black stallion endowed, according to his biographer, with the "haunches of a rugbyman and head carriage of an aristocrat."[35] Their backward canter dances recur in all the works in which this duo appears together, including *Cabaret Equestre*, *Mazeppa*, and *Eclipse*, and they are prominently excerpted in Bartabas's more recently released retrospective film, *Galop Arrière* (2010), whose title becomes the very term he uses to summarize his whole career. His partner Quichotte descends from the Turkish and North African Barb-derived black Lusitano horses of the Coudelario Ortigão Costa stud farm north of Lisbon, Portugal.[36] Bred originally for bullfighting for their beauty, impressive movement, strength, maneuverability, and gentle personalities and tractability, these animals also excel in dressage. Like many of his horses, Quichotte came to Bartabas relatively cheaply as a reject, in this case because his famous *corrida* rider, Manuel Jorge de Oliveira, did not like him, did not understand him, and found him "too cold."[37] But Bartabas managed to suss out his personality and arouse his extraordinary talents to achieve the *galop arrière*, which, unlike other dressage moves that extend the horse's natural movement, is considered "unnatural"—i.e., purely the result of human training and riding. It cannot come from force, but only from the subtlest, most delicate, ergonomically coordinated interspecies communication. As such, it is the supreme example of giving in to in order to get more from the horse, of attaining total dominance through submission. To use Bartabas/Franconi's fornication analogy, if the Mazeppa ride is "taking it up the rear" entirely at the whim of a "wild" low Other, the reverse canter is being "on top" of the embodied black Orient in the most dexterous of ways.

Understanding how the two bodies articulate together in this imperial conjugal relation requires some technical knowledge of equine movement. As prey animals, horses are built to run; the gallop is ordinarily their fastest, most forward-moving, ground-covering gait. In most riding situations, the fast gallop is impractical; the three basic gaits for nonracing horse sports are the walk, trot, and canter, which is a more modulated, controlled gallop. At the canter (or gallop), the horse is said to be "leading" with either his left or right front leg. The terminology is confusing because the leading leg is actually the last to hit the ground in the horse's stride. Since the motive power originates from the hind end, a horse cantering "on the left lead" strikes the ground first with his right hind leg, then with his left hind and right front paired diagonally, then lastly with the left front, making the canter a three-beat gait. There is a split second in which all four legs are off the ground as the right hind comes forward again to start the next stride.[38] Horses can modulate their speed to some degree within each gait by slowing the rhythm and shortening the stride, but to slow down markedly from a gallop or canter, a horse would naturally "break gait" and drop into a trot or walk where the legs hit the ground in different beats. They have least versatility in reverse, and generally will only back up at the walk; when frightened, their preferred mode is to pivot on a dime and bolt forward in the opposite direction, as countless riders who have been left sitting in the dirt from horses darting out from under them can attest.

Because of how the horse moves, it is far easier for the rider to get him to gallop with extreme speed than to canter with extreme slowness. Maintaining the canter, a modulation of his most forward-moving gait, while slowing the horse's speed to the points where he would naturally trot, walk, and halt is a tremendous riding and training challenge, increasing in magnitude of difficulty with increasing slowness and reaching mind-boggling near-impossibility when carried into reverse. This is why Bartabas/Franconi bases his superior mastery on perfecting the canter and achieving slowness rather than eliciting faster speed. To slow the speed progressively while maintaining the canter, the rider cannot simply keep urging forward with the legs and seat while pulling back harder on the reins, which can lead to stiffness, resistance, and frustration. Horse and rider need to train into what the French call *rassembler*, which Fillis defines as "the complete equilibrium of the horse in all his movements." In the *rassembler*, the horse's and rider's centers of gravity are perfectly aligned; the horse's hind end is well under him, providing impulsion; his back is relaxed; and he is not pulling on the rider's hands but is carrying himself light on the reins with his neck arched, forehead at or just above the vertical, jaw soft and chewing on the bit, responsive to the rider's slightest indication.[39] To achieve and sustain the *rassembler*, the rider's seat must maintain full and supple contact with the horse through the saddle, for it is the subtle shifts in weight coordinated with the leg aids that most effectively communicate. Sociologist and equestrian Ann Game describes how the rider must absorb the bounding movement of the canter in order to stay deeply seated:

> Unless you allow for the connection you cannot do it. If the body is not to bump, it must be relaxed, open and receptive to the rhythm. It feels as if you are soaking the movement up as you drop into it, drop into the horse, as the horse rises into you, rise and fall now contained within your body, within your horse-human body, the very connection generating the movement. The implications of this process are wondrous, even though the riding manuals studiously avoid the obvious sexual connotations of the relation. With echoes of Leda and the Swan, riding involves an "absorption" of movement with "loins" and "seat": absorbing horse, taking horse into your body.[40]

The slower the canter, the deeper and more subtle that absorption as the rider spreads what Fillis delicately calls "the fork," the area comprising the pubic and seat bones and inner thighs, further over the saddle, while dexterously applying the legs to get the horse to shorten his stride without breaking gait. With supple, rhythmic, and precise squeezes down around the horse's sides, the lower legs not only create impulsion but effectively pull the horse further up into the rider, where he is being controlled by the seat and not the hands. The shorter the horse's stride becomes, the less ground he covers until, with gradual training, he canters in place.

The movement from cantering in place to cantering in reverse is where the horse-rider communication becomes the most subtle and mutually sensitive. Fillis writes:

> [W]hen my horse is cantering on one spot, with such ease and lightness that I have no need for the reins, I try to bring him back an inch or two by my seat and legs and not the reins. While my legs are raising the horse, I seize the moment when he is in the air to carry my seat back. I change the position of my seat, and not that of the upper part of my body, by taking nearly all my weight off my stirrups to put it on my buttocks. The movement of the horse is so great, at a moment when he is in suspension, that a movement of the rider is sufficient to make him gain a little ground to the rear, which is enough to begin the canter to the rear. By repeating and gradually increasing these effects every day, we succeed in obtaining the canter to the rear as I have described.[41]

Fillis concentrates on using that crucial moment of suspension between strides of the canter when all four of the horse's legs are off the ground: "It can be seized only with great difficulty, and then we can get everything out of a horse, because he is in the air. A puff of wind can displace him."[42] In that crucial moment of suspension, the horse is simultaneously most up into and most susceptible to the rider; it is the very pinnacle, for the rider, of attaining dominance through submission.

Bartabas shows off these techniques in a stunning flashback in *Mazeppa*, where Mouste recalls how Franconi won her when he was young and still had a face. He wagers with her army officer father that he can canter so slowly it will take one hour to cross a courtyard expanse that is less than fifty yards wide. The scene was filmed in the famous Colbert courtyard of France's premiere national stud farm, the Haras National du Pin in Orne, Normandy, which was originally commissioned by Louis XIV. [43] The façade of the historic neoclassical chateau of this "Versailles for Horses" serves as the scene's backdrop. A large clock mounted in the façade's central peak ticks loudly overhead while Mouste watches from an upstairs window, and her father and other mounted cavalry officers stand sternly abreast in the courtyard below. Resplendent in Napoleonic military regalia astride Quichotte, Bartabas/Franconi, takes the full hour to make the cross in front of this line-up by delicately controlling the canter to gain only a few inches per stride. The officers' begrudging admiration turns to dumbfounded awe when he then exceeds the terms of what seemed an impossible bet by moving back across the same width of the courtyard at the reverse canter. A long cavalry line enters in formation, and riders salute the conquering hero as he and Quichotte exit toward the camera through the military ranks.

This demonstration of supreme masculine equestrian prowess becomes more legible as a "clandestine act of love between man and animal" when Bartabas and Quichotte dance the slow perfection of their canter on the seminal circle in the penultimate scene of *Cabaret Equestre*. The scene is structured in several movement sequences framed by the slow-tempo sounds of music from instruments connected to horses' bodies: a hammer striking a blacksmith's anvil like a chime and a horsehair bow drawn languorously across the strings of a cello. In each movement sequence, Bartabas and Quichotte turn in from the larger arena circle onto a smaller circular wooden dance floor, barely ten feet in diameter, laid down in the center and connected to the entrance by a flat hanamichi-like wooden ramp. The primary sounds during the dancing, apart from the clicking of the horse chewing his bit, are those of the horse's metal-shod hooves striking the wooden floor. Usually in dressage, the horse dances on soft, loose footing; we see the precision of the leg movements but do not hear them. Here the sharp sounds of the hoof strikes accentuate that precision and its virtuosity. In the first of two canter sequences, he enters on the right lead, each hoof striking in the proper order with exquisite visible and audible clarity: left hind, then right hind and left front in a diagonal pair, then right front—three beats in each stride, da-da-dum. After circling to the right, he turns through the circle center and changes leads to the left lead, shifting to strike first with the right hind, then left hind and right front in a diagonal pair, then left front. To cue the change of leads at the moment of suspension between strides, Bartabas deftly applies his lower legs to specific pressure points on Quichotte's sides with a corresponding almost imperceptibly light shift in pressure on the bit in the horse's mouth through the reins. Keeping the same rhythm, he turns the horse tighter and tighter to the left in the small circle until Quichotte is pirouetting on the left hind hoof in the circle center. He then gently pushes the horse to the small circle's edge and turns him up the circle's center line, shortening the stride until Quichotte is cantering in place.[44] Bartabas so absorbs the horse's movement in his erect but supple body that his seat hardly leaves the saddle. Of Moorish-derived Iberian design, his saddle lacks the wooden or metal trees of most modern saddles, which brings his flesh closer to his mount's to increase mutual sensation. As his pelvis undulates with the rhythm, and his "fork" rubs subtly and deeply into Quichotte's back through the leather, a hot, highly communicative friction passes between rider and horse.

In the final canter sequence of this scene, Bartabas and Quichotte enter on the left lead da-da-dum, da-da-dum, da-da-dum, down the hanamichi to the far edge of the wooden circle and then, astoundingly, without breaking gait or lead, move in reverse to exit retracing their steps back up the ramp: *galop arrière*. (See Clip 39.3 for the canter in place and the backward canter.) Bartabas starts the reverse motion of each backward stride by sliding his buttocks to the rear and pulling the horse up into his fork with his lower legs squeezing farther back on the roundest part of Quichotte's barrel. As Fillis described, this movement of the rider brings the horse's right hind leg backward instead of forward, followed by the backward steps of the diagonally paired left hind and right front, with the "leading" left front leg stepping back last. Taking the horse into himself to the fullest possible extent in this *gallop arrière*, Bartabas melds with Quichotte's powerfully pulsing ebony body whose exotically long, wavy mane and tail accentuate his Orientalized beauty. When the pair reenters to take a bow, Bartabas, on foot carrying the saddle, turns and dips his head to his belabored and glistening partner, who stands still chewing and attentive to his master with steam rising from his hot back where the saddle was. The man gestures in gratitude for what the horse has given, his total obedience to the subtlest of signals, his whole self.

Lest there be any doubt, after this steamy equestrian encounter, about confusion of love objects and loss of self in the Other, Bartabas immediately follows with an overtly sexualized display of cross-species dominance. He stages a mating dance with a pretty, finely boned, dished-faced grey mare, probably of Arab extraction. She waits in the arena led by the same blond male company member who played the anvil for the *galop arrière*, which visually links this sequence with the previous scene. Bartabas enters, still in riding costume, leading an excited, prancing mahogany stallion, another well-bred Oriental Barb-type horse, on a long line and works the animal around him in a circle until he will stand and listen for The Master's signal. That obedience achieved even at the height of a stallion's arousal, Bartabas nods for the mare to be led closer and then lets the stallion approach her. The stallion sniffs her nostrils delicately as though to kiss her hello and caresses her neck with his chin before rearing up and walking on his hind legs to mount her from the rear, while the camera recedes on their highly orchestrated copulation. In the interview accompanying the film, Bartabas touts this sequence as an extraordinary theatrical achievement:

> [W]hat happened was an incredible phenomenon. The stallion was mild enough, not really violent, and the mare who was tireless, shall we say, understood that this was her work, her role, and let herself, not be mated every day because when she wasn't in heat she didn't let herself be mated, but let herself be mounted by the stallion. This is completely unique because when

CLIP 39.3 Bartabas and Quichotte dancing two canter sequences on the circular wooden floor in *Cabaret equestre* [videorecording], originally filmed in 1990, published in DVD in 2004.

a mare isn't in heat, the stallion doesn't approach her . . . . [The mounting in performance] is a phenomenon that remains for me a . . . moment when you have the impression that the horse is really a part of the company, who understands at a certain level what we ask of it.[45]

Exceeding the stallion handler's pride in his horse's potency in the Haras Nationaux breeding barn, Bartabas boasts that his horses know their roles and will enact fornication night after night, like human actors in a porn show. Indeed, he singles out this instance as one in which the two primary species comprising his company are most alike. The ability to demonstrate mastery of the body, epitomized and elaborated through equestrian control of the sexualized, orientalized Other, whether human or equine, sustains his white masculine dominance as an impresario.

The ultimate test of that impresarial mastery happens in Théâtre Equestre Zingaro's live, rather than filmed, shows staged in the round, where neither retakes nor stage tricks are possible, and actors of both species must perform on command in the moment in full view of the audience. As circus historian Anthony Hippisley-Coxe points out about live equestrian acts in the ring, "the encircling audience can be assured that a difficult feat has been performed."[46] Audiences of *Cabaret Equestre* in Théâter Equestre Zingaro's home theater in Fort d'Aubervilliers do more than bear witness to these feats; they consume the spectacle as congregants in a quasireligious ceremony as they partake of the bread and wine the company members serve them at their cabaret tables. While eating and drinking, they also ingest the smells, sounds, and energies as well as sight of biped and quadruped performers working at close proximity. They breathe air carrying the dust kicked up by the aroused, prancing stallion and the steam rising off of Quichotte's sweaty back. This communal sharing makes them highly complicit in what they have witnessed: the ultimate contemporary reenactment of the core dance of imperial conquest, that of humans and horses. Experiencing such extraordinary equestrian display amid such closeness of moving bodies and exchange of bodily sensations, the congregants, along with the performers, encounter a breaking down of the human/animal binary that challenges biped superiority and enlarges understanding of what was and is possible between these two species.

While the congregants can return home to a world where human dominance is taken for granted, Bartabas must remain immersed in his interspecies compound asserting and reasserting his impresarial authority. In this endeavor, the films of his live performances become his means of controlling how his work will be remembered. Significantly, the performance of Théâtre Equestre Zingaro's seminal *Cabaret Equestre*, as memorialized on film, does not end with a company bow after the final mating dance, but with the camera panning Bartabas's trailer walls thick with antiquarian artifacts and memorabilia of his shows. The closing shot rests on his face in a mirror as he sits at his desk planning his next imperial equestrian adventure. He reinscribes himself as The Master artist; the humans and, primarily, the horses he works with are his fleshly instruments. Ironically, he has resorted to the visual medium of film, descendant of the technologies decried in *Mazeppa*, to extend his work in and beyond the circle. Thus constituting further circus echoes, his films both give him another auteur arena and archive his work with horses whose lives are relatively fleeting, lasting, on average, twenty-five to thirty years, but allowing only about eight peak years (roughly ages ten to eighteen) for an *haute-école* dressage horse. Zingaro, Vinaigre, and Quichotte are long since retired and probably all gone by now.[47] When a horse dies, according to Bartabas, "it's not only an emotional thing—it also means you lose years of work. Every horse is special, it can do things no other horse can. When he goes, you lose part of yourself. It's like losing an arm or a leg. You can never have it back."[48] But the need to re-member himself through a necessarily different relationship with another horse persists, circling back from the memorializing films into the live arena, where his equine communion plays into his interpersonal relationships, as he continues to bring crucial historical dynamics into the present for public consumption. That embodied connection between species, with all of its complexly raced and gendered passions and identifications, so intensely exemplified in Bartabas's equestrian dance theater, makes horses the necessary third party for historians to consider in studying imperial relations among humans of horse-powered eras.

Notes

1. *Eclipse* was imported from France for the BAM 1998 Next Wave Festival. The company included twelve riders, acrobats, and dancers and twenty-six equine performers. I saw the show in October. I have also viewed film of the performance. See Bartabas, *Eclipse* [videorecording]. Théâtre Equestre Zingaro made a third US appearance—in 2002 in Los Angeles with *Triptyk* for the Eclectic Orange Festival. See Oestreich.
2. At age eighteen in 1976, Clément Marty dropped his given name: "I wanted to take an artist's name as a way of saying my work was my life. It meant I wasn't just Bartabas for an hour on the stage." Quoted in Mackrell.
3. See http://www.bartabas.fr/en/Zingaro/spectacles for a full listing.
4. Before Bausch died in 2009, she and Bartabas had become close, and they were planning a collaboration. See Mackrell. The Bausch dancer Quincella Swyningham appeared in Zingaro's *Eclipse* in New York 1998.
5. See Rockwell.
6. Riding, "Dance: Using the Horse to Hold a Mirror to the Human."
7. Quoted in Riding, "Majestic Prancing Steeds, Actors All."
8. Quoted in Bartabas, "Preface: Entretien avec Bartabas." Translated with the help of Heidi Collins.
9. For example, in popular discourse surrounding the Civil War sesquicentennial, the magnitude of equine sacrifice is rarely mentioned, yet twice as many equines died as humans. The War Horse Memorial dedicated in 1997 that stands in front of the Virginia Historical Society in Richmond is inscribed with the best documentable estimate of 1.5 million horse and mule deaths from combat and disease in the war. See Schofield. The best estimate of the human toll is 750,000. See Hacker.
10. *Cabaret Equestre* [videorecording]. Translation from Bartabas's website: http://www.bartabas.fr/en/Zingaro/spectacles-7/Cabaret-Equestre (accessed September 7, 2012).
11. Bartabas quoted in Lam.
12. Riding, "Dance: Using the Horse to Hold a Mirror to the Human."
13. Garcin, 78.
14. Quoted in Shine, 10.
15. From Bartabas, "Making of *Mazeppa*."
16. Interview with Bartabas by Karine Ciupa, "Bartabas: Des chevaux et des hommes," *Cipria Magazine* (July–August, 1997): 79, quoted in Williams, 32.
17. Sirven-Gualde.
18. Ibid.

19. Laurent.
20. Williams, 36.
21. Quoted in Bartabas, "Preface: Entretien avec Bartabas," the interview that accompanies *Cabaret Equestre* [videorecording]. Translated with the help of Katharine Sherman.
22. Riding, "Majestic Prancing Steeds, Actors All."
23. See, for example, Nauleau and Céline Sirven-Gualde.
24. Riding, "Majestic Prancing Steeds, Actors All."
25. From English subtitles of the film *Mazeppa* (1993).
26. Williams, 36.
27. Dressage riders especially prefer stallions, whereas show jumpers, hunter riders, and three-day eventers, as well as their forebears in the cavalry, prefer geldings or mares, who are less excitable and easier to handle around other horses. Significantly, equestrian statues invariably depict the human, usually a (male) ruler or military figure, atop a stallion, regardless of the sex of the horse the person actually rode, to convey the equine potency arrogated to the rider.
28. Miller and Lamb, 100–101.
29. See Miller and Lamb, Chapter 6 "Why [NH] Works and Why It's Better," 87–115.
30. Hyland, 2–3.
31. From Bartabas, "Making of *Mazeppa*," translated by Heidi Collins.
32. Byron, "Mazeppa."
33. See *Géricault*, 197. Images of this painting are also available on numerous websites, including http://www.wikigallery.org/wiki/painting_253352/Theodore-Gericault/The-Page-Mazeppa (accessed June 15, 2014).
34. For a filmic recreation of these late nineteenth-century staging practices, see *Heller in Pink Tights*.
35. Garcin, 216.
36. Williams, 37. For more on the bloodlines of these horses and the current breeding stock, see http://lusitanosmarket.com/coudelaria/ortigao-costa-stud-farm/ (accessed February 10, 2013).
37. See Garcin, 216–17. Bartabas purchased Quixote as a five-year-old for 30,000 francs or about $6,000 from Oliveira, which is quite inexpensive for a horse of this caliber.
38. At the faster gallop, the diagonally paired left hind and right front actually hit the ground in sequence to make a beat of four-time rather than three, but these two legs still remain on the ground together before the strike of the leading front leg. Stop-action photography and slow-motion film have made it possible to analyze the horse's gaits with precision, starting with Eadweard Muybridge's famous photo sequences of Leland Stanford's horses in California in 1878.
39. The chewing of the jaw signifying relaxation and submission derives from the acceptance and trust the horse grants to the rider as his surrogate leader; in the wild, horses can eat when their leader signals that it is safe enough to stop running and put their heads down to chew grass. See Miller and Lamb, 99.
40. Game, 16, quoting from *Manual of Equitation: The Complete Training of Horse and Rider*, published by the British Horse Society (London: Threshold Books, 1990).
41. Fillis, 322.
42. Ibid.
43. http://www.haras-national-du-pin.com/en/le-haras-national-du-pin-se-devoile/history.html (accessed January 15, 2014).

44. In the canter in place and the backward canter, the diagonally paired legs of the stride hit the ground in sequence rear to front, as they do in the fast gallop, rather than simultaneously, as in the forward-moving canter. This makes the canter in place and the backward canter technically four beats rather than three, but the fourth beat is hardly perceptible, so the sound of three beats remains dominant on the wooden dance floor. For these movements to qualify as a canter, the key is that the diagonally paired legs, even though they come down separately, remain on the ground together before the leading leg strikes. See Fillis, 319.

45. Quoted in Bartabas, "Preface: Entretien avec Bartabas," the interview that accompanies *Cabaret Equestre* [videorecording]. Translated with the help of Heidi Collins.

46. Hippisley-Coxe, 110.

47. Zingaro actually died at seventeen in a veterinary hospital in New Jersey of an illness contracted during the 1998 New York run of *Eclipse*. The performance I saw turned out to be one of his last. See "Star Horse Dies."

48. Mackrell.

Bibliography

Bartabas. *Cabaret Equestre* [videorecording]. Performance filmed in May 1990, at Fort d'Aubervilliers, France. Published in DVD, 2004, by MK2 Editions.

Bartabas. *Eclipse: Equestrian Theater by Zingaro* [live performance]. Conception and artistic direction by Bartabas. Brooklyn Academy of Music. New York, New York. October 1998.

Bartabas. *Eclipse* [videorecording]. Originally produced as a motion picture in 1998, published in DVD, 2004, by MK2 Editions.

Bartabas. *Galop Arrière: Un Film de Bartabas*. MK2TV. Théâtre Zingaro. 2010. DVD.

Bartabas. "Making of Mazeppa" or "Bartabas, de la piste à l'écran" (from arena to screen), an interview with Bartabas accompanying the film *Mazeppa* (1993). Available on the 2005 DVD version.

Bartabas. *Mazeppa* (1993). Originally produced as a motion picture in 1993, published in DVD in 2005 by MK2 Editions.

Bartabas. "Preface: Entretien avec Bartabas." Interview with Bartabas accompanying *Cabaret equestre* [videorecording]. MK2 Editions, 2004.

Bartabas Website. Accessed June 14, 2014. http://www.bartabas.fr.

Byron, George Gordon. "Mazeppa." In *The Works of Lord Byron. A New, Revised and Enlarged Edition, with Illustrations*, edited by Ernest Hartley Coleridge [and R. E. Prothero]. New York and London: John Murray and Charles Scribner's Sons, 1898–1904. Electronic version in *Literature Online*. Cambridge, UK: Chadwyck-Healey, 1992.

Fillis, James. *Breaking and Riding, with Military Commentaries*. Translated by M. H. Hayes. New York: Scribner's, 1902.

Game, Ann. "Riding: Embodying the Centaur." *Body and Society* 7, no. 4 (2001): 1–12.

Garcin, Jérôme. *Bartabas, Roman*. Paris: Gallimard, 2006.

Géricault. Catalogue de l'exposition Géricault aux Galeries Nationales du Grand Palais, Paris, 10 octobre 1991–6 janvier 1992. Paris: Réunion des Musées Nationaux, 1991.

Hacker, J. D. "A Census-Based Account of the Civil War Dead." *Civil War History* 57, no. 4 (2011): 306–47.

Haras National du Pin. Accessed January 15, 2014. http://www.haras-national-du-pin.com/en/le-haras-national-du-pin-se-devoile/history.html.

Heller in Pink Tights (1960). Paramount Home Entertainment, videorecording, 2005.

Hippisley-Coxe, Anthony. "Equestrian Drama and the Circus." In *Performance and Politics in Popular Drama: Aspects of Popular Entertainment in Theatre, Film, and Television, 1800–1976*, edited by D. Bradby, L. James, and B. Sharratt, 109–18. Cambridge: Cambridge University Press, 1980.

Hyland, Ann. *The War Horse, 1250–1600*. Stroud, UK: Sutton, 1998.

Lam, Chris. "All the Pretty Horses," *bc magazine* [Hong Kong], Issue 247, 3 January 2008.

Laurent, Anne. "Zingaro," Program Note for *Eclipse* Program, BAM bill, 1998, Next Wave Festival.

Mackrell, Judith. "Bartabas: Dances with Horses," *The Guardian*, February 21, 2011. Accessed June 15, 2014. http://www.theguardian.com/stage/2011/feb/21/bartabas-zingaro-dance-horses-interview.

Miller, Robert M., and Rick Lamb. *The Revolution in Horsemanship and What It Means to Mankind*. Guilford, CT: Lyons Press, 2005.

Nauleau, Sophie. "The Horses: The Other Bartabas." Accessed September 26, 2012. http://www.bartabas.fr/en/Bartabas/les-chevaux.

Oestreich, James R. "A Hybrid Style: Equine-Modern." *New York Times*, September 8, 2002.

Ortigao Costa Stud Farm. Accessed February 10, 2013. http://lusitanosmarket.com/coudelaria/ortigao-costa-stud-farm/.

Riding, Alan. "Dance: Using the Horse to Hold a Mirror to the Human." *New York Times*, September 6, 1998.

Riding, Alan. "Majestic Prancing Steeds, Actors All." *New York Times*, September 15, 1996.

Rockwell, John. "France's Summer Hit Is a Circus, Sort Of," *New York Times*, August 8, 1994.

Schofield, Arnold W. "Battlefield Dispatches No. 208 'War Horses,'" *Fort Scott Tribune* [Kansas], April 2, 2010. Accessed September 19, 2012. http://www.fstribune.com/story/1623063.html.

Sirven-Gualde, Céline. "L'ombre du chef" ["The Shadow of the Chief]. *Le Point*, October 24, 2003. Accessed September 24, 2012. http://www.lepoint.fr/actualites-economie/2003-10-2 4/l-ombre-du-chef/916/0/118975.

Shine, Clare. "Animal Magic; French Performer Bartabas Puts On Unique Shows Using Horses on Stage Alongside Actors." *Financial Times* (London, England), February 19, 2011.

"Star Horse Dies." *New York Times*, December 4, 1998.

Williams, David. "The Right Horse, The Animal Eye—Bartabas and Théâtre Zingaro." *Performance Research* 5, no. 2 (2000): 29–40.

CHAPTER 40

···

CAPITAL CITY CAMP
Gay Carnival and Capitalist Display

···

NEAL HEBERT

WHETHER one examines Attic Greek performance, the staging practices of Noh drama, the drama of the English Renaissance, or contemporary performance, female impersonation (or drag performance) is a performance practice that has embodied contradictions and slippages of gendered meanings throughout the history of Western performance traditions. In the contemporary academy, however, not all drag is created equal—or, at least, not all drag performances have been equally theorized within the field of performance studies. Although much attention has been paid to drag revues, comparatively little scholarly attention has been directed at the decades-long tradition of "drag Carnival" in the Louisiana region.[1] This chapter is dedicated to one such performance, performed by one such Krewe: The Krewe of Apollo – Baton Rouge's January 16, 2010, performance of Bal Masque XXIX.

For the uninitiated, a Bal Masque is a yearly event organized by at least one local Mardi Gras krewe. A Mardi Gras krewe is a traditionally heterosexual organization specifically dedicated to sponsoring a ticketed formal Mardi Gras celebration each year (or Bal Masque); a krewe can accept anywhere between dozens or hundreds of paid members depending on the size of either the krewe or its intended event. These Bal Masques typically combine elements of a formal dance (in some ways an amalgamation of a debutante ball and a high school prom) with a raucous celebration of decadence and licentiousness. Although this practice is common in (and, at least in the North American zeitgeist, often associated with) the city of New Orleans, Mardi Gras is not only practiced within New Orleans; rather, it is a season of celebrations throughout Louisiana (and neighboring states) that culminates in the famous parades and aforementioned Bal Masques.[2] The Krewe of Apollo – Baton Rouge is Baton Rouge's oldest still-existent gay Mardi Gras krewe, and its Bal Masque XXIX was marketed to the local community as an evening of performances presented within the oeuvre of Mardi Gras performance; the event promised performances that were performed, produced, designed and created by the most visible members of the gay male community in the city-parish of East Baton Rouge.[3]

The Bal Masque is an example of a performance practice that has, for three decades, provided gay krewe members with a thrilling (and historically dangerous)[4] opportunity to perform their identities within the context of Carnival celebration. In this article I provide a tour of the Krewe of Apollo – Baton Rouge's Bal Masque XXIX by describing the event as a whole (and several of the performances in detail). Because this event features drag performances by gay performers, it would be easy to conclude that it fits neatly into other specifically gay visibility-oriented performances such as a traditional drag show. After all, this performance occurs in Baton Rouge, the capitol of the traditionally conservative state of Louisiana; while New Orleans may be known for its licentiousness, Baton Rouge's exceedingly poor track record on gay rights and assorted other Gay, Lesbian, Transgender, and Queer (GLBTQ) issues could appear to militate in this conclusion's favor.[5] I argue, however, that the fusion of class, Camp(s), and capital inherent in the spectacular Baton Rouge Bal Masque complicates such a reading. That is, instead of preaching tolerance through visibility or attempting to perform gay citizens' resistances to the City-Parish's status quo, Bal Masque XXIX is a gay performance that argues for gay participation within the City-Parish of Baton Rouge without ever appearing to make an argument—and without ever formally acknowledging the divisive political dimension of the performance in question.

I also demonstrate that Bal Masque XXIX relies on nested Camp and Pop camp performance tactics to mask the performances of gay identity that undergird the krewe's drag performances; moreover, it uses the license of Carnival to obscure the krewe's attempts to perform members' current inclusion into the patriarchal/capitalist ruling class of the City-Parish. This reading relies on Moe Meyer's distinction between Camp and Pop camp (as formulated within his 2010 monograph *The Achaeology of Posing*); for Meyer, Camp refers to specifically gay significations that enact and allow individuals to perform gay identities despite these significations' nesting within (and role in critiquing) heterosocial culture, while Pop camp refers to nongay appropriations of Camp signification.

Where Meyer focuses on the performer's intent to establish whether a performer is engaging in Camp or Pop camp, I suggest that the leveraging of these significations in performance at Bal Masque XXIX reveals that Pop camp and Camp are easier to separate in theory than they are in practice. Audience interpretation, as much as a performer's intent, plays a role in ascribing Camp status to a performance; without an audience's awareness of the history behind a specifically gay signification, a performer's intention to create a Camp performance can be obscured or masked as Pop camp fun. As I demonstrate later in this essay, the potential for play between Camp and Pop camp is, far from a limiting factor, a further opportunity for performative critique. I further complicate this Camp reading within the performance of Bal Masque XXIX by invoking Kate Davy's critiques of the classist appeals on which all iterations of Camp and camp depend (as in Meyer, *The Politics and Poetics of Camp*). By using multiple (and multiply interpretable) Camp and camp appeals, the Krewe of Apollo reveals to its audience that gay citizens do not need to be integrated into the City-Parish—the approval of public officials and their participation in the economic life of the city through Carnival celebration reveals an already integrated present and gives both performers and audience an experience of how the community could grow after the performance ends.

THE KREWE OF APOLLO – BATON ROUGE

In order to understand The Krewe of Apollo – Baton Rouge's Bal Masque XXIX, however, it is necessary to historicize the social club that sponsors the ball.[6] The Krewe of Apollo – Baton

Rouge today is a 501(c) nonprofit corporation in the state of Louisiana; it runs a charity and produces a yearly Mardi Gras ball, with a slate of officers democratically elected by the corporation's membership.[7] A cursory review of any of the programs produced for their yearly Mardi Gras balls reveals an impressive number of local corporate and community sponsors for their yearly Bal Masques.[8] Visitors to the City-Parish or nonresidents might be inclined to see these sponsorships and conclude that the City-Parish is progressive, or at least remarkably gay-friendly for an area of the geographic south of the United States; such a view would be mistaken, given recent political history.[9]

Antigay sentiment, according to older members of the Krewe who have lived in the City-Parish for decades, is old hat. Of the Krewe of Apollo – Baton Rouge's eight founding members, only one still lives: Larry Fremin, the krewe's first president and king. Before I began interviewing Fremin about the krewe's history in 2009, no documentation of the krewe's early history existed. Indeed, even interviewing Fremin was a challenge; given krewe members' past (and present) experiences of marginalization because of their sexual orientation within the City-Parish, members were hesitant to allow an outsider such as myself access to Fremin's story or the organization's history. Fremin himself, as well as several of the younger members of the krewe curious about the krewe's history, were forced to put the matter up for a vote before the entire krewe before my interviews could proceed. Although, to an outside observer, resolution occurring through democratic process may seem to be a matter of course, in Louisiana Carnival practice many (if not most) krewes eschew democratic organization in favor or private or individual control. According to Fremin, The Krewe of Apollo – Baton Rouge was organized around member-driven democracy rather than the fiat of private charter owners.[10]

Interviews with Fremin reveal that the Krewe of Apollo – Baton Rouge is simply the lone local satellite of New Orleans's historically gay Mystic Krewe of Apollo. The Mystic Krewe of Apollo was formed in New Orleans by Roland Dobson in 1969 as an exclusively gay Mardi Gras Krewe: a trait that all krewes deriving from Dobson's Krewe retain.[11] The Mystic Krewe of Apollo de Lafayette[12] launched as a satellite Krewe in 1975. The Baton Rouge, Shreveport, and Birmingham, Alabama, satellites all launched in 1981; the Baton Rouge charter was formed by eight former members of the Mystic Krewe of Apollo de Lafayette, all of whom resigned their membership from the Lafayette Krewe to devote themselves to launching a successful Baton Rouge satellite. This was viewed as a risky business proposition, given that two prior attempts to form a Baton Rouge branch of the Mystic Krewe had gone bankrupt due to lack of community support and insufficient fundraising.[13] Fremin, as the principal member of the first Krewe, was the Bal Masque's first captain (read as: organizer) and was elected its first king; Fremin has served as captain more than eight times since the organization's inception. Membership disagreements in 1991, however, caused The Mystic Krewe of Apollo – Baton Rouge's name to be contested.[14] Rather than fight a legal battle over the name, Fremin and other krewe members formed a new charter with a new name: The Krewe of Apollo – Baton Rouge, the name under which the krewe exists today.

Membership of the krewe is not afforded to every gay man in the city who wants to join; rather, members must pay dues to be a member in good standing. Dues for krewe membership, as of this writing, cost more than $500 annually, a hefty figure that obscures additional, hidden costs active krewe members incur. The price of being a krewe member—both in terms of dues paid for membership and in terms of additional expenses—necessarily limits who is included within the krewe. Krewe members assert that this exclusion is not intentional, but a fact of operation given that the club's primary purpose is to put on a yearly Bal Masque. In 2010, this Bal Masque's budget was approximately $100,000.

Although $100,000 may appear to be a large sum of money, it is worth taking a moment to pause and analyze exactly what this $100,000 actually pays for. This cost accounts for building rentals, insurance, set design, technical crew, and assorted other building fees; it decidedly does not account for how much additional money is spent on each of the individual numbers, or the food and drink consumed by guests and performers. A person who is royalty, such as the king or queen, might well, at the time of this writing, to spend up to $30,000 for a particularly lavish costume and parade; as Fremin remarked to me, being Apollo royalty "is a big monetary investment—and of course, it is in any carnival" (Fremin, 2009). Each costume worn by a krewe member or back-up dancer in the performance is constructed at the expense of the krewe member or members who sponsored that performance. For performances featuring dozens of back-up dancers in addition to floats and costumes with backpieces and props, this expense can quickly become formidable, given that all materials are expected to be purchased in the event that donations are impossible to obtain; in Louisiana, many "necessities" of Carnival performance simply must be purchased, such as beads, custom-made backpieces, materials for floats, rhinestones, and the like. It would not be unreasonable, based on the quality and number of costumes in the assorted numbers throughout the show, to assume that at least another $100,000 was spent by the members of the krewe performing within the show. This is a shocking expense in the City-Parish of Baton Rouge. Recent Census data indicates that 18.3 percent of all citizens live at or below the poverty line. Per capita income from 2007 to 2012 was estimated to be $26,714, while median household income was estimated to be $46,838.[15]

Corporations and individuals who believe they are being gay friendly by supporting the Krewe of Apollo – Baton Rouge may be guilty of buying into an (unintentionally) mainstreamed image of what it means to be gay in Baton Rouge. Census data also indicates that the middle-class, mostly white men who are economically able to join the Krewe of Apollo – Baton Rouge are not, demographically speaking, particularly representative of the metropolitan area. According to the most recent US census data, 45.5 percent of the City-Parish is African American, while white citizens account for only 50 percent of the total population. A full 24.3 percent of citizens aged 18 through 65 live at or below the poverty line, and it would be irresponsible to assume that none of these people are, themselves, gay (census. gov).[16] Although the krewe has an open-door membership policy to any man (cisgender or transgender) interested in joining and who can afford the dues irrespective of his sexuality, women currently cannot be members.[17]

While it would be inaccurate to state that all of the above is evident to all spectators of the performance of Bal Masque XXIX, many of these facts inform engaged spectatorship of the Bal Masque. Women who perform onstage are specifically designated as nonmembers of the krewe in the program for the performance, for example, and the fact that this is the case certainly challenges krewe claims that the social club is a democracy in the ordinary sense of the term. Although much of the Krewe of Apollo – Baton Rouge's history has been left untold and is not public knowledge, audience members are typically the family and friends of various members of the krewe. Given the club's existence throughout the past three decades, it would be shocking to discover that any adult watching the show is completely ignorant of the City-Parish's past and present cultural transgressions against GLBTQ citizens. Indeed, even the name change from The Mystic Krewe of Apollo – Baton Rouge to the Krewe of

Apollo – Baton Rouge is apparent to anyone who examines the program of the event. The organization's history may not be a formal text of the performance in question, but for any Bal Masque bearing a Roman numeral (such as X, XV, or, in this case, XXIX) the event is explicitly positioned within the organization's history. Although Bal Masque XXIX may not be a performance of history, a krewe's Bal Masque is always a performance with history. This positioning calls attention, either subtly or overtly, to the political events that have produced or constrained these performances. Participation in Mardi Gras's formal events is to engage in a history-laden spectatorship; the presence of performances past weighs on present performances.

THE KREWE OF APOLLO – BATON ROUGE'S BAL MASQUE XXIX

It is January 16, 2010, the night of the Krewe of Apollo – Baton Rouge's Bal Masque XXIX. The Baton Rouge River Center has been converted into a giant thrust stage; a catwalk extends 100 yards down the center of the arena, bisecting the thousand spectators who are divided among several hundred tables. The loudspeakers blare dance remixes of Lady Gaga, Madonna, and other pop songs as the spectators loudly talk and drink.

At a traditional Bal Masque, spectators would expect a rather stately affair, at least by Mardi Gras standards. While there would be dancing, food, and alcohol, a Bal Masque is a far more muted affair than attending a parade on the city streets of many Louisiana cities—and certainly more so than the famous parades of New Orleans. Attendees of a Mardi Gras parade may dress as they please, consume alcohol publically, and can expect each float[18] to boast performers throwing colorful beads to the spectators. Unlike parade-goers, however, guests at a Bal Masque are expected to wear their finest attire, dance with their dates during those times proscribed for dancing, and rest comfortably in the assurance that bead-throwing will happen at the end of the celebration. At the Krewe of Apollo – Baton Rouge's Bal Masque XXIX, however, the evening's entertainment is anything but traditional. Rather than a progressive series of dances that leads to the parade of the year's newly crowned royalty and court, the Krewe of Apollo's Bal Masque XXIX turns the parade of the year's royalty and court into a sort of anticlimax: The principle draw to the Bal Masque is the opportunity for guests to see the more than a dozen drag routines performed, designed, costumed, and directed by members of the krewe (either singly or in groups).

Although the entertainments throughout the evening are not traditional Bal Masque fare, the guests' attire certainly is. The men's tuxedos boast vests the colors of the rainbow, ranging from traditional midnight black to more opulent gold-sequined affairs. The women, too, dress to impress: they wear gowns and heels of all colors. Some audience members don half-masks, while others eschew the Mardi Gras custom of Carnival masks—an eschewal many of the Krewe of Apollo's performers have adopted this evening. Although this deviation from Carnival tradition has become relatively common in contemporary Carnival celebrations within Louisiana, for the Krewe of Apollo – Baton Rouge this omission has a historical resonance. At the first Bal Masque sponsored by the krewe in 1981, all members of the royalty and court were required by the krewe to be masked. Larry Fremin explained the reason for this custom:

> Our very first ball, the only way I could get anyone to participate in the ball was that I guaranteed that everybody onstage would be masked. To many people, they had to have some secrecy about it. [One of our members] was a businessman here in town—his father owned a construction company, he worked for his father—and he thought, "If it came out that I was gay, it could literally cost my family hundreds of thousands of dollars in contracts or something." Back then there was reason to be so protected. (Fremin, 2009)

Although Fremin publicly unmasked as soon as the first Bal Masque ended (while onstage, no less), the guarantee of a kind of anonymity during the performance was the only way Fremin could get local men to agree to be Royalty for the first Bal Masque. The abolition of required masking is one of the aspects of the Krewe of Apollo's growth throughout the past three decades that Fremin finds most gratifying.

The Bal Masque is spectacular, in multiple senses of the word. As noted, the attendees are dressed formally—with modern, Carnival-tinged touches (such as gaudy plastic beads, scepters, or stage jewelry) to accentuate their outfits. Tables, at the Krewe of Apollo – Baton Rouge's Bal Masque, can cost hundreds of dollars; the choicest tables, such as those closest to the stage, are frequently reserved for the friends and family of officers or royalty within the producing krewe. The large production numbers, costumed at the expense of krewe members in excess of their yearly membership fees to the Krewe of Apollo – Baton Rouge, can sometimes involve costuming more than twenty people in addition to the sponsoring krewe member's lavish costumes (featuring backpieces that weigh up to fifty pounds and extend up to twenty feet above the krewe member so accoutered). Although members of the krewe, such as Fremin, frequently point out that deserving men have been elected king or queen despite not having the money to purchase a "royalty-appropriate" costume, usually through the largesse and generosity of the wealthier members of the krewe, a spectator who knows nothing of the krewe's history and merely shows up to Bal Masque XXIX would likely believe that the evening's entertainments were designed by the affluent and wealthy for an audience of affluent and wealthy citizens within the City-Parish. The fact that almost all krewe members were white performers would, perhaps, reinforce the above supposition.

Despite Baton Rouge's reputation for being a relatively conservative city in an extremely conservative state, the Bal Masque's crowd is filled to capacity and surrounded by banners of the numerous local businesses and national corporations sponsoring the lavish event (Tullier, 2010). This is due, in large part, to the transgressive nature of Mardi Gras and its position within the larger oeuvre of Carnival performances: Indeed, this transgressive sponsorship locates the Bal Masque as a performance event that, like most Carnival performance, fits firmly within Mikhail Bakhtin's concept of the carnivalesque.[19] As Bakhtin notes, the carnivalesque "celebrated temporary liberation from the prevailing truth and the established order; it marked the suspension of all hierarchical rank, privileges, norms, and prohibitions" (Bakhtin, 10). Although throughout the normal course of the year a religious organization sponsoring a GLBTQ event would clearly violate the social order of the City-Parish, during Louisiana's Mardi Gras season cultural norms are given license to be suspended; during Carnival it is simply a given that licensed transgressions of this sort are, by convention, not transgressions at all.

This idea of licensed transgression is concretized once the Bal Masque proper begins. The performance proper opens with the introduction of the krewe's current president, Lester Mut, who performs his introduction in drag as "Jennifer Marlowe." Mut's introduction as president is the first drag number presented to the audience. His use of drag effectively queers Bal Masque XXIX from the moment it begins, and contrasts the traditional presentation of the next event: the introduction of the krewe's founder and first king Larry Fremin, who is attended by the krewe's color guard.[20] After the introduction of the color guard, Sharon James, a local singer, is introduced to the crowd while the krewe's president requests that partygoers stand for the singing of the national anthem. As the final notes of the song hang in the air, the thousand attendees of the Bal Masque explode into applause, seemingly grateful that the licentiousness to come is foregrounded by an appeal to (or acknowledgment of) patriotism.

The evening's patriotic appeal is further reinforced when Kip Holden, the Democratic mayor-president of East Baton Rouge Parish, is given the opportunity to speak to the thousands of citizens in attendance. Holden praises the scale of the event, positions himself as a frequent attendee of the yearly Apollo Bal masques (highlighting his bona fides to speak to the quality of the spectacles audience members are about to see), and thanks the Krewe of Apollo for the members' charitable fundraisers throughout the year in the City-Parish (specifically mentioning the krewe's AIDS-Crisis fund dedicated to helping those diagnosed with HIV).[21] Just as the "normal" rules of sponsorship can be suspended during Carnival, so, too, can the City-Parish's political conservatism be suspended; the national anthem and Holden's presence both work to legitimize—and, in Holden's case, personify—the fact that, for the next four hours, different social norms will be operative in this corner of the City-Parish.

While this staging of political presence within the performance of the Bal Masque defines the performance as an explicitly patriotic act, it also represents a break from Bakhtinian Carnival practice. Per the Bakhtinian reading of Carnival, the legitimizing and normalizing moves that accompany the carnivalesque are frequently tacit; Carnival was explicitly allowed by the ruling classes of the medieval era, and these performances represented a "temporary suspension, both ideal and real, of hierarchical rank" (Bakhtin, 10). But during Bal Masque XXIX, although the City-Parish's social conservatism (as can be seen through the event's sponsors) is suspended, its political hierarchy is preserved and highlighted during the course of the performance to the vocal approval of the Bal Masque's guests. The reaction of the audience to these events as spectators—a spectatorship certainly informed by the Bal Masque's choice to incorporate the newly ascendant Mayor-President Kip Holden into the performance while displaying his attendance to the event—suggests that the effect of these explicit political legitimations needs further analysis.

Mayor-President Kip Holden's inclusion in the Bal Masque is a strong statement to residents of the City-Parish. Holden, a Democrat, was first elected mayor-president in 2004, his third attempt at the office, with 54 percent of the vote. In addition to being the first Democrat elected mayor-president since 1989, Holden also holds the distinction of being the first African American to ever win the office of mayor-president of East Baton Rouge Parish. By Bal Masque XXIX, Holden's legacy as a local politician was secure, having recently won his first reelection without losing a single district of the City-Parish.[22] Holden's status within the local community as a Democratic politician who had won reelection to office while advocating for the politically divisive "One Baton Rouge" initiative to promote GLBTQ diversity within the City-Parish makes him a figure doubly historic to guests: the first African

American mayor-president, and the first mayor-president to publicly support the gay community. Furthermore, Holden's success speaks to the possibility of progress for minority members of the City-Parish, and his extreme popularity within the City-Parish speaks to the possibility of minority acceptance (rather than tolerance or token diversity).

With the patriotic pump primed and the subtext of the evening's performances laid out, it is time for the unveiling of the evening's master of ceremonies: Elvira, the Mistress of the Dark.[23] Elvira enters the arena on a palanquin born by bare-chested men. Combining off-the-cuff political humor with an R-rated comedy routine, Elvira grounds the ball and literalizes its theme of "Tales from the Dark." Her presence primes the audience for the mingling of drag and horror elements in the fourteen drag performances that fill the majority of the event's four hour duration. The event culminates in the revelation of the king and queen, and their grand march is the ending parade for which Bal Masques are famous.

Even for a Krewe of Apollo – Baton Rouge bal masque, Bal Masque XXIX is unique: according to Bal Masque XXIX Captain Corey Tullier and Co-Captain John Deshotel, the theme and scale of the event is the most ambitious attempted by the Krewe of Apollo – Baton Rouge in memory. Although on that evening I took them at their word given that Bal Masque XXIX was the first Krewe of Apollo – Baton Rouge bal masque I had attended, my attendance to subsequent bal masques has borne out both men's assessment of the event's iconoclasm. Krewe of Apollo – Baton Rouge Bal Masque XXX in 2011, the ninth Bal Masque for which Larry Fremin served as captain, was a comparatively conservative affair: Its classic Hollywood theme of "Apollo Revealed" resulted in a largely traditional formal event, where City-Parish Carnival traditions were occasionally disrupted by moderately risqué drag numbers. Bal Masque XXXI's "Disco Ball," organized by Captain Lester Mut and Co-Captain Stephen McCants, was a much wilder affair than Bal Masque XXX, albeit less raucous than XXIX; the 1970s theme allowed for disco wildness (and requisite Village People–themed performances that wowed audiences), but there was no Elvira figure lending her larger-than life celebrity to the event as Mistress of the Dark nor did any numbers ever approach the dangers of horror explored in Bal Masque XXIX. Aside from the drag routines and the size of the arena hosting the event, subsequent Apollo Bal Masques more closely resemble the sorts of events put on by traditionally heterosexual Mardi Gras krewes than the bacchanal, celebrity-studded celebration of licentiousness put on by Tullier and Deshotel in 2010.

Several earlier performances, however, demand further scrutiny. The presentation of the captain and co-captain of Bal Masque XXIX were the first performances by krewe members to deeply engage with the evening's unifying theme of "Tales from the Dark." Corey Tullier, appearing as Frank N Furter from *The Rocky Horror Picture Show* began the krewe-coordinated performances, and his choice of character and songs from the show established the drag queen as a figure of both power and fun: Tullier, a former athlete, stands more than 6 feet tall, and his embodiment of Frank N Furter provokes laughter from the audience given his physicality. Tullier's partner and co-captain, John Deshotel, appears as the Werecat with a troupe of back-up dancers—scantily-clad men who gyrated behind Deshotel's lip-synching. When Tullier and Deshotel's performances were complete, they retired to an oversized stage-right throne built for two. The two remained onstage throughout the entire Bal Masque, reclining decadently as co-audiences-in-chief for all subsequent performances, entreating nearby tables to ensure that their oversized gothic chalices were never empty of hard liquor between drag routines. As performances came and went throughout the evening, Tullier and Deshotel would embody the active, licentious spectatorship desired by the krewe members; both men loudly exhorted the audience to follow their example between acts.

Both Tullier and Deshotel's performances highlight the role of theatricality within Bal Masque XXIX.[24] Tullier and Deshotel, as the captain and co-captain of this Bal Masque, were responsible for selecting the evening's theme, and both chose iconic exemplars from cult horror films as the subject of their routines despite the fact that neither, physically, resembled the performers whose works were reappropriated for the evening. Indeed, this miscasting (at least by traditional theatrical standards) of both Tullier and Deshotel was written in to their performances; given the crowd response to these performances, part of the appeal relied on the fact that, when Tullier and Deshotel first appeared on stage, their physicality did not reveal the subject of their coming drag routines. Moreover, the sheer enthusiasm of the crowd's responses to the source material—Tullier's Frank-N-Furter was an obvious homage to *Rocky Horror*, while Deshotel's dance numbers incorporated Michael Jackson's pop standard "Thriller"—suggests that, to this crowd on this night, Dehotels and Tullier's miscasting allowed audiences to see how the performers celebrated the iconic theme of the evening. Their physicality called attention to the excesses of the event, of drag, and reinforced the artificiality at the heart of Carnival.

Another noteworthy routine is Ernest Ourso's performance themed around *The Exorcist*. The piece began with frightening mood music and the revelation of an actual Mardi Gras float being pulled onto the River Center's giant runway: a bed containing a frightened little girl. As the music grew darker and more intense a chorus of dancing demons entered the runway to "terrify" the girl, and at the music's crescendo the foot of the bed erupted as the covers were revealed to be a piece of a demon's costume. Ourso, the demon, tormented the girl as the float-bed was revealed to be a giant revolve capable of spinning a full 360 degrees, allowing the entire audience to see all aspects of his costume and act (as well as the child performer's mimed terror). As the music wound down, all performers engaged in a tableau that was only broken by Ourso's split-second costume change: His demonic attire was ripped away to reveal an emerald green evening gown underneath a blonde bouffant. Legion became Venus Envy, Ourso's drag persona (who would, incidentally, be Miss National Apollo 2011 the following year). Ourso launched into performances of Madonna and Lady Gaga before the dazzled crowd—his drag persona serving to supplant audience members' awareness of the "terrified" little girl tormented only moments before. Bal Masque XXIX's theme might have been "Tales from the Dark," but the only horrors fit to be staged throughout the evening were either "B" horror movies or, as in the case of Ourso's performance, classics of the Hollywood horror canon that could be defanged through Pop camp appeals—usually literalized in the incorporation of female impersonation, the drag queen as camp figure par excellence.

But more on Camp and Pop camp in the next section.

All of the performances that constitute the Bal Masque were united in two respects. First, Elvira provided a visual reminder of the B-movie tradition that spawned her celebrity and inspired the evening's spectacles. More troubling, however, was the way that the presences of Elvira and other "real" women on stage provided a clue to the real role of women within the show: subordinated beneath the actual male members of the Krewe of Apollo – Baton Rouge. Elvira's position of prominence as master of ceremonies masked the position of all other women within the evening's other performances: Her position of prominence was a function of her celebrity and the fact that the krewe licensed her to be the evening's MC.

Other women in the show received neither prominence nor license to be more than objects of the spectators' gazes; indeed, backup dancers helped the drag performers' pieces remain spectacular without stealing focus away from the drag performances around which the show was marketed. At all moments during the Bal Masque, effort was expended ensuring that the men on stage—even those wearing women's clothes—assumed positions of patriarchal power within the performance. But even Elvira's masking of women's importance within the Bal Masque was only a temporary masking: As the show ended, Elvira was literally upstaged by the king and queen's parade. Before the evening would end, Elvira would prostrate herself before both King and Queen Apollo XXIX. Bal Masque XXIX ended with Elvira, obscured by the costumes of the king and queen, calling crowd members onstage via microphone to receive trinkets; the remainder of the court, all of whom were onstage, tossed beads to the remaining spectators insufficiently privileged by the krewe to be called from their place on the floor to the stage itself.

CAMP

As I noted earlier, Bal Masque XXIX is a Mardi Gras performance that relies on Carnival expectations while nonetheless challenging traditional aspects of Mardi Gras performance. But thus far only cursory attention has been paid to the performance tactic that allowed these transgressions to be integrated into the performances of the Bal Masque: multivalent Camp performances. The appeal of Bal Masque XXIX—and, although substantiation of this claim falls outside the purview of this article, other Krewe of Apollo – Baton Rouge Bal Masques—relies on the combination of Carnival pageantry with drag performance: in other words, the wink of Camp combined with camp appeals. Like Moe Meyer,[25] I hold that conversations about Camp throughout the scholarly discourse of the past few decades are actually complex attempts to narrow and specify the ways in which Camp has been invoked at alternate times throughout the discourse; these arguments occur given the different ways Camp is leveraged in performance. I retain Meyer's sense that Camp operates in two senses. The first sense, called Camp, refers to a "suppressed and denied oppositional critique embodied in the signifying practices that processually constitute gay identities" (Meyer, *The Archaeology of Posing*, 39). This results in a Camp that is political and functions within an explicitly gay discourse and as cultural critique available to gay men. Moreover, Camp should be understood as "the total body of performative practices and strategies used to enact a gay identity, with enactment understood as the production of social visibility" (Meyer, *The Archaeology of Posing*, 40). The second sense, designated Pop camp, involves "all ungay activities that have been previously accepted as 'camp,' such as Pop culture expressions" (Meyer, *The Archaeology of Posing*, 39); Meyer asserts that these camps are the result of appropriations of gay culture and gay praxis of identity formation, and are definitionally not Camp. Throughout this article, I have followed Meyer's suggestion to label what, for Meyer, constitutes authentic Camp with a capital *C* (Camp); all nongay appropriations are marked with a lowercase *c* (camp).

Meyer spends much time in his definition of Camp focusing on the individual who performs a Camp identity and locates the distinction between Camp and Pop camp in the intention of the performer. I posit, however, that emphasis must also be placed on the spectator of these sorts of performances; an audience that mistakes the performer's intent will mistake Camp for Pop camp (as well as the opposite). The spectator of a Camp performance can be mistaken about that which they have witnessed, and this mistake could result in a Camp performance being read as devoid of gay signification: Camp performance becomes Pop camp performance through no fault of the performer.

Consider the figure of Judy Garland: Garland's celebrity in the Golden (and post-Golden) age of Hollywood renders her a figure ripe for appropriation.[26] A Camp reading of Garland would involve understanding Garland as a potentially performed representation with a specifically gay meaning. Such a performed appropriation might involve a performer in some way embodying the traces of Judy Garland: This could be accomplished through a set of gestures associated with Garland, songs Garland famously sang in any of her films, or mimetically through costume and makeup. To an audience capable of interpreting Garland's utility in gay signification, the Camp inherent in a performance that incorporates elements of Garland would be extremely clear; an audience ignorant of Garland's gay signifying potential, however, would be forced to read a performance of Garland as an example of Pop camp irrespective of the performer's intent. Furthermore, there is no such guarantee that *any* performed representation of Garland would be Camp; Garland could be appropriated in a nongay way, and remain a bearer of Pop camp meaning. Such an appropriation might be identical in form to a Camp performance. Thus, I would modify Meyer's distinction between Camp and Pop camp to accommodate both the transmission of a performer's intentions as well as an audience's reception of that meaning: A performance is Camp if and only if (1) a performance is a gay signification of gay identity and (2) an audience can correctly perceive the differences between a gay signification and a nongay signification.

Although many of the performances within Bal Masque XXIX satisfy condition (1), it is unreasonable to conclude that all citizens numbered among the thousands in attendance were sufficiently aware of gay performance practice (either in terms of knowledge or in terms of sobriety) to clearly satisfy condition (2). In Ourso's performance of *The Exorcist*, for example, an audience could read the transition from Legion to Venus Envy as solely a nongay appropriation; Ourso's drag persona was styled in the manner of a Hollywood icon, and the split-second costume change's spectacularity could easily be interpreted by an audience as a nongay signification. Alternatively, however, an audience member who sees in Venus Envy's costume elements of Judy Garland and numerous other gay icons could see the totality of Ourso's performance as a metaphor for the positionality of gay men within the City-Parish: The figure of horror gives way to the iconic, visible, and (above all else) safe figure of the drag queen. Both readings could well be considered accurate to different segments of the audience given that not all citizens in attendance would be equally fluent within gay discourse or performance practice.

Meyer's totalizing framework is useful insofar as it clearly delineates the fractious discourse on Camp into identifiable categories.[27] It resists Susan Sontag's assertion in her influential essay "Notes on Camp" that Camp is indefinable—a contentious claim given that so many scholars throughout the discourse on Camp responding to Sontag have seemingly done just that—while retaining her intuition that the Camp aesthetic (be it Pop or otherwise) combines elements of class, taste, and affluence. More importantly, it accommodates the lexical usage of Camp as something that is specifically associated with tactics of gay visibility, something that happens both on and through the bodies of gay performers, while retaining the historical associations of Camp with the gay community.[28]

The presence of Camp and Pop camp within the Bal Masque is not solely the result of misinterpretations of the performances; it is clear that both Pop camp and Camp performance elements are intentionally threaded throughout the Krewe of Apollo – Baton Rouge's Bal Masque XXIX. Elvira, Mistress of the Dark, and the B-movie inspiration of all the skits, grounds the event in Pop camp, celebrating the kitsch of contemporary American cinema: Characters from the *Rocky Horror Picture Show* were merely the appetizer to prepare audiences for a parade of pop culture references that included *Beetle Juice*, *Ghostbusters*, *Little Shop of Horrors*, *Dracula*, *Buffy the Vampire Slayer*, *The Munsters*, and *The Exorcist*.[29] The scope of the films parodied let audiences in on the joke, and the krewe's members went big and bold in their skits to ensure that audiences would "get" the parodies.

Even Bal Masque XXIX's theme of "Tales from the Dark" is a clear play on Pop camp; these words printed across a ticket promise an evening filled with the schlocky fun and cultural detritus of yesteryear, material ripe for the lampooning promised by the drag queen in performance. An audience not clued in to the political valences of Camp performance or the importance of Camp to gay history is left in exactly the sort of situation David Román describes, wherein

> The social significance of camp and drag, available to gay men and lesbians, may not be apparent to a mainstream audience. Mainstream spectators, some with no sense of gay and lesbian history, may leave with such predictable impressions that simply identify gay men as entertainments. (Román, 314)

Audiences at the Krewe of Apollo – Baton Rouge's Bal Masque XXIX might find drag queens dressing up like '70s horror pinups and lampooning horror culture wildly entertaining without knowing anything about gay history. There is no spectatorship test that audiences must meet to enjoy watching Ourso satirize *The Exorcist*, Tullier's Frank N Furter, or Deshotel's parody of Michael Jackson's "Thriller." Drag can be fun simply because it traffics in Pop camp appropriations; and at Bal Masque XXIX, the presence of Pop camp fun was used to great effect to mask the deeper Camps playing out on stage.

This sense of Camp was obvious to every spectator sufficiently positioned to receive the message sent by its deployment in performance: Gay men were showcased on stage as performers, participating in an event designed to make them visible as gay performers. Although drag performances obviously fit into this formulation of Camp, it is worth noting that men not in drag participated equally in this discourse: Appearing on stage at a gay Mardi Gras Bal fulfills Meyer's requirement that Camp be "the total body of performative practices and strategies used to enact a gay identity" (Meyer, *An Archaeology of Posing*, 40). As Fremin noted to me, the Bal Masques put on by the Krewe of Apollo – Baton Rouge are more than just drag shows: "I'm not a female impersonator so I don't do drag costumes. I've always been more on the masculine side. And we need a mix of both of those things in the ball. If we were all just female impersonators, then we'd [only] be a big drag show" (Fremin, 2009). People remember drag queens because they are funny and outrageous, but their popularity with the audience should not be taken to be the entirety of the ball's appeal.

For audiences aware of gay history—either in the City-Parish or the overarching narrative of Western articulations of GLBTQ struggles—the deeper Camp resonances of the performances were quite striking. Each of the three men singled out above—Corey Tullier, John Deshotel, and Ernest Ourso—grew up in the aftermath of the Stonewall riots.[30] All three men are also too young to have witnessed firsthand the original activism of ACT UP in the wake of HIV/AIDS during the 1980s. None of these men were around at the formation of the Mardi Gras krewe to which they belong. But by stepping onstage and engaging in the sorts of cultural appropriations that, to a certain segment of the audience, seems to be Pop camp, these men are reenacting in the present the sorts of processual identifications that so many gay men before them went through in the time before Stonewall; their experiences occur within the confines of the present, but, given the Camp symbolism of the act and the gay discourse within which Camp operates, these men can gain an appreciation for a history they never lived while being a part of a historical performance.

The distinction between Camp and Pop camp also reveals the differing modes of spectatorship operative within the Bal Masque's audience. The Camp discourse offers, for the gay performers and clued-in spectators, a way to engage in a political act without recourse to formal argumentation—and the Carnival context within which this specific performance of Camp occurs allows these performers a safe-space and safe-time within the City-Parish for exactly these sorts of performances. The Pop camp context of Bal Masque XXIX—and the promise of drag performance in general—masks that the above sorts of identity performances are occurring at all; the humor of the event, its fun and spectacle, offers plausible deniability that anything outside the licensed licentiousness of Carnival is occurring at the ball. The wink of Camp invites the City-Parish to close its eyes to exactly what is going on onstage at the Baton Rouge River Center each year, allowing a segment of the citizenry to willfully blind themselves to the possibility that the message they receive from the performance might differ from the messages being sent by the performers to other audience members.

But as useful as Meyer's move is to distinguish between camp (Pop culture appropriations of gay taste) and Camp (the process of suppressed/resistant gay identity formation), Meyer's distinction remains silent on the ways in which Camp itself bears the traces of a bourgeois identification (although it does speak to bourgeois appropriations of gay identity). As Steve Vallochi notes, the origins of Camp's synonymy with gay identity coincides with the time period wherein the concept of what it meant to be gay was in flux; to identify Camp with the process of gay identity in the aftermath of World War II yet prior to the Stonewall riots is to make claims that have a specific racial and classist connotation. In the aftermath of World War II, the term "homosexual" was forced on people who experienced same-sex attraction rather than to people who articulated their gender's performance in countercultural ways; to be a gay man, at this time, ceased to be a statement about one's gender stylings (masculine or effeminate) and became a statement of sexual orientation. As this shift occurred in the 1950s through 1960s, differences between the race, ethnicity, affluence, and taste of these men were considered of less import than matters of same-sex desire: This new definition ignored the differences in the subcultures and included everyone in its chilling embrace (Valocchi, 215). To be gay, at this point, was not to be black *and* gay, or white *and* gay; rather, the sorts of identifications that we now view as important to and partially constitutive of contemporary identities—especially subaltern identities—were flattened and homogenized into one totalizing label. Whether intentional or unintentional, this designation resulted in a whitewashing of what it meant to be gay: Racial differences were downplayed, and the sorts of tastes described by Sontag—with their affluent connotations—became an imposed false universal of gay experience.

Perhaps it is in this phenomenon that we can begin to come to an explanation as to why the Krewe of Apollo – Baton Rouge is so disproportionately Caucasian. Krewe members' protestations that the club is egalitarian are likely true; but the mixture of Camp and Pop camps on display in a performance of the Bal Masque may well mean differently to nonwhite gay men within the City-Parish than it does to the predominately white membership of the Krewe. Indeed, the Pop camps on display throughout the Bal Masque are the sorts of loaded cultural appropriations labeled the "camp effect" by Andrew Ross:

> The camp effect, then, is created not simply by a change in the mode of cultural production (and the contradictions attendant on that change), but rather when the products (stars, in this case) of a much earlier mode of production which has lost its power to produce and dominate cultural meanings, become available, in the present, for redefinition according to contemporary codes of taste. (quoted in Kleto, 312)

While Pop camp remains an operation of taste, as Ross notes above, taste is not universal; to understand taste one absolutely must understand the cultural production that gave rise to this taste as well as the ability of capitalist culture to then market things to this taste. If Pop camp traffics in reappropriation, it is important to keep in mind the fact that not all reappropriations are of interest to all performers.

Although Meyer's distinction between Camp and Pop camp is the formulation that I find most useful in making sense of the Krewe of Apollo – Baton Rouge's Bal Masques, it is important to note that Meyer's formulation is far from the definitive word on the subject.[31] Although much of this scholarship falls outside the purview of this chapter, I do rely on Davy's contention, articulated in her 1994 essay "Fe/Male Impersonation: The Discourse on Camp," that "the wink of Camp (re)assures its audience of the ultimate harmlessness of its play, its palatability for bourgeois sensibilities" (quoted in Meyer, *The Politics and Poetics of* Camp, 145). Despite the intensity of the pushback against Sontag's 1964 essay, few have argued against her observations regarding the codependence of camp and (specifically Western) affluence; and Davy's intuition harnesses Sontag's observations into a useful corrective to the discourse.

The audience of Bal Masque XXIX can absolutely enjoy the performances without understanding the role Camp and drag performance plays in the signification of gay identity. Moreover, as was demonstrated earlier with the discussion of Judy Garland, it is plausible to contend that, for some audience members, these Camp performances of gay signification can be (mis)interpreted as simple Pop camp appropriations. The political nature of Camp identity performance is elided behind the wink of Camp; the performances are so entertaining and spectacular that it is entirely possible for an audience to effectively miss the fact that these significations are sending a different message to audience members aware of gay history than to audience members without this awareness.

This potential for misreading is exactly why Camp implies both in-the-know performers and in-the-know spectators. For Meyer, the signs must necessarily point to something intrinsic to gayness: the potential for political action. For others, the signs are not necessarily grounded in gayness but in different varieties of selectivity. As seen above, Davy contends that, often, the selectivity of camp—the wink—is specifically of/by/for a group privileged in terms of gender and class—not just sexuality. The Krewe of Apollo Bal Masque XXIX's effect on its audience relies on the combination of Camp and Pop camp with the Mardi Gras traditions that allow the display of excess. For some spectators, the trappings of Pop camp make the evening enjoyable; gay men are entertaining because, well, *drag queens!* For other spectators, the wink of Camp speaks to past articulations of gay identity while arguing for a different present and future informed by the mass appeal of gay visibility. The presence of both of these meanings throughout the performance, irrespective of whether every audience member can consciously receive the messages being sent, is necessary for the celebratory atmosphere of Bal Masque XXIX. Both Camp and Pop camp come together in the promise for a different, more tolerant, and never-explicitly-argued-for future of the City-Parish.

CAPITALIST CAMP, PATRIARCHAL CAMP

Beneath the Bal Masque's appearance of countercultural decadence, however, lies a normalizing dramaturgy that relies on this blend of Camp, Pop camp, and Carnival to create a space wherein present cultural mores within the City-Parish are no longer operative. In so doing, Bal Masque XXIX uses its performance to articulate the ways that the Bal Masque's display of capital demonstrates its constituent members' status (be they aspirational or existent) within the City-Parish; or, as Davy argues, "male camp tends to reinscribe, rather than undermine, the dominant culture paradigms it appropriates for its farce and means to parody" (as in Meyer, *The Politics and Poetics of Camp*, 145). In many ways, the success and acceptance of the Bal Masque in particular (and the Krewe of Apollo – Baton Rouge in general) struck me as a deft disruption of the assumed heterosexuality of the City-Parish of East Baton Rouge. That being said, at the end of the ball I marveled at the event's efficacy in situating the gay male subject into a position of patriarchal and capitalistic power within the community. The costumes were spectacular. The performances were exhaustingly well rehearsed. The building within which the event was held is, perhaps, the most expensive performance space found in the City-Parish. Even the program highlights that the "ball this evening was made possible by a group of hard working men, the members of the Krewe, and financial supporters" (Mut and Tullier, 3).

For many households, participation in something like Bal Masque XXIX as a performer is an impossible luxury given the annual dues required to be a member of the krewe in addition to the masked costs of putting on a respectable performance. Fremin, however, thinks of his own spending in the following terms:

> Let me put it into perspective for you: You make this much a year. Decent salary. I'm not rich by any means. I'm self-employed. I've worked for every dollar, but you know, with what I make, in five years I should be able to save up enough to take a trip to Europe. Go to Europe for three or four weeks. Or I could wear it in one costume for one night and be just as happy. Well, I haven't seen Europe, my friend—but I'm just as happy. (Fremin, 2009)

While Fremin's view of performance in a Bal Masque as a culmination of five years' savings is certainly one valid way of justifying the cost, not all Krewe members approach the Bal Masque in this way. Bal Masque XXIX is not the only Krewe of Apollo – Baton Rouge Bal Masque that I have attended during my time in Baton Rouge. Although there are certainly some performers who, like Fremin, only perform on special occasions, there are other krewe members who stage full numbers with a full complement of backup dancers on a yearly basis both before and after they join the krewe's royalty club. Given City-Parish census data regarding the affluence of the average citizen, it is not unreasonable to conclude that the Krewe of Apollo – Baton Rouge, like many other Mardi Gras krewes throughout Louisiana, stages its own affluence. Although the Pop camp and Camp appeals make the nontraditional Bal Masque extremely entertaining and viable as a public performance to audiences of all stripes, the amount of money on display each year surrounding these Camp and camp performances are the clear draws to the event. Given the scale and scope of these performances, much of the performance's spectacularity relies on the staggering amounts of capital underwriting these performances.

Despite the fact that the Krewe of Apollo is a gay Mardi Gras krewe and presumably uninterested in women as sexual objects, the sum total of the Bal Masque's performances situated the gay male transvestite subject as the proper vessel for the display of femininity; this fact of performance, coupled with the classist and affluential aspects of the performance, positions the krewe as being entitled to the very privileges afforded to straight men in the community. The opulent display performed by men and women at traditional Mardi Gras Bal Masques is resituated onto the transvestite or gay body of a krewe member, and the display is only made available to audiences affluent enough to buy a ticket to see this spectacle. For Bal Masque XXIX, a table at the Bal costs $800; balcony seating is $50 per person; access to the floor seating surrounding the stage is limited to those the krewe members invite to the event.

While the above prices might not seem particularly high to residents of cities such as Los Angeles or New York City, remember the demographic information provided near the beginning of this chapter; in the Baton Rouge community, median household income is less than $50,000 per year. A ticket to Swine Palace Productions, the only equity theater in Baton Rouge, costs only $28.00 for a single adult ticket (season tickets run an adult $85.00). Louisiana State University's Theatre Department sells tickets $18.00 per adult, while the average price of a ticket to the cinema is $9.00, with cheaper prices available for a matinee showing. The price for a ticket to the Krewe of Apollo's Bal Masque decidedly does not include dinner, attire, or drinks; guests must provide their own alcohol, purchase dresses and tuxedos, and typically eat before attending. For a couple to attend the Bal Masque, the real cost of attending the event is likely between $250.00 and $300.00—more than what a single Louisiana citizen earning minimum wage would earn after taxes are deducted from a full week's pay of $7.25 an hour for forty hours' worth of work.

In real life, I can imagine little that would be more gauche than to pay several hundred dollars to watch wealthy people throw multiple hundreds of thousands of $1 bills in the air and roll around in it while an appreciative audience roared its approbation. But in Mardi Gras practice, this is, ultimately, an element put on display for crowds at *any* Bal Masque. Although the wink of Camp turns this deadly serious element of a traditional Bal Masque into something wickedly funny at Bal Masque XXIX, the fact remains that some would find this behavior despicable outside the Carnival context (consider the ramifications of this behavior at an Occupy Wall Street protest, for example). It is worth noting, here, that the above characterization of Carnival display is something that most krewes would vociferously deny if asked this in a public forum: they would appeal to Louisiana tradition and cite the storied history of Carnival practice as the draw of a Bal Masque. Regardless, there are no notable Bal Masques where spectacular effects and extravagant displays are not the draw: Although parades celebrate licentiousness and establish the misrule of the carnivalesque, it is at a Bal Masque where ornate costumes are given center stage for one night.

Only that's not quite the case at Bal Masque XXIX. Rather, it is in the layering of Camp and Pop camp appeals that this Bal Masque distinguishes itself. At a traditional heterosexual Bal Masque, participation in the Bal Masque as royalty or a member is frequently an affirmation of a family's wealth or position within the community; at Bal Masque XXIX, an event sponsored by a gay Mardi Gras krewe, the members' minority status gives these displays of wealth a different meaning than that normally seen at numerous heterosexual Mardi Gras balls. Because of the City-Parish's contentious attitude toward GLBTQ issues and its history of discrimination, the displays of wealth that would affirm a heterosexual family's affluence and status within the community becomes, for the Krewe of Apollo, a chance to display their bona fides in the community. That no one notices the effect of these repeated, yearly performances is unsurprising: As David Roman argues, "The survivalist quality that so marks camp and drag for the gay spectator is reconfigured and depoliticized in the commodification process" (Román, 314). Krewe members get to perform their success, participate in patriarchy, and demonstrate all of the ways krewe members almost, but not quite, belong to the privileged class of the City-Parish.

The reason the above is possible lies in the ball's use of Camp as part of its performance; the wink of Camp makes the audaciousness of the Bal Masque palatable within the City-Parish as both a Bal Masque and as a gay event. Carnival tradition, as noted earlier, allows this event to occur; the given social order is suspended, and the illicit is licit during Carnival season. But the appeal and power of these performances lies in the twin messages being sent out to spectators in attendance: Camp in the political sense (which speaks to the citizens in attendance knowledgeable of gay history, an appeal that works in part through the Bal Masque's history in the City-Parish) and Pop camp (aimed at and subtly lampooning audiences clueless about Camp's political dimension). Although gay performances are common in metropolises across the United States, Baton Rouge only gets one event of this scope each year. Fremin and numerous other members of the Krewe of Apollo – Baton Rouge may contend that the group is apolitical, but the by-product of the Krewe's goal to produce a Bal Masque is that they inadvertently create an event that provides affluent gay members of the City-Parish visibility. The krewe may be nonpartisan, but their mission to put on a gay-themed Bal Masque nonetheless retains a political valence despite the absence of explicit political argument. The entire point of the Bal Masque, according to krewe members, is to have a good time: That it also allows the gay men who promote and fund the krewe to be seen as gay men fortunate enough to be part of a Mardi Gras krewe is simply lagniappe. As I hope is now clear, what Bal Masque XXIX actually does is combine the commercial viability of Pop camp to the historically gay processes of identity creation that mark Camp to create an event wherein the performer, by participating in gay performance, displays the ways in which these displays of capital, power, and taste already incorporate this particular segment of the gay male population into the prevailing City-Parish status quo. If money and patriarchal power are required to run a conservative city, these yearly performances, licensed by the tradition of Carnival, allow for a specific minority within the City-Parish to demonstrate their participation in the very status quo that would (incorrectly) label them subaltern.

Finally, operating underneath both Pop camp and Camp proper lies the real appeal: For one night, thousands of people in Baton Rouge were at a gay event, marveling at the productive power of one specific segment of the gay community. This spatial transformation is, in some ways, unremarkable: a simple fact of people showing up, in the same way that going to a gay bar, a gay pride march, or a gay political event involves going to a gay space devoted to promoting gay visibility. The intermingling of Pop camp and Camp elements in the context of Louisiana Carnival practice ensured the attendance of numerous people to the event and solicited the participation of numerous people in the event in numbers that far exceed the attendance and support of other events devoted solely to the production of gay visibility. The fun and games of Bal Masque XXIX elided the transfiguration of the Baton Rouge River Center (a space that is the home of numerous industrial shows and family entertainments the other 364 days each year) into a gay space, even if that transfiguration is a transfiguration that can only last one night each year.

I believe that Bal Masque XXIX provides a template, rough and imperfect as it might be, for how different types of Camp (be it capitalized or no) can work in concert to create events that are far more mainstream than traditional gay events, such as pride marches or overtly political rallies. Perhaps this is true because of the wink of gay Camp, as Davy contends, or, instead, because the traditions of Carnival ensure that this can only happen one night each year in the City-Parish of East Baton Rouge. But something has happened in Louisiana. Despite the strength of conservative politics and religious fundamentalism in the city, the Krewe of Apollo – Baton Rouge has been able to market itself as a viable player in the free-market economy of contemporary Louisiana by virtue of the quality of its yearly performances. Corporate sponsors line up to give away money even as businesses ask the krewe to send drag queens to corporate parties throughout the year. According to Larry Fremin, 30 to 40 percent of the thousands who attend the Apollo Ball are heterosexual, a number he contends is significantly higher than the number of heterosexuals who frequent other gay spaces (Fremin, 2009). I believe it is the plausible deniability of Pop camp—a camp that masks the Camp of the Krewe's Bal Masque—that has allowed the krewe to insinuate itself into the business of the city more and more each year, to combine Camp performance with spectacular displays of capital. Bal Masque XXIX's overt mixing of Pop camp and Camp demystified the ways in which the Krewe of Apollo – Baton Rouge has winked its way into the good graces of the City-Parish, and invited citizenry to close its eyes to fact that, in many of the ways that matter, the gay men who make up the Krewe of Apollo – Baton Rouge have already arrived.

But this wink is not without its own complexities. On the one hand, attention must be paid to the thirty-year history of the Krewe of Apollo – Baton Rouge and the strides it has made in producing an authentically gay performance event: Conceived of, funded by, and performed by gay members of the City-Parish community, the expensive spectacle is frequently the most extravagant local performance in the Baton Rouge River Center each year. But on the other hand, every social club without open membership, even a club like the Krewe of Apollo – Baton Rouge, which requires only dues to be paid, is necessarily exclusionary: even if, in this case, members who cannot pay simply cannot be members of the krewe for years that they do not pay their dues. Despite the krewe's efforts in creating a safe space for gay men at its yearly Bal Masque, the Bal Masque's performances, as a consequence of its exclusionary membership policies, perform a vision of gay life that is intimately entangled with issues of class, sex, race, and privilege. These observations are not meant to belittle or minimize the numerous barriers through which the Krewe of Apollo – Baton Rouge has already broken within its thirty-year history: They should remind us that, despite the progress that has been made, perhaps there is more progress yet to come.[32]

NOTES

1. For readers curious about Mardi Gras as a performance practice, a good primer is William Jankowiak and C. Todd White's "Carnival on the Clipboard: An Ethnological Study of

New Orleans Mardi Gras," *Ethnology* 38, no. 4 (1999). Although the authors focus specifically on New Orleans Mardi Gras practice, key concepts such as Bal Masques and existing research trends surrounding Mardi Gras are explained in great detail. Even though there is no scholarship focusing on Baton Rouge gay Mardi Gras to date, there are two scholars in particular who have done work similar to my own: Jonathan Bollen in "Sexing the Dance at Sleaze Ball 1994," *TDR* 40, no. 3 (1996) and Vicki Mayer in "Letting It All Hang Out: Mardi Gras Performances Live and on Video," *TDR* 51, no. 2 (2007). Bollen's article focuses on the phenomenon of gay disco in Sidney, Australia, and links gay practice to issues of class and capitalism. Mayer's essay addresses the link between Mardi Gras practice—in both New Orleans and Brazil—to the advent of soft- and hard-core pornography industry based around selling Mardi Gras as a location of carnivalesque sexual license (which is complicated by the unspoken class- and race-based rules of transgression of New Orleans).

2. For those curious about the specialized terms used in Mardi Gras practice, Hennig Cohen's "The Terminology of Mardi Gras," *American Speech* 26, no. 2 (1951), contains a great deal of information still relevant today.

3. Some notes on Louisiana-specific terminology. The state of Louisiana is the only state within the United States of America to organize itself into "parishes" rather than "counties" (or, in Alaska's case, "boroughs" and census areas). This nomenclature can be traced back to Louisiana's status as a French and Spanish territory during the sixteenth, seventeenth, and eighteenth centuries; both France and Spain were, at that time, Catholic nations. The 1811 constitutional convention that was organized to prepare for the Louisiana territory's admission to the United States of America legitimized the nomenclature of "parish" first established by the 1807 territorial legislature as the term used to divide the territory of Louisiana into smaller areas for local governments. The city of Baton Rouge is part of East Baton Rouge Parish; in 1947, the citizens of the city of Baton Rouge and the parish of East Baton Rouge voted to consolidate the government into a single, local entity. This combined the office of the mayor of Baton Rouge with the president of East Baton Rouge Parish—and further consolidation has continued throughout the six decades since the merger. Throughout this piece, I use the term "city-parish" to reflect the consolidation of government into one homogeneous entity.

4. Older krewe members, like Larry Fremin, all have stories about past harassment outside the venues of early Bal Masques (Fremin, 2009).

5. This poor track record extends back decades and is well documented by various GLBTQ watchdog groups as well as the City-Parish's newspaper, *The Baton Rouge Advocate*. In the final three months of 2012 alone, the East Baton Rouge Democratic Parish Committee—the leadership council of the area's Democratic Party made local headlines when members of the committee attempted to censure local attorney and fellow Committee member Donald Hodge; Hodge had requested that local Democrats who sought the EBRDPC's endorsement should be required to back the United States' national Democratic Party's platform supporting marriage equality for same sex couples. The motion to censure Hodge was abandoned after Hodge sued the committee. Joe Gyan Jr., "EBR Democrats Won't Censure Hodge," *The Advocate*, December 10, 2012. This local issue is indicative of the sorts of issues facing GLBTQ citizens in the City-Parish: As of January 2013, the Human Right's Campaign's awarded the City-Parish of Baton Rouge a score of 2 out of 100 in its Municipal Equality Index.

6. One need not go so far as to subscribe to Dickie's institutional theory of art or even Noel Carroll's historical theory of art to agree with this. One can argue, for example, that recognizing even aesthetic properties proper (such as "beauty") requires careful attention to the kind of contextual details raised by philosophers such as Carroll or Dickie. For an excellent discussion, see Noel Carroll, *Philosophy of Art* (New York: Routledge, 1999).

7. The organization's membership consists only of men, almost all of whom identify themselves as gay men. Visitors to the Krewe of Apollo – Baton Rouge's website might miss this fact; barring pictures of members in drag as current or past royalty, no text exists that broadcasts or highlights the fact that this is a gay social organization.

8. Ads for Gerry Lane Enterprises (a Baton Rouge car dealership), After Five Tuxedo Company, Greenoaks Funeral Home, and Renaissance Funeral Services are displayed within the program alongside ads from the Metropolitan Community Church of Baton Rouge ("You don't have to be straight to be straight with God!"), La Mestizo Louisiana/ Mexican Cuisine, and Dow Louisiana Federal Credit Union, to list only a few. It is worth noting that, in New Orleans Carnival praxis, corporate sponsorships are forbidden by law.

9. For the curious, City-Parish Mayor-President Kip Holden, in partnership with local business leaders, attempted to launch what he called the "One Baton Rouge" initiative in 2007. The One Baton Rouge initiative was a tourism and immigration policy designed to (1) create the impression that Baton Rouge was progressive and welcoming for both minority and GLBTQ individuals as a place to visit by (2) creating government policies that actually made the City-Parish a minority- and GLBTQ-friendly city. Despite Holden's popularity as a mayor (which is addressed and expanded on later in this chapter), the City-Parish's Metro Council opposed this initiative. The initiative finally died in 2010: Local pastors throughout the City-Parish purchased numerous advertisements slamming the policy, and their attempts to lobby the Metro Council to cut the One Baton Rouge initiative's funding bore fruit. For those who wish to see the Metro Council meeting where this was admitted, WBRZ Baton Rouge has made the video available on their website ("'One Baton Rouge' Resolution Dead").

10. "I said, 'This [private charter fiat] will never work in the gay community. This club will fold as so many other gay clubs around us have done. I want to see us form something that the members are going to control; if we don't like you as captain for this year we've just got to put up with you for nine more months because we're going to elect somebody else.'"— Interview with Larry Fremin, November 25, 2009.

11. It is something of a tradition in Louisiana that successful Mardi Gras krewes can effectively give birth to satellite krewes in different cities. Thus, Dobson's Mystic Krewe of Apollo is the "mother" krewe of all the krewes listed in this section because all of the krewes were spun off from or inspired by Dobson's Mystic Krewe. That the Krewe of Apollo – Baton Rouge is the only krewe to eschew the word "mystic" in its title will be addressed later in this section.

12. Lafayette, Louisiana, is a medium-sized city approximately 60 miles west of Baton Rouge. Given the city's proximity to Baton Rouge—commutes to Lafayette routinely take 30 to 45 minutes less than a commute to New Orleans—it was natural for men to commute to Lafayette rather than New Orleans.

13. Interview with Larry Fremin.

14. Fellow founder (and Queen Apollo I) Earl Reed disagreed with Fremin's organization of the Mystic Krewe of Apollo – Baton Rouge as a democracy, and wanted to take more direct control over the direction of the krewe. Reed gained control of the "Mystic Krewe

of Apollo – Baton Rouge" name; all other members of the krewe resigned and reincorpo-
rated under the name of "Krewe of Apollo – Baton Rouge." The Krewe of Apollo – Baton
Rouge promptly erased Reed from krewe history, a fact apparent to all individuals who
go to the krewe's website. The krewe's archives list all past kings and queens as part of the
krewe's "Royalty Club." Reed's erasure has caused King Apollo I, Larry Fremin, to be listed
as the only King Apollo without a queen.

15. This information, provided by the US Census, contains numerous demographic facts that
help put the expense of the Bal Masque in perspective; for instance, the City-Parish is 50%
Caucasian and 45.5% African American, but krewe membership does not distribute in
numbers anywhere close to the demographic make-up of the city.

16. I cite Steve Valocchi's arguments in "The Class-Based Nature of Gay Identity," *Social
Problems* 46, no. 2 (1999), to this effect in the section "The Krewe of Apollo – Baton Rouge's
Bal Masque XXIX."

17. This practice became common because of the krewe's informal prohibition on allowing
women to join the krewe. A careful review of the krewe's Constitution and Bylaws will
reveal that there is no explicit rule forbidding women (excluding the usage of the masculine pronoun "he" in all instances, which possesses plausible deniability given the common usage of this in other legal documents). Instead, the Bylaws reveal only one specific
reference to women: the chartering of a "Women's Auxiliary," which shall maintain a separate set of Articles and Bylaws—but that is guaranteed a single table at the Apollo Ball
each year. Fremin confirms that this ambiguity is intentional; as founder, he did not want
to preclude female membership as a matter of course. Instead, he chose to leave this up to
the membership of the krewe to decide democratically. Thus far, no attempts to change the
informal prohibition of female membership have been successful (nor, for that matter, are
any such attempts documented).

18. A float is a platform pulled by a car, decorated and costumed by the performers who sponsored the float's inclusion in the parade.

19. Much of the academic discourse surrounding Mardi Gras works within an explicitly
Bakhtinian understanding of these celebrations. Those curious about other applica-
tions of Bakhtin's carnivalesque to Mardi Gras celebrations should refer to Vicki Mayer's
aforementioned article "Letting It All Hang Out: Mardi Gras Performances Live and On
Video," as well as Carolyn Ware's "Anything to Act Crazy: Cajun Women and Mardi Gras
Disguises," *Journal of American Folklore* 114, no. 452 (2001); Marcia Gaudet's "The World
Downside-Up: Mardi Gras at Carville," *Journal of American Folklore* 111, no. 439 (1998);
Carl Lindahl's "Bakhtin's Carnival Laughter and the Cajun Country Mardi Gras," *Folklore*
107 (1996); and Mary Russo's "Female Grotesques: Carnival and Theory," in Theresa
de Lauretis, ed., *Feminist Studies/Critical Studies* (Bloomington: Indiana University
Press, 2009).

20. The military reference is no accident; in Mardi Gras tradition, color guards bear the "flag"
of the individual krewe.

21. According to the Baton Rouge AIDS Society (http://www.batonrougeaidssociety.org/),
"Baton Rouge ranks 4th for AIDS case rates among the largest metropolitan areas in the
United States." In Louisiana, Baton Rouge has the highest rate of AIDS cases; the state is
the fifth highest in terms of AIDS cases and twelfth in number of diagnoses. Interestingly,
however, HIV and AIDS disproportionately affects the African American community;
while this in no way diminishes the Krewe of Apollo's efforts to combat HIV/AIDS, it is
interesting that the community most in need of assistance in the City-Parish is not well

represented within the krewe. According to the Centers for Disease Control, Baton Rouge was the leader of per capita diagnoses of HIV/AIDS in 2010, the year of Bal Masque XXIX.

22. Holden received 71 percent of the City-Parish vote, winning every district in the City-Parish. This election was among the more contentious in recent City-Parish history: Holden was the subject of an intense smear campaign. While the state of Louisiana is no stranger to smear campaigns and attack advertisements, the employment of these tactics in a local race against a politician as popular as Holden was unusual. This particular campaign featured the distribution of anonymous advertisements bearing doctored pictures of Holden's face wherein Holden had suffered multiple black eyes and bruises "supposedly caused by an angry husband for [Holden's] indiscretions with the man's wife." Tyana Williams, "Councilman Sharper Denies Responsibility for Flyer about Mayor Holden," WAFB (Baton Rouge, LA), August 4, 2008.

23. Although there is a surprising dearth of scholarly work surrounding Elvira, I encourage readers to visit http://modlife.com/elvira, Elvira's website, to see how little her appearance has changed since her heyday as a feature film star.

24. Please note that the discourse on "theatricality" is fractious, frequently prey to Eurocentrisms, and, at least in performance studies and theater history, invites disagreement. My own usage of the term, here, is consonant with Janelle Reinelt's description of an "uncritical" usage: It denotes "aspects of texts or performances that gesture to their own conditions of production or to metatheatrical effects; these usages are generally clear enough and forthright, if imprecise." Janelle Reinelt, "The Politics of Discourse: Performativity Meets Theatricality," 206.

25. Meyer published two editions of his essay "Reclaiming the Discourse of Camp": one in his 1993 anthology *The Politics and Poetics of Camp* (New York: Routledge, 1993), and one in his 2010 monograph *The Archaeology of Posing* (Madison, WI: Macater Press, 2010). In his 2010 essay, Meyer notes that he received editorial pressure in 1993 to define camp as "queer parody" rather than his preferred "gay parody"—a decision motivated by the ascendance of queer studies. Meyer asserts that this was never a good fit for what he was trying to articulate: that Camp is a specifically gay discourse and praxis. As such, I will defer to Meyer's assessment of his scholarship and refer only to the 2010 publication.

26. In post–World War II vernacular, a "Friend of Dorothy" was slang for a gay man. Refer to Andrew Ross, "Uses of Camp," in Fabio Cleto's *Camp: Queer Aesthetics and the Performing Subject: A Reader* (Ann Arbor: University of Michigan Press, 1999).

27. One can refer again to Cleto for a sense of exactly how fractious this discourse is. Typically, camp scholars locate Oscar Wilde (Shugart and Waggoner), J. Redding Ware's 1909 dictionary *Passing English of the Victorian Era* (Meyer, *Archaeology of Posing*), and Christopher Isherwood's novel *The World in the Evening* (London: Methuen, 1954) as all being instrumental in the early theorizing and history of the term. Subsequent articulations of camp differ in terms of analytical approach, objects defined as camp, and numerous other particulars.

28. This emergence of camp is ineluctably tied to the development of post–World War II, pre-Stonewall gay male identity. As Alan Berubé notes in *Coming Out under Fire: The History of Gay Men and Women of World War Two* (New York: Plume Books, 1990), before Pride marches and other visibility-oriented political protest became widespread, camp "could simultaneously distance [gay men] from the humiliation they endured as social outcasts while creating an alternative moral order and culture in which gay men were in control . . . These styles reflected the self-consciousness of some gay men as sexual

or gender outsiders and helped them define themselves as 'insiders' of their own secret world" (86–87).

29. For an excellent treatment on kitsch and its relation to camp, refer to Chuck Kleinhans's essay "Taking Out the Trash: Camp and the Politics of Parody" (in Meyer, 1993).

30. The Stonewall riots occurred on June 28, 1969, in Greenwich Village, New York City. These spontaneous, unplanned riots occurred when members of the gay community violently responded to police raids of gay establishments. Scholars position the Stonewall riots as being the catalyst for the gay liberation movement, and an important predecessor to pride marches and other, visibility-centric political protests.

31. Scholars interested in the possibilities of lesbian camp can refer to the work of Kate Davy, Judith Halberstam, Sue-Ellen Case, and numerous other writers.

32. I'd like to thank Leigh Clemons, Jon Cogburn, John Fletcher, Alan Sikes, and Les Wade for their advice on earlier drafts of this chapter. Special appreciation is extended to Shaye Anderson, Michelle Bart, Billy Bryan, David Coley, Maia Elgin, Jennie Garland, Skylar Gremillion, Emma Harvey, Macy and Russell Jones, Mark Lance, John Mabry, Cara Melvin, Piper Nosal, John Protevi, Francois Raffoul, James and Mona Rocha, Daniel Ruiz, Caroline Russell, Mark Silcox, Lauren Stefanski, Wiliam Thomas, and Joshua Zuckerman for helpful discussions about the issues addressed in this chapter.

BIBLIOGRAPHY

Bakhtin, Mikhail. *Rabelais and His World*. Translated by Helene Iswolsky. Bloomington: Indiana University Press, 1984.

"Baton Rouge AIDS Society: National Statistics." Baton Rouge AIDS Society. Accessed January 12, 2013. http://www.batonrougeaidssociety.org/.

Berubé, Alan. *Coming Out under Fire: The History of Gay Men and Women in World War Two*. New York: Plume Books, 1990.

Bollen, Jonathan. "Sexing the Dance at Sleaze Ball 1994." *TDR* 40, no. 3 (1996): 166–91.

Butler, Judith. "Performative Acts and Gender Constitution: An Essay in Phenomenology and Feminist Theory." *Theatre Journal* 40 (1988): 519.

Case, Sue-Ellen. "Classic Drag: The Greek Creation of Female Parts." *Theatre Journal* 37, no. 3 (October 1985).

Cohen, Hennig. "The Terminology of Mardi Gras." *American Spéech* 26, no. 2 (1951): 110–15.

Davis, Kristy. " 'One Baton Rouge' Resolution Dead." WBRZ (Baton Rouge, LA), July 28, 2010.

Department of Health and Human Services: Centers for Disease Control. "Basic Statistics." Accessed January 15, 2013. http://www.cdc.gov/hiv/topics/surveillance/basic.htm.

Fremin, Larry. Personal interview. November 25, 2009.

Gaudet, Marcia. "The World Downside-Up: Mardi Gras at Carville." *Journal of American Folklore* 111, no. 439 (Winter 1998), 23–38.

Gyan, Joe Jr. "EBR Democrats Won't Censure Hodge." *The Advocate* (Baton Rouge, LA), December 10, 2012. http://theadvocate.com/home/4597551-125/ebr-democrats-wont-censure-hodge.

Human Rights Campaign. "Municipal Equality Index." Accessed January 15, 2013. http://hrc.org/apps/mei/profile.php?id=14#.UQB7dInjmXR.

Isherwood, Christopher. *The World in the Evening*. London: Methuen, 1954.

Jankowiak, William, and C. Todd White. "Carnival on the Clipboard: An Ethnological Study of New Orleans Mardi Gras." *Ethnology* 38, no. 4 (1999): 335–49.

Krewe of Apollo – Baton Rouge. Constitution and Bylaws.

Krewe of Apollo – Baton Rouge. "Krewe Archives." Accessed January 15, 2013. http://www.apollobatonrouge.com/Archives.html.

Lindahl, Carl. "Bakhtin's Carnival Laughter and the Cajun Country Mardi Gras." *Folklore* 107 (1996): 57–70.

Mayer, Vicki. "Letting It All Hang Out: Mardi Gras Performances Live and on Video." *TDR* 51, no. 2 (2007): 76–93.

Meyer, Moe, ed. *The Politics and Poetics of Camp*. New York: Routledge, 1993.

Meyer, Moe. *An Archaeology of Posing: Essays on Camp, Drag, and Sexuality*. Madison, WI: Macater Press, 2010.

Mut, Lester, and Tullier, Corey. "Tales from the Dark—Bal Masque XXIX: Apollo's Horror, 2010." Baton Rouge: Krewe of Apollo – Baton Rouge, 2010.

"One Baton Rouge." One Baton Rouge. Accessed May 11, 2010. http://onebatonrouge.com/.

Reinelt, Janelle. "The Politics of Discourse: Performativity Meets Theatricality." *SubStance* 31, no. 2/3 (2002): 201–15.

Reinelt, Janelle, and Joseph R. Roach. *Critical Theory and Performance*. Revised and enlarged edition. Ann Arbor: University of Michigan Press, 2007.

Roberts, Robin. "New Orleans Mardi Gras and Gender in Three Krewes: Rex, the Truck-Parades, and Muses." *Western Folklore* 65, no. 3 (Summer 2006), 303–28.

Román, David. " 'It's My Party and I'll Die if I Want To!': Gay Men, AIDS, and the Circulation of Camp in U.S.Theatre." *Theatre Journal* 44, no. 3 (October 1992): 305–27.

Russo, Mary. 1986. "Female Grotesques: Carnival and Theory." In *Feminist Studies/Critical Studies*, edited by Teresa de Lauretis, 213–29. Bloomington: Indiana University Press.

Sontag, Susan. *Against Interpretation and Other Essays*. New York: Picador, 1966.

Shugart, Helene, and Catherine Egley Waggoner. *Making Camp: Rhetorics of Transgression in U.S. Popular Culture*. Tuscaloosa: University of Alabama Press, 2009.

Tullier, Corey. Personal interview. April 21, 2010.

US Census. "Baton Rouge City, Louisiana." http://factfinder2.census.gov/faces/nav/jsf/pages/searchresults.xhtml.

Valocchi, Steve. "The Class-Inflected Nature of Gay Identity." *Social Problems* 46, no. 2 (May 1999): 207–24.

Ware, Carolyn. "Anything to Act Crazy: Cajun Women and Mardi Gras Disguise." *Journal of American Folklore* 114, no. 452 (Spring 2001).

Williams, Tyana. "Councilman Sharper Denies Responsibility for Flyer about Mayor Holden." WAFB (Baton Rouge, LA), August 4, 2008.

SECTION X

INFECTION

CHAPTER 41

···

BORROWED CROWDS
The Living Theatre's Contagious Revolution

···

MIRIAM FELTON-DANSKY

IN the late fall of 1964, the Living Theatre attempted to stage Artaud's plague. The company was touring Europe, having fled the United States the year before, following dramatic show-downs with the IRS and New York City police, which had resulted in expulsion from their theater building on Fourteenth Street in downtown Manhattan. Now, in Europe, the company planned to present productions of two plays by Jean Genet, and was in the process of raising the necessary funds. In the meantime, intending to experiment with their newest, most radical staging ideas, and in the process to create a touring production that would bring in ticket sales, the members of the Living Theatre composed a performance piece that came to be called *Mysteries and Smaller Pieces* (fig. 41.1). *Mysteries*, which premiered in Paris that October, would become a part of the Living Theatre's tours for at least the next five years—and would represent a turning point in the company's approaches to dramaturgy, staging, and audience participation.

The form of this new piece was a departure for the Living Theatre, which had, until that point, primarily based their productions on written scripts: first, after Judith Malina and Julian Beck founded the group in 1947, by staging the language play of high modernist poets such as T. S. Eliot and Gertrude Stein. In the 1950s and early 1960s, the company drew on Malina's experiences studying with Brecht's early collaborator Erwin Piscator, and intro-duced American audiences to several Brecht dramas, including *In the Jungle of Cities* and *Man Is Man*. During that same era, between 1959 and 1963, the company produced premieres of formally adventurous, frame-breaking new plays by American writers: Jack Gelber's *The Connection*, a palimpsest layering multiple realities over a *Godot*-like tale of addicts awaiting a fix; and Kenneth Brown's *The Brig*, in which the company enacted the horrific daily brutali-ties attending life in an American Marine brig.

Mysteries, by contrast, was a theatrical collage, sampling iconic scenes and images from the Living Theatre's previous productions—*The Brig*'s harsh military choreography made several appearances—and combining them with new movement sequences and perfor-mances of poetry and ritual. Before long, one scene from *Mysteries* had become iconic in its own right: the final sequence, an attempt to physically enact the metaphysical plague that Antonin Artaud had described thirty years earlier, in his famous essay "The Theater and the

Plague." Beck had conceived the idea for this scene, taking inspiration from Artaud's poetic description of the affinities between theatrical performance and mercilessly contagious epidemic. Onstage, Beck's concept unfolded in graphically literal terms: members of the company dispersed themselves through the auditorium, then pretended to expire in gruesomely close proximity to the audience—writhing, suffering paroxysms, and collapsing, sometimes in spectators' laps. When all "life" among the acting company had been extinguished, two performers moved through the crowd, stacking the stiff bodies in a pyramid onstage.

Frequently—and significantly, for the purposes of this chapter—this body pile included more than just the members of the Living Theatre. In many, if not most, of the places across Europe where the Living Theatre performed *Mysteries*, audience members took a cue from the performers and "caught" their plague—dramatically dying alongside them, then accompanying them onstage to create a pyramid of bodies, a heap of flesh in which spectators' and performers' limbs and torsos were crushed together into a single unit, intermingled until audience and actors were virtually indistinguishable.

The body pile scene from *Mysteries* constituted the first of many attempts by the Living Theatre to stage contagion: to transform metaphorical and philosophical notions of theatrical communicability into physical and affective infection, to create onstage a performance so irresistibly replicable that spectators would feel compelled to join the action. Most significantly, the body pile scene set a precedent for the specific types of contagion—political, emotional, and physical—that the company staged in one of the major theatrical works that followed *Mysteries*, their best-known and most notorious performance piece, 1968's *Paradise Now*. In that piece, the company expanded their contagious dramaturgy from the strategies developed in *Mysteries*, no longer seeking only to make gestures communicable but also to render those gestures revolutionary—to make worldwide, pacifist-anarchist revolution contagious.

This chapter charts the Living Theatre's efforts, in *Paradise Now*, to stage contagion—to make the plague revolutionary, and to make anarchist revolution contagious. The Living Theatre's relationship with Artaud's theatrical philosophy serves as an important point of origin for the company's experiments with infectious performance (though Artaud is not the only influence at work here: Brecht's very different model for politically communicative theater also played an essential role). In *Paradise Now*, the Living Theatre sought to create a performance that would physically and emotionally infect their audiences, and that would eliminate boundaries between performers and spectators, overtaking audiences' minds and bodies during the piece's four- to five-hour performances, and leaving cells of revolutionary agitators in their wake.

The Living Theatre's vision for these revolutionaries—and for the new society they would build—was complex, constantly under revision, and the subject of heated debate among the members of the company.[1] Nonetheless, a few influences, and a few elements of the company's collective political vision, were consistent: Pacifism and anarchism constituted the central social and political aims of *Paradise Now*, along with an end to the Vietnam War, and to colonialist violence more broadly. Beck and Malina had protested with Dorothy Day in New York in the 1950s, and her pacifism proved influential to them, as did the anarchist philosophies of Paul Goodman and the spiritual writings of Martin Buber and Eric Gutkind. They maintained contacts with revolutionary groups in Europe and the United States—the French student protesters of May 1968, representatives from Students for a Democratic Society, the Black Panthers—and spoke frequently about abolishing the capitalist system and achieving a radical redistribution of wealth. But the company's vision of a utopian society was frequently articulated in the negative (the abolition of capitalism, the end of war) and in general terms (a society of love and freedom) rather than as a concrete and programmatic image of the postrevolutionary world. *Paradise Now* placed more emphasis on provoking spectators to collective action than on outlining the precise organization of the new society the company hoped their contagious dramaturgy would create.

To describe the ways in which the Living Theatre attempted to stage contagion, I will first return to the "body pile" scene from *Mysteries*. I see this sequence as a primary origin of the contagious strategies and participatory dramaturgies that would recur in *Paradise Now*. I will then draw on two elements of historical context—the language of Cold War containment doctrine, and the historical context offered by twentieth-century crowd theory—to situate the Living Theatre's approach to Artaudian theatrical metaphysics in its political and cultural surround. In doing so, I will propose *Paradise Now* as a politically charged instance of contagious dramaturgy, developed with the intention of spreading emotions, gestures, and actions to its audiences in order to enact anarchist-pacificist revolution. In a sense, the Living Theatre's piece "went viral" decades before the contemporary concept existed. *Paradise Now*'s contagious dramaturgy offers a new means of understanding the particular aims and effects—more deliberate than are often recognized—of the company's revolutionary performance in their own time. More than this, viewing the piece through this lens helps to illuminate the significance that concepts of contagion came to hold for theater artists both in the Living Theatre's era and beyond.

FIGURE 41.1 *Mysteries and Smaller Pieces*, Brooklyn Academy of Music, New York, 1968. Photo: Gianfranco Mantegna. Yale Collection of American Literature, Beinecke Rare Book and Manuscript Library.

ARTAUD'S PLAGUE

Malina and Beck first read Artaud's writings in 1958. Mary Caroline Richards, an acquaintance of the pair, was working on the first English translation of the essay collection *The Theater and Its Double*, and insisted that the Living Theatre's two founders read her manuscript—believing, correctly, that Beck and Malina would discover intense artistic affinities with Artaud's thought. "When Judith Malina and I first encountered [Artaud's] principal work," writes Beck in *Theandric*, a collection of theater theory and notes on the Living Theatre's work, "we felt that we had suddenly found an organized compendium of things we had been thinking but which we had not realized constituted a theory."[2] And Malina, interviewed in person in April 2011, remembered experiencing a similar epiphany upon discovering Artaud: "The moment we read it," she says of *The Theater and Its Double*, "we were overwhelmed with the reality that Artaud showed us, that theater is about the relationship of cruelty to art, of art to cruelty, of our political position and our dramatic position being equivalent."[3] Beck and Malina identified with Artaud's predilection for spectacle and his approach to performing violence, as well as his desire to create a theater that could transcend stage fictions and eliminate the need for written text. Artaud's insistence that unraveling the modern human psyche was a prerequisite to reinventing society echoes in the Living Theatre's efforts to commandeer its audiences' spiritual lives—even as they evinced far more interest than he did in engaging with the realities of political struggle. "Artaud is political and who masks his politics misrepresents his theory," concluded Beck.[4]

Artaud's famous essay comparing the theater to the plague is part metaphysical formula and part graphic epidemiological account. Alongside declarations that "the essential theater is like the plague,"[5] the essay contains detailed descriptions of the violence that the plague wreaks on both the bodies and societies under its sway. Though the link between performance and deadly epidemic is most often interpreted as a metaphorical one, Artaud himself offered the Living Theatre a precedent for staging the comparison physically. During his famous 1933 lecture-demonstration at the Sorbonne, he recited the essay aloud—and, simultaneously, pretended to suffer gruesome physical symptoms, culminating in paroxysms on the stage. It is impossible to know whether Julian Beck knew of Artaud's lecture-demonstration when he suggested to the company that they stage physically the comparison that Artaud had articulated, but the scene that was ultimately created had much in common with the earlier one. This time, though, the plague was not just public but also participatory.

Indeed, the Living Theatre's "body pile" scene, as it came to be called, was designed for mass participation. Its stark, nonverbal staging helped to eliminate potential language gaps between the company members and their audiences as they traveled through Europe, and its frantic energy and easily imitated gestures invited spectators to join the action. Accordingly, the scene inspired noteworthy responses among many of its European audiences. Saul Gottlieb, a friend and follower of the Living Theatre, chronicled a succession of infectious responses to the scene as *Mysteries* toured:

> The plague scene has had a most violent effect on audiences. Most people get out of their seats, mill about, laugh, cry, shout, touch the bodies of the actors, pull and push them, and even sometimes beat them. Some people die with the actors, and permit themselves to be put in

the body-pile—in Brussels, fifty people took part in the scene. In Trieste the show was banned after one performance, which included the nude appearance of one actor for three seconds during the tableaux vivants, as well as the audience's refusal to leave the theatre on the orders of police while the plague-deaths were going on. It was also banned after the first performance in Vienna's elegant old Theater An Der Wien, when the fire department rang down the curtain in the middle of the scene because twenty Viennese student-actors had gone on stage to join the dying. In Rome, a fist-fight and general pandemonium broke out during the scene. Most recently, police in Venice had to stop a brawl between pro- and anti-Mysteries people in the audience.[6]

The Living Theatre had seized on Artaud's elusive metaphorical description of the plague's affinity to performance, and rendered that likeness luridly literal. This approach made the performers' actions tangible and succinct—intentionally available for mimicry and replication. Because the "plague" was so clearly visible, its throes so concretely enacted, spectators were able to join in the suffering with no barrier of preparation or comprehension between the performers and themselves.

Or, at least, spectators were allowed to attempt to participate, and to believe they had comprehended the scene's meaning. Though less explicitly tied to a vision for social change than the scenes of contagion that the company would develop for *Paradise Now*, the body pile suggested all sorts of metaphorical social commentary—images of helpless dead bodies, a silent division between live spectators and frozen performers—and different audiences interpreted this differently, a response that was welcomed by the artists. "In Europe," Malina told Richard Schechner, in a 1969 *TDR* interview, "it is always assumed to be Auschwitz or Hiroshima. Except in Vienna, where, of course, they always thought it was a sex orgy."[7]

"Here in America," Schechner replied, "nobody died with you because Americans don't really like to think of death." (Rather than joining the body pile onstage, he remarked, American audiences tended to spring up and attempt to comfort the "dying" performers—again, creating a scene of mass participation, if less violently than audiences in Europe did.) Yet American audiences, too, saw a broad social commentary in the scene. In his essay on the Living Theatre's late-1960s tour, in which the company presented *Mysteries* alongside their productions of *Frankenstein, Antigone*, and *Paradise Now*, Richard Gilman pointed to the social implications of *Mysteries*' concluding gesture:

> The last piece of action, a long mimesis of our social despair and the horrors of our impersonality, in which members of the group "die" in agony at various points in the theater and are carried stiff and strangely remote by others in the company to be piled in a pyramid on stage, was solemn and affecting, and, what's more, a true theatrical action, a new one.[8]

Part of the scene's participatory ethos, then—part of what made it irresistibly catching—was the interpretive flexibility it offered spectators: It could be understood as Hiroshima in Brussels, the Holocaust in France, and the alienating angst of American politics in New York.

And yet participation in the plague was not quite as uninhibited as it might sound: the Living Theatre's epidemic was physically strenuous to perform, and not all of the spontaneous participants were allowed to follow the scene to completion. In fact, as *Mysteries* toured, Beck, Malina, and their collaborators began to employ the scene as a barometer of sorts, measuring the readiness of the Living Theatre's audiences to join corporeally and emotionally in the stage action. "We have a test for them," Malina told Schechner in their 1969 interview. "We pick them up by their neck and ankles. If they're stiff, they get carried up [to the stage]; if they fold, then we put them down."[9]

It wasn't only an exterior physical commitment to reenacting Artaud's plague that the Living Theatre looked for—they were seeking, in their company and in their spectators, an emotional dedication as well. Describing the company's initial development of this scene, Malina and Beck explicated an approach to performing plague that sounds surprisingly reminiscent of Stanislavsky (or, in fact, the acting approaches of American Method teachers Stella Adler and Lee Strasberg, who had been among the faculty at the New School, where Malina had studied):[10]

> Beck: We keep talking about the plague, for instance, as an exercise in locating the pain and watching the pain travel around the body, feeling it . . .
> Malina: The first time we did it, it was just as intense [as in later public performances]. There were some people who didn't do it well and we worked with them . . . Mostly they were not finding specific enough pain or not taking it out far enough.[11]

In conclusion, Malina adds, the Living Theatre, which was then attracting a steady stream of would-be company members, sought only to recruit "a certain kind of person; that kind of person can do this dying."[12] In other words, only those spectators who not only sympathized with the Living Theatre's broad theatrical and political goals but also possessed the physical stamina and the rigorous emotional presence to enact the Living Theatre's scene on a moment's notice, were allowed to join in the action, as the pile of stiff "corpses" onstage grew and grew. The Living Theatre, then, intended to create a contagious stage performance—but one that was contagious within defined gestural limits, one in which spectators replicated a particular stage action and transmitted it to other spectators, using principles of skilled performance to create clear, comprehensible, communicability. The Living Theatre wanted to create a performance that could be repeated precisely, in order to create a performance that would be repeated contagiously—believing that rigorous participation in revolutionary performance would lead to rigorous performance of revolutionary action.

PARADISE NOW

These principles of highly directed participation resurfaced in *Paradise Now* (fig. 41.2), in which the company pursued further their rebellion against conventional distinctions between stage and auditorium; their impulse toward overt enactment of metaphysical concepts; and particularly, their efforts to embody notions of contagion through their audiences. This time, though, contagion figured as not only an aesthetic concern, but as the means of implementing a large-scale social agenda.

The Living Theatre developed *Paradise Now* between February and May of 1968, while housed in an off-season tourist resort in Cefalú, Sicily. Over months of participation in heated debates, acting exercises, and research into sources of inspiration as disparate as the Zohar and the artistic philosophies of John Cage, the company began to construct an ambitious theater piece that echoed the devised dramaturgy of *Mysteries* but added to it a detailed sequence of rituals intended to stage a world-historical saga culminating in real-world revolution. The company, by necessity, depended on spectators' willing cooperation in order to

FIGURE 41.2 *Paradise Now.* Photo: Desdemone Bardin. Yale Collection of American Literature, Beinecke Rare Book and Manuscript Library.

achieve this goal, and rehearsal conversations frequently revolved around methods of wresting audiences out of their habitual modes of passive spectatorship—and particularly, around ways to make the performance physically infectious.

"We want to find something that will change 500 people a night," announced actor Rufus Collins to his collaborators in February 1968, early in *Paradise Now*'s development. During another rehearsal, he declared his intentions even more violently: "I want them [the audience] to be trapped into it," he explained, adding that "I think that in 6 minutes the A[udience] will be in a point of hysteria." William Shari, another performer, agreed that the actors' primary objective in *Paradise Now* was to "infect the people nearest you to do something."[13] And in discussion during a subsequent rehearsal, two company members explicitly established the connection between contagion and dramatic form: When performer Jenny Hecht announced that she hoped the new piece, the embryonic *Paradise Now*, would move beyond the format of *Mysteries*, another actor, Henry Howard, proposed that it would do so by striving "Not just to be/but to communicate/to make it catching like the plague."[14]

Artaudian metaphysics, then, remained a central point of inspiration for the Living Theatre four years after the premiere of *Mysteries*—but, in developing *Paradise Now*, the company merged this metaphorical image with real-world goals for mobilizing and organizing audiences. Suddenly, spectators were not only susceptible witnesses to mass destruction, as they had been in the final scene of *Mysteries*; they were also protagonists of the action, both artistic representations of fictive masses and living members of the real revolutionary crowds the company hoped to inspire. Beck and Malina cast their audiences as the creators of local "cells," which would, in turn, manufacture a new society. The company's ultimate goal, as Collins pointed out in one rehearsal session, was "to do something in *Paradise Now* in which the cooperation of the audience is essential to the completion of the act."[15]

That "act" ultimately became a complex series of rituals, performance exercises, and political statements, organized into a progression of "rites" and "rungs"—turning four- to five-hour performances into teleological sequences designed to lead performers and spectators "up" a spiritual ladder toward paradise. Each performance of *Paradise Now* began with the confrontation that would become one of its most iconic scenes, the "Rite of Guerrilla Theater" (to which I will return in detail later). In this first "rite," performers moved through the crowd, challenging spectators directly by reciting statements about political and social restriction. "I'm not allowed to travel without a passport," they said, and "I'm not allowed to smoke marijuana." They hoped, through this discussion of impediments to personal freedom, to arouse such livid frustration in their audiences that spectators would join in the action for the rest of the hours-long performance.

Subsequent sections of the piece surveyed scenes of protest and revolution around the world: students staging sit-ins at Columbia University, Bolivian rebels hiding in the mountains, Palestinians and Israelis facing off in the Middle East. World histories, in microcosm, mingled with meditative mantras, expressions of physical and spiritual love for each other and for their audiences, and other ritualized stagings of repression and revolt. The Living Theatre often incorporated current or local events, or exhorted spectators to join them at real-world protests after the show. The end of each performance, and the section that frequently resulted in the arrest of members of the company, was a scene in which, after repeating all of the historical and political "lessons" learned over the previous hours, actors invited spectators to march with them out of the theater, often carried on performers' shoulders. After breaking down barriers between performers and spectators, the Living Theatre sought to burst the boundaries of the theater itself.

CONTAINMENT

"Containment is our greatest enemy, much more dangerous than the helmeted cops that meet us at the demonstrations," argued Judith Malina, in her 1969 interview with Richard Schechner. She added that if "it can be contained, then its value is not revolutionary."[16] Here, she was explaining the company's decision to withdraw from the 1968 Avignon Festival, where *Paradise Now* had recently premiered and then quickly been banned, along with street performances of any kind. The "it," in Malina's declaration, was the company's theatrical work as a whole: Avignon city authorities had asked the company to substitute their production of *Antigone* for the banned work, believing it would be less incendiary, but the Living Theatre had refused, releasing a statement of principles instead.[17] "When our art becomes acceptable, we have to take it where it's not acceptable because that's the only way we can destroy the established culture in order to set up a new one," Malina explained, describing the Living Theatre's decision not to acquiesce to authorities' request.[18]

Despite the distinction that Malina drew between "containment"—meaning, here, ideological co-option by any source of authority—and the physical clashes between the Living

Theatre and their adversaries in law enforcement, the "helmeted cops" also constituted a form of literal containment that the company regularly confronted. Police frequently surrounded buildings where the Living Theatre performed, arresting audience members who joined the raucous culminating march into the street. Many manifestations of "containment"—co-option and coercion, and, beyond them, the term's geopolitical significance during the heightened years of the Cold War—framed performances of *Paradise Now* as it toured between 1968 and 1970. The Cold War–era implications surrounding the notion of "containment," both as Malina uses it in the quotation above, and in its broader sense, are essential to elucidating the particular significance that a dramaturgy of contagion would have had when the Living Theatre developed and performed *Paradise Now*. I turn here to a brief overview of the ways in which the terminology of contagion and containment intertwined in Cold War–era rhetoric—context that adds political dimension to the Living Theatre's metaphorical staging of the plague.

The notion of contagion constituted, during the Cold War era, the frightening inverse of the doctrine of containment that reached its disastrous apotheosis in the Vietnam War. Initially articulated by American diplomat George F. Kennan in a (then anonymous, now infamous) 1947 *Foreign Affairs* article, containment offered a strategy for keeping the threat of international Communism—and devastating nuclear war—at bay. Hovering alongside containment, in policy and the public imagination, was its opposite: international Communist contagion, represented by the "domino theory," which held that once any single country fell to Communist domination, it would infectiously incite its neighbors to Communist revolution as well.

In his writings on Cold War politics, for instance, former secretary of state Dean Acheson describes the "domino theory" in language that reveals the ideas of contagious transmission at its center. Speaking of his attempts to avert a Communist Greece, he writes, in his memoirs:

> Like apples in a barrel infected by one rotten one, the corruption of Greece would infect Iran and all to the east. It would also carry infection to Africa through Asia Minor and Egypt, and to Europe through Italy and France, already threatened by the strongest domestic Communist parties in Western Europe.[19]

Propelled by the rhetoric of international epidemic, containment provided the template for American policy over the course of several decades, not only defining the United States' stance toward other nations but also inspiring corresponding anxieties in public attitudes toward cultural life. As Alan Nadel argues in his study *Containment Culture*, prevailing assumptions and political pressures "equated containment of communism with containment of atomic secrets, of sexual license, of gender roles, of nuclear energy, and of artistic expression."[20] And in his study of postwar theater, Bruce McConachie directly links notions of containment to American theatrical production, writing that containment came to represent a "cognitive schema" shaping American theatrical culture, both overtly and implicitly, during the first two decades of the Cold War.[21]

The "cognitive schema" represented by containment, and by Cold War ideology more broadly, permeated *Paradise Now* in many ways. The company viewed the performance as a means of breaking down every sort of barrier that could "contain" them: stage fictions, theater buildings, legal restrictions, social inhibitions, and the historical present tense. They preferred to present *Paradise Now* in theaters without traditional separations between audience and actors—in college gymnasiums, as well as ballrooms and amphitheaters.[22] Recalling months of touring the performance piece, Beck told Schechner in 1969 that "the most beautiful place we worked in was the Sports Palace in Geneva, which had tiers on all four sides, a huge playing space for us."[23]

Paradise Now's onstage narrative was also directed toward contesting containment: In writing and rewriting the piece, the Living Theatre attempted to link the struggles of repressed peoples the world over, connecting geographically disparate conflicts in a hypo-thetical inversion of the nightmare scenario posed by the domino theory. In the philoso-phy represented by Kennan, Acheson, and their contemporaries, a liberation struggle in Southeast Asia could topple regimes across a vast geographical region, resulting in the Communist takeover of an entire continent. In the Living Theatre's worldview, the Palestinian struggle for self-determination, similarly, was inextricably intertwined with the political projects of Bolivian guerrilla fighters, Czech protestors, and Parisian and American students marching in the streets. Though the Living Theatre did not explicitly subscribe to the politics of international Communism, they created the piece with the idea of promot-ing peaceful anarchist revolution around the world, contagiously overtaking cities, regions, countries, and continents.

This anticontainment narrative was, in performance, also not to be contained by stage fictions. The Living Theatre combined scenes from a world-historical liberation story with rituals in which spectators were called on to enact their own liberation (from inhibition, from clothing, from local laws) right there and then. One particular performance exercise, proposed to the group by performers Jim Anderson and Rufus Collins in March 1968, offers a tangible instance of this participatory ethos, and evokes the Dionysian aesthetic guid-ing *Paradise Now*'s infectious dramaturgy. The idea was simple: The actors suggested that *Paradise Now* would open in silence. The company would wait until they heard an audience vocalization of any kind—an accidental sniffle, a nervous hum—then amplify it, voice over voice, until sounds filled the room. "When it gets to a/Point at which/It reaches blossom," adds Collins, "The lights go on."[24] "We have to hold back on our desire to create and let the A. [audience] be the creator," he warned in another rehearsal session.[25] This scenario was similar to an older "chord" exercise practiced by the company—Pierre Biner credits Joseph Chaikin with introducing it into the Living Theatre's repertoire—but, significantly, Collins's new version of "the chord" centered fully on the audience, making spectators' vocalizations the company's aural guides.[26] Even in rehearsal settings, the company found the "chord" ecstatically powerful, and the specter of chaos hovered around the exercise. "As audience member I was afraid of riot," observed Malina, after one practice session.[27]

The idea that sounds could be infectious—even dangerously, rebelliously infectious—was not unique to the Living Theatre. In his article "The Red Mask of Sanity," which details Paul Robeson's HUAC trials more than a decade earlier, scholar Tony Perucci argues that, in the context of Cold War culture, vocal expression itself was frequently understood to be sub-versive. Sounds, he explains, can travel through walls and across borders, escaping through fissures and overriding the boundaries that the ideology of containment was intended to reinforce. To Robeson's prosecutors, Perucci writes, "the mere hearing of Robeson's singing turned one into a Communist. Indeed, the incendiary infectiousness of 'emancipation utter-ances' had to be contained, as the act of collective hearing threatened the status quo and the believability of American stagecraft."[28] Collins's variation on the "chord" exercise, promptly enshrined as an enduring feature of the group's repertoire, enacted precisely that: a scene of "collective hearing" and mass vocal expression that recruited audiences' voices and ears. The scene offered a central image for the Living Theatre's contagious dramaturgy; it drew energy from spectators, blurring distinctions between practiced performers and spontaneous participants, individuals and crowds, personal intonations and collective cries.

As a whole, this newest Living Theatre production was so threatening that it was frequently performed not only in the presence of police, but also with plainclothes officers actually standing onstage or joining in the performance among the spectators. This resulted in the permeation of *Paradise Now* with Cold War ideological preoccupations in another way: After many encounters with the police, the Living Theatre began to replicate, on a small scale, the era's obsessions with infiltration and ideological betrayal. Malina's diary, for instance, reports an instance in which the Living Theatre conducted a workshop with students at Vincennes. As the performers and collaborators planned their political actions, Malina was moved to warn her young comrades not to take revolutionary actions too far, as it was impossible to say which of the workshop participants were true revolutionaries: "I make a speech saying that we can't plan anything together that is against the law as we are aware that some of us in the room are policemen," she recalled in her diary. "Those who want to do anything against the law must know everyone in their group or they will be busted."[29]

Notions of containment and contagion, both conceptual and corporeal, thus suffused the development of *Paradise Now*. In a bid for contagious revolution, the Living Theatre attempted to forge an infectious dramaturgy that they could transmit in highly particular form to their spectators, hoping that it would leap from stage to auditorium, and out into the streets, leaving a changed society in their wake.

Rehearsing Apocalypse

In *Stages of Emergency*, her 2007 study arguing for an understanding of Cold War domestic nuclear defense tactics as theatrical behavior, Tracy Davis describes the procedures of civilian preparation for a hypothetical nuclear attack as "rehearsals." The oft-repeated rituals Davis outlines—preparing and tracing escape routes, practicing emergency drills—were, she explains, acts of preparation that looked toward "an eventual—though perhaps perpetually deferred—performance."[30] These trial runs, she argues, constituted a kind of mass choreography, in which citizens learned roles in an apocalyptic drama they hoped never to really enact. This idea, the concept that citizens and members of the public could be mobilized toward a world-changing performance, that large-scale national calamity could be rehearsed, constitutes a second historical model, on which I build here, for understanding the ways in which *Paradise Now* attempted to intervene in Cold War society. Rather than rehearsing preparedness, Beck and Malina reversed Davis's schema, choreographing revolutionary performances that would not defer social crisis, but rather, would catalyze contagious revolution.

The Living Theatre had reason to believe, in 1968, that large-scale revolution was imminent. Historic student protests that had convulsed the streets of Paris in May, when Beck and Malina joined a group of Parisian students in occupying the Odéon Theatre—a place that constituted, for the French protestors and for the Living Theatre's leaders, a historic center of the older, liberal, more socially acceptable forms of European counterculture. The Odéon, a place where the works of great modernists such as Genet and Beckett had been staged, was seen as a site against whose less threatening politics the radical new movements could stand out in stark relief. "It was important to occupy the Odéon just because it was *le Théatre de France* where the government gave the Barrault-Renaud Company the chance to do Beckett and Adamov and Ionesco and Genet," wrote Beck, after the fact, adding that "the students and their comrades were refusing to grant the government the privilege of flattering both itself and the public into believing that the state maintains reputable avant-garde *contra-sistemo* art."[31]

After occupying the Odéon, and after marching in the streets of Paris and enduring often-violent confrontations with French police, Beck and Malina came to understand May 1968 as a turning point in their efforts to incite, stage, and participate in sweeping societal change. (Beck's account of this time of upheaval, in his memoir, *The Life of the Theatre*, also reveals how thoroughly the language of plague and contagion had permeated the company's thinking about revolutionary struggle. "So powerful the germs of corruption," he wrote, describing the forces of French government authority, then explained, of the students participating in the uprising, that, "We are fighting a plague."[32] *Paradise Now* was to be contagious "like the plague," then, even as the French authorities were infected with the "germs of corruption"—a comment that demonstrates the significance of the contagious metaphor for the Living Theatre, and its broad applicability to every aspect of their struggle.) Even long after *Paradise Now*'s last performance, members of the Living Theatre viewed the Paris protests as a historic turning point for the French counterculture and for their own art. In 2011, Judith Malina reflected on the heady events of that spring, affirming her belief that the student uprisings constituted an essential shift in her generation's historical consciousness. "We did get rid of the idea that these [social] structures are inevitable and immutable," she recalled. "We passed into another phase of history. A lot of hope was created."[33]

Onstage, *Paradise Now* was constructed with the intention of leading the Living Theatre's audiences, too, into another phase of history. To layer on top of collective exercises such as the "chord," Beck, Malina, and their collaborators conceived a complex, world-historical plot, one that was aimed at placing spectators at a crucial historical juncture—at situating them to enact, as Collins had said, the piece's "completion." By aggregating religious and spiritual history, local political struggle, and autobiography, the company hoped to propel their proposed revolution out of fictional narratives and into spectators' bodies. One page from Beck's 1968 notebooks demonstrates this aspiration graphically, listing two columns of political and theatrical tasks. The first is labeled "A Demonstration of how it will be at this point in the future/Seen now," and the second, "A Demonstration of what we can practically do at this moment, in history this moment of being to bring it about."[34] Laid out side by side, these two timelines—cosmic and contemporary, mythical and mundane—are twinned in *Paradise Now*, the idealized future coexisting with the pragmatics of the present.

The play's text contains a highly structured series of historical scenes, from the immediate—the company researched socioeconomic conditions in each city they visited—to the broadly imaginative, like a scene of the "Discovery of the North Pole," which employed documentary material from a British expedition to the Arctic. Other "historical" scenes lingered in the realm of exotic generalization, like a scenario of Bolivian "revolutionaries" plotting an uprising from their jungle lair—which was, at a later point, replaced by language about the 1968 Soviet occupation of Prague. These "historical" sequences were as diverse as the group's array of artistic inspirations: in one scene, performers mutated through a portrayal of the development of multicellular life out of prehistoric amoebic entities.

Notes from a rehearsal in early 1968 report an exercise in which the group split into "teams" representing a mismatched series of historical "eras": the "Ice Age"; the "Italian Renaissance"; the "Egyptians"; "Hitler." This sequence of rehearsal notes concludes with the instructions that "Each Team works out its stuck."[35] Though they do not explicitly dub these sequences *Lehrstücke*—Brecht's term for his "learning plays" or "didactic plays," which were meant to be performed by and for small audiences of workers—the company's use of the German word for "skit" is a reminder of Beck's and Malina's Brechtian heritage. Imagining these scenes as miniature *Lehrstücke* can help illuminate their purpose in the context of *Paradise Now*. As deliberately schematic renderings of world history, *Paradise Now*'s historical sequences were intended to shrink the past into comprehensible form, opening spaces for audiences to step in and change its course. If Brecht hoped his audiences would rise from performances of *Lehrstücke* with newfound Marxist consciousness, the Living Theatre hoped that spectators would understand *Paradise Now* as a rehearsal for a new anarchist-pacifist society.

Though their proposed revolution was compiled from a mosaic of anarchism, pacifism, and broad, sometimes contradictory, commitments to individual freedom and collective responsibility,[36] the Living Theatre held many goals in common with the *Lehrstücke*. Both dramaturgies imagine borrowing the bodies of nonactors, forging crowds of workers (in Brecht's case) and spectators (in the Living Theatre's) into revolutionary masses, the crowd in the theater serving as synecdoche for vast populations outside. In sympathy with Brecht's model, Beck and Malina envisioned each performance leaving a lasting trace in the form of a revolutionary cell—a direct descendent of the shapeless primordial "cells" depicted earlier in the performance. Beck, in rehearsal conversations, proposed that *Paradise Now*'s finale should consist of "the formation of cells/the Distribution of the Revolutionists Handbook"; to account for language barriers as they toured, he suggested that each actor "go to the audience with the Revolutionists Handbook" and then "ask for interpreters."[37] Malina's notebook lists "Ten Political Rites for the Audience," the third of which is "The Rite in which the People Join Together (in Cells)."[38] And Beck's own notebook suggests placing a screen onstage, behind which audience members could disappear to exchange contact information toward the establishment of local cells.[39]

The mundane and practical was thus bound inextricably together with the apocalyptic and spiritual in *Paradise Now*—and examining the result of the project while it was still in the midst of its touring life, in the spring of 1969, Beck and Malina understood these recruiting methods to be successful: The company, they explained, boasted an enormous following of potential participants, future members of the very revolutionary cells the Living Theatre hoped to create. "We have about 2,000 people who want to join the Living Theatre, of whom, I would guess, about two or three hundred would be terrific," noted Malina, in her interview with Schechner. "About two years ago," added Beck, "we started saying, 'Don't travel with us . . . Better form your own group.' The extraordinary thing is that there are now about 11 itinerant groups in Europe that are creating plays collectively, that live as communities in Italy, Belgium, France, Switzerland."[40]

Crows

Paradise Now thus summoned into being—in the form of live audiences, and in the enormous public that the company addressed, cajoled, and provoked in the process of performing

the piece across Europe and the United States—a constellation of revolutionary and potentially revolutionary crowds. In doing so, they drew on a long history of twentieth-century
mass performance, a legacy that, both deliberately and implicitly, shaped the Living Theatre's
assumptions about contagion and their attitudes toward the bodily participation of gathered spectators. In her landmark study *Theatre, Sacrifice, Ritual*, Erika Fischer-Lichte traces
the rise of mass political performances in the early twentieth century: works that assembled
large groups of spectators, or that employed vast numbers of performers, overwhelming and
frequently incorporating their audiences. From the large-scale Soviet spectacle *The Storming
of the Winter Palace* to Nazi *Thingspiele* to the first modern Olympics, Fischer-Lichte argues
that modern mass performances functioned, in various ways, as methods of reviving and
reinforcing mass identification and national or communal sentiment. Central to these
approaches to mass performance, Fischer-Lichte argues, is the assumption that actions,
affects, and ideologies are more readily disseminated—in other words, that they are particularly contagious—among a live, gathered crowd. Fischer-Lichte explains that in these early
twentieth-century mass spectacles:

> [T]heatre appeared to be capable of transforming individuals into members of a community,
> albeit only temporarily, by focusing on the bodily co-presence of actors and spectators, on the
> physical acts of the actors and their capacity to "infect" the spectators as well as on the "conta-
> gion" occurring among the spectators.[41]

Though *Paradise Now* was created explicitly to counter established governments and
nation-building projects, it, too, participated in eschatological narratives meant to galvanize
audiences and fuse them into a single, collective entity, using the power of crowd dynamics.
Crowd theory—as formulated by early-to-mid-twentieth-century thinkers culminating in
the work of Elias Canetti—thus plays an essential role in elucidating the type of contagious
spectacle to which Beck and Malina aspired. It also helps place *Paradise Now* in the context
of the other types of crowds, artistic and political, in which its creators participated.

The study of crowd dynamics—pioneered in the early twentieth century by Gustave
LeBon and a number of intellectual followers—had reactionary origins, stemming from
fin-de-siècle fears of restless, irrational mobs, unmoored from traditional cultural affiliations
and uprooted from places of origin by a rapidly industrializing society. As the early twentieth century turned into the era of Italian Fascism, Nazi Germany, and World War II, crowd
theorists turned their focus from the danger of the mob to the seemingly vast influence that
demagogues and totalitarian leaders could wield over impressionable mass gatherings. In
1962, Elias Canetti, often considered the century's most significant crowd theorist, offered a
comprehensive taxonomy of crowds in *Crowds and Power*, which attempted to explain, cen-
trally among other phenomena, the paradoxes of mass behavior under totalitarian regimes.
Essential to his theory of crowd behavior (and to most midcentury writings on the subject)
was the assumption that people behave differently when surrounded by vast numbers of
strangers than they do alone—that they relinquish their individual moralities and rational
wills in the context of a crowd, and that crowd behavior is, in some way, contagious.

Just as the interwar period was a time in which gathered masses held great political
and cultural significance in Europe, 1968 was an important year for American crowds, a
high-water mark for the hope and violence that emerged from demonstrations of the civil
rights movement, students' movement, and antiwar movement, among others, and their

frequently violent suppression. In 1968, notes Erika Munk, "Martin Luther King and Robert Kennedy were assassinated. The Chicago police savagely attacked protesters at the August Democratic Convention, igniting a division of the American New Left, with one part moving toward armed action. The Vietnam War continued. The Living Theatre came to America to tour four of its European productions."[42] Protest movements of that year offered a form of real-life corollary to the Living Theatre's participatory stagings, drawing masses of bodies together to agitate directly for change. If LeBon's crowds were the newly urbanized turn-of-the century poor, and Canetti's crowds were participants in the fascist rallies of interwar Germany and Italy, the Living Theatre's crowds were the protesters marching through the Paris and Chicago streets in 1968.

Though Beck and Malina never explicitly subscribed to the thinking of crowd theorists, their approaches to guiding audiences' actions frequently parallel midcentury thinking on mass behavior—and it's no accident that they came into contact with such modes of thought. The Living Theatre's philosophical and artistic allegiance to Artaud's writings on theater would have led them directly to these assumptions about crowd behavior. Artaud emphasized notions of mass ecstasy in ways that echo the writings of crowd theorists (and particularly, Canetti's descriptions of the powerful sway that fascist leaders held over European crowds).

I am indebted here to Kimberly Jannarone, who writes persuasively in *Artaud and His Doubles* of the affinities between Artaud's descriptions of his ideal theater of cruelty, and the approaches to controlling crowd behavior employed by Fascist and Nazi leaders in the interwar period. She argues that crowd theory "helps us see that the Theater of Cruelty envisions the audience in many of the same ways people's theaters in Italy and Germany did, and as demagogic political leaders elsewhere in Europe were also doing: as a group of people they would make feel liberated and exalted while keeping it under tight control.[43] Jannarone goes on to suggest that Artaud had a particular idea about how crowds would be influenced by his theater of cruelty: They would not simply be driven to ecstatic ritual expression but would also be led toward a new world order.[44]

It is disturbing to note how closely the Living Theatre's vision for persuasively funneling crowds toward revolution echoes this imagery: They hoped that their revolution would be participatory and ecstatic, but they also hoped that spectators would follow them precisely, and would participate in disseminating the gestures and ideologies they sought to promote. Beck and Malina even attempted to formulate equations for the exact transmission of their ideas in the context of an excited crowd. "To make the People aware," said Malina in one of the Living's rehearsal-discussions, "that 10% of the population can paralyze the structure . . . 10 poets obstruct less than 10 working men but 10 poets inspire 100." This observation inspired Malina to a form of viral arithmetic:

> so if you have 10 poets
> +10 working men
> 100 influenced[45]

Like Artaud, Beck and Malina intended their performances as a first stage in systematically remaking society—ten, then one hundred, then (as Collins had asserted early on) five hundred people at a time. Like Artaud, they attempted a form of contagion that was ecstatically oriented toward mass identification, both in performance and beyond the theater.

The Living Theatre's approach to crowd behavior was not only theoretical: as *Paradise Now* toured, the Living Theatre's leaders applied their ideas to real audiences, attempting to generate passionately frenzied masses of spectators, and then attempting to channel their unruly emotions toward a political agenda. This was not an easy task: in performance, the presence of emotional crowds, and the corresponding presence of police officers attempting to control those crowds, frequently threatened to derail the company's careful plans for corralling their audiences toward revolution—or even for presenting the performance piece at all. Sometimes, this was the result of police presence; other times, it was the result of the Living Theatre's broad alliances with many radical political groups, and their audiences' differences with them. The Living Theatre's audiences, as Malina's diary recounts, were often as angry at the theater company's particular brand of anarchist revolution as they were at the failures of Western society at large. In fact, as they toured, the company frequently ran up against deep divisions among the European and American student left. In her diaries from the *Paradise Now* tour, Malina observed that while some student radicals, the Marxist-Leninists, rejected the idea that sexual revolution could precede the elimination of the class system, others, such as the "American hippie" population, couldn't accept class struggle without sexual liberation. In many cases, the Living Theatre's concurrent blend of anarchism, pacifism, and sexual rebellion proved repellant even to spectators who shared their desire for large-scale revolution and their opposition to the Vietnam War.[46]

At one performance in fall 1969, in Urbino, Italy, Malina recalled facing a room packed with students angry both at their own society and at the Living Theatre: "vehement, violent radical students, angry faces, harsh voices, great fervor," she wrote.[47] More students stood raging outside, angry at being excluded from the performance, even as the audience members gathered inside accused the performers of "finking" by refusing to begin the show. Eventually, the Living Theatre allowed hundreds of protestors in from the rain; once inside, they disrupted the performance so completely—repeatedly chanting "Ho Chi Minh" over the actors' voices, thus declaring their allegiance to a different brand of revolutionary action than the one the Living Theatre was offering—that several sections of the hours-long drama had to be skipped. "The din is terrific, the crush incredible," reported Malina. "300 people all shouting."[48] These competing performances of revolution veered toward chaos: "The dance + the song continue for 2 or 3 hours," wrote Malina. "I am carried away/I let myself be carried away/into a strong + frenzied place."[49]

Despite the tumultuous atmosphere these descriptions might suggest, *Paradise Now* was far from unstructured in performance—in fact, it was carefully conceived to build on the contagious potential of crowds, even as it sought to test its audiences' stamina and their commitment to the Living Theatre's particular revolutionary ideal, much as *Mysteries'* "body pile" scene had done. In an essay about the Living Theatre's four-production tour during the fall and winter of 1968—during which the company presented *Antigone, Frankenstein*, and *Mysteries* alongside *Paradise Now*—Stefan Brecht described his experiences attending multiple performances of *Paradise Now*. In particular, he observed that each segment of the marathon performance had been carefully subdivided into three types of action. First, the "'rites,'" he explained, "seem suggestions as to what we all can & should do, now & as the revolution develops. The 'visions' are poetic metaphors of revolution as markstone modes of life, abrupt qualitative transformations into opposites by which life realizes itself."

Finally, Brecht points out that at each juncture, the Living Theatre offered its audience "examples": "The 'examples,'" he says, "point out contemporary more or less exemplary revolutionary situations (New York City), exhorted revolutions (The Street), revolutions going wrong (Jerusalem)."[50] Malina and Beck had also described these scenes, with their local variations, as an integral aspect of *Paradise Now*'s dramatic structure: "There's another place [in the production], which we call the Brooklyn scene, which is always the city where the play is being played, so Brooklyn is ... Avignon, or New Haven, or wherever," explained Malina in the 1969 interview with Schechner. "Sometimes we substitute some of the rungs for what we call the horror city of the week—wherever there's any kind of terrible action happening, we try to take that one to Paradise because it needs it."[51]

That this repeated sequence of three segments—"rite," "vision," and "examples"; or, in Malina's words, "horror cities"—left a clear impression on Brecht, and that it did so despite the fact that, earlier in the same essay, he reports being unable, after attending *Paradise Now* twice, to "draw from [his] memory any outline of content or structure"—suggests the performances were actually as carefully structured and controlled as was the highly stratified text. The Living Theatre deliberately configured *Paradise Now*'s dramatic structure around what they perceived to be their spectators' own realities—with current events, or the company's current location, frequently featured as the third and final element in the rite-vision-example sequence. Not only did the company attempt to channel its audiences' energies by telling spectators the stories of their own cities—the company also sought, through contagious crowd dynamics, to pass along both highly specified forms of emotional affect and political gesture to the observer-participants that attended *Paradise Now*.

Nowhere is this more evident than in the section of the performance that, in criticism and reports about *Paradise Now*, became the most memorably replicable, the most infectiously confrontational, scene in the production—the infamous "Rite of Guerrilla Theater," which began each presentation of the piece. In this sequence, actors confronted individual members of the audience with impassively blunt assertions of social and political restrictions, from those governing large-scale political action ("I don't know how to stop the wars") to those dictating the artistic and social confines of the *Paradise Now* performances themselves ("I'm not allowed to take my clothes off," "I'm not allowed to smoke marijuana.")[52]

Stage directions in the printed version of *Paradise Now* clarify the company's efforts, through this initial sequence, to directly implicate their spectators in the frustration and agony these restrictions created—while, at the same time, denying spectators agency in the performance unfolding around them. Here is how they suggested performers respond to spectators' efforts to participate in the dialogue that the "Rite" appeared to be initiating:

> If the spectator addresses him [the actor], he listens to the spectator but repeats only this phrase. The spectator may mock him, encourage him, question him. The spectator may be passive, sympathetic, superficial, witty, profound, cynical, hostile. The actor uses this response to increase his expression of the frustration at the taboos and inhibitions imposed on him by the structure of the world around him ... He experiences the spectators' growing frustration at the sense of a lack of communication.[53]

When I interviewed Malina, I asked her to describe the function of that iconic scene, and she affirmed its importance in *Paradise Now*'s dramaturgy. Describing spectators' centrality to the Rite, she explained the sequence was meant

> To get them roused up to talk! To get them to understand that it was a play not about some abstract reality, but about them! It's about you! It was a question really of making them feel involved.[54]

And yet the Living Theatre did not want to foster any type of "involvement" among their audiences; they wanted spectators, particularly, to feel precisely the same emotional frustration that the performers worked up to in their delivery of the Rite's expressions of helplessness and rage. In his observations on the four Living Theatre productions that he saw on the company's tour, Stefan Brecht described the performers' approach to rousing audiences' outrage and angst, using language that seems to echo the thinking of the company members themselves. "The audience's spontaneity is to be triggered," he wrote, "if necessary by provocation into antagonism or defense: the volitional energy mobilized might disintegrate the ego, might mobilize the natural spiritual powers."[55]

This idea of inspiring spectators to "spontaneity," of summoning forth their "natural spiritual powers," by staging a scene of truncated communication, usually resulting in disappointment and anger, was frequently understood to be a contradiction in terms—even a terrible miscalculation on the performers' part. Many spectators responded with confusion or outrage to the contradiction between the Living Theatre's apparent interest in open conversation and their subsequent refusal to actually engage in it. Erika Munk, in an essay on the Living Theatre and its audiences, summarizes this ambiguously counterproductive effect:

> The opening "Rite of Guerrilla Theater" ... became every critic's paradigmatic, usually enraging, Living Theatre moment... Reading the description, one can easily imagine a true communication of the impossibility of communication. What occurred instead, not only the three times I saw it but from all reports at most performances, was a psychodrama of scorn and hostility.[56]

Though he does not cite the Rite of Guerrilla Theater by name, Richard Gilman's assessment of this element of *Paradise Now*, objected, in similar terms, to the disjuncture between the performers' rhetoric about participation and the actual dynamic that spectators experienced in the auditorium. He condemns what he refers to as the company's "pompous, self-righteous, clichéd talk," which he goes on to describe as talk "that separates and kills as effectively among leftists and radicals as among the 'enemy,' the talk that reinforces complacency at the very moment it's trying to unsettle and prod, that brings the darkness closer through its utter blindness to the political and social realities, that says what we already know, what we've found useless *as talk*."[57]

Talk, though, wasn't what Beck and Malina wanted their spectators to engage in—as with *Mysteries*' "body pile" scene, and as with the "tree of knowledge" sequence at *Paradise Now*'s conclusion (to be discussed shortly), they wanted to make their own emotions contagious. If spectators had been granted the opportunity to engage in dialogue with performers about the various social restrictions and obstacles mentioned during the Rite of Guerrilla Theatre—the impossibility of living without money, the social and legal obstructions barring public nudity, the necessity of carrying passports when traveling—then their energies might have been channeled into conversation, even into potentially satisfying agreement with the performers. Individual performers and spectators would have remained individuals, and uncontrolled eruptions of emotion might have been contained.

But the Living Theatre did not want spectators' feelings to respond to, or complement, their own—they wanted spectators' feelings to precisely match their own. ("The actor's direction," Beck had said, "is not to go around and announce it like someone on a picket line but as if he were literally driven crazy from it"[58]; in other words, the performers' slogans were not intended to rouse inspiring political agreement, but rather, intolerable anger.) Emotions would be more contagious if they were communal, and nothing could be transmitted from performer to spectator so quickly as the frustration of a dramatic event that appeared to thwart the very goals it had set out for itself. The Rite, then, was not only designed to foster communicable rage through the contents of the actors' speech, but also through its deliberately frustrating form.

This frustration was not intended to remain so for long. The Rite of Guerrilla Theatre led directly into the first instance of a recurring device the Living Theatre employed throughout *Paradise Now*, which the company referred to as a "flashout." Repeated at regular intervals in the performance, "flashouts" were conceived as instants of ecstatic rupture—moments when the performers were to have generated so much frenetic energy that a break in the action became necessary. "Whenever this [flashout] happens in the play," they write in the performance's published text, "the actor by the force of his art approaches a transcendent moment in which he is released from all the hangups of the present situation."[59] Beck, Malina, and their collaborators imagined that these revelations would inspire spectators by revealing to them the constrained nature of their everyday lives, and that the flashouts' repetition would galvanize audiences into joining together in revolutionary action.

Canetti's ideas of crowd behavior, though, suggest an even more particular function that the flashouts might have been meant to serve. Early in *Crowds and Power*, Canetti proposed the idea of the "discharge," which, he explained, constituted the moment of transformation, the shift in energy, which forges a collection of assorted individuals into a united crowd. In the moment of "discharge," Canetti argues, members of a group relinquish their individual wills to fuse emotionally with those surrounding them. Social inhibitions fall away at this moment, removing habitual barriers to mass physical contact and even rendering the crush of strangers' bodies ecstatically desirable.[60] "This is the moment," Canetti writes, "when all who belong to the crowd get rid of their differences and feel equal."[61] Though Canetti wrote these words nearly a decade before *Paradise Now* began touring, they offer a compelling description of the Living Theatre's aims in the "flashout" sections of their piece. The Rite of Guerrilla Theater was intended to be as frustrating as possible—in order to make the emotional release of the "flashout" that followed as contagious as possible. The Living Theatre's intention of freeing the performers (and spectators) from their "hangups" closely resembles the phenomenon Canetti describes, of "discharging" their individual consciousnesses—fusing them together, in order to ready them for a euphoric journey toward paradise.

Only after this transferal of affect, and after the repeated efforts to fuse together the gathered crowd through "flashouts," did the Living Theatre envision passing along particular gestures to their audiences and ultimately dismantling the barrier between spectators and performers permanently. The company concluded *Paradise Now* with a sequence entitled "The Tree of Knowledge," in which they recapitulated, in brief, the historical tales that had been imparted over the performance's previous hours. "The tree contains all of the information contained in the play," they assert in *Paradise Now*'s written text.[62] Reprising the rituals and actions played out in the piece's successive "rungs," the company also allowed for the possibility that performers would want to incorporate unexpected discoveries from each individual performance into this recapitulation. They note, accordingly, that "The Text and Action maybe be altered at any performance to include significant text and/or action created by actors or public in the preceding stages of the voyage."[63]

The "tree of knowledge" section led directly into *Paradise Now*'s infamous ending (and the actions that frequently caused actors' and spectators' arrests) in which the company invited spectators to ride on their shoulders out of the theater and into the streets. Distinctions between actor and audience member, theater and real world, between fictive performance and real revolution, were to be rendered obsolete; spectators were subsumed into the action, carrying the company's recapitulated ideas with them as they physically reentered the real world. Beck mused, in his notebook, that the piece concludes "with a dissolve of actors and Audience, you can't tell the difference, from the theatre into life."[64] Finally, then, after a carefully constructed, highly theatrical sequence of Rites and flashouts, physical gestures and physical contact, the creators of *Paradise Now* imagined that the performance would burst out of the theater's containment and transform the real world of the streets.

AFTERWARD

Once the performers and spectators left the theater, bursting into the real world of the streets—what then? What, if anything, was transformed in the end? Looking back at *Paradise Now* from a forty-five-year remove, it is impossible to avoid the ways in which the piece did not, of course, transform the streets as the Living Theatre had hoped it would, did not leave active revolutionary cells across the United States and Europe, did not result in the anarchist-pacifist revolution the company so ardently hoped to catalyze. The year 1968, rather, constituted in many ways a high-water mark for the countercultural movements of the era, and in the years following their *Paradise Now* tour, the Living Theatre itself transformed, disbanding into four separate groups that dispersed to different countries and continents, reflecting the increasingly disparate spiritual, theatrical, and political priorities of different members of the company.

But to view *Paradise Now* exclusively, or even mainly, in terms of failure is to miss its significance. The piece is widely acknowledged as a dramaturgical landmark: cited, remembered, discussed, and dissected with nostalgia and irritation, frustration and awe, but frequently viewed as one of the most significant theatrical performances to register and stage the vision of the late 1960s American and European counterculture. As I see it, a central aspect of this legacy—a primary reason for *Paradise Now*'s persistence—is its contagious dramaturgy. In creating *Paradise Now*, the Living Theatre drew on and transformed historically charged ideas about contagion, infectiousness, and performance. It addressed pressing contemporary questions about containment and crowd dynamics, and it did so by weaving together a vast array of philosophical, spiritual, political, and social sources and influences. The Living Theatre's goal for its audiences, if impossible, was visionary—and was, as is less frequently acknowledged, highly structured and particular, due to the company's specific dramaturgical innovations as they attempted to make sounds, gestures, and emotions contagious. If the plague was not infectious precisely the way the Living Theatre had planned, it nonetheless made *Paradise Now* into a groundbreaking model for revolutionary performance.

And even if the specific tactics deployed in *Paradise Now* have given way to other radical theater forms, the contagious metaphor lived on long after the piece ceased touring. It persisted in the political theater of artists like Augusto Boal and Marc Estrin—both of whom took inspiration from the Living Theatre and created "invisible" performances meant to infiltrate society infectiously, one spectator-participant at a time. It lived on into the era of the HIV/AIDS epidemic, finding form in the work of artists like General Idea, who declared themselves "viral" artists, not only because they took on the subject matter of real disease but also because they attempted to infiltrate the mass media and spread their images and ideas contagiously. And, of course, the concept of contagious culture returned with a vengeance in the age of the Internet, when corporations and artists alike imagine their work in the language of the viral, thinking of ideas and images in terms of their capacity to spread. Contagious performance surged through the 1960s, found groundbreaking expression in *Paradise Now*—and continued to new artists, new audiences, and new revolutionary fights.

NOTES

1. For instance, during the rehearsal period for *Paradise Now*, Judith Malina wrote in her diary, "The Company is intensively committed, but it is not clear yet what revolution is meant, or how literally it is meant" (Judith Malina's Diary, 39).
2. Julian Beck, *Theandric: Julian Beck's Last Notebooks*, ed. Erica Bilder (Philadelphia: Harwood Academic, 1992), 121.
3. Judith Malina, interview with author, April 17, 2011.
4. Ibid., 122.
5. Antonin Artaud, "The Theater and the Plague," in *The Theater and Its Double*, trans. Mary Caroline Richards (New York: Grove Press, 1958), 30.
6. Saul Gottlieb, "The Living Theatre in Exile: 'Mysteries, Frankenstein,'" *Tulane Drama Review* 10, no. 4 (Summer 1966): 145.
7. Judith Malina, Julian Beck, and Richard Schechner, "Containment Is the Enemy," *The Drama Review: TDR* 13, no. 3 (Spring 1969): 35.
8. Richard Gilman, "The Living Theatre on Tour," in *The Drama Is Coming Now: The Theater Criticism of Richard Gilman, 1961–1991* (New Haven, CT: Yale University Press, 2005), 123.
9. Malina, Beck, and Schechner, 35.
10. John Tytell, *The Living Theatre: Art, Exile, and Outrage* (New York: Grove Press, 1995), 30.
11. Malina, Beck, and Schechner, 35–36.
12. Ibid., 36.
13. *Paradise Now*, Notebook #2, 58.
14. Ibid., 62.
15. *Paradise Now*, Notebook #1, 81.
16. Malina, Beck, and Schechner, 44.
17. Company of the Living Theatre, "Avignon Statement," July 28, 1968, published in *The Drama Review: TDR* 13, no. 3 (Spring 1969): 45.
18. Malina, Beck, and Schechner, 43–44.
19. Dean Acheson, *Present at the Creation: My Years in the State Department* (New York: Norton, 1969), 219.
20. Alan Nadel, *Containment Culture: American Narratives, Postmodernism, and the Atomic Age* (Durham, NC: Duke University Press, 1995), 5–6.
21. Bruce McConachie, *American Theater in the Culture of the Cold War: Producing and Contesting Containment* (Iowa City: University of Iowa Press, 2003), 11.
22. In the records of their American tour during 1968 and 1969, the Living Theatre perform *Paradise Now* in college gymnasiums all over the country (see Company of The Living

Theatre, Living Theatre Records). In Beck and Malina's 1969 interview with Schechner, Malina notes that the company prefers to work in ballrooms and amphitheaters.

23. Malina, Beck, and Schechner, 34.

24. *Paradise Now*, Notebook #1, 14.

25. *Paradise Now*, Notebook #2, 14–20.

26. Ibid., 64.

27. Ibid., 19.

28. Tony Perucci, "The Red Mask of Sanity: Paul Robeson, HUAC, and the Sound of Cold War Performance." *TDR* 53, no. 4 (Winter 2009): 36.

29. Judith Malina's Diary, 75.

30. Tracy Davis, *Stages of Emergency: Cold War Nuclear Civil Defense* (Durham, NC: Duke University Press, 2007), 2.

31. Julian Beck, *The Life of the Theatre* (San Francisco: City Lights, 1972), section 91, pages not numbered.

32. Beck, *The Life of the Theatre*.

33. Judith Malina, interview with author, April 17, 2011.

34. Julian Beck's *Paradise Now* notebook, IV-23-313.

35. *Paradise Now*, Notebook #1, 73.

36. The company drew inspiration, for instance, from the theatrical philosophies of both Brecht and Artaud, from spiritual writings from Martin Buber to the I Ching, from John Cage to Karl Marx.

37. *Paradise Now*, Notebook #3, 16.

38. Judith Malina's *Paradise Now* notebook, 74.

39. Julian Beck's *Paradise Now* notebook, VIII-27-574.

40. Malina, Beck, and Schechner, 36.

41. Erika Fischer-Lichte, *Theatre, Sacrifice, Ritual: Exploring Forms of Political Theatre* (New York: Routledge, 2005), 30.

42. Erika Munk, "Only Connect: The Living Theatre and Its Audiences," in *Restaging the Sixties: Radical Theaters and Their Legacies*, ed. James Harding and Cindy Rosenthal (Ann Arbor: University of Michigan Press, 2006), 45.

43. Kimberly Jannarone, *Artaud and His Doubles* (Ann Arbor: University of Michigan Press, 2010), 116–17.

44. Artaud, "The Theater and the Plague," 32.

45. *Paradise Now*, Notebook #3, 21–22.

46. Judith Malina's Diary, 18.

47. Ibid., 15.

48. Ibid., 16.

49. Ibid., 16.

50. Stefan Brecht, "Revolution at the Brooklyn Academy of Music," *The Drama Review: TDR* 13, no. 3 (Spring 1969): 57.

51. Malina, Beck, and Schechner, 31.

52. Company of the Living Theatre, *Paradise Now: Collective Creation of the Living Theatre* (New York: Random House, 1971), 16–17.

53. Ibid., 15.

54. Judith Malina, interview with author, April 17, 2011.

55. Brecht, 57.

56. Munk, 46–47.

57. Gilman, 122.

58. Malina, Beck, and Schechner, 29.
59. Company of the Living Theatre, *Paradise Now*, 16.
60. Elias Canetti, *Crowds and Power* (New York: Viking Press, 1962), 17–19.
61. Ibid., 17.
62. Company of the Living Theatre, *Paradise Now*, 136.
63. Ibid., 84.
64. Julian Beck's *Paradise Now* notebook, X-5-689–X-6-690.

BIBLIOGRAPHY

Acheson, Dean. *Present at the Creation: My Years in the State Department.* New York: Norton, 1969.

Artaud, Antonin. *The Theater and Its Double.* Translated by Mary Caroline Richards. New York: Grove Press, 1958.

Beck, Julian. *The Life of the Theatre.* San Francisco: City Lights, 1972.

———. *Theandric: Julian Beck's Last Notebooks.* Edited by Erica Bilder. Philadelphia: Harwood Academic, 1992.

Brecht, Stefan. "Revolution at the Brooklyn Academy of Music." *TDR: The Drama Review* 13, no. 3 (1969): 46–73.

Canetti, Elias. *Crowds and Power.* New York: Viking Press, 1963.

Davis, Tracy. *Stages of Emergency: Cold War Nuclear Civil Defense.* Durham, NC: Duke University Press, 2007.

Fischer-Lichte, Erika. *Theatre, Sacrifice, Ritual: Exploring Forms of Political Theatre.* New York: Routledge, 2005.

Gilman, Richard. "The Living Theatre on Tour." In *The Drama Is Coming Now: The Theater Criticism of Richard Gilman, 1961–1991,* 119–24. New Haven, CT: Yale University Press, 2005.

Gottlieb, Saul. "The Living Theatre in Exile: 'Mysteries, Frankenstein.'" *Tulane Drama Review* 10, no. 4 (1966): 137–52.

Jannarone, Kimberly. *Artaud and His Doubles.* Ann Arbor: University of Michigan Press, 2010.

Company of The Living Theatre. "Avignon Statement." *TDR: The Drama Review* 13, no. 3 (1969): 45.

———. Living Theatre Records. Yale Collection of American Literature, Beinecke Rare Book and Manuscript Library.

———. *Paradise Now: Collective Creation of the Living Theatre.* New York: Random House, 1971.

Malina, Judith. Interview with author, April 17, 2011.

Malina, Judith, Julian Beck, and Richard Schechner. "Containment Is the Enemy." *TDR: The Drama Review* 13, no. 3 (1969): 24–44.

McConachie, Bruce. *American Theater in the Culture of the Cold War: Producing and Contesting Containment.* Iowa City: University of Iowa Press, 2003.

Munk, Erika. "Only Connect: The Living Theatre and Its Audiences." In *Restaging the Sixties: Radical Theaters and Their Legacies,* edited by James Harding and Cindy Rosenthal. Ann Arbor: University of Michigan Press, 2006.

Nadel, Alan. *Containment Culture: American Narratives, Postmodernism, and the Atomic Age.* Durham, NC: Duke University Press, 1995.

Perucci, Tony. "The Red Mask of Sanity: Paul Robeson, HUAC, and the Sound of Cold War Performance." *TDR* 53, no. 4 (2009): 18–48.

Tytell, John. *The Living Theatre: Art, Exile, and Outrage.* New York: Grove Press, 1995.

CHAPTER 42

THE SALOME EPIDEMIC
Degeneracy, Disease, and Race Suicide

MARLIS SCHWEITZER

ON August 30, 1908, the *Baltimore Sun* alerted readers to a peculiar series of events. "An epidemic of 'Salomes' has struck the world," the paper declared. "Almost as naked as truth, and concealing principally by gauze and ropes of jewels [. . .], a host of great dancers are going through sinuous movements to show the daughter of Herodias in her extreme moment of ecstasy."[1] Though varying in talent and looks, the "host of great dancers" shared certain distinctive features: bared feet, exposed midriffs, jewel-encrusted tops, gauze skirts, sensual choreography, and the severed head of John the Baptist. Appearing in vaudeville, musical comedy, and burlesque, they presented a collective spectacle of writhing female desire that delighted some and outraged many.

Theatrical fads were hardly unusual in early twentieth-century theater culture, especially in the intensely competitive world of American vaudeville, where performers engaged in all manner of artistic theft. What distinguished the Salome "epidemic" from earlier dance crazes, however, was the "amazing rapidity" with which it crossed geographic and generic boundaries, from European spas and music halls to North American vaudeville theaters, burlesque halls, and dime museums.[2] Less than a week after American mimic Gertrude Hoffman introduced New York audiences to "A Vision of Salome"—an act closely modeled on, if not outright stolen from, "The Vision of Salome" staged at London's Palace Theatre by Canadian dancer Maud Allan—female performers were filling the boards with their own interpretations of the biblical princess.[3] By July 18, a "chorus girl" speaking to a journalist for the *Evening World* noted that "The only other topic in our set [chorus girls] is the Salome craze. You can't book an act now unless you have a Salome dance featured in it in some way . . . straight, imitation or burlesque."[4] The *Baltimore Sun* agreed: "Actresses and singers, [as] well as dancers, who made their living in other kinds of work have found out that if they want to stay in the game successfully they must learn how to do the 'Salome' act."[5]

The *Baltimore Sun* was not the only newspaper to equate the Salome dance with the discourses of disease and contagion. The word "epidemic" and invented terms such as "Salomania" appeared frequently in reviews and editorials as the dance moved across the continent. Though some writers used the terms jokingly, others found little humor in the dance's disease-like mobility. These critics warned that the proliferation of scantily clad

Salomes would pollute the contained, corseted bodies of respectable women and corrupt the minds of men. Others worried that the vulgar dance would encourage the spread of immoral thoughts and behavior among immigrants, urban youth, and those vulnerable to cheap amusement.[6] Still others maintained that the Salome dance would damage dancers' internal organs and make them susceptible to hysteria, which in turn would induce similar forms of mental distress in female spectators.

Such arguments point to a complicated understanding of the relationship between moral, physical, and cultural contagion, one that imagined germs moving along the same channels as bad behavior, degenerate affects, and performing bodies. Intriguingly, many of these arguments resonate with recent scholarship on the transmission of affect, which acknowledges the dynamic, relational, and physiological aspects of affective experience. In looking broadly at the association between disease and Salomania, this chapter considers how dance exposed the porous boundaries between self and other, individual and community, American and foreigner at the turn of the twentieth century.

"Salomania" has reemerged in recent years, not on vaudeville stages but in academic circles, where it has become a favorite subject of historians of gender, culture, and performance. These scholars have subjected the dance to a wide range of sophisticated analyses, reading it by turns as an Orientalist fantasy, an exercise in anti-Semitism, an exploitative act of cultural imperialism, a feminist celebration of authorship and self-pleasure, a racialized performance comparable to other forms of minstrelsy, and an exploration of cosmopolitan subjectivity.[7] For the most part, however, scholars have overlooked the discourse of disease pervasive in descriptions of "Salomania." One notable exception is cultural historian Mary Simonson, who argues that the characterization of the Salome dance as a foreign, communicable disease reveals early-twentieth century American anxieties about women's incursions into public space, their desire for less restrictive clothing, and their demands for "suffrage, reproductive rights, and greater opportunities in the public sphere."[8]

Simonson's argument is persuasive and compatible with feminist scholarship on the transformation of gender roles in early twentieth-century American society. I nevertheless hesitate to read the fierce backlash against the Salome dance and the repeated use of such words as "epidemic" and "disease" as exclusively rooted in gender anxiety. Rather, I argue that in addition to highlighting changing definitions of female agency, the discourse of contagion and decay surrounding the Salome dance exposed deep-seated fears about a broader range of issues. These included concern about "race suicide," the much-discussed decline of white America heralded by declining birth rates among WASPS and the dangerous influence of "diseased" immigrants arriving from eastern and southern Europe; anxiety about theater's role in the moral contamination of the youth, especially immigrant youth; and (following Simonson) fear about the sexual power of the female body, freed from the tight constraints of the corset and thus capable of expressing sexual desire through unfettered movement and sweating, jiggling flesh.

In *Contagious: Cultures, Carriers, and the Outbreak Narrative*, cultural studies scholar Priscilla Wald defines "outbreak narratives" as formulaic stories of contagion that identify an emerging infection, trace its movement through local as well as global networks, and detail efforts to ensure the containment and eventual eradication of the disease. These narratives appear in the popular press as well as in mainstream Hollywood films (e.g., *Invasion of the Body Snatchers, Outbreak, Contagion, World War Z*) and help to make the invisible (contagious viruses and bacteria) visible and intelligible. A further characteristic of the "outbreak

narrative" is general antipathy toward immigrants and other foreigners, who are often identified with the initial outbreak and its subsequent dispersal.[9]

The rhetoric of disease and contagion surrounding the Salome dance followed the general
structure of the "outbreak narrative" described by Wald. Those who condemned the dance,
from government censors and vice boards to church ministers and social workers, often referenced its origin in the play by known-"degenerate" Oscar Wilde, as well as its association
with dancer Maud Allan, the sister of an executed murderer. "The vulgarization of Salome by
music-hall dancers of all descriptions is the poetic vengeance which the fates have granted
to the spurned composer [Strauss] and the dead poet [Wilde]," the literary journal *Current
Literature* proclaimed in its October 1908 issue.[10] Through publications and public speeches,
opponents of the Salome dance sought to contain the leaky, desiring bodies of its hosts.
A study of Salomania thus exposes the social dis-ease that insisted on equating the dance
with physical, sexual, racial, and spiritual contagion.[11]

Yet the Salome "outbreak" was about more than disease/dis-ease. Indeed, as the playful tone of newspaper reviews and editorials suggest, Salomania was also a celebration, an
exuberant expression of female agency and sexuality transmitted from body to body and
through the pages of mass circulation newspapers. In this respect, the "carriers" of Salomania
rejected the negative associations of the "outbreak narrative" and promoted a very different
view of the modern female body. Moving along a variety of theatrical circulatory networks,
the viral dance presented new opportunities for performers hoping to make names for themselves and to demonstrate their embrace of modern values.

To get at the complicated, at times contradictory, aspects of the Salome dance and the
Salomania it inspired, I trace the dance's transmission path, across borders of nation, genre,
and body. I begin with its initial contact with US audiences in January 1907 following the
New York debut of Strauss's opera *Salomé*, which incited heated debate in the pages of the
city's most respected papers. I then examine the dance's return to New York the following summer in the body of dancer Gertrude Hoffman, the primary vector of Salomania,
who acquired (or stole) Maud Allan's interpretation through lengthy exposure to the latter's London act. From there, I investigate the dance's disease-like spread throughout the
United States via the circuitry of vaudeville, musical comedy, and burlesque, focusing on
the many performers who embraced the dance and its risqué costume. Finally, I explore the
various attempts to contain Salomania, situating anti-Salome rhetoric within larger social
and cultural debates about women, sexuality, immigration, race, and morality. Ultimately,
Salomania was about much more than sweating, scantily clad bodies onstage; it was about
the future of American society and culture.

FIRST CONTACT: SALOME, SYPHILIS, DEGENERATION

The Salome dance entered the United States from Europe heavily pregnant with contradictory meanings shaped by anti-Semitic, homophobic assumptions about the degeneracy
of Jewish sexuality. European interest in Salome as a biblical figure dates back to the 1830s
and 1840s, when noted writers such as Jacob Grimm and Heinrich Heine invigorated New

Testament accounts of the unnamed "daughter of Herodias," who performs the "Dance of the Seven Veils" for her stepfather Herod in exchange for the head of John the Baptist. In their accounts, the newly christened Salome emerged as a seductive virgin passionately in love with the Baptist, who exacts terrible vengeance at her mother's bidding. Later representations of Salome by writers and painters including Gustave Flaubert, Gustav Moreau, Henri Regnault, and J. K. Huysman reinforced the gory eroticism of the story.[12] But it was Oscar Wilde's 1892 symbolist drama *Salomé* that came to haunt all subsequent representations of the biblical princess, including the 1905 Strauss opera of the same name. In Wilde's version, Salome lusts after Jokanaan (John the Baptist), who has been imprisoned in a well for condemning her mother's marriage to Herod; when he rejects her declarations of love, she spitefully decides to perform the dance that guarantees his death. The play ends with Salome speaking lovingly to Jokanaan's decapitated head before raising it to her lips to kiss. Repulsed by her deviancy, Herod calls on his guards to kill her and she is crushed beneath their shields.[13]

Wilde's *Salomé* was originally scheduled for an 1892 opening at the Palace Theatre in London with Sarah Bernhardt in the title role; however, its forthright treatment of biblical characters and its none-too-subtle depiction of deviant sexuality caught the attention of the Lord Chamberlain's office and the play was denied a license for performance. *Salomé* eventually opened in Paris in 1896, after Wilde's sodomy trial had made him a cause célèbre, followed by a critically acclaimed Berlin production in 1903 staged by Max Reinhardt.[14]

In Germany, as cultural historian Sander Gilman has persuasively shown, critical reception of Wilde's *Salomé* was informed by homophobic reactions to Wilde, the celebrity "pervert." Critics and censors saw the play as a celebration of sexual pathology, a "morally repugnant" representation of "perverted sensuality," rife with diseased and corrupted characters. In a close reading of Richard Strauss's operatic treatment of Wilde's play, Gilman argues that the unholy alliance of deviancy, perversion, and disease was mapped onto the character of Salome, whose unnatural desires led to her death. Even the French novelist Romain Rolland warned his friend Strauss that the material had "a nauseous and sickly atmosphere [. . . .] Wilde's Salome, and all those who surround her are unwholesome, unclean, hysterical or alcoholic beings, stinking of sophisticated and perfumed corruption."[15] Gilman suggests that such reactions were informed by contemporary German accounts of the Salome story, many of which reinforced stereotypical images of the sexually aggressive, syphilitic Jewess. In the most extreme example, Oskar Panizza's 1895 play *The Council of Love*, a sensual Salome communes with the Devil and bears a daughter who "is syphilis incarnate."[16] The daughter, identified only as "The Woman," infects non-Jewish men through her beautiful, leaky, diseased body, presaging the destruction of the Aryan race.[17]

Gilman and Anne L. Seshardi maintain that German audiences, as well as audiences elsewhere, would have recognized Salome's perverse desires as signs of hysteria, a disease that clinical psychiatrists associated with Jews and saw as an external manifestation of incest.[18] In Wilde's play and Strauss's opera, Salome's sexual obsession is matched by that of her stepfather, Herod, who lusts hungrily after her virginal body. Audiences would therefore have understood Salome's hysteria as emerging from Herod's incestuous passion. The lingering question was whether Salome's hysteria could be cured and her body cleansed through communion with the Baptist. In Wilde's play the answer is definitively no: The play concludes with Salome in a state of hysterical ecstasy before her body is crushed. But Strauss's opera suggests otherwise. As Seshardi argues, Strauss's opera shows Salome as remorseful and spiritually transfigured after the Baptist's death. Her "desire for atonement" is consistent with the imperialist "conversion project," whereby all heathens, including Jews, would be converted to Christianity.[19] In other words, Strauss's Salome is a much more sympathetic character because she ultimately supports white Christian hegemony.

Questions about the nature of Salome's degeneration and perversion accompanied Strauss's opera across the Atlantic to New York City in the early winter of 1907, when the German American impresario Heinrich Conried staged *Salome* at the Metropolitan Opera.[20] Although the critic for the *New York Times* declared the opera a "remarkable work" and celebrated the "superb impersonations" of its stars, the opening night audience was repulsed by the "Dance of the Seven Veils" and Salome's passionate kiss with the Baptist's head. In keeping with operatic tradition trained ballet dancer Bianca Froelich, not diva Olive Fremstad, performed the "Dance of the Seven Veils." "It was the dance that women turn away from, and many of the women in the Metropolitan Opera House last night turned away from it," the *Times* reported. Dressed in a revealing costume, Froelich rolled her hips and slithered across the stage seductively, much to the discomfort of the men in the audience, many of whom "decided to go to the corridors and smoke."[21] Those who remained were further outraged by the scene following the "Dance of the Seven Veils," in which Fremstad "crouch[ed] over the dissevered head of the prophet" and sang to it "in terms of reproach, of grief, of endearment and longing" before "press[ing] her teeth into the gelid flesh" and kissing the "bloody lips."[22] At this point, entire rows and theater boxes began to empty, while those in the galleries, presumably representatives of a lower class, stood on their seats to get a closer look.

A series of letters published in the *New York Times* demonstrates how varying interpretations of Salome's degeneracy became entangled with discussions of the opera's artistic merit. On January 24, a man claiming to have spent twenty years treating "nervous and mental diseases," especially among "degenerates (using that word in its biological sense to designate those who do not conform to the moral, mental and physical standard to which we have reached in evolutionary progress entitles them)," condemned *Salome* as "a detailed and explicit exposition of the most horrible, disgusting, revolting and unmentionable features of degeneracy (using the word now in its customary, sexual significance) that I have ever heard, read of, or imagined."[23] Distinguishing between degeneracy as a biological condition and degeneracy as perverse sexual practice, the author (writing under the pseudonym "Imparo Ancora" or "I am still learning") warned that the opera's graphic portrayal of "perversion, lust, and murder" sung to "emotion-liberating music" threatened to corrupt "our women, our children." Although as a doctor he felt great sympathy for those whose biological disposition impeded their "evolutionary progress," he feared that the representation of degeneracy would promote dangerous ideas among otherwise healthy Americans. He concluded by calling on the members of a "society too young and lusty to show evidence of decay" to resist the production and call for its immediate closure.[24]

Imparo Ancora's references to decline and decay echoed the rhetoric of President Theodore Roosevelt, who in a series of public lectures and articles, expressed concern that declining birth rates among America's WASP population, coupled with the arrival of thousands of immigrants from southern and eastern Europe, many of them carrying dangerous diseases, would culminate in "race suicide." The image of the disease-ridden immigrant dominated the American cultural imaginary during the height of mass immigration between 1880 and 1920, when approximately twenty-three million people from eastern and southern Europe, entered the United States. Nervous that immigrant diseases would spread to the rest of the population, the government subjected new arrivals to emotionally stressful and physically invasive screenings at ports of entry.[25] Many immigrants, especially Jews, fled persecution in Eastern Europe only to be blamed by American officials for outbreaks of cholera in the 1890s and the spread of highly contagious eye and scalp diseases (trachoma and favus) in the early 1900s.[26] At Ellis Island, immigrant bodies were choreographed along specific "courses" of steep staircases and narrow passageways, designed to help medical examiners identify physically disabled bodies prior to conducting a physical exam. These exhausting and often invasive screening measures treated immigrant bodies as legible texts that could be made to speak through sufficient probing and prodding.[27]

Roosevelt and others likewise lamented the debilitating effects of "overcivilization" on white men and women. Responding to a perceived increase in cases of "neurasthenia" (a kind of mental prostration or nervous exhaustion associated with fast-paced urban life), Roosevelt encouraged the development of the "strenuous life," a masculinist program of sporting activities and outdoor excursions designed to equip the next generation of American men with the necessary leadership qualities to realize the nation's potential.[28] For Roosevelt, as for Imparo Ancora, future American prosperity required assisting those who suffered from biological degeneration while forestalling the transmission of degenerate ideas to healthy men and women. *Salome*, a foreign import based on the degenerate writing of a known pervert and thus tainted by provocative content and emotionally manipulative music, threatened to undermine these efforts.

Others disagreed with this perspective, rejecting the pathologization of *Salome* and Wilde. The day after the first letter appeared, a writer identified as C.I.H. critiqued Imparo Ancora for his overblown rhetoric, pointing out that advance publicity "left no doubt in the minds of readers that the spectacle itself must be the apotheosis of lust." C.I.H. further questioned whether any members of the audience would have interpreted the performance "from a pathological point of view," noting that *Salome* was hardly alone in the operatic canon for its portrayal of deviant sexuality.[29] "Sancta Simplicitas" shared this perspective, claiming that "Every man or woman who 'assisted' at this performance knew exactly what he or she was going to see and went there to see it." This writer rejected Impara's characterization of Salome as a degenerate, arguing that "Salome's extravagances" were better interpreted as the "manifestations of a passionate Oriental's half mad, half hysterical remorse."[30] For this writer, then, Salome's behavior was not unnatural, degenerate, or "hideous" but rather the natural display of a particular ethnic sensibility coupled with genuine remorse.[31] Like many German audiences, Sancta Simplicitas understood Salome as a sympathetic character capable of conversion; her hysteria and degeneracy were the product of her Jewishness and therefore posed no threat to morally sound Christians.

As the debates over Salome's degeneracy waged in the pages of the *New York Times*, the directors of the Metropolitan Opera House and Real Estate Company met to discuss whether to allow the production to continue. Under pressure from society figures, including Anne Morgan, daughter of financier J. P. Morgan, they ultimately decided to withdraw their support, claiming that it would not be "advisable for [the Company] to be directly or officially associated with any such performances in this city."[32] Though Conried briefly considered moving the opera to the New Amsterdam Theatre, his ailing health and the pressure of the directors proved too daunting and he was forced to close the production.[33] To all appearances the Salome threat had been contained.[34]

But this was not the case. The following spring, the Salome dance returned in all of its menacing glory to the United States, hidden in the body of an American mimic.

THE CONTAGIOUS DANCE: MIMICRY AND MOVEMENT'S CONTAGION

If, as Carrie Noland observes in *Migrations of Gesture*, to gesture is to carry meaning in the body—following the Latin root of the word "gesture" is *gerere*, meaning to carry, to act, or to do—then to carry *learned* gestures in the body is to transport meaning from one location to another, from one body to another in the manner of a contagious disease.[35] By 1908 female performers had titillated audiences for well over a decade with their interpretations of eroticized oriental dance,[36] but it was a single event—Gertrude Hoffman's July 1908 debut of Maud Allan's "Vision of Salome"—that sparked "Salomania."

Born in Toronto and raised in California, Maud Allan traveled to Germany in 1895 to pursue a career as a concert pianist. After several years of conservatory training, she turned her attention toward dance and began performing interpretations of classical music in artists' salons. In April 1906, while in Berlin, Allan attended Max Reinhardt's celebrated production of Wilde's *Salomé* and was inspired to create her own version of the story. On December 26, 1906, she premiered "The Vision of Salome" in Vienna before an audience of invited guests, who were at once delighted and scandalized by her erotic dance and midriff-baring costume. The following year, after performances in Budapest, Berlin, and other European cities, Allan presented the dance at a special soiree in the spa town of Marienbad, where the vacationing Edward VII was so impressed that he urged her to contact Alfred Butt, the manager of the Palace Theatre in London. Butt could hardly refuse an endorsement from the king, and Allan's "The Vision of Salome" opened at the Palace on March 6, 1908, to great critical and popular acclaim.[37]

Allan was but one of a growing number of young white, predominantly North American women filling the music halls and salons of Europe. Indeed, her touring schedule often coincided with those of fellow dance innovators Ruth St. Denis, Isadora Duncan, and Mata Hari, among others.[38] Criss-crossing the continent, these women offered a "broad panoply of non-European dances, including incense rites, Indian Nautch dances, 'Oriental,' 'Arab,' and occasionally 'African' dances, incongruously set to a specific group of baroque, classical, romantic, and contemporary composers."[39] Most historians interpret the proliferation of these racialized dances via "allegedly foreign bodies" as evidence of heightened European anxiety about the slow unraveling of the colonialist project. The repeated experience of seeing attractive, young white women play out Orientalist fantasies of the mysterious, sexually voracious colonial woman temporarily assuaged fears of colonial unrest and the "threat of the racial Other."[40] It is certainly no surprise that the most famous dancers of the period played before royalty and other high-ranking members of society. Cultural historian Amy Koritz argues that in creating her "Vision of Salome," Allan carefully negotiated early-twentieth-century British orientalist fantasies such that her performance affirmed "some essential 'truth' about the East" at the same time as it distanced the white dancer from "the explicit expression of sexuality assumed to characterize Eastern dance as practiced in

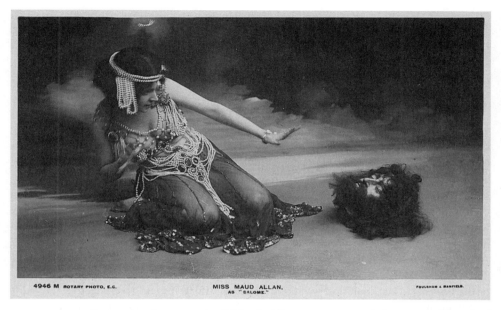

FIGURE 42.1 Promotional postcard of Maud Allan encountering the severed head of John the Baptist in "The Vision of Salome." Courtesy: Dance Collection Danse.

Cairo or Tangier."[41] According to Koritz, most London critics did *not* view the dance as particularly transgressive or degenerate in spite of her bare feet and exotic costume.[42] Judith Walkowitz makes a similar observation, noting how British critics rose up to defend Allan against her detractors by emphasizing the dancer's whiteness, her Delsartean technique (based on the expressive movement training of the François Delsarte), and her extensive research into the history of dance and visual art.[43]

If Allan simultaneously embodied yet disavowed Salome's destructive, degenerate sexuality by "displacing it onto an Oriental woman," and not just any Oriental woman but one closely entangled with anti-Semitic stereotypes of the diseased Jewess, did Gertrude Hoffman enact a similar disavowal of Orientalist sexuality when she staged her version of Allan's "Vision of Salome" in New York? And if this was Hoffman's intention, did audiences perceive it as such? To answer these questions, I look at the circumstances surrounding the transmission of the "Vision" from one body to another before turning to reviews of Hoffman's performance and the epidemic that followed.

Unlike her other impersonations, vaudeville mimic Gertrude Hoffman was commissioned to "get" the Salome dance by the enterprising theater manager Willie Hammerstein at the urging of his agent Morris Gest.[44] In April 1908, American newspapers disclosed that Maud Allan was the sister of infamous "Belfry Murderer" Theodore Durrant, a man convicted and executed for the brutal rape and murder of two women in San Francisco in the late 1890s.[45] Eager to exploit the scandalous news, Gest suggested hiring someone to extract the dance from the dancer by means of mimicry. Importing the "Vision of Salome" in another performer's body, he argued, would allow Hammerstein to capitalize on the notoriety of the dance while avoiding lengthy and expensive negotiations with its originator.

Gest and Hammerstein had good reasons for pursuing the Salome dance. The previous season, a brief but intense "vaudeville war" had placed a premium on importing high caliber acts from European cultural centers and salaries for guaranteed hits had reached record heights. In the spring and summer of 1907, agents for the "Advanced Vaudeville" circuit run by Abraham Erlanger and Marc Klaw participated in a major hunt for foreign talent, contracting hundreds of performers from Europe and elsewhere. But by November 1907, Klaw and Erlanger realized the folly of their venture and conceded defeat, agreeing to leave vaudeville for at least a decade. Through a special arrangement with the victorious United Booking Office (UBO) led by B. F. Keith, they transferred responsibility for all contracted performers to the UBO. The result was a major talent glut that sent ripples throughout the entire theater industry. Small-time performers had to rethink their acts to attract notice from booking agents. Headliners likewise felt pressure to compete with other headliners, especially in double-booking situations when two or more headliners appeared on the same bill.[46] In late winter of 1908, Hoffman herself was caught up in an intense rivalry with fellow vaudevillian Eva Tanguay, whereby each sought to out-imitate the other in a bid for fame and fans.[47] Although the intensity of the "vaudeville war" was cooling by the spring of 1908, vaudeville and musical comedy managers continued to vie for hot acts, and Allan was certainly one of the hottest.[48] Gest's solution was therefore straightforward and cost-effective. Gertrude Hoffman's unique range of abilities as a highly skilled mimic, an experienced stage director, and a choreographer made her an ideal candidate for the job.[49] On April 23, she departed for London, accompanied by her husband Max, with the specific goal of getting Allan's dance.[50]

Hoffman's thieving actions were not unique to vaudeville or musical comedy. Dancers, comics, singers, and other performers frequently lifted material from one another; in fact, Hoffman titled her vaudeville act "The Borrowed Art of Gertrude Hoffman" as an overt advertisement of her mimetic abilities. Well-versed in the intricacies of copyright law through previous run-ins with proprietary impresarios,[51] she likely knew that dance originators like Allan could do little to prevent others from stealing their choreography because international copyright law had yet to recognize dance. In 1892, dancer Loie Fuller's request for an injunction against a rival performer who had copied "The Serpentine Dance" was denied by the New York Circuit Court because it did not conform to the definition of "dramatic composition." As the judge's decision outlined, "a stage dance illustrating the poetry of motion by a series of graceful movements combined with an attractive arrangement of drapery, lights, and shadows, but telling no story, portraying no character, and depicting no emotion, is not a 'dramatic composition' within the meaning of the Copyright Act."[52] Although Allan's dance *did* tell a story, portray a character, and depict emotion, the absence of spoken dialogue and a straightforward narrative made it vulnerable to theft, especially by someone like Hoffman.

Hoffman's undetected appropriation of Allan's dance raises intriguing questions about the transmission of dance from stage performer to spectating body. Unlike situations where choreographed movement is transmitted through specific instruction and direct physical contact—as in a formal dance class or rehearsal—Hoffman learned Allan's dance by *watching* it from her seat in the Palace auditorium. In her essay "Movement's Contagion," dance scholar Susan Leigh Foster draws an explicit connection between dance and contagion, arguing that the very act of seeing dance affects the bodies of those watching: "Viewers' bodies, even in their seated stillness, nonetheless feel what the dancing body is feeling—the tensions of expansiveness, the floating or driving momentums that compose the dancer's motion."[53] Drawing on recent work in cognitive neuroscience, specifically research on "mirror neurons," Foster describes how seated viewers can also feel "the choreographer's desires and intentions" by experiencing the muscular sensations of the dance. In this respect, dance and the emotional states associated with it move like a disease from body to body via physical exposure, often without the knowledge or awareness of those "simply" observing.[54]

If, as Foster maintains, dance moves between bodies by stimulating neurocognitive activity, it is hardly surprising that Hoffman was able to "catch" the "Vision" after multiple visits to the Palace—in interviews, she claimed that she had watched Allan fourteen times.[55] Already skilled in the art of reproducing other performers' voices, postures, and gestures, she had only to see Allan's choreography to transform herself from a seated spectator into a "carrier" of the Salome dance. Of course, Hoffman must also have rehearsed the performance in the privacy of her hotel room between each of the fourteen performances she attended, notating it in some way or working methodically through each step and gesture so that she could accurately reproduce the choreography once she returned to the United States. Nevertheless, it would appear that the real site of transmission was the Palace auditorium.

Second Contact: The "Vision" and the Vector

Gertrude Hoffman's "A Vision of Salome" premiered on July 13, 1908, before an audience of New York critics and theatergoers eager to see the dance that everyone had read about. Recognizing that transparency about Hoffman's debt to Allan was critical to the act's success, Hammerstein and Gest emphasized that she wasn't performing just *any* Salome dance but rather an "accurat[e] and cleverly reproduced" version of "Maud Allan's celebrated 'The Vision of Salome.'"[56] In the lead-up to the opening, Gest built audience expectations with "planted" stories about the near-incineration of Hoffman's costume in a streetcar fire and public sightings of the prop head.[57] By July 13, New York was well primed for the American premiere of Hoffman's "faithful copy" of Allan's provocative dance.[58]

Hoffman did not disappoint. Although, as the *New York World* took pains to point out, "Miss Hoffman is a mimic, not a poetic dancer or great actress," she succeeded in "arous[ing] the audience to a high pitch [. . .] because of wondrous scenic investiture, dreamy, sensuous music composed by her husband and magnificent stage management."[59] An orchestra of thirty musicians led by Max Hoffman set the mood for the act with "eerie," "trembling" music. Slowly the drop curtain rose to "disclos[e] the rich tableau curtains that parted slowly on a production, beautiful, complete and possessing a sort of barbaric grandeur."[60] Like the lifting of a veil or the removal of a costume, the opening of the two curtains played up the erotic aspect of the performance and drew attention to the dimly lit garden setting. Columns flanked the side of the stage and a painted drop of a desert stretched across the back, marking the locale as vaguely Middle Eastern.[61] After several moments, Hoffman emerged through "blood crimson curtains" to the sound of a crashing cymbal. Standing in a blue light, her body "gleaming white," she began a series of "sinuous" arm movements "of the Oriental order," which extended from the shoulder down the arms to the fingertips.[62]

Running under twenty minutes, the Allan/Hoffman "Vision" used the convention of the "dream vision" to telescope two scenes from Wilde's *Salome* into one, thereby eliminating the need for other characters to appear onstage.[63] The act begins not with the "Dance of the

Seven Veils," as one might expect, but in the moments immediately following the dance, when Salome has retreated from Herod and the court. Through pantomimic movements, she expresses "joy at the victory she ha[s] achieved for her mother, Herodias, in the death of John the Baptist."[64] Her celebration is interrupted, however, by the arrival of the Baptist's head on a salver. At first Salome recoils from the gruesome spectacle, horrified by the evidence of her deviancy and sin. But gradually her shock subsides and she is overcome with desire. She inches slowly toward the head, moving across the floor in a languid, serpentine manner, until finally she grasps and fondles it in her hands (Figure 42.1). Rising from the floor, she then dances "around it in wild excess," "whirling till her slight skirt rose in the air and giving full vent to the emotion of the theme," before again dropping to the floor to crawl "toward it snakelike." As her excitement builds, Salome lifts the Baptist's head to her mouth and kisses it passionately before collapsing to the floor in exhaustion.[65]

Like Wilde's play, the Allan/Hoffman "Vision" depicted Salome in a state of hyperarousal without any lingering expressions of remorse. In this respect, it supported stereotypical depictions of Salome as a degenerate hysteric tainted by her Jewish blood and the incestuous lust of her stepfather. But whereas Wilde's play ends with Salome's body being crushed by soldiers' shields, "A Vision of Salome" concludes with Salome's sexual awakening. This Salome is not ashamed of her sexuality or body but rather delights in new discoveries.

Hoffman reproduced the narrative and choreography of Allan's original (as a comparison with descriptions of Allan's dance clearly shows),[66] yet she also adapted the dance to accord with her own personality and the expectations of the Victoria Roof Garden audience. In fact, when interviewed, Hoffman insisted that the act was not an imitation but an original creation. "I saw Miss Allan about fourteen times and am indebted to her for the general spirit of the act but I worked it out for myself," she told journalist Heywood C. Broun in a July 1908 interview. "I never saw her any nearer than the back of the orchestra." Hoffman maintained that while she used the overall shape and narrative of Allan's dance, she had incorporated more of Wilde's interpretation into her piece, introduced poses inspired by Aubrey Beardsley's illustrations for the 1896 published version of the play, and used music composed specifically for her "Vision" by her husband Max. In addition to these aesthetic innovations, Hoffman had also adapted certain sections of the dance in recognition of vaudeville's insistence on speed and variety. "She [Allan] spends more time in the preliminary arm motions than I do," she explained to Broun. "You see it is hard to draw a man's attention away from his beer and cigar up there on the Roof, and I have to get down to cases very rapidly. Miss Allan does a great deal of juggling with the head of John which people wouldn't stand here so I am only able to suggest that."[67] Hoffman bridled when Broun implied that the performance was dance, insisting that it was "pantomimic acting." "I try to think I am really Salome and act the way Salome would," she explained. "I have not done the dance the same way any two nights running."[68]

Cultural historian Susan Glenn reads Hoffman's commentary on the difficulty of performing for beer-drinking, cigar-smoking patrons as evidence of the mimic's transgressive and satirical interpretation of the Oriental dance and its high art originator: "Deliberately keeping her critics off balance, she milked Salome's potential to offend public taste while defending her performance as 'artistic' expression."[69] Mary Simonson shares Glenn's view, arguing that "more than anything else the dance was a dramatic spectacle of Hoffman's (re)creation: it was her moving body and affect, her artistry, and above all, her sense of

FIGURE 42.2 Gertrude Hoffman in costume for "A Vision of Salome," which she trans-planted from London to New York after watching Maud Allan perform her "Vision" in London. Courtesy: Dance Collection Danse.

humor . . . . simultaneously an imitation and another unique original in itself."[70] I find these readings compelling, but I also wonder whether they overstate Hoffman's use of humor. With the notable exception of critic Ashton Stevens, who claimed to have seen Hoffman smile satirically before kissing the Baptist's head, no other account implies that Hoffman was caricaturing Allan or Salome.[71] On the contrary, many critics expressed surprise at her skillful execution of the dance, commenting on how different it was from her previous vaudeville performances.[72] Moreover, Hoffman's proto-Stanislavsian comments to Broun about her artistic exploration of Salome's psychology suggest that rather than disavowing the Orientalist sexuality of the piece, Hoffman reveled in it. According to critic Charles Darnton, she seemed to "strain every muscle to give you the horrors. Hers is the most vicious Salome in town."[73] This and other accounts of Hoffman's raw physicality stand in stark contrast to descriptions of Allan's more delicate approach to the character, supporting Hoffman's contention that the dance was her own.

But if Hoffman entertained artistic ambitions, she was stymied by factors beyond her control. Whereas Allan had managed to strike a delicate balance between eroticism and artistry in London, Hoffman was unable to do the same in New York. Her association with Allan, now known to most Americans as a tabloid sensation; the spatial dynamics of the Victoria Roof Garden, which encouraged a more intimate interaction between spectators and performers; and the talent glut plaguing American vaudeville, firmly planted Hoffman in the world of sensationalism, spectacle, and Salomania.

OUTBREAK!

Eager to capitalize on the buzz surrounding Allan/Hoffman, vaudeville headliners Lotta Faust, La Petite Adelaide, and Eva Tanguay were among the first to take on the Salome dance. "I had never known that Miss Lotta Faust was a dancer, and after seeing her at the Casino [at West 39th and Broadway] I am still in ignorance of the fact," critic Charles Darnton quipped.[74] Although her performance consisted "principally of poses more or less delsartian [sic], and the kissing of the grewsome [sic] wax work representing the head of John the Baptist," Faust appears to have reproduced the "Vision of Salome" with some degree of accuracy, as the following description suggests:[75]

> Her undulation becomes more riotous as the dance continues, and a moment later she falls upon her knees and drags herself toward the head of John upon the charger, which has been pushed through the black curtain. This she accepts at first in horror, then she kisses it, and then she dances with something of the abandon of degeneracy with it held in front of her. Finally she lays it again upon the ground, twists her way around it, and falls in a heap at its side.[76]

All elements of Allan/Hoffman's "Vision" are present here: the accelerating undulations, the crawling across the floor, the kiss, the degenerate dance, and the final orgasmic collapse into a heap. Accounts of La Petite Adelaide's dance in Baltimore offer similar evidence of fidelity to the "Vision":

> She begins the willowy dance with a slow swinging movement that gradually waxes faster and faster as the dancer loses herself in the dance. Her arms twine sinuously and her whole body keeps in movement to the music. The head of John the Baptist, demanded by her mother, appears on a platter, and with the gory object in her hands she dances deliriously, finally falling senseless to the carpet as shame and horror overcome her.[77]

Though there is no evidence to indicate whether Faust and La Petite Adelaide lifted their choreography from Hoffman directly or if they simply worked from descriptions of the dance, the resemblances between the acts suggests an eagerness to reproduce the same gestural vocabulary and narrative intensity as the original.

As the Salome dance spread from body to body, performers continued to reproduce the general shape of the dance, despite variations in technical execution. The electric Eva Tanguay, one of vaudeville's biggest headliners and Hoffman's archrival, offered an impassioned, if artistically deficient, interpretation of the dance at the Alhambra Theatre in

Harlem that left writers scrambling for words. Opening with her signature song, "I Don't Care," she danced and hopped about the stage "as though some one had built a fire under her."[78] The *Dramatic Mirror* "commended [Miss Tanguay] for her ambition," but suggested that "her admirers would much prefer her in her regular line of work in which she is unapproachable."[79] Another critic described her act as "the war dance of an apache or the fetish of a South African Savage," evoking a different colonial context than the one most frequently associated with the dance.[80] Though Tanguay lacked the technical skill to offer a convincing reproduction of the "Vision," her boundless energy and enthusiasm delighted audiences.[81]

The relative fidelity observed by other Salomes made the variation introduced by La Sylphe (Edith Lambelle) much more notable (Figure 42.3). According to press accounts, the American-born La Sylphe had introduced her Salome at the Folies Bergère, a full year before Maud Allan's 1906 Parisian debut. Incorporating her skills as a contortionist into an act titled "The Remorse of Salome," she left critics at Keith & Proctor's 125th Street Theatre wondering

FIGURE 42.3 Contortionist "La Sylphe" offers her very unique interpretation of the Salome dance, c. 1908. Schwimmer-Lloyd collection, Manuscripts and Archives Division, The New York Public Library, Astor, Lenox and Tilden Foundations.

"what she has done with her bones."[82] Unlike Allan and Hoffman, who depicted Salome in an obsessive, lustful, half-mad state following the death of John the Baptist, La Sylphe represented Salome as "a dejected, remorseful, desolate being," who "cast[s] herself in a despairing effort of soul sacrifice at the feet of the Monolith [of Dead Faiths]."[83] Whereas the Allan/Hoffman "Vision" climaxed with Salome's kiss, La Sylphe "omitted the head in favor of a nighttime ritual of 'soul sacrifice,'" creating a sympathetic portrayal that hinted at Salome's spiritual "transfiguration."[84] Such an emphasis on remorse and transfiguration challenged prevailing assumptions about Salome's degeneracy, showing instead how deeply she had been influenced by her encounter with the Baptist. In this respect, La Sylphe's act worked much like Strauss's opera to represent Salome's transfiguration as part of a larger "conversion project—the global civilizing mission—that was dedicated to transforming the earth into a single pedigree of history and a universal standard of cultural value, defined and maintained by Christian Europeans."[85] Though it is doubtful that audiences read this deeply into La Sylphe's act, especially while watching her contort her body in all directions, the subtext worked against associations of Salome with degeneracy and disease, suggesting instead that she could be assimilated into dominant white society.

Other dancers, including La Belle Zola at the Dewey Theatre and several unnamed "ten-cent" Salomes appearing at a Fourteenth Street dime museum, presented much tamer interpretations of the dance despite their less auspicious surroundings. Unlike the "Skin Salomes" headlining theaters uptown (Hoffman, Faust, Tanguay), these small-time Salomes were "eminently respectable when it [came] to a question of comparative clothing."[86] They nevertheless drew large crowds and fueled the public appetite for more. By September 1908, press reports estimated that anywhere between twenty-four and thirty women in New York alone had joined the Salome craze, including Bianca Froelich, the premiere danseuse of the Metropolitan Opera, who had so outraged audiences in the 1907 Strauss production.[87] Inside and outside New York, burlesque, drag, and musical comedy performers offered their own variation of the "Vision" to curious audiences.[88] Through their collective reproduction of the dance and its revealing costume, these Salomes offered a powerful image of female sexual desire and abandon that critics of the dance seized on as evidence of moral degeneracy and disease.

EXPOSED SKIN, TAINTED SOULS

Not surprisingly, one of the most shocking features of "Salomania" was the costume, an Orientalized fantasy inspired by the Salome of Gustav Moreau, among others. With minor exceptions (as noted earlier), most performers adopted some variation of Hoffman's costume, itself an almost identical copy of the one designed by Maud Allan (compare Figures 42.1 and 42.2).[89] Worn without a body stocking ("fleshlings"), it consisted of a transparent black skirt made of gauze with gold embroidery along the hem and "ropes of pearls, emeralds and diamonds around the waist, underneath which Hoffman wore a pair of short "silk trunks." Her breasts, though concealed, were accentuated by a bodice "made up of a network of jewels" and pearls artfully arranged in a swirling pattern topped by two prominent red stones in the place of nipples.[90] Had the costume been worn by a stationery performer, it would have been startling; worn as it was by a dancing performer flailing her body about the stage and across the floor, the effect was understandably shocking. Critics described moments when Hoffman's legs appeared "rigid and skirtless" as she crawled across the floor and others when the skirt rose up in the air as she leaped around the head. "The skirt disclosed with unmistakable exactness the extent of the rest of the costume," the *New York Times* quipped.[91] Although such accounts say nothing about the movement of the bodice, it is difficult to imagine the heavy, jewel-encrusted top remaining in place throughout the act, especially when Hoffman (and her imitators) bent down to grasp the Baptist's head.

Some critics argued that the exposure of the dancer's belly, arms, legs, and feet was entirely appropriate when viewed within the context of the act. "The naked feet, limbs and torso fitted into the picture to such an extent that they lost much of their startling effect until they were considered afterwards," claimed the *New York World*.[92] For others, however, it was too much. Of course, performers (and producers) had flirted with onstage nudity for decades. In the mid-nineteenth century, impresarios skirted decency laws by staging *tableaux vivants* (living pictures) inspired by classical statuary, in which performers assumed a variety of stationery poses wearing skin-tone fleshlings and artfully placed props or fabric. These spectacles coincided with the rise of "leg shows" in the 1860s and 1870s featuring large choruses of women dressed in short skirts and breeches designed to enhance their shapely legs. Originating in ballet, this "convention of 'clothed nudity'" quickly spread to other genres including burlesque, music hall, and pantomime such that "[t]he female leg, naked in tights, became synonymous with the female performer, with enjoyment, and with the theatre itself."[93] By the turn of the century, tights were a standard costuming item for all chorus girls, soubrettes, and ballet dancers, much to the disgust the popular musical comedy singer Marie Cahill, who in 1906 lobbied theater managers to stop making short skirts and pink tights a requirement of a job.[94] Cahill's lobbying efforts ultimately failed: New York law permitted the wearing of tights and managers saw little incentive for lengthening skirts. But uncovered legs, bared midriffs, and barely contained breasts were impossible to ignore.

Conservative opposition to the recent Parisian Directoire or "sheath gown" undoubtedly fueled reaction to the Salome costume. Indeed, the Salome "epidemic" coincided with a major aesthetic revolution in women's fashion that provoked similar fears about moral decay and female susceptibility to foreign influence. In April 1908, mere weeks after Maud Allan's London debut, Parisian couturiers introduced the controversial sheath or Directoire gown, a form-fitting style that dramatically reworked the female silhouette by abandoning the prevailing S-shaped corset in favor of a more tubular style evocative of the Directoire (or Napoleonic) period. One of the most shocking characteristics of the new gown was a large side slit that exposed the thigh and made it possible for women to move in a much less constricted way along city streets and on public transportation. As I've argued elsewhere, this combination of sexual provocation and heightened mobility drew considerable fire from conservative observers in Europe and the United States, who feared that the moral corruption of modern womanhood signaled the decline of Western civilization. In many respects, then, the Salome costume represented a more extreme version of the sheath gown, transforming the mobile female body into a fierce symbol of sexual desire and liberation.[95]

Salomania also marked a turning point in the long-standing debate about the health benefits of the corset. Although sheath-wearing women did not abandon the corset completely, the modified garment worn beneath the sheath was much less restrictive than the S-curve corset, which bent the female body into an approximation of the letter 'S'. For decades, fashion reformers had called for looser clothing styles worn with a modified corset or without one altogether. Throughout the 1880s, the female members of the aesthetic movement wore long flowing gowns modeled on medieval art as part of their ongoing efforts to transform themselves into beautiful *objets d'art*. Fittingly, the infamous Aubrey Beardsley illustrations that accompanied the 1896 published edition of Wilde's play include several of Salome dressed in loose, flowing garments undoubtedly inspired by the aesthetic movement that Wilde himself had actively promoted in the 1880s.[96]

Rejecting the claims of fashion reform, corset apologists insisted that corseting the female body was imperative for physiological reasons. Sexologist Havelock Ellis argued that the need for corsetry arose from the evolution of the human species: "It is because the fall of the viscera in woman when she imitated man by standing erect induced such profound physiological displacements . . . that the corset is morphologically essential."[97] Others argued that some form of physical containment protected women's internal organs and helped sustain muscular strength for the whole body.[98] Women who rejected the corset jeopardized their own health and the health of their children (born and unborn); in so doing, they undermined the foundation of civil society, which relied on white women to raise strong (white) leaders and maintain domestic harmony.

In light of ongoing debates about the morality of tights onstage and the sheath gown offstage, the spectacle of the Salome dancer's bared feet, legs, and midriff was shockingly transgressive. Multiplied twenty or forty or one hundred times over, it became altogether frightening. Historian Paul DiMaggio contends that "barefoot dancers" like Hoffman and her imitators were threatening because they signaled the "further breaking down of those barriers that separate the audience from the performer upon the stage." When Hoffman as Salome slithered her way across the floor, flashing her calves and thighs at roof garden patrons, she crossed a metaphorical threshold that jeopardized hegemonic social values. Uncontained by tights or fleshlings, her sweating, jiggling, desiring flesh exposed audiences to new definitions of morality that, as one commentator put it, "decreas[ed] the average efficiency of the individual citizen" and made "the spectator less able to enjoy genuine dramatic art."[99] In other words, exposure to the Salome dancer's skin threatened to suck the moral marrow from the bones of American men.

CONTAINING THE EPIDEMIC

Critics initially understood the Salome epidemic as a localized phenomenon, a symptom of the moral decline and decadence that arose from fast-paced urban life. In July, a writer for the *Washington Post* asserted that declining morality among New Yorkers in the wake of the Harry Thaw murder trial was responsible for the "epidemic of Salomes" "overrun[ing]" the city. After months of reading explicit details about Thaw's victim, architect Stanford White, and his sexual conquest of Thaw's young wife, Evelyn Nesbit, "the public consciousness" had become accustomed to all "things salacious." "A public that has gorged itself almost to repletion on the Thaw scandal, and then accepts the Salome dance for dessert will not be shocked at anything," the writer argued. Rejecting claims that the dance was art and should be appreciated as such, the writer insisted that it was "a moral disease [. . .] the expression of something hideous, loathsome, unclean. [. . .] It arouses not one strain of noble feeling or sentiment. It ought to be abolished and chloride of lime spread over every spot where it has dragged its pollution."[100] Referring specifically to a chemical treatment [chloride of lime] used to prevent the spread of contamination, this writer equated the Salome dance with other forms of contagion.[101]

Other conservative authorities used similar language to voice their objections. At the invitation of the *New York World,* evangelist Reverend Dr. D. C. Hughes claimed that the Salome dance had "demoralizing effects not only upon the youth of our cities, of both sexes, but also of their effects upon all who are drawn to witness such demoralizing sights." Although he admitted that he had not seen Hoffman dance, he had seen her promotional photographs, and therefore felt the need to call on local authorities to curtail the immoral act lest it infect the moral virtues of others. "Should a state be less interested in the exclusion of moral poison from the body politic, so far as it is in its power so to do, than in the creation and enforcement of the Pure Food Law?" Equating an anti-Salome stance with progressive health reform, Hughes urged his fellow citizens to clean up the filth associated with vaudeville and protect the body politic.[102]

Hill's rhetoric resembled that of other progressive reformers, likewise anxious about the spread of moral contagion among American youth. Between 1908 and 1914, businessmen, church leaders, and feminists formed a strange alliance in a wide-ranging crusade to eliminate vice from the urban environments, targeting dance halls, vaudeville theaters, and other sites of public amusement. Through graphic accounts of white women forced into prostitution by "dark and sinister alien-looking figure[s]," they alerted upstanding middle-class Americans to the dangers of "white slavery," casting much of the blame on ethnic minorities and other immigrants. Their insistence that the contagion came from without rather than within was further corroborated by government studies. For example, a 1909 report to the US Senate claimed that "[t]he vilest practices are brought here from continental Europe, the most bestial refinements of depravity."[103] Such depravity led not only to the sexual enslavement of white women but also to the spread of sexually transmitted diseases through the bodies of unsuspecting American men and women.

Some critics took a more whimsical approach to the Salome epidemic. In mid-August, the *New York Times* published a tongue-in-cheek article on the "Salomania" raging through New York, observing that the management at the New Amsterdam Theatre, one of Broadway's most elegant theaters and home of the hugely successful Viennese operetta *The Merry Widow* "ha[d] been exceptionally active in guarding against outbreaks of Salomania among members of the [*Merry Widow*] company. As soon as any chorus girl shows the very first symptoms of the disease she is at once enveloped in a fur coat—the most efficacious safeguard known against the Salome dance—and hurriedly isolated."[104] Drawing on common stereotypes of the gold-digging chorus girl, for whom a fur coat was a necessary sign of status, the *Times* suggested that the contagion associated with the wriggling, scantily clad body of the Salome dancer could be contained by wrapping young women in luxury fashion and isolating them from their peers.

But others found little to laugh at. Echoing Hill's emphasis on the dance's threat to the nation's moral and physical health, the *New York World* asked medical professionals and other authorities to share their thoughts on the "insidious" and "dangerous" dance as it affected both performer and spectator. Claude M. Alviene, former ballet master at La Scala, argued that Eva Tanguay's "daring undress" led to "morbid, dark brown thoughts."[105] Though offering no explanation of what these "dark brown" thoughts might entail, Alviene's racialized metaphor hints at underlying anxieties about miscegenation. Indeed, while much of the anti-Salome discourse can be read in light of anti-Semitic sentiment, animosity toward other racial groups, most notably African Americans, also lurks beneath the "Salomania" back-lash. African American dancer Aida Overton Walker implicitly recognized this animosity when she offered her interpretation of Salome during the August 27, 1908, performance of the musical comedy *Bandanna Land* at the Grand Opera House in Brooklyn. Through ele-gant costuming (no bared midriff or flashing bare legs) and intricate choreography, she dis-tanced herself from dominant stereotypes of black women as wild, animalistic, and sexually voracious by offering a dignified, sympathetic Salome.[106]

Despite these efforts, negative racial stereotypes pervaded the discourse surrounding the dance. Two weeks before Walker introduced her Salome, Dr. Sarah J. MacNutt, "[a] woman physician who has practised [*sic*] among New York women for years and who is one of the most prominent club workers in the city," warned that the Salome dance would have debili-tating physical and mental effects on white American women. According to MacNutt, con-tortionist dancing did not threaten the health of actual "Oriental" dancers because they were trained from childhood and felt "no symbolism, no passion in the dance." By contrast, con-tortionist dancing was "most dangerous physically and morally" for "high-strung" American girls because it "congests those organs most immediately and intimately connected with the nervous system, resulting in hysteria and all forms of nervous diseases." More alarmingly, Dr. MacNutt warned, the "intense abnormal passion" embodied by the dancer onstage "must reach across the footlights and react on the nervous system of women in the audience."[107] In other words, the mere sight of the Salome dance was contagious.

Dr. MacNutt's analysis is significant not just because of its racist commentary or because it offers a rare example of a female medical perspective but also because it grounds anxiet-ies about the Salome dance in the medical knowledge of the period. Like corset apologists who argued that without a corset a woman's internal organs would shift inside her body with disastrous, long-term effects, MacNutt warned that contortionists like La Sylphe would suffer organ and nerve damage culminating in hysteria. This equation of dance with hysteria was hardly unusual. As dance historian Felicia McCarren writes, "[i]n the West, dance has largely been considered either a representation of madness [. . .] or a manifestation of order, through individual or social control of the body."[108] Yet for MacNutt, dance was more than a repre-sentation of madness; it was the very *cause* of madness, not just for the performer but for the female spectator as well. Whereas the dancer injured herself through bodily contortions, the spectator disrupted her nervous system in watching spectacles of "intense abnormal passion."

Although MacNutt's comments may strike the contemporary reader as antifeminist, racist, and scientifically unsound, they nevertheless anticipate recent developments in cognitive neu-roscience, which (as discussed above) have shown how those *watching* a dance experience the very same mental processes as those *executing* it. MacNutt's observations also resonate with the work of affect theorists such as Teresa Brennan, who argues that human sensitivity to the hor-monal secretions of others can help to explain the transmission of affect. "By the transmission of affect," Brennan writes, "I mean simply that the emotions or affects of one person, and the enhancing or depressing energies these affects entail, can enter into one another."[109] Arguing against the modern notion of the self-determining, contained individual, Brennan maintains that "the biochemistry and neurology" of the human body is changed, if only briefly, by the transmission of affect between individuals. Brennan's work emphasizes the leakiness of human bodies (male as well as female) and suggests that what we feel emotionally and physically is often a response to what those around us are feeling. In light of such arguments, MacNutt's warning that La Sylphe's hysterical performance would somehow provoke hysterical reactions in female spectators is worth reconsidering. Although I doubt that it was hysteria that moved between La Sylphe and her female spectators, I expect that *something* moved between them. And this something was cause for alarm among those who wanted to keep white female bodies contained lest their excessive displays of affect contaminate male bodies as well.

Though lacking MacNutt's medical knowledge, the actress Marie Cahill similarly invoked the language of contagion to urge politicians to take decisive action against Salomania. On August 24, a week after the publication of MacNutt's letter, Cahill wrote to President Roosevelt and other influential politicians, pleading for the outright censorship of the Salome dance. If such "vulgar exhibitions" continued unabated, Cahill warned, they would not only lead to the "poisoning of that great teaching institution—the drama" but would also contaminate the minds of "the large body of foreign youths and girls" who attended vaudeville and other theatrical entertainments.[110] Tapping into growing anxieties about the effect of mass immigration on "native," i.e. white, American culture and society—anxieties that Roosevelt himself had articulated in speeches about impending "race suicide"—Cahill implied that widespread moral contamination among foreign youth would eventually cross class and ethnic barriers, infecting all Americans.

Despite Cahill's efforts, the Salome epidemic showed no signs of stopping, and the authorities stepped in with uneven results. In early September, the *Dramatic Mirror* reported that "Orders were issued to several police captains on Saturday to send detectives to the various theaters at which Salome dancers are appearing and to forward reports concerning the costumes of the performers. The action was taken it is said on the account of a complaint made to the police commissioner concerning the dresses, or lack of them, used by the dancers."[111] In response to the police crackdown, most Salome dancers donned tights and fleshlings, at least until they knew that they were no longer under surveillance. But the morality squad could do little to contain the epidemic, and the fall season approached with news that numerous touring productions would feature a Salome act.[112]

As the Salome dance moved outside New York City, it faced new opposition from ministers and community organizations who viewed it as a threat to the peace, order, and morality of good, upstanding (read: white) citizens. Touring productions of musical comedies with a Salome dance "special" faced protests and petitions from those unwilling to allow the contagion to infiltrate their homes and communities. In March 1909, for example, ten thousand men and women in Kansas City led by the British evangelist Rodney "Gipsy" Smith signed a petition calling for local officials to stop Hoffman, the woman responsible for Salomania, from performing the Salome dance in *The Mimic World*, a revue produced by the Shubert brothers. Ironically, widely distributed promotional posters showing Hoffman as Salome gave local authorities "conclusive" proof of the moral contamination of dance and dancer.[113] Despite the attempted intervention of the tour managers and Hoffman's insistence that the dance was not filth but art, the local judge disagreed, ruling in favor of her opponents.[114] Once again, the Salome dance was contained, but only temporarily.

THE END OF SALOMANIA

By 1910, the Salome "epidemic" was waning and with it the high-blown rhetoric. In fact, when Maud Allan finally crossed the Atlantic in the early winter of 1910 and danced her original "Vision of Salome" at Carnegie Hall, New York audiences were intrigued but under-whelmed. A writer for the *Dramatic Mirror* observed that her Salome was "girlishly fascinating without showing the peculiarly erotic fervour that has marked its exposition by other dancers here."[115] Others simply found it passé. Social reformers nevertheless maintained their vigilant watch over both theatrical entertainment and the behavior and movement of immigrant bodies.

Intriguingly, the "outbreak narrative" associated with the Salome dance eerily anticipated (and in some cases overlapped with) the public hysteria that surrounded Irish immigrant Mary Mallon ("Typhoid Mary") when her case became public in the summer of 1909. Two years earlier, Dr. George A. Sopher had uncovered "a trail of typhoid epidemics that tracked her through her domestic engagements" and concluded that Mallon was 'a living culture tube and chronic typhoid germ producer.' "[116] When Sopher finally found her in a rooming house on Third Avenue in New York City and informed her of her status as a carrier, she refused to believe him and denied his requests to be tested for the typhoid bacillus. Sopher ultimately had to call in public-health officials to forcibly remove her to a hospital for testing. Despite these measures, Mallon continued to resist the medical authorities and in June 1909 took her case to court, where she was declared a threat to public health and forced to return to the Riverside Hospital for observation.[117]

The discovery of "Typhoid Mary" radically transformed the field of epidemiology and challenged, in a greatly distressing manner, accepted views of human contagion and the transmission of disease. Priscilla Wald writes:

> [T]he discovery of microorganisms allowed scientists to chart contacts that would otherwise have been invisible to all participants. When people became ill with typhoid, it meant that they had ingested someone else's bodily excretions . . . The connections were more than imagined; typhoid made gruesomely literal the material relations of, and intimate contact with, strangers in the industrial, immigrant city. The discovery of human vectors of disease fleshed out the contours of contact phobias, explaining the easy enlistment of typhoid (among other diseases) in the discourse of "race suicide," the sociological and political laments that the white race was facilitating its own demise.[118]

In other words, the discovery of Typhoid Mary undid modern assumptions about the containability of the human body by testifying to its unbounded leakiness and susceptibility to the leakiness of others. The same might be said of the Salome dance. Though it would be stretching the limits of believability to associate George Sopher's discovery of Mary Mallon in 1907 with the eruption of "Salomania" in the summer and fall of 1908, the similarities in the public discourse surrounding the two events are illuminating. Just as the spectacle of the naked, sweaty, sexually aroused Salome dancer prompted fears about the spread of moral, physical, and mental contagion, Mallon's mysterious status as a "healthy carrier" of typhus played into anxieties about dissolving social boundaries. At the center of each "outbreak narrative" stood the frightening, contaminated female body and the equally frightening spectacle of the "great unwashed" waiting to be admitted to the United States.[119]

Yet while much of the anxiety surrounding the Salome dance emerged from the dance's rapid and apparently undetectable movement from body to body—i.e., vice officers couldn't prevent women from learning the dance or predict where the next Salome dancer would appear—nervous theatergoers could nevertheless protect themselves from exposure to the dance's contagion by staying at home or leaving the theater when a Salome dancer appeared onstage. Unlike Mary Mallon, who showed no outward signs of the death she carried within, Gertrude Hoffman, Eva Tanguay, La Petite Adelaide, and La Sylphe were visible and thus (theoretically) containable threats. The challenge for church leaders, political figures, and other opponents to the dance, however, was the number of people who embraced "Salomania" and actively pursued contamination. The spectacle of the writhing, naked, female body was undeniably attractive for many. And as the images and descriptions of Salome dancers circulated in the popular press and moved along theatrical circuits, they radically challenged traditional assumptions about dance, the body, and female sexual desire. By 1910, Salome was passé not because the dance itself was boring or the dancers unskilled but because the ideas it promoted no longer seemed particularly shocking or transgressive to American audiences. In effect, through lengthy exposure, these audiences had become inoculated to the effects of the dance.

NOTES

1. "Now the Daring Salome Dance Rages through the World Like an Epidemic," *The Sun (Baltimore)*, 30 Aug. 1908, 24.
2. Ibid.
3. Hoffman's name also appears as "Hoffmann" in some accounts.
4. Roy L. McCardell, "The Chorus Girl Squanders a Bunch of Thought on 'Salome' and the Close-Lidded Race Track," *The Evening World*, 18 July 1908.
5. "Now the Daring Salome Dance," 24.
6. "The Salome Dance Gets into Politics," *New York Times* [hereafter *NYT*], 24 Aug. 1908, 2.
7. Some of the most recent work on Salome includes: Amy Koritz, "Dancing the Orient for England: Maud Allan's 'The Vision of Salome,'" *Theatre Journal* 46 (1994): 63–78; Susan Glenn, *Female Spectacle: The Theatrical Roots of Modern Feminism* (Cambridge, MA: Harvard University Press, 2000); Judith R. Walkowitz, "The 'Vision of Salome': Cosmopolitanism and Erotic Dancing in Central London, 1908–1918," *American Historical Review* 108, no. 2 (Apr. 2003): 337–76; Larry Hamberlin, "Visions of Salome: The Femme Fatale in American Popular Songs before 1920," *Journal of the American Musicological Society* 59, no. 3 (Fall 2006): 631–94; Mary Simonson, "'The Call of Salome': American Adapatations and Re-creations of the Female Body in the Early Twentieth Century," *Women and Music* 11 (2007): 1–16; Sunaina Maira, "Belly Dancing: Arab-Face, Orientalist Feminism, and U.S. Empire," *American Quarterly* (2008): 317–45; Sharon Marcus, "Salomé!! Sarah Bernhardt, Oscar Wilde, and the Drama of Celebrity," *PMLA* 126.4 (2011): 999–1021; Petra Dierkes-Thrun," in *Salome's Modernity: Oscar Wilde and the Aesthetics of Transgression* (Ann Arbor: University of Michigan Press, 2011).
8. Simonson, "'The Call of Salome,'" 9–10.
9. Priscilla Wald, *Contagious: Cultures, Carriers, and the Outbreak Narrative* (Durham, NC: Duke University Press, 2007), 1–28.
10. "The Vulgarization of Salome," *Current Literature*, 1 Oct. 1908, 437. See also "The Salome Pestilence," *NYT*, 3 Sept. 1908, 6.
11. Articles with titles such as "The Muckraker in the Playhouse," make the theater an explicit target of progressive concern. See *Current Literature* 45, no. 5 (May 1909), 537–40.

12. Sander L. Gilman, "Strauss, the Pervert and Avant Garde Opera of the Fin de Siècle," *New German Critique* 43 (Winter 1988): 35–68, 37–38. See also Gilman, "Sarah Bernhardt and the 'Modern Jewess,'" *German Quarterly* 66, no. 2 (Spring 1993): 195–211.

13. Oscar Wilde, *Salomé* (Boston: Brandon, 1989).

14. Gilman, "Sarah Bernhardt," 203; Marcus, "Salomé!!," 1012.

15. Rolland, quoted in Gilman, "Strauss, the Pervert," 52.

16. Gilman, "Sarah Bernhardt," 200.

17. Gilman, "Sarah Bernhardt," 199, 200, 201. On stereotypes of the dangerous Jewess, see also Harley Erdman, *Staging the Jew: The Performance of an American Ethnicity, 1860–1920* (New Brunswick, NJ, Rutgers University Press, 1997), 40–62; and Bram Dijkstra, *Evil Sisters: The Threat of Female Sexuality in Twentieth-Century Culture* (New York: Henry Holt, 1996), 261–309.

18. Gilman, "Strauss, the Pervert," 54.

19. Anne L. Seshadri, "The Taste of Love: Salome's Transfiguration," *Women and Music* (2006): 24–44; 38, 44.

20. Most of the American primary sources I consulted use the Anglicized spelling *Salome*, rather than *Salomé*, so I have opted to use the American spelling here for the 1907 Met production.

21. "Strauss's 'Salome' the First Time Here," *NYT*, 23 Jan. 1907, 9. See also Daria Santini, "'That invisible dance': Reflections on the 'Dance of the Seven Veils' in Richard Strauss's *Salome*," *Dance Research* 29, no. 2 (2011): 223–45.

22. Henry Krehbiel, "The 'Salome' of Wilde and Strauss," *New York Tribune*, 23 Jan. 1907, quoted in Joseph Horowitz, "Critic Henry Krehbiel Excorciates Richard Strauss's Salome (1907)," *Journal of the Gilded Age and Progressive Era* 8, no. 2 (2009), http://www.shgape. org/critic-henry-krehbiel-excoriates-richard-strausss-salome/ (accessed 12 June 2014).

23. Imparo Ancora, "'Salome' Condemned," *NYT*, 24 Jan. 1907, 8. For a similar argument see "Concerning Depravity," *The Independent* 62, no. 3035 (31 Jan. 1907), 277.

24. Ibid.

25. Alan M. Kraut, *Silent Travelers: Germs, Genes, and the 'Immigrant Menace'* (Baltimore: Johns Hopkins University Press, 1994), esp. 31–49.

26. Kraut, *Silent Travelers*, 105–135; Krista Maglen, "Importing Trachoma: The Introduction into Britain of American Ideas of an 'Immigrant Disease', 1892–1906," *Immigrants and Minorities* 23, no. 1 (March 2005): 80–99.

27. Kraut, *Silent Travelers*, 105–135; Wald, *Contagious*, 16, 68–113.

28. On Roosevelt's theories see Thomas G. Dyer, *Theodore Roosevelt and the Idea of Race* (Baton Rouge: Louisiana State University Press, 1980); on "overcivilization" see T. J. Jackson Lears, *No Place of Grace: Antimodernism and the Transformation of American Culture, 1880–1920* (Chicago: University of Chicago Press, 1994). I have found no direct evidence to suggest that Roosevelt weighed in on the Salome debates, though his ideas certainly percolate beneath it.

29. C. I. H. "Another View of 'Salome,'" *NYT*, 25 Jan. 1907, 8.

30. Sancta Simplicitas, "Theories as to 'Salome,'" *NYT*, 26 Jan. 1907, 8.

31. Ibid.

32. "'Salome' Withdrawn; Conried Fully Yields," *NYT*, 31 Jan. 1907, 3; see also "No Decision on 'Salome'; Seats Are Still on Sale," *NYT*, 28 Jan. 1907, 3.

33. "Fight to Keep 'Salome' from Another Theatre," *NYT*, 30 Jan. 1907, 3.

34. In July, *The Follies of 1907* featured a burlesque of the Salome dance with dancer Mlle. Dazie doubling as Fremstad. Elizabeth Kendall, *Where She Danced: The Birth of American Art-Dance* (Berkeley and Los Angeles, London: University of California Press, 1979), 75.

35. Carrie Noland, "Introduction," in *Migrations of Gesture*, eds. Carrie Noland and Sally Ann Ness (Minneapolis: University of Minnesota Press, 2008), xi.

36. See, for example, the popularity of "Little Egypt" at the Colombian Exhibition in Chicago in 1893. Donna Carlton, *Looking for Little Egypt* (Bloomington, IL: International Dance Discovery, 1995).

37. For detailed analyses of Allan's dance see Koritz, "Dancing the Orient for England," 63–78; Walkowitz, "The 'Vision of Salome,'" 337–76; Felix Cherniavsky, *The Salome Dancer: The Life and Times of Maud Allan* (Toronto: McClellan and Stewart, 1991); Cherniavsky, *Maud Allan and Her Art* (Toronto: Dance Collection Danse, 1998); Toni Bentley, "Maud Allan: The Cult of the Clitoris," in *Sisters of Salome* (Lincoln: University of Nebraska Press, 2002), 47–84.

38. Walkowitz, "The 'Vision of Salome,'" 342; Alexandra Carter, "London, 1908: A Synchronic View of Dance History," *Dance Research* 23, no. 1 (Summer 2005): 36–50. Other key sources on early twentieth-century art dance include Bentley, *Sisters of Salome*; Wendy Buonaventura, *Something in the Way She Moves: Dancing Women from Salome to Madonna* (Cambridge, MA: Da Capo Press, 2003); and Kendall, *Where She Danced*.

39. Michelle Clayton, "Touring History: Tórtola Valencia between Europe and the Americas," *Dance Research Journal* 44, no. 1 (Summer 2012): 29–49; 30.

40. Koritz, "Dancing the Orient for England," 76.

41. Koritz, 70.

42. Koritz, 65.

43. Walkowitz, 352.

44. Unpublished manuscript, Folder: MS: Act II, Sc. 7: "Salome from San Francisco," and Folder: Gest/Ms. Notes from Mr. Gest, Box 5 Morris Gest Collection, Harry Ransom Center, University of Texas at Austin.

45. "Mysterious 'Salome' Dancer of Paris Has Revealed Her Identity," *Evening World*, 20 Apr. 1908, 3; Cherniavsky, *Maud Allan and Her Art*, 19–22.

46. Marlis Schweitzer, "A Failed Attempt at World Domination: 'Advanced Vaudeville,' Financial Panic, and the World Wide Trust," *Theatre History Studies* 32 (2012): 53–79.

47. On the Tanguay/Allan showdown and other examples of female mimicry see Glenn, *Female Spectacle*, 74–95.

48. The list of impresarios to approach Allan in the spring of 1908 included B. F. Keith, head of the United Booking Office; Marc Klaw, producing partner of Abraham Erlanger and a highly influential member of the Theatrical Syndicate; Florenz Ziegfeld, producer of the *Ziegfeld Follies*; and William Morris, the independent talent agent who had formerly booked acts for the Victoria Roof Garden until Willie Hammerstein abandoned him to become part of the United Booking Office run by Keith. "Maud Allan Wants to Capture America," *Chicago Daily Tribune*, 5 July 1908, G2; "Maude [*sic*] Allan's Dance Here," *NYT*, 8 July 1908: 7.

49. In 1903, Hoffman became the first female stage manager/dance director on Broadway when she was hired to stage *Punch and Judy* for Hammerstein's Paradise Roof Garden Theatre. In addition to training and choreographing sixty chorus women, she was responsible for arranging "all the 'business' for the ensemble work and the various stage pictures that go toward making a pleasing spectacle of the operetta." *New York World*, 6 July 1903, quoted in Barbara Naomi Cohen [Stratyner], "The Borrowed Art of Gertrude Hoffmann," *Dance Data* 2 (1977): 2–11, 2. Between 1903 and 1906, Hoffman continued to stage musical comedies and operettas and began directing acts for vaudeville performers including juvenile mimic Elsie Janis and the dancer "Le Domino Rouge." By the fall

of 1906, she decided to venture into vaudeville herself with an act titled "The Borrowed Art of Gertrude Hoffman," a series of imitations of famous headliners, dance numbers, and songs from recent Broadway shows. She next appeared in Florenz Ziegfeld's production of *The Parisian Model*, where she delighted audiences with her impersonation of its star, Anna Held. After an early departure from the show, prompted by Held's jealousy, Hoffman returned to vaudeville, where she challenged several headliners, including the feisty Eva Tanguay, to imitation duels. Stratyner, 2, 3. Another helpful source on Hoffman is Claudia B. Stone, "Gertrude Hoffmann: Artist or Charlatan?" MA thesis, New York University, 1987.

50. "To See Allan Dance Here," *NYT*, 13 July 1908.

51. In April 1908, impresario Henry Savage issued a restraining order against Hoffman for imitating the costumes, dances, and songs from *The Merry Widow*, claiming that her mimetic act violated his exclusive producing rights to the operetta. Hoffman, with some musicological support from her husband, responded by claiming "that the opera was not original with Victor Leon and Leo Stein, but was an adaptation of a play entitled 'L'Attache d'Ambassade,' and was produced in Paris at the Theatre du Vaudeville on or about March 12, 1861." Savage's claims to the operetta were therefore irrelevant because it was not an original work. The judge decided in Hoffman's favor, and she was allowed to continue the act. "Merry Widow an Elderly Dowager," *NYT*, 8 Apr. 1908, 7; "The Dubious Past of the 'Merry Widow,'" *Current Literature*, 1 June 1908, 65–66.

52. Quoted in Anthea Kraut, "Race-ing Choreographic Copyright," in *Worlding Dance*, ed. Susan Leigh Foster, 76–97 (London: Palgrave Macmillan, 2009), 79.

53. Susan Leigh Foster, "Movement's Contagion: The Kinesthetic Impact of Performance," in *The Cambridge Companion to Performance Studies*, ed. Tracy C. Davis, 46–59 (New York: Cambridge University Press, 2008), 49.

54. Ibid.

55. Heywood C. Broun, "Gertrude Hoffman Will Try for Greater Things Than 'Salome,'" *Morning Telegraph*, 19 July 1908. Folder: Gest/MS Act II, sc. 7 Notes, Morris Gest Collection, Harry Ransom Center.

56. Advert for Hammerstein's Roof. *The Sun*, 28 Aug. 1908, 6. Though possibly an error, with the use of the indefinite singular article "a" in place of the definite article "the," as in "A Vision of Salome," Gest and Hammerstein marked the difference between the two "Visions," implying that Hoffman's "Vision" was *not* "the" original. Hoffman's act almost didn't open. By the summer of 1908, Willie Hammerstein's father, opera impresario Oscar Hammerstein I, was preparing for his own production of Strauss's *Salome* with the Manhattan Opera Company, which he had formed in 1906 to rival Conried's Metropolitan Opera. Angry to learn that his son was planning to stage "A Vision of Salome" at the Victoria Roof Garden, he insisted that the act be cancelled lest it damage his own production. But while Oscar Hammerstein wanted to protect his interests, he was not averse to advance publicity. After reflecting on the matter for several days, he reversed his position and gave his son permission to stage the Salome dance at the Victoria. Folder: Gest/Ms. Notes from Mr. Gest, Box 5 Morris Gest Collection, Harry Ransom Center, University of Texas at Austin.

57. Cohen Stratyner, "The Borrowed Art," 5.

58. Hoffman first presented the act at a matinee in Hammerstein's Theatre, and repeated it that night at the Victoria Roof Garden. According to the *New York Times*, the special scenery for the act "showed to more advantage in the theatre than on the Roof Garden." "A 'Salome' Dance by Miss Hoffman," *NYT*, 14 July 1908, 5.

59. "Atlanta Favorite Gives New Thrill to New York," *The Atlanta Constitution*, 18 July 1908, 6. This article included a reprint of the review from the *New York World*.

60. Sam M'Kee for the *New York Telegraph*; quoted in Stratyner, "The Borrowed Art," 6.

61. Ibid.

62. "Atlanta Favorite, 6; See also "A 'Salome' Dance," 5.

63. Walkowitz, "The 'Vision of Salome,' " 352.

64. *New York World*, quoted in "Atlanta Favorite," 6.

65. Broun, "Gertrude Hoffman Will Try," quoted in "Atlanta Favorite," 6; "A 'Salome' Dance by Miss Hoffman," *NYT*, 14 July 1908, 5. Interestingly, the *New York Times* describes a different ending for the act, in which Hoffman "flung [the head] into the well." No other reviews refer to a well, which suggests that a well set piece was cut for the roof garden performance. The *Times* review also mentions Hoffman kissing the head multiple times and pressing it to her bosom, details that do not appear in other accounts.

66. By way of example, here is a description of Allan's dance from the *Neues Wiener Journal* (Vienna), 29 Dec. 1906: "Miss Allan starts to dance, and she does so in a fashion similar to Miss [Isadora] Duncan; she turns, she drags and jumps, bends the upper body in all its curves, lifts her slender arms very dramatically but always, always moves her hands, which she turns as in a battle to the outside and inside (this is really disturbing). A terrible wax skull of John lies on the stage. She pulls it up to her knees, kisses it and dances around it. Salome's Vision." Quoted in Cherniavsky, *Maud Allan and Her Art*, 38.

67. Broun, "Gertrude Hoffman Will Try for Greater Things."

68. Ibid.

69. Glenn, *Female Spectacle*, 104.

70. Simonson, " 'The Call of Salome,' " 8.

71. "Ashton Stevens Says: Salome 'Vision' Saved from Nightmare by Miss Hoffman's Humor," *Evening Journal*, 14 July 1908, clipping, Folder: Gest/MS Act II, sc. 7 Notes, Morris Gest Collection, Harry Ransom Center, University of Texas at Austin.

72. "Atlanta Favorite," 6. Charles Darnton, "The Visitation of Salome," *New York World*, 8 Aug. 1908, 2.

73. Darnton, "The Visitation of Salome," 2.

74. Ibid.

75. "Wears Cosmetics as Tights," *Chicago Daily Tribune*, 10 Sept. 1908, 3.

76. "Salome Dance is Unveiled," *Chicago Daily Tribune*, 9 Sept. 1908, 3.

77. "Salome Dance Here," *The [Baltimore] Sun*, 8 Sept. 1908, 7.

78. Darnton, "The Visitation of Salome, 2." For other accounts of these dancers see Frances Beck Barnes, "Dance into the Star Class," *Chicago Daily Tribune*, 13 Sept. 1908, H4; Franklyn Fyles, "New York Is Dancing Mad," *Salt Lake Herald*, 26 July 1908; "Now the Daring Salome Dance," 24.

79. "Still Another Salome," *New York Dramatic Mirror*, 15 Aug. 1908, 14.

80. Quoted in Glenn, *Female Spectacle* 108.

81. In fact, Tanguay tried to copyright the dance for herself and supposedly contacted Oscar Wilde's estate about the matter. "Eva Tanguay Makes Bold Claim," *New York Dramatic Mirror*, 26 Sept. 1908, 17.

82. Darnton, "The Visitation of Salome," 2.

83. "La Sylphe in New Salome Dance," *Dramatic Mirror*, 8 Aug. 1908, 14.

84. Quoted in Simonson, " 'The Call of Salome,' " 6.

85. Seshadri, "The Taste of Love," 44.

86. Darnton, "The Visitation of Salome," 2.

87. "Girls and the Salome Dance," *The Freeman*, 26 Sept. 1908, 2; "The Vulgarization of Salome," 437–41; "Bertha Froelich as Salome," *NYT*, 9 Aug. 1908, 9; "Chooceeta Again in Law's Clutch," *Chicago Daily Tribune*, 29 Aug. 1908, 1.

88. "Chooceeta Again in Law's Clutch," 1; Julie Jones Jr., "Chicago Show Shop," *The Freeman*, 3 Oct. 1908, 5; "Lind as Salome," *New York Dramatic Mirror*, 29 Aug. 1908, 14; " 'The Call of Salome,' " SM4.

89. For a detailed analysis of Allan's costume, now held in the collections of Dance Collection Dance in Toronto, please see Marlis Schweitzer, " 'Nothing but a strong of beads': Maud Allan's Salome Costume as a 'choreographic thing,' " in *Performing Objects & Theatrical Things*, eds. Marlis Schweitzer and Joanne Zerdy (Basingstoke: Palgrave Macmillan, 2014), 36–48.

90. Broun, "Gertrude Hoffman Will Try for Greater Things."

91. "A 'Salome' Dance by Miss Hoffmann," 5. See also Darnton, "The Visitation of Salome," 2.

92. "Atlanta Favorite," 6.

93. Tracy C. Davis, *Actresses as Working Women: Their Social Identity in Victorian Culture* (London and New York: Routledge, 1991), 105–136; 135. Robert C. Allen, *Horrible Prettiness: Burlesque and American Culture* (Chapel Hill: University of North Carolina Press, 1991).

94. "Marie Cahill Dies; Famed in Theatre," *NYTI*, 24 Aug. 1933, 15.

95. On the politics of the sheath gown, see Marlis Schweitzer, *When Broadway Was the Runway: Theater, Fashion, and American Culture* (Philadelphia: University of Pennsylvania Press, 2009), 143–54.

96. Illustrations in Wilde, *Salome*. Most of Beardsley's other images show Salome in a state of undress, if not entirely naked. On Wilde's promotion of aesthetic fashion see Patricia A. Cunningham, *Reforming Women's Fashion, 1850–1920: Politics, Health and Art* (Kent, OH: Kent State University Press, 2003), 137.

97. Quoted in Jill Fields, *An Intimate Affair: Women, Lingerie, and Sexuality* (Berkeley and Los Angeles: University of California Press, 2007), 49. See also Valerie Steele, *The Corset: A Cultural History* (New Haven, CT: Yale University Press, 2001).

98. Fields, *An Intimate Affair*, 57.

99. Twentieth Century Club, quoted in Paul DiMaggio, "Cultural Boundaries and Structural Change: The Extension of the High Culture Model to Theater, Opera, and the Dance, 1900–1940," in *Cultivating Differences: Symbolic Boundaries and the Making of Inequality*, ed. Michèle Lamont and Marcel Fournier, 21–67 (Chicago: University of Chicago Press, 1992), 24.

100. "The Salome Dance," *Washington Post*, 12 July 1908, 6.

101. " 'The Call of Salome,' " SM4.

102. Roy L. McCardell, " 'Salome Dances,' Now Being Given in New York, Denounced by the Rev. Dr. David C. Hughes—the Governor's Father—as Demoralizing," *New York World*, 16 July 1908, 1.

103. John D'Emilio and Estelle B. Freedman, *Intimate Matters: A History of Sexuality in America*, 2nd ed. (Chicago and London: University of Chicago Press, 1997 [1988]), 209.

104. " 'The Call of Salome,' " SM4.

105. "The Shocking Costumes and Grotesque Contortions in the 'New' Dances Condemned by the Ballet Master, the Artist and the Physician—What the Wrenching of the Spine Means to the Performer," *New York World*, 16 Aug. 1908, 7.

106. For further discussion of Aida Overton Walker's Salome, see Richard Newman, " 'The Brightest Star': Aida Overton Walker in the Age of Ragtime and Cakewalk," *Prospects*

18 (1993): 465–81; David Krasner, "Black *Salome:* Exoticism, Dance, and Racial Myths," in *African American Performance and Theater History: A Critical Reader,* ed. Harry J. Elam and David Krasner, 192–211 (Oxford and New York: Oxford University Press, 2001); Daphne Brooks, *Bodies in Dissent: Spectacular Performances of Race and Freedom* (Chapel Hill: University of North Carolina Press, 2006), 333–34; and Glenn, *Female Spectacle,* 112–17.

107. Sarah J. MacNutt, "Abnormal Dancing as the Physician Sees It," *New York World,* 16 Aug. 1908, 7.

108. Felicia McCarren, "The 'Symptomatic Act' Circa 1900: Hysteria, Hypnosis, Electricity, Dance," *Critical Inquiry* 21, no. 4 (Summer 1995): 748–74; 748.

109. Teresa Brennan, *The Transmission of Affect* (Ithaca, NY: Cornell University Press, 2004), 3, 74–96.

110. "The 'Salome' Dance Gets into Politics," 2. "Attacks the Salome Craze," *Washington Post,* 24 Aug. 1908, 4.

111. "Salomes under Observation," *New York Dramatic Mirror,* 5 Sept. 1908, 19.

112. "Now the Daring Salome Dance," 24.

113. "The Moral Wave in Kansas City," *St. Louis Post-Dispatch,* 21 Mar. 1909, B3.

114. "The Moral Wave in Kansas City," B3; "Court Order Stops Salome," *Kansas City Journal,* 2 Mar. 1909, http://www.vintagekansascity.com/100yearsago/labels/arts.html. By this point Hoffman had left the Victoria Roof Garden and signed a contract with the Shubert brothers to headline their revue comedy. See correspondence between road manager Zweifel and the Shuberts, Gen. Correspondence, 1908–1910, Box 100, Shubert Archives. I detail the events surrounding this injunction in Schweitzer, *Transatlantic Broadway: The Infrastructural Politics of Global Performance* (Basingstoke: Palgrave Macmillan, 2015), ch. 4.

115. Judith Walzer Leavitt, "Maud Allan," *New York Dramatic Mirror,* 5 Feb. 1910, 9.

116. Wald, *Contagious,* 68.

117. Mallon was permitted to leave the hospital the following year after a change in administration as long as she reported to the department of health on a regular basis. Once again, Mary refused to accede to such requests, assumed an alias and disappeared, only to be rediscovered in 1915. Wald, *Contagious,* 68–113; Leavitt, "Maud Allan," 9.

118. Wald, *Contagious,* 80.

119. Ibid.

BIBLIOGRAPHY

Advert for Hammerstein's Roof. *The (New York) Sun,* August 28 1908, 6.

Allen, Robert C. *Horrible Prettiness: Burlesque and American Culture.* Chapel Hill: University of North Carolina Press, 1991.

"Ashton Stevens Says: Salome 'Vision' Saved From Nightmare by Miss Hoffman's Humor." *Evening Journal* July 14, 1908. Clipping, Folder: Gest/MS Act II, sc. 7 Notes, Morris Gest Collection, Harry Ransom Center, University of Texas at Austin.

"Atlanta Favorite Gives New Thrill to New York." *Atlanta Constitution,* July 18, 1908, 6.

"Attacks the Salome Craze." *Washington Post,* August 24, 1908, 4.

Bentley, Toni. *Sisters of Salome.* Lincoln: University of Nebraska Press, 2002.

"Bertha Froelich as Salome," *New York Times,* August 9, 1908, 9.

Barnes, Frances Beck. "Dance into the Star Class," *Chicago Daily Tribune,* September 13, 1908, H4.

Brennan, Teresa. *The Transmission of Affect*. Ithaca, NY: Cornell University Press, 2004.

Brooks, Daphne. *Bodies in Dissent: Spectacular Performances of Race and Freedom*. Chapel Hill: University of North Carolina Press, 2006.

Broun, Heywood C. "Gertrude Hoffman Will Try for Greater Things Than 'Salome.'" *Morning Telegraph*, July 19, 1908. Folder: Gest/MS Act II, sc. 7 Notes, Morris Gest Collection, Harry Ransom Center.

Buonaventura, Wendy. *Something in the Way She Moves: Dancing Women from Salome to Madonna*. Cambridge, MA: Da Capo Press, 2003.

Carlton, Donna. *Looking for Little Egypt*. Bloomington, IL: International Dance Discovery, 1995.

Carter, Alexandra. "London, 1908: A Synchronic View of Dance History," *Dance Research* 23, no. 1 (Summer 2005): 36–50.

Cherniavsky, Felix. *Maud Allan and Her Art*. Toronto: Dance Collection Danse, 1998.

———. *The Salome Dancer: The Life and Times of Maud Allan*. Toronto: McClellan and Stewart, 1991.

"Chooceeta Again in Law's Clutch." *Chicago Daily Tribune*, August 29, 1908, 1.

C.I.H. "Another View of 'Salome.'" *New York Times*, January 25, 1907, 8.

Clayton, Michelle. "Touring History: Tórtola Valencia between Europe and the Americas." *Dance Research Journal* 44, no. 1 (Summer 2012): 29–49.

"Concerning Depravity." *The Independent* 62, no. 3035 (January 31, 1907): 277.

"Court Order Stops Salome." *Kansas City Journal*, March 2, 1909. http://www.vintagekansascity.com/100yearsago/labels/arts.html.

Cunningham, Patricia A. *Reforming Women's Fashion, 1850–1920: Politics, Health and Art*. Kent, OH: Kent State University Press, 2003.

Darnton, Charles. "The Visitation of Salome." *New York World*, August 8, 1908, 2.

Davis, Tracy C. *Actresses as Working Women: Their Social Identity in Victorian Culture*. London and New York: Routledge, 1991.

D'Emilio, John, and Estelle B. Freedman. *Intimate Matters: A History of Sexuality in America*. 2nd ed. Chicago and London: University of Chicago Press, 1997 [1988].

Dierkes-Thrun, Petra. *Salome's Modernity: Oscar Wilde and the Aesthetics of Transgression*. Ann Arbor: University of Michigan Press, 2011.

Dijkstra, Bram. *Evil Sisters: The Threat of Female Sexuality in Twentieth-Century Culture*. New York: Henry Holt, 1996.

DiMaggio, Paul. "Cultural Boundaries and Structural Change: The Extension of the High Culture Model to Theater, Opera, and the Dance, 1900–1940." In *Cultivating Differences: Symbolic Boundaries and the Making of Inequality*, edited by Michèle Lamont and Marcel Fournier, 21–67. Chicago: University of Chicago Press, 1992.

"The Dubious Past of the 'Merry Widow.'" *Current Literature*, June 1, 1908, 65–66.

Dyer, Thomas, G. *Theodore Roosevelt and the Idea of Race*. Baton Rouge: Louisiana State University Press, 1980.

Erdman, Harley. *Staging the Jew: The Performance of an American Ethnicity, 1860–1920*. New Brunswick, NJ, Rutgers University Press, 1997.

"Eva Tanguay Makes Bold Claim." *New York Dramatic Mirror*, September 26, 1908, 17.

Fields, Jill. *An Intimate Affair: Women, Lingerie, and Sexuality*. Berkeley and Los Angeles: University of California Press, 2007.

"Fight to Keep 'Salome' from Another Theatre." *New York Times*, January 30, 1907, 3.

Foster, Susan Leigh. "Movement's Contagion: The Kinesthetic Impact of Performance." In *The Cambridge Companion to Performance Studies*, edited by Tracy C. Davis, 46–59. New York: Cambridge University Press, 2008.

Fyles, Franklin. "New York Is Dancing Mad." *Salt Lake Herald*, July 26, 1908.

Gilman, Sander L. "Sarah Bernhardt and the 'Modern Jewess.'" *German Quarterly* 66, no. 2 (Spring 1993): 195–211.

———. "Strauss, the Pervert and Avant Garde Opera of the Fin de Siècle." *New German Critique* 43 (Winter 1988): 35–68, 37–38.

"Girls and the Salome Dance." *The Freeman*, September 26, 1908, 2.

Glenn, Susan. *Female Spectacle: The Theatrical Roots of Modern Feminism*. Cambridge, MA: Harvard University Press, 2000.

Hamberlin, Larry. "Visions of Salome: The Femme Fatale in American Popular Songs before 1920." *Journal of the American Musicological Society* 59, no. 3 (Fall 2006): 631–94.

Horowitz, Joseph. "Critic Henry Krehbiel Excoriates Richard Strauss's Salome (1907)." *Journal of the Gilded Age and Progressive Era* 8, no. 2 (2009). Accessed June 12, 2014. http://www. shgape.org/critic-henry-krehbiel-excoriates-richard-strausss-salome/.

Imparo Ancora, "'Salome' Condemned." *New York Times*, January 24, 1907, 8.

Jones, Julie Jr. "Chicago Show Shop." *The Freeman*, October 3, 1908, 5.

Kendall, Elizabeth. *Where She Danced: The Birth of American Art-Dance*. Berkeley, Los Angeles, and London: University of California Press, 1979.

Koritz, Amy. "Dancing the Orient for England: Maud Allan's 'The Vision of Salome.'" *Theatre Journal* 46 (1994): 63–78.

Krasner, David. "Black *Salome*: Exoticism, Dance, and Racial Myths." In *African American Performance and Theater History: A Critical Reader*, edited by Harry J. Elam and David Krasner, 192–211. Oxford and New York: Oxford University Press, 2001.

Kraut, Alan. *Silent Travelers: Germs, Genes, and the 'Immigrant Menace.'* Baltimore: Johns Hopkins University Press, 1994.

Kraut, Anthea. "Race-ing Choreographic Copyright." In *Worlding Dance*, edited by Susan Leigh Foster, 76–97. Basingstoke, UK: Palgrave Macmillan, 2009.

"La Sylphe in New Salome Dance." *New York Dramatic Mirror*, August 8, 1908, 14.

Leavitt, Judith Walzer. "Maud Allan." *New York Dramatic Mirror*, February 5, 1910, 9.

Lears, T. J. Jackson. *No Place of Grace: Antimodernism and the Transformation of American Culture, 1880–1920*. Chicago: University of Chicago Press, 1994.

"Lind as Salome." *New York Dramatic Mirror*, August 29, 1908, 14.

McCardell, Roy L. "The Chorus Girl Squanders a Bunch of Thought on 'Salome' and the Close-Lidded Race Track." *The Evening World*, July 18, 1908.

———. "'Salome Dances,' Now Being Given in New York, Denounced by the Rev. Dr. David C. Hughes—the Governor's Father—as Demoralizing." *New York World*, July 16, 1908, 1.

McCarren, Felicia. "The 'Symptomatic Act' Circa 1900: Hysteria, Hypnosis, Electricity, Dance." *Critical Inquiry* 21, no. 4 (Summer 1995): 748–74.

MacNutt, Sarah J. "Abnormal Dancing as the Physician Sees It." *New York World*, August 16, 1908, 7.

Maglen, Krista. "Importing Trachoma: The Introduction into Britain of American Ideas of an 'Immigrant Disease', 1892–1906." *Immigrants and Minorities* 23, no. 1 (March 2005): 80–99.

Maira, Sunaina. "Belly Dancing: Arab-Face, Orientalist Feminism, and U.S. Empire." *American Quarterly* 60, no. 2 (2008): 317–45.

"Marie Cahill Dies; Famed in Theatre." *New York Times*, August 24, 1933, 15.

Marcus, Sharon. "Salomé!! Sarah Bernhardt, Oscar Wilde, and the Drama of Celebrity." *PMLA* 126, no. 4 (2011): 999–1021.

"Maud Allan Wants to Capture America." *Chicago Daily Tribune*, July 5, 1908, G2.

"Maude [*sic*] Allan's Dance Here." *New York Times*, July 8, 1908: 7.

"Merry Widow an Elderly Dowager." *New York Times*, April 8, 1908, 7.

"The Moral Wave in Kansas City." *St. Louis Post-Dispatch*, March 21, 1909, B3.

"The Muckraker in the Playhouse." *Current Literature* 45, no. 5 (May 1909): 537–40.

"Mysterious 'Salome' Dancer of Paris Has Revealed Her Identity." *Evening World*, April 20, 1908, 3.

Newman, Richard. "'The Brightest Star': Aida Overton Walker in the Age of Ragtime and Cakewalk." *Prospects* 18 (1993): 465–68.

"No Decision on 'Salome'; Seats Are Still on Sale." *New York Times*, January 28, 1907, 3.

Noland, Carrie, and Sally Ann Ness. *Migrations of Gesture*. Minneapolis: University of Minnesota Press, 2008.

"Now the Daring Salome Dance Rages through the World Like an Epidemic." *The Sun (Baltimore)*, August 30, 1908: 24.

"A 'Salome' Dance by Miss Hoffman." *New York Times*, July 14, 1908, 5.

"The Salome Dance." *Washington Post*, July 12, 1908, 6.

"The Salome Dance Gets into Politics." *New York Times*, August 24, 1908, 2.

"Salome Dance Here." *The [Baltimore] Sun*, September 8, 1908, 7.

"Salome Dance Is Unveiled." *Chicago Daily Tribune*, September 9, 1908, 3.

"The Salome Pestilence." *New York Times*, 3 Sept. 1908, 6.

"Salomes under Observation." *New York Dramatic Mirror*, September 5, 1908, 19.

"'Salome' Withdrawn; Conried Fully Yields." *New York Times*, January 31, 1907, 3.

Sancta Simplicitas. "Theories as to 'Salome.'" *New York Times*, January 26, 1907, 8.

Santini, Daria. "'That invisible dance': Reflections on the 'Dance of the Seven Veils' in Richard Strauss's *Salome*." *Dance Research* 29, no. 2 (2011): 223–45.

Schweitzer, Marlis. "A Failed Attempt at World Domination: 'Advanced Vaudeville,' Financial Panic, and the World Wide Trust." *Theatre History Studies* 32 (2012): 53–79.

———. "'Nothing but a string of beads':" Maud Allan's Salome Costume as a 'choreographic thing.'" *Performing Objects & Theatrical Things*. Ed. Marlis Schweitzer and Joanne Zerdy. Basingstoke: Palgrave Macmillan, 2014. 36–48.

———. *Transatlantic Broadway: The Infrastructural Politics of Global Performance*. Basingstoke: Palgrave Macmillan, 2015.

———. *When Broadway Was the Runway: Theater, Fashion, and American Culture*. Philadelphia: University of Pennsylvania Press, 2009.

Seshadri, Anne L. "The Taste of Love: Salome's Transfiguration." *Women and Music* 10 (2006): 24–44.

"The Shocking Costumes and Grotesque Contortions in the 'New' Dances Condemned by the Ballet Master, the Artist and the Physician—What the Wrenching of the Spine Means to the Performer." *New York World*, August 16, 1908, 7.

Simonson, Mary. "'The Call of Salome': American Adapatations and Re-creations of the Female Body in the Early Twentieth Century." *Women and Music* 11 (2007): 1–16.

Stratyner Cohen, and Barbara Naomi. "The Borrowed Art of Gertrude Hoffmann." *Dance Data* 2 (1977): 2–11.

Steele, Valerie. *The Corset: A Cultural History*. New Haven, CT: Yale University Press, 2001.

"Strauss's 'Salome' the First Time Here." *New York Times*, January 23, 1907, 9.

"Still Another Salome." *New York Dramatic Mirror*, August 15, 1908, 14.

Stone, Claudia B. "Gertrude Hoffmann: Artist or Charlatan?" MA thesis, New York University, 1987.

"To See Allan Dance Here." *New York Times*, July 13, 1908.

Unpublished manuscript, Folder: MS: Act II, Sc. 7: "Salome from San Francisco," and Folder: Gest/Ms. Notes from Mr. Gest, Box 5 Morris Gest Collection, Harry Ransom Center, University of Texas at Austin.

"The Vulgarization of Salome." *Current Literature*, October 1, 1908, 437.

Wald, Priscilla. *Contagious: Cultures, Carriers, and the Outbreak Narrative.* Durham, NC: Duke University Press, 2007.

Wilde, Oscar. *Salomé.* Boston: Brandon Publishing, 1989.

Walkowitz, Judith R. "The 'Vision of Salome': Cosmopolitanism and Erotic Dancing in Central London, 1908–1918," *American Historical Review* 108, no. 2 (April 2003): 337–76.

"Wears Cosmetics as Tights." *Chicago Daily Tribune*, September 10, 1908, 3.

CHAPTER 43

CHOREOGRAPHING A CAUSE
Broadway Bares as Philanthroproduction and Embodied Index to Changing Attitudes toward HIV/AIDS

VIRGINIA ANDERSON

THE stuff of erotic nightmares. As awareness of the sexually transmitted potential of HIV expanded throughout the 1980s and 1990s, perception and depiction of the sensual body on the Broadway stage changed from alluring to dangerous. Viewed by many in the 1970s as a political claim to personal identity, sex came to signify a threat to survival. In those early years of the AIDS epidemic, the popular media largely presented the HIV-positive individual as isolated, emaciated, and otherwise physically and socially outcast. For over twenty years, however, director and choreographer Jerry Mitchell has gathered a community of the most physically fit and conventionally beautiful dancers on Broadway to fight AIDS as a medical and social disease through what I term a "philanthroproduction": Broadway Bares.[1]

The economic implications of Broadway Bares as a philanthroproduction provide an ideal site for combining analysis of dance, theater, and an evolving medical, social, and political reality to illuminate the history of the AIDS epidemic in the United States. This chapter begins by defining the philanthroproduction, a unique expression of philanthropy and ideology through fully produced performance. The philanthroproduction is then proven to be a highly relevant form through its exploration within the parameters characterizing Broadway and the age of AIDS respectively. Finally, as a case study, Broadway Bares finds definition with essential traits and community placement and analysis through a lens of cultural synchronicity.

THE PHILANTHROPRODUCTION: A DEFINITION

An alternative genre of performance within the Broadway theater community, philanthroproductions found considerable representation in the face of the AIDS epidemic.

As I define the term, philanthroproductions are professionally produced, fully mounted performance events developed exclusively to raise money for nonprofit services.[2] Such events have three defining components: philanthropy, largely original production elements presented with artistic integrity, and the presence of both ideological and artistic spines.[3]

Like plays and musicals, the evolution of philanthroproductions reflects changing attitudes concerning AIDS over the course of the epidemic. They find further definition in their distinction from these forms: sometimes eclectic in content and style and ranging from sketch comedy to intricately choreographed dances, philanthroproductions are neither plays, nor musicals, nor concerts, though they may contain elements of each.

Furthermore, philanthroproductions may be distinguished from the "special events" that serve as fundraisers for nonprofit organizations. Set apart by the high caliber of artistic integrity and production value, philanthroproductions in fact operate as extensions of special events. Kim Klein explains that special events, "often called 'fundraising benefits,' are social gatherings of many sorts that expand the reputation of the organization, give those attending an amusing, interesting, or moving time, and possibly make money for the organization sponsoring the event."[4] Klein articulates the risks associated with special events: "An organization that wants to raise its profile, bring in new people, and possibly make money will find a special event an ideal strategy. In many cases special events can lose money or barely break even and still be successful because of the publicity and visibility they produced."[5] Perhaps with this in mind, philanthroproductions rely almost entirely on donated resources and personnel. And while the risk Klein describes is true of philanthroproductions in general, such a financial risk is minimized by the popularity among participants and audience members alike of the four primary philanthroproductions produced by Broadway Cares/Equity Fights AIDS (BC/EFA): The Easter Bonnet Competition, Gypsy of the Year, Broadway Backwards, and Broadway Bares.

The artistic and ideological spines, or through-lines, of philanthroproductions may sometimes range from the tenuous to the obvious, but there is always an artistic coherence driving each philanthroproduction from start to finish. There is also an implicit acknowledgment of, as well as an explicit statement concerning, the cause for which the participants strive to raise funds. While such recognition for the cause may be overtly represented through a direct audience appeal, it more importantly emerges through the very nature of the production itself. In their own ways, each of the philanthroproductions benefiting BC/EFA counters the stigma and ignorance that historically has encompassed HIV/AIDS.

Like many plays and musicals, philanthroproductions feature leading, or star performers, often celebrities. Whether in featured or ensemble roles, performers in philanthroproductions for BC/EFA reinforce identification with their "home" Broadway productions. While charitable in nature, philanthroproductions can serve a commercial purpose as well; audience members attracted to certain performers during a philanthroproduction may wish to prolong their association with them by attending the for-profit production with which the performers are affiliated. Indeed, over the course of the AIDS epidemic, Broadway philanthroproductions have generated publicity and funds for BC/EFA and increased the visibility of not only the organization but participating productions and performers.[6]

PHILANTHROPRODUCTION AND THE BROADWAY COMMUNITY

In order to understand philanthroproduction, we must consider the ideas behind philan-thropy and related notions of community. With etymological roots in Greek terms indicat-ing "love of people,"[7] philanthropy refers to a fundamental goodwill or humanitarianism, "often expressed in donations of property, money, or volunteer time to worthy causes."[8] "Community," in turn, involves self-identification in relation to others. Drawing on the research of multiple social scientists, Emily Barman explains two divergent approaches to defining community that more deeply explore notions of community:

> *Community of place*: Community occurs when residence in a common locale results in shared sentiments and goals among members. Community, at the most basic level, entails place; it refers to a locality, bounded space, a limited geography.[9]
>
> *Community of the mind:* Members must embrace a common good: a set of shared values, ide-als, and expectations that exist outside the specific and oft divergent interests of individuals. This common faith is reinforced by common narratives, collective ways of doing, and a com-munal history.[10]

To be sure, the spirit of philanthroproduction throughout the AIDS epidemic emerges from Broadway's communities of space and mind.

Put another way, the notion of a Broadway theater community combines both the geo-graphical and ideological aspects of community. Geographically, most of these theaters of 500 or more seats are situated within a short radius of one another on the west side of Manhattan between 41st and 54th Street. Ideologically, membership within the "Broadway community" may serve as a point of pride for those who achieve the perceived status asso-ciated with performing in a Broadway show. Barman emphasizes that "community is gen-erated from a shared sense among members of the 'we' and the 'they,' of an inside and an outside, and of association and disassociation. Ideologically, these social borders serve a dual purpose: they not only mark the commonalities of a group but also intensify them by emphasizing their inherent distinctness from others."[11] Broadway, while often associated with commercialism,[12] is culturally defined by its status; it is broadly perceived to be the best of the best, perhaps due in part to higher guaranteed salaries than those offered through off-Broadway counterparts, larger budgets, and popular recognition through the televised Antoinette Perry (Tony) Awards. To be a part of the Broadway theater community is, often in the eyes of the general public, to have established oneself in a notoriously competitive field.

Deep roots of identity enmeshed in Broadway culture find emphasis through philanthro-productions as community performance. As Jerry Mitchell, the creator of Broadway Bares, indicates, "once a [Broadway] gypsy, always a gypsy."[13] Director, performer, and choreog-rapher Denis Jones further illustrates this point: "In a way I've kind of ghettoized myself in that all of my friends are in the business, you know, my whole social life, really, it's just so show-business intensive. That's my community, that's my family, that's my *city*."[14] Yet, the benefits of belonging to a community involve more than identification alone; according to Barman, community also implies support in challenging times "and assistance as [individu-als within the community] pursue their own goals. In turn, the presence of shared networks and meanings further solidifies social connectedness, generating intensified feelings of trust and reciprocity."[15] Community identification thus reduces feelings of isolation that, especially in the early years of the AIDS crisis, often proved devastating. It is clear, then, that the Broadway community serves as a key component of the successes of the BC/EFA philanthroproductions.

Broadway Philanthroproduction in the Age of AIDS

Equity Fights AIDS had been established in 1986 by Colleen Dewhurst and others within the Actors Equity Association, to be followed shortly thereafter by Broadway Cares. Although the two organizations did not merge to form Broadway Cares/Equity Fights AIDS until 1992 (and is now often referred to simply as "Broadway Cares"), the philanthroproductions that have come to represent the combined organization were established long before they joined forces. The BC/EFA philanthroproductions now employ hundreds of volunteers from within the Broadway theater community including actors, directors, stage managers, wardrobe and hair personnel, ushers and front of house staff, technicians, stagehands, musicians, producers, company managers, and concessionaires. While in its current iteration events put on by BC/EFA are large in scale, such events were born out of small community moments. BC/EFA Executive Director Tom Viola acknowledges, "the success of Broadway Cares is in fact in that incremental growth. All of these events which have extraordinary range right now all really grew from small ideas. Our ability to produce them grew as they grew."[16] Viola further explains that the timing of each event is carefully orchestrated to keep the community engaged and to keep volunteer efforts from becoming onerous; for example, no philanthroproductions are produced in the period between the announcement of Tony nominations and the award show itself when, as Viola explains, everyone's attention—hopes, dreams, and anxieties—are focused there.[17] In effect, through such sensitivity, these philanthroproductions strengthen ties among members of the Broadway theater community as they serve those in need within and beyond it.

Philanthroproductions have been crucial to the organization's success, financially and ideologically. While BC/EFA remains inextricably linked with the Great White Way, it incorporates the fundraising activities of many touring companies of Broadway shows and off-Broadway companies. It has been described as "the on-going, committed response from the American theater community to an urgent worldwide health crisis. By drawing upon the talents, resources and generosity of participants, BC/EFA raises funds for AIDS-related causes across the United States."[18] Howard Sherman observed to BC/EFA president Tom Viola, "you are not only social service providers, you are not only fundraisers. You are producers."[19]

In the earliest years of the epidemic, funding for AIDS service organizations was relatively limited due to the lack of public concern and the slow response of government officials. The development of charitable organizations and programs over the years correlated with the number of AIDS-reported cases and the consequent recognition of the need for more prevention and services.[20] Susan Chambré reinforces the importance of this context by suggesting that the year 1986

> represents a major turning point in the development of HIV/AIDS policy at the local level and the growth of public contracts with nonprofit organizations. Growing public awareness and concern were evident in increased attention by the mass media, which was fueled by a growing sense that the epidemic was involving "innocent victims," including children and hemophiliacs, and by the death of screen actor Rock Hudson [in October of 1985], the first person many Americans had heard of who had died of AIDS.[21]

Such identification was important for the establishment of the immediacy of the epidemic in the popular imagination.

Recognition of the epidemic, however, came with its own dangers; as early as 1988, psychologists acknowledged the consequences of the dominant, if misinformed, attitudes toward people with AIDS. Gregory Herek and Erik Glunt argued for the importance of addressing the issue:

> AIDS-related stigma is a problem for all of society. It imposes severe hardships on the people who are its targets, and it ultimately interferes with treating and preventing HIV infection. By attacking AIDS-related stigma, we create a social climate conducive to a rational, effective, and compassionate response to this epidemic.[22]

Philanthroproductions by BC/EFA, then, were established not only to raise funds but also to join in this counteroffensive against the stigma Herek and Glunt describe.[23] Director and choreographer Jerry Mitchell suggests this dual purpose: "There's no other community where it can work. I'm certain of it. Because it stretches beyond just raising money. It's a bigger deal."[24] Indeed, the first Broadway philanthroproduction to raise money for AIDS services and prevention was a significant development, emerging in the midst of this public anxiety. The inaugural event took place in 1987 when the cast of *La Cage aux Folles* presented the first Easter Bonnet Competition, raising $21,000 for the National AIDS Network.[25] A year later, the event was produced as a benefit for BC/EFA for the first time, raising $51,000, a significant amount of money to be raised in just one night, equal to approximately 5 percent of that year's federal budget for HIV/AIDS-related services.[26]

BROADWAY BARES

Since its inception in 1992, founder Jerry Mitchell and other creators of Broadway Bares have brought together volunteers from across the Broadway theater community to create an unparalleled event both to raise money for AIDS service organizations and to celebrate life through sexual expression, even when it was unpopular to do so. Broadway Bares thus serves as a prime illustration of philanthroproduction, for it encompasses record-setting financial characteristics, significant production quality, and a strong ideological message. Like plays, musicals, and other philanthroproductions, Broadway Bares has evolved with shifting perceptions of the epidemic—particularly regarding perceptions of the sexual body.

In the early years of the epidemic, the distortion of the healthy body resulting from opportunistic infections, which often marked the shift from HIV to AIDS, contributed to a plague metaphor that would come to dominate public discourse and perception. Cultural critic, activist, and literary icon Susan Sontag explains, "the most feared diseases, those that are not simply fatal but transform the body into something alienating, ... are the ones that seem particularly susceptible to promotion to 'plague.'"[27] The image of the plague victim, expertly analyzed by Sander Gilman, highlights his or her skeletal frame and dark spots. Graphic accounts from the period describe high fevers, loss of bowel control, and puss-filled boils covering the body—symptoms comparable to those experienced by the untreated AIDS patient in the 1980s. While those living with HIV may show no symptoms for years, in the first decade of the AIDS crisis, opportunistic infections quickly consumed their untreated hosts. Kaposi's sarcoma lesions, often the first marker of the illness, were compared to the marks of the "spotty monster" of the fourteenth century. Bodies similarly wasted away, leaving emaciated frames where muscular forms once stood.

Overturning both "victim mentality" and the fear associated with "plague," Broadway Bares offers a fiercely determined celebration of sexuality through carefully choreographed music and dance performance. Mitchell emphasizes its purpose: "Broadway Bares always was built for the community and celebrating life *now*, not wanting death, but celebrating the life you have now and learning to live with your life *now*. That's what it was, that's what it *is*."[28] In fact, Broadway Bares is a fully mounted burlesque extravaganza centering on dance and music, employing the donated resources and talent of the Broadway theater community to raise money for BC/EFA. While a narrative has been a regular feature of Broadway Bares since its earliest years, the show has always been less about story and more about the celebration of the human body. The demanding and often sexually suggestive choreography, combined with the revealing costumes (or lack thereof), showcase the physical fitness of the performers on display for the viewing pleasure of the paying audience.

THE BIRTH OF BROADWAY BARES: A BRIEF HISTORY

Having grown up in Paw Paw, Michigan, Jerry Mitchell came to New York in 1980, a time when the sexual revolution of the post-Stonewall years was still in full swing. As the years progressed and the epidemic took hold of the city and particularly the performing arts community, the epidemic acquired a personal dimension. He explains:

> Imagine going to college and bonding with ten friends during that all-important first step away from home. Now imagine it's eight years later, and all but two of those college friends are, for all intents and purposes, in heaven. That's not the way it's supposed to work. At the age of twenty-six I had established myself as a Broadway gypsy working alongside Michael Bennett, whom we would also later lose to AIDS, dreaming of choreographing a Broadway show and searching for an outlet to express my personal loss.[29]

After a period working in London, Mitchell returned to New York City in 1990 and joined his friends volunteering for Gay Men's Health Crisis (GMHC). "So I go and I'm licking stamps and licking envelopes and doing what I can because I can't afford the $500 ticket to [a benefit]. I don't have that kind of money, but I'm getting involved in any way I can, volunteering." Mitchell, then thirty, had just ended a relationship and experienced first-hand the fear-stricken dating world of the AIDS era. "I was responding to the AIDS crisis in my own way. When I created Broadway Bares, it was 1992, I was single, and I was dating, and I found that people were afraid to date . . . and afraid to be intimate. I was trying to promote intimacy with responsibility. That was one of the goals."[30] The event's creation came from his experience of Broadway audiences responding to a nearly naked body.

Mitchell was performing as a featured dancer, "the Indian of the Dawn" in *The Will Rogers Follies* on Broadway, a role that required him to dance in a loincloth on a large drum. He was consistently surprised by the power he felt over his captivated audiences. Like Ziegfeld girls of yesteryear, he even received extravagant gifts in his dressing room in honor of his display. Mitchell and dressing roommates Jason Opsahl, Troy Johnson, John Ganun, and Jack Doyle had been brainstorming ideas for raising money for the Easter Bonnet competition, a previously established philanthroproduction:

> We were always brainstorming ways to raise money for the Easter Bonnet and Gypsy of the Year. *New ways.* Everybody did bake sales. Everybody did calendars. Everybody did cookbooks. Everybody did backstage tours. We were trying to think of a *new* way to raise a lot of money. And Jason said "Why don't you go dance on the bar and go go dance and raise money—get money in your g-string!"[31]

Opsahl had planted a pivotal idea in Mitchell's head: Pointing out that his loin-cloth costume for the *Follies* required him to be nearly naked as it was, he suggested that Mitchell capitalize on his assets by dancing for a cause. Admitting that he was "in the best shape of [his] life," Mitchell "called five guys I knew who were in incredible shape and appearing in Broadway musicals, and in ten days, I put together a little show with an opening number, individual strips and go-go dancing for tips."[32] Broadway Bares was born. The first show took place on April 8, 1992, at Splash, a Manhattan gay bar long known for its driving beat and go go dancers until it closed in 2013. The event has grown considerably since its first performance; from one individual's brainchild raising $8,000 gathered in a famously beer-soaked pillowcase in 1992 to its ownership by the Broadway community, Broadway Bares has raised more than one hundred fifty times its first collected amount, $1,386,105 in 2014. In fact, through its first 23 iterations, Broadway Bares has raised more than 11.3 million dollars for BC/EFA.

LOCATION, COMMUNITY, AND CASTING

The event itself took place in a variety of locations before it found its longterm home at the Roseland Ballroom in the heart of the Broadway theater district.[33] Mitchell insists that its various moves were intended to accommodate the growing crowds, a trend foreshadowed the night of the first Broadway Bares when a second performance was added after a large crowd wrapped around the exterior of Splash to see the event. Progressing from Splash to Shout to Bump and ultimately to the Palladium, the show then moved to Webster Hall, where a runway was added, changing the dynamics of the interior space to maximize audience interaction. Mitchell explains, "Palladium had a lot of upstairs space, but not a lot of space downstairs, where the people who gave a lot of money wanted to be close. So we needed to find a place where we could do that, where we could serve two masters."[34] After the Palladium, Roseland, located on West 52nd Street between Broadway and Eighth Avenue, brought Broadway Bares to the heart of the community.

On a theoretical level, these locational changes reflect the acceptance and ultimately the adoption of the event by the Broadway community as a whole; Broadway Bares began at the periphery before moving to a place of geographical and cultural centrality. On a practical level, the long-term location at Roseland allowed stagehands and performers to get to rehearsals easily from their evening matinee and evening performances. Mitchell conjoins space and community in his description of the space: "What Roseland affords us is a theatre in the neighborhood. It makes it very comfortable . . . because more peo-ple feel like its *their* show and they can get there and work for an hour or volunteer for two hours, they can show up and it makes it feel like . . . it strengthens the *community* feel of the event."[35] Years before it was known that Roseland would close, Denis Jones corroborated,

> I love that it's at Roseland because Roseland is right in the heart of it. I love that it's right in the hub of the theatre community because it is such a *Broadway* event . . . I do think there is some-thing particularly *right* about its location now. I like that it's nestled across the street from and right next to Broadway theatres—not only for logistical reasons (it's easier to get people over there on time—it's right there)—it just *feels* like it *should* be in the theatre district. Roseland is perfect. I think it's got to stay there, unless it turns into something else entirely.[36]

Jones's comment points to the intrinsic cultural nature of the event, inextricably tied to loca-tion as representative of community.

The space is, for now, established, and so, too, are the participants. That is, as the num-ber of participants has grown, restrictions have been put in place to limit who may partici-pate in the event. Jones emphasizes that the ranks are usually filled by current Broadway performers and those "grandfathered" in: "If you're not in an off-Broadway or Broadway show and haven't been in the show, we can put you on a wait list—Priority casting goes to the other tier." He continues, "Casting is really a very, very tricky process . . . You just hate turning people away—whatever their motivation, they show up and want to be a part of this thing. Of course you want to use them if you can."[37] Mitchell insists that he never held auditions, but community identification was a requirement: "If you're in a Broadway show, we have to find a place for you. Because ultimately, the money is being raised by the Broadway community for the entire world."[38] Once again, Broadway represents com-munal as well as geographic ideology, and Mitchell sought to enrich and enforce such identification.

This community of mind is further established through the participation of stars, which also adds to the perceived legitimacy and status of Broadway Bares the philanthroproduction as a Broadway production. Like most Broadway productions, Broadway Bares features well-known actors: the cast grew from a small group of Broadway gypsies to include A-list celebrities including Nathan Lane, Alan Cumming, David Hyde Pierce, Jane Krakowski, and many oth-ers. Mitchell observes, "The stars? If they do it once they'll do it again. They love the kids in the show, and the audience loves them and responds to them in a way that is worship worthy! And rightfully so. But the bigger thing is everyone is taking part in a community effort."[39]

IDEOLOGICAL TRANSFORMATION WITHIN
AND BEYOND THE BROADWAY COMMUNITY

The reinforcement of the Broadway community Mitchell describes may be seen through the exponential increase in the size of the event, growing from eight performers in 1992 to over 240 in 2008 and beyond. Participants return year after year. Like the emotional link to space felt by Broadway actors, there appears to be a metaphysical component found through performing in the event. Denis Jones explains:

> I think a lot of people come to the event as performers because they hear that it's so much fun and they want to take off their clothes, and I think a lot of them come because they want to meet Jerry or they want to meet these other choreographers. There's certainly more than a few of them that come to it with business on the brain a little bit, but I think they end up having an experience that transcends that. I'm not saying it's changing everybody's life who's involved, but I think for more than a few of them, they go out having an experience that is much larger than the one they expected to have.[40]

Whatever their motivation, through their act of service, participants often develop a meaningful connection to their community. Michael Graziano, one of the producers of Broadway Bares, noted that performers have "such a profound experience with it that, in a way, it is their doorway to activism [within the community]. They get involved with this event and then become *more* involved with this event and *other* events because they got to know the organization [Broadway Cares/Equity Fights AIDS]."[41] This link to social activism finds reflection in the philanthroproduction, drawing on popular ideology for creative inspiration in order to transcend and reform it.

Broadway Bares was created to insist on such ideological transformation: the right of individuals to embrace sexuality at a time when doing so was considered deadly. As the epidemic has changed through better treatment and more compassionate public perception, the goals remain largely the same and just as urgent. Mitchell explains,

> Broadway Bares exists because it is important to remind everyone to live, to love and to cherish life! And be safe, and take care of yourself and each other! . . . I see a younger generation who needs our advice and we need to find ways to share it that is welcoming and not off-putting from an older perspective. Broadway Bares is the perfect tool. We put on a show. A damn sexy show. If in that show we can say be sexy, be cool, be hot and just be safe . . . that's a start. And a message worth repeating year after year after year. Can't say it enough, especially to the young-uns. But it's our responsibility to share whatever we can to keep everyone safe. It was one of the original goals of this strip show to make people feel good again about being intimate. To feel good and be safe![42]

The resonance of this message is rooted in the historical component of the AIDS epidemic and its effect on the Broadway theater community. Broadway Bares continues to represent and affect ideological transformation with each iteration.

The Broadway community was undeniably affected by the disease throughout the 1980s and 1990s; the consequent culture that fosters philanthroproduction represents the "aggregate of what human beings inherit from previous generations: representations, knowledge, values, ideas and types of sensitiveness.["43] These values within the Broadway culture may be transmitted from generation to generation through various events supporting Broadway Cares/Equity Fights AIDS, which often rely on the donated efforts of community members. Denis Jones observes:

> Broadway Bares is amazing, but Broadway Cares does all kinds of events that are amazing and these performers work year round volunteering for the organization, raising money and doing these things. So many of these people really haven't been affected by the AIDS crisis at all—even less so than I! I hope it is on their radar enough that they are behaving themselves accordingly, but they came to New York recently and at the time when it was already very much treatable. You just weren't seeing people walking around with emaciated faces and you weren't hearing about friends who were diagnosed. It has been so much less a part of their lives than myself or people who are ten years older than me and they still constantly volunteer and still raise money and have a great time doing it. It's beautiful.[44]

To be sure, Broadway Cares/Equity Fights AIDS brought the community together in a time of crisis and continues to nurture the community, which has grown with the knowledge and values acquired during this crucial period. The dancer of the present moment in Broadway Bares confronts specters of the past. This link between past and present finds expression through music and dance in Broadway Bares.

ANALYZING PERFORMANCE: CULTURAL SYNCHRONICITY

Even while moving forward, past productions of Broadway Bares, when read closely, offer evidence of synchronicity with the cultural moment from which each production emerged. Social concerns, stigma, and even the state of medical treatment of the epidemic find what may be subconscious expression through dance. Broadway Bares thus engenders empowerment by linking the present with issues of the past to confront the future through Joel Bonnemaison's theory of custom:

> Custom . . . and authenticity . . . stand as political/cultural phenomena that emphasize not the precedence of the past over the present, or that of tradition over modernity, but the link between one and the other. Such phenomena always involve reinvention and reconstruction as well as renewed focus on a certain vision of the past. In turn, this vision brings more strength to the collective ability of a community to face the future and the outside world. A type of syncretism evolves, which blends the old with the new.[45]

In order to define these sometimes subtle changes in ideological transformation, one must first consider the following constants within a Broadway Bares philanthroproduction:

1. **Its celebration, rather than condemnation, of the body.** Broadway Bares exemplified fierce determination to subvert contemporary associations linking sex and death.
2. **Its materials/sponsorship donations.** Every component of the Broadway Bares event is donated. Performers, designers, make-up artists, even union stage crew and press

photographers volunteer their time and skills without financial compensation. For services such as delivery of donated lighting equipment, funds from sponsors are employed, ranging from cosmetic to pharmaceutical companies.

3. **Its community ownership.** Broadway Bares emerges directly from the Broadway community; this community identification is reflected in space, spirit, and practice.

4. **Its ritualized format, including a rotation.** Over time, many core components of Broadway Bares have emerged. A central theme links the numbers, and the show always contains elements of comedy and satire. An aerial act performs over the heads of the audience. Since composer/lyricist Andrew Lippa wrote "The Barest Show on Earth," the opening number for Broadway Bares in 1997, there has always been an original number written for the show. Celebrities appear alongside Broadway gyp-sies. There is always at least one acrobatic number and one "art" number ("to keep the cops out," Denis Jones jests). A rousing dance with the full company on stage closes the structured portion of the show. Finally, following acknowledgments, the com-ponent most identified with Broadway Bares: rotation. Since the first event in 1992, the evening has concluded with the performers lining up on stage and go-go dancing free-style in a procession along the runways, collecting cash in their g-strings from the eager audience members engulfing them.

While the defining features of Broadway Bares are important factors in the analysis of the event, the subtle changes in its performance history reveal mutual cultural resonance. Reflecting developments in society, medicine, and politics, the musical numbers and chore-ography evolved from sensual, yet often mournful melodies and movement to consistently celebratory mixes. Mitchell reflects on this synchronous development:

> It was subliminal—it was subconscious . . . It's weird to think that . . . the show was reflecting what was going on in the community. I think that's because I was a big part of the community. I was a single guy in the early 90s and I was in the community, and I was *living* in the com-munity and I meeting people in the community, and having sex with people *in the community*, and I was sort of letting that dictate the way I responded in dance in numbers that I picked.[46]

In the absence of a text, reading the choreography of Broadway Bares requires interpreting cultural lexicons, idioms, and tropes as embodied gesture.[47] By considering symbolic ges-tures and physical positions found elsewhere within popular culture, one may interrogate a dance's reinforcement or subversion of associated signification.

While the significance of the choreography within these dances cannot be overstated, music, or its representation, also plays a crucial role in Broadway Bares, stirring performer and viewer. Patrice Pavis explains:

> Music is asemantic, or at least nonfigurative; unlike words, it does not represent the world. Located within a performance, it radiates, without us knowing precisely what it is that is given off. It influences our overall perception, but it is difficult to say exactly what meanings it gives rise to. It creates an atmosphere that makes us particularly receptive to the performance. It is as if the soul's light stirs inside us.[48]

Music, then, offers *evocation* rather than *signification*. Within Broadway Bares, music, like costume and scenic elements, also serves to locate the performance distinctly within the present; musical numbers are built around songs that are current popular hits, even when the theme of a show may suggest another era (such as the 2008 show, constructed around the 1865 story of Alice in Wonderland). Music becomes representative of fashion, placing the production in the present. Mitchell emphasizes this point: "I've always used the fashion—what's happening—the fashion of the time to help explain the show. To stay contemporary—to stay *right now*, to deal with what's going on *right now* in our community. It's always been on my mind in every aspect. That's probably why there's been some synchronicity between what's happening in the world and what's happening on our stage."[49] In effect, music, like dance, provides a synchronizing effect, reinforcing and commenting on the present cultural moment.

Just as the choreography and music of each production of Broadway Bares have evolved with changing cultural circumstances, so, too, has the scenic design. Although a given year's design may depend on the theme, a marked shift in iconic signification reflects changing public attitudes toward the epidemic. For example, in the early years of Broadway Bares, the red ribbon, introduced in 1991 at the peak of the AIDS crisis and symbolizing compassion and awareness, frequently appeared within the stagecraft of the event, ranging from scenic details to glittering red ribbon pasties covering the nipples of a performer. Over time, the red ribbon went from frequent inclusion to nearly complete omission in the look of Broadway Bares, reflecting that, with the development of life-prolonging and life-enhancing medication, AIDS was perceived to be less of a crisis situation.

A CASE STUDY: BROADWAY BARES III (1993)

Taking choreography, music, and stagecraft into consideration, a close reading of any Broadway Bares performance illuminates its relationship to the past, the present, and the future. In 1993, AIDS had been a part of the social landscape for a dozen years, and in that time it led to waves of media attention and stigma-driven attacks on the afflicted. The virus had spread rapidly in urban areas such as New York, and in 1992, AIDS had become the number one cause of death for men between the ages of 25 and 44.[50] The arts community had been severely affected, acknowledged through the annual Day Without Art which commenced in 1989. Discrimination was rampant during this time, leaving people living with HIV without insurance, jobs, and long-held friendships while being ostracized by their communities.

The images used to convey information regarding public health concerns captured and often directly influenced popular perceptions of AIDS. In his essay "The Beautiful Body and AIDS: The Image of the Body at Risk at the Close of the Twentieth Century," Sander Gilman critically examines the iconography of international public health campaign posters over the course of the epidemic.[51] Gilman concludes that the posters he studied "attempt to simplify the lived complexity of disease through the use of highly constructed visual images,"[52] noting their intended public display and direct communication of specific information to a mass audience. Contextualizing his iconographic analysis, he writes,

> The posters presume a certain level of awareness of AIDS; therefore reading the posters provides an index of awareness of the disease, the images used to evoke the disease, the visual and verbal language employed to characterize those who have or are at risk from the disease, and an index of how the disease was understood over time and in various visual cultures.[53]

Gilman's assessment proves equally valuable when applied to additional visually based forms of communication, such as the public service announcement (PSA) and, of course, the choreography and design of *Broadway Bares*.

Public service announcements from the period from which *Broadway Bares* emerged reflect a widespread fear of the AIDS body as well as the stigma imposed on those who were HIV positive. In 1992, the same year as the first *Broadway Bares* performance, a PSA produced for MTV and filmed at an AIDS hospice in San Antonio captures the shame and isolation associated with AIDS. Filming in black and white, the camera haunts largely empty, dark hallways, passing rooms with solitary figures standing at a window or sitting on a bed, until one slowly stands to close the curtains. The PSA represents the HIV-positive individual as isolated, lonely, and ultimately walking alone toward a symbolic exit sign.

Another PSA from this period exacerbates the fear wrought by popular images and reports of the AIDS epidemic in the United States. It features a camera voyeuristically entering a hospital room in which an emaciated young man covered in Kaposi's sarcoma lesions, apparently oblivious to the camera's voyeuristic gaze, stares straight ahead, wheezing for breath as the viewer circles his bed. A young man's voice offers the following commentary:

> This is someone who has AIDS. Take a good look. Before AIDS kills him, it can give him a fever that won't go away. Purple sores that won't go away. And then maybe pneumonia, or a brain tumor or something even worse that won't go away. Then finally, he'll go away. That's all. *This is AIDS.* Look at it. You can get AIDS by having sex or sharing a needle with someone who has the AIDS virus. So don't. Don't ask for AIDS.

At this point the boy's hand reaches up to the camera. The voice concludes: "Don't get it."

In addition to such broadcast messages, cultural events contributing to the negative signification of these representations include the arson attack on the home of the Ray family in Florida—three of their hemophiliac boys were HIV positive, as well as the story of Kimberly Bergalis—the young woman who was said to have been infected by a vilified homosexual dentist and who insisted before congress that she did nothing to *deserve* her condition, implying the guilt of others. And of course, the popular media similarly seized on Jerry Falwell's language of deserving behavior—"AIDS is not just God's punishment for homosexuals; it is God's punishment for the society that tolerates homosexuals."[54] Each of these stories and figures contributed to a public fascination with and fear of AIDS—fanning the flames of stigma that came to encompass the AIDS body.

Nevertheless, as demonstrated by the "die-in" protests sponsored by the AIDS Coalition to Unleash Power (ACT UP), the body was a site of political resistance. So was the case with *Broadway Bares*. As if in direct response to the PSA's call "Don't ask for AIDS," Jerry Mitchell in *Broadway Bares III* insists on the right of individuals to embrace sexuality; he describes the ideological spine of *Broadway Bares*, "It was one of the original goals of this strip show to make people feel good again about being intimate. To feel good and be safe!" In 1993 guilt-laden messages about physical intimacy bombarded the public, and through its very production, *Broadway Bares* argued against such attacks on the body and the mind.

Reflecting Mitchell's intentions, the performed "AIDS body" is recognized within the choreography of *Broadway Bares* in 1993 and other years in which AIDS was most present in the public consciousness. In his outstanding study, *How to Make Dances in an Epidemic*, David Gere begins by grappling with the question, "How can you tell that a dance is *about* AIDS?" He establishes the following three criteria:

1. First, the dance must depict gayness—the gay man is abject . . . marginalized outside the mainstream.
2. The depiction . . . of homosexual desire.
3. It must depict some form of mourning. (12)

Gere's reliance on gayness may appear to be problematic given the universality of possible HIV transmission, and even Gere admits, "I am not pleased with myself for having arrived at this conclusion, for these three preconditions serve to reinforce . . . the conflation of gay male identity, gay erotics, and death." Still, early popular perceptions of AIDS were only sometimes linked to truth; Gere points out that "as a result of popularly held conceptions that are reinforced in dance and choreography, it appears . . . that only gay men—or men who appear to be gay—signify as having HIV or AIDS in dance."[55] Gere's assertion acquires additional support in the context of an event designed to raise funds and awareness for AIDS services and prevention.

Through stagecraft, choreography, and music, Broadway Bares III responded not only to recent history, but the history that preceded it, the history in which bathhouses were sites for the expression of a newly acquired sexual freedom for the gay community in the 1970s and early 1980s. For example, a key scenic element was offered by a mylar curtain, evocative of the one famously used by Boris Aronson in the original set design for *Cabaret*, signifying the Emcee's command to "leave your troubles outside." In addition, Broadway Bares III visually carried forth the message of remembrance and compassion represented by the red ribbon, itself introduced to the public through the televised broadcast of Broadway's Tony Awards in 1991. The event began with the stately entrance of dancers costumed as medieval knights (although not for long, as they would soon strip to the slightest of undergarments) carrying banners—one emblazoned with a red ribbon—as if to suggest that sexiness will win the confrontation against the stigma and fear attached to the disease. Further suggesting the sexual "battleground," XXX was boldly printed on the stage, serving as the foundation on which the dances took place.

An early, sexually charged number that year was "Rain," by Madonna. Men in bathrobes dance seductively together to the sensually slow song. The bathrobes are soon reduced to towels, creating an atmosphere evocative of the bathhouse, yet viewed through a lens of nostalgia. The choreographic link to the present may be perceived through the fact that the men never actually touch one another. Their yearning is palpable, but physical separation is always maintained, creating an aura of isolation within the large group of physically attractive young men dancing the number. The lyrics to the popular contemporary song also reflect the cultural moment of the dance; the chorus expresses a feeling shared across the stage:

> *Rain, wash away my sorrow*
> *Take away my pain*
> *Your love's coming down like rain*

The sense of loss is escalated through the song's lyrics for the performed dance in Broadway Bares. The lyrics of "Rain" continue in a verse that reflects the loss felt by each individual on stage and in the audience, underscoring a shared desire to end the epidemic:

> *When you looked into my eyes*
> *And you said goodbye could you see my tears*

> *When I turned the other way*
> *Did you hear me say*
> *I'd wait for all the dark clouds bursting in a perfect sky*
> *You promised me when you said goodbye*
> *That you'd return when the storm was done*
> *And now I'll wait for the light, I'll wait for the sun*
> *Till I feel your* [rain].

Lyrics work with music and choreography to evoke – and capture – an emotional response at the heart of the Broadway cultural community.

In another number, "Fever," the relationship between past, present, and future alters its meaning, perhaps inadvertently. Mitchell, often inspired by music, selected the song for its sex appeal—an aspect certainly emphasized by the sultry choreography and alluring costume worn by dancer Cynthia Rubia and designed by Kevin Draves. "It was just really sexy," Mitchell recalls. "I love that number. It was probably that classy, sort of burlesque-Vegas strip."[56] Even within this classic form, coupled with the song lyrics of "Fever," the choreography of this number suggested contagion and dying linked to sexual intimacy. Several bare chested men in form fitting black pants part ways for Rubia as she struts toward the audience to begin the number. Group by group they mimic her steady kicks, falling into a phalanx behind her before she parts them with one powerful gesture. In the dance that follows, the men channel sexual energy toward her with their focused attention and movements as she leads and dominates them. She begins a pattern and one by one they replicate it as if to suggest contagion. The men then form a ring around Rubia with their arms overlapping, supporting one another as they ease their way to the ground as one unit. Their pelvises rise as she begins a slow, classic strip tease in the middle of the circle. One by one, she moves between the men as they take their turn in a featured dance with her until they all join in, removing more layers of clothing for her until she is suddenly lifted above their heads in a horizontal position. After she is set down, the men move nearly in unison once more behind her until the final moments of the song when they lift her up to the waiting arms of two bare chested men waiting for her in a window opening above the stage, evocative of an ascent to others waiting to receive her in heaven.

With feverish night sweats as a widely known symptom of HIV, the interplay between the song's lyrics and the cultural moment further conjoins sex appeal with contemporary dangers:

> *You give me fever*
> *When you kiss me*
> *Fever when you hold me tight*
> *Fever*
> *In the morning*
> *Fever all through the night*
> *. . .*
> *Everybody's got the fever*
> *That is something you all know*
> *Fever isn't such a new thing*
> *Fever started long ago.*

These lyrics, paired with the number's choreography, present layers of meaning, recognizing associated symptoms of HIV while celebrating the sexiness of physical intimacy.

With its celebratory significance, Broadway Bares has always offered a message from, within, and directed toward its community to bring about an end to the damaging associations between sexual expression and stigmatized death. The penultimate act of Broadway Bares III is a prime example. The act consists of two men in street clothes (sweat shirts, shorts, and sneakers), costumes in sharp contrast to the overtly sexy, elaborately designed costumes of other acts. Providing the cheering audience with this means of immediate identification, the performers gradually strip one another to dance belts and perform sensual, acrobatic feats that suggest distorted sexual acts, their movements growing synchronized and culminating in the suggestions of a stylized orgasm, followed by a lingering kiss that delighted the vocal audience. The men look out to the audience, still embracing one another, and then, as if having made a decision, slowly part together while holding hands, through the mylar curtain as the cheering audience erupts into applause.

This number reaches heightened significance because the song, "Don't Give Up," immediately follows as the finale. Danced by a group of stripping newspaper boys, the focus is placed on a featured dancer whose primary prop is a messenger bag boldly emblazoned with a red ribbon. The images and gestures within the dance communicate a message of hope and a call to spread the word, made all the more powerful through subversion: newspapers so regularly spread stories that propagate fear of HIV like those discussed earlier. At the end of the act, the full company, many undressed and many wearing large Broadway Bares t-shirts, joins the newsboys. This continued shift away from stylized costumes provides a somewhat alienating effect, reminding the audience that they have been watching a performance with the reality of the epidemic waiting for them just beyond the club walls. However, the go-go dance continues to the refrain, "hold on, don't give up," further suggesting that the celebration of sexual expression need not be lost with the end of the show. This dance culminates in a message of hope as the company forms a final tableau of flesh wrapped in an enormous sheath of red ribbon.

Evolving with an Epidemic

If creator Jerry Mitchell directed Broadway Bares in response to his own experience of the epidemic, then so, too, did Denis Jones, his successor.[57] Jones explains, "By the time I had arrived on Broadway [in 1996], I felt like with the amount of education that was out there and already the amount of treatment that was out there, [the AIDS epidemic] seemed to be less in the public eye." Indeed, messages found within the show have evolved from the promotion of safe sex and intimacy in the era of AIDS to more generalized themes of the importance of love over sex (Broadway Bares XVII) and the idea that "it's okay to have questions, it's okay to feel like an outsider, 'cause there are all kinds of outsiders out there" (Broadway Bares XVIII). Jones notes that such themes don't "directly relate to the epidemic, but they . . . have a larger sort of relevance in the context of the event—I love to turn people on. I want to get people all sexed up. That's the nature of the game. That's what we do. But there's an opportunity to communicate a larger idea." [58] That larger idea evolved as the epidemic reached its peak, a breakthrough, and a consequent turning point in public consciousness.

Alongside its enduring celebration of sexual expression and fantasy, the Broadway Bares of 1995 offered some of the most somber choreography of the philanthroproduction's history.

The FDA approved protease inhibitors, medications that would alter the course of the epidemic in the United States (and would greatly lessen the presence of AIDS within popular public consciousness) with its wide release the following year. The consequent "Lazarus Effect" as it was described, offered life to HIV-positive individuals and gave new hope for long-term survival.

The darkness before that dawn finds synchronous representation within the 1995 edition of Broadway Bares, which is especially important when one considers its economic component. To be in attendance that year and thus contributing financially to that new hope was surely significant. Leading up to this breakthrough, however, people living with HIV were still associated with tremendous suffering. Whether in newspaper and magazine articles about the epidemic or well-intended public awareness campaigns, popular media both reflected and *reinforced* the HIV-positive experience through iconography used to represent the depressed, isolated male, joining together image, connotation, and disease. Such imagery was even employed by the widely distributed advertising for *Angels in America, Part One: Millennium Approaches*,[59] noted in press coverage for being a play "about AIDS."

This image also appears in a number for the 1995 Broadway Bares, "I Don't Know How to Love Him," taken from Andrew Lloyd Webber's *Jesus Christ Superstar*, and, considering all of its signifying elements, the number provides the most direct commentary on the epidemic. A man, wearing only a sheet (signifying the bedroom and its accompanying activities), slowly crosses the stage and sits, providing the primary stage picture: that of an isolated man, sitting on a chair in a pose directly evocative of the image used to advertise *Millennium Approaches*. A female ballet dancer, Nina Goldman, wearing only a man's white tuxedo shirt, moves freely about the space, functioning in the number as his "muse en pointe," as Mitchell described her. While the man sits still, in isolation, pairs of male ballet dancers, first draped in white bed sheets and later wearing only fitted white briefs, dance together around him. "It was about them having intimate moments with each other and how it was either working for them or not working for them," Mitchell explains. One pair ends in a tender embrace before they separate and leave through different doors, evoking a sense of partners separated by AIDS-related death. The solitary man then rises with the bed sheet around his waist. Another man, his partner, emerges and removes the sheet from around the man, leaving him in white briefs. The partner then wraps the bed sheet around the man again but holds it out to the sides, evoking angels' wings. At this moment, in a marked change of facial expression, the man smiles peacefully. The partner then slides the man's underwear down, leaving him naked—but vulnerable rather than "sexy." They hold one another as other couples around the stage do the same. This embrace suggests the possibility of happiness and support through a disease so clearly associated with depression and isolation.

Considering the cultural climate of AIDS in 1995, the choreography of the number as well as the song's lyrics present a story of an HIV-positive man faced with a new loving relationship. Mitchell recalls, "It was taking that song which was written for a musical and [using] it for something completely different. The lyrics were so . . . If you'd asked someone to write a song for Broadway Bares—it could have been written for Broadway Bares *in that period*."[60] Indeed, the song seems to tell the commonly shared story of a previously confident and beautiful "swinger" struck by the disease and caught off guard by a newly formed emotional attachment to a man, perhaps HIV negative, whom he does not want to infect and hurt:

I don't know how to love him.
What to do, how to move him.
I've been changed, yes really changed.
In these past few days, when I've seen myself,
I seem like someone else.
I don't know how to take this.
I don't see why he moves me.
He's a man. He's just a man.
And I've had so many men before,
In very many ways,
He's just one more.
. . .
Yet, if he said he loved me,
I'd be lost. I'd be frightened.
I couldn't cope, just couldn't cope.
I'd turn my head. I'd back away.
I wouldn't want to know.
He scares me so.
I want him so.
I love him so.

It is important to note that unlike in most other numbers in Broadway Bares, in this number the musicians were made visible, drawing extra attention to the song itself. Billy Porter sang the song live on stage accompanied only by Mark Oka, who himself was apparently naked, playing a cello.[61] Patrice Pavis explains the impact of this staging choice:

> The decision to make musical sources visible, or on the other hand to conceal them, has significant repercussions in determining the nature of dynamic relations between the music and the rest of the mise-en-scène, particularly the space and the acting. It is not only a matter of the emotional influence of the music on the theater performance, but also of the impact of the stage on the music and the ways in which it is perceived.[62]

This staging of the number keeps the song's original, musical theater, context at a distance, thus allowing the song to take on a new layer of meaning through its performed signification. Because of its resonance, the inclusion of this dance within the context of Broadway Bares meaningfully contributes to a chronicle of the epidemic.

The same edition demonstrated marked determination to keep a sense of humor. In "Lick It," a man in pajamas goes to a refrigerator for a midnight snack. A cast of characters emerges from the refrigerator and he is stripped and turned into a hot fudge sundae. Mitchell explains, "it was just me wanting to be silly and fun and say 'You know what? Let's have *fun* with this, too. You can have *fun* having sex. Fantasies *do* happen. Fantasies are *good*'."[63] The number made an impression. In fact, years later, a man in line for another Broadway Bares installment excitedly recalled, "There was one a couple years ago—they had whipped cream and cherries and strawberries and they covered the guy in all the sauces—it was the hottest number."[64] The participants in Broadway Bares acknowledged the past experiences of the community even while reframing the experience of the contemporary moment, prompting not only survival, but quality of life, through the celebration of sexuality and the human body.

Further suggesting cultural synchronicity, while choreographers indeed captured the emotional trauma of this period, such numbers are now few and far between, resting only in the earliest years of Broadway Bares. Put another way, since the medical breakthrough of 1995, there has been a clear shift in the content and style of choreography seen within Broadway Bares. Most numbers offer sex appeal and a great deal of humor, even as they set out to recast light on the epidemic. As time passed, the perceived seriousness of the epidemic changed. The balance between past and present was weighed specifically in 2002, ten years after Broadway Bares debuted, when the theme of the show was "Doctor's Orders." Sensitivity coming from cultural knowledge generated through past trauma raised some concern for Denis Jones as he assumed the role of director.[65] Handed a theme built around a song and a recurring doctor/nurse routine, Jones recalls,

> I was kind of mortified when he told me that that's what we were doing ... I kind of thought "Oh God!" My knee-jerk was "what a terrible idea!" It just seemed so insensitive. . . it's one thing to have a burlesque show that raises money for AIDS organizations—I think that's fine and I think that it's so sexually charged—even so, raising money for a disease that is by and large transmitted sexually—I'm with it, I'm cool, I'm still fine, but then on top of it to have a medical theme—I just thought "My God, I can't believe this!"

Ultimately, Jones elected to stay far away from depicting situations that would feel familiar to those with vivid memories of hospital stays related to HIV. Instead, light and comedic numbers were built around cosmetic surgeries and Frankenstein-like fantasies. Jones acknowledged the elephant in the room, however, by inviting none other than sex-expert Dr. Ruth to appear toward the end of the evening to provide a brief message encouraging safe sex. The moment stands out from the burlesque comic exchanges and sexualized dance numbers. Jones recalls, "It was actually a 'hey guys, by the way, put on a condom.' It was simply stated. For that kind of theme it was fine—almost mandatory."[66] Such messaging has since become more subtle in its representation; yet the self-awareness of each production in its social context remains.

As the perceived sense of urgency surrounding AIDS has broadly diminished, the choreography of Broadway Bares has evolved to suit popular tastes and thereby serve the ultimate purpose of the philanthroproduction: to raise money for Broadway Cares/Equity Fights AIDS. Perhaps mirroring the decreased presence of the epidemic within the mainstream media, the performances within Broadway Bares now almost never directly address HIV. In fact, maintaining the sexual celebration of the show and perhaps reflecting renewed behavioral trends, numbers have sometimes suggested aggressive sexual promiscuity.[67] One such number in the 2009 Broadway Bares, "Click It," riffed on the phrase associated with internet and e-mail provider America Online, "you've got mail." A line of male dancers wearing ultimately nothing but mailboxes around their groin areas danced one by one with a suggestive and aggressive mail/male delivery man who seemed to surprise each one with a pelvic thrust to his backside.

The show continues to evolve and reflect the current sociopolitical conversations surrounding gay culture. Developed during a year of social and political upheaval leading up to the June 2012 performance, Broadway Bares XXII: Happy Endings offered a political emphasis that catered to the convictions of the largely gay and gay-friendly audience. Just after the previous Broadway Bares in 2011, gay marriage was legalized in New York State. The celebratory air clearly informed the production concept for the show ahead, which centered on the refrain of the opening number: "everyone deserves a happy ending." A white proscenium frames the stage, conspicuously less decorated than those from Broadway Bares of years past. A young man (Kyle Dean Massey) wonders if he'll ever find someone with whom to settle down, his true prince charming. His fairy godmother (Miriam Shor) appears and encourages him to read through a book of fairy tales to find his own happy ending. As should be expected, an evil step mother (played by Jennifer Tilly) appears, her evil nature signified by her dark costume and curses of marriage equality (met with thunderous booing from the audience). The philanthroproduction concludes with the young man finding his prince and Roseland ballroom is quickly transformed into a wedding chapel for the show's finale. The crowd of predominantly gay men and supporters alike warmly embraced the politically charged story arc. The emphasis on love and marriage, rather than on survival, made Broadway Bares the most politically charged it has been in years, but may have been so in order to make it all the more successful in its fundraising efforts. And successful it was: the 2012 Broadway Bares shattered fundraising records, making over one and a quarter million dollars for BC/EFA. While dancers received a letter from BC/EFA Executive Director Tom Viola emphasizing the history and present circumstances of living with HIV, AIDS was publicly mentioned only during rotation as the crowd was reminded why it was important to tip the dancers, just as they were reminded in the next breath to stand up and shout for marriage equality beyond New York.

Conclusion

As a performance genre, the philanthroproduction offers rich material for interdisciplinary analysis. Drawing on not only established forms of theater, dance, and music, it is also heavily informed by the economics, politics, and popular perceptions of the cause it supports. It is necessarily an artistic form with implicit social activism, and should be studied as such.

A leading example of the philanthroproduction, Broadway Bares has used song, dance, and comedic sketches to affect behavior and attitudes about the AIDS epidemic, raising money and awareness for its philanthropic cause while reflecting the changing medical, social, and political reality of the disease and those whose lives are affected by it. Through the creation of a joyous atmosphere that celebrates the human body and sexuality, Broadway Bares worked to diminish pervasive fears and continues to do so. Subverting early popular media messages condemning homosexuality and sexual expression, the event has affirmed cultural and political identity while affecting public attitudes toward mortality. Broadway Bares empowers those infected and *affected* by the disease to savor each moment as individuals and to take care of one another. As an event rooted in dance and theater, produced by and for the community, these philanthroproductions find their geographical and cultural location within the heart of Broadway, itself representing both territory and ideology within the performing arts landscape.

Notes

1. This chapter builds on and departs from my previous work concerning Broadway Bares, "Plagues and Performance: Broadway Bares as *Danse Macabre*," published in *Text and Presentation*, ed. Kiki Gounaridou (Boston: McFarland, 2010), and is developed from

my doctoral dissertation, "Beyond Angels: Broadway Theatre and the AIDS Epidemic, 1981–2006," advised by Barbara Wallace Grossman of Tufts University. I wish to thank my committee, Robert Vorlicky, Laurence Senelick, and Downing Cless, for their critical insights, and the American Society for Theatre Research for opportunities to share this work in various stages of development. This chapter is heavily informed by the insightful analysis of David Román in theater studies, David Gere in dance, and Sander Gilman in cultural iconography. I am indebted to BC/EFA Executive Director Tom Viola, former Producing Director Michael Grazziano, Jerry Mitchell, Denis Jones, and Peter Gregus, for candidly sharing their intentions and memories.

2. Philanthroproductions are thus distinct from benefit performances of extant Broadway productions. Far from unique to the AIDS epidemic, there is a long history of philanthroproductions, including those created to raise funds for the Red Cross during World War I. For an example, on October 15, 1917, a philanthroproduction raised $50,000 for the American Red Cross. The so-called pageant was served by a book at its core, included performances by John and Ethel Barrymore, and was professionally directed and designed. "The result was a pageant of rare beauty and dramatic worth, as well as of historic accuracy and patriotic inspiration." Describing the production, Evan Evans suggests its spine: "The Prologue announces the theme of the Pageant and calls upon the audience to follow her to the high court, where the Allied Nations plead their cause—the Court of Truth, Liberty and Justice." Each nation finds representation through a dance, dramatic scene, or musical interlude. The production closes as "America enters, saluting her allies, and pledging her sword to their common cause." See Evan Evans, "Red Cross Pageant," *Harper's Bazaar* 52 (December 1917): 54–55, 130.

3. Broadway performers, in addition to stars of opera and film, had come together before to raise money for AIDS charities; in 1985, stars performed in an event called "The Best of the Best," but the material performed was not created specifically for the event (though it should be noted that Stephen Sondheim provided new lyrics for "Together" for the event). Still, as "the brainchild of members of the Actors Equity Council who wanted their union to become involved with AIDS research," the event provided valuable inspiration for the philanthroproductions that soon followed. See Stephen Holden, "AIDS Benefit Show at the Met Opera," *New York Times*, November 4, 1985, http://www.nytimes.com/1985/11/04/arts/aids-benefit-show-at-the-met-opera.html?sec=health (accessed April 15, 2014).

4. Kim Klein, *Fundraising for Social Change* (San Francisco: Jossey-Bass, 2000), 89.

5. Ibid., 90.

6. Ibid., 89.

7. Ibid., 5.

8. Ibid.

9. Emily Barman, *Contesting Communities: The Transformation of Workplace Charity* (Stanford, CA: Stanford University Press, 2006), 5.

10. Ibid., 6. Howard Lune counters, "technically, there are no criteria for establishing the boundaries of a community, counting its members, or even knowing whether you yourself are a part of one. On the other hand, a community is real if the people in it see themselves as such." Howard Lune, *Urban Action Networks: HIV/AIDS and Community Organizing in New York City* (Lanham, MD: Rowman & Littlefield, 2006), 10. Lune provides an excellent overview of the organizations that emerged from the AIDS epidemic in New York City throughout the 1980s and early 1990s, arguing that "The scope and urgency of the crisis fostered an accelerated, strategically directed, and relatively unimpeded development of

community-based work" (12). I am confident that his work would prove pivotal to anyone pursuing further documentation of the formation and efforts of BC/EFA.

11. Barman, *Contesting Communities*, 7.

12. Despite its frequent association with commercialism, it is important to note that "Broadway" includes three nonprofit companies: Lincoln Center Theater, Manhattan Theater Club, and Roundabout Theater Company.

13. Jerry Mitchell, Interview by the author, 42nd Street Studios, New York City, August 20, 2008.

14. Denis Jones, Interview by the author, by telephone, August 31, 2008. Emphasis added.

15. Barman, *Contesting Communities*, 6.

16. Tom Viola and Joseph P. Benincasa, Interview by John VonSoosten and Howard Sherman, *Downstage Center*, episode 131, The American Theatre Wing, December 22, 2006, http://americantheatrewing.org/downstagecenter/detail/actors_fund_and_broadway_cares_equity_fights-aids (accessed May 10, 2009).

17. Ibid.

18. David Lotz, "Gypsy of the Year: Raises Astonishing $2,754,631 To Benefit Broadway Cares/ Equity Fights Aids." *Actors' Equity Association*. December 8, 2004. http://www.actorsequity.org/newsmedia/archive/04_12_8_GypsyRobeOfTheYear.html. (accessed April 15, 2014)

19. Viola and Benincasa, Interview.

20. Susan M. Chambré, "The HIV/AIDS Grants Economy in New York City, 1983–1992." *Health Affairs* 15, no. 3 (1996): 256.

21. Ibid.

22. Gregory M. Herek and Erik K. Glunt, "An Epidemic of Stigma: Public Reactions to AIDS," *American Psychologist* 43, no. 11 (1988): 890.

23. Although other events such as the annual flea market and grand auction continue to raise millions of dollars for BC/EFA, it is the philanthroproductions that most heavily inform public perceptions of the disease and the obligations of a community to respond.

24. Mitchell, Interview by the author.

25. Both the Easter Bonnet and Gypsy of the Year are fully produced each year (Gypsy in the fall, Bonnet in the spring) and bring in considerable additional funds through tickets sold to eager Broadway aficionados. Both comprise songs, original dances and comedic sketches; the primary difference is that the pieces comprising the Easter Bonnet competition culminate in the presentation of the often elaborate bonnets designed and hand-assembled by their casts and crews. The content of both philanthroproductions range from spoofs to dances conveying emotional artistry. The considerable production qualities that define them as philanthroproductions even catch the eye of critics. Matt Windman observed, "I won't lie—there is often more stunning work being done in the Gypsy of the Year or Easter Bonnet skits than you will find in many a Broadway season. That is not to say that all the skits are good—some are bores, like most of the dance stuff, or shamelessly self-promotional . . . but some are damn brilliant" (Windman). Both competitions mark the culmination of intensive six-week fundraising campaigns for BC/EFA conducted by the companies of primarily Broadway, but also off-Broadway and touring Broadway productions. Through curtain speeches, auctions, cabaret performances, the sale of autographed merchandise, and other creative endeavors, companies raise hundreds of thousands of dollars in the weeks leading up to the competition at the heart of the philanthroproduction. At the end of both philanthroproductions, awards are presented to the companies who raised the most money over the preceding six weeks as well as to

the best performance. Unique to the Easter Bonnet competition, additional awards are given to the best bonnets. The Gypsy of the Year competition, meanwhile, celebrates the chorus members of Broadway shows, and, as in the Easter Bonnet competition, company members devise and perform original numbers as they celebrate the previous six weeks of fundraising appeals for BC/EFA.

26. Judith A. Johnson, *AIDS Funding for Federal Government Programs: FY1981–FY1999 (CRS Report for Congress)*, Updated March 31, 1998. www.law.umaryland.edu/marshall/crsreports/.../96-293_SPR.pdf (accessed May 27, 2013).

27. Susan Sontag, *Illness as Metaphor and AIDS and Its Metaphors* (New York: Picador, 1990), 133.

28. Mitchell, Interview by the author.

29. Jerry Mitchell, "Sass, Class, and Ass," *Broadway Bares: Backstage Pass* (New York: Universe, 2008) 4.

30. Mitchell, Interview by the author.

31. Ibid.

32. Jerry Mitchell. "Jerry Mitchell: The Naked Truth about Broadway Bares." *Broadway.com*. http://www.broadway.com/gen/Buzz_Story.aspx?ci=549515 (accessed May 19, 2008).

33. The Roseland Ballroom hosted Broadway Bares from 2001–2013 until the historic building was closed permanently. In 2014 Broadway Bares was held at the Hammerstein Ballroom, where the philanthroproduction is set to be produced again in 2015.

34. Mitchell, Interview by the author.

35. Ibid., emphasis added.

36. Dennis Jones, Interview.

37. Ibid.

38. Jerry Mitchell, Interview by the author.

39. Jerry Mitchell, Interview with Duane Wells, "Sex on Stage: A Backstage Pass to Broadway Bares," *GayWired.com*, June 19, 2008, http://www.247gay.com/article.cfm?ArticlePage=1&Section=67&id=19338 (accessed May 15, 2009).

40. Denis Jones, Interview by the author.

41. Ibid., Emphasis added.

42. Mitchell, Interview with Wells.

43. Joël Bonnemaison, *Culture and Space: Conceiving a New Cultural Geography*, trans. Josée Pénot-Demetry (New York: I. B. Taurus, 2005), 59.

44. Denis Jones, Interview by the author.

45. Bonnemaison, 69.

46. Mitchell, Interview by the author.

47. Julia Kristeva provides useful analysis of the semiotics of gesture in *Desire in Language: A Semiotic Approach to Literature and Art*, trans. Thomas Gora (New York: Columbia University Press, 1980), further considered by Patrice Pavis in "Problems of a Semiology of Theatrical Gesture," *Poetics Today* 2, no. 3 (Spring 1981): 65–93.

48. Patrice Pavis, *Analyzing Performance: Theater, Dance, and Film*, trans. David Williams (Ann Arbor: University of Michigan Press, 2003), 140.

49. Mitchell, Interview by the author.

50. Kaiser Family Foundation, *Global HIV/AIDS Timeline*, http://www.kff.org/hivaids/timeline/hivtimeline.cfm (accessed May 15, 2009).

51. Gilman examined and categorized 700 posters from a collection of 3,500 images and 1,100 posters dealing specifically with AIDS and HIV infection at the National Library of Medicine at Bethesda, Maryland. Sander L. Gilman. *Diseases and Representation: Images of Illness from Madness to AIDS* (Ithaca, NY: Cornell University Press), 1988.

52. Ibid., 115.
53. Ibid., 116.
54. Jerry Falwell, quoted in Bill Press, "The Sad Legacy of Jerry Falwell," *Milford* (Mass.) *Daily News*, May 18, 2007.
55. David Gere, How to Make Dances in an Epidemic: Tracking Choreography in the Age of AIDS, Madison: University of Wisconsin Press, 2004, 14.
56. Mitchell, Interview by the author.
57. Jodi Moccia, Mitchell's longtime assistant, took over the reins for one year in 2004. Jones, however, directed the next four Broadway Bares productions.
58. Denis Jones, Interview by the author.
59. The angel in the poster design, encased in a golden halo, signifies goodness, a blessing, and the afterlife—connotations which themselves were far removed from the popular media's negative portrayal of the disease. The angel's body position, however, subverts the positive message through its suggestion of weeping and/or depression. Although it may have been far from the designer's intention, the imagery used to advertise the first part of *Angels in America* reinforces the association between AIDS, isolation and depression, which had become common visual tropes. Nevertheless, the depiction of an angel served as a powerful graphic counterpart to the conservative right's loudly voiced stance that people with AIDS are sinners who brought the disease on themselves.
60. Mitchell, Interview by the author.
61. The cello's uniquely somber and mournful tones have been noted by many composers In the realm of musical theater, this link may have been made most memorably by Stephen Sondheim, who, in *A Little Night Music*, provides the extremely serious Henrik with a cello to vent his sexual and emotional longing.
62. Pavis, 141.
63. Mitchell, Interview by the author.
64. Unidentified man. "Burlesque Is Back." *Broadway Beat*. www.broadwayworld.com. (accessed April 10, 2009)
65. Jerry Mitchell continues to serve as executive producer of Broadway Bares but devotes most of his energy to additional production work. He recently directed and choreographed *Kinky Boots* and *Legally Blonde: The Musical* and choreographed *Catch Me If You Can, Dirty Rotten Scoundrels*, and many other Broadway productions.
66. Jones, Interview by the author.
67. In December 2008, Richard Wolitski, acting director of the Division of HIV/AIDS Prevention at the Centers for Disease Control and Prevention, attributed an increase in infection rates among gay men to "'prevention fatigue,' confidence in new antiretroviral drugs, the use of methamphetamines and the arrival of a generation of young men who did not experience the ravages of the 1980s." Ceci Connoly, "Renewed AIDS Threat Seen in Gay Community," *Washington Post*, August 8, 2008, http://www.boston.com/news/world/latinamerica/articles/2008/08/08/renewed_aids_threat_seen_in_gay_community (accessed April 10, 2009).

BIBLIOGRAPHY

Adler, Steven. *On Broadway: Art and Commerce on the Great White Way*. Carbondale: Southern Illinois University Press, 2004.
Aronowitz, Stanley. "Forward." In *Performance as Political Act: The Embodied Self*, by Randy Martin, vii–xii. New York: Bergin and Garvey, 1990.

Barman, Emily. *Contesting Communities: The Transformation of Workplace Charity.* Stanford, CA: Stanford University Press, 2006.

Bonnemaison, Joël. *Culture and Space: Conceiving a New Cultural Geography.* Translated by Josée Pénot-Demetry. New York: I. B. Taurus, 2005.

Broadway Cares/Equity Fights AIDS. *Easter Bonnet Competition.* http://www.broadwaycares.org/easterbonnet2014.

Chambré, Susan M. *Fighting for Our Lives: New York's AIDS Community and the Politics of Disease.* New Brunswick, NJ: Rutgers University Press, 2006.

Connoly, Ceci. "Renewed AIDS Threat Seen in Gay Community." *The Washington Post,* August 8, 2008. http://www.boston.com/news/world/latinamerica/articles/2008/08/08/renewed_aids_threat_seen_in_gay_community.

Crimp, Douglas. "AIDS: Cultural Analysis/Cultural Activism." *October* 43 (1987): 3–16.

———. *Cultural Analysis/Cultural Activism.* Boston: MIT Press, 1988.

———. *Melancholia and Moralism: Essays on AIDS and Queer Politics.* Cambridge, MA: MIT Press, 2002.

Crimp, Douglas, and Adam Rolston. *AIDS Demo/graphics.* Seattle: Bay Press, 1990.

Evans, Evan. "Red Cross Pageant." *Harper's Bazaar* 52 (December 1917): 54–55, 130.

Gere, David. *How to Make Dances in an Epidemic: Tracking Choreography in the Age of AIDS.* Madison: University of Wisconsin Press, 2004.

Gilman, Sander L. *Disease and Representation: Images of Illness from Madness to AIDS.* Ithaca, NY: Cornell University, 1988.

———. *Picturing Health and Illness: Images of Identity and Difference.* Baltimore: Johns Hopkins University Press, 1995.

Herek, Gregory M., and Erik K. Glunt. "An Epidemic of Stigma: Public Reactions to AIDS." *American Psychologist* 43, no. 11 (1988): 886–91.

Holden, Stephen. "AIDS Benefit Show at the Met Opera." *New York Times,* November 4, 1985. http://www.nytimes.com/1985/11/04/arts/aids-benefit-show-at-the-met-opera.html?sec=health.

Johnson, Judith A. *AIDS Funding for Federal Government Programs: FY1981–FY1999 (CRS Report for Congress),* Updated March 31, 1998. Accessed 27 May, 2013. www.law.umaryland.edu/marshall/crsreports/.../96-293_SPR.pdf.

Jones, Denis. Telephone interview with the author. August 31, 2008.

Kaiser Family Foundation. *Global HIV/AIDS Timeline.* http://www.kff.org/hivaids/timeline/hivtimeline.cfm.

Klein, Kim. *Fundraising for Social Change.* San Francisco: Jossey-Bass, 2000.

Kristeva, Julia. *Desire in Language: A Semiotic Approach to Literature and Art.* Translated by Thomas Gora. New York: Columbia University Press, 1980.

Lotz, David. "Gypsy of the Year: Raises Astonishing $2,754,631 To Benefit Broadway Cares/Equity Fights Aids." *Actors' Equity Association.* December 8, 2004. http://www.actorsequity.org/newsmedia/archive/04_12_8_GypsyRobeOfTheYear.html.

Lune, Howard. *Urban Action Networks: HIV/AIDS and Community Organizing in New York City.* Lanham, MD: Rowman & Littlefield, 2006.

Mitchell, Jerry, ed. *Broadway Bares: Backstage Pass.* New York: Universal, 2008.

———. Interview by the author. August 20, 2008, 42nd Street Studios, New York City.

Mitchell, Jerry. Interview by Duane Wells. *247gay.com,* June 19, 2008. http://www.247gay.com/article.cfm?ArticlePage=1&Section=67&id=19338.

———. (April 2, 2008) (transcript). *An Interview with "Step It Up & Dance"'s Jerry Mitchell*. Interview with John Polly. *AfterElton*. http://www.afterelton.com/people/2008/4/ jerrymitchell?page=0%2C2. Retrieved 2009-01-27.

———. Interview by John von Soosten and Howard Sherman. *Downstage Center*. May 11, 2007. http://www.americantheatrewing.org/downstagecenter/detail/jerry_mitchell (accessed May 10, 2009).

———. "Jerry Mitchell: The Naked Truth about Broadway Bares." *Broadway.com*. http://www. broadway.com/gen/Buzz_Story.aspx?ci=549515.

Pavis, Patrice. *Analyzing Performance: Theater, Dance, and Film*. Translated by David Williams. Ann Arbor: University of Michigan Press, 2003.

———. "Problems of a Semiology of Theatrical Gesture," *Poetics Today* 2, no. 3 (Spring 1981): 65–93.

Román, David. *Acts of Intervention: Performance, Gay Culture, and AIDS*. Bloomington: Indiana University Press, 1998.

———. " 'It's My Party and I'll Die If I Want To!' Gay Men, AIDS, and the Circulation of Camp in U.S. Theatre." *Theatre Journal* 44, no. 3 (1992): 305–27.

———. "Not about AIDS." *GLQ: A Journal of Lesbian and Gay Studies* 6, no. 1 (2000): 1–28.

———. "Performing All Our Lives: AIDS, Performance, Community." In *Critical Theory and Performance*, edited by Janelle Reinelt and Joe Roach, 208–21. Ann Arbor: University of Michigan Press, 1992.

Sontag, Susan. *Illness as Metaphor and AIDS and Its Metaphors*. New York: Picador, 1990.

Treichler, Paula. "AIDS, Africa, and Cultural Theory." *Transition* 51 (1991): 86–103.

———. "AIDS, Gender, and Biomedical Discourse: Current Contests for Meaning." In *AIDS: The Burdens of History*, edited by Elizabeth Fee and Daniel M. Fox. Berkeley: University of California Press, 1988.

———. *How to Have Theory in an Epidemic: Cultural Chronicles of AIDS*. Durham, NC: Duke University Press, 1999.

Viola, Tom, and Joseph P. Benincasa. Interview by John VonSoosten and Howard Sherman. *Downstage Center*. The American Theatre Wing. December 22, 2006.

Windman, Matt. "Gypsy of the Year—Monday Afternoon at the New Amsterdam." *A.M. New York*, quoted in *The Leonard Bernstein Forums*, January 1, 2008. http://bernstein.client-sandbox.com/forums/viewtopic.php?p=4611&sid= a001406ac4785e2269a7ee6620f6c03f.

CHAPTER 44

···

DANCE AND THE PLAGUE
Epidemic Choreomania and Artaud

···

MICHAEL LUEGER

ANTONIN Artaud's "Theatre and the Plague" begins with an anecdote of a Sardinian viceroy who supposedly averted an outbreak of the plague because he had communicated with the approaching pestilence in a dream. So forewarned, he prevented the ship that would have brought the disease to his shores from docking. The story helps Artaud to establish some of the metaphorical similarities between his ideal theater and the actual plague, as well as his skepticism about the germ theory of contagion, which had become well established by the time he first delivered this manifesto in lecture form.[1] Artaud seems to have been unaware of another historical phenomenon, almost as obscure as his Sardinian anecdote but possessing a much more literal correspondence to the notion of theater as a spreading plague capable of overturning established social order and bringing to light the hidden desires and fears of those affected by it. This phenomenon was epidemic choreomania, often referred to as the dancing plague. In its most extreme manifestations, epidemic choreomania affected hundreds (perhaps thousands) of people in one place at the same time, causing them to dance in public uncontrollably for days or even weeks on end. Since attempts to categorize and explain this strange illness first began in the mid-nineteenth century, it has hitherto been treated primarily as a subject for medical and psychological discourse. In this chapter, I will attempt to examine epidemic choreomania as performance—indeed, I will question whether such a bizarre occurrence can even be properly deemed a performance. I will also seek to investigate how it speaks to Artaud's notion of theater-as-plague, particularly with regard to some of the less progressive and more disturbing potential implications and uses of Artaud's theories. Simply stated, epidemic choreomania can be seen as a phenomenon by which bodies in motion expressed not so much a desire for social or political liberation as a call for the renewed efficacy of more traditional forms of authority and control.

It is first necessary to briefly review the medical literature on this phenomenon in order to define precisely what I mean by the phrase "epidemic choreomania." The disorder shares a number of attributes with phenomena ranging from trance performance in Bali to religious revivals in America, and many of the most important accounts of epidemic choreomania treat it within this wider context rather than as a unique case. Furthermore, the very definition of choreomania is somewhat slippery: Isolated instances of small outbreaks appear in medieval European chronicles, in nineteenth-century travelers' accounts of Ethiopia, and perhaps most famously in the roots of the tarantella, which seems to have originated in southern Italy as either an effect of or cure for (perhaps both simultaneously) the bite of a reputedly poisonous spider. As with the tarantella, a number of instances of choreomania that may have begun as spontaneous occurrences gradually evolved into something with a more rigid set of rules governing its appearance and manifestation, particularly in the decades after the last epidemic European outbreak in 1518. Finally, choreomania should not be confused with chorea, which entails the inability to control one's movements and stems from altogether different causes. Although past accounts of choreomania have tried to make the case that it represented a massive manifestation of either chorea or some other purely physical cause such as a symptom of ergotism, these theories are now generally discredited as possible causes of choreomania in both individuals and on an epidemic scale.

I am adopting the definition of choreomania used by one of the most recent medical articles on the phenomenon, which draws on earlier accounts to define "the essential features of the disorder" in the following terms:

> [Choreomania] could occur sporadically or in epidemics; it was a psychophysical disease distinguishable from modern chorea, and from organic nervous diseases; it was always characterised by an uncontrollable impulse to dance, and a morbid love of music; physical contact with an affected person was not a prerequisite for contracting the disease (the sight or sound of someone already affected could be sufficient); in its epidemic form the attack was generally preceded by premonitory nervous symptoms; and the disease was commonly manifest by physical symptoms, including death.[2]

It is the epidemic form of choreomania in which I am almost exclusively interested here, primarily because its sheer scale and the way it spread makes its connection with Artaud's plague-theater—as well as the underlying social and political conditions that helped to cause it—much clearer. This means that Tarantism and the smaller-scale manifestations of choreomania in medieval Europe and Ethiopia, while nonetheless fascinating, are beyond the present scope of this essay. Instead, I will focus on the three historical instances of epidemic choreomania that represent the major outbreaks of the disorder in its most pronounced form and which are indeed worthy of the title of "dancing plagues."

There is an immediate and obvious parallel between Artaud's idealized plague and epidemic choreomania in that both contagions are "a kind of psychic entity" rather than the result of some purely physical cause such as germs, which Pasteur's theory had established as the source of disease.[3] Furthermore, epidemic choreomania, like Artaud's ideal theater and "like the plague, is a delirium and is communicative."[4] Artaud's notion of plague as an entity able to both communicate and infect at long distance and through nonmechanistic means occasionally chimes with J. F. C. Hecker's classic account of the history of dancing plagues in an eerily resonant manner: The German physician describes a "morbid sympathy" that leads to a malady "propagated by the sight of the sufferers" and by means of which "[s]ecret desires were excited."[5] Indeed, Stanton Garner's exploration of Artaud's attitude toward germ theory notes that he was sympathetic toward "pre-modern (and pre-scientific) views of the bubonic plague" whereby the disease "was understood in terms of divine intervention."[6] The medieval and early modern European victims of epidemic choreomania would have found such a notion quite familiar.

Although isolated instances of choreomania appear in European chronicles starting from the early eleventh century,[7] the first epidemic case occurred in 1374. This was perhaps the most geographically widespread of all recorded cases, extending from the foot of the Alps down through the Rhine Valley to modern-day Belgium. The chronicler Peter of Herental described what transpired:

> At that time . . . a strange sect, comprising men and women, from various parts of Germany, came to Aachen, and they went as far as Hennegau and France. This was their condition. Both men and women were abused by the devil to such a degree that they danced in their homes, in the churches and in the streets, holding each other's hands and leaping in the air. While they danced they called out the names of demons, such as Friskes and others, but they were unaware of this nor did they pay attention to modesty even though people watched them. At the end of the dance, they felt such pains in their chest, that if their friends did not tie linen clothes tightly around their waists, they cried out like madmen that they were dying. In Liège they were freed of their demons by means of exorcisms such as those employed before baptism. Those who were cured said that they seemed to have been dancing in a river of blood, which is why they jumped into the air.[8]

This brief account is important for our purposes, as it introduces a number of elements that would recur in the major dancing plagues and which I will deal with in due course. Obviously, dancing was the choreomaniacs' primary activity, but as Peter of Herental mentions, some dancing occurred in their homes, raising the issue of what is at stake when such an event brings crowds of people out into public to enact their inner conflicts. In addition, the mention of the dancers calling on demons without being aware of their doing so raises a number of questions, as does the use of exorcisms to bring the dancing to an end.

The next epidemic manifestation of choreomania occurred in Strasbourg in 1518. This is perhaps the best-documented of the major outbreaks because it occurred at the beginning of that era we now tend to refer to as "early modern." It was also the last major outbreak in Europe. Indeed, the Strasbourg outbreak is so well documented that we can identify the first victim of the dancing plague by name: Frau Troffea, a woman of lower-class status who began to dance uncontrollably for six days beginning on July 14, 1518.[9] Her affliction quickly spread, with one family chronicle reporting thirty-four people affected by July 18, and possibly as many as four hundred within four weeks.[10] At the height of the outbreak, as many as two hundred people may have been dancing at any one time in the guildhalls and marketplaces, which the town council had designated for them in an ill-conceived attempt to confine the disorder.[11] The casualties began to mount, with the highest contemporary estimate claiming some fifteen deaths every day. The figure seems high, but historian John Waller claims that it is not inconceivable that this was indeed the toll during the few days that constituted the peak of the plague. If we accept that figure in tandem with the high-end estimate of some four hundred individuals overall who were affected by the disorder, he says, "then there could certainly have been several dozen deaths" as a result of the dancing plague.[12] Throughout this crisis, the city council made a number of disastrous decisions that actually fueled the spread of the plague, and it was not until August 10 that they managed to bring the epidemic under control by decreeing a general penance and arranging for the dancers to be brought to a nearby shrine of St. Vitus, where a ritual was performed that managed to bring the surviving dancers out of their state of seeming possession.[13]

The Strasbourg dancing plague may have been the last outbreak of epidemic choreomania in Europe, but one final case that occurred in Madagascar in 1863 presents some striking parallels with the two European epidemics—as well as some intriguing differences. This case also presents something of a problem for the historian, as our primary source for it comes from an article in the *Edinburgh Medical Journal* for July to December of 1867 written by Dr. Andrew Davidson, who had witnessed the outbreak but processed it through some marked biases. Known as the Imanenjana, the Malagasy dancing plague began with rumors in the capital of disturbances in the outlying villages in February; by March, dancers had practically taken over the streets in the capital and spread all over the island.[14] Davidson observed that

> The patients usually complained of a weight or pain in the praecordia, and great uneasiness, sometimes a stiffness about the nape of the neck . . . . [T]hey became increasingly restless and nervous, and if excited in any way, more especially if they happened to hear the sound of music or singing, they got perfectly uncontrollable, and, bursting away from all restraint, escaped from their pursuers, and joined the music, when they danced sometimes for hours on end with amazing rapidity . . . They thus danced to the astonishment of all, as if possessed by some evil spirit, and, with almost superhuman endurance, exhausting the patience of the musicians . . . then fell down suddenly, as if dead . . . After being completely exhausted in this way, the patients were taken home, the morbid impulse apparently in many cases destroyed. Sometimes the disease, thus stopped, never recurred; but more frequently there was a return.[15]

The symptoms described in Davidson's article bear some obvious correspondences to the accounts of choreomaniacs in the medieval chronicles, such as the complaints of pain (albeit preliminary ones in this case), the rapid spread of the disorder through sight or even sound, and the amazing endurance displayed by the dancers. There are other parallels with the European cases, having to do with the sociopolitical background to the dancing plagues, which we will consider in due course.

Obviously, one must approach these varying accounts of the different outbreaks with differing degrees of skepticism. The Strasbourg outbreak seems to be the only European one documented by multiple reliable sources, and some of the claims made in records of the earlier medieval cases are most likely exaggerated, such as the story of the crowd of five thousand choreomaniacs who supposedly camped around a chapel in the forest outside of Trier in search of a cure. As for Davidson's account of the Madagascar outbreak, one must keep in mind that, as a Westerner and particularly as a missionary, he was not necessarily in a position to appreciate or fully comprehend the rich cultural and historical backdrop to the Imanenjana. Nevertheless, the fact that, at least in the case of the European episodes of choreomania, the same phenomenon kept recurring within a limited geographic area (the Rhine River valley) suggests that there was some collective cultural memory of an event that, however distorted and exaggerated it might have been in the intervening years, had actually occurred. Indeed, as we shall see, the fact that these earlier episodes may have been wildly exaggerated may well have made later outbreaks all the more potent.

These three cases of epidemic choreomania bring us to the question of whether or not this phenomenon can be treated as "performance," an admittedly slippery term for which I have chosen to adopt Erving Goffman's definition of "all the activity of an individual which occurs during a period marked by his continuous presence before a particular set of observers and which has some influence on the observers."[16] It may be worthwhile here to once again point out that the dancing plagues have often been discussed as historical instances of larger phenomena ranging from religious revival meetings to lycanthropy; obviously, not everything that falls on this spectrum necessarily meets the criteria of a performance. Rather than attempt to draw any pat conclusions by attempting to shoehorn epidemic choreomania into the framework of any one theory, I will instead merely attempt to outline some of the general attributes of its major manifestations in 1374, 1518, and 1863 as a way of establishing some parallels with phenomena from other cultures that are already widely accepted as performance. I will begin by briefly considering the sort of dances performed by the choreomaniacs in all three major cases.

There are few detailed descriptions of the sort of dances performed by those affected by the 1374 and 1518 dancing plagues. E. Louis Backman's useful (if notably flawed) account of the history of the choreomania notes that both of these major outbreaks included a common folk dance referred to as "two-and-one," in which a single woman is flanked by two men.[17] He points to a number of examples from artists of the seventeenth century who illustrated this dance, most notably Pieter Brueghel the Elder, whose sketch of a smaller-scale outbreak of choreomania in the 1560s depicts a number of women dancing in a state of what seems like a combination of rapture and agony. Each woman is flanked by two men, one to each side, with a number of musicians interspersed among them. This depiction points to the fact that cases of choreomania came to be associated most frequently with women, as well as the channeling of the disorder into a more regular form that gave the dancers (or at least their friends and family members) some control over delivering themselves from their delirious state. In addition, the center-right trio's dance seems to involve some degree of skipping or hopping, bringing to mind Peter of Herental's description of the leaping choreomaniacs of 1374.

Andrew Davidson provides a description of the Malagasy dancers that he witnessed in 1863:

> They moved the head from side to side with a monotonous motion, and the hands, in the same way, alternately up and down. The dancers never joined in the singing, but frequently uttered a deep sighing sound. The eyes were wild, and the whole countenance assumed an indescribable, abstracted expression, as if their attention was completely taken off what was going on around them. The dancing was regulated very much by the music, which was always the quickest possible—it never seemed to be quick enough. It often became more of a leaping than a dancing.[18]

Without getting too far into the details of the particular dances or trying to draw misleading parallels between the leaping observed in both the European or Malagasy dancers, I believe it is sufficient to note here that in all three cases the dancers were actually dancing, not merely moving about at random or in some other uncontrolled fashion that would be indicative of a purely physiological affliction. Certainly the Malagasy dancers (if Davidson's account is to be taken as largely accurate) all seem to have been performing the same dance, one that worked in tandem with the music being played at the site of the dance.

Although the dances that took place in each of these cases were preexisting dances that were presumably associated with happier, more festive times, there was, as John Waller notes, "nothing even remotely pleasurable in the dancing plague. Chroniclers tell us that those who were momentarily roused from their trances [a word I will return to in a moment] screamed for help from bystanders, God, and the saints."[19] Certainly the dancers of 1374 described by Peter of Herental, with their complaints of severe pain and their frequent invocation of frightening devils, do not seem to have enjoying themselves. These observations call to mind Gregory Bateson's often-quoted "Theory of Play and Fantasy," which posits a metacommunicative dimension to playful activity that signals that, "These actions in which we now engage do not denote what those actions *for which they stand* would denote."[20] The intriguing thing about the dancing plague is that the reactions of those who suffered from it seem to provide a sort of mirror image of Bateson's paradigmatic statement. Dancing, an activity which the inhabitants of medieval and early modern Germany would generally have considered playful, suddenly began occurring in a context that seems to have signaled to its audience the precise opposite: "this is *not* play." This fact calls to mind Bateson's acknowledgment of the oftentimes slippery nature of play, in which the play frame can break down and suddenly become deadly serious. It may also be appropriate to refer to Goffman's notion of the "front," which is "that part of the individual's performance which regularly functions in a general and fixed fashion to define the situation for those who observe the performance."[21] The fact that the dancers' actions were not apparently undertaken voluntarily, and indeed represented something far more serious than the merriment one would normally associate with a large number of people performing a folk-dance in a public space, serves to further complicate the question of just how we can approach epidemic choreomania in terms of its being a performance.

One way of further sharpening our understanding of the dancing plagues as performances comes from the apparent consensus in recent scholarly literature on their immediate cause: trance. Judith Becker defines trance "as a bodily event characterized by strong emotion, intense focus, the loss of the strong sense of self" and as "an event that accesses types of knowledge and experience which are inaccessible in nontrance events, and which are felt to be ineffable, not easily described or spoken of."[22] As a corollary to this loss of a sense of self, "Many trances involve the penetration or invasion of the body by another self, an alien spirit, the 'Holy Spirit,' a deity or devil."[23] Trance can also endow individuals with incredible endurance, something that would adequately account for the amazing anecdote—recorded by Felix Platter and mentioned by Davidson in his preliminary overview of the history of choreomania—of one Strasbourg dancer who "continued [dancing] above four weeks, when she fell down exhausted, and was carried to an hospital where she recovered."[24]

The prevalence in medieval and early modern Europe of belief in the possibility of possession by either demons or vengeful, disapproving saints was widespread, and it seems the most likely explanation for the epidemics that occurred in both 1374 and 1518, as well as numerous smaller outbreaks at other times. St. Vitus' dance is a disorder with which we are still familiar today, and it was widely believed that that saint could and did curse people to dance uncontrollably. As Waller notes, "In times of acute hardship, with physical and mental distress leaving people more than usually suggestible, his [St. Vitus'] specter could quickly return. All it then took was for one or a few people, believing themselves to have been cursed by St. Vitus, to slip into a hysterical trance. Then they would unconsciously act out the part of the accursed: dancing wildly and uncontrollably for days on end."[25] Further, the state of trance would render the dancers oblivious to the need for food, water, and rest, which would account in large part for the high casualty figures in the Strasbourg outbreak.

With regard to the Madagascar case, Davidson's description of the dancers' "indescribable, abstracted expression" would seem to indicate that they were in a similar though not necessarily identical state. Without delving too deeply into the nuances and potential pitfalls of intercultural comparisons, it is worth remembering that each of these discrete instances of epidemic choreomania, and indeed of trance phenomena in general, share certain similarities but are ultimately uniquely determined by the culture in which they appear. As Becker notes, "Trance experiences are socially constructed and personally experienced within a particular religious cosmology which encourages some kinds of feelings and some kinds of bodily attitudes, and constrains others. Trance processes are embedded within worldviews . . . and interpreted by the trancer in a way that is congruent with the understanding of her social group."[26] Although the similarities between each of these particular cases of epidemic choreomania make it worthwhile to study them in relation to each other, Becker's observation is a useful caveat to keep in mind.

The note of caution on comparing the states of trance experienced by the European and Malagasy dancers brings up some important points about how other cultures' traditions regarding trance can be helpful when compared with the dancing plagues. Jane Belo's observations on "Trance Experience in Bali" offers some important clues as to why the European outbreaks seem to have been particularly deadly, while the choreomaniacs in Madagascar do not seem to have suffered such widespread harm. Belo notes that

> trancers in any individual culture learn to perform from each other, they observe the trance behavior of their fellows before they ever themselves fall into trance—hence the distinct cultural patterning of the behavior in the somnambulistic states—and, when they are themselves asked to describe their feelings, they cannot help giving answers based upon their observation of their fellows and the conception of the trance phenomena accepted by the culture.[27]

The Balinese audiences share this "conception of trance phenomena" and help to shape the trajectory of the individual trancer's experience by singing, goading on the trancer, and by finally restraining him and allowing him to work his way out of the trance. All of this, as Becker observes at the very beginning of her book, "is practiced within a communal framework."[28] It would seem that the European dancers' problem was that they belonged to a culture whose belief in possession could lead to spontaneous manifestations of trance but which had not developed any prescribed means of bringing dancers either into or out of the state. In both the 1374 and 1518 outbreaks, the initial cases seem to have had a suggestive power that soon resulted in hundreds of people being afflicted with the urge to dance nonstop, largely oblivious to what they were doing. By contrast, even though the epidemic in Madagascar overtook a significant portion of the island, Davidson notes that the "few cases of death" which did occur only did so "when the patient was restrained from joining in the dances."[29] This observation tracks with Lesley Sharp's more contemporary research on Malagasy spirit possession, which finds that, "Should a person show signs of . . . possession, she must accept it, for if she resists the spirit, it may cause her great physical harm."[30] The crucial difference was that the Malagasy already possessed a tradition of trance performance which presumably gave them a context even for such a large and apparently unprecedented outbreak of choreomania as the one that occurred in 1863.

Belo's observations on trance in Bali are especially relevant to our consideration of the Madagascar case, since there is a clear historical connection between the island and what is now Indonesia. The Malagasy people are unique in that they trace their origins to Austronesia as well as the African mainland. As Maurice Bloch notes, "the Southeast Asian element is particularly strongly marked"[31] in the Merina, the dominant subgroup of the Malagasy, among whom the 1863 outbreak primarily occurred. The specific origin of the Merina seems to be southern Borneo, but, as Ann Kumar notes, there are a considerable number of Malay and Javanese words in the Malagasy language, just as there are in the Balinese, suggesting that, to a degree, they shared some cultural origins.[32] Although I am not aware of another outbreak on the scale of the Imanenjana, Malagasy culture has long included trance phenomena as a crucial element. Indeed, Lesley Sharp speaks of the "*assumed centrality* of possession in the local culture" (original emphasis) in the work of scholars investigating trance and possession in the context of social and economic changes.[33] There was in Malagasy culture, then, the preexisting "communal framework" that Becker identifies as part of the development and context of trance rituals and that was lacking in the medieval and early modern European contexts.

Both Becker and Gilbert Rouget have discussed at length the deep connection between music and trance while also cautioning their readers that "There is nothing intrinsic to the music that can cause trancing. The relationship between music and trance is not causal or deterministic."[34] This is an important point for any study of epidemic choreomania to take into consideration, since the role of music in the dancing plagues is rather difficult to define with any certainty. The idea that music could excite the "dancing fit" was reflected in contemporary bans against the playing of instruments in both 1374 and 1518, and it has played an important role in explanations of choreomania since the first attempts at comprehensive accounts were written in the 1830s.[35] Even the most recent scholarship on dancing plagues has largely repeated this assertion, despite the warnings of Rouget and Becker. The fact is that there is no hard evidence to suggest that the initial sufferers of choreomania in the Strasbourg outbreak (and probably in the 1374 epidemic as well) required music to cue their dancing. Musicians were later provided by local authorities in the misguided belief that this would help the dancers to work whatever was afflicting them out of their system more quickly, but since the manifestations of choreomania were probably not part of any preexisting ceremony, the role (if any) that they played in furthering the disorder's spread is unclear.

Despite the lack of any preexisting script that would determine the course of the European outbreaks, ritual nevertheless came to play the crucial role in causing the cessation of the epidemic. One chronicle of the 1374 outbreak records that as many a horde of people decamped to "a deserted old chapel" in the forest near Trier, where "they were possessed by demons and greatly tormented by them" until they "were brought to churches and shrines . . . after the prayers and alms of the people, by means of the exorcisms of the priests."[36] The Strasbourg plague was brought to an end in a similar fashion. The chronicler Daniel Specklin recorded that the dancers in that city were gathered onto large wagons, which carried them to a shrine to St. Vitus in the nearby countryside. There, he says,

> They fell down dancing before his image. So then a priest said Mass over them, and then they were given a little cross and red shoes, on which the sign of the cross had been made in holy oil, on both the tops and the soles. In St. Vitus' name they were sprinkled with holy water. It helped many, and they gave a large contribution. This is why it is called St. Vitus' dance.[37]

Finally, in the case of the Malagasy Imanenjana, Davidson notes that many of the dancers congregated at "a sacred stone below the city [the capital, Antananarivo] where many of the kings of Madagascar have been crowned . . . They danced for hours on end, and concluded by placing sugarcane, as a sort of offering, upon the stone."[38]

The fact that all three of these dancing plagues seem to have ended entirely or in large part through the means of some ritual raises the question of whether or not the dancers in each case were following a "script" of some sort. This is an important question to resolve, as it is another crucial point to consider in determining whether or not these epidemic outbreaks of choreomania can be said to constitute a performance. As I noted earlier, the fact that many of the dancers seem to have danced involuntarily and—at least in the European cases—without any sort of preexisting scenario in mind casts doubt on whether or not this phenomenon can even be considered in terms of performance. However, I would contend that the consistency with which ritual managed to calm and eventually cease these separate outbreaks suggests that the dancers were indeed following a sort of "script," albeit a somewhat impromptu one that they could not necessarily articulate in a conscious way. Furthermore, the fact that the choreomaniacs were following some sort of scenario, however ill-defined, that necessitated the involvement of religious figures brings in the crucial factor of audience. Even though they might not have done so consciously, the choreomaniacs seem to have been expressing the need for and indeed inviting the intervention of a group separate from themselves in order to undertake some efficacious action.

Dancing plagues appear to have been very public events that were capable of drawing—and subsequently infecting—a large crowd of observers. The relationship between dancers and observers was an ill-defined one; Hecker's account of the Strasbourg case speaks of "innumerable spectators attracted by curiosity."[39] Backman makes note of a chronicle of the 1374 epidemic which recounts how many choreomaniacs demanded that bystanders join in their dancing, although he also expresses the suspicion that in many cases "quite healthy people would often join in a dance to help their sick friends or relations or to protect themselves against the disease."[40] There were even a number of individuals who feigned the symptoms of choreomania; in the Strasbourg case, some of the more desperate denizens of the city may have faked their affliction in order to partake of the food and water supplied by the local authorities to the dancers.[41] At any rate, the dancing plagues' high visibility served to make them even more contagious. In order to counteract this, city councils in both 1374 and 1518 attempted to confine the dancers to less-visible venues, although this was accomplished through different means and with varying success. An edict issued by the magistrates of Maastricht in 1374 that banned anyone from dancing in public seems to have been more effective than the Strasbourg city council's attempt to confine the dancers to a number of guildhalls and market areas that were nevertheless still too prominent, as well as being important for the economic well-being of the city.[42]

I mentioned early in this essay the importance of the distinction between public and private in understanding the effects of outbreaks of epidemic choreomania, and the various efforts made to contain the dancers and stop the spread of their activity raises this issue again. The presence of a significant number of people dancing in a fairly visible public space, such as the market of Strasbourg, brings into play the dynamics of the crowd, a concept which in some ways did not fully emerge until the late nineteenth century but which is nevertheless relevant to epidemic choreomania in terms of the power these conglomerations of people can possess and project. As Kimberly Jannarone summarizes it, a "cumulative look" at writings on crowd theory leads to a few conclusions: "They are violent, contagious, and extraordinarily powerful; they operate by emotion rather than reason; they respond to images and archetypes rather than arguments; they will gladly surrender themselves to higher powers and forceful figures. In a crowd, suggestion replaces discussion . . . things become possible in crowds that otherwise individuals never would or could achieve."[43] Furthermore, "Immersion in a crowd means loss of consciousness and openness to suggestion; the consequences can be violent or heroic, but they are, in all cases, unrational and uninitiated by the individual."[44] All of these characteristics, which for Jannarone pertain to the mass political movements of the early twentieth century as well as Artaud's ideal theater, are also evident in the outbreaks of epidemic choreomania. The environment created by these outbreaks, then, was one in which large numbers of people developed a similar, highly irrational response to a set of circumstances that had plunged them into personal crisis, establishing a volatile situation in which the afflicted dancers formed a unified crowd with immensely disruptive potential.

In order to understand just who the dancers seemed to be addressing, it is necessary to understand more fully the social and political situations that underlay each particular case of epidemic choreomania. As George Rosen notes in his survey of the major European cases, "[s]ituations of stress" are a common factor in practically every noteworthy manifestation of choreomania, epidemic or otherwise.[45] Sharp echoes this finding, saying that "it is well documented that the incidence of spirit possession often rises dramatically in times of social disruption and crisis."[46] The 1374 outbreaks, for instance, occurred within memory of the devastation wrought by the Black Death, and the fact that both 1373 and 1374 saw further damage caused by major flooding may have been enough to create an environment in which fears of divine displeasure and the plague of possession by either vengeful saints or malicious spirits ran rampant. By the same token, the history of Strasbourg in the decades preceding its dancing epidemic reads like a seemingly endless chronicle of catastrophe, with famine, bloodily abortive attempts to organize peasant uprisings, and outbreaks of both syphilis and actual plague wearing down the populace.[47] The Madagascar case also occurred at a time of widespread suffering and profound social turmoil. The bloody reign of the ruthless Queen Ravanalona had recently ended, and while the new king, Radama II, was a well-meaning ruler with modernizing impulses, he was also apparently a dissipated one whose inept handling of the political situation raised fears of both the erasure of traditional culture and the possibility of foreign domination at the hands of either France or Great Britain.[48]

In all three cases, women and the poor seem to have been particularly hard-hit by the prevailing conditions and more likely to succumb to the urge to dance uncontrollably. In the European cases, we must rely on the spotty record provided by the chronicles to give us some vague idea of the gender and socioeconomic status of those afflicted; this can, at best, merely provide us with a few names, such as Frau Troffea's in the case of the Strasbourg outbreak. Luckily, with regard to Madgascar, Lesley Sharp's investigation of contemporary trance and possession among the Sakalava people of the northern coast provides a somewhat deeper understanding of how gender, in particular, functions in these cases. Sharp notes that virtually all of those she encountered who had been possessed were women: "The reasons given for this by the living (and by the spirits as well) is that women are more susceptible to possession because they are 'weak' (*malemy*) and it is difficult for them to resist the advances of spirits, in contrast to men who are 'strong' (*hery*)."[49] However, the implications of this for the status of women in this society should not necessarily be taken as entirely negative. After all, the roots of possession in Madagascar lie in a process by which deceased (male) rulers would speak through female mediums, thereby making them a conduit for dead royalty to continue communicating with their people. "Thus," says Sharp, "in the precolonial context, possession . . . was not evidence of marginal status . . . Instead, it was a central institution associated with adult female status."[50] In light of this, it seems noteworthy that the Imanenjana involved large numbers of people claiming possession by a recently deceased *female* ruler, which may have accounted for the apparently abnormal nature and scale of this particular case of epidemic choreomania, occurring as it did in a culture that knew about and understood how to channel smaller versions of this form of trancing.

In each case, the dancing plagues seem to have expressed uncertainty or a lack of confidence in traditional sources of authority. This was especially pronounced in the European outbreaks; the Madagascar epidemic had strong religious overtones, but the immediate crisis was more overtly political than in the case of the European dancing plagues. A lack of confidence in the efficacy and moral standing of the ecclesiastical authorities seems to have been a primary factor in both 1374 and 1518, and the importance of ritual in bringing about the cessation of the plagues suggests that they were on one level an appeal for more efficacious spiritual leadership. This obviously put the clergy in a position that was paradoxically both dangerous and authoritative at the same time. Hecker observes that the choreomaniacs of 1374 "took possession of religious houses," and that in the city of Liège,

> the priests had recourse to exorcisms, and endeavored, by every means in their power, to allay an evil which threatened so much danger to themselves; for the possessed assembling in multitudes, frequently poured forth imprecations against them, and menaced their destruction . . . Some of the affected had indeed themselves declared . . . that if the demons had been allowed only a few weeks more time, they would have entered the bodies of the nobility and princes, and through these have destroyed the clergy.[51]

The situation in Strasbourg was just as fraught, with ecclesiastical courts persecuting peasants unable to pay for their use of church lands and banned books that fantasized about "the holy slaughter of parasitic clergymen" circulating in secret.[52] In both cases the despair over the venality and corruption of the clergy contributed to a sense that they would neither be able to avert divine wrath nor protect their flock from the depredations of demonic forces.

Given the dire state of affairs that preceded all three epidemic cases of choreomania, we can attempt to draw some conclusions about whom the dancers imagined as their audience and what they hoped to achieve by means of their performance. In treating the dancing plagues as a means of expression, I am following H. C. Erik Midelfort's suggestion that phenomena such as demonic possession "provided troubled persons with the means of expressing their often guilty and morally straining conflicts, a vocabulary of gestures, grimaces, words, voices, and feelings with which to describe their sense that they were not fully in charge of their lives or their own thoughts."[53] Rosen observes that "dance frenzies and related occurrences . . . represent reactions to stress and are attempts to manage stressful situations. The consequences may be a re-establishment of a pre-existing equilibrium, failure to adapt in some way, or the achievement of fresh potentials for action."[54] To view the dancing plagues in these terms would suggest that the choreomaniacs were trying to express a sense of powerlessness and abandonment in the midst of severe crises that were straining the very fabric of their society and which their political and spiritual leadership seemed unable to effectively address.

Here we see the dancing plagues speak to Artaud's ideas on another level through their status as an embodied enactment of inner feelings and stresses. Garner observes that "Artaud's plague, like his theatre, manifests itself in a performative spectacle that physicalizes its spiritual operations. The plague is efficacious, exteriorizing psychic states, changing the nature of the real, and re-embodying metaphysics in transformative theatricality."[55] It was in just such a manner that the choreomaniacs of 1374 and 1518 or the Malagasy dancers of 1863 gave outward expression to the spiritual, cultural, and political conflicts playing out within their society and within their own individual consciousness. The mention of efficaciousness calls to mind the response that the dancers subconsciously hoped to evoke by enacting their sense of powerlessness in the face of widespread social disruption. To put it in Artaud's terms, "we can comprehend the troubled body fluids of the victim [of bubonic plague] as the material aspect of a disorder which, in other contexts, is equivalent to the conflicts, struggles, cataclysms and debacles our lives afford us." This physicalized, exterior display of inner disorder subsequently feeds the contagion, just as "the external events, political conflicts, natural cataclysms, the order of revolution and the disorder of war, by occurring in the context of the theater, discharge themselves into the sensibility of an audience with all the force of an epidemic."[56]

What is so fascinating about the dancing plagues—and what I find particularly significant with regard to Artaud—is the fact that each of these cases seems to have ended not with the overthrow of the old political or spiritual order, but with a reassertion of that old order's continued efficacy. In each case, the dancing seems to have been calmed by the first of Rosen's possible outcomes, namely the "re-establishment of a pre-existing equilibrium," whether that equilibrium meant the spiritual authority of the clergy in the case of the European epidemics or the overthrow of the less traditionally minded (and pro-Christian, pro-Western) regime in Madagascar.[57] The latter case in particular provides a clear-cut example of the political orientation and reverberations of the unrest brought about by the choreomaniacs; at one point Radama II actually had to flee his palace when it was invaded by a group of dancers, and he would soon be executed by forces sympathetic to those who danced in the Imanenjana.[58] The two European cases are perhaps not as clearly delineated in terms of their immediate political impact—Strasbourg would be engulfed by the turmoil of the Reformation and the Peasants' War not long after its dancing plague had died down—but one can nevertheless state with a fair degree of confidence that the decisive factor in ending the epidemics was a demonstration that the priesthood could, at least for the moment, continue to provide spiritual guardianship for the laity.

In a similar way, Artaud's theater of cruelty stems, as Kimberly Jannarone has recently observed in *Artaud and His Doubles*, from a period of intense conflict and disruption. Furthermore, it may lend itself more to an assertion of repressive authority than the pathway to liberation that admirers such as Peter Brook, Judith Malina, and Julian Beck have perceived. After all, she points out, "Artaud conceived of his theatrical project in the aftermath of World War I, when feelings of alienation and a deep yearning to belong to something larger than the self organized the social and aesthetic dimensions of much of European mass culture."[59] This was an era that saw "large swaths of Western Europe entertaining apocalyptic fantasies fueled by violent metaphysical pessimism," fantasies reflected in Artaud's scenarios for depictions of cataclysms such as the conquest of Mexico by Cortes.[60] The end result of this environment was the rise of fascism, which, although admittedly a much more radical solution in political terms than the "pre-existing equilibrium" to which the post-epidemic choreomania societies returned, nevertheless represented a yearning for a return, in this case to an imagined unifying cultural essence that predated developments such as the Enlightenment. Significantly, the turn to a single figure of unlimited political power entailed by the fascist program was reflected in Artaud's desire for total control over his audience: "*The Theater and Its Double* proposes nothing for the spectator, society, or mankind except for the opportunity to submit. The Theater of Cruelty concerns itself above all else with the exercise of power, with what a director—filled with messianic zeal—can do."[61]

All this brings to mind Goffman's observation that, in performance, "if the individual's activity is to become significant to others, he must mobilize his activity so that it will express *during the interaction* what he wishes to convey."[62] All three epidemics of choreomania appear to have represented an acting-out of a widespread feeling that the inadequacy of the long-established order left them vulnerable to the depredations of exterior mystical forces that could only be calmed or expelled with the reassurance that that order was still capable of functioning. Schechner notes that the European Middle Ages in particular were a period when performances were especially concerned with efficacy and were "allegorical, ritualized, tied to a stable established order."[63] The dancing plagues correspond in large part to this description, functioning as a performance that conveyed the dancers' sense that they fundamentally lacked spiritual guidance and protection and were therefore vulnerable in a highly visible and public way to the depredations of malignant metaphysical forces.

Artaud's emphasis on the exterior "conflict, struggles, cataclysms" and so forth that correspond to the workings of the plague on the body raises what is perhaps the most difficult and potentially troubling aspect of the relationship between theater-as-plague and epidemic choreomania. Our present-day conception of Artaud has, of course, been shaped to a large degree by the enthusiastic embrace of his manifestoes by the theatrical avant-garde of the 1960s. Therefore, when he describes a plague-ridden city in which "all social forms disintegrate" and "[o]rder collapses" or a theater which "disturbs the senses' repose, frees the repressed unconscious, incites a kind of virtual revolt (which moreover can have its full effect only if it remains virtual), and imposes on the assembled collectivity an attitude that is both difficult and heroic," his words seem to bear the indelible imprint of a progressive politics.[64] However, we have seen how in every case of epidemic choreomania the general thrust of the situation was toward a decidedly conservative resolution that reaffirmed the heretofore-uncertain authority of the old order. It is worth noting, for instance, that the Strasbourg outbreak occurred just one year after the peasant leader Joss Fritz launched his third failed attempt at fomenting a peasants' revolt that proclaimed its desire to exterminate the entire class of nobles and clergy who were contributing to the miserable lot of the lower classes.[65] A radical (if patently hopeless) and practical outlet for the sufferings and frustrations of the Strasbourg choreomaniacs therefore existed, but the dancers instead launched on a performance that ended when they obtained the attention and ministrations of the same clergy that Fritz hoped to wipe out. If there is anything positive to be said about the way in which the dancers may have affected the power dynamic between themselves and the clergy, it is perhaps to be found in the implicit threats of violence mentioned earlier, which likely played a part in forcing the religious hierarchy to pay closer heed to the spiritual needs of the people, if not their material ones.

Artaud noted that, "Like the plague, the theater is a formidable call to the forces that impel the mind by example to the source of its conflicts." In the same fashion, "The plague takes images that are dormant, a latent disorder, and suddenly extends them into the most extreme gestures; the theater also takes gestures and pushes them as far as they will go."[66] Both theater and the plague lead to acts whose "gratuitousness . . . appears infinitely more valid than that of a feeling fulfilled in life."[67] The dancing plagues were just such a gratuitous act, a phenomenon that on the surface appeared to be a singularly inappropriate expression of carnivalesque abandon at times of deep and widespread suffering. However, the "conflicts" and "latent disorder" that gave rise to the "extreme gestures" of the choreomaniacs ultimately appear to have been resolved (albeit in a temporary fashion) by recourse to the preexisting hierarchy. In a similar manner, Artaud's idea of a "spiritual transformation of a crowd based on a one-way exercise of power grounded in an aggressively dark view of the universe enacted through the use of immersion, unreason, emotion, and myth" was vulnerable to co-option by the forces of a decidedly nonprogressive force in twentieth-century politics, as evidenced by the similarities between his ideal theater and the fascist spectacles of the 1930s.[68] Artaud proclaims that "The theater, like the plague . . . releases conflicts, disengages powers, liberates possibilities, and if these possibilities and these powers are dark, it is the fault not of the plague nor of the theater, but of life," and that like the plague it is "a crisis which is resolved by death or cure."[69] As the historical record of epidemic choreomania show, the powers and possibilities unleashed by such a plague can indeed be, in Artaud's words, "dark"—and perhaps not always the ones that most of us would like to imagine being released in performance.

NOTES

1. Stanton B. Garner Jr. "Artaud, Germ Theory, and the Theatre of Contagion," *Theatre Journal* 58 (2006): 10.
2. L. J. Donaldson, J. Cavanagh, and J. Rankin, "The Dancing Plague: A Public Health Conundrum," *Public Health* 11 (1997): 201.
3. Antonin Artaud, *The Theater and Its Double*, trans. Mary Caroline Richards (New York: Grove Press, 1958), 18.
4. Ibid., 27.
5. J. F. C. Hecker, *The Dancing Mania of the Middle Ages*, trans. B. G. Babington (New York: Franklin, 1970), 34, 1, 3.
6. Garner, 10.
7. Hecker, 8.
8. Quoted in George Rosen, *Madness in Society: Chapters in the Historical Sociology of Mental Illness* (Chicago: University of Chicago Press, 1968), 196–97.
9. John Waller, *The Dancing Plague: The Strange, True Story of an Extraordinary Illness* (Naperville, IL: Sourcebooks, 2009), 1, 75.
10. H. C. Erik Midelfort, *A History of Madness in Sixteenth-Century Germany* (Stanford, CA: Stanford University Press, 1999), 33.
11. Waller, 148–49.
12. Ibid., 139.
13. Midelfort, 36.
14. Andrew Davidson, "Choreomania: An Historical Sketch, with Some Account of an Epidemic Observed in Madagascar," *Edinburgh Medical Journal* 13 (1867): 131.
15. Ibid., 132.
16. Erving Goffman, "Performances," in *Ritual, Play, and Performance: Readings in the Social Sciences/Theatre*, ed. Richard Schechner and Mady Schuman (New York: Seabury Press, 1976), 91.
17. E. Louis Backman, *Religious Dances in the Christian Church and in Popular Medicine*, trans. E. Classen (London: Allen & Unwin, 1952), 275.
18. Davidson, 132.
19. Waller, 87.
20. Gregory Bateson, "A Theory of Play and Fantasy," in *Ritual, Play, and Performance*, 69.

21. Goffman, 91.

22. Judith Becker, *Deep Listeners: Music, Emotion, and Trancing* (Bloomington: Indiana University Press, 2004), 43.

23. Ibid., 14.

24. Davidson, 128.

25. Waller, 97.

26. Becker, 27.

27. Jane Belo, "Trance Experience in Bali," in *Ritual, Play, and Performance*, 159.

28. Becker, 1.

29. Davidson, 134.

30. Lesley A. Sharp, *The Possessed and the Dispossessed: Spirits, Identity, and Power in a Madagascar Migrant Town* (Berkeley: University of California Press, 1993), 123.

31. Maurice Bloch, *From Blessing to Violence: History and Ideology in the Circumcision Ritual of the Merina of Madagascar* (Cambridge: Cambridge University Press, 1986), 12.

32. Ann Kumar, "'The Single Most Astonishing Fact of Human Geography': Indonesia's Far West Colony," *Indonesia* no. 92 (October 2011), 63.

33. Sharp, 16.

34. Becker, 25.

35. For which see Hecker, 13.

36. Quoted in Backman, 207.

37. Quoted in Midelfort, 36.

38. Davidson, 133.

39. Hecker, 4.

40. Backman, 201.

41. Waller, 133.

42. Backman, 201; Waller, 131–32. Eventually, the Strasbourg council came to the same conclusion as the Maastrich authorities in 1374, banning both public dancing and music.

43. Kimberly Jannarone, *Artaud and His Doubles* (Ann Arbor: University of Michigan Press, 2010), 117.

44. Ibid., 121.

45. Rosen, 200.

46. Sharp, 12.

47. For an assessment of the state of affairs in Strasbourg immediately prior to the beginning of the dancing plague, see Waller, 76–77.

48. Mervyn Brown, *Madagascar Rediscovered: A History from Early Times to Independence* (Hamden, CT: Archon Books, 1979), 195–96.

49. Sharp, 122.

50. Ibid., 174.

51. Hecker, 2–3.

52. Waller, 32, 47.

53. Midelfort, 14.

54. Rosen, 224.

55. Ibid., 11.

56. Artaud, 25–26.

57. The fact that resentment against European influence was a major factor in the Imanenjana further complicates our understanding of this particular case of choreomania by bringing

in issues pertaining to colonialism, specifically the brutal French conquest of the island, which would take place some thirty years later.

58. Brown, 196–97.
59. Jannarone, 96.
60. Ibid., 35.
61. Ibid., 186.
62. Goffman, 94.
63. Richard Schechner, "From Ritual to Theatre and Back," in *Ritual, Play, and Performance*, 209.
64. Ibid., 15, 28.
65. Waller, 56.
66. Artaud, 27–28.
67. Ibid., 25.
68. Kimberly Jannarone, "Audience, Mass, Crowd: Theatres of Cruelty in Interwar Europe," *Theatre Journal* 61, no. 2 (May 2009): 211.
69. Artaud, 31.

BIBLIOGRAPHY

Artaud, Antonin. *The Theater and Its Double*. Translated by Mary Caroline Richards. New York: Grove Press, 1958.

Backman, E. Louis. *Religious Dances in the Christian Church and in Popular Medicine*. Translated by E. Classen. London: Allen & Unwin, 1952.

Becker, Judith. *Deep Listeners: Music, Emotion, and Trancing*. Bloomington: Indiana University Press, 2004.

Bloch, Maurice. *From Blessing to Violence: History and Ideology in the Circumcision Ritual of the Merina of Madagascar*. New York: Cambridge University Press, 1986.

Brown, Mervyn. *Madagascar Rediscovered: A History from Early Times to Independence*. Hamden, CT: Archon Books, 1979.

Davidson, Andrew. "Choreomania: An Historical Sketch, with Some Account of an Epidemic Observed in Madagascar." *Edinburgh Medical Journal* 13 (1867): 124–36.

Donaldson, L. J., J. Cavanagh, and J. Rankin. "The Dancing Plague: A Public Health Conundrum." *Public Health* 11 (1997): 201–4.

Garner, Stanton B., Jr. "Artaud, Germ Theory, and the Theatre of Contagion." *Theatre Journal* 58 (2006): 1–14.

Hecker, J. F. C. *The Dancing Mania of the Middle Ages*. Translated by B. G. Babington. New York: Franklin, 1970.

Jannarone, Kimberly. *Artaud and His Doubles*. Ann Arbor: University of Michigan Press, 2010.
———. "Audience, Mass, Crowd: Theatres of Cruelty in Interwar Europe." *Theatre Journal* 61, no. 2 (May 2009): 191–211.

Kumar, Ann. " 'The Single Most Astonishing Fact of Human Geography': Indonesia's Far West Colony." *Indonesia* no. 92 (October 2011): 59–95.

Midelfort, H.C. Erik. *A History of Madness in Sixteenth-Century Germany*. Stanford, CA: Stanford University Press, 1999.

Rosen, George. *Madness in Society: Chapters in the Historical Sociology of Mental Illness*. Chicago: University of Chicago Press, 1968.

Schechner, Richard, and Mady Schuman, eds. *Ritual, Play, and Performance: Readings in the Social Sciences/Theatre*. New York: Seabury Press, 1976.

Sharp, Lesley A. *The Possessed and the Dispossessed: Spirits, Identity, and Power in a Madagascar Migrant Town*. Berkeley: University of California Press, 1993.

Waller, John. *The Dancing Plague: The Strange, True Story of an Extraordinary Illness*. Naperville, IL: Sourcebooks, 2009.

INDEX

Page numbers followed by *f* indicate figures. Numbers in italics indicate photographs and videos. Numbers followed by n indicate endnotes.